Litigation Library

COMMERCIAL LITIGATION: PRE-EMPTIVE REMEDIES

AUSTRALIA
LBC Information Services
Sydney

CANADA and USA
Carswell
Toronto, Ontario

NEW ZEALAND
Brooker's
Auckland

SINGAPORE and MALAYSIA
Thomson Information (S.E. Asia)
Singapore

LITIGATION LIBRARY

COMMERCIAL LITIGATION: PRE-EMPTIVE REMEDIES

Third Edition

By

Iain S. Goldrein, M.A. (Cantab.)
Barrister, Northern Circuit
Sir Jack Jacob Visiting Professor of Litigation,
Nottingham Law School

His Honour Judge Kenneth Wilkinson

His Honour Judge Kershaw, Q.C.,
Mercantile Judge

Assisted by
Titus Gibson, M.A.
Barrister, Northern Circuit

With A Foreword By
The Right Honourable The Lord Woolf, M.R.

LONDON
SWEET & MAXWELL
1997

First Edition 1987
Second Edition 1991

Published in 1997 by Sweet & Maxwell Ltd of
100 Avenue Road, London, NW3 3PF
Typeset by Selwood Systems, Midsomer Norton
Printed and bound in Great Britain by Butler and Tanner Ltd,
Frome and London

No natural forests were destroyed to make this product;
only natural timber was used and re-planted.

A CIP catalogue record for this book is available from the
British Library

ISBN 0 421 53660 8

FOREWORD

Previous editions of this valuable book have established its high reputation. The many practitioners who have taken assistance from **Pre-emptive Remedies** already will not be disappointed by this latest edition.

The costs and delays of civil justice in general have highlighted the advantages of being able to obtain a pre-emptive remedy. In many fields of litigation in practice, this can determine the outcome of the proceedings. As there is rarely oral evidence given in pre-emptive proceedings, it is essential that before the hearing of the application for the pre-emptive order, a litigant has his tackle in order, irrespective of whether he is appearing to support or oppose the application. This is where this book is so helpful. It clearly warns of the dangers which lie in wait for the unprepared litigator and as to how the dangers can be avoided. The editors now include Judge Kershaw who has great experience of commercial litigation. They have, either in a judicial or professional capacity, had to deal with the problems which can arise personally. They are therefore able to give advice which is extremely useful to practitioners.

I have long held the view that the influence of our procedures and remedies upon our substantive law is much greater than is generally appreciated. This book will not only assist the practitioner to advance his clients interests, it will provide him with greater understanding of substantive English law.

I commend this book to all those who become engaged in civil litigation.

The Right Honourable The Lord Woolf, M.R.

FOREWORD TO THE FIRST EDITION

Not the least interesting feature of this work is the use of the word "pre-emptive" in its title. It is a word which I associate with a financial context, as in "pre-emptive bid" or a military context as in "pre-emptive strike". And I have long railed against practitioners who regarded litigation as a species of warfare or even a game of chess. "Pre-emptive" coupled with "Remedies" was clearly something new.

Now I have to confess that as a Judge I have come to think of interlocutory proceedings as merely a means to an end, which is the orderly trial of the action, any prior disposal being a highly desirable bonus, but not usually an end in itself. But the authors have made me think again and I have studied the latest Commercial Court's statistics which are for the year 1985–6. These show that for that and the preceding few years, the Court heard and disposed of something of the order of 130 cases. By contrast it heard between 2,000 and 2,500 summonses. Accepting, as I do, that there would be several summonses in each case that came to trial, it is nevertheless clear that most commercial cases never do come to trial, which of course I knew, and that interlocutory proceedings play a very significant part in ensuring this result, which I certainly had not fully appreciated.

Whilst not every interlocutory proceeding has a pre-emptive character, those that do acquire a very special importance. It is, therefore, somewhat surprising that this seems to be the first attempt to study them as a major means of disputes settlement. Now that it has been done, it is a pleasure to welcome it and to pay tribute to the expertise of the authors. It is an essentially practical work which approaches the matter from the point of view of the busy practitioner in both branches of the profession. Thus where there are pre-conditions for the grant of relief, they are set out clearly, often in the form of a check-list. Where authorities are cited, there is no mere reference to law reports to be found and consulted, but full citation of the relevant passages from the judgments or speeches. And whilst pointing out the advantages of adopting a particular course, the dangers and disadvantages are brought clearly to the attention of the reader.

May I wish it and its authors every success. They deserve it.

May 1987

Sir John Donaldson
The Master of the Rolls

PREFACE

The commercial world and its mirror image, the commercial litigator, was agog in the 1980s with its new products: The *Mareva* and the *Anton Piller*.

The pattern of their application in the legal world reflected so clearly the pattern of a new pharmaceutical product in the medical world.

For the first few heady years, the product is perceived as the universal panacea.

Then as the ramifications of the remedy begin to assert themselves long term, there is a drawing back from their use with reaction against them.

And gradually, a balance is struck from wisdom and experience.

The First Edition of this work was published in the heady days of what we now look back on as the 1980s boom era, when these pre-emptive remedies were invoked with all the enthusiasm which greets the new wonder drug.

The Second Edition arrived on the market as a recession hit the market place as powerful as the boom, coinciding with a drawing back by the judiciary from universal acclaim for the broad use of these remedies.

And this, the Third Edition, arrives on the litigator's desk as a balance is struck and the true relevance of pre-emptive relief can be seen dispassionately and assessed in context.

The context of course is the reforms conceived by Lord Woolf when heading the Access to Justice committee and which are shortly to be with us.

We should look at his reforms, not just through the matrix of procedure, but also through the matrix of funding. Increasingly, litigants are demanding that litigation should be to a pre-determined budget.

This book is designed to facilitate that end, by providing a clear exposition of the law, coupled with a practical analysis of how the law is to be applied to a dispute to be resolved.

We are honoured by the preparedness of Lord Woolf M.R. to provide the Foreword. We hope that the efforts we have made to help the legal profession provide a cost-effective product in the field of pre-emptive relief are worthy of the reforms which he conceived as a Law Lord, and which he ushers into the world of practice through his role as head of the Civil Division of the Court of Appeal.

Iain S. Goldrein
K.H.P. Wilkinson
Michael Kershaw
July 1996

CONTENTS

Chapter 3: *Anton Piller* Orders

Chapter 6: Judgment in Default of Defence

Chapter 7: Dismissal

PART D

I. *Cyanamid*—Case File

TABLE OF CASES

[The references in **bold** type indicate material set out in Part D]

xlix

l

TABLE OF STATUTES

TABLE OF STATUTORY INSTRUMENTS

TABLE OF RULES OF THE SUPREME COURT (S.I. 1965 No. 1776)

TABLE OF RULES OF THE COUNTY COURT

PART A

Quick Access Summary

CYANAMID—MAREVA— ANTON PILLER: A Quick Access Summary

OVERVIEW

A The interlocutory armoury

1. Objectives of pre-emptive relief
 (a) Don't litigate if it can be avoided.
 (b) As a general rule, try and avoid getting to court for a full hearing.
 (c) If litigation is required, then try and resolve the litigation as cheaply as possible and with maximum expedition.
 (d) Consider the "preservative" remedies, all of which are different sorts of interlocutory injunction. Thus:
  (i) Preserve your opponent's cash.
  (ii) Preserve your opponent's documents.
  (iii) Preserve the status quo pending trial.
  (iv) Preserve the subject-matter of the action.
There will be many actions in which it is inappropriate to seek such preservative relief. Applications for interlocutory injunctions can be expensive and time consuming. Be vigorous but keep it in perspective.

2. Jurisdiction Supreme Court Act 1981, s.37; County Courts Act 1984, s.38. *Note*: No *Mareva* or *Anton Piller* in the County Court.
 Consider speedy trial: see also R.S.C., Ord. 29, r.5 for injunction/speedy trial/directions interface. Also consider the injunction/counterclaim interface: *Marcus Publishing plc v. Hutton-Wild Communications Ltd* [1990] R.P.C. 576. An injunction must support a legal right: *Associated Newspapers Group v. Insert Media* [1988] 1 W.L.R. 509. An interlocutory injunction is not a cause of action in itself: *The Siskina* [1979] A.C. 210. Therefore the writ must be indorsed with a claim for substantive relief. The court also has jurisdiction to grant an injunction on a counterclaim even if the counterclaim has yet to be served: *Marcus Publishing plc v.*

1

Hutton-Wild Communications Ltd (*ibid.*) In such circumstances, the court must obtain an undertaking from the defendant either to issue a separate writ or to serve a counterclaim once the plaintiff has served his statement of claim.

3. The Crown See Crown Proceedings Act 1947, s.21(1)(a) and *R. v. Licensing Authority, ex p. Smith Kline and French Laboratories Ltd (No. 2)* [1989] 2 W.L.R. 378. Also, see *R. v. Secretary of State for Transport, ex p. Factortame Ltd. (No. 2)* [1990] 3 W.L.R. 818.

4. Interlocutory relief Interlocutory relief is exceptional and discretionary— not granted as of right.

5. Types of interlocutory injunction

(a) *Mandatory:* (requiring the performance of an act). For example, in an industrial dispute—to withdraw instruction and notify Press Association, or delivery up of goods, when no arguable defence: *Locobail International Finance v. Agroexport* [1986] 1 W.L.R. 657. Also see *Elliot v. Islington London Borough Council, The Times,* July 6, 1990, where a mandatory injunction was granted requiring the defendant borough council to remove a tree which was growing on its land and causing damage to the plaintiff's property.

(b) *Quia timet: Redland Bricks Ltd v. Morris* [1970] A.C. 652 at 668. Conditions precedent:
  (i) Threatened wrong or continuing wrong.
  (ii) Plaintiff must aver and prove that what is going on is calculated to infringe his rights.

6. The "half-way house" injunction For example, passing off—where the defendant is restrained from using a particular name without making it clear that it is different from the plaintiff. See also *Nationwide Building Society v. Nationwide Estate Agents Ltd* [1987] F.S.R. 579.

7. Interlocutory and interim injunctions Orders to preserve a particular set of circumstances.

(a) *Interim:* Only for a few days—until named date or further order.
(b) *Interlocutory:* Q.B.D.—until further order. Ch.D.—until trial or further order.

Also note that *Mareva* and *Anton Piller* orders can be made in aid of execution.

8. Other orders

(a) The safe custody of the subject matter of the order pending trial: Ord. 29, r.2.

(b) Intermediate delivery up of goods, *e.g.* under section 4 of the Torts (Interference with Goods) Act 1977.

(c) The immediate sale of perishable or deteriorating property.

(d) The inspection of documents/property.

(e) Binding the plaintiff:

    (i) Expedition: *Newson v. Pender* (1884) 27 Ch.D. 43 at 63.

    (ii) Payment in: *Cavenagh v. Coker* (1919) 147 L.T. 252; *Jones v. Pacaya Rubber & Produce Co. Ltd* [1911] 1 K.B. 455.

(f) Binding the defendant:

    (i) Undertaking in lieu: *Clarke v. Clarke* (1864) 13 W.R. 133.

    (ii) Taking account of profits, etc.: *Rigby v. G.W.R.* (1849) 2 P.L. 44.

    (iii) Notice before doing a particular act: *Smith v. Baxter* [1900] 2 Ch. 138.

    (iv) Demolition of property: *Ford v. Gye* (1858) 6 W.R. 235.

    (v) Making admissions: *Hilton v. Granville (Lord)* (1841) Cr. & Ph. 283.

9. Examples

(a) To restrain infringement of intellectual property and similar rights, *e.g.*:

    (i) Valid covenants in restraint of trade.

    (ii) Confidential information. But note *Re A Company's Application* [1989] 3 W.L.R. 265—where disclosure to F.I.M.B.R.A. not restrained.

    (iii) Passing off (by restraining use of business name).

    (iv) *Anton Piller*—delivery up of chattels/documents (held in violation of intellectual property rights).

(b) Trespass:

    (i) to property;

    (ii) unlawful eviction.

(c) Defamation, etc. (remembering the defence of plea of justification).

10. Drafting the order

(a) *Don't prejudge the issue: Hepworth Plastics Ltd v. Naylor Bros. (Clayware) Ltd* [1979] F.S.R. 521. Order should be directed to specific conduct, <u>not</u> restrain *e.g.* a "passing off".

(b) *Need for precision*—especially in confidentiality cases: *Potters-Ballotini v. Weston Baker* [1977] R.P.C. 202 at 206.

11. Drafting the writ See commentary in *The Supreme Court Practice 1995*, at Vol. 1, para. 29/1/ 9. The plaintiff should indorse his writ with a claim for an injunction if the obtaining of it is a substantial object of his claim: *Colebourne v. Colebourne* (1876) 1 Ch. D. 690; and the purpose for which it is claimed must be stated: *Re Myer's Patent* (1882) 26 S.J. 371.

12. Summary Interlocutory injunctions are targeted at preservation, namely preserving:
   (a) Status quo (*Cyanamid*).
   (b) Cash (*Mareva*).
   (c) Documents, subject-matter of action (*Anton Piller*).

B The injunction/undertaking interface

1. Breach of undertaking Sanction identical to breach of injunction.

2. After trial Usually injunction even if undertaking volunteered: *Royal Insurance Co. Ltd v. G. & S. Assured Investment Co. Ltd* [1972] 1 Lloyd's Rep. 267.

C Vitiating factors

1. Fraud and unclean hands

(a) Deliberate wrongdoing: *Woollerton and Wilson v. Costain Ltd* [1970] 1 W.L.R. 411.
(b) Morality: *Church of Scientology of California v. Miller, The Times,* October 23, 1987.
(c) Agent provocateur—trap orders: *Walt Disney Productions Ltd v. Gurvitz* [1982] F.S.R. 446.
(d) Companies used as a cloak for fraud: *Idmac Industrial Designers v. Midland Bank Ltd, The Times,* October 8, 1981.
(e) Commercially disreputable transactions: *Wilton Group plc v. Abrams; Abrams v. Samuelson* [1990] BCC 310.

2. Failure to fully disclose material facts

(a) *Ex parte—utmost good faith:* Note: duty to make sufficient inquiries. Tell court if defendant has given notice of intention to defend. Court will look closely at time at which the plaintiff first had notice of the act complained of.
(b) *Where non-disclosure is error of judgment/non-deliberate:* court can still discharge *Mareva: Thermax Ltd v. Schott Industrial Glass Ltd* [1981] F.S.R. 289. See also below; under "*Mareva*".

(c) *But failure must be only as to material facts, not peripheral matter: Gallery Cosmetics Ltd v. Number 1* [1981] F.S.R. 556.

(d) *Defendant's failure to disclose can strengthen plaintiff's hand: Dunhill (Alfred) Ltd v. Sunoptics S.A.* [1979] F.S.R. 337 at 476.

3. Acquiescence

(a) *Meaning:* Passive conduct on the part of the plaintiff which induces the defendant to believe that he had given consent: *Davies v. Marshall* (1861) 10 C.B. (N.S.) 697 at 710D.

(b) *Criterion:* Has defendant changed position by reason of the acquiescence?

(c) *Acquiescence:* No bar to an injunction if it can be satisfactory explained.

(d) *Practice tips:*
 (i) Acquiescence by one plaintiff may bar other plaintiffs: *Marker v. Marker* (1851) 9 Hare 1 at 15.
 (ii) Irrelevant that plaintiff a company: *Laird v. Birkenhead Railway Co.* (1859) John 500.

4. Delay

(a) *Principle:* If matter is genuinely urgent, no reason to delay. Delay would probably be fatal to application for *ex parte* relief: *Bates v. Lord Hailsham* [1972] 1 W.L.R. 1373.

(b) *Examples—where delay fatal:*
 (i) One year: *Borough of Morecambe and Heysham v. Mecca Ltd* [1962] R.P.C. 145.
 (ii) Five months: *Shepherd Homes Ltd v. Sandham* [1971] Ch. 340.
 (iii) Six weeks: *E.A.R. Corporation v. Protector Safety Products (U.K.) Ltd* [1980] F.S.R. 574.
 (iv) Three months: *Kentex Chemicals Inc. v. Kenitex Textured Coating Ltd* [1965] 2 F.S.R. 109; *Bravingtons Ltd v. Barington Tennant* [1957] R.P.C. 183—delay unexplained.
 (v) Five months: *Century Electronics Ltd v. CVS Enterprises Ltd* [1983] F.S.R. 1. (Defendant lulled into a false sense of security, expanded business.)
 (vi) *Church of Scientology of California v. Miller, The Times,* October 23, 1987—application only made after preparation of book far advanced. If publication restrained to trial, publishers would be exposed to considerable losses.

(c) *Examples—where delay not fatal:*
 (i) Two months: *Radley Gowns Ltd v. Costos Spyrou* [1975] F.S.R. 445—but defendant had not materially changed his position for the worse.

5

(ii) One month: *Curson & Poole v. Rash* (1982) 263 EG 518 (no detriment, only four weeks).

(iii) Two months: *Carroll v. Tomado Ltd* [1971] F.S.R. 218. (Patent— plaintiff reasonably waited until it inspected a copy of defendant's article.)

(iv) *United Telephone Co. v. Equitable Telephone Association* (1888) 5 R.P.C. 233. (Plaintiff's solicitor advised not to commence action until the defendant appeared to be financially able to manufacture infringing article.)

(v) Two months: *CPC (United Kingdom) Ltd v. Keenan* [1986] F.S.R. 527 (plaintiff spent time seeking to negotiate amicable solution in alleged trade mark infringement/passing off).

(d) *Status quo and delay: Note*: If other factors are equally balanced, the court will prefer to preserve the status quo (*American Cyanamid Co. Ltd v. Ethicon Ltd* [1975] A.C. 396 at 408G). The longer the delay, the longer the *status* has had a chance to become *quo*. See also *Unigate Dairies Ltd v. Bruce, The Times*, March 2, 1988: the position to be maintained was that as it had been before the alleged breaches began, not as at the date of hearing.

D Practice and procedure—*ex parte*

1. Generally

(a) *Urgency:* Note the need for urgency emphasised in the commentary to *The Supreme Court Practice 1995*, Vol. 1 at para. 29/2–3/6. In *Lock International plc v. Beswick* [1989] 1 W.L.R. 1268, Hoffman J. said that the making of an *Anton Piller* order is only justified when there is a paramount need to prevent a denial of justice to the plaintiff, which cannot be met by an order for delivery up or preservation of the documents. *Anton Piller* orders are often sought in actions against former employees who have joined competitors or begun competing businesses; there is a strong incentive for employers to launch a pre-emptive strike to crush the unhatched competition in the egg by causing severe strains on the financial and management resources of the defendants. Even in cases where the plaintiff has strong evidence that an employee has taken specific confidential information, the court must employ a graduated response; there must be proportionality between the perceived threat to the plaintiff's rights and the remedy granted. The fact that the defendant has behaved wrongfully in his commercial relationships does not necessarily justify an *Anton Piller* order; in many cases it will be sufficient to order delivery up of the plaintiff's documents pending further order, or to allow the plaintiff's solicitor to make copies. In this case, Hoffman J. discharged a fully executed *Anton Piller* order.

(b) *Indorsement—the injunction: Colebourne v. Colebourne* (1876) 1 Ch.D. 690. Should follow exactly terms of relief sought: *Re Myer's Patent* (1882) 26 S.J. 371.

(c) *Which division:*
    (i) If the matter is specifically assigned to a particular division of the High Court, the application must be made in that division: Supreme Court Act 1981, Sched. 1.
    (ii) Chancery Division—open court (but can sit *in camera* if application made, in appropriate circumstances).
    (iii) Q.B.D.—chambers (solicitors have rights of audience).

(d) *To whom? Judge—unless:*
    (i) Parties are agreed on terms—Master/District Judge;
    (ii) The injunction is ancillary or incidental to a charging order: Ord. 50, r.9; or to the appointment of a receiver by way of equitable execution: Ord. 51, r.2.

(e) *Enforcement—conditions precedent:*
    (i) Must be indorsed with a penal notice.
    (ii) Personal service (companies—on appropriate office): Ord. 45, r.7.
    (iii) If order prohibitory and not mandatory—need to prove notice: *Ronson Products Ltd v. Ronson Furniture Ltd* [1966] Ch. 603.

(f) *Note: Practice Direction(Judge in Chambers: Procedure)* [1983] 1 W.L.R. 433.

(g) *When?*
    (i) Waiting for *inter partes* hearing would result in irreparable damage. But be reasonable. Try and negotiate before having recourse to the courts.
    (ii) Secrecy: *Mareva, Anton Piller.*
    (iii) Pressure of court business precludes a full hearing: *Beese v. Woodhouse* [1970] 1 W.L.R. 586.

(h) *Setting down:* If return date given:
    (i) serve notice of motion, and
    (ii) set down.

(i) *Duration:*
    (i) *Ch.D.*: First motion day for which defendant can be properly served: *Ex p. Abrams* (1884) 50 L.T. 184.
    (ii) *Q.B.D./Com.Ct.*: "Until after the trial of this action (or until judgment in this action) or until further order," or "until further order," or "until the hearing of the summons *inter partes*," etc.

(j) *Application can be made ex parte* **to vary or discharge:** *London City Agency (J.C.D.) Ltd v. Lee* [1970] 1 Ch. 597 at 599 H—600A.

(k) *Costs:* generally—reserved. But see *Pickwick International Inc. (G.B.) Ltd v. Multiple Sound Distributors Ltd* [1972] 1 W.L.R. 1213.

(l) *Appeals:* if first instance *ex parte* application refused, time frame for appeal is within seven days: R.S.C., Ord. 59, r.14(3).

2. London

(a) *Where?*
   (i) *Generally*: Court
   (ii) *Urgency*: Judge's home.
   (iii) *Dire emergency*: Telephone—see *Allen v. Jambo Holdings Ltd* [1980] 1 W.L.R. 1252. Tel.: 0171–936–6199. The judge is not to be telephoned except after reference to the clerk and it should be only by counsel.
(b) *Applications during Court hours:* The Courts will hear *ex parte* applications at the following times—save where circumstances do not permit.
   (i) *Q.B.D*: 10.00 a.m. and 2.00 p.m. (See *Practice Direction (Judge in Chambers: Procedure)* [1983] 1 W.L.R. 433.) Papers must be lodged by 3.00 p.m. on the day before the application. If very urgent, produce papers at 9.30 a.m. (for 10.00 a.m. hearing) or 12.30 p.m. (for 2.00 p.m. hearing) together with certificate signed by counsel that matter is urgent.
   (ii) *Ch. D*: 10.30 a.m. and 2.00 p.m. (See *Practice Direction (Chancery Division: Motions Procedure)* [1980] 1 W.L.R. 751.) Applications should be notified (by telephone, if necessary) to the clerk to the motions judge or, if he cannot be reached, the clerk of the Lists.
   (iii) *Com. Ct.*: 10.30 a.m. and 1.45 p.m. (follow Q.B.D. *Practice Direction*, above).
(c) *Where to lodge, etc. Royal Courts of Justice:*
   (i) *Q.B.D.*: Room 549.
   (ii) *Ch.D.*: Room 413. Not later than 12 noon on the working day before the date for which notice of motion has been given.
   (iii) *Com.Ct.*: Room 193.
(d) *What to lodge:*
   (i) *Q.B.D.*: Writ, affidavit, draft. *Note*: if interlocutory injunction is substantial object of the action, it should be indorsed on the writ: *The Supreme Court Practice 1995*, Vol. 1, para 29/1/9.
   (ii) *Com. Ct.*: Minute of order.
   (iii) *Ch.D.*: Two copies of writ, two copies of order sought, best estimate of time that counsel can give. This must be done no later than 12 noon on the day before the date for hearing.
   If real emergency, writ can be in draft; and affidavit entitled: "In the matter of an intended action. ..." See *Refson & Co. Ltd v. Saggers* [1984] 1 W.L.R. 1025.

(e) *Undertakings:*
  (i) As to damages.
  (ii) To notify the defendant of terms.
  (iii) To pay reasonable costs of third parties, if a *Mareva*.
  (iv) Exceptionally, to issue/swear affidavit. *Note*: failure is a grave breach of a solicitors' duty: *Refson & Co. Ltd v. Saggers (ibid.)*.

3. Provinces

(a) *Note*: No duty judge (but see Northern Circuit, below).
(b) Court administrator should issue the police and the secretary of the local law societies with the telephone number of the chief clerk. He will require:
  (i) Cause of action.
  (ii) That the proposed application is within the jurisdiction of the court.
  (iii) Telephone number of solicitor, applicant and (if appropriate) counsel.
(c) Northern Circuit Mercantile Court: see below.

4. Affidavit practice

See R.S.C., Ord. 41. In particular note that the contents for an interlocutory injunction must embrace:
(a) Full and frank disclosure.
(b) Facts generating a cause of action.
(c) Facts generating a claim for injunctive relief.
(d) Facts justifying an *ex parte* application and/or any notice given (and if not, why not) and/or notice of intention to defend.
(e) Any explanation (if *ex parte*) of what the other side's defence may be and/or if they have given notice of intention to defend.

E. Practice and procedure—*inter partes*

1. Commencement

(a) *Ch.D.:* Notice of motion not issued by the court. Unless time abridged by leave, two clear days notice: Ord. 8, r.2(2).
(b) *Q.B.D.:* Summons must be issued prior to service (Room 549). Unless time abridged by leave, two clear days' notice: Ord. 32, r.3.
(c) *Clear days:* The following do not count as "clear days": Saturdays, Sundays, Bank Holidays, Christmas Day and Good Friday.
(d) *Leave:* Only a judge can grant—not a master/district judge, even in long vacation: *Conacher v. Conacher* (1881) 29 W.R. 230. If notice/service is short—must specifically so state.

2. Venue

(a) *Q.B.D.*: Room 98 (*Note*: Queues, delays).
(b) *Ch.D.*: Motions Judge (less delay than Q.B.D.).
(c) *Com.Ct.*: Commercial Judge in Chambers (less delay than Q.B.D. but must be able to justify choice of Com. Ct.).

3. Practice

(a) *Ch.D.* (See *Practice Direction (Chancery Division: Motions Procedure)* [1980] 1 W.L.R. 751.)
 (i) *Two hours*: Adjourn to come on as a motion by order.
 (ii) *Generally*: Counsel will open on day specified in notice.
 (iii) *Saving*: Motions can be saved without mention, if by consent. If motion by special leave, it cannot be saved without leave of the court: *Arthur v. Consolidated Collieries Corporation* (1905) 49 S.J. 403; *Max Factor & Co. Ltd v. M.G.M./U.A. Entertainment Company* [1983] F.S.R. 577.
(b) *Q.B.D.*: Special appointment if likely to take more than 30 minutes (thus elect for Ch.D. if possible, if hearing likely to last for more than 30 minutes but less than two hours).

4. Essential documents for the court

(a) *Q.B.D.*:
 (i) Pleadings, affidavits, summons.
 (ii) File summons in Room 549 indorsed with estimated length of hearing. These documents must be lodged not later than 12 noon on the day before the date for which the notice of motion has been given (or Friday if the motion date is on the following Monday). The clerk should also be notified immediately if a motion goes "short", *i.e.* if it will take less than five minutes. (The two days is extended to five days in special appointment cases).

(b) *Ch.D.*:
 (i) Two copies of writ.
 (ii) Two copies of notice of motion.
 (iii) Best estimate of time that counsel can give.
Documents to be lodged with the Clerk of the Lists, Room 412, not later than noon on the day before the date for which the notice of motion has been given (unless Friday, in which case—for Monday). The defendant can in turn file an affidavit in answer and so forth. If motion "goes short" (less than five minutes) clerk should be notified immediately.

5. **Essential documents for service on the defendant:**
    (a) Writ, and any pleading.
    (b) Notice of the hearing.
    (c) Copy affidavit.
    (d) If previously ordered—a copy of the *ex parte* injunction.

6. **Interlocutory consent orders** *Chanel Ltd v. Woolworth & Co.* [1981] 1 W.L.R. 485. Must show a change in circumstances (fact not law). *Note*: Seek to include in order "Liberty to apply with or without change in circumstances." If interlocutory order not by consent, court may vary: *Pfizer Corporation v. Inter-Continental Pharmaceuticals Ltd* [1966] R.P.C. 565. The court may grant an extension of time for compliance with an interlocutory consent order: *Siebe Gorman & Co. v. Pneupac Ltd* [1982] 1 W.L.R. 185, but not where it is effectively a contract also with the other side: *Tigner-Roche & Co. v. Spiro* (1982) 126 S.J. 525. Where a motion is adjourned generally (and not stood over to trial) upon undertakings given by the defendant, there is no limitation to his right to seek their discharge: *Butt v. Butt* [1987] 1 W.L.R. 1351.

7. **Problems of disclosure—secret processes, trade secrets, etc.**
    (a) Do not disclose to judge, but fail to disclose to other side's solicitor/counsel: *W.E.A. Records Ltd v. Visions Channel 4 Ltd* [1983] 1 W.L.R. 721.
    (b) Suggestion: two affidavits—both for the judge and other side's counsel and solicitor. But that in which secret information referred to, to be withheld from defendant.

F The undertaking as to damages

1. **The undertaking as to damages—a hedge against the court getting it wrong** *Rigby v. Great Western Railway Co.* (1849) 2 Ph. 44 at 50. Designed as far as possible to compensate the respondent: *Fletcher Sutcliffe Wild v. Burch* [1982] F.S.R. 64. Also see *Rochdale B.C. v. Anders* [1989] 3 All E.R. 490.

(a) *Applies also to legally aided plaintiffs: Allen v. Jambo Holdings* [1980] 1 W.L.R. 1252. But if the plaintiff cannot financially honour his undertaking as to damages, and the defendant is likely to sustain significant damage, then an injunction will probably be refused: *Morning Star Co-operative Society Ltd v. Express Newspapers Ltd* [1979] F.S.R. 113. Also see *Oxy Electric Ltd v. Zainuddin* [1991] 1 W.L.R. 115 (injunctions to restrain development on land—requirement of cross-undertaking in damages—impecunious plaintiff).

(b) *Ch.D.:* Automatic; where the defendant consents to an undertaking to the court in lieu of an interlocutory injunction: *Practice Note* [1904] W.N. 203.

(c) *Q.B.D.:* must be expressly inserted.

2. Practice points

(a) *Security:* The court can order a sum to be paid into joint account of solicitors to "fortify the undertaking" (*The Supreme Court Practice 1995*, Vol. 1, para. 29/1/12).

(b) *Enforcement—by whom?* Any defendant—not just those actually restrained by the order: *Tucker v. New Brunswick Trading Company of London* (1890) 44 Ch.D. 249. Also see recent case where the principle confirmed: *Dubai Bank v. Galadari (No. 2)* [1990] 1 W.L.R. 731.

(c) *What if plaintiff outside jurisdiction? Harman Pictures N.V. v. Osborne and Others* [1967] 1 W.L.R. 723—security.

(d) *The Crown?—usually no: Secretary of State for Trade and Industry v. Hoffman-La Roche & Co. A.G.* [1975] A.C. 295, but yes, if a proprietary or contracted right was asserted—as in *Att.-Gen. v. Wright* [1988] 1 W.L.R. 164, where in part the Attorney-General was asserting the proprietary rights of a charity.

(e) *By whom is undertaking given?*
 (i) Counsel: *Manchester & Liverpool Banking Co. v. Parkinson* (1888) 60 L.T. 47.
 (ii) A local authority: *East Molesey Local Board v. Lambeth Waterworks Co.* [1892] 3 Ch.D. 289.

3. When enforceable

(a) *Ushers Brewery Ltd v. King (P.S.) & Co. Finance Ltd* [1972] Ch 148.
 (i) Failure on merits at trial.
 (ii) Established before trial, that injunction should not have been granted.
 (iii) Established after trial, by unsuccessful defendant, that injunction should not have been granted: *Barclays Bank Ltd v. Rosenberg* (1985) 135 New L.J. 633.

(b) Liability on the cross-undertaking—not a counterclaim (either in contract or tort).

(c) An inquiry as to damages will always be ordered unless:
 (i) There has been delay.
 (ii) Trivial loss: *Smith v. Day* (1880) 13 Ch.D. 651.
 (iii) An inquiry would be fruitless, *i.e.* the prospects of recovering significant damages was too slight to justify an inquiry: *McDonald's Hamburgers Ltd v. Burgerking (U.K.) Ltd* [1987] F.S.R. 112.

4. Quantum
(a) Contract measure.
(b) Damages can be "aggravated": *Columbia Picture Industries Inc. v. Robinson* [1987] Ch.38.

G Appeals

1. *Ex parte* injunctions can be made pending appeal *Erinford Properties Ltd v. Cheshire County Council* [1974] Ch. 261. But *note*: *London Underground Ltd v. National Union of Railwaymen* [1989] IRLR 341.

2. The approach of the appellate court
(a) Limited right to interfere: *Hadmor Productions Ltd v. Hamilton* [1983] 1 A.C. 191. But *note*: *Associated British Ports v. T.G.W.U.* [1989] 1 W.L.R. 939, H.L.
(b) Concessions made at first instance usually bind interlocutory appeal: *Bryanston Finance v. de Vries (No. 2)* [1976] 1 Ch. 63.
(c) Take a note of first instance decision: *Dellborg v. Corix Properties and Blissfield Corporation N.V.* (1980, June 26, C.A.T. No. 541).

3. The appeal/application to discharge interface See *London Underground Ltd v. N.U.R. (No. 2)* [1989] IRLR 343: There were certain circumstances in which an enjoined party could apply for discharge rather than an appeal. However, even assuming that the High Court had jurisdiction to hear such an application, it was inappropriate for it to do so where justice between the parties could be achieved as readily by pursuing an appeal. The application to discharge was refused.

H American Cyanamid—outline

1. Court retains overriding discretion
Hubbard v. Vosper [1972] 2 Q.B. 84.

2. That discretion—guided by four (flexible) criteria
(a) Is there a serious issue to be tried? If the answer is "No", the application fails: *C.B.S. Songs v. Amstrad Consumer Electronics* [1988] A.C. 1013. *Note*: the mirror image of this criterion is, is there an arguable defence? *Patel v. Smith* [1987] 1 W.L.R. 853.
(b) Are damages an adequate remedy? (*Note*: If damages are an adequate remedy, the absence of an arguable defence will not justify an injunction). A defendant's ability to pay may be relevant—such ability to pay is not a rich man's charter. *Evans Marshall v. Bertola SA* [1973] 1 W.L.R. 349. *Note*: In cases where an interlocutory

13

injunction was sought by employers to enforce a restrictive covenant in a contract of employment, the principles laid down in *American Cyanamid Co. Ltd v. Ethicon Ltd* [1975] A.C. 396 were to be applied. Also contrast, for example, *Potters-Ballotini v. Weston-Baker* [1977] R.P.C. 202—damages not an adequate remedy where the effect on defendant would have been "catastrophic" if had to close down before trial.

(c) Where does the balance of convenience lie? Arises if there is doubt as to the adequacy of the respective remedies in damages. *Note:* If there is no arguable defence, this criterion does not fall for consideration: *Bradford Metropolitan City Council v. Brown* (1987) 19 H.L.R. 16.

(d) Are there any special factors?

If, in a *Cyanamid* situation, the court fails to consider these criteria, the exercise of its discretion may be vitiated, thereby justifying an appeal *Porter v. National Union of Journalists* [1980] IRLR 404.

3. Serious issue to be tried—meaning

(a) *"Prima facie case" criteria—no: Cyanamid* at 410 D.

(b) *Not frivolous or vexatious: Cyanamid* at 407 D, but see Sir Robert Megarry's reservation as to such criterion: *Mothercare Ltd v. Robson Books Ltd* [1979] F.S.R. 466.

(c) *Not a trial on affidavits:* Court should generally abstain from expression opinion on the merits: *Wakefield v. Duke of Buccleugh* (1865) 12 L.T. 628. But sometimes, can be helpful to test the direction of the judicial wind: *Conder International Ltd v. Hibbing Ltd* [1984] F.S.R. 312. Also see *R. v. Westminster City Council, ex p. Costi, The Independent*, March 12, 1987.

(d) *Must be some evidence: Tetrosyl Ltd v. Silver Paint & Lacquer E.C. Ltd* (1979, C.A.T. No. 599).

Odds against success do *not* defeat plaintiff, unless his expectation of success is no more than a hope: *Mothercare Ltd v. Robson Books Ltd* [1979] F.S.R. 466.

4. Balance of convenience

(a) *Meaning?* Balance of risks of doing an injustice: *Cayne v. Global Natural Resources plc* [1984] 1 All E.R. 225 at 237 H.

(b) *The "balance of convenience" regulator*—status quo:
   (i) All things being equal, maintain status quo: *Cyanamid*: 408G.
   (ii) *Note:* the "status" which is "quo" is "ante"; the "existing state of things."
   (iii) When is the "quo" "ante"? The state of affairs immediately

preceding writ or motion, assuming it be more than minimal; see *Unigate Dairies Ltd v. Bruce, The Times*, March 2, 1988. One cannot contrive the "quo" *Shepherd Homes Ltd v. Sandham* [1971] Ch. 340.

(c) *The regulator of last resort—merits: Cyanamid* at 409 A–C. See also *R. v. Westminster City Council, ex p. Costi, The Independent*, March 12, 1987; *Cambridge Nutrition Ltd v. B.B.C.* [1990] 3 All E.R. 523. Also— the public interest criterion: *Megaphone International Ltd v. British Telecommunications Ltd, The Independent*, March 1, 1989. Public interest factors also the regulator in *Roussel Uclaf v. Searle (G.D.) & Co.* [1978] R.P.C. 747—life saving drug/alleged patent infringement.

Also *note*: Supreme Court Act 1981, s.50: *Shelfer v. City of London Electric Lighting Co.* [1895] 1 Ch. 287; *Att.-Gen. v. Wimbledon Home Estate Co. Ltd* [1904] 2 Ch.34; *Kennaway v. Thompson* [1981] Q.B. 88 and *Leeds Industrial Co-operative Society v. Slack* [1924] A.C. 851.

5. Special factors These factors have resulted in the Courts applying *Cyanamid* in a particular way in:
  (a) Passing off.
  (b) Patent.
  (c) Copyright.
  (d) Trade disputes. See *British Railways Board v. National Union of Railwaymen* [1989] I.C.R. 678.
  (e) Where the decision on the injunction proceedings would have the effect of being final, *e.g.* restraint of trade cases: *Lawrence David Ltd v. Ashton* [1989] I.C.R. 123.
  (f) Injunctions to thwart winding-up petitions.
  (g) Impossibility of phrasing injunction order.
  (h) Conflict between public and private interest.
  (i) Covenants in restraint of trade.
  (j) Mandatory interlocutory injunctions.
  (k) No dispute on the evidence.
  (l) Documentary credits and performance bonds.
But it is not a relevant factor that the defendant has other business interests which he could pursue pending trial: *Conder International Ltd v. Hibbing* [1984] F.S.R. 312.

6. Costs
  (a) Plaintiff wins—plaintiff's costs in the cause: *Steepleglade Ltd v. Stratford Investments Ltd* [1976] F.S.R. 3.
  (b) Plaintiff fails—defendant's costs in the cause: *Steepleglade* (*ibid.*).
  (c) Make provision for contingency that action may never come to trial—if appropriate, *e.g.* costs reserved: See *Stratford (J.T.) & Son*

Ltd v. Lindley (No. 2) [1969] 1 W.L.R. 1547; *The Supreme Court Practice 1997*, Vol. 1 Ord. 62.

MAREVA

A *Mareva* check-list

1. Is the *Mareva* really necessary?
That is:

(a) Has the plaintiff a good arguable case?
(b) Are there assets?
(c) Is there a risk of dissipation—if yes, on what grounds?
(d) Is there an alternative? *Seven Seas Properties Ltd v. Al-Essa* [1988] 1 W.L.R. 1272.

2. Consider
(a) How broad need be the terms of the proposed injunction, to safeguard the plaintiff's claim?
(b) To what particular assets of the proposed defendant should the injunction be applied—identifying same?
(c) If it is known that assets are in the hands of third parties, *e.g.* in particular banks, everything should be done to define their location to the greatest possible extent, *e.g.*:
  (i) Which bank(s).
  (ii) Address of relevant branch.
  (iii) Account numbers—if possible.

3. As to issue/service of the writ/affidavit—and the injunction if it is granted
(a) How soon can the affidavit/writ be sworn/issued (if yet to be issued)?
(b) How soon can the defendant be (i) given notice and (ii) served?
(c) In what manner can the defendant be served as quickly as possible?
(d) Upon which third parties is it reasonably necessary to serve a copy of the injunction.
(e) The following undertakings, as appropriate, will *inter alia* be included in the order.
(f) If there is a return date, notice/summons *must* be served.

4. Documents
(a) Full and frank disclosure in affidavit (including any criminal charge

or conviction against applicant. *Block v. Nicholson* [1987] C.L.Y. 3064).

(b) Draft order.

5. Expedition *Lloyds Bowmaker Ltd v. Britannia Arrow Holdings* [1988] 1 W.L.R. 1337. A plaintiff who succeeded in obtaining a *Mareva* injunction is under an obligation to press on with his action as rapidly as he can so that if he should fail to establish liability in the defendant, the disadvantage which the injunction imposed on the defendant would be lessened so far as possible.

Similarly in *Town and Country Building Society v. Daisystar Ltd* (1989) 139 New L.J. 1563, C.A., it was held that a litigant who had obtained a *Mareva* injunction had a duly to press on with his claim. If for any reason he did not wish to proceed with the claim even temporarily, he should then seek to discharge the injunction. It was an abuse of process to obtain an injunction and then wait for the opportunity of starting the action afresh in an attempt to get security ahead of others through the use of the injunction on assets not included in the injunction. The injunction was accordingly discharged.

6. Change in circumstances If after an *ex parte* injunction there has been a change in circumstances, the duty of full disclosure requires the plaintiff to return to the court: *Commercial Bank of the Near East v. A.B.C. & D.* [1989] 2 Lloyd's Rep. 319 (ditto in an *Anton Piller* context: *O'Regan v. Iambic Productions Ltd* (1989) 139 New L.J. 1378).

B Introduction of *Mareva* jurisdiction

1. Origins

(a) *Traditional view:* —Lister & Co. v. Stubbs (1890) 45 Ch.D. 1 (Such a injunction is equivalent to security—"that would be wrong in principle".)

(b) *Mareva:* "A telephone call or telex message could within seconds of the service of a writ ... put all liquid assets out of the reach of the creditor ...": *Third Chandris Shipping Corporation v. Unimarine S.A.* [1979] Q.B. 645 at 671. "The *Mareva* injunction was brought into use to make this kind of behaviour in commercial cases unprofitable." Now see section 37(3) of the Supreme Court Act 1981.

(c) *"Freezure":* Creates no rights *in rem*; although equivalent, when served on a bank: *SCF Finance Co. Ltd v. Masri* [1985] 1 W.L.R. 876 at 884.

(d) *Caution:*
(i) Not to be abused.
(ii) Not a punishment: £100 per week spending limit for wealthy

man—wholly unrealistic. *PCW (Underwriting Agencies) Ltd v. Dixon* [1983] 2 All E.R. 158. *Mareva* orders should always make provision for living expenses unless it was known that a defendant had the funds. The order should also make provision for him to pay his ordinary debts as they become due. There should also be an allowance for legal costs *Campbell Mussells v. Thompson* (1984) 81 L.S. Gaz 2140 Also see *Investment and Pensions Advisory Service Ltd v. Gray* [1990] BCLC 38.

   (iii) Third parties must not be unfairly prejudiced: *Unicorn Shipping v. Demet Navy Shipping Co.* [1987] FTLR 109. Similarly injunction lifted where it froze a legitimate established trading account: *Avant Petroleum Inc. v. Gatoil Overseas Inc.* [1986] 2 Lloyd's Rep 236, C.A. But note the risk of a potentially collusive relationship between agent and principal: *Atlas Maritime Co. S.A. v. Avalo Maritime Ltd (The Coral Rose)* [1990] 2 Lloyd's Rep. 258, C.A.

(e) *Arbitration:* Whether pending—or to enforce: *The Rena K* [1979] Q.B. 377; *Siporex Trade SA v. Comdel Commodities Ltd* [1986] 2 Lloyd's Rep. 428.

(f) *Costs:* To restrain disposal of assets pending taxation on an interlocutory order for payment of taxed costs: *Panton (Faith) Property Plan Ltd v. Hodgetts* [1981] 1 W.L.R. 927.

(g) *Mareva and the police: Chief Constable of Kent v. V* [1983] Q.B. 34; *Chief Constable of Hampshire v. A* [1985] Q.B. 132.

(h) *As an aid to execution: Stewart Chartering Ltd v. C. & O. Management SA* [1980] 1 W.L.R. 460. (*Mareva* ordered to be continued after judgment). In *Maclaine, Watson & Co. Ltd v. International Tin Council* [1989] Ch. 253, the defendant was ordered to disclose its assets worldwide in aid of execution of an arbitration award.

(i) *Prison for contempt: Pospischal v. Phillips, The Times,* January 20, 1988; flagrant breaches of a *Mareva* should be met with an immediate term of imprisonment.

2. Practice and procedure—an outline

(a) *Essential ingredients:*
   (i) Speed.
   (ii) *Ex parte.*
(b) *When does it take effect?* From pronouncement.
(c) *Courts?*
   (i) High Court.
   (ii) County Court, by County Court Remedies Regulation 1991 as amended by the County Court Remedies (Amendment) Regulations 1995: in very limited circumstances—in practice, post-judgment *Mareva* if judgment obtained in the County Court, and generally in

Central London County Court Business List (apply to a nominated judge).

(d) *Ancillary orders:* To prevent a *Mareva* being nugatory.

   (i) Discovery: But unless exceptional circumstances, only as to present assets: *Bekhor & Co. Ltd v. Bilton* [1981] 1 Q.B. 923. However in *Reilly v. Fryer* [1988] 2 FTLR 69, the Court of Appeal held that where an order was made in respect of assets within the jurisdiction, it would only be in exceptional circumstances that discovery would be ordered in respect of assets abroad. But risk of self-incrimination under foreign law will not justify the discharge of a *Mareva: Arab Monetary Fund v. Hashim* [1989] 1 W.L.R. 565. There was concern that third parties might be exposed to criminal proceedings in Iraq as a result of information. In consequence, part of the order was limited to disclosing information to solicitors acting for the plaintiff, and not to the plaintiff itself.

   (ii) Interrogatories.

   (iii) Delivery up of chattels: *C.B.S. United Kingdom Ltd v. Lambert* [1983] Ch. 37—motor vehicles purchased out of the proceeds of sale, by the defendant, of articles which infringed the plaintiff's copyright.

   (iv) Cross-examination: Cross-examination refused in *Allied Arab Bank Ltd v. Hajjar* [1988] Q.B. 787: disclosures already made by defendant as to assets within the jurisdiction not so deficient.

   (v) Anton Piller: "Piling *Piller* on *Mareva*": *Bekhor & Co. Ltd v. Bilton* [1981] 1 Q.B. 923 at 955: *C.B.S. United Kingdom Ltd v. Lambert* [1983] Ch. 37—copyright/piracy.

   (vi) Delivery up of passport: *Bayer AG v. Winter (No. 2)* [1986] 1 W.L.R. 540. Contrast writ *ne exeat regno*. For the interaction of a *Mareva* and the writ *ne exeat regno*, see: *Al Nahkel for Contracting and Trading Ltd v. Lowe* [1986] Q.B. 235. See *Re Oriental Credit* [1988] Ch. 204 where a order under section 37 of the 1981 Act was made restraining a company director from leaving the jurisdiction to bolster an order made under section 561 of the Companies Act 1985, for his private examination. *Note:* Writ *ne exeat regno* should be issued to the tipstaff rather than the sheriff.

(f) *Defences:*

   (i) No good arguable case.

   (ii) Failure to disclose.

   (iii) Set-off.

   (iv) Insufficient evidence of risk.

   (v) Variation of order.

(g) *"Before and after" remedy:* In addition to being used to freeze assets prior to trial, the *Mareva* can be invoked also after judgment or registration of a foreign judgment, in aid of execution. *Orwell Street (Erection and Fabrication) v. Asphalt and Tarmac (U.K.) Ltd* [1984] 1 W.L.R. 1097. Orders freezing a defendant's foreign assets may be expected to be made with less hesitation, after judgment *Babanaft International Co. S.A. v. Bassatne* [1989] 2 W.L.R. 232.

3. Mareva—its limits

(a) *No priority:* The *Mareva* jurisdiction is not intended to re-write the English law of insolvency: *Bekhor & Co. Ltd v. Bilton* [1981] 1 Q.B. 923. Also note the proprietary injunction, where the defendant has misappropriated or dealt improperly with the plaintiff's money. If tracing, etc. sought, ensure that writ claims proprietary (as opposed to personal) relief. Thus in *Investment and Pensions Advisory Services Ltd v. Gray* [1990] BCLC 38, it was held that where a *Mareva* injunction was granted the court would normally allow a variation of the injunction to permit the defendant to pay debts which were genuine and currently payable if the source of the payment was property which was not subject to any proprietary claim by the plaintiff.

(b) *No bar to a judgment creditor:* (*Note*: Seek judgment and execution with all dispatch).

(c) *No bar to a pre-existing creditor:*
   (i) Banks honouring cheques supported by a guarantee card.
   (ii) Debenture holder. (even though charge crystallises after *Mareva* injunction).
   (iii) Company creditor: However, the principle that required the variation of injunctions to permit the making of payments in good faith did not extend so far as to require the court to permit a subsidiary to pay to its principal sums which represented not ordinary trading debts but capital by means of which the principal traded through the subsidiary: *Atlas Maritime Co. S.A. v. Avalon Maritime Ltd The "Coral Rose" (No. 1)* [1991] 4 All E.R. 769.

(d) *Mareva* and bill of exchange:
   (i) Beware the *Mareva* technique in support of a counterclaim as a means of circumventing the rule on defences to bills and bonds: *Montecchi v. Shimco (U.K.) Ltd* [1979] 1 W.L.R. 1180.
   (ii) Up-hill task for defendant. Defendants failed in *Montecchi*. Italian plaintiff was financially sound and judgment could be enforced in Italy.

(e) *Letters of credit: Intraco Ltd v. Notis Shipping Corporation (The Bhoja Trader)* [1981] 2 Lloyd's Rep. 256:
   (i) A *Mareva* does not operate to freeze payment by a bank to third parties under irrevocable security documents.
   (ii) When a *Mareva* is granted over the proceeds of a letter of credit

or similar document, the order can be made in anticipation of the moneys falling in.

4. Acting for plaintiff How to avoid limits of *Mareva* jurisdiction
  (a) Seek from defendant a consideration for discharge of *Mareva*
    (i) Paying money into court.
    (ii) Providing a bond or guarantee that the plaintiff's debt will be met. See for an example, the actual result in *The Assios* [1979] 1 Lloyd's Rep. 331.
  (b) Availability of such security—relevant to the exercise of the court's discretion.
  (c) The garnishee problem:
    (i) If the funds in the hands of the garnishee are subject to a *Mareva*, he should apply to the court for leave to pay the garnishor—the *Mareva* has no priority over the order absolute.
    (ii) Insolvent defendant—discretion over garnishee order absolute.

5. Full and frank disclosure

(a) *The principle: Bank Mellatt v. Nikpour (Mohammed Ebrahim)* [1985] F.S.R. 87. The plaintiff must disclose:
  (i) Nature of his case.
  (ii) Any defence which the defendant has indicated in correspondence or elsewhere.
In summary: Probe and dig into client's dealings with defendant. Details of any relevant criminal charges or convictions should also be given: *Block v. Nicholson* [1987] C.L.Y. 3064. This duty must be discharged even if the plaintiff's case might be prejudiced by such disclosure: *Guinness plc v. Saunders* [1988] 1 W.L.R. 863. It has been held that where a *Mareva* injunction has been obtained on the basis of fabricated evidence, the costs of both the application for the injunction and the application for its subsequent discharge should be paid by the plaintiff immediately on an indemnity basis, even where it is not yet established that the plaintiff was involved in the fabrication of the evidence.
(b) *Mistake in framing cause of action—not automatically fatal: Hispanica v. Vencedora Oceanica Navegacion S.A. (The Kapetan Markos)* [1986] 1 Lloyd's Rep. 211.
(c) *Brink's-Mat Ltd v. Elcombe:* [1988] 1 W.L.R. 1350: The following principles were laid down by the Court of Appeal:
  (i) It was the duty of the plaintiffs to make full and frank disclosure of the material facts in applying for the injunction.
  (ii) Materiality was to be decided by the court and not the plaintiffs or their advisers.
  (iii) The duty of disclosure applied to material facts known to the

21

plaintiffs and any additional facts which would have been known had proper inquiries been made.

(iv) The extent of those inquiries depended on all the circumstances of the case.

(v) It must be ensured that the party obtaining the injunction was deprived of any advantage derived from a breach of the duty of disclosure.

(vi) The question whether a fact not disclosed was sufficiently material to justify the immediate discharge of the injunction depended on the importance of the fact to the issues to be decided.

(vii) The court had a discretion to continue the injunction or grant a new one. See also *Behbehani v. Salem* [1989] 1 W.L.R. 723. An *ex parte* order discharged for non-disclosure will not be regranted if material non-disclosure due to deliberate lack of candour or lack of due care.

(d) *Cases on the disclosure duty:*

(i) *Ali & Fahd Shobokshi Group Ltd v. Moneim* [1989] 1 W.L.R. 710. Where a plaintiff had obtained *ex parte* a *Mareva* order preventing dissipation of assets without proper disclosure the court, on an *inter partes* motion, must refuse to continue the order if the non-disclosure complained of by the defendant could not be regarded as innocent and the order could not properly have been granted if full disclosure had been made. Where, however, the non-disclosure was innocent and the order could have been granted on full disclosure, the court could exercise its discretion whether or not to refuse *Mareva* relief. Further, it would not be right to require a defendant to wait until after trial to seek damages for non-disclosure and he should be at liberty to require the discharge of an *ex parte Mareva* order (without its immediate re-imposition) as soon as he could show non-disclosure of a substantial kind.

(ii) *Commercial Bank of the Near East v. A.B.C. & D.* [1989] 2 Lloyd's Rep. 319—the duty of a plaintiff to return to court arose where the court had been misinformed or been given incomplete information at the time of the initial *ex parte* application. There was also a continuing need to disclose any change in circumstances while the proceedings remained on an *ex parte* basis.

C. Practice and procedure—detailed

1. The six-hurdle test

(a) There must be a legal or equitable right: see *Securities and Investments Board v. Pantell S.A.* [1989] 3 W.L.R. 698, where it was held that a public body had a cause of action despite not having a beneficial interest in the sums claimed.

(b) Jurisdiction: For example, the court has jurisdiction over assets within the jurisdiction owned by an American company which was continuing as a going concern under the supervision of a creditors committee and the court: *Felixstowe Dock & Railway Co. v. United States Lines Inc.* [1987] 2 All E.R. 77. The Civil Jurisdiction and Judgments Act 1982, s.25(1)(a) gave the High Court power to grant interim relief where proceedings had been or were to be commenced in a contracting state other than the United Kingdom. Although the plaintiffs were not seeking any substantive relief in England, the English courts thus had jurisdiction to grant the interlocutory relief sought by them: *Republic of Haiti v. Duvalier* [1989] 2 W.L.R. 261. Also note that a pre-trial *Mareva* can be ordered even in respect of defendants domiciled in a non-convention country: *X v. Y* [1989] 3 W.L.R. 910. Also see *House of Spring Gardens v. Waite* [1984] F.S.R. 277 where there was *Mareva* relief in two jurisdictions.

(c) A good arguable case.

(d) Assets: they can be tangible or intangible. Includes land, bank accounts (including accounts in overdraft), aeroplanes, ship's bunkers, machinery, time charterer's bunkers and cargo, stamps, business goodwill. They must be within the legal or beneficial ownership of the defendant. They must not be subject to legal or equitable interests of third parties to the extent that they would not be available on execution of a judgment. The assets must be held by the defendant *qua* defendant—not in any other capacity: *Roberts v. Death* (1881) 8 Q.B.D. 319. Assets may be "after acquired." A debt owing to a defendant by an English company payable in America, is an asset within the English jurisdiction; *Deutsche Schachtbau-und Tiefbohrgesellschaft m.b.H. v. R'As al-Khaima National Oil Co. Ltd* [1987] 3 W.L.R. 1023. As to assets appearing to belong to a third party, see *SCF Finance Co. Ltd v. Masri* [1985] 1 W.L.R. 876. *Note: Bank Mellat v. Kazmi* [1989] 1 Q.B. 541; *Mareva* against social security claimant Held: where a debtor had notice of a probability that the money would, if paid to the defendant direct, be disposed of in breach of the injunction, the court had to take action to subject the money effectively to the operation of the injunction. That would normally be achieved by payment into court. In the present case it was preferable to pay the money into the defendant's frozen bank account.

(e) Risk of dissipation. The mere fact that the defendant is foreign or abroad is not sufficient: *Third Chandris Shipping Corporation v. Unimarine S.A.* [1979] 1 Q.B. 645. Consider: origins; business domicile; length of time in business; cross-firing between accounts; known assets; circumstances in which dispute has arisen. If, after inquiry, nothing can be found out about the defendant, that by itself may be enough to justify a *Mareva* injunction. Plaintiffs should seek to establish in particular that the defendants are "debt dodgers," or that they have a bad reputation in the trade, that they are difficult to track down, or that they are notoriously fallible in providing assets to meet large adverse judgments; and/or that there exists no mechanism for enforcement of awards in the defendant's country.

(f) Consent to undertakings: *Note*: If defendants want to strengthen the undertaking as to damages with security, they should apply therefore at the outset: *Commodity Ocean Transport Corporation v. Basford Unicorn Industries Ltd* [1987] 2 Lloyd's Rep. 197:

    (i) On the application to discharge the *Mareva* injunction, it is for the court to which the application is made to decide whether the injunction was rightly granted and whether there should be an inquiry as to damage.

    (ii) There must be loss warranting compensation.

    (iii) Clean hands (*e.g.* no delay).

    Note:

    (i) The cross-undertaking as to damages can be limited: *Re D.P.R. Futures Ltd* [1989] 1 W.L.R. 778. Ordinarily the limit would be fixed by reference to a reasonable estimate of what losses might be suffered by the party or parties covered by the undertaking.

    (ii) The plaintiff may still be liable on his cross-undertaking even if his action is successful. The issues are different: *Barclays Bank v. Rosenberg* (1985) 135 New L.J. 633.

In *Sabani v. Economakis, The Times*, June 17, 1988 (a case about failure to comply with undertaking concerning notification) the plaintiff through an oversight failed to observe an undertaking. Potter J. held that there was a clear duty to carry out such undertakings to the letter but in the present case there was no suggestion that the undertakings were given other than honestly and genuinely. Further in *Financiera Avenida S.A. v. Shiblaq, The Times*, January 14, 1988, it was held that where a defendant seeks damages arising out of a cross-undertaking given by the plaintiff when granted a *Mareva*, the burden of proof rests on the defendant to show that the damage suffered would not have occurred were it not for the injunction.

2. Risk of dissipation—burdens of proof

(a) Defendant has no obligation to disclose its financial affairs, *merely* to answer a challenge from a plaintiff which is unsupported by solid evidence.

(b) Only if an inference is raised by the plaintiff should the defendant answer a challenge—and then, only for the purpose of displacing that inference.

3. Overcoming these hurdles—not necessarily enough The court retains

an overriding discretion. As to the weight to be attached to the competing interest of a foreign court, see: *Felixstowe Dock & Railway Co. v. U.S. Lines Inc.* [1988] 2 All E.R. 77. Hirst J. declined to treat the U.S. bankruptcy proceedings and the wish of the defendants to make English assets available to be dealt with in the bankruptcy as a paramount or overriding factor inconsistent with the grant of *Mareva* relief.

4. Assets outside the jurisdiction Subject to affording protection to third parties and to protecting the defendants against abuse, it can be proper to embrace within the freezing order, foreign assets: *Republic of Haiti v. Duvalier* [1989] 2 W.L.R. 261, C.A., is authority for the principle that the discretion to grant a *Mareva* injunction over assets worldwide would be more readily exercised where the plaintiff's claim was a proprietary claim for the return of specific assets or a tracing claim against assets representing assets allegedly misappropriated, than where the plaintiff sought a money judgment only; though it may be more accurate to describe relief in a tracing claim as akin to Mareva: see *Polly Peck International plc v. Nadir* [1992] 4 All E.R. 769 at 776e. Further in *Derby & Co. Ltd v. Weldon (Nos. 3 and 4)* [1989] 2 W.L.R. 412, C.A., it was held that although orders were normally limited to assets within the jurisdiction, the fact that assets were not held within the jurisdiction was not a bar to granting a *Mareva* injunction. Changing circumstances now meant that it was necessary to state unequivocally that in an appropriate case the court would grant a worldwide interlocutory injunction. The principal requirement of the order was that it would be made in accordance with the rationale of previous cases. The absence of assets within the jurisdiction could of itself create the necessity for protective measures. On the facts of that case there was to be no distinction between the E.E.C. and the Panamanian company relating to the granting of a *Mareva* injunction. Although the order against the Panamanian company could not be specifically enforced, a sanction existed in that should the company fail to comply, the court could bar the right to defend. Against that backdrop, the headnote in *Derby & Co. Ltd v. Weldon, The Times*, August 2, 1988, falls into perspective.

> "The court would order a pre-judgment world-wide *Mareva* injunction to freeze a party's assets, in an exceptional case so long as, by undertaking or proviso or a combination of both; (a) oppression of the defendants by way of exposure to a multiplicity of proceedings was avoided, (b) the defendants were protected against the misuse of information gained from the ordinary order for disclosure in aid of the *Mareva* and (c) the position of third parties was protected."

Also note Derby v. Weldon (No. 6) [1990] 1 W.L.R. 1139.

25

D Maximum sum orders

1. Fixing the maximum sum

(a) Liquidated claims: the sum claimed.

(b) Unliquidated claims: the maximum amount will be that which the plaintiff will reasonably anticipate recovering.

2. Banks

(a) *A compromise:* Draft the order in such terms that any third party on which it is served is only obliged to freeze whatever assets of the defendant it may hold up to the maximum sum specified in the order.

(b) *Check list:*

    (i) "a net value of £. ..." (to hedge against the defendant having assets but denuding their value by running up debts charged against them).

    (ii) Allow for legal advice: but see *National Bank of Greece v. Constantinos Dimitriou, The Times,* November 16, 1987, where the defendant's application for partial release of assets within the jurisdiction, for the purposes of paying legal fees was refused where he had (previously undisclosed) unfrozen assets abroad and *Atlas Maritime Co S.A. v. Avalon Maritime Ltd The "Coral Rose" (No. 1)* [1991] 4 All E.R. 769: the Court may, without piercing it, lift the corporate veil.

    (iii) Consensual written variation provision without recourse to the court.

    (iv) Living expenses/transactions in the ordinary course of business; including ordinary debts as they become due: *Law Society v. Shanks* (1987) 131 S.J. 1626 (also, defendant's employer not prevented from paying defendant on gratuity).

3. Ancillary problems

(a) *Maximum sum orders and chattels:* Generally—order does not restrain chattels, unless specifically identified. *Z. v. A–Z and AA–LL* [1982] Q.B. 558

(b) *Joint accounts:*

    (i) Should be frozen only in "rare" cases; *Z v. A–Z (ibid.)*

    (ii) If frozen, all account holders should be served.

    (iii) See *Allied Arab Bank Ltd v. Hajjar* [1988] Q.B. 787. Wife's account not frozen though the defendant had authority to draw on it.

(c) *Letters of credit:* To be frozen only if paid into account(s) the subject matter of the *Mareva.*

(d) *Bank guarantee cards:*

    (i) Bank must honour the guarantee contained in a "cheque card."

    (ii) Solution: cancel the card.

4. Summary re *Mareva* **and banks** A *Mareva* served on a third party, (*e.g.* bank) should:

(a) bind the defendant in relation to his assets generally to the extent to which this is reasonably necessary; and

(b) provide expressly to what extent assets in the hands of third parties are affected by the generality of the first part of the order.

5. Protecting banks—practice points The order should:

(a) Clearly identify the assets covered, and to what extent, *e.g.*

(i) The location of the money.

(ii) The bank which holds it, and which branch.

(iii) The number and type of account.

(b) The order must make clear whether the order covers all assets held by the bank (including chattels) or just monies. If the plaintiff is unsure of the extent of the defendant's assets, the better course may be:

(i) To include all assets in the order.

(ii) To ask the court to order the defendant to swear an affidavit listing his assets and their value.

(c) If the bank is holding the money in a foreign currency, the *Mareva* can still attach. Upon being served with the order, the bank should convert the credit balance into sterling at the buying rate to the extent necessary to meet the sum stated in the order, and then put a stop on the account to this extent, as with garnishee orders: *Choice Investments Ltd v. Jeromnimon* [1981] 1 Q.B. 149.

(d) Banks and expense:

(i) Problem: If an account is not identified in the order banks are put to the expense of seeking to identify it: *Searose Ltd v. Seatrain U.K. Ltd* [1981] 1 W.L.R. 894.

(ii) Solution: The plaintiff must give an undertaking at the *ex parte* hearing to reimburse any third party as to expense resulting fro the order. *Note*: The courts demonstrate an increasing tendency to require security to be put up in support on an undertaking to reimburse third parties.

(e) Service: Notify bank prior to defendant.

ANTON PILLER

A Introduction

1. Characteristics

(a) "Seizure."

(b) The orders are largely mandatory.

(c) *Ex parte.*

(d) Irrevocable—the defendant is confronted with a *fait accompli.*
But not a search warrant—entry only by consent: *Anton Piller K.G. v. Manufacturing Process Ltd* [1976] Ch. 55.

2. Contrast: *Mareva/Anton Piller*

(a) *Anton Piller*:
   (i) The conduct sought to be restrained is always alleged to be wrong (infringement of copyright, etc.).
   (ii) The order is substantially mandatory.
(b) *Mareva*:
   (i) The conduct sought to be restrained is not of itself a wrong (dissipation of assets).
   (ii) The order is substantially prohibiting.

3. Caution

(a) There must be full and frank disclosure: including the need for the plaintiff to make sufficient inquiry.
(b) Must be grave danger that vital evidence will be destroyed, lost or hidden: (consider engaging commercial inquiry agents—but *note*: duty of full and frank disclosure will probably require the revealing of how the agent came by the information).
(c) An exceptional remedy: *Booker McConnell v. Plascow* [1985] R.P.C. 425. But trap orders by an *agent provocateur*—permitted, if disclosed on application: *Walt Disney Productions Ltd v. Gurvitz* [1982] F.S.R. 446.
(d) Such orders were being granted too readily: *Columbia Picture Industries Inc. v. Robinson* [1987] Ch. 38, *per* Scott J. Sufficient consideration should be given to the interest of the defendant.
(e) Further—*Columbia*:
   (i) The order should be no wider than absolutely necessary.
   (ii) Once documents have been seized, they should be copied and the originals returned, a detailed record being kept of all documents seized.
   (iii) Where ownership of the property seized is disputed, it should not be retained by the plaintiff's solicitors (Scott J. suggested deposit of the goods into the hands of a neutral officer appointed by the court or alternatively, delivery up to the defendant's solicitor with an undertaking for its safe custody).
(f) Summary: Because of potentially disastrous consequences for the defendant, the plaintiff's solicitor is under a very strict duty to act scrupulously and give full and frank disclosure.

4. What information is usually sought by *Anton Piller* order?
(a) Names and addresses.
(b) Places of manufacture.
(c) Supplier.
(d) Distributors.
(e) Retailer.
(f) Customers.
(g) Places of storage.
(h) Invoices and records.
Note: The applicant will usually undertake not to allow any person (including the Customs and Excise) to have access to the goods and documents seized, without the leave of the court. But the plaintiff can sue third parties on the basis of documents seized: *Roberts v. Jump Knitwear Ltd* [1981] F.S.R. 527.

5. What can be taken?
(a) Illicit material (*e.g.* infringing copyright).
(b) Chattels.
(c) Computerised records.
(d) Filing cabinets.
(e) Essential evidential documents.
See *Crest Homes plc. v. Marks* [1987] A.C. 829, and *Piver (L.T.) Sarl v. S. & J. Perfume Co.* [1987] F.S.R. 159.
But *note*: subject to leave of the court.:
(a) One of the main purposes of the *Anton Piller* order was to obtain information from the defendant upon which one could pursue one's claims against other parties.
(b) Information obtained by an *Anton Piller* order could be used against third parties implicated in the same wrongful handling of the same infringing goods.
(c) The information could also be used to bring criminal proceedings against third parties outside the jurisdiction.

6. *Anton Piller* may include a "batch" of orders
(a) An injunction to restrain:
  (i) Particular activities (precisely defined) alleged to constitute a tort.
  (ii) The warning of third parties.
(b) An order immediately to disclose the names and addresses of third parties "mixed up" in the allegedly tortuous activities, for example, suppliers and customers.
(c) An order directing the defendant:
  (i) to permit a search of its premises and the removal of particular items;
  (ii) immediately to disclose the whereabouts of illicit material.

29

7. Controlling the *Anton Piller* jurisdiction Four hurdles:
  (a) A *very* strong prima facie case.
  (b) Risk of damage—must be very serious.
  (c) Possession of the relevant material. The court must be able properly to infer that the defendant has in his possession incriminating documents or relevant evidence.
  (d) Risk of disposal. Not if defendant acts openly. In *Yousif v. Salama* [1980] 1 W.L.R. 1540—evidence of a forgery in the endorsement of a cheque, sufficient.

8. Full and frank disclosure
  (a) Probe and dig (previous convictions, etc.).
  (b) The problem of informants—*W.E.A. Records Ltd v. Visions Channel 4 Ltd* [1983] 1 W.L.R. 721. The judge will have to decide to what extent he is prepared to rely upon information coming from anonymous and unidentifiable sources.

9. What can be taken?
  (a) Illicit material, for example, material infringing the plaintiff's copyright.
  (b) Chattels.
  (c) Computerised records (take to premises a computer hacker?).
  (d) Filing cabinets (removals van?)
  (e) Essential evidential documents: *Yousif v. Salama* [1980] 1 W.L.R. 1540.

10. Judicial control over delivery up of chattels—*C.B.S. United Kingdom v. Lambert* [1983] Ch. 37
  (a) Tainted property and risk of dissipation.
  (b) Not all chattels (*e.g.* personal effects).
  (c) Order must definite chattels.
  (d) Not a search warrant—must be permission.
  (e) Delivery up—order must specify to whom (solicitor or a receiver appointed by the court).
  (f) Liberty to apply. (As to judicial control over "discharge" of an *Anton Piller* see *Booker McConnell v. Plascow* [1985] R.P.C. 425). If there has been material non-disclosure, application to discharge should normally be made at trial and not at interlocutory hearing.
  (g) Supervised by an "outside" solicitor who reports to the Court.

11. The order must be meticulously executed As to service, the order must:
  (a) Provide for service by an outside solicitor who is experienced in supervising the service of such order.
  (b) Identify the individuals who will attend.

(c) Identify precise premises.

(d) Anticipate defendant's absence—order should provide for execution on "the person appearing to be in charge."

(e) Specify times and days on which order may be executed.

Note: No forcible entry.

12. Practical check list

(a) Check the premises.

(b) If potentially aggressive reaction—Sentries? Video film? Police—breach of peace?

(c) If defendant has solicitors—inform them just prior to service (Cellnet, Vodaphone).

(d) If more than one location involved—synchronise.

(e) If several involved in service/execution—brief them all first.

(f) Supervising solicitor must explain to defendant *clearly*—everything in layman's language, with tact. Defendant may be off balance.

(g) When searching, do *not* go outside the order of *A.B. v. C.D.E.* [1982] R.P.C. 509:

"some documents were taken away which were outside the ambit of the order altogether."

(h) Supervising solicitor will have to report to court, so contemporaneous note—tape-recorder?

1. Interlocutory Injunction—Practice and Procedure

2. *Mareva*—Practice and Procedure

3. *Anton Piller* Orders

4. Order 14: Summary Judgment

5. Judgment in Default of Notice of Intention to Defend Action

6. Judgment in Default of Defence

7. Dismissal

8. Security for Costs

CHAPTER 1

Interlocutory Injunctions—Practice and Procedure

A: THE NATURE OF INTERLOCUTORY EQUITABLE RELIEF

1 Jurisdiction

1. Introduction An injunction is an order of the court directing a party to the proceedings to do or to refrain from doing a specified act. It is granted in cases where monetary compensation would afford an inadequate remedy to an injured party. The High Court has power by order, whether interlocutory or final, to grant an injunction in all cases in which it appears to the court to be just and convenient to do so: section 37(1), Supreme Court Act 1981. Such an order may be made either unconditionally or on such terms and conditions as the court thinks just: section 37(2). These provisions cover all applications for interlocutory injunctions including *Mareva* and *Anton Piller* orders (see pp. 175 and 280).

2. County court An essentially parallel jurisdiction is afforded to the county courts by section 38 of the County Courts Act 1984.

Note:
   (a) *Mareva* and *Anton Piller* relief have been removed from the remit of the county court: section 38(3)(6), the County Courts Remedies Regulations 2(a) and 2(b) and article 3 of the High Court and County Courts Jurisdiction Order 1991.
   (b) Because of the absence of any monetary limit on the jurisdiction of the county court in relation to actions in contract and tort there is no reason why more injunctions cannot be brought in the county court (which otherwise would have been brought in the High Court). See section 15 of the County Courts Act 1984, and section 1 of the Courts and Legal Services Act 1990 together with article 7 of the High Court and County Courts Jurisdiction Order 1991.

3. The interlocutory injunction—what is it? Spry, *Equitable Remedies* (4th ed. 1990), at p. 437 advances the following definition:

"An interlocutory injunction is an injunction that is limited so as to apply only until the final hearing or final determination by the court of the rights of the parties; and accordingly it issues in a form that requires that, in the absence of a subsequent order to the contrary, it should continue up to but not beyond the final hearing of the proceedings."

In other words, the purpose of an interlocutory injunction is to regulate the position of the parties pending trial whilst avoiding a decision on issues which could only be resolved at trial. They are either prohibitory (not to perform certain specified acts) or mandatory (directed to performance of specified acts).

4. There must be a cause of action This has the following consequences:
  (a) Without a writ (or default or other originating summons), there can be no cause of action.
  (b) The cause of action must be justiciable in England and Wales, which in turn generates consideration of the following:
    (i) the domicile of the defendant;
    (ii) if the defendant is not domiciled in England and Wales, whether the Civil Judgments and Jurisdiction Act 1982 or the Lugano Convention legislation make the action justiciable in England and Wales;
    (iii) failing that, does section 25 of the Civil Judgments and Jurisdiction Act 1982 apply, which empowers the English court to grant relief ancillary to court proceedings in Brussels Convention or Lugano Convention countries?
    (iv) Where a defendant is foreign, and the action is not justiciable in England under the above statutory provisions, consider invoking procedure under R.S.C., Ord. 11, and combine the application for leave to issue the writ and serve out the jurisdiction with the application for the injunction.
    (v) *Note:* Section 12(6)(e) and (h) of the Arbitration Act 1950 permit of applications for interlocutory injunctions ancillary to an arbitration.

5. The application for the interlocutory relief is not in itself a cause of action The right to interlocutory relief is not a cause of action in itself (despite what Lord Denning M.R. said in *Chief Constable of Kent v. V.* [1983] Q.B. 34). As Lord Diplock said in *The Siskina* [1979] A.C. 210 at 256:

"A right to obtain an interlocutory injunction is not a cause of action. It cannot stand on its own. It is dependent upon there being a pre-existing cause of action against the defendant arising out of an invasion, actual or threatened by him, of a legal or equitable right of the plaintiff for the enforcement of which the defendant is amenable to the jurisdiction of the court. *The right to obtain an interlocutory injunction is merely ancillary and incidental to the pre-existing cause of action.* [Editors' emphasis.]"

Developing this theme, in *Channel Tunnel Group Ltd v. Balfour Beatty Construction Ltd* [1993] A.C. 334, Lord Mustill said at 360–362:

"Although the words of s. 37(1) and its forebears are very wide it is firmly established by a long history of judicial self-denial that they are not to be taken at their face value and that their application is subject to severe constraints: see *The Siskina* [1979] A.C. 210 ... the doctrine of *The Siskina,* put at its highest, is that the right to an interlocutory injunction *cannot exist in isolation, but is always incidental to and dependent on the enforcement of a substantive right, which usually although not invariably takes the shape of a cause of action.* . . . [Editors' emphasis.]"

6. When can it lie? In *American Cyanamid Co. Ltd v. Ethicon Ltd* [1975] A.C. 396, Lord Diplock, discussing the principles to be applied and matters to be taken into consideration when an interlocutory injunction is sought, referred at 406C, to:

"... an application for an interlocutory injunction to restrain the defendant from doing acts alleged to be in violation of the plaintiff's legal rights."

In interpreting this passage, Buckley L.J. said in *Bryanston Finance v. de Vries (No. 2)* [1976] 1 Ch. 63 at 76E:

"His attention was addressed to the kind of action in which issues relating to the existence of a right claimed by the plaintiff and the existence or threat of some infringement by the defendant of that right are for the time being uncertain but will be investigated and determined at the trial."

7. The relevant date. The court must consider all the evidence, not just by reference to the date of the alleged infringement of the plaintiff's right but by reference to all the relevant evidence at the time the injunction is sought: *Comet Radiovision Services Ltd v. Farnell-Tandber Ltd* [1971] 1 W.L.R. 1287, *per* Goulding J.

8. A discretionary remedy The discretionary nature of the remedy was emphasised by Lord Diplock in *American Cyanamid Co. Ltd v. Ethicon Ltd* [1975] A.C. 396 at 405G:

"The grant of an interlocutory injunction is a remedy that is both temporary and discretionary."

9. An exceptional remedy? In *Landi den Hartog N.V. v. Sea Bird (Clean Air Fuel Systems) Ltd* [1975] F.S.R. 502, Whitford J. said at 504:

"... relief by way of injunction is relief which is *never lightly granted* and in interlocutory proceedings the court in any event must be satisfied that there is a *real apprehension* that if steps be not taken to preserve a party's interest in property, then *irreparable damage* may be done. [Editors' emphasis.]"

In other words, the plaintiff must show that he would suffer substantial prejudice or hardship in a material respect if he were confined to other remedies, such as damages. And as Whitford J. said in *Celanese Corporation v. Akzo Chemie U.K. Ltd* [1976] F.S.R. 273 at 275:

"... the grant of interlocutory relief has always been considered the grant of relief of a *somewhat exceptional character*, and it is inappropriate to grant relief of this nature unless it is *absolutely vital* in order *to protect the legitimate interests* of the plaintiff that such relief be granted. [Editors' emphasis.]"

10. Proportionality The need for the proposed order and its terms have to be weighed very carefully. Hoffman J. said in *Lock International v. Beswick* [1989] 3 All E.R. 373 at 384:

"... the court must employ a graduated response. To borrow a useful concept from the jurisprudence of the European Community, there must be proportionality between the perceived threat to the plaintiff's rights and the remedy granted. The fact that there is overwhelming evidence that the defendant has behaved wrongfully in his commercial relationships does not necessarily justify an *Anton Piller* order. People whose commercial morality allows them to take a list of customers with whom they were in contact will not necessarily disobey an order of the court requiring them to deliver it up. Not everyone who is misusing confidential information will destroy documents in the face of a court order requiring delivery of them."

"Proportionality" was the basis of the ruling of Robert Walker J. in *Anglia Oils v. Procter & Gamble Ltd*, December 11, 1995. On a "confidential information" issue, the court was very restrictive in the terms of the order restricting disclosure.

11. Law enforcement by a local authority Exceptional circumstances warranting injunctive relief were held to have arisen in *City of London*

Corporation v. Bovis Construction Ltd (1988) 84 L.G.R. 660, C.A. where a local authority obtained an interlocutory injunction to restrain breaches by the construction managers of a development site of a notice served on them under the Control of Pollution Act 1974, s. 60 to control nuisance by noise (contravention of the notice without reasonable cause being a crime). The same principle was considered by the Court of Appeal in *Portsmouth City Council v. Richards* (1989) 87 L.G.R. 757, C.A. In that case a local authority successfully brought proceedings to close down a "sex shop". The following principles for the grant of such an injunction emerge from the cases:

(a) The court would only buttress the criminal law in exceptional circumstances. Such circumstances were not by reference to the nature of the breach (*e.g.* flagrant or deliberate), but by reference to the criteria as to whether the inference was to be drawn that unlawful operations would continue unless restrained by injunction.

(b) Emergency situations where the court must intervene to prevent irreversible events.

(c) Where enforcement and stop notices have been ignored, and criminal proceedings proved ineffective, it is not unreasonable for an authority to issue civil proceedings under section 222(1) of the Local Government Act 1972: *Waverley Borough Council v. Hilden* [1988] 1 W.L.R. 246.

However the Court will grant an interlocutory injunction preventing a public authority from enforcing an existing law if there appears to be a strong case that the law is in breach of the provisions of the EEC Treaty: *R. v. Secretary of State for Transport, ex p. Factortame (No. 2)* [1990] 3 W.L.R. 818.

12. Representative injunctions Where in proceedings there was a clear conflict of interest between persons belonging to or affiliated with an unincorporated association, it was inappropriate to sue selected individual members as representing all other members: *United Kingdom Nirex Ltd v. Barton, The Times,* October 14, 1986.

13. Effect on third parties Interlocutory relief can have effect over and beyond the ambit of the immediate dispute. Thus where there were in existence interlocutory injunctions restraining newspapers from publishing information in a book called *Spycatcher*, the stocking and lending of the book by a public library would be a contempt of court: *Att.-Gen. v. Observer: Application by Derbyshire County Council* [1988] 1 All E.R. 385, Knox J. Thus, an act in breach of an injunction by a person who was not the subject of that injunction could still amount to a contempt of court if, in carrying out the act, the person intended to impede or prejudice the administration of justice. Similarly in *Att.-Gen. v. Newspaper Publishing,* *sub nom. Att.-Gen. v. The Independent* [1987] 3 All E.R. 276, the Court of Appeal held that the publication by those newspapers of material derived from Peter Wright, and obtained by him in his capacity as a member of the British Security Service, could constitute contempt of court in relation to the injunction restraining two other papers from publishing such material. By granting the interlocutory injunctions against the two newspapers, the court had made it clear that its chosen method of administering justice was to preserve the confidentiality of the information in question pending trial, and the three newspapers could not have been in any doubt that this was the case. Whilst in all the circumstances the three newspapers did not fall within the "strict liability rule" set out in the Contempt of Court Act 1981, there was an express saving in section 6(c) in respect of conduct intended to impede or prejudice the administration of justice, *i.e.* of conduct specifically intended to do so. It was not necessary that this should be the sole intention of the contemner. However, a person who hands an asset to a party subject to a *Mareva* does not ordinarily assist him in dissipating it: *Law Society v. Shanks* (1987) 131 S.J. 1626. In that case the defendant, the subject of the *Mareva*, received a gratuity and pension upon leaving his employment.

14. Leave to appeal Leave to appeal is required from the grant or refusal of an interlocutory order: R.S.C. Ord. 59, r.1B(f). In *Moran v. University College, Salford, The Times*, October 27, 1993, C.A., the headnote reads:

> "On an application for leave against the refusal by a deputy High Court judge on October 8, 1993 to grant a mandatory injunction on an interlocutory application to compel the university to admit the applicant, the court allowed the application but dismissed the appeal. It then gave guidelines with regard to recent changes in the rules concerning leave to appeal."

15. Mercantile lists Note the availability of specialist commercial judges in Manchester, Liverpool, Birmingham and Bristol.

2 Principles

1. How untrammelled is the court's discretion? There is an issue (not yet resolved) as to how untrammelled the discretion should be:

(a) *South Carolina Insurance Co. v. Assurantie Maatschappij* [1987] A.C. 24 *per* Lord Brandon at 39–40:

> "In considering the question which I have formulated, it will be helpful in the first place to state certain basic principles governing the

grant of injunctions by the High Court. The first basic principle is that the power of the High Court to grant injunctions is a statutory power conferred on it by section 37(1) of the Supreme Court Act 1981, which provides that 'the High Court may by order (whether interlocutory or final) grant an injunction in all cases in which it appears to the court to be just and convenient to do so'.... The second basic principle is that, although the terms of section 37(1) of the Act of 1981 and its predecessors are very wide, the power conferred by them has been circumscribed by judicial authority dating back many years. The nature of the limitations to which the power is subject has been considered in a number of recent cases in your Lordships' House.... The effect of these authorities, so far as material to the present case, can be summarised by saying that the power of the High Court to grant injunctions is, subject to two exceptions to which I shall refer shortly, limited in two situations. *Situation (1) is when one party to an action can show that the other party has either invaded, or threatens to invade, a legal or equitable right of the former for the enforcement of which the latter is amenable to the jurisdiction of the court. Situation (2) is where one party to an action has behaved, or threatens to behave, in a manner which is unconscionable.* The third basic principle is that, among the forms of injunction which the High Court has power to grant, is an injunction granted to one party to an action to restrain the other party to it from beginning, or if he has begun from continuing, proceedings against the former in a foreign court. Such jurisdiction is, however, to be exercised with caution because it involved indirect interference with the process of the foreign court concerned." [Editors' emphasis.]

(b) *Pickering v. Liverpool Daily Post* [1991] 2 A.C. 370: The House of Lords confirmed the approach it had taken in the *South Carolina* case.
(c) *Channel Tunnel Group Ltd v. Balfour Beatty Construction Ltd* [1993] A.C. 334: Lord Mustill did not accept without more, the dicta of Lord Brandon in the *South Carolina* case. At 363 he said *inter alia*:

"... I prefer not to engage the question whether the law is now firmly established in terms of Lord Brandon's statement, or whether it will call for further elaboration to deal with new practical situations at present unforeseen. For present purposes it is sufficient to say that the doctrine of the *Siskina*, put at its highest, is that the right to an interlocutory injunction cannot exist in isolation, but is always incidental to and dependent on the enforcement of a substantive right, which usually although not invariably takes the shape of a cause of action. *If the underlying right itself is not subject to the jurisdiction of the English court, then that court should never exercise its power under section 37(1) by way of interim relief.* If this is a correct appreciation of the doctrine, it does not apply to the present case...." [Editors' emphasis.]

(d) *Kirklees B.C. v. Wickes Building Supplies Ltd* [1993] A.C. 227: Lord Goff said *inter alia* at 270–271:

"... There are cases in which an interlocutory injunction has been granted, despite the fact that the defendant was raising a defence to the alleged crime. In *Portsmouth City Council v. Richards* [1989] 87 L.G.R. 757, the Court of Appeal upheld the grant of an interlocutory injunction restraining the operation of sex shops, despite the fact that the defendant had raised a defence under article 30 of the Treaty. In *City of London Corporation v. Bovis Construction Ltd*, 86 L.G.R. 660, the Court of Appeal upheld the grant of an interlocutory injunction restraining a breach of the Control of Pollution Act 1974, notwithstanding an alleged defence invoked by the defendant which had not been disposed of. Furthermore, the submission of Mr Collins ignores the fact that, since an injunction may be granted in an emergency to restrain an infringement of the law, for example the cutting down of a tree in breach of a trees preservation order ... it may well be impossible in such circumstances to resolve the issue of a possible defence on the application for an interlocutory injunction. Mr Collins sought to accommodate such cases by recognising them as an exception to his suggested rule. I cannot think that this is right. *The power to grant injunctions, which now arises under section 37 of the Supreme Court Act 1981, is a discretionary power, which should not as a matter of principle by fettered by rules. In my opinion, the existence of an alleged defence is a matter to be taken into account in the exercise of the court's discretion, when deciding whether it is just and convenient that interlocutory relief should be granted.*" [Editors' emphasis.]

2. "Status quo" These words are a term of art, and are considered in greater detail at p. 161 below. The usual purpose of an interlocutory injunction is to preserve the status quo until the rights of the parties have been determined in the action. This is consistent with the proposition that a court had jurisdiction to make such an injunction, even if such an order would not be appropriate at final trial: *Fresh Fruit Wales v. Halbert, The Times*, January 29, 1991. The case involved Rugby Union football tickets for a season, in circumstances where the trial over the right to use such tickets would be heard only after the season had ended.

3 Examples

1. Extent of jurisdiction

(a) *Restraining the publishing of State Secrets in another jurisdiction: Lord Advocate v. Campbell, The Times,* March 17, 1988, where an interdict was made in Scotland under section 27 of the Civil Jurisdiction and Judgments Act 1982 protecting proceedings commenced but not concluded in England.

(b) *To protect the rights of creditors against an unincorporated association: Maclaine Watson & Co. v. International Tin Council (No. 2)* [1988] 3 W.L.R. 1190; [1988] 3 All E.R. 257, to plug the gaps left by R.S.C., Ord., 48, 4. 1 which sets out the policy of the law to assist judgment creditors but may not apply to unincorporated associations (which the Tin Council was).

(c) *Restraint as to leaving the jurisdiction:* The flexibility of the injunctive jurisdiction of the court is again demonstrated by the case of *Re Oriental Credit* [1988] Ch. 204; [1988] 2 W.L.R. 172. The case is authority for the principle that the court has jurisdiction to issue an injunction restraining a director who has been ordered to attend for examination from leaving the country. Harman J. held, refusing the application, that although the order for A to attend created no cause of action or legal or equitable right in the liquidators, the court had jurisdiction under section 37 of the Supreme Court Act 1981 to ensure that its orders were complied with, and the injunction was valid.

(d) *French Laboratories (No. 2)* [1989] 2 W.L.R. 378: It was held that under Ord. 53, r.3(10) the High Court can grant an injunction or stay of proceedings against the Crown or a minister of the Crown on an application for judicial review. This was also the ruling of the House of Lords in *M. v. Home Office* [1994] 1 A.C. 377; [1993] 3 W.L.R. 433.

(e) *Misleading advertisements:* An interlocutory injunction may be granted to restrain misleading advertisements when there is strong prima facie evidence that the advertisements make false claims on behalf of a product that might induce the public to buy it. *Director General of Fair Trading v. Tobyward* [1989] 1 W.L.R. 517; [1989] 2 All E.R. 266.

(f) *Health authorities*

    (i) *In Re C. (Adult: Refusal of Medical Treatment)* [1994] 1 W.L.R. 290 *per* Thorpe J.: The schizophrenic plaintiff could not elicit from his doctors an undertaking that his leg would not be amputated at some time in the future. The headnote *inter alia* reads:

        "... that an individual was entitled to access to judicial determination by the court under its inherent jurisdiction by way of injunction or declaration that an individual was capable of refusing or consenting to medical treatment; that there was no reason why such relief should not extend to future circumstances; and that, accordingly, the applicant was entitled to an injunction to prevent the amputation of his leg by the hospital, or any other hospital to which he might be transferred in the future, without his written consent."

(ii) *In Re J. (A Minor) (Child in Care: Medical Treatment)* [1993] Fam. 15, Balcombe L.J. said at 29:

"... I can conceive of no situation where it would be a proper exercise of the jurisdiction to make such an order as was made in the present case: that is to order a doctor, whether directly or indirectly, to treat a child in a manner contrary to his or her clinical judgment. I would go further. I find it difficult to conceive of a situation where it would be a proper exercise of the jurisdiction to make an order positively requiring a doctor to adopt a particular course of treatment in relation to a child, unless the doctor himself or herself were asking the court to make such an order. Usually all the court is asked, or needs, to do is to authorise a particular course of treatment where the person or body whose consent is requisite is unable or unwilling to do so."

2. Limits to jurisdiction However, jurisdiction was held not to lie in:

(a) *Fennbend v. Millar* (1988) 20 H.L.R. 19, C.A.: Unsuccessful application by landlord in possession proceedings to restrain a tenant from disposing of alternative accommodation available to him.

(b) *Associated Newspapers Group v. Insert Media Ltd* [1988] 1 W.L.R. 509, *per* Hoffman J.: It was held that possible damage to a plaintiff's business and goodwill, unfair trading, and the fact that an injunction is "just convenient" are not *per se*, sufficient grounds for granting an injunction. In that case, the plaintiff brought a passing-off action against the defendant for having advertising leaflets inserted in the plaintiff's newspapers. All was not lost to the plaintiff, however, because of the interlocutory relief which it had already been granted earlier: see *Associated Newspapers Group plc v. Insert Media Ltd; Express Newspapers plc v. Arnold* [1988] 1 W.L.R. 509, where Roch J. held that there was a serious issued to be tried, namely passing off (based on the submission that the advertiser misrepresented to the reader of the publications that they had the authority of the proprietor to insert the advertisements).

(c) *Ali v. Southwark London Borough Council* [1988] I.C.R. 567; [1988] IRLR 100, *per* Millet J.: Plaintiff employee failed to restrain defendant employer from hearing disciplinary proceedings against her. This was because the court would not restrain a domestic tribunal which had not completed a hearing unless it had acted improperly or it was inevitable that it would do so. A not dissimilar constellation of facts arose in *Walsh v. National Union of Public Employees, The Times*, March 22, 1988. An injunction had been granted to restrain the disciplinary committee of the defendant tribunal from hearing a complaint against the plaintiff. A judge refused to continue the injunction until trial of the action. On appeal against the refusal the Court of Appeal held that an interlocutory injunction would not lie in such circumstances unless the complaint to be considered was one which no reasonable tribunal properly directed could find proved, or the tribunal was clearly biased or prejudiced, or relevant rules had already been misapprehended or misapplied and it was likely that they would again.

(d) *Normid Housing Association v. Ralphs* [1989] 1 Lloyd's Rep. 265: Clients of a firm of architects who were suing the firm for defective work were held not to be entitled, as third parties, to an injunction restraining the firm from reaching a settlement with their insurers in respect of claims which they had made under the professional indemnity insurance policy.

(e) *Warren v. Mendy* [1989] 1 W.L.R. 853: A boxer had signed a management agreement with the plaintiff but due to differences between them, the boxer had issued a writ against the plaintiff making claims based *inter alia*, on, constructive trust. At that time, the boxer asked the defendant to advertise and manage his career. The plaintiff commenced proceedings to restrain the defendant from inducing a breach of the management contract. The plaintiff appealed against refusal of his application for interlocutory injunctions. The Court of Appeal refused to grant such injunctions as they would have had the effect of compelling the boxer to comply with an agreement to be managed by the plaintiff.

(f) *National Dock Labour Board v. Sabah Timber Co. Ltd, The Times*, January 5, 1988: An interlocutory injunction was granted to restrain an alleged breach by the defendants of the Dock Worker Employment Scheme 1967. An industrial tribunal subsequently decided that the defendant was not in breach of the scheme. The plaintiff intended to appeal against that decision and contended that the injunction should be continued on the basis that the plaintiff continued to argue that the defendants were in breach of the scheme. The Court of Appeal held that the industrial tribunal was the body specifically charged with deciding such questions. The issue had been decided in the defendant's favour and the Court of Appeal discharged the interlocutory injunctions.

(g) *Bullivant v. Ellis* [1987] I.C.R. 464, C.A.: This case is authority for the principle that when the court makes an order restricting a defendant's freedom to do business so as to prevent him from acquiring an unfair advantage in starting up in competition with the plaintiff through misuse of the plaintiff's confidential information, it should limit the order to the period that the advantage might reasonably have been expected to last. In this case the plaintiff, who specialised in under-pinning buildings, employed the defendant as managing director under a contract of employment which restrained him for 12 months after termination from doing business with any person who had done business with the plaintiff during a period of 12 months before termination. The Court of Appeal held that since the contract con-templated that any benefit from the confidential information would have ceased by 12 months after termination, the injunction should have been limited to that period. This decision has been followed by Carnwath J. in *CBT Systems UK Limited v. Campopiano* [1995] July 25 citing also *PSM International plc v. Whitehouse* [1992] IRLR 279.

(h) *C.B.S. Songs v. Amstrad Consumer Electronics plc* [1988] 3 W.L.R.144, C.A. (affirmed by H.L. [1988] A.C. 1013): This is authority for the principle that the alleged incitement to commit an offence under section 21(3) of the Copyright Act 1956 does not give rise to an equitable right for injunctive relief to prevent such alleged incitement.

(i) *Restraint against gypsies trespassing and committing nuisance on land within its area, some of which was privately owned: Bradford Metro-politan City Council v. Brown* (1987) 19 H.L.R. 16.

4 Drafting the order

1. Definition of terms—how wide? In *Hubbard v. Pitt* [1976] Q.B. 142, C.A., which was in the nature of a "picketing" case, counsel for the unsuccessful defendant argued that the terms of the injunction were too wide, in that it would prevent the defendants from doing that which (as was claimed) it was not unlawful for them to do, namely, to assemble outside the plaintiff's premises for the sole purpose of imparting or receiving information. Accepting for the purpose of the argument the validity of such claim by counsel, Orr L.J. held at p. 190 E-H:

> "I accept that the court must be careful not to impose an injunction in wider terms than are necessary to do justice in the particular case; but I reject the argument that the court is not entitled, when satisfied that justice required it, to impose an injunction which may for a limited time prevent the defendant from doing that which he would otherwise be at liberty to do.... In the present case, because it is important that interlocutory injunctions should not be too widely worded, we pressed Mr Turner-Samuels to suggest some alternative wording which would give proper protection to the plaintiffs, but the

only suggestion he was able to make, and I do not criticise him for failure to suggest a better, was that the defendants should be restrained from assembling outside the plaintiffs' premises otherwise than 'for the purposes of' or 'with a view to' imparting or receiving information. In my judgment, however, an injunction in such a form would be insufficient to do justice between the parties in that the issue to be decided on a complaint of breach of such an injunction would be the very issue to be decided at the trial, namely, with what purpose or what view the defendants have assembled."

(Note: Questions relating to picketing were considered by Scott J. in Thomas v. National Union of Mineworkers (South Wales Area) [1986] Ch. 20, which is authority for the proposition that mass picketing amounted to tortious intimidation. And in News Group Newspapers Ltd v. Society of Graphical and Allied Trades [1986] IRLR 337, Stuart-Smith J. held that dismissed employees picketing outside the new premises of their former employers were not at their place of work under section 15 of the Trade Union and Labour Relations Act 1974, and thus could not come within its immunity.)

2. Pre-judging the issue—an avoidable risk In *Hepworth Plastics Ltd v. Naylor Bros. (Clayware) Ltd* [1979] F.S.R. 521, Graham J. granted the following injunction:

"To restrain the defendants until judgment or further order from

(i) the manufacture, use sale or supply or offer for sale or supply of manhole inspection chambers substantially the same as exhibited as 'A H B 3' to the Affidavit of Andrew Hamilton Bell sworn herein or from otherwise infringing letters patent No. 1,447,227;

(ii) the sale or supply or offer for sale or supply in conjunction with chambers manufactured, sold or supplied by the defendants or any of them of manhole covers marked 'Plastidrain' or with any mark substantially the same thereas."

On appeal Buckley L.J. held:

"The injunction will not contain the phrase 'or otherwise infringing it'; it will be just the specific injunction in the form that we have agreed. The appellant will pay the respondents' cost of the appeal."

His rationale was (at p. 522):

"I would have thought that it was right to leave out the words 'or otherwise infringing,' because after all, you are seeking an interlocutory injunction to prevent a particular thing occurring pending trial; it is

47

not interlocutory relief to prevent any form of infringement pending trial."

In Staver Company Inc. v. Digitext Display Ltd [1985] F.S.R. 512, Scott J. had originally ordered that the defendants be restrained from "infringing the plaintiffs' copyright in six specified drawings." After the order the defendants redesigned certain units and sought, inter alia, a declaration that their units now fell outside the scope of the injunction. Scott J. observed at p. 521:

> "The discussion in this case has satisfied me that there are grave objections in principle to the granting of interlocutory injunctions in a form that appears to anticipate the plaintiffs' success at trial. In my view *interlocutory injunctions ought in cases like the present, and perhaps in many other types of case, to identify the prohibited acts in a manner which is not dependent on the resolution of factual triable issues.*" [Editors' emphasis.]

3. Problems with bad drafting—the standard of proof on the application to commit On an application to commit for breach, not only will the plaintiff have to prove that there was copyright infringement, he will have so to prove to the criminal burden of proof: *Deborah Building Equipment Ltd v. Scaffco Ltd, The Times*, November 5, 1986. It is in this context that the following ruling can be interpreted, set out in the headnote to *Chelsea man Plc v. Chelsea Girl Ltd* [1988] F.S.R. 217 at 218:

> "Where it was alleged that the defendant had broken the terms of an injunction or undertaking to the court, the requirement of proof beyond reasonable doubt related only to the allegation that the defendant had committed the acts complained of. It did not relate to the different question whether those acts, if proved to have been committed by the defendant, constituted a breach of the injunction or undertaking. Accordingly, the question whether the signs were capable of being read as CHELSEA MAN was not one which required or was susceptible of proof beyond reasonable doubt. It was a question of impression and was for the court, not witnesses, to decide."

Deborah Building Equipment Ltd v. Scaffco Ltd (ibid.) is also authority for the principle that unless the terms of the order were absolute and unqualified, a breach would not be proved unless the plaintiff also established that the defendant's disobedience to the order was wilful and deliberate. In *Re W. (Minors), The Times*, April 30, 1988, a local authority unsuccessfully applied to commit publishers and editors of newspapers for contempt of court, in publishing the name of two wards, because it could not establish, on the criminal standard of proof, that they had the requisite knowledge of the injunction.

4. Example of a difficulty in drafting the order—the terms of an advert In *Director General of Fair Trading v. Tobyward Ltd* [1989] 2 All E.R. 266, Hoffman J. ruled *inter alia* at 271 in the context of allegedly misleading advertisements:

> "In a case like this the formulation of the injunction must avoid extremes on either side. On the one hand it must not be so specific that by a small variation in the terms of the advertisement the advertiser can escape its effect and publish an advertisement which is nevertheless misleading in the same kind of way. On the other hand, it must not be in terms so general that the advertiser does not have a clear idea of what he is not allowed to do."

5. Summary A party who was subject to an interlocutory injunction should know what he could and could not do pending trial. As Lord Denning M.R. said in *Potters-Ballotini Ltd v. Weston-Baker* [1977] R.P.C. 202 at 206:

> "So there seems to me to be a great difficulty in defining what are the items of confidential information to which Potters would be entitled. We are given by Mr Leggat a most useful table showing 13 items. Some of them he had to acknowledge could not be said to be confidential although they were items which had been copied. But he pointed to others which were confidential, particularly part of the furnace and how it was made. He may succeed upon some items eventually, but it must be remembered that the injunction which is sought is in the most general terms. It is sought to restrain the defendants from using information, and so forth, obtained during their employment as to the workings of any processes, as to know-how and the like. That is uncertain in that extreme. *It is well established that an injunction ought to be such that the party affected can known with certainty what he is or is not allowed to do. There is no such certainty here.*" [Editors' emphasis.]

The importance of specifying in the injunction precisely what steps are to be restrained features predominantly in "confidentiality" cases—specifically what it is that the defendant is not to divulge. Similarly, in cases of alleged libel, the court has to know the words targeted, *inter alia*, to enable it to frame an injunction defining with reasonable precision what the defendant is to be restrained from publishing: *British Data Management plc. v. Boxer Commercial Removals plc. and Todd*, February 22, 1996, C.A. (unreported).

6. Duration Where an injunction is granted to extend over a certain day or until further order, the injunction can be dissolved at a date earlier than the date limited. But it cannot continue beyond such date without a fresh order: *Bolton v. London School Board* (1878) 7 Ch.D. 766.

5 The nature of a discretionary remedy

1. The law/equity distinction An injunction is an equitable remedy. Unlike the case of infringement of a right at common law, recourse to equitable relief does not automatically warrant remedy, even where it is proved or admitted that rights have been infringed. Whether the court will exercise its discretion to grant relief turns on a variety of factors.

2. The primary hurdles In most applications for interlocutory relief the plaintiff will have to surmount the following hurdles:
   (a) He must establish as a triable issue, the infringement of a right.
   (b) He must go on to show that the defendant threatens and intends, unless restrained, to continue to infringe that right.
   (c) He must prove that if such right is further infringed he will suffer injury for which damages are not a complete remedy.
In certain circumstances, even surmounting these hurdles may not be sufficient for the exercise of the court's discretion. For example, in defamation (and other cases akin, such as malicious falsehood) an injunction will not lie unless:
   (a) there is no real doubt that the words are defamatory; and
   (b) the defendant does not swear that he will be able to justify the words complained of; and
   (c) the defendant does not swear that he intends to rely on any other recognised defence, such as privilege (unless the evidence of malice is so overwhelming that the judge is driven to the conclusion that no reasonable jury could find otherwise, *i.e.* that it would be perverse to acquit the defendant of malice).

6 Factors affecting the exercise of the court's discretion

The cases reveal that the exercise of the court's discretion is affected by the following vitiating factors.
   (a) Fraud and "unclean hands"—see p. 61 *et seq.*
   (b) Acquiescence and delay. See p. 70 *et seq.*

7 Types of interlocutory injunctions

1. Interlocutory injunctions and interim injunctions These phrases are often used interchangeably. However, they may be interpreted thus.

(a) *Interlocutory injunction:* An order to preserve a particular set of circumstances pending full trial of the matters in dispute.

(b) *Interim injunction:* An order in the nature of an "interlocutory injunction" but restraining the defendant only until after a named day or further order (usually no more than a few days). Such an injunction remains in force until a named day, the order (for example) running thus: "Until 10.30 a.m. on Wednesday August 10 or so soon thereafter as counsel may be heard".

(*Note: In Savings & Investment Bank Ltd v. Gasco Investments (Netherlands) B.V.* (No. 2) [1988] Ch. 422, it was held that although in general, interlocutory proceedings were proceedings other than the trial of the action or its equivalent, an application to commit for breach of an injunction would be an interlocutory proceeding whether the injunction itself was interlocutory or final.)

2. The flexibility of the relief Depending on circumstances, the jurisdiction of the court may be invoked in the following instances:
    (a) after damage or *quia timet*;
    (b) "half-way house" injunctions;
    (c) for mandatory interlocutory injunctions.

3. *Quia timet* explored *Quia timet* actions are broadly applicable to the following types of case, *per* Lord Upjohn in *Redland Bricks Ltd v. Morris* [1970] A.C. 652 at 665:
    (a) Where the defendant has as yet done no hurt to the plaintiff but is threatening and intending (so the plaintiff alleges) to do works which will render irreparable harm to him or his property if carried to completion.
    (b) The type of case where the plaintiff has been fully recompensed both at law and in equity for the damage he has suffered but where he alleges that the earlier action of the defendant may lead to future causes of action—e.g., where the defendant has withdrawn support from his neighbour's land or where he has so acted in depositing his soil from his mining operation as to constitute a menace to the plaintiff's land.

4. "Timeo!"—is that enough? No:

> "But no one can obtain a *quia timet* order by merely saying 'Timeo'; he must aver and prove that what is going on is calculated to infringe his rights." (*Per* Lord Dunedin in *Att.-Gen. for Dominion of Canada v. Ritchie Contracting and Supply Co. Ltd* [1919] A.C. 999 at 1005.)

The principle to be distilled from the authorities is that an injunction *quia timet* will be granted only to restrain an apprehended or threatened injury where the injury is certain or very imminent, or where mischief of an overwhelming nature is likely to be done, such as destructive operations.

5. The "half-way house" injunction This reflects the inherent flexibility of the remedy, appropriate to "passing-off" actions:

(a) *First option:* Refusal of an injunction *with or without an order for speedy trial.* Falconer J. demonstrated the approach in *M.S. Associates v. Power* [1988] F.S.R. 242 at 252:

> "... I have come to the conclusion that the balance of convenience is against the grant of an injunction now. I am fortified in that view in that both parties are anxious to have a speedy trial and, if so asked, I will give the appropriate directions."

(Note: The ordering of a speedy trial does not prevent the grant of an interlocutory injunction: *Alfa Laval v. Wincanton Engineering* [1990] F.S.R. 583.)

(b) *Second option:* The grant of an injunction, which generally resolves the entirety of the proceedings.

(c) *Third option:* The middle course where, for example, the defendant is restrained from using a particular name without making it clear that it is different from the plaintiff. A not dissimilar approach was suggested by Sir Nicholas Browne-Wilkinson V.-C. in *Nationwide Building Society v. Nationwide Estate Agents Ltd* [1987] F.S.R. 579.

6. Mandatory interlocutory injunctions These are positive rather than negative orders, requiring the taking of certain steps. In *Locabail International Finance Ltd v. Agroexport* [1986] 1 W.L.R. 657, Mustill L.J. said at p. 663, citing from the 4th. ed. vol. 24 of Halsbury's *Laws of England*:

> "A mandatory injunction can be granted on an interlocutory application as well as at the hearing, but, *in the absence of special circumstances, it will not normally be granted.* However, if the case is clear and one which the court thinks ought to be decided at once, or if the act done is a simple and summary one which can be easily remedied, or if the defendant attempts to steal a march on the plaintiff ... a mandatory injunction will be granted on an interlocutory application." [Editors' emphasis.]

The court's reluctance to grant "mandatory" relief is reflected in the Court of Appeal decision in *Gooden v. Kelly*, February 29, 1996, (unreported), relating to the issues of "nuisance" and trespass to land.

7. Examples The following situations may warrant application for a mandatory interlocutory injunction.

(a) *If there is no arguable defence:* An order for delivery up of goods (see p. 297. See also *Films Rover International Ltd v. Cannon Films Sales Ltd* [1987] 1 W.L.R. 670).

(b) *In an industrial dispute case:* Ancillary to the order restraining conduct, a mandatory order requiring the union to withdraw such instructions which it has given and to publish such withdrawal and in urgent cases to give notice to the Press Association that such instructions have been withdrawn. A not dissimilar type of relief emerges from the case of *Sealink UK v. National Union of Seamen, The Times*, February 5, 1988. Despite the grant of a injunction on February 1, 1988 ordering the defendant to call off a strike, the strike went ahead on February 2. The plaintiff obtained leave to serve a motion for sequestration of the union's assets. The motion was adjourned on February 4, on the defendant's undertaking to instruct its members to call off the strike. The issue resolved itself to the penalty to be imposed on the defendant for its delay in obeying the order to call off the strike. Michael Davies J. held that the court must consider whether the union had done enough, had acted quickly enough and whether what it had done was genuine. He was of the view that the defendant's instructions were not merely play-acting. He took the view that such instructions were effective and immediately effective. The penalty thus had to reflect the two to three-day delay from the making of the order until steps were taken to call off the strike, the fact that the defendant's officials had made imprudent comments, that the defendant had made a full and frank apology and would pay costs on an indemnity basis. The fine was ordered to be £7,500.

(c) *In clear cases:* Either where the court thought that the matter ought to be decided at once, or where the injunction was directed at a simple and summary act which could easily be remedied or where the defendant had attempted to steal a march on the plaintiff: *Locobail International Finance v. Agroexport* [1986] 1 W.L.R. 657, C.A.; [1986] 1 Lloyd's Rep. 317. But such relief is generally not appropriate to unpaid wages: *Jakeman v. South West Thames Regional Health Authority* [1990] IRLR 62.

8. Standard of proof in applications for the mandatory order Since a mandatory injunction is likely to be more drastic in its effects than a prohibitory injunction, the case has to be unusually strong and clear, even if it is sought to enforce a contractual obligation. This is a different and higher standard than was required for a prohibitory injunction: *Leisure Data v. Bell* [1988] F.S.R. 367 C.A. and *Jakeman v. South West Thames Regional Health Authority* [1990] IRLR 62. This standard was reached in *Harrington v. Polytechnic of North London* [1984] 1 W.L.R. 1293, where it was held that the court did have jurisdiction to require 14 named members of the polytechnic staff to swear affidavits as to whether they could or could not identify persons photographed whilst such persons were engaged in preventing the plaintiff (by reason of his political beliefs) from obtaining access to the polytechnic.

9. Form of order A mandatory injunction must be expressed in such a form that, except in very exceptional circumstances, the person against whom it is granted knows exactly in fact what he has to do: *Redland Bricks Ltd v. Morris* [1970] A.C. 652. Where, however, the evidence establishes that a trade secret has been wrongfully taken, the injunction should not be limited to precise formulations, since the restraint may then be avoided by small variations: *Johnson & Bloy (Holdings) Ltd v. Wolstenholme Rink Plc* [1989] F.S.R. 135 C.A. On the other hand, an injunction simply restraining the use of the plaintiff's secrets will be too vague. The terms of any injunction must be framed in sufficient detail to enable the defendant to know exactly what information he is not free to use: *Lock International Plc v. Beswick* [1989] 3 All E.R. 373.

10. Duration of interlocutory orders and undertakings Orders (and undertakings in lieu) remain in force until discharged by the court. An order made by a court of unlimited jurisdiction, even though irregular, must be obeyed unless and until it is set aside, and therefore disobedience to an interlocutory injunction which is irregular amounts to a contempt of court: *Isaacs v. Robertson* [1985] A.C. 97. Whereas in the Queen's Bench Division one can give an undertaking "until further order," in the Chancery Division, it is "until trial or further order." In this context it should be noted that in *Kangol Industries Ltd v. Alfred Bray & Sons Ltd* [1953] 1 All E.R. 444, where in interlocutory proceedings the defendants gave an undertaking to deliver up confidential documents, the court ordered an affidavit verifying compliance.

8 Interactions

1. Undertakings and injunctions The sanction for breach of an undertaking is identical to that of an injunction. Thus if the plaintiff consents, the court may accept an undertaking by counsel or solicitor on behalf of the defendant in lieu of an injunction in the terms of the interlocutory injunction sought.

2. The interface between application for an interlocutory injunction application and final orders If the parties so desire and consent, the summons for an interlocutory injunction may be treated as the trial of action and the agreed terms may be embodied in a consent judgment or order.

3. Interlocutory injunction applications and directions for trial The judge may order an early or speedy trial if he grants the interlocutory injunction. He has a similar jurisdiction even when the injunction is refused: Ord. 29, r.5. In such circumstances the judge will give the necessary directions for the further conduct of the action, such as:

(a) the service of pleadings (or ordering the affidavits to stand as the pleadings);
(b) an order for the exchange of lists of documents and exceptions;
(c) directions to setting down and application being made to the Clerk of the Lists for a fixed date for the trial.

Note: The ordering of a speedy trial does not prevent the grant of an interlocutory injunction: *Alfa Laval v. Wincanton Engineering* [1990] F.S.R. 583.)

4. Final orders At the full trial (if the plaintiff so wishes) a court may be expected to make an injunction order even if the defendant is content to volunteer an undertaking: *Royal Insurance Co. Ltd v. G. & S. Assured Investment Co. Ltd* [1972] 1 Lloyd's Rep. 267. Furthermore, a court is justified in granting an injunction to restrain an obvious and admittedly actionable wrong, even if the defendant offers an undertaking to continue in a way which was not contrary to the law: *Solihull Metropolitan Borough Council v. Maxfern* [1977] 1 W.L.R. 127.

9 Affidavit practice

1. Affidavits-a vehicle for facts, not law Roskill L.J. gave guidance in *Alfred Dunhill Ltd v. Sunoptics S.A.* [1979] F.S.R. 337 at 352:

> "I hope it is not out of place to say at this stage that the affidavits filed on both sides are in at least two cases very much too long. Affidavits are designed to place facts, whether disputed or otherwise, before the tribunal for whose help they are prepared. They are not designed as a receptacle for or as a vehicle for legal arguments. *Draftsmen of affidavits should not, as a general rule, put into the mouths of the intended deponents legal arguments of which those deponents are unlikely ever to have heard.* Legal arguments, especially in interlocutory proceedings, should come from the mouths of those best qualified to advance them and not be put into the mouths of the deponents. There has been much unnecessary paper in this case brought about by the inclusion of legal arguments in affidavits." [Editors' emphasis.]

2. Riposte of the court to such affidavits *Per* Browne L.J. in *Alfred Dunhill* (*ibid.*) at p. 373:

"There is one feature of this barrage and counter-barrage of affidavits on which I think that comment ought to be made. Some of the affidavits, in particular the second defendant's first affidavit, have been made the vehicle for numerous submissions of law and for forensic argument, wholly out of place in an affidavit, as it would be in the oral evidence of the witness. If such a document were to be admitted at all, there might be much to be said for giving the Court power (perhaps the Court has inherent power) to treat the affidavit as though it were a party's brief to the Court in United States procedure: with the consequence that Counsel's time for oral argument would be drastically restricted."

3. "Hearsay"

(a) *R.S.C., Ord. 41, r.5:* (i) Subject to Ord. 14, r. 2(2) and 4(2) to Ord. 86, rule 2(1) to paragraph (2) of this rule and to any order made under Ord. 38, rule 3, an affidavit may contain only such facts as the deponent is able of his own knowledge to prove. (ii) An affidavit sworn for the purpose of being used in interlocutory proceedings may contain statements of information or belief with the sources and grounds thereof.

(b) *Reason for allowing hearsay:* The purpose of rule 5(2) was explained by Peter Gibson J. in *Savings and Investment Bank Ltd v. Gasco Investments (Netherlands) BV* [1984] 1 W.L.R. 271 at 282 F-G:

"To my mind the purpose of rule 5(2) is to enable a deponent to put before the court in interlocutory proceedings, frequently in circumstances of great urgency, facts which he is not able of his own knowledge to prove but which, the deponent is informed and believes, can be proved by means which the deponent identifies by specifying the sources and grounds of his information and belief. What the sub-rule allows the deponent to state that he has obtained from another must, in my judgment, be limited to what is admissible as evidence."

(c) *Hearsay—meaning:* Peter Gibson J. made clear that hearsay must be first-hand—second-hand hearsay falls outside the rule. See, however, the dicta of Phillips J. in *Deutsche Ruckversichering Aktiengesellschaft v. Wallbrook Insurance Co. Ltd and Others, The Times,* May 6, 1994 at 58.

(d) *Importance of compliance:* Inclusion of hearsay in an affidavit without reference to source of information and grounds for belief is inadmissible and liable to be struck out: *Re Young J.L. Manufacturing Co. Ltd* [1900] 2 Ch. 753. Rigby L.J. said at 754–755:

"In the present day, in utter defiance of the order (Rules of the

Supreme Court, 1883, Order XXXVIII., r.(3)(1)), solicitors have got into a practice of filing affidavits in which the deponent speaks not only of what he knows but also of what he believes, without giving the slightest intimation with regard to what his belief is founded on. Or he says, 'I am informed,' without giving the slightest intimation where he has got his information. Now, every affidavit of that kind is utterly irregular, and, in my opinion, the only way to bring about a change in that irregular practice is for the judge, in every case of the kind, to give a direction that the costs of the affidavit, so far as it relates to matters of mere information or belief, shall be paid by the person responsible for the affidavit. At any rate, speaking for myself, I should be ready to give such a direction in any such case. The point is a very important one indeed. I frequently find affidavits stuffed with irregular matter of this sort. I have protested against the practice again and again, but no alteration takes place. The truth is that the drawer of the affidavit thinks he can obtain some improper advantage by putting in a statement on information and belief, and he rests his case upon that. I never pay the slightest attention myself to affidavits of that kind, whether they be used on interlocutory applications or on final ones, because the rule is perfectly general-that, when a deponent makes a statement on his information and belief, he must state the ground of that information and belief."

And Vaughan-Williams L.J. added at 755:

"With regard to affidavits of the sort before us, it is not quite a sufficient or satisfactory remedy to throw upon the party upon whose behalf such affidavits are put forward the liability of paying the costs of those affidavits. The only more satisfactory remedy is one which I am aware is difficult, if not impossible, to apply as the law stands: namely, that no one should pay for these affidavits at all, and that the solicitor who has drawn these affidavits and made copies of them, and so forth, should be left out of pocket thereby."

(e) *Striking out—when?* In a clear and obvious case, the court may be prepared to strike out improper hearsay, on the grounds of "manifest convenience", as Peter Gibson J. said in *Savings and Investment Bank Ltd v. Gasco Investments (Netherlands) BV (ibid.).*

(f) *Instead of striking out—why not just ignore?* Peter Gibson J. said at 278 C–F:

"I shall deal with Mr Parker's last point first, as if correct it would absolve me from the task of considering this application further. Mr Lindsay explained the reasons why he has applied to strike out as twofold. First the defendants need to know before the effective hearing of the motion whether they should go to the expense and trouble of putting in a large amount of additional evidence to counter what is contained in the report. He points out that a decision on this point may assist the plaintiff as well, which may wish, if the passages are struck out, to put in admissible evidence to prove what it now seeks to show by way of reference to the inspectors' reports. Secondly for a judge other than the judge hearing the motion to strike out the passages in the affidavit would avoid the motions judge having to perform the mental gymnastics of putting out of mind the lengthy inadmissible passages to which he would have been referred. In my judgment on both of those grounds it is right for me to deal with this application now. I keep well in mind that I am not hearing the motion, and in the circumstances I think that I should only strike out if satisfied that this is a plain and obvious case for doing so. Judges frequently have to take decisions on evidence in advance of a main hearing to be determined by another judge, and there is a manifest convenience in the course on which the defendants have embarked. It is of course true that judges are accustomed to put out of mind matters which they have seen or heard and judged to be inadmissible, but the greater the amount of such material the more desirable it seems to me to have the question of striking out determined in advance."

4. Affidavit practice points

  (a) The affidavit must point out clearly the alleged right infringed or threatened.
  (b) A reference to "information and belief" is misconceived if not accompanied by a statement as to the source of the information and grounds for the belief: See R.S.C. Ord. 41, r.5. But the reference need not be to an original source. In *Deutsche Ruckversichering Aktiengesellschaft v. Walbrook Insurance Co Ltd and Others*, *The Times*, May 6, 1994, Phillips J. *inter alia* said:

> "While agreeing with the judge in *Gasco* that the purpose of rule 5(2) was to enable a deponent to put before the court, frequently in circumstances of very great urgency, facts which he was not able of his own knowledge to prove, his Lordship could not conclude that, at the interlocutory stage, a deponent must identify as the source of his information or belief an original source of evidence which would be admissible at the trial.
>
> The object of the rule militated against placing that restriction upon the natural meaning of its words. In a situation of urgency a plaintiff might well not have time to identify or trace evidence which would be admissible at the trial.

If he had learned of facts via an intermediate source which there was good reason to believe would itself have had access to primary sources of information, his Lordship could see no good reason for precluding the plaintiff relying upon that intermediate source as a ground for seeking interlocutory relief.

Perhaps the most important form of interlocutory relief was the injunction. The power of the court to grant an interlocutory injunction was one that should be flexible and not fettered by the technical rules of admissibility of evidence that applied at trial.

An original source would normally carry much more weight than an intermediate source, and where original sources were known, they had to be identified. But it did not follow that intermediate sources could not be referred to or relied upon.

Ultimately, it had to be for the court to weigh all the material to decide whether the applicant had made out his case." [Editors' emphasis.]

(c) An injunction granted prior to the statement of claim will probably be discharged if the statement of claim is inconsistent with the affidavits upon which the injunction was granted.

(d) Affidavits should be sworn after the writ is issued: *Silber v. Lewin* (1889) 33 S.J. 757. But where the affidavit was sworn two days before the issue of the writ, an order was made on the plaintiff's undertaking to have the affidavit resworn and filed: *Green v. Prior* (1886) W.N. 50. However, where an *ex parte* injunction was obtained on the terms that the writ should be amended by adding a plaintiff, in order that an undertaking, as to damages, might be given on his behalf, and it appeared, on motion to dissolve the injunction, that some days had elapsed without the writ being amended, the court at once dissolved the injunction, on the ground that the plaintiff had not fulfilled the condition on which it was granted: *Spanish General Agency Corporation v. Spanish Corporation* (1891) 63 L.T. 161.

(e) An affidavit filed on behalf of a plaintiff should depose to the ability of the plaintiff to pay pursuant to an undertaking as to damages: *Intercontex v. Schmidt* [1988] F.S.R. 574.

5. *Ex parte* affidavits—the need to demonstrate promptitude Since the granting of an *ex parte* injunction is the exercise of a very extraordinary jurisdiction, the court will look closely at the time at which the plaintiff first had notice of the act complained of. The court's purpose is to prevent an improper order being made against a party in its absence. The affidavit should therefore state the precise time at which he or those acting for him became aware of the threatened injury and go on to show why the court should grant the order before service on the defendant. In this context, Ord. 8, r.2(1) sets out motion procedure *ex parte*. Thus in *Morny Ltd v.*

Ball & Rogers (1975) [1978] F.S.R. 91, Goulding J. said at 94:

> "Further, the plaintiff appears to have acted promptly as soon as the gift pack appeared in advertisements and the preference given in the Cyanamid speeches to preserving the status quo again turns, like the financial comparison, in favour of granting relief at this stage. Except where an application by motion may properly be made *ex parte*, no motion shall be made without previous notice to the parties affected thereby, *but the court, if satisfied that the delay caused by proceeding in this ordinary way would or might entail irreparable or serious mischief may make an order* ex parte *on such terms as to costs or otherwise....*" [Editors' emphasis.]

10 An overview of the flexibility of interlocutory relief and related orders

1. Avoiding tunnel vision The problem occasioned by unduly detailed analysis of a particular remedy (*e.g. Mareva*) is that potentially it tunnels the vision to the extent of concealing its relationship with other forms of relief; such as:

(a) *the interaction of a* Mareva *and Ord. 13:* — *Stewart Chartering Ltd v. C & O Management S.A.* [1980] 1 W.L.R. 460 (Practice Note);

(b) *the interaction of a* Mareva *and Ord. 14* — for example, a defendant's summons in the Commercial Court to discharge may in appropriate circumstances be matched by a plaintiff's Ord. 14 summons.

2. The general protective powers of the court Quite apart from the jurisdiction of the court to grant *Mareva* injunctions (including the power of delivery up (see *CBS United Kingdom Ltd v. Lambert* [1983] 1 Ch. 37 discussed at p. 175) and the jurisdiction in relation to *Anton Piller* orders), the court has other protective powers which may be of use as a pre-emptive tactic.

3. Specific powers Thus, the court has jurisdiction in relation to the following:

(a) the safe custody of the subject matter of the action pending trial under Ord. 29, r. 2 (Interim Preservation Order): see p. 292.

(b) The interim delivery up of goods which are the subject of a claim under section 4 of the Torts (Interference with Goods) Act 1977 under Ord. 29, r.2(A) (Interim Delivery of Goods): see p. 29.

(c) The immediate sale of perishable or deteriorating property other than land prior to trial under Ord. 29, r.4 (Sale of Perishable or Deteriorating Property).

(d) The inspection of documents/property: sections 33–35 of the Supreme Court Act 1981; Ord. 24, r.7 and Ord. 29, rr. 2, 3 and 7(a).

B: VITIATING FACTORS

1 Fraud and unclean hands

1. The Church of Scientology cases
  (a) In *Hubbard v. Vosper* [1972] 2 Q.B. 84 at 101A, Megaw L.J. gave as the reason for refusing the Church of Scientology an interlocutory injunction restraining publication by a former disciple of its confidential tracts, the fact that:

   "... there is here evidence that the plaintiffs are or have been *protecting their secrets by deplorable means* such as evidenced by this code of ethics; and that being so, they do not come with clean hands to this court in asking this court to protect those secrets by the equitable remedy of an injunction. [Editors' emphasis.]"

  (b) *Church of Scientology of California v. Miller, The Times,* October 23, 1987, the plaintiff applied for an interlocutory injunction to restrain publication of a biography of the church's founder, submitting that the church owned the copyright in particular photographs featuring in the work and that it contained confidential information communicated to an employee of the church. The Court of Appeal refused the injunction and held:
   (i) Delay—the church had not made its application until the preparations for publication of the book were far advanced.
   (ii) Motive—the intention of the church was to cause maximum embarrassment and disruption.
   (iii) Loss—if publication was restrained until trial, the publishers would be exposed to considerable losses.
   (iv) Public interest—the public interest in exposing the assertions made by the church's founder to public scrutiny far outweighed any duty of confidentiality which might attach to the information.

2. The Tower Crane case In *Woollerton and Wilson v. Costain Ltd* [1970] 1 W.L.R. 411, for the facts of which see p. 976, Stamp J. said at 416B–C:

   "... but if I had thought that the defendant in this case had deliberately

61

proceeded upon the footing that the importance of the work would prevent the court from granting an injunction, I would have made [a different] order...."

The actual decision in the Tower Crane case was doubted in *Charrington v. Simons & Co. Ltd* [1971] 1 W.L.R. 598.

3. Agent provocateur In *Walt Disney Productions v. Gurvitz* [1982] F.S.R. 446, Vinelott J. held that the plaintiff was entitled to place trap orders with a defendant with a view to proceeding with discovery, even after that defendant in *Anton Piller* proceedings had given an undertaking not to deal in the illicit materials.

4. Companies used as a cloak for fraud In *Idmac Industrial Designers and Management Consultants B.V. v. Midland Bank Ltd, The Times,* October 8, 1981, C.A., Templeman L.J. is reported as saying:

"... revelling in its own fraud Idmac had the impertinence to come to a court of equity claiming relief. It was high time that all clearing banks looked very carefully at all their subsidiaries in the Channel Islands and the Isle of Man to ensure that there was no longer any scope for those *companies being used as a cloak for fraud.* It also seemed to his Lordship that it was time that the Government should look into the position. Following the *American Cyanamid* decision [1975] A.C. 396 it will still open to the court to take an equitable view and to refuse to grant an injunction where the merits were one way and where the case put forward by a plaintiff asking for relief was unmeritorious or lacking in substance." [Editors' emphasis.]

The rationale for this approach goes back long into the history of the Court of Equity, and is well expressed by Kekewich J. in *Williams v. Quebrada Railway, Land and Copper Co.* [1895] 2 Ch. 751 where he said at 755:

"... where there is anything of an underhand nature or approaching to fraud, especially in commercial matters, where there should be the veriest good faith, *the whole transaction should be ripped up and disclosed in all its nakedness to the light of the court....* Then it is alleged that the company was insolvent, and that they found it useless for them to continue to carry on business and they had to stop, but that in order to prevent for a time this inevitable result they gave a charge in favour of their agents, and, as the plaintiff alleges, they did it in such a way as to defeat the holders of first debentures. That is what I understand the plaintiff's case to be, and it is said that is not a charge of fraud. It is difficult to say it is not commercial dishonestly.

It is, in my opinion, commercial dishonesty of the very worst type; and that is fraud." [Editors' emphasis.]

And see *A.B. v. C.D.E.* [1982] R.P.C. 509.

2 Failure fully to disclose material facts

1. The principle Suppression of a material fact may also taint the hands of an applicant for equitable relief. This was the position in *Ross v. Buxton* [1888] W.N. 55, and led to the discharge of an *ex parte* injunction. In *R. v. Kensington Income Tax Commissioners, ex p. Princess Edmond de Polignac* [1917] 1 K.B. 486 at 509, *per* Warrington L.J.:

> "It is perfectly well settled that a person who makes an *ex parte* application to the court—that is to say, in the absence of the person who will be affected by that which the court is asked to do—*is under an obligation to the court to make the fullest possible disclosure of all material facts within his knowledge*, and if he does not make that fullest possible disclosure, then he cannot obtain any advantage from the proceedings and he will be deprived of any advantage he may have already obtained by means of the order which has thus wrongly been obtained by him. That is perfectly plain and requires no authority to justify it. [Editors' emphasis.]"

Similarly, Davies L.J. said in *Beese v. Woodhouse* [1970] 1 W.L.R. 586 at 590:

> "The second point is that it is fundamental to any *ex parte* application for an injunction that the party applying for it should show the utmost good faith in making the application, and that the doctrine of *uberrimae fidei* in effect applies. There is no doubt that that is so. We were referred to two authorities in support of it, which clearly establish that proposition: *Dalglish v. Jarvie* (1850) 2 Mac. & G. 231, where the proposition is clearly stated by Rolfe B., at p. 243, and that passage is adopted and followed in *Rex v. Kensington Income Tax Commissioners, ex p. Princess Edmond de Polignac* [1917] 1 K.B. 486, 505." [Editors' emphasis.]

One reason for the principle of disclosure is the issue of prejudice to the defendant. Saville J. said in *Commercial Bank v. A* [1989] 2 Lloyd's Rep 319:

> "The second factor was that the plaintiff should have disclosed the preliminary step which it had taken to obtain security in Greece. I agree that this should have been but was not disclosed. In my view, however, *no prejudice was caused to the second defendant in this respect*

since those applications were in their initial stages and the failure to disclose is not (to my mind) anything like sufficiently grave to cause the Court to discharge the order...." [Editors' emphasis.]

2. Dig and probe The duty to make full disclosure in appropriate cases requires that the plaintiff makes sufficient enquiries before making his application. The legal advisers should probe and dig into the background of the case. This is particularly so in the case of *Mareva* and *Anton Piller* orders. In *Jeffrey Rogers Knitwear Productions Ltd v. Vinola (Knitwear) Manufacturing Co Ltd* [1985] F.S.R. 184, an *Anton Piller* order was set aside with costs on a common fund basis because insufficient enquiries had been made by the plaintiff.

3. Full and frank—what does it mean in practice? In *Sumitomo Heavy Industries Ltd v. Oil and Gas Natural Commission* [1994] 1 Lloyd's Rep. 45, Potter J. described what he wanted in an affidavit with the phrase "reasonably detached appreciation of the case."

4. Full disclosure does not mean overloading the court There is a difference between disclosing material facts, and flooding the court with unnecessary documents. Lloyd L.J. said in *National Bank of Sharjah v. Dellborg*, *The Times*, December 24, 1992:

> "The material facts at the *ex parte* stage were those which were necessary to enable the judge to exercise his discretion properly and fairly between the parties, bearing in mind that he had not at that stage heard the defendants' side of the case, and bearing also in mind the hardship and inconvenience which a *Mareva* injunction caused.
>
> But *the place to disclose the facts, both favourable and adverse, was in the affidavit and not in the exhibits.* No doubt it would usually be convenient to exhibit a few key documents where it was necessary to do so to explain the case.
>
> But the recent tendency to overload the case at the *ex parte* stage and to burden the judge with masses of documents in case something was left out ought to be firmly resisted.
>
> If the facts were not fairly stated in the affidavit it would not assist the plaintiff to be able to point to some exhibit from which the fact might be extracted." [Editors' emphasis.]

5. Brevity and public policy This was emphasised by Staughton L.J. in *Derby & Co. Ltd v. Weldon (No. 6)* [1990] 1 W.L.R. 1139 at 1153:

> "The growth of pre-trial restraint over the past 15 years has had a number of consequences. The most obvious, although not perhaps the most important, is an increasing demand on the time of the courts

and judges. No doubt it is desirable that our judicial system should include measures to ensure that judgments, when eventually given, are enforceable; and it can be argued that the resources of the system must be increased so as to make such measures available. But the amount that the country can spend on courts and judges is finite, just as is the amount that it can spend on the National Health Service. Since pre-trial business tends to have priority, an increase in it may result in additional delay for widows and orphans and claims for damages, and for persons waiting to be tried for crime."

A reflection of this same theme, brevity, is to be distilled from the following dicta of Slade L.J. in *Normid Housing v. Ralphs* [1989] 1 Lloyd's Rep. 265 at 254:

"As a general rule I think it would be most undesirable if on *Mareva* applications the Court began to concern itself with the merits or otherwise of proposed settlements of claims against third parties unless there were clear prima facie evidence that the settlements would be in bad faith or would be collusive."

6. Disclosure—A *Mareva* example The point arose for consideration also in *Bank of Mellat v. Nikpour* [1985] F.S.R. 87. In *ex parte* proceedings: (a) The original writ disclosed no cause of action; (b) the first amendment pleaded a "loan"; (c) the second amendment pleaded that moneys had been wrongfully credited to the defendant (a former chief executive of the plaintiff bank). The injunction was discharged on the grounds that there had not been full and proper disclosure on the original *ex parte* application. Sir John Donaldson M.R. said:

"This principle that no injunction obtained *ex parte* shall stand if it has been obtained in circumstances in which there was a breach of the duty to make the fullest and frankest disclosure is of great antiquity. Indeed, it is so well enshrined in the law that it is difficult to find authority for the proposition; we all know it; it is trite law. But happily we have been referred to a dictum of Lord Justice Warrington in the case of *R. v. Kensington Income Tax Commissioners, ex p. Princess Edmond de Polignac* [*ibid.*], at 509. He said:

'It is perfectly well settled that a person who makes an *ex parte* application to the court—that is to say, in the absence of the person who will be affected by that which the court is asked to do—is under an obligation to the court to make the fullest possible disclosure of all material facts within his knowledge, and if he does not make that fullest possible disclosure, then he cannot obtain any advantage from the proceedings, and he will be deprived of any advantage he may have already obtained by means of the order which has thus wrongly been obtained by him.' "

See also *Block v. Nicholson* [1987] C.L.Y. 3064.

7. Disclosure—An *Anton Piller* example In *Thermax Ltd v. Schott Industrial Glass Ltd* [1981] F.S.R. 289, the plaintiffs obtained an *Anton Piller* order, on the basis of their fear that the defendants were infringing their registered design and would suppress evidence of such infringement. The plaintiffs, *inter alia*, deposed to the fact that the defendant company was run by three ex-directors of the plaintiffs and against whom the plaintiffs had already commenced separate proceedings for breach of confidence. What the plaintiffs failed to do was disclose the following material facts.

   (i) The defendant company was a member of a group of companies controlled by the Carl Zeiss Foundation.
  (ii) In correspondence relating to the earlier proceedings between the parties' respective solicitors, the plaintiffs had sought and been refused inspection of the defendants' premises. Browne-Wilkinson J. set aside the mandatory provisions of the *Anton Piller* order, holding that on an *ex parte* application the party seeking relief must make full disclosure to the court of all matters within his knowledge and that if he fails to do so, even where that failure was an error of judgment only and not deliberate, the order must be discharged without investigating its merits.

8. A "piling *Mareva* on *Piller*" example In *International Bank & Trust Corporation Ltd v. Joacs Luis Perestrello* (1985, C.A.T. October 15), there was a major international battle for the control of the management of the bank. *Anton Piller* and *Mareva* orders were discharged on appeal through material non-disclosure. Slade L.J. explained the principle thus:

> "The grounds of the appeal are in effect that in its evidence before Mr Justice Tudor Price the bank failed to disclose highly material facts within its knowledge, and that in the circumstances and in accordance with well established principles Mr Justice Drake was bound to discharge the *ex parte* injunction without further enquiry into its merits. The relevant principles are, or should be, well known to all practitioners. The leading case on the subject of non-disclosure in this case is the decision of this court in *The King v. Kensington Income Tax Commissioners* [1917] 1 K.B. 486. Lord Justice Warrington stated the principles thus (at 509):
>
>> 'It is perfectly well settled that a person who makes an ex parte application to the Court—that is to say, in the absence of the person who will be affected by that which the Court is asked to

do—is under an obligation to the Court to make the fullest possible disclosure of all material facts within his knowledge, and if he does not make that fullest possible disclosure, then he cannot obtain any advantage from the proceedings, and he will be deprived of any advantage he may have already obtained by means of the order which has thus wrongly been obtained by him.'

Lord Cozens-Hardy M.R. (at 505) stated that in such a case where there has not been full disclosure:

'... the court ought not to go into the merits of the case, but simply say "we will not listen to your application because of what you have done."

'The particular relief claimed in the present case, as stated previously, included an *Anton Piller* order. Mr Justice Browne-Wilkinson had some pertinent comments to make in this context in *Thermax Ltd v. Schott Industrial Glass Ltd* [1981] F.S.R. 289. He said (at 298):

'As time goes on and the granting of Anton Piller orders becomes more and more frequent, there is a tendency to forget how serious an intervention they are in the privacy and rights of defendants. One is also inclined to forget the stringency of the requirements as laid down by the Court of Appeal. In my judgment, the rule of full disclosure to the court is almost more important in Anton Piller cases than in other ex parte applications. Since Anton Piller orders give compulsory rights of inspection, once those inspections have taken place, the information procured from it is in the hands of the other side and the situation is irreversible. I therefore think it is very important indeed that in making applications it should be in the forefront of everybody's mind that the court must be fully informed of all the facts that are relevant to the weighing operation which the court has to make in deciding whether or not to grant the order.'

I would respectfully agree with these comments. I also think that the learned judge's reference to the 'weighing operation' provides helpful guidance as to what are the material facts which have to be disclosed on an *ex parte* application. If the facts are likely to be relevant to the relevant weighing operation which the court has to make, then they are in my opinion material facts. Mr Justice Goulding applied much the same test in *Wardle Fabrics Ltd v. G. Maristis Ltd* [1984] F.S.R. 263, which is another case concerning an application for an *Anton Piller* order. He held that, on an *ex parte* application for such an order, the court must be fully informed of all the facts that are relevant to the weighing operation referred to by Mr Justice Browne-Wilkinson.

He made another important point—that is that the absence of any intention on the part of the plaintiff or its advisers positively to mislead or unfairly influence the court by suppression of material facts would not relieve the plaintiff from the usual consequence of a breach of the duty of disclosure."

9. But not all facts are material In the *Anton Piller* case of *Gallery Cosmetics Ltd v. Number 1* [1981] F.S.R. 556 (European Ct.), Nourse J. held:

(i) A statement in an affidavit sworn on May 18 that the plaintiffs had been informed by customers "in the past few days" of the defendants' intention to produce the perfumes complained of did not amount to a material non-disclosure, since it was apparent on a fair reading of the plaintiffs' evidence that the matter had in fact first come to their attention at about the beginning of May.

(ii) Neither the fact that the parties had traded in the past nor a dispute between them concerning the alleged poaching of a secretary, were sufficiently material that the omission to mention them required the order to be discharged.

(iii) Where freehold owners were subject to a mortgage of about £100,000, this did not mean that part of the plaintiffs' evidence was not as full and frank as it ought to have been, when it appeared that the premises were worth about £170,000 and the quantifiable damage suffered by the defendants as a result of the execution of the order was about £6,000 or £7,000. "The points taken by the defendants were not sufficient, either individually or cumulatively, to entitle them to have the order set aside."

10. The defendant also should disclose Similarly, a failure to be candid on the part of the defendant may render the court more amenable to the plaintiffs' application. In the passing-off case of *Dunhill (Alfred) Ltd v. Sunoptics S.A.* [1979] F.S.R. 337 at 476, Megaw L.J. on appeal said:

"It is, of course, for the plaintiffs to make out their case for an interlocutory injunction. But when, on these questions of balance of convenience, it emerges that the *evidence adduced by the defendants is so defective in such important respects*, and the court below appears in some respects to have been misled thereby, that is a factor which cannot be said to be irrelevant in assessing the balance of convenience. It must at least reduce the reluctance which this court would feel in departing from the decision of the court below on a matter of this nature." [Editors' emphasis.]

11. Bad drafting not necessarily fatal In *I.T.C. Film Distributors Ltd v.*

Video Exchange Ltd (No. 2) (1982) 126 S.J. 672, the plaintiffs obtained an *Anton Piller* order, having, *inter alia*, mentioned to the court through counsel, that the police were interested in the defendants in relation to "adult films," and that they proposed a "visitation at about the same time" as it was intended to serve the *Anton Piller* order. In fact the police executed a search warrant concurrently with the execution of the *Anton Piller* order, prompting an application to vary or discharge the order by reference to the court having been deceived. Lawton L.J. held:

> "It should be stressed that those who swore such affidavits must take the greatest care to ensure that what was said was accurate. However, it did not follow that, because the affidavit was sloppily drafted, the plaintiffs were excluded from relief."

12. *Ex parte* cases generally On an application for an *ex parte* injunction, the plaintiff should inform the court if the defendant has given notice of intention to defend: *Mexican Co. v. Maldonado* [1890] W.N. 8 referring to *Harrison v. Cockerell* (1817) 3 Mer. 1. Note, however, the reaction of the Court of Appeal in *Re All Starr Video Ltd, The Times*, March 25, 1993, C.A. in the context of a *Mareva* injunction which had been applied for *ex parte* on the eleventh day of an *inter partes* hearing. Dillon L.J. said, *inter alia*:

> "The deputy judge granted the injunction. The applicant's counsel informed the respondent's counsel of the order just before the *inter partes* hearing resumed that morning.
>
> It was wholly wrong that the application should have been made *ex parte* during the course of the trial. The result was that counsel obtained an unfair advantage.
>
> If the *Mareva* injunction was necessary during the continuance of the trial, the application should have been made in open court in the presence of counsel for the respondent."

13. Applying to discharge for non-disclosure Hoffman J. observed in *EMI Records Ltd v. The CD Specialists Ltd* [1992] F.S.R. 70 at 74 that there is no format for applying to discharge for non-disclosure:

> "The application for discharge is made on the ground of non-disclosure. There is at present no procedure for requiring a party to give notice of the precise non-disclosures upon which he intends to rely. I think that this is unfortunate. In this case, although some of the matters of complaint were elicited in correspondence between David Jeacock ('Mr Jeacock'), C.D. Record's solicitor, and Messrs. Hamlin Slowe ('Hamlin Slowe') for the plaintiffs, they underwent substantial change before and even during the hearing of the motion.

In the event this has made no difference to the outcome, but it could easily have required an adjournment to allow the plaintiffs a chanced to deal with the new allegations. *In my view a party moving to discharge an interlocutory order should give the other side as much notice as the circumstances will allow of the precise grounds upon which the application is made.*" [Editors' emphasis.]

(*Note:* In *Re Capital Expansion and Development Corporation Ltd*, *The Times*, November 30, 1992, Millet J. held:

"His Lordship said that it reflected no credit on the administration of justice that the court should be unable to make time available for an application to discharge, where it had made time available for the grant of the *ex parte* injunction.

If the court granted time for an expeditious hearing for an application for an *ex parte* injunction it should likewise grant an expeditious hearing for an application to discharge it.

That was particularly the case on the grant of an injunction restraining a secured creditor from enforcing his security; for the grant of such an injunction was dependent on the balance of convenience and for an *ex parte* application a critical factor in the equation was the time gap before any hearing of an application to discharge the injunction. . .")

3 Acquiescence and delay-inter partes applications

1. Introduction As with all equitable relief, delay is a relevant factor in interlocutory proceedings for injunctive relief: *vigilantibus non dormientibus jura subvenient*—a plaintiff should not sleep on his rights. Usually the problem faced by a defendant is not the dormant plaintiff, but a plaintiff affected by a bout of forensic hyperactivity. Thus rarely has the problem been reported in cases touching upon interlocutory relief: see *Comet Radiovision Ltd v. Farnell-Tandberg* [1971] 1 W.L.R. 1287, *per* Goulding J., and *Super-Rax v. Broadfoot* [1961] R.P.C. 61, *per* Cross J. In this context a distinction can technically be drawn between two closely related, yet distinct concepts:
  (i) acquiescence;
  (ii) delay (which in turn covers delay in bringing action, and delay in the prosecution of the action. They are dealt with separately.)

2. Acquiescence This is passive conduct on the part of the plaintiff (*e.g.* sitting back) which has led the defendant to labour under the misapprehension that no objection will be taken if he changes or worsens his position. As Erle C.J. said in *Davies v. Marshall* (1861) 10 C.B. (N.S.) 697 at 710:

> "The plea does allege that the plaintiff so conducted himself so as induce the defendant to believe that he had given his consent to the alterations she was making, and to induce her to lay out money on the strength of such consent."

Similarly, in *Dalgety Spillers Foods Ltd v. Food Brokers Ltd*, *The Times*, December 2, 1993, Blackburn J. *inter alia* said:

> "But there was a further heavy factor: the plaintiff's failure to respond to the letter of October 21, 1992. Between then and the plaintiff's opening shot in the action almost a year had elapsed, during which the defendants had collectively embarked on a considerable programme of planning and expenditure in the UJ.
>
> In taking the legal advice on which they had written that letter, the defendants had demonstrated a wish to act with proper regard to the rights of others and warned the plaintiff that the container in question would be used.
>
> The plaintiff had ignored that warning and in the meantime the defendants had expended time, trouble and expense in launching its product in that container...."

The weight to be attached to the period which had elapsed must largely depend upon the degree of additional prejudice an injunction would occasion by virtue of such change in his position.

3. Delay in bringing action Delay, even if not amounting to acquiescence, may deprive a plaintiff of equitable relief, on the ground that if the matter was so urgent, application for an interlocutory injunction would have been made earlier.

4. Defence to an assertion of acquiescence A plaintiff is not barred by acquiescence if it can be accounted for. The following decisions are to be interpreted in that context.

(a) *Bankart v. Houghton (1860) 27 Beav. 425:*
   (i) "Acquiescence in the erection of noxious works, while they produce little injury, does not warrant the subsequent extension of them to an extent productive of great damage."
   (ii) "It may well be, that a person's assent is given under an erroneous opinion and view and in ignorance of the consequences. Is that mistake of fact to bind him thenceforward and for ever? I think not. The court holds, in cases of election that a man is

not to be considered bound by an election which he has made in ignorance or mistake of the real facts of the case."

(b) *Greenhalgh v. Manchester and Birmingham Railway Co.* (1838) 3 My. & Cr. 783: The headnote reads:

"The owner of land, upon which a railway company empowered by Parliament are about to enter, is not entitled to an interlocutory injunction to restrain them from so entering, if, by his silence and conduct, he has permitted the company to carry on their works upon the supposition that they were entitled to enter on and take the land in question."

Cottenham L.C. added at 791:

"In considering how far a party has, by his own conduct, lost the benefit of an equity to which he was once entitled, it is obvious that very different considerations attach to a case in which a party has been all along cognizant of his rights, from those which attach to a case in which he was not so cognizant. *If the case should arise in which both parties were ignorant of the right which one of them, had he been aware of it, might have asserted, it might be open to considerable question how far that ignorance ought to prejudice him.*" [Editors' emphasis.]

(c) *Att.-Gen. v. Council of the Borough of Birmingham* (1858) 4 K. & J. 528: The plaintiff was not barred from claiming an injunction where he had been led to believe by the defendant that the evil would be remedied:

"... although the plaintiff had submitted to the injury for nearly four years, *trusting to the assurance of the council* that they were carrying out a scheme of sewage by which eventually the evil would be removed, he was not precluded on the ground of laches from now applying for an injunction." [Editors' emphasis.]

(d) *Davies v. Marshall* (1861) 10 C.B. (N.S.) 697: Plaintiff held entitled to an injunction where the defendant had falsely represented that the injury complained of would not result from his operation.

(e) *Gordon v. Cheltenham and Great Western Union Railway Co.* (1842) 5 Beav. 229: Lord Langdale M.R. said at 283–289:

"Then it is said that there was a delay in filing the bill. Was that a delay which gave the defendants any right, or deprived the plaintiff of any? He saw something going on which he objected to, which he considered to be a violation of his rights under the Act of Parliament. He was told in the month of September that it was a temporary eviction only. Would it then have been correct on his part, or right in him immediately to have commenced litigation on the subject? Or rather, was it not a part of his moderation, and desire to accommodate the company, when he acquiesced in what he was led to consider a mere temporary violation of his rights, in the expectation that it would only last for a short time."

(f) *My Kinda Town Ltd (t/a Chicago Pizza Pie Factory) v. Lauren Sabin Soll and Grunts Investments Ltd (t/a L.S. Grunts Chicago Pizza Co.)* [1981] Com. L.R. 194: The approach of Slade J. was reported at 196:

"The judge said that the attitudes and activities of the plaintiffs up to and including the opening of Grunts indicated that they had done something beyond mere delay to encourage the defendants to believe that they did not intend to enforce any rights which they might have had to prevent use by the defendants of the words 'Chicago Pizza' as part of their name. The judge said that the test applicable was that in *Shaw v. Applegate*; whether in the circumstances it had become unconscionable for the plaintiffs to rely on their legal rights. He held that *the defendants had not shown that the plaintiffs were fully aware of the nature and extent either of the risk* of confusion arising from their activities or of the plaintiffs' legal right against them until much later in the year. The full nature and extent of the risk of confusion only gradually dawned on the plaintiffs after the first incident was followed by others. Slade J. held that there was insufficient acquiescence on the part of the plaintiffs, and accordingly granted an injunction to restrain the defendants from carrying on business under or by reference to any name including the phrase '*Chicago Pizza*,' and from representing that their trading name included the phrase. [Editors' emphasis.]"

(g) *Smith (T.J.) & Nephew Ltd v. 3M United Kingdom plc* [1983] R.P.C. 92, *per* Dillon L.J. at 104:

"Mr Gratwick argued further that the plaintiffs' entitlement to an interlocutory injunction was barred by laches. He said that the plaintiffs should have issued their proceedings in the United Kingdom either in July 1981 when they first learned that there was clinical testing of Tegaderm in Aberdeen or at the beginning of October 1981 after their first meeting with the defendants' representatives in New York or at latest in the middle of February 1982 after the meeting in London when any tentative negotiation, or the possibility of negotiation, broke down. I do not see that the plaintiffs' claim is barred in that way at all. At the end of the meeting of February 10, 1982 the plaintiffs' Chairman, Mr Kemp, is reported in the defendants' representatives' note of the meeting as stating 'that the "Op-Site"

73

product was S & N's "crown jewel"' and that the plaintiffs would have to defend their patent position. Following that, the defendants were, on the evidence, warned off in South Africa and New Zealand and when they started marketing their products in Australia they met with an immediate application for an interlocutory injunction, which was granted and still stands. Mr Gratwick says that nonetheless, when these proceedings were started in September 1982 as soon as the defendants began marketing Tegaderm in this country, it was cheating for the plaintiffs to go for an interlocutory injunction after what had passed between the parties. It seems to me that the defendants were amply warned by Mr Kemp in February 1982 and by what had happened since. They went ahead knowing that there were patents, desiring to challenge those patents, but they have only themselves to thank if they did not envisage the possibility of an application being made for an interlocutory injunction. I therefore reject that ground also."

(h) *Foseco International Ltd v. Fordath Ltd* [1975] F.S.R. 507, *per* Foster J. at 512:

"Counsel for Fordath strongly contended that FI had disentitled itself to its remedy, owing to its delay. It was pointed out that, in a letter dated August 13, 1973 and was reiterated in a letter of February 14, 1974, Fordath asserted that it was proposing to start selling core binders abroad, and that as long ago as July 25, 1973 Hepworth, in a letter to FI, had asserted that the agreement was a non-exclusive agreement. Since, however, negotiations, which I think may have been purposely prolonged to enable Fordath to establish itself abroad independently of FFAG, did not finally end until November 1974, I do not think that FI had been guilty of any inexcusable delay so as to disentitle it to interlocutory relief."

5. Acquiescence—practice points

(a) Acquiescence on the part of one of several plaintiffs may well preclude the grant of interlocutory relief: *Marker v. Marker* (1851) 9 Hare 1, at 15. Also see: *Rundell v. Murray* (1821) Jac. 311 at 316; *Saunders v. Smith* (1838) 3 My. & Cr. 711 at 730.

(b) The effect of knowledge and acquiescence is the same in the case of a company as in the case of a private individual: *Laird v. Birkenhead Railway Co.* (1859) John 500.

6. Delay in bringing action—the approach of the court

(a) *Société Française d'Applications Commerciales et Industrielles Sàrl v.*

Electronic Concepts Ltd [1976] 1 W.L.R. 51: The following *obiter dicta* at p. 56 B–D reflect the attitude of the courts:

"He drew my attention to a number of cases supporting the well-known rule that delay in launching proceedings for interlocutory relief may be fatal, and in particular, to *Kentex Chemicals Inc. v. Kenitex Textured Coating Ltd* [1965] 2 F.S.R. 109, where a delay of some three months was considered fatal, and a similar case, *Bravingtons Ltd v. Barrington Tennant* [1957] R.P.C. 183, where again there was an unexplained three months' delay which was considered fatal. He submits—and I think this must be right—that there is no real distinction to be drawn between a case where a plaintiff delays in instituting the relevant proceedings and the case of a plaintiff who institutes the relevant proceedings and then delays in prosecuting them. Indeed, he drew my attention to *Burgess v. Burgess* (1853) 22 L.J. Ch. 675, where a six months' delay in prosecuting an appeal was considered to be a fatal stumbling block. He has also drawn my attention to the well-known line of cases starting with *Allen v. Sir Alfred McAlpine & Sons Ltd* [1968] 2 Q.B. 229 and the three factors which were considered to be relevant in the judgment of Salmon L.J. in that case."

(b) *Radley Gowns Ltd v. Costos Spyrou* [1975] F.S.R. 445; *per* Oliver J.:

"I should finally, I think, deal with one other aspect of the matter. Some criticism has been directed—and I think rightly—at the time-table here. It is pointed out that the letter of complaint was over six weeks after the test purchase, and there was then a delay of two months before the writ was issued. The delay from November to January can, I think, be clearly accounted for by a not altogether unnatural preoccupation with the Christmas selling season. I cannot however express myself as wholly satisfied with the explanation which has been advanced for a delay of two months before seeking the intervention of the court. Mr Laddie has prayed in aid the fact that when the proceedings were commenced the plaintiffs came to court with their tackle already in order. I observe only as to this that the initial tackle, which consisted of three affidavits and exhibits, does not seem to have been in a very good order even after two months. In the first place, as I have already observed, the original sketches were neither exhibited nor accounted for as they should have been. In the second place, Mr White, who swore the principal affidavit, got the story wrong so far as the evolution of style 1441 was concerned. *There seems to me to be some force in Mr Davies's comment that the plea in Mr White's affidavit pressing me for interlocutory protection seems strangely at variance with what I might, I think, not unfairly describe as a somewhat leisurely stroll to the door of the court.* I have had to consider rather carefully whether I ought to refuse this motion on the ground of unreasonable delay. *Had there been any evidence that the defendant had materially changed his position for the worse on the strength of it, it might well prove fateful.* I find no evidence of this, and on the whole I do not think the delay of two months by itself is of such a serious order that I ought to refuse the plaintiffs the relief which they seek." [Editors' emphasis.]

(c) *Netlon v. Bridport-Grundy Ltd* [1979] F.S.R. 530, *per* Goff L.J. at 543 (for facts see p. 790):

"Now, if there were any evidence that the appellants had sat down whilst any considerable volume of offending netting was being imported by others, that no doubt might have formed a reason on the ground of delay for not granting relief. But there is no evidence that anyone was involved other than the respondents and Permac, and the appellants say the previous Permac figures had been much smaller than the estimate of what they intended to sell in the coming year— and that as soon as they discovered there was serious competition by allegedly infringing material on the part of Permac they commenced proceedings against them and I do not think even this addition is sufficient for the respondents' purposes. In my judgment, therefore, relief ought not to be refused on the ground of delay, and I then turn my mind to the balance of convenience..."

7. Delay in bringing action—examples

(a) *One month:* In *Curson and Poole v. Rash* [1982] 263 EG 518, Vinelott J. discounted a delay of one month in launching proceedings to enforce a covenant in restraint of trade, because: (i) of itself, one month was not undue delay; and (ii) the defendant had suffered no detriment.

(b) *Six weeks: E.A.R. Corporation v. Protector Safety Products (U.K.) Ltd* [1980] F.S.R. 574 at 577:

"The history of the matter, as far as the defendants are concerned, is that they started accepting orders for plugs in March 1980 and the plaintiffs got to hear of them and tried to get samples, which they were unable to do until late March. They had ordered plugs on March 11, 1980 and they were not delivered until March 28. Tests were promptly carried out. It was presumably thought that they infringed the plaintiffs' claim and a writ was issued on April 10. At one point there was a suggestion that the plaintiffs had delayed in bringing their action but I am satisfied on those facts that there was no unreasonable delay."

(c) *Five months:* In *Shepherd Homes Ltd v. Sandham* [1971] Ch. 340, Megarry J. refused a mandatory interlocutory injunction, *inter alia*, by reason of the plaintiff's delaying for five months before moving to have pulled down a garden fence erected in breach of a restrictive covenant.

(d) *Five months: Century Electronics Ltd v. CVS Enterprises Ltd* [1983] F.S.R. 1. A delay of five months prior to the launching of a motion for interlocutory relief was held to be prejudicial, in that during that time the defendant contended that they had been expanding their business and that they had been lulled into a false sense of security.

(e) *One year:* In the same vein, Wilberforce J. refused an injunction in the "Miss Great Britain" case of *The Borough of Morecambe and Heysham v. Mecca Ltd* [1962] R.P.C. 145, where the delay had effectively been for over a year.

(f) *Eighteen months:* Where the plaintiffs delayed for about 18 months before seeking a removal on a stay of an injunction, the court allowed the stay to remain for a further two months so as not to cause undue difficulties to the defendants: *Pfizer Corporation v. InterContinental Pharmaceuticals Ltd* [1966] R.P.C. 565

8. Not all delay is bad Some delay may be inevitable. For example, in the patent case of *Carroll v. Tomado Ltd* [1971] F.S.R. 218, the defendant commenced manufacturing in August 1970 and started to advertise its products a month later. It was not, however, until about the middle of November 1970 that the plaintiffs first heard of the defendant's article. The plaintiffs immediately gave instructions to obtain one of the defendant's articles but this was not obtained until January 11, 1971. Instructions were thereupon given to start the present proceedings and the motion was dated January 21, 1971. Graham J. held:

> "In my judgment it would have been unreasonable to expect the plaintiffs to start an action until they had actually been able to inspect a copy of the defendants' article particularly having regard to the fact that in correspondence between the parties on the subject in December 1970 the defendants were apparently taking the point that there was something special about the fact of the feet of their article which would take it out of the plaintiffs' claim. In such circumstances *it was, in my judgment, quite reasonable that the plaintiffs should wait until they had been able to inspect the article.* I do not therefore think that there is anything in the point that the plaintiffs have been guilty of such delay that they should be deprived of the injunction. [Editors' emphasis.]"

Similarly, delay was satisfactorily explained in *United Telephone Co. v.*

77

Equitable Telephone Association (1888) 5 R.P.C. 233, where the plaintiffs'
solicitor advised them not to commence an action until the defendant
appeared to be in a condition of sufficient financial soundness to undertake
manufacture of the infringing articles.

9. Delay may not, on closer examination, be culpable In *Quaker Oats
Co. v. Alltrades Distributors Ltd* [1981] F.S.R. 9, the plaintiffs brought
proceedings for an interlocutory injunction for alleged infringement of
copyright. The calendar of events was:

(a) The defendants displayed the items at three fairs, in November 1978,
January 13, 1979 and at Olympia, at the end of January 1979.

(b) On April 10, 1979, the plaintiffs discovered that the defendants were
dealing in these articles.

(c) On April 11, 1979, the defendant ordered 300 dozen more items for
Hong Kong.

(d) On May 4, 1979, the defendants ordered a further 300 dozen.

(e) On May 10, 1979, the defendant placed a third order for 480 dozen.

(f) The plaintiffs first corresponded with the defendants as to the alleged
infringement, on June 6, 1979.

(g) The plaintiffs issued a writ on June 26, 1979, and launched the
motion for interlocutory relief on June 27, 1979.

In substantially exonerating the plaintiffs, Buckley L.J. said at 12:

> "I have stated the three dates of the three orders placed by the
> defendants after the date upon which the plaintiffs first became aware
> of what the defendants were doing; an earlier notification by the
> plaintiffs would have served no useful purpose unless it was one made
> before May 10, because that was the date when the last order was
> placed, and the defendants have not been in any way prejudiced by
> any delay which has taken place after May 10; and the period from
> April 10 to May 10 does not seem to me to be an unreasonably long
> time for the plaintiffs to have devoted to the problem of discovering
> just where they themselves stood with regard to the copyright in their
> own product, bearing in mind that the English plaintiff company is a
> subsidiary of an American corporation and that the information all
> had to be sought in the United States of America, and that the
> organisation is evidently a large one and consequently communications
> are bound to take time in being transmitted from one part of the
> organisation to another for ascertaining facts of this sort."

But Buckley L.J. went on to suggest:

> "So for my part I do not think the plaintiffs here were guilty of any
> delay although, as it turns out, it would of course have been more
> helpful to all concerned, including the plaintiffs, I think, if they had

written a letter of a warning character saying, in effect, 'We find that you are selling a toy medical kit which is virtually identical with a toy medical kit which we are selling; we think it right to warn you that we may perhaps be bringing proceedings against you in copyright.' If they had done that, it seems to me most probable that from the receipt of such a warning letter the defendants would certainly have been put upon their guard and probably would have taken what steps they could to limit their liability; indeed, they might themselves have made enquiries of their suppliers in Hong Kong as to what the position was or they might, in respect of subsequent orders, have armed themselves with an indemnity from their suppliers in Hong Kong—it seems to me that there were a number of steps that they might have taken which might have made the position less difficult than it is today. Nevertheless, as I say, it does not seem to me that the plaintiffs could be charged with having been guilty of such delay as to disentitle them to interlocutory relief if on other grounds this is an appropriate case to grant it."

Further, in *CPC (United Kingdom) Ltd v. Keenan* [1986] F.S.R. 527, Peter Gibson J. exonerated those who spent some months seeking to negotiate an amicable solution to a trade mark infringement/passing-off claim, particularly since the defendants took two months to respond to correspondence. Invoking *Legg v. Inner London Education Authority* [1972] 1 W.L.R. 1245 at 1259–1260, *per* Megarry J., he held the test to be not so much the length of the delay, but whether such delay made it unjust to grant the injunction. At 534, he said:

"I do not regard it as wrong for plaintiffs, particularly a large corporation, when faced with a person trading either as a sole trader or with her husband, to seek to arrive at a solution out of court. There was the period during which Mrs Keenan and the plaintiffs corresponded in without prejudice correspondence. It would not have been unrealistic of the plaintiffs to take the view that the court would be unlikely to stifle a defendant at short notice at the most important period of the defendant's trade, that is to say at Christmas time."

Similarly in *Mirage Studios v. Counter-Feat Clothing Company Limited* [1991] F.S.R. 145 Sir Nicholas Browne-Wilkinson V.C. said at 153:

"The defendants say that the plaintiffs have been guilty of delay. Although they knew what the defendants were up to in mid-May the notice of motion was not served until August. I would agree that, if that delay was unexplained, it would be a major factor especially as the defendants say that during that time they had been lulled into a sense of security and decided to concentrate on their one new turtle line. However, I do not think that that is a proper reflection of what

79

occurred in this case. The plaintiffs were seeking to enforce their rights, as they thought them to be, through the trading standards authorities. The defendants were well aware of that and when that proved to be abortive then no further delay, as far as I can see, occurred. *I do not think the defendants were entitled to feel secure when they were in fact being pursued through the trading standards authorities' route.*" [Editors' emphasis.]

10. Status quo and delay In *Shepherd Homes Ltd v. Sandham* [1971] Ch. 340, the defendant was the purchaser of a plot of land on a large housing estate on which he built his home. In breach of a restrictive covenant (designed to maintain the open-planned concept) the defendant erected a front garden fence. His motive was to restrain the repeated incursions of sheep. The defendant did not heed a letter from the plaintiff's solicitor dated September 11, 1969 to remove the fence. This prompted the plaintiff to launch proceedings on October 23, 1969. But then the plaintiff did nothing until he gave notice of motion for a mandatory interlocutory injunction on February 25, 1970. Megarry J., *inter alia*, held:

"Furthermore, the status quo for any reasonable period prior to the service of the notice of motion is that of the defendant's fence being *in situ*, so that the injunction sought will disturb rather than preserve anything that can fairly be called the status quo. In *Agbor v. Metropolitan Police Comr.* [1969] 1 W.L.R. 703, I may say, continuation in possession for four weeks was treated as the status quo that was to be preserved, and a mandatory injunction was granted on an application made the very day that the status quo was disturbed."

Megarry J., it should be noted, also gave leave on the defendant's cross-motion, to apply to the Lands Tribunal for the modification of the covenant, together with a stay of all further proceedings pending determination of the application.

11. The costs sanction for delay In *Société Française v. Electronic Concepts Ltd* [1976] 1 W.L.R. 51, Oliver J. penalised the plaintiff in costs. He said at 58G:

"As it seems to me, in the ordinary way I would accede to the plaintiff's application and stand the motion for trial reserving the costs. But I think that they, when it was clear that their invitation issued very late in January, to stand the motion on terms of the costs being reserved, was not acceptable to the defendants, ought to have brought the matter back to the court then; and I think that in the circumstances the right course is that the costs of the motion should be the defendants' costs in the cause because of the delay which has occurred. In doing that, I am following what Pennycuick J. did in the case to which I have already referred: but I think that the defendants should have the costs of the restored hearing today in any event."

12. Delay in context of *ex parte* cases contrasted with the position at the full hearing of the application for *inter partes* relief A delay by the plaintiff prompted Slade J. to refuse *ex parte* relief in a passing-off action: *Wilmot-Breedon Ltd v. Woodcock Ltd* [1981] F.S.R. 15. At 16 he said:

"The evidence, without going into details, clearly, I think, shows that the plaintiffs have been somewhat tardy in making this application. It may well be that their tardiness will not deprive them of their right to have interlocutory relief on an *inter partes* hearing. In my judgment, however, particularly in the face of this tardiness, for the court to make an order against the defendant of this kind, before the defendants have the opportunity to say anything in answer to the plaintiff's claim, would not be just."

13. Delay in prosecuting the action In *Lloyds Bowmaker Ltd v. Britannia Arrow Holdings plc* [1988] 1 W.L.R. 1337, Glidewell L.J. said in relation to a *Mareva* that a plaintiff who has succeeded in obtaining such an injunction is:

"... in my view under an obligation to press on with his action as rapidly as he can so that if he should fail to establish liability in the defendant the disadvantage which the injunction imposes upon the defendant will be lessened so far as possible."

The following cases illustrate the same point.

(a) *Hong Kong Toy Centre Ltd v. Tomy (UK) Ltd*, *The Times*, January 14, 1994: Aldous J. said:

"By their nature, *ex parte* orders should only be made for a limited period, until the matter could be fully considered. Therefore a plaintiff who got such an order was not entitled to sit back and let things drift. Having got interlocutory relief, he had a particular duty to push things forward to the appropriate hearing.

Save in exceptional circumstances, it was right that inexcusable and inordinate delay in carrying out that duty should be visited with dismissal of the action."

(b) *Newsgroup Newspapers Ltd v. The Mirror Group Newspapers (1986) Ltd* [1991] F.S.R. 487: Hoffman J. discharged interlocutory injunctions due to delay. He said at 489:

"The plaintiffs' delay in proceeding with the action since the grant of the interlocutory injunction in July 1988 has been, in my judgment, inordinate and inexcusable. Notwithstanding that delay, there can in my view be no question of striking out the action because the limitation period has not expired and in any event the plaintiffs would be free to commence fresh proceedings to seek injunctive relief with regard to any future advertisements. *The more serious question is whether the interlocutory injunction should be maintained.* An interlocutory injunction is an order which restricts a defendant's liberty at a time when there had been no finding of wrongdoing by the court. It is done in order to preserve the position, pending a determination of the merits, in cases when the court thinks that justice so requires. In my judgment *it is incumbent on a plaintiff whose position has been protected in that way by an interlocutory injunction to proceed with the action with due diligence* so as to limit as far as possible the period during which the defendant's liberty is restricted without there having been any determination of the merits ... [then citing from the *Lloyds Bowmaker* case].

A *Mareva* injunction is a particularly onerous form of restriction on the defendant's liberty and to that extent the obligation upon a plaintiff to bring on the action as soon as possible is the stricter, but in principle it seems to me that the considerations to which the learned Lords Justices referred also apply to other forms of interlocutory relief which prevent the defendant from doing what he would otherwise be free to do. *A plaintiff who has obtained an interlocutory injunction is not in my view entitled simply to rest upon that injunction,* to assume, as the plaintiff in this case expressly said he assumed, that in the absence of complaint the defendant is content to treat the injunction as permanent without any further steps having to be taken and to wait until the defendant finds the situation sufficiently burdensome to prompt him to make an application for variation of its terms. [Editors' emphasis.]"

(c) *Hytrac Conveyors Ltd v. Conveyors International Ltd* [1983] 1 W.L.R. 44: The Court of Appeal refused leave to appeal against an order dismissing the plaintiffs' claim against defendants, on the basis that the plaintiffs had failed to serve a statement of claim within the time limited by Ord. 19, r.1, despite it having executed an *Anton Piller* order. Lawton L.J. held at 47A–B, C–D and H:

"We have been told by counsel that there has grown up in the Chancery Division a practice that, when an application is made for an interlocutory injunction, a statement of claim is not served. It may be that an application for an interlocutory injunction is a good reason why the court should give an extension of time, but it is not a good reason why the Rules of Court should be disregarded. If the idea is getting around that, as the result of service of a notice of motion asking for an interlocutory injunction, no statement of claim should be delivered, then the sooner that idea is dissipated the better, because often it is essential for the purposes of seeing whether an interlocutory injunction should be granted that the court should know what is the nature of the allegations which the plaintiff is making. In *R.H.M. Foods Ltd v. Bovril Ltd* [1982] 1 W.L.R. 661, 665 I pointed out that until at least a statement of claim has been delivered the court can seldom know what are the matters in question in the action. It has to be remembered by all concerned that we do not have in this country an inquisitorial procedure for civil litigation. *Our procedure is accusatorial. Those who make charges must state right at the beginning what they are and what facts they are based upon. They must not use* Anton Piller *orders as a means of finding out what sort of charges they can make. They must deliver their statement of claim within the time specified in the rules, unless the court orders otherwise.* [Editors' emphasis.]"

The mirror image of the decision in *Hytrac* is the principle laid down by the Court of Appeal in *Town and Country Building Society v. Daisystar Ltd* (1989) 139 New L.J. 1563, *per* Dillon L.J.:

"[It is] not ... right that a litigant who obtained a *Mareva* injunction, and in the light of information it obtained as a result of that *Mareva*, concluded that the party against whom the injunction was obtained was not worth pursuing, could then sit back without giving up the *Mareva* when challenged and have the injunction continued indefinitely."

Farquharson L.J. added:

"... it was the duty of a litigant where a *Mareva* had been granted, to press on with his claim so that the other party was subject to the order for the minimum amount of time necessary and not kept in limbo.

If such a litigant did not for any reason wish to proceed with his claim, even temporarily, than he ought of his own motion to seek the discharge of the injunction from the court."

C: PRACTICE AND PROCEDURE

1 Introduction

1. R.S.C. Order 29, rule 1

"(1) An application for the grant of an injunction may be made by any party to a cause or matter before or after the trial of the cause or matter, whether or not a claim for the injunction was included in that party's writ, originating summons, counterclaim or third party notice, as the case may be. (2) Where the applicant is the plaintiff and the case is one of urgency such application may be made *ex parte* on affidavit but, except as aforesaid, such application must be made by motion or summons. (3) The plaintiff may not make such an application before the issue of the writ or originating summons by which the cause or matter is to be begun except where the case is one of urgency, and in that case the injunction applied for may be granted on terms providing for the issue of the writ or summons and such other terms, if any, as the Court thinks fit."

2. "Any party to a cause or matter"—meaning Not only the plaintiff, but also the defendant can apply for interlocutory relief, for example in the following circumstances (as is clear from the last words of the rule):

(a) pursuant to a counterclaim; and

(b) in third party proceedings.

However, the defendant's rights are subject to the following restrictions.

(a) He must have given notice of intention to defend: see *The Supreme Court Practice* 1997, Vol. 1, commentary at 29/1/7.

(b) He cannot apply *ex parte*: Ord. 29, r.1(2).

(c) The defendant who has not filed a counterclaim cannot apply for an injunction against the plaintiff, unless the relief sought by the injunction is incidental to or arises out of the relief sought by the plaintiff. If the defendant applies for any other relief before the time arrives for delivery of the counterclaim, he must issue a writ in a cross-action: *Carter v. Fey* [1894] 2 Ch. 541, *Marcus Publishing plc v. Hutton-Wild Communications Ltd,* [1990] R.P.C. 576 (and see section 2 below, p. 89).

3. "Before or after trial"—meaning Instinctively, one regards interlocutory relief as being a pre-trial remedy. However, it is also, in exceptional circumstances, available after trial, such as by way of *Mareva* order to protect assets after judgment, pending enforcement.

4. "Writ, originating summons, counterclaim or third party notice"—meaning Ord. 5, r.4(2) provides:

"Proceedings—(a) In which the sole or principal question at issue is, or is likely to be, one of the construction of an Act or of any instrument made under an Act or of any deed, will, contract or other document, or some other question of law, or (b) In which there is unlikely to be any substantial dispute of fact, ... are appropriate to be begun by originating summons unless the Plaintiff intends in those proceedings to apply for judgment under Order 14 or Order 86 or for any other reason considers the proceedings more appropriate to be begun by writ."

5. Indorsement of writ If the obtaining of the injunction is the substantial object of the action, the plaintiff should indorse the writ with a claim for the injunction: *Colebourne v. Colebourne* (1876) 1 Ch. D. 690. Ideally the exact terms should be adopted in which it is desired that the final order granting the injunction should be framed: see *Re Myer's Patent* (1882) 26 S.J. 371. Thus if the application relates to breach of a restrictive covenant, it should follow the actual terms of the covenant. Similarly, physical details of any relevant parcel of land or building should be defined with reasonable particularity in the writ, even if at a later stage full plans may be introduced in evidence and possibly referred to in the judgment.

6. To whom? Applications for injunctions must as a general rule be made to the judge; Ord. 32, r. 11(1)(d). But in the following circumstances, the application can be made to a master/district judge.
   (a) If the parties are agreed as to the terms:
      (i) *Queen's Bench Division*: the master/district judge may grant an injunction in terms agreed by the parties to the proceedings in which it is sought; Ord. 32, r.11(2).
      (ii) *Chancery Division*: The master may grant an injunction in a consent order but only if the parties or one of them is unwilling to consent to an undertaking in lieu thereof; Ord. 32, r. 14.
   (b) The injunction is ancillary or incidental to a charging order; Ord. 50, r.9.
   (c) The injunction is ancillary or incidental to the appointment of a receiver by way of equitable execution; Ord. 51, r.2.

7. Which division of the High Court? Schedule 1 to the Supreme Court Act 1981 provides:

"(1) To the Chancery Division are assigned all causes and matters relating to—(a) the sale, exchange or partition of land, or the raising of charges on land: (b) the redemption or foreclosure of mortgages; (c) the execution of trusts; (d) the administration of the estates of deceased persons; (e) bankruptcy; (f) the dissolution of partnerships or the taking of partnerships or other accounts; (g) the rectification, setting aside or cancellation of deeds or other instruments in writing; (h) probate business, other than non-contentious or common form business; (i) patents, trade mark, registered designs or copyrights; (j) the appointment of a guardian of a minor's estate; (k) replacing executor, (section 50 of the Administration of Justice Act 1985); and all causes and matters involving the exercise of the High Court's jurisdiction under the enactments relating to companies. Passing-off cases should also be brought in the Chancery Division by virtue of the particular expertise of the Chancery judges in such field.

[Copyright and passing off cases should also be conducted in the Chancery Division: *Swedac Ltd v. Magnet & Southerns Plc* [1989] F.S.R. 243; *APAC Rowena Ltd v. Norpal Packaging Ltd* [1991] F.S.R. 273.]

(2) To the Queen's Bench Division are assigned—(a) applications for writs of habeas corpus, except applications made by a parent or guardian of a minor for such a writ concerning the custody of the minor; (b) applications for judicial review; (c) all causes and matters involving the exercise of the High Court's admiralty jurisdiction or its jurisdiction as Prize Court; and (d) all causes and matters entered in the commercial list."

To the Commercial Court are assigned any cause arising out of the ordinary transactions of merchants and traders and, without prejudice to the generality of the foregoing words, any cause relating to the construction of a mercantile document, the export or import of merchandise, affreightment, insurance, banking, mercantile agency and mercantile usage.

8. Procedure—the difference Applications for interlocutory relief to the Chancery Division differ from such applications in the Queen's Bench Division in that:

(a) *Chancery Division:* Motion in open court before the motions judge.

(b) *Queen's Bench Division:* Before the judge in chambers.

(c) *Commercial Court:* Before the commercial judge in chambers, in the Commercial List. Thus a desire for publicity would generate an inclination to the Chancery Division, and vice versa. But even in the Chancery Division, hearings will be in camera if circumstances warrant, as with a *Mareva* or *Anton Piller* order.

9. Service Before an interlocutory injunction to do any act can be enforced, the following conditions precedent must be satisfied.
   (a) If possible—the order must be indorsed with a penal notice.
   (b) It must be served on the appropriate individual personally in accordance with Ord. 45, r.7 (if a company—on the appropriate officer). If the order is prohibitory rather than mandatory then it can be enforced if the notice of the making of the order can be proved: *Ronson Products Ltd v. Ronson Furniture Ltd* [1966] Ch. 603.

10. Practice Directions—essential reading Reference should in particular be made to the important Q.B.D. Practice Direction reported at [1983] 1 W.L.R. 433, and particularly at 435 at 435C set out in Part E. The thrust of these Directions is to ensure that the requisite papers are lodged with the clerk to the judge in chambers before the hearing in order to give the judge a reasonable, or at any rate some opportunity to read them first. If the requisite documents are not or cannot be lodged with the clerk to the judge in chambers on the day before the hearing but can only be lodged on the morning or during the day of the hearing, a certificate of extreme urgency must be made by counsel or solicitor if counsel is not instructed. If the case is of such urgency that the requisite papers cannot be lodged at all, the judge will hear the application at once, interrupting his list if necessary, but in such a case, the counsel or solicitor must be prepared to justify this exceptional course. In all *ex parte* cases, counsel's clerk or the solicitor should endeavour to apprise the judge in chambers that the application is on its way. In *Allied Arab Bank Ltd v. Hajjar* [1988] Q.B. 787; [1988] 2 W.L.R. 942, Leggat J. said at 797 H:

> "I am more than usually grateful to leading counsel for their assistance in this matter. But if ever there was a case which called for compliance with Lord Lane C.J.'s practice direction, *Practice Direction (Evidence: Documents)* [1983] 1 W.L.R. 922, this was it. Ten lever arch files containing nearly 4,000 pages could then have been reduced to the 100 or so documents to which counsel found it necessary to refer. For the purposes of these applications, the rest were otiose."

A warning against prolixity was sounded also by Dillon L.J. in *Dubai Bank Ltd v. Galadari and Others* [1990] I Lloyd's Rep. 120 at 125:

> "These matters decided by the Judge, in a very careful judgment of some 62 pages in which he goes through the evidence and the relevant authorities, are in my judgment pre-eminently matters involving the exercise of the Judge's discretion. In those circumstances the function of this Court, on an appeal against a decision made by a Judge in the exercise of his judicial discretion, are very limited. The limits are clearly set out and explained by Lord Diplock in *Hadmor Productions Ltd v. Hamilton* [1983] 1 A.C. 191 and—*pace* leading Counsel for DBL on the present appeal—I had thought that those limits were by now well known to the profession. *The hearing of the appeal is* **not** *simply a rehearing such that this Court is free to substitute its own view for the view taken by the Judge below on any question that may arise.* I would also wish to endorse as strongly as I can the observations of Lord Justice Parker in *Derby & Co. Ltd v. Weldon* [1989] 1 Lloyd's Rep. 122 at 126; [1989] 2 W.L.R. 276 at 283G to 284 where he said: 'More recently, in relation to an application under R.S.C. Ord. 12, r.8

to set aside service of a writ outside the jurisdiction Lord Templeman in *Spiliada Maritime Corporation v. Cansulex Ltd* [1987] 1 Lloyd's Rep. 1; [1987] A.C. 460, said that such cases should be measured in hours, not days, that appeals should be rare and that this court should be slow to interfere. These observations, in my view, also apply to cases such as the present. Mr Heslop for the defendants has, however, sought to go yet again into large parts of the evidence in order to persuade us that the Judge's finding that there is a high risk of dissipation of assets, both here and overseas, should be reversed in respect of overseas assets. *In essence he sought to persuade us to attempt to resolve conflicts of fact going to the merits of the claim, but which were also important on the question of risk of dissipation. This is no part of this Court's function* any more than it is the function of the Court at first instance. He also sought to show that the plaintiffs in the present case have no proprietary claim. His submissions in this behalf depended on the resolution both of disputed detailed and complex fact and of difficult questions of law requiring mature consideration. The function of this Court is again mis-appreciated. Then a little later he [Mr Heslop] said:

'... *if such attempts are made, they can and should be discouraged by appropriate orders as to costs.*'

In the present case the hearing of the appeals and cross-appeals was estimated for seven days. Leading Counsel for DBL, however, in opening the main appeal alone took until 3.30 in the afternoon of the sixth day. There are 19 black ring folders of affidavits and other documents before the Court. I interject that in our discretion we refused an application on behalf of DBL to admit a further five folders of documents by way of additional evidence for the appeal. Leading Counsel took us to a large number of pages in these bundles and sought to persuade us from these references that on virtually every question to which the Judge directed his mind, the Judge got the emphasis wrong or got the balance wrong. So, it was said, the Judge's decision on all these points was wrong and should be corrected by this Court. I find this exercise misconceived and very sterile. It is easy to show that on very many of the questions he considered, the Judge could legitimately have taken a different view. But that falls miles short of showing that it was not open to the Judge to take the view he did on such questions. *The relevant discretion is that of the Judge, not that of this Court.* In these circumstances I do not propose to go into very great detail on the issues argued for DBL on the main appeal." [Editors' emphasis.]

In similar vein, Ralph Gibson L.J., in *Powell v. Brent London Borough Council* [1988] I.C.R. 176 at 186C, referred to the words of Lord Diplock in the American Cyanamid case [1975] A.C. 396 at 407:

> "It is no part of the court's function at this stage of the litigation to try to resolve conflicts of evidence on affidavits as to facts on which the claims of either party may ultimately depend nor to decide difficult questions of law which call for detailed argument and mature consideration. These matters are to be dealt with at the trial."

2 Cross-applications for an injunction

1. The problem Can a defendant who has not filed a counterclaim apply for an injunction against the plaintiff in the plaintiff's proceedings?

2. *Carter v. Fey* In this case, reported at [1894] 2 Ch. 541, C.A., the plaintiff, who had been in partnership with the defendant, gave notice of motion for an interlocutory injunction to restrain the defendant from carrying on directly or indirectly the business of a wine, ale and spirit merchant in the city of Winchester or within a radius of two miles. The defendant appeared to the writ, and on April 7, no statement of claim having been filed and no defence or counterclaim having been put in, he gave cross-notice of motion for an interlocutory injunction restraining the plaintiff from using the name of the defendant on vans, signboards, or labels or otherwise, in carrying on his business.

3. The legal issue defined Lindley L.J. said at 543:

> "The question is whether a defendant who is in a hurry is entitled to apply by way of motion in the plaintiff's action for an injunction without waiting to deliver a counter-claim or issuing a writ in a cross-action, where the relief which he seeks is not in any way comprised in or incidental to the plaintiff's cause of action."

4. The decision *Carter v. Fey* (*ibid.*) is authority for the principle that a defendant who has not filed a counterclaim cannot apply for an injunction against the plaintiff, unless the relief sought by the injunction is incidental to or arises out of the relief sought by the plaintiff. Lindley L.J., *inter alia*, said at 544:

> "In the present case the cross-notices have nothing to do with each other, except that they are both based upon covenants contained in the same deed; but the covenants are quite distinct."

But of course, the court does have jurisdiction to grant an injunction to a defendant upon his undertaking to file a counterclaim. (In the interests of completeness it should be noted that in *Sargant v. Reed* (1876) 1 Ch. D. 277, the defendant was held entitled to apply for an interlocutory injunction in the plaintiff's action, after giving notice of intention to defend. But there, the relief claimed by the defendant was incidental to the plaintiff's cause of action.)

5. In what order should counsel move? In cases involving motions and cross-motions, the plaintiff should move his motion first, dealing also, unless the defendant objects, with the cross-motion. If the defendant objects, the plaintiff can leave it to the defendant to open the cross-motion when he presents his own case on the plaintiff's motion. And this applies even if defence counsel is senior to the plaintiff's counsel: *Fior (London) Ltd v. Eric Schemilt Designs Ltd* [1976] F.S.R. 107. Dillon J.: "I do not know how far logic and Chancery procedures are related." Brightman Q.C.: "Chancery procedure, unless anything is laid down, depends on the Bench, does it not?"

3 Ex parte applications

1. When? *Ex parte* procedure will only be appropriate, either where the delay occasioned by notifying the defendant may cause to the plaintiff irreparable damage, or where secrecy is essential. As Megarry J. said in *Bates v. Lord Hailsham of St Marylebone* [1972] 1 W.L.R. 1373:

> "*Ex parte* injunctions are for cases of real urgency, where there has been a true impossibility of giving notice of motion."

The following are examples.
  (a) *Mareva* and *Anton Piller* applications.
  (b) To restrain defamation and similar torts, such as malicious falsehood (*e.g.* where a newspaper is about to go to press).
  (c) To restrain demolition/construction of a building.
  (d) Where, without fault of either party, pressure of court business does not permit of an *inter partes* hearing: *Bese v. Woodhouse* [1970] 1 W.L.R. 586; but before doing so it must consider the balance of convenience and where the major risk of damage lies.
  (e) If, when the motion is brought on, it has to stand over to enable either party to answer affidavits, and the defendant will not give an undertaking, the court will, if the party moving can make out a case of urgency, grant an interim order over to the day to which the motion stands adjourned. Generally, however, such an injunction will only be granted in cases of real emergency, where property is in danger of being lost or destroyed.

Hoffman J. forcefully set out the criteria warranting *ex parte* relief in *Re First Express Ltd*, *The Times*, October 10, 1991, which passage was approved by the Court of Appeal in the unreported case of *TRP Ltd v. Thorley*, July 13, 1993:

"... he was firmly of the view that it was wrong for the application to have been made *ex parte*. It was a basic principle of justice that an order should not be made against a party without giving him an an opportunity to be heard. The only exception was when two conditions were satisfied. First, that giving such an opportunity appeared likely to cause the applicant injustice, by reason either of delay or action which it appeared likely the respondent or others would take before the order could be made, *and* second, when damage to the respondent was compensatable under a cross-undertaking or when the risk of uncompensatable loss was clearly outweighed by the risk of injustice to the applicant if the order were not made.

Applicants tended to think that a calculation of the balance of advantage and disadvantage in accordance with the second condition was sufficient to justify an *ex parte* order. That attitude should be discouraged. One did not reach any balancing of advantage and disadvantage unless the first condition had been satisfied.

The principle *audi alteram partem* did not yield to a mere utilitarian calculation and could be displaced only by invoking the overriding principle of justice which enabled the court to act at once when it appeared likely that otherwise injustice would be caused...."

2. Delay—fatal Since *ex parte* injunctions are cases for real urgency where there has been a true impossibility of giving notice of motion, an *ex parte* order after a delay is a contradiction in terms. Unless the plaintiff has an overwhelming case on the merits, or the delay can be properly explained, *ex parte* relief will not be granted; see *Bates v. Lord Hailsham* (above). Furthermore, to justify granting *ex parte* relief, the applicant must satisfy the court that the delay caused by awaiting *inter partes* proceedings would or might entail irreparable or serious mischief, and the evidence alleged in support of the application should show this accordingly.

3. Urgent cases—the duty to be reasonable Whereas the essence of *Mareva* and *Anton Piller* applications is secrecy, other circumstances of urgency potentially necessitating *ex parte* relief do not militate against alerting the proposed defendant. In such cases, since the nature of the remedy is equitable (thus justifying, *inter alia*, an attitude of reasonableness on the part of the plaintiff) steps should be taken if possible to achieve the result of an *ex parte* order without the need for applying—by asking the defendant (or if represented, his solicitor) for an undertaking, by telephone or telex.

4. Special rules for industrial action cases Section 221 of the Trade Union and Labour Relations (Consolidation) Act 1992 provides:

"(1) Where—

(a) an application for an injunction or interdict is made to a court in the absence of the party against whom it is sought or any representative of his and

(b) he claims, or in the opinion of the court would be likely to claim, that he acted in contemplation or furtherance of a trade dispute,

the court shall not grant the injunction or interdict unless satisfied that all steps which in the circumstances were reasonable have been taken with a view to securing that notice of the application and an opportunity of being heard with respect to the application have been given to him.

(2) Where—

(a) an application for an interlocutory injunction is made to a court pending the trial of an action, and

(b) the party against whom it is sought claims that he acted in contemplation or furtherance of a trade dispute,

the court shall, in exercising its discretion whether or not to grant the injunction, have regard to the likelihood of that party's succeeding at the trial of the action in establishing any matter which would afford a defence to the action under section 219 (protection from certain tort liabilities) or section 220 (peaceful picketing).

This subsection does not extend to Scotland."

But do these provisions apply where there can be no "trade dispute" defence? For example:

(a) where the action complained of was secondary action not statutorily protected; or

(b) where the action complained of was trespass to which "trade dispute" would not be a defence; or

(c) where there has been no ballot, contrary to section 10 of the Trade Union Act 1984.

5. Setting down If on the *ex parte* hearing, a return date is given, solicitors should remember, in addition to serving the notice of motion/summons, to set the matter down.

6. Duration

(a) *Chancery Division:* It is usual to order it to run until the first motion day for which the defendant can be properly served: *Ex p. Abrams* (1884) 50 L.T. 184.

(b) *Queen's Bench Division/Commercial Court:* It is usual for it to provide that the order take effect "until after the trial of this action (or until judgment in this action) or until further order" and the order may go on to provide that the defendant "be at liberty to discharge it less than two clear days' notice:" Ord. 8, r. 2(2). This shifts the burden to the defendant to apply to discharge or vary the order, which he may choose not to do, but leaves the plaintiff with the burden of applying to the court to continue the injunction in aid of execution or until execution or satisfaction of the judgment. In *PCW (Underwriting Agencies) Ltd v. Dixon* [1983] 2 All E.R. 158, Lloyd J. said at 160E:

"Only a very small proportion of *Mareva* injunctions granted *ex parte* come back for hearing before the court. In many cases, that will be because the terms of the original order have proved appropriate. Where the terms of the original order have proved inappropriate they are usually varied or discharged by consent. Consent orders are placed before the judge for initialling; no court appearance is necessary; little time is taken up. But there are exceptional cases where a further hearing is necessary, either because the jurisdiction has been abused, or for some other reason."

The position, however, is inherently flexible. For example, to avoid further expense, costs and labour, the judge may initially order the *ex parte* injunction to take effect simply "until further order." Alternatively, he may (having regard to the particular circumstances) order that the *ex parte* injunction should not take effect until a specified date or take effect until the hearing of the summons *inter partes* to continue the injunction returnable on a specified date or until further order. In such a case, the burden will be on the plaintiff to issue and serve the summons to continue the *ex parte* injunction until after the trial of the action or until further order.

7. Applying *ex parte* to vary or discharge If the circumstances warrant, an application can be made *ex parte* to vary or discharge an order which was itself made *ex parte: London City Agency (J.C.D.) Ltd v. Lee* [1970] Ch. 597. Megarry J. said at 599H–600A:

"The court will grant an interlocutory injunction on an *ex parte* application if a case of sufficient cogency is made, and no reason has been suggested why, if an application *ex parte* to discharge or vary such an injunction is supported by sufficiently cogent grounds, the court should not do what is sought. If time permits, it is plainly preferable that any such application should be made upon due notice; but in a case of sufficient urgency, I do not see why an injunction granted *ex parte* should be immune from being varied or discharged upon an *ex parte* application. I cannot believe it to be the law that however clearly it has been established that it would be wrong for the injunction to continue in force unchanged, the court is impotent to discharge or vary it until notice of motion has been given and has expired, especially where (as here) counsel for those entitled to the injunction has in fact been present on the hearing of the *ex parte* application for the discharge or variation."

The law on this point was further considered by Simon Brown J. in *London Underground Ltd v. National Union of Railwaymen* [1989] IRLR 341. He *inter alia* said:

"Before embarking on the application to discharge the injunction, it was necessary first to decide whether or not I could entertain it at all. Mr Burke, for the plaintiffs, submitted that I have no jurisdiction to do so, being long since *functus*; alternatively, that even if strictly there is jurisdiction to hear such an application, I should not in my discretion do so.

There is a somewhat want of authority, let alone any direct rule of court, governing this point. In certain circumstances it is plainly open to a party enjoined to apply to discharge that injunction rather than appeal against it. Most obviously this is so:

(1) when the injunction against him was obtained strictly *ex parte*. Indeed, in that situation, as Sir John Donaldson MR said in *WEA Records Ltd v. Visions Channel 4 Ltd* (1983) 1 W.L.R. 721 at 727:

'It is difficult, if not impossible to think of circumstances in which it would be proper to appeal to this Court [the Court of Appeal] against an *ex parte* order without first, giving the judge [an opportunity to discharge it]';

(2) when the injunction was obtained *ex parte* on notice, the defendant not having filed evidence: see *Hunter & Partners v. Wellings & Partners* (1987) F.S.R. 83, where the Court of Appeal observed that it was in general most unsatisfactory for the Court of Appeal to be asked to adjudicate on such appeals when only one side's evidence had been filed, and that the more appropriate procedure would be to stand over the plaintiff's original motion for subsequent *inter partes* hearing when the evidence of both sides was before the Court;

(3) when the sole, or at least the main, basis for seeking the discharge is that there has been a material change of circumstance since the injunction was first granted, *i.e.* a crucial new factual development;

(4) when after the injunction is granted it becomes apparent that it was founded on an erroneous view of the law: see for instance *Regent Oil Company Ltd v. JT Leavesley (Lichfield) Ltd* (1966) 1 W.L.R. 1210.

(*Note:* The Court of Appeal does not have the jurisdiction to entertain an application to discharge an interlocutory injunction which it had granted, on a successful appeal by a plaintiff from the court below. The defendant's application to discharge has to be made to the judge at first instance: *Ocean Software Ltd v. Kay* [1992] Q.B. 583.)

8. Costs

(a) *General rule:* Reserved.
(b) *Defendant attends:* If the defendant attends the *ex parte* hearing and the plaintiff loses, the plaintiff may be ordered to pay the defendant's costs, notwithstanding that he was under no obligation to attend: *Pickwick International Inc. (G.B.) Ltd v. Multiple Sound Distributors Ltd* [1972] 1 W.L.R. 1213.

4 Ex parte applications—London

1. Hearing—where?

(a) *Usually:* Court.
(b) *In cases of real necessity:* The Judge's home.
(c) *As a last resort:* telephone. (The telephone number of the Security Office of the R.C.I. is 0171 936 6260.) *Allen v. Jambo Holdings Ltd* [1980] 1 W.L.R. 1252, is an example, as Lord Denning M.R. explained at 1254H–1255A:

> "There was an inquest. It was held on March 1, 1979. The coroner found a verdict of accidental death. As soon as the inquest ended, the pilot told the solicitor for the widow that he intended to fly the aircraft back to Nigeria immediately. The solicitor was afraid that any claim by the widow for damages would be fruitless if the aircraft was flown back to Nigeria. It would be very difficult to enforce any judgment in Nigeria. The solicitors tried to discover whether the aircraft was insured with an English insurance company, but they failed. So on the next day they took steps immediately. They instructed counsel. Counsel telephoned Drake J. and explained the circumstances to him. The judge granted a *Mareva* injunction to restrain the Nigerian company and the pilot from removing the aircraft from the jurisdiction until after the hearing of a summons. The aircraft has remained at Leavesden aerodrome ever since. The injunction was continued by agreement."

Also see *Barretts & Baird (Wholesale) Ltd v. Institution of Professional Civil Servants*, [1987] 1 FTLR 121, where *ex parte* injunctions granted by Jupp

J. on October 26, in an industrial dispute context were discharged by Henry J. on November 17, 1986.

2. Applications during Court hours The Courts will hear *ex parte* applications at the following times, save where circumstances do not permit.

(a) *Queen's Bench Division:* 10.00 a.m. or 2.00 p.m. (See Practice Direction [1983] 1 W.L.R. 433.). Listing office for the Q.B.D. General List is Room W15, Royal Courts of Justice: tel. 0171 936 6009/fax 0171 936 6724.

(b) *Chancery Division:* 10.30 a.m. or 2.00 p.m. (See Practice Direction [1980] 1 W.L.R. 751; 2 All E.R. 750). Listing office for the Ch. D. is located in Rooms 813/814, Thomas More Building, R.C.J., tel. 0171 936 6816.

(c) *Commercial Court:* 10.30 a.m. or 1.45 p.m. Note: Usually, application is made to the Commercial Court for a *Mareva* injunction in aid of arbitration proceedings. Commercial Court Office is Room E201, R.C.J., tel. 0171 936 6826; fax: 0171 936 6245. Fax for issue of writs outside court hours: 0171 936 6667.

3. Outside Court hours The position (for really urgent applications) is:

(a) *Queen's Bench Division:* The judge sitting in Room E101 is on duty overnight. If he sits on Friday, he is on duty over the weekend. In vacation, the vacation judge is on call throughout his tour of duty.

(b) *Chancery Division:* Essentially the same as the Q.B.D.

(c) *Commercial Court:* Application is made to the Q.B.D. judge on duty. The duty Judge (be he *Q.B.D.* or *Chancery Division*) must not be contacted outside normal Court hours, without first going through the sift, which is:

   (i) Room E101 (Q.B.D.)/Room 413 (Ch.D.), Royal Courts of Justice, Strand, London WC2A 2LL, or—if closed:

   (ii) the officer on 24-hour duty on the main gate: 0171 936 6199. N.B. Clerk of the Rules: 0171 936 6000.

4. Where to lodge? Application for a hearing should be made to the Royal Courts of Justice as follows:

(a) *Queen's Bench Division general list:* to Room 549, R.C.J.: tel. 0171 936 6009 (the listing office for the Judge in Chambers).

(b) *Chancery Division:* Clerk to the Lists, Room 413, R.C.J.: tel. 0171 936 6690.

(c) *Commercial Court:* Room 193, R.C.J. (the Commercial Court Office). The Commercial Court Listing Office can be contacted by telephone at 0171 936 6826.

5. What to lodge? The essential documents for *ex parte* injunction applications are:

(a) *Queen's Bench Division and Commercial Court:*
  (i) Writ.
  (ii) Affidavit.
  (iii) A draft minute of the order sought stating precisely the relief the court is asked to grant. Although the application for a *Mareva* may be made after the issue and service of the writ or (like any other application for an interlocutory injunction) at any time while the proceedings are pending, a *Mareva* can be applied for and granted before the issue of the writ. Thus the Practice Direction regulating *ex parte* applications applies with especial force to *Mareva* relief. It should be applied scrupulously, particularly as regards the contents of the supporting affidavit and the undertakings which the plaintiff will usually be required to give. Note: if an interlocutory injunction is a substantial object of the plaintiff's action, it should be indorsed on the writ: *The Supreme Court Practice* (1997), Vol. 1, para. 29/1/9.

(b) *Chancery Division:*
  (i) Two copies of the writ.
  (ii) Two copies of the order sought.
  (iii) The best estimate of time that counsel can give.

6. Real emergency

(a) *What documents?* If the case is one of real emergency, when time is of the essence, then if the plaintiff has not had time to issue the writ:
  (i) he can produce a draft writ at the *ex parte* hearing together with an affidavit headed "In the matter of an intended action between A and B"—which upon the making of the order are kept by the Court and passed on to the Central office or Chancery Chambers at the earliest opportunity, with instructions to treat them as issued and filed as of the time when they passed into official custody (see *Re N. (Infants)* [1967] Ch. 512);
  (ii) if the affidavit is yet to be sworn, an order can be made *ex parte* upon the giving of undertakings to swear and file (and if the circumstances are dire, a telegram may suffice, to be verified by affidavit as soon as the writ is issued).

(b) *Procedure to be adopted:* In *P.S. Refson & Co. Ltd v. Saggers* [1984] 1 W.L.R. 1025, Nourse J. held that if an application was made *ex parte* for an injunction prior to the issuing of proceedings, the following procedure should be adopted.
  (i) Wherever possible there should be put before the court the draft

97

of an indorsement on the writ and preferably an engrossed writ ready for issue. In cases where relief was sought over the telephone the part or parts of the draft indorsement should normally be read to the judge. Only in cases of very exceptional urgency should the court be asked to act without a sight or hearing of a material part or parts of the draft indorsement.

(ii) Although there is no difference in meaning or effect between an obligation to issue a writ "forthwith" or "as soon as practicable" or "as soon as reasonably practicable," the first of those formulae was to be preferred and should normally be adopted. Further, the writ should normally be expressed to be *"in the form of the said draft writ or summons"* or to claim *"relief substantially similar to that hereinafter granted"* as the case may be. Note: To serve a writ five or six days after issue, in the face of an undertaking to serve as soon as issued, is a serious matter: *Manor Electronics Ltd v. Dickson* [1988] R.P.C. 618.

(iii) As was the case with any other undertaking relating to the conduct of proceedings, it was the duty of a solicitor acting for an intended plaintiff on whose behalf an undertaking was given to the court to issue a writ, to see that it was properly and expeditiously implemented; and counsel who was instructed to give such undertakings might sometimes regard it as his duty to remind his solicitor of this.

(*Note:* The affidavits should be sworn after the writ is issued: *Silber v. Lewin* [1889] 33 S.J. 757. But where the affidavit had been sworn two days before the issue of the writ, an order was made on the plaintiff's undertaking to have the affidavit re-sworn and filed: *Green v. Prior* [1886] W.N. 30.)

(c) *An example:* In *W.E.A. Records Ltd v. Visions Channel 4 Ltd* [1983] 1 W.L.R. 721, Sir John Donaldson M.R., *inter alia* recorded, at 724D–F:

"The history of the matter is as follows. The plaintiffs suspected that the defendants were actively engaged in what is popularly known as 'video piracy'—making or selling unauthorised copies of films or video tapes in breach of copyright. They made inquiries, including the keeping of observation on certain premises, and came to the conclusion that it was an appropriate case in which to apply *ex parte* for an *Anton Piller* order immediately before, or simultaneously with, an application to issue a writ claiming injunctive relief, delivery up of offending material and an inquiry as to damages. *Such was thought to be the urgency of the situation that counsel was asked to appear before Mervyn Davies J. armed only with a draft writ and instructions as to the nature and results of the plaintiffs' inquiries. No affidavit evidence was produced, nor had counsel the advantage of being able to produce unsworn draft affidavits.*" [Editors' emphasis.]

5 The significance of undertakings

1. Relief on terms—source of jurisdiction R.S.C. Ord. 29, r.1(3) provides:

"The plaintiff may not make such an application before the issue of the writ or originating summons by which the cause or matter is to be begun except where the case is one of urgency, and in that case the injunction applied for may be granted on terms providing for the issue of the writ of summons and such other terms, if any, as the Court thinks fit."

2. Relief on terms—the court's options In the event of the Court giving interlocutory relief, it may be expected to be on some or all of the following terms (wherever relevant).
   (a) An undertaking in damages.
   (b) To notify the defendant of the terms of the order forthwith.
   (c) In an application of the *Mareva* type, to pay the reasonable costs and expenses incurred in complying with the order by any third party to whom notice of the order is given.
   (d) In the exceptional case where proceedings have not been issued, to issue the same forthwith.
   (e) In the exceptional case where a draft affidavit has not been sworn, or where the facts have been placed before the Court orally, to procure the swearing of the affidavit, or the verification on affidavit of the facts outlined orally to the Court. (But see *Siporex Trade S.A. v. Banque Indosuez* [1986] 2 Lloyd's Rep. 146.)

3. Relief on terms in practice In the event that an interlocutory order is made before issue of proceedings, the writ and affidavit are retained by the judge, and are sent forthwith to the Central Office or Chancery Chambers with instructions that they are to be issued and filed on the day when they pass into the custody of the Court. After the writ of summons is issued, the affidavit is filed in the action, and the writ of summons and an office copy of the affidavit are produced to the associate before the order is passed and entered. Clearly, when the plaintiff seeks leave to issue out of the jurisdiction, he will only be in a position to supply a draft writ. If the intended writ cannot be left with the judge (*e.g.*, when it has yet to be drawn up), terms should be imposed requiring the writ to be so drawn that if it had been issued the injunction could have been granted.

4. Compliance with undertakings Undertakings should be meticulously complied with. However, where the plaintiff's solicitors had failed to comply, by an honest and genuine oversight, with undertakings given on the granting of a *Mareva* injunction, it was not discharged at the defendant's request: *Sabani v. Economakis, The Times,* June 17, 1988, Potter J. Sight, however, should not be lost of the fact that breach of an undertaking is a contempt of court, which can bring in its wake orders for costs personally against the solicitor (as officer of the court) and even disciplinary sanctions under the Solicitors Act 1974. Thus where a solicitor gives an undertaking which becomes impossible to perform, the court will not make an order for performance in vain, but it may use its discretion to order compensation: *Udall v. Capri Lighting (In Liquidation)* [1988] Q.B. 907; [1987] 3 W.L.R. 465, C.A. The Court of Appeal held, *inter alia*, that where the solicitor's conduct merited reproof, the court could use its discretion to order compensation, and the case would be remitted for consideration of that question. The Court went on to hold that the court had power to make a compensatory order of a disciplinary nature. Finally in this context, the Court of Appeal ruled in *Sinclair-Jones v. Kay* [1988] 2 All E.R. 611 that a finding of gross misconduct was not a prerequisite to an order requiring a solicitor to pay costs personally. An order could be made if costs had been incurred unreasonably or improperly by failure to conduct proceedings with reasonable competence.

6 Sunday applications

1. Is Sunday a *dies non juridicus*? No-not as far as injunctions are concerned: *Re N. (No. 2)* [1967] Ch. 512, *per* Stamp J. The first limb of the headnote reads:

> "... in a case of emergency, as the present case was, an interlocutory injunction being an act in exercise of the equitable jurisdiction originally of the Lord Chancellor, could be granted validly on a Sunday, although that day was a *dies non juridicus*, as the granting of an injunction was within the class of judicial acts which were expected from the general rule of the common law that a judicial act could not be done on a Sunday."

2. But on what date should the originating process be taken as being issued? Stamp L.J. at 572G in *Re N. (ibid)* said:

> "... the judges ... have adopted the ... practice ... of requiring an undertaking to issue the writ (or originating summons) immediately it is possible to do so without the writ coming into the custody of the judge or registrar and, in those cases, the practice has been, so I am told, at any rate in the Queen's Bench Division, to date the writ with

the date on which it is actually issued and to add a note that it is to be treated as issued as at the date of the undertaking."

In that context the following dicta of Nourse J. in *P.S. Refson & Co. Ltd v. Saggers* [1984] I W.L.R. 1025 at 1028F fall into perspective:

"The current practice in [the Chancery Division] is in general accordance with [Stamp J.'s observations in *Re N. (Infants)* [1967] Ch. 512, at 527–528], although I should emphasise that the writ is dated with the date on which it is actually issued and without the addition of any note that it is to be treated as if issued as at the date of the undertaking."

7 Ex parte applications-provinces

1. Introduction Save on the Northern Circuit, there is no duty judge system as in London. During term, the High Court Judge will be approached through the local listing clerk. Where no High Court Judge is available, recourse must be had to London. The telephone number for a Northern Circuit emergency application is 0161 834 7717.

2. Emergency procedure Solicitors should have available the telephone number of the chief clerk—usually issued by the court administrator's office to secretaries of the local law societies and to the police. The chief clerk will require: (a) the cause of action; (b) that the proposed application is within the jurisdiction of the court; (c) the telephone number and location of solicitor, applicant (and, if appropriate, counsel).

3. Documentation, etc. As in London.

8 The "opposed ex parte motion"

1. What is it? As in *London City Agency (J.C.D.) Ltd v. Lee* [1970] 1 Ch. 597, so in *Pickwick International Inc. (G.B.) Ltd v. Multiple Sound Distributors Ltd* [1972] 1 W.L.R. 1213 the defendant was present at the plaintiff's *ex parte* application. Megarry J. said at 1214E–G:

"At this stage I may mention a procedural point upon which there appears to be no reported authority. Both before me and before the Court of Appeal the defendants were present at the hearing of the *ex parte* application, and took part in it in order to assist the court. *The* ex parte *motion thus became what may be termed an opposed* ex parte *motion. The fact that this is a contradiction in terms ought not to be allowed to obscure the utility of the process.* The practice seems to be of comparatively recent origin, though it has been pointed out to me that at least to some extent it may be a reversion to a procedure in the early part of the last century, which, if not usual, was at least permissible: see *Acraman v. Bristol Dock Co.* (1830) 1 Russ. & M. 321. The practice supplements, without supplanting, the former practice of moving *ex parte*, with the party moved against being silently present and taking no part in the proceedings unless an injunction was granted, in which case he thereupon moved *ex parte* to vary or discharge that injunction. Of course, if the party moved against is not present he can similarly move *ex parte* to vary or discharge the injunction when he learns of it." [Editors' emphasis.]

2. Problem—which procedure? The problem then arises, which procedure should be adopted: the older one (where the respondent sits back quietly to see if the *ex parte* order is made, and if it is, launches forth to seek to vary or discharge it); or the more modern procedure, with the cut and thrust of argument? The nature of the difference was explained by Megary J. in *Pickwick* (*ibid.*):

"... there is a considerable practical difference between the ebb and flow of argument in *inter partes* proceedings and the still life of hearing all that one side has to say, reaching a decision, and then hearing separately all that the other side has to say. There can be no doubt, too, that proceedings *inter partes* usually make it possible for the real points to emerge more quickly, and thus save time."

The fact that the courts prefer the more modern approach was clear from the judgment of Megarry J. at 1215D:

"The two procedures, ancient and modern, thus co-exist. In the present case I ventured to laud the present procedure as being a comparatively recent practice which has much to commend it. Indeed, in most cases it seems to be the practice which the court will encourage. In the Court of Appeal in this case I observe that Russell L.J. referred to it as being 'the modern and very sensible practice'...."

3. Advantages of having the respondent present These were enumerated by Megarry J. in *Pickwick International Inc. Ltd v. Multiple Sound Distributors Ltd* (*ibid.*) at 1214G:

(a) *For the court:* In most cases it would be assisted in deciding whether or not to grant the *ex parte* injunction by knowing what contentions may be advanced against the grant, and what is the general line of evidence in opposition that is likely to be fled when the applicant later moves on notice.

(b) *To the applicant:* The court, having heard what there is to be said in opposition to the grant of the injunction, may sometimes be encouraged to grant an injunction that otherwise would be refused, and the applicant may escape an avoidable liability on his undertaking in damages.

4. The modern approach—disadvantages The modern approach is not without its disadvantages, as Megarry J. explained at 1215B–C:

(a) *To the applicant:* There is the risk that if the application fails he may be ordered to pay the costs of the party who has successfully opposed the application:

> "In the present case, as in a number of other recent cases, I have held that the court has jurisdiction to make an order for costs against the applicant in such cases, whether in the cause or in any event. It cannot be right that the applicant should issue an express or tacit invitation to be present to the party whom he is seeking to enjoin, and then deny him any claim to the costs of what has proved to be a successful opposition. I say nothing about cases in which there has been no such invitation."

(b) *To the respondent:* He may go to the trouble of preparing and advancing contentions at short notice in a case in which a truly *ex parte* application would have failed in any event, and on the older procedure he could have gone silently away, with no *ex parte* injunction in existence which he need move to vary or discharge.

5. Discharging *ex parte*—what if the defendant is not present? Can a court discharge an *ex parte* order even if the defendant to the order had not entered an appearance? Yes, *per* Kerr J. in *Harbottle (R.D.) (Mercantile) Ltd v. National Westminster Bank Ltd* [1978] Q.B. 146 at 157D–F, and 158D–E:

> "Why then should this court not have power to discharge all the injunctions, now that these actions are again before it? Injunctions, as here, are frequently granted *ex parte* on the basis of hurried applications against persons before they have any notice of the application. They are not bound to enter an appearance when they are served, but they would be guilty of a contempt of court if they disobey the injunction. When the matter comes back before the court to continue the order and can be fully considered and at greater leisure, why should the court not have inherent jurisdiction to discharge its prior discretionary order if it appears to it right to do so, even though the persons concerned have not entered an appearance and therefore do not themselves apply for the discharge of the injunction? Why should the court be bound to leave its discretionary order in force when it

considers that the order should not have been made, or should not have been continued, and when disobedience to the order is a contempt of court? I cannot believe that this can be right.... *The courts have a discretion to grant interlocutory injunctions whenever it is just or convenient to do so. They must equally have an inherent jurisdiction to discharge them on the same basis when the matter comes back to them for a further order.* If in the present case it is right to discharge the injunctions against the bank, then the fact that the Egyptian defendants have taken no part in the proceedings cannot possibly be a good ground for maintaining them against the bank. Further, since I am now convinced that at least equally strong considerations apply in favour of the discharge of the injunctions against the Egyptian defendants, their failure to participate in these proceedings should not deter me from discharging them, and I do not consider myself precluded by any authority." [Editors' emphasis.]

6. Hearing opposed *ex parte* appeals Although the Court of Appeal has jurisdiction to hear an appeal from the grant of interim interlocutory injunctions on an "opposed *ex parte*" hearing, such appeals were to be deprecated: *Hunter and Partners v. Welling and Partners* [1987] F.S.R. 83. The usual procedure should be to allow the *ex parte* motion to stand over to a subsequent *inter partes* hearing when both sides' evidence would be before the court, the party aggrieved by the order on that hearing could then appeal without leave under section 18(1)(h) of the Supreme Court Act 1981. May L.J. is reported as saying at 87–88:

"... on a strict analysis, the opposed *ex parte* hearing consisted of an *ex parte* motion by counsel for the plaintiffs for interim interlocutory injunctions. The judge having indicated directly or indirectly that he was minded to grant such injunctions, counsel for the defendants must be taken then to have moved *inter partes* to have those injunctions discharged. In this [counsel] failed. Accordingly if [counsel] were to seek to challenge the learned judge's decision in this court, the proper procedure was by way of an appeal against the judge's dismissal of [counsel's] *inter partes* motion to set aside the interim interlocutory injunctions.... Having made what we think is the correct procedural analysis of what occurred at first instance, we wish to make it clear that we deprecate appeals to [the Court of Appeal] at this stage in matters of this nature. It is in general most unsatisfactory for [the Court of Appeal] to be asked to adjudicate upon such appeals when only one side's evidence had been filed."

The Court of Appeal does not have the jurisdiction to entertain an application to discharge an interlocutory injunction which it had granted, on a successful appeal by a plaintiff from the court below. The defendant's application to discharge has to be made to the judge at first instance: *Ocean Software Ltd v. Kay* [1992] Q.B. 583.

9 Procedure-inter partes

1. Introduction
(a) Whereas in the Chancery Division, notice of motion is not issued by the court, in the Queen's Bench Division the summons for the *inter partes* hearing must be issued (Room ***) prior to service.
(b) Procedure for *inter partes* applications: The following Practice Directions (to which reference should be made) regulate how applications for injunctions *inter partes* are to be made:
  (i) Queen's Bench Division;
  (ii) Chancery Division;
  (iii) Commercial Court.

2. Notice of motion—abridging time limits

(a) *Queen's Bench Division:* Ord. 32, r.3:

> "A summons asking only for the extension or abridgment of any period of time may be served on the day before the day specified in the summons for the hearing thereof but, except as aforesaid and unless the Court otherwise orders or any of these rules otherwise provides, a summons must be served on every other party not less than two clear days before the day so specified."

(b) *Chancery Division:* Ord. 8, r.2(2):

> "Unless the Court gives leave to the contrary, there must be at least two clear days between the service of notice of a motion and the day named in the motion for hearing the summons."

(c) *Do holidays, etc., stop the clock?* In the computation of two clear days, Saturdays, Sundays, bank holidays, Christmas Day and Good Friday are not reckoned: Ord. 3, r.2.
(d) *Leave:* In a proper case the court will grant leave to abridge time limits. In this regard only the judge can grant leave—not a master (even in the long vacation: *Conacher v. Conacher* (1881) 29 W.R. 230). The court may disregard irregularity and hear the motion on its merits, where leave to serve short notice is irregularly obtained: *Dawson v. Beeson* (1882) 22 Ch.D 504, C.A.; (R.S.C., Ord. 2, r.1). The headnote, *inter alia*, reads:

> "Where a party applies for special leave to serve short motion he must distinctly state to the court that the notice applied for is short;

105

and the same fact must distinctly appear on the face of the notice
served on the other party."

The position is now covered by Ord. 8, r.3(1).

3. Venue

(a) *Queen's Bench Division:* Room E 101.

(b) *Chancery Division:* Motions Judge (where the application is heard and
decided on affidavit evidence in open court). Motions in actions and
matters relating to patents are made to the Patents Court.

(c) *Commercial Court:* Commercial Judge in Chambers in the Commercial
Court.

4. Summons practice in the Queen's Bench Division
(a) The hearing of a summons may be adjourned from time to time,
either generally or to a particular date, as may be appropriate: Ord.
32, r.4(1).
(b) If the hearing is adjourned generally, the party by whom the summons
was taken out may restore it to the list on two clear days' notice to
all the other parties upon whom the notice was served: Ord. 32,
r.4(2).

5. Motion practice in the Chancery Division If a hearing is likely to be
protracted, the Judge may on application fix a special day for opening the
motion, or alternatively, adjourn the motion to a special day (if a motion
is estimated to last for more than two hours, it will be adjourned to come
on as a motion by order). It is usual for counsel for the plaintiff to open
the motion to the Court on the day specified in the notice of motion.
However, assuming the other side consents, the practice is that motions
can be saved without mentioning to the Court. But where the motion is
by special leave, it cannot be saved without the leave of the Court: *Arthur
v. Consolidated Collieries Corporation* (1905) 49 S.J. 403. Similarly, if
(instead of opening the motion) counsel for the applicant wants to save
the motion for a subsequent motion day or to the trial, he must mention
it to the judge, who has a discretion as to whether or not it should be
saved: *Max Factor & Co. v. MGM (UA Entertainment Company)* [1983]
F.S.R. 577. In this context, it should be noted that a motion may be stood
over in the Chancery Division by a Registrar or on postal application that
all parties agree and certain conditions are satisfied: see the Practice
Directions [1976] 1 W.L.R. 441; [1977] 1 W.L.R. 228 and [1983] 1 W.L.R.
4. But this only applies if no undertakings or injunctions are incorporated
in the order.

6. Essential documents-*inter partes*

(a) *Queen's Bench Division:* Pleadings, affidavits and summonses. Summonses are to be indorsed with estimated length of hearing. Any alteration or settlement should be notified forthwith.

(b) *Chancery Division:* Unless the following documents are lodged with the Clerk of the Lists, who enters the motions by noon on the day before the effective date of hearing, the motion will not be entered in the Motions Book: (Room 813/814) Chancery Chambers, Royal Courts of Justice:
  (i) two copies of the writ;
  (ii) two copies of the notice of motion;
  (iii) the best estimate of duration that counsel can give signed by counsel for the applicant.

(c) *Commercial Court:* The main pleadings and affidavits.

7. Essential documents to be served on the defendant
  (a) Writ, and any pleadings.
  (b) Notice of the hearing.
  (c) Copy affidavit.
  (d) If previously ordered, a copy of the *ex parte* injunction.

10 Interlocutory consent orders

1. Can a court vary an interlocutory consent order? The problem arose in *Chanel Ltd v. Woolworth & Co.* [1981] 1 W.L.R. 485. The first sentence of the headnote reads:

> "The plaintiffs, an English company, brought an action for infringement of trade marks of which they were the registered proprietors and for passing-off against the importers and retailers of foreign products, bearing the plaintiffs' trade mark."

Buckley L.J. took up the facts at 491C–D:

> "They [the plaintiffs] moved *ex parte* for interlocutory relief by way of an *Anton Piller* order and injunctions, and obtained *ex parte* relief on March 29, 1979. Before the motion came on *inter partes* the second defendants, Three Pears Wholesale Cash and Carry Ltd, believing that the only defence available to them was one under European Community law, felt constrained to give undertakings until judgment or further order in the terms of the notice of motion. Accordingly, when the motion came before the court *inter partes*, the defendants tendered such undertakings. The plaintiffs were content, upon the defendants'

giving those undertakings, to their motion being stood over until the trial. Accordingly, on April 6, 1979, the motion was disposed of in that manner by consent without its being opened to the court and without the evidence being read."

2. The *Revlon* case And that would probably have been the end of the matter as far as the astute law reporter would have been concerned, but for a decision of the Court of Appeal several months later, namely *Revlon Inc. v. Cripps & Lee Ltd* [1980] F.S.R. 85. Buckley L.J. described the essence of the claim in that case, at 491G:

"The plaintiff company sued for passing-off Revlon goods, manufactured in the United States of America by a Revlon company operating in the United States, as Revlon goods manufactured in the United Kingdom by another Revlon company operating in the United Kingdom."

3. *Revlon* failed—why? The Court of Appeal took the point that the marks or get-up had been developed as a house mark distinctive of the whole group and that every company in the group was to be taken to have consented to the marks being used by every other company of the group to designate the products so marked as products of the group as a whole.

4. The link-up with the *Chanel* case It was the decision in the *Revlon* case which put into legal perspective the results of certain company searches which the defendants, Woolworth and Co. Ltd had made months before, on May 2–10, in connection with the claim by Chanel Ltd. As Buckley L.J. explained in the *Chanel* case at 491E–F:

"Subsequently the defendants made certain company searches on May 2 to 10. These disclosed certain apparent organisational links between the plaintiff company and the other companies (which were in fact foreign companies) through whom the goods which are the subject matter of the alleged infringements and passing-off were acquired by the defendants. These links suggest that there may exist a group structure embracing both the plaintiff company and the foreign companies from or through whom the defendants acquired the goods. The defendants also discovered other evidence, in the form of advertising material and the like, suggesting the existence of a group structure of that kind."

5. The *Chanel* case—against the *Revlon* backrop So it was that Woolworths applied to discharge their undertakings. This prompted two issues: (a) Did the court have jurisdiction? (b) If yes, should such jurisdiction be exercised?

6. The first issue—jurisdiction Buckley L.J. held at 492D–E:

> "In my judgment, an order or an undertaking to the court expressed to be until further order, by implication gives a right to the party bound by the order or undertaking to apply to the court to have the order or undertaking discharged or modified if good grounds for doing so are shown. Such an application is not an application to set aside or modify any contract implicit in the order or undertaking. It is an application in accordance with such contract, being an exercise of a right reserved by the contract to the party bound by the terms of the order or undertaking."

7. The second issue—should jurisdiction be exercised? Buckley L.J. ruled against the defendants on the basis that they were in reality seeking two bites at the cherry. There had been nothing to prevent them taking the *Revlon* point six months earlier, before that case was decided:

> "Accordingly, with deference to Foster J., I take a different view from that which he took on his first ground for rejecting the defendants' application. When the motion for an injunction came before the judge *inter partes*, the defendants did not seek any adjournment to permit them to put in evidence in answer to the plaintiff's evidence. They might then have asked for a sufficiently long adjournment to permit them to make the company searches they made in May, and possibly to search for corroborative evidence in the form of advertising material and so forth, to build up a case for saying that a relevant group structure existed in this case. They did not do so, probably because it had not then occurred to their advisers that evidence of this kind might assist them in accordance with the reasoning on which the *Revlon* decision was based. The fact that the *Revlon* decision had not then taken place is, in my view, no ground for saying that the defendants might not have succeeded in resisting the motion successfully on parallel reasoning."

8. The jurisdiction to vary—when exercised? In the *Chanel* case, Buckley L.J. gave some guidance as to when the court would exercise its jurisdiction to vary a consent order/undertaking, at 492H–493A:

> "... in interlocutory matters a party cannot fight over again a battle which has already been fought unless there has been some significant change in circumstances, or the party has become aware of facts which he could not reasonably have known, or found out, in time for the first encounter."

These dicta further explain the judgment of Whitford J. in *G.C.T. (Management) Ltd v. Laurie Marsh Group Ltd* [1972] F.S.R. 519.

9. G.C.T. (Management)—the facts The plaintiffs managed a cinema in Curzon Street, London, known as the Curzon Cinema. As Whitford J. explained:

"They originally brought a motion seeking relief substantially in the same terms which came before Megarry J. in May of this year. The basis of their complaint was that the defendants, who had originally operated a cinema in the King's Road, Chelsea, as the Essoldo Cinema, had changed the name of that cinema to the Curzon Cinema, with the consequent likelihood of confusion between the defendants' cinema and the plaintiffs' cinema which, I am told, has been operated as the Curzon Cinema in Curzon Street for a good many years. At the hearing of the motion before Megarry J., an undertaking was offered by the defendants which was substantially in terms that, until judgment or further order, the defendants would change their name and would call their cinema Classic Curzon Chelsea. It was apparently anticipated that this would be a sufficient change of name to obviate any possibility of confusion pending the final determination of the matters in dispute between the parties and the plaintiffs accept on this present application that, the undertaking having been offered, it was accepted by them."

10. G.C.T. (Management) launch a second motion Several weeks later, by notice of motion dated July 3, 1972 (nine weeks after the writ) the plaintiffs asked for an order restraining the defendants until judgment or further order:

"... from using the words Curzon or any other name so closely resembling the name of the plaintiffs' Curzon cinema as to be likely to deceive or cause confusion as the name or part of the name of their cinema previously known as the Essoldo Cinema in the King's Road, Chelsea."

The reason for the second motion was that although the defendants had changed the name pursuant to their undertaking, confusion was alleged still to be occurring.

11. Relief refused—merits irrelevant Before getting to the issue whether there was such confusion (which the defendants denied) Whitford J. refused relief. His judgment can be analysed thus:

(a) *First:* He stated the principle:

"It is inevitably always an important question in cases of this kind whether or not the public are being confused, because the court, apart from deciding the conflict that there is between the parties, has always got to have the interests of the public in mind and it is highly

110

undesirable that in the field of businesses, as much as it is in the field of trade marks for goods, the public should be put in a position where they are likely to be deceived or confused. That, however, is a matter which has finally to be determined on the final hearing of the action, that is to say, the position as regards the public. The point of interlocutory relief is basically to protect the position of the plaintiffs who fear that unless some interlocutory relief be granted to them they will suffer damage and will not be adequately compensated in damage if they eventually succeed in the action."

(b) *Secondly:* He explained the basis of the plaintiffs' acceptance of the defendants' original undertaking:

"When they made their first application the plaintiffs were in fact prepared to accept that the possibility of serious damage pending the final determination of the action would be sufficiently obviated if they accepted the undertaking which the defendants offered, and they accepted the undertaking upon this basis. It seems to me that, in those circumstances, it would be wholly wrong for them now if perhaps they feel, or circumstances would appear to indicate, that they wrongly estimated what the result of the change of name would be, to reopen the matter...."

(c) *Thirdly:* Against that backdrop, he summarised his reason for refusing further relief:

"Before getting to that [the extent of the confusion] a question arose as to whether in all the circumstances the plaintiffs were entitled to bring this motion for further relief at all. As I see it, they are not. They are, as I have already said, now seeking to have a second bite at the same cherry. Their original contention was that the defendants should be restrained from using this name Curzon, upon an interlocutory basis. When the undertaking was offered they were prepared to accept it. Obviously now they think that the change of name which has already been effected is insufficient and I will assume for present purposes that the evidence to which they wish to direct my attention is adequate to establish some degree of confusion in the minds of the public."

12. But the position is different if the interlocutory order is not by consent The Chanel case should be contrasted with *Pfizer Corporation v. Inter-Continental Pharmaceuticals Ltd* [1966] R.P.C. 565. There, Lloyd-Jacob J. had stayed an injunction granted on the plaintiffs' application to restrain infringement of a drug patent, because the defendants had made an application to the Comptroller for a compulsory licence under the patent. Days later, in *Hoffman La Roche & Co. A.G. v. Inter-Continental*

111

Pharmaceuticals Ltd [1965] Ch. 795, the Court of Appeal expressed disapproval of allowing an application to the Comptroller to thwart an
otherwise effective injunction application. On further application by the
plaintiffs, Lloyd-Jacob J. removed the stay—but by virtue of the plaintiffs'
delay of 18 months, he ordered the stay to be removed only after the
expiration of two months:

> "The evidence appears to indicate that from time to time when orders
> are placed with their manufacturing suppliers, to the time when they
> have cleared the product from their shelves, a period of some 15 or
> 16 weeks may elapse. I think that would be an unduly long period in
> which to provide that the removal of stays should not be operative. I
> realise that it is to a certain extent a matter of guess-work, but I
> cannot help thinking that by showing all reasonable diligence in
> communicating with the manufacturers as a matter of urgency a
> certain amount of that time can be trimmed off."

In other words a court has power, on the application of the defendant by
motion or summons as the case may be, to dissolve or discharge an
injunction which the plaintiff has obtained otherwise than by consent, if
it subsequently becomes apparent that the injunction was founded on a
decision which was wrong in law: *Regent Oil Co. Ltd v. J.T. Leavesley
(Lichfeld) Ltd* [1966] 1 W.L.R. 1210.

13. The "consent" order parallel Although an order can be made "by
consent", the court still has a discretion under Ord. 3, r. 5(1) to grant an
extension of time for compliance with it: *Siebe Gorman & Co. v. Pneupac*
[1982] 1 W.L.R. 185. But where a consent order embodies an agreement
which amounts to a contract between parties, the court will only interfere
with it on the same grounds as it would with any other contract. Where
it is clear that the order embodies the negotiations between the parties, the
court will give effect to it where one party is in breach and not vary it by,
for example, giving extra time to perform its terms: *Tigner-Roche & Co.
v. Spiro* (1982) 126 S.J. 525, C.A.

14. Practitioners! How to avoid the *Chanel* trap To seek to avoid the
Chanel trap, application should be made for there to be included in the
order containing the undertaking: "Liberty to apply with or without change
in circumstances." In the same vein, Knox J. said in *Raindrop Data Systems
Ltd v. Systemics Ltd* [1988] F.S.R. 354 at 366:

> ". . . my intention is that the plaintiffs should have made available to
> them the software; and the argument is particularly centred around
> the source code; I have heard very little about the object code. It is
> my intention that the plaintiffs should have available to them what is

needed in that respect to comply with contractual obligations. But I do so on their undertaking to make those payments and on terms that both parties are to be at liberty to apply. I wish to make it quite clear that the liberty to apply is meant to be a general one and is not governed by such considerations as were ventilated by the Court of Appeal in the case of *Chanel Ltd v. F. W. Woolworth & Co. Ltd* [1981] 1 W.L.R. 485; [1981] F.S.R. 196, whereby a serious change of circumstances has to occur before an application can be made."

15. Applying to vary or discharge an undertaking In *Cutler v. Wandsworth Stadium Ltd* [1945] 1 All E.R. 103, it was held that if a party to litigation seeks to vary an undertaking he has already given, the procedure is to apply for a release from that undertaking coupled with (if appropriate) the offer of a different undertaking. *Chanel Ltd v. Woolworth & Co. (ibid.)* was distinguished in *Butt v. Butt* [1987] 1 W.L.R. 1351, C.A. The headnote, *inter alia*, reads:

"... where a motion for an interlocutory injunction was adjourned generally or *sine die* upon the giving of an undertaking by the defendant it was not dealt with or disposed of, but that the order itself contemplated an application for the matter to be re-opened before trial; that, moreover, the undertaking had been given on the express understanding that the defendant might apply for its variation or discharge; and that, accordingly, the defendant did not have to show good grounds, consisting of a significant change in circumstances or the discovery of new evidence which was not reasonably available before the undertaking had been given, before applying to modify the terms of the undertaking or discharge it."

11 Problems of secret processes, trade secrets, etc.

1. Type of problem Where the court is satisfied that there is a secret process, and that the ex-servant has learnt a material part of it during his employment, and has made an improper use of the knowledge so obtained, can the court grant an injunction despite the fact that the actual details of the secret process have not been disclosed?

2. *Amber Size & Chemical Co. Ltd v. Menzel* [1913] 2 Ch. 239 Yes. Astbury J. said at pp. 247–248:

"I have been somewhat troubled during the course of this case in making up my mind what the court ought to do where it is perfectly satisfied that there is a secret, and that the defendant has learnt a material part of it during his employment and has since made an

113

improper use of the knowledge so obtained, but where the court does not (at this stage of the action) know the full nature and extent of the secret process. Now the court will not and ought not to make an order performance of or obedience to which it cannot enforce. *But in the event, which I trust will not occur, of any breach of the order I propose to make taking place on the part of the defendant there will be no difficulty in the plaintiffs supplying the court, under proper safeguards protecting them from disclosure, with the details of their process in the event of their alleging disobedience to my order*, and I do not think I am prevented by anything said by Lord Eldon L.C. in *Newbery v. James* from making the order I propose to make." [Editors' emphasis.]

3. The trade secrets and duty of disclosure conflict The more draconian the order, the greater the obligation to disclose. But what if the information which would help strengthen an application for an *Anton Piller* order is secret to the extent that the defendants should remain in ignorance of it? In *W.E.A. Records Ltd v. Visions Channel 4 Ltd* [1983] 1 W.L.R. 721, the judge had been given oral information of (so the plaintiffs contended) a confidential nature which had not later been incorporated into affidavits in support of the motion. Sir John Donaldson M.R. said at 726G:

"I fully appreciate the problem which faced Peter Gibson J. when he learned that the original order had been granted after Mervyn Davis J. had been given confidential information which could not be disclosed to the defendants. I have already said that such a situation should never be allowed to arise. But, it having arisen, *there was no possible justification for this information being revealed to the defendants' counsel, but not to their solicitors.* Solicitors are officers of the court and are to be trusted to exactly the same extent as counsel. Any breach of that trust would be visited with the direst consequences and it is immaterial that the machinery involved might, but would not necessarily, differ according to whether the transgressor was counsel or a solicitor." [Editors' emphasis.]

And the Master of the Rolls continued at 728D:

"However that may be, there remains the problem of the confidential information disclosed to Mervyn Davies., and, I think, to Warner J. and Peter Gibson J. and eventually, of course, disclosed to the defendants' counsel and solicitors but not to the defendants. Understandably Mervyn Davies J. felt difficulty in dealing with the matter further if this information could not be passed to the defendants. Clearly the matter has to be considered solely on the basis of evidence which is known to both parties, and insofar as any judge concerned has other evidence or information he must ignore it. This is a difficult exercise and in the circumstances it may be thought better that some judge other than these three judges be seized of the action for the future. If the transcript of what was said to Mervyn Davies J. is considered to be relevant, it should be edited by counsel and solicitors on both sides in order to remove confidential matter which cannot be disclosed to the defendants. If there is any dispute as to the right of the defendants to be informed of any particular matter put before Mervyn Davies J., then this should be decided either by that judge, Warner J. or Peter Gibson J. as they already have that information from the transcript."

(Note: Evidence obtained on an *Anton Piller* order which has been discharged on the grounds of non-disclosure may be used in support of an application for an interlocutory injunction only for good and compelling reasons: *Guess Inc. v. Lee Seck Mon* [1987] F.S.R. 125.)

4. Exhibits in patent applications On a motion to restrain infringement, a copy of the plaintiff's specification should be exhibited where the defendant does not appear on the motion: *British Thomson-Houston v. Mandler* [1927] W.N. 152.

D: STANDING MOTIONS OVER

1 The problem

1. The *Pictograph* case The nature of the problem was referred to in *Pictograph Ltd v. Lee-Smith Photomechanics Ltd* [1964] 1 W.L.R. 402 where the plaintiff launched a motion in passing-off proceedings and the defendant filed evidence which raised a direct conflict of fact. When the plaintiff sought to have the motion stood over until trial, the defence argued:

"It is admittedly within the discretion of the court whether or not it will stand a motion over to the trial. It does not follow that because evidence is given on the motion which raises a conflict of evidence the court cannot deal with it at the trial. *But it would be wrong if a plaintiff could launch a motion which never had a chance and then, having seen that the evidence put in by the defence raises a direct conflict of fact, ask for the motion to be stood over to the trial without putting in his own evidence in reply.* The question is not simply one of costs. If that were allowed the motion would be no more than a fishing expedition on the part of the plaintiff; the defendant is entitled to fish in the same waters. It would be a great advantage to the plaintiff to see what was the defendant's evidence before drafting his statement of claim, and without himself answering the evidence on oath until trial." [Editors' emphasis.]

2. What did Pennycuick J. do? In the event, it was held that the plaintiff must either abandon the motion, or move it on the evidence as it then stood, or file further evidence in reply and then move. On March 3, 1964, approximately two weeks later, the motion was heard and no order was made on the motion, save that costs were ordered to be the defendant's costs in the action. The report, at [1964] R.P.C. 376, misleadingly says in the headnote: "Held: That the motion should be dismissed with defendant's costs in the cause."

2 Is Pictograph right?

1. The *Simon Jeffrey* case The approach of Pennycuick J. in the *Pictograph* case was reviewed by Walton J. in *Simon Jeffrey Ltd v. Shelana Fashions Ltd* [1977] R.P.C. 103. Already in the proceedings, an *ex parte* injunction granted on the application of the plaintiffs had been discharged and prior to the motion coming before Walton J. in the reported hearing, it had been stood over on several occasions. On the application of the plaintiffs, Walton J. stood the motion over to trial. Hours later, the defendant came before the same court and effectively asked for a *Pictograph* order as made by Pennycuick J. and reported at [1964] 1 W.L.R. 403, see above.

2. Walton J. disagreed with Pennycuick J. In response to the defendant's application, Walton J. said at 104(10–25):

"I have always been brought up to believe that in this Division a person moving a motion who has not opened that motion—and obtaining an *ex parte* injunction is not for this purpose to be equated with opening motion—is entitled as of right to stand that motion to the trial. The reason for that practice and procedure, which to my knowledge has obtained for many years in the Chancery Division, is obvious. A plaintiff launches a motion to which, so far as he can see, there is no answer. He is then met with an answer which shows that there is an actual conflict of fact. What is he to do? If he goes on with the motion he is almost certainly bound to fail. But it may nevertheless turn out when the matter is fully investigated at the trial that the evidence put in raising these disputes of fact is shown to be a complete fabrication. I am not for one moment suggesting that this is so in the present case. I am not dealing with the merits of the present case. So as a speedy way of relieving the lists of a motion which is not now going to be moved but to preserve both parties' positions as to costs, the practice grew up, and I have found it in operation for many years, of the mover of the motion being entitled to stand the motion to the trial. If he had opened it in any way it would have been different, because he has then elected to have the matter tried. Similarly, of course, if the defendant elects to fight the motion without putting in evidence—that is, to say it is completely misconceived on the plaintiff's own evidence—then the right to stand the motion to the trial never arises."

With regard to the *Pictograph* decision, Walton J. said at 104(20):

"... the decision of Pennycuick J. in *Pictograph Ltd v. Lee-Smith Photomechanics Ltd* [1964] 1 W.L.R. 402 came as something of a shock to the profession because it appeared to say this was not in fact the practice. It may well be that there were circumstances in that case which justified a departure from practice. But if that decision is intended to say that the old practice does not apply, I must respectfully decline to follow it because in my view it has always been done.... I still have an absolute discretion [to stand over to trial]."

3. The "fishing risk" The judgment of Walton J. was not delivered oblivious to the "fishing risk". He said at 104(45)–105(5):

"The whole point of standing the motion over is to save time and costs for everybody. I may respectfully quarrel with the views expressed by Mr Settle and Mr Monckton in the case above cited that it is only a matter of costs. It is only a matter of costs because the suggestion that it would be wrong if a plaintiff could safely launch a motion which never did have a chance of succeeding merely for the purpose of obtaining his opponent's evidence which then raises direct conflict of fact is misconceived. If anybody, plaintiff or defendant, wishes to fight along those lines they can do so and nothing can stop them. The only sanction that would be applied to such fishing would be that at some stage it would become an expensive method of proceeding. It may well be that if it does turn out at the trial of the action that the plaintiff is proved wrong this proceeding will prove expensive for them. I cannot see that a person who is intent on using the interlocutory motion procedure for fishing is going to be deterred by an immediate order for costs (usually payable later) as distinct from a deferred order for costs payable later."

4. Summary of Walton J.'s view Standing the motion over to trial, Walton J. said at 105(15):

"If you like to put it in bold terms, it is whether an order for costs should be made now on the basis of imperfect information or by the

117

judge at the trial on the basis of perfect information, as far as the court is ever going to have it...."

5. The Court of Appeal—ambivalent After hearing counsel for both parties in the Simon Jeffrey case, the Court of Appeal refused leave to appeal but indicated that in so doing it was not to be taken as endorsing the view taken by Walton J. Similarly, in *Simons Records Ltd v. W.E.A. Records Ltd* [1980] F.S.R. 35, Brightman L.J. said at 39:

> "In the circumstances, it is not appropriate that I should express any view on the correctness of the decision of Walton J. in *Simon Jeffrey Ltd v. Shelana Fashions Ltd* [1976] F.S.R. 54 in which the learned judge considered that an applicant had an absolute right to have his motion stood over to the trial of the action, where he had read no evidence. The point does not arise."

3 Chronology—what happened next?

1. *Pictograph* not followed Walton J. followed his decision in the *Simon Jeffrey* case in *Gloverall Ltd v. Durworth Ltd and Bodner Elan Ltd* [1976] F.S.R. 543.

2. *Gloverall*—the attitude of counsel for the plaintiff The motion moved on behalf of the plaintiff sought to restrain alleged passing-off in relation to duffel costs. However, when the matter came before Walton J., counsel for the plaintiff indicated that he did not intend to move the motion. This was because various allegations made in the evidence in answer led the plaintiffs to the conclusion that it would not be proper to seek an interlocutory injunction at that stage but rather risk for a speedy trial.

3. What did Walton J. do? Having refused to order a speedy trial Walton J. first stood the motion to trial and made no further order upon it, following *Simon Jeffrey Ltd v. Shelana Fashions Ltd* [1977] R.P.C. 103.

4. Costs—what happened? Walton J. secondly turned to the question of costs. He distinguished the instant case from that where the motion was hopeless as it stood, without the need for any defence evidence.

(a) *As to the instant case he said:*

> "... the whole matter left in the motion at this stage, because it is not now going to be moved, is costs. If I make an order as to costs, I am in fact dealing with the whole motion, and that is precisely and exactly what I do not propose to do. I do not propose to do so because evidence has been filed by both sides.... Once there is evidence

in on both sides, so that there is something, and I care not what it is, which is in issue between the parties, then the position changes. Under those circumstances, in my judgment, as I have already expressed in the case to which I have referred, the plaintiff has an absolute right to have the motion stood to the trial, because at that stage all that is left in it is the matter of costs, and the trial judge will be in a much better position, a very much better position than any interlocutory judge would ever be to decide whether the motion ought to have been brought into court in the first place...."

(b) *As to the other type of case, Walton J. said:*

"It may well be that if defendants to a motion are in a position to stand up and say 'we have not answered the evidence, the motion is hopeless as it stands,' the judge is then bound to deal with it and dismiss the motion."

In this context, it was held in *Kickers International SA v. Paul Kettle Agencies Ltd* [1990] F.S.R. 436 that where a plaintiff seeks an interlocutory injunction but decides, after seeing the defendant's evidence, not to proceed with the application for interlocutory relief, it may be a proper exercise of the court's discretion to award the defendant his costs of the application in any event and, in appropriate circumstances, to order taxation of the costs forthwith.

4 Summary

1. *Pictograph* and *Simon Jeffrey*—is there a reconciliation? In Société Française v. Electronic Concept Ltd [1976] 1 W.L.R. 51, Oliver J. said at 57D-H:

"It appears in fact that the decision of Pennycuick J. (in *Pictograph*) was not really fully reported in the All England Reports and I have been referred to a fuller report in [1964] R.P.C. 376. ... [It] does not appear to me ... that the report of the case in the All England Reports is sufficiently full.... Indeed, it does not appear to me that there is any necessary conflict between that case (*Pictograph*) and the decision of Walton J. in *Simon Jeffrey Ltd.* ... I think that in truth the court always has a discretion whether it will stand the motion to the trial on the plaintiff's application and that, in appropriate circumstances, where the court finds that it is necessary to determine issues of fact and is unable to do so on affidavits alone, that course will be taken on such terms as may be appropriate in the particular case."

2. **A synthesis** The court has a discretionary power to stand the motion

or summons over to trial. This is the course of action the court will usually follow (on such terms as it seems are just) where it is necessary to determine issues of fact which do not lend themselves to resolution on affidavit evidence alone: see *Simons Records Ltd v. W.E.A. Records Ltd* [1980] F.S.R. 35 at 36–37, for an example. But if the plaintiff wishes to apply to stand the motion over, he should give prior notice to the other side. Thus in *Max Factor & Co. v. MGM/UA Entertainment Co.* [1983] F.S.R. 577, Vinelott J. held that the court had a discretion whether the motion should be saved or not, and that the plaintiffs should in this case, having given no prior notice to the defendant of their intention to ask for the matter to be stood over, elect whether to move their motion on existing evidence, or abandon it. See also *Kodak Ltd v. Reed International* [1986] F.S.R. 477, which is authority for the proposition that if there is no point in standing over a motion to trial and the defendant has not wasted any costs, the better course is to dispose of the motion by making no order on it and granting the defendant costs in the cause. However, if an undertaking is given pending the hearing of the motion, and the plaintiff thereafter decides not to proceed for an injunction until trial, the defendant will have an unanswerable case for release from his undertaking: *Woodcock v. Denton Tackle Co. Ltd* [1978] F.S.R. 548.

E: ANCILLARY ORDERS

1 The plaintiff's cross-undertaking as to damages

1. Introduction An undertaking by the plaintiff as to damages ought to be given on every interlocutory injunction, though not where the order is in the nature of a final order: *Fenner v. Wilson* [1893] 2 Ch. 656. Except under special circumstances, effect ought to be given to it: *Graham v. Campbell* [1878] 7 Ch. D. at 490 *per* James L.J. The plaintiff should in the affidavit supporting the injunction depose to both his willingness to volunteer, and his ability to honour an undertaking as to damages: *Intercontex v. Schmidt* [1988] F.S.R. 574.

2. Purpose The cross-undertaking in damages is that in the event of the interlocutory injunction being discharged, the person obtaining the injunction undertakes to pay such damages as the court may be of the opinion compensates the other party for the loss suffered as a result of the grant of the injunction: *Fletcher Sutcliffe Wild v. Burch* [1982] F.S.R. 64, *per* Gibson J. at 68. In other words, the court seeks to ensure that the order for the injunction is so framed that neither party will be deprived of the benefit he is entitled to, if in the event it turns out that the party in whose favour it was made is in the wrong (see dicta of Cottenham L.C. in *Rigby v. Great-Western Railway Co.* (1849) 2 Ph. 44 at 50). Thus where a material fact has been withheld on an *ex parte* application, the defendant was held entitled to an inquiry as to damages, although the order *ex parte* containing the undertaking has been discharged by order made on notice: *Ross v. Buxton* [1888] W.N. 55.

3. The principle The jurisprudential nature of the undertaking was explained by Turner L.J. at 290 in *Newby v. Harrison* (1861) 3 De G.F. & J. 287:

"The true principle appears to me to be this, that a party who gives an undertaking of this nature puts himself under the power of the court, not merely in the suit but absolutely; that the undertaking is an absolute undertaking that he will be liable for any damages which the opposite party may have sustained, in case the court shall ultimately be of opinion that the order ought never to have been made."

Thus, the undertaking is not between the parties, but between the party giving the undertaking and the court. Hence the following part of the sidenote in that case reads:

"An undertaking given by a plaintiff upon obtaining an injunction, to abide by any order the court may thereafter make as to any damages that may be occasioned to the defendants by the injunction, remains in force notwithstanding the dismissal of the bill. An inquiry as to damages will in such a case be granted where the plaintiff's case failed by reason of his having no right to interfere with the act which he seeks to restrain, though the defendant was a mere trespasser."

4. When? An undertaking by the plaintiff as to damages ought to be given on every interlocutory injunction, though not where the order is in the nature of a final order: *Fenner v. Wilson* [1893] 2 Ch. 656 and (except under special circumstances) effect ought to be given to it, *per* James L.J., *Graham Campbell* (1878) 7 Ch.D. 490: and see note by Jessel M.R. in [1879] W.N. 74; *Newcomen v. Coulson* (1878) 7 Ch.D. 764.

5. Legally aided plaintiffs, etc. This principle applies, even if the plaintiff has no assets and is legally aided: *Allen v. Jambo Holdings Ltd* [1980] 1 W.L.R. 1252, C.A. It can be argued that in such circumstances, the undertaking is an empty shell and should not be exacted: equity does nothing in vain. But the counter-argument is that such a plaintiff may win damages at trial and yet have wrongly obtained an injunction as in *Barclays Bank Ltd v. Rosenberg* (1985) 135 New L.J. 633. If awarded damages, assets would be available to meet liability on the undertaking. Nonetheless, the court must take into account all factors when assessing the merits of the injunction application and hence the importance of the applicant giving full disclosure of his financial resources.

6. What if funds available to plaintiff of limited value, or nil? The court will not generally deny the plaintiff an interlocutory injunction to which he would otherwise be entitled simply on the ground that his cross-undertaking in damages would be of limited value. Thus in *Allen v. Jambo Holdings Ltd* [1980] 1 W.L.R. 1252, the Court of Appeal held that when granting a *Mareva* injunction, a cross-undertaking in damages could properly be taken from the plaintiff despite his being legally aided. This was attributed to the proposition that questions of financial ability ought not to affect the position in regard to what is the essential justice of the case. This may be interpreted as the principle underpinning the decision of the Court of Appeal in *Southway Group Ltd v. Wolff*, *The Times*, May 21, 1991, where Nourse L.J. held that where an application had been made for a *Mareva* injunction and it had been contended that an undertaking should be fortified by a guarantee for a certain amount, it was not for the judge to decide the matter upon a consideration that an amount of security greater than that which had been suggested by the interested party was necessary.

Note: Different criteria apply to *Anton Piller* orders.)

7. What if the defendant agrees to an undertaking in the terms of the injunction sought? The defendant should stipulate as a precondition that the plaintiff reciprocates by way of an undertaking as to damages. Curiously, it is only in the Chancery Division that (unless otherwise expressly provided) a cross-undertaking as to damages is automatically inserted where the defendant consents to an undertaking to the court in lieu of an interlocutory injunction: Practice Note [1904] W.N. 203 at 208, and *Oberrheinische Metallwerke v. Cocks* [1906] W.N. 127.

8. By whom can a plaintiff's undertaking as to damages be enforced? Loss occasioned by compliance with an injunction granted to a plaintiff can be claimed by all the defendants—not just those actually restrained by the order: *Tucker v. New Brunswick Trading Company of London* (1890) 44 Ch.D. 249, C.A. Thus in *Dubai Bank v. Galadari (No. 2)* [1990] 1 W.L.R. 731, Morritt J. held that when a plaintiff obtains an injunction against one of several defendants, and gives an undertaking in damages, that undertaking applies to all the other defendants as well. The rationale is that it may not be clear which of the defendants are liable to suffer loss as a result of the injunction being granted, particularly in the context of complex litigation. He further held that it would be a complete waste of the court's time to seek to determine at an early stage of the proceedings which defendants would be likely to be affected by the injunction, since damages would only ultimately be payable where damage had actually been suffered.

9. Security A difficulty may arise if the plaintiff is outside the jurisdiction. What security is there then for the undertaking? This problem confronted Goff J. in *Harman Pictures N.V. v. Osborne & Others* [1967] 1 W.L.R. 723. He said at 739C–D:

> "I must, however, impose terms for the protection of the defendants, and that is indeed conceded by Sir Andrew. As the plaintiffs are not within the jurisdiction, I must require them to give security towards implementing any liability they may incur under their cross-undertaking in damages. It is impossible to quantify that at this stage, but they have offered £10,000, which is the figure I had independently conceived in my own mind. The injunction will therefore be conditional upon the plaintiffs giving security in that amount to the satisfaction of the master within 21 days or such further time, if any, as the parties may agree or the master direct. Further, the defendants will have liberty to apply to discharge the injunction at any time."

Security will not, however, be ordered *ex post facto*: *Commodity Ocean Transport Corporation v. Basford Unicorn Industries Ltd (The Mito)* [1987] 2 Lloyd's Rep. 197. Hirst J. *inter alia* said:

> "Of course, Mr McClure accepts, as he must, that the Court has no power to impose an undertaking on the plaintiffs; and here I think that if I were to make this order I would in essence, *ex post facto*, be imposing an additional term to the undertaking, without any knowledge one way or the other as to what the situation would have been if it had been sought by the defendants in the first place. That is something which I think it is wrong in principle to do. The addition cannot be shrugged off by the defendants as being merely ancillary, as Mr McClure suggested, since it would have been, in my judgment, an important and substantive extra burden over and above the undertaking in fact given. A further aspect which seems to me to be important is this: now that the *Mareva* injunction is gone I would not be fortifying the undertaking at all, but in reality granting security to the defendants at the present stage for their potential damages on the cross-undertaking: and just as this is not the purpose of the Court when granting *Mareva* injunctions, so, in my judgment, it should not be the purpose of the Court in the present context. If, of course, the defendants could establish a *Mareva*-type situation here, namely, the presence of assets in this country belonging to the plaintiffs, a *Mareva* application might well be appropriate, but that is not the case."

10. Fortifying the undertaking In a proper case a plaintiff may be ordered to fortify his undertaking, *e.g.* by paying a sum into the joint names of the solicitors for each party: *Baxter v. Claydon* [1952] W.N. 376. The following practice points are generated by the cases.

(a) Where a defendant desires that a plaintiff should give security to fortify a cross-undertaking as to damages, he should apply for the security at the time when the injunction is granted and the cross-undertaking given.

(b) Such an application will not be entertained subsequently, particularly where the security relates to a cross-undertaking given upon the grant of a *Mareva* injunction which has been discharged: *Commodity Ocean Transport Corporation v. Basford Unicorn Industries Ltd; The Mito* [1987] 2 Lloyd's Rep. 197.

(c) Before an application to fortify an undertaking can succeed, a likelihood of a significant loss arising as a result of the injunction and a sound basis for belief that the undertaking will be insufficient must be shown: *Bhimji v. Chatwani; Chatwani v. Bhimji (No. 2)* [1992] 1 W.L.R. 1158, [1992] 4 All E.R. 705.

11. Interaction of undertakings and the perpetual injunction Quite frequently a plaintiff who is claiming a perpetual injunction, *e.g.* to restrain the defendant from proceeding with a major construction project, chooses not to apply for an interlocutory injunction because of the high cost of compensating the defendant for delay in completing the work in the event of the plaintiff not establishing his case at trial. The defendant for his part cannot risk going on with the works in case the plaintiff succeeds at the trial, but as no undertaking in damages has been given, he will obtain no recompense for his inevitable loss if the plaintiff's claim fails at the trial. Exceptionally, a plaintiff in such a case may be forced by the court to elect between applying for interlocutory injunction on the usual terms or having his claim for a final injunction struck out: *Blue Town Investments Ltd v. Higgs & Hill plc* [1990] 1 W.L.R. 696. *Oxy Electric Ltd v. Zainuddin* [1991] 1 W.L.R. 115 went the other way. The plaintiff sought a perpetual injunction (but not an interlocutory injunction) to enforce a restrictive covenant, which would have the effect of prohibiting the construction of a mosque and community centre. The defendant applied to strike out the statement of claim. Hoffman J. held:

> "Mr Cherryman's main submission was that the plaintiff was not bringing the action in its own interest but on behalf of its paymaster, Gallaghers. Mr Stapleton admits, as I have said, that he could not have contemplated bringing proceedings without Gallagher's financial support. He regarded himself as representing not only his own interests and that of Gallaghers but also those of adjoining owners who were

opposed to the scheme, but he insisted that the plaintiff was seeking to protect its own interests as it saw them. It had from the start been opposed to the scheme and had contributed to a legal fighting fund set up by local residents and industrial owners to mount resistance, unsuccessfully as it turned out, to the application for planning permission. I see no reason to treat this statement on affidavit as being made otherwise than in good faith. If the plaintiff has the benefit of the covenant and does not want to allow an infringing development I do not see that it needs any further justification for attempting to enforce it. In my view therefore the financial support of Gallaghers, which it is not suggested would contravene the doctrine of maintenance so far as it has survived, is irrelevant. I must look at the plaintiff's case for a permanent injunction on its own merits, and as it appears to me to give rise to issues which can only properly be determined at the trial, the motion to strike out the claim for injunctive relief must be dismissed."

12. Undertaking—by whom? The undertaking is properly given by the plaintiff's counsel, even though the plaintiffs are a limited company: *Manchester and Liverpool Banking Co. v. Parkinson* (1888) 60 L.T. 47; and a local authority may give the undertaking itself: *East Molesey Local Board v. Lambeth Waterworks Co.* [1892] 3 Ch.D. 289.

13. Undertaking enjoys life after death Where, after an interlocutory order for an injunction with the usual undertaking as to damages, the defendant died intestate as to his real estate, and his heir and executor were made defendants, and the action was dismissed, an inquiry was granted whether the deceased defendant and his heirs had sustained any damages: *Sheppard v. Gilmore* [1887] W.N. 242. Furthermore, the discontinuance of the action will not prevent the cross-undertaking being enforced.

14. Can a cross-undertaking be enforced if the defendant has consented to the injunction? The defendant's entitlement to damages under the cross-undertaking was not prejudiced by their consent to the granting of the injunction: *Universal Thermosensors v. Hibben* [1992] 1 W.L.R. 840. Sir Donald Nicholls V.C. also set out, at 580, a succinct summary of the law relating to that confidential information which the courts will protect.

2 Cross-undertakings as to damages—the position of the Crown and public authorities

1. The issue The problem arises, what if the plaintiff is the Crown? Should the Crown be required to give an undertaking? The question arose in

Secretary of State for Trade and Industry v. F. Hoffman-La Roche & Co. A.G. [1975] A.C. 295.

2. Facts of *Hoffman* Both Houses of Parliament approved an order laid before them by the Secretary of State pursuant to his powers under section 3(4) of the Monopolies and Mergers Act 1965, directing Hoffmans to reduce the price of their manufactured drugs. Hoffmans declared it to be their intention to disobey the order on the basis that it was *ultra vires* and invalid. Invoking section 11(2) of the Monopolies and Restrictive Practices (Inquiry and Control) Act 1948, the Secretary of State applied by notice of motion for an interim injunction to restrain Hoffmans from charging any prices in excess of those stipulated by the order.

3. Ruling in *Hoffman* The House of Lords held that by reason of the Crown Proceedings Act 1947 the Crown would in principle be required to give an undertaking. However, before such an undertaking would have been required on the facts of the instant case, Hoffmans would have had to show very good reason, e.g. where such relief might operate harshly against a defendant if it were ultimately successful at trial.

4. Rationale The justification for such a heavy burden of proof was that the Crown was not seeking to enforce its property rights, but rather to enforce what was prima facie the law of the land. The House of Lords, on the facts, came down in favour of not requiring an undertaking. Similarly, the injunction in *Director General of Fair Trading v. Tobyward Ltd* [1989] 1 W.L.R. 517 was not made subject to the usual cross-undertaking as to damages because the Director-General was enforcing the law on behalf of the Crown and also, given the strong prima facie case, there was no reason to require a cross-undertaking.

5. What if the Crown seeks to enforce proprietary rights? However, where the Crown otherwise applies for an interlocutory injunction, it will ordinarily be required to give an undertaking in damages just as a subject: *F. Hoffman-La Roche A.G. (ibid.)* at 318, *per* Lord Denning M.R., and Crown Proceedings Act 1947, s. 21. The generic issue of a cross-undertaking by the Crown arose also in *Att.-Gen. v. Wright* [1988] 1 W.L.R. 164; [1987] 3 All E.R. 579. The Attorney-General in an action brought against trustees of an educational charity, sought an interlocutory injunction to restrain the defendant from disposing of certain assets. Hoffman J. held that since the Crown was asserting proprietary rights on behalf of the charity, it was right to protect the defendant's interests by a cross-undertaking. There were difficulties about requiring such an undertaking from the Attorney-General, but the receiver of the charity was in a position to give the cross-undertaking. The cross-undertaking by the receiver was justified, in that:

(a) in so far as the Crown sought to recover property alleged to belong to the charity, it was, on behalf of the charity, asserting property rights; (b) there was no presumption that the first defendant had acted unlawfully and there remained serious issues to be tried.

6. When the plaintiff is a local authority A local authority can be required at the court's direction to give a cross-undertaking in damages where, although it has power to enforce the provisions of a statute by criminal prosecution for breach, it opts to seek an injunction: *Rochdale Borough Council v. Anders* [1983] 3 All E.R. 490, *per* Caulfeld J., distinguishing *F. Hoffman-La Roche & Co. A.G. v. Secretary of State for Trade and Industry* (*ibid.*). By reference to the same approach, the Court of Appeal under section 222 of the Local Government Act 1974 held in *City of London Corporation v. Bovis Construction Ltd* [1992] 3 All E.R. 697 that an injunction was properly granted even though it was not established that contravention of a notice under pollution legislation was a criminal offence and there had been a deliberate and flagrant flouting of that notice. The test was whether it could be inferred that the unlawful operations would continue unless and until restrained by an injunction. Lord Goff articulated the rationale in *Kirklees MBC v. Wickes Building Supplies Ltd* [1993] A.C. 227 at 274:

> "... Yet I do not read the speeches in the *Hoffman-La Roche* case as conferring a privilege on the Crown in law enforcement proceedings. On the contrary, I read them as dismantling an old Crown privilege and substituting for it a principle upon which, in certain limited circumstances, the court has a discretion whether or not to require an undertaking in damages from the Crown as law enforcer. *The principle appears to be related not to the Crown as such but to the Crown when performing a particular function.* It is true that, in all the speeches in that case, attention was focused upon the position of the Crown, for the obvious reason that it was the position of the Crown which was in issue in that case. But the considerations which persuaded this House to hold that there was a discretion whether or not to require an undertaking in damages from the crown in a law enforcement action are equally applicable to cases in which some other public authority is charged with the enforcement of the law. ... In the circumstances, *I find it difficult to understand why the same principle should not, in similar circumstances, apply to other public authorities when exercising the function of law enforcer in the public interest.*" [Editors' emphasis.]

Similarly, in *Securities and Investments Board v. Lloyd-Wright* [1994] BCLC 147 it was held that the court had a discretion not to require a cross-undertaking in damages when granting a *Mareva* injunction to a designated

127

agency which was seeking to discharge functions exercisable pursuant to statutory delegation. The fact that a worldwide *Mareva* injunction was draconian in nature did not prevent the granting of an injunction being law enforcement, but merely reflected the fact that the activities of the defendants might be worldwide.

3 Enforcing the undertaking

1. When does the undertaking become enforceable? In *Ushers Brewery Ltd v. P.S. King & Co. Finance Ltd* [1972] Ch. 148 at 154C, Plowman J. identified the following sets of circumstances which are capable of rendering the undertaking enforceable, by way of inquiry as to damages, namely: (a) the plaintiff has failed on the merits at the trial, or (b) it is established before trial that the injunction ought not to have been granted in the first instance, or (c) it is established, after trial, by an unsuccessful defendant, that the injunction ought not to have been given: *Barclays Bank Ltd v. Rosenberg* (1985) 135 New L.J. 633. However, an undertaking as to damages cannot be enforced if the defendant admits liability and pays money into court which the plaintiff accepts without going on to claim a perpetual injunction: *Wiltshire Bacon Co. v. Associated Cinema Properties Ltd* [1938] Ch. 268.

2. Before trial—how? The question thus arises: in what circumstances may it be established before trial that the injunction ought not to have been granted? The following authorities provide guidance, recited by Plowman J. at p. 155 (*ibid.*).
  (a) A decision of the House of Lords in another case decisively concluding the case against the plaintiff: *Novello v. James* (1854) 5 De G.M. & G. 876.
  (b) The plaintiff discontinuing his action before trial: *Newcomen v. Coulson* (1878) 7 Ch.D. 764.
  (c) Where a plaintiff obtains an *ex parte* injunction improperly, which is discharged at the *inter partes* interlocutory hearing: *Ross v. Buxton* [1888] W.N. 55, a case involving suppression of a material fact.

3. No counterclaim in contract The corollary of the principle that the cross-undertaking is not a matter of contract between the parties to the litigation is that there is no cause of action on which a party to the litigation can sue until such time as the court has made an award of damages pursuant to the undertaking in that person's favour: *Fletcher Sutcliffe Wild Ltd v. Burch* [1982] F.S.R. 64. Thus a claim in respect of a cross-undertaking in damages should not be pleaded by way of counterclaim before the court has decided whether or not the interlocutory injunction should continue permanently and before the court has exercised its discretion whether or not to order payment of damages on the cross-undertaking: *Fletcher Sutcliffe (ibid.), per* Gibson J.

4. No counterclaim in tort Gibson J. also rejected the "tort" contention in Fletcher Sutcliffe (*ibid.*) at p. 70:

> "In my judgment this is not a contractual matter, nor in my judgment is there anything that could be said to amount to a tort when a plaintiff obtains an injunction from the Court but subsequently fails to persuade the Court to grant a permanent injunction. Again, I would find it astonishing if this were to give rise to a claim in damages on the footing that the plaintiff had acted tortiously. True it is that the basis of an award of damages pursuant to the undertaking is to recompense that person affected by the injunction from being kept out of his money, but in my judgment that does not amount to a tort in respect of which that person can sue independently of seeking the assistance of the Court to enforce the undertaking."

5. Even in *Anton Piller* cases, the defendant's relief is limited In *Digital Equipment Corporation v. Darkcrest Ltd* [1984] Ch. 512, a defendant, having been subjected to an *Anton Piller* order, sought to argue that the plaintiffs had misled the court. As a vehicle for that argument, they counterclaimed in relation to the following causes of action:

(a) abuse of the process of the court;
(b) negligence;
(c) trespass.

Falconer J. held that such parts of the counterclaim were properly struck out, in that:

(a) there had not been an abuse of the process of the court, namely:
  (i) the defendants did not allege that the plaintiffs sought the *Anton Piller* for an improper motive;
  (ii) the court retained control over proceedings arising out of the *Anton Piller* orders, thus providing the defendants with full protection under the cross-undertaking;
(b) the plaintiffs did not owe a duty of care to the defendants giving rise to an action in negligence;
(c) there was no trespass because the plaintiffs' entry into the defendants' premises was with the defendants' permission pursuant to the order. Thus, no cause of action lay in trespass and any damage which arose from the entry would be compensated by the plaintiffs' cross-undertaking.

6. Fault irrelevant It is irrelevant to the inquiry as to damages that the plaintiff was without fault in his application for the injunction, as the headnote in *Griffth v. Blake* (1884) 27 Ch.D. 474, makes clear:

> "*Per* Baggallay, Cotton and Lindley L.JJ., where an interlocutory injunction has been granted on the usual undertaking as to damages, if it afterwards is established at the trial that the plaintiff is not entitled to an injunction, an inquiry as to damages may be directed, though the plaintiff was not guilty of misrepresentation, suppression, or other default in obtaining the injunction."

Analogously, a solicitor was ordered to pay costs as between solicitor and client and an assessed sum for damages where an undertaking proved worthless because the solicitor (without mala fides) had suppressed the fact that bankruptcy proceedings were pending: *Schmitten v. Faulkes* [1893] W.N. 64.

7. Inquiry as to damages—always? Will the court always order an inquiry as to damages if the plaintiff fails? No—the court has a discretion: *Smith v. Day* (1882) 21 Ch.D. 421, *per* Cotton L.J. at 430. In this regard, the following dicta of Cotton L.J. in *Griffith v. Blake* (*ibid.*) at 477 are material:

> "... the rule is, that whenever the undertaking is given, and the plaintiff ultimately fails on the merits, an inquiry as to damages will be granted unless there are special circumstances to the contrary."

In other words there is a presumption in favour of such an inquiry but it is rebuttable by reference to special circumstances. This principle was reasserted by the Court of Appeal in *Cheltenham & Gloucester Building Society v. Ricketts* [1993] 4 All E.R. 276 at 281 *per* Neill LJ:

> "From the authorities the following guidance can be extracted as to the enforcement of a cross-undertaking in damages.
>
> (1) Save in special cases *an undertaking as to damages is the price which the person asking for an interlocutory injunction has to pay for its grant.* The court cannot compel an applicant to give an undertaking but it can refuse to grant an injunction unless he does.
> (2) The undertaking, though described as an undertaking as to damages, *does not found any cause of action.* It does, however, enable the party enjoined to apply to the court for compensation if it is subsequently established that the interlocutory injunction should not have been granted.
> (3) The undertaking is not given to the party enjoined but to the court.
> (4) In a case where it is determined that the injunction should not

have been granted the undertaking is *likely to be enforced*, though the court retains a discretion not to do so.

(5) The time at which the court should determine whether or not the interlocutory injunction should have been granted will vary from case to case. It is important to underline the fact that *the question whether the undertaking should be enforced is a separate question from the question whether the injunction should be discharged or continued.*

(6) In many cases injunctions will remain in being until the trial and in such cases the propriety of its original grant and the question of enforcement of the undertaking will not be considered before the conclusion of the trial. Even then, as Lloyd L.J. pointed out in *Financiera Avenda v. Shiblaq, The Times,* November 21, 1988 the court may occasionally wish to postpone the question of enforcement to a later date.

(7) Where an interlocutory injunction is discharged before the trial the court at the time of discharge is faced with a number of possibilities.

(a) The court can determine forthwith that the undertaking as to damages should be enforced and can proceed at once to make an assessment of the damages. It seems probable that it will only be in *rare cases* that the court can take this course because the relevant evidence of damages is unlikely to be available. It is to be noted, however, that in *Columbia Pictures Industries Inc. v. Robinson* [1987] 3 All E.R. 338, [1987] Ch. 38 Scott J. was able, following the trial of an action, to make an immediate assessment of damages arising from the wrongful grant of an *Anton Piller* order. He pointed out that the evidence at the trial could not be relied on to justify *ex post facto* the making of an ex parte order if, at the time the order was made, it ought not to have been made (see [1987] 3 All E.R. 338 at 378, [1987] Ch. 38 at 85).

(b) The court may determine that the undertaking should be enforced but then *direct an inquiry as to damages* in which issues of *causation* and *quantum* will have to be considered. It is likely that the order will include directions as to pleadings and discovery in the inquiry. In the light of the decision of the Court of Appeal in *Norwest Holst Civil Engineering Ltd v. Plysious Ltd* [1987] C.A.T. 644 the court should not order an inquiry as to damages and at the same time leave open for the tribunal at the inquiry to determine whether or not the undertaking should be enforced. A

131

decision that the undertaking should be enforced is a pre-condition for the making of an order of an inquiry as to damages.

(c) The court can adjourn the application for the enforcement of the undertaking to the trial or further order.

(d) The court can determine forthwith that the undertaking is not to be enforced.

(8) It seems that damages are awarded on a similar basis to that on which damages are awarded for breach of contract. This matter has not been fully explored in the English cases though it is to be noted that in *Air Express Ltd v. Ansett Transport Industries (Operations) Ltd* (1979) 146 C.L.R. 249 Aicken J. in the High Court of Australia expressed the view that it would be seldom that it would be just and equitable that the unsuccessful plaintiff *'should bear the burden of damages which were not foreseeable from circumstances known to him at the time'*. This passage suggests that the court in exercising its equitable jurisdiction would adopt similar principles to those relevant in a claim for breach of contract." [Editors' emphasis.]

Note:

(a) In the *Financiera* case (*ibid.*) the Court of Appeal held that where a plaintiff gave a cross-undertaking in damages on the grant of a *Mareva* injunction, preventing the defendant's dissipation of assets, ordinary principles of the law of contract applied both as to causation and to *quantum* when it was sought to enforce the cross-undertaking.

(b) In *Balkanbank v. Taher and Others (No. 2), The Times*, December 1, 1994, the Court of Appeal held that when a consent order approved by a judge provided for an enquiry as to damages "which the plaintiff ought to pay", the question of discretion as to the enforcement of liability remained to be decided by the holder of judicial office who held the enquiry. In the course of his judgment Staughton L.J. referred to the *Financiera* case (*ibid.*)

(c) *Norwest Holt (Ibid.)* is also reported, *The Times*, July 23, 1987.

8. Burden of proof *Financiera Avenida SA v. Shiblaq, The Times*, November 21, 1988: Where a defendant seeks damages arising out of a cross-undertaking given by a plaintiff when granted a *Mareva* injunction, the burden of proof rests upon the defendant to show that the damage suffered would not have occurred were it not for the injunction. The defendant need not deal with every possible minor cause of the damage; however, he must establish a prima facie case that the injunction was the exclusive cause of the damage. The absence of evidence to the contrary will enable the court to infer that the damage would not have occurred, but for the injunction.

9. Inquiry—before whom? In both the Chancery Division and the Queen's Bench Division the inquiry is usually held before a master, though in some cases it is referred to an official or special referee.

4 Quantum

1. How much? As to the measure of damages, Brett L.J. explained the position in *Smith v. Day* (1882) 21 Ch.D. 421 at 428:

> "Now in the present case there is no undertaking with the opposite party, but only with the Court. There is no contract on which the opposite party could sue, and let us examine the case by analogy to cases where there is a contract with, or an obligation to the other party. *If damages are granted at all, I think the Court would never go beyond what would be given if there were an analogous contract with or duty to the opposite party.* The rules as to damages are shewn in *Hadley v. Baxendale....* If the injunction had been obtained fraudulently or maliciously, the Court, I think, would act by analogy to the rule in the case of fraudulent or malicious breach of contract, and not confine itself to proximate damages, but give exemplary damages. In the present case there is no ground for alleging fraud or malice. The case then is to be governed by analogy to the ordinary breach of a contract or duty, and in such a case the damages to be allowed are proximate and natural damages arising from such breach, unless as in *Hadley v. Baxendale*, notice had been given to the opposite party, of there being some particular contract which would be affected by the breach. [Editors' emphasis.]"

Similarly Lord Diplock said in *Hoffman-La Roche v. Secretary of State for Trade and Industry* [1975] A.C. 295 at 361E:

> "The assessment is made upon the same basis as that upon which damages for breach of contract would be assessed if the undertaking had been a contract between the plaintiff and the defendant that the plaintiff would not prevent the defendant from doing that which he was restrained from doing by the terms of the injunction...."

2. Who pays? An interesting point arises as to the costs of the inquiry. Some light has been shed on this issue by Stirling J. in *Ross v. Buxton* [1888] W.N. 55:

> "Stirling J. ... was of the opinion that though he had discharged the

order of January 12, he could direct an inquiry as to damages, as the plaintiff in giving an undertaking when the order was made put himself within the power of the court; but the defendant would take the inquiry at his own risk. The costs of the motion the plaintiff must pay in any event, and the costs of the inquiry would be reserved."

3. What category of damages? Falconer J. said in *Digital Equipment Corporation v. Darkcrest Ltd* [1984] Ch. 512 at 516G:

"The judgments in *Griffith v. Blake* referred to the earlier case of *Smith v. Day* (1882) 21 Ch.D. 421, and it is to be observed that in *Smith v. Day* Brett L.J., referring to a plaintiff's cross-undertaking as to damages when granted an interlocutory injunction, expressed the view, at p. 428, that, *if the injunction was obtained fraudulently or maliciously, the court would not confine itself to proximate damages, but would give exemplary damages.* Indeed, in the present case in their application to discharge the *Anton Piller* order, stood over by Goulding J. to the trial, the defendants have applied for an order for exemplary and/ or aggravated damages." [Editors' emphasis.]

Aggravated damages were awarded in *Columbia Picture Industries Inc. v. Robinson* [1986] 3 W.L.R. 542.

4. The duty to mitigate There is an onus on respondents to a *Mareva* to take such steps as are reasonable to mitigate such loss as may flow from the injunction. This principle, not expressed judicially in so many words, is reflected in the following dicta of Millet J. in *Re D.P.R. Futures Ltd* [1989] 1 W.L.R. 778 at 786–787:

"It is important to remember that it is not the purpose of a *Mareva* injunction to prevent a defendant from carrying on business or living his life normally pending the determination of the proceedings. It is not the purpose of the present injunctions to deprive the respondents of the use of their assets for reasonable purposes. At their request, and without any objection from the joint liquidators, I propose to add words to the order which will permit them freedom to vary or transpose assets with the prior written consent of the joint liquidators' solicitors or the leave of the court. In my judgment, and in the absence of wholly unforeseen circumstances, a cross-undertaking of £2m. is more than sufficient to cover any realistic estimate of the loss likely to be suffered by the respondents from the continuation of the injunctions. If this proves not to be the case the respondents can always apply, with proper evidence to support their claim, for an increase in the amount of the cross-undertaking, and the court will then consider whether to require fortification in an appropriate amount. The respondents may also make such an application if the company's assets are increased by recoveries, including, for example, repayment of the loans made to Mr Page and Mr Rycott. With these safeguards, I have no doubt that the balance of convenience requires the continuance of the injunctions."

5. Costs? It is contrary to the practice of the court to give as damages the difference between party and party and a higher scale of costs: *Harrison v. McSheehan* [1885] W.N. 207.

6. Interest? An award of damages ensuing from the cross-undertaking attracts, it is submitted, the jurisdiction of the Court to award interest under section 35A of the Supreme Court Act 1981.

5 Special circumstances barring action on the cross-undertaking

1. Are they defined? There is no all-embracing definition of such circumstances. The cases, however, shed light upon the attitude of the courts; for example, in relation to:
  (a) delay;
  (b) trivial loss.
As to the exercise of the court's discretion relating to whether such an inquiry should be ordered, Brett L.J. said in *Smith v. Day (ibid.)*:

> "Again, I am strongly of opinion that the question whether an inquiry as to damages should be granted is within the discretion of the judge who originally tries the case, and that his discretion ought not lightly to be interfered with. In exercising this discretion the court should act as nearly as may be on fixed rules or by analogy to fixed rules."

2. Delay The reason why delay should be avoided is to enable the court to be in a position accurately to remember the circumstances. In *Smith v. Day (ibid.)* and *Re Wood, ex p. Hall* (1883) Ch.D. 644, the plaintiff failed at the trial of the action and on appeal, but the inquiry was refused as a matter of discretion on the ground of delay. In the former case the delay was eight months without any explanation as to why. This should be compared with *Newby v. Harrison* (1861) De G.F. & J. 287, where the delay was four months, in relation to which Jessel M.R. said in *Smith v. Day (ibid.)* at 426:

> "After a lapse of time the statement of counsel is not enough; there must be evidence that damages have been incurred. In *Newby v. Harrison* an inquiry was directed after four months, and I do not say

that special circumstances might not induce the court to allow more, but had it not been for that case I should have thought four months too long."

See also *Schlesinger v. Bedford* [1893] W.N. 57.

3. But not all delay is bad An example of such "special circumstances" justifying lengthy delay me be found in *Newcomen v. Coulson* (1878) 7 Ch.D. 764, where Malins V.-C. said, at 765:

"I was at first struck by the delay on the part of the defendants, but there was a delay of four months in *Newby v. Harrison* which was not considered too much, and perhaps a year may not be considered too long to wait. Here there has been a delay of 11 months, during which negotiations probably went on. There must be a reference as to damages in the ordinary way."

4. Trivial loss Trivial loss will not justify an inquiry, as Jessel M.R. explained in *Smith v. Day (ibid.)* at 425:

"Then, again, the court must have regard to the amount of the damage; if it be trifling or remote the court would not be justified in directing an inquiry as to damage, though the damage might not be so remote that an action would not lie."

Because it would have proved to be fruitless, an inquiry into damages was refused in *McDonald's Hamburgers Ltd v. Burgerking UK Ltd* [1987] F.S.R. 112.

6 Inquiry

1. When does the defendant apply to the court for an inquiry? This problem does not lend itself to easy resolution, as the following dicta show (recited verbatim by Plowman J. in *Ushers Brewery v. King & Co.* [1972] Ch. 148 at 155H–156E, the actual dicta deriving from Smith v. Day):

"Then again the time at which the application is made is material. Having regard to the decision, we are not entitled to say that the application for an inquiry must be made either when the injunction is dissolved or at the trial. One of these must be the most proper time. The application may be made when the injunction is dissolved, but if made then it probably will be ordered to stand over till the trial."

Sir George Jessel M.R. in *Smith v. Day* went on to say at 426:

"Suppose the court doubts which side is really in the right, but considers that it is a case for an interlocutory injunction before the trial, and grants an injunction until the trial. *In such a case the application for an inquiry as to damages would most properly be made at the trial if the result of the trial is favourable to the defendant.* [Editors' emphasis.]"

Then Brett L.J. on this subject said at 427:

"As regards the time when the application ought to be made, I do not think that we ought to lay down that it must be made at the time when the injunction is dissolved. I do not think that the applicant is necessarily to be allowed to postpone it till the trial, nor do I say that he never can successfully make the application after the trial. *I think that he ought to make it within a reasonable time after the dissolution of the injunction, and that what is a reasonable time depends on the circumstances of the case.*" [Editors' emphasis.]

2. Adjournment to trial—an example In the *Ushers Brewery* case (*ibid.*), Plowman J. stood the application for an inquiry as to damages over until the trial of the action because even though he dissolved the injunction, it had not at that stage been established that the injunction should not have been granted in the first instance.

3. Preparing the ground If a defendant acquiesces in the continuance of an injunction wrongly granted, he may prejudice an application at the end of the trial, for an inquiry as to damages. Thus a motion to discharge an *ex parte* injunction on the ground of its having been obtained by misrepresentation may be proper, though the injunction is about to expire. This is consistent with the principle that an application to recover damages pursuant to an undertaking should be made promptly, and where the undertaking is dissolved at or before the trial, should be made then.

7 Other ancillary orders

1. Introduction Although the cross-undertaking in damages is the virtually inevitable partner of an interlocutory injunction, it is not unique as an order which the court has power to make, conditional upon the grant of an injunction.

2. Ancillary orders binding the plaintiff As a condition of granting the injunction the court may require of the plaintiff:

(a) *Expedition:* To undertake to prosecute the action with due diligence: *Newson v. Pender* (1884) 27 Ch.D. 43 at 63.

(b) *Payment-in:* If the plaintiff's claim is, *inter alia*, for a liquidated or unliquidated sum, an injunction can be granted conditional upon a payment of money into court: *Cavenagh v. Coker* (1919) 147 L.T. 252, where upon payment into court of the amount claimed to be owing, the court restrained a sale by a moneylender of goods pledged to him: *Jones v. Pacaya Rubber & Produce Co. Ltd* [1911] 1 K.B. 455, C.A., the headnote reads:

"If, while an action is pending against a company for the rescission of a contract to take shares, the company gives notice to the plaintiff to forfeit the shares in consequence of non-payment of calls, the court will, on the plaintiff paying into court the amount of the call with interest, restrain the company until the trial of the action from forfeiting the shares."

3. Ancillary orders binding the defendant Similarly, as a condition of withholding an injunction, the court may require of the defendants:

(a) *Undertaking in lieu:* To give an undertaking in lieu of an injunction: *Clarke v. Clark* (1864) 13 W.R. 133. (In that case the undertaking was subsequently discharged because the plaintiff broke the terms of the arrangement pursuant to which it was made.)

(b) *Account:* To undertake to keep an account, (*e.g.* of profits) and in the event of the plaintiff establishing his case to pay such sum as the court directs: *Rigby v. Great Western Railway Co.* (1846) 2 Ph. 44 at 50, *per* Cottenham L.C. (An account may also be ordered to be kept in any case where an interlocutory injunction is refused, or when an injunction is stayed pending an appeal.) In *Warren v. Mendy* [1989] 1 W.L.R. 853, the Court of Appeal held *inter alia* that it would be open to a court to refuse injunctive relief at the interlocutory stage on an undertaking by the defendant to keep full and proper accounts of his receipts.

(c) *Notice, etc.: Smith v. Baxter* [1900] 2 Ch. 138, *per* Stirling J. at 148:

"If I thought that when this action was brought the defendant actually threatened and intended to raise a building 60 feet high in the position in which that hoarding was placed, I should consider the plaintiffs entitled to an injunction in the ordinary *Yates v. Jack* ((1866) L.R. 1 Ch. 295) form. But I think, upon looking at the correspondence, that the object of the defendant was rather to ascertain what the plaintiffs' rights were rather than to infringe them. If, therefore, the defendant is willing to undertake to give the plaintiff reasonable notice of his intention to build, and at the same time to produce to the plaintiff upon request his building plans, it seems to me that the rights of the plaintiffs would be amply protected by reserving them liberty to apply hereafter for an injunction."

(d) *Demolition:* As to pulling down the structure complained of, the order made in *Ford v. Gye* (1858) 6 W.R. 235:

> "The defendant undertaking to abide by any order the court may make as to pulling down that portion of the north wall of the theatre opposite the plaintiff's premises, erected after January 8, 1858...."

(e) *Admissions:* To make certain admissions for the purposes of trial: *Hilton v. Granville (Lord)* (1841) 4 Beav. 130, the headnote of which reads:

> "An injunction to restrain the working of valuable mines refused, under the circumstances, on condition of the defendant's making certain admissions for the purpose of enabling the plaintiff to bring an action, although there was reason to apprehend that if the working was continued, the plaintiff's houses upon the surface would be totally destroyed or irreparably damaged before the legal right could be decided."

F: APPEALS

1 Ex parte injunctions pending appeal

1. Leave Leave is required to appeal from the grant or refusal of an interlocutory injunction: R.S.C. Ord. 59, r.1B(f).

2. Is there jurisdiction to grant injunction pending appeal? The court does have jurisdiction to grant on *ex parte* application a limited injunction preserving the status quo pending appeal, notwithstanding its having dismissed an application for an interlocutory injunction: *Erinford Properties Ltd v. Cheshire County Council* [1974] Ch. 261, Megarry J. explained the position thus at 267H–268H:

(a) First, he distinguished between interlocutory injunctions, final injunctions and injunctions pending appeal:

> "Putting it shortly, on a motion the question is whether the applicant has made out a sufficient case to have the respondent restrained pending trial. On the trial, the question is whether the plaintiff has sufficiently proved his case. On the other hand, *where the application is for an injunction pending an appeal, the question is whether the judgment that has been given is one upon which the successful party ought to be free to act* despite the pendency of an appeal." [Editors' emphasis.]

(b) He then justified the jurisdiction he declared the court had, to grant an injunction pending appeal:

"One of the important factors in making such a decision, of course, is the possibility that the judgment may be reversed or varied. Judges must decide cases even if they are hesitant in their conclusions; and at the other extreme a judge may be very clear in his conclusions and yet on appeal be held to be wrong. No human being is infallible, and for none are there more public and authoritative explanations of their errors than for judges. *A judge who feels no doubt in dismissing a claim to an interlocutory injunction may, perfectly consistently with his decision, recognise that his decision might be reversed, and that the comparative effects of granting or refusing an injunction pending an appeal are such that it would be right to preserve the status quo pending the appeal.* I cannot see that a decision that no injunction should be granted pending the trial is inconsistent, either logically or otherwise, with holding that an injunction should be granted pending an appeal against the decision not to grant the injunction, or that by refusing an injunction pending the trial the judge becomes *functus officio quoad* granting any injunction at all." [Editors' emphasis.]

(c) He set out the principles on which a court should act when deciding whether or not to accede to an application to grant an injunction pending appeal:

"There will, of course, be many cases where it would be wrong to grant an injunction pending appeal, as where any appeal would be frivolous, or to grant the injunction would inflict greater hardship than it would avoid, and so on. But subject to that, the principle is to be found in the leading judgment of Cotton L.J. in *Wilson v. Church (No. 2)* (1879) 12 Ch.D. 454, where, speaking of an appeal from the Court of Appeal to the House of Lords, he said, at 458, '... *when a party is appealing, exercising his undoubted right of appeal, this court ought to see that the appeal, if successful, is not nugatory.*' That was the principle which Pennycuick J. applied in the *Orion* case [1962] 1 W.L.R. 1085; and although the case had not then been cited to me, it was on that principle, and not because I felt any real doubts about my judgment on the motion, that I granted Mr Newsom the limited injunction pending appeal that he sought. This is not a case in which damages seem to me to be a suitable alternative." [Editors' emphasis.]

(d) He then confirmed that, initially, application should be made to the trial judge:

"I accept, of course, that convenience is not everything, but I think that considerable weight should be given to the consideration that any application for a stay of execution must be made initially to the trial judge. He, of course, knows all about the case and can deal promptly with the application. The Court of Appeal will not be troubled with it unless one of the parties is dissatisfied with the decision of the judge, in which case the Court of Appeal will at least have whatever assistance is provided by knowing how the judge dealt with the application."

(e) Finally, he drew the parallel between applying for an injunction pending appeal and a stay pending appeal:

"Although the type of injunction I have granted is not a stay of execution, it achieves for the application or action which fails the same sort of result as a stay of execution achieves for the application or action which succeeds. In each case the successful party is prevented from reaping the fruits of his success until the Court of Appeal has been able to decide the appeal. Except where there is good reason to the contrary (and I can see none in this case), I would apply the convenience of the procedure for the one to the other."

A variation on this can be perceived in the dicta of Croom-Johnson L.J. in the unreported case of *Fairley v. McLean & Others* (December 21, 1987):

"This is an application by the plaintiff against an order made by Sir Neil Lawson, sitting as a Deputy Judge of the High Court, on Friday last, 18th December, when he ordered that a *Mareva* injunction should be discharged but granted the plaintiff a stay of execution until 4 o'clock today, Monday 21st December 1987, in order either, first, to get an extension of the stay if he was able to do so and, secondly, to put in hand proceedings to appeal against the deputy judge's order discharging the *Mareva* injunction."

Note: Before the court will make a mandatory injunction pending appeal, there must be a strong prima facie case that the appeal will be successful: *R. v. Westminster City Council, ex parte Augustin* [1993] 1 W.L.R. 730.)

3. Appeal to the House of Lords The Court of Appeal has a jurisdiction similar in principle, in respect of an appeal pending to the House of Lords. In *Sturla v. Freccia* (1879) 1 Ch.D. 438, Cotton L.J. said at 446:

"The only question we have to consider is, whether or not the Court has jurisdiction in a proper case to stay all dealings with a fund pending an appeal to the House of Lords although the Court has

141

decided against the title of the plaintiff and dismissed the action. I see no difference in principle between staying the distribution of a fund to which the Court has held the plaintiff not to be entitled, and staying the execution of an order by which the Court has decided that a plaintiff is entitled to a fund. In that case, as in this case, the Court, pending an appeal to the House of Lords, suspends what it has declared to be the right of one of the litigant parties. On what principle does it do so? It does so on this ground, that when there is an appeal about to be prosecuted the litigation is to be considered as not at an end, and that being so, if there is a reasonable ground of appeal, and if not making the order to stay the execution of the decree or the distribution of the fund would make the appeal nugatory, that is to say, would deprive the appellant, if successful, of the results of the appeal, then it is the duty of the Court to interfere and suspend the right of the party who, so far as the litigation has gone, has established his rights. That applies, in my opinion, just as much to the case where the action has been dismissed, as to the case where a decree has been made establishing the plaintiff's title."

4. The risk of abuse In the *Sturla* case, James L.J. recognised the risk of the court's jurisdiction being abused. He said at 445:

"I had when the case was before us on the former occasion some misgiving which has led to this further argument today, and I am not yet entirely free from misgiving, not so much as to whether it is right or wrong to make an order in the present case, but as to whether the making of such an order may not be a dangerous precedent and likely to lead to great mischief. What I have been afraid of is that it may be said to be a precedent for holding that if anyone applies for an injunction and obtains it the injunction ought to be kept up as long as he can keep the litigation alive."

5. Recognising the risk—how should the court exercise its jurisdiction? Jessel M.R. said at 444, in the *Sturla* case:

"The terms in which the jurisdiction is conferred are general and unlimited. How that jurisdiction should be exercised is a question of judicial discretion which must be guided by proper rules founded on principle. It is not every case in which the Court or Judge should interfere. It is not to be said that when a party litigant has succeeded in two Courts he is to be in the same position as if had never succeeded at all. In my opinion it requires a stronger and more special case to induce the Court to interfere against him on behalf of the other party than would have been required if there had not been any trial of the action. I am by no means disposed to lay down the rule that this

Court should interfere pending an appeal to the House of Lords, simply because it would be the duty of the Court of first instance to interfere before the action was tried at all."

James L.J., at 446, emphasised the same point, but perhaps went further than the Master of the Rolls:

"If, however, it is distinctly understood that, as stated by the Master of the Rolls, *the granting of such an injunction pending an appeal is a thing to be done only under very special and exceptional circumstances*, then probably the danger that I have been afraid of will not exist." [Editors' emphasis.]

2 The approach of the appellate court

1. The limited right to interfere In *Hadmor Productions Ltd v. Hamilton* [1982] 2 W.L.R. 322 at 325E, Lord Diplock said:

"The function of the appellate court is initially one of review only. It may set aside the judge's exercise of his discretion on the ground that it was based upon a misunderstanding of the law or of the evidence before him or upon an inference that particular facts existed or did not exist, which, although it was one that might legitimately have been drawn upon the evidence that was before the judge, can be demonstrated to be wrong by further evidence that has become available by the time of the appeal; or upon the ground that there has been a change of circumstances after the judge made his order that would have justified his acceding to an application to vary it. Since reasons given by judges for granting or refusing interlocutory injunctions may sometimes be sketchy, there may also be occasional cases where even though no erroneous assumption of law or fact can be identified the judge's decision to grant or refuse the injunction is so aberrant that it must be set aside upon the ground that no reasonable judge regardful of his duty to act judicially could have reached it."

Lord Diplock reaffirmed this principle in *Garden Cottage Foods Ltd v. Milk Marketing Board* [1984] A.C. 130. And in *Elan Ditigal Systems Ltd v. Elan Computers Ltd* [1984] F.S.R. 373, Sir John Donaldson M.R. said at 384:

"*I think it should be said, and said with great volume and clarity, that this court does not exist to provide a second bite at each interim cherry in the sense that it is open to parties, having failed in front of the learned judge, simply to start again and have a* de novo *hearing in the hope that they will succeed in front of the Court of Appeal. We are a court of* appeal, and particularly in the field of interim injunctions it is primarily the trial judge who is appointed to decide whether or not an injunction should be granted. This is not of course to say that there is no right of appeal, but there is a heavy burden on the appellant to show that the learned judge has erred in principle, and that in exercising his discretion there is either an error of principle or—which is the same thing in a different form—he exercised his discretion in a way which no reasonable judge properly directing himself as to the relevant considerations could have exercised it." [Editors' emphasis.]

Thus the Court of Appeal dismissed an appeal against a refusal to stay proceedings on the basis of *forum non conveniens*—in that pursuant to *Hadmor* the finding of the Court of Appeal was one of review only: *Hawke Bay Shipping Co. Ltd v. The First National Bank of Chicago* [1986] 1 Lloyd's Rep. 244, C.A.

2. What weight is to be attached to the evidence on appeal? In *Scott Ltd v. Nice-Pak Products Ltd* [1988] F.S.R. 100, Fox L.J. held at 111:

"On the hearing of an appeal concerning the grant of an interlocutory injunction, it is not for me to say whether I accept or reject the plaintiff's evidence as to what was the direction and slant of its advertising. I content myself by stating that this evidence by itself is not strong enough to establish that there was a serious issue to be tried."

3. Time estimate and size of core bundle on appeal In *Dubai Bank v. Galadari* [1990] 1 Lloyd's Rep. 120 Dillon L.J., *inter alia*, said at 125:

"... such cases should be measured in hours, not days, that appeals should be rare and that this court should be slow to interfere.... In the present case the hearing of the appeals and cross-appeals was estimated for seven days.... Leading Counsel took us to a large number of pages in these bundles and sought to persuade us from these references that on virtually every question to which the Judge directed his mind, the Judge got the emphasis wrong or got the balance wrong. So, it was said, the Judge's decision on all these points was wrong and should be corrected by this Court.

I find this exercise misconceived and very sterile. It is easy to show that on very many of the questions he considered, the Judge could legitimately have taken a different view. But that falls miles short of showing that it was not open to the Judge to take the view he did on such questions. The relevant discretion is that of the Judge, not of this Court."

4. How should the appellate court view fresh evidence? In *Hadmor*, Lord Diplock said at 325H:

"I cannot agree that the production of additional evidence before the Court of Appeal, all of which related to events that had taken place earlier than the hearing before Dillon J., is of itself sufficient to entitle the Court of Appeal to ignore the judge's exercise of his discretion and to exercise an original discretion of its own. The right approach of an appellate court is to examine the fresh evidence in order to see to what extent, if any, the facts disclosed by it invalidate the reasons given by the judge for his decision. Only if they do, is the appellate court entitled to treat the first evidence as constituting in itself a ground for exercising an original discretion of its own to grant or withhold the interlocutory relief."

5. Concessions made at first instance—do they bind on interlocutory appeal? Generally yes—held Buckley L.J. in *Bryanston Finance Ltd v. de Vries (No. 2)* [1976] 1 Ch. 63 at 77C–F:

"Mr Bateson says that this concession was made for the purposes of the hearing before the judge only and should not bind him in this court. This is not, in my opinion, a tenable position. On an interlocutory application a party can, of course, make a concession limited to the purposes of that application. This is often done where a party does not wish at an interlocutory stage to incur the expense and delay that might attend the investigation of some disputed issue. But such a concession must, I think, be made for the purposes of that application in its entirety. If the interlocutory order be appealed, the party having made the concession below cannot resile from it in the appellate court, at any rate without the leave of the court. The primary function of the appellate court is to decide whether the judge at first instance has reached the right conclusion on the material before him. This material must include any concession made before him. If the appellate court were to be satisfied that the concession was made as a result of some misunderstanding or that for some other reason justice required that the party should be allowed to withdraw it, it might allow the withdrawal of the concession. Otherwise the concession must hold. It cannot be equated with the reservation of a point of law for argument in the appellate court which is not open in the lower court."

6. The need for a note of the first instance reasons The problem is well illustrated by the following dicta of Lawton L.J. in *Dellborg v. Corix Properties and Blissfeld Corporation N.V.* (June 26, 1980, C.A.T. No. 541):

"But I had to remind myself that this is an appellate court and all these matters were canvassed before the judge at chambers. The parties were represented by experienced counsel; the hearing occupied one and half hours. According to the recollection of counsel, what happened was this: As counsel put forward their arguments, Mr Justice Jupp from time to time made comments, as judges often do, which revealed how his mind was working. At the end of the argument, again according to the recollection of two of the three counsel who were putting forward submissions to him, he said, 'The applications are dismissed.' That way of dealing with an appeal is one commonly followed by judges sitting in chambers. I make no criticism of it. We have, however, been confronted with a difficulty. Whether or not to grant a *Mareva* injunction is a matter of discretion and this court ought not to interfere with the discretion of the judge at chambers unless it is sure that he either misdirected himself as to the law, or took into account matters which he ought not to have taken into account, or failed to take into account matters which he should have taken into account. In a case of this kind, the court likes to know what led the judge at chambers to make the order he did. As a result of that desire, this court has been saying now for some time that when there is an appeal to the judge in chambers, counsel should make note of the reasons the judge gave for making the order he did."

As to the extent of that note and the need for reasons by the first instance judge, in the unreported case of *KiMiS Advertising plc & Another v. Singer* (March 24, 1988) the Court of Appeal *inter alia* said:

"In my judgment the judge is not under any duty, when sitting as a judge in chambers hearing a contested *Mareva* application or an application to discharge a *Mareva* injunction on voluminous evidence, to include in his judgment a detailed analysis of the evidence giving the full reasons which bring him to the conclusion that there is, or is not, a real risk of the defendant disposing of his assets. If he does not analyse the evidence, or if he does not indicate the reasons for his conclusion, it may be that this court would reach the conclusion that he must have overlooked some important aspect of the evidence. But here the case for the *Mareva* is overwhelmingly put on the strength of the case of fraud against the defendant, Mr Singer. I cannot conceive that the learned deputy judge could have overlooked that that was the nature of the case that was being put forward, when he says that the evidence before him does not. . . ."

G: *AMERICAN CYANAMID*—AN ANALYSIS

1 Introduction

1. Background *American Cyanamid Co. v. Ethicon Ltd* [1975] A.C. 396

was a patent case. The general principles for which it is authority should be read in the context of the following dicta of Whitford J. in *Celanese Corporation v. Akzo Chemie U.K. Ltd* [1976] F.S.R. 273 at 276–277:

> "The plaintiffs move for an interlocutory injunction to restrain infringement of two letters patent. For many years a plaintiff in a patent action seeking interlocutory relief was in a rather disadvantageous position, which arose from this fact: that the courts took the view that, unless the patent were what is referred to in the old cases as 'an established patent'—that is, a patent of long standing which was generally recognised or had been tested as to its validity in the courts—if on an application for an interlocutory injunction a challenge was made to validity, then it would not be right to grant relief by way of interlocutory injunction, having regard for the uncertainties which it was felt must attach to the validity of any patent. In recent years there has been a considerable change of attitude. It is still open to anybody to sue for infringement of letters patent and to anybody who is brought to this court faced by an application for an interlocutory injunction to defend himself upon the basis that the patent is invalid; and, again, until relatively recently, although a mere challenge was not sufficient, as it had been in previous times, if a fairly formidable case could be made out—something in the nature of a prima facie case at least—there was a period during which it was almost impossible for a patentee to secure interlocutory relief. At this time on applications for interlocutory injunctions, there was sometimes something almost approaching a preliminary trial on the issue of validity, and it may have been sometimes even to the advantage of the parties that the matter could be tested in this way, because they might at the end of the interlocutory proceedings be in a better position to see the strength of their respective cases. All that has now, however, gone by the board, and the position so far as applications for interlocutory injunctions in respect of alleged infringement of letters patent is concerned has been made quite clear by the House of Lords in an opinion of Lord Diplock, which received the unanimous assent of the rest of their Lordships."

2. Cyanamid's four criteria When deciding whether to grant an application for an interlocutory injunction the decision of the House of Lords in *American Cyanamid v. Ethicon Ltd* [1975] A.C. 396 stipulates that the court should as a general rule have regard only to the following criteria.

(a) Is there a serious issue to be tried?
(b) Are damages an adequate remedy?
(c) Where does the "balance of convenience" lie?
(d) Are there any "special factors?"

3. The criteria are not infexible These criteria are analysed below, but they should be read in the context of the principle that the discretion of the court should not be fettered by laying down any rules which would have the effect of limiting the flexibility of the remedy: *Hubbard v. Vosper* [1972] 2 Q.B. 84 cited with approval in *Cyanamid* at 407D in the judgment of Lord Diplock.

2 Guidelines—must be allowed to guide

1. The duty to invoke. The *American Cyanamid* criteria must, whenever appropriate, be invoked. This was emphasised by the House of Lords in *Porter v. The National Union of Journalists* [1980] IRLR 404, which, *inter alia*, involved an interpretation of the defendant union's rules. At 406(7) Lord Diplock held that the case fell within the ambit of the Cyanamid guidelines:

> "My Lords, at no stage in these proceedings has this been a case where grant or refusal of an interlocutory injunction, would have the effect of disposing of the action finally in favour of whichever party was successful upon the application, as was the case in *N.W.L. Ltd v. Woods* [1979] IRLR 478. The strike itself was over before the proceedings were begun. The only question was whether the plaintiffs could lawfully be expelled, or otherwise penalised, for having refused to take part in it; and it was unlikely, as subsequent events have shown, that either side would throw in their hands at the interlocutory stage of the action. So it was a case that fell within the normal rule laid down by the House in *American Cyanamid Co v. Ethicon Ltd* [1975] A.C. 396. Slade J. however, although he did refer to *American Cyanamid*, did not in his judgment consider the balance of convenience at all. His failure to do so, in my view, vitiated any purported exercise of his discretion."

2. Consequence of failure to invoke—delay and expense The failure of the court at first instance to apply the guidelines prompted Lord Diplock in the *Porter* case (*ibid.*) at 407(11) to say:

> "My Lords, the ruling by the Court of Appeal as to the meaning of rule 20(a) and (b) was made by a court of three after full argument and was not expressed, even parenthetically, to be provisional. If left undisturbed, the judge at the trial would regard himself as bound by it; and, on the undisputed facts, it would be decisive of the action in favour of the plaintiffs. In view of this and of the wide disparity between the Court of Appeal's interpretation and the interpretation put upon it, with equal confidence, by Slade J. (which, on the

undisputed facts, would have been decisive of the action in favour of the NUJ), the Appeal Committee of this House thought it right to give the NUJ leave to appeal from the order of the Court of Appeal despite the fact that technically it was only interlocutory and had involved an exercise by that court of a discretion which the judge in whom it was originally vested had failed to exercise himself. I cannot refrain from pointing out that all the delay and expense involved in these successive appeals have resulted from the judge's disregard of the guidance given by this House in *American Cyanamid* by setting out to decide in interlocutory proceedings a doubtful question of interpretation of the Rules and leaving out of all account the question of the balance of convenience."

3 What is "a serious issue to be tried"?

1. The condition precedent In any application for an interlocutory injunction the first issue before the court has to be: *Is there a serious issue to be tried?* If the answer to that question is "no", the application fails *in limine*. (See *C.B.S. Songs v. Amstrad* [1988] A.C. 1013.)

2. What does it mean? Lord Diplock explained in *American Cyanamid* at p. 407D: "The court no doubt must be satisfied that the claim is not frivolous or vexatious...."

In *Mothercare Ltd v. Robson Books Ltd* [1979] F.S.R. 466, Sir Robert Megarry V.-C. observed:

"In view of the possibilities of misunderstanding that the term 'frivolous or vexatious' appears to offer unless accompanied by explanatory words. I would hope that it might disappear from general use in this context."

3. How much investigation? The court should not undertake an investigation in the nature of a preliminary trial of the action upon evidential material different from that upon which the actual trial will be conducted. It is no part of the court's function at this stage of the litigation to try to resolve conflicts of evidence on affidavit as to facts on which the claims of either party may ultimately depend nor to decide difficult questions of law which call for detailed argument and mature considerations: 407G–H. One of the reasons for the introduction of the practice of requiring an undertaking as to damages upon the grant of an interlocutory injunction was that "it aided the court in doing that which was its greatest object, *viz.* abstaining from expressing any opinion on the merits of the case until the hearing": *Wakefeld v. Duke of Buccleugh* (1865) 12 L.T. 628 at 629.

4. Deciding whether the question to be tried is serious—how? It is open to the court to decide that there is not a serious issue to be tried if the material available at the interlocutory hearing fails to disclose that the plaintiff has any real prospect of succeeding in his action for a permanent injunction at the trial: p. 408A. And in this context, Lawton L.J. said in *Tetrosyl Ltd v. Silver Paint and Lacqueur Co. Ltd* [1979] C.A.T. No. 599, reported in New L.J. August 28, 1980: "A serious question ... can only arise if there is evidential backing for it."

5. How serious is "serious"? Sir Robert Megarry V.-C. said in *Mothercare Ltd v. Robson Books Ltd* [1979] F.S.R. 466 at 474:

> "The prospects of the plaintiff's success are to be investigated to a limited extent, but they are not to be weighed against his prospects of failure. All that has to be seen is whether the plaintiff has prospects of success which, in substance and reality, exist. Odds against success no longer defeat the plaintiff, unless they are so long that the plaintiff can have no expectation of success, but only a hope. If his prospects of success are so small that they lack substance and reality, then the plaintiff fails, for he can point to no question to be tried which can be called 'serious' and no prospect of success which can be called 'real'."

Similarly, Megaw L.J. said in Alfred Dunhill Ltd v. Sunoptics S.A. [1979] F.S.R. at 373:

> "It is *irrelevant* whether the court thinks that the plaintiff's chances of success in establishing liability are *90 per cent or 20 per cent*." [Editors' emphasis.]

6. Should the concept of a "prima facie case" be invoked? No: The use of such expressions as "a probability," "a prima facie case," or "a strong prima facie case" in the context of the exercise of a discretionary power to grant an interlocutory injunction leads to confusion as to the object sought to be achieved by this form of temporary relief: *Cyanamid* at p. 407G. Moreover, to express at the interlocutory stage an opinion as to the prospects of success of either party would only be embarrassing to the judge who would ultimately try the case: *Cyanamid* at 410D.

7. "Serious issue to be tried"—in the context of the defence It is implicit in the dicta of Lord Diplock that whether or not there is a defence must also be taken into account—for it is only against that anvil that the court can hammer out:

(a) whether or not the issue raised by the plaintiff is serious; or indeed

(b) whether it is going to be tried.

Inevitably, if there is no arguable defence, the question of the balance of convenience does not arise: *Bradford Metropolitan City Council v. Brown* (1987) 19 H.L.R. 16, C.A. Also see *Official Custodian for Charities v. Mackey* [1985] Ch. 151 at 187 C–F and *Sheppard Cooper Ltd v. TSB Bank*, February 26, 1996, C.A. (unreported), where it was held that if, prima facie, the plaintiff is entitled to an injunction restraining the defendant, it is irrelevant to consider the question of the balance of convenience.

But of course, if damages are an adequate remedy, the absence of an arguable defence will not justify an injunction. In this context, reference should also be made to *Patel v. Smith* [1987] 1 W.L.R. 853. In this case the plaintiff and the defendant were freehold owners of adjoining properties which once had been in common ownership. There was a right of way in favour of the defendant over the plaintiff's yard, plus the right to park for the purpose of loading and unloading. For 30 years the defendant had used the yard for general parking. The plaintiff commenced proceedings to restrain that use. The defendant claimed a prescription right by virtue of a lost modern grant or 20 years' user as of right. The judge refused an interlocutory injunction. The Court of Appeal held, allowing the appeal, that where title was not in issue, a landowner was prima facie entitled to an injunction to restrain a trespass even if the trespass did not harm him. Only if the defendant could show an arguable case that he had a right to do what the plaintiff sought to prevent, should the court go on to consider the balance of convenience, the preservation of the status quo and the adequacy of damages as a remedy. There was no such arguable case, and the injunction would be granted. The case is also authority for the principle that a landowner is prima facie entitled to an injunction to restrain trespass on his land where title is not in issue even if he suffers no harm, unless the defendant can show an arguable case that he has the right to enter. However, in the interest of completeness, it should be noted that a court may, by injunction, control the detailed use of a right of way in order to prevent excessive and unreasonable use and possible nuisance: *Rosling v. Pinnegar* (1987) 54 P. & C.R. 124, C.A.

8. Is it open to express a view on merits? Perhaps. In *Conder International Ltd v. Hibbing Ltd* [1984] F.S.R. 312, Whitford J. at first instance had said:

> "... whatever the ultimate position so far as infringement is concerned, and I was not impressed by counsel for the defendants saying that the plaintiffs' case was unarguable, although he said ultimately he would so submit, so far as the issue of validity is concerned, although it would be wholly inappropriate for me to come to anything like a concluded opinion on evidence which has not been tested by cross-

examination, I must say that I do not think that the plaintiffs' case on Patent No. 1,430,930 is a strong one."

On appeal, Buckley L.J. said at 314–315:

"It appears to me that all the learned judge is saying in that passage is that although he does not think the plaintiffs' case is a strong one, he does think that it is proper to regard it as an arguable one, and that indeed is the first matter which has to be considered on an application for an interlocutory injunction when applying the principles discussed in *American Cyanamid v. Ethicon* reported in [1975] A.C. 396. I do not see in the learned judge's judgment a just ground for saying that he allowed his view of the strength of the plaintiffs' case in that respect unduly to influence his decision."

See also *R. v. Westminster City Council, ex p. Costi, The Independent,* March 12, 1987.

9. Equity does nothing in vain The court refused an application for permanent injunctions preventing the publication of information even though it might originally have been disseminated in breach of a duty of confidence where widespread publication had already taken place and the purpose of the injunction sought would be nugatory: *Att.-Gen. v. The Observer* [1988] 3 W.L.R. 776.

10. Simple point of construction Though it was said in *Cyanamid* that at the interlocutory stage it is no part of the court's function "to decide difficult questions of law which call for detailed argument and mature consideration" (at [1975] A.C. 396 at 407) a court may grant or refuse interlocutory relief without applying the Cyanamid guidelines if the action is concerned only with a simple question of constructing a statute or document, *e.g.* a lease or a contract. *Fellowes & Son v. Fisher* [1976] Q.B. 122 at 141; *Associated British Ports v. T.G.W.U.* [1989] 1 W.L.R. 939 at 979, 980.

4 "Serious issue to be tried"–how much evidence does one adduce?

1. The problem One party adduces evidence and bundles of documents indicating a serious issue to be tried. The other side rejoins by documents of equal weight. The plaintiff, concerned lest he has failed to get over the first *Cyanamid* hurdle, calls for more documents.

2. Consequence The result of such caution can result in the court—through the back door, as it were—being seised of sufficient material to answer the forbidden question: What are the chances of success at trial? Browne L.J. explained the point in *Alfred Dunhill Ltd v. Sunoptics S.A. (ibid.)* at 373:

"The massiveness of the evidence and the length of the argument on this issue as to the chances of the plaintiffs' success—the forbidden issue—have come about without any impropriety on the part of either party in their general approach to this application for an interlocutory injunction. They have come about because, first, as I suppose is only natural, the plaintiffs, in putting forward their claim, were concerned to omit nothing that might assist to show that they had at least a good arguable case. The defendants then sought to show that the plaintiffs did not have even an arguable case. Whether or not in the circumstances that was realistic, the defendants were entitled, under the *American Cyanamid* doctrine, to seek to show, if they could, that there was no real cause to meet. So they, in their turn, deployed lengthy affidavits, with exhibits, in support of that contention. The plaintiffs, in their turn, replied with much further material in answer."

3. Rationale The problem for the practitioner is that the conduct of application for interlocutory injunctions necessarily brings him into the arena where there is a virtual conflict of duties:

   (a) On the one hand there is the overriding duty for the court to comply with the *Cyanamid* guidelines.

   (b) On the other hand, there is the duty to the client—which entails recognition of what is the reality, namely that most interlocutory judgments are decisive of the action as a whole. Thus, inevitably, the plaintiff seeks to strike hard and fast (hence the title to this book—*Pre-emptive Remedies*) to achieve a favourable judgment and/or settlement whereas the defendant's strategy must be to stave off the plaintiff whereby he will ultimately tire of the action.

Yet the burden on the defendant may not be unduly onerous. In *Smith (T.J.) and Nephew Ltd v. 3M United Kingdom plc* [1983] R.P.C. 92, (for the facts of which see below, pp. 801–805). Lawton L.J. said at 101(5):

"... in this class of case [patent infringement], although the defendants, according to the circumstances, will have to show that they do genuinely intend to defend the action and are not merely playing for time so as to get a further opportunity of infringing the plaintiffs' patent, it is not necessary for them to reveal in detail what the case is."

And Dillon L.J. continued at 103(25–40):

"As to the first point, it seems to me that it amply appears from the circumstances of this case, whether or not it was strictly necessary for

153

the defendants to make it apparent, that the defendants have points which they genuinely might wish to urge by way of defence to this action. In these circumstances, it was, in my judgment, wholly unnecessary for them to put in elaborate evidence which the court could not have assessed on motion. The question how far a defendant who faces an application for an interlocutory injunction has to show his hand and disclose his evidence is one which may have important implications in other cases and I would not wish to say more than is necessary for the decision of this particular case, as the answer may often depend upon the particular facts of the case. Here I do not feel able to support the judge's view that it was necessary for the defendants to put in evidence to substantiate their assertion that their Tegaderm does not infringe the plaintiffs' patents or their assertion that the plaintiffs' patents are invalid."

Similarly in *Celanese Corporation v. Akzo Chemie U.K. Ltd* [1976] F.S.R. 273 at 276, Whitford J. aired the following view:

"Where questions of infringement of patent arise and proceedings are started on a motion for an interlocutory injunction, having regard to the position that is now established by the authority of *American Cyanamid v. Ethicon*, the parties would be well advised to see whether they cannot agree that it would be a waste of time to deal with the question of the issues of infringement and validity in cases where it is apparent to the advisers on both sides that there must be an arguable case, so as to save altogether the time which is lost in pursuing those matters."

5 Damages an adequate remedy?

1. The second criterion Once the court has found that there is a serious issue to be tried, it should go on to consider the adequacy of the respective remedies in damages available for either party. In this regard the cases should be read in the context of the following dicta of Sachs L.J. in *Evans Marshall & Co. Ltd v. Bertola S.A.* [1973] 1 W.L.R. 349 at 379 H:

"The standard question in relation to the grant of an injunction— 'Are damages an adequate remedy?'—might perhaps, in the light of recent authorities of recent years, be rewritten—'Is it just, in all the circumstances, that a plaintiff should be confined to his remedy in damages?' "

2. Why have that criterion? Buckley L.J. explained the rationale in *Polaroid Corporation v. Eastman Kodak Co.* [1977] R.P.C. 379 at 395:

"... but in every case of an application for an interlocutory injunction until trial the court must, in my judgment, approach the case with the object of making whatever order will be likely best to enable the trial judge to do justice between the parties, whichever way the decision goes at the trial. Their freedom of action should only be interfered with to an extent necessary to this end. This, as I understand the decision in the case of *American Cyanamid Company v. Ethicon Limited* [1975] A.C. 396 is the reasoning underlying the decision of the House of Lords in that case. Accordingly, if the plaintiff can be compensated in damages for anything he may wrongfully suffer between the date of the application and the trial, the defendant should not be restrained, save in exceptional circumstances."

3. Establishing whether damages an adequate remedy—how? When considering the adequacy of the respective remedies in damages available for either party, the court adopts the following approach:

(a) The court asks whether, if the plaintiff were to succeed at trial in establishing his right to a permanent injunction, he would be adequately compensated by an award of damages for the loss he would have sustained as a result of the defendant's continuing to do what was sought to be enjoined between the time of the application and the time of trial. If damages in the measure recoverable at common law would be an adequate remedy and the defendant would be in a financial position to pay them, no interlocutory injunction should normally be granted, however strong the plaintiff's claim appeared to be at that stage: *American Cyanamid* at 408C–D. This was held to be the position in *Hodge Clemco Ltd v. Airblast Ltd* [1995] F.S.R. 806 *per* Jacob J., a passing-off action where the defendant's manufactured items were said "to suit" the plaintiff's product.

(b) If, on the other hand, damages would not provide an adequate remedy for the plaintiff in the event of his succeeding at the trial, the court should then consider whether, on the contrary hypothesis that the defendant were to succeed at the trial in establishing his right to do that which was sought to be enjoined, he would be adequately compensated under the plaintiff's undertaking as to damages for the loss he would have sustained by being prevented from doing so between the time of the application and the time of trial. If damages in the measure recoverable under such an undertaking would be an adequate remedy and the plaintiff would be in a financial position to pay them, there would be no reason on this ground to refuse an interlocutory application: 408D–E. By way of example, damages were held not to be an adequate remedy in *Re Gillen's Application* [1988] N.I.J.B. 47 D.C. Gillen had been arrested

155

on suspicion of terrorist offences and detained for questioning. His counsel applied for a writ of habeas corpus to obtain his release on the ground that his retention was rendered unlawful by reason of police ill-treatment. It was held that:

   (i) Gillen had established a strong prima facie case that he had been assaulted by the police in the course of interviews to extract a confession from him.

  (ii) Although Gillen's detention was initially lawful it became unlawful when the police tried to extract a confession from him by assaulting him.

 (iii) An injunction to restrain the police from further assaulting or questioning Gillen would not adequately protect him.

  (iv) The right to receive damages for assault was not an adequate remedy.

   (v) A writ of habeas corpus would issue unless it was proved that Gillen had not been seriously assaulted. As the Chief Constable did not produce such proof Gillen was released by the police from custody.

4. Damages an adequate remedy—the ability of a party to pay In *Evans Marshall v. Bertola* [1973] 1 W.L.R. 349, C.A., for the facts of which see pp. 637–638, there fell for consideration the question whether the defendant could satisfy a judgment in the event that the court refused an injunction, on the basis that damages were an adequate remedy. Sachs L.J. said at 380H:

> "So far the question of *adequacy of damages* has been discussed on the footing that if judgment was recovered the sum awarded would be paid. But whenever the adequacy of damages falls to be considered in this class of case, there arises the further question—*are the defendants good for the money*? Also (if they are abroad), will their government's exchange control permit the payment? In other words, will the judgment be satisfied? Bertola being a wholly owned subsidiary of unknown financial status in Spain, and I.S.I. a company with a £5,000 share capital, the chances of a judgment for sums such as have just been mentioned being satisfied by them cannot be rated as other than questionable. So on that ground, too, damages would prima facie in this case not be an adequate remedy." [Editors' emphasis.]

5. Is "ability to pay" a rich man's charter? Surely not—as Sir Robert Megarry V.-C. said in *Vernon & Company (Pulp Products) Ltd v. Universal Pulp Containers Ltd* [1980] F.S.R. 179:

> "It would be intolerable if the *Cyanamid* case was allowed to become a charter of success for all the rich companies who seek interlocutory

injunctions against poor companies in cases in which damages would be an adequate remedy, enabling them to obtain an injunction merely on showing that there is a serious question to be tried."

And indeed, the Vice-Chancellor demonstrated the danger of allowing "ability to pay" to weigh unduly in the balance:

"If the defendants are in a precarious financial state, the grant of an injunction against them to restrain them from carrying on the activity which they hope will restore them to prosperity may of itself drive them into insolvency and liquidation, and so leave the plaintiffs in undisputed possession of the field. Accordingly, I think the court has to be astute to prevent this sort of unfairness if this can be done without injury to the plaintiffs."

However, these dicta should be contrasted with those of Buckley L.J. in *Standex International Ltd v. C.B. Blades and C.B. Blades Ltd* [1976] F.S.R. 114 at 122 (for the facts, see pp. 910–913):

"There is a further consideration whether, if at the trial the plaintiffs were to succeed and the defendant had not been restrained in the meanwhile, the defendants would be good for any damages to which the plaintiffs might then be entitled in respect of what had occurred between the present time and the trial of the action. The defendant company has a paid-up capital of just under £3,000. It has not been long in business. There seems to me to be no ground for supposing that it has had an opportunity to build up any substantial financial reserves. It must have had to expend a considerable part of the proceeds of its paid-up capital in acquiring the capital assets required to carry on the business or, if it has not spent the paid-up capital, it must have incurred liabilities which would reduce the net value of the company's assets. I do not see any substantial grounds for supposing that the defendant company would be in a position to pay substantial damages."

6. How can a defendant circumvent the "ability to pay" problem?

(a) *Security:* One way of avoiding the particular problem facing a defendant outside the jurisdiction would be to provide security to the satisfaction of the court for damages up to a stipulated sum. In the context of a case such as *Evans Marshall v. Bertola*, that would have involved dealing in proper detail not only with the form of the undertaking but also with the safeguards offered to the plaintiffs in order to secure its fulfilment. Similarly, in *Re DPR Futures Ltd* [1989] BCLC 634 at 639–640, [1989] 1 W.L.R. 778 at 785–786, Millet J. *inter alia* said:

"Although theoretically unlimited, the value of the cross-undertaking

157

was in reality limited to the value of the company's assets. This made it necessary for the court to make a realistic estimate of the potential loss which might be suffered by the defendant as the result of the grant of an injunction, and where the company's assets were insufficient to support an adequate cross-undertaking the court would require it to be fortified by a bond or payment into court. The cross-undertaking would still in practice be limited in amount; that is to say, to the amount of the company's assets together with the amount of the bond or payment into court. The court would not require the creditors, still less the liquidator to provide an unlimited guarantee that the defendant would suffer no less from the granting of the injunction....

... any such estimate can be reviewed from time to time and further fortification required if necessary. If fortification cannot be obtained this will affect the balance of convenience between granting or refusing the injunction. But the court cannot abdicate its responsibility for deciding where the balance of convenience lies." [Editors' emphasis.]

But defendants who invoke the assistance of third parties not before the court, in making an offer as to security, attract a certain judicial cynicism: As Sachs L.J. said at 381E:

"It is, however, as well to observe that *offers of guarantee by a third party not before the court are indeed a novelty*; and if designed to stave off an injunction must be looked at with considerable caution."

(b) *Joint bank account:* In a breach of copyright/patent type case, the technique adopted by the solicitors in *Coco v. A.N. Clark (Engineers) Ltd* [1969] R.P.C. 41 at 54 may be invoked, namely: that an injunction would not be granted on the basis that the respondents to the proceedings would set aside appropriate sums in the nature of royalties in a bank account in the joint names of the solicitors for each side on trusts that will protect those sums if financial disaster were to overtake such respondents. The order actually made in the *Coco* case reads:

"... AND the plaintiff by his Counsel undertaking to abide by any Order as to damages this Court may make in this case if it shall hereafter be of opinion that the Defendants shall have sustained any by reason of any of the undertakings on their part hereinafter contained. AND the Defendants by their Counsel undertaking as follows that is to say: (1) that they will on or before the seventh day of every month pay into a bank deposit account in the joint names of the Solicitors for the plaintiff and for the defendants the sum of five shillings sterling for each 'SCAMP' engine which shall have been made by the defendants during the previous month every such sum to be held in trust to follow the directions of this Court in this Action, and (2) that they will on or before the seventh day of every month give to the solicitors for the plaintiff an account for the total number of such engines made in the preceding month the solicitors for the plaintiff by Counsel for the plaintiff being their Counsel for this purpose undertaking not to divulge the said account to the plaintiff or to any one (other than to the plaintiff's Counsel upon his giving an under-taking not to divulge the said account to the plaintiff or to any one (other than to the plaintiff's Counsel upon his giving an undertaking not to divulge the said account to anyone) without the consent of the defendants or of this court. THIS COURT DOTH NOT think fit to make any order upon the said motion BUT DOTH ORDER that the costs of the said motion are to be costs in the cause."

7. Assessing the damages—a passing off example In *Granada Group Ltd v. Ford Motor Co. Ltd* [1972] F.S.R. 103, as to the facts of which see p. 924, Graham J. dismissed the motion, but went on to say at 109:

"Furthermore, it seems to me that, if it ultimately turns out that I am wrong and the plaintiffs are right, the plaintiffs can be adequately compensated by damages, which would probably be based on the notional cost of a licence to use the plaintiffs' name Granada in the way the defendants seek to use it."

8. Damages—an adequate but not a complete remedy Save in the simplest cases, the decision to grant or refuse an interlocutory injunction will cause to whichever party is unsuccessful on the application some disadvantages which his ultimate success at the trial may show he ought to have been spared. Such disadvantage may be such that the recovery of damages to which he would then be entitled either in the action or under the plaintiff's undertaking would not be sufficient to compensate him fully for all of them. The extent to which the disadvantages to each party would be incapable of being compensated in damages in the event of his succeeding at the trial is always a significant factor in assessing where the balance of convenience lies: *Cyanamid* at 408H–409A.

9. The adequacy of damages/injunction interface It is open to the court to refuse injunctive relief at the interlocutory stage on an undertaking by the defendant to keep full and proper accounts of income received from the wrong complained of: *Warren v. Mendy* [1989] 1 W.L.R. 853.

10. Evidence When applying for an interlocutory injunction it is usually incumbent on the plaintiff to tender in evidence particulars of his financial position. In *Brigid Foley Ltd v. Ellott* [1982] R.P.C. 433, Sir Robert Megarry V.-C. said at 435 (40–50)–436(5):

"One must add to that that although in this case the first defendant raised in her affidavit of August 18 the question of the financial position of the plaintiff, and gave some evidence as to her own financial position the plaintiff, in its affidavit in reply, sworn on August 22, gave no information as to its financial position, save a statement to its turnover. I have allowed Mr DeLacey to mention some figures in an unaudited balance sheet to December 31 last for the plaintiff from which it appears that the plaintiff is a substantial company with a substantial sum of net current assets. I should have been reluctant to dismiss the motion simply on the grounds of a failure to put in evidence that balance sheet; but I would emphasise that in applications for injunctions, especially since *Cyanamid*, one of the important matters always to be dealt with is the ability of a plaintiff to meet an undertaking in damages."

6 Balance of convenience

1. The third criterion It is where there is doubt as to the adequacy of the respective remedies in damages available to either party or to both that the question of "balance of convenience" arises.

2. *"Balance of convenience"*—a term of art May L.J., mirroring the view expressed by Sir Robert Megarry V.-C. at first instance, explained in *Cayne v. Global Natural Resources plc* [1984] 1 All E.R. 225 at 237H:

> "That [the 'balance of convenience'] is the phrase which, of course, is always used in this type of application. It is, if I may say so, a useful shorthand but in truth, ... the balance that one is seeking to make is more fundamental, more weighty, than mere 'convenience.' I think that it is quite clear from both cases that, although the phrase may well be substantially less elegant, the 'balance of the risk of doing an injustice' better describes the process involved."

Sir John Donaldson M.R. expanded on the same theme thus, in *Francome v. Mirror Group Newspapers* [1984] 1 W.L.R. 892 at 898E:

> "I stress, once again, that we are not at this stage concerned to determine the final rights of the parties. Our duty is to make such orders, if any, as are appropriate pending the trial of the action. It is sometimes said that this involves a weighing of the balance of convenience. This is an unfortunate expression. Our business is justice, not convenience. We can and must disregard fanciful claims by either party. Subject to that, we must contemplate the possibility that either party may succeed and must do our best to ensure that nothing occurs pending the trial which will prejudice his rights. Since the parties are usually asserting wholly inconsistent claims, this is difficult, but we

have to do our best. In so doing, we are seeking a balance of justice, not convenience."

3. "Balance of convenience"—what should be taken into account? The question is not readily susceptible of answer. As Lord Diplock said at 408F in *Cyanamid*:

> "It would be unwise even to attempt to list all the various matters which may need to be taken into consideration in deciding where the balance lies, let alone to suggest the relative weight to be attached to them. These will vary from case to case."

4. Status quo—its significance If other factors are equally balanced, it is a counsel of prudence to take such measures as are calculated to preserve the status quo: *Cyanamid* at 408G. The rationale is that if the defendant is enjoined temporarily from doing something that he has not done before, the only effect of the interlocutory injunction in the event of his succeeding at the trial is to postpone the date at which he is able to embark upon a course of action which he has not previously found it necessary to undertake. On the other hand to interrupt him in the conduct of an established enterprise would cause much greater inconvenience to him since he would have to start again to establish it in the event of his succeeding at trial: *Cyanamid* at 408G–H.

5. The problem—When is the *"Status"* to be fixed as *"Quo"*? In *Dunhill (Alfred) Ltd v. Sunoptics* [1979] F.S.R. 337, Megaw L.J. explained at 376 the difficulty of pin-pointing when precisely *"ante"*, the "status" was "quo":

> "I do not think that any assistance is to be derived in this case from consideration of the 'status quo' which is referred to in *American Cyanamid*. Like all Latin terms used in a legal context, it is necessary to try to see what, in English, the Latin term is intended to convey. 'Status quo', or, more fully, 'status quo ante', means simply 'the existing state of things'—existing before a particular point of time. For that to be of any help, it is necessary to answer the question: Existing when? Before what point of time? For the answer may be different, according as you look at the existing state of things at the date when the defendant did the act, or the first act, which is alleged to have been wrongful; or the date when the plaintiff first learned of that act; or the date when the plaintiff first complained to the defendant; or the date when he issued his writ. I think the relevant point of time for purposes of the 'status quo' may well vary in different cases. [Editors' emphasis.]"

161

In *Graham v. Delderfield* [1992] F.S.R. 313 Dillon L.J. *inter alia*, said in the context of a "confidential information" case:

"With all respect to Lord Diplock, it would seem that it must be the service rather than the issue of the writ that fixes the status quo where, as here, there was no letter before action and there was delay after the issue of the writ before service. The issue of a writ does not tell the defendants of the existence of the writ or indicate to them in any way that a claim is being made against them."

In the same case at 318, Butler-Sloss L.J. said:

"In considering the principles enunciated in Lord Diplock's speech in *American Cyanamid*, despite considerable sympathy for the appellant, I am driven to the conclusion that the judge was right not to grant an injunction. The effect of delay in bringing the matters to court is to place the status quo at the period in the Autumn of 1990; see Lord Diplock in *Garden Cottage Foods Ltd v. Milk Marketing Board* [1984] 1 A.C. 130 at 140. By the Autumn of 1990, the respondents had completed their first contract in August and had other contracts in existence and their business was up and running. In my view the judge was right to take the view that it was far too late to grant a springboard injunction, to bring to a halt an existing business and there has not been sufficient evidence presented to us to warrant a conclusion as to whether a perpetual injunction is likely to be granted at the trial."

6. Status quo—a definition from the House of Lords It was held *per curiam* in *Garden Cottage Foods Ltd v. Milk Marketing Board* [1984] A.C. 130 that for the purpose of deciding whether an interlocutory injunction should be granted to preserve the status quo, the status quo is the state of affairs existing during the period immediately preceding the issue of the writ, and in respect of a motion for an interlocutory injunction, the period immediately preceding the motion. Lord Diplock went on to add at 140D:

"The duration of that period since the state of affairs last changed must be more than minimal, having regard to the total length of the relationship between the parties in respect of which the injunction is granted; otherwise the state of affairs before the last change would be the relevant status quo."

7. Status quo—working examples

(a) *The* "school case": In *Thompson v. Park* [1944] 1 K.B. 408, the parties, each of whom owned a school, agreed to amalgamate. Pursuant to that, the defendant and 25 of his pupils were licensed to enter upon and to use the plaintiff's premises. The parties fell out and the plaintiff revoked the licence, thus prompting the defendant into a forcible re-entry. The Court of Appeal granted an interlocutory injunction excluding the defendant from the premises, Goddard L.J. expressing the position thus at 409:

"Having got back into the house, to use the words of the statute of 5 Rich. II, c. 7, 'with strong hand' [and] with 'multitude of people,' he has established himself in the house, and he then says: 'I ought not to have an injunction given against me to make me go out because I got back here and got my boys back and, therefore, I want the status quo preserved.' The status quo that could be preserved was the status quo that existed before these illegal and criminal acts on the part of the defendant. It is a strange argument to address to a court of law that we ought to help the defendant who has trespassed and got himself into these premises in the way in which he has done and to say that that would be preserving the status quo and a good reason for not granting an injunction."

The *"licence"* aspects of the judgment in *Thompson v. Park* (*ibid.*) were criticised by Megarry J. in *Hounslow London Borough Council v. Twickenham Garden Developments Ltd* [1971] Ch. 233, but this does not touch upon the "status quo" issue.

(b) *Standex International Ltd v. C.B. Blades & C.B. Blades Ltd* [1976] F.S.R. 114: Scarman L.J. said at 127:

"Like my Lord, I see the formidable difficulties facing the defendant and his company if this relief is granted, but on that aspect of the case I would make two comments. First of all, at an interlocutory stage, the court is well advised to make orders maintaining the status quo. It would be wrong to think of the status quo, as Mr Francis has submitted we should consider it, as being a situation, which he says was obtaining on October 3, at the date of issue of the writ, of the defendant and his company being in active business as mould engravers. In my judgment one has to look at the position as it was at the end of July when the plaintiffs for the first time obtained the evidence suggesting that the defendant and his company had entered or were entering the business of mould engraving. At that time the defendant and his company were disturbing the state of affairs which had previously existed; and it was a disturbance to the detriment of the plaintiffs to the order that I have sought to describe."

(c) *Fellowes v. Fisher* [1975] 3 W.L.R. 184: Sir John Pennycuick said at 199H–200A:

"By the expression 'status quo' I understand to be meant the position prevailing when the defendant embarked upon the activity sought to be restrained."

(d) *CPC (United Kingdom) Ltd v. Keenan* [1986] F.S.R. 527: (for the facts, see pp. 743–748 below). Peter Gibson J. rejected the argument in favour of maintaining the status quo, saying at 534–535:

"I must also bear in mind the question of the status quo. Mr Hill-Smith has urged on me that this necessitates that there should be no injunction. The business, however, of the defendant is an expanding business and she has been for some time aware of the dangers posed by the attitude of the plaintiffs."

(e) *Harrods Ltd v. Schwartz-Sackin & Co. Ltd* [1986] F.S.R. 490: Warner J. said at 498 in reference to defence counsel's "delay" argument:

"First, he pointed to the delay that had elapsed between 25 January 1985 when Mr Sackin first wrote to Mr Drewitt telling him what the defendant intended to do, and this month, when I am at last hearing this motion. He said that delay was unreasonable and that, in view of it, I should not grant an injunction. But it seems to me that the delay up to the issue of the writ and the notice of motion is fully explained in paragraph 3 of Mr Drewitt's second affidavit; and that the delay since then is explained by the course taken by the proceedings of this court, not least by the fact that time had to be found for this motion to be heard as a lengthy motion by order."

(f) *Unigate Dairies Ltd v. Bruce, The Times,* March 2, 1988, C.A.: The Court of Appeal held that an interlocutory injunction to restrain alleged breaches of a covenant restricting an employee's activities after the end of his employment, should preserve the status quo as it had been before the breaches, not as at the date of hearing. In that case, the plaintiff alleged that the defendant milkman, the plaintiff's former employee, was in breach of a covenant not to serve the plaintiff's customers after the termination of his employment. An interlocutory injunction to restrain alleged breaches of covenant pending trial should preserve the status quo. The position to be maintained was that as it had been before the alleged breaches began, not as at the date of hearing. The appeal was allowed because to allow the defendant to continue to do acts alleged to be in breach of covenant was both inconsistent and contradictory with the decision that an injunction was necessary to restrain further alleged breaches.

8. The strengths of the respective cases—a criterion of last resort If the extent of the uncompensatable disadvantage to each party would not differ widely, it may not be improper to take into account in tipping the balance the relative strength of each party's case as revealed by the affidavit evidence adduced on the hearing of the application. For an example relating to computer software, see *Series 5 Software Ltd v. Clarke and others, The Times*, January 19, 1996, *per* Laddie J.; and *Simtech Advanced Training and Simulation Systems Ltd v. Jasmin Simtech Ltd* [1995] F.S.R. 475 *per* Chadwick J. The court is not justified in embarking upon anything resembling a trial of the action upon conflicting affidavits in order to evaluate the strength of either party's case: *Cyanamid*, p. 409A–C. See also *R. v. Westminster City Council, ex p. Costi, The Independent*, March 12, 1987. Nor, if possible, should the court attempt to resolve complex issues of disputed fact or law: *Series 5 Software Ltd v. Clarke* [*ibid.*].

9. Ancillary matters The following have been held (in the context of breach of a tenancy agreement, in keeping a dog) not to be factors relevant to the exercise of discretion in deciding whether to grant an injunction:
(a) The order of the court would be disobeyed.
(b) The unlikelihood of a defendant being sent to prison or being fined.
(c) That the plaintiff could issue possession proceedings.
However, the case was decided in the context of the fact that the order sought would not require close supervision: *Sutton Housing Trust v. Lawrence* (1988) 55 P. & C.R. 320, C.A. Also see *Clarkson v. Bransford* [1987] C.L.Y. 1166 (injunction in a domestic context restraining the keeping of snakes and monitor lizards)

7 "Special factors"

1. The fourth criterion Lord Diplock in *Cyanamid a priori* emphasised the importance of applying the criteria, listed above. However, he went on to introduce a measure of flexibility by saying in *Cyanamid* at 409C:

> "I would reiterate that, in addition to those to which I have referred, there may be many other special factors to be taken into consideration in the particular circumstances of individual cases."

In the same context, Kerr L.J. said in *Cayne v. Global Natural Resources plc* [1984] 1 All E.R. 225 at 234F–G:

> "Nor do I regard that decision [*Cyanamid*] as going further than to lay down guidelines in situations where two prerequisites are present. The first, as stated by Lord Diplock, is that the question whether to grant or refuse an interlocutory injunction has been placed into a state of balance to the extent that the court can see that the plaintiff's case raises a serious issue to be tried. If the plaintiff fails at that point, then clearly there is no case of an injunction, and obviously the *Cyanamid* guidelines cannot come into play. The second prerequisite,

as it seems to me, is that a trial is in fact likely to take place, in the sense that the plaintiffs' case shows that they are genuinely concerned to pursue their claim to trial, and that they are seeking the injunction as a means of a holding operation pending the trial. It is only in such cases, in my view, that the decision is any guide, though undoubtedly a valuable one, to the problem whether or not the plaintiffs should be protected by an injunction; and it is to be noted that this was indeed the position in the *Cyanamid* case itself. It must also be remembered that the grant or refusal of an injunction is ultimately a matter of statutory discretion, and that the powers of the courts in this regard cannot be fettered by decisions in general terms, when the facts of the cases will vary infinitely."

2. "Special factors"—what are they? There is no definition, but for ease of handling the vast case law material, the following categories of suit appear to fall within the spirit of his dicta.

(a) *Passing off:* (a plaintiff in a passing off case must show more than an arguable case, as the injunction will often be final in effect: *Parnass Pelly Ltd v. Hodges* [1982] F.S.R. 329).

(b) *Patents.*

(c) *Copyright.*

(d) *Trade disputes:* this is a special case by virtue of the terms of section 221(2) of the Labour Relations (Consolidation) Act 1992. It is a prerequisite for the application of the guidelines laid down in the *Cyanamid* case "that a trial is in fact likely to take place, in the sense that the plaintiff's case shows that they are seeking the injunction as a means of holding operation pending the trial": *Cayne v. Global Natural Resources plc* [1984] 1 All E.R. 225 at 234, *per* Kerr L.J. Accordingly, where the grant or refusal of an interlocutory injunction will have the practical effect of putting an end to the action (as frequently occurs in labour disputes) "the degree of likelihood that the plaintiff would have succeeded in establishing his right if the action had gone to trial is a factor to be brought into the balance by the judge in weighing the risks that injustice may result from his deciding the application one way rather than the other." (*N.W.L. Ltd v. Woods* [1979] 1 W.L.R. 1294 at 1307, *per* Lord Diplock.)

(e) *Where the decision on the injunction proceedings would effectively end the action:* (such as where the subject matter of the application is the transmission of a broadcast or the publication of an article, the impact and timing of which depends on the timing of the transmission or publication).

(f) *Injunctions to thwart winding up petitions.*

(g) *Impossibility of phrasing the injunction order.*

(h) *Conflict between public and private interests.*

(i) *Trade secrets/confidential information:* this is a classic category of case where damages will probably not be an adequate remedy. The *American Cyanamid* criteria apply unless the action cannot be tried before the covenant expires or has nearly done so: *David (Lawrence) Ltd v. Ashton* [1991] 1 All E.R. 385. Frequently an order for a speedy trial will be appropriate: *David (Lawrence) (ibid.).* Where a covenant is not limited territorially, and provided that it cannot be attacked for obscurity, illegality or on public policy grounds such as being in restraint of trade, it may be enforced by an interlocutory injunction having world-wide effect: *Att.-Gen v. Barker* [1990] 3 All E.R. 257 C.A. But if a covenant is void and of no effect (as being too wide), it is not permissible for the Court to give it effect by granting an injunction which is reasonable because narrower than the covenant: *JA Mont (UK) Ltd v. Mills* [1993] F.S.R. 557. This was also the position in *Lansing Linde Ltd v. Kerr* [1991] 1 W.L.R. 251, where Staughton L.J. said at 258:

> "If it will not be possible to hold a trial before the period for which the plaintiff claims to be entitled to an injunction has expired, or substantially expired, it seems to me that justice requires some consideration as to whether the plaintiff would be likely to succeed at the trial. In those circumstances it is not enough to decide merely that there is a serious issue to be tried. The assertion of such an issue should not operate as a *lettre de cachet*, by which the defendant is prevented from doing that which, as it later turns out, he has a perfect right to do, for the whole or substantially the whole of the period in question. On a wider view of the balance of convenience it may still be right to impose such a restraint, but not unless there has been some assessment of the plaintiff's prospects of success. I would emphasise 'some assessment,' because the courts constantly seek to discourage prolonged interlocutory battles on affidavit evidence.... Where an assessment of the prospects of success is required, it is for the judge to control its extent."

(j) *Mandatory interlocutory injunctions:* the court has jurisdiction to grant a mandatory injunction on an interlocutory application, but will very rarely do so. The court usually requires a high degree of assurance that at the trial it will appear that the injunction was rightly granted. The principles were fully discussed in *Nottingham Building Society v. Eurodynamic Systems Plc* [1993] F.S.R. 468 where the order was for the handing over of computer software.

(k) *Defamation (including malicious falsehood, unlawful interference with trade etc.).* The court will not ordinarily restrain publication of a defamatory statement, whether relating to the plaintiff personally or to his trade which the defendant genuinely intends to justify at the trial, since to do so would interfere with freedom of speech: *Femis-Bank (Anguilla) Ltd v. Lazar* [1991] Ch. 391. The court will however restrain the publication of obvious lies: *Bestobell Paints Ltd v. Bigg* [1975] F.S.R. 421, where the cases are reviewed. The public interest in preserving freedom of speech will also be an important factor to be taken into account where the cause of action is conspiracy to injure the plaintiff by publishing allegations against him that he is financially unsound and dishonest: *Femis-Bank (Anguilla) Ltd v. Lazar* [1991] 2 All E.R. 865.

(l) *No dispute on the evidence.*

(m) *Documentary credits and performance bonds.* In the absence of a clear case of fraud or the like, an injunction should not ordinarily be granted to interfere with bankers' irrevocable credits: *Discount Records Ltd v. Barclays Bank Ltd* [1975] 1 W.L.R. 315; [1975] 1 All E.R. 1071; *Bolvinter Oil S.A. v. Chase Manhattan Bank* [1984] 1 W.L.R. 392 C.A.

Such categorisation, however, is open to criticism, in that:
(a) it is not recognised as such by the House of Lords, and
(b) like all categorisations, it is artificial in that questions of "balance of convenience," "adequacy of damages", etc. cross the boundaries of such categories;
(c) such categories are not closed—see *R. v. Westminster City Council, ex p. Sierbien* (1987) 151 L.G.R. 888, for the "public interest" factor. However, sight should not be lost of the fact that such special factors still operate against the *Cyanamid* backdrop. Thus in *Lawrence David Ltd v. Ashton* [1989] I.C.R. 123, C.A., A was employed as the plaintiff company's sales director, under a contract which contained a clause prohibiting him from disclosing to any person at any time "any information relating to the company or its customers or any trade secrets of which he becomes possessed while acting as sales director." The contract also contained a covenant effectively restricting him from being employed for a period of two years in any competing business. A was dismissed and accepted an offer of employment from a competitor, although this offer was subsequently withdrawn. The company sought an interlocutory injunction to enforce both the contractual restrictions and the covenant. The High Court, disapproving *Fellowes & Son v. Fisher* [1976] Q.B. 122 at 133,

134, dismissed the application and the company appealed. It was held, allowing the appeal in part and granting an interlocutory injunction enforcing the restrictive covenant pending trial, that the High Court had erred in failing to apply the principles of *American Cyanamid v. Ethicon*. These principles applied whenever there was either an unresolved dispute on affidavit evidence or there was a question of law to be resolved. It applied equally to restraint of trade cases. The present case disclosed serious issues of law and fact to be tried and the injunction in respect of the restrictive covenants should therefore be granted. The High Court had not erred, however, in refusing to grant an injunction in respect of the clause relating to disclosure of information, since this was too widely framed and incapable of being interpreted with the requisite precision. Similarly in *Dairy Crest Ltd v. Pigott* [1989] I.C.R. 92, it was held that interlocutory injunctions which are sought to enforce a covenant in restraint of trade do not constitute a special category of case which is exempt from the principles.

H: INTERLOCUTORY COSTS

1 The court's options

1. **"Costs in the cause"** The costs of those interlocutory proceedings are to be awarded according to the final award of the costs in the action. If the plaintiff wins and gets an order for his costs, he gets those interlocutory costs as part of his costs of the action against the defendant. Vice versa, if the defendant wins and gets an order for his costs, he gets those interlocutory costs as part of his costs of the action against the plaintiff.

2. **"Plaintiff's costs in the cause"** If the plaintiff wins, he gets the costs of the interlocutory proceedings; but, if he loses, he does not have to pay the other side's costs of them.

3. **"Plaintiff's costs in any event"** No matter who wins or loses, when the case is decided, or settled, the plaintiff is to have the costs of those interlocutory proceedings—but only on final taxation.

4. **"Plaintiff's costs"** The plaintiff is to have the costs of the interlocutory proceedings, with immediate taxation: *Allied Collection Agencies v. Wood* [1981] 3 All E.R. 176, *per* Neill J. But this order should be made only in exceptional cases. (For the avoidance of doubt, if this is the intention, the right for immediate taxation should be made expressly.)

169

These orders for costs are now defined in R.S.C. Ord. 62, r.3(6).

2 Cyanamid and costs

1. The problem What interlocutory order for costs should be made: (a) when a plaintiff succeeds on an application for interlocutory relief, and (b) when a plaintiff fails in an application for interlocutory relief? In other words, after *Cyanamid*, do costs follow the event?

2. Plaintiff succeeds The usual order is "plaintiff's' costs in the cause": *Steepleglade Ltd v. Stratford Investments Ltd* [1976] F.S.R. 3.

3. Plaintiff fails The usual order is "defendant's costs in the cause": *Steepleglade (ibid.)*.

4. Why? In the *Steepleglade* case, the discussion ran as follows (Jacob Q.C. acting for the unsuccessful plaintiffs): Jacob Q.C.:

> "I would seek to address your Lordship on the question of costs. The normal rule as to costs prior to *American Cyanamid* was that the successful party got its costs in the cause. I apprehend that the only sensible reason one can think of for such a rule is that, broadly speaking, it looked as though the plaintiff, if he got his costs in the cause, had a good strong case. But now, following *American Cyanamid*—and your Lordship has no doubt followed that case in this judgment—when the matter turns on balance of convenience is there any rational reason why, I ask forensically, if it turned out at the trial that I was right and I ought to have had an interlocutory injunction as well as the final injunction, I should be precluded from the costs of these proceedings? I say no. I say that the proper order is either costs reserved or costs in the cause as is the practice in the Queen's Bench Division. . . . But I do say that it is a very odd situation, if it turns out that I should have had an injunction and this was a wrongful act by the defendants right from the beginning, that I should be precluded from getting the costs of an attempt to stop them."

Oliver J.:

> "Yes; I see the force of that; but the practice is a very well-established one. I am not myself convinced that the *Cyanamid* case produced a totally different approach in practice to the granting or withholding of interlocutory injunctions. Of course, there is not any rule which binds this court to deal with costs in any particular way. The matter is one of discretion. I can readily conceive that there may well be cases where the consideration is not only on balance of convenience

but possibly, also, the merits may be such that the court might think the matter so finely balanced that costs in the cause was the right order. That is not the view I take about the present case and, in my view, the order which I have indicated is the right order and the one which I propose to make."

5. Indemnity costs? Where a *Mareva* injunction has been obtained on the basis of fabricated evidence, the costs of both the application for the injunction and the application for its subsequent discharge should be paid by the plaintiff immediately on an indemnity basis, even where it is not yet established that the plaintiff was involved in the fabrication of the evidence: *Bir v. Sharma, The Times*, December 7, 1988, Vinelott J.

3 The contingency that the action may never come to trial

1. The problem What is the position as to costs if after the grant of an interlocutory injunction, nothing further happens? As Winn L.J. said in *Stratford (J.T. & Son Ltd v. Lindley (No. 2)* [1969] 1 W.L.R. 1547 at 1554E:

"Supposing that nothing whatsoever had thereafter happened with regard to this action, if it had simply lain like a dead pigeon in the street, then it would have been impossible to suggest that either the plaintiff or the defendant could have enforced any order for costs against the opposite party."

Stratford was followed in *Allied Collection Agencies v. Wood* [1981] 3 All E.R. 176.

2. The background Lord Denning M.R. explained the background to the Stratford case at 1552F–H:

"There was an important case in 1964 called *Stratford (J.T.) & Son Ltd v. Lindley* [1965] A.C. 269. A watermen's union had a dispute with Stratford & Son Ltd, the plaintiffs, about recognition of the union. Some of the union officials placed an embargo on Stratford's barges. It was likely to injure Stratford's business irreparably. Stratford's brought an action against the union officials, Mr Lindley and others, the defendants, seeking an injunction to restrain them from enforcing the embargo. Marshall J. granted an interim injunction against the union officials. He made the costs before him 'costs in the cause.' The union officials appealed. This court allowed the appeal [1965] A.C. 269, 276, and awarded the union officials the 'costs' of the appeal 'in any event.' Stratford's appealed to the House of Lords. The House allowed the appeal [1965] A.C. 269, 320. They granted an interim injunction. Stratford's asked for the costs in any event in the

> House of Lords and in the Court of Appeal. But the House of Lords, after considering the matter, made an order, see pp. 325, 339, that the costs in the House of Lords and in the Court of Appeal were to be 'costs in the cause,' just as the costs before Marshall J. were. So all the costs of the interlocutory proceedings were 'costs in the cause.' "

There was a long delay. The action never came to trial. No costs had ever been awarded in the action.

3. How was the costs issue resuscitated? In order to bring matters to a head, the defendants took out a summons to dismiss the action for want of prosecution and they asked for all the costs to be paid by the plaintiffs to the defendants including the "costs in the cause" ordered by the House of Lords. They invoked Ord. 25, r.1(5):

> "On an application by the defendant to dismiss the action under paragraph (4) the court may either dismiss the action on such terms as may be just or deal with the application as if it were a summons for directions."

The summons prompted the plaintiffs to seek leave to discontinue and they further asked either that the defendants should pay the plaintiffs' costs or at any rate that each side should pay its own costs. They invoked Ord. 21, r. 3(1):

> "... a party may not discontinue an action ... without the leave of the court, and the court ... may order the action ... to be discontinued ... on such terms as to costs, the bringing of a subsequent action or otherwise as it thinks just."

4. What did the Court of Appeal do? Lord Denning M.R. treated the application as to costs as if the original order had been "costs reserved." Because the case had initially been finely balanced, the court put aside the respective merits of the dispute. It then went on to allow the plaintiff's summons to discontinue, rejected the defendants' summons to strike out and ordered that each side should bear its own costs throughout the proceedings including those of the instant appeal.

5. What if costs are reserved? In *Computer Machinery Company Ltd v Drescher* [1983] 1 W.L.R. 1379, the defendant gave undertakings in response to the plaintiff's motion, until judgment or further order, the costs of the motion being reserved. Some time later the defendant made a payment into court and in a letter, stated to be "without prejudice save as to costs" offered to submit to permanent injunctions in the same terms as those sought by the plaintiff "with taxed costs relating thereto" as if Ord. 62, r.10(2) applied. The plaintiff accepted the offer, the money was paid into

172

court, and the action never proceeded to trial. The question whether the taxed costs included the costs reserved in respect of the interlocutory motions was referred to the court. On the hearing of that question the plaintiff sought to adduce certain documents which it had obtained on discovery after the hearing of the motions in order to show that the evidence relied on by the defendants in their affidavits was false. The defendant contended that the documents were not admissible because only evidence used at the hearing of the motions could be admitted for deciding the question of costs. Sir Robert Megarry V.-C. held: (a) There was no rule that on the issue of costs evidence is inadmissible even though relevant, unless it has previously been adduced. (b) *Per curiam:*

> "Where a defendant offers to submit to an injunction, or to give an undertaking or afford other relief, and the offer is made 'without prejudice' or 'without prejudice save as to costs,' the courts ought to enforce the terms on which the offer is made so as to encourage compromises and shorten litigation. If the offer is made 'without prejudice as to costs,' this has the added advantage of preventing the offer from being inadmissible as to costs, thereby assisting the court towards justice in making the order as to costs. This principle is of perfectly general application and is in no way confined to matrimonial costs. Dicta in *Calderbank v. Calderbank* [1976] Fam. 93, C.A. applied."

6. Summary If interlocutory costs are orders to be in the cause, it is wise to make provision for the contingency that the action may never come to trial. (See also *The Supreme Court Practice* 1997, Vol. 1, Ord. 62.

Practice Check List:

1. Jurisdiction? Check:
(a) Cause of action?
(b) Justiciable in England?
(c) In the relevant court?
(d) Writ issued?

2. Need?
(a) What damage is feared? Irreparable?
(b) Terms of injunction sought? Too wide? Too narrow?
(c) Could such terms be enforced (*e.g.*, by committal or sequestration of assets)?
(d) How much hardship if awarded/not awarded? Damages an adequate

remedy? What about alternative relief—*e.g.* voluntary undertaking to keep an account of profits?

3. Full and frank disclosure? Probe and dig. The duty is not limited to material facts known to the plaintiff, but also to facts which should have been known if proper inquiry were made.

4. Affidavit Check—must cover the following:
  (a) Facts generating the cause of action,
  (b) Why interlocutory relief is necessary, including:
      (i) damages not an adequate remedy for the plaintiff;
      (ii) status quo;
      (iii) prejudice/hardship.
  (c) Full and frank disclosure as to what the other side's defence is likely to be, and the merits of that defence.
  (d) Precisely the relief sought.

5. Enforcement Ensure that the provisions of R.S.C. Ord. 45 regarding penal notices are scrupulously complied with, otherwise the court will not make an order of committal or sequestration. On service, the defendant should be shown the penal notice, and this should be recorded in any affidavit of service.

6. Acting for a defendant Be reasonable:
  (a) Make sure correspondence shows the "upside" of the defendant's position—so that this has to be disclosed to the court by the plaintiff.
  (b) If possible, volunteer limited undertakings.
  (c) Come over as candid, to avoid interpretation of having something to conceal.
  (d) Check (with commercial enquiry agent?):
      (i) plaintiff's ability to pay;
      (ii) plaintiff's conduct (delay—prejudice as a result? Unclean hands?);
      (iii) directions for the early service of pleadings.

CHAPTER 2

Mareva—Practice and Procedure

A: INTRODUCTION

1 Origins and jurisdiction

1. The traditional view Cotton L.J. in *Lister & Co. v. Stubbs* (1890) 45 Ch.D. 1 at 14 said:

> "But here, if the money sought to be recovered is not the money of the plaintiffs, we should be simply ordering the defendant to pay into Court a sum of money in his possession because there is a prima facie case against him that at the hearing it will be established that he owes money to the plaintiffs. In my opinion, that would be wrong in principle ... if we were to order the defendant to give the security asked for, it would be introducing an entirely new and wrong principle—which we ought not to do, even though we might think that, having regard to the circumstances of the case, it would be highly just to make the order."

2. The traditional view overturned—why? Lawton L.J. explained in *Third Chandris Shipping Corporation v. Unimarine S.A.* [1979] Q.B. 645 at 671A:

> "Once a writ is issued, a debtor who intends to default will do what he can to avoid having to meet his obligations. The British defaulter may try to dissipate his assets; he may succeed to some extent but retribution in the form of either bankruptcy or liquidation will probably come about one day. Until recently the prospects for the defaulting foreigner were much better. A telephone call or telex message could within seconds of the service of a writ, or knowledge that a writ had been issued, put all liquid assets out of the reach of the creditor...."

Lawton L.J. further explained the position in *CBS United Kingdom Ltd v. Lambert* [1983] Ch. 37 at 42A–B:

> "On the facts put before us this was not a case of a plaintiff seeking to freeze a defendant's assets pending trial in anticipation of getting

175

judgment. It was one which seemed to us to show that the first defendant was conducting his affairs with intent to deprive anyone who got judgment against him of the fruits of victory. The *Mareva* injunction was brought into use to make this kind of behaviour in commercial cases unprofitable."

These dicta explain the rationale for the actual decision in *Mareva Compania Naviera S.A. v. International Bulkcarriers S.A.* [1975] 2 Lloyd's Rep. 509; [1980] 1 All E.R. 231, C.A.

3. The "nuclear" *Mareva*—what does it do? The *Mareva* injunction has been described as one of the nuclear weapons of law: *Bank Mellat v. Mohammed Ebrahim Nikpour* [1982] Com.L.R. 158 at 159, *per* Donaldson L.J. And together, *Mareva* and *Anton Piller* have been described helpfully as "Freezure and Seizure." Lord Denning described how it works in *Z Ltd v. A–Z and AA–LL* [1982] Q.B. 558 at 573C:

> "It enables the seizure of assets so as to preserve them for the benefit of the creditor: but not to give a charge in favour of any particular creditor."

In other words, unlike the position when a ship is arrested, a *Mareva* does not create rights *in rem: Cretanor Maritime Co. Ltd v. Irish Marine Management Ltd* [1978] 1 W.L.R. 966; *Bank Mellat v. Kazmi* [1989] Q.B. 541. Accordingly, it creates no property or security in the frozen assets and generates exclusively rights *in personam* rendering a breach, merely a contempt of court. But, when served on a bank, a *Mareva* is tantamount to a right operating *in rem: per* Webster J. at first instance in *SCF Finance Co. Ltd v. Masri* referred to at [1985] 1 W.L.R. 876 at 884.

4. Not restricted to foreigners Originally, *Mareva* relief extended to freezing only the assets of foreigners. Now it extends to the assets of anybody, foreign or otherwise; whether the risk is as to dissipation of assets in the jurisdiction, or elsewhere: Supreme Court Act 1981, s.37. As Kerr L.J. explained in *Z Ltd v. A–Z and AA–LL* [1982] Q.B. 558 at 584E:

> "When the [*Mareva*] procedure was first sanctioned by this court in 1975, residents of this country were subject to Exchange Control. With the abolition of Exchange Control it was therefore logical to extend the jurisdiction to residents."

5. Statutory recognition Section 37 of the Supreme Court Act 1981 provides:

> "(1) The High Court may by order (whether interlocutory or final) grant an injunction or appoint a receiver in all cases in which it appears to the court to be just and convenient to do so.

(2) Any such order may be made unconditionally or on such terms and conditions as the court thinks just.

(3) The power of the High Court ... to grant an interlocutory injunction restraining a party to any proceedings from removing from the jurisdiction of the High Court, or otherwise dealing with, assets located within that jurisdiction shall be exerciseable in cases where that party is, as well as in cases where he is not, domiciled, resident or present within that jurisdiction."

Note:

(a) The words "dealing with" include disposing of, selling, pledging or charging; and there are no limitations put on the word "assets" from which it follows that this word includes chattels such as motor vehicles, jewellery, *objets d'art* and other valuables as well as choses in action: *C.B.S. United Kingdom Ltd v. Lambert* [1983] Ch. 37.

(b) As to the appointment of a receiver: the court may invest the receiver with such powers as it thinks necessary for the preservation of property: *Hart v. Emelkirk* [1983] 1 W.L.R. 1289. In that case it was held that where a landlord refuses or neglects to collect the rents due under a lease and refuses or neglects to perform the covenants in the lease to repair and insure the property, the court may appoint a receiver to receive and give a good receipt for the rent, profits and all other moneys payable under a lease of property in accordance with the rights and obligations of the reversioner. Other situations which may invite the appointment of a receiver include where an asset needs to be managed (*e.g.* a controlling shareholding in a company) or where the asset is wasting and needs to be exploited. Further, *Derby & Co. Ltd v. Weldon (Nos. 3 & 4)* [1989] 2 W.L.R. 412, is authority for the principle that assuming it is just and equitable so to do, section 37 of the Supreme Court Act 1981 enables a court to appoint a receiver before judgment.

6. But note—the abiding need for propriety This chapter should be read against the backdrop of the following dicta of Lord Denning M.R. in *The Assios* [1979] 1 Lloyd's Rep. 331 at 334:

"The judge said that caution should be used in granting *Mareva* injunctions. I agree with him. The *Mareva* injunction has proved most valuable in practice to the City of London and to all those who operate in the shipping world and elsewhere. But we must be careful that it is not stretched too far, else we should be endangering it. It must be kept for proper circumstances and not extended so far as to be a danger to the proper conduct of business. So, while supporting it wholeheartedly for all proper cases, we must be careful that it is not extended too far."

And these dicta are confirmed by the ruling *per curiam* in *Ninemia Maritime Corporation v. Trave Schiffahrtsgesellschaft mbH und Co. K.G.* [1983] 1 W.L.R. 1412:

> "The *Mareva* jurisdiction cannot be invoked simply for the purpose of providing plaintiffs with security for claims, even when these appear likely to succeed and even when there is no reason to suppose that an order for an injunction, or the provision of some substitute security by the defendants, would cause any real hardship to the defendants."

In this context, the following dicta of Glidewell L.J. fall into perspective in *Lloyd's Bowmaker Ltd v. Britannia Arrow Holdings plc* [1988] 1 W.L.R. 1337 at 1347A–C:

> "Mr Burke argues, however, that it is at this stage that delay does become relevant. He points out that it is now over two and a half years since the third party proceedings were commenced, and, although the summons for directions was over two years ago, neither the action nor the third party proceedings have been set down for trial. I agree with him that this is a most relevant consideration. A *Mareva* injunction, as Donaldson L.J. in *Bank Mellat v. Nikpour* [1985] F.S.R. 87, 92, said, is a draconian remedy. It is intended as an adjunct to the action itself, not as a substitute for relief to be obtained on trial. In other words, a plaintiff who succeeds in obtaining a *Mareva* injunction is in my view under an obligation to press on with his action as rapidly as he can so that if he should fail to establish liability in the defendant the disadvantage which the injunction imposes upon the defendant will be lessened so far as possible. There is no sign that the defendants in the present case have been active in pressing ahead with these proceedings."

And in the same case, Dillon L.J. said at 1349G–1350A:

> "But in the present case a further important factor comes in at this stage. The *Mareva* injunction was granted on August 20, 1984. It is a very onerous injunction which has hung over the third party for two and a half years, with the attendant expense of applying from time to time for relaxations, but the action is not yet set down. The defendants say that that is in part due to delay or prevarication on the part of the third party in answering interrogatories in aid of discovery as to what has happened to money he received from the plaintiffs in respect of equipment which he, or his company, supplied to the defendants. But the directions for setting down were given before 1984 expired. They have been ignored; nothing has happened. The defendants have been content to leave the third party tied up indefinitely in the toils of the *Mareva* injunction. For a plaintiff to do that when an *Anton*

Piller order had been obtained was strongly disapproved in *Hytrac Conveyors Ltd v. Conveyors International Ltd* [1983] 1 W.L.R. 44, a decision of this court affirming a decision of Whitford J. Precisely the same considerations, in my judgment, apply in relation to a *Mareva* injunction; where a party has obtained a *Mareva* injunction, that party is bound to get on with the trial of the action—not to rest content with the injunction. The injunction is merely ancillary to the trial of the action to hold the position until the action comes on for trial."

7. Not a punishment It should be appreciated that a *Mareva* is not conceived as punishing or penalising. As Lawton L.J. said in *C.B.S. United Kingdom v. Lambert* [1983] Ch. 37 at 43F (although of course implicitly recognising the presumption of innocence):

"Even if a plaintiff has good reason for thinking that a defendant intends to dispose of assets so as to deprive him of his anticipated judgment, the court must always remember that rogues have to live and that all orders, particularly interlocutory ones, should as far as possible do justice to all parties."

In a similar vein, Lloyd J. in *PCW (Underwriting Agencies) Ltd v. Dixon* [1983] 2 All E.R. 158, said at p. 162F–G; and at 162J–163A:

"I am not going to attempt to define in this case what is meant by dissipating assets within the jurisdiction or where the line is to be drawn; but wherever the line is to be drawn this defendant is well within it. It could not possibly be said that he is dissipating his assets by living as he has always lived and paying bills such as he has always incurred ... [W]hat concerns me more in this case is why the figure of £100 was ever put forward by the plaintiffs in the first place. Here was a man who was known to be wealthy. He had been a founder member and chairman of the plaintiff company. The plaintiffs must have known his salary. No doubt it was considerable. They must therefore have known that the figure of £100 a week put forward was wholly unrealistic if he was to maintain his standard of living. Inevitably I have been led to wonder whether the real purpose in putting forward so low a figure and in failing or refusing to agree any increase was to exert pressure on the first defendant to settle the action. If so then this case would fail within one of the two abuses mentioned by Kerr L.J. in *Z Ltd v. A.*"

And Lloyd J. continued at 164G–H:

"All injunctions are of course in the end discretionary. I would regard it as unjust in the present case if the defendant were compelled to

179

> reduce his standard of living, to give up his flat or to take his children away from school, in order to secure what is as yet only a claim by the plaintiffs."

However, these principles should not be confused with the fact that flagrant breaches of a *Mareva* injunction should be met with an immediate term of imprisonment: *Pospischal v. Phillips, The Times*, January 20, 1988. The Court of Appeal *inter alia* said:

> "But the plaintiff is not the only interested party. The public is an interested party, because it is and it should be known that it is of the highest importance that orders as serious as *Mareva* injunctions made by the court are there to be obeyed and not flouted. It is quite apparent, and Mr Goodman has not sought to argue to the contrary, that this order was deliberately flouted by the defendant."

As to the considerations which arise where a person who is in flagrant contempt of court makes an application to the court, see *Hadkinson v. Hadkinson* [1952] P. 285; [1952] 2 All E.R. 567.

8. Arbitration awards A *Mareva* may be granted in aid of intended or pending arbitration proceedings or for an order to enforce an award of the judgment and to enter judgment under section 26 of the Arbitration Act 1950: *The Rena K* [1979] 1 Q.B. 377. See also *Siporex Trade S.A. v. Comdel Commodities Ltd* [1986] 2 Lloyd's Rep. 428; (1986) 136 New L.J. 538. A *Mareva* may also be granted where leave has not been given under section 26: *Gidrxslme Shipping Co. Ltd v. Tantomar-Transportes Maritimos Lda* [1994] 4 All E.R. 507. Such applications for a *Mareva* injunction are usually made to the Commercial Court. At first instance in *Cretanor Maritime Co. Ltd v. Irish Marine Management Ltd* [1978] 1 W.L.R. 966 Mocatta J. made a *Mareva* order, to continue "until 14 days after the publication of the award in any arbitration between the (owners) and the (charterers) or further order." In *The Rena K* [1979] Q.B. 377, Brandon J. said at 408F–409C:

> "Although I cannot, for the reasons which I have given, accept that section 12(6)(f) of the Arbitration Act 1950 covers the arresting of a ship, or the keeping of a ship under arrest, it appears to me that both section 12(6)(f) and (h) cover the granting of a *Mareva* injunction, and so give the court the same power to grant such an injunction for the purpose of and in relation to an arbitration as it has for the purpose of and in relation to an action or matter in the court.
>
> As to the question whether the court can exercise such power not only once the arbitration concerned has been commenced but also in anticipation of its commencement, it is to be observed that R.S.C., Ord. 29, r.1(3), gives the court power to grant interim injunctions, for

the purpose of and in relation to an action or matter in the court, before the writ or originating summons by which the cause or matter is to be begun has been issued, and, in such cases, to impose terms providing the issue of the writ or originating summon, together with such other terms as it thinks fit.

It follows, in my view, that the court has power under section 12(6)(f) and (h) to grant a *Mareva* injunction for the purpose of and in relation to an arbitration which has not yet been commenced, and to do so to a term providing for the arbitration to be commenced within a specified time, together with such other terms, if any, as it thinks fit. Various arguments were advanced for the shipowners against the application of the procedure of *Mareva* injunctions to ships. First, it was said that, because the Administration of Justice Act 1956 provided for the arrest of ships in Admiralty actions *in rem*, it impliedly excluded ships from the categories of chattels in respect of which a *Mareva* injunction could be granted under section 45 of the Supreme Court of Judicature (Consolidation) Act 1925. If that were not so, it was said, a plaintiff with a maritime claim might obtain a *Mareva* injunction in respect of two or more ships, or proceed *in rem* against one ship and obtain a *Mareva* injunction in respect of one or more other ships, and by these means obtain security for a larger amount than he could by proceedings *in rem* against a single ship (which was all he was allowed to do) under the Administration of Justice Act 1956."

9. *Mareva*, "freezure" and the police *Chief Constable of Kent v. V.* [1983] Q.B. 34 is authority for the following propositions:
  (a) that it is the duty of a chief constable to use his best endeavours to recover stolen property and return it to its rightful owner; and
  (b) that he has a right to seize goods which he had reasonable grounds for believing to be stolen in pursuance of that duty; and
  (c) that a similar right exists in respect of money standing to the credit of a bank account to the extent that it can be shown to have been obtained from another in breach of the criminal law.

However, whereas Lord Denning M.R. justified such propositions by recourse to *Mareva* principles, Donaldson L.J.'s approach reflected in *Chic Fashions (West Wales) Ltd v. Jones* [1968] 2 Q.B. 299. In the *Kent* case, Donaldson L.J. expressly left open the question whether such right to freeze could be extended to a case in which the criminal takes tangibles, converts it into money by selling it, and banks the money. But in a case where the proceeds of crime could not realistically be traced with any degree of accuracy, the Court of Appeal refused an injunction: *Chief Constable of Hampshire v. A. Ltd* [1985] Q.B. 132.

10. A pre-emptive remedy—but not too pre-emptive Lord Donaldson M.R. said in *Derby & Co. Ltd v. Weldon (Nos. 3 & 4)* [1989] 2 W.L.R. 412 at 419D:

> "The fundamental principle underlying this jurisdiction is that, within the limits of its powers, no court should permit a defendant to take action designed to ensure that subsequent orders of the court are rendered less effective than would otherwise be the case. On the other hand, it is not its purpose to prevent a defendant carrying on business in the ordinary way or, if an individual, living his life normally pending the determination of the dispute, nor to impede him in any way in defending himself against the claim. Nor is it its purpose to place the plaintiff in the position of a secured creditor."

11. No *Mareva* if a tracing claim In *Polly Peck International plc v. Nadir (No. 2)* [1994] 4 All E.R. 769 C.A. Scott L.J. said:

> "Equitable tracing leads to a claim of a proprietory character. A fund is identified that, in equity, is regarded as a fund belonging to the claimant. The constructive trust claim, in this action at least, is not a claim to any fund in specie. It is a claim for monetary compensation. The only relevant interlocutory protection that can be sought in aid of a money claim is a *Mareva* injunction, restraining the defendant from dissipating or secreting away his assets in order to make himself judgment proof. But if identifiable assets are being claimed, the interlocutory relief sought will not be a *Mareva* injunction but relief for the purpose of preserving intact the assets in question until their true ownership can be determined. Quite different considerations arise from those which apply to Mareva injunctions."

2 Practice and procedure—the rudiments

1. *Mareva*—the overriding procedural requirements In all *Mareva* applications, the following overriding factors should be borne in mind:
  (a) Speed: *Mareva* relief should be applied for with all despatch.
  (b) *Ex parte*: It is, in the very nature of things, applied for *ex parte* (in the first instance). Secrecy from the defendant is essential.

2. When does it take effect? The defendant is bound by the negative provisions of a *Mareva* injunction as soon as he has notice of them, even though the order has not been drawn up or served upon him. Any third party who is aware of the injunction is also guilty of contempt of court if he does anything to assist the defendant to disobey the injunction. Lord Denning M.R. said in *Z Ltd v. A–Z and AA–LL* [1982] Q.B. 558 at 572H:

"As soon as the judge makes his order for a *Mareva* injunction restraining the defendant from disposing of his assets, the order takes effect at the very moment that it is pronounced [references are given]. Even though the order has not then been drawn up—even though it has not then been served on the defendant—it has immediate effect on every asset of the defendant covered by the injunction."

3. How does it take effect? It is an order prohibiting the defendant from doing something. Giving the judgment of the Court of Appeal in *Cretanor Maritime Co. Ltd v. Irish Marine Management Ltd* [1978] 1 W.L.R. 966 Buckley L.J. said at 974A:

"... [I]t is, I think, manifest that a *Mareva* injunction cannot operate as an attachment. 'Attachment' must, I apprehend mean a seizure of assets under some writ or like command or order of a competent authority, normally with a view to their being either realised to meet an established claim or held as a pledge or security for the discharge of some claim either already established or yet to be established. An attachment must fasten on particular assets ... A *Mareva* injunction, however, even if it relates only to a particularised asset ... is relief *in personam* ... All that the injunction achieves is in truth to prohibit the owner from doing certain things in relation to the asset."

4. Which court? The jurisdiction extends to the High Court and Central London County Court Business List only. County courts do not have jurisdiction to grant a *Mareva* order, except in aid of execution (see the County Court Remedies Regulations 1991).

5. No automatic right to intervene A *Mareva* injunction granted to a creditor or alleged creditor by which the defendant in an action is prevented from dealing with an asset does not of itself create "a question or issue arising out of or relating to or connected with" another action in which the defendant is a party so as to provide jurisdiction for joining the creditor as a party to the second action under R.S.C., Ord. 15 r.6(2)(b)(ii): *Sanders Lead Co. Inc. v. Entores Metal Brokers Ltd* [1984] 1 W.L.R. 453, C.A. See also *Woodstock Shipping Co. v. Kyma Compania Naviera S.A. (The "Wave")* 1 Lloyd's Rep. 521.

6. The *Mareva*/security for costs connection *Mareva* injunctions are designed to improve the lot of plaintiffs, or claimants. On the other hand, security for costs is relief sought by defendants, or respondents. There can, therefore, be no interaction unless there is a counterclaim: *Hitachi Shipbuilding & Engineering Co. Ltd v. Viafel Compania Naviera S.A.* [1981] 2 Lloyd's Rep. 498, C.A. In the event of such interaction arising from a counterclaim, the following should be noted:

(a) If the plaintiff to the claim obtains a *Mareva* he is not obtaining security for that claim. All the plaintiff achieves is the prevention of the defendant from dissipating his assets thereby to deprive the plaintiff of the fruits of any judgment or award which he may thereafter obtain.

(b) If such a plaintiff is defendant to a counterclaim, he may be able to claim security for costs: Ord. 23. But it is well settled that an order for security for costs will not be made against a foreign plaintiff who has substantial property within the jurisdiction, provided that the property is permanently here and will be available to satisfy any order for costs which is made against the plaintiff: *Re Apollinaris Company's Trade Mark* (1891) 1 Ch. 1; *Hitachi (ibid.)*.

7. Orders capable of being made ancillary to a *Mareva* So as to render the *Mareva* effective, it is open to the courts, in appropriate circumstances, to have recourse to the following ancillary order:

(a) discovery: see p. 258.

(b) discovery by interrogatories: see p. 261.

(c) oral examination and cross-examination: see p. 266.

(d) delivery up of chattels: see p. 271.

(e) *Anton Piller* (thereby to "pile *Piller* on *Mareva*": see p. 270).

As Lawton L.J. said in *C.B.S. United Kingdom Ltd v. Lambert* [1983] Ch. 37 at 42G–H:

> "A jurisdiction to grant *Mareva* injunctions, however, it is not likely to be of any use to a plaintiff who believes that he is suing a defendant who intends to deal with his assets in such a way as to deprive him of the fruits of any judgment he may obtain unless there is some means of making the defendant disclose what his assets are and whereabouts they are to be found."

8. Discharge or variation The defendant to a *Mareva* may:

(a) apply for it to be discharged on the basis of the provision of security for the amount of the plaintiff's claim;

(b) apply for it to be discharged because the risk of dissipation has disappeared, *e.g.* because administrative receivers have been appointed: *Capital Cameras Ltd v. Harold Lines Ltd and others (National Westminster Bank plc intervening)* [1991] 3 All E.R. 389;

(c) apply for it to be discharged on the basis that it should not have been made:

    (i) because the plaintiff does not have a good arguable case. (But note that the question is whether the plaintiff has a good arguable case, not whether the defendant has a good arguable defence);

(ii)   because the defendant has a defence by way of set off;

(iii) because there is insufficient evidence of risk. A defendant may be able to show that the plaintiff had no reasonable grounds to aver risk, particularly if he can annex documents to his affidavit showing a steady level of assets. But note—the burden here has shifted. The defendant must provide his solicitor with full instructions: *Third Chandris* [1979] Q.B. 645 at 664–666;

(iv)   failure to disclose. (It may well be that in the urgency of the application, the plaintiff has omitted some salient fact; and note—a defendant does not have to establish that the non-disclosure was *mala fides: Thermax v. Schott Industrial Glass* [1981] F.S.R. 289). See also *Lloyd's Bowmaker Ltd v. Britannia Arrow Holdings plc* [1988] 1 W.L.R. 1337. (However, defendants must be scrupulous not to abuse this line of defence. As the Court of Appeal said in *Ali Mohamed Shorafa Al Hamadi & Another v. Tarik Alfred Abu Samra & Another* (December 17, 1987, unreported):

"I should also say that whilst it is important that full disclosure should be made, it is equally important that immaterial non-disclosure should not be made available to defendants as a means of escaping from a *Mareva* injunction which would otherwise be more than fully justified. There has been a tendency for the defendants to raise non-disclosure on many occasions, and on many occasions those attempts have turned out in the end to be wholly unjustified.");

(d) apply for variation of order: see p. 247.

3 The "before and after" remedy

1. As an aid to execution The *Mareva* can be used to freeze assets prior to trial, and also after judgment or registration of a foreign judgment, in support of execution: *Stewart Chartering v. C. & O. Managements S.A.* [1980] 1 W.L.R. 460 (*Mareva* ordered to be continued after judgment); *Hill Samuel & Co. v. Littaur* (1985) 129 S.J. 433; *Orwell Steel v. Asphalt & Tarmac (U.K.) Ltd* [1984] 1 W.L.R. 1097 (*Mareva* granted between judgment and execution).

2. Rationale—*per* Farquharson J. The decision of Farquharson J. in the *Orwell* case (*ibid.*) at 1100 may be analysed thus:

(a) *Justification for extending operation of court's power:*

"If there is such a power, there seems to be no logical reason why a

Mareva injunction should not be used in aid of execution. Indeed, in one sense it could be said that there is greater justification for restraining a defendant from disposing of his assets after judgment than before any claim has been established against him."

(b) *Supplements other "execution" remedies:*

"It is true that there is a variety of methods for enforcing execution as set out in R.S.C. Ord. 45, r.1 and once the plaintiff has obtained judgment it may be said that he should pursue the remedies provided by the rules rather than extend the application of *Mareva* injunctions still further. The answer to that objection is that, as has been frequently pointed out, the *Mareva* injunction acts *in personam* on the defendant and does not give the plaintiff any rights over the goods of the defendant nor involve any attachment of them. In this context it would have the effect of preserving the defendant's goods until execution could be levied upon them; and the remedies of injunction and execution can take effect side by side. Such was the view of Robert Goff J. in *Stewart Chartering Ltd v. C. & O. Managements S.A.* [1980] 1 W.L.R. 460 where he continued a *Mareva* injunction granted before judgment in aid of execution."

(c) *In support of execution—when?*

"Plainly an injunction will only be granted where the plaintiff can adduce evidence of a kind which normally supports an application for a *Mareva* injunction, namely, that there are grounds for believing that the judgment debtor will dispose of his assets to avoid execution. Perhaps such grounds may be more readily established after judgment than before it. The present application was therefore granted."

3. Rationale—*per* Bingham J. Bingham J., in following Farquharson J., summarised the principle in *Hill Samuel Co. (ibid.).* (The notation has been added only for ease of exposition.)

(a) *Only interlocutory:*

"That an injunction is to be regarded as interlocutory, whether given before judgment or after, if it is not finally determinative of the rights of the parties but is merely in aid of the court's procedure and safeguarding the rights of the parties in the proceedings. If, however, I am wrong and a *Mareva* injunction to take effect after judgment is to be regarded as final, then I regard that as permitted by section 37(1) of the 1981 Act and not forbidden by section 37(3)."

(b) *Creates no rights in rem:*

"The grant of a *Mareva* injunction in aid of execution does not attach any fund, does not interfere with the ordinary law of insolvency, does not convert the beneficiary of such an injunction into a secured creditor, or in any way infringe the well-known purposes for which such injunctions are permitted."

However, Mareva relief can be sought cumulatively with other relief: The Rena K [1979] 1 Q.B. 377, per Brandon J.

(c) *Vulnerability:*

"It would, in my judgment, expose the administration of the law to justified reproach if a fund were to be protected by *Mareva* injunction until the moment of greatest vulnerability and then to be entrusted to the unfettered control of a defendant who is *ex hypothesi* regarded as likely to remove or dissipate it."

(d) *Does not fly in the face of authority:*

"There is nothing in the existing practice of extending *Mareva* injunctions in aid of execution which is, as I conclude, contrary to either statutory authority or judicial authority or principle ... injunction continued."

4. Phrasing the order A *Mareva* granted in aid of execution of any money judgment may be expressed to take effect "until after execution (or satisfaction) of the judgment entered herein."

5. How the court exercises its discretion In principle, a court will be the readier to grant a *Mareva* injunction in aid of execution, just as it will be less amenable in such circumstances to an application by the debtor to vary the injunction to enable him to pay outstanding debts. However, the plaintiff must in such circumstances demonstrate that he will not sit back, but rather make anxious efforts to pursue his judgment. Open to him will be remedies such as:

(a) execution;
(b) bankruptcy;
(c) winding up.

Thus, it is open to a court to conclude that if a judgment creditor does not (for example) proceed to wind up a judgment debtor, there is no reason why the court should interfere to prevent that debtor from continuing to pay his ordinary business debts. The dicta of Lord Donaldson M.R. in *Deutsche Schachtbau-und Tiefbohrgesellschaft m.b.H v. R'As al Khaimah National Oil Co.* [1987] 3 W.L.R. 1023 provide some basis for that proposition (unaffected by the subsequent appeal to the House of Lords). However, there may be exceptional circumstances where even if enforcement of a judgment could reach a particular asset, the court would still refuse a *Mareva* injunction over that asset: *Deutsche Schachtbau-und Tiefborhrgesellschaft v. Shell International Petroleum Co. Ltd* [1988] 3 W.L.R. 230. The plaintiff had obtained a *Mareva* injunction to preserve the position pending the commencement of garnishee order proceedings to enforce a judgment debt. The House of Lords discharged the *Mareva* because it held it to be inequitable to make a garnishee order absolute where there is a real risk that the garnishee will be required to pay the garnisheed debt a second time by a foreign court notwithstanding that the foreign court had no jurisdiction so to require.

B: *MAREVA*—ITS LIMITS

1. Introduction

1. No priority Because it creates no priority, limits to *Mareva* relief necessarily emerge. As Ackner L.J. said in *Bekhor & Co. Ltd v. Bilton* [1981] 1 Q.B. 923 at 942A:

> "The *Mareva* jurisdiction was not intended to re-write the English law of insolvency in this way. The purpose of the *Mareva* jurisdiction was not to improve the position of claimants in an insolvency, but simply to prevent the injustice of a defendant removing his assets from the jurisdiction which might otherwise have been available to satisfy a judgment. It is not a form of pretrial attachment, but a relief *in personam* which prohibits certain acts in relation to the assets in question."

2. Does not block a judgment creditor A judgment creditor can enforce a judgment against frozen assets—the *Mareva* is not a barrier: *Iraqi Ministry of Defence v. Arcepey Shipping Co. S.A. (Gillespie Brothers & Co.), The Angel Bell* [1980] 2 W.L.R. 488. Thus the plaintiff to a *Mareva* application should seek judgment and enforcement with all despatch—in the race against other potential judgment creditors.

3. Does not block a pre-existing creditor Even if not enforceable, pre-existing liabilities incurred in good faith by the defendant to third parties will be honoured, especially in the case of banks. Thus:

(a) *Banks:* A bank is not in contempt of court by honouring cheques backed by a guarantee card, and indeed, honouring other guaranteed debts such as irrevocable letters of credit: *Cretanor Maritime Co. Ltd v. Irish Marine Management Ltd* [1978] 1 W.L.R. 966; *Intraco Ltd v. Notis Shipping Corporation* [1981] 2 Lloyd's Rep. 256 and *Power Curber International Ltd v. National Bank of Kuwait S.A.K.* [1981] 1 W.L.R. 1233. (But a *Mareva* can apply to the proceeds of a letter of credit or a bank guarantee as and when received by and for the defendant: *Z Ltd v. A–Z and AA–LL* [1982] 1 Q.B. 558.)

(b) *Debenture holder:* A *Mareva* does not prevail as against a debenture holder where the floating charge crystallises after the injunction has been granted: *Cretanor Maritime Co. Ltd v. Irish Marine Management Ltd* [1978] 1 W.L.R. 966. This is because the rights of a debenture holder over the deposited fund stem from the creation of the debenture, and not from the appointment of the receiver which merely crystallises the existing equitable charge.

(c) *Company creditor:* A *Mareva* should not block a company creditor. Goff J. said in *Iraqi Ministry of Defence v. Arcepey Shipping Co. S.A. (Gillespie Bros. (intervening))* [1980] 2 W.L.R. 488 at 495A:

> "I find it difficult to see why, if a plaintiff has not yet proceeded to judgment against a defendant but is simply a claimant for an unliqui-dated sum, the defendant should not be free to use his assets to pay his debts. Of course, if the plaintiff should obtain a judgment against a defendant company, and the defendant company should be wound up, its previous payments may thereafter be attacked on the ground of fraudulent preference, but this is an entirely different matter which should be dealt with at the stage of the winding up."

4. The problem of banks—an outline Eveleigh L.J. summarised the position in *Z Ltd v. A–Z and AA–LL* [1982] Q.B. 558 at 583G–H:

> "The fact that the bank is under an obligation to others to make a payment should be strong evidence that the bank was not con-tumacious where that obligation emanates from a relationship between the bank and such other people as was established before the making of the order. Thus to honour a cheque drawn with the support of a banker's card should not be treated as contempt because before the order is made the bank will have made it known, as banks already have, that they will honour cheques up to a certain amount when supported by such a card. Where after the order is made some positive step from the bank is necessary before it then incurs liability to a third party, then, of course, it should refrain from taking that step because the court would then not regard its obligation to a third party as an excuse for contributing to the disobedience of the court's order."

The position of banks is considered in greater detail at p. 235.

5. The position of the spouse A *Mareva* injunction does not of itself freeze the assets of the defendant's spouse, unless there is good evidence that these assets are in fact the defendant's: *Allied Arab Bank Ltd v. Hajjar* (1989) Fam.Law 68, C.A. The plaintiff bank claimed over £4m. against guarantors of certain loans and obtained *Mareva* injunctions against them. The Court of Appeal held that there could not be brought within the ambit of the *Mareva* two bank accounts belonging to the defendant's wife, against which he had authority to draw. The plaintiff had failed to show that the monies in those accounts were assets of the defendant. In *Mercantile Group (Europe) AG v. Aiyela and others* [1994] Q.B. 366, C.A. the plaintiff had started an action against Mr Aiyela, his wife and several companies. The action was compromised by a Tomlin order by which Mr Aiyela agreed to pay $2.2m. by a certain date, in default of which the plaintiff was to be at liberty to enter judgment against him. The plaintiff abandoned its causes of action against all the other defendants. Mr Aiyela paid only $388,000. The plaintiff entered judgment against him for the balance. It was held that an interlocutory injunction is incidental to and dependent on the enforcement of a substantive right, which will usually be but is not necessarily a cause of action, that the enforcement of the judgment was a substantive right, and on the basis of evidence that Mrs Aiyela was frustrating the enforcement of the judgment and was still a party to the action, the court had jurisdiction to make a post-judgment *Mareva* against Mrs Aiyela, even though the plaintiff had no cause of action against her.

6. Equity's darling The bona fide purchaser for value or assignee for value or chargee of assets without notice of the injunction gets good title to assets the subject-matter of a *Mareva*. Despite the contempt of court necessarily involved by the party parting with the property, in not having *mens rea* the purchaser is not party to the contempt.

2 The *Cretanor* case—a good working example of the limits of a *Mareva*

1. The facts In *Cretanor Maritime Co. Ltd v. Irish Marine Management Ltd* (above) the plaintiff owners of the Cretan Harmony chartered her to the defendants. Thereafter, the defendant executed a debenture in favour of a U.S. bank creating a first floating charge for all moneys due or to become due, and conferring on the debenture holder a right to appoint a receiver with powers to collect property charged by the debenture.

2. *Mareva* discharged A receiver so appointed applied successfully, in the capacity of agent of the debenture holder, to have discharged a *Mareva* granted to the plaintiffs, resulting from disputes under the charterparty.

3. **Why?** The reasoning of the Court of Appeal was:

(a) The debenture holder was an equitable assignee of a deposited fund in a bank within the jurisdiction.

(b) That fund was the defendant's only asset.

(c) On the evidence there was no prospect of any surplus becoming available for unsecured creditors in the liquidation of the defendants after the satisfaction of the claims of preferential creditors and the debenture holder.

(d) The *Mareva* gave the plaintiffs no present right against the fund.

3 *Mareva* and the bill of exchange

1. **Background** A buyer may accept a bill of exchange in a sale of goods contract, on delivery of the goods. In the event of dishonour, the seller can seek summary judgment under Ord. 14.

2. **The problem** But what if the defendant has a valid counterclaim? The answer is: if necessary, the defendant can freeze in the plaintiff's hands the proceeds of the bill by a *Mareva*.

3. **Plaintiffs—beware** Thus, plaintiffs should beware the *Mareva* technique in support of a counterclaim as a means of circumventing the rule on defences to bills and bonds: *Montecchi v. Shimco (U.K.) Ltd* [1979] 1 W.L.R. 1180, C.A.

4. **Policy—the defendant's uphill struggle** However, it may be anticipated that defendants to such Ord. 14 proceedings will have an uphill struggle in persuading a court to grant a *Mareva* thereby apparently to defeat the commercial autonomy of a bill of exchange. And apart from that policy factor, such a defendant will have to show a "good arguable" case and "risk of dissipation."

5. ***Montecchi*—reasons for failure** In *Montecchi (ibid.)* the defendants failed because there was no evidence to suggest that the Italian plaintiffs were other than persons of perfectly sound financial standing in Italy against whom the defendants, in the event of success, could enforce their judgment in Italy under the Foreign Judgments (Reciprocal Enforcement) Act 1933. (And see now the Convention on Jurisdiction and the Enforcement of Judgements in Civil and Commercial Matters 1968, Art. 31.)

4 Documentary credits and *Mareva: The Bhoja Trader* [1981] 2 Lloyd's Rep. 256

1. The facts At the beginning of April 1981, the sellers sold their vessel *Bhoja Trader* (formerly *Notis*) to the buyers. The contract was in the Norwegian sale form which included clause 9, lines 82–89, a guarantee that the vessel at the time of delivery was free from all encumbrances and maritime liens or other debts whatsoever and further provided an indemnity in respect of the consequences of any such claim incurred prior to the time of delivery. The purchase price was $810,000 with $41,000 being paid as a deposit, $369,000 payable in cash on delivery and the balance of $400,000 being paid within 90 days of delivery by means of a bank guarantee which provided, *inter alia*, for payment to "M/S Notis Shipping Corporation of Liberia ... upon receipt of tested telex of Citibank NA Piraeus ... Piraeus Greece of the sellers' simple demand stating the amount due and also that such amount has not been paid by the buyers M/S Intraco Ltd. and confirm that they have in their possession protocol of receipt of delivery executed as above." Delivery took place in Calcutta on April 16 and shortly after the vessel was arrested. The buyers had to provide security of $200,000 to obtain her release and consequently alleged that they had suffered large losses due to cancellation of cargo bookings for the vessel. The buyers claimed against the sellers for breach of contract.

2. What did the buyers do? Save for their rights under the bank guarantee, the sellers had no assets within the jurisdiction. The buyers accordingly applied *ex parte* (and successfully) to Goff J. for an injunction restraining the sellers from calling upon the bank to make payment. At the *inter partes* hearing Staughton J. refused to continue the injunction restraining the sellers from calling upon the bank to make payment under the guarantee, but granted a *Mareva* injunction restraining the sellers:

> "Until further order from removing from the jurisdiction or otherwise disposing of any of their assets and in particular moneys payable under a guarantee given by the Banque de l'Indochine et de Suez dated April 14, 1981 in favour of the defendants, save insofar as the same exceed the sum of U.S. $50,000."

3. Why did Staughton J. vary the order? In refusing to interfere with the sellers' right to call upon the bank to make payment under its guarantee, Staughton J. acted in conformity with the well-established principle that the court will not grant such an injunction unless fraud is involved (see *Richardson (Howe) Scale Co. Ltd v. Polimex-Cekop* [1978] 1 Lloyd's Rep. 161, C.A.). This approach was confirmed by Sir John Donaldson M.R. at the appeal in *The Bhoja Trader*:

"In refusing to interfere with the sellers' right to call upon the bank to make payment under its guarantee, the learned Judge acted in conformity with the well-established principle that the court will not grant such an injunction unless fraud is involved (see *Richardson (Howe) Scale Co. Ltd v. Polimex-Cekop* [1978] 1 Lloyd's Rep. 161). We agree with him. Irrevocable letters of credit and bank guarantees given in circumstances such that they are the equivalent of an irrevocable letter of credit have been said to be the life blood of commerce. Thrombosis will occur if, unless fraud is involved, the courts intervene and thereby disturb the mercantile practice of treating rights thereunder as being the equivalent of cash in hand."

4. Should Staughton J. have discharged the order? Yes—because the guarantee must be treated as cash in Greece, not in London. As Sir John Donaldson M.R. explained at 258:

"The learned Judge went on to say that this did not prevent the court, in an appropriate case, from imposing a *Mareva* injunction upon the fruits of the letter of credit or guarantee. Again we agree. It is the natural corollary of the proposition that a letter of credit or bank guarantee is to be treated as cash that when the bank pays and cash is received by the beneficiary, it should be subject to the same restraints as any other of his cash assets. Enjoining the beneficiary from removing the cash asset from the jurisdiction is not the same as taking action, whether by injunction or an order staying execution, which will prevent him obtaining the cash (see *Montecchi v. Shimco (U.K.) Ltd* [1980] 1 W.L.R. 1180).

If therefore this bank guarantee had provided for payment in London, we should have agreed wholly with the learned Judge's judgment, subject to any argument upon the amount to which the injunction should apply. But this guarantee did not provide for payment in London, and we do not think that the significance of this aspect was ever really to be brought to the learned Judge's attention."

5. The buyers' arguments—which failed The following arguments were unsuccessfully advanced on behalf of the buyers:
  (a) First:
    (i) *Case for buyer:* Properly analysed, the bank's obligation was to pay in London and transfer to Greece.
    (ii) *Ruling:* No—the obligation was solely to pay in Greece and the bank could achieve this result how it liked—by drawing on funds already in Greece, by transfer from a third country such as France (where the bank was incorporated), or by transfer from London.

(b) Secondly:
  (i) *Case for buyer:* The assets is a "chose in action" whose *situs*, under English rules of conflict of laws, is in London.
  (ii) *Ruling:* Yes, in principle—but in practice, this would then involve interfering with the rights and obligations of the bank *vis-à-vis* the beneficiary of its guarantee.

6. Summary
  (a) A *Mareva* does not operate to freeze payment by a bank to third parties under irrevocable security documents.
  (b) It is implicit in the judgment of Donaldson L.J. in *The Bhoja Trader (ibid.)* that when a *Mareva* is granted over the proceeds of a letter of credit or similar document, the order can be made in anticipation of the moneys falling due (*cf. Ninemia Maritime Corporation v. Trave Schiffahrtsgesellschaft gmbH und Co. K.G.* [1938] 1 W.L.R. 1412 where Mustill J. refused a *Mareva* until the cause of action had crystallised).

5 The *Mareva* limits—how to avoid them

1. Techniques The inherent weaknesses of a *Mareva* order are: from the plaintiffs point of view the ultimate sanction is committal for contempt, not financial security; and from the defendant's point of view that whatever protection may be built into the order so as to allow him to continue trading and to pay his debts, notification of a *Mareva* to his bank is likely to affect his creditworthiness. These can be avoided, to the advantage of both, if agreement can be reached that in consideration for discharging the injunction:
  (a) paying money into court, or
  (b) providing a bond or guarantee that the plaintiff's debts will be met.
In such circumstances, the plaintiff can apply on notice (but without the attendance of the defendant) for the discharge of the *Mareva* order. It is essential in such circumstances for the plaintiff to explain all the material facts and also to set out whether any third party served with the order has suffered any damages which are still to be assessed and awarded. The defendant should however avoid any discharge of the plaintiff's original undertaking as to damages.

2. What is the effect of these techniques? These techniques have the effect of elevating the plaintiff to the rank of the defendant's secured creditors. As Donaldson L.J. said in *Hitachi Shipbuilding & Engineering Co. Ltd v. Viafel Compania Naviera S.A.* [1981] 2 Lloyd's Rep. 498 at 509:

"Curiously enough, the substitution of a bank guarantee for an asset may improve the position of a plaintiff, since he then obtains a chose in action which is earmarked for the satisfaction of his claims and which can be used for no other purpose. In particular, the plaintiff need no longer fear the competing claims of other creditors. However, this does not affect the principles involved."

3. Availability of such security—relevant to the exercise of the court's discretion In *Allen v. Jambo Holdings Ltd* [1980] 1 W.L.R. 1252, Lord Denning M.R. expressly referred to the desirability of putting up security to achieve the release of an aircraft. And in *Dellborg v. Corix Properties and Blissfield Corporation N.V.* (1980, June 26, C.A.T. No. 541), Lawton L.J. said:

"[Mr Justice Jupp] then asked himself what the effect of a *Mareva* injunction would be, and he seems to have come to the conclusion that the effect would be to stop the two companies from carrying out the purposes for which they had been incorporated, namely, the making of profits and getting those profits out of the United Kingdom. That, of course, would be the consequence of a *Mareva* injunction if it were not modified in any way.

But commercial experience has been that when *Mareva* injunctions are made the parties often cope with the problem which Mr Justice Jupp had in mind, by arranging for security to be given. Mr Goldblatt invited the court's attention to the analogy of what happens in the Admiralty jurisdiction of this court when a ship is arrested. The same kind of approach is possible in this class of case. We do not know what the profits are likely to be from these two developments; all we have are the figures which have been given us by Corix Properties ltd. Clearly the profits are going to be substantial and more than enough to meet any claims by the plaintiffs.

In my judgment Mr Justice Jupp failed to appreciate that the operation of a *Mareva* injunction in practice would not inhibit the very objects for which the companies had been incorporated."

4. Such techniques—and the effect on third parties Whether or not a defendant puts up such security should not be a factor which is allowed to affect third parties: *Zephyros Maritime v. Mineral Import/Export and Navron Roumanian Shipping (Intervening Respondents)* (1981, C.A.T. No. 534). In that case the plaintiffs obtained *Mareva* injunctions in respect of the cargoes of two vessels. The cargoes belonged to the defendants; the ships to the interveners. The interveners successfully applied to discharge the injunctions on the grounds that they adversely affected their trading assets (since the effects of the *Mareva* would have been to detain the vessels in dock for an indefinite period of time which would have caused a loss of $10,000 a day as the vessels were on voyage charters). On appeal, the court rejected the plaintiff's argument which relied on the fact that the defendants had been poised to provide a bankers' guarantee that would have released the vessels in the same way as the discharge of the injunction would, since the court held that whether or not a guarantee would be forthcoming was of no concern to the interveners.

6 Plaintiffs and the "garnishee" problem

1. Usual sequence of events:
   (a) With a judgment, a creditor may apply for a garnishee order against the debtor: Ord. 49, r.1.
   (b) Service of a garnishee order nisi operates as an equitable charge on the property.
   (c) On the order being made absolute the garnishee's obligation to pay the garnishor crystallises (see, by analogy, the significance of the appointment of a receiver in *Cretanor Maritime Co. Ltd v. Irish Marine Management Ltd* [1978] 1 W.L.R. 966; and *Rekstin v. Severo, Sibersko and the Bank for Russian Trade Ltd* [1933] 1 K.B. 47).
   (d) If the funds in the hands of the garnishee are subject to a *Mareva*, he should apply to the court for leave to pay the garnishor—the *Mareva* has no priority over the order absolute. (However, there is an argument that since the obligation to pay the garnishor is by order of the court, payment does not constitute breach of the injunction: see *Iraqi Ministry of Defence v. Arcepey Shipping Co. (the "Angel Bell")* [1981] Q.B. 65 at 72, *per* Robert Goff J. and *A v. B (X. Intervening)* [1983] 2 Lloyd's Rep. 532 at 534 which dicta constitute authority for the proposition that a judgment creditor does not need to seek a variation of a *Mareva* order before executing judgment on the assets.)

2. What if defendant insolvent? In considering whether or not to exercise its discretion to make absolute a garnishee order, the court must bear in mind, not only the position of the judgment creditor, the judgment debtor and the garnishee, but also the position of other creditors of the judgment debtor and must have regard to the fact that proceedings are on foot for ensuring the distribution of the available assets of the judgment debtor among the creditors *pari passu: Wilson (D.) (Birmingham) Ltd v. Metropolitan Property Developments Ltd*, Court of Appeal Transcript No. 383A of 1974, following *Hudson's Concrete Products Ltd v. Evans (D.B.) (Bilston) Ltd* (1961) 104 S.J. 281, C.A. and cited in *Rainbow v. Moorgate Properties Ltd* [1975] 1 W.L.R. 788. Thus:
   (a) If the *Mareva* plaintiff's claim is for a liquidated sum, it is open to

the court to decline to make a garnishee order absolute, with the result that the plaintiff would continue to enjoy a limited protection.

(b) If the *Mareva* plaintiff's claim is for an unliquidated sum the court may ignore that claim when assessing whether the defendant is insolvent.

In the latter example, the plaintiff should seek to protect himself by crystallising his claim under a judgment debt with all expedition. In the interests of completeness it should be noted that it is inequitable to make a garnishee order absolute where there is a real risk that the garnishee will be required to pay the garnisheed debt a second time by a foreign court notwithstanding that the foreign court had no jurisdiction so to require: *Deutsche Schachtbau-und Tiefbohrgesellschaft v. Shell International Petroleum Co. (T/A Shell International Trading Co.)* [1988] 3 W.L.R. 230, H.L.

C: EVIDENCE—THE DUTY OF FULL AND FRANK DISCLOSURE

1 Full and frank disclosure—what it means in practice

1. The principle As with all cases of injunctive relief, coming to equity carries with it the obligation to have clean hands. And the more draconian the relief sought, so the greater the obligation of "cleanliness," as Lord Denning M.R. said in *Bank Mellat v. Nikpour (Mohammad Ebrahim)* [1985] Com.L.R. 158:

"I would like to repeat what has been said on many occasions. When an *ex parte* application is made for a *Mareva* injunction, it is of the first importance that the plaintiff should make full and frank disclosure of all material facts. He ought to state the nature of the case and his cause of action. Equally, in fairness to the defendant, the plaintiff ought to disclose, so far as he is able, any defence which the defendant has indicated in correspondence or elsewhere. It is only if such information is put fairly before the court that a *Mareva* injunction can properly be granted. We stated the guidelines in 1979 in *Third Chandris Shipping Corporation v. Unimarine S.A.* at 668: 'The plaintiff should make full and frank disclosure of all matters in his knowledge which are material for the judge to know.' I think the judge in this case was well justified on the material before him in refusing to grant a new *Mareva* injunction."

Donaldson L.J. summed up the position at 159:

"It was so well enshrined in the law that no injunction obtained *ex*

197

parte should stand if it had been obtained in circumstances in which there had been a breach of duty to make the fullest and frankest disclosure that it was difficult to find authority for the proposition; it was trite law. Happily the court had been referred to the dictum of Warrington L.J. in *R. v. Kensington Income Tax Commissioners, ex p. Princess Edmond de Polignac* at 509, where it was said that if a person did not make the fullest possible disclosure he would be deprived of any advantage he might have already obtained by means of the order."

In the same case *Donaldson L.J.* categorised the *Mareva* injunction and the *Anton Piller* order together as the law's two "nuclear" weapons, so it is worth remembering that in *Columbia Picture Industries Inc. v. Robinson* [1987] Ch. 38 Scott J. said that the affidavit evidence in support of an application for an *Anton Piller* order should err on the side of excessive disclosure, and to apply the same approach to an application for a *Mareva*. The operation of the principle of full and frank disclosure resulted in discharge of *Mareva* and *Anton Piller* orders in *International Bank & Trust Corporation Ltd v. Joao Luis Perestrello* (1985, October 15, C.A.T.). Reference should also be made to *Eastglen International Corporation v. Monpare S.A.* (1987) 137 New L.J. 56, the head-note of which reads:

> "The fact that a *Mareva* injunction is obtained by the non-disclosure of material facts will not result in automatic discharge of the injunction when the non-disclosure is brought to the court's attention and nor will it prevent a new application being made for a fresh injunction. However, where a *Mareva* injunction had been improperly obtained because of material non-disclosure on the part of the plaintiffs' solicitor and the plaintiffs as a result had had the very considerable advantage of the continuance of a *Mareva* injunction to which they were not entitled, it was held that a fresh application had not cured the position and accordingly an injunction granted *ex parte* on the fresh application was ordered to be discharged."

It should also be noted that this duty to make full and frank disclosure also requires the plaintiff to make sufficient enquiries before launching the application: *Bank Mellat (ibid.)*.

2. A continuing duty The plaintiff has an obligation to furnish the court with the full facts after an *ex parte* injunction has been granted if new matters become known to him or if circumstances alter in any material way: *Commercial Bank of the Near East v. A.* (1989) 139 New L.J. 648, Saville J. Similarly, a party who has obtained an *Anton Piller* order has a continuing duty of disclosure to the court, so that the court can decide whether the order should be continued: *O'Regan v. Iambic Productions* (1989) 139 New L.J. 1378.

3. Does a mistake sully the plaintiff's hands irrevocably? No—not necessarily, as Lord Denning M.R. explained, also at 159:

> "There may sometimes be a slip or a mistake—in the application for a *Mareva* injunction—which can be rectified later. It is not for every omission that the injunction will be automatically discharged. A *locus pœnitentiae* may sometimes be afforded; but not in this particular case. It is quite clear that the plaintiffs themselves had the greatest difficulty in showing what their cause of action was. At first they did not show any cause of action. Next they claimed that the moneys had been loaned to Mr Nikpour. Finally they said against Mr Nikpour that he had wrongly credited the sums to his account. It seems to me that, in all the circumstances, the judge was quite entitled to say that the injunction was not properly obtained: and that it was not a case where the plaintiffs should be given any *locus pœnitentiae* to come in."

However, *Eastglen International Corporation v. Monpare S.A.* (1986) 137 New L.J. 56, is authority for the proposition that where a plaintiff obtains a *Mareva* injunction based on non-disclosure the court will not automatically discharge it if the non-disclosure had been caused entirely through the fault of his solicitor. But where a significant failure to disclose fully and fairly how matters stood according to a reasonably detached appreciation by the applicant and its legal advisers, a *Mareva* injunction will be discharged: *Siporex Trade S.A. v. Comdel Commodities Ltd* [1986] 2 Lloyd's Rep. 428. Bingham J. *inter alia* said at 438:

> "While I am quite sure that there was no intention to mislead the Judge, I think that he must have received an altogether too rosy view of Comdel's litigious position..."

4. Mistake in framing cause of action—automatically fatal? No. In *Hispanica v. Vencedora Oceanica Navegacion S.A. (The Kapetan Markos N.L.)* [1986] 1 Lloyd's Rep. 211, it was held that such a mistake did not justify subsequent discharge of a *Mareva*, when the factual substance of the case remained unaltered. This, however, should be read in the context of the dicta of Slade L.J. in *Bank Mellat (ibid.)* at 159:

> "No amount of urgency or practical difficulties could justify the making of a *Mareva* injunction unless the applicants had first made serious attempts to ascertain the relevant cause of action and to identify for the court the principal facts that would be relied on. It was the applicants' duty on any such application to state any defence which they anticipated would be relied upon by the other side."

5. *The Assios* [1979] 1 Lloyd's Rep. 331 By a contract of sale on the Norwegian Sale form dated August 31, 1978, the sellers agreed to sell *The*

Assios to the buyers for $1,900,000, of which 10 per cent was to be paid into a joint account pending completion of the sale, which was to be by September 30, following. Clause 17 provided:

> "Vessel to be delivered in substantially the same condition as when inspected at Rosario 22/6/78 fair wear and tear excepted with her present class fully maintained free of recommendations free of average damages affecting class, and with all continuous survey cycles up to date without any extensions."

Inspection at port of delivery (Rotterdam) revealed damage to the ship's bottom, which may have constituted a breach of clause 17. And this prompted the buyers to devise the following plan: that the ship be handed over to the buyers pursuant to the contract, but the proceeds of the sale be immediately frozen in the hands of the sellers, to provide the buyers with security in respect of litigation touching upon clause 17. As Lord Denning M.R. summed up the position at 333:

> "In getting the injunction the object of the buyers was to have security for their honest and bona fide claim for damages because the vessel was not up to contract."

6. Why did Mocatta J. initially grant the *Mareva*? All Mocatta J. knew was:
  (a) The estimate for repairs and loss of use came to $600,000.
  (b) The sellers were a "one-ship" company, which, it was argued, might disappear with the money.
And the injunction provided in substance for the following:
  (a) Freezing of the $190,000 deposit.
  (b) Freezing of the balance of the purchase moneys.
That injunction, it should be noted, was granted on the date fixed for deliver, September 21, nine days before the final date by which completion under the contract had to be effected.

7. Mocatta J. subsequently discharged the injunction—why? He took the view that by virtue of his not being apprised of "the plan," there had not been full and frank disclosure. The Court of Appeal agreed—and confirmed the discharge.

8. What did the buyers do that was wrong? The Court of Appeal identified the following factors as constituting a breach by the buyers of their duty to the court.
  (a) Non-disclosure of plan to judge.
  (b) Non-disclosure of the injunction to the sellers, prior to handing over of documents transferring the ship.

As Lord Denning M.R. said at 333:

> "The judge felt that [the] plan should have been disclosed to him at the time the *Mareva* injunction was granted. If he had been told that that was the plan, he might never have granted the injunction at all. Another part of the plan, which I think the judge did not think was quite fair, was that the buyers did not tell the sellers about the injunction before the exchange was made in that afternoon. They did not say to the sellers, 'We have an injunction against you, so it is no good your thinking you are going to get these moneys for your own use. We have an injunction to stop you dealing with them.' If they had been told, it seemed to the judge and it seems to me that the sellers might well have said, 'We are not going on with this deal in this way. We are not going on unless we get the money in hand as contemplated.'"

9. Would it have made any difference to sellers if they had known? Perhaps, for they had a further nine days before which they were contractually bound to complete the sale, in that time they might have repaired the ship.

10. Did the buyers lose all? No—The sellers volunteered on undertaking that they would not remove the amount of the deposit ($190,000) from the account with the National Bank of Greece—except on two clear business days' notice so as to allow the plaintiffs to apply for an injunction as regards that sum as security for their damages (and indeed, the Court of Appeal said that but for the undertaking, it might have ordered it anyway). Reference should also be made to *Ninemia Maritime Corporation v. Trave Schiffahrtsgesellschaft gmbH und Co. K.G.* [1983] 1 W.L.R. 1412.

11. Summary thus far Kerr L.J. summarised the need for full and frank disclosure in *Z Ltd v. A–Z and AA–LL* [1982] Q.B. 558 at 585A–E:

> "However, the jurisdiction must not be abused. In particular, I would regard two types of situations as an abuse of it."

(a) *First type of abuse:*

> "This increasingly common one, as I believe, of a *Mareva* injunction being applied for and granted in circumstances in which there may be no real danger of the defendant dissipating his assets to make himself 'judgment-proof'; where it may be invoked, almost as a matter of course, by a plaintiff in order to obtain security in advance for any judgment which he may obtain; and where its real effect is to exert pressure on the defendant to settle the action."

(b) *Second type of abuse:*

"The second, and fortunately, much rarer, illustration of what I would regard as an abuse of this procedure, is where it is used as a means of enabling a person to make a payment under a contract or intended contract to someone in circumstances where he regards the demand for the payment as unjustifiable; or where he actually believes, or even knows, that the demand is unlawful; and where he obtains a *Mareva* injunction *ex parte* in advance of the payment, which is then immediately served and has the effect of 'freezing' the sum paid over. Thus, we are told by Mr Slowe that payments are sometimes made for premiums which are required illegally on the assignment of leases, and which are then 'frozen' immediately as soon as the payment has been made. In effect, this amounts to using the injunction as a means of setting a trap for the payee."

(c) *Example of second type of abuse:*

"A reported instance of such a case (though not in a context of alleged illegality) was *Negocios Del Mar S.A. v. Doric Shipping Corporation S.A.* [1979] 1 Lloyd's Rep. 331, where the injunction was set aside because the plaintiff had not disclosed to the court that he intended to use the order for this purpose."

(d) *Would full and frank disclosure have been enough?*

"However, in my view even the disclosure of the intention should not suffice to obtain the injunction in such cases. If a person is willing to make such a payment, appreciating the implications, the courts should not assist him to safeguard the payment in advance by means of a *Mareva* injunction. However, this is a special type of situation, and, like all others in this field, ultimately a matter for the discretion of the judge to whom the application is made. Accordingly, I say no more about it."

12. The recent authorities

(a) *Lloyd's Bowmaker Ltd v. Britannia Arrow Holdings plc.* [1988] 1 W.L.R. 1337; [1988] 3 All E.R. 178, C.A., where it was held:

   (i) On an application to discharge a *Mareva* injunction for failure to make full and frank disclosure, the court had a discretion to grant a second injunction in the light of the full facts.

   (ii) The applicant was under a duty to give full and frank disclosure of all material facts including potential defences and/or explanations of the defendant to the applications.

   (iii) A *Mareva* injunction was a draconian order. Where such an order was obtained, the applicant was under a duty to press on with the litigation as quickly as possible so that the issues between the parties could be resolved.

Dillon L.J. said at 1348F:

> "The applicant owes a duty of fullest and frankest disclosure: if he puts in matters of prejudice he must put them in as fully as is necessary to be fair. He cannot pile on the prejudice and then when it is pointed out that he has told only half the story and has left out matters which give a quite different complexion, say 'Oh, well, it is not material. It is only prejudice, and so, on a strict analysis of the pleadings, does not have to be regarded.'"

  (b) *Brinks-Mat Ltd v. Elcombe* [1988] 1 W.L.R. 1350, C.A., where it was held:

    (i) A *Mareva* injunction granted upon the application of a plaintiff who failed to make full and frank disclosure could be continued notwithstanding the plaintiff's failure.

    (ii) Facts were material if they were relevant to the judge to know in dealing with the application.

    (iii) The plaintiff was bound to make proper inquiries before making his application and thus under a duty to disclose material facts that proper inquiries would reveal.

    (iv) The fact that non-disclosure was innocent was an important albeit not a decisive factor as to whether the plaintiff ought to be deprived of the injunction he had obtained.

    (v) The court retained a discretion where non-disclosure was established to discharge or continue the injunction or make a new order on terms.

    (vi) On the facts of the case: the plaintiff was guilty of an innocent non-disclosure of material facts in the evidence initially put before Roch J. Even if those facts had been put before Roch J. he would have been entitled to make the order that he did. To make an order discharging the injunction would amount to punishing the plaintiff for its innocent non-disclosure.

    (vii) *Per* Balcombe L.J. at 1358, that the discretion to maintain an order, or to make a new one in the same terms, after a non-disclosure is to be exercised "sparingly".

  (c) *Ali and Fahd Shobokshi Group v. Moneim Ltd* [1989] 1 W.L.R. 710; [1989] 2 All E.R. 404, *per* Mervyn Davies J.:

    (i) Where a plaintiff obtains a *Mareva* injunction *ex parte*, without proper disclosure of material facts, the court will refuse to continue the order if the non-disclosure is not innocent.

    (ii) The *ex parte* order could not properly have been granted if full disclosure had been made.

    (iii) Thus on the facts the court had no power to exercise its discretion and was obliged to refuse to continue the *Mareva* injunction and to refuse to hear an application for its immediate re-imposition.

   (iv) *Per curiam*: "Damages for non-disclosure awarded after trial may be an entirely inadequate remedy for a defendant who has had to suffer the oppression of a *Mareva* order up to trial."

(d) *Behbehani v. Salem* [1989] 2 All E.R. 143. The Court of Appeal held that failure to disclose the existence of proceedings in another jurisdiction when applying *ex parte* for a *Mareva* injunction, is sufficiently serious to prevent fresh injunctions being granted.

(e) *O'Regan v. Iambic Production* (1989) 139 New L.J. 1378. Peter Pain J. said:

> "It is clearly the duty of Counsel and of the solicitor to point out to the Judge any points which are to their clients' disadvantage, which the Judge should take into account in considering whether or not to grant the injunction. It is difficult for a Judge upon an *ex parte* application at short notice to grasp all the relevant points. In this context it is prudent to remind myself of the following dicta of Bingham J. in *Siporex Trade S.A. v. Comdel Commodities Ltd* [1986] 2 Lloyd's Rep. 428 at 437:
>
> > '[The applicant must] identify the crucial points for and against the application, and not rely on the mere exhibiting of numerous documents.' "

As to the responsibility of a solicitor to ensure full and frank disclosure, see *O'Regan v. Iambic Productions (ibid.)* at 1379, *per* Peter Pain J. [Interestingly, in the *Anton Piller* case of *Swedac v. Magnet and Southerns* [1989] F.S.R. 243, Harman J. ruled that solicitors should not pay costs personally despite their having made a serious misjudgment.]

   (f) *Bir v. Sharma, The Times*, December 7, 1988, *per* Vinelott J. Where a plaintiff obtained a *Mareva* injunction based on false evidence, he would be ordered to pay the costs incurred in connection with the injunction forthwith even where it had not yet been established whether or not the plaintiff personally knew of the falsity of the evidence.

   (g) *Dubai Bank Ltd v Galadari & Others* [1990] 1 Lloyd's Rep. 120, where it was *inter alia* held that on an *ex parte* application to the court *uberrimae fidei* was required. The applicant had a duty to put before the court all matters within his knowledge which were material to the consideration of the court in relation to his application. Even if there had been material non-disclosure the court had a discretion whether or not to discharge an order obtained *ex parte* and a discretion whether or not to grant fresh injunctive relief. Discharge of an order was not automatic on any non-disclosure being established of any fact known to the applicant which was found to be material by the court.

2 Failure to make full and frank disclosure—a working example

1. *Ninemia Marine Corporation v. Trave Schiffahrtsgesellschaft gmbH und Co. K.G.* [1983] 1 W.L.R. 1412 At the *inter partes* hearing, Mustill J. discharged the *Mareva*—his decision being upheld on appeal. The proceedings arose out of a sale by the defendants to the plaintiffs of a vessel which the plaintiffs claimed was in a condition which constituted a breach of clause 18 of the sale form requiring the vessel to be "free of average damages affecting class."

2. *The Assios*—in the wings Clearly mindful of the strictures of the Court of Appeal in *The Assios* [1979] 1 Lloyd's Rep. 331, the deponent to the plaintiffs' *ex parte Mareva* affidavit deposed thus:

"I verily believe that if the plaintiffs take delivery of the ship and pay the whole of the price to the sellers they will have no security for legitimate claims. The vessel is under steam, her class certificates are in order and a notice of readiness has been issued. Accordingly, the plaintiffs are effectively put in the position of being obliged to take delivery though knowing that the vessel is defective. The defendants are a West German corporation who are selling both of their only two vessels. The defendants have an account with Citibank, London, W.C.2, *i.e.* within the jurisdiction of this Honourable Court. The moneys payable under the [memorandum of agreement] are to be paid into such account. I verily believe that on closing such moneys as held in such account will be removed very quickly so that the defendants will have no assets in this country against which the plaintiff buyers would be able to enter any award or judgment. I am pessimistic about the prospects of the defendants honouring any award or judgment unless they are forced to keep sufficient assets in this country. A request was made by telex dated March 4, 1983, to the sellers that they should undertake to indemnify the buyers in respect of further leakages when steam was raised but such request was ignored ... Finally, I should mention that it would be the intention of the plaintiffs not to disclose the existence of any injunction that the court may make until immediately after closing and delivery of the ship. If the defendants are notified of the injunction beforehand, the plaintiffs fear that the defendants will sell the vessel elsewhere or may seek to assign the proceeds of sale to a third party . ...."

3. Grounds for criticism of the plaintiff That affidavit was considered to be open to criticism in that:

(a) It made no reference to the fact that the defendants formed part of the Oldendorff group of companies, who were well known in shipping circles generally: 1418G.

(b) The plaintiffs adduced no evidence about the defendants—let alone the group—to support the deponent's expression of pessimism about the prospects of the defendants honouring any award or judgment, other than what was stated in the passage quoted above: 1418H.

(c) The non-disclosure to the seller. Kerr L.J. said at 1419B–C:

"... there was the fact that the plaintiffs were proposing to use the machinery of a *Mareva* injunction in order to 'freeze' the price of the vessel as soon as it was paid over, unbeknown to the sellers. In this connection the judge referred to a passage in the judgment of Kerr L.J. in *Z Ltd v. A–Z and AA–LL* [1982] Q.B. 558 at 585, with which Eveleigh L.J. agreed at p. 584, and expressed reservations about this conduct on the part of the plaintiffs even though their intentions in this regard had of course been fully disclosed in Mr Nott-Bower's affidavit. However, given the fact that a plaintiff's intention in this regard is fully disclosed to the court, as it must be, we do not think that it would be desirable to express any views about this aspect. We agree with the judge when he said:

'There is something unattractive about the idea of a buyer, who is ostensibly paying the full price of a chattel, preparing himself behind the seller's back to deprive him of part of the price. This gives the buyer the best of both worlds.'

This factor should certainly be borne in mind by the court when it arises, and it may well militate against the exercise of the discretion to grant the injunction in such cases. However, in other cases the circumstances might well be such as to justify a *Mareva* injunction even in the face of this factor. In our view it would not be appropriate to seek to lay down any guidelines about it."

4. *The Ninemia*—injunction discharged—why? The injunction was discharged, in the face of the following factors advanced by the plaintiffs:

(a) In an affidavit sworn by a partner of the firm of solicitors acting for the plaintiffs there was reference to Embiricos Shipping Agency having made some vague attempt to obtain bank references in respect of the defendants and that these "had produced little useful information": 1421A.

(b) Upon Citibank in London being requested that the defendants should provide "a corporate guarantee," this had met with a firm refusal: 1421B.

(c) The defendant company was a limited partnership with a share capital of only D.M. 20,000: 1421B.

(d) There was evidence that the plaintiffs offered to consider the discharge of the injunction by consent on the basis of a bank guarantee or a guarantee from a major company in the group, which was refused: 1421C.

(e) Two press cuttings from Lloyd's List newspaper referring to a dispute in March 1975 between the Oldendorff group and a German shipyard about the possibility of cancelling or varying a contract for the construction of two vessels against the background of the shipping slump.

Facts as additionally advanced by the defendants to defeat the injunction were:

(a) The plaintiffs did not depose to the defendants as being "debt dodgers": 1424E.

(b) The plaintiffs did not speak of any bad reputation in the trade: 1424F.

(c) The plaintiffs did not say, and in the case of a company incorporated in the Federal Republic of Germany, could not say that companies registered there are difficult to track down, or are notoriously fallible in providing assets to meet large adverse judgments: 1424F.

(d) The plaintiffs did not say, and could not say, that there existed no mechanism for enforcement of awards in the sellers' country of incorporation—for the Federal Republic (unlike the Republic of Liberia, in which the buyers were incorporated) was a party to the New York Convention on the Recognition and Enforcement of Foreign Arbitral Awards: 1424. (*Cf. Allen v. Jambo Holdings Ltd* [1980] 1 W.L.R. 1252M–1254H *per* Lord Denning M.R.: "It would be difficult to enforce any judgment in Nigeria"): 1424G.

In other words, the fuller the disclosure, the less evidence there would have been as to risk of dissipation.

D: PRACTICE AND PROCEDURE

1 Introduction

1. The six-hurdle test To establish a claim in principle to *Mareva* relief, there must be evidence as to the following:

(a) The existence of a legal or equitable right: see p. 208.

(b) The English court must have jurisdiction in relation to that right: see p. 211.

(c) A good arguable claim for a certain or approximate sum: see p. 214.

(d) Assets (which need not necessarily be within the jurisdiction): see p. 218.

(e) Risk of dissipation, *i.e.* that a refusal of an injunction would involve a real risk that a judgment or award in the plaintiff's favour would remain unsatisfied. (N.B. the charging of assets may constitute dissipation: *Faith Panton Property Plan Ltd v. Hodgetts* [1981] 1 W.L.R. 927. Also see p. 223.

(f) Consent to an undertaking as to damages save in very exceptional circumstances: see p. 233.

2. Overcoming the hurdles—not necessarily enough Being a discretionary remedy, a court may refuse a *Mareva* even if the plaintiff apparently qualifies for its grant, if the injustice to the defendant would outweigh the justice to the plaintiff. A good working example of this principle is provided by *Rasu Maritima S.A. v. Perusahaan* [1978] Q.B. 644. In that case, the Court of Appeal refused a *Mareva* in respect of goods lying in the West Gladstone Dock in Liverpool, on the basis that:

(a) The "cleanliness" of the plaintiff's hands was open to question.

(b) The goods were parts of equipment needed for constructing a fertiliser plant in Indonesia.

(c) There was lack of certainty as to the title of the goods.

(d) The value of the goods, though $12m. to the owners, would, if seized and sold as scrap have realised only $350,000.

As Lord Denning M.R. said at 663C:

> "That is only a 'drop in the ocean' compared to the immense claim which Rappoport is making. And security would only be for that sum."

As to the weight to be attached to the competing interest of a foreign court, see *Felixstowe Dock & Railway Co. v. United States Lines Inc.* [1989] 2 W.L.R. 109.

3. Evidence The plaintiff is under a duty of full and frank disclosure, more fully explored at p. 197.

2 Legal or equitable right

1. An agency example There was held to be no legal or equitable right in *Man (E. D. & F.) (Sugar) Ltd v. Evalend Shipping Company S.A.* [1989] 2 Lloyd's Rep. 192. The plaintiff agreed to purchase sugar. The plaintiff's brokers, and X who purported to act on the defendant's behalf, agreed by telex on the provision of tonnage to carry the sugar. The plaintiff's brokers prepared a liner booking note, copies of which were sent to the plaintiff, and to the defendant via X. for signature. The plaintiff commenced arbitration proceedings against the defendant pursuant to the arbitration clause in the booking note. The plaintiff obtained a *Mareva* injunction against the defendant in that arbitration. The defendant sought to set aside the proceedings on the basis that they were not parties to any contract with the plaintiff. Rokison Q.C. held that on the facts, the defendant had never authorised X to contract on their behalf, and that therefore the *Mareva* should be set aside.

2. A potential future right is not sufficient In *Steamship Mutual Underwriting Association (Bermuda) v. Thakur Shipping Co.* [1986] 2 Lloyd's Rep. 439, there was no existing cause of action other than for a declaration that in event of (i) the plaintiffs' club having to honour a guarantee given by it; (ii) the defendant shipowners being called upon the pay the plaintiffs under their undertaking to them; and (iii) the defendants not meeting their obligation, the defendants would be liable to the plaintiffs. The Court of Appeal held that a *Mareva* injunction was not available to support such declaratory relief. What the plaintiffs really wanted was security for a future cause of action which would give entitlement to monetary relief. Granting a *Mareva* in these circumstances would be contrary to a long line of authority which said that section 37 of the Supreme Court Act 1981, which gave jurisdiction to the court, was to be used in support of an existing legal or equitable right. Reference should also be made to *The Niedersachsen* [1983] 2 Lloyd's Rep. 600 at 602, 613, and to *Siporex Trade S.A. v. Comdel Commodities Ltd* [1986] 2 Lloyd's Rep. 428. In the latter case, Bingham J. held that when the *Mareva* was granted, the defendant in whose favour it was made had no existing legal or equitable right. The only relief which at that stage the defendant was able to seek was a declaration of the plaintiff's duty upon receiving payment from a bank to pay over any excess to the defendant after compensating themselves for their own loss. The limit to this principle however was demonstrated in *A. v. B.* [1989] 2 Lloyd's Rep. 423. The case is authority for the proposition that the court will grant conditional *Mareva* relief in circumstances where no cause of action has yet arisen, if the plaintiff can show that it would be appropriate to give a *Mareva* when the cause of action arose. The *Mareva* could not take effect until the cause of action did arise. The facts were that the plaintiff had paid money into a joint account as a deposit on the purchase of a ship from the defendant. They had reason to suspect that the ship would not be in good condition on delivery and thus sought a *Mareva* injunction to freeze the account. The plaintiff had no cause of action against the defendant until the ship was delivered. It was held that if material was produced to the court which showed that it would be appropriate to grant a *Mareva* when the cause of action arose, then there was no reason why a conditional *Mareva* should not be granted in advance to come into effect as and when the vessel was delivered. The draft *Mareva* order should be so phrased as not to result in refusal of an injunction at the *ex parte* stage and/or discharge at the *inter partes* stage.

3. Interlocutory injunction In *Mercantile Group (Europe) AG v. Aiyela and others* [1994] Q.B. 366 C.A. the plaintiff had started an action against Mr Aiyela, his wife and several companies. The action was compromised by a Tomlin order by which Mr Aiyela agreed to pay $2.2m. by a certain date, in default of which the plaintiff was to be at liberty to enter judgment against him. The plaintiff abandoned its causes of action against all the other defendants. Mr Aiyela paid only $388,000. The plaintiff entered judgment against him for the balance. It was held that an interlocutory injunction is incidental to and dependent on the enforcement of a sub-stantive right, which will usually be but is not necessarily a cause of action, that the enforcement of the judgment was a substantive right, and on the basis of evidence that Mrs Aiyela was frustrating the enforcement of the judgment and was still a party to the action, the court had jurisdiction to make a post-judgment *Mareva* against Mrs Aiyela, even though the plaintiff had no cause of action against her.

4. Foreign restraint—does it negative legal or equitable rights? A U.S. court order restraining litigation by creditors of a U.S. company pending its re-organization was held not to prevent the English court from freezing the company's U.K. assets in ancillary English proceedings. *Felixstowe Dock & Railway Co. v. United States Lines Inc.* [1989] 2 W.L.R. 109. In that case the defendant company was a U.S. incorporated shipping line who were also registered in England as an overseas company under section 691 of the Companies Act 1985. The defendant company found themselves in severe financial difficulty, and filed "Chapter 11" bankruptcy proceedings in the U.S.A. This had the effect of freezing all claims against the defendant company, allowing them to restructure under the supervision of the court. A number of English plaintiffs obtained *Mareva* injunctions to prevent the withdrawal of the defendant company's assets from the jurisdiction. The defendant company applied to have the injunctions set aside on the grounds that the English court should recognise the order of the U.S. Bankruptcy Court and allow the court to administer the defendant company's assets. Hirst J. held that the Chapter 11 proceedings were only one of the considerations. Irreparable harm might be done to U.K. creditors if the defendant company's assets were removed from the country and the defendant company had shown an intention to withdraw from its European operations, whereas the injunctions did not grant priority and the assets were in safe hands. In that case Hirst J. considered:

(a) the *Mareva* injunction;
(b) comity under English law;
(c) English bankruptcy procedures;
(d) the relevant United States authorities on comity and bankruptcy procedure;
(e) contempt in the United States.

Moreover a court has jurisdiction to grant *Mareva* relief on the application of the Securities and Investment Board, restraining a company under investigation by the S.I.B. from dissipating its assets notwithstanding that the S.I.B. had no beneficial interest in those assets. *Securities and Investment Board v. Pantell S.A.* [1989] 3 W.L.R. 698, *per* Browne-Wilkinson V.-C., who *inter alia* said at 703E:

> "... But in my judgment the statutory right of action for the benefit of investors conferred on the S.I.B. by Section 6 [of the Financial Services Act 1986] is as much a right of action as any normal right of action in common law."

Following on from this, "victims" of a transaction defrauding creditors can found a cause of action on sections 423, 424 and 425 of the Insolvency Act 1986.

3 Jurisdiction

1. Introduction There will be jurisdiction over a dispute if there is a cause of action triable in the English courts. That can arise if:

(a) the cause of action is justiciable in England, or
(b) an overseas judgment is enforceable in the jurisdiction.

2. No cause of action in the jurisdiction—no *Mareva*? *The Siskina* [1979] A.C. 210, H.L.:

(a) *The facts:* The plaintiffs, cargo owners in Saudi Arabia, sued the defendant shipowners, a Panamanian company. The bill of lading issued on shipment of the cargo in Italy conferred exclusive jurisdiction on the courts of Genoa; the ship was registered in Panama; the claim was in respect of the discharge of the cargo in Cyprus. The dispute thus had no connection with England; but *The Siskina*, the defendants' sole asset, had subsequently sunk and the insurance money was payable in London.

(b) *Held:* That there was no cause of action triable in the English courts, and that the plaintiffs were accordingly not entitled to an injunction restraining the removal of the insurance money from the jurisdiction.

3. *The Siskina*—its significance The principles flowing from the decision were:

(a) *First:* the injunction cannot stand alone under Ord. 11, but has to be linked to substantive relief within the Order, and

(b) *Secondly:* the presence of moneys or assets within the jurisdiction of the court did not without more give jurisdiction to the court (in contrast to the presence of an aircraft or ship for an action *in rem*).

The Siskina was followed by Sheen J. in *The Stolt Filia* (L.M.L.N.—Issue No. 15, 1980). The plaintiffs had provided spare parts and rendered services to the vessel following serious heavy weather damage, for which the owners had not paid. Mortgagees had subsequently arrested the vessel and it appeared that from the proceeds of judicial sale, nothing would be left for the plaintiffs. But the weather damage had resulted in hull and machinery insurance proceeds in London, which the plaintiffs sought to freeze. The court refused to continue a *Mareva* because:

(a) all the plaintiff had was an action *in rem* against the ship (which was probably valueless to them), and

(b) the plaintiffs conceded that they could not obtain leave to serve out of the jurisdiction because their claim did not fall within Ord. 11.

4. *The Siskina* and the Act of 1982 *The Siskina* ruling is reversed, initially as regards proceedings pending in other EEC countries, by section 25 of the Civil Jurisdiction and Judgments Act 1982. This empowers the English court to grant interim relief in certain circumstances, though it may refuse to do so in circumstances where jurisdiction depends on section 25 and it is thought inexpedient to make an order. Section 24 of the Act provides for the grant of interim relief pending the trial (in England) of an issue relating to the court's jurisdiction to entertain the proceedings. (Section 25 applies to proceedings of a civil or commercial nature, save for actions relating to the status or legal capacity of natural persons, rights in property arising out of a matrimonial relationship, wills and succession; bankruptcy, proceedings relating to the winding-up of insolvent companies or other legal persons, judicial arrangements, compositions and analogous proceedings; social security and arbitration.)

5. Reciprocal enforcement conventions, etc. Registration in England of a foreign judgment pursuant to one of the conventions, affords the court jurisdiction (whereby the foreign judgment creditor can enforce it as an English judgment). For example:

(a) Administration of Justice Act 1920, s.9—discretionary registration.

(b) Foreign Judgments (Reciprocal Enforcement) Act 1933—mandatory registration.

(c) Arbitration Acts 1950 and 1975—arbitral awards. Thus, where a party to an arbitration agreement which contains a choice of law clause in favour of non-English law obtains an award he will be entitled to leave to enforce the award here as a judgment provided (i) the parties intended to create legally enforceable rights and obligations; (ii) the agreement was sufficiently certain to constitute enforcement; and (iii) there are no public policy objections to enforcement. If a debt is enforceable within the jurisdiction it constitutes an asset to which a *Mareva* jurisdiction can attach; *Deutsche Schachtbauund Tiefbohrgesellschaft mbH v. Ras Al Khaimah National Oil Co.* [1987] 3 W.L.R. 1023, C.A. In that case D.S.T. and R entered into an agreement to explore for oil, which included a term providing for arbitration in Geneva according to a proper law adopted by the arbitrators. Later D.S.T. referred a claim to arbitration and received a substantial award, while R obtained rescission of the agreement and damages from a court in a Gulf State. Neither party took part in the proceedings instituted by the other. D.S.T. later discovered that an English company, S, had bought oil from R and obtained leave to enforce the arbitration award in England as a judgment, together with a *Mareva* injunction. R obtained leave to serve a writ out of the jurisdiction on D.S.T. claiming enforcement of its judgment. The Court of Appeal held that D.S.T.'s *Mareva* injunction and leave should not be discharged, while R's leave should be. The choice of law clause was effective because the parties had intended to create legally-enforceable rights and obligations, the agreement was sufficiently certain as to constitute a contract and enforcement would not be contrary to public policy. Further, the *Mareva* injunction was valid despite the fact that S's indebtedness to R would normally be settled in U.S. dollars in New York, since in default it could be enforced within the jurisdiction.

(d) See Civil Jurisdiction and Judgments Act 1982 and Article 31(2) of the Convention, pursuant to which enforcement takes place through registration when the foreign judgment is from one of the EEC countries. Judgments are enforced under section 18 of the Civil Jurisdiction and Judgments Act 1982. (Thus for example, a plaintiff can enforce a judgment against a defendant's assets in London, having obtained a judgment in Rome.)

6. Order 14 Summary proceedings in respect of a foreign judgment for a liquidated claim are available to the judgment creditor.

7. Costs The court may grant an injunction restraining disposal of assets pending taxation on an interlocutory order for payment of taxed costs, under section 45(1) of the Supreme Court of Judicature (Consolidation) Act 1925: *Panton (Faith) Property Plan Ltd v. Hodgetts* [1981] 1 W.L.R. 927, C.A. In that case the plaintiffs claimed against the defendant for passing

213

off. The defendant gave an undertaking in interlocutory proceedings. The plaintiffs then moved to commit the defendant for breach of the undertakings. The judge ordered the defendant to pay the costs of the motion to be taxed on full indemnity basis. That sum was likely to amount to some £12,000, but could not be taxed for some five months. The defendant had been heard to state that he was going to sell his assets and go bankrupt. The Court of Appeal held that it had a discretion to grant the injunction—which it exercised in the plaintiff's favour.

8. Other circumstances founding jurisdiction

(a) A successful application for leave to issue and serve out of the jurisdiction, under R.S.C., Ord. 11: application can then be made for a *Mareva* order to freeze the defendant's assets which can in turn be rendered subject to enforcement if the plaintiff is in a position to enter judgment in default. In this context *The Siskina* [1979] A.C. 210 remains good authority for the principle that an application for a *Mareva* injunction cannot stand alone under R.S.C., Ord. 11 but has to be linked to substantive relief within the Order.

(b) Submission to the jurisdiction:
  (i) a plaintiff so submits if he sues within the jurisdiction: *High Commissioner for India v. Ghosh* [1960] 1 Q.B. 134;
  (ii) Entering an appearance to contest the jurisdiction of/or to apply to discharge a *Mareva* order is *not* such a submission to the jurisdiction; see, for example, *Re Dulles' Settlement (No. 2)* [1951] Ch. 842.

4 A "good arguable case"

1. Meaning "'A good arguable case' is no doubt the minimum which the plaintiff must show in order to cross what the judge rightly described as the 'threshold' for the exercise of the jurisdiction. But at the end of the day the court must consider the evidence as a whole in deciding whether or not to exercise the statutory jurisdiction": *The Ninemia* [1983] 1 W.L.R. 1412. In *The Niedersachsen* [1983] 2 Lloyd's Rep. 600, it was defined at 605 as "a case which is more than barely capable of serious argument, and yet not necessarily one which the judge believes to have a better than 50 per cent chance of success."

2. The necessity for sufficient evidence—an "agency" example In *The Tatiangela* [1980] 2 Lloyd's Rep. 193, the plaintiff, *inter alia*, sought to show that although the vessel was apparently chartered to Messrs Al Naseem Trade Bureau of Jeddah, the plaintiff was, as undisclosed principal, the time charterer. Parker J. held at 197:

"I have no doubt that the evidence presently before the court is inadequate. There is no scrap of documentary evidence of agency or of transactions which would normally flow from an agency if there was one. Nor is there any information shown to have been given by either of the parties to any oral agency or by someone present at the time. These matters are of great importance, particularly in the case of an alleged undisclosed principal where, since ratification cannot arise, the date of the alleged agency is or can be crucial. The plaintiff must, it is common ground, show a good arguable case. He has not in my judgment done so and I decline the invitation to make a conditional order. Had the point been raised late, such an order or an adjournment, might well have been appropriate, but the plaintiff has had three months in which to produce adequate evidence. He has failed to do so and his whole case depends upon his being the charterer this is sufficient to dispose of both applications for it must follow that the injunction should be discharged and the proceedings set aside."

3. The *Dakota* case *Visionair International Inc. v. Euroworld California Inc. and Exeter Airport Ltd* (unreported) came before the Court of Appeal on November 30, 1979. Euroworld applied for discharge of an injunction to enable them to fly out three aircraft lying at Exeter Airport which Visionair claimed to own—the title to which had been purportedly transferred to one Browd (an attorney) as trustee for Visionair. The court held that Visionair had not established a good arguable case as to title. Lord Denning M.R. said at p. 3 of the transcript:

"Having examined all the circumstances, it seems plain that neither Mr. Browd, Mr. Hawke, nor Visionair can really show any beneficial title in these aircraft whatsoever: and there is a query as to whether these transcriptions were valid in any way at all. At all events, no good arguable case is made out for preventing Euroworld California Inc. from removing this aircraft from Exeter. There is no reason whatsoever why their pilots should not fly them out. It would be very wrong for any threats to be made against the pilots or anyone else so as to prevent their departure."

Goff L.J. went on to explain that the evidence failed to substantiate the endorsement on the writ:

"So when you get further evidence it is perfectly plain that on the plaintiffs' own showing they are not seeking a declaration that Visionair are the sole owners of the aircraft. What they are saying is that they are mortgagees of the aircraft under a security which they have chosen without the knowledge of the mortgagor to create for themselves."

215

4. A "good arguable case" where there is a counterclaim The point was considered by the Court of Appeal on *inter partes* argument (because the defendant was seeking discharge of a *Mareva* because of a counterclaim) in *Avant Petroleum Inc. v. Gatoil Overseas Inc.* [1986] 2 Lloyd's Rep. 236. Neill L.J. said

> "In order to obtain an injunction, the plaintiff must show as a minimum that he has a good arguable case. ... It seems to me ... that where the defendant is relying on a set-off or a counterclaim which can be used by way of an equitable set-off, the Court should consider whether, looking at the matter as a whole, it is a case where the jurisdiction should be exercised."

He then cited words of Kerr L.J. in *Z Ltd v. AZ and AA–LL* [1982] Q.B. 558 at 585F:

> "It follows that in my view *Mareva* injunctions should be granted, but granted only when it appears to the Court that there is a combination of two circumstances. First, when it appears likely that the plaintiff will recover judgment against the defendant for a certain or approximate sum ...".

5 The good arguable case criterion—and shipping cargo claims

1. The authority The problem was (albeit *obiter*) explored in *The Tatiangela* [1980] 2 Lloyd's Rep. 193.

2. The issue The vessel sank when carrying a cargo of coffee owned by the plaintiffs. The plaintiffs argued that where a charter had lost his goods and the vessel had been sunk, he can (when applying for a *Mareva*) do no more than rely on his prima facie case unless and until he has obtained from the owners full particulars and discovery both documentary and by interrogatories of the details of what happened and what precautions the defendants had taken, because all such knowledge was in the owner's possession.

3. The terms of the charterparty That argument was based upon the following premises:

(a) *Clause 13 of the charterparty:*

> "The owners only to be responsible for ... loss or damage to goods on board, if such delays or loss has been caused by want of due diligence on the part of the owners or their manager in making the vessel seaworthy and fitted for the voyage or of any other personal act or omission or default of the owners or their manager. The owners

216

not to be responsible in any other case nor for damage or delay whatsoever and howsoever caused even if caused by the neglect or default of their servants." (at 198)

(b) *Effect of clause:* That clause puts the burden on the shipowner to establish that the loss was not due to want of due diligence by the owners or their manager to make the vessel seaworthy or to any other personal act or omission or default of the owners or their manager: *The Roberta* (1938) 60 Ll.Rep. 84.

(c) *Court must also look at defendant's case:* The unreported Court of Appeal decision of April 10, 1979, in *Fary-Jones (Insurance) Ltd v. I.F.M. Funding GmbH* establishes (1) that, in order to obtain or retain, the grant of a *Mareva* injunction the plaintiff must, as in the case of leave to serve out, show that he has a good arguable case on the merits, and (2) that the court which deals with the matter is both entitled and bound to consider the strength or weakness of the plaintiff's and defendant's case.

4. The argument—rejected Parker J. rejected the plaintiff's argument on three grounds: In summary, his rationale was that the plaintiffs were hoist by the petard of their own argument, namely, that since all the relevant information was then in the hands of the defendants, the defendants were in a better position to show that the plaintiffs had no good arguable case. The three grounds may be summarised thus—but are particularised below:
  (a) A prima facie case was not a good arguable case.
  (b) As a matter of policy the *Mareva* jurisdiction should not be extended to prima facie cases.
  (c) Cargo owners seeking a *Mareva* should pursue all reasonably available lines of enquiry.
These grounds for the court's decision are explored immediately below.

5. First ground—a prima facie case is not a good arguable case

"In a case such as the present, where the burden is upon the defendant, the strength or weakness of the plaintiff's case depends essentially upon the strength or otherwise of (a) the defendants' evidence that there was no personal fault and (b) any evidence that the plaintiff may produce setting up a particular alleged fault. The position must be judged at the stage when the matter is before the Court. In the present case the plaintiff sets up nothing more than the actual loss. This establishes, I accept, a prima facie case but it does no more. It does not show that the plaintiff has good, good arguable, weak or bad prospects or in any way reveal the quality of his case. The question must therefore depend upon any assessment of the defendants'

217

evidence. They have put before me a body of evidence that all proper steps were taken to see that the vessel was in every respect seaworthy and properly equipped, that she was subject to thorough surveys and drydocking only some three weeks before the loss, that certificates given as late as December 18, 1978, had covered her fire-fighting equipment, that the master and crew were properly and carefully selected and that no one had made any suggestion that the owners of Mr. Pefanis or indeed anyone else were in any way to blame for the loss." (at 198).

6. Second ground—the policy behind not extending the *Mareva* jurisdiction to prima facie cases

"The *Mareva* injunction is a useful and very powerful remedy, but its grant is a serious matter which may do the defendants great damage, and in *The Genie* [1979] 2 Lloyd's Rep. 184, Lord Denning M.R., observed at p. 189 that it must not be stretched too far. It would in my judgment be stretching it too far to allow it in cases where a shipowner had advanced cogent evidence of lack of personal fault and the cargo owner had neither put in countervailing evidence nor advanced some credible hypothesis as to what, involving personal fault, had happened or might reasonably be inferred to have happened." (at 198.)

7. Third ground—the need for a cargo owner to make enquiries

"Furthermore, although at the *ex parte* stage it may be sufficient simply to set up the loss, I do not consider that this will always be so, for I am unable to see how, if he has made no enquiries at all, a cargo owner can properly submit that he has a good arguable case. He simply does not know and he has made no attempt to find out. It may be different if he has made inquiries and met with no answers or evasive answers. It may be that in that case it would be right to invite the Court to infer that there was a good arguable case, but it would in my judgment imperil the continued existence of the *Mareva* injunction if it were granted on loss of cargo without more. I cannot consider it to be just and convenient to expose foreign shipowners to having assets here frozen on such material alone." (at 198–9.)

6 Assets (which need not necessarily be within the jurisdiction)

1. Defining the assets liable to "freezure"
(a) They can be tangible or intangible.
(b) They must be within the legal or beneficial ownership of the

defendant. Thus for money in a joint bank account to be covered by a *Mareva* order, it must be expressly included—and see in this context *S.C.F. Finance Co. Ltd v. Masri* [1985] 1 W.L.R. 876, C.A.

(c) They must not be subject to legal or equitable interests of third parties to the extent that they would not be available on execution of a judgment.

(d) The assets must be held by the defendant *qua* defendant—and not in any other capacity: *Roberts v. Death* (1881) 8 Q.B.D. 319.

(e) Section 13(2)(a) of the State Immunity Act 1978 forbids the giving of relief against a State by way of injunction save with the written consent of the State concerned, which may be contained in a prior agreement.

2. Must assets be within the jurisdiction? No. If the defendant's assets within the jurisdiction are insufficient to meet the claim the court can make a *Mareva* order in respect of the defendant's dealings with his assets outside the plaintiff. Note that at one time it was thought that the answer to this question is "Yes", and any authorities prior to *Babanaft International Co. S.A. v. Bassatne* [1990] Ch. 13 and *Derby & Co. Ltd v. Weldon (Nos. 3 & 4)* [1990] Ch. 65 should be ignored. The effect of the authorities on the so-called *Babanaft* proviso is now incorporated in the standard form of world-wide *Mareva* at Annex 2 to the Practice Direction [1994] 4 All E.R. 52. In *Rosseel N.V. v. Oriental Commercial Shipping (U.K.)* [1990] 1 W.L.R. 1387, the Court of Appeal held that the High Court will not make orders which extend beyond its territorial jurisdiction except in exceptional circumstances. In that case the judge at first instance had declined to grant relief in respect of assets outside the jurisdiction where the plaintiff sought a worldwide *Mareva* injunction against the defendant pending proceedings to enforce an arbitration award made in New York. This application of the brake on world-wide *Mareva* applications should not, however, be interpreted as blighting proper claims. Thus it has been held that the English courts have unlimited jurisdiction *in personam* over every person who has properly been a party to pending English proceedings. The court therefore has power to order the transfer of assets from one foreign jurisdiction to another: *Derby v. Weldon (No. 6)* [1990] 1 W.L.R. 1139, C.A.

3. After acquired assets? Yes—A *Mareva* covers assets acquired after date of order: *T.D.K. Tape Distributor (U.K.) Ltd v. Videochoice Ltd* [1986] 1 W.L.R. 141. In that case the defendant's solicitors appropriated towards their outstanding fees the proceeds of an insurance policy which had matured upon the death of the defendant's wife, after the grant of the *Mareva*. Skinner J. held:

(a) Such proceeds were not in fact after-acquired assets because the

219

entitlement under the insurance already existed at the time of the *Mareva* order. It was simply the wife's death which crystallised the actual right to payment.

(b) If that approach was wrong, then a *Mareva* also applied to after-acquired assets:

> "A *Mareva* injunction is looking to the future and is dealing with the situation between the obtaining of the judgment and its eventual execution, and it will cover any assets which are acquired between the granting of the order and the eventual execution of any judgment obtained in the action in question."

7 What categories of assets are included?

1. Land Selling of land may be part of the evidence of risk of dissipation. In theory, land can be included (*Kirby v. Banks* (1980) C.A.T. No. 624, but in practice a court is likely to regard an injunction which might prevent a possible sale as unfairly and unnecessarily onerous. The standard orders in the Annex to the Practice Direction [1994] 4 All E.R. 52 permit sale but restrain disposal of the net proceeds of sale, and in an appropriate case the plaintiff may be permitted to interrogate the defendant as to the identity of an estate agent and solicitor or licensed conveyancer who is acting for him, so that notice of the *Mareva* can be given to him. A defendant can be restrained from charging his land. A *Mareva*, being an order *in personam*, cannot be registered as a land charge.

2. Bank accounts As to locating such accounts, one example is provided in *Third Chandris Shipping Corporation v. Unimarine S.A.* [1979] Q.B. 645. The deponent to the first plaintiffs' affidavit said:

> "I am advised by the plaintiffs' Protection and Indemnity Club that they have made inquiries which have revealed that the defendants have a bank account at the Bank of Credit and Commerce, 100 Leadenhall Street."

3. Accounts in overdraft A *Mareva* can be granted even if the account is an overdraft. As Lawton L.J. said at 673A–C:

> "The only evidence which the owners produced of the existence of assets within the jurisdiction was that the charterers had an account with an English branch of a Luxembourg bank. The charterers claim, and their bankers support them in this, that when the *Mareva* injunction was granted this account was overdrawn. They submitted that without proof of assets within the jurisdiction a *Mareva* injunction should not be granted. I agree; but it does not follow that the

existence of an overdraft establishes that there are no assets within the jurisdiction. Large overdrafts, such as commercial undertakings have, are almost always secured in some way. The collateral security may represent substantial assets. The charterers' evidence makes no reference to the existence or absence of collateral security. This omission leads me to conclude that the existence of the bank account, albeit in overdraft, is some evidence of assets within the jurisdiction."

4. Specific assets

(a) *Aeroplane: Allen v. Jambo Holdings* [1980] 1 W.L.R. 1252 and also see the unreported case of *British Air Ferries Ltd v. Svenska Aktiebolaquet für Direkta Kompenstionsaffarer* (1987, April 22, C.A.).

(b) *Ship's bunkers: Sanko Steamship Co. Ltd v. D.C. Commodities (Australasia) Pty Ltd* (1980) W.A.R. 51.

(c) *Ship: The Rena K* [1979] Q.B. 377; *Clipper Maritime Co. of Monrovia v. Mineralimportexport, The Marie Leonhardt* [1981] 1 W.L.R. 1262. The advantage of a *Mareva* in the Admiralty jurisdiction is that the plaintiff is not limited to looking to only one ship.

(d) *Machinery: Rasu Maritima S.A. v. Purusahaan Pertambangan Minyak Dan Gas Bumi Negara (Pertamina)* [1978] Q.B. 644.

(e) *Time charterer's bunkers and cargo: Clipper Maritime (supra)*.

(f) *Stamps:* In *Johnson v. L & A Philatelics* [1981] F.S.R. 286 the plaintiff claimed that the defendants, stamp dealers, owed him £21,700 for services rendered. He sought an injunction restraining the defendants from removing from the jurisdiction or dealing with their stamps or other assets and an order requiring the defendants to permit the plaintiff's solicitors to search for and take the stamps. Robert Goff J. granted the order, because there was good evidence that the defendants were closing down their business and leaving the jurisdiction. The actual order, *inter alia*, provided:

  (i) That the defendants permit the plaintiffs to enter specified premises to search for and seize stamps and documents relating to stamps.
  (ii) That the defendants disclose the whereabouts of stamps and cars belonging to the defendants.
  (iii) That the defendants deliver up forthwith all stamps in their immediate personal possession.

But see *C.B.S. United Kingdom Ltd v. Lambert* [1983] 1 Ch. 37 below at p. 271.

5. Business goodwill *Darashah v. UFAC U.K. Ltd, The Times*, March 30, 1982: Lord Denning M.R. held that there was a good arguable case for

substantial damages, because the goodwill of a company can be a very valuable commodity. That decision is of particular significance because it avoided the effect of the dicta of Kerr L.J. in *Z. Ltd v. A–Z and AA–LL* [1982] Q.B. 558, that a *Mareva* should only be granted where it was likely that a plaintiff would receive judgment for a "certain or appropriate" sum. (This was also the position in *Dellborg v. Corix Properties and Blissfield Corporation N.V.* (1980, June 26, C.A.T. No. 541)). In the *Darashah* case, the plaintiff was summarily dismissed in alleged breach of his service contract and there was evidence to suggest that in order to avoid the consequence of such breach the defendant company was contemplating a scheme which would have the effect of divesting itself of its principal asset—its goodwill.

6. Choses in action A chose in action can form the subject-matter of a *Mareva* order—the simplest example is a bank account. Further, as Ralph Gibson L.J. said in *Maclaine Watson & Co. Ltd v. International Tin Council* [1989] Ch. 253 at 271 in relation to the corresponding power to appoint a receiver:

> "If Maclaine Watson are right, the assets which the receiver would be appointed to collect would include sums owing by the Crown in right of the United Kingdom. An alternative procedure for dealing with the situation where money is due from the Crown, is made available by section 27 of the Crown Proceedings Act 1947 by which the Court may, in accordance with rules, make an order restraining a creditor of the Crown from receiving money owed to him and directing payment of it to a receiver. Maclaine Watson, upon objection taken by the I.T.C., applied for the appropriate order under section 27 of the Act of 1947 so far as concerns any claims of the I.T.C. against the Crown. The point has no relevance to the substantial issues raised in the appeal."

Perhaps the ruling in *Normid Housing Association Ltd v. Ralphs & Mansell* [1989] 1 Lloyd's Rep. 265 suggests a distinction between a chose in action and a cause of action. That case is authority for the proposition that the courts will never allow a *Mareva* injunction to inhibit the ordinary course of business or to interfere with a defendant's ordinary transactions, especially where third parties are involved. The court refused to order an injunction to prevent a defendant reaching a bona fide settlement with his insurers of a claim against him by a plaintiff. Lloyd L.J. said at 275:

> "Mr Colman, supported by Mr Stitcher, submitted by way of answer that there is a crucial distinction between disposing of a tangible asset such as a house or a car at an under-valuation and disposing of a chose in action at an under-valuation. This would, he said, be the

first case in which the Court had ever been asked to regard a pending claim against a third party as an asset in a *Mareva* application. If a Court is to investigate the merits of a claim against a third party in order to determine whether the proposed settlement is reasonable or not that would, says Mr Colman, lead to insuperable practicable difficulties ... Mr Colman's distinction between the disposal of a tangible asset and the disposal of a chose in action may or may not be correct. It is unnecessary for us to decide."

It should be also noted, for completeness, that the insurers in *Normid* further argued that the plaintiff would have a remedy under section 423 of the Insolvency Act 1983 whereunder the transaction could be impugned. Whilst the Court of Appeal did not adjudicate on this, it may in other cases be a factor relevant to the exercise of the court's discretion.

8 Risk of dissipation—the principles

1. An overview In *Third Chandris Shipping Corporation v. Unimarine S.A.* [1979] Q.B. 645 at 669A–D, Lord Denning M.R. said in the context of applications against foreigners:

"The plaintiff should give some grounds for believing that there is a risk of assets being removed before the judgment or award is satisfied. The mere fact that the defendant is abroad is not by itself sufficient. No one would wish any reputable foreign company to be plagued with a *Mareva* injunction simply because it has agreed to London arbitration. But there are some foreign companies whose structure invites comment. We often see in this court a corporation which is registered in a country where the company law is so loose that nothing is known about it—where it does no work and has no officers and no assets. Nothing can be found out about its membership, or its control, or its assets, or the charges on them. Judgment cannot be enforced against it. There is no reciprocal enforcement of judgments. It is nothing more than a name grasped from the air, as elusive as the Cheshire Cat. In such cases the very fact of incorporation there gives some ground for believing there is a risk that, if judgment or an award is obtained, it may go unsatisfied. Such registration of such companies may carry many advantages to the individuals who control them, but they may suffer the disadvantage of having a *Mareva* injunction granted against them. The giving of security for a debt is a small price to pay for the convenience of such a registration. Security would certainly be required in New York. So also it may be in London. Other grounds may be shown for believing there is a risk. But some such should be shown."

Inevitably, therefore, an application for a *Mareva* against a reputable bank will almost certainly be doomed to failure: *Etablissement Esefka International Anstalt v. Central Bank of Nigeria* [1979] 1 Lloyd's Rep. 445. See also *Polly Peck International plc v. Nadir* [1992] 4 All E.R. 769.

2. The principles distilled In *Third Chandris Shipping Corporation v. Unimarine S.A.* [1979] Q.B. 645 at 671–672, Lawton L.J. explained the problem facing those acting for the plaintiffs:

(a) *Being "foreign" does not constitute evidence of risk:*

"The mere fact that a defendant having assets within the jurisdiction of the Commercial Court is a foreigner or a foreign corporation cannot, in my judgment, by itself justify the granting of a *Mareva* injunction."

(b) *The criterion of commercial judgment:*

"There must be facts from which the Commercial Court, like a prudent, sensible commercial man, can properly infer a danger of default if assets are removed from the jurisdiction."

(c) *The relevant lines of enquiry:*

"For commercial men, when assessing risks, there is no commercial equivalent of the Criminal Records Office or Ruff's Guide to the Turf. What they have to do is to find out all they can about the party with whom they are dealing, including origins, business domicile, length of time in business, assets and the like; and they will probably be wary of the appearances of wealth which are not backed up by known assets."

(d) *The particular skills of the Commercial Court:*

"In my judgment the Commercial Court should approve application for *Mareva* injunctions in the same way. Its judges have special experience of commercial cases and they can be expected to identify likely debt dodgers as well as, probably better than, most businessmen."

(e) *Guidance to the commercial court:*

"They should not expect to be given proof of previous defaults or specific incidents of commercial malpractice."

(f) *The contents of supporting affidavits:*

"Further they should remember that affidavits asserting belief in, or fear of, likely default have no probative value unless the sources and grounds thereof are set out: see Ord. 41, r.5(2). In my judgment an affidavit in support of a *Mareva* injunction should give enough particulars of the plaintiff's case to enable the court to assess its strength and should set out what enquiries have been made about the defendant's business and what information has been revealed, including that relating to its size, origins, business domicile, the location of its known assets and the circumstances in which the dispute has arisen. Default is most unlikely if the defendant is a long established, well-known foreign corporation or is known to have substantial assets in countries where English judgments can easily be enforced either under the Foreign Judgments (Reciprocal Enforcement) Act 1933 or otherwise. But if nothing can be found out about the defendant that by itself may be enough to justify a *Mareva* injunction."

3. How relevant is fraud—does it have to be pleaded? In *Guinness plc v. Saunders and Another, The Independent*, April 15, 1987, Sir Nicholas Brown-Wilkinson said:

"... Guinness in pleading the statement of claim alleged fraud. Whether or not at that stage Guinness had considered what was going in the statement of claim I know not. But Mr Heslop's submission to me is based on the proposition that the question whether *Mareva* relief should be granted is closely linked to the nature of the cause of action pleaded in the case. If fraud is pleaded, *Mareva* relief, it is said, is more likely to be awarded than if it is not. In my judgment that is a misconceived submission. In many cases involving dishonesty it is unnecessary to plead fraud ... Guinness do not require at this stage to prove fraud. They do allege lack of bona fide belief and it was not necessary for them to go further in the pleading. In my judgment dishonest behaviour is relevant to *Mareva* relief not by reference to what is pleaded but by reference to the possibility or likelihood of it existing. Whether or not pleaded, if there is dishonesty or suspicion of dishonesty, that will be an important ground on which *Mareva* relief can be obtained."

4. The significance of reciprocal enforcement agreements The existence of such agreements may be expected to render a court less willing to grant a *Mareva*. This was indeed one of the factors which led to the discharge of the injunction in the *Ninemia* case—see above p. 205. However, it is only a factor—which may be overborne by evidence as to risk of dissipation in the reciprocal jurisdiction. As Lawton L.J. said in *Dellborg v. Corix Properties and Blissfield Corporation N.V.* (1980, June 26, C.A.T. No. 541):

"Mr Morrison went on to say that there is this further aspect of the Blissfield case; the affidavits sworn on their behalf by the solicitors representing them in these proceedings stated that there was $100,000 on deposit in the Dutch Antilles. Mr Morrison pointed out that an Order in Council has been made under the Foreign Judgments Act 1933, which has provided reciprocity for the enforcement of judgments between the United Kingdom and the Dutch Antilles and that that is a factor which we should take into account (and I do take it into account) in deciding whether it is appropriate to make a *Mareva* injunction. But the assets which are available in the Dutch Antilles are on deposit in a bank, and as has been pointed out in a number of these *Mareva* injunction cases, assets which are on deposit in a bank account can be moved out in a matter of seconds to other parts of the world, and when they have been moved, creditors may have great difficulty in discovering where they have been moved to."

9 Burdens of proof

1. General principle The judge who heard the proceedings *inter partes* must decide on all the evidence laid before him. Against that principle, the following propositions may be advanced, distilled from the judgments of Mustill J. and Kerr L.J. in *Ninemia Maritime Corporation v. Trave Schiffahrtsgesellschaft mbH und Co. K.G.* [1983] 1 W.L.R. 1412.

(a) *No automatic obligation to disclose:* The defendants have no obligation to disclose their financial affairs, simply to answer a challenge from the buyers which is unsupported by solid evidence: p. 1425. Note that the standard forms annexed to the Practice Direction [1994] 4 All E.R. 52 provide for disclosure by the defendant of his assets.

(b) *A priori—must be an inference to be rebutted:* The evidence adduced for the defendant will normally be looked at for the purposes of deciding whether it is enough to displace any inferences which might otherwise be drawn from the plaintiff's evidence. But there must be an inference to be displaced, if the injunction is to stand, and comment on the defendant's evidence must not be taken so far that the burden of proof is unconsciously reversed: 1424B and D.

2. Absence of evidence may rebound However, at the risk of rendering the principle "circular," the absence of evidence from a defendant may strengthen the inferences which a plaintiff seeks to draw. As Lawton L.J. said in *Dellborg v. Corix Properties and Blissfield Corporation N.V.* (1980, June 26, C.A.T. No. 541):

"That prima facie case could have been destroyed by evidence given on behalf of Corix Properties Ltd. No such evidence has been put before the court. I have reminded myself that the absence of evidence proves nothing. On the other hand, the fact that there is no evidence from one side makes it easier to draw inferences from the evidence which is already before the court; and the evidence before the court as against Corix Properties Ltd is that there has been a scheme to make access to the profits of this development difficult for the Inland Revenue."

3. Inference—a good working example Such an inference was generated by the plaintiffs in *Allen v. Jambo Holdings Ltd* [1980] 1 W.L.R. 1252 where Lord Denning M.R. was less than flattering as to the quality of the defendant's evidence in rebuttal.

(a) First he pointed to the inadequacy of the 'insurance' averment:

> "The Nigerian company now come here and ask that the injunction be discharged. They do it on these grounds. First, they say in their affidavit: '... the first defendant'—that is, the Nigerian company— 'is insured against claims of this nature under Policy No. MA/AHL/78/HL/0004 issued by the National Corporation of Nigeria of 118, Broad Street, P.O. Box 1100, Lagos, Nigeria, upon whose instructions the first and second defendants' solicitors herein are acting.' That is all we are told. Nothing is said about whether the insurance company have accepted responsibility. Nothing is said as to their stability or their backing or as to reinsurance or anything of that kind. Until more is known about it, it seems to be that the mere assertion of insurance is not sufficient ground for discharging the injunction. If there had been an undertaking by an English insurance company of standing, it would be different. But no such undertaking has been offered." (at 1256B–D.)

(b) Secondly, he deprecated the financial effect of the *Mareva* to which the defendant deposed:

> "The affidavit goes on to say that this is a new aircraft which was made in the United States from where it was exported in February 1978. It was intended to register it in Nigeria. It was worth half a million pounds, which is far more than what might be awarded on any claim. No doubt that is true. But then it goes on to say that, if this injunction remains, the Nigerian company would suffer great loss. They are a big industrial group, and if they were deprived of the use of this aircraft they would have to employ a further 20 senior managers at £50,000 pounds a year each; and this would raise the group's overheads by £1m. a year. That is difficult to swallow." (at 1256D–F.)

(c) Thirdly, he drew a shipping parallel:

> "So the affidavit does not impress me in the least. I can see no

227

reason in this case, as is done in shipping cases all over the world, why security should not be given in the way of a bond or an undertaking by a reputable company or concern in England so as to ensure that any award of damages to the plaintiffs would be met. If the Nigerian company are of such high standing, as we are now told they are, if they are ready to accept any liability, as we are told they will, it seems to me that a bank or an insurance company of standing in this country would back the Nigerian company by way of security without any difficulty whatsoever. No such security is forthcoming or is mentioned in the affidavit." (at 1256F–G).

(d) Fourthly, he disputed that ships were different:

"We were told, 'Ships are different. They have their protection and indemnity clubs, whereas aircraft have not.' I would expect that insurance policies nowadays would cover the provision of security. But, even if they do not, the sooner they do the better. As with ships, so with aircraft. The situation is so parallel, the one with the other, that even though this is a new case, it seems to me that it would be right to continue the *Mareva* injunction in the expectation that the aircraft will be released at any moment as soon as security is provided." (at 1256H.)

4. *Third Chandris*—inference not rebutted Similarly, the inference as to the risk of dissipation was not rebutted in *Third Chandris Shipping Corporation v. Unimarine S.A.* [1979] 1 Q.B. 645 at 665A–E, *per* Lord Denning M.R.:

(a) First, he identified the extent of the defendants' evidence:

"Before us further evidence was adduced. There was, in particular, a letter from the bankers of Unimarine, saying that the account was sometimes in overdraft. Written on April 9, 1979, from their London office, their Luxembourg branch said:

'We write to confirm that Unimarine S.A. are one of our most valued customers and have been since 1972. We have no doubt that they would be in a position to meet liabilities arising, in the normal course of business, for arbitration awards against them as operators of time charter tonnage.

We have been asked to reveal in this letter the present state of their account with us at Friday, April 27, 1979, to date. During this period of time, having overall regard to their trade patterns, they have been in overdraft with us. Naturally, as valued customers, this is quite acceptable to us, as the income from freight in any one month is very substantial.'"

(b) Secondly, he explained the limitation of that evidence:

"That letter tells nothing of the assets of Unimarine S.A. Unimarine S.A. gave no other evidence of assets anywhere. No director or officer of the company gave any evidence. Ince & Co. made inquiries of their correspondent lawyers in Panama. It showed that Unimarine S.A. were engaged only in off-shore operations and had no property in Panama. It had no obligation to file statements, returns, or other financial information with the local authorities in Panama; nor to keep its books in the Republic of Panama. Consequently, it was not possible to determine its financial status."

(c) Thirdly, he highlighted the significance of the "Baltic Exchange":

"It is further pointed out that, unlike most large chartering organisations, Unimarine S.A. are not members of the Baltic Exchange. So the informal procedure (by posting in the Exchange) is not available to enforce an award."

5. The "Luxury flats" case *Dellborg v. Corix Properties and Blissfield Corporation N.V.* (1980, June 26, C.A.T. No. 541) is a good example of the interaction of inferences and burdens of proof. The plaintiff tenant sought a *Mareva* against defendant builders, who were incorporated "off-shore" as part of a tax avoidance scheme. The claim was in respect of substantial damages for "nuisance." The court accepted that the plaintiff had made a good arguable case despite their inability to qualify loss. Lawton L.J. said:

"In my judgment, the fact that Corix Properties Ltd have behaved in the way they have (*i.e.* a scheme to make access to profits difficult for the Inland Revenue), and have not seen fit to put any information before the court as to the commercial experience and assets of those who are behind them, leads me to the inference that there is a risk— I put it no higher than that—that at the end of the litigation the plaintiffs may have difficulty in getting the fruits of judgment, if judgment is given in their favour."

And as to the second defendants, Lawton L.J. said:

"So far as the issue of risk to the plaintiffs is concerned, the situation is this: Blissfield Corporation N.V. were incorporated in the Dutch Antilles. The probabilities are—and Mr Morrison accepted this on behalf of his client—first, that the incorporation was a part of a tax avoidance scheme, just as in the case of Corix Properties Ltd; and secondly, that as also in the case of Corix Properties the company was incorporated solely for the purpose of this development. The directors of Blissfield Corporation N.V. are said to be two persons

229

resident in the Dutch Antilles and someone resident in Switzerland. Their names were revealed to the solicitors acting for J. M. L. Stone & Co. Ltd, but nothing more is known about these directors. They are represented in these proceedings by a well-known firm of solicitors practising in the City of London. A partner in that firm deposed that Blissfield Corporation N.V. had no intention of avoiding their just liability. But he did not say who told him that, and there is no affidavit from any director or officer of the company. The court is wholly ignorant as to who is behind the company. All we do know—and it is an inference rather than a firm fact—is that whoever it is caused the company to be incorporated for the purposes of ensuring that no part of the profits made in carrying out this redevelopment should get into the hands of the Inland Revenue in the United Kingdom."

10 Risk of dissipation—examples

1. Introduction *Ninemia Maritime Corporation v. Trave Schiffahrts-gesellschaft mbH und Co. K.G.* [1983] 1 W.L.R. 1412 is authority for the principle that as to risk of dissipation the plaintiff must show that a refusal of an injunction would involve a real risk that a judgment or award in his favour would remain unsatisfied. In defining the principle, Kerr L.J. drew on the following authorities, at 1423:

(a) *Etablissement Esefka International Anstalt v. Central Bank of Nigeria* [1979] 1 Lloyd's Rep. 445 at 448, *per* Lord Denning M.R.:

> "The *Mareva* injunction is only to be granted where there is a danger of the money being taken out of the jurisdiction so that if the plaintiffs succeed they are not likely to get their money."

Note that this was said in 1979. In *Rahman (Prince Abdul) bin Turki al Sudairy v. Abu-Taha* [1980] 1 W.L.R. 1268 (c) below, the Court of Appeal for the first time extended *Mareva* to dissipation of assets within the jurisdiction.

(b) *Third Chandris Shipping Corporation v. Unimarine S.A., The Genie* [1979] Q.B. 645: Lord Denning M.R. said at 669:

> "In such cases the very fact of incorporation there gives some ground for believing there is a risk that, if judgment or an award is obtained, it may go unsatisfied."

(c) *Montecchi v. Shimco (U.K.) Ltd* [1979] 1 W.L.R. 1180 at 1183, *per* Bridge L.J.:

> "The basis of the *Mareva* injunction is that there has to be a real reason to apprehend that if the injunction is not made, the intending

plaintiff in this country may be deprived of a remedy against the foreign defendant whom he seeks to sue."

(d) *Barclay-Johnson v. Yuill* [1980] 1 W.L.R. 1259 at 1265, *per* Sir Robert Megarry V.-C.:

"It must appear that there is a danger of default if the assets are removed from the jurisdiction. Even if the risk of removal is great, no *Mareva* injunction should be granted unless there is also a danger of default."

The following additional dicta are also of note, at 1265E–G:

"A reputable foreign company, accustomed to paying its debts, ought not to be prevented from removing its assets from the jurisdiction, especially if it has substantial assets in countries in which English judgments can be enforced."

(e) *Rahman (Prince Abdul) Bin Turki v. Abu-Taha* [1980] 1 W.L.R. 1268 at 1273, *per* Lord Denning M.R.:

"So I would hold that a *Mareva* injunction can be granted against a man even though he is based in this country if the circumstances are such that there is a danger of his absconding, or a danger of the assets being removed out of the jurisdiction, or otherwise dealt with so that there is a danger that the plaintiff, if he gets judgment, will not be able to get it satisfied."

In the *Rahman* case, the defendants claimed to have accumulated great wealth during their short time in business, but neither gave their home address nor said where their assets were. Moreover their business concern in Lichtenstein had been wound up.

(f) *Law Society v. Shanks* (1987) 131 S.J. 1626: The *Mareva* was set aside on the basis that the defendant (subject to an order for costs) had not evinced an intention to dissipate his funds despite his unwillingness, and failure, to discharge the judgment debt.

2. Working examples of evidence of risk

(a) *Nippon Yusen Kaisha v. Karageorgis* [1975] 1 W.L.R. 1093: In granting what is now called a *Mareva* injunction, the Court of Appeal took into account the following:
   (i) The defendants had not paid the charter hire. They said that they had transmitted it to New York, but the money had never been received.
  (ii) Attempts to find the defendants had proved unsuccessful.
 (iii) The defendants' office in Piraeus was closed.

On this case it is interesting to read the foreword by Lord Denning to the first edition (reprinted in subsequent editions) of *Mareva Injunctions and Anton Piller Relief*, by Steven Gee Q.C.

(b) *Allen v. Jambo Holdings Ltd* [1980] 1 W.L.R. 1252: The evidence as to risk was explained by Templeman L.J. at 1258:

> "The pilot's employers are a foreign corporation with no assets in this country except the aircraft. They resist liability for the death of Mr Allen; and through counsel they complain that their one asset in this country, the aircraft, has been frozen. They produce evidence, although months have gone by, merely making the bland statement that the pilot's employers are solvent and have assets sufficient to satisfy a judgment. They produce the bland statement that they are insured against claims of this nature. They do not explain why they have not taken what would be the normal precautions to reassure the widow and executors in the circumstances, namely of producing an undertaking by insurers who are resident in this country or by producing a bond or some form of security. Instead of that they have put forward the proposition that if an injunction is granted and they have to do without the aircraft for a long period they will require 20 senior managers at £50,000 a year, raising their overheads by £1m. a year. I am not impressed either by what they have not said, or by what they have said."

(c) *C.B.S. United Kingdom Ltd v. Lambert* [1983] Ch. 37: Lawton L.J. at p. 42A–B held that the evidence seemed to show that the first defendant was conducting his affairs with intent to deprive anyone who got judgment against him of the fruits of victory. In this case of alleged breach of copyright in tape-recording, that evidence was:
  (i) The first defendant's council house had recently been the subject of expensive improvement.
  (ii) He was claiming to be unemployed and in receipt of state benefits.
  (iii) He had apparently lied as to the origin of certain cassettes.
  (iv) The police had found 15,000 labels at his home—of a kind which had previously been affixed to counterfeit cassettes.
  (v) He had apparently told the police he was a "record pirate".
  (vi) He was apparently the owner of several expensive motor vehicles which, the court inferred, could easily be hidden from creditors and disposed of for case if the need arose.

3. "Risk of dissipation"—check list Thus when taking instructions on the risk of dissipation, consider:
  (a) The origins of the defendant (what is the defendant's commercial "character" and trading history?).

(b) The defendant's business domicile.

(c) Of what assets are the plaintiffs aware? Are accounts of the defendant available? If there is a legal obligation to file accounts, has the defendant complied with it? Do they generate an impression of wealth? If yes, is that impression contrived, *e.g.* by cross-firing between accounts thereby to generate an impression of wealth? For an example of such "cross-firing", see *Barclays Bank Ltd v. Rosenberg* (1985) 135 New L.J. 633, *per* Anthony Evans J.

(d) Has there been previous default? (If yes—give particulars.)

(e) How has the dispute arisen?

(f) What is the defendant's length of time in business?

(g) May an adverse inference properly be drawn from incorporation in a tax/finance haven?

(h) Has the defendant assets which he has apparently fraudulently failed to disclose? In *Kirby v. Banks* (1980, C.A.T. No. 624) the defendants were legally aided yet an inquiry agent located property of the defendants offered for sale in the sum of £60,000.

11 Plaintiff's undertaking as to damages

1. Introduction In *Z Ltd v. A–Z and AA–LL* [1982] Q.B. 558 Lord Denning M.R. said at 577E:

"The plaintiff who seeks a *Mareva* injunction should normally give an undertaking in damages to the defendant, and also an undertaking to a bank or other innocent third party to pay any expenses reasonably incurred by them. The judge may, or may not, require a bond or other security to support this undertaking: but this may not be insisted on when the is legally-aided: see *Allen v. Jambo Holdings Ltd* [1980] 1 W.L.R. 1252. But the undertakings only cover damages or expenses reasonably incurred. If the defendant or third party could have reduced it by taking reasonable steps, it is his duty to do so: see *Smith v. Day* (1882) 21 Ch.D. 421 and *Allen v. Jambo Holdings Ltd* [1980] 1 W.L.R. 1252 at 1256F–H."

The wording of the Practice Direction [1994] 4 All E.R. 52 assumes that an undertaking as to damages will be required.

2. Evidence of financial status In *Manor Electronics v. Dickson* [1988] R.P.C. 618 (an *Anton Piller* case, but the difference is for present purposes immaterial), Scott J. said that if a plaintiff makes no reference to his financial status it is open to the court to assume that the plaintiff's financial status is adequate for the purpose of the cross-undertaking. However, it is suggested that if a plaintiff makes no reference to his financial status it

233

would be equally open to the court to infer that the plaintiff is being coy. The modern practice is to expect a plaintiff to provide evidence (which must be as full and frank as all evidence in *ex parte* applications) about his means to satisfy any order made against him.

3. Legally aided plaintiffs A legally aided plaintiff, even one with a nil contribution, can be required to give an undertaking as to damages: *Allen v. Jambo Holdings Ltd* [1980] 1 W.L.R. 1252.

4. Reinforcing the undertaking The plaintiff may be required to pay money into court or to his solicitor, to be held by the solicitor as an officer of the court pending further order or to provide a bond by an insurance company (see the Practice Direction [1994] 4 All E.R. 52 para. (3)(A)2, and one of these forms of security is likely to be required of a plaintiff from out of the jurisdiction who does not have assets within the jurisdiction.

In *Re D.R.P. Futures Ltd* [1989] 1 W.L.R. 778 at 786D, Millett J. said (in a passage sometimes not quoted beyond the first two sentences):

> "In my judgment, a liquidator cannot be criticised for refusing to risk his personal assets by giving an unlimited cross-undertaking. It is right to require him to give an undertaking of an amount commensurate with the size of the company's assets and to take the risk that he may not be authorised by the court to have recourse to them to meet his liability. If the value of such an undertaking is considered insufficient in any particular case he should be required to fortify it by obtaining a bond or an indemnity from a substantial creditor, but in either case of a fixed amount. The court cannot avoid the need to make an intelligent estimate of the likely amount of any loss which may result from the grant of the injunction. There is nothing unusual in this. It is so in every case where the balance of convenience has to be considered. A plaintiff's resources are not infinite. But any such estimate can be reviewed from time to time and further fortification required if necessary. If fortification cannot be obtained this will affect the balance of convenience between granting or refusing the injunction. But the court cannot abdicate its responsibility for deciding where the balance of convenience lies."

E: "MAXIMUM SUM ORDERS"

In the first *Mareva* injunctions no limit was placed on the amount of the defendant's assets to be frozen. There followed a period in which there were cases on whether and when a maximum sum should be specified in the order. These, and the treatment of them in previous editions of this work, are now of no more than historical interest. The practice, reflected in the wording of the standard form in the Annex to the Practice Direction [1994] 4 All E.R. 52, is to stipulate a maximum sum.

When showing a good arguable case it is for the plaintiff to show the amount of his claim in debt or by way of liquidated damages and the approximate amount of his claim for unliquidated damages. If he does this, it is then difficult to see any reason why the defendant's freedom to deal with his own property should be restricted to any greater extent.

In the case of post-judgment *Marevas*, the defendant's liability may have been quantified by the judgment; if the judgment is for damages to be assessed a plaintiff seeking a post-judgment *Mareva* should provide evidence upon which the court can fix a maximum sum. (A plaintiff who obtains judgment for damages to be assessed is likely in any event to make an application for an interim payment, for which purpose the same evidence will be required, but of course if there is a risk of dissipation the plaintiff will need to have the evidence available for an immediate application to the judge for a *Mareva* rather than assemble it for a later application to a master or district judge for an interim payment.)

F. THE POSITION OF BANKS

1. Consequences of the standard orders

Twenty years of experience have identified various problems and the best practicable solutions have been worked out for most of them and incorporated in the standard orders annexed to the Practice Direction [1994] 4 All E.R. 52 which form a useful agenda for consideration of points which can arise in the preparation for an application for a *Mareva*, the application to the court and the making of an order.

Banks are innocent third parties. The court will do its best to protect them from the trouble and expense which arise when they are given notice of a *Mareva*. Therefore the standard orders provide:

(a) *For particular bank accounts to be specified:* The plaintiff should identify any bank accounts of the defendant known to them with as much precision as possible: name of bank, branch, type of account and account number: *Searose Ltd v. Seatrain (U.K.) Ltd* [1981] 1 W.L.R. 894 at 897 *per* Robert Goff J.; *Z Ltd v. A–Z and AA–LL* [1982] Q.B. 558 at 575D–F *per* Lord Denning M.R.

(b) *For the plaintiff to undertake that his solicitors (and the same would apply to a plaintiff acting in person will give a copy of the order to anyone notified of it:* The reason is so that third parties such as banks know with precision what the order is. A breach of this, like a breach of any undertaking, is a contempt of court punishable by imprisonment in the case of an individual and sequestration of assets in the case of a limited company or other body.

(c) *That the plaintiff must undertake to pay the reasonable costs of anyone other than the defendant incurred as a result of the order, including the costs of ascertaining whether that person holds any of the defendant's assets:* If there is any reason to wonder whether a plaintiff knows what expense this undertaking may entail, and whether the plaintiff may be able to afford it, the court may ask the plaintiff's solicitor or counsel what the anticipated expense will be. (Banks may be willing to give an approximate figure, depending on the number of accounts and branches involved.) Irrespective of what it does about reinforcing the plaintiff's undertaking as to damages suffered by the defendant, the court may well require the plaintiff to pay money into court or lodge money with his solicitor as an officer of the court within a short time to secure the payments due to banks and other third parties.

(d) *That if the order causes any other loss to a third party and the court decides that the third party should be compensated for that loss, the plaintiff undertakes to comply with any order which the court may make.*

(e) *That the injunction does not prevent any bank from exercising any right of set-off it may have in respect of any facility which it gave to the defendant before it was notified of the order.*

(f) *That no bank need inquire as to the application or proposed application of any money withdrawn by the defendant if the withdrawal appears to be permitted by the order:* The reason is that the order will permit certain expenditure by the defendant even if he thereby reduces his assets below the specified figure: a specified sum per week for the ordinary living expenses of a human defendant; dealing with or disposing of assets in the ordinary and proper course of business by a human or corporate defendant in business; and, usually, a specified (or a reasonable) sum on legal advice and representation. A bank could not know, and cannot be expected to threaten its commercial relationship with its customer by being placed in a position whereby it must enquire of him what a particular cheque or cash withdrawal is for.

Moreover, by the terms of the standard orders, any spending limits specified in a *Mareva* may be varied by agreement in writing between the defendant and the plaintiff's solicitors. Although the standard orders do not say so, if such an agreement is made it would be prudent for the plaintiff's solicitors to notify any banks which have been notified of the original order of any variation, and to provide a copy of the written variation agreement. A defendant would have a legitimate grievance against the plaintiff if his bank dishonoured a cheque, although there were funds in his account to meet it, on the basis that the withdrawal did not appear to be permitted by the order in its original terms but would clearly have been permitted by the order as varied.

2. Other points

(a) *Foreign currency accounts:* In *Z Ltd v. A–Z and AA–LL* [1982] Q.B. 558 at 593B, Kerr L.J. said:

"Of the problems debated before us this then leaves only the relatively simple one when the order is expressed in one currency and is made applicable expressly to bank accounts, but where a bank served with the order discovers that it holds an account in another currency. It seems to me that this problem should be resolved in the same way as was held by this court in relation to garnishee orders in *Choice Investments Ltd v. Jeromnimon* [1981] Q.B. 149: upon being served with the order, the bank should convert the credit balance into sterling at the then buying rate to the extent necessary to meet the sum stated in the order, and then put a stop on the account to this extent."

It is suggested that Kerr L.J. cannot have intended to suggest that if its customer has, for his own reasons, which may be good commercial reasons, a foreign currency account the bank should in breach of contract convert it into a sterling account; he must have intended that upon service of the order the bank should calculate the equivalent in the currency of the account of the sterling sum in the order and put a stop on the foreign currency account at that level.

It is further suggested that if a plaintiff has any reason to think that the defendant has accounts in two or more currencies, this is a matter which he should disclose so that the court can attempt to devise an order which will cater for the easy calculation by the bank of the specified sum on a once and for always basis which does not involve daily recalculations as exchange rates fluctuate. This is to enable the court to make life as easy as possible for the innocent third party, even if the defendant's possession of a foreign currency account is not something upon which the plaintiff wishes to rely as a factor on the question of risk of removal of assets from the jurisdiction.

(b) *Defendant's chattels:* If the plaintiff has any reason to think that the defendant's bank has in its possession any chattels belonging to the defendant (*e.g.* bearer securities), that fact should be disclosed to the court, both so that the court can tailor the order appropriately so that the innocent bank knows what it must not do and in the plaintiff's own interest so that the bank does not have to apply to the court for clarification (the costs of which would probably be ordered against the plaintiff). On the importance of getting *Mareva* orders right first time if possible, see Kerr L.J. in *Z Ltd v. A–Z and AA–LL* [1982] Q.B. 558 at 587F–588D (considered at p. 000 below).

(c) *Garnishee orders:* If, after a bank receives notice of a *Mareva* against its customer, a third party obtains a judgment against the defendant in other proceedings and a garnishee order nisi over the defendant's account at the bank, the bank will probably apply to the court which granted the *Mareva* for authority to pay the judgment creditor if and when the garnishee order nisi is made absolute.

G: THE POSITION OF THIRD PARTIES OTHER THAN BANKS

1 When is intervention warranted?

1. Unwarrantable interference A third party can properly interfere if its rights are substantially and unwarrantably interfered with: *Galaxia Maritime S.A. v. Mineralimportexport* [1982] 1 W.L.R. 539. That case is authority for the principle that courts will always be astute to ensure that third party rights are fully protected, and that where this cannot be done by an effective undertaking, or where for whatever reason an undertaking is inappropriate, the rights of the third party must prevail over the rights of the plaintiff. In this context, it should be noted that a state-owned trading corporation has been held for *Mareva* purposes to be entirely independent of a state-owned shipping company, and thus entitled to assert an independent right to assets: *Zephyros Maritime v. Mineralimportexport (Nayron Rumanian Shipping intervening)* (1983) 133 New L.J. 254.

2. *Galaxia Maritime*—what happened? The plaintiff shipowners, who were claiming demurrage under a charterparty against the defendants, obtained a *Mareva* which covered, *inter alia*, a cargo of coal belonging to the defendants loaded on a third party's vessel in port elsewhere. This other vessel was chartered under a voyage charter, and if it was prevented from sailing forthwith, its trading activities would have been adversely affected, as would the crew's personal arrangements for Christmas.

3. The Court of Appeal discharged the injunction—why? Notwithstanding that the plaintiff undertook to indemnify the third parties affected by the order, the Court of Appeal discharged the injunction. Its reasons for doing so were:

(a) A plaintiff could not buy off a third party's rights by order:

"The effect of this present injunction, insofar as the owners of the

Eleftherios are concerned, is to interfere with their trading assets. Mr Simon has submitted to this court that that is a matter which should not affect the final outcome because, as he says, his clients have given a guarantee. For myself, I do not believe that when the third party protests, the fact that a guarantee has been given should be decisive in the matter at all. A third party is entitled to freedom of action and he is entitled to trade freely. I do not think that a plaintiff has the right to a 'compulsory purchase' of the rights of a third party and that is what it amounts to in this case ... I regard it as absolutely intolerable that the fact that one person has a claim for a debt against another, that third parties should be inconvenienced in this way, not only to affect their freedom of trading but their freedom of action generally speaking." (*Per* Eveleigh L.J. at 541G–542A.)

(b) The distinction between banks and bailees on the one hand, and shipowning third parties on the other, *per* Kerr L.J. at 542D–F:

    (i) *The measure of the abuse*: "To allow a plaintiff to serve a *Mareva* injunction on a shipowner in relation to cargo, which is owned or alleged to be owned by the defendant and which is on board pursuant to a voyage charter concluded between the shipowner and the defendant, in order to seek to prevent the ship from sailing out of the jurisdiction with the cargo, appears to me to be a clear abuse of this jurisdiction, because it involves an unwarrantable act of interference with the business of the third party, the shipowner."

   (ii) *Indemnity—not sufficient*: "A plaintiff seeking to secure an alleged debt or damages due from the defendant, by an order preventing the disposal of assets of the defendant, cannot possibly be entitled to obtain the advantage of such an order for himself at the expense of the business rights of an innocent third party, merely by proffering him an indemnity in whatever form.

    In this connection, it is crucial to bear in mind not only the balance of convenience and justice as between plaintiffs and defendants, but above all also as between plaintiffs and third parties."

 (iii) *The position of banks/bailees—in contrast*: "Where assets of a defendant are held by a third party incidentally to the general business of the third party—such as the accounts of a defendant held by a bank, or goods held by bailee as custodian, for example in a warehouse—an effective indemnity in favour of the third party will adequately hold this balance, because service of the injunction will not lead to any major interference with

239

the third party's business. But where the effect of service must lead to interference with the performance of a contract between the third party and the defendant which relates specifically to the assets in question, the right of the third party in relation to his contract must clearly prevail over the plaintiff's desire to secure the defendant's assets for himself against the day of judgment."

4. Distinguishing Clipper Maritime—how? In distinguishing the not dissimilar case of *Clipper Maritime Co. Ltd of Monrovia v. Mineralimportexport* [1981] 1 W.L.R. 1262, Kerr L.J. said at 542H:

"In this case the effect of the service of the injunction prevents the third party from sending its ship on a voyage out of the jurisdiction under a previously concluded contract between the third party and the defendants. In my view, this is a clear case of an abuse of this jurisdiction. It is said that the jurisdiction was exercised in a similar manner in the *Clipper Maritime* case [1981] 1 W.L.R. 1262. However, it is not clear whether the shipowners objected in that case. Furthermore, that was a case of a time charter (with these same defendants), so that the financial consequences of delay would be more likely to have fallen on the defendants and not on the shipowners, as here."

5. Time charter—would it really have made a difference? Kerr L.J. said at p. 543A:

"However, even in the cases of time charters, disputes might well arise as to whether or not the vessel remained on hire during the consequent delay. A plaintiff is not entitled, in my judgment, to expose the third party to the risk of such disputes merely by the offer of an indemnity. He cannot, merely in order to secure a benefit for himself, coerce the third party into a serious risk of litigation or arbitration with the defendant, and thereafter possibly also with himself under the terms of the proffered indemnity."

See also Unicorn Shipping v. Demet Navy Shipping Company [1987] 2 Lloyd's Rep. 404. In that case P obtained a *Mareva* injunction against C time charterers which attached to the bunkers on a vessel owned by five shipowners. The vessel was consequently unable to sail from harbour in England. S intervened to seek the discharge of the injunction since the vessel was their only trading asset, running costs were accruing and a further charter was imperilled by the restriction. The injunction restraining a time charterer from removing bunkers from the jurisdiction was discharged where it would detain the vessel after the charter period causing loss to innocent shipowners.

6. Third parties and the problem of contempt The mere notice of the existence of a *Mareva* injunction cannot render it a contempt of court for a third party to make over an asset to a defendant direct. Only the third party's notice of a probability that the assets will be disposed of or dealt with in breach of it would render such an act a contempt of court, *per* Nouse L.J. in *Bank Mellat v. Kazmi* [1989] 1 Q.B. 541 at 547. However, the question arises—is the position different if the *Mareva* extends to a particular asset? Lord Denning M.R. said in *Z Ltd v. A–Z and AA–LL* [1982] Q.B. 558 at 574:

> "I have confirmed my observations to banks and bank accounts. But the same applies to any specific asset held by a bank for safe custody on behalf of the defendant. Be it jewellery, stamps or anything else. And to any other person who holds any other asset of the defendant. If the asset is covered by the terms of the *Mareva* injunction, that other person must not hand it over to the defendant or do anything to enable him to dispose of it. He must hold it pending further order."

However, in *The Law Society v. Shanks* [1988] 1 FLR 504, Lord Donaldson M.R. (with whom the other members of the court agreed), refused to follow these dicta. He said:

> "... I know of no authority other than this particular passage [*i.e.* the passage at 574E] for the proposition that [the injunction] prevents anybody handing the asset over to the owner of the asset, in this case the defendant. That does not amount to a dissipation or a disposal of any kind whatsoever. In special circumstances, where it is known that the sole purpose of requiring the asset to be handed over to the defendant is to facilitate a dissipation of that asset, different considerations may arise ... That would be a very peculiar case indeed.
>
> ... [W]hilst [the two passages] are entitled to the greatest possible respect as coming from Lord Denning, they do not in my judgment represent a general statement of the law which is applicable in any ordinary case."

The position however, may not be so clear cut, as Nourse L.J. explained in *Bank Mellat v. Kazmi* [1989] 1 Q.B. 541 at 547:

> "... Mere notice of the existence of a *Mareva* injunction cannot render it a contempt of court for a third party to make over an asset direct. Otherwise it might be impossible, for example, for a debtor with notice to pay over to the defendant even the most trivial sum

without seeking the directions of the court. A distinction must be drawn between notice of the injunction on the one hand and notice of a probability that the asset will be disposed of or dealt with in breach of the order on the other. It is only in the latter case that the third party can be in contempt of court. No general test can be propounded for the latter class of case, although the facts here suggest that it may not be quite as peculiar as Sir John Donaldson M.R. thought."

The potential problem generated for creditors by these cases may be resolved by the introduction of wording into the original *ex parte* order, restraining the debtor from receiving such moneys.

2 Investigating third parties

1. The situation covered Where a third party asserts rights to an asset frozen by a *Mareva* injunction, the court may inquire into the assertion, either by ordering it to be tried as a preliminary issue, or by awaiting the result of the trial: *SCF Finance Co. Ltd v. Masri* [1985] 1 W.L.R. 876. In *Allied Arab Bank v. Hajjar* [1988] Q.B. 787, the Court of Appeal held that a *Mareva* injunction does not also freeze the assets of the defendant's spouse, unless there is good evidence that these assets are in fact the defendant's. *Inter alia*, Nicholls L.J. said:

> "... he must surmount the 'Niedersachsen' threshold. Until he has done that it will not normally be just and convenient to put the defendant to the difficulty and inconveniences which can be expected to flow from the grant of a *Mareva* injunction. Likewise, it seems to me, justice and convenience point to the need normally for a plaintiff to cross a similar threshold before he can subject a third party to the difficulties and inconveniences which can be expected to flow from the grant of a *Mareva* injunction against an asset which apparently belongs to the third party and not to the defendant."

2. *SCF Finance*—what was the issue? It was defined thus:

> "What happens when there is a dispute between the plaintiff and a third party as to the ownership of assets within the jurisdiction? What happens if the plaintiff says that the assets belong to the defendant, and the defendant says that they do not. Or if a third party claims they belong to him?" (at 879F.)

3. What approach should the court adopt? Lloyd L.J. summarises the position thus, at 884B–D:

(a) *Weighty evidential burden on plaintiff:*

> "Where the plaintiff invites the court to include within the scope of a *Mareva* injunction assets which appear on their face to belong to a third party, *e.g.* a bank account in the name of a third party, the court should not accede to the invitation without good reason for supposing that the assets are in truth the assets of the defendant."

(b) *The evidential burden on the defendant:*

> "Where the defendant asserts that the assets belong to a third party, the court is not obliged to accept that assertion without inquiry, but may do so depending on the circumstances. The same applies where it is the third party who makes the assertion, on an application to intervene."

(c) *The option of trying the issue*

> "In deciding whether to accept the assertion of a defendant or a third party, without further inquiry, the court will be guided by what is just and convenient, not only between the plaintiff and the defendant, but also between the plaintiff, the defendant and the third party … Where the court decides not to accept the assertion without further inquiry, it may order an issue to be tried between the plaintiff and the third party in advance of the main action, or it may order that the issue await the outcome of the main action, again depending in each case on what is just and convenient."

3 Third parties (other than banks) and payment of outstanding debts

1. The "bank"/"other third party" distinction In dealing with interveners other than banks, Parker J. said at 534 in *A v. B (X. intervening)* [1983] 2 Lloyd's Rep. 532:

> "It is of course clear that the court must carefully guard the rights of third parties but it cannot be right that the court can or should dispense with the need to be satisfied as to the justification for a variation, when a defendant says to a third party that he is willing to pay and leaves it to the third party to apply."

2. What must the court know? In such circumstances, Parker J. went on at 534 to stipulate the information of which the court should be apprised:

> "In my judgment, however, whether the application is made by the defendant or his creditor the court should, save in the cases already mentioned, be fully acquainted with the position and be satisfied by

243

evidence that in allowing the payment to be made out of assets caught by the injunction it is sanctioning no more than a payment which would normally have been made out of such assets had there been no injunction."

The court learnt the full facts in *Atlas Maritime Co. S.A. v. Avalon Maritime Ltd* [1990] 2 Lloyd's Rep. 258. In that case the defendant company agreed to sell a ship, its only asset, to the plaintiff. When the defendant subsequently sold the ship elsewhere, the plaintiff issued proceedings for breach of contract. The plaintiff obtained a *Mareva* injunction to prevent the defendant from disposing of or dealing with the proceeds of the sale. The defendant sought a variation order which would permit it to pay the proceeds to its parent company Marc Rich, claiming that any money it had was owed to the parent company and that the relationship with the parent company was only one of debtor and creditor. Hobhouse J. held that:

(a) The principle that a *Mareva* injunction could be varied to permit the making of payments in good faith and in the ordinary course of business did not extend so as to require the court to permit an agent to pass over to its principal assets without which the agent would be unable to meet its liability incurred in the course of that agency.

(b) On the facts and the evidence the plaintiffs had a good arguable case that the relationship between the defendants and Marc Rich was one of agent and principal.

(c) On the material before the court and having regard to all the circumstances including those relating to Marc Rich, the court would not exercise its discretion in favour of the defendants so as to vary the injunction and allow the payment over to Marc Rich of the sole remaining funds held by the defendants.

(d) If the relationship of the defendant company to Marc Rich was one of agent and principal, then Marc Rich would not be entitled to look to the defendants to reimburse Marc Rich in respect of the liability incurred to third parties in the performance of the agency; the defendants' application for the variation and/or discharge of the injunction would be dismissed.

Hobhouse J. went on to say at 264:

"Accordingly, I consider that the principle in the *Angel Bell* requiring the variation of *Mareva* injunctions to permit the making of payments in good faith and in the ordinary course of business does not extend so as to require the court to permit an agent to pass over to its principal assets without which the agent would be unable to meet its liability to another incurred in the course of that agency.

... In the present case I consider that the plaintiffs are right to say that, on the material placed before the court, the court should not exercise its discretion to vary the injunction. It would not be right for the court to exclude a relationship of agent and principal or a relationship sufficiently close to one of agency so as to give rise to an abuse falling within the exception to the *Angel Bell* principle which I consider exists."

This decision was upheld by the Court of Appeal: *The Times*, December 4, 1990.

The *Angel Bell* is reported under *Iraqi Ministry of Defence & Others v. Arcepey Shipping Co. S.A. & Another* [1981] Q.B. 65, *per* Robert Goff J. In this case, the defendant's creditors, who had obtained leave to intervene in the action, successfully applied for an order that the injunction be varied to enable the defendant ship owners to pay back an advance of £200,000, which they claimed had been secured on the proceeds of insurance policies on the vessel, amounting to £240,000.

3. From where should the information come? As to the source of the evidence of which the court should be seised, Parker J. in *A v. B* added:

"In the present case I have no evidence upon which I could be so satisfied. If the defendant wants to make the payment he can make an application himself or possibly provide X. *Ltd* with the necessary evidence. Alternatively X. *Ltd* could proceed to judgment, in which case they would have no difficulty in executing upon any assets within the jurisdiction which they might find."

4. Was there enough evidence to justify payment of £6,700? The interveners were claiming £400,000, cheques therefore having already been dishonoured on September 15. On October 19, the credit balance on the relevant account was £6,700. So the question arose—could the interveners at least recover the sum? No—held Parker J. at 534–5, his reasoning being founded on lack of relevant evidence:

"There remains the question of the moneys which at the date of the defendant's affidavit were standing to the credit of the bank account on which the cheques in favour of the interveners were drawn. It appears to me that if cheques are drawn on an account which is in credit at the date of the injunction there is no reason why, if the defendant desires that the cheques should be met or met to the extent that the credit allows, an injunction should not in most cases at any rate be varied to allow the payment to be made from that account. If the cheques are drawn before action and injunction there is no question of this defeating the underlying purpose of the injunction. At the time it was granted the creditor had an existing right to be paid from that particular source. In the present case, however, there is no evidence

245

of the state of the account as at the date of the injunction. All that is known is that the cheques were returned by the bank on September 15 marked 'Refer to drawer,' and that on October 19 the credit balance was £6,700. That is in my judgment not sufficient to justify a variation on the evidence as it now stands."

4 Expense of third parties other than banks

1. An example A working example of problems facing non-banking third parties is provided by *Clipper Maritime Co. Ltd of Monrovia v. Mineralimportexport* [1981] 1 W.L.R. 1262, *per* Goff J.

2. The order The injunction restrained, on certain undertakings and other terms, the defendants from disposing of or dealings with their assets within the jurisdiction or from removing such assets from the jurisdiction, and in particular cargo or bunkers being the property of the defendants loaded on board a vessel called the *Marie Leonhardt*, so as to reduce the value of those assets below the sum of U.S.$123,026.40 (at 1263G).

3. The evidence founding the injunction The evidence before the court at the time of the application was that the *Marie Leonhardt* was on time charter to the defendants, and that the defendants were likely to be loading her at the port of Barry in Wales with a cargo of coke for discharge at Constanza.

4. The threat to third parties In these circumstances there was held to be a danger that the injunction might have some effect upon the movements of a ship within the port, and might also have some adverse effect upon the port authority of Barry, a third party having no interest in the dispute between the plaintiffs and the defendants (at 1263)

5. Protecting the port authority Goff J. said at 1264A–C:

> "In these circumstances, consistent with the recent decisions of this court in *Searose Ltd v. Seatrain U.K. Ltd* [1981] 1 W.L.R. 894, I imposed certain conditions upon the grant of the injunction with a view to preventing it bearing harshly upon the port authority. The particular matters I had in mind were as follows.
>
> (1) The vessel may be docked at a heavily used and high-income-producing berth; and, until the port authority can make satisfactory arrangements to move the vessel without infringing the terms of the injunction, income from that berth may be lost.
>
> (2) The port authority may in any event incur administrative costs as a consequence of the granting of the injunction.

"(3) It may be necessary for the port authority to move the vessel in the ordinary course of good administration of the port; and in cases of danger it may be necessary for the port authority to move her outside the confines of the port, and possibly even outside the injunction of the court."

6. Reimbursing the port authority Goff J. continued at 1264C:

"To take account of these contingencies I required, as a condition of granting the injunction, an undertaking by the plaintiffs to pay the actual income lost to the port authority controlling the port of Barry in South Wales and the administrative costs incurred by that port authority as a consequence of the granting of the injunction: and I also qualified the injunction by making it subject to the proviso that the port authority should always have a discretion for operational reasons to move or order the movement of the vessel within the area of the jurisdiction of the High Court or, in the event of danger, to move or order the movement of the vessel within the area of the jurisdiction of the High Court if a place within the jurisdiction was not available, and that the defendants should have liberty to comply with such an order."

7. Summary

"This court will in future, on other *ex parte* applications for *Mareva* injunctions which may affect ships in port, impose similar terms, subject always, of course, to the particular circumstances of the case." (at 1264F.)

H: VARIATIONS OF A *MAREVA*

1 General principles

1. In what circumstances? Application may be made to vary in the following circumstances:
- (a) In favour of a third party intervener.
- (b) To enable the defendant to discharge certain liabilities or expenses.
- (c) To clarify, at the behest of third parties.
- (d) In favour, exceptionally, of the plaintiff. As Ackner L.J. said in *Bekhor (A.J.) & Co. Ltd v. Bilton* [1981] 1 Q.B. 923 at 945A:

"The order of April 28 varying the *Mareva* injunction and allowing the defendant to remove £1,250 per month from the jurisdiction

247

appears to have been obtained without proper disclosure to the court of the true position of the defendant's assets. The plaintiffs could have applied for the withdrawal, and the judge of his own initiative could have withdrawn from the defendant the permission to remove any further money from the jurisdiction unless and until he made a full and proper disclosure of those matters which the court thought were necessary to establish the true nature of his assets, and he had given a proper explanation of his conduct between the material dates."

2. Variation?—Prevention is better than cure In *Z Ltd v. A–Z and AA–LL* [1982] Q.B. 558 at 587F–588D, Kerr L.J. explained the importance of having *ex parte* orders correctly phrased:

(a) *Subsequent variations—only a fall back:*

"Any subsequent hearing, when adjustments of the original order may be made, should in my view only be regarded as a fall-back position. Thus, it should not be the practice as I believe it to be at present, at any rate to some extent that relatively little thought is given to what should be the appropriate terms of the order at the stage of the *ex parte* application, because it is felt that these can always be adjusted subsequently. Although this undoubtedly provides a crucial safeguard, it should not be allowed to overshadow the original application."

(b) *Try not to fix a return date:*

"While subsequent hearings *inter partes* may be unavoidable in many cases, these involve additional time for the court and costs for the parties, and also for any possible interveners, such as banks. For this reason I feel doubtful whether it should become the practice in every case to fix a return date at once. It seems to me that such a practice would have two undesirable consequences."

(c) *First undesirable consequence:*

"First, it would tend to lessen the degree of thought which should be given to ensuring, so far as is then foreseeably possible, that the appropriate order is made on the *ex parte* application."

(d) *Second undesirable consequence:*

"Secondly, return dates given as a matter of routine will clutter up the courts, and in particular the Commercial Court, with hearings on *Mareva* injunctions to an even greater extent than is already happening. Moreover, in most cases where return dates are given on the original application I think that it will be found that this will usually be followed by an application for an adjournment, often by the consent of both parties, and it then takes further time on the part of the listing officer, and often of the court itself, to deal with such applications."

(e) *The additional difficulty of a foreign defendant:*

"In this connection it should also be borne in mind that in many cases of *Mareva* injunctions the defendant may be outside the jurisdiction or otherwise difficult to serve expeditiously, and that thereafter further time will usually be needed by both parties to consider whether, and if so to what extent, the original order requires adjustment and whether or not any contested hearing *inter partes* is necessary for this purpose."

(f) *The advantage of consent variation orders:*

"Consent orders varying or discharging the original order, on the other hand, could no doubt usually be submitted to the court for initialling without the need of any appearance on behalf of the parties."

(g) *Summary—terms should be appropriate* ab initio:

"Accordingly, I am of the view that, while it must of course always be clear that it is open to the defendant, or any third party affected by the order, to apply to have it varied or discharged on short notice, and even *ex parte* in extreme cases, reliance on such means of adjustment should only be a secondary consideration. The primary consideration should be at the stage of the *ex parte* application, and what then appears to be the appropriate order."

3. Fixing of return date Note, however, in relation to 2(b) above that the standard forms in the Practice Direction [1994] 4 All E.R. 52 provide for a return date to be fixed, though there is no reason why the dictum of Kerr L.J. should not continue to be followed in cases in which it seems the better course for the reasons given by him.

2 Variations of order at behest of defendant

1. The principle A *Mareva* is not conceived as punishing or penalising: *Rasu Maritima S.A. v. Perusahaan* [1978] 1 Q.B. 644. This was clear from *Iraqi Ministry of Defence v. Arcepey Shipping Co. S.A.* [1981] 1 Q.B. 65 at 71E:

"It does not follow that, having established the injunction, the court should not thereafter permit a qualification to it to allow a transfer of assets by the defendant if the defendant satisfies the court that he

249

requires the money for a purpose which does not conflict with the policy underlying the *Mareva* jurisdiction."

2. What sort of purpose? Lloyd L.J. said in *SCF Finance Co. Ltd v. Masri* [1985] 1 W.L.R. 876 at 880G:

"It is now well settled that an injunction will be varied where necessary so as to enable a defendant to pay his ordinary trading debts as they fall due, or to meet his ordinary living expenses. If there is a dispute as to the extent of his living expenses, or as to whether the defendant has other assets out of which he ought to pay his debts, there is a ready solution. Such disputes are resolved everyday in the Commercial Court or by the judge in chambers."

Similarly in Law Society v. Shanks [1987] 131 S.J. 1626; [1988] 1 FLR 504, the Court of Appeal held that *Mareva* injunctions should always make provision for living expenses unless it was known that a defendant had other funds. Furthermore, in general, there should be provision for him to pay his ordinary debts as they fell due. It was not the purpose of a *Mareva* injunction to establish the plaintiff as a primary creditor. However, a line was drawn in *National Bank of Greece v. Dimitriou, The Times*, November 16, 1987. The defendant's assets within the jurisdiction were subject to a *Mareva* injunction. Contrary to an affidavit he had made earlier in the proceedings, he also held undisclosed assets outside the jurisdiction and these were not subject to the *Mareva* injunction. He appealed against a decision of the High Court that he was not entitled to have part of the frozen assets released in order to pay his solicitors. The Court of Appeal held that although the defendant's case was advanced as a plea on behalf of his solicitors, in reality it was an appeal by the defendant who was attempting to preserve his overseas assets. The defendant was abusing the process of the court and was in contempt. The court would not assist him.

3. Examples of proper expenditure Thus the defendant is entitled to an allowance for:

(a) *Living expenses or payment of debts: PCW (Underwriting Agencies) Ltd v. Dixon* [1983] 2 All E.R. 158. This case is authority for the proposition that a defendant was not dissipating his assets by living as he had always lived and paying bills such as he had always incurred. Justice requires that he should be allowed the means of defending himself even if it could be said that the plaintiff had laid claim to the whole of his assets as a trust fund. Costs of paying a Queen's Counsel privately for a criminal trial would *not*, however, fall within the definition of an existing allowance for living expenses or for legal costs of defending the civil proceedings in question. This case is of note also because one of the grounds for the plaintiff's opposition to the proposed variation for living expenses was that the money (the subject-matter of the *Mareva*) was subject to a proprietary claim. On appeal (see [1983] 2 All E.R. 697) it was ordered that the drawing of money should first be made against funds indisputably the defendant's, and not impressed with any equitable interest of the plaintiffs or other persons; secondly, against funds reasonably believed to be free of such beneficial interest; and thirdly, against funds the defendant did not know were impressed with such a beneficial interest. In *Law Society v. Shanks* [1988] 1 FLR 504 Lord Donaldson M.R. said:

"... saying that he will be sent to prison if he does not comply ... this would have prevented Mr Shanks from buying himself a loaf of bread or indeed incurring any expenditure at all in the course of his ordinary life. It is plainly wrong in that respect. *Mareva* injunctions addressed to natural persons should always make provision for the defendant's living expenses unless there is reason to believe that the defendant has other assets to which the order does not attach and which would be available for that purpose.

Furthermore, there should always be provision for the payment of ordinary debts as they become due, because the purpose of a *Mareva* injunction is not to establish a potential or actual judgment creditor as a priority creditor. Its purpose is solely to prevent the defendant evading the due processes of execution by salting away assets ...

I come back to this position. The *Mareva* injunction has deprived Mr Shanks of his pension; it has deprived him for the time being of his gratuity; it makes no provision for his living expenses at all or for the payment of any other debts. It is faulty on all those grounds."

(b) *Listed trade creditors:* In *K/S A/S Admiral Shipping v. Portlink Ferries Ltd* [1984] 2 Lloyd's Rep. 166, the defendants successfully applied to vary an *ex parte Mareva* to enable them to pay trade creditors. This was despite the fact that the defendants were apparently running down their business and transferring their assets to another company, with the result that the remaining assets were probably only sufficient to pay their ordinary trade creditors. This would result in there being nothing left to meet the plaintiff's claim if and when it was established. Sir John Donaldson M.R. is reported as saying:

"Since a company cannot be wound up on the basis of a disputed claim for unliquidated damages, the plaintiffs were said to be faced with grave injustice. The judge on the basis of *Iraqi Ministry of Defence v. Arcepey Shipping Co. S.A., The Angel Bell* [1981] Q.B. 65 had said that it was not the function of the courts to rewrite the established law of insolvency (see, *per* Robert Goff L.J. at 69F–G, 72F–G). The court should not make an order which would produce the quasi winding-up of the defendants in circumstances in which the law did not permit that course."

In the *K/S* case, the plaintiff of course did not have a judgment; hence the Court of Appeal setting its face against a "quasi winding-up" of the defendants.

Not dissimilarly, it was held that an injunction was improperly granted which had prevented the defendant from using London bank accounts for the purposes of their trade. The injunction was varied to the extent that such accounts were used purely for the established course of trade: *Avant Petroleum Inc. v. Gatoil Overseas Inc.* [1986] 2 Lloyd's Rep. 236. O'Connor L.J., *inter alia*, said at 243:

> "In my judgment the learned Judge erred in principle in that the form of the order which he was asked to vary would operate, for the reasons given in the affidavit, really to close down the use of the credits in London. That was recognised to some extent by the amendment which was made to the original order to allow Banque Paribas to set off sums received from individual transactions concerned with the purchase and sale of cargoes of oil in the operation of the facility insofar as those transactions preceded the injunction. It is because of that that I agree with my Lord that some further variation to the injunction is necessary, and I propose that, if Counsel cannot agree appropriate terms, the matter should come back to us perhaps later today for argument."

(c) *Partner in insolvent firm wishing to spend own moneys on legal costs:* In *Investment & Pensions Advisory Services v. Gray* [1990] BCLC 38, G was a partner in IPAS, a firm of financial intermediaries involved in the introduction of business to the collapsed Barlow Clowes group of companies. In October 1988 the official receiver was appointed as provisional liquidator of IPAS. Proceedings were commenced against G seeking to recover commissions improperly paid to G by Barlow Clowes. Early in those proceedings a *Mareva* injunction was granted against G. G applied to vary the injunction to permit him to pay legal expenses in connection with the proceedings to wind up IPAS and certain claims being made against him by IPAS clients and to pay his accountants. He wished to pay those debts out of assets of £138,000 into which it was agreed the official receiver could not trace any claim. Morrit J. held, allowing the variation, that the official receiver's argument that the variation ought not to be allowed because it would diminish the assets of G to which the insolvent firm's creditors would have recourse, failed. G was, subject to the *Mareva* injunction, entitled to deal with his assets as he saw fit unless and until a bankruptcy order was made. There were no insolvency proceedings against G. The debts were genuine and presently payable. G proposed to pay them from assets to which the official receiver had no proprietary claim. The payments were proper payments that G was entitled to make.

4. What if the outstanding debt is unenforceable? A variation will probably still be allowed even if the indebtedness is for some reason not enforceable, so long as the transaction generating the debt was bona fides: *The Angel Bell* [1981] Q.B. 65. As Goff J. said at 72H–73C:

> "No doubt the court will not enforce, directly or indirectly, an illegal contract; but by lifting the *Mareva* injunction in the present case to enable the defendants to repay to the interveners the loan they have received would not be to enforce the transaction, even indirectly. A reputable businessman who has received a loan from another person is likely to regard it as dishonourable, if not dishonest, not to repay that loan even if the enforcement of the loan is technically illegal by virtue of the Moneylenders Acts. All the interveners are asking is that the defendants should be free to repay such a loan if they think fit to do so, not that the loan transaction should be enforced. For a defendant to be free to repay a loan in such circumstances is not inconsistent with the policy underlying the *Mareva* jurisdiction. He is not in such circumstances seeking to avoid his responsibilities to the plaintiff if the latter should ultimately obtain a judgment; on the contrary, he is seeking in good faith to make payments which he considers he should make in the ordinary course of business. I cannot see that the *Mareva* jurisdiction should be allowed to prevent such a payment. To allow it to do so would be to stretch it beyond its original purpose so that instead of preventing abuse, it would rather prevent businessmen conducting their business as they are entitled to."

5. What if the outstanding debt may be unlawful? This was the position (*obiter*) in *The Tatiangela* [1980] 2 Lloyd's Rep. 193, *per* Parker J. where Parker J. would have been prepared to vary a *Mareva* to allow payment under a guarantee, the terms of which may have been unlawful under Greek law.

3 Defendant's application to vary—must he prove no other available assets?

1. The problem The authorities have thrown up a conflict of opinion: *A. v. C. (No. 2)* [1981] 2 W.L.R. 654; [1981] 2 All E.R. 126, *per* Goff J. is authority for the proposition that a defendant cannot claim to reduce funds frozen when he can meet his liabilities in other ways. The ruling in the All E.R. headnote reads:

"Although the court had jurisdiction to qualify a *Mareva* injunction
where the defendant satisfied the court that assets subject to the
injunction were required for a purpose which did not conflict with
the policy underlying the *Mareva* jurisdiction, in order to satisfy that
burden the defendant had to go further than merely to state that he
owed money to someone, and had to show that he did not have any
other assets available out of which the debt would be paid. Since the
defendants had failed to adduce evidence to show that they had no
other assets out of which they could pay the legal costs, their
application would be dismissed."

2. The Court of Appeal disagrees However, the apparent rigour of *A. v.
C. (No. 2) (ibid.)* should be read against the more recent judgment of the
Court of Appeal in *Campbell Mussels v. Thompson* (1985) 81 L.S. Gaz.
2140. In that case the first defendant successfully made application to
Bingham J. for an injunction to enable provisions to be made for the needs
of his family and for his legal representation. The plaintiffs appealed on
the basis that apparently contrary to the dicta of Goff J. in *A. v. C. (No.
2) (ibid.)* the defendant had made insufficient disclosure of his assets. In
dismissing the appeal, Sir John Donaldson M.R. is reported as saying:

"What *A. v. C. (No. 2)* was said to decide was stated in the Supreme
Court Practice 1981, Seventh Cumulative Supplement, para. 29/1/11F,
to be that although the court had power 'to qualify a *Mareva*
injunction . . . such a qualification will not be made unless the defendant
satisfied the court not merely that he owed money to someone but
also that he did not have any other assets available out of which that
the debt would paid . . .' If *A. v. C. (No. 2)* did so decide, it decided it
wrongly. Every case had to be dealt with on its own merits. The
'fundamental purpose' of the *Mareva* injunction was stated in *A. v.
C. (No. 2)* at 692 in the quotation from *Iraqi Ministry of Defence v.
Arcepey Shipping Co. S.A.* [1981] Q.B. 65 at 70. The *Mareva* jurisdiction had never been intended to allow a plaintiff to put himself
in the position of a secured creditor. *A. v. C. (No. 2)* illustrated that
judges should have a healthy scepticism in dealing with parties to
whom *Mareva* injunctions applied. Bingham J. had exercised his
discretion when he made the variation."

3. The real issue—motive In other words the issue was not "assets"—but
motive, and thus when considering motive, availability of other assets may
be (but not necessarily is) a relevant criterion. As Griffiths L.J. is reported
to have said:

"The note (29/1/11F) in the supplement to the White Book [1981
edition] did not fairly represent the rationale in *A. v. C. (No. 2)* which

was merely pointing out that it was essential for applicants seeking to vary a *Mareva* injunction to satisfy the court by full disclosure of their needs that there was no ulterior motive involving the removal of undisclosed assets from the jurisdiction."

4. Motive and "balance of convenience" If the hardship of the grant of such an injunction to the defendant would outweigh the advantage to the plaintiff then the "balance of convenience" would militate against grant. As Stamp J. said in the unreported case of *Cybil Inc. of Panama v. Timpuship* (1978, C.A.T. No. 478):

"On behalf of the defendant it is said—and it would seem to be almost inevitable—that as a result of the injunctions which were obtained by the plaintiffs the defendant company's overdraft facilities have been frozen in the accounts of the Habib Bank and Qatar National Bank, and it is pointed out that, without overdraft facilities at these banks, the company is unable to continue its business as charterers and the company is suffering, and will continue to suffer, financial loss and injury to its commercial reputation."

In *PCW (Underwriting Agencies) Ltd v. Dixon* [1983] 2 All E.R. 697, the Court of Appeal, *inter alia*, ordered that the defendant be entitled to withdraw up to £1,000 per week in respect of reasonable living expenses, such drawings to be:
(a) against funds indisputably his own money and not impressed with any equitable interest of the plaintiff or others;
(b) against funds which the defendant reasonably believed not to be impressed with such beneficial interest; and
(c) against funds which the defendant did not know to be impressed with such beneficial interest.
And in *Bakarim v. Victoria P Shipping Co. Ltd* [1980] 2 Lloyd's Rep. 193, *per* Parker J. *obiter* at 199:

"If a defendant outside the jurisdiction desires to use money within the jurisdiction to make a payment to or for the benefit of someone else within the jurisdiction and there is no question of the payment being a disguised method of removing assets from the jurisdiction, he is prima facie entitled to do so and is not bound to justify it up to the hilt."

5. Transfer of funds to parent company In *Atlas Maritime Co. SA v. Avelon Maritime Ltd The "Coral Rose" (No. 1)* [1991] 4 All E.R. 769 the defendant was a "one-ship" company, a subsidiary of a Swiss company. The plaintiff obtained a *Mareva* injunction against the defendant. The defendant applied to the court to discharge or vary the *Mareva* so that it could transfer money to its parent in order to pay a debt *Held*: "lifting the corporate veil without piercing it", the court would examine the commercial reality. On doing so, the "debt" was not an ordinary business debt but the entire trading capital of the defendant, through which the parent was trying to achieve its own commercial aims. The application was refused. In *Atlas Maritime Co. SA v. Avalon Maritime Ltd The "Coral Rose" (No. 3)* [1991] 4 All E.R. 783 the defendant applied for a variation in order to use funds to meet legal expenses. This was refused on the basis that the parent had full financial and managerial control over the defendant: throughout the life of the defendant all its receipts had been passed straight to the parent and the parent had provided money to meet specific liabilities of the defendant; there was a probability that if the application was refused the parent would provide money for the legal expenses.

6. Summary In order to show a bona fide application to vary, a defendant should show how the expense which he wishes to pay was incurred, the trading background between himself and the creditor, and relevant documents including an invoice and letter before action—in short, sufficient information to show that the defendant's motive in making the application is not to reduce those assets otherwise available to the plaintiff. Further, costs can be reduced by the provision in the standard forms permitting the plaintiff's solicitor to consent in writing to variations proposed by the defendant, without the need for recourse to the court.

4 Intervention by third parties—practice

1. Introduction When drawing up the *Mareva* order it is open to the court to embrace the interests of third parties (*e.g.* rights of set-off for a bank), despite their not being parties to the action. But if a third party seeks variation or discharge of the order, it will generally have to intervene in the proceedings in which the *Mareva* application is made. But not always—see paragraph 3 below.

2. Jurisdiction Ord. 15, r. 6(2) provides:

> "(2) Subject to the provisions of this rule, at any stage of the proceedings in any cause or matter the Court may on such terms as it thinks just and either of its own motion or on application—
> (a) order any person who has been improperly or unnecessarily made a party or who has for any reason ceased to be a proper or necessary party, to cease to be a party;
> (b) order any of the following persons to be added as a party, namely—
> (i) any person who ought to have been joined as a party or

whose presence before the Court is necessary to ensure that all matters in dispute in the cause or matter may be effectually and completely determined and adjudicated upon, or

(ii) any person between whom and any party to the cause or matter there may exist a question or issue arising out of or relating to or connected with any relief or remedy claimed in the cause or matter which in the opinion of the Court it would be just and convenient to determine as between him and that party as well as between the parties to the cause or matter."

3. Cretanor In *Cretanor Maritime Co Ltd v. Irish Marine Management Ltd* [1978] 1 W.L.R. 966, Buckley L.J. said at 978F–H:

"For reasons which I have stated when dealing with the owner's first head of argument I do not think that the receiver in his capacity as agent of the charterers can obtain the discharge of the injunction, but I see no reason why the debenture holder should not apply for this. Where an injunction has been granted in an action which affects someone who is not a party to the action, he can apply in the action for the discharge of that injunction without himself being made a party to the action (*Bourbaud v. Bourbaud* (1864) 12 W.R. 1024; *Daniell's Chancery Practice*, 8th ed. (1914), p. 1343 and *Kerr on Injunctions*, 6th ed. (1927), p. 662). Where the interest of the applicant is clear, he may make such application by motion in the action (see *Jones v. Roberts* (1841) 12 Sim. 189) and in my opinion can equally well do so by summons. If it were necessary, it seems to me that probably there would be power under R.S.C. Ord. 15, r. 6(2)(b)(ii), to add the debenture holder as a party, but in the circumstances I do not consider that this is necessary. The question whether, as between the owners and the debenture holder, the injunction should be discharged can be adequately brought before the court by amendment of the summons so as to make the debenture holder an additional applicant. I would give leave for such an amendment to be made subject to any question as to costs."

4. Interveners and costs The costs of an innocent third party's application to vary a *Mareva* injunction may be ordered to be taxed on an indemnity basis. In *Project Development Co. Ltd S.A. v. K.M.K. Securities Ltd* [1982] 1 W.L.R. 1470, at 1473E, Parker J. said:

"It should, I think, be stressed that a plaintiff who resorts to the *Mareva* jurisdiction must expect to pay, and should in justice pay, all reasonable expenses and all reasonable costs to which innocent third parties may be put by his actions."

5. Summary It is submitted that the principle applying to a variation at the behest of a defendant operates equally in the context of such applications made by third parties—see, for example, *A v. B (X. intervening)* [1983] 2 Lloyd's Rep. 532, *per* Parker J., and *Bakarim v. Victoria P Shipping Co. Ltd (The Tatiangela)* [1980] 2 Lloyd's Rep. 193.

I: ORDERS ANCILLARY TO A *MAREVA*

1 Discovery

1. Background It was explained by Ackner L.J. in *Bekhor (A.J.) & Co. Ltd v. Bilton* [1981] 1 Q.B. 923 at 931B:

> "The essential point raised by this appeal is whether and to what extent an order for discovery can be made in relation to matters which relate, not to the issues in the action, but to the operation of a *Mareva* injunction granted against the defendant restraining him from removing from the jurisdiction of the High Court or otherwise dealing with certain of his assets."

And in the same case at 949A, Griffiths L.J. said:

> "If the court has power to make a *Mareva* injunction it must have power to make an effective *Mareva* injunction. If the injunction will not be effective it ought not to be made."

2. The problem Are R.S.C., Ords. 24 and 26 the sole sources of authority with regard to discovery? The problem can be explained thus:

(a) The Rules providing for discovery are Ord. 24 and Ord. 26 (discovery by interrogatories).

(b) The documents which can be made the subject of discovery must relate to "matters in question in the action": Ord. 24, r.1(1). As to interrogatories, the power to grant them is similarly circumscribed, for Ord. 26 provides that a party to the cause or matter may apply to the court for an order, giving him leave to serve on any other party, interrogatories relating "to any matter in question between the applicant and that other party in the cause or matter": Ord. 26, r.1(3).

(c) It will usually be the case that if an applicant for a *Mareva* seeks, *inter alia*, discovery of documents (*e.g.* bank statements), such documents will not relate to matters in question in the action, etc.— but rather to assist the court in securing its objective of preventing the defendant defeating a judgment. As Griffiths L.J. said in *Bekhor (A.J.) & Co. Ltd v. Bilton* [1981] 1 Q.B. 923 at 948G:

"The phrases 'matters in question in the action' and 'matters in question ... in the cause or matter' have for generations been understood to refer to the issues to be decided in the litigation. The present existence and whereabouts of the defendant's wealth are not such an issue; they are relevant only to the defendant's ability to satisfy judgment if the 'matters in question in the action' are resolved in the plaintiffs' favour."

3. Solution The court has inherent jurisdiction to make all such ancillary orders, including an order for discovery, as appears to the court to be just and convenient in order to ensure that the exercise of the *Mareva* jurisdiction is effective to achieve its purpose: see *Bekhor Ltd (ibid.)* at 949, *per* Griffiths L.J.

4. Solution—its limits In *Bekhor Ltd (ibid.)* Parker J. at first instance was faced with the following problems:
(a) A *Mareva* had been granted in March 1980.
(b) The defendant obtained variations of that order. The applications for variation were supported by affidavits which revealed, *inter alia*, that he had misled the court about his residence abroad, had concealed the transfer abroad of the sale proceeds of his farm, had been evasive about his assets generally and, despite his undertaking to the court, had removed some of his assets out of the jurisdiction with the result that the assets remaining were insufficient to produce the income he had been permitted to take out for living expenses.
(c) In November 1980 the defendant sought a further variation so as to be allowed to meet certain expenses within the jurisdiction. The plaintiffs in turn gave notice that they would seek discovery.

5. What was Parker J.'s reaction? He made an order requiring the defendant to swear an affidavit to disclose the full value of his assets within the jurisdiction as at specified dates, to identify the nature of his assets, to disclose their present whereabouts and manner of any charge or disposal and to verify documents relevant to the value of assets, their distribution and disposal or change between specified dates.

6. Overturned on appeal—why? The Court of Appeal held that he went too far. Ackner L.J. said at 945C–D:

"In short, while fully endorsing and approving the judge's desire to put an end to the defendant's evasiveness and to establish to what extent if at all there had been non-compliance with his order or breaches by the defendant of the undertaking, I do not consider that he had the jurisdiction to achieve it by the order which he made.

Having regard to the existence of the remedies available to the plaintiffs to police the order that they had obtained, it would, in my judgment, be quite wrong to seek to create new machinery which could have far-reaching and undesirable consequences and which are quite unnecessary for the proper operation of the *Mareva* jurisdiction."

And Stephenson L.J. added at 955B–D:

"Parker J. described the plaintiffs' application and his order for discovery as an aid or support of the *Mareva* injunction and so in a sense they were. But in so far as they relate to the defendant's assets at past dates as distinct from their present whereabouts their purpose seems to be not so much to help the court or the plaintiffs to locate and freeze particular assets now, as to open the way to incriminating and ultimately punishing the defendant for contempt of court in formerly disobeying the *Mareva* injunction and/or breaking his undertaking. This purpose emerges not only from the wide terms of the order but from the judge's comments at the end of his judgment. To that extent the order goes beyond the legitimate purpose of an order for discovery in aid of a *Mareva* injunction and Robert Goff J.'s order in *A v. C* and is not necessary for the proper and effective exercise of the *Mareva* injunction."

7. What is the use of *Mareva* discovery? Goff J. explained in *A v. C (Note)* [1981] Q.B. 956 at 959H–960B and 961B–C:

(a) *Ignorance of assets defeats Mareva jurisdiction:*

"Now the exercise of this jurisdiction may lead to many problems. The defendant may have more than one asset within the jurisdiction— for example, he may have a number of bank accounts. The plaintiff does not know how much, if anything, is in any of them; nor does each of the defendant's bankers know what is in the other accounts. Without information about the state of each account it is difficult, if not impossible, to operate the *Mareva* jurisdiction properly."

(b) *Examples of problems caused by ignorance:*

"For example, if each banker prevents any drawing from his account to the limit of the sum claimed, the defendant will be treated oppressively, and the plaintiff may be held liable on his undertaking in damages. Again, there may be a single claim against a number of defendants; in that event the same difficulties may arise. Furthermore, the very generality of the order creates difficulty for the defendant's bankers, who may, for example, be unaware of the existence of other assets of the defendant within the jurisdiction."

(c) *Knowledge can protect the defendant's bankers:*

> "Indeed, if a more specific order is possible, it may give much needed protection for the defendant's bankers, who are after all simply the innocent holders of one form of the defendant's assets ... Furthermore, for the purposes of the *Mareva* jurisdiction, since this is a case involving a number of defendants, it is necessary for the proper exercise of that jurisdiction to know how much money is standing in the identified bank account; if, for example, that account should be unencumbered and in excess of the plaintiffs' claim, the *Mareva* injunction can be restricted to that amount."

8. Disclosure of foreign assets This question, and previous authorities on it, were considered by Colman J. in *Gidrxslme Shipping Co. Ltd v. Tantomar-Transportes Maritimos Lda* [1994] 4 All E.R. 507. He held:

(a) That a disclosure order ancillary to a *Mareva* injunction cannot be more extensive than the injunction itself, and the court has no power to order disclosure of assets outside the jurisdiction in an order ancillary to a *Mareva* which is limited to assets within the jurisdiction.

(b) That the court has power to order disclosure against a defendant against whom judgment has been given. Therefore post-judgment discovery of assets out of the jurisdiction can be ordered, though a *Mareva* injunction is limited to assets within the jurisdiction or even if there is no *Mareva* at all.

(c) The position is the same if an arbitral award has been converted into a judgment, and if there has been an arbitral award which had not been converted into a judgment.

If a defendant applies to vary a *Mareva* limited to assets within the jurisdiction he may be well advised to disclose his assets outside the jurisdiction and to show how they could if necessary be attacked if he were to fail to honour a judgment against him.

2 Discovery by interrogatories

1. Jurisdiction It is clear from *Bekhor Ltd v. Bilton* [1981] 1 Q.B. 923 that the court has the power to give leave to interrogate a defendant, in order to make a *Mareva* effective. As Goff J. said in *A. v. C. (Note)* [1981] 1 Q.B. 956 at 959D:

> "In an action in which the plaintiff seeks to trace property which in equity belongs to him, the court not only has jurisdiction to grant an injunction restraining the disposal of that property; it may in addition, at the interlocutory stage of the action, make orders designed to ascertain the whereabouts of that property. In particular, it may order

a bank (whether or not party to the proceedings) to give discovery of documents in relation to the bank account of a defendant who is alleged to have defrauded the plaintiff of his assets; and it may make orders for interrogatories to be answered by the defendants or their employees or director."

2. Trust funds—the distinction from discovery in aid of a *Mareva* The distinction is summarised in the judgment of Scott L.J. in *Polly Peck International plc v. Nadir (No. 2)* [1992] 4 All E.R. 769. At p. 776E he said:

"Equitable tracing leads to a claim of a proprietory character. A fund is identified that, in equity, is regarded as a fund belonging to the claimant. The constructive trust claim, in this action at least, is not a claim to any fund in specie. It is a claim for monetary compensation. The only relevant interlocutory protection that can be sought in aid of a money claim is a *Mareva* injunction, restraining the defendant from dissipating or secreting away his assets in order to make himself judgment proof. But if identifiable assets are being claimed, the interlocutory relief sought will not be a *Mareva* injunction but relief for the purpose of preserving intact the assets in question until their true ownership can be determined. Quite different considerations arise from those which apply to *Mareva* injunctions."

As Lloyd J. explained in *PCW (Underwriting Agencies) Ltd v. Dixon* [1983] 2 All E.R. 158 at 164E–F:

"The distinction between the ordinary *Mareva* plaintiff (to use Ackner L.J.'s phrase) and the case where the plaintiff is laying claim to a trust fund on the so-called wider ground, is thus clear. In the latter case the whole object is to secure the trust fund itself so that it should be available if the plaintiff should prove his claim. In the former case by contrast the plaintiff is not entitled to any security. The purpose of the jurisdiction, as is now clearly established, is not to provide the plaintiffs with any form of pre-trial attachment. It is simply to prevent the injustice of a defendant removing or dissipating his assets so as to cheat the plaintiff of the fruits of his claim."

3. *Bankers Trust Co. v. Shapira* [1980] 1 W.L.R. 1274 This was a tracing case. The Court of Appeal upheld the following order:

"(1) Against the first, second and third defendants that each of them do disclose to the plaintiffs forthwith the sums or balances at present standing in any account in either of the names of the first or second defendants at the third defendants.
(2) Against the third defendants [*i.e.* Discount Bank (Overseas) Ltd]

that they do disclose to the plaintiffs forthwith and permit the plaintiffs to take copies of the following documents:

(i) All correspondence passing between the third defendants and the first and second defendants relating to any account at the third defendants in the names of either the first and/or second defendants from September 20, 1979 onwards.

(ii) All cheques drawn on any account at the third defendants in the names of either the first and/or the second defendants from September 20, 1979 onwards.

(iii) All debit vouchers, transfer applications and orders and internal memoranda relating to any account at the third defendants in the names of either the first and/or second defendants from September 20, 1979 onwards."

4. The "bankers trust" order—why so powerful? The significance of that order emerges from the following dicta of Waller L.J. at 1282H–1283E:

(a) *Strong evidence of fraud:*

"I only add a word or two about three points which were made by [counsel] appearing on behalf of [Discount Bank (Overseas) Ltd] and taking, so far as he could, a neutral attitude in this matter. He, first of all, emphasised that where the other two parties had not been served, it was very strong action on the part of the court to order the bank to break their duty of confidentiality. It was going further, he said, than an *Anton Piller* order because, when an *Anton Piller* order is made, there remains the opportunity of disobeying it or appealing against it.

Clearly it is undesirable that an order such as this should be lightly made. But the answer to this part of [counsel's] submission, in my judgment, is that here there is very strong evidence indeed of fraud on the part of the other two defendants—the first and second defendants. They presented two forged cheques, each for $500,000, and as a result a total of $1m. was transferred to accounts in their names or from which they would benefit."

(b) *Fraud—delay accentuates the need for speed:*

"Secondly, [counsel for Discount Bank] submitted that, having regard to the amount of time which had gone by, there was no case for making this order now; it could wait until the normal time for discovery; and indeed Mustill J. in his decision adverted to that. But again, in my opinion, where you have a fraud of this nature, although it may be late and although much or perhaps all of the money may now have gone, the sooner that steps are taken to try and trace where

263

it is the better. If steps are going to be taken, it is important that they should be taken at the earliest possible moment."

(c) *Tracing—a remedy that requires full information:*

"Thirdly, [counsel for Discount Bank] expressed concern at the wideness of the order which it was sought to make—one which required the bank to permit the plaintiffs to take copies of all correspondence, for example, all debit vouchers, transfer applications and orders, and internal memoranda. He submitted that the breadth of that order went far beyond disclosure which would have to be made under the Bankers' Books Evidence Act 1879. Again, in my opinion, an order of that breadth is completely justified in a case of this sort because, unless there is the fullest possible information, the difficulties of tracing the funds will be well-nigh impossible."

5. Tracing technique In *PCW (Underwriting Agencies) Ltd v. Dixon* the Court of Appeal in the Note reported at [1983] 2 All E.R. 697 made the following order:

"(i) ... the instruction of a specified firm of chartered accountants to prepare a schedule setting out the identity and whereabouts of all assets, property and moneys wherever located held or retained by the first defendant in his sole name or in joint names with another or others or in his direct or indirect control representing in whole or in part or deriving from premiums paid in respect of contracts of reinsurance of risks originally written by any Lloyd's syndicate managed by the plaintiffs, (ii) to require the plaintiffs and the first defendant to afford that firm such co-operation as it might reasonably require in connection therewith, and (iii) to require the plaintiffs to pay that firm's fees ..."

6. *Mareva*/interrogatories/the problem of self-incrimination Ackner L.J. dealt *obiter* with this problem in *Bekhor Ltd v. Bilton* [1981] 1 Q.B. 923 at 945E–946B (see also p. 266 below).

(a) *The general rule:*

"It has long been established that the fact that the answer to interrogatories sought to be administered would or might tend to incriminate the party interrogated, is no ground to objecting to leave being given to administer them: see *Fisher v. Owen* (1878) 8 Ch.D. 645 and the other cases cited in *The Supreme Court Practice* 1979, at p. 450. The objection to answer on this ground must be taken in the answer. The only exception to this general rule arises in an action to recover a penalty: see *Hunnings v. Williamson* (1883) 10 Q.B.D. 459."

(b) *"Rank"—an exception to the general rule?*

"I do not consider that *Rank Film Distributors Ltd v. Video Information Centre* [1980] 3 W.L.R. 487 in any way detracts from the general rule referred to above. In that case the plaintiffs, who were film companies owning the copyright to films produced and made by them, believed the defendants were pirating copies of those films and recording and selling unauthorised video cassettes of them. They obtained *Anton Piller* orders which went beyond requiring the defendants to permit forthwith representatives of the plaintiffs to enter premises occupied by the defendants for the purpose of inspecting and removing any unauthorised films. The orders further required three of the defendants to disclose: (a) the names and addresses of persons who supplied the cassettes and customers who bought them; (b) all invoices and other documents relating to the cassettes; and (c) the whereabouts of all pirate cassettes and master copies known to the defendants.

These were peremptory orders for discovery and interrogation requiring instant obedience and the defendants were informed by the penal notice on the order that disobedience would expose them to penal consequences. This was, therefore, no ordinary order for discovery or interrogatories where the party interrogated has the opportunity to consider and take legal advice before deciding whether to comply with the order: *per* Templeman L.J., at p. 515. It was, accordingly, held by the majority of the Court of Appeal that that part of the orders requiring disclosure was contrary to the well-established principle of privilege against self-incrimination and would accordingly be expunged."

7. Residual factors In the interests of completeness the following points relate to matters touched upon by Waller L.J.:

(a) *The Bankers' Book Evidence Act 1879:* It applies to both criminal and legal proceedings, and by section 7 allows the court to make an order permitting any party to a legal proceeding to inspect and take copies of entries in a bankers' books, so long as the inspection is in furtherance of the proceedings. "Books" includes microfiche, magnetic tapes and other data retrieval systems: *Barker v. Wilson* [1980] 1 W.L.R. 884. If there is a risk of dissipation, relief is by recourse to a *Mareva*—not section 7 of the Act.

(b) *The implied undertaking:* Lord Diplock said in *Home Office v. Harman* [1983] A.C. 280 at 304G:

"... an order for production of documents to a solicitor on behalf of a party to civil litigation is made upon the implied undertaking given by the solicitor personally to the court (of which he is an officer) that

265

he himself will not use or allow the documents or copies of them to be used for any collateral or ulterior purpose of his own, his client or anyone else; and any breach of that implied undertaking is contempt of court by the solicitor himself."

And as Waller L.J. said in the *Bankers Trust* case (*ibid.*):

"On the other side of the coin in relation to that, there must be an implied undertaking on the part of the plaintiffs that the information which they obtain will only be used for the purposes of this action and of course will not be disclosed otherwise." (p. 359A.)

3 Oral examination

1. When If in the proper exercise of its discretion the court considers such form of order just and convenient as ancillary to *Mareva* relief.

2. Authority *House of Spring Gardens Ltd v. Waite* [1985] F.S.R. 173, *per* Slade L.J.:

"... it is by no means inconceivable that cases, albeit perhaps rare cases, could arise where the court could properly take the view (1) that the defendant in an action appeared determined both to put or keep his assets beyond the reach of the plaintiff, and to conceal the true nature and extent of these assets from the court; and (2) that, in the particular circumstances of the case, an immediate order for oral examination or cross-examination of the defendant was the only 'just and convenient' way of ensuring that he would not deal with his assets so as to deprive the plaintiffs in the future of the fruits of any judgment. In such a case I consider it reasonably clear that section 37 would be wide enough to give the court the requisite power to make an immediate order obliging the defendant to give oral evidence, as 'just and convenient' relief ancillary to the *Mareva* order."

3. Ambit The subject-matter of the examination relates *not* to the subject-matter of the action, but to ensure compliance with the *Mareva* order.

4 Cross-examination

1. "Policing the order"—the principle In an appropriate case, the court may order a defendant to be cross-examined to ensure that a *Mareva* order is effective. As Ackner L.J. said in *Bekhor Ltd v. Bilton* [1981] 1 Q.B. 923 at 944G:

"If the plaintiffs, or the court of its own volition desired to 'police its order,' then the plaintiffs could have applied for an order for the cross-examination of the defendant on his affidavit, or the court itself could have made such an order: see Ord. 38, r.2."

2. "Policing"—when? *House of Spring Gardens Ltd v. Waite* [1985] F.S.R. 173, C.A. is authority for the following:

> "In the case where the defendants to an action seem determined to put their assets beyond the reach of the plaintiffs, the High Court had jurisdiction to order a cross-examination upon the affidavits of defendants who were subject to the *Mareva* injunctions, for the purpose of ascertaining the true extent and location of their assets."

In that case, Slade L.J. said that, as was pointed out by the Court of Appeal in *CBS United Kingdom Ltd v. Lambert* [1983] Ch. 37, the jurisdiction to grant *Mareva* injunctions was not likely to be of any use unless there were some means of making the defendant disclose his assets and their whereabouts. It should be noted however that:

(a) the order as to "cross-examination" was made by consent; and
(b) there is no reported case where the order has been made otherwise than by consent.

3. A "policing" order—practice and procedure Where the court took the view that:

(a) The defendant appeared determined to put or keep his assets beyond the plaintiffs' reach.
(b) He wished to conceal the true nature and extent of those assets from the court.
(c) That in the particular circumstances of the case an immediate order for oral examination or cross-examination was the only "just and convenient" way of ensuring that he would not deal with his assets in such a way as to deprive the plaintiffs of the fruits of any future judgment; then,

section 37 of the Act of 1981 was wide enough to give the court jurisdiction to make the requisite order. And Cumming-Bruce L.J. added that the court had the power as well as the duty to take such steps as were practicable to procure that where the defendants had been ordered to identify and disclose the whereabouts of their assets, that order was able to have effect as completely and successfully as possible. An order to cross-examine upon an unsatisfactory affidavit already filed was one of the courses that the court had jurisdiction to take. When such cross-examination took place, it was entirely a matter for the presiding judge properly to control it, even to the extent of not requiring further recourse to the court consequent upon such cross-examination: *House of Spring Gardens Ltd v. Waite* [1985] F.S.R. 173, C.A.

4. *House of Spring Gardens*—not a ticket to Star Chamber It may be proper to assert that *House of Spring Gardens Ltd v. Waite* [1985] F.S.R. 173 is the high-water mark of the court's willingness to "police" orders. In *Bayer A.G. v. Winter (No. 2)* [1986] 1 W.L.R. 540, Scott J. was alert to point out that in *House of Spring Gardens*:

(a) the court merely recognised that it had jurisdiction to make such order; and

(b) the order was in fact made by consent.

He went on to say at 544D–F:

> "The view was expressed by Cumming-Bruce L.J. in *House of Spring Gardens Ltd v. Waite* [1985] F.S.R. 173 that in appropriate circumstances, it may be the duty of the court to police its own orders. I would respectfully accept that the court has, through its *in personam* jurisdiction, power to subject citizens to an interrogatory process designed to enforce court orders. In the *House of Spring Gardens* case the defendant had consented to the order for his cross-examination. So the court did not have to decide whether, as a matter of discretion, the order was one which it would be right to make. For my part I find it very difficult to envisage any circumstances in which, as a matter of discretion, it would be right to make such an order as is sought in the present case and as was made by consent in the *House of Spring Gardens* case.
>
> Star Chamber interrogatory procedure has formed no part of the judicial process in this country for several centuries. The proper function of a judge in civil litigation is to decide issues between parties. It is not, in my opinion, to preside over an interrogation."

In this context, the following dicta indicate a wariness at first instance of allowing "draconian remedies" to apply to situations which do not truly warrant them:

(a) *Per* Falconer J. in *C.B.S. United Kingdom Ltd v. Perry* [1985] F.S.R. 421, citing an unreported decision of Peter Gibson J.:

> "Inevitably if cross-examination is ordered and information is elicited there is likely to be some information which will go to questions of contempt and to the subject-matter of the litigation. The court must, I think, be alive to the dangers that an order for cross-examination brings. Mr Platts-Mills accepted that the court should not make an order for cross-examination unless satisfied that there was a reasonable likelihood that the person sought to be cross-examined had information which should have been disclosed pursuant to the order for disclosure and which would lead to the fulfilment of the purpose of such an order, that is to say disclosure of sources and ascertaining the whereabouts of illicit goods. In my judgment Mr Platts-Mills was

plainly right to accept that that was a proper limitation on the court's power to order cross-examination. It cannot be right to allow a plaintiff the opportunity of a roving cross-examination merely because the plaintiffs harbour suspicion that the person sought to be made the subject of the order has not been entirely open in his disclosure. It will be apparent that in every *Anton Piller* case there will be grave suspicions about the persons served with the order. Some inconsistencies may well become apparent between what is said when they are taken by surprise when confronted with the order and what is said on affidavit, but it would be in my view quite wrong if it became the norm for an *Anton Piller* order to be followed by applications for cross-examination."

(b) *Per* Scott J. in *Bayer A.G. v. Winter (No. 2) (ibid.)* at 543D–H, to 544A:

"Mr Prescott made clear that the purpose of his proposed cross-examination of the first defendant is a free-ranging one. He proposes to question him as to the whereabouts of his assets world-wide. He proposes to question him as to his knowledge of and part played in transactions in counterfeit Baygon wherever they may have happened.

I am doubtful whether orders of this sort are justifiable in this case or in any other. I am not doubting the jurisdiction of the court to make *in personam* orders in any case where the *in personam* order is thought right. The question whether in a particular case a particular *in personam* order to be made is always in the end one of discretion. As Mr Prescott pointed out to me, there has been a recent tendency on the part of the courts to make more and more Draconian, more and more interrogatory types of interlocutory orders in order to try to combat the rising level of international fraud, and, in particular, international fraud relating to abuse of intellectual property rights. That tendency seems to have resulted in *ex parte* orders of an increasingly extensive sort being made. In my view, the basis on which *ex parte* orders can properly be made requires to be very carefully examined. Defendants are entitled, prima facie, not to have assumptions made against them and orders made against them without a hearing at which they can be represented and can put forward their case. If the evidence is as plain as Mr Prescott's submissions suggest it is and shows that the first defendant is bound to be found liable of selling counterfeit Baygon, there is nothing to prevent the plaintiffs obtaining final relief under R.S.C., Ord. 14 procedure for an inquiry as to damages and whatever other orders are appropriate to be made. So far, however, there has been no proper opportunity for the first defendant to answer the case made against him. The plaintiffs have obtained an order on an *ex parte* application made *in camera*. The first defendant is here to resist a further extension of that *ex parte* order. The cross-examination that Mr Prescott has in mind would, it seems to me, cover almost the whole area on which the first defendant would be cross-examined at trial. The trial will be concerned with transactions in counterfeit Baygon and may be concerned with the whereabouts of the ill-gotten gains of the sales of counterfeit Baygon. Mr Prescott wants to conduct this wide ranging cross-examination in the advance even of service of a statement of claim. He justifies his application to cross-examine on the footing that the first defendant has made inadequate compliance with the court order. He has in mind that following the cross-examination committal applications for contempt based upon the first defendant's answers given in cross-examination may then be brought against him."

5 Anton Piller

1. Principle In an appropriate case the court can "pile *Piller* on *Mareva*". That phrase was first aired, *obiter* in *Bekhor Ltd v. Bilton* [1981] 1 Q.B. 923 at 955.

2. The *CBS* case—its significance *C.B.S. United Kingdom Ltd v. Lambert* [1983] Ch. 37 was, primarily, an *Anton Piller* (copyright/piracy) case. It assumed significance in two respects:
   (a) it was the first authoritative case where *Piller* was piled on *Mareva*; and
   (b) it is the first reported decision involving "delivery up".
"Delivery up" is considered below. What follows turns exclusively upon the *Piller/Mareva* juxtaposition.

3. *Mareva* ordered—why? Lawton L.J. explained at 43G–44B:

"On the evidence put before us *ex parte* in this case there was reason to think that the first defendant had put such profits as he had made from infringing the plaintiffs' copyrights into easily removable and disposable chattels such as motor vehicles. There is no reason at present to think that he uses the motor vehicles he owns for the purposes of earning his living; indeed, he claims to be unemployed. Neither he nor his wife will suffer hardship pending trial if his motor vehicles are kept in a garage chosen by the plaintiffs' experienced solicitors. Further, a man who can buy expensive motor cars, as the first defendant is alleged to have done, must have access to money and it is improbable that he has confined his buying for the purpose of acquiring easily disposable assets exclusively to cars. It follows, in our judgment, that this is the kind of case in which both defendants should be ordered to disclose the value, nature and whereabouts of their assets, including bank or other accounts."

6 *Mareva* and delivery up

1. Introduction A court may order the disclosure of the value, nature and whereabouts of assets—but if such assets could be readily hidden and/or disposed of for cash if the need arose, such disclosure would be nugatory. The courts have thus recognised themselves as having the power—in exercise of the statutory jurisdiction under the Supreme Court Act 1981, to make an order for delivery up of assets.

2. "Deliver up" orders—when? The *locus classicus* is *CBS United Kingdom Ltd v. Lambert* [1983] Ch. 37. Lawton L.J. postulated at 44B–45C the following "guidelines" (and in so doing, said, "Guidelines are guidelines; they are not rules of court and the spirit of them and not the letter should be kept in mind": at 45C).

(a) *Risk of dissipation/nexus with claim:*

"There should be clear evidence that the defendant is likely, unless restrained by order, to dispose of or otherwise deal with his chattels in order to deprive the plaintiff of the fruits of any judgment he may obtain. Moreover, the court should be slow to order the delivery up of property belonging to the defendant unless there is some evidence or inference that the property has been acquired by the defendant as a result of his wrong-doing. In the present case, for example, the inference is that the motor vehicles which the defendants own could only have been purchased out of the proceeds of sale by the defendants of articles which infringe the plaintiffs' copyright. The inference is also that, if the defendants are forewarned or left in possession of the motor vehicles, those vehicles will be sold and the proceeds of sale dissipated or hidden so that the plaintiffs would be deprived not only of damages but also of the proceeds of sale of infringing articles which belong to the plaintiffs."

(b) *Exclude personal necessaries:*

"No order should be made for the delivery up of a defendant's wearing apparel, bedding, furnishings, tools of his trade, ... [or other goods] which it is likely he uses for the purposes of a lawful business. Sometimes furnishings may consist of *objets d'art* of great value. If the evidence is clear that such objects were bought for the purposes of frustrating judgment creditors they could be included in an order."

(c) *Try if at all possible to identify the chattels:*

271

"All orders should specify as clearly as possible what chattels or classes of chattels are to be delivered up. A plaintiff's inability to identify what he wants delivered up and why is an indication that no order should be made."

(d) *No licence to enter:*

"The order must not authorise the plaintiff to enter on the defendant's premises or to seize the defendant's property save by permission of the defendant. In *Anton Piller K.G. v. Manufacturing Processes Ltd* [1976] Ch. 55 Lord Denning M.R. emphasised that the order in that case at p. 60:

'. . . does not authorise the plaintiffs' solicitors or anyone else to enter the defendants' premises against their will . . . It only authorises entry and inspection by permission of the defendants. The plaintiffs must get the defendants' permission. But it does do this: It brings pressure on the defendants to give permission. It does more. It actually orders them to give permission . . .' "

(e) *Authorised recipient:*

"No order should be made for delivery up to anyone other than the plaintiff's solicitor or a receiver appointed by the High Court. The court should appoint a receiver to take possession of the chattels unless satisfied that the plaintiff's solicitor has, or can arrange, suitable safe custody for what is delivered to him."

(f) *Protecting third parties:*

"The court should follow the guidelines set out in *Z Ltd v. A–Z and AA–LL* [1982] Q.B. 558 in so far as they are applicable to chattels in the possession, custody or control of third parties."

(g) *Liberty to apply:*

"Finally, provision should always be made for liberty to apply to stay, vary or discharge the order."

7 Delivery up of passport, etc.

1. Meaning In *Bayer A.G. v. Winter (No. 2)* [1986] 1 W.L.R. 540, the Court of Appeal had previously ordered that the defendant be restrained from leaving England and Wales without the leave of the court for a period of two days after service of the order on him, and secondly, it ordered him to deliver up his passport to the solicitor who should serve the order upon him, with a requirement that the passport be returned on the expiry of the two days in question. Scott J. said at 542B:

"The reason, as I understand it, behind the restriction on the liberty of the first defendant to leave England and Wales, which is, in my experience, unprecedented, was that it was thought that his obligation to disclose information to the plaintiffs might be evaded by the simple device of his leaving the country. It was, therefore, thought right that he should be prevented from leaving the country for a period sufficient to enable the plaintiffs to ensure that he complied with the disclosure order."

2. Contrasting the writ *ne exeat regno* This writ is aimed at assisting the plaintiff in obtaining a judgment the terms of which were in a form which could be properly executed: *Lipkin Gorman (A Firm) v. Cass, The Times,* May 29, 1985, *per* Walton J. In this case, the plaintiff sought to recover stolen money and therefore needed an inquiry into any monetary accounts with building societies, banks and other depositees the defendant might have had. The writ was therefore to assist the plaintiff in obtaining an effective tracing remedy. (The writ, however, was never executed as it transpired that the defendant was already in custody in another connection and the writ was discharged before he was released.) The question of the existence and scope of the writ was discussed in *Felton v. Callis* [1969] 1 Q.B. 200, 211 by Megarry J. who specified the four following conditions which had to be met:
  (a) The action was one in which the defendant would formerly have been liable to arrest at law.
  (b) A good cause of action for at least £50 was established.
  (c) There was probable cause for believing that the defendant was about to quit England unless he was arrested.
  (d) The absence of the defendant from England would materially prejudice the plaintiff in the prosecution of his action.
In summary:
  (a) The writ is a means of coercing a defendant to give bail on pain of arrest; and
  (b) the writ is marked with a specific sum upon payment of which the defendant avoids arrest pursuant to the order.

3. How the *Mareva* injunction and the writ *ne exeat regno* interact In *Allied Arab Bank Ltd v. Hajjar* [1988] 2 W.L.R. 942, the first defendant, a Jordanian citizen, was one of the guarantors of substantial sums lent by the plaintiffs to the tenth defendant, a company in liquidation. The plaintiffs elected to bring an action against him and the other defendants for fraudulent conspiracy. Upon learning that the first defendant had entered the country, they successfully applied to Hirst J. for a writ *ne exeat regno* marked for bail in the sum of £36 million. Unable to raise that sum, the first defendant was arrested and brought before the court. Being satisfied that the plaintiffs had substantial grounds for seeking discovery which would not be available if the first defendant was permitted to leave the country, Hirst J.:

(a) granted a *Mareva* injunction restraining the first defendant dealing with assets within the jurisdiction;

(b) made an order "for the purpose of tracing assets which may already have been dissipated" that the first defendant disclose on affidavit his assets within the jurisdiction and those of the other proposed defendants of which he had knowledge.

The defendant applied to have the writ *ne exeat regno* set aside on the ground that it had been wrongly issued and an inquiry as to the damage he had suffered thereby. Leggat J. granted the application, *inter alia* setting out:

(a) *The historical context:* At 946H–947A:

"The efficacy and scope of the writ *ne exeat regno* were considered by Megarry J. in *Felton v. Callis* [1969] 1 Q.B. 200. It originated in the 13th century as a prerogative writ. By Stuart times it had been adapted by equity as a means of coercing a defendant to give bail on pain of arrest in cases where the debt was equitable and he was not liable to arrest on mesne process. At least from that time judges have emphasised the need for caution in the grant of the writ. In 1838 arrest on mesne process was abolished except in certain cases in which the debtor could be arrested by order of a judge. The Court of Chancery exercised an analogous jurisdiction. Finally, in 1869 the Debtors Act still further limited the power of arrest on mesne process, and the courts of equity once more followed the analogy."

(b) *The principles presently applying:* At 947B–C he went on to explain how they related to the instant case:

"The practice was thus established whereby the writ would not be issued except in cases in which, though the debt was not a legal debt, the four conditions stipulated by section 6 of the Debtors Act 1869 were satisfied. They were summarised thus by Megarry J. in *Felton v. Callis*, at 211:

'(1) The action is one in which the defendant would formerly have been liable to arrest at law. (2) A good cause of action for at least £50 is established. (3) There is "probable cause" for believing that the defendant is "about to quit England" unless he is arrested. (4) "The absence of the defendant from England will materially prejudice the plaintiff in the prosecution of his action."'

There is here no dispute about conditions (2) and (3)."

274

(c) *The plaintiff's argument:* At 947D–F:

"For the plaintiffs Mr Wadsworth argues that the fourth condition is satisfied, because the 'prosecution' of the action may include obtaining discovery, interrogatories and a *Mareva* injunction. He accepts that the writ must be subordinate to some other part of the claim, but contends that it may issue, for example, to make an injunction effective. In *Al Nahkel for Contracting & Trading Ltd v. Lowe* [1986] Q.B. 235 Tudor Price J. concluded his judgment by saying, at 239:

'I was satisfied that in the present case all the four conditions set out above are satisfied and that it was a proper exercise of discretion to give leave to issue the writ. In my judgment this ancient remedy, or "tool of the law" as Megarry J. called it, is available in support of the modern *Mareva* injunction to prevent a defendant fleeing the jurisdiction with assets in order to frustrate a lawful claim before the court.'

He relied on a note of a judgment by Evans J. to which, because judgment was given in chambers, I do not regard it as appropriate to refer."

(d) *Limited approval to the Al Nahkel case:* At 947G Leggat J. said:

"Since Tudor Price J. held that in the case before him the four conditions were satisfied, there can be no quarrel with the issue of the writ in that case. His conclusion that the writ can issue in support of a *Mareva* injunction may have been intended to refer only to those cases in which both remedies may properly issue, with the result that the arrest of the debtor may incidentally prevent him from breaching the *Mareva* injunction. But if it was intended to go further and to suggest that the writ may be ordered for the purpose of enforcing a *Mareva* injunction, I disagree: for that purpose the appropriate remedy is an injunction to restrain the defendant from leaving the jurisdiction."

(e) *He went on to explain how condition (4) was not satisfied:* At 947H– 948A–B:

"A *Mareva* injunction issues for the purpose of preserving within the jurisdiction of the court assets against which a creditor may have recourse, provided that he is successful in obtaining judgment. The remedy is in aid of execution, and constitutes an exception to the principle enunciated in *Lister & Co. v. Stubbs* (1890) 45 Ch.D. 1. It is not part of the prosecution of the action. If the claim is a proprietary claim, or a tracing claim, it may well be appropriate for a writ to issue as well as a *Mareva* injunction. But in every case the question must be asked, 'For what purpose is the issue of the writ required?'

275

Here the primary purpose suggested it to require the first defendant to identify assets in relation to which the *Mareva* injunction would operate. That is not part of the *prosecution* of the action. It follows that condition (4) is not satisfied. I would add that in so far as the issue of the writ was sought to be justified in aid of discovery of what may for convenience be termed the *Norwich Pharmacal* [*Norwich Pharmacal Co. v. Custom and Excise Commissioners* [1974] A.C. 133] type I do not consider that, if the point had been determinative, the need for this discovery would have been of such importance as would have justified the issue of the writ."

(f) *He then went on to explain how condition (1) was not satisfied:* At 948C–E:

"With regard to condition (1), it is plain that a debtor was never liable to arrest at law except for a debt certain, and equity followed the law in this respect: *Colverson v. Bloomfield* (1885) 29 Ch.D. 341. The plaintiffs are prosecuting their claim in this action for damages, having refrained from proceeding upon the debt arising under the guarantees. In my judgment under condition (1) the first defendant would not have been liable to arrest at law, since the claim effectively being prosecuted is not the claim for debt; or alternatively, in so far as it is, it is not for the purpose of prosecuting that part of the claim that the writ was sought. The cause of action on the guarantees was not one for the prosecution of which the presence of the first defendant in England was required. Conversely, his absence will not materially prejudice the plaintiffs in the prosecution of that claim. The joinder in one action of a cause of action in respect of which a defendant would have been liable to arrest at law with one in respect of which he would not, cannot possibly entitle the plaintiff to procure the latter cause of action."

(g) *Leggat J. went on to buttress his ruling by showing that a condition precedent to issue of the writ was the existence of an equitable debt:* At 948E–949B:

"The scope of the writ was in any event confined to equitable claims. None of the plaintiffs' claims in this action is equitable. Mr Wadsworth argues that because the forms of action are no longer observed, the writ ought no longer to be confined to equitable claims. He cites *Parker v. Camden London Borough Council* [1986] Ch. 162 in which Sir John Donaldson M.R. said, at 173:

'For my part I do not accept that the pre-Judicature Act practices of the Court of Chancery or any other court still rule us from their graves.'

The Master of the Rolls was there concerned with a statute which gave in terms an unqualified power to appoint a receiver, and was meeting the submission that the power ought only to be exercised in circumstances in which the Court of Chancery would have before 1873. Understandably he rejected that submission. What I am concerned with is a power to issue a writ which is itself a survival. It does not seem to me that I am entitled on that account to extend its application. The logic of Mr Wadsworth's argument appears to be that because there was power under the Debtors Act 1869, and still is since the statute has not been repealed, to arrest for legal debt, and because equity followed the law in relation to equitable debt, the courts ought since the fusion of law and equity to apply the equitable remedy indifferently. I find this argument unappealing. It is true that any court can now apply the remedy. But it does not follow that that remedy is to be treated as having a wider application than it formerly had. In any event, the Court of Appeal in *Drover v. Beyer* (1879) 13 Ch.D. 242 decided that since the debt there in question was a mere legal demand, for which the plaintiff could not before the Judicature Act have sued in the Court of Chancery, the defendant could only be prevented from leaving England under section 6 of the Debtors Act 1869. That decision is binding on me, and in my judgment on that ground also the plaintiffs were not entitled to the issue of the writ."

(h) *Summary:*

   (i) For the issue of a writ *ne exeat regno*, it had to be shown that the absence of the defendant from the jurisdiction would materially affect the plaintiff in the prosecution of the action.

   (ii) A *Mareva* injunction was a remedy in aid of execution, and not part of the prosecution of a claim.

   (iii) In *Hajjar* the primary purpose of requiring the issue of the writ was to require the defendant to identify assets in relation to which the *Mareva* injunction would operate. That was not part of the prosecution of the action.

   (iv) A writ *ne exeat regno* could not be issued for the purpose of enforcing a *Mareva* injunction.

J: SOLICITORS' *MAREVA* QUESTIONNAIRE AND CHECK LIST

1 Source

The following questionnaire and check list is inspired by the judgment of Kerr L.J. in *Z Ltd v. A–Z and AA–LL* [1982] 1 Q.B. 558 at 558–9.

1. Is the *Mareva* really necessary? That is:
  (a) Has the plaintiff a good arguable case?
  (b) Are there assets within the jurisdiction?
  (c) Are they sufficient to meet the claim (and interest and costs)?
  (d) If the answer to (c) is "no", are there assets out of the jurisdiction?
  (e) Has the client grounds to argue that the proposed defendant may well take steps designed to ensure that assets are no longer available or traceable when judgment is given against him?

2. Consider:
  (a) How broad need be the terms of the proposed injunction, to safeguard the plaintiff's claim?
  (b) To what particular assets of the proposed defendant should the injunction be applied?—such assets to be identified.
  (c) If it is known or suspected that assets are in the hands of third parties, in particular of banks, everything should be done to define their location to the greatest possible extent, *e.g.*:
    (i) Which bank or banks hold the account in question?
    (ii) At what branches?
    (iii) If possible, under what account numbers?

3. As to issue/service of the writ/affidavit—and the injunction if it is granted:
  (a) If the writ is not issued, how soon can it be issued? Note that the Practice Direction [1994] 4 All E.R. 42 (see above) provides: "Where practicable the papers to be used on the application should be lodged with the judge at least two hours before the hearing." This is to enable him to read them before the hearing starts, which will shorten the hearing without extending the period before which the order is made. The two-hour period should normally enable the writ to be issued, even if the papers lodged with the judge contain only a draft writ.
  (b) If the affidavit(s) is not/are not sworn, how soon can they be sworn? See (a) above on two-hour period.
  (c) If an order is made, how can the defendant be given notice of it as soon as possible? Fax?
  (d) How can the order and other documents (writ, affidavits, summons (if in Queen's Bench Division or Admiralty and Commercial Court) or notice of motion (if in Chancery Division) be served on the defendant as quickly as possible? Engage process server?
  (e) Explain to the client (written explanation advisable) undertakings as to damages and as to expense/loss incurred by third parties. Get information on client's means, with documents if possible (*e.g.* latest audited accounts if a company or trader) and exhibit to affidavit.

(f) Prepare draft order in form annexed to the Practice Direction (Annex 2 world-wide *Mareva*; Annex 3 *Mareva* with effect only to assets within the jurisdiction).

4. Documents

(a) There must be full and frank disclosure in the affidavit. (This includes reference to any criminal charge or conviction against the applicant: *Block v. Nicholson* [1987] C.L.Y. 3064.)

(b) The application should be supported by a full draft order for consideration by the judge, *i.e.* one which contains all the undertakings on the part of the plaintiff and which gives effect to the appropriate injunction in terms which are adapted to the particular circumstances of the case.

5. Getting on with the action. *Lloyd's Bowmaker Ltd v. Britannia Arrow Holdings plc* [1988] 1 W.L.R. 1337 is authority for the following propositions:

(a) A plaintiff who has obtained a *Mareva* injunction is under a duty to get on with the action.

(b) Failure to get on with the action is relevant to an application to discharge the injunction.

(c) Failure to get on with the action is also relevant to whether a *Mareva* injunction should be discharged on the ground of failure to disclose and, if it is discharged, to whether a further *Mareva* should be granted.

CHAPTER 3

ANTON PILLER Orders

A: INTRODUCTION

1 What is an *Anton Piller* order?

The *Anton Piller* order takes its name from the case *Anton Piller K.G. v. Manufacturing Process Ltd* [1976] Ch. 55, the first reported case in which its use was sanctioned by the Court of Appeal. The nature of the basic *Anton Piller* order is best explained in the words of Lord Denning M.R. in that case, at 60:

> "... the order sought in this case is not a search warrant. It does not authorise the plaintiffs' solicitors or anyone else to enter the defendants' premises against their will. It does not authorise the breaking down of any doors, nor the slipping in by a back door, nor getting in by an open door or window. It only authorises entry and inspection by the permission of the defendants. The plaintiffs must get the defendants' permission. But it does do this: It brings pressure on the defendants to give permission. It does more. It actually orders them to give permission—with ... the result that if they do not give permission, they are guilty of contempt of court."

In *Thermax Ltd v. Schott Industrial Glass Ltd* [1981] F.S.R. 289 Browne-Wilkinson J. said at 291:

> "The procedure is very obviously draconian in its results. It is quite rightly said that it is not a search warrant in the sense that if the defendant refuses to obey the order and allow the plaintiff and his representatives to enter and search no force can be used against such defendant. But its effect is often very similar."

2 *Anton Piller* order distinguished from an order under R.S.C., Order 29, rule 2(2)

Ord. 29, r.2 provides:

> "(1) On the application of any party to a cause or matter the Court

280

may make an order for the detention, custody or preservation of any property which is the subject-matter of the cause or matter, or as to which any question may arise therein, or for the inspection of any such property in the possession of a party to the cause or matter.

(2) For the purpose of enabling any order under paragraph (1) to be carried out the Court may by the order authorise any person to enter upon any land or building in the possession of any party to the cause or matter."

(a) An order under Ord. 29, r.2(2) authorises a person to enter onto any land or building; an *Anton Piller* order does not: it operates *in personam*, *i.e.* it orders the occupier to permit entry.

(b) An order can only be made under Ord. 29, r.2(2) on summons or on a notice under the summons for directions (Ord. 29, r.2(5)). Therefore it can only be made if the other party has had notice that it will be sought and has had a chance to object in advance. An *Anton Piller* order is made *ex parte*, often before the writ is served and occasionally even before the writ is issued.

(c) An order under Ord. 29, r.2(2) may provide for the detention, custody or protection of property; under a basic *Anton Piller* order the property is normally returned after a short interval for inspection.

3. Why the adjective "basic" in relation to *Anton Piller* orders?

Because in practice other orders are often combined with the "basic" order to the defendant to permit entry and search.

B: THE REASONS FOR AN *ANTON PILLER* ORDER

(a) To enable the plaintiff to discover and preserve evidence against the defendant which is in the possession of the defendant and is likely to be destroyed or concealed by him.

(b) To identify and to obtain evidence against others who have been involved with the defendant in tortious activities, under the principle first enunciated in *Norwich Pharmaceutical Co. v. Customs and Excise Commissioners* [1974] A.C. 133.

(c) To prevent the defendant from warning others (who may not already be named as defendants or proposed defendants) to destroy or conceal evidence.

(d) To prevent further damage to the plaintiff, including, in an appropriate case, identification of the assets of a defendant against whom judgment has already been given.

C: WHAT THE PLAINTIFF MUST SHOW

1 Their origin

In the *Anton Piller* case, Ormrod L.J. said at p. 62 that there are three essential preconditions. By 1987 *Anton Piller* orders had become frequent. *Columbia Picture Industries Inc. v. Robinson* [1987] Ch. 38 was described by the judge, Scott J., as the first case in which the propriety of the obtaining and execution of an *Anton Piller* order was considered otherwise than in interlocutory proceedings. He expressed "very grave disquiet" at what he found:

> "[a] procedure which, on a regular and institutionalised basis, is depriving citizens of their property and closing down their businesses by orders made *ex parte*, on applications of which they know nothing and at which they cannot be heard, by orders which they are forced, on pain of committal, to obey, even if wrongly made."

Such judicial disquiet, and judicial response to public concern, led to the setting up of a committee under the chairmanship of Staughton L.J. Its report suggested that there should be a fourth precondition—that the harm likely to be caused by the execution of the *Anton Piller* order to the respondent and his business affairs must not be excessive or out of proportion to the legitimate objects of the order, especially when the effect of the order will be the seizure of trading stock or the perusal by the plaintiff of the defendant's confidential commercial documents. Seizure or trading stock is an example of an order sometimes made at the same time as a "basic" *Anton Piller* order.

2 The four preconditions

An order will not be made because the four preconditions are fulfilled, but is most unlikely to be made unless they are fulfilled, so far as is relevant.

1. An extremely strong prima facie case An *Anton Piller* order will not be made to enable a plaintiff to fish for evidence in order to justify mere suspicion, but wrongdoing which will justify an *Anton Piller* order—e.g. pirating of copyright material—is likely to be of the type which is committed deliberately, repeatedly and surreptitiously. The plaintiff's case when he applies for an *Anton Piller* order may therefore be based wholly or largely on circumstantial evidence, and the plaintiff may be unaware of the scale of the defendant's wrongdoing. To obtain and preserve evidence when there is material from which the court can infer a serious risk that the evidence might be concealed or destroyed by the defendant is a legitimate purpose of an *Anton Piller* order: *Yousif v. Salama* [1980] 1 W.L.R. 1540.

2. Serious damage The damage, potential or actual, must be very serious for the applicant.

3. Incriminating material The plaintiff must produce clear evidence that the defendant has in his possession incriminating documents or things and that there is a real possibility that the defendant may destroy such material before any *inter partes* application can be made. In *Booker McConnell Plc v. Plascow* [1985] R.P.C. 425 the Court of Appeal stressed the difference between "a real possibility" and "the extravagant fears which seem to afflict all plaintiffs who have complaints of breach of confidence, breach of copyright or passing off."

The *Anton Piller* case was about "incriminating documents or things". It is clear, however, that an *Anton Piller* order can be made even after judgment, when liability is no longer in issue, in order to obtain documents essential to execution of a judgment if there is a serious risk that a defendant will remove or destroy them in order to frustrate enforcement of a judgment: *Distributori Automatici Italia SpA v. Holford General Trading Co. Ltd* [1985] 1 W.L.R. 1066.

4. Harm caused must not be excessive The harm likely to be caused by the execution of the *Anton Piller* order to the respondent and his business affairs must not be excessive or out of proportion to the legitimate object of the order. This, it is suggested, means that if the three original *Anton Piller* preconditions are satisfied and the court would otherwise make an order in terms which it has decided are appropriate, it must first balance the harm likely to be caused by the execution of an order *in those terms* against the object which it has already decided to be legitimate. For example, if the order which would otherwise be made would permit the removal from business premises of documents for copying, followed by their swift return, but not the indefinite removal of the defendant's stock in trade which is the subject of an alleged infringement of copyright or execution of an order at the defendant's home, it is the harm likely to be caused by the execution of that order which is to be weighed.

D: PRACTICE AND PROCEDURE

1 The court

An application may be made in any division of the High Court, though *Anton Piller* orders are rarely granted in the Family Division (*Emanuel v.*

Emanuel [1982] 1 W.L.R. 669). In the Queen's Bench and Family Divisions the hearing is in chambers; in the Chancery Division it is in court, but the court will usually sit *in camera*. The county court does not have jurisdiction.

2 The evidence

1. The duty of full and fair disclosure As in all *ex parte* applications, there is a duty to make full and frank disclosure of all material facts: *R. v. Kensington Income Tax Commissioners, ex parte Princess Edmond de Polignac* [1917] K.B. 486. It is a duty owed to the court, not to the defendant. The duty is to identify any possible defences or weak points, and not merely to exhibit documents in which defences or weak points lurk and might be discovered: *Siporex Trade SA v. Comdel Commodities Ltd* [1986] 2 Lloyd's Rep. 428 (*A Mareva* case). The duty is not merely to disclose all material facts known to the plaintiff but also to make such enquiries as are reasonable in the circumstances and to disclose material facts revealed by such enquiries: *Bank Mellat v. Nikpour* [1985] F.S.R. 87. In *Columbia Picture Industries Inc. v. Robinson* [1987] Ch. 38, Scott J. said (1) that the affidavit evidence in support of an application for an *Anton Piller* order should err on the side of excessive disclosure and (2) that if there are two or more plaintiffs the duty of disclosure is owed by each of them and breach of the duty by any of them prejudices all.

The plaintiff should be very careful to disclose and bring to the attention of the court anything which might give rise to a possible claim by the defendant to privilege against self-incrimination. See below.

2. Means The plaintiff will be required to give an undertaking as to damages and should provide evidence (which must also be full and frank) about his means to satisfy any order made against him. The plaintiff may be required to pay money into court or to his solicitor, to be held by the solicitor as an officer of the court pending further order, or to provide a bond by an insurance company (see the Practice Direction [1994] 4 All E.R. 52 para. (3)(A)2 (see above), and one of these forms of security is likely to be required of a plaintiff from out of the jurisdiction who does not have assets within the jurisdiction.

3. Supervising solicitor There must be evidence of the identity and experience of the proposed supervising solicitor and his/her familiarity with the operation of *Anton Piller* orders, either from that solicitor or, if it is not practicable to have an affidavit sworn by that solicitor (or at least a draft affidavit) in time for the hearing, there should at least be affidavit evidence from someone who can testify from his own knowledge as to experience of the proposed supervising solicitor and his/her familiarity with the operation of *Anton Piller* orders. If for any reason the judge will be asked not to provide that the order be served by an independent supervising solicitor there should be evidence to justify the request (which may not, of course, be granted).

3 Form of the order

1. Standard form The standard form is clear and self-explanatory.

2. Order served—independent supervising solicitor? If the judge orders that the order need not be served by an independent supervising solicitor, his reasons for doing so should be expressed in the order and the solicitors and counsel for the plaintiff owe a duty to the court to bring this to his attention if the judge overlooks it.

3. Privilege against self-incrimination It used to be thought that an *Anton Piller* order could not be made if the complaint against the defendant included a conspiracy allegation. In *Tate Access Floors Inc. v. Boswell* [1991] Ch. 512 at 532 Sir Nicholas Browne-Wilkinson V.-C. said:

> "But if, as is likely to be too often the case, there is a real risk of a conspiracy charge, the judge will not be able to make an *Anton Piller* order at all and in consequence vital evidence will be destroyed."

However, in *IBM United Kingdom Ltd v. Prima Data International Ltd* [1994] 1 W.L.R. 719, Warner J. made an order, and Sir Mervyn Davies refused to set aside the material part, in which a proviso was included in the following terms:

> "[B]efore any persons enter [address] pursuant to this order the supervising solicitor shall offer to explain to the second defendant the meaning and effect of this order in everyday language and shall also advise the second defendant of his right to obtain legal advice for permitting entry provided such advice is obtained at once (such advice to include an explanation that the second defendant may be entitled to avail himself of the privilege against self-incrimination); and so that the provisions of paragraphs (1), (2), (3) and (4) of the order shall have effect only in so far as such privilege is not claimed by the second defendant."

Sir Mervyn Davies said:

> My conclusion from the foregoing is that an *Anton Piller* order may properly be made in the terms of paragraph (1) with its provisos. The order may be served but may not be executed until (a) the defendant is told of his privilege right and (b) the defendant then expressly

declines to claim that right. In short, the order means that the supervising solicitor must say to the defendant, "I have a search order but I cannot execute it if you tell that the search may result in disclosing matters showing that you have been involved in a conspiracy." It seems to me that the form of order adequately protects the defendant's privilege while at the same time allowing search if privilege is not claimed. Of course that is not the end of the story. Defendants are bemused by the appearance of solicitors bearing 13 page orders in legal language. A supervising solicitor must ensure that the defendant properly understands his rights as preserved by the order, *i.e.* that there will be no entry if the defendant claims privilege and the meaning of privilege must be explained. Everyday language must be used—see proviso (i)."

In "intellectual property" cases (which are cases to which *Anton Piller* orders are particularly appropriate), the privilege against incrimination of a person or his or her spouse has been partly removed by statute, the Supreme Court Act 1981 s.72, with a corresponding restriction upon the right to use statements and admissions in criminal proceedings (see s.72(3) and (4) sub sections 72(1), (2) and (5) provide:

"(1) In any proceedings to which this subsection applies a person shall not be excused, by reason that to do so would tend to expose that person, or his or her spouse, to proceedings for a related offence for the recovery of a related penalty
    (a) from answering any question put to that person in the first-mentioned proceedings; or
    (b) from complying with any order made in those proceedings.
(2) Subsection (1) applies to the following civil proceedings in the High Court, namely—
    (a) proceedings for infringement of rights pertaining to any intellectual property or for passing off;
    (b) proceedings brought to obtain disclosure of information relating to an infringement of such rights or to any passing off; and
    (c) proceedings brought to prevent any apprehended infringement of such rights or any apprehended passing off.
(5) In this section "intellectual property" means any patent, trade mark, copyright, registered design, technical or commercial information or other intellectual property."

The definitions of "related offence" and "related penalty" mean that only. the privilege against incrimination of "intellectual property" offences has been removed. (In *Universal City Studios Inc. v. Hubbard* [1984] Ch. 225, a copyright case, the manufacture of pornographic films came to light.)

286

4. Penal notice By R.S.C., Ord. 45, r.7(4),

"There must be prominently displayed on the front of the copy of an order served under this rule a warning to the person on whom the copy is served that disobedience to the order would be a contempt of court punishable by imprisonment, or (in the case of an order requiring a body corporate to do or abstain from doing an act) punishable by sequestration of the assets of the body corporate and by imprisonment of any individual responsible."

In order to be able to take enforcement proceedings against a director or officer of a corporate body he must be served with a copy of the order. The penal notice would read "If A.B. Plc/Ltd neglect to obey this order you X.Y.Z a director (or officer) may be held to be in contempt of Court and liable to imprisonment."

4 Execution of the order

The order will be in the standard form (see the Practice Direction [1994] 4 All E.R. 52 Annex 1) or based on that form with any necessary variations. The directions as to when and how it is to be served must be followed scrupulously.

5 Appeal

Under R.S.C., Ord. 59, r.14(3) when an *ex parte* application has been refused by the Court below, an application for a similar purpose may be made to the Court of Appeal *ex parte* within seven days after the date of the refusal.

The hearing will normally be in open court but may be *in camera*: see Practice Note (Court of Appeal: *Anton Piller* Orders) [1982] 1 W.L.R. 1420.

E: SEARCH AT PREMISES OUT OF JURISDICTION

In *Altertext Inc. v. Advanced Data Communications Ltd and Others* [1985] 1 W.L.R. 457 there were six defendants, of which the sixth was a company incorporated in Belgium which had no business premises in England. The plaintiff sought an *Anton Piller* order against all of them. Scott J. said that because an *Anton Piller* order is an *in personam* order it can only be made against a person within the jurisdiction of the court, *i.e.* someone who can be served within the jurisdiction, someone who submits to the jurisdiction or someone over whom the court assumes jurisdiction by permitting service out of the jurisdiction. At. 462G–H he said:

> "If the order is sought *ex parte* before service of the writ and against a foreign defendant in respect of foreign premises, an essential requirement must be that the case is one in which leave under Order 11 for service out of the jurisdiction ought to be given. Otherwise the court has no jurisdiction over that defendant. But since the initial application is *ex parte* and since the foreign defendant may seek to have the leave under Order 11 set aside, the assumption by the court of jurisdiction is, in a sense, provisional only. In my view, where an *Anton Piller* order against a foreign defendant has to be accompanied by leave under Order 11 for service abroad, the *Anton Piller* order ought not to be executed until the foreign defendant has been given the opportunity to apply to set aside the Order 11 leave.

In that case the Belgian company was controlled by two of the other defendants who lived and carried on business in England. Scott J. refused to make an order against them requiring them to permit entry to the premises of the Belgian company. He seems to have concluded that he had jurisdiction to do so but based his refusal on discretion. "I can see the attraction of that approach but it cannot be right for me to do indirectly what I do not think it right to do directly, and I therefore decline to follow it."

A detailed exposition of the Civil Jurisdiction and Judgments Act 1982 (which was not in force at the time of *Altertext Inc. v. Advanced Data Communications Ltd and Others*) is outside the scope of this work. Note, however, that by virtue of that Act, as amended by the Civil Jurisdiction and Judgments Act 1991, there are many cases in which it is possible to serve writs and other process out of the jurisdiction without leave.

In *Cook Industries Incorporated v. Galliher* [1979] 1 Ch. 439 the plaintiff was the assignee of judgments of courts in the USA against a Mr Sarlie, the second defendant. The first defendant, Mr Gilliher, acquired a flat in Paris. The plaintiff alleged that he had acquired it on behalf of Mr Sarlie and that it contained pictures and works of art which Mr Sarlie had acquired with the proceeds of his frauds upon the assignor and brought from the USA or which he had purchased with the proceeds of sale of such assets. The plaintiff issued a writ and on the same day obtained *ex parte* a *Mareva* injunction restraining the first defendant from disposing of or removing any of the contents of the flat. The first defendant was served in England with the writ, the injunction and notice of motion seeking orders that he should disclose the contents of the flat on affidavit and allow inspection of the flat by a named French advocate (who was also a member of the English bar). Thus, unusually, the application for an order requiring the first defendant to permit access to his flat was heard *inter partes* and the first defendant was represented by counsel. Templeman J. held that he had jurisdiction to make the order and as a matter of discretion made it.

F: SEARCH OF PREMISES IN ENGLAND AND WALES BY WAY OF INTERIM RELIEF IN THE ABSENCE OF SUBSTANTIVE PROCEEDINGS

Practitioners may be asked by lawyers outside England and Wales to apply for an *Anton Piller* order in England or may want an *Anton Piller* order in England for purposes connected with litigation outside of England and Wales. Under section 25 of the Civil Jurisdiction and Judgments Act 1982:

> "(1) The High Court in England and Wales or Northern Ireland shall have power to grant interim relief where
>
> (a) proceedings have been or are to be commenced in a Contracting State other than the United Kingdom or in a part of the United Kingdom other that that in which the High Court in which the High Court in question exercises jurisdiction; and
>
> (b) they are or will be proceedings whose subject-matter is within the scope of the 1968 Convention as determined by Article 1 (whether or not the Convention has effect in relation to the proceedings).
>
> (2) On an application for any interim relief under subsection (1) the court may refuse to grant that relief if, in the opinion of the court, the fact that the court has no jurisdiction apart from this section in relation to the subject-matter of the proceedings in question makes it inexpedient for the court to grant it.
>
> (7) In this section "interim relief", in relation to the High Court in England and Wales or Northern Ireland, means interim relief of any kind which that court has power to grant in proceedings relating to matters within its own jurisdiction, other than—
>
> (a) a warrant for the arrest of property; or
>
> (b) provision for obtaining evidence."

The 1982 Act is extended by the Civil Jurisdiction and Judgments Act 1991.

Subsection (7)(b) renders section 25 of limited use in the context of *Anton Piller* orders, though such orders may be made in connection with the enforcement of judgments, as opposed to obtaining evidence: see *Cook Industries Incorporated v. Galliher* [1979] 1 Ch. 439, at p. 288 above.

G: DISCHARGE AND VARIATION

1 *Ex parte* application to discharge or vary

An application to discharge or vary an *Anton Piller* order made *ex parte* should be made to the court which made it, not by way of appeal to the Court of Appeal. In *WEA Records Ltd v. Visions Channel 4 Ltd* [1983] 1 W.L.R. 721 at 727B–C and F, Sir John Donaldson

> "... it is difficult, if not impossible, to think of circumstances in which it would be proper to appeal to this court against an *ex parte* order without first giving the judge who made it or, if he was not available, another High Court Judge an opportunity of reviewing it in the light of argument from the defendant and reaching a decision. This is the appropriate procedure even when an order is not provisional, but is made at the trial in the absence of one party: see R.S.C., Ord. 35, r.2(1), and *Vint v. Hudspith* (1889) 29 Ch. 322 to which Mr Tager very helpfully referred us this morning.
>
> ... In terms of jurisdiction, there can be no doubt that this court can hear an appeal from an order made by a High Court Judge upon an *ex parte* application. This jurisdiction is conferred by section 16(1) of the Supreme Court Act 1981. Equally there is no doubt that the High Court has power to review and to discharge or vary any order which has been made *ex parte*. This jurisdiction is inherent in the provisional nature of any order made *ex parte* and is reflected in R.S.C., Ord. 32, r.6."

An appeal may be made to the Court of Appeal against the refusal of the judge at first instance to discharge or vary.

2 Application to discharge or vary before the order is executed

The standard form prescribed by the Practice Direction [1994] 4 All E.R. 52 provides:

> "Before permitting entry to the premises by any person other than the Supervising Officer and the plaintiff's solicitors, the defendant or other person appearing to be in control of the premises may seek legal advice, and apply to the Court to vary or discharge this order, provided that he does so at once. While this is being done, he may refuse entry to the premises by any other person, and may refuse to permit the search to begin, for a short time (Not to exceed two hours, unless the supervising solicitor agrees to a longer period.)"

This provision is drawn to the attention of the defendant by wording under the heading "IMPORTANT: NOTICE TO THE DEFENDANT", which is part of the standard form but which precedes the order itself. The provision therefore clearly envisages that an application to vary or discharge may be made before the search is carried out. It is suggested that it will seldom be possible in practice to produce at very short notice evidence which is uncontroversial and which would justify an immediate discharge (an indisputable conviction of the plaintiff for a serious offence of fraud which was not disclosed?) and that the better course would be to apply for a variation whereby for a short time the search is suspended on terms which will protect the plaintiff in the meanwhile, such as the supervising solicitor (and perhaps other suitable people in rotation) remain on the premises to prevent removal or destruction of documents and other material so that the defendant can make an effective application for discharge or variation on the basis of all relevant evidence in affidavit form.

3 Applications to discharge or vary after order executed

The tenor of the judgments of the Court of Appeal in *Booker McConnell plc v. Plascow* [1985] R.P.C. 425 is that an application to discharge a "basic" *Anton Piller* order (the mandatory order to allow a search) should be dealt with at trial, when any conflicts of fact in the affidavits can be resolved after cross-examination, and that any negative injunctions granted *ex parte* at the same time and incorporated in the order will be for a limited period until the return date, when the plaintiff may apply for them to be continued and the defendant can oppose such an application.

That case must now be read in the light of the provisions of the Practice Direction [1994] 4 All E.R. 52:

> "(3)(A)3 So far as practicable, any application for the discharge or variation of the order should be dealt with effectively on the return date.
>
> (4) If an *Anton Piller* order or Mareva injunction is discharged on the return date, the judge should also consider whether it is appropriate that he should assess damages at once and direct immediate payment by the applicant."

These provisions give effect to the judicial disquiet described at p. 288 above and to a recommendation of the Staughton Committee. If documents are removed only for a short time to be copied, and no other goods are removed, the execution of an *Anton Piller* order will often occasion little or no financial loss which needs to be scheduled by the defendant, checked by the plaintiff and proved by the defendant unless admitted. In *Columbia Pictures Industries Inc. v. Robinson* [1987] Ch. 38 at 87C–F Scott J.

suggested, *obiter*, that aggravated or exemplary damages could be awarded. Whether that is so, particularly in the light of the wording of the plaintiff's undertaking as to damages, remains to be decided. It is worth remembering that the evil which the *Anton Piller* order was originally designed to combat was copyright piracy; that in such cases the plaintiff may well be a foreign corporation; that a foreign corporation which seeks an *Anton Piller* order may well be required to provide (and, necessarily, at short notice) an insurance company bond to secure its undertaking as to damages; that foreign corporations might find it difficult to obtain such a bond if there was a risk of an award of aggravated or exemplary damages; and therefore that the salutary punishment of those who misuse the *Anton Piller* remedy might operate to the detriment of other innocent plaintiffs.

H: INTERIM PRESERVATION ORDERS

1 Scope

1. R.S.C., Order 29, rule 2(1) It provides:

> "2.—(1) On the application of any party to a cause or matter the Court may make an order for the detention, custody, or preservation of any property which is the subject-matter of the cause or matter, or as to which any question may arise therein, or for the inspection of any such property in the possession of a party to the cause or matter."

2. When? This protective measure extends to every case in which the courts sees that as between the parties something ought to be done for the security of the property in question: *Chaplain v. Barnett* (1912) 28 T.L.R. 256. So, for example, in an action for the recovery of jewellery which the plaintiffs alleged belonged to them and which was in the defendant's possession, the court made an order that the jewellery should be delivered up to an officer of the court to abide the event of the action: *Velati & Co. v. Braham & Co.* (1987) 46 L.J.P.C. 415.

3. Who may apply? Although the rule says that "any party" may apply, that expression really means "any opposite party": Shaw v. Smith (1886) 18 Q.B.D. 193. Thus, a plaintiff may seek an order against a defendant and vice versa, but:
  (a) defendants cannot generally seek an order against each other, and
  (b) neither can plaintiffs seek an order against one another,
unless they can demonstrate that there are rights which have to be adjusted between them in the action and where an order may be material in the determination of that adjustment.

4. Against whom? The court will not make an interim preservation order against a party unless it is shown that he has the thing in his possession or under his control: *Wilder v. Wilder* (1912) 56 S.J. 571. It would be unjust to make such an order under which a party may be committed for contempt for failure to hand over the property when he has neither got it nor got control over it.

5. What is "property"? The only property which can be made the subject of the order under Ord. 29 is property which is either the subject-matter of the action or as to which a question may arise in the action. The property normally sought to be protected or inspected is the physical subject-matter of the action such as a car of jewellery. It only covers tangibles. The definition does not extend to the inspection of a manufacturing or packaging process: *Tudor Accumulator Co. Ltd v. China Mutual Co.* [1930] W.N. 201. Machinery used to carry out the process is "property" within the rule: *Unilever plc v. Pearce* [1985] F.S.R. 475.

6. Money "Property" extends to money—that is a specific fund which is in dispute in the action: Ord. 29, r.2. The court has the power to order the fund to be paid into court or otherwise secured—as, for instance, by the payment into an account in the joint names of the parties' solicitors pending trial.

7. Documents "Property" has also been held to extend to documents. Thus in *Re Saxton, (dec'd)* [1962] 1 W.L.R. 859, the plaintiffs claimed to be entitled to the whole of the deceased's estate which was being administered by the defendants. The plaintiffs alleged that certain assets belonging to the deceased had been excluded by the defendants from the administration. The defendants contended that by a written agreement the deceased had given the assets during his lifetime to the second defendants and that consequently those assets did not form part of the deceased's estate. The plaintiffs challenged the authenticity of the agreement. Clearly, although the agreement was not the subject-matter of the action, it was "property" as to which a question may arise. Wilberforce J. held that the rule was sufficiently widely drawn to authorise him to make an order for the delivery up of the written agreement to an expert for inspection so that he could give evidence upon it.

8. Medium or message? Whether documents can be "property" fell to be considered by Hoffmann J. in *Huddleston v. Control Risks Information Services Ltd* [1987] 1 W.L.R. 701, in the context of an application under the Supreme Court Act 1981, s.33(1) and (2) and Ord. 29, r.7A (pre-action inspection of property and discovery of documents). He concluded (at 703F–H):

"It seems to me that a written instrument or any other object carrying information such as a photograph, tape recording or computer disc can be both 'property' for the purposes of section 33(1) of the Act and a 'document' for the purposes of section 33(2). Whether for the purposes of a particular case it is one or the other depends on the nature of the question which it is said may arise. In my judgment Parliament intended, whatever Marshall McLuhan might have said, to distinguish between the medium and the message. If the question will be concerned with the medium, the actual physical object which carries the information, the application is to inspect 'property' within section 33(1). If the question will be concerned with the message, the information which the object conveys, the application is for discovery . . ."

On this basis in the context of an application for a preservation order, if the importance of a document were attributable to its message, it would not be classified as "property" and would thus be outside the scope of the rule.

2 "Subject-matter of the cause or matter"

1. The "police" cases In *West Mercia Constabulary v. Wagener* [1982] 1 W.L.R. 127, the first defendant was arrested in connection with an alleged fraud. The second defendant had a bank account containing sums believed to be the proceeds of the alleged crimes. The police applied by originating summons for an injunction restraining the second defendant from making withdrawals from the account. Forbes J. held that since magistrates were not empowered to issue a warrant in respect of moneys in a bank account, the High Court could fill that gap by using its powers under Ord. 29, r.2(1) because the police had a common law right to seize and preserve property which is the subject of crime for the purpose of preserving material evidence and enabling the proceeds to be returned to their rightful owner.

2. The principle for which *West Mercia* is authority The High Court has power on the application of the police to grant an injunction under Ord. 29, r.2(1) to preserve the proceeds of the alleged crime. The police have the power to seize goods reasonably believed to have been stolen without the need to obtain an order in civil proceedings: *Chic Fashions (West Wales) Ltd v. Jones* [1968] 2 Q.B. 299.

3. Order 29 and section 37 of the Supreme Court Act 1981 In *Chief Constable of Kent v. V* [1983] 1 Q.B. 34, V had been arrested and charged with a number of offences the proceeds of which were believed to have

294

been paid into certain bank accounts. In order to prevent removal of those moneys the plaintiff sought interlocutory injunctions, restraining V and the bank from dealing with the moneys. The Court of Appeal held that it had jurisdiction to grant the injunctions, and that it would do so in the circumstances, on the basis that a Chief Constable is under a duty to recover, if possible, stolen goods and that gives him the interest required for an injunction under section 37 of the Act of 1981.

4. The principle for which the *Kent* **case is authority** An applicant for an injunction, which the court has a power to grant wherever just and convenient, must show a right or an interest, whether legal or equitable, which requires the making of an injunction and the enforcement or protection it provides. A Chief Constable who believes on reasonable grounds that a sum of money in a bank account represents the fruits of crime does have such an interest. But, of course, the court will not exercise that jurisdiction if the proceeds of the crime cannot be identified or are incapable of separation from legitimate funds: *Chief Constable of Hampshire v. A Ltd* [1985] Q.B. 132; and see *Malone v. Metropolitan Police Commissioner* [1980] 1 Q.B. 49. Nor will the court grant the police an injunction restraining a defendant from dealing with profits made from the sale of property obtained by dishonest means: *Chief Constable of Leicestershire v. M* [1988] 3 All E.R. 1015; but see now Drug Trafficking Offences Act 1986 and Criminal Justice Acts 1988 and 1993 and the Criminal Justice (International Co-operation) Act 1990 for powers of court to restrain dispositions of assets suspected of being derived from dealing in indictable offences.

3 "... as to which any question may arise therein..."

1. The nexus between the property and the cause or matter Assuming that the property does not form the subject-matter of the action, an interim preservation order may still be made under Ord. 29, r.2 if it can be demonstrated that a question may arise about it in the action. But the property must have more than a vague and tenuous connection with the action.

2. Example *Scott v. Mercantile Accident Insurance Co.* (1892) 8 T.I.R. 320. A jeweller sued his insurers when they refused to pay out under an insurance policy following an alleged burglary at the jeweller's shop. The insurers argued that there had been no burglary. Some time later a parcel containing some of the jewellery was found and handed to the police. The plaintiff asked the Chief Constable to return it to him, as no one disputed that the jewellery belong to him. The defendant sought an order preserving it until trial. Cave J. described the defendant's application as absurd:

"It is admitted that the property is not the subject-matter of the action; but that only a question may arise about it in the cause or matter ... The defendants have got all they are entitled to as they have a description and valuation of the goods which has been admitted."

The application was refused.

4 Usual orders and conditions

1. Jurisdiction Under Ord. 29, r.2(4) the court may attach conditions to the making of an interim order. For example, in the *Saxton* case, (see p. 293) Wilberforce J., *inter alia*, held that the court could authorise the carrying out of modern scientific tests on the document in order to determine its authenticity.

2. Safe custody—etc. The order may lay down conditions for the safe custody of the property. So, for example, a motor car, the subject-matter of the action, may be ordered to be held in storage at some specified commercial garage (subject of course to the consent of the garage) on terms that the applicant for the order should be responsible pending trial for insuring it in a specified sum with a reputable insurer against loss or damage by specified risks.

3. Valuables and documents The usual form of order provides for valuables or documents to be:
  (a) deposited with the solicitor for one of the parties to be held in safe custody to the court's order pending trial for further order; or
  (b) alternatively, that they be deposited with a specified bank.
It is not usual to order valuables or documents to be lodged in court pending trial.

4. Bulky items These may be ordered to be kept at some suitable repository, although it is as well for the applicant to ascertain beforehand the trade conditions on which the repository is willing to accept them. If no satisfactory arrangements for the safe keeping of the property can be laid before the court by the applicant's solicitor, consideration should be given to an application for the appointment of an interim receiver to take care of them pending trial. The court will generally be most reluctant to order the property to be kept by the plaintiff himself by way of interim preservation.

5 Practice and procedure

1. Time for application The plaintiff may apply for an interim preservation order under Ord. 29, r.2 as soon as he issues the proceedings. If he has no time to issue before making an application, he should consider making an *ex parte* application under Ord. 29, r.2A if the claim is for wrongful interference with goods (see below) or for an *ex parte* injunction. The defendant may only apply for an interim preservation order once he has acknowledged service, unless the court otherwise directs.

2. Mode of application There are two ways of making the application for an interim preservation order:
- (a) By summons supported by affidavit returnable either in the Queen's Bench or Chancery Divisions before the master or district judge.
- (b) If the application also includes injunctive relief under Ord. 29, r.1, the summons must go before the judge since the master or district judge has no power to grant an injunction: Ord. 32, r.11(1)(d), except by consent; Ord. 32, r.11(2).

3. The hearing On the hearing the court has power to give directions as to the further proceedings of the action; Ord. 29, r.7—even before the summons for directions in most writ actions.

I: INTERIM DELIVERY OF GOODS

1 Jurisdiction

1. The Act of 1977
Section 4(2) of the Torts (Interference with Goods) Act 1977 enables the High Court on an application of any person in accordance with the rules of the court to make an interlocutory order providing for the delivery up of any goods:

> "... which are or may become the subject-matter of subsequent proceedings in the court or as to which question may arise in the proceedings."

2. The R.S.C. controls Ord. 29, r.2A narrows the scope of the statute by limiting any such application to proceedings which have been commenced rather than to proposed proceedings: Ord. 29, r.2A says:

> "**2A.**—(1) Without prejudice to rule 2, the court may, on the application of any party to a cause or matter, make an order under

297

section 4 of the Tort (Interference with Goods) Act 1977 for the delivery up of any goods which are the subject-matter of the cause or matter or as to which any question may arise therein.

(2) Paragraphs (2) and (3) or rule 1 shall have effect in relation to an application for such an order as they have effect in relation to an application for the grant of an injunction."

3. County court C.C.R., Ord. 13, r.7(1)(d) adopts all the provisions of the R.S.C. in proceedings for wrongful interference in the county court.

4. The condition precedent—proceedings for wrongful interference The protective remedy of interim delivery is only available in proceedings for wrongful interference with goods. This means actions for:
  (a) conversion of goods;
  (b) trespass to goods;
  (c) negligence insofar as the negligence results in damage to goods or to an interest in goods;
  (d) any other tort insofar as that tort results in damage to goods or to an interest in goods.

5. Goods—meaning The goods targeted for protection must form the subject-matter of the action. "Goods" includes all chattels personal other than things in action and money: Torts (Interference with Goods) Act 1977, s.14(1). So, the remedy is not available in copyright actions as such, although infringing copies of works subject to copyright may be the subject of an action for wrongful interference.

6. Delivery up The power to order delivery up of goods is wide enough to cover an order requiring a defendant to allow the plaintiff to collect for himself goods which the defendant is unwilling or unable to deliver to him in the sense of collecting and transporting them. The expression includes the process of merely transferring authority over something *in situ*: *Howard Perry & Co. Ltd v. British Railways Board* [1980] 1 W.L.R. 1375.

7. Practice Application is by summons to the master or district judge. Where the applicant is the plaintiff and the case is one of urgency, the application may be made *ex parte* on affidavit: Ord. 29, r.2A and Ord. 29, r.1(2). In urgent cases, application may be made before the commencement of the action on terms as to the issue of proceedings and any other relevant terms: Ord. 29, r.2A(2) and Ord. 29, r.1(3) and *Re N* [1967] Ch. 512.

8. A discretionary remedy The court has a discretion—to be exercised on well-established principles—whether to make an interlocutory order for delivery up of the goods (see Robert Megarry V.-C. in the *Howard Perry* case [1980] 1 W.L.R. 1375 at 1382). The discretion will normally be refused in the case of goods which are ordinary articles of commerce with no special value or interest if damages will fully compensate the plaintiff: *Whitely v. Hilt* [1918] 2 K.B. 808; *General and Finance Facilities Ltd v. Cooks Cars (Romford) Ltd* [1963] 1 W.L.R. 644.

9. Effectively—supersedes *replevin* *Replevin* is a summary process exclusive to the county court under which, prior to commencing any proceedings, a person who alleges that he has been wrongfully deprived of possession of his goods can go to the district judge for an order for *replevin* which, subject to him giving satisfactory security, entitles him to the immediate return of the goods pending trial of the subsequent action to determine the respective rights of the parties. However, C.C.R. 1981 does not prescribe any forms or procedure, presumably because it was anticipated that the power to make interlocutory orders for delivery of the goods (without security) under the Act of 1977 would supersede this remedy.

CHAPTER 4

Order 14: Summary Judgment

A: INTRODUCTION

1 Origins

1. The incentive to delay In times of relatively high interest rates and economic depression, there may be a strong incentive to a defendant who has cash-flow problems to keep his creditor waiting rather than borrow money to pay off the debt at a commercial rate of interest from a bank or finance house. So it was in the middle of the last century.

2. The problem which precipitated change A defendant trader would take delivery of goods and then dishonour the cheque or other bill of exchange on some spurious pretext that the goods were faulty. In general, there is no defence to a dishonoured cheque: *Fielding & Platt Ltd v. Selim Najjar* [1969] 1 W.L.R. 357. Nevertheless, the mid-nineteenth century plaintiff was driven to prosecute his action against the defendant to trial. Shortly before the case was called the defendant would offer to settle. He had achieved his objective—an interest-free period of credit.

3. "Keating's Act" There was an outcry in the City of London and this resulted in the Summary Procedure on Bills of Exchange Act 1955 (popularly known as "Keating's Act"). Under the Act, the defendant was only allowed to defend the action if he either paid the money allegedly due into court or set up his proposed defence in an affidavit.

4. Summary procedure—extended The popularity and success of Keating's Act was such that its scope was successively extended in 1873, 1883, 1937 and 1964 by which time it covered all actions (with certain exceptions which we shall discuss below) begun in the Queen's Bench Division or Chancery Division by writ. This summary procedure, regulated by R.S.C., Ord. 14, was extended not only to part of a claim as well as a whole claim but also to a defendant's counterclaim.

5. How does it work? Trial, as a rule, must precede judgment. Ord. 14

provides an extraordinary procedure in certain cases. It is a procedure in which, instead of trial first and then judgment, there is judgment at once and never a trial: *Symon & Co. v. Palmer's Stores (1903) Ltd* [1912] 1 K.B. 259, *per* Buckley L.J. at 266. The policy of Ord. 14 is to prevent delay in cases where there is no defence. So, where the plaintiff can satisfy the court that he has a clear case against the defendant which the defendant cannot answer, the court should give the plaintiff judgment forthwith without the expense and delay which would otherwise be involved in letting the case go on to trial in the ordinary way.

6. It should not be overworked In *Jacobs v. Booth's Distillery Co.* (1901) 85 L.T. 262, H.L., Lord Halsbury L.C. gave a defendant leave to defend an action brought on two promissory notes. The case for the defendant was that he had been told that he would incur no liability by signing. Right up to the House of Lords the defendant had summary judgment recorded against him. Lord Halsbury said:

> "I am somewhat surprised at the decision which has been arrived at by tribunals before whom this question has come. I think that if this is an example of the mode in which Ord. 14 is administered, it would be desirable for the legislature to consider whether that Order should continue to be put in force. People do not seem to understand that the effect of Ord. 14 is that, upon the allegation of the one side or the other, a man is not permitted to defend himself in court; that his rights are not to be litigated at all. There are some things too plain for argument; and where there were pleas put in simply for the purpose of delay, which only added to the expense, and where it was not in aid of justice that such things should continue, Ord. 14 was intended to put an end to that state of things, and to prevent sham defences from defeating the rights of parties by delay and at the same time causing great loss to the plaintiffs who are endeavouring to enforce their rights. But when in such a case as this, Ord. 14 is applied, there are a great many things to be said. I do not propose to enter into the merits of the case or the comprehension of it, which is necessary to some extent in order to deal with the merits. That question would have to be dealt with when the case is tried. But I am bound to say that it startles me to think that in a case of this sort an order should be made, the effect of which is that the defendant is not to be heard to make his defence."

7. A modern restatement Recently the Court of Appeal has sounded a warning reminiscent of the views expressed by Lord Halsbury in *Jacobs*. Bingham L.J. said in *Crown House Engineering v. Amec Projects Ltd* (1990) 6 Const.L.J. 141 at 154:

"The high cost of litigation, and the premium on holding cash when interest rates are high, greatly increase the attractiveness to commercial plaintiffs of procedural shortcuts such as are provided by Ord. 14 and Ord. 29, r.12. A technical knock-out in the first round is much more advantageous than a win on points after 15. So plaintiffs are understandably tempted to seek summary judgment or interim payment in cases for which these procedures were never intended. This is a tendency which the courts have found it necessary to discourage: *Home and Overseas Insurance Company Ltd v. Mentor Insurance Company (UK) Ltd* [1989] 3 All E.R. 74; *British and Commonwealth Holdings plc v. Quadrex Holdings Incorporated* [1989] Q.B. 842.

These cases emphasise that Ord. 14 is for clear cases, that is, cases in which there is no serious material factual dispute and, if a legal issue, then no more than a crisp legal question as well decided summarily as otherwise. Ord. 29, r.12 enables the court to order payment to a plaintiff to the extent that a claim, although not actually admitted, can scarcely be effectively denied. The procedure is entirely inappropriate where the plaintiff's entitlement to recover any sum is the subject of any serious dispute, whether of law or fact. This is not to say in either case that a defendant with no or no more than a partial defence can cheat a plaintiff of his just deserts by producing hefty affidavits and voluminous exhibits to create an illusion of complexity where none exists. Where the point at issue is at heart a short one the court will recognise the fact and act accordingly no matter how bulky its outer garments. But it does mean that where there are substantial issues of genuine complexity the parties should prepare for trial (perhaps, as here, with trial of preliminary issues) rather than dissipate their energy and resources on deceptively attractive short-cuts."

See also *Banque de Paris et des Pays-Bas (Suisse) S.A. v. Costa de Naray* [1984] 1 Lloyd's Rep. 21, C.A.; *National Westminster Bank plc v. Daniel* [1994] 1 All E.R. 156; *Bhogal v. Punjab National Bank* [1988] 2 All E.R. 296 at 303, *Balli Trading v. Afalone Shipping, "The Coral"* [1993] 1 Lloyd's Rep 1, C.A.

2 Present scope

1. The rule Ord. 14, r.1:
"(1) Where in an action to which this rule applies a statement of claim has been served on a defendant and that defendant has given notice of intention to defend the action, the plaintiff may, on the ground that that defendant has no defence to a claim included in the writ,

or to the particular part of such a claim, or has no defence to such a claim or part except as to the amount of any damages claimed, apply to the court for judgment against that defendant.

(2) Subject to paragraph (3), this rule applies to every action begun by writ in the Queen's Bench Division (including the Admiralty Court) or the Chancery Division other than:

    (a) an action which includes a claim by the plaintiff for libel, slander, malicious prosecution or false imprisonment;

    (b) [Revoked], or

    (c) Admiralty action *in rem*.

(3) This order shall not apply to any claims to which Ord. 86 applies."

2. Examples The extent of the ambit of Ord. 14 today can best be illustrated by listing some examples:

    (a) Goods supplied; work done; services rendered (see p. 310).

    (b) Bills of exchange (see p. 313).

    (c) Negligence (see p. 325).

    (d) Specific performance outside Ord. 86 (see p. 321).

    (e) Injunctions (see p. 322).

    (f) Letters of credit; performance bonds; guarantees (see p. 326).

    (g) Possession of land (see p. 330).

3. Actions involving trial by jury It will be seen that the exceptions contained in Ord. 14, r.1(2)(a) are those actions which by virtue of section 69 of the Supreme Court Act 1981 give rise to a right to trial by judge and jury.

4. Counterclaiming a "jury" cause of action What if the defendant counterclaims for libel, slander, malicious prosecution or false imprisonment? The wording of Ord. 14, r.1(2)(a) refers to "a claim by the plaintiff." In *Rotherham v. Priest* (1879) 28 W.R. 277 the plaintiff was allowed to enter summary judgment under Ord. 14 in an action for rent but it was held that the defendant could not set up a counterclaim for damages for libel not connected with the subject-matter of the action.

5. Personal representatives Order 14 proceedings may be brought against personal representatives in respect of a claim against the estate of the deceased, but if the administration has already been completed, the most that the plaintiff can expect to get is a *Millar v. Keane* ((1889) 24 L.R.Ir. 49) order whereby he should be at liberty to sign final judgment against the personal representatives for the sum claimed with costs, to be levied off the estate and effects of the deceased which shall thereafter come into the personal representatives' hands to be administered and a further order that the plaintiff should pay the personal representatives' costs of the action.

6. Commercial Court Ord. 14 applies to a Queen's Bench action in the Commercial List begun by writ just as to other actions in that division. In London, the application is heard by the judge (Ord. 72, r.2). In the provinces, it is made in the first place to the district judge who may deal with it himself or refer it to the judge (Ord. 72, r.3). Although the Commercial List comprises a list of actions arising out of the ordinary transactions of merchants and traders, it was never intended to embrace the usual debt case. But in proceedings relating to the construction of mercantile documents, international trade, banking, insurance or mercantile customs, Ord. 14 proceedings are relevant despite the inherent complexities. (See the revised guide to Commercial Court Practice of March 9, 1990.)

7. "Commercial action"—restrictive definition In the past, when the Commercial Court was not as busy as now, the practice was to interpret the definition of "commercial action" widely. Now that the volume of work in the Commercial Court has increased the modern tendency is for the judges to interpret it restrictively: see *Zakhem International Construction Ltd v. Nippon Kokkan K. K. (No. 2)* [1987] 2 Lloyd's Rep. 661. In a Practice Statement of 10 December, 1993 ([1994] 1 W.L.R. 14; [1994] 1 All E.R. 34), Cresswell J., whilst emphasising the primary role of the Commercial Court as a forum for deciding commercial cases, encouraged the use of alternative dispute resolution as a possible additional means of resolving disputes.

8. Mercantile list: Manchester and Liverpool On April 24, 1990 two new Queen's Bench Lists in the district registries of Manchester and Liverpool were created [see *Practice Note (Practice: Commercial Cases: Northern Circuit)* [1990] 1 All E.R. 528]. Its business is considerably wider than that of the Commercial Court since it covers actions relating to business and commercial transactions in a broad sense (*e.g.* sale of goods, hire purchase, agency, banking, carriage of goods, etc.). A designated circuit judge hears all interlocutory applications and tries the actions. Ord. 14 summonses are a common feature of this system. The primary purpose was to create a new and improved structure for the hearing of cases of a commercial or business character on the Northern Circuit. On June 29, 1992, the Lord Chief Justice issued a Practice Direction (Commercial Lists: Manchester and Liverpool) [1992] 1 W.L.R. 726; [1992] 3 All E.R. 375, the effect of which was to change the name of the lists from "Commercial Lists" to "Mercantile Lists" and the description of the judges in charge of them from "Circuit Commercial Judges" to "Mercantile Judges". The object was to avoid confusion with the Commercial List within the scope of Ord. 72.

9. Birmingham and Bristol Similar Mercantile Lists have now been created in Birmingham and Bristol: see Practice Direction (Mercantile List: Birmingham) [1993] 1 W.L.R. 1401; [1993] 4 All E.R. 381: and Practice Direction (Mercantile Court Bristol) [1993] 1 W.L.R. 1522; [1993] 4 All E.R. 1023.

10. The Crown The Crown may apply for summary judgment under Ord. 14 whether on its claim as a plaintiff or on its counterclaim as a defendant. Ord. 14 is not, however, available against the Crown (Ord. 77, r.7).

11. Partnerships and companies Ord. 14 applies also to claims against partnerships and limited companies: *Lysaght v. Clarke & Co.* [1891] 1 Q.B. 552; Ord. 81, r.3(1)(a); and *Muirhead v. Direct U.S. Cable Co. Ltd, The* (1879) 27 W.R. 708; *Shelford v. Louth & East Coast Railway Co.* (1879) 4 Ex.D. 317. And judgment may be given under Ord. 14 against a firm even if one of its partners is an infant: *Harris v. Beauchamp (No. 1)* [1893] 2 Q.B. 534.

12. Fraud Until 1992, the plaintiff was prohibited by Ord. 14, r.1(2)(b) from seeking summary judgment in action which included a claim by him based on the allegation of fraud. As from April 1, 1992 Ord. 14, r.1(2)(b) was revoked so that an application for summary judgment can now be made in an action in which the plaintiff alleges fraud. It is thus no longer necessary to consider the nature, extent or meaning of "fraud" in the context of Ord. 14.

3 Foreign judgments

1. The situation The plaintiff may have obtained a judgment abroad against the defendant which remains unsatisfied. If there is no convention between this country and the foreign country providing for the reciprocal enforcement of judgments it may be necessary for the plaintiff to bring an action against the defendant on the foreign judgment in the English courts.

2. Convention and non-Convention cases—a difference A difference of approach may be emerging in the way English courts treat the registration of Convention foreign judgments compared with the treatment of non-Convention foreign judgments. The principles applicable to the recognition of Convention foreign judgments are regulated by the Civil Jurisdiction and Judgments Acts 1982 and 1991, the Brussels, Lugano and other Conventions, all of which are outside the scope of this work. The principles—including those under Ord. 14—which regulate non-Convention foreign judgments are discussed below.

3. Conditions precedent to Order 14 The plaintiff can seek judgment under Ord. 14. English courts will uphold the foreign judgment so long as:
- (a) there is no suggestion that the foreign judgment was obtained by a fraud;
- (b) the foreign judgment is final and conclusive;
- (c) the foreign judgment was not contrary to English public policy;
- (d) the cause of action giving rise to the foreign judgment is known to English law.

4. Fraud—a conflict of principles In the last decade of the nineteenth century a conflict emerged between two principles of English law. The first was that a party to an action could impeach the judgment in it on the ground of fraud. Whether the judgment was English or foreign mattered not. The second was that when you brought an action on a foreign judgment you could not go into the merits which had been tried by the foreign court.

5. Fraud—the question posed The question was: how were the courts to apply these two conflicting rules in a case where you could not go into the alleged fraud without going into the merits? (*Per* Lindley L.J. in *Vadala v. Lawes* (1890) 25 Q.B.D. 310 at 316.)

6. Abouloff in *Abouloff v. Oppenheimer & Co.* (1880) 10 Q.B.D. 259 the plaintiff sued the defendant in Russian for non-delivery of goods. Having obtained judgment there, he sought to enforce it in England by bringing an action on it. The defendant alleged that the plaintiff had fraudulently misled the Russian Court into believing that he had not received the goods when, in fact, he had.

7. Abouloff—the conflict resolved Lindley L.J., in *Vadala v. Lawes* (above at 316) expressed the *ratio* in Abouloff in the following way:

> "I cannot read the judgments [in *Abouloff*] without seeing that they amount to this: that if fraud upon the foreign court consists in the fact that the plaintiff has induced that court by fraud to come to a wrong conclusion you can re-open the whole case even although you will in this court have to go into the very facts which were investigated and which were in issue in the foreign court."

8. Fraud—its effect A foreign judgment obtained by fraud is thus vitiated by the fraud: *Manger v. Cash* (1889) 5 T.L.R. 271.

9. Fraud—English and foreign judgments—a difference The resolution in this way of the conflict of these two principles was at odds with the principle of estoppel *per rem* judication which applied to English judgments where fraud was alleged. Although the law had long permitted the party against whom an *English* judgment had been given to bring an independent action to set the judgment aside for fraud, strict limits were imposed in order to preserve the principle that a judgment which brings litigation to an end should not be too easily disturbed. In particular in the case of an action on an *English* judgment, the court would not permit the new action to proceed unless fresh evidence, discovered since the first trial and which could not have been produced with reasonable diligence, was put forward and which, if it had been put forward at trial would probably have resulted in a different conclusion: see, *e.g. Boswell v. Coaks* (1894) 6 R. 167.

10. Fraud—policy and expediency It is clear that considerations of policy and expediency arising from the lack of confidence by the nineteenth century High Court judges in the variable standards of foreign justice caused a departure in the case of actions on foreign judgments attacked for fraud from the strict rules applicable to actions brought on English judgments attacked for fraud.

11. Abouloff—not to be extended In *House of Spring Gardens v. Waite* (1990) 3 W.L.R. 347, the plaintiffs sued on a judgment given by the Irish Supreme Court. The defendants sought to raise the defence that the Irish judgment had been obtained by fraud. They had, however, unsuccessfully argued this point in a second Irish action in which they had sought to set aside the first Irish judgment. The Court of Appeal held that the second Irish judgment estopped the defendants from raising the issue of fraud in England. Stuart-Smith L.J. said about *Abouloff* and *Vadala* (above at 355):

> "These cases have been considerably criticised over the years; they were decided at a time when our courts paid scant regard to the jurisdiction of other countries. Nevertheless we are bound by them and they were recently followed in this court in *Jet Holdings Inc v. Patel* [1990] 2 Q.B. 355. But in my judgment the scope of these decisions should not be extended."

12. An invitation to overrule *Abouloff* declined In *Owens Bank Ltd v. Bracco* [1992] A.C. 443 the House of Lords had the opportunity to consider the rule in *Abouloff*. The plaintiff's bank had obtained judgment for Sw. Fr 9m in the High Court of St Vincent. The defence had been that the documents relied on by the bank were forgeries. Having succeeded in St Vincent, the bank sought to enforce their judgment by registration under section 9 of the Administration of Justice Act 1920. Section 9 (2)(d) provides that no judgment shall be ordered to be registered if it was obtained by fraud. The defendant resisted the plaintiff's application to register the St Vincent judgment on the ground that it had been obtained by fraud. The plaintiffs invited the House of Lords to overrule *Abouloff*. The House of Lords declined the invitation, saying that it could now only be altered by statute, since s. 9 (2)(d) of the 1920 Act had given statutory force to the common law as it existed in 1920, including the rule in *Abouloff's* case. Lord Bridge, who gave the only speech, concluded (at p.489) that enforcement of overseas judgments is now primarily governed by the statutory codes of 1920 and 1933 (Foreign Judgments (Reciprocal Enforcement) Act 1933). In *Owens Bank Ltd v. Etoile Commerciale S.A.* [1995] 1 W.L.R. 44, the Privy Council, whilst not suggesting that *Bracco* was wrongly decided, did not regard the decision in *Abouloff* with any enthusiasm and, as we shall see in the next paragraph, sought by other means to close the gap.

13. English and foreign judgments—an attempt to close the gap In *Owens Bank Ltd v. Etoile Commerciale S.A. (supra)* the Privy Council held that every court of justice has an inherent power to prevent misuse of its process, whether by a plaintiff or a defendant. Accordingly, there is nothing to preclude a party from obtaining summary judgment where the defendant alleged fraud. Where the allegation of fraud has been made and determined abroad, summary judgment in subsequent proceedings is an appropriate remedy in the absence of plausible evidence disclosing at least a prima facie case of fraud. On the facts, the Privy Council concluded that the Saint Vincent Court of Appeal had been right to conclude that the defence of fraud put forward by the appellants was an abuse of process and should be struck out.

14. Fraud and fraud Attempts have been made to justify the rule in *Abouloff* on the basis that a distinction should be drawn between a judgment procured by the plaintiff's deception of the foreign court and a judgment granted by the foreign court after the defendant's allegation that the plaintiff has behaved fraudulently towards him has been ventilated in that foreign court. This argument has been criticised as "technical": see *Owens Bank Ltd v. Bracco (The Times*, April 15, 1991, C.A.) *per* Parker L.J.; *Interdesco v. Nullifire* [1992] 1 Lloyd's Rep. 180 *per* Phillips J. Certainly where registration of a Convention judgment is challenged on the ground that the foreign court has been fraudulently deceived, *Nullifire* decided that the English Court should first consider whether a remedy lies in the foreign jurisdiction in question. If so, it will normally be appropriate to leave the defendant to pursue his remedy in that jurisdiction. If the fraud alleged falls into the second category above, the rule in *Abouloff* does not apply in a Convention case: see generally *Nullifire* (above).

15. Fraud alleged—the approach of the court on an Order 14 application In *Codd v. Delap* (1905) 92 L.T. 510, H.L., Lord Linley said:

> "When an application is made under Ord. 14 for a judgment on a foreign judgment and an affidavit is put in to the effect that the foreign judgment is impeachable for fraud, the greatest possible caution is required in proceeding further; and, unless it is obvious that the allegation of fraud is frivolous and practically moonshine, Ord. 14 ought not to be applied."

16. Final and conclusive—minor irregularities The fact that the defendant alleges some minor procedural irregularities under the local law will not prevent the foreign judgment from being treated as final and conclusive so long as English views of substantial justice are not offended: *Pemberton v. Hughes* [1899] 1 Ch. 781; *Israel Discount Bank of New York v. Hadjipteras* [1984] 1 W.L.R. 137; *Williams and Humbert Ltd v. W. & H. Trade Marks (Jersey) Ltd* [1986] A.C. 368.

17. Final and conclusive foreign judgment—meaning What is meant by a final and conclusive foreign judgment? Lord Herschell said in *Nouvion v. Freeman* (1890) 15 App.Cas. 1 at 9:

> "The principle on which I think our enforcement of foreign judgments must proceed is this: that in a court of competent jurisdiction, where according to its established procedure the whole merits of the case were open, at all events, to the parties, however much they may have failed to take advantage of them, or may have waived any of their rights, a final adjudication has been given that a debt or obligation exists which cannot thereafter in that court be disputed and can only be questioned in an appeal to a higher tribunal. In such a case it may well be said that giving credit to the courts of another country, we are prepared to take the fact that such adjudication has been made as establishing the existence of the debt or obligation."

So, in that case, where the plaintiff had obtained what was called a "remate" judgment in the courts of Spain under which a defendant had been restricted in the nature and number of defences that he was permitted to raise, the English courts decided that the Spanish judgment was not *res judicata* between the parties and thus not final and conclusive.

18. Suing on an earlier English judgment It may seem surprising that a plaintiff, having obtained final judgment in an English court, should wish to commence a second action in England on that earlier judgment. That was what the plaintiff sought in *E.D. & F. Man (Sugar) Ltd v. Haryanto*, *The Times*, November 24, 1995 P.C. The judgment in the first action had

309

remained outstanding for nearly six years. The defendant had failed to satisfy that judgment. The Plaintiff brought the second action to alleviate the effect of the six-year time limit for suing on a judgment imposed by the Limitation Act 1980, s.24. Longmore J. held that although the plaintiff was not entitled as of right to bring a second action, the court had a discretion to entertain one. In the circumstances, he granted summary judgment under Ord. 14. (But see *Lowsky v. Forbes, The Times*, April 5, 1996.)

B: CLAIMS IN CONTRACT OTHER THAN BILLS OF EXCHANGE

1 Goods sold; work done; services rendered

The bulk of Ord. 14 applications relate to money allegedly due to the plaintiff for goods sold, work done or services rendered. The approach of the court in deciding whether to give judgment for the plaintiff or grant the defendant leave to defend in this type of case is discussed fully later. The extent to which contractors in the building industry may use Ord. 14 so as to secure prompt payment of monies due under architects' certificates is discussed at p. 374.

2 The special case of solicitors' claims for fees

1. The situation A solicitor sues his client for unpaid costs and seeks judgment under Ord. 14. The client may contend that he acknowledges the retainer—but that the fees claimed are exorbitant. The client has a right to ask for a taxation (Solicitors' Act 1974, s.70) but suppose that he has not exercised that right by the time the Ord. 14 summons is heard?

2. The *Smith v. Edwardes* order The order is derived from the case of *Smith v. Edwardes* [1882] 2 Q.B.D. 10, the terms of which were that:
  (a) The bill of costs on which the action is brought should be referred to the taxing master pursuant to the Solicitors' Act 1974.
  (b) The plaintiff should give credit at the time of taxation for all sums of money received by him from or on account of the defendant.
  (c) If the defendant does not within the time specified in the order lodge the bill of costs for taxation and obtain a taxation appointment, the plaintiff may enter final judgment for the amount endorsed on the writ (with interest, if any) and costs.

3. Interim payment The solicitor should consider whether it is appropriate to couple the Ord. 14 application with an application for an interim payment where the defendant concedes some liability. If, however, the defendant raises objection to specific items (*e.g.* an expert's fees) there would seem to be no good reason why the plaintiff should not have Ord. 14 judgment for the undisputed part of the bill and the defendant leave to defend by a taxation reference of the disputed part.

4. The "negligence" counterclaim Suppose, however, that the client alleges that the solicitor has been negligent in the conduct of the client's affairs and that that negligence gives rise to an alleged counterclaim by a client against the solicitor. In *Slater v. Cathcart* (1891) 8 T.L.R. the solicitor had secured the defendant's eventual release from a lunatic asylum, only to be told that he had done it negligently. The court made a *"Smith v. Edwardes"* order, but ordered a stay on the proceedings on the bill after taxation until the trial of the counterclaim.

3 Accounts

1. General If the evidence suggests that the taking of accounts is necessary in order to establish liability and its extent, Ord. 14 is inappropriate. The plaintiff should consider making application under Ord. 43 for a summary order for an account to be taken: see, for example, *Newton Chemical Ltd v. Arsenis* [1989] 1 W.L.R. 1297. The application can be made at any time after the issue of the writ and is made on summons supported by affidavit or other evidence returnable before the master. Where it is apparent that there is some indebtedness the plaintiff may also consider coupling an application for an interim payment (see Ord. 29, r. 12(a)) to the application for the taking of accounts. The position which sometimes arises on the Ord. 14 summons where it becomes clear that the defendant admits to some indebtedness to the plaintiff is fully discussed at p. 348.

2. Solicitors' accounts If the relationship of solicitor and client exists or has existed, the client or his personal representatives may seek an order for the delivery by the solicitor of a cash account. Ord. 14 is inappropriate here, too. Application must be made by originating summons and the procedure is regulated by Ord. 106, r.3.

4 Wrongful interference with goods

1. Jurisdiction Ord. 14, r.9 recognises the right of the plaintiff to seek summary judgment for the specific return of goods by providing that:

"9. Where the claim to which an application under rule 1 or rule 5 relates is for the delivery of a specific chattel and the court gives judgment under this order for the applicant, it shall have the same

311

power to order the party against whom judgment is given to deliver up the chattel without giving him an option to retain it on paying the assessed value thereof as if the judgment had been given after trial."

2. Relief—when goods not in possession of defendant Detinue, as such, was abolished by section 2(1) of the Torts (Interference with Goods) Act 1977 and absorbed along with conversion into the new single tort of "wrongful interference with goods." Where the goods are no longer in possession of the defendant, the form of relief to which the plaintiff is entitled is judgment for damages only for a single sum of money of which the measure is generally the value of the chattel at the date of the conversion together with any consequential loss flowing from wrongful interference.

3. Relief—when goods are in possession of defendant Where, however, the goods are still in the possession or control of the defendant, the plaintiff has a choice of relief which he may seek not only at trial but under Ord. 14. He may seek:

(a) An order for the specific return of the goods and in addition damages for its wrongful retention. This form of relief is not usual where there is a ready market for the goods which have been detained since damages would be regarded as sufficient remedy (for an example of such an order see *Hymas v. Ogden* [1905] 1 K.B. 246). Whether to grant such an order is a matter for the court's discretion.

(b) An order for the specific return of the goods or in the alternative the recovery of their value as assessed and damages for their wrongful detention. The second form of order gives the plaintiff a choice of enforcing the money judgment (for the value of the goods) or issuing enforcement for the return of the goods themselves.

(c) An order for damages alone representing the value of the goods together with damages for its wrongful detention. The third kind of order is usually made when the goods are in common form; see, for example, *Whiteley v. Hilt* [1918] 2 K.B. 808.

Under the first form of order the court will not be required to assess the value of the goods. In the other two cases, the court will have to assess not only the value of the goods as at the date of assessment but also quite separately and distinctly, damages for wrongful detention of the goods up to the date of assessment: see *General & Finance Facilities Ltd v. Cook Cars (Romford) Ltd* [1963] 1 W.L.R. 644. (See Part C, section 2, Form P, at p. 565 for specimen forms of summons.)

C: BILLS OF EXCHANGE

1 The agreed rule

1. The problem S supplies goods to B. Payment is by bill of exchange. On presentation the bill is dishonoured. B says that the goods supplied by S are defective. S sues on that dishonoured bill. Should he be entitled to judgment under Ord. 14 or should the court refuse him the relief sought on the ground that he may be subject to a valid counterclaim?

2. Two contracts—not one In considering the cases, it is important to understand that the court is being asked to consider two contracts not one. The bill of exchange itself constitutes one entire contract on its own. Then there is the underlying mercantile contract for the supply of goods.

3. The general rule As long ago as 1806 in *Morgan v. Richardson* (1806) 7 East 482n, it was held that the alleged inferior quality of the goods afforded no defence to an action on a bill of exchange. A long line of cases since then has confirmed this rule: *Trickey v. Larne* (1840) 6 M. & W. 278; *Jackson v. Murphy* (1887) 4 T.L.R. 91; *Anglo Italian Bank v. Davies* (1878) 38 L.T. 197; *Lamont v. Hyland* [1950] 1 K.B. 585; *Fielding & Platt Ltd v. Selim Najjar* [1969] 1 W.L.R. 357; *Brown Shipley & Co. Ltd v. Alicia Hosiery Ltd* [1966] 1 Lloyd's Rep. 668; *Nova (Jersey) Knit Ltd v. Kamngarn Spinnerel Ltd GmbH* [1977] 1 W.L.R. 713; *Case Poclain Corporation Ltd v. Jones* [1986] E.C.C. 569; *Montecchi v. Shimco Ltd* [1980] 1 Lloyd's Rep. 50; [1979] 1 W.L.R. 1180; *Montebianco v. Carlyle Mills* [1981] 1 Lloyd's Rep. 509.

4. The rule—a modern restatement The rule was succinctly stated by Bridge L.J. in *Montecchi v. Shimco Ltd* [1980] Lloyd's Rep. 50 at 51; [1979] 1 W.L.R. 1180 at 1183:

> "It is elementary that as between the immediate parties to a bill of exchange, which is treated in international commerce as the equivalent of cash, the fact that the defendant may have a counterclaim for unlimited damages arising out of the same transaction forms no sort of defence to an action on the bill of exchange and no ground on which he should be granted a stay of execution of the judgment in the action for the proceeds of the bill of exchange."

5. Policy The rule is so important that the courts are extremely reluctant to contemplate any but the rarest exceptions. The reason, as Sachs L.J. said in *Cebora S.N.C. v. S.I.P. Industrial Products Ltd* [1976] 1 Lloyd's Rep. 271, is that the courts should be careful not to:

"... whittle away a rule of practice by introducing unnecessary exceptions to it under influence of sympathy-evoking stories, and should have due regard to the maxim that hard cases can make bad law. Indeed, in these days of increasing international interdependence and increasing need to foster liquidity of resources, the rule may be said to be of special import to the business community. Pleas to leave in court large sums to deteriorate in value while Official Referee scale proceedings are fought out may well to that community seem rather divorced from business realities, and should perhaps be examined with considerable caution."

6. Exceptional cases The result is that Ord. 14 procedure is particularly tailor-made for an action on a dishonoured bill of exchange. There are, however, some exceptional circumstances where it would not be proper for the court to grant Ord. 14 judgment on a dishonoured bill of exchange. The existence of such circumstances was recognised by Lord Denning M.R. in *Brown Shipley & Co. Ltd v. Alicia Hosiery Ltd* [1966] 1 Lloyd's Rep. 668:

"I do not say that there may not be some cases in which the court may in its discretion grant a stay of execution. I think it is possible, but, as Sir George Jessel M.R. said in an earlier case (*Anglo Italian Bank v. Wells (and Davies)* (1878) 38 L.T. 197), that is only in exceptional circumstances."

2 Bills of exchange—the bankruptcy exception

1. Section 323 Insolvency Act 1986 and section 612 Companies Act 1985 Section 323 of the Insolvency Act 1986 (applied to liquidated companies by section 612 of the Companies Act 1985) provides:

"323—(1) This section applies where before the commencement of the bankruptcy there have been mutual credits, mutual debts or other mutual dealings between the bankrupt and any creditor of the bankrupt proving or claiming to prove for a bankruptcy debt.

(2) An account shall be taken of what is due from each party to the other in respect of the individual dealings and the sums due from one party shall be set off against the sums due from the other.

(3) Sums due from the bankrupt to another party shall not be included in the account taken under subsection (2) if that other party had notice at the time they became due that a bankruptcy petition relating to the bankrupt was pending.

> (4) Only the balance (if any) of the account taken under subsection (2) is provable as a bankruptcy debt or, as the case may be, to be paid to the trustee as part of the bankrupt's estate."

This statutory provision effectively re-enacts and replaces section 31 of the Bankruptcy Act 1914.

2. A working example In *Willment Bros. Ltd v. North West Thames Regional Health Authority* (1984) 26 Build.L.R. 51, C.A., the plaintiffs were building contractors under a contract to build, for the defendants, a new wing at the West Middlesex Hospital. The contract contained the usual terms for stage payments as certified by the architect and on November 12, he issued a certificate for £132,000, the plaintiffs being entitled to payment within 14 days. On November 29, 1982, the defendants drew a cheque in payment and sent it by first-class post to the plaintiffs. At 10.00 a.m. on November 30, 1982, the plaintiffs appointed a liquidator. The defendants learned of this at 11.00 a.m. and immediately stopped the cheque. The plaintiffs sued the defendants on the cheque and not otherwise. In Ord. 14 proceedings the plaintiffs contended that the cheque was to be treated as cash.

3. *Willment Bros.*—the case for the defendants The defendants contended, *inter alia*:
  (a) that under section 31 of the Bankruptcy Act 1914 (the then relevant statutory provision) they had a statutory right to set off their counterclaim against the plaintiffs' claim; and
  (b) under the terms of the contract the effect of the plaintiffs' insolvency was that they were entitled to withhold payment until the account had been taken and that the account would show a large balance in their favour.

5. The issue—resolved in favour of the defendants Did the general rule that a cheque is to be treated as cash prevail or were the defendants able to rely on section 31? O'Connor L.J. said at 59:

> "The words of the section are clear and unambiguous. There are three prerequisites to the operation of the section: (i) a debtor against whom a receiving order has been made, (ii) a person proving or claiming to prove a debt under the receiving order, (iii) some mutual dealings between those two persons. What meaning is to be given to 'debt' in the phrase 'proving or claiming to prove a debt'? The answer is found in section 30 of the Act where, among others, a contingent liability is deemed to be a debt proveable in bankruptcy. I can see no reason

315

whatsoever for limiting 'debt' in section 31 to any particular classes of debt proveable in bankruptcy."

So the defendants were entitled by reason of section 31 to set off their claim against the plaintiffs' claim and the general rule that cheques are to be treated as cash was displaced. The corresponding provision to section 30 of the 1914 Act is section 323 of the 1986 Act.

5. No contracting out O'Connor L.J. further held in the *Willment Bros.* case (*ibid.*) that section 31 was mandatory in the sense that it was not permissible to contract out of its provisions, relying on *National Westminster Bank Ltd v. Halesowen Presswork and Assemblies Ltd* [1972] A.C. 785 and *Rolls Razor Ltd v. Cox* [1967] 1 Q.B. 552 at 570. There is no reason to believe that section 323 of the 1986 Act will be treated any differently.

6. Section 323—restricted to immediate parties It should be stressed, however, that this section only arises between immediate parties to a bill. Where the plaintiff and defendant are intermediate parties, the principle, that between the immediate parties contractual rights and liabilities and equities can be raised between them on the bill does not arise. Intermediate parties who take the bill for value as holders in due course will not find themselves subject to any of the contractual rights or liabilities and equities that affect the value of the bill between immediate parties: *Jade International v. Robert Nicholas Ltd* [1978] 1 Q.B. 917.

3 Bills of exchange—the "fraud, duress and illegality" exception

1. The issue Is the plaintiff in proceedings brought on a dishonoured cheque entitled to judgment under Ord. 14 where the defendant alleges the bill is affected by fraud, duress or illegality?

2. The initial burden of proof In the first place, it is for the defendant to establish a prima facie case of fraud, etc. Section 30(2) of the Bills of Exchange Act 1882 provides:

> "(2) Every holder of a bill is prima facie deemed to be a holder in due course; but if in an action on a bill it is admitted or proved that the acceptance, issue or subsequent negotiation of the bill is affected with fraud, duress or force and fear of illegality, the burden of proof is shifted, unless and until the holder proves that, subsequent to the alleged fraud or illegality, value has in good faith been given for the bill."

Denham J. in *Tatam v. Haslar* (1889) 23 Q.B.D. 345 said:

"The words of section 30(2) 'if it is admitted or proved' mean no more than that some evidence of circumstances in the nature of fraud must be given sufficient to [require a trial]."

3. If the burden shifts to the plaintiff? Cairns L.J. explained the position once the burden has shifted to the plaintiff, in *Bank Für Gemeinwirtschaft Aktiengesellschaft v. City of London Garages Ltd* [1971] 1 W.L.R. 149 at 155D–G:

"It is clear that if the fraud is proved the holders have the onus of proving that they, or the previous holders who indorsed to them, took the bills in good faith and for value. Since in Order 14 proceedings, the defendant cannot be required to establish his defence (it being sufficient for him to show that he has some ground which would constitute a defence if what he alleges were proved at the trial) it must follow that in an action on a bill of exchange he is entitled to leave to defend if he sets up a case of fraud affecting the bill, unless the plaintiff in his turn can establish that the bill was taken in good faith and for value ... I readily accept that if on Order 14 proceedings there is a real issue as to whether the bills were taken in good faith and for value, and that issue cannot be resolved at that stage leave to defend must be given. But if there is clear evidence of value given in good faith, and no grounds shown on which that evidence can be challenged, then the defendant's allegation of fraud does not constitute material which would afford a defence."

4. Plaintiff discharging burden of proof—how? The plaintiff does not, however, discharge the onus on him by the mere assertion in affidavit that he has given value in good faith: *Fuller v. Alexander* (1883) 52 L.J.Q.B. 103 and *Polish Bank v. Paros* [1932] 2 K.B. 353. Davis L.J. in the *Bank Für Gemeinwirtschaft* case (*ibid.*) said at 159H:

"The authorities cited under Order 14 ending with the *Polish Bank* case [1932] 2 K.B. 353, as to bills of exchange really amount to no more than that the bare assertion of being a bona fide holder for value is not enough, just as the bare allegation of fraud is not enough on the other side, and that if there is no more than such an allegation by the plaintiff the case should go for trial. But, in my opinion, that cannot apply when the claim to be a bona fide holder for value is supported by unchallenged or unchallengeable contemporary documents."

So, the court must ask itself whether the account given by the plaintiff standing together with all other evidence put before it, can be said to establish good faith and the giving of value with such a degree of probability that if the case went to trial the defendant's defence of fraud would have no real chance of success.

5. A recent example The plaintiff obtained judgment against the defendant under Ord. 14 for £58,000 on a dishonoured cheque given in purported payment of a quantity of scrap metal delivered by the plaintiff to the defendant. The defendant appealed and was given leave to adduce further evidence to the effect that over a considerable period of time, as a result of defalcations by the plaintiff's employers, the defendant had lost over £250,000 by reason of short deliveries of scrap metal and so started separate proceedings against the plaintiff for breach of contract and fraud. The defendant's appeal was allowed. The Court of Appeal held that although the plaintiff's claim was on a dishonoured cheque, under Ord. 14 the court was given a wide discretion to stay execution and justice demanded that there should be a stay of execution. The Ord. 14 judgment was upheld but stayed pending disposal of the proceedings by the defendant against the plaintiff and the defendant was required to bring into court the whole of the Ord. 14 judgment debt: *Cobury v. Wolverhampton Metal* (February 18, 1987, C.A.T. No. 187).

6. Summary as to the shifting burdens of proof It is for the defendant to raise a prima facie case of fraud, etc., and having done so he will normally be allowed to defend the action unless the plaintiff can establish clearly that he gave value honestly without notice of the fraud etc. in which event the plaintiff is entitled to judgment under Ord. 14 without a stay.

4 Bills of exchange—a possible "misrepresentation" exception

1. The issue What is the effect so far as Ord. 14 proceedings are concerned, of an alleged misrepresentation on a bill of exchange?

2. The authority In *Clovertogs Ltd v. Jean Scenes Ltd* [1982] Com.L.R. 88, the defendants were retailers of ladies' clothes. It was agreed that the plaintiffs would purchase and import a range of clothes to be made in South Korea and sell them to the defendants for retail sale in their various shops in the United Kingdom. The defendants paid £52,750 in instalments to the plaintiffs and then stopped payment of two further cheques for £5,500. The defendants alleged that:

    (a) It was part of the deal that before shipment from South Korea a representative of the plaintiffs would inspect the clothes and issue a certificate of satisfaction whereupon they would be shipped to the United Kingdom.

    (b) The plaintiffs represented to them that the inspection and certification had been carried out by the plaintiffs' representatives whereas in fact nothing of the sort had taken place and the representation was accordingly false.

3. "Misrepresentation"—a triable issue The Court of Appeal, in giving the defendant leave to defend said:

"... it seems to me that the effect of misrepresentation upon a bill of exchange is a matter on which it is not easy to discover the law. That being so, I would have thought that indeed there can be an arguable point of law on that matter, but its force would clearly depend upon very nice findings of fact." (*Per* Eveleigh J.L. at p. 89.)

4. The Court of Appeal later doubts itself In *Famous Ltd v. Ge.Inn Ex Italia S.R.L.*, *The Times*, August 3, 1987, the defendants obtained summary judgment under Ord. 14 on a counterclaim on two cheques given to them by the plaintiffs for goods sold and delivered. The plaintiffs alleged that the reason why the had caused the cheques to be dishonoured was because they contended that they had a valid claim in misrepresentation against the defendants. *Clovertogs* was distinguished on its facts but May L.J. (who also sat in *Clovertogs*) said that he had no recollection of *Clovertogs*, had not seen a detailed transcript and concluded that on its face *Clovertogs* was a surprising decision save to the extent that it was decided on its own facts.

5 Bills of exchange—the "no consideration" exception

1. Consideration—the prerequisite A bill of exchange (other than an accommodation bill) is a contract which must be supported by consideration.

2. No consideration—no summary judgment The plaintiff will not be entitled to Ord. 14 judgment on a dishonoured cheque if the defendant can establish that he received no consideration for the cheque. In *Wing v. Thurlow* (1893) 10 T.L.R. 53, the defendant alleged that he had not received any consideration for his acceptance of the bill of exchange and was given leave to defend.

3. Past consideration is, unusually, good consideration Unlike other contracts at common law however, valuable consideration for a bill includes not only any consideration sufficient to support a simple contract but also an antecedent debt or a liability: Bills of Exchange Act 1882, s. 27(1).

319

4. The consideration—can be retrospective Where value has at any time been given for a bill, the holder is deemed to be a holder for value as regards the acceptor and all parties to the bill prior to the time when value was given (section 27(2)). Further, a holder in due course has the right to enforce payment against all prior parties since he is completely unaffected by the absence of consideration between the parties (section 29(3)).

5. Accommodation bills—are different The position is different, however, in the case of the acceptor of an accommodation bill who, by definition, is a person who has not received value and only lends his name on the bill to enable someone else to raise temporary finance on it (Bills of Exchange Act 1882, s. 28). So in *Charles v. Marsden* (1808) 1 Taunt. 224 the defendant had accepted an accommodation bill and was sued by the plaintiff, and indorsee. The defendant's contention that he had received no value for the bill was rejected and the plaintiff was entitled to judgment.

6 Bills of exchange—banks and their customers

1. The bank's right of set-off—the basic rule Suppose a bank has a customer with one account in credit and another in debit. Has the bank a right to combine the accounts so that he can set-off the debit against the credit and be liable only for the balance? The answer is: Yes; *Halesowen Presswork & Assemblies Ltd v. Westminster Bank Ltd* [1971] 1 Q.B. 1; and see *Hong Kong and Shanghai Banking Corporation v. Kloeckner & Co. A.G.* [1989] 2 Lloyd's Rep. 323.

2. *Bhogal v. Punjab National Bank*—suspected nominee accounts Suppose that a bank entertains suspicions that a number of accounts in the names of different customers are in reality nominee accounts belonging to one and the same person. Suppose further that some of the accounts are in credit and some overdrawn. Is it permissible for the bank to refuse to honour cheques drawn on the accounts in credit unless and until monies are transferred from those accounts so as to bring the overdrawn accounts into credit? Can the bank plead in an action brought on the dishonoured cheques a defence by way of equitable set off? That was the position in *Bhogal v. Punjab National Bank* [1988] 2 All E.R. 296.

3. Banks treated no differently The Court of Appeal held in *Bhogal* that a banker is required to pay all cheques drawn by a customer in accordance with the mandate given to him if he has funds belonging to the customer, and he was not entitled without warning to refuse to honour a customer's cheque when there was money in the account to cover it, merely on the suspicion that the account was held by a customer as nominee for a third party who was indebted to the bank. Clear and indisputable evidence is required that the customer held his account as a nominee or bare trustee for the third party before the bank could set-off the credit in one account against the debit in another (see also *Uttamchandani v. Central Bank of India* (1989) 133 S.J. 262).

D: TYPES OF RELIEF AVAILABLE OTHER THAN CLAIMS IN DEBT OR DAMAGES

1 Specific performance

1. Order 86 We have seen that Ord. 14, r. 1(3) provides that the summary procedure shall not apply to a claim to which Ord. 86 applies. Ord. 86, r.1(1) says:

> "**1.**—(1) In any action in the Chancery Division begun by writ indorsed with a claim:
>
> (a) for specific performance of an agreement (whether in writing or not) for the sale, purchase, exchange, mortgage or charge of any property, or for the grant or assignment of a lease of any property, with or without an alternative claim for damages, or
> (b) for rescission of such an agreement, or
> (c) for the forfeiture or return of any deposit made under such an agreement,
>
> the plaintiff may, on the ground that the defendant has no defence to the action, apply to the court for judgment."

2. Order 86—does not oust specific performance under Order 14 Application can be made under Ord. 14 for specific performance and rescission of contracts other than those recited in Ord. 86: (For an example—where application was refused on the facts—see *S.K.F. Laboratories Ltd v. Harris Pharmaceuticals Ltd* (1991) B.M.L.R. 119).

3. Specific performance of a licence to use land In *Verrall v. Great Yarmouth Borough Council* [1981] 1 Q.B. 203, the defendants agreed to the hiring of their hall to the National Front for its annual conference in 1979. Following a change in its political control before the conference took place, the Council repudiated the contract of hire. The National Front brought an action for specific performance of the contract and took out an Ord. 14 summons in which they sought summary relief by way of specific performance. The judge set aside the master's order for interlocutory judgment with damages to be assessed and granted an order for specific performance,

321

and he upheld an appeal. The defendants had argued, amongst other things that the case ought not to be dealt with under Ord. 14. Lord Denning M.R. said at 215C–D:

> "I reject that point. In many cases now, when all issues are clear and the point of substance can be decided as well now as hereafter, we have repeatedly decided matters under the Order 14 procedure." (See also *Beswick v. Beswick* [1968] A.C. 58; *Posner v. Scott-Lewis* [1986] 3 W.L.R. 531.)

2 Injunctions

1. The original approach At one time it was thought that an injunction could not be granted in an Ord. 14 application because the master or district judge before whom an Ord. 14 summons is generally taken, does not ordinarily have the power to grant injunctions: Ord. 32, r.11(1)(d); except in agreed terms, Ord. 32, r.11(2).

2. By-passing the master's jurisdiction In *Shell Mex and B.P. Ltd v. Manchester Garages Ltd* [1971] 1 W.L.R. 612, the plaintiffs issued a writ claiming an injunction restraining the defendants from continuing to use a filling station and they took out an Ord. 14 summons for an injunction. Lord Denning M.R. said at p. 615D:

> "It is true that a master has no power to grant an injunction. But the judge has ample power. I see no reason whatever why a plaintiff cannot go straight to a judge and ask for a summary judgment under Order 14 for an injunction. If and in so far as that note (in the 1970 *Supreme Court Practice*) suggests to the contrary, it is wrong. Shell Mex were quite entitled to go under Order 14 to the judge for an injunction."

3. An example—breach of covenant The defendant had a lease of a house from the plaintiff. The lease contained a covenant not at any time during the term of the lease to cut or injure any of the walls, timbers or roof of the house and not to alter its plan, height or layout. Despite being warned against doing so, the defendant lowered a parapet wall in flagrant breach of the negative covenant. The Court of Appeal confirmed the judge's order granting a mandatory final Ord. 14 injunction for reinstatement of the wall: *Cadogan v. Muscatt, The Times*, May 15 1990; (1990) 35 EG 63.

4. Moral Where an injunction is sought under Ord. 14, the summons should be returned before the judge rather than the master or district judge. See Form R, p. 566.

5. *Cyanamid* and Order 14 Most plaintiffs seeking relief do so under the provisions of Ord. 29 in the form of an interlocutory injunction pending trial or further order. Ord. 14 is used only infrequently. But when the plaintiff has included a claim for an injunction in his statement of claim and the circumstances are such that it is perfectly clear that the defendant is in breach of some statutory or common law duty imposed on him, there would appear to be every advantage in proceeding under Ord. 14 rather than Ord. 29. Such advantages are:

(a) The Ord. 14 injunction would be final, not interlocutory.

(b) The "balance of convenience" test laid down in *American Cyanamid v. Ethicon Ltd* [1973] A.C. 396, it is submitted, would be inapplicable: see *Macmillan Publishers Ltd v. Thomas Reed Publications Ltd* (1993) F.S.R. 455.

(c) The plaintiff would not need to give an undertaking as to damages since such an undertaking is only required on the grant of an interlocutory injunction: *Fenner v. Wilson* (1893) 2 Ch. 656.

(d) The plaintiff would normally get his costs of the action.

(e) There would appear to be no obstacle in the way of the plaintiff seeking additional relief (for example, an order for possession as well as an injunction on the Ord. 14 summons. See, for example, the dicta of Lord Diplock in *Manchester Corporation v. Connolly* [1970] Ch. 420 at 429C).

If, however, the plaintiff wanted to hedge his bets just in case he failed to secure his injunction under Ord. 14, there would appear to be nothing improper in his combining his Ord. 14 summons with a summons under Ord. 29 for an interlocutory injunction. (See Form R, p. 566.) The application would have to go to the judge for the reasons set out below (see para. 2(1)).

3 Declarations

1. The power Ord. 15, r.16 now provides that "no action or other proceedings shall be open to objection on the ground that a merely declaratory judgment is sought thereby and the court may make binding declarations of right whether or not any consequential relief is or could be claimed."

2. A discretionary power The court has a discretion whether to grant a declaration: *Russian Commercial & Industrial Bank v. British Bank for Foreign Trade* [1921] 2 A.C. 438.

3. Conditions precedent to the exercise of discretion—proper argument It will not, however, make a declaration unless it has heard proper argument.

It follows that declaratory relief will not be granted on admissions contained in the pleadings or by consent of the parties or in default of defence: *Wallersteiner v. Moir* [1974] 1 W.L.R. 991 and *Metzger v. Department of Health and Social Security* [1978] 1 W.L.R. 1046.

4. A discretion cautiously to be exercised The Ord. 14 jurisdiction should be exercised with great caution: *Russian Commercial and Industrial Bank (ibid.).* The declaration must be final and not in the nature of interim relief: *International General Electric Company of New York Ltd v. Commissioners of Customs and Excise* [1962] Ch. 784 at 789–790.

5. But not too cautiously Examples:

(a) *Copyright:* In *Leco Instruments (U.K.) Ltd v. Land Pyrometers Ltd* [1982] R.P.C. 133, the plaintiffs under threat of an allegation that they had broken the defendants' copyright in some drawings relating to thermocouples, sought a declaration that they (the plaintiffs) were entitled to import and deal in thermocouples and that "the same were no infringement of the copyright of the defendants." The judge granted the relief sought. The Court of Appeal reversed his decision but only on the ground that "I say only that in my judgment the defendants have disclosed a defence which it is right should be considered at a trial and not by summary process. In my view the case is essentially one for trial and not for disposal on summary application." *Per* Fox L.J. at 144. See also *Centrovincial Estates plc v. Merchants Investors Assurance Co. Ltd* [1983] Com.L.R. 158).

(b) *Lady Anne Tennant v. Associated Newspapers Group Ltd* [1979] F.S.R. 298: A copyright infringement action relating to four photographs taken by the plaintiff, two being of Her Royal Highness Princess Margaret and two of a friend, Mr Roddy Llewellyn. The plaintiff's son sold the photographs to the *Daily Mail* without the plaintiff's permission and they were later published. The plaintiff applied under Ord. 14 for, *inter alia*, a declaration that the defendants had infringed the plaintiff's copyright in the photographs and wrongfully converted the infringing copies to their own use. Megarry V.-C. said at 303:

"[Counsel for the plaintiffs] indicated that he did not wish to press for an injunction if he obtained the declarations that he sought and I think that I ought to make these, both as to infringement of copyright and as to conversion."

E: DAMAGES CLAIMS OTHER THAN CONTRACT

1 Negligence

1. Three ingredients Given that:
- (a) the three ingredients of the tort of negligence—duty of care, breach of the duty and damages flowing from that breach—are present;
- (b) the existence and breach of that duty are unarguable; and
- (c) the only remaining issue is simply the quantum of damages,

there is no reason why the plaintiff should not seek interlocutory judgment under Ord. 14 with damages to be assessed. The damages are generally assessed by the master or district judge (except in more complicated cases) and that normally means an assessment by appointment—a quicker and cheaper method of getting damages than setting down for trial as to damages only. The primary merit of this form of summary procedure is that it produces an early confrontation of the parties, an object which it is desirable, wherever possible, to achieve: Pearson Commission, paragraph 230. (See Form O, p. 565.)

2. Particular example: personal injury claims It is permissible to proceed under Ord. 14 in personal injury actions when there is no defence except as to quantum:

> "Looking at the substance of the matter, it seems to me to be reasonably plain that in truth there is in this case no defence on the issue of liability, and if there is no defence, then it seems to me eminently desirable that costs should be saved by going straight to the issue of the quantum of damages." (*Per* Jenkins L.J. in *Dummer v. Brown* ([1953] 1 Q.B. 710 at 720–21); and see *Bhowmick v. Ward* (December 14, 1981, C.A.T. No. 512; unreported).)

3. Contributory negligence Contributory negligence goes to the issue of liability not to quantum and so judgment under Ord. 14 should not be given where it is a live issue.

4. No assessment on hearing The actual assessment of the damages pursuant to the interlocutory judgment obtained on the Ord. 14 summons is not carried out on the Ord. 14 hearing (see *Yarnold v. Radio Wyvern* (1985, C.A.T. No. 194; unreported). A further summons under Ord. 37 must be taken out before the master unless some other method is ordered.

5. Judgment interest Interest payable under section 17 of the Judgments Act 1838 is payable, not from the date of entry of interlocutory judgment, but from the date when the damages are assessed pursuant to interlocutory judgment: *Thomas v. Bunn* [1991] 2 W.L.R. 27.

2 Copyright, trade marks, passing off

1. Commercial piracy A comparatively recent but growing use of Ord. 14 proceedings is apparent in the field of commercial piracy.

2. Examples Actions for damages for breach of copyright, for the infringement of trade marks and for passing off may be the subject of an Ord. 14 summons: see, for example, *Sony Corporation v. Anand (No. 2)* [1982] F.S.R. 200; *Academy Sound and Vision Ltd v. W.E.A. Records Ltd* [1983] I.C.R. 586.

F: THE SPECIAL REGIME OF DOCUMENTARY CREDITS

1 Letters of credit

1. What are they? An irrevocable credit constitutes a definite undertaking of the issuing bank, provided that the terms and conditions of the credit are complied with:
- (a) to pay, or that payment will be made, if the credit provides for payment, whether against a draft or not;
- (b) to accept drafts if the credit provides for acceptance by the issuing bank or to be responsible for their acceptance and payment at maturity (see article 3a of the Uniform Customs and Practice for Documentary Credits (1974) Provision).

2. General rule—inviolability The English courts have recognised that the inviolable characteristic of the undertaking given in a letter of credit is of fundamental importance to the commercial world. It is irrelevant that behind the letter of credit stands the commercial contract for the supply of goods and services or whatever is the subject of the dispute between the parties to that contract. (See, for example, *Forestal Mimosa Ltd v. Oriental Credit Ltd* [1986] 1 W.L.R. 631.)

3. Order 14 It is because it is hardly ever possible for the defendant to seek to justify its failure to honour a letter of credit according to its terms that the plaintiff is on strong ground in asking for judgment under Ord. 14.

4. Letters of credit and Order 14—a working example In *Power Curber*

International Ltd v. National Bank of Kuwait SAK [1981] 1 W.L.R. 1233, the plaintiffs, American sellers, exported goods from the United States to buyers in Kuwait. They were to be paid by a letter of credit issued by the National Bank of Kuwait, the defendants. The bank, which wanted to honour its obligations under the letter of credit, was forbidden to do so by an order of the courts in Kuwait. The plaintiffs brought an action in England on the letter of credit. In allowing the plaintiffs to have judgment under Ord. 14 without a stay of execution against the bank, Lord Denning M.R. said at [1981] 1 W.L.R. 1241A:

> "... I must draw attention to the importance of letters of credit in international trade. They are the means by which goods are supplied all the world over. It is vital that every bank which issues a letter of credit should honour its obligations. The bank is in no way concerned with any disputes that the buyer may have with the seller. The buyer may say that the goods are not up to contract. Nevertheless, the bank must honour its obligations. The buyer may say that he has a cross-claim in a large amount. Still the bank must honour its obligations. A letter of credit is like a bill of exchange given for the price of goods. It ranks as cash and must be honoured. ... If the court of any other countries should interfere with the obligations of one of its banks (by ordering it not to pay under a letter of credit) it would strike at the very heart of that country's international trade. No foreign seller would supply goods to that country on letters of credit—because he could no longer be confident of being paid. No trader would accept a letter of credit issued by a bank of that country if it might be ordered by its courts not to pay. So it is part of the law of international trade that letters of credit should be honoured." (And see *Forestal Mimosa Ltd v. Oriental Credit* (above).)

5. No right of set-off against bank Because credits are by their nature separate transactions from the sales and other contracts on which they are based and so are in no way concerned with or bound by them, the banks are immune to claims of set-off, counterclaim or injunctive relief sought to be raised against them in letters of credit actions: see, for example, *Malas & Sons v. British Imex Industries Ltd* [1958] 2 Q.B. 127; *Hong Kong and Shanghai Banking Corporation v. Kloeckner & Co. A.G.* [1989] 2 Lloyd's Rep. 323.

6. But the bank has a right of set-off Where, however, the bank is liable under a letter of credit, it may enforce a set-off against the person to whom it is indebted under the letter of credit, thus only being liable for the balance: *Hong Kong and Shanghai Banking Corporation v. Kloeckner & Co. A.G.* (above).

327

2 Performance bonds

1. What are they? A performance bond or guarantee is a guarantee by a bank for a specified sum that a party to a contract will carry out his obligations under the contract with the other contracting party.

2. Proof of damage required Until recently, it was generally thought that, although the bond is called a guarantee, it was not really a guarantee at all, but was more in the nature of a promissory note payable by the bank on demand. In *Trafalgar House Construction (Regions) Ltd v. General Surety & Guarantee Co. Ltd*, [1995] 3 All E.R. 737, H.L., the House of Lords held that a bond entered into by sub-contractors with provision for the payment of damages sustained by the main contractor up to the amount of the bond amounts to guarantee by the surety under which proof of damage and not mere assertion thereof is required before liability under the bond arises. Lord Jauncey therefore concluded that he had no hesitation in concluding that the surety would be entitled to raise all questions of sums due and cross-claims which would have been available to the sub-contractors in any action against them for damages.

3. The letter of credit parallel In *Edward Owen Engineering Ltd v. Barclays Bank International Ltd* [1978] 1 Q.B. 159, the Court of Appeal held that such a bond or guarantee stands on the same footing as a letter of credit and a bank must honour it according to its terms. As with letters of credit generally the bank is not concerned:
  (a) with the underlying mercantile contract between supplier and buyers;
  (b) nor with the question whether the supplier has performed his contractual obligations;
  (c) nor with the question whether the supplier is in default or not.
The bank must pay according to its guarantee, on demand, if so stipulated, or (if it be the case) on the happening of the event upon which its obligation under the bond has arisen: *per* Roskill L.J. in *Howe Richardson Scale Co. Ltd v. Polimex-Cekop & National Westminster Bank Ltd* [1978] 1 Lloyd's Rep. 161, C.A. and see *Potton Homes Ltd v. Coleman Contractors (Overseas) Ltd* (1984) 128 S.J. 282.

4. Fraud The only exception to the rule that letters of credit and per-formance bonds or guarantees must be honoured according to the terms is where there is clear evidence of fraud of which the issuing bank has notice. So that where, for instance, the unscrupulous supplier has forged documents or has intentionally purported to sell non-existent goods and his fraud has been drawn to the attention of the issuing bank before the draft and the accompanying documents have been presented for payment, the bank, it would seem, is under no obligation to pay and would get leave to defend in Ord. 14 proceedings.

5. The evidence must be clear In *Tukan Timber Ltd v. Barclays Bank plc* [1987] 1 Lloyd's Rep. 171, Hirst J., in stressing the autonomous nature of a letter of credit in the sense that the bank is not concerned with the merits or demerits of the underlying transaction, held that only in "the most extremely exceptional circumstances" should the court interfere with the paying bank honouring a letter of credit in accordance with its terms. Only if the bank has notice of a clear fraud committed by the beneficiary is the court entitled to interfere.

3 Guarantees

1. Liability must be clear Order 14 has been successfully invoked by plaintiffs against sureties and guarantors: see, for example, *Hyundai Heavy Industries Co. Ltd v. Papadopoulos* [1980] 1 W.L.R. 1129; *Lloyds Bank Ltd v. Ellis-Fewster* [1983] 1 W.L.R. 559; *Den Norske Creditbank v. The Sarawak Economic Development Corporation* [1989] 2 Lloyd's Rep. 35. In order to succeed, however, the liability of the guarantor must be quite clear and, if not, the guarantor will be entitled to go to trial. (See, *e.g. Midland Bank Ltd v. Phillips, The Times*, March 28, 1986.)

2. The *Ogle* case—an example of liability not being clear In *Lloyds Bank & Co. v. Ogle* (1876) 1 Ex.D. 263 the defendant stated that although he was aware that there was a running account between the principal debtor and the plaintiffs which he had guaranteed in principle, he was unable to ascertain whether anything was due on the guarantee and believed that nothing was due and further that he had not received any statement of account. The judgment of Bramwell B. at 263–4 may be analysed thus:

(a) *First*—he explained the policy of the summary judgment procedure:

"... the power to sign judgment was, in my opinion, intended to apply to those cases which almost on the admission of the defendant are undefended and not to cases in which the defendant might reasonably say, 'I do not know if your case is well founded or not, but I require you to prove it.'"

(b) *Secondly*—he demonstrated where summary judgment could be proper:

"I by no means say that under no circumstances, in an action on a guarantee, could security be required, because it is quite possible to imagine a case in which the defendant might only put in a plea

329

for the purpose of delay, knowing his indebtedness, and having acknowledged it."

(c) *Thirdly*—he showed how the plaintiffs could have succeeded:

"If the plaintiffs had sworn that the debt had been admitted by the company, and that the defendant had been informed of the amount, and had not dissented or in any other way denied his liability, it would seem to me that he could only defend the action for the purpose of delay ... but where a guarantor bona fide says that he does not know that the debt is due, and that he requires it to be proved, I think the statute was not intended to operate to take that right from him."

3. Guarantees and a triable issue—a working example So, for instance, a receiver realising assets under the debenture owes a duty not only to the borrower but to the guarantor of the debt to take reasonable care to obtain the best price and to exercise care in choosing the time of sale. In *Standard Chartered Bank Ltd v. Walker* [1982] 1 W.L.R. 1410; the court refused Ord. 14 judgment and allowed the defendant guarantor unconditional leave to defend when he alleged that those duties had been broken; and see *Morgan Guaranty Trust co. v. Hadjantonakis* [1988] 1 Lloyd's Rep. 381. (As to guarantor's cross-claims see *Continental Illinois National Bank and Trust Co. of Chicago v. Papanicolaou* [1986] 2 Lloyd's Rep. 441 and at p. 378.)

G: SUMMARY JUDGMENT FOR POSSESSION AND RELIEF AGAINST FORFEITURE

1 Introduction

1. Forfeiture A claim for possession of a dwelling house under Ord. 14 will only be entertained if the court is satisfied that the defendant is not entitled to the protection of the Rent Act: *Peachey Property Corporation v. Robinson* [1967] 2 Q.B. 543; Rent Act 1977, s.4. A claim by a landlord for the possession of premises other than residential premises is permissible under Ord. 14 (see Form Q, p. 565). A mortgagee seeking possession should do so under Ord. 88 rather than Ord. 14. Again, a judgment creditor seeking to enforce a charging order should look to Ord. 88, r.5A rather than Ord. 14.

2. Relief against forfeiture In Ord. 14 proceedings, r.10 provides for relief against such forfeiture:

"**10.** A tenant shall have the same right to apply for relief after judgment for possession of land on the ground of forfeiture for non-payment of rent as has been given under this Order as if the judgment had been given after trial."

3. Relief—statutory basis Relief for non-payment of rent may be sought under sections 210 to 212 of the Common Law Procedure Act 1852 and section 38 of the Supreme Court Act 1981. As to relief against forfeiture in the county court, see section 138 of the County Courts Act 1984; *U.D.T. Ltd v. Shellpoint Trustees Ltd* (1993) 4 All E.R. 310; *Escalus Properties Ltd v. Robinson* [1995] 3 W.L.R. 524, C.A.

2 The Act of 1852

1. Section 210—post-judgment relief—the true limits Section 210 in the 1852 Act in effect provides that a landlord has the right to re-enter the property when there are at least six months' rent owing but that any claim to relief must be made by the tenant within six months after execution of the judgment in respect of which relief is sought. So a time limit is set.

2. Section 211—stipulates conditions precedent to relief Section 211 of the Act enables the court to grant relief against forfeiture of the lease only on payment of everything that is due to the landlord for rent, arrears and costs.

3. Section 212—a pre-trial relief Section 212 differs from the other two sections in that it enables the relief to be granted before trial (or the hearing of an Ord. 14 summons) by providing that on payment of all rent, arrears and costs, the proceedings shall be discontinued.

4. Section 38 of the Act of 1981 The Act of 1852 cannot be invoked by the tenant where there are less than six months' arrears of rent: *Standard Pattern Co. Ltd v. Ivey* [1962] 1 Ch. 432. In that situation, the tenant must rely on section 38 of the Supreme Court Act 1981 which provides that:

> "38.—(1) In any action in the High Court for the forfeiture of a lease for non-payment of rent, the court shall have power to grant relief against forfeiture in a summary manner, and may do so subject to the same terms and conditions as to the payment of rent, costs or otherwise as could have been imposed by it in such an action immediately before the commencement of this Act.
>
>   (2) Where the lessee or a person deriving title under him is granted relief under this section, he shall hold the demised

premises in accordance with the terms of the lease without the necessity of a new lease."

3 The ambit of the court's discretion

1. The general rule The approach of the court in the exercise of this jurisdiction is conveniently summed up by Jenkins L.J. in *Gill v. Lewis* [1956] 2 Q.B. 1 at 13:

> "As to the conclusion of the whole matter, in my view, save in exceptional circumstances, the function of the court in exercising this equitable jurisdiction is to grant relief when all that is due for rent and costs has been paid up, and (in general) to disregard any other causes of complaint that a landlord may have against the tenant. The question is whether, provided all is paid up, the landlord will not have been fully compensated; and the view taken by the court is that if he gets the whole of his rent and costs then he has got all he is entitled to as far as rent is concerned, and extraneous matters of breach of covenant, and so forth, are, generally speaking, irrelevant.
>
> But there may be very exceptional cases in which the conduct of the tenants has been such as, in effect, to disqualify them from coming to the court and claiming any relief or assistance whatsoever. The kind of case I have in mind is that of a tenant falling into arrears with the rent of premises which he was notoriously using as a disorderly house."

2. For any breach of covenant No distinction is to be drawn in the exercise of this jurisdiction between cases of relief against forfeiture for non-payment of rent and other cases where relief against forfeiture is sought: *Starside Properties Ltd v. Mustapha* [1974] 1 W.L.R. 816.

3. Relief—may only be in part The court may grant relief against forfeiture of part of the demised premises in an appropriate case: *GMS Syndicate v. Gary Elliott Ltd* [1982] 1 Ch. 1.

4. The position of the sub-lessees It would appear that relief against forfeiture for non-payment of rent would also be available in Ord. 14 proceedings to the sub-lessee: *cf. Cadogan v. Dimovic* [1984] 1 W.L.R. 609 (in which case the sub-lessee should take out a summons for leave to intervene for the purpose of making the application for relief).

5. Relief—the effect of the order Relief against forfeiture restores the lease as if it had never been forfeited: *Dendy v. Evans* [1909] 2 K.B. 1894.

332

H: ACTING FOR THE PLAINTIFF

1 Introduction

1. The rule Ord. 14, r.2 provides:

"**2.**—(1) An application under rule 1 must be made by summons supported by an affidavit verifying the facts on which the claim, or part of the claim, to which the application relates is based and stating that in the deponent's belief there is no defence to that claim or part, as the case may be, or no defence except as to the amount of any damages claimed."

2. Conditions precedent to summary judgment The combined effects of Ord. 14, r.2(1) and Ord. 14, r.1(1) (as to which see p. 302) mean that, before the plaintiff can attend the hearing of an Ord. 14 summons with confidence, he must be able to satisfy the court that:

(a) the defendant has given notice of intention to defend the proceedings;
(b) he has served his statement of claim on the defendant;
(c) his Ord. 14 summons has been duly issued and served;
(d) the supporting affidavit is in required form and has been served with the summons;
(e) in his belief, the defendant has no defence.

2 Notice of intention to defend

1. Significance of such notice If the defendant has failed to return the acknowledgment of service or filed an acknowledgment of service indicating that he does not intend to contest the proceedings, the plaintiff can enter judgment in default under Ord. 13.

2. Several defendants If an action is brought against several defendants, Ord. 14 can be invoked against any one who was given notice of intention to defend. Ord. 13 can be invoked against those defendants who have not.

3. Partnerships In an action against partners sued as a firm, an acknowledgment of service by one partner indicating an intention to defend is an acknowledgment of the firm enabling judgment under Ord. 14 to be obtained against the firm: *Lysaght v. Clarke & Co.* (1891) 1 Q.B. 552; and see Ord. 81, r.3(1)(a).

4. What if a defence in fact delivered? The application under Ord. 14 need not necessarily be made before the defendant has delivered his defence. However:

(a) If the application is made thereafter, the plaintiff must show circumstances which justify the delay: *McLardy v. Slateum* (1890) 24 Q.B.D. 504.

(b) If the plaintiff has already received the defendant's defence, he may find himself unable to swear that there is no defence—unless, of course, he contends that the so-called defence is in reality no defence at all.

5. Does defence have to be delivered after issue of Order 14 summons? Suppose, after issue of the Ord. 14 summons and having given notice of intention to defend, the defendant fails to serve his defence within the time allowed. Can the plaintiff enter judgment in default of defence under Ord. 19? In *Hobson v. Monks* [1884] W.N. 8, Pearson J. said:

> "It seems to me that it would be an absurdity to hold that the defendant must put in a defence when the plaintiff is asking for final judgment on the ground that there is no defence. What is the use of the defendant's delivering a defence while the question is pending whether he is to be allowed to defend? My strong opinion is that when a summons is taken out under Order 14, the defendant ought not to put in a defence. When the summons is heard, the master can take all the circumstances into consideration and give what time he considers necessary."

So, the time for service of the defence does not run between the time of issue and the time of hearing of the Ord. 14 summons (see Ord. 18, r. 2(2)). Notwithstanding the dicta of Pearson J. however, about not putting in a defence, it is excellent practice to exhibit a draft defence to the defendant's affidavit lodged in an answer to the Ord. 14 summons.

6. How late in the day can an Order 14 summons be issued? In *Bath Press Ltd v. Rose*, *The Times*, July 13, 1987, the Court of Appeal held that where the court is satisfied that there is no defence to the plaintiff's claim, the fact that the plaintiff had not applied for summary judgment until after issuing a summons for directions following the close of pleadings does not raise any estoppel or technical objection which would prevent the plaintiff succeeding under Ord. 14. Indeed, in *Brinks Ltd v. Abu-Saleh* [1995] 4 All E.R. 65 it was held that delay in applying for an Ord. 14 judgment is not of itself a relevant matter in determining the application in circumstances where there is no defence to the claim. In certain cases, the use of a late Ord. 14 application might be commendable as saving both extra costs and time involved in a full trial. In that case it was estimated that 70 counsel would be appearing at trial.

7. A second Ord. 14 application? A second application under Ord. 14 is permissible provided that the legal or factual basis of the claim in the second application is separate from that relied on in the pleading underlying the first application: *Bristol & West of England Building Society v. Brandon, The Times*, March 9, 1995. A second application is, however, considered impermissible if the defendant has been granted unconditional leave to defend on the merits: *Fox v. Fontana Holdings Inc.* (C.A.T.) March 5, 1991 (unreported).

3 Applications for transfer

1. The problem If (a) the defendant does not reside or carry on business or have its registered office in the district of the registry in which the action is proceeding and (b) the cause of action did not arise within that district, the defendant may, on his acknowledgment of service, apply for the action to be transferred to the Royal Courts of Justice or another district registry (Ord. 4, r.5(3)). The plaintiff may object to that application. If he does, a hearing date is given. The plaintiff's Ord. 14 summons may also be due to be heard. Which application should be taken first?

2. A tactical device It is not unknown for a defendant, whose position in the action is hopeless, to use Ord. 4, r.5 as a tactical delaying device. If he succeeds in persuading the court to take his application first and succeeds on it—the Ord. 14 hearing is vacated and the plaintiff must seek a fresh Ord. 14 return date in the Royal Courts of Justice or in a new district registry.

3. The usual arguments The solicitor for the plaintiff usually contends that:
    (a) it is his prerogative to issue a Queen's Bench writ in London or any district registry;
    (b) that prerogative is given to him because he is responsible for the overall conduct of the action and so makes most of the running;
    (c) in order to create and sustain the momentum of the action, convenience dictates the retention of the action in the place of issue.
The defendant's solicitor usually counters that:
    (a) the action has no or only the most tenuous connection with the district in whose registry it was issued—the plaintiff's solicitor practises in that district;
    (b) the convenience of witnesses attending the trial demands a transfer;
    (c) it is in the interest of justice that the action be removed to that court where there will be the trial so that it will be one and the same court that determines both interlocutory matters and the trial itself.

4. The test-balance of interlocutory convenience Each case will necessarily turn on its own facts but in each case the court will have to consider the balance of convenience in relation to the *interlocutory* proceedings (see the unreported decisions of *Holden v. Trent Regional Health Authority* (November 17, 1980; unreported); *Schofield v. River Don Stamping Ltd and Woodhouse & Rixon Ltd* (Lincoln J. at Cardiff, December 12, 1980); *Grey v. Durham County Council* [1987] C.L.Y. 3109; *Fyffes Group Ltd v. T. L. Onions Ltd*, Kennedy J. at Liverpool, July 11, 1990).

5. A good working rule As a general rule, it is thought better to deal with the Ord. 14 summons first because, if the plaintiff succeeds, there may be no action to transfer. (See also *Smith v. Hurley* (1884) W.N. 99.)

4 Service of a statement of claim

1. In what form? The statement of claim may be indorsed on the writ (Ord. 6, r.2) or served separately either with the writ or at any time within 14 days of the defendant giving notice of intention to defend the action (Ord. 18, r.1).

2. Purpose of the form In either case the statement of claim must give sufficient particularity to enable the defendant to know the nature of the claim he is faced with and to enable him to give his solicitor proper instructions.

3. Defective form—fatal? A defect in the statement of claim cannot be cured by a simple averment in the plaintiff's Ord 14 affidavit: *Sheba Gold Mining Co. Ltd v. Trunshawe* [1892] 1 Q.B. 674.

4. Defective form—the plaintiff's cure A plaintiff is entitled to amend the writ and statement of claim once without leave prior to close of pleadings (Ord. 20, rr. 1 and 3) and afterwards with leave. So, he may amend between issue and the hearing of the Ord. 14 summons without issuing a fresh summons. Unless the defendant consents to the Ord. 14 hearing proceeding on the original return date, the plaintiff should obtain a fresh hearing date for the summons, warn the defendant not to attend on the original hearing, give him notice of the new hearing date and serve a copy of the amended statement of claim: *Satchwell v. Clarke* (1892) 66 L.T. 641 and *Bradley v. Chamberlyn* [1893] 1 Q.B. 439.

5 Issue and service of Order 14 summons

1. Pre-issue checks Before issuing the Ord. 14 summons, the plaintiff should make sure that:

(a) the action is not excluded from the Ord. 14 provisions (for example, under Ord. 14, r.1(2); Ord. 86 or Ord. 77, r.7);

(b) the defendant has given notice of intention to defend (or if more than one, that those against whom the Ord. 14 summons is issued have given such notice);

(c) the statement of claim has either been indorsed on the writ or if not has been served separately;

(d) the affidavit in support complies with Ord. 41 (see p. 341);

(e) the form and content of the summons are correct (see below, para. 5(2));

(f) if more than one year has expired since the acknowledgment of service filed, notice of intention to proceed has been given (Ord. 3, r. 6).

2. Summons—form and content The summons must:

(a) be correctly intituled;

(b) state that it relates to:

(i) the whole of the plaintiff's claim; or

(ii) part or parts of the plaintiff's claim (in which case it should identify the part or parts to which it relates), or

(iii) one or more of the several claims in the writ (in which case it should identify those claims to which it relates);

(c) (if there is more than one plaintiff) state by which of the plaintiffs it is brought;

(d) (if there is more than one defendant) state against which of the defendants it is brought;

(e) contain a notice to the following effect (see *Practice Direction (Order 14 Return Date)* [1970] 1 W.L.R. 258):

"Take notice that a party intending to oppose this application or to apply for a stay of execution should sent to the opposite party or his solicitor to serve him not less than three days before the date above-mentioned, a copy of any affidavit intended to be used."

(f) contain the name and address for service of the issuing solicitor;

(g) contain the name and address for service of the party against whom it was issued. (See Form N, p. 564.)

In addition, if the Ord. 14 application is to be combined with an application for an interim payment it must:

(a) include such an application;

(b) specify the grounds on which it is made.
(For precedent see Form M, p. 564.)

3. Requirements on issue

(a) *London—Q.B.D.:* Short Ord. 14 summonses are heard by Q.B. masters in chambers in the General List in Rooms E102, E103 and E110. The first summons issued in the action is assigned by the issuing officer to a named master who thereafter remains the assigned master for that action. The summons is issued in the Action Department of the central office. See Practice Direction 3(13), *The Supreme Court Practice* (1997) Vol. 2.

(b) *London—Q.B.D.—private room appointments:* If the Ord. 14 hearing is estimated to last longer than 20 minutes, the summons will be dealt with as a private room appointment. Private room appointments are obtained through the Master's Secretary's department or by going before the master who keeps his own diary for these appointments. The applicant must:
  (i) consult with all other parties as to inconvenient dates and the estimated length of hearing *before* making the private room appointment application;
  (ii) submit the appropriate application form (see *The Supreme Court Practice* (1997) Vol. 2, para. 711 for the form);
  (iii) the original summons;
  (iv) a certificate that the defendant has duly given notice of intention to defend. Postal applications may be sent to the Master's Secretary's department together with the appropriate fee (£20). (See Practice Direction 3(13) *The Supreme Court Practice* (1997) Vol. 2, para. 708.)

(c) *London—Q.B.D.—Senior Master's List:* In addition, Ord. 14 summonses of approximately 30 minutes' duration may be placed in the Senior Master's List which is taken each Wednesday and Thursday in term in Room E119. Appointments are obtained in Room E116 on any business day.

(d) *London Queen's Bench Division: Commercial List:* The plaintiff should seek a hearing date from the Clerk of the Commercial Court in Room E201, Royal Courts of Justice (tel. 0171 936 6826), by producing the summons (indorsed with time estimate) and the notice of intention to defend. The Clerk should be told immediately of any revision of that time estimate (by either party) for the more efficient conduct of judicial business (see *Practice Direction (Commercial Court: Urgent Matters)* [1981] 3 All E.R. 864). By *Practice Note (Commercial Court: Interlocutory Proceedings)* [1987] 3 All E.R. 799, the Commercial Court Judges prescribed stricter control of time limits for interlocutory hearings by directing the clerk not to accept estimates which in the case of Ord. 14 summonses exceed four hours. A longer time can only be obtained by counsel applying in writing to the judge in charge of the Commercial List. The Ord. 14 hearing takes place before the judge in chambers: see generally *The Supreme Court Practice* notes.

(e) *Mercantile Lists: Manchester and Liverpool:* Application for a hearing date should be made to the Mercantile List Listing Officer at the appropriate registry and the following should be lodged:
   (i) two copies of the summons indorsed with an estimate of the length of hearing (combined where appropriate, with an application for interim payment);
   (ii) the supporting affidavit;
   (iii) the affidavit in support of any application for an interim payment (where appropriate);
   (iv) a fee of £20 payable to H.M. Paymaster General.

All interlocutory summonses are returnable before the Circuit Mercantile Judge in chambers.

(f) *London Chancery Division:* The plaintiff should lodge with the county Clerk, the Chancery Chambers Registry, Room TM3.07, Thomas More Building Royal Courts of Justice, London WC2A 2LL:
   (i) two copies of the summons (indorsed with an estimate of the length of hearing);
   (ii) the supporting affidavit;
   (iii) the affidavit in support of any application for an interim payment;
   (iv) a fee of £20 payable to H.M. Paymaster General.

Reference should also be made to *Practice Direction (Chancery 5/92)* (1993) 1 All E.R. 359.

(g) *District Registry: Queen's Bench Division and Chancery Division:* The plaintiff should lodge at the district registry the documents listed in (e) above, together with the appropriate fee. The hearing takes place before the District Judge in chambers.

4. Service The Ord. 14 summons:
   (a) must be served within 14 days of its issue;
   (b) must be served not less than 10 clear days before the return date;
and any affidavit evidence relied on in support of the application must be served with the summons: Ord. 14, r.2(3) and Ord. 32, r.3 as substituted by R.S.C. (Amendment) 1994, r.7.

5. Mode of service The summons can either be served:
   (a) personally, or
   (b) by post, or

   (c) by delivery by hand at the proper address in the acknowledgment of
      service, or
   (d) through a document exchange in accordance with Ord. 65, r.5(2A),
      or
   (e) by fax in accordance with Ord. 65, r.5(2B).

6. Usual methods If personal service is effected it is likely that the enquiry
agent's costs will be disallowed unless there are exceptional circumstances.
Until changes were introduced on February 1, 1991, the almost invariable
method of service was by post. Now it is anticipated that service by
document exchange and fax will become the norm. So a word or two
about each method may assist.

7. Document exchange service The summons may be served through a
document exchange where either:
   (a) the proper address for service includes a numbered box at an
      approved document exchange; or
   (b) a DX box number is to be found on the writing paper of the person
      to be served (if he is acting in person) or on his solicitor's writing
      paper (if he is acting by solicitor); and
   (c) the party to be served or his solicitor (as the case may be) has not
      indicated in writing to the serving party that he is unwilling to accept
      DX service. So, if the letterhead contains a DX number, any document
      left at the DX is deemed to have been served on the second business
      day following the day on which it is left unless the contrary is
      proved.

8. Service by fax For the first time service by fax of documents (other than
writs and other originating process) is permitted by the R.S.C. which
followed hot on the heels of *Hastie & Jenkerson v. McMahon* [1990] 1
W.L.R. 1575, C.A., which had upheld service by fax. This method of
service is, however, more restrictive and is permissible only where:
   (a) the party serving the document acts by a solicitor;
   (b) the party to be served acts by a solicitor;
   (c) service is effected by faxing the document to the business address of
      the solicitor who acts for the party to be served;
   (d) that solicitor has indicated in writing to the solicitor serving the
      document that he is willing to accept service by fax at a specified
      fax number and the document has been sent to that number;
   (e) on the same day as the document is faxed, the solicitor for the party
      serving it serves another copy on the solicitor for the party served
      by any other method of ordinary service (post; DX). If he fails to
      do so, the document is deemed never to have been served.
For purposes of (d) above, the fact that the solicitor's notepaper contains

a fax number is treated as an indication of his willingness to accept service by fax at that number unless he states otherwise in writing.

A fax transmitted on a business day before 4.00 p.m. is deemed to have been served on that day unless the contrary is proved. If transmission takes place after 4.00 p.m. it is deemed to have taken place on the following business day. "Business day" means any day other than Saturday, Sunday, Christmas Day, Good Friday or a Bank Holiday.

9. Postal service—the service period problem If postal service is chosen, particular care should be taken in reckoning the service period. In order to avoid uncertainty as to the date of service, the court will presume (unless the contrary is established) that:
  (a) if the summons is sent by first-class post, it will be deemed to have arrived (and thus served) on the second working day after posting;
  (b) if sent by second-class post, on the fourth working day after posting (see Practice Direction No. 41 S.C.P. (1997) Vol. 2, para. 754).
"Working days" are Monday to Friday. They do not include Bank Holidays.

10. Calculating service period As the service period is over seven days, Saturdays and Sundays and other days mentioned in Ord. 3, r.2(5) are included in the reckoning. Thus:
  (a) If personal service—subtract 11 days from the return date as being the last day of service.
  (b) If first-class post—subtract 13 days.
  (c) If second-class post—subtract 15 days.
Remember also that if service of the summons is effected after 4.00 p.m. on a weekday, it counts as service on the following day. And service of a document on a Saturday after noon (including all day Sunday) counts as service on the following Monday (Ord. 65, r.7, and Ord. 65, r.10). so it will be seen that reckoning the service period may well be affected by the day of the week on which the summons is issued.

11. August The summons may be served in August because time for service of the defence does not run pending the determination of the Ord. 14 summons: *Hobson v. Monks* [1884] W.N. 8.

6 The plaintiff's affidavit

1. General It is of fundamental importance that the form and contents of the affidavit are correct—so important, that the rules regulating them are set out in *Practice Direction (Evidence Documents)* [1983] 1 W.L.R. 992, to which reference should be made. Reference should also be made to the

341

requirements of R.S.C. Ord. 41 and the new C.C.R., Ord. 20, r.10(3). In *Barclays Bank plc v. Piper, The Times,* May 31, 1995, the Court of Appeal held that if the affidavit is defective and a second affidavit which purported to cure the defects in the first affidavit conceded the defects in the first affidavit without correcting them, the court could not grant an order for summary judgment. So the plaintiff's failure to identify the deponent's source of information and belief in either affidavit was fatal to the application.

2. Prerequisites The plaintiff's affidavit must:
   (a) verify the facts on which the claim (or relative part) is based;
   (b) assert that there is no defence (either as to a part or to the whole or accept as to damages, as appropriate).

3. Hearsay It may contain statements of information and belief in which case it must state the sources and grounds of that information and belief: Ord. 14, r.2(2). If the affidavit fails to do so, the conditions imposed by the rule have not been fulfilled and the court has no jurisdiction to make an order: *Lagos v. Grunwaldt* [1910] 1 K.B. 41, C.A. In such a case it has been held that where the affidavit is insufficient so as to require a dismissal of the summons, the defendant is entitled to an order for payment of the costs of the application forthwith rather than waiting until the end of the action: *Symon & Co. v. Palmers' Stores (1903) Ltd* [1912] 1 K.B. 259.

4. Can defects be cured? The court has the power to allow the plaintiff to cure defects in the affidavit by allowing him to file a supplemental affidavit; *Begg v. Cooper* (1878) 40 L.T. 29; and *Les Fils Dreyfus v. Clarke* [1958] 1 W.L.R. 300; (but see *Barclays Bank plc v. Piper,* above).

5. Verification One of the functions of the plaintiff's affidavit is to verify the cause of the action. Such verification may be made in general terms by reference to the statement of claim: *May v. Chidley* [1894] 1 Q.B. 451, even when the particulars have been added by amendment: *Roberts v. Plant* [1895] 1 Q.B. 597, C.A. In other words it need not state or verify each (or any) of the particulars contained in the statement of claim.

6. Who swears? The affidavit must be made either by the plaintiff himself or someone whom he authorises to make it.

7. An employee? Yes—for example a clerk employed by the defendant in a responsible position may depose. In such circumstances the deponent should state that:
   (a) he is authorised by his employers to swear the affidavit, and
   (b) that it is within his knowledge that the debt was incurred, and

(c) that to the best of his knowledge and belief the debt still remains unpaid: *Pathe Freres Cinema Ltd v. United Electric Theatres Ltd* [1914] 3 K.B. 125, C.A.

8. A solicitor? Yes: *Chirgwin v. Russell* (1910) 27 T.L.R. 21, C.A. and his clerk: *Hallett v. Andrews* (1898) 42 S.J. 68. In ordinary commercial debt cases, it is quite unusual for the plaintiff's solicitor or the solicitor's clerk to swear on information and belief. But in a case which is out of the ordinary, it is prudent for the deponent to be the plaintiff or someone else with first hand knowledge.

9. "No defence" It is quite sufficient for the deponent to assert that there is no defence to the action; or to the part of the action with which the Ord. 14 summons is concerned; or save as to the quantum of damages.

10. Forms For specimen forms of supporting affidavits see Form B, p. 558 and Form S, p. 566.

I: ACTING FOR THE DEFENDANT

1 The defendant showing cause

1. Burden of proof—on the defendant Ord. 14, r.3 says that the court may give judgment for the plaintiff "unless on the hearing of an application under rule 1 either the court dismisses the application on the defendant satisfies the court with respect to the claim, or part of the claim, to which the application relates that there is an issue or question in dispute which ought to be tried or that there ought for some other reason to be a trial of that claim or part. . . ."

2. How high is the hurdle The hurdle which the defendant must surmount before being allowed to defend the case is modest. The height of the hurdle has, however, been raised and lowered at different times over the last century, perhaps reflecting changes in judicial policy objectives which reflect the variable pressures of commerce and litigation. In 1905, Lord Lindley said in *Codd v. Delap* (1905) 92 L.T. 510 H.L. that unless the alleged defence is practically moonshine, the defendant should be given leave to defend.

3. The modern low-water mark The low-water mark in modern times was reached in 1993 when, in *Paclantic Financing Co. Inc. v. Moscow Narodny Bank Ltd* (1983) 1 W.L.R. 1063, Webster J. concluded (at 1067) in a case

343

where the affidavits gave completely conflicting accounts of a transaction:

> "But in the absence of an opportunity to test the defendant's veracity, it seems to me that the court should never give summary judgment for the plaintiff where, upon the evidence before it, even a faint possibility of a defence exists."

4. Banque de Paris A year later, in 1984, the Court of Appeal by necessary inference rejected Webster J.'s test. In *Banque de Paris et des Pays-Bas (Suisse) SA v. de Naray* (1984) 1 Lloyd's Rep. 21, Ackner L.J. had this to say (at 23):

> "It is of course trite law that Ord. 14 proceedings are not decided by weighing the two affidavits. It is also trite that the mere assertion in an affidavit of a given situation which is the basis of a defence does not, *ipso facto*, provide leave to defend; the court must look at the whole situation and ask itself whether the defendant has satisfied the court that there is a fair or reasonable probability of the defendants' having a real or bona fide defence." (See also *Standard Chartered Bank v. Yacoub* (1990) C.A.T. 699).

5. The test today The *Banque de Paris* test was adopted in preference to the *Paclantic* test by the Court of Appeal in *National Westminster Bank plc v. Daniel* (1994) 1 All E.R. 156, another case in which the affidavits revealed conflicting accounts of a transaction. After a chronological review of the modern cases, Glidewell L.J. concluded (at 160):

> "I regard the test formulated by Webster J. [in *Paclantic*], with respect to him, as being too narrow and restrictive. I think it right to follow the words of Ackner L.J. in the *Banque de Paris* case, or indeed those which amount to much the same thing (as I see it) of Lloyd L.J. in *Standard Chartered Bank v. Yacoub*; is there a fair and reasonable probability of the defendants having a real or bona fide defence? Lloyd J. posed the test: is what the defendant says credible? If it is not, there is no fair or reasonable probability of him setting up a defence."

6. Showing cause—how? Ord. 14, r.4 provides:

> "**4.**—(1) A defendant may show cause against an application under rule 1 by affidavit or otherwise to the satisfaction of the court.
>
> (2) Rule 2(2) applies for the purposes of this rule as it applies for the purposes of that rule."

7. Ways of showing cause The defendant who seeks to oppose an application for judgment under Ord. 14 will have to do so in one or other of the following ways:

(a) On a preliminary technicality (see p. 345); or

(b) by showing that he has a clear defence (see p. 347); or

(c) by showing that there is a serious issue of fact to be tried (see p. 361); or

(d) by showing that there is an arguable point of law (see p. 363); or

(e) (in certain circumstances) by raising a prima facie set-off or counter-claim (see p. 370); or

(f) by showing the court that for some other reason there ought to be a trial (see p. 379).

2 The defendant's affidavit

1. The general rule The method by which the defendant should seek to show cause is by affidavit. Reference should be made to p. 347.

2. Time for service? Ord. 14 does not provide for service of a copy of the defendant's affidavit on a plaintiff.

3. The Practice Direction of 1970 Nevertheless, the Ord. 14 summons must contain a notice "that a party intending to oppose this application ... should send to the opposite party or his solicitor, to reach him not less than three clear days (before the return date) a copy of any affidavit intended to be used": *Practice Direction (Order 14: Return Date)* [1970] 1 W.L.R. 258.

4. Non-compliance—consequences If, as a result of the defendant's failure to comply with the Practice Direction, the hearing has to be adjourned, it is likely that the defendant will be condemned in costs. (See also *Fowkes v. Duthie* [1991] 1 All E.R. 337 on solicitor's liability.)

5. Information or belief Just as the affidavit sworn by or on behalf of the plaintiff may contain statements of information or belief together with the sources and the grounds, so also may the affidavit sworn or on behalf of the defendant: Ord. 14, r.2(2) as applied by Ord. 14, r.4(2).

3 Preliminary technicalities

1. Technicality—should the defendant serve an affidavit? If the defendant intends to base his opposition solely on a technicality, there is strictly no need for him to file an affidavit in opposition to the Ord. 14 summons: see *Bradley v. Chamberlyn* [1893] 1 Q.B. 439. However, if he intends to raise other grounds of opposition on the merits, he should file an affidavit dealing with those merits otherwise he may well be told on the hearing that it is too late. In *Bradley v. Chamberlyn* (above), Collins J. said dismissively:

> "The defendant has come to the court without an affidavit of merit, relying solely on his legal position, and it is now too late, after relying merely on legal technicalities, to turn round and ask for leave to make an affidavit of merits."

2. Claims outside Order 14 The most effective technical way of showing cause against an Ord. 14 summons is to show that Ord. 14 does not apply. So, for instance, the summons will be dismissed if a defendant establishes that the action is:

(a) an action attracting the right to trial by jury (see Ord. 14, r. 1(2)(a));

(b) an Admiralty action *in rem* (see Ord. 14, r.1(2)(c));

(c) an action to which Ord. 86 applies (see Ord. 14, r.1(3));

(d) an action involving the Crown in which application is sought against the Crown for Ord. 14 judgment (see Ord. 77, r.7);

(e) an action to enforce a mortgage (which is regulated by Ord. 88);

(f) a summary revenue application by the Crown under section 14 of the Crown Proceedings Act 1947 (see Ord. 77, r.8);

(g) a form of proceedings not regulated by the Rules of the Supreme Court such as for example, proceedings in bankruptcy; company winding-up proceedings; non-contentious or common form probate actions; proceedings under the Prize Courts Act 1894; Mental Health Act 1983 proceedings; Matrimonial proceedings in general (see Ord. 2, r.1).

3. Matrimonial proceedings Generally, Ord. 14 will not be appropriate in matrimonial proceedings. However, there is the "arrears of maintenance" exception. This was the position in *Temple v. Temple* [1976] 1 W.L.R. 701. The wife issued a writ against the husband in the Queen's Bench Division for arrears under a maintenance agreement, and applied for summary judgment. The Court of Appeal held that although there was jurisdiction for proceedings issued in the Queen's Bench Division to be transferred to the Family Division as she ought not to be deprived of the opportunity of obtaining summary judgment.

4. Statement of claim disclosing no cause of action For example, the assignee of a debt or other legal chose in action must bring himself within section 136 of the Law of Property Act 1925. That means that his statement of claim must expressly aver:

(a) an absolute assignment in writing, to him, of the chose in action, and

(b) that notice of the assignment has been given in writing to the defendant.

If the assignee cannot do so, he has not title to sue: *Read v. Brown* (1888) 22 Q.B.D. 128. In this context it should be remembered that the plaintiff may amend once without leave prior to close of pleadings.

5. Defect in plaintiff's affidavit Reference should be made to p. 341 where the matter is discussed more fully. In summary if the affidavit is defective, the plaintiff will normally be granted leave to file further evidence to cure the defect, subject to the possibility of being penalised in costs thrown away by amendment.

4 Establishing a defence

1. General denial—not sufficient It is inadequate for the defendant to restrict himself to a general denial in his affidavit: in *Re General Railway Syndicate, Whiteley's Case* [1900] 1 Ch. 365. Quite apart from other considerations, such a general denial excites the suspicion that the defendant himself cannot really believe that he has a defence since, if he had, he would have set it down in some detail. As Lord Blackburn said in *Wallingford v. Mutual Society* (1880) 5 App.Cas. 685 at 704:

"I think that when the affidavits are brought forward to raise a defence they must, if I may use the expression, condescend upon particulars. It is not enough to swear, 'I say I owe the man nothing.' Doubtless, if it was true, that he owed the man nothing, as you swear, that would be a good defence. But that is not enough. You must satisfy the judge that there is reasonable ground for saying so. So again, if you swear that there was fraud, that will not do. It is difficult to define it, but you must give such an extent of definite facts pointing to the fraud as to satisfy the judge that those are facts which make it reasonable that you should be allowed to raise that defence. And in like manner as to illegality, and every other defence that might be mentioned." (And see *Banque de Paris v. Costa de Naray* [1984] 1 Lloyd's Rep. 21, C.A. and also *Potato Marketing Board v. Drysdale* [1986] C.M.L.R. 331, C.A.; *Bremar Holdings Ltd v. De Roth* (1984) 134 New L.J. 550.)

2. Exhibiting draft defence It will undoubtedly help the defendant in his attempt to convince the court of his bona fide if he exhibits to his affidavit a draft of the intended defence but such a course is not an essential requirement of Ord. 14.

3. Hardship—no defence Hardship to the defendant does not amount to a defence: *Earl of Desart v. Townsend* (1887) 22 L.R.Ir. 389. If the defendant finds himself defenceless and penniless, it is in his interest to keep the costs down. Thus he should not make an issue of liability under Ord. 14 but rather consent to judgment being entered and state his intention to seek a stay of execution on the judgment. He can do this either in the Acknowledgment of Service or, if he has passed up that opportunity, by issuing a summons under Ord. 47 supported by affidavit setting out details of his means and making some offer to discharge the debt by instalments.

4. Liability of third party—no defence It may happen that the defendant acknowledges that as between him and the plaintiff he has no defence but that the law allows him to pass the liability down the line to someone else against whom he, in turn, has a cause of action. This, too, affords no ground for opposing judgment under Ord. 14 (but see *Pinemain Ltd v. Welbeck International Ltd* (1985) 129 S.J. 66).

5. Admission of part liability only Suppose that the defendant can set up a defence to part only of the plaintiff's claim? Ord. 14, rr.3 and 8 enable the court to give the plaintiff judgment on the admitted part and the defendant leave to defend as to the balance. What it will not generally do, is to give the defendant leave to defend the disputed part only on condition that he pays the admitted part into the court or to the plaintiff direct: *Dennis v. Seymour* (1879) Ex.D. 80; *Lazarus v. Smith* [1908] 2 K.B. 266, C.A.

6. But what if the defendant does not put a figure on the part of the claim admitted? Suppose that the plaintiff claims a liquidated sum and that the defendant, although acknowledging that he owes something, declines to put a figure on it. Should the court refuse to give judgment to the plaintiff under Ord. 14? Should the court allow the defendant to obtain any advantage on that account? Should he be allowed to pay nothing? In *Ellis Mechanical Services Ltd v. Wates Construction Ltd* [1978] 1 Lloyd's Rep. 33, Bridge L.J. said:

> "To my mind, the test to be applied in such a case is perfectly clear. The question to be asked is: is it established beyond reasonable doubt by the evidence before the court that at least £X is presently due from the defendant to the plaintiff? If it is, the judgment should be given for the plaintiff for that sum whatever X may be, and in a case where, as here, there is an arbitration clause, the remainder should go to arbitration. The reason why arbitration should not be extended to cover the area of the £X is indeed because there is no issue, or difference, referable to arbitration in respect of that amount." (But

cf. Hayter v. Nelson (1990) 23 Con LR 88; *Thyssen v. Higgs* (1990) 23 Con LR 101).

In the same case Lawton L.J. gave this as the reason for that approach:

"If the [defendant] can turn round, as [he] has done in this case and say: 'Well, I don't accept your account; therefore there is a dispute,' that dispute must be referred to arbitration and the arbitration must take its ordinary long and tedious course. Then the sub-contractor is put into considerable difficulties; he is deprived of his commercial lifeblood. It seems to me that the administration of just in our courts should do all it can to restore that lifeblood as quickly as possible. ... In my judgment it can be avoided if the courts make a robust approach, as the Master did in this case, to the jurisdiction under Order 14."

7. A frequent problem in the building industry The *Ellis* case was concerned with a problem which frequently arises in the construction industry and which is a fruitful source of litigation—the architect's certificate. The architect issues a certificate that a specific sum representing the value of the work done by the plaintiff contractor is due to him from the defendant employer. The defendant refuses to pay contending that the work has been overvalued. As was seen in the *Ellis* case, it is not good enough for the defendant simply to say: "The certificate is overvalued. I want to investigate the accounts." He must demonstrate by affidavit (if necessary, backed up by authenticated expert calculations of an architect or quantity surveyor) that there is sufficient material on which the court is entitled to conclude that the defendant has a bona fide arguable contention that the certificate is open to challenge. Once the defendant does that, the plaintiff is not entitled to immediate payment and summary judgment unless the contract expressly says so. If, as is usually the case, the building contract contains an arbitration clause, the defendant is entitled to have the issue arbitrated: *Pillings (C.M.) & Co. Ltd v. Kent Investments Ltd* (1985) 30 Build. L.R. 80. If, however, it is clear that the defendant does owe the plaintiff something under the certificate, the court, it seems, has the power (after inviting counsel to make representations as to the amount) to order the defendant to provide the plaintiff with some security, such as a bank guarantee, for a certified sum as a condition of staying the proceedings and allowing the dispute to go to arbitration (*ibid.*); but see *The World Star* [1986] 2 Lloyd's Rep. 274, where it was held that it was not open to the court to impose conditions upon which a stay under section 1 of the Arbitration Act 1975, is imposed.

8. What if the court cannot summarily assess a sum which is indisputably due? Despite it being clear that the plaintiff will recover something,

349

summary judgment will not be entered if there is no quantified or definable part of the claim which is indisputably due: *Associated Bulk Carriers Ltd v. Koch Shipping Inc.; The Fuohsan Maru* [1978] 2 All E.R. 254. In this case the plaintiff, a shipowner, let a bulk carrier to the defendant on a time charter for five years in 1974. During the period of the charter, the tanker market collapsed precipitating the defendants into wrongfully repudiating the charterparty. The plaintiff brought an action claiming damages for $4,000,000 representing the estimated loss of hire, and applied for summary judgment. The defendants admitted liability for wrongful repudiation but denied that the plaintiff was entitled to the amount claimed. They said that there was a dispute which should be referred to arbitration. *Obiter* the Court of Appeal held that the plaintiffs were not entitled to summary judgment under Ord. 14 for it was impossible to identify or quantify any particular part of their claim which was indisputably due or in respect of which there was no defence. Geoffrey Lane L.J. went on to say that in any event, the plaintiff must assert and prove what he alleged to be the moneys indisputably due (but see *Welling Private Hospital v. Baum* [1988] C.L.Y. 2940, and p. 000 below). This was one of the problems facing the plaintiff in *Ochse v. Duncan* (1887) 3 T.L.R. 220 where an allegation made apparently in good faith that the claim was excessive was one of the reasons for allowing the defendant unconditional leave to defend. Similarly, if the evidence discloses the need for the taking of account to decide whether some (and if so, what) amount has been paid in respect of sums claimed in the action, the defendant will be given leave to defend: *Lynde v. Waithman* [1895] 2 Q.B. 180.

9. The defendants admit £X "or thereabouts" In *Contract Discount Corporation v. Furlong* [1948] 1 All E.R. 274, two of the defendants filed an affidavit in Ord. 14 proceedings in which they said: "We admit that we are indebted to the plaintiffs but we say that to the best of our knowledge, information and belief such amounts will be found, upon full investigation, to be £10,000 or thereabouts." The plaintiffs' claim for £19,000 under a guarantee. The Court of Appeal held that the defendants' admission was qualified by the words "or thereabouts" and might be read as "£10,000 with a reasonable margin" for which allowance ought to be made. It varied the judge's order so that the defendants were given liberty to defend as to the whole claim subject to payment into court of £8,000 and in default of such payment the plaintiffs were to have liberty to sign judgment for £8,000 and the defendants would have liberty to defend as to the residue of the claim.

10. Defence of tender Where the defendant pleads tender before action the court will allow him to defend the action on payment within a specified time of the amount alleged to have been tendered and it will order that the amount paid in shall be treated as if paid into court with a plea of tender. If the defendant fails to make the payment into court within the prescribed time, the plaintiff is entitled to judgment for the sum claimed. But if it is clear on the Ord. 14 summons that the defendant's plea of tender before action accompanied by a payment into court in satisfaction is correct, the court will dismiss the Ord. 14 summons and order the plaintiff to pay the defendant's costs because he should never have sued in the first place: *Griffiths v. School Board of Ystradyfodwg* (1890) 24 Q.B.D. 307.

11. Multiple defendants If it happens that the master is satisfied that the first defendant has an arguable defence but the second defendant has not, he may give summary judgment against the latter and allow the action against the former to proceed to trial: Ord. 14, r.8.

12. Joint defendants Judgment, whether in tort or contract or otherwise, against one defendant jointly liable to the plaintiff does not operate as a bar to continuing against the remainder: Civil Liability (Contribution) Act 1978, s.3.

13. An exception: alternative defendants If the plaintiff sues the first and second defendant and only one of them can be liable in law to the plaintiff but not both (as, for instance, if the first defendant is allegedly the second defendant's principal), he cannot seek Ord. 14 judgment against one and proceed to trial against the other. He issues his summons and takes his chance since judgment against the one operates as a bar to proceedings against the other: *Morrell Bros. v. West Moreland* [1903] 1 K.B. 64, C.A. Moreover, the plaintiff cannot seek to set aside the judgment against the one in order to remove the bar on proceedings against the other: *Cross v. Matthews* (1904) 91 L.T. 500; but see *City of Westminster v. Reeme Construction Ltd* (1990) 20 Con LR 44.

5 The interim payment palliative

1. Interim payments defined An interim payment is a payment on account of any damages, debt or other sums (excluding costs) which a defendant may be held liable to pay to or for the benefit of the plaintiff: Ord. 29, r.9.

2. No inherent power The power to make rules of court to enable courts to make interim payment orders was first conferred by section 20 of the Administration of Justice Act 1969. The court has no inherent power to order an interim payment: *Moore v. Assignment Courier* [1977] 1 W.L.R.

638. Prior to 1980, the problem was that the power to order interim payment was restricted to fatal accident and personal injury claims and actions for possession of land.

3. *Associated Bulk Carriers*—problem overcome The problem facing the plaintiffs in *Associated Bulk Carriers* (above) has since been alleviated by the extension of Ord. 29 relating to interim payments so as to give the court power to make a payment on account of any damages, debt, or other sum which a defendant may be held liable to pay to or for the benefit of the plaintiff. The object of the power to order interim payments is simply to ensure that money which the court is satisfied rightfully be in the plaintiff's pocket is not retained by the defendant in his pocket. Ord. 29 specifically recognises the plaintiff's right to couple an application for an interim payment with an Ord. 14 summons: Ord. 29, r.10(2): see also *Messenger Newspapers Group Ltd. v. National Graphical Association* [1984] I.C.R. 345 and *Halvanon Insurance Co. v. Central Reinsurance Corporation* [1984] 2 Lloyd's Rep. 420. The merit of combining the two is that if summary judgment is refused, the court may order an interim payment.

4. Damages and debts—separate codes? Ord. 29, r.11 requires the court to be satisfied that if the action proceeded to trial the plaintiff would obtain judgment for substantial damages. Ord. 29, r.12 deals with claims other than for damages. There the court must be satisfied that if the action proceeded to trial, the plaintiff would obtain judgment for a substantial sum of money apart from damages. In *Shearson Lehman Brothers Inc. v. MacLaine, Watson & Co. Ltd* [1987] 1 W.L.R. 480, the plaintiffs claimed payment of liquidated sums and in the alternative unliquidated damages for breach of contract. The judge was satisfied that the plaintiff would recover either £5.2m. as damages or £7.2m. as a liquidated sum at trial but, because he could not be satisfied which—liquidated or unliquidated— he refused the application. The Court of Appeal held that he had erred in his approach.

5. Rules 11 and 12 form a single code Lloyd L.J. resolved the apparent dichotomy thus (at 485G):

> "The solution lies, as so often, in the way the question is asked. By asking two separate questions you create the difficulty. By asking a single question the difficulty disappears. Still on the assumption that all the sub-paragraphs had been contained in a single rule, if you ask, 'Am I satisfied that the plaintiff will succeed under (a)?,' the answer would be 'No' if he were equally likely to succeed under (b). If you were then to ask, 'Am I satisfied that the plaintiff will succeed under

(b)?,' the answer would again be 'No,' because he would be equally likely to succeed under (a). But if you were to ask the single question, 'Am I satisfied that he will succeed under (a) or (b)?,' the answer would be a resounding 'Yes.' There is nothing in the *language* of rule 11 (still on the same assumption) that would compel you to ask two questions rather than one."

And so he concluded (at 487A):

"So I would read rule 11(1)(c) and rule 12(c) together in the following way: 'If, on the hearing of an application under rule 10 in an action for damages, the court is satisfied that ... the plaintiff would obtain judgment for substantial damages ... or that ... the plaintiff would obtain judgment ... for a substantial sum of money apart from damages ... the court may, if it thinks fit, and without prejudice to any contentions of the parties as to the nature or character of the sum to be paid by the defendant, order the defendant to make an interim payment...' "

6 The court's approach to interim payments

1. A two-stage exercise Whether the application is made under r.11 or r.12 or both, the court has to embark on a two-stage exercise. First, it must be satisfied of the existence of one of the three requirements set out in paragraph 3 below. Secondly, and only if the plaintiff gets over stage one— the court may, if it thinks fit, proceed to order an interim payment of such an amount as it thinks fit.

2. No necessity to show need or prejudice It is not necessary for the plaintiff to establish the need for an interim payment nor that if one is not made he will suffer hardship or prejudice: *Schott Kem Ltd. v. Bentley* [1991] 1 Q.B. 61; *Stringman v. McArdle, The Times*, November 19, 1993. It is, however, customary in personal injury claims for interim payments to be limited to sums for which the plaintiff can show a need because large interim payments in such cases may lead to difficulties if an order for repayment is made under Ord. 29, r.17.

3. What the plaintiff must establish—damages claims A plaintiff seeking an interim payment against a defendant against whom he is claiming damages must satisfy the court that:
(a) that defendant has admitted liability; or
(b) he has obtained interlocutory judgment against the defendant for damages to be assessed; or
(c) if the action proceeded to trial he would obtain judgment for

substantial damages against that defendant or where there are two or more defendants, against any of them: Ord. 29, r.11(1).

4. Personal injury cases In addition, in personal injury cases, the defendant against whom an interim payment order is sought must either be:
(a) insured against the plaintiff's claim, or
(b) a public authority, or
(c) a person whose resources are such as to enable him to make the interim payments (Ord. 29, r.11(2)).

See also *Powney v. Coxage, The Times,* March 8, 1988; *cf. O'Driscoll v. Sleigh* (November 20, 1984, C.A.T. No. 510; unreported).

5. Other money claims A plaintiff seeking an interim payment on account of monies claimed other than damages may satisfy the court that:
(a) he has obtained an order for an account to be taken as between himself and the defendant and for any amount certified as due on the account to be paid; or
(b) in land possession claims, if the action proceeded to trial the defendant would be liable to pay money to the plaintiff for the defendant's use and occupation of during the pendency of the claim; or
(c) if the action proceeded to trial, the plaintiff would obtain judgment against the defendant for a substantial sum of money apart from any damages or costs.

6. "Satisfied"—standard of proof In *Shearson Lehman Brothers Inc. v. MacLaine, Watson & Co. Ltd* (above), Lloyd L.J. said ([1987] 1 W.L.R. 480 at 489):

> "Something more than a prima facie case is clearly required, but not proof beyond reasonable doubt. The burden is high. But it is a civil burden on the balance of probabilities, not a criminal burden. This involves no lasting hardship on the defendants, since there is provision for readjustment at the trial in the case of an overpayment."

7. "Satisfied"—Ord. 14 and Ord. 29 contrasted How, it may be asked, can the court, on the hearing of an Ord. 29 summons, be satisfied that the plaintiff would obtain judgment for a substantial sum against the defendant if the action proceeded to trial, and at the same time conclude, on the hearing of a combined Ord. 14 summons, that the apparent strength of the defendant's case is such as to warrant the court granting him unconditional leave to defend? Are interim payments possible where the defendant is granted unconditional leave to defend?

8. Conflict in the Court of Appeal In *Shanning International Ltd v. George Wimpey International Ltd* [1989] 1 W.L.R. 981, the judge granted the defendant unconditional leave to defend and then made an order for an interim payment in favour of the plaintiff. On appeal, the Court of Appeal was faced with the rhetorical question posed in the last paragraph. Glidewell L.J. after reciting counsel's submission that the test under Ord. 29 is less stringent than under Ord. 14 said (at 990):

"... Shanning, in order to bring itself within r.12(c), in order to satisfy the first stage, must satisfy the court on the balance of probabilities but to a high standard. Once it accepts that Wimpey has a genuinely arguable claim for an amount which may equal or exceed its admitted claim ... it cannot in my view satisfy this burden."

Three weeks later, in *Ricci Burns Ltd v. Toole* [1989] 1 W.L.R. 993, another division of the Court of Appeal had to consider the very same point. In that case, the Court of Appeal held that an order granting the defendant unconditional leave to defend and an order for an interim payment were not mutually incompatible.

9. *British and Commonwealth Holdings plc v. Quadrex Holdings Inc.* Yet another division of the Court of Appeal had the identical point raised again. After considering *Shanning*, *Ricci Burns* and *Gibbons v. Wall, The Times*, February 24, 1988 Browne-Wilkinson V.-C. stated in *British and Commonwealth Holdings plc v. Quadrex Holdings Inc.* [1989] Q.B. 842 that he could see no reconciliation between *Shanning* and *Ricci Burns* and concluded (at 745D):

"For myself, I find it an impossible concept that the same court can be simultaneously 'satisfied' that the plaintiff *will* succeed at trial and at the same time consider that the defendant has an arguable defence sufficient to warrant unconditional leave to defend. If there is a distinction between the two concepts which I have failed to detect, such distinction must in my judgment be the result of 'an uncommon nicety of approach' which the requirements of certainty in the law would make it undesirable to recognise. In my judgment, therefore, it is impossible to make an order for interim payment where unconditional leave to defend has been given."

10. *Andrews v. Schooling* It now seems to be generally accepted that *Quadrex* is to be preferred to *Ricci Burns*. In *Andrews v. Schooling* [1991] 1 W.L.R. 783, the Court of Appeal held that an order for an interim payment was inconsistent with an order granting unconditional leave to defend. A perceived exception may occur where the plaintiff applies for interlocutory judgment in a personal injury action and the defendant is given unconditional leave to defend on account of the plaintiff's alleged contributory negligence.

11. "Satisfied"—"likely to succeed" not enough In *Andrews*, the judge had asked himself whether the plaintiff could satisfy him that he was likely to succeed at trial. Balcombe L.J. said that "likely to succeed" is not enough. He quoted from the judgment of Sir Nicolas Browne-Wilkinson V.-C. in *Quadrex* (at (1989) Q.B. 842 at 865–866):

> "But Order 29 (as construed by this court in the *Shearson Lehman Brothers Inc v. Maclaine, Watson & Co. Ltd* [1987] 1 W.L.R. 480) requires the court, at the first stage, to be satisfied that the plaintiff *will* succeed and the burden is a high one: it is not enough that the court thinks it likely that the plaintiff will succeed at trial." (See also *Gibbons v. Wall, The Times*, February 24, 1988).

12. Satisfied—relevance of plaintiff's resources Whilst, as we have seen, the plaintiff does not have to establish the need for an interim payment, his financial position may have some relevance. In *Smallman Construction Ltd v. Redpath Dorman Long Ltd* (1989) 5(62) Const.L.J. 62, Bingham L.J. considered it a matter of ordinary common sense that the greater the doubt about the plaintiff's ability to repay an interim payment if required to do so, the greater the need to be satisfied that repayment would not be called for.

13. Complex cases In *Crown House Engineering Ltd v. Amec Projects Ltd* (1989) 48 B.L.R. 32 Bingham L.J. emphasised that Ord. 29, r. 12 enables the court to order payment to a plaintiff to the extent that a claim, although not actually admitted, can scarcely be effectively denied. The procedure was, he said, entirely inappropriate where the plaintiff's entitlement to recover any sum is the subject of any serious dispute whether of law or fact. This was said in the context of a large mechanical and electrical contract which was part of a large design and construction project and has been interpreted as suggesting that large construction cases may be unsuitable for Ord. 29. Certainly there is a danger in the case of difficult questions of law that real embarrassment could be caused if the trial judge reached a different conclusion on the law than that reached by the master or district judge on the interim payments application.

7 Other points of substance

1. Conditional leave to defend It is clear that where the court entertains sufficient doubt as to the genuineness of the defence to grant only *conditional* leave to defend, it may order an interim payment if in all the circumstances such a payment appears to be sensible: *British and Commonwealth Holdings plc v. Quadrex Holdings Inc.* (above). In *Andrews* (above) the defendant was ordered to make an interim payment as a condition of being granted leave to defend.

2. Arguable point of law Where there is an arguable point of law an interim payment order is inappropriate: *Crown House Engineering v. Amec Projects Ltd* (1990) 6 Const.L.J. 141, C.A.

3. Impact of cross-claims and contributory negligence In deciding whether the plaintiff would recover substantial damages or a substantial sum of money if the action proceeded to trial, the court has to take account of any contributory negligence, set-off, cross-claim or counterclaim: Ord. 29, r.11(1) and r.12. But at what stage—the stage when it is determining whether the plaintiff will get judgment? Or at the second stage when fixing the amount of the interim payment? The answer is that it must do so at both stages. In *Shanning* (above) Glidewell L.J. put it thus (at 989D–G):

> "I agree with the judge that it was correct for him to consider the matter arising on the application for an interim payment in two stages. The first stage was to answer the question, was he satisfied that, if the action proceeded to trial, the plaintiff would obtain judgment for a substantial sum? If the action did proceed to trial, the court would, of course, have to rule on the defendant's counterclaim and set-off. As I have said, if the amount set-off exceeded the amount found to be due to the plaintiff in the first instance, there would be no judgment for the plaintiff. In my judgment, on the wording of the rule it is inescapable that, at stage 1, the likelihood of the set-off or any other defence succeeding must be considered by the court.
>
> If, but only if, the court is satisfied at stage 1, then it proceeds to consider at stage 2 whether, in its discretion, it should order an interim payment and, if so, of what amount. At that stage the rules again require the court to take any set-off claimed by the defendant into account or any counterclaim arising out of some other transaction and not available as a defence and, in an application under rule 11, any alleged contributory negligence."

(See also Imodco Ltd v. Wimpey Major Projects Ltd (December 18, 1987, C.A.T. No. 1312); *Smallman Construction Ltd v. Redpath Dorman Long Ltd* (1989) 5 Const.L.J. 62; *Old Grovebury Manor Farm v. W. Seymour Ltd* [1979] 1 All E.R. 573.)

4. Defendant's resources We have seen (at p. 354) that in personal injury cases, the plaintiff needs to establish that the defendant is insured; or a public authority; or whose resources are such that he can afford to make an interim payment. In non-personal injury cases there is no such requirement yet as the power to order an interim payment is discretionary, even in non-personal injury cases, and so the defendant's financial resources are relevant. In *Quadrex* (above) the court rejected an argument that they were irrelevant but accepted that they were not decisive. The test is that if a defendant's resources are such that an interim payment order would cause immediate harm which cannot be made good by an eventual repayment, that is a very relevant factor to be taken into account in fixing the amount of any interim payment: *per* Sir Nicholas Browne-Wilkinson V.-C. in *Quadrex* (at [1989] 3 W.L.R. 746; see also *Newton Chemicals Ltd v. Arsenis* [1989] 1 W.L.R. 1297 C.A.).

5. Instalments Should the defendant plead poverty, the plaintiff would do well to bear in mind that the court has the power to order an interim payment to be made "in one sum or by such instalments as the court thinks fit": Ord. 29, r. 13(3).

6. Ord. 29 and stay of proceedings Suppose that the plaintiff applies for an interim payment and the defendant issues a cross summons seeking a stay of proceedings in order that the dispute might be referred to arbitration. If the court is minded to grant the stay, has it the power before doing so to make an interim payment order? After all, it may be argued, the court can hardly be satisfied that the plaintiff will recover substantial damages if the action proceeded to trial, when the court knows full well that there may well not be a trial once it has imposed a stay. In *Imodco* (above) the Court of Appeal held that the court has jurisdiction to order an interim payment in such a situation.

7. Multiple defendants The plaintiff seeking an order for an interim payment against a number of defendants on the grounds that if the action were to proceed to trial he would obtain substantial damages against one or some of them, must satisfy the court, with a high degree of proof and beyond merely making out a prima facie case, that he will be likely to recover against a particular defendant before the court will make an order against the defendant. It is not sufficient for the plaintiff to prove that he will succeed against some unspecified defendant: see *Breeze v. McKinnon (ibid.)*. An order may be made against two or more defendants in respect of the same sum and the same liability if the court is satisfied as to the liability of each such defendant. Again, an order may be made against multiple defendants for different fractions of the total amount thought to be just so long as it's made clear that the interim sum could not exceed (a) if the aggregate of the fraction exceeded "the just amount," that amount, and (b) in the case of a claim for damages, the "reasonable proportion" of the damages: *Schott Kem Ltd v. Bentley* [1991] 1 Q.B. 61.

8. Appeals and interim payments The fact that the defendant informs the court that he intends to appeal against the order for summary judgment is no reason for refusing the plaintiff's application for an interim payment: *Halvanon Insurance Co. Ltd v. Central Reinsurance Corporation* [1984] 2 Lloyd's Rep. 420.

9. Interest The court has power to award interest on an interim payment; *I.B.A. v. EMI Electronics Ltd* (November 13, 1981; unreported). The rate and amount of the interest should be shown in the order together with the dates from and to which it is calculated. In personal injury cases, the order should make it clear whether the payment is on account of general or special damages because of the different interest rates applicable to each.

10. Repayment with interest In ordering a plaintiff to repay an interim payment pursuant to section 32(3) of the Supreme Court Act 1981, the court has power under Ord. 29, r.17 to order the payment of interest on the sum: *Wardens and Commonalty of the Mystery of Mercers of the City of London v. New Hampshire Insurance Co.* [1992] 1 Lloyd's Rep. 431.

11. Motor Insurers' Bureau The court has no jurisdiction to make an interim payments order against the M.I.B. which has been joined in an action for personal injuries since the plaintiff has no cause of action against the Bureau and could not get judgment against it at trial: *Powney v. Coxage, The Times*, March 8, 1988.

12. Compensation Recovery Unit An interim payment falls within the definition of a compensation payment under section 81(1) Social Security Administration Act 1992. The defendant should thus obtain a certificate of total deduction under section 84 unless the amount of the interim payment is an exempt payment under section 81(3)—at present "small payments", *i.e.* those not exceeding £2,500, are exempt. There would appear to be no reason why an interim payment order should not refer to the C.R.U. deduction being taken into account as long as the court is aware of the amount of the certificate before fixing the amount of the payment. Any benefits recouped at the interim payment stage will be taken into account when the action is concluded.

13. Legal Aid Board—statutory charge The Legal Aid Board's statutory charge created by section 16(6) Legal Aid Act, 1988 does not apply to interim payments, whether paid under an order or voluntarily: Civil Legal Aid (General) Regulations, 1989, regulation 94(a).

14. Payments in and interim payments There is no objection to the court being informed, at the hearing of the application, of any payment into court: *Fryer v. London Transport Executive, The Times*, December 4, 1982. If an order is made, it usually contains a direction for the payment to be met out of the money in court.

15. Non-disclosure of interim payment order The existence of an interim payment order must not be pleaded nor disclosed to the trial judge until all questions of liability and quantum have been decided: Ord. 29, r.15.

8 Interim payments—procedural requirements

1. Time Application may be made against any defendant who has been served with the writ and whose time for acknowledging service has expired.

2. Mode Application is by summons which, as is recognised by Ord. 29, r.10(2), may be included in an Ord. 14 summons. Fee £20.

3. Supporting affidavit—Ord. 14 and Ord. 29—different requirements The affidavit in support of the plaintiff's application under Ord. 29 must comply strictly with Ord. 29, r.10(3) by verifying the amount claimed, the grounds of the application and exhibiting the documentary evidence relied upon. So the common form of affidavit used in Ord. 14 proceedings is not sufficient for the purpose of an application under Ord. 29: *Breeze v. McKinnon (R.) & Son* (1986) 130 S.J. 16.

4. Personal injury claims The supporting affidavit should:
   (a) confirm that the defendant is within Ord. 29, r.11(2)—see paragraph 6.4 (at p. 354);
   (b) exhibit any relevant medical report;
   (c) give particulars of any special damages and past and future loss of earnings;
   (d) although not strictly necessary, set out any special needs or hardship.

5. The service period The service period of 10 clear days is the same as for the Ord. 14 summons (see p. 341 for a detailed discussion of the service rules). Although the initial supporting affidavit has to be served at least 10 clear days before the return date, it is not necessary for supplemental affidavits to be so served: *Barstow v. Roberts & Co. (Building)* (June 11, 1985, C.A.T. No. 272; unreported).

6. Forum Normally the hearing takes place before the master or district judge in chambers. A High Court Judge has power to hear the application:

Smith v. Glennon, The Times, June 26, 1990. In the Manchester and Liverpool Commercial Lists, the Circuit Commercial judge hears all inter-locutory applications (including applications for interim payments).

9 Triable issues of fact

1. Order 14—not a trial on affidavits It very rarely occurs that the defendant establishes a quite conclusive and incontrovertible defence on an Ord. 14 summons so as summarily to curtail the proceedings. Generally he will only be able to say at best "I do not honestly believe that the plaintiff's claim is valid. There is a genuine and serious disagreement between us on the facts. The plaintiff contends one view of the facts. I take an entirely different view. My liability to the plaintiff depends upon the view of the facts taken by the judge after he has heard all the evidence. If the judge finds against me on the facts, it is likely I will be found to be liable to the plaintiff. If he finds for me on the facts, my defence is likely to succeed." In such circumstances, the defendant ought never to be denied a trial: *per* Baron Pollack in *Saw v. Hakim* (1889) 5 T.L.R. 72. Thus, it is not the aim of Ord. 14 to secure a trial on summons in chambers.

2. The Proper Order 14 test Reference should be made to p. 344 for the proper test to be applied in determining whether the defendant should be allowed to defend the action.

3. The problem of the "shadowy defence" Very often, the master or district judge will have serious doubts of the defendant's chance of succeeding in resisting the plaintiff's claim. He may very well say to himself, "I am strongly of the opinion that the defendant is unlikely to succeed. I think his so-called defence is weak and 'shadowy.'" Yet he will then say, "But I am at a disadvantage. I haven't seen all the documents. I haven't listened to any of the witnesses. I have not had the chance of observing their general demeanour in the witness-box. In short, I am not in a position to make any final judgment." So the defendant would generally be given the chance to defend: see for example, *Paclantic Financing Co. Inc. v. Moscow Narodny Bank Ltd* [1984] 1 W.L.R. 931; and see *Refidian Bank v. Agom Universal Sugar Trading Co. Ltd, The Times,* December 23, 1986; *Midland Bank v. Phillips, The Times,* March 28, 1986; *Banque de Paris v. de Naray* [1984] 1 Lloyd's Rep. 21. C.A.; *National Westminster Bank plc v. Daniel* [1994] 1 All E.R. 156.

4. A "shadowy" defence may be no defence In *Lady Anne Tennant v. Associated Newspapers Group Ltd* [1979] F.S.R. 298, Sir Robert Megarry

V.-C. said of the defendants' attempts to persuade him that there was a triable issue, at 302:

> "Now under Ord. 14, r.3 I must refuse to enter judgment of the plaintiff if the defendants satisfy me that there is 'some issue or question in dispute which ought to be tried or that there ought for some other reason to be a trial of the action.' [Counsel for the defendant] addressed me at some length, but from the first to last he failed to make it clear to me what issue or question there was in dispute that ought to be tried."

And then a little later on at 303 he continued:

> "The desire to investigate alleged obscurities and the hope that something will turn up on the investigation cannot, separately or together, amount to sufficient reason for refusing to enter judgment for the plaintiff. You do not get leave to defend by putting forward a case that is all surmise and Micawberism ... accordingly, I think that the plaintiff is entitled to judgment. In my view, when stripped of [counsel for the defendants'] ingenuity, this is a plain case."

See also *Bremar Holdings Ltd v. de Roth* (1984) 134 New L.J. 550.

5. Re-running the criminal defence In *Brinks Ltd v. Abu-Saleh* (No.1) [1995] 4 All E.R. 65, the plaintiffs were bailees of over £27m worth of gold. The gold was stolen from Heathrow airport. The plaintiffs brought civil proceedings against a number of the alleged robber's handlers, those converting the gold into money and innocent converters. There were 57 defendants in all. A number of the robbers and handlers were caught, tried and convicted. Just before the civil trial it occurred to the plaintiffs that they should seek Ord. 14 judgment against the convicted criminal defendants. Some of those defendants had served terse defences in the civil action putting the plaintiff to proof and asserting their innocence. Was this enough to raise triable issues of fact?

6. Civil Evidence Act 1968 Section 11 of the Civil Evidence Act 1968 provides firstly that the fact that a person has been convicted of an offence is admissible in evidence in later civil proceedings as proof of his conviction. Secondly, once the conviction is proved in those civil proceedings, he is to be taken to have committed that offence unless the contrary is proved.

7. What has to be established? In *Brinks*, Jacob J. said (at 69h):

> "For the defendants to suceed they need more than simply a retrial in the civil action on essentially the same evidence as was called at the criminal trial. A hope that the civil judge will take a different view

from a jury who found the case proved beyond a reasonable doubt does not justify a civil trial relitigating the same issues as were tried criminally. A trial on such a basis would be an abuse of process ... To relitigate the matter now they need to show at least that new evidence not called at the criminal trial will be called at the civil trial. Such evidence must not only be new but must 'entirely change the aspect of the case'. That this is so is apparent from *Hunter v. Chief Constable of West Midlands* [1982] A.C. 529, [1981] 3 W.L.R. 906, H.L., where convicted criminals were not permitted to relitigate matters determined against them in criminal proceedings ... In the case of Ord. 14 therefore, a defendant cannot show that there is an issue which ought to be tried if he has lost that issue in a criminal trial and is simply seeking its relitigation on essentially the same evidence. This defence would be an abuse of process". (See also *Ladkarn Holdings Ltd v. Summit Property Developments Ltd* 32 Con LR 66.)

10 An arguable point of law

1. Arguing the unarguable If the legal point taken on behalf of the defendant is quite clearly unarguable, the court has precisely the same duty under Ord. 14 as it has in any other case: *Carol v. Casey* [1949] 1 K.B. 474. In that case involving a claim for possession of a dwelling house (as being outside the scope of the Rent Restriction Acts) Lord Greene M.R. said:

"The only point is that, as everybody knows, the Rent Restriction Acts are complicated Acts. They contain a number of difficult matters and there are a number of authorities decided upon them, but it is not sufficient under an Order 14 case to flourish the title of the Rent Restriction Acts in the face of the court and say that it is enough to give leave to defend. If the point taken under the Rent Restriction Acts is quite obviously an unarguable point, the court has precisely the same duty as it has in any other case. It may take a little longer to understand the point ... but when the point is understood and the court is satisfied that it is really unarguable, the court has the duty to apply the rule." (See also *Customs & Excise Commissioners v. Holvey* [1978] 1 Q.B. 311.)

2. Argument on law—forum? On the Ord. 14 summons or at trial? In *Verrall v. Great Yarmouth Borough Council* [1981] Q.B. 202 Roskill L.J. gives the following answer:

"We have often said in this court in recent years that where there is a clear cut issue raised in Order 14 proceedings, there is no reason why the judge in chambers—or, for that matter, this court—should not deal with the whole matter at once. Merely to order a trial so that the matters can be reargued in open court is to encourage the law's delays which in this court we are always trying to prevent." (See *Forestal Mimosa Ltd v. Oriental Credit Ltd* [1986] 1 W.L.R. 631 at 636C; *S.L. Sethia Liners Ltd v. State Trading Corporation of India Ltd* [1985] 1 W.L.R. 1398 at 1401).

3. Simple points of construction So, in *Coastal (Bermuda) Ltd v. Esso Petroleum Ltd* [1984] 1 Lloyd's Rep. 11, where the dispute was over a pure question of construing the legal effect of documents in such a way as to give effect to the true commercial intent of the parties, the court held that the plaintiff was entitled to summary judgment. The result is that if the defendant raises a point of law which the court feels able to consider without reference to contested facts simply on the submissions of the parties, it is now settled that in applications for summary judgment under Ord. 14, the court will do so in order to see whether there is in any substance in the proposed defence. If it concludes that the point, though arguable, is bad, it will give judgment for the plaintiff there and then.

4. Limits Yet this principle must not be taken too far. Although, where the defendant seeks to set up a point of law which has no real substance to it, it is the policy of the court to decide that point of law finally under the Ord. 14 summons, in all other circumstances, the better view is that argument should be left to trial: see *Zakhem International Construction Ltd v. Nippon Kokkan K.K.* [1987] 2 Lloyd's Rep. 596; *Systems Control v. Monro Corporate* [1990] BCC 386; *Crown House Engineering Ltd v. Amec Projects Ltd* (1989) 48 B.L.R. 32; *Home and Overseas Ins. Co. Ltd v. Mentor Ins. Co. (UK) Ltd* [1989] 3 All E.R. 73. So in *Pinemain Ltd v. Welbeck International Ltd* (1985) 129 S.J. 66, Kerr L.J. said that the point of law in that case was delivered by the judge in a 17-page judgment after he had considered a number of cases, statutes and textbooks. That was not a desirable course. Having concluded (as he had done) that there was an arguable defence, the judge should at once have given leave to defend: and see *Hoffman-La Roche (F.) & Co. A.G. v. Harris Pharmaceuticals Ltd* [1976] F.S.R. 154; *S.L. Sethia Liners Ltd v. State Trading Corporation of India Ltd* [1985] 1 W.L.R. 1398; and *Heyes v. Derby* (1984) 272 EG 939. In *Schindler Lifts (Hong Kong) Ltd v. Shui On Construction Co. Ltd* (1984) 29 Build.L.R. 95, although the questions in issue on the Ord. 14 summons were questions involving the legal construction of contract documents, the case was held not appropriate for decision under Ord. 14. There was a complex chain of building contracts binding the employer, main contractor and sub-contractors.

5. A recent restatement In *Carter (R.G.) Ltd v. Clarke* [1990] 1 W.L.R. 578, Lord Donaldson M.R. summarised the current state of the law when the court takes the view on an Ord. 14 summons that there is a triable issue of law (at 584F):

> "If a judge is satisfied that there are not issues of fact between the parties, it would be pointless for him to give leave to defend on the basis that there was a triable issue of law. The only result would be that another judge would have to consider the same arguments and decide that issue one way or another. Even if the issue of law is complex and highly arguable, it is far better if he then and there decides it himself, entering judgment for the plaintiff or the defendant as the case may be on the basis of his decision. The parties are then free to take the matter straight to this court, if so advised. This was the situation in the classic case of *Cow v. Casey* [1949] 1 K.B. 474. But it is quite different if the issue of law is not decisive of all the issues between the parties or, if decisive of part of the plaintiff's claim or of some of those issues, is of such a character as would not justify its being determined as a preliminary point, because little or no savings in costs would ensue. It is an *a fortiori* case if the answer to the question of law is in any way dependent on undecided issues of fact."

11 The new Order 14A

1. The rule stated On February 1, 1991 the scope of Ord. 14 was extended by the introduction of a rule giving the court wider powers summarily to determine questions of law and construction. Ord. 14A, r.1 provides:

> "1.—(1) The Court may upon the application of a party or of its own motion determine any question of law or construction of any document arising in any cause or matter at any stage of the proceedings where it appears to the Court that—
> (a) such question is suitable for determination without a full trial of the action, and
> (b) such determination will finally determine (subject only to any possible appeal) the entire cause or matter or any claim or issue therein.
>
> (2) Upon such determination the Court may dismiss the cause or matter or make such order or judgment as it thinks just.
>
> (3) The Court shall not determine any question under this Order unless the parties have either—
>
> (a) had an opportunity of being heard on the question, or
> (b) consented to an order or judgment on such determination.

(4) The jurisdiction of the Court under this Order may be exercised by a master.

(5) Nothing in this Order shall limit the powers of the Court under Order 18, rule 19 or any other provision of these rules."

2. Its purpose The purpose of the change is to provide a form of summary judgment additional to those which already exist. By this new provision, the court is empowered to give judgment in favour of a defendant as well as a plaintiff in all cases where a question of law or construction is thought suitable for determination without a full trial and where the determination will finally dispose of the entire case (or an issue in it).

3. Its Scope The Scope of Ord. 14A was considered by the Court of Appeal in *Korso Finance Establishment Anstalt v. Wedge* (1994) C.A.T. February 15 (unreported). Leggatt L.J. made the following points of principle. Firstly, the construction of a document is well capable of constituting an issue under Ord. 14A. Secondly, an issue may be said to be a disputed point of fact or law relied on by way of claim or defence. Thirdly, ". . . the judge was, in effect, saying that the Court should not entertain the application [under Ord. 14A] unless determination of the issue of construction would finally determine the entire matter. That was plainly wrong, both as an interpretation of the Order and as an exercise of discretion. In my judgment, having rightly decided that the issue could be properly disposed of without evidence and discovery, if he decided on the side of the plaintiffs, it would determine the action. In any event the question of construction was a dominant feature of the case and the judge ought to have proceeded to determine that issue." Fourthly, when the court is, to the knowledge of all the parties, being invited to construe a document and the parties think that there are circumstances which the court should take account of in performing that task, the parties are entitled to adduce evidence about them. For example, in *Korso* the draftsman of the document might have been expected to explain the circumstances in which he prepared it, yet he remained silent. What respondents are not entitled to do is contend that they should be allowed to hunt around for evidence or that something might turn up on discovery which will explain or modify the meaning of the document. In the absence of any such evidence the court should not refrain from dealing with the application. See also *Prenn v. Simmonds* [1971] 1 W.L.R. 1381; [1971] 3 All E.R. 257 H.L.; *E. v. Dorset C.C.* [1994] 3 W.L.R. 853; *X. v. Bedfordshire C.C.* [1995] 152 at 175.

4. Procedural defect cured Before this change it sometimes became clear during the course of the hearing of an Ord. 14 summons that not only did the defendant have an arguable defence on a point of law but that the defence was a good one. As things stood, the court was powerless to give judgment for the defendant and so there was nothing to prevent the plaintiff from ploughing on to trial. Ord. 18, r. 19(1) is only available in the clearest cases and in any event could not be invoked by the court of its own motion. The rule enables the court to give judgment there and then either way on application or of its own motion.

5. Application—when? The greatest flexibility is permitted since application can be made by summons or on motion or orally in the course of any interlocutory application to court.

6. The Crown No application can be made under Ord. 14A against the Crown.

7. Ord. 14A—requirements If Ord. 14A is to be invoked:
   (a) the defendant must have given notice of intention to defend. If he has not done so, judgment in default may be entered under Ord. 13;
   (b) the question of law or construction must be suitable for summary determination. In this context reference should be made to the section "An arguable point of law" in this chapter (p. 363 *et seq.*);
   (c) the determination of the point of law or construction must be determinative of the entire action. It is not appropriate to determine preliminary issues for which Ord. 33, r.3 is intended;
   (d) the parties must either:
      (i) have had an opportunity of being heard on the point of determination; or
      (ii) have consented to judgment or an order on the determination.

8. Practice The application should normally be made by summons specifying the point of law or construction upon which a decision, determinative of the action, is sought. Affidavit evidence of the material facts should be filed. The application may be combined with an application under Ord. 14. The court does have the power, however, to determine issues at any stage of the proceedings and can do so of its own motion as well as on application. It follows that Ord. 14A can be invoked orally and during the course of another interlocutory application.

12 Foreign law, criminal law and arbitration stays

1. Foreign law The courts have shown a marked reluctance to determine points of foreign law summarily. For example, in *Western National Bank of New York v. Perez, Triana & Co.* (1891) 6 T.L.R. 366 Lord Coleridge L.C.J. said it was impossible for the court to try a question as to the law of New York on affidavits under Ord. 14. The defendant was entitled to defend the action. *Cf. Israel Discount Bank of New York v. Hadjipateras* [1984] 1 W.L.R. 137; *Williams and Humbert Ltd v. W. and H. Trade Marks (Jersey) Ltd* [1986] A.C. 368.

2. European law Matters of construction of the provisions of the Treaty of Rome—to the extent that they relate to anti-competition practices—are not designed for Ord. 14 procedure: *Dymond v. Britton & Sons (Holdings) Ltd* [1976] F.S.R. 330 and see *Potato Marketing Board v. Drysdale* [1986] C.M.L.R. 331.

3. The civil law/criminal law interface In *Jefferson v. Bhetcha* [1979] 1 W.L.R. 898 the plaintiffs employed the defendant as an accounts clerk. Following her dismissal, it was discovered that some cheques appeared to have been misappropriated and paid into the defendant's bank account. The plaintiffs sued her for those moneys and issues an Ord. 14 summons. The defendant swore an affidavit in which she stated that she was being prosecuted for offences connected with the cheques and that if she were required to swear an affidavit for the purposes of Ord. 14 she would be required to disclose her defence in criminal proceedings. Forbes J. ordered the Ord. 14 proceedings to be adjourned until the conclusion of the criminal proceedings. On appeal, Megaw L.J. held that there was no established principle of law that the defendant was entitled to be excused from taking in the civil action any procedural steps resulting in the disclosure of her defence in the criminal proceedings. The court had a discretion to order a stay (under section 41 of the Supreme Court Act 1981) of the civil action if it appeared to the court that the balance of justice between the parties so required, having regard to the concurrent criminal proceedings and the "right of silence" of the defendant. But the so-called "right of silence" did not extend as a matter of right so as to prevent a plaintiff in a civil action from pursuing his remedy in the ordinary way. The Court of Appeal concluded that the justice of the case required the restoration of the Ord. 14 summons.

4. The arguable point of law and the arbitration clause The contract contains an arbitration clause referring all disputes to arbitration. The plaintiff issues proceedings and takes out an Ord. 14 summons. The defendant issues a cross summons for a stay of proceedings under section 4(1) of the Arbitration Act 1950 or section 1 of the Arbitration Act 1975. Should the court proceed to hear the Ord. 14 summons or grant the stay? That was the issue in *S.L. Sethia Liners v. State Trading Corporation of India* (above). The Court of Appeal held that under Ord. 14 proceedings where the defence depended on an arguable point of law on which the plaintiff was clearly right, the court would give judgment for the plaintiff and dismiss any cross-application for a stay, since there was no dispute to go to arbitration. But if the plaintiff was not clearly right, the court would grant leave to defend without determining the point of law and would be bound to grant an application to stay and refer the matter to arbitration (unless the parties agreed that the court should determine the point of law and waive any arbitration agreement in its entirety); see also *Schindler Lifts (Hong Kong) Ltd v. Shui On Construction Co. Ltd* (above); *Archital Luxfer v. Dunning & Son* [1987] 1 FTLR 372—summary judgment on part of claim—balance to arbitration. In *Chatbrown Ltd v. Alfred McAlpine Construction (Southern) Ltd* (1986) 35 Build.L.R. 44, it was expressly held that in applications for summary judgment under Ord. 14 the court will deal with questions of law (in that case the construction of clause 15(2) of FASS blue form) if it can properly do so and the position is no different where there is an arbitration clause.

5. Arbitration "disputes" The question posed here is: when is a dispute not a dispute? One view is that there is a dispute until the defendant admits that the sum claimed is due and payable (see *e.g.* Templeman L.J. in *Ellerine v. Klinger* [1992] 1 W.L.R. 1375 at 1383; *Hayter v. Nelson* (1990) 2 W.L.R. 265; *The M Enegli* [1981] 2 Lloyd's Rep. 169; *Douglas Construction v. Bass Leisure* (1990) 53 B.L.R. 119; and *Smith Ltd v. H & S International* [1991] 2 Lloyd's Rep. 127; and *Thyssen Engineering GmbH v. Higgs & Hill plc* 23 Con LR 101). This view defines "dispute" in a subjective sense so that only in the simplest and clearest cases where it is readily and immediately demonstrable that the defendant has no good grounds at all for disputing the claim should he be deprived of his right to arbitrate.

6. "Disputes"—the objective view Another line of authority would adopt a more objective approach by asking whether the plaintiff's claim is genuinely disputable (see, *e.g. Sethia* (above); *The John C. Helmsing* (1990) 2 Lloyd's Rep. 290—where Bingham L.J. reviews the relevant authorities). The divergence of view remains, as yet, unresolved. Whether there is also a difference of substance in the wording of section 4(1) Arbitration Act 1950 and section 1 Arbitration Act 1975 also remains to be resolved.

7. Arbitration and stay: step in action It is well established that the defendant is precluded from applying for arbitration if he takes a step in the action before he applies for arbitration. That principle applies even if, when he takes that step in the action, he does not realise that there is an arbitration clause. The step in the action which would preclude an application for a stay does not have to be an application to the court by the defendant. It is sufficient if the defendant consents to an application to the court made by the plaintiff: *County Theatres & Hotels Ltd v. Knowles* [1902] 1 K.B. 480 and *Richardson v. Le Maitre* [1903] 2 Ch. 222; and see *Marzell Investment v. Trans Telex* (June 25, 1986 C.A.T. No. 587;

369

unreported). Thus, where the plaintiff issues an Ord. 14 summons and, before applying for arbitration the defendant filed an affidavit in reply to the Ord. 14 proceedings in which, *inter alia*, he invited the court to consider whether it would be more appropriate to refer the matter to arbitration, that course of action would constitute a step in the action and preclude the application for a stay: *Turner & Goudy v. McConnell* [1985] 1 W.L.R. 898. Where in Ord. 14 proceedings the defendant alleges an agreement not to sue in England and the question of a stay of proceedings arises, the correct approach is to determine the question of stay before dealing with the Ord. 14 summons. *Morgan Guaranty Trust Co. v. Hadjantonakis* (No. 2) [1988] 1 Lloyd's Rep. 375.

8. Stay on terms In *Pillings (C.M.) Co. Ltd v. Kent Investments Ltd* (1985) 30 Build.L.R. 80 the plaintiffs, as contractors, entered into a building contract *(J.C.T. Fixed Fee Form of Prime Cost Contract 1967*, ed. 1976 revision). The architect issued a certificate for £110,000 but revised it to £101,529. This sum was not paid by the defendant employer. The plaintiffs sought summary judgment under Ord. 14 and the defendant applied for a stay so that the matter could be referred to arbitration. At the hearing the judge decided that there was a dispute which entitled the defendants to have leave to defend and that they were entitled to a stay. On appeal, the Court of Appeal held that under that form of contract there was no right to immediate payment since the employer was entitled to challenge the correctness of the certificate by arbitration without first having made payment thereunder. However, as the case was a borderline case in which no clear-cut challenge to the certificate had been established, the plaintiffs should have some security for the sum which had not been paid. Subject to hearing counsel, security in the sum of £70,000 was ordered by means of a bank guarantee (but see *The World Star* [1986] 2 Lloyd's Rep. 274 where it was held that it was not open to the court to impose conditions upon which a stay under section 1 of the Arbitration Act 1975 is imposed).

13 Cross-claims—the general rule

1. Set-off—the general rule The right of a defendant either at law or in equity to offset the plaintiff's claim by a monetary cross-claim generally amounts to a defence in its own right to the extent of the amount found due under a set-off: *Banks v. Jarvis* [1903] 1 K.B. 549, *per* Channell J. at 553. This is because the existence and the amount of the set-off must be taken to be known by the plaintiff who should give credit for it in his action against the defendant: *Stooke v. Taylor* (1880) 5 Q.B.D. 569 at 576. To the extent of his set-off the defendant is entitled to unconditional leave to defend: *United Overseas Ltd v. Robinson Ltd* (unreported) (1991) C.A.T.

March 26; it is for the court to determine whether the defendant's claim to set-off is arguable or not. In *Hargreaves v. Action 2000* 62 B.L.R. 72 C.A., however, it was held that a set-off at common law is available only if the claims on both sides are in respect of liquidated debts or money demands which can readily and without difficulty be met. It has been said that there is a case for reform of the law, which has been described as unsatisfactory: *Axel Johnson Petroleum AB v. M. G. Mineral Group* [1992] 1 W.L.R. 270 at 274 and 276.

2. The reason The historical reason for the general rule is that the old courts of Chancery would not allow the plaintiff to proceed with his claim where the defendant could establish that it would be unconscionable to allow him to do so. As was said in *Rawson v. Samuel* (1841) Cr. & Ph. 161 the defendant's equitable right undermined the plaintiff's legal demand; see also *Hanak v. Green* [1958] 2 Q.B. 9. Perhaps more to the point, the original purpose of section 13 of the Insolvent Debtors Relief Act 1729, which allowed mutual debts to be set off between plaintiffs and defendants, was to prevent debtors from being cast in to prison for failure to meet a judgment when, on a full taking of accounts, they might not be indebted at all.

3. Set-off—the classic definition Whether a cross-claim by the defendant falls within the description of a legal set-off depends on Cockburn C.J.'s classic definition in *Stooke v. Taylor (supra)* (at 575) when he said that "this plea is available only where the claims on both sides are in respect of liquidated debts or money demands which can be readily and without difficulty ascertained".

4. Readily ascertainable—what does it mean? To be within the definition, is the proper approach to ask whether the cross-claim is arithmetically easy to quantify; or should the focus be the defendant's claim to see if it is a liquidated one, no matter whether there may be disputed issues as to quantum? In *Aectra Refining and Marketing Inc. v. Exmar NV* [1995] 1 All E.R. 641, a claim under a charter party for the stipulated daily rate of hire in respect of specific off-hire periods was held to be a liquidated debt which was capable of being a legal set-off against the plaintiff's claim in an unrelated dispute notwithstanding that disputed issues as to the quantum of the defendant's claim had been raised by the plaintiff and remained unresolved.

5. The general rule—a working example In *Morgan & Son Ltd v. S. Martin Johnson & Co. Ltd* [1949] 1 K.B. 107, the plaintiffs as bailees claimed charges in respect of the storage of the defendant's vehicles. The defendant deposed:

"I admit that the plaintiffs stored vehicles and that, but for the matters hereinafter referred to the amount claimed in the writ would be due from the defendant to the plaintiffs but I say that the plaintiffs in breach of their duty as bailees of the defendant of a certain Dodge vehicle either delivered up the said vehicle to someone without the authority of the defendant or, alternatively, kept so inefficient a watch on the said vehicle that it was stolen."

On the hearing of the Ord. 14 summons the court gave judgment to the plaintiffs on the claim in view of the defendant's admission but stayed execution pending the determination of the defendant's cross-claim, and it was this which was the subject-matter of the appeal to the Court of Appeal. That tribunal gave the defendant unconditional leave to defend the whole action.

6. *Morgan & Sons*: leave to appeal—why? The master and judge at first instance failed to appreciate that the defendant's unliquidated cross-claim was a defence in its own right. It should be noted that a set-off frequently consists of a liquidated claim but in *Morgan's* case the set-off consisted of a claim to unliquidated damages; see also Ord. 18, r.17 and section 49(2) of the Supreme Court Act 1981; *Liverpool Properties v. Oldbridge Investments* (1985) 276 E.G. 1352, C.A.; *Sable Contractors Ltd v. Bluett Shipping Ltd* [1979] 2 Lloyd's Rep. 33; *Rapid Building Group Ltd v. Ealing Family Housing Assoc. Ltd* (1984) 29 Build.L.R. 5; *Dole Dried Fruit & Nut Co. v. Trustin Kerwood Ltd* [1990] 2 Lloyd's Rep. 309.

7. Connected counterclaim A second class of case—the first class comprising set-off—is where the defendant sets up a bona fide counterclaim arising out of the same subject-matter as the claim and connected with the grounds of the defence. In this case the order should not be for judgment on the claim subject to a stay of execution pending trial of the counterclaim but should be for unconditional leave to defend even if the defendant admits the whole or part of the claim: *United Overseas Ltd v. Robinson* (above); *A. B. Contractors Ltd v. Flaherty Bros. Ltd* (1978) 16 B.L.R. 8; *Drake & Fletcher Ltd v. Batchelor* (1986) 83 L.S.G. 1232; *Dole Dried Fruit & Nut Ltd v. Trustin Kerwood* [1990] 2 Lloyd's Rep. 309.

8. Admitted claim—arguable counterclaim A third class of case arises where the defendant has no defence to the plaintiff's claim but sets up a plausible counterclaim for an amount not less than the plaintiff's claim. Here the plaintiff should not be put to the trouble and expense of proving his claim. In such a case the order should not be for leave to defend but should be for judgment for the plaintiff on the claim and costs with a stay of execution pending trial of the counterclaim: *Sheppards & Co. v.*

Wilkinson & Jarvis (1889) 6 T.L.R. 13; *United Overseas Ltd v. Robinson* (above).

9. Unconnected counterclaims The fourth class of case is where the counterclaim arises out of a quite separate and distinct transaction or is wholly foreign to the claim. Here the proper order is for judgment for the plaintiff with costs without stay: *United Overseas Ltd v. Robinson* (above); *Rotherham v. Priest* (1879) 28 W.R. 277: see also *Redpath Dorman Long Ltd v. Tubeworking Ltd* C.A.T. (unreported) March 15, 1984; *Anglian Building Products v. French Construction Ltd* (1972) 16 B.L.R. 1; *Shell International Petroleum Co. Ltd v. Transnor (Bermuda) Ltd* (1987) 1 Lloyd's Rep. 363.

10. Set-off and arbitration It has been said that to be available as a set-off, a cross-claim must be capable of being litigated in the court where the set-off is pleaded. If so, would it follow that a cross-claim does not qualify for set-off if the parties to the plaintiff's litigation have agreed that the defendant's claim should be submitted to the decision of an arbitrator? New judicial terminology was introduced by Hoffman L.J. in *Aectra Refining v. Exmar NV* [1995] 1 All E.R. 641 in order to resolve the matter.

11. *Aectra*—the facts The plaintiff chartered two vessels from the defendant. "M.T. Pacifica" was chartered under the first charterparty. "M.T. New Vanguard" was chartered under the second. Both charterparties led to disputes which were referred to arbitration. The "New Vanguard" arbitration was settled, the defendant agreeing to pay the plaintiff $U.S. 120,000. In the Pacifica arbitration the arbitrator made an interim award to the defendant of $U.S. 42,000 as being indisputably due. The rest remained in dispute. The defendant's solicitor then wrote to the plaintiff's solicitor suggesting that they should deduct the $U.S. 42,000 due to the defendant from the $U.S. 120,000 due to the plaintiff. The plaintiff agreed to that proposal, but the defendant's solicitor also asked whether they could hang on to the $U.S. 78,000 as security for the remaining claims of the defendant in the unresolved Pacifica arbitration instead of *Marevaring* it. The plaintiff rejected the proposal, issued proceedings for the $U.S. 78,000 and applied for Ord. 14 judgment. The defendant resisted the application on the ground that its unresolved Pacifica arbitration claims for hire and bunkers were liquidated claims capable of set-off at common law. The Court of Appeal accepted that argument; but the plaintiff further contended that the defendant's claim did not qualify as a set-off since it had been to arbitration by agreement.

12. "Independant" and "transaction set-off" Hoffman L.J. found that there was no authority on the point and went back to first principles. He drew a distinction between "independent set-off" and "transaction set-off". The former does not require any relationship between the transactions out of which the parties' cross-claims arise. The only requirements are that they must both be due and payable and either liquidated or capable of being quantified by reference to ascertainable facts which do not in their nature require estimation or valuation. "Transaction set-off", on the other hand, is a cross-claim arising out of the same transaction or one so closely related that it operates in law or in equity as a complete or partial defeasance of the plaintiff's claim. The authorities are, he said, in favour of allowing transaction set-off to be pleaded even though it had been submitted to arbitration or to a different jurisdiction on the ground that it obviously makes good sense. But, he continued, the argument is not nearly so strong in the case of independent set-off which is not a substantive defence to the claim but a procedure for taking account of the balance due between parties. Nevertheless he concluded that as a basic rule it is of the essence of independent set-off in English law that the defendant should be entitled to have the merits of his cross-claim tried by the court in which he has been impleaded. He reminded himself thus, however; what the defendant in this case was seeking was leave to defend the plaintiff's action. That necessarily involved the right of the defendant to have his cross-claim adjudicated by the court. But the defendant had no such right because he has agreed to the jurisdiction of another tribunal and so could not assert an independent set-off.

13. Cross-claims in the building industry

(a) *R.I.B.A. contracts:* There is no special set of rules applicable to cross-claims in the building industry. Some doubt as to whether the defence of set-off applied to the R.I.B.A. and other known forms of building contracts and sub-contracts was cast in 1971 in the case of *Dawnays Ltd v. F. G. Minter Ltd* [1971] 1 W.L.R. 1205. That doubt was dispelled in *Modern Engineering (Bristol) Ltd v. Gilbert-Ash (Northern) Ltd* [1974] A.C. 689 by Lord Salmon at 726H–727B:

> "I have no doubt that the standard forms of R.I.B.A. main contract and the standard forms of sub-contract, despite certain obscurities, work well enough in practice. The provisions relating to interim certificates as a rule ensure a steady cash flow in normal conditions, which is what I think they are designed to do. When, however, a bona fide dispute arises, I do not think the contract is designed to put the plaintiff contractors or sub-contractors in a fundamentally better position than any ordinary plaintiffs nor the defendants in any worse position than any ordinary defendants. I can find nothing in any of the standard forms which support the view that the defendants are deprived of their ordinary rights of set-off. Indeed, the arbitration

clause in the main contract form and in what is called the 'green form' of sub-contract respectively allow the building owners and the contractors to attack an architect's interim certificate during the currency of the work on the ground that it is not in accordance with the contractual conditions and then have the dispute referred to arbitration. This strongly supports the view that the right to hold up payment pending decision still remains and that the ordinary rights of set-off have not been eroded.''

(b) *Pay now—arbitrate later? An all-too-familiar problem:* The plaintiff is a builder. He is under contract with the defendant employer to construct certain building works. The architects issues a certificate stating the amount payable to the builder from the employer. The contract provides that the plaintiff shall be entitled to payment from the defendant within the period for honouring certificates (frequently 14 days). The contract contains an arbitration clause. The employer wishes to challenge the correctness of the certificate by referring the dispute to arbitration. Can the plaintiff say to the defendant on the Ord. 14 summons: "Pay now: arbitrate later?" Or can the defendant say to the plaintiff: "You have no right to immediate payment since I am entitled to challenge the correctness of the certificate by arbitration without first having made payment?" (See Kerr C.J. in *Pillings (C.M.) & Co. Ltd v. Kent Investments Ltd* (1985) 30 Build.L.R. 80.)

(c) *The answer depends:* As always, the answer depends upon the actual terms of the contract. The first question to which the court will address itself is whether the defendant's challenge to the correctness of the certificate raises a bona fide triable issue. If the court finds against the defendant on that point, that is the end of the matter and the plaintiff is entitled to summary judgment. If, however, the defendant establishes a triable issue, the decision in *Gilbert-Ash* (above), is that in order to exclude the right to assert cross-claims admissible as equitable set-offs and thus to exclude the rights of deduction or non-payment of certified amounts based on such cross-claims, it is necessary to find some clear and express provision in the contract which has that effect. In *Pillings* and *Gilbert-Ash*, the plaintiff was not entitled to summary judgment because there were arguable cross-claims and the contract in each case did not exclude or restrict the right to assert them by way of set-off.

(d) *Restricting the cross-claim—an example:* In *Tubeworkers Ltd v. Tilbury Construction Ltd* (1986) 4 ConLR 13, the contract did expressly restrict the defendants' right of set-off by stipulating that they could only make a deduction from sums due under the architect's certificate if (i) they obtained a certificate of the plaintiff's delay from the architect, (ii) they quantified their set-off in detail with reasonable accuracy and (iii) they gave 17 days' notice to the plaintiff of their intention to set off the amount so quantified from the amount due to the plaintiff. As the defendants failed to do so, the plaintiff was entitled to summary judgment for the full amount payable under the architect's certificate without deduction.

(e) *The defendant takes a second point:* Having failed to block the plaintiff in his attempt to get summary judgment, the defendants asked the court to stay execution on it pending the determination of the arbitration of their cross-claim. The judge granted the request. The Court of Appeal reversed the judge.

(f) *The court will not modify contractual rights:* Kerr L.J. had this to say about the judge's decision ((1986) 4 ConLR 13 at 21):

"So what it comes to is this that, without there being any possibly relevant circumstances concerning the plaintiff, the judge's order of a stay has had the effect of setting aside the terms of clause 11 (b) whereby the plaintiffs were entitled to immediate payment on October 4, 1983. Indeed by this order he has put the plaintiffs in a worse position than they might possibly have been in if the defendants had been able to invoke and had invoked the machinery of clause 13A [*the restricted right of set-off provisions*]. The reason is that, in that event, the immediate decision as to what was to happen pending arbitration would have gone to an adjudicator under clause 13B and he might possibly have ordered that all or part of the money certified as being payable to the plaintiffs was to be paid to them. Under the judge's order, on the other hand, none of it was to be paid until further order, which in practice meant that payment would have to await events in the arbitration ... So what the judge has done, in effect, is that he has replaced the contractual machinery agreed between the parties by the process of the courts in ordering a stay under Ord. 47. In my view, this is prima facie wrong, I say prima facie because as already mentioned there might be exceptional circumstances to justify it."

As Dunn L.J. said in *Northern Regional Health Authority v. Derek Crouch Construction Co. Ltd* [1984] Q.B. 644 at 664:

"Where parties have agreed on machinery of that kind for the resolution of disputes, it is not for the courts to intervene and replace its own machinery for the contractual machinery agreed by the parties."

(g) *Is that the end of the road for the defendant?* It would appear not. In *Acsim (Southern) Ltd v. Dancon Danish Contracting and Development Co. Ltd.* [1990] 19 Con LR 1, the Court of Appeal held that although, under the FASS/MFBTE standard form of sub-contract [the Blue Form] the contractor's right of set-off is governed exclusively by the express provisions of the sub-contract itself, those provisions do not contain the exclusive machinery by which a contractor can challenge a sub-contractor's right to a payment on account if the reason for non-payment is that the work has not been properly executed or that sum claimed includes the value of work not in fact done, or that there is an error in the calculation of the value of the work done or that the part of the work done is worth less than the agreed price by reason of the contractor's breach of the sub-contract. In so finding, the Court of Appeal held that the decision in *BWP (Architectural) Ltd v. Beaver Building Systems Ltd* (1988) 42 Build.L.R. 86, which had reached a contrary conclusion—was wrong. It is perhaps worth recording that the decision in *Tubeworkers* was not referred to in the decision in *Acsim*.

14 Cross-claims—exceptions to the general rule

1. Freight It has been established since at least 1814 that a cross-claim in respect of cargo cannot be asserted in order to diminish or extinguish a claim for freight: *Sheels v. Davis* (1814) 4 Camp. 119; *Aries Tanker Corporation v. Total Transport Ltd* [1977] 1 W.L.R. 185 at 190; and see *Henriksens Rederi A/S v. T.H.Z. Rolimpex; The Brede* [1974] Q.B. 233. The *Aries Tanker* case concerned the carriage of goods by sea. The same exception to the general rule applies to freight arising from the carriage of goods by road (*R.H. & D. International Ltd v. IAS Animal Air Services Ltd* [1984] 1 W.L.R. 573; *United Carriers Ltd v. Heritage Food Group (U.K.) Ltd* [1995] 4 All E.R. 95. For a case in which cross-claims against freight were successful, see, *e.g. Colonial Bank v. European Grain Ltd; The Dominique* [1988] 3 W.L.R. 60).

2. Cross-claims and dishonoured cheques A further exception to the general rule that a monetary cross-claim may amount to a defence or may afford a stay of execution occurs where the defendant seeks to set up a cross-claim in an action brought by a plaintiff on a dishonoured bill or cheque. In the absence of fraud or a total failure of consideration, the courts have consistently treated bills of exchange as cash. Judgment on the plaintiff's claim will not be delayed by virtue of a set-off or counterclaim which the defendant might assert—even a cross-claim relating to the specific subject-matter of the contract (see the cases referred to at pp. 313 *et seq.*). Such an alleged cross-claim does not even afford a ground for staying execution of the judgment on the plaintiff's claim. In *Bhogal v. Punjab National Bank* [1988] 2 All E.R. 296, the Court of Appeal re-affirmed the established rule that a banker is required to pay all cheques drawn by a customer in accordance with the mandate given to him if he had funds belonging to the customer and he is not entitled to refuse to honour a customer's cheque when there was money in the account to cover it, merely on the basis of a suspicion that the account was held by the customer as nominee for a third party whose account with the bank was overdrawn. The bank had no right to raise the defence of equitable set-off.

3. Commercial guarantees and letters of credit The courts have consistently and steadfastly refused to grant a stay of execution on a summary judgment based on commercial guarantees and letters of credit pending the determination of the defendant's counterclaim. In *Continental Illinois National Bank and Trust Co. of Chicago v. Papanicolaou* [1986] 2 Lloyd's Rep. 441, the court said that the purpose of a guarantee was to ensure immediate payment if the principal debtor did not pay. It would defeat the whole commercial purpose of the transaction, would be out of touch with business realities and would keep the plaintiff bank waiting for a payment which both the borrowers and the guarantors intended that it should have, while protracted proceedings on the alleged counterclaims were litigated. Doubtless the court had a discretion to grant a stay but it should rarely, if ever, be exercised. Commercial guarantees were the equivalent of letters of credit, the court said, and only in exceptional circumstances should the court exercise such a discretion. The fact that a counterclaim is likely to succeed would not of itself be enough. It might be that the existence of a counterclaim coupled with cogent evidence that the plaintiff would, if paid, be unable to meet the judgment on the counterclaim would suffice. (See also *Intraco v. Notis Shipping Corporation* [1981] 2 Lloyd's Rep. 256; *Nova (Jersey) Knit Ltd v. Kammgarn Spinnerei GmbH* [1977] 1 W.L.R. 713; *Montecchi v. Shimco (U.K.) Ltd* [1979] 1 W.L.R. 1180; *Cebora S.N.C. v. S.I.P. Industrial Products Ltd* [1976] 1 Lloyd's Rep. 271; *Aries Tanker Corporation v. Total Transport Ltd* [1977] 1 W.L.R. 185).

4. Bankruptcy exception Reference has already been made (at p. 000) to the provisions of section 323 of the Insolvency Act 1986 (applied to liquidated companies by section 612 of the Companies Act 1985) under which there is a statutory right of mutual set-offs between the bankrupt and a creditor covering mutual dealings between them prior to the bankruptcy.

5. Only net balance assignable In *Stein v. Blake* [1995] 2 W.L.R. 710, the plaintiff justified proceedings against the defendant for breach of contract and the defendant counterclaimed for damages for misrepresentation. Before trial the plaintiff was adjudicated bankrupt. The plaintiff's trustee in bankruptcy purported to assign to the plaintiff the right of action against the defendant. The plaintiff applied for a stay and succeeded before the master and the judge on the ground that the plaintiff's claim and the defendant's counterclaim fell to be dealt with by way of set-off under section 323 and until the trustee had taken an account under that section, there was nothing to assign. The Court of Appeal allowed the plaintiff's appeal. The defendant appealed to the House of Lords which dismissed his appeal and held that on the bankruptcy the choses in action represented by the cross-claims were extinguished and thus no longer capable of being assigned. All that was assignable was the amount due. Also the mandatory account under section 323 has been taken, namely a claim to the net balance. So the trustee was entitled to assign the net balance like any other chose in action and accordingly the action was to be restored.

15 Trial for some other reason

1. *Miles v. Bull*—the "conspiracy" defence The final way in which a defendant may be given leave to defend the action occurs where, although he cannot satisfy the court that there is an issue or question in dispute which ought to be tried, nevertheless there ought for some other reason be a trial. *Miles v. Bull* [1969] 1 Q.B. 258 is a case in point. Mr and Mrs Bull separated. Mrs Bull continued to live in the family home which Mr Bull then proceeded to sell to the plaintiff. The plaintiff took proceedings against her for possession and sought summary judgment under Ord. 14. Mrs Bull failed to establish that she had any defence to the plaintiff's claim but she contended that the whole transaction between her estranged husband and the plaintiff was a conspiracy to get her evicted. Megarry J. gave leave to defend. ([1969] 1 Q.B. 265):

> "If the question is whether or not the defendant had an arguable defence to the claim, I would have to answer no; for as matters stand I can perceive no such defence. All that can be said is that this is a transaction which ought to be scrutinised with some care; for plainly it bears something of the appearance of a device to evict the defendant. ... Order 14 is for the plain and straightforward, not for the devious and crafty."

2. Other reasons In *Bank für Gemeinwirtschaft v. City of London Garages* [1971] 1 W.L.R. 149, Cairns L.J. suggested the following further examples of cases which were not appropriate for summary judgment even if there was apparently no defence, at p. 158F:
  (a) The defendant being unable to get in touch with some material witness who might be able to provide him with material for a defence.
  (b) If the claim were of a highly complicated or technical nature which could only be properly understood if oral evidence were given.

(See also *Messenger Newspapers Group Ltd v. National Graphical Association* [1984] I.C.R. 345.)

(c) If the plaintiff's case tended to show that he had acted harshly and unconscionably and it was thought desirable that if he were to get judgment at all it should be in the full light of publicity: see *Harrison v. Bottenheim* (1878) 26 W.R. 362 at 363; *Bhogal v. Punjab National Bank* [1988] 2 All E.R. 296 at 305D; *Hereford and Worcester County Council v. N.A.S., The Times,* March 26, 1988; *Morgan Guaranty Trust Co. v. Hadjantonakis* (No. 2) [1988] 1 Lloyd's Rep. 375. For a building case where the defendant in good faith and on reasonable grounds challenged the architect's certificate without being able to show an arguable defence, see *Douglas Const. v. Bass Leisure Ltd* (1991) 53 B.L.R. 119; and see *Trafalgar House Construction (Regions) Ltd v. General Surety and Guarantee Co Ltd,* [1995] 3 W.L.R. 204; [1995] 3 All E.R. 737.

J: THE HEARING

1 Motion or summons—judge or master?

1. General rule An application for summary judgment under Ord. 14, whether in the Queen's Bench Division or Chancery Division, should be made by summons returnable before the master or a district judge. The summons is returnable before the judge rather than the master or district judge if, and only if:

(a) an injunction is sought (a master has no power generally to grant injunctions—see *Shell-Mex and B.P. Ltd v. Manchester Garages Ltd* [1971] 1 W.L.R. 612, *per* Lord Denning at 615); or,

(b) the action is in the London Commercial List, see Ord. 72, r.2(3) and p. 310; or,

(c) the action is in the Manchester, Liverpool, Birmingham or Bristol Mercantile Lists.

2. Exceptionally—motion In the Chancery Division applications to a judge for injunctive relief under Ord. 14 may be made on motion but only in exceptional circumstances: see Supreme Court Practice (1995) Vol. 2, Ch. Pract. Direction Summary Judgements. In *Sony Corporation v. Anand (No. 2)* [1982] F.S.R. 200 at 202–203 Walton J. explained the practice in the Chancery Division as follows:

"[Counsel for the plaintiffs] claims the right to proceed under Order 14 by way of motion in the Chancery Division, notwithstanding that the provisions of Order 14 direct that an application under rule 1 of that Order is to be made by summons supported by an affidavit. As long as I have been at the Chancery Bar it has been accepted by all concerned that anything which can be done by summons, whether under the rules or otherwise, can always be done in the Chancery Division by motion.

The fact that things normally done by summons can be done by motion is not, however, an invitation to everybody so to proceed, otherwise of course the motions judge would be totally overwhelmed by applications so brought because of the speed with which one can get on a motion as compared to the speed with which one can get on a summons. Therefore, the fact that this is possible as a matter of Chancery procedure is qualified by the fact that a plaintiff, or for that matter a defendant, will only be allowed to proceed in that way where there is some very good reason indeed for so proceeding. The normal reason for so proceeding is of course a question of speed. Where it is absolutely vital that matters should be done urgently then of course a motion is appropriate." See also *Wilkinson v. Telephone Information Services plc, The Times*, November 1, 1991.

2 The court's options

(a) dismiss the summons;
(b) give summary judgment to the plaintiff;
(c) grant unconditional leave to the defendant to defend;
(d) grant conditional leave to the defendant to defend;
(e) additionally now, under Ord. 14A, give summary judgment to the defendant on the plaintiff's summons.
(a)–(d) are dealt with in detail at pp. 384 *et seq.* below. (e) is dealt with at p. 365 above.

3 The absent defendant

1. Where the defendant has acknowledged receipt of the summons If the defendant does not attend on the hearing of the summons, the first task of the court is to satisfy itself that the summons has been duly served. Where the defendant has acknowledged receipt of the summons either to the plaintiff or to the court, the production of his letter of acknowledgment will be sufficient to enable the application to proceed in his absence and the summons will be marked "Dispense with affidavit of service".

2. Where the defendant has not acknowledged receipt of the summons If the defendant has not acknowledged receipt of the Ord. 14 summons, the practice of the courts varies. Some courts require an affidavit of service to be handed in at the hearing. If none has been sworn, any judgment given is made only on the subsequent production of the affidavit of service or a letter received late from the defendant acknowledging the receipt of the summons. The Ord. 14 summons is then marked "On filing of affidavit of service or letter of acknowledgment." Other courts are less stringent, simply requiring production of a carbon copy letter written by the plaintiff's solicitor to the defendant enclosing a copy of the Ord. 14 summons by way of service. The Ord. 14 summons would then be marked "defendant absent but having been duly served." It is considered the better procedure to require an affidavit of service or letter of acknowledgment as the Ord. 14 procedure involves the giving of judgment against a person in his absence.

3. Form A form of affidavit of service of a summons through the document exchange is to be found in Form S, p. 566.

4. The absent defendant—setting aside judgment Ord. 14, r.11 says:

> "**11.** Any judgment given against a party who does not appear at the hearing of an application under rule 1 or rule 5 may be set aside or varied by the court on such terms as it thinks just."

The principle on which the court may set aside the judgment given in the absence of the defendant was stated by Lord Atkin in *Evans v. Bartlam* [1937] A.C. 480 as follows:

> "The principle obviously is that unless and until the court has pronounced a judgment on the merits or by consent, it is to have the power to revoke the expression of its coercive power where that has only been obtained by a failure to follow any of the rules of procedure."

If the defendant can show that he has never received notice of the Ord. 14 proceedings, he is entitled to have the judgment set aside *ex debito justitiae* and without terms. In other cases, it is a matter of discretion and the court may impose terms. The judgment may be set aside as to part only: *Mosenthal, ex p. Marx* (1910) 54 S.J. 751, C.A.

4 Evidence

1. Oral evidence—only exceptionally The master will consider the contents of the affidavits filed in support of and in opposition to the summons. He will also pay careful attention to the submissions of those representing the parties. What he will not do is to allow oral evidence to be called save in the most exceptional circumstances. Ord. 14, r. 4(4) says:

"(4) On the hearing of [an application for summary judgment] the court may order a defendant showing cause...

(a) to produce a document;

(b) if it appears to the court that there are special circumstances which make it desirable that he should do so, to attend and be examined on oath."

2. Why only "exceptionally"? Ord. 14 provides machinery for summary judgment without trial, not judgment by summary trial. The admission of oral evidence would lead not only to great expense but also to actions being tried on the Ord. 14 summons—and that was never the intention: *Millard v. Baddeley* [1884] W.N. 96. Megarry J. explained the rationale in *Sullivan v. Henderson* [1973] 1 W.L.R. 333 at 338A—a case under Ord. 86 but where exactly the same rule applies:

"... the present case seems to me to illustrate the difficulties that may arise if leave to cross examine a witness on his affidavit is given in cases under Order 86. The summary process under Order 86 is one thing, and the trial of an action is another: a hearing under Order 86 with oral evidence is liable to become neither one nor the other, and to share the disadvantages of each. The hearing ceases to be summary, and the absence of pleadings and discovery, for example, prevents the hearing from achieving the exhaustiveness of a trial. The court may be put in the position, at the end of a two-day hearing, of saying that there ought to be a trial of the action in which case there will then be the repetition of much that has occupied the court and the parties during the hearing under Order 86. ... There may be cases where it is right to give leave to cross-examine, perhaps limited to a single point, though this has its own problems both for counsel and for litigants who are bursting to reveal all; and in any case I would expect cases in which it would be desirable for such leave to be given to be a comparatively rare occurrence."

Although, as can be seen from Ord. 14, r.4(4)(a), the court has power to order a defendant to produce documents, it rarely does so for similar reasons.

5 Affidavit evidence

1. The *Paclantic* case In *Paclantic Financing Company Ltd v. Moscow Narodny Bank Ltd* [1984] 1 W.L.R. 930 the defendants sought summary judgment under Ord. 14 on their counterclaim. The plaintiff adduced evidence in two affidavits in support of allegedly arguable issues of fact and law. The defendants alleged that the evidence was incredible and should be rejected. The judge assumed that, in such circumstances, a court was entitled to reject the plaintiff's affidavit evidence only if it was irrelevant or inherently unreliable through self-contradiction, or where it was unequivocally inconsistent with other evidence admitted by the plaintiff or unchallengeable by him, or no plausible explanation was given for the inconsistency; but that a court should not reject evidence found to be incredible or almost incredible by reason of its inherent implausibility or inconsistency with other evidence. In the circumstances the judge held that while the plaintiff's evidence on most of the factual issues was almost entirely incredible, the court was not entitled to reject it on any one issue and that having regard to the issues raised by the plaintiff's affidavits, an arguable, albeit shadowy, defence to the counterclaim existed. Accordingly, he granted leave to defend the counterclaim conditional on the payment into court of $3.5m.

2. What happened on appeal On appeal by the plaintiff against the imposition of the condition, the Court of Appeal held that in all the circumstances of the case, and having regard to all the documents concerned, the plaintiff's case against the defendants was properly described as "shadowy"; that was therefore a proper case for leave to defend to be made conditional upon a payment into court of at least a substantial part of the sum at stake, and that accordingly, since no criticism had been made of the amounts of the payment in ordered by the judge, his order should stand. See also *Bremar Holdings Ltd v. de Roth* (1984) 134 New L.J. 550 and *Midland Bank v. Phillips, The Times*, March 28, 1986.

3. Paclantic not followed In *National Westminster Bank plc v. Daniel* [1994] 1 All E.R. 156, Glidewell L.J. rejected the test formulated by the judge at first instance as set out above. He said that it was too narrow and restrictive. The proper test is to ask: is there a fair or reasonable probability of the defendants having a real or bona fide defence? Is what the defendant says credible? If it is not, then there is no fair or reasonable probability of him setting up a defence: see also *Banque de Paris v. de Naray* [1954] 1 Lloyd's Rep. 21; *Standard Chartered Bank v. Yacoub* (1990) C.A.T. 699.

6 Dismissal of summons

1. Technicality Where the defendant successfully takes a preliminary technicality, the correct order (unless the technicality can be cured) is for the summons to be dismissed. We have already discussed Ord. 14 technicalities at pp. 345 *et seq*.

2. "No defence"—when there is a defence If the plaintiff pursues an Ord.

14 application in circumstances where he knew very well that the defendant had an arguable defence, his summons will be dismissed and he will render himself liable to pay the defendant's costs. He should never have issued the summons in the first place: *Warner v. Bowlby* (1882) 9 T.L.R. 13. And in *Pocock v. A.D.A.C. Ltd* [1952] 1 T.L.R. 29, Lord Goddard said at p. 34:

> "I wish it to be known as a practice rule that the proper course for a master to take if he considers that in a summons under Order 14 it is clear that the plaintiff knew that there was an arguable defence to the claim, is to dismiss the summons with costs. Masters should use their powers under Order 14 much more freely."

3. Costs—when defendant has not served defence It is considered that the dicta of Lord Goddard above apply even if the defendant has not served a defence, so long as he has made the plaintiff aware in some detail that there was an arguable defence to the claim.

4. Order 14—not to be abused In *Dott v. Brown* [1936] 1 All E.R. 543 Scott L.J. said at 545:

> "I feel personally a little doubt as to whether it is right to take out a summons under R.S.C., Ord. 14 where there is really no possibility of obtaining a judgment. I am not sure that it is a satisfactory use of R.S.C., Ord. 14 that it should be employed purely for tactical purposes...."

Vaughan Williams L.J. in *Symon & Co. v. Palmers' Stores (1903) Ltd* [1912] 1 K.B. 259 expressed himself more robustly at p. 264:

> "Order 14 makes, no doubt, a very salutory provision for the purpose of preventing a defendant, who knows perfectly well that he owes the sum claimed, from postponing the time of payment and putting the plaintiff to further expense in a litigation which ought never to have taken place; but on the other hand Order 14 is an order which can be, and often is, abused. A plaintiff's legal adviser may advise him that, though there is not much prospect of him getting judgment under Order 14, and the defendant will probably get unconditional leave to defend, the defendant may have to swear an affidavit in answer to an application for judgment, in which he will have to disclose on oath what defence he is going to set up, and that may be a great assistance to the plaintiff at the trial, and therefore such an application should be made. I hope that this does not often occur, but I think that such a course is sometimes taken, and in my opinion that is a manifest abuse of the process of the court."

In that case the plaintiff was made to pay the defendant's costs of the application forthwith rather than at the end of the proceedings.

5. Costs—immediate Ord. 4, r.7(1) provides if the plaintiff makes an application under rule 1 where the case is not within this Order or if it appears to the court that the plaintiff knew that the defendant relied on a contention which would entitle him to unconditional leave to defend, then, without prejudice to Ord. 62, and, in particular, to Ord. 62, r.8(1)–(3) the court may dismiss the application with costs and may, if the plaintiff is not an assisted person, require the costs to be paid to him forthwith.

6. Dismissal—form of order For form of order on dismissal, see Form J, p. 563. If the order provides for the "defendant's costs to be paid forthwith" the defendant may tax his costs of the Ord. 14 proceedings straightaway without waiting for the outcome of the action but otherwise the costs of the Ord. 14 summons cannot be taxed until the conclusion of the proceedings: Ord. 62, r.8(1).

7. Dismissal—consequences On dismissal of the summons the parties revert to the position they were in before its issue. Ord. 18, r. 2(2) provides that the defendant must serve his defence within 14 days of the date of the order or such other period as specified in the order.

7 Order for summary judgment

1. The court's duty If it is quite clear—and only if it is quite clear—to the master that there is no fairly arguable point which the defendant may take or that there is no other reason for a trial, it is his duty to give summary judgment to the plaintiff. The court approaches the matter not on the basis of whether there is an arguable defence but whether, after argument, there remains a good defence: *I.R.C. v. Aken* [1988] 1 All E.R. 69; and see also *Nichimen Corporation v. Gatoil Overseas Inc.* [1987] 2 Lloyd's Rep. 46.

2. Common forms of judgment Among the more common forms of summary judgment are:
  (a) Judgment for the plaintiff for the whole or part of a liquidated claim against one or more defendants.
  (b) Interlocutory judgment for the plaintiff with damages to be assessed.
  (c) Judgment for the plaintiff for the delivery of goods with or without giving the defendant the option of paying their value and for damages for their wrongful detention.
  (d) Judgment for the plaintiff for the recovery of land.
  (e) Judgment for solicitor's costs in *Smith & Edwardes'* form.
  (f) Judgment for an injunction.

See generally Part C for forms and precedents.

3. No assessment on Order 14 hearing Where damages or the value of some property fall to be assessed under a summary judgment obtained under Ord. 14, the assessment does not generally take place on the Ord. 14 hearing. Unless some other method of assessment is directed, the plaintiff should take out a further summons under Ord. 37 returnable before the master for assessment.

4. An exception In special cases where the facts are clear and the likely result of the assessment is instantly apparent, the court has the power on an Ord. 14 summons so to assess and order judgment for a liquidated sum. But in the great majority of cases, the proper order must be a judgment for damages to be assessed later: *Yarnold v. Radio Wyvern* (1985, C.A.T. No. 194; unreported).

5. Order 14 and speedy trials If the plaintiff has already obtained an order for speedy trial, any application for summary judgment under Ord. 14 should normally be refused: *Fabre (Pierre) S.A. v. Ronco Teleproducts* [1984] F.S.R. 148.

6. Summary judgment on counterclaim Just as the plaintiff has the right to seek summary judgment against the defendant on his claim, so the defendant may seek summary judgment against the plaintiff on his counterclaim (Ord. 14, r.5). The rules applicable to plaintiffs apply equally with appropriate modifications to defendants. The defendant cannot issue an Ord. 14 summons until he has served his counterclaim. He may seek judgment on part of the counterclaim and also against one or more of several plaintiffs.

7. Summary judgment on counterclaim against co-defendant or additional party Where a defendant makes a counterclaim against the plaintiff and a co-defendant or person not already a party to the action, he is entitled to apply for summary judgment under Ord. 14 on his counterclaim against that co-defendant or added party: Ord. 15, r.3(5A) (negativing *Heath v. Ceram Holding Co.* [1988] 1 W.L.R. 1219, C.A.).

8 Judgment in a foreign currency

1. Terms of order Where appropriate, a judgment under Ord. 14 for a liquidated sum may be entered in foreign currency: *Miliangos v. George Frank (Textiles) Ltd* [1976] A.C. 443. The judgment will read:

"It is this day adjudged that the defendant do pay the plaintiff [state

387

the sum in foreign currency for which the court has ordered judgment to be entered] or the sterling equivalent at the time of payment and £— costs (or costs to be taxed)."

2. Satisfying foreign judgments If the plaintiff wishes to ensure that an English judgment in an action to enforce a foreign judgment will have the effect of transferring to the foreign jurisdiction sufficient funds to satisfy the judgment there, he should set out in his pleadings, or in some other way bring to the court's attention before judgment the full extent of his claims. Prima facie if the plaintiff enters judgment, for example, for $1,000 or its sterling equivalent, there is no reason why the defendant should not be able to satisfy that judgment by paying $1,000 forthwith—even though that amount has been devalued by fluctuations in the exchange rate since the date of the foreign judgment such that that judgment is still not entirely discharged by the payment. (See *Mechanical & Electrical Engineering Contracts Co. v. Christy & Norris Ltd* (1984) 134 New L.J. 1017; *Thynne v. Thynne* [1955] P. 272.)

3. Costs The amount of the fixed costs (see below) will be calculated on the sterling equivalent of the amount of the foreign currency claimed as indorsed and certified on the writ unless the court otherwise orders.

4. Judgment—interest A judgment entered in foreign currency will carry the statutory rate of interest on the amount of the judgment in foreign currency and such interest will be added to the amount of the judgment itself for the purpose of enforcement of the judgment: *Practice Direction (Judgment: Foreign Currency)* [1976] 1 W.L.R. 83.

5. Unliquidated damages Summary judgment may also be given under Ord. 14 for unliquidated damages to be assessed in a foreign currency.

9 Interest under Order 14

1. Pre-judgment interest

(a) *The claim:* The court has a discretion to award interest to the plaintiff on money adjudged to be due to him in Ord. 14 proceedings provided he has specifically pleaded his claim to interest whether pursuant to section 35A of the Supreme Court Act 1981 or otherwise. If the claim to interest is alleged to be under a contract, a statute or under some commercial practice, the relevant facts and matters relied on as giving rise to the claim must be pleaded: see generally *Practice Note (Claims for Interest) (No. 2)* [1983] 1 W.L.R. 377.

(b) *The principle:* The object is not to compensate the plaintiff for any damage done, but for him being kept out of his money: *London, Chatham and Dover Railway Co. v. South Eastern Railway Co.* [1893] A.C. 429 at 437.

(c) *The rate:* Not one but several different rates may be given according to the circumstances. The more usual are:

   (i) Judgment debt rate—the rate payable on judgment debts pursuant to section 17 of the Judgments Act 1838. Recent rates are:
   From 10.11.82—12 per cent.
   From 16.4.85—15 per cent.
   From 1.4.93—8 per cent.

  (ii) Special investment account rate:
   From 1.1.87—$12\frac{1}{4}$ per cent.
   From 1.4.87—$11\frac{3}{4}$ per cent.
   From 1.11.87—$11\frac{1}{4}$ per cent.
   From 1.12.87—11 per cent.
   From 1.5.88—$9\frac{1}{2}$ per cent.
   From 1.8.88—11 per cent.
   From 1.11.88—$12\frac{1}{4}$ per cent.
   From 1.1.89—13 per cent.
   From 1.11.89—$14\frac{1}{4}$ per cent.
   From 1.4.91—12 per cent.
   From 1.10.91—$10\frac{1}{4}$ per cent.
   From 1.2.93—8 per cent.

 (iii) Commercial rate—how much did the plaintiff have to pay on borrowing the money or would he have had to pay had he borrowed it?

 (iv) Investment rate—how much would his return have been had the plaintiff invested the money?

  (v) Foreign interest rate—the going rate of interest of the country in whose currency the judgment is given.

(d) *The period:* Interest is normally payable on:
   (i) liquidated claims—from the date when the money should have been paid;
  (ii) personal injury claims—from the date of service of the writ;
 (iii) economic loss claims—from the date of the loss or the date on which the cause of action arose.

(e) *Damages already paid:* Suppose the defendant sends a cheque to the plaintiff in full and final settlement of the claim for damages. He accepts it but then asks: "What about the interest?" Payment in full of the amount of damages still leaves the court with power to give interlocutory judgment on liability and assess damages and interest, taking into account the fact that there has been a payment and acceptance on account of an amount equal to the full amount of damages: *Edmunds v. Lloyds Italico S.p.A.* [1986] 1 W.L.R. 492.

(f) *Liquidated debt already paid:* On the other hand, payment of a liquidated debt in full extinguishes the cause of action and would leave the court with no basis for giving any judgment but for the provisions of section 35A(3) of the Supreme Court Act 1981 which reads:

"(3) Subject to rules of court, where—

(a) there are proceedings (whenever instituted) before the High Court for the recovery of a debt; and
(b) the defendant pays the whole debt to the plaintiff (otherwise than in pursuance of a judgment in the proceedings),

the defendant shall be liable to pay the plaintiff simple interest at such rate as the court thinks fit or as rules of court may provide on all or any part of the debt for all or any part of the period between the date when the cause of action arose and the date of payment."

So, if the debt is paid *after* the issue of proceedings, interest may be claimed under section 35A(3). If the debt is paid *before* issue, then, in the absence of any contractual right to interest, there is no power to award interest either at common law or under section 35A(3): *Edmunds v. Lloyds Italico S.p.A.* (above).

2. Post-judgment interest

(a) *Section 17, Judgments Act 1838:* By this section every High Court judgment debt (which includes an Ord. 14 judgment debt) carries interest from the date of the judgment until payment.
(b) *Final, not interlocutory judgment:* "Judgment" in section 17 contemplates a single, final judgment for a quantified sum rather than an interlocutory judgment which merely establishes the defendant's liability. So, interest runs under the section from the judgment assessing the damages not from the date of interlocutory judgment: *Thomas v. Bunn* [1991] 2 W.L.R. 27.

10 Costs under Order 14

1. General rule—fixed costs Fixed costs are the norm in unopposed or virtually unopposed Ord. 14 proceedings for a liquidated sum, or the recovery of land. If the writ was indorsed for a claim for a debt or liquidated demand only of £600 or more and the plaintiff obtains Ord. 14

judgment for £600 or more, he will be entitled to fixed costs under Ord. 62, Appendix 3.

2. Taxed costs Costs are always at the discretion of the court: Ord. 62, r.3(2). thus in appropriate cases—usually where there is some substance to the application—the court frequently orders the costs to be taxed if not agreed.

3. Summary judgment for part of claim only—costs The master will make the appropriate order for costs of the Ord. 14 application after the exercise of a judicial discretion on ordinary principles and then usually order that the costs of the balance of the claim shall be in the cause.

11 Entering Order 14 judgment

1. Carriage The order made on the summons is usually drawn up by the plaintiff as being the party having the custody of the summons (Ord. 42, r.5) unless the summons has been dismissed in which case the defendant should draw it up. If the party who has the carriage of the order fails to draw it up within seven days after it is made, any other party affected by it may draw it up (Ord. 42, r. 4).

2. Requirements when summary judgment granted The plaintiff should draw up and lodge two top copies of the form of judgment. No fee is payable.

3. Requirements of the court The court staff will check that:
  (a) The parties are properly named on the form of judgment.
  (b) The judgment debt agrees with the amount for which judgment is given.
  (c) That the correct figure for costs (if fixed) has been entered.
  (d) That the judgment is dated on the day on which it was given.
  (e) If the Ord. 14 judgment is marked "on filing of affidavit of service or letter of acknowledgment" (see p. 382), the affidavit or letter has been filed.
Both forms of judgment are sealed with the court seal and one is returned to the plaintiff's solicitor. No leave is required to enter judgment under Ord. 14.

12 Stay of execution

1. Jurisdiction Ord. 14, r.3(2) reads:

> "(2) The court may by order, and subject to such conditions, if any, as may be just, stay execution of any judgment given against a defendant under this rule until after the trial of any counterclaim made or raised by the defendant in the action."

2. Stay on terms—mode of security The defendant may wish to appeal against the Ord. 14 judgment and seek a stay of execution pending the hearing of the appeal. If the court is minded to grant a stay on terms that the defendant provides security, the usual mode of security is by the payment into court of a specified sum of money to bide the appeal. But so long as the plaintiff can be adequately protected, it is proper that the security should be given in a way which is least disadvantageous to the defendant: *Rosengrens Ltd v. Safe Deposit Centres Ltd* [1984] 1 W.L.R. 1334. It may take many forms. Bank guarantees would be an alternative mode as would a solicitor's undertaking (*ibid.*).

13 Leave to defend

1. The general principles The general principles on which the defendant ought to be given leave to defend have already been discussed (see pp. 343 *et seq.*).

2. Any defence The position of the plaintiff seeking leave to defend a counterclaim is identical to that of a defendant seeking leave to defend a claim: *Paclantic Financing Company Inc. v. Moscow Narodny Bank Ltd* [1984] 1 W.L.R. 930.

14 Conditional leave to defend

1. Jurisdiction Given that the defendant should be granted leave to defend, should any conditions be attached to the order granting leave? Ord. 14, r.4(3) is the enabling power. It reads:

> "(3) The court may give a defendant against whom such application is made leave to defend the action with respect to the claim, or the part of the claim, to which the application relates either unconditionally or on such terms as to giving security or time or mode of trial or otherwise as it thinks fit."

2. Conditions—must be reasonable Just as it is important for the court to ensure that a defendant is not deprived of his right to defend if he has an argument, so it is equally important not to deprive him of that same right by imposing conditions on the grant of leave with which he is quite unable to comply: *Ward v. Plumbley* (1890) 6 T.L.R. 198.

3. Legal aid—not necessarily a bar to giving security In *Yorke (M.V.) Motors v. Edwards* [1982] 1 W.L.R. 444, the plaintiff claimed £21,500 against a car dealer who had sold him a vehicle without title. The defendant obtained a legal aid certificate with a nil contribution to defend the action. In Ord. 14 proceedings, the master had given the defendant unconditional leave to defend the action. On appeal, Boreham J. varied the order attaching a condition of the defendant's leave to defend that he brought £12,000 into court within 28 days. The Court of Appeal reduced the sum to £3,000. The House of Lords refused to interfere with the Court of Appeal's decision. There was evidence before the court that the defendant had been engaged in buying and selling secondhand cars for cash. Lord Diplock quoted with apparent approval at p. 449H Brandon L.J.'s comment in the Court of Appeal:

> "The fact that the man has no capital of his own does not mean that he cannot raise any capital; he may have friends, he may have business associates, he may have relatives, all of whom can help him in his hour of need."

4. How does a defendant prove his impecuniosity? If the court's grant of leave to defend on condition that money is paid is foreseeable and the defendant contends that he has no money with which to comply with the condition, it is not sufficient for him merely to say "I'm broke"—unless, of course, the plaintiff accepts that he is. In *Yorke's* case (*ibid.*) Lord Diplock showed what the defendant should do by citing with approval written submissions made on behalf of the plaintiff. They read as follows:

> "(i) Where a defendant seeks to avoid or limit a financial condition by reason of his own impecuniosity the onus is upon the defendant to put sufficient and proper evidence before the court. He should make full and frank disclosure.
> (ii) It is not sufficient for a legally aided defendant to rely on there being a legal aid certificate. A legally aided defendant with a nil contribution may be able to pay or raise substantial sums.
> (iii) A defendant cannot complain because a financial condition is difficult for him to fulfil. He can complain only when a financial condition is imposed which it is impossible for him to fulfil and that impossibility was known or should have been known by the court by reason of the evidence placed before it."

The evidence will almost invariably be in affidavit form supported by documentation.

5. How much security—a balancing act On the one hand, the court will assess the total amount for which the plaintiff is on risk—capital sum claimed, plus interest, plus costs. On the other hand, it will bear in mind the rule already referred to of not fixing such a sum as makes it effectively impossible for the defendant to defend the action. Each case must necessarily turn on its own facts: see *Conti Commodity Services Ltd v. Athos Philalithis* (C.A.T., June 6, 1980; unreported).

6. Mode of security Almost invariably, the plaintiff's position is secured by an order requiring the defendant to pay a specified sum into court. Nevertheless there would seem to be no objection to other forms of security which have a similar effect but are more convenient to the defendant, such as a bank guarantee or a solicitor's undertaking: see *Rosengrens Ltd v. Safe Deposit Centres Ltd* [1984] 1 W.L.R. 1334—a case concerned with the provision of security on a stay of execution pending appeal, but where the principle is thought to be the same. In *Pillings (C.M.) & Co. Ltd v. Kent Investments Ltd* (1985) 30 Build.L.R. 80, the Court of Appeal, considering the defendants' contentions "somewhat shadowy, but just sufficient," ordered them to provide security for the plaintiff's claim to the extent of £70,000 by way of bank guarantee as a condition of staying proceedings pending the determination of the dispute by arbitration.

15 Conditional leave to defend—when?

1. General rule The starting point is *Jacobs v. Booth's Distillery Co.* (1901) 85 L.T. 262, H.L. That case is generally taken as House of Lords authority for the proposition that where there are issues to be tried, the defendant ought not to be put on terms but should be given unconditional leave to defend. Accordingly, in *Lloyd's Bank Co. v. Ogle* (1876) 1 Ex.D. 263, it was said that conditions "should only be applied when there is something suspicious in the defendant's mode of presenting his case."

2. A change in the legal climate For many years the approach in *Jacobs (ibid.)* prevailed. However, from 1961 a change of approach is to be perceived. In *Fieldrank Ltd v. Stein* [1961] 1 W.L.R. 1287, Devlin L.J. said, in a case in which it was conceded that there was a triable issue and the only question was whether it was a proper exercise by the judge of his discretion in the circumstances that he should have imposed a condition of payment into court, at 1289:

"For my part, I should be very glad to see some relaxation of the strict rule in *Jacobs v. Booth's Distillery Co.* I think that any judge who has sat in chambers to hear summonses under Order 14 has had the experience of a case in which, although he cannot say for certain that there is not a triable issue, he is nevertheless left with a real doubt about the defendant's good faith, and would like to protect the plaintiff, especially if there is no great hardship on a defendant being made to pay money into court. For my part, I should be prepared to accept that there has been a tendency in the last few years to use this condition more often than it has been used in the past, and I think that that is a good tendency."

3. Change in the climate—why? Other reasons which are notable for their absence at the time when *Jacobs* was decided, such as high interest rates and inflation, have caused a further relaxation in the *Jacobs* approach. In the *Yorke* case, Lord Diplock said:

"The facts in *Jacobs v. Booth's Distillery Co.* were complex and its value as an authority against giving unconditional leave to defend may not be as great as had been thought; but, quite apart from this, an expression of opinion by this House as to the way a judicial discretion ought to have been exercised in circumstances as they existed many years ago ought not to be regarded as immutable when circumstances have altered radically from those current when the judgment containing that expression of opinion was delivered. To depart from it in the changed circumstances does not involve any question of overruling a previous decision of the House."

4. The more "shadowy" the defence—the greater the security In *Ionian Bank Ltd v. Couvreur* [1969] 1 W.L.R. 781, the Court of Appeal, satisfied that the defence raised by the defendant was not a sham, nevertheless took the view that it had little or no substance in it and "the case is almost one in which summary judgment should be ordered" (*per* Davis L.J. at 788) and was described as so "shadowy" that the judge was right in giving leave to defend only on condition on the full amount being brought into court" *per* Denning L.J. at 787 (see *Van Lynn Developments Ltd v. Pelias Construction Co. Ltd* [1969] 1 Q.B. 607). The defendant was thus required to bring the full amount into court as a condition of being granted leave to defend. See also *Midland Bank v. Phillips*, *The Times*, March 28, 1986.

5. The defendant's alter ego—whose debt? Frequently, in an action for goods sold, work done or services rendered, the defendant says: "It is not I who owe the money to the plaintiff. It is my company." Inevitably, the company has gone into liquidation. The Ord. 14 investigation may well involve questions of fact and law and so it is not possible to lay down any general rule on the approach of the courts. Where, however, the Court of Appeal had substantial doubts about the ultimate success of the defence which it described as "shadowy to say the least"; was satisfied that the work had been done; which meant the defendant or his companies had had the benefit of it; and that the defendant "an experienced financier" could, if he set his mind to it, find an appropriate amount of cash, it granted him leave to defend conditional upon his bringing into court the whole of the amount of the claim inclusive of interest: *Dumfrey Construction Ltd v. Childs, The Times*, July 12, 1985.

6. Section 394(4), Companies Act 1985 The plaintiff, faced with the company alter ego defence, will do well to remember section 394(4) of the Companies Act 1985 under which an officer of a company is personally liable on any bill of exchange, note or order for money or goods signed by him on which the corporate name is not stated in legible characters.

7. Both cases "shadowy" What is the position where there are features of both the claim and the defence which the court finds disturbing because, for instance, they bear the appearance of falsity and disreputable dealing? In *Extrakionstechnik Gesellschaft für Anlagenbau GmbH v. Oskar* (1984) 128 S.J. 417, the Court of Appeal granted unconditional leave to defend.

8. Both cases "shadowy"—the approach of the courts Watkins L.J. said that it was proper to look first at the defence in isolation, to see whether there was a lack of good faith or whether the defence was a sham. But if one of those flaws in the defence was found, the decision as to the imposition of a condition could not properly be made before an examination was also undertaken of the plaintiff's case, having regard to any attack made on it by the defendant. If that examination aroused suspicions that the claim might be made in bad faith, or there was a shadowy aspect to it, or that it might be tainted with illegality, the defendant should be granted unconditional leave to defend. No measuring, however approximate, of the respective degrees of possible bad faith should be made, nor should any opinion be expressed, however tentative, as to which case appeared to be stronger at the time.

9. In the result The position would appear to be that the imposition of terms as a condition of the defendant being granted leave to defend is more frequent nowadays than used to be the case. Conditions will be imposed where the court takes the view that the defence is so shadowy that the court is very nearly ready to give the plaintiff Ord. 14 judgment or is surrounded by suspicion of bad faith. Conditions should not however be imposed where the result will be to deprive the defendant of his right to defend: *Manger v. Cash* (1888) 5 T.L.R. 271.

10. Forms For forms of order giving leave to defend—reference should be made to Part C, Forms D, H, I, K at pp. 559, 562 and 563.

16 Costs on granting leave to defend

1. Unconditional leave The usual order here is for the courts to be in the cause. If the action is transferred to the county court the usual order is for costs to be in the discretion of the county court. The county court judge has power to award costs on the High Court scale instead of a county court scale in a transferred action: *Forey v. London Buses Ltd* [1991] 1 W.L.R. 327.

2. Conditional leave Assuming that the defendant is given leave to defend on condition that he brings money into court to bide the event, the order for costs will normally be expressed in the alternative—one order for costs covering the situation where he complies with the condition and the other where he fails to comply with the condition. If he brings the money into court, costs will be "in the cause." If he fails to do so, the plaintiff may sign judgment for the sum indorsed on the writ, interest (if any) and costs of the action.

3. Powers of trial judge The trial judge cannot disturb an order that the costs be in the cause made on the Ord. 14 summons even though he feels that the action should have never been brought: *Koosen v. Rose* (1897) 76 L.T. 145. If the master, having made an order for costs in the cause transfers the action to the county court, the county court judge's discretion over the costs of the action is not restricted: *Forey v. London Buses Ltd* (above).

17 Directions

1. General rule Whenever the court gives leave to defend or gives judgment but orders a stay of execution, it must (subject to paragraph 3 below) give directions for the further conduct of the action and treat the Ord. 14 summons as if were a summons for directions: Ord. 14, r. 16.

2. Time for defence Time for service of the defence is 14 days from the date of the Ord. 14 order, or such other period as the court directs on the Ord. 14 hearing: Ord. 18, r. 2(2).

3. No directions If the master decides to refer the action to the Official Referee or to the London Commercial List or to transfer it to the county court, the usual practice is not to give directions.

4. Usual directions Provision may be made for the service of the defence if more or less time is required than is provided for in Ord. 18, r.2(2); for discovery and inspection of documents; for medical and/or other experts' reports and for the place and mode of trial (*i.e.* as if it were the summons for directions).

5. Mode of trial—general powers The master or district judge has power to direct that the action shall be tried by himself or another master or district judge but only where all the parties consent. Ord. 14, r.6 and Ord 36—the advantages—an early and economic disposal on a fixed appointment. The master has all the powers of a High Court judge (except the power to commit). Appeal is direct to the Court of Appeal: Ord. 58, r.2(1). The action may be such as is within the jurisdiction of the county court in which case the master may transfer it to the appropriate county court: section 40 of the County Courts Act 1984 (as amended by section 2 of the Courts and Legal Services Act 1990). The question of costs up to transfer can be dealt with by the master or left to be dealt with by the county courts at the conclusion of the proceedings: section 45 of the County Courts Act 1984. In London, if the master considers the action suitable for the commercial or arbitration list he should adjourn the summons to enable the application to be made to the judge in charge of the commercial list. In the provinces, the district judge has the power to transfer to the commercial court: Ord. 72, r.3(1), but not to the Manchester and Liverpool Mercantile Lists. Such orders can at present only be made by the Mercantile Circuit Judges.

6. Mode of trial—London In London cases, the master can direct the case to be set down in the non-jury list. If the estimated length of hearing does not exceed four hours, he may direct the action to be tried by the judge in the short cause list. The master cannot, however, restrict the right of the defendant to raise such defences as he can: *Langton v. Roberts* (1894) 10 T.L.R. 492. In other words, it is open to the defendant to raise defences at the trial which he has not raised on the Ord. 14 summons. In order to ensure that all defences are raised well in advance of hearing in the short cause list, the order will normally say:

> "1. The defendant's affidavit shall stand as his defence but he may within the next four days serve on the plaintiff written particulars of any further defence or counterclaim not disclosed in his affidavit and may rely thereon at the trial.
>
> 2. Save with the leave of the trial judge, the defendant shall not raise any further defence or counterclaim." (See generally *Practice Direction (Trials in London)* [1981] 1 W.L.R. 1296.)

As a further alternative, if he is of the view that the action ought to have an early trial, the master may make an order for speedy trial. He achieves this by directing that an application be made to the clerk of the lists to fix a date for the hearing. The application must be made within a week of setting the action down.

7. No directions on dismissal of Order 14 summons The court will not, however, give further directions where the Ord. 14 summons is dismissed. It was said in *Symon & Co. v. Palmer's Stores (1903) Ltd* [1912] 1 K.B. 259 at 265 that there is no jurisdiction to do so.

8. Judgment for plaintiff—no directions given for disposal of counterclaim In *CSI International Co Ltd v. Archway Personnel (Middle East) Ltd* [1980] 1 W.L.R. 1069, the plaintiff obtained an Ord. 14 judgment against the defendant which appeared not to have asked for directions for the disposal of its counterclaim. The defendant paid the money due under the judgment and later attempted to serve its counterclaim on the plaintiff. The Court of Appeal held that, after the satisfaction of the plaintiff's judgment, there was no continuing action which could be the subject of the defendant's counterclaim.

K: APPEALS UNDER ORDER 14

1 From master or district judge to High Court judge

1. Regulation Appeals from a master or district judge to a High Court judge under Ord. 14 are regulated by Ord. 58.

2. Leave Any party may appeal against the decision of a master or district judge to a High Court judge in chambers without leave: Ord. 58, r.1.

3. Time limit The time allowed for notice of appeal is five days from the date of a master's decision appealed against or seven days in the case of an appeal from the decision of a district judge: Ord. 58, r. 3(2).

4. Time limit—extended The master or district judge may within the time allowed for an appeal, extend that time under Ord. 3, r.5. After the time for appeal has expired, application to extend the time must be made to a High Court judge in chambers: see *Burke v. Rooney* (1897) 4 C.P.D. 226. Application to extend time for appeal may be included in the notice of appeal. There must be a good explanation for any delay in giving notice of appeal: *Revici v. Prentice Hall Inc.* [1969] 1 W.L.R. 157.

5. Appeal—not a stay The lodgement of a notice of appeal does not operate as a stay of the proceedings except so far as the master or district judge may otherwise direct, Ord. 58, r.1(4).

2 Procedural requirements on appeal

1. Documents The appellant should lodge two copies of the notice of appeal and a fee of £20. A specimen form of notice of appeal is set out in Form C, p. 559.

2. London In London this is done in Room 549, Judge in Chambers' Department, Royal Courts of Justice.

3. Provinces In a district registry case notice of appeal must bear the title of the district registry in which the action is proceeding but should be issued in the district registry at the place at which it is to be heard: *Practice Direction (Judge in Chambers: Outside London) (No. 3)* [1976] 1 W.L.R. 246.

4. Pressure of business The appellant should enquire before issue in a district registry whether the state of business will permit the matter to be heard there.

5. Transfer A notice of appeal issued in the district registry may be transferred for hearing to a High Court judge in chambers sitting in London or at another place outside London either on the application of a party or by the court of its own motion. Similarly, a London appeal can, if thought convenient, be heard out of London (*ibid.*).

6. Service The service period of the notice of appeal is two clear days before the hearing or three days in a district registry case: Ord. 58, r.1(3) and r. 3(2).

3 Judge's papers—London actions

1. Which lists All appeals to a High Court judge in chambers are initially entered in a general list.

2. "Over 30 minute" appeals Those with an estimated length of hearing of more than 30 minutes are transferred to a Chambers Appeals list.

3. Duties of the parties In order to ensure that a complete set of papers is available for perusal by the judge before hearing the appeal, the parties must, not later than 48 hours after the appeal has been warned for hearing, comply with the following requirements:

(a) each party must bespeak the affidavits already filed which that party proposes to use;

(b) each party must lodge in Room 549 Royal Courts of Justice, the exhibits in the affidavit referred to in (a); and

(c) each party must lodge in Room 549 a paginated bundle of the pleadings, affidavits, notice of appeal and relevant orders.

4. Warning Except with the leave of the High Court judge no document may be adduced in evidence or relied on unless it has been bespoken or lodged: *Practice Direction (Judge in Chambers: Amended Procedure)* [1989] 1 W.L.R. 359.

4 Judge's papers—provincial actions

1. What needs to be lodged A bundle, properly paged in order of date and indexed, must be lodged containing the following documents:

(a) the notice of appeal;

(b) the pleadings, if any;

(c) copies of all affidavits (together with exhibits) upon which any party intends to rely;

(d) any relevant order made in the action;

(e) notes (if any) of reasons given by the district judge, prepared by the district judge, counsel or solicitors.

2. Where? The bundle, which should be agreed, must be lodged at the civil listing office of the trial centre concerned.

3. When? If a date for hearing has been fixed, the bundle has to be lodged not later than three clear days before the fixed date. If the hearing date had not been fixed, it must be lodged within 24 hours of the parties being notified that the appeal is to appear in the warned list or, if that is impossible, as soon as is practicable thereafter.

4. Limit placed on documents Except with the judge's leave, no document can be adduced in evidence or relied on unless it is in the bundle lodged. The bundle should contain copies not originals. The originals should be bespoken or produced on the appeal hearing.

5. Skeleton argument In cases of complexity, a skeleton argument or, where it would be helpful, a chronology, should be lodged at the same time as the bundle: *Practice Direction: Appeals from District Judges (Q.B.D.)* [1991] 3 W.L.R. 534.

5 The hearing of the appeal

1. Forum The hearing before the High Court judge takes place in chambers.

2. Procedure It is a rehearing. The judge is in no way fettered by the decision of the master. His own discretion is intended to determine the parties' rights. He is therefore entitled to exercise it as though the matter came before him for the first time: *Evans v. Bartlam* [1937] A.C. 473: *Europa Property and Finance Services Ltd v. Stubbert, The Times,* November 25, 1991, C.A.

3. Weight to be attached to master's decision Of course, the judge in chambers will give the weight it deserves to the master's decision (*ibid.*).

4. Further evidence Apart from the restriction contained in the Practice Directions above, there would appear to be no restriction on a party filing further affidavits prior to the hearing of the appeal before the judge in chambers in order to try to strengthen his case. As we shall see, the position is different on appeals to the Court of Appeal. It is common practice to let in additional evidence on appeals to the judge, subject to costs, unless the judge in his discretion considers that there are special reasons to exclude the evidence: *Kiu May Construction Co. Ltd v. Wai Cheong Co. Ltd* (1983) 29 Build.L.R. 137 (Hong Kong). In *Wales Tourist Board v. Roberts, The Times,* January 10, 1987, it was held that the court has no power to refuse to consider fresh evidence adduced on the appeal on the basis that it could reasonably have been but had not been adduced before the district judge. All relevant evidence which first appeared at a late stage would be looked at with circumspection.

5. The judge's options Because the hearing before the judge in chambers is in the nature of a rehearing, the judge has the same options open to him as were open to the master or district judge on the initial hearing (see p. 381).

6. Costs The costs normally follow the event on the appeal so that a successful appellant will get his costs of the appeal and of the hearing before the master or district judge. If the judge considers that matters turned on fresh evidence filed after the date of the master's decision, he may leave the master's order for costs intact and make a separate order for the costs of the appeal.

6 Appeals to the Court of Appeal

1. Jurisdiction Appeals from a High Court judge in chambers to the Court of Appeal are regulated by Ord. 58, r.6 and Ord. 59.

2. Supreme Court Practice Reference should be made to *The Supreme Court Practice* for the detailed practice and procedural requirements of Ord. 59 and the notes and to the important Practice Direction which came in to effect on September 4, 1995, reported at [1995] 1 W.L.R. 1191. An outline is set out below.

3. Leave to appeal Leave to appeal is required under Ord. 59, r.1B(1)(f) against interlocutory orders and interlocutory judgments (save for certain irrelevant exceptions).

4. Which orders are interlocutory? The list of interlocutory orders is to be found in Ord. 59, r.1A(6) as amended by R.S.C. (Amendment) 1993. The position now is that *any* order made on an application for summary judgment either under Ord. 14, Ord. 86 or C.C.R. Ord. 9, r.14 is interlocutory.

5. Need for leave to appeal The result is that leave to appeal is now required whatever the outcome of an application for summary judgment and whoever the appellant, be he plaintiff or defendant: Ord. 59, r.1B(1)(f) combined with the amended Ord. 59, r.1A(6)(aa).

6. Interim payments Any order for or relating to an interim payment is interlocutory: Ord. 59, r.4 and so leave to appeal is required.

7. Appeals from official referees

(a) *On facts:* Since October 1, 1988 Ord. 58, r.4(b) allows appeals against any finding of fact by an official referee but only with his leave or the leave of the Court of Appeal.

(b) *Leave to appeal on fact—the test:* The test is whether the ground of appeal which it is sought to argue has a reasonable prospect of success. If it has, leave should be granted; if not, it should be refused: *Virgin Group Ltd v. De Morgan Group plc, The Times*, March 9, 1994.

(c) *An uphill task:* An intending appellant will have difficulty in satisfying that test if he seeks to challenge:
    (i) an official referee's findings of primary fact based on his evaluation of oral evidence;
    (ii) the fine details of an official referee's factual investigations;

(iii) findings of fact falling within an official referee's area of specialised expertise.

(d) *Fact/law connection:* The appellant's task will be easier if the challenge on fact is closely bound up with an issue of law for which leave to appeal is not required (see below). In any event, applications should always be considered with reference to specific issues of fact. So, leave should be refused unless the challenge, if successful, will affect the official referee's overall decision (*ibid.*).

(e) *Leave hearing—fresh evidence:* In *Edmund Nuttal Ltd v. Weatherwise Ltd* 51 B.L.R. 118, Ralph Gibson L.J. sitting as a single judge on the leave application, refused the intending appellant's application to admit fresh evidence since it had been readily available and its significance should have been appreciated before the time of the original trial.

(f) *On law:* No leave is required on appeal to the Court of Appeal from an official referee on a point of law.

(g) *Costs only:* Leave is generally required (where section 18(1)(f) of the Supreme court Act 1981 applies).

8. No leave—no appeal Where leave to appeal to the Court of Appeal is required, that leave must be obtained before notice of appeal is given. The notice of appeal cannot incorporate an application for leave. If it does, it is not a valid notice of appeal: *Cumbes v. Robinson* [1951] 2 K.B. 83. The Court of Appeal will raise the question of the necessity of leave of appeal of its own motion where it considers leave is necessary because it has no jurisdiction to hear the appeal otherwise: *White v. Brunton* [1984] Q.B. 570.

9. Setting aside the grant of leave to appeal In *The Iran Nabuvat* [1990] 1 W.L.R. 1115 the Court of Appeal said that where a single Lord Justice had decided that the grounds of appeal are arguable, to succeed on an application to have the grant of leave to appeal set aside, a respondent would have to be able to point to a statutory provision or a binding authority which the single Lord Justice had overlooked or to a factor not brought to his attention which would be decisive of the proposition that the appeal would inevitably fail.

10. Time and mode of appeal An appeal to the Court of Appeal is by notice of motion (usually referred to as "notice of appeal"). The notice of appeal must be served on all parties to the proceedings in the court below who are directly affected by the appeal: Ord. 59, r. 3(5), within four weeks from the date on which the Ord. 14 judgment was perfected; Ord. 59, r.4. Service may be effected by fax in accordance with Ord. 65, r.5(2B). In a

London Chancery division case, the judgment is perfected by sealing in the Chancery Registry; in a London Queen's Bench case it is perfected by being signed, entered and sealed with the seal of the central office and in a district registry case it is perfected by being sealed at the district registry.

11. Extending time for appeal The Court of Appeal has an unfettered discretion to extend time for appealing beyond the normal four-week period and that discretion will normally be exercised in favour of the applicant where the delay is very short and there is an acceptable excuse: *Palata Investments v. Burt & Sinfield* [1985] 1 W.L.R. 942; *Nestlé v. National Westminster Bank, The Times*, March 23, 1990, (longer delay); see also *Norwich & Peterborough Building Society v. Steed* (1991) 1 W.L.R. 449; and *Mallory v. Butler* (1991) 1 W.L.R. 458.

12. Form of notice of appeal A specimen form of notice of appeal is set out in Part C at p. 558.

13. Subsequent procedural requirements Reference should be made to *The Supreme Court Practice 1995*, Vol. 1. pp. 961 *et seq*.

14. Hearing The hearing takes place before the Lords Justices (usually three) sitting in open court. It is by way of rehearing: Ord. 59, r.3(1). The court has the power to receive further evidence on questions of fact on appeals under Ord. 14; Ord. 59, r.10; *Langdale v. Danby* [1982] 1 W.L.R. 1123.

15. Fresh evidence Further evidence can only be put before the Court of Appeal in three restricted situations:
  (a) where "special circumstances" are established: Ord. 59, r.10(2); and see paras. 16 and 17 below;
  (b) where the appeal is one of the exceptional cases where fresh evidence is permitted (*e.g.* judicial review). Ord. 14 appeals are not exceptional for this purpose;
  (c) where the evidence relates to matters which have occurred *after* the original hearing. This exception does not cover evidence which came to light after the original hearing of matters which occurred *before* the original hearing.

16. Special circumstances It would be wrong to think that either party has the freedom to lodge further affidavits to bolster his case before the Court of Appeal whenever it is thought convenient. Denning L.J. said in *Krakaeur v. Katz* [1954] 1 W.L.R. 278 at 279:

   "A preliminary point has arisen whether in an interlocutory matter this court can and should admit further affidavits on behalf of the defendant. It was suggested that an appellant on an interlocutory matter had a right in this court to adduce further evidence by affidavit. I am clearly of the opinion that he has no such right. It is a matter of discretion in this court whether or not further evidence by affidavit should be admitted."

17. Three conditions The special circumstances will only be established if three conditions are satisfied. It must be shown that the further evidence:

(a) could not have been obtained with reasonable diligence for use before the judge in chambers;

(b) is such that, if given, it will probably have an important influence on the outcome, though it need not be decisive; and

(c) must be apparently credible: *Ladd v. Marshall* [1954] 1 W.L.R. 1489; *Skone v. Skone* [1971] 1 W.L.R. 812; *Langdale v. Danby* (above) and *K/S A/S Oil Transport v. Saudi Research & Development Corporation Ltd* [1984] 1 Lloyd's Rep. 5; *Nash v. Rockford R.D.C.* [1917] 1 K.B. 384 at 393.

18. A less stringent rule for Order 14 appeals? The application of these three conditions (which are of general application in relation to the reception of fresh evidence before the Court of Appeal) may require some modification in Ord. 14 appeals to the Court of Appeal. In *Langdale v. Danby* (above) Lord Bridge said at 1133D:

"It may well be that the standard of diligence required of a defendant preparing his case in opposition to a summons for summary judgment, especially if under pressure of time, will not be so high as that required in preparing for trial. The second and third condition will no doubt be satisfied if the further evidence tendered is sufficient, according to the ordinary principles applied on applications for summary judgment, to raise a triable issue. But I can see no injustice at all in requiring a defendant to use such diligence as is reasonable in the circumstances to put before the judge on the hearing of the summons, albeit in summary form, all the evidence he relies on in defence, whereas it would be a great injustice to the plaintiff to allow the defendant to introduce for the first time on appeal evidence which was readily available at the hearing of the summons but was not produced."

19. Special exceptions Whether the three conditions are as laid down in *Ladd's* case are exhaustive or subject to the proviso that if special grounds can be shown for the admission of the further affidavits they will be admitted, remains to be seen. In the *Saudi Research* case (above) the defendant sought to adduce further evidence before the Court of Appeal in spite of the fact that it could with reasonable diligence have been made available to the judge on the Ord. 14 hearing. The defendant said that there were special grounds for its admission. These were the large sums involved, the presence of a fine element and the fact that negotiations were in progress right up to the date of hearing. Ackner L.J. pointed out however that the sum of money involved could not serve to lower the standard of diligence required of a defendant to such an action. It could be said, moreover, of many modern commercial cases that a fine element was present. The negotiations between the parties indicated that the possibility of their concurrence in a form of settlement was far from being a real one. Accordingly, the defendant's attempt to introduce new evidence was refused. The Court of Appeal did not consider that the facts of the case provided any justification for relaxing a requirement which is not a procedural technicality but which is based upon the public interest that finality in litigation should be achieved. On the other hand, where the judge had found the defendant's story incredible from which there was a necessary inference to be drawn that the defendant, an established leading underwriter, was deliberately deceiving the court, the Court of Appeal exceptionally allowed the defendant the chance to explain the situation more fully by admitting fresh evidence: *Compton v. Hussey* (September 30, 1987, C.A.T. No. 933; unreported).

20. Unusual speed In *Messenger Newspapers Group v. National Graphical Association* [1984] I.C.R. 345, the plaintiffs produced a formidable body of affidavit evidence in support of their Ord. 14 application. That evidence was not dealt with in substance by the defendants in their affidavit in reply. In the Court of Appeal, the defendants were permitted to put in further affidavits—affidavits which should have been before the judge— because of the unusual speed with which the proceedings had moved in the courts below.

21. Approach of the Court of Appeal Some of the older cases dealing with the approach of the Court of Appeal need to be treated with a certain amount of circumspection because until 1981 the plaintiff had no right to appeal against an order giving a defendant unconditional leave to defend. Nowadays, the plaintiff is in the same position as the defendant when considering the possibility of an appeal. It was said in *Wardens of St Saviour's Southwark v. Gery* (1887) 3 T.L.R. 667 (at a time when appeal lay from the divisional court to the Court of Appeal) that:

"... when the divisional court had in a matter under Order 14 allowed a case to go on and had permitted a defendant to defend, the Court of Appeal would not interfere with their decision, unless they were absolutely certain that the divisional court was wrong. If the divisional court had shut out a defendant from defending an action, then the court, considering the rule a hard one, would look if there were any plausible defence to the action; but the case was different whether the defendant was allowed to defend." (See also *Ludford v. Rymill* (1888) 4 T.L.R. 693.)

22. The modern re-statement—questions of fact Echoes of the *Wardens of St Saviour's* case can be heard in the decisions of the Court of Appeal in the 1980s. This is perhaps best illustrated by a passage from a decision dealing with questions of fact. In *European Asian Bank AG v. Pubjab and Sind Bank (No. 2)* [1983] 1 W.L.R. 642, Robert Goff L.J. said (at 654B):

> "If a judge has already decided, on the evidence, that there is a very triable issue on a question of fact, it must in the very nature of things be unlikely that this court will interfere with his decision and decide that no trial shall take place; because, where such a conclusion has already been reached by a judge, this Court will be very reluctant to hold that there is no issue or question to be tried."

(See also dicta of Sir John Donaldson M.R. in *Lloyds Bank Ltd v. Ellis-Fewster* [1983] 1 W.L.R. 559 at 562B, and see *Alliance and Leicester Building Society v. Ghahremani*, [1992] RVR 198.)

23. A softer approach for the defendant appellant Still dealing with appeals on questions of fact, the Court of Appeal has shown itself less reluctant to interfere with the judge's decision to grant the plaintiff summary judgment. In *Pumfrey Construction Ltd v. Childs, The Times*, July 12, 1985, May L.J. said:

> "However, when the judge has decided that there is no triable issue and given judgment to the plaintiff, the position is different. Although the learned judge will have had to weigh up the evidence in the affidavits filed on both sides, and to that extent will have been exercising a judicial discretion, if then he gives judgment for a plaintiff, I do not think that this court should be as reluctant to disturb his decision as it would be had this been to the effect that there was a triable issue. Of course, this court should and will pay the greatest respect to the views of the judge below, but save in the exceptional case the evidence before us will be the same as that which was before him. Further, a case in which judgment has been signed does I think merit different consideration from one in which leave to defend has been given. In these cases, I think that this court is entitled to and should have a fresh look at the affidavits and exhibits and then reach its own conclusion, albeit with the assistance of the views of the judge below, as to whether a triable issue has been shown.

In the result it would appear, therefore, that the plaintiff may have a harder task in seeking to persuade the Court of Appeal to reverse the judge who has found that there are triable issues of fact than the defendant who is seeking to persuade the same court to be allowed to defend the action. It is respectfully suggested that this must be correct for one is reminded of the words of Lord Halsbury L.C. in *Jacobs v. Booth's Distillery Co.* [1901] 85 L.T. 265, H.L. when he said:

> "People do not seem to understand that the effect of Order 14 is that, upon the allegation of the one side or the other, a man is not permitted to defend himself in court; that his rights are not to be litigated at all."

24. Questions of law To the extent that the question arising under Ord. 14 depends wholly or partly on law, it has been said by the Court of Appeal (in the *Pumfrey Construction* case (*ibid.*)) that the duty of that court is to come to a decision as to the law and apply it to the facts. It is not open to the Court of Appeal to adopt the approach that the law is arguable, thereby to leave it to be argued at trial: and see now Ord. 14A.

25. Money in—money out Where the defendant who has paid money into court pursuant to an order giving him leave to defend, succeeds on appeal in getting unconditional leave to defend, he is entitled to the repayment of his money out of court (and that remains so even though the plaintiff is appealing the order giving the defendant unconditional leave to defend)— *Yorkshire Banking Co. v. Beatson* (1879) 4 C.P.D. 213.

26. Costs in the Court of Appeal The Court of Appeal has jurisdiction not only over the costs of the appeal to its own court, but over the costs below (section 51 of the Supreme Court Act 1981 to be substituted by section 4 of the Courts and Legal Services Act 1990 when operative). As always, costs are in the discretion of the court. They normally follow the event.

27. Carriage of order The order of the Court of Appeal is drawn up by the Associate of the Court of Appeal rather than the party who would normally have carriage of the order.

28. Appeal from the Court of Appeal to House of Lords Appeal lies from the Court of Appeal to the House of Lords. The rights to and procedure for appeal are governed by the Administration of Justice (Appeals) Act 1934, Procedural Directions and Standing Order to which reference should be made in *The Supreme Court Practice 1995*, Vol. 2, Part 16.

7 The county court

1. An analogous remedy The County Court Rules 1981 provide a similar procedure for summary judgment by C.C.R., Ord. 9, r.14.

2. Broadly analogous restrictions The summary county court remedy is available in all actions except those concerning:
  (a) small claims (*i.e.* those automatically referred to arbitration under Ord. 19, r.2(3));
  (b) possession of or title to land:
  (c) defamation, malicious prosecution and false imprisonment;
  (d) fraud;
  (e) admiralty action *in rem.*

3. Other restrictions The procedure cannot be invoked if the defendant has not filed a defence. However, in such a situation, the plaintiff may enter judgment in default of defence under Ord. 9, r.6.

4. Procedure Application is made on notice supported by affidavit which must:
  (a) verify the facts on which the claim or the party of it to which the application relates is based; and
  (b) state that, notwithstanding the delivery of a defence, the defendant has no defence to the claim or the particular part to which the application relates.
No fee is payable.

5. Service period Notice of the application and a copy of the supporting affidavit and exhibits must be served on the defendant not less than seven days before the date fixed for the hearing of the application: Ord. 9, r.14(3).

6. Hearing date This is normally the date fixed for the pre-trial review.

7. Showing cause The provisions of R.S.C. as to the defendant showing cause are adopted in the county court: Ord. 9, r.14(5).

8. Court's powers The county court has exactly the same powers as the High Court when dealing with an application for summary judgment: Ord. 9, r.14(5). A defendant who, having obtained leave to defend unconditionally upon the payment of money into court and who, as a consequence of his failure to comply with the condition, has judgment entered against him, cannot apply under C.C.R., Ord 37, r.4 for the judgment to be set aside: *Markholme Ltd v. Braithwaite* (April 14, 1985; unreported).

CHAPTER 5

Judgment in Default of Notice of Intention to Defend Action

A: GENERAL PRINCIPLES

1 The basic rule

1. The defendant at risk A defendant in a writ action who fails to give notice of his intention to defend the action within the prescribed time runs the risk of the plaintiff entering judgment against him by default.

2. A plaintiff's weapon The advantage to the plaintiff is that he succeeds in obtaining judgment against the defendant without the bother and expense of proving his claim at the trial of the action. This summary procedure is regulated by Ord. 13. It is perhaps worth noting in passing that if there is material before the court to suggest that a default judgment might well not be of any value to the plaintiff, (as, for example, where such a judgment might not be enforceable in a foreign jurisdiction where the defendant is reasonably believed to have assets) the plaintiff has a right to proceed to trial, although where he could have entered judgment in default he will get no more costs by going to trial than he would have recovered under default judgment unless the court otherwise orders.

3. Claims within Order 13 The plaintiff who can satisfy the qualifying requirements referred to below may seek a default judgment under Ord. 13 against a defendant in one or other of the following forms:
  (a) Final Judgment for a liquidated sum.
  (b) Interlocutory judgment for unliquidated damages.
  (c) Judgment for wrongful interference with goods which may be either:
      (i) interlocutory judgment for the value only of the goods to be assessed (and damages for consequential loss); or
      (ii) interlocutory judgment for delivery of the goods or their value to be assessed (and damages for consequential loss); or
      (iii) final judgment for specific delivery of the goods (and damages

412

for consequential loss) [but in this case only, application is
made by summons].

(d) Final judgment for possession of land (subject to para. 5(b) below).

(e) Where the claim is for a combination of claims within (a)–(d) above,
such judgment as is appropriate to those claims.

Each of these kinds of judgment will be discussed in detail later.

4. Claims outside Order 13 If the claim is not of a kind encompassed by
Ord. 13, rr.1–4 it is not possible to sign judgment in default under that
Order. The following is an illustrative, not exhaustive, list of actions and
claims outside the scope of Ord. 13:

(a) Admiralty actions *in rem* (where judgment can be obtained on motion
in default of acknowledgment of service but only by satisfying the
court that the claim is well founded—Ord. 75, r.21).

(b) Mortgage actions—*i.e.* those in which relief of a kind covered by
Ord. 88 is sought.

(c) Probate actions (Ord. 76, r.6(1)).

(d) Actions commenced otherwise than by writ. So, for instance, a
plaintiff who commences an action by originating summons cannot
secure judgment by default under Ord. 13.

(e) Counterclaims (save for a minor and rare exception contained in
Ord. 15, r.3).

(f) A claim for accounts to be taken.

(g) Injunctions.

(h) Declarations.

(i) Specific performance.

(j) Rectification of documents.

(k) Actions in which provisional damages are claimed (Ord. 37, r.8(5)—
and see *Practice Direction (Provisional Damages)* [1988] 1 W.L.R.
654).

(l) Actions to enforce agreements regulated by the Consumer Credit Act
1974 or linked transactions which by section 141 of that Act must
be brought in the county court. (When an action which ought, by
virtue of that section, to have been brought in the county court is
wrongly commenced in the High Court, the court must of its own
motion set aside any default judgment and transfer it to the appropriate county court: *A.A. Financial Services Ltd v. Docherty* (Scott J.,
November 10, 1987; unreported)).

5. Claims within Order 13 but only with leave Six kinds of action, although
within Ord. 13, are subject to the rule that the plaintiff can only enter
judgment in default with leave of the court. They are:

(a) actions in tort between husband and wife brought during the
subsistence of the marriage (see Ord. 89, r.2);

413

(b) actions for the recovery of possession of a dwelling house whose rateable value does not exceed £1,500 in Greater London and £750 elsewhere (Ord. 13, r.4(2) (see Ord. 77, r.9));

(c) actions against the Crown (see Ord. 77, r.9);

(d) actions in which the debtor has served notice of a wish to re-open a credit agreement under section 139(1)(b) of the Consumer Credit Act 1974 (see Ord. 83, r.3);

(e) actions in which the defendant is a State (see Ord. 13, r.7A);

(f) actions in which default judgment is sought under the Civil Jurisdiction and Judgment Act 1982 (see Ord. 13, r.7B).

2 Qualifying requirements

1. When? The plaintiff may only seek default judgment under Ord. 13 if:

(a) The action is a writ action.

(b) The claim on the writ is of a kind within the Scope of Ord. 13.

(c) The writ has been duly served.

(d) The defendant has failed to return the form of acknowledgment to court within the prescribed time, or he has returned it to court but has stated in it that he does not intend to contest the proceedings.

(e) Service of the writ can be proved either by reference to the defendant's filed acknowledgment of service; affidavit of service or production of the defendant's solicitor's indorsement of acceptance of service.

(f) In claims for possession of land, no relief is claimed of a kind specified in Ord. 88 relating to mortgages.

If the defendant can show that any of these qualifying requirements has not been complied with, the judgment is irregular and may be set aside.

2. The defendant disputes the jurisdiction It would seem that if the defendant disputes the jurisdiction of the court to entertain the action and has issued a summons to stay further proceedings on the writ for that reason, entry of judgment in default by the plaintiff prior to the determination of the defendant's application would amount to an abuse of the process of the court and would be set aside for irregularity; *Bankers Trust Co. v. Abdul Gatif Galadari* [1987] Q.B. 222.

3. The importance of the "acknowledgment of service" form The writ must be accompanied by a prescribed form of acknowledgment of service in which the title and the title number of the action are filled in (Ord. 10, r.1(6)). Prescribed Form 14 (*The Supreme Court Practice (1997)*, Vol. 2, para. 9) is used where proceedings are commenced by writ. Attached to and forming part of the form are printed directions for acknowledging service and notes for guidance.

4. The importance demonstrated In *Westpile v. Collins (A.D.) Site Developments* [1989] C.L.Y. 3100, the notes for guidance accompanying the acknowledgment of service form, contrary to Prescribed Form 14, did not include in the margin a warning that the rules as to deemed service by post were not applicable to a defendant company. The company's director erroneously thought that he had 18 days in which to acknowledge service when in reality he only had 13. Judge Fox-Andrew Q.C. sitting as an Official Referee held that the notes for guidance are a vital element of the prescribed form rendering the writ defective and any judgment obtained on it irregular thereby entitling the defendant to have it set aside (but see *Bondy v. Lloyds Bank plc* (1991) 135 S.J. 412; where writ served on experienced solicitors a day before expiry of limitation period—proceedings not set aside).

5. Lost and spoilt forms If a defendant loses or spoils the form, he may obtain another form from the court office.

3 Multiple defendants

1. Judgment against one does not stop claim against other
Ord. 13 makes it quite clear that where the plaintiff sues several defendants in the same action, he may enter judgment against any defendant who has failed to give notice of intention to defend and proceed to trial in the action against the other defendants who have indicated an intention to defend (See Ord. 13, rr.191), 2, 3(1) and 4(1)).

2. But what is some defendants not served? The position is the same where some defendants have been served with the writ and some have not been served. The plaintiff may proceed to judgment against any served defendant who has not indicated an intention to defend and leave action against the others in abeyance for the time being.

3. Does it matter where liability is joint or several? No—it is irrelevant whether the liability of the defendants is joint or joint and several. However, the plaintiff cannot get paid twice over for the same debt irrespective of the number of default judgments he may enter, so long as the whole or part of the debt remains unsatisfied the plaintiff is entitled to go on and obtain judgment against any of the defendants; *Weall v. James* (1893) 68 L.T. 515, C.A.; *Pim Bros. Ltd v. Coyle* [1903] 2 K.B. 457; and see Civil Liability (Contribution) Act 1978, s.3.

4. Claims in the alternative—the significance of "election" If the plaintiff's claim is against one of two defendants in the alternative (such as in the case of agent and principal) he must make his choice, *i.e.* "elect"—if he is considering entering judgment by default. Once he enters judgment against one defendant, he is barred from proceeding against the other: *Morel v. Earl of Westmorland* [1903] 1 K.B. 64. For example in *Cross v. Matthews and Wallace* [1904] 91 L.T. 500, Cross sued Matthews for £311 for goods supplied. Cross signed judgment against Matthews in default of appearance and the action proceeded against Wallace to trial. The judge found as a fact that the debt was contracted by Matthews solely as an agent for Wallace. The judge then adjourned the case to enable an application to be made to set aside the default judgment against Matthews. That being done the case was relisted before the judge. No evidence was offered against Matthews and judgment was entered against Wallace. The divisional court allowed an appeal by Wallace. Lord Alverstone C.J. said:

> "The case coming before the judge on February 29, he would then have given judgment for the plaintiffs upon his findings of fact but it was brought to his knowledge that a judgment had been signed against Matthews. That being so he ought to have given judgment for the defendant Wallace, because the fact of the judgment having been signed against Matthews showed an election on the part of the plaintiffs to accept the liability of the agent ... I am of opinion that the county court judge ought to have given judgment for the defendant on the grounds that the plaintiffs had conclusively elected to enforce their remedy against Matthews."

5. Does the plaintiff "elect" when he enters interlocutory judgment against one defendant? The answer would seem to be "No." In *City of Westminster v. Reema Construction Ltd and others* (1990) 20 Con LR 44, the plaintiffs employed the fourth and seventh defendants to carry out remedial works to their blocks of flats. Some work was done by the fourth defendants and some by the seventh defendants. These defendants were apparently related in some way as there had been some name-swapping between them. A winding up order was made against the seventh defendants and the action was brought against them by leave of the court. As a result, the plaintiffs sought to make the fourth defendants responsible for the whole of the work done severally by the fourth and seventh defendants. Later, the plaintiffs entered judgment in default against the seventh defendants. Later still, the plaintiffs applied for leave to set aside the judgment. The fourth defendants resisted the application on the ground that the plaintiffs' judgment was an irrevocable election to proceed against he seventh defendants to the exclusion of the fourth defendants. Judge Peter Bowsher Q.C. sitting as an Official Referee held that an interlocutory judgment for damages to be assessed was not an irrevocable election, but was only conditional until the damages had been assessed and the judgment completed.

4 Time limits

1. Acknowledging service in England and Wales—by when? The defendant, if in England and Wales, has 14 days after the writ has been served on him (including the day of service) in which to return the acknowledgment of service to court (Ord. 12, r.5). If the last day for acknowledging service falls on a Saturday, Sunday or any other day on which the court office is closed, he has all the next day on which the court office is open in which to return his acknowledgment of service to court (Ord. 3, r.4). Thus, if the last day for acknowledging falls, say, on a Saturday, the plaintiff cannot enter judgment in default until the following Tuesday morning.

2. Acknowledging service outside England and Wales—by when? The court has power to extend the time for acknowledging service. If the writ is served out of the jurisdiction, the effect of Ord. 12, r.5 is to allow a longer time for acknowledging service by reference to the Extra Jurisdiction Tables (see *The Supreme Court Practice 1995*, Vol. 2, para. 902).

3. What if the defendant tarries? The defendant may, however, return his acknowledgment of service even after the 14 day period has expired so long as judgment has not been entered against him (Ord. 12, r.6). In that situation, however, he is not allowed to serve his defence any later than if he had acknowledged service within the 14 day period unless the court so orders (Ord. 12, r.6(2)).

4. What if judgment already entered? The defendant is not allowed to file an acknowledgment of service in which he indicates an intention to defend the action once judgment has been entered. He may apply to have the judgment set aside if he wishes to defend the action. (For procedure for setting aside judgment in default see pp. 450 *et seq.*)

5. What if the plaintiff tarries? Suppose the plaintiff having issued the writ, refuses or neglects to serve it on the defendant? Under Ord. 12, r.8A, the defendant may serve a notice on the plaintiff requiring him either to serve the writ or discontinue the action within a specified time not being less than 14 days after service of the notice. If the plaintiff fails to do one or the other, the court may, on application by the defendant, dismiss the action or make such other order as it thinks fit. Application is made by summons supported by affidavit which must,

    (a) verify the facts on which the application is based; and

(b) state that the defendant intends to defend the proceedings.

A copy of the affidavit must be served with the summons on the plaintiff.

6. Defendant applies to set aside writ renewal/service A writ is valid in the first instance for four months from the date of its issue (six months where leave to serve out of the jurisdiction is required).

The period of the validity of the writ may be extended by order following an *ex parte* application by the plaintiff under Ord. 6, r.8(2). The principles on which extensions are granted were stated in *Kleinwort Benson Ltd v. Barbak Ltd "The Myrto" (No. 3)* [1987] A.C. 597; [1987] 2 W.L.R. 1053, H.L.; and *Waddon v. Whitecroft-Scovill Ltd* [1988] 1 All E.R. 996, [1988] 1 W.L.R. 309, H.L. The defendant may apply to discharge the *ex parte* order for renewal and to set aside service under Ord. 32, r.6 but should give notice of his intention to defend before issuing the application, which must be issued within the time limited for defence: Ord. 12, r.8(1)(a) and (d); see also *Waid-Lee v. Linehan* [1993] 2 All E.R. 1006; [1993] 1 W.L.R. 754, C.A.; and *Lawson v. Midland Travellers Ltd* (1993) 1 All E.R. 989, [1993] 1 W.L.R. 735, C.A.; *Sage v. Double A Hydraulics Ltd, The Times,* April 2, 1992, C.A.

B: SERVICE OF PROCESS

1 Introduction

1. The significance of service Time begins to run against the defendant from the date of service of the writ.

2. What is service? Service is construed so as to involve both sender and recipient. "Serve" means the whole process of transmission. So, a writ is not served until it is actually received, or deemed to have been received under the provisions of the rules: *per* May L.J. in *Austin Rover Group Ltd v. Crouch Butler Savage Associates* [1986] 1 W.L.R. 1102; [1986] 3 All E.R. 50; and see *Forward v. West Sussex County Council* [1995] 2 W.L.R. 1469.

3. The varieties of service Various methods of service and the date when service is deemed to have taken place are summarised immediately below.

4. Differences The essential difference between personal service and other forms of service (at any rate, so far as service on individuals is concerned) is that, since service is only effected when the proceedings are actually brought to the notice of the defendant and not on mere delivery of the writ to his last known address, personal service is the only method of service which guarantees that the proceedings have been brought to the defendant's attention. In all other forms of service, there is an element of risk that the defendant has not actually received the writ and hence has not had the proceedings brought to his notice. The real test is one of notice, not delivery. It follows that in all but cases of personal service the plaintiff runs the risk of the defendant rebuffing the presumption that he has received notice of the proceedings. if he does so, the plaintiff has to go back to "square one" and effect service properly. By that time the plaintiff may be in serious trouble with limitation issues or problems concerning the period of validity of the writ. For these reasons, it is always safer to effect personal service, if possible.

5. How Long? The defendant usually has 14 days to return the acknowledgment of service—but 14 days from when? This is dealt with at pp. 427 *et seq.*

6. Service in August It has always been permissible to serve a writ in August. Until R.S.C. (Amendment No. 2) 1990 (S.I. 1990 No. 1689), pleadings could not be served in August by virtue of Ord. 18, r.5. That rule has now been revoked so that time for service of any pleading runs in August. A writ is not a pleading even if it is indorsed with a statement of claim: *Murray v. Stephenson* (1887) 20 Q.B.D. 60.

7. Sealed service copies only A writ is issued when it is sealed at the court office. Every service copy must be sealed with the court seal and be accompanied by the prescribed form of acknowledgment of service (Ord. 10, r.1(6)).

8. Admiralty and Commercial Registry In 1987, this Registry was created at the R.C.J. so as to provide a more efficient administrative structure there for the processing of Admiralty and Commercial Court actions. Although the general rules, set out at p. 418, as to sealing and service, apply to these actions, it is now permissible to issue writs by fax in that Registry when it is closed. The writ must be indorsed with a prescribed form of certificate before being faxed. The issue of the writ takes place when the fax is recorded at the Registry and has the same effect "for all purposes" as a writ issued under Ord. 6, r.7. So, exceptionally, a writ, properly issued by fax there, may be served even though not bearing the court seal. It is treated as if it were sealed. But the issuing solicitor must attend the Registry when it is next open to get the writ sealed and pay the issue fee. If he fails to do so, the writ is treated as never having been issued (Ord. 6, r.7A). See also *Practice Direction (Commercial Court: Writ—Issue by Fax)* [1991] 3 All E.R. 448.

2 Individuals

1. Personal service Service of the writ may be effected personally on the defendant, by physically handing it to him. It should not be in an envelope. It may be served at any time of the day or night but not on a Sunday except by leave of the court. *Murray v. Stephenson (ibid.)*; Ord. 65, r.10. (As the service copy of the writ is sealed, the former rule whereby the defendant was entitled to be shown the original by the plaintiff so as to satisfy himself that the action was genuine, no longer applies.) If the defendant refuses to accept the writ the process server should apprise him of its contents, leave it with him and if necessary, even throw it at his feet.

2. Postal service As an alternative to personal service, the writ may be sent to an individual by ordinary first-class post at his usual or last known address (Ord. 10, r.1(2)(a)). This method is only permitted if the individual defendant is within the jurisdiction. It cannot be used if the defendant's usual or last-known address is abroad. "Ordinary first-class post" means pre-paid post or post in respect of which there is an arrangement under which no prepayment is necessary. Thus registered or second-class post does not qualify.

3. No service on defendant's insurers In *Towers v. Morley* [1992] 1 W.L.R. 511 the plaintiff issued a writ against the defendant claiming damages for personal injuries, a copy of which was sent to the defendant's insurer's by the plaintiff's solicitors for information. Although the defendant was not served with the writ, his solicitors filed an acknowledgement of service indicating an intention to defend and made a payment in to court. Over a year later the plaintiff's solicitor indicated a willingness to accept the payment in. The defendant's solicitor then took the point that the action was now dead for want of service of the writ and issued a summons to strike out the action. The Court of Appeal held that, as the writ had not been served on the defendant, the plaintiff could not rely on the defendant's act in acknowledging service; and that her payment in did not stop her from asserting that the writ had not been served. The action was struck out. (See also review of some Court of Appeal cases concerning service of county court summons, *Supreme Court Practice News 8/95*.)

4. Which address? In a case concerning the meaning of "address" in C.C.R. Ord. 7, r.10(1)(b), it was held that "address" was to be given its ordinary meaning, namely a place at which to a greater or lesser extent a person was present to receive delivery of written communications. It did not include a flat of which the defendant was the lessee but at which he had never resided; at which he was never present; and at which the service of the summons did not come to his notice: *Willowgreen Ltd v. Smithers* [1994] 2 All E.R. 533; see also *White v. Weston* [1968] 2 All E.R. 842; and *Al Tobaishi v. Aung* (1994) L.S.G. March 30; and *Supreme Court Practice News Issue 8/95, "Recent Cases on Service of Originating Process by Post".*

5. Letter-box service This is an alternative to personal and postal service. It may be effected on an individual defendant by inserting the writ through his letter-box (Ord. 10, r.1(2)(b)). Again, this method only applies to a defendant within the jurisdiction. If the defendant has no letter-box, "letter-box" service is inapplicable. (Thus, a writ cannot be pushed under his front door, handed to his wife, the caretaker or a cleaner, etc.) See also *India Videogram Ass. Ltd v. Patel* [1991] 1 All E.R. 214.

6. Document exchange and fax Although Ord. 65, r.5 permits service of other documents by document exchange and fax, neither of these methods of service is permissible in the case of originating process.

3 Service on limited companies

1. Statutory provisions Section 725 of the Companies Act 1985 applies. (Ord. 10, r.1 does not apply to limited companies.)

2. How? Documents (including writs) are served on a company by leaving it at or sending it by post to its registered office. First-class, second-class or registered post are all permissible.

3. Defective service A writ served on a limited company elsewhere than at its registered office is insufficient to render the proceedings a nullity so as to entitle the defendant to have them set aside *ex debito justitiae*. Where the defendant is in no doubt as to whom the plaintiff intended to sue, Ord. 2, r.1 gives the court power to cure the irregularity and Ord. 13, r.9 enables the court to set aside any judgment on terms: *Singh v. Atombrook Ltd* [1989] 1 W.L.R. 810; *Golden Ocean Assurance Ltd v. Martin; The Goldean Mariner* [1990] 2 Lloyd's Rep. 215.

4. Overseas companies Overseas companies with a place of business in Great Britain must deliver a return to the Registrar of Companies in prescribed form containing the name and address of a person resident in Great Britain authorised to accept on the company's behalf service of process and any notices required to be served on it: Companies Act 1985 s.691(1)(b)(ii). By section 695 of the same Act, any process required to be served on an overseas company is sufficiently served if addressed to that person whose name and address are on the Companies Register pursuant

421

to section 691. What happens if the proposed defendant overseas company has never filed the return; or has done so but the person is now dead or has ceased to reside at the address supplied; or refuses to accept service on the company's behalf; or for any other reason cannot be served with the writ? Section 695 authorises the plaintiff to serve it on the company by leaving it at, or sending it by post to any place of business established by the company in Great Britain. (See *Boocock v. Hilton International Co.* [1993] 1 W.L.R. 1065.)

4 Other corporate bodies

1. What? Service on other corporate bodies such as building societies, charities and local authorities may be served on one or other of the officers specified under Ord. 65, r.3(1).

2. Upon whom? Mayor, Chairman, President, Town Clerk, Secretary, Treasurer "or other similar officer thereof."

3. How? In the same way as for individuals (*i.e.* personal, postal or insertion through letter-box).

5 Patients and minors

1. No difference in principle Service of the writ may be effected in the same way as for an individual, save for particular modifications, explained below.

2. Infants In the case of an infant who is not also a patient, service must be effected upon his father or guardian if he has none, or on the person with whom he resides or in whose care he is (Ord. 80, r.16(1)).

3. Patients In the case of a patient, on the person (if any) authorised under Part VII of the Mental Health Act 1983 to conduct the proceedings on the patient's behalf or if there is no one authorised, on the person with whom he lives or in whose care he is.

6 Service on firms

1. General rule If the defendant firm has not been dissolved to the knowledge of the plaintiff before the action is started, service may be effected:
    (a) personally, by handing it to a partner or,
    (b) by handing it personally at the firm's principal place of business

within the jurisdiction to any person having control or management of the business (Ord. 81, r.3) or,

(c) by ordinary first-class post to the principal place of business within the jurisdiction (as to which see *Austin Rover Group Ltd v. Crouch Butler Savage Association* [1986] 1 W.L.R. 1102).

(d) pursuant to agreement between the parties under Ord. 10, r.3(1). An agreement includes an *ad hoc* agreement between, for example, the plaintiff's process-server acting as the plaintiff's agent and a partner in the defendant firm: *Kenneth Allison Ltd v. A. E. Limehouse & Co* [1992] A.C. 105, H.L.

Each person served should also be given an acknowledgment of service, and a written notice, the importance of which is explained below.

2. Ineffective service Service on a firm cannot be effected by insertion through its letter-box. (See also *Marsden v. Kingswell Watts* [1992] 2 All E.R. 239.)

3. The significance of the written notice If personal service on a firm is effected, a written notice should be given to the person to whom the writ is handed, stating whether he is served as a partner or a person having the control or the management of the business or both (Ord. 81, r.3(4)).

4. What if no notice given? If no notice is given, the person served is deemed to be served as partner. The result is that if a partner is served, the failure to serve an accompanying notice is of no consequence.

5. What if service upon non-partner without written notice? If a non-partner manager is served with the notice, service of the writ is bad.

6. Postal service—written notice required? No such accompanying notice is required if service is by post.

7. Firm out of jurisdiction? These methods of service relating to firms only apply to firms carrying on business within the jurisdiction. Where the firm does carry on business here, the methods of service apply even though the partners reside abroad. Thus, a partner resident abroad and her temporarily on a business trip may be served effectively (*Lysaght v. Clark* [1891] 1 Q.B. 552).

8. What if firm dissolved? If the defendant partnership has been dissolved prior to the plaintiff commencing the action, the writ must be served on every person within the jurisdiction sought to be made liable. The methods of service then are those for an individual.

7 Service on foreign states

1. How? Service of the writ on a foreign state is effected by transmission through the Foreign and Commonwealth Office to the Ministry of Foreign Affairs of the proposed defendant state.

2. When? Service is deemed to have been effected when the writ is received by that Ministry (section 12(1) of the State Immunity Act 1978).

3. Procedure The procedure is regulated by Ord. 111, r.7. The plaintiff must lodge in the Central Office (*not* the Foreign and Commonwealth Office):
   (a) A request for service to be arranged by the Secretary of State (no form).
   (b) The sealed copy of the writ and an extra copy.
   (c) A translation of the writ in the official language or one of the official languages of the state.
   (d) The acknowledgment of service and a copy.
Provision is made under section 12(6) of the State Immunity Act 1978 for a foreign state to agree a different method of service than that set out above, in which case either method may be used (Ord. 11, r.7(4))—that is the transmission method in paragraph 6(1)–(3) above or the agreed different method.

8 H.M. Forces

1. Source material For detailed information reference should be made to the memorandum on service of legal process on members of H.M. Forces issued by the Lord Chancellor's Department on July 26, 1979. Provision is made for the plaintiff's solicitor to find out where the serviceman is serving if he does not already know by writing to the appropriate officer of the Ministry of Defence.

2. The solicitor's undertaking The plaintiff's solicitor is supplied with the serviceman's address against an undertaking of non-disclosure.

3. And then? Once the plaintiff's solicitor has learned the serviceman's address he may use it as the address for service by post. If the serviceman is out of the United Kingdom, the plaintiff's solicitor will be told of the approximate date of his likely return.

9 Crown

1. The rule Service of a writ on the Crown is regulated by Ord. 77, r.4.

2. Personal service No: personal service is not required (Ord. 77, r.4(1)).

3. Service—how? Service is effected either by leaving it at the office of or by posting it to the person to be served in the appropriate Government Department or by posting it in a pre-paid envelope addressed to the person who is to be served (Ord. 77, r.4(2)(b)).

10 Service in actions for possession of unoccupied land

1. How? Where a writ is indorsed with a claim for the recovery of land, the court may order service of the writ on the defendant by fixing a copy to some conspicuous part of the land if it is satisfied that there appears to be no one in possession and there is no other effective method of service. Special service rules apply in actions under Ord. 113 for the summary recovery of possession of land.

2. Retrospective validation If service has already been effected in such a way without an order, the plaintiff may seek an order that such service is good (Ord. 10, r.4).

3. Procedure Application is made *ex parte* supported by affidavit showing the efforts made to effect service on the defendant and that the land appears unoccupied or even deserted.

11 Substituted service

1. The rule Ord. 65, r.4 makes provision (by way of an order for substituted service) for the situation where it appears impracticable to serve the writ in the manner prescribed by the rules.

2. Substituted service—what is it? It is an order that the plaintiff should take such steps as the court may direct to bring the writ to the notice of the defendant. For example, the order can require postal service on the defendant at some address other than his usual or last-known address (such as, for example, the address of his solicitor) where it is thought that the writ will come to his notice.

3. Substituted service on M.I.B. A frequent example of substituted service occurs in personal injury claims arising out of a road traffic accident where the defendant cannot be traced. The master or district judge may make an order for substituted service through the post on the defendant's insurers or the M.I.B. (Motor Insurance Bureau) (*Gurtner v. Circuit* [1968] 2 Q.B. 587).

4. How is the application made? Application for substituted service is made by:
  (a) supporting affidavit together; and
  (b) a draft form of order in duplicate; and
  (c) a copy of the writ and acknowledgement of service for sealing; and
  (d) a self-addressed envelope, if application is made by post.

5. What should go into the affidavit? The supporting affidavit must show what steps have been taken to effect personal service and why it is not practicable to effect service by any of the prescribed methods (see *Afro Continental Nigeria v. Meridian Shipping Co. S.A., The Vrontados* [1982] 2 Lloyd's Rep. 241; *Paragon Group Ltd v. Burnell* [1991] 2 W.L.R. 854).

12 Service on defendant's solicitor

1. The significance of the solicitor's indorsement Where a defendant's solicitor indorses on the writ a statement that he accepts service of the writ on behalf of that defendant, the writ shall be deemed to have been duly served on that defendant on the date on which the indorsement was made: Ord. 10, r.1(4).

2. Is service good on the defendant's duly authorised agent other than his solicitor? No, except where it has been expressly provided for in a contract between the parties: *Kenneth Allison Ltd v. A. E. Limehouse & Co.* [1990] 2 All E.R. 723, C.A.; and see *Towers v. Morley* [1992] 1 W.L.R. 511.

3. What does the solicitor do? The defendant's solicitor merely writes "I accept service of this writ on behalf of the defendant", followed by the date, his signature and his address.

4. Drawbacks There are drawbacks to the defendant in this method of acknowledging service, namely:
  (a) As it is not necessary for an acknowledgment of service to be filled in and sent back, the defendant runs the risk that the plaintiff may enter judgment in default of notice of intention to defend.
  (b) The defendant cannot indicate any wish to protest the jurisdiction or to raise objections as to irregularity on issue or service of the writ.

426

5. This method of service—best ignored The defendant's solicitor is well advised to ignore this method and simply fill in and return the acknowledgment of service in the normal way since he has authority to accept service on behalf of his client.

C: WHEN DOES TIME BEGIN TO RUN?

1 Individuals

1. Introduction In the case of personal service on an individual, the date on which the writ is served is the date of service.

2. Post/letter-box service In the case of service on an individual either by first-class post or by insertion through the letter-box, the date of service is deemed to be the seventh day after the date on which the writ was posted or put through the letter-box unless the contrary is proved.

3. Do Saturdays and other holidays count? Yes—Saturdays, Sundays, Bank Holidays, Christmas Day and Good Friday are included. The date on which the letter was posted or put through the letter-box is excluded.

4. What if the defendant received writ within seven days? If the writ, served by post, is admittedly received by the defendant within the seven-day period after it was posted, it is treated as having been served on the date of its actual receipt: *Hodgson v. Hart District Council* [1986] 1 W.L.R. 317; [1986] 1 All E.R. 400, C.A.

5. Postal service—generates only a rebuttable presumption The provisions as to postal service in other respects only raise a rebuttable presumption of service seven days after posting or putting through the defendant's letter-box. The defendant may be able to establish either that he never received the writ at all or at any rate that he has not received it within the seven days' period in which case the presumption of service under Ord. 10, r.1(3)(a) would have been rebutted.

6. What if the defendant acknowledges service when writ not properly served? Again, there is a rebuttable presumption that the writ has been properly served on the date when the defendant acknowledged service. So, if the writ was sent "for information only" to the defendant, his acknowledgment will not have the effect of deeming the writ to have been duly served on him: *Abu Dhabi Helicopters Ltd v. International Aeradio plc* [1986] 1 W.L.R. 312.

427

7. What if the defendant acknowledges service of the writ before its actual service? There is nothing to prevent him from doing so: Ord. 10, r.1(5): *The Gniezno* [1968] P. 418; [1967] 3 W.L.R. 705. The date of service will be deemed to be the date of receipt of the acknowledgment of service at the court office.

8. Patients and minors Time runs against patients and minors in exactly the same way as with ordinary "individuals". But if no acknowledgment of serve is filed for such a person, the plaintiff cannot take any steps to enter judgment (or indeed take any other steps) Until he has applied to the court for the appointment of a guardian *ad litem* (Ord. 80, r.6(1)). The application must be supported by evidence showing:
  (a) that the applicant is a person under disability;
  (b) that the proposed guardian *ad litem* is willing to act as such and has no adverse interest;
  (c) due service of the writ on the person under disability;
  (d) due service of the notice of application on the proposed guardian *ad litem* (Ord. 80, r.6(5)).

9. Illustration of entering default judgment The plaintiff sends the writ by first-class post on Friday, November 1. The writ is treated as having been served on Saturday, November 9, since in reckoning the seven day service period, the date of posting is excluded. The last day for acknowledging service is 14 days after that including the day of service, Saturday, November 23. Since the court office is not open on a Saturday, the defendant can lodge his acknowledgment of service in court at any time on Monday, November 25. The earliest day on which the plaintiff can enter judgment in default of notice of intention to defend is on the morning of Tuesday, November 26.

2 Limited companies

1. The presumption In the case of first-class postal service on a limited company, service is deemed to have been effected on the second working day after posting.

2. That presumption—rebuttable It is open to the company to prove to the contrary; section 725 of the Companies Act 1985 and *Practice Direction (Q.B.D.) (Service of Documents)* [1985] 1 W.L.R. 489; *Press Construction v. Pilkington Bros.* (1987) 7 Con LR 80.

3 Foreign states

1. From when time runs The time for acknowledging service by foreign state begins to run two months from the date on which the writ is deemed to have been served on that state's Ministry of Foreign Affairs (State Immunity Act 1978, s.12(2)).

2. Note—three periods of time to aggregate So, one first of all ascertains the date of deemed service under Ord. 10 then one adds two months to that date. Finally, one adds the service period prescribed by the Extra Jurisdiction Table (*The Supreme Court Practice* (1997), Vol. 2, para. 901).

4 Crown

1. Order 10—irrelevant Ord. 10 does not apply to service of originating process on the Crown (see Ord. 77, r.4).

2. Irrelevance—the procedural consequence Thus, it would appear that the date of service in the case of service by first-class mail will be taken to be the second working day after posting and in the case of second-class mail on the fourth working day after posting unless the contrary is proved: Interpretation Act 1978, s.7; *Practice Direction (Q.B.D.) (Service of Documents)* [1985] 1 W.L.R. 489.

3. "Working days"—meaning "Working days" are Monday to Friday but excluding any Bank Holiday.

D: LIQUIDATED DEMANDS

1 Introduction

1. For what? In a claim for a liquidated sum of money, the plaintiff can enter final judgment under Ord. 13 for:

(a) *The sum claimed:* Irrespective of whether the currency claimed is U.K. or foreign; and

(b) *Interest:* Ord. 13, r.1(2) provides that a claim will not be prevented from being treated as a claim for a liquidated demand by reason only that part of the claim is for interest under section 35A of the Supreme Court Act 1981 at a rate which is not higher than that payable on judgment debts at the date of the writ (the calculation of interest is dealt with at p. 433); and

(c) *Costs:* The costs recoverable on a liquidated claim are fixed in accordance with Ord. 62, Appendix 3 unless the court otherwise orders (Ord.
62, r.32(4)).

2. **Specimens** Specimen forms of judgment appear at p. 571.

2 What is a liquidated demand?

1. **Must be capable of calculation** A liquidated demand is a claim for a
specific sum of money. If the demand is for any amount which has not
already been calculated but is merely a matter of arithmetic, the demand
is still for a liquidated sum. A claim for unliquidated damages is not a
liquidated demand because the quantum of the claim requires judicial
assessment beyond mere arithmetical calculation: *Knight v. Abbott* (1883)
10 Q.B.D. 11.

2. **Liquidated demands and penalty clause** If a contract stipulates the
payment of a specified sum by way of damages in the event of a breach
of the contract, a claim for that specified sum amounts to liquidated
damages if the sum represents a genuine pre-estimate of the damages which
would probably have arisen in any event on breach. Against that, however,
if the pre-estimate is not a genuine attempt to assess damages in advance
or amounts to a stipulation *in terrorem* it is not only not liquidated but
irrecoverable: *Dunlop Pneumatic Tyre Co. v. New Garage & Motor Co.*
[1915] A.C. 79; *Campbell Discount Co. Ltd v. Bridge* [1962] A.C. 600.

3. **Liquidated demands and *quantum meruit*** A claim for a specific sum of
money which is intended to represent reasonable remuneration, such as
for solicitors' costs, constitutes a liquidated demand. If the defendant fails
to indicate his intention to defend the action, the presumption is that he
acknowledges the reasonableness of the sum claimed and final judgment
can be entered for the sum claimed. It is not necessary for the writ to have
been indorsed with a statement of claim nor for a separate statement of
claim to have been served.

3 Final judgment for liquidated sum

1. **Practice requirements** The plaintiff must produce (or send by post—see
Queen's Bench Practice Direction No. 3(12): The Supreme Court Practice
(1997) Vol. 2, Para. 70):
   (a) The original writ.
   (b) An affidavit of due service of the writ (Forms B–E, pp. 570–571).
       (N.B. This is not necessary where either the defendant has returned

the acknowledgment or service to court or the defendant's solicitor has indorsed his acceptance of the writ on the defendant's behalf on the plaintiff's copy of the writ and the plaintiff produces it to the court clerk.) It must state by whom the writ was served, the day of the week and the date of service and where and how it was served (Ord. 10, r.1(2)(b)). These requirements under Ord. 10, r.1(2)(b) are mandatory. If there is no such affidavit or the affidavit is defective in the sense that it fails to comply with Ord. 10, r.1(2)(b), the writ has not been validly served: *India Videogram Assoc. Ltd v. Patel* [1991] All E.R. 214.

(c) Two top copies of the completed form of proposed judgment showing the amount for which judgment is requested to be entered; the amount, if any, which has been received since the issue of the writ and the amount of fixed costs; stating that the defendant against whom judgment is requested has failed to give notice of intention to proceed.

(d) Self-addressed envelope (if by post).

(e) Notice of intention to proceed, where appropriate. (*N.B.* If 12 months or more have elapsed since service of the writ and no further steps have been taken in the action, the plaintiff must give every other party not less than one month's notice of his intention to proceed (Ord. 3, r.6) before entering judgment in default.) No form of notice is prescribed—a letter will suffice. Production to the court clerk of the carbon copy of the original will suffice.

2. Entry of judgment The court clerk will:

(a) Check that no notice of intention to defend has been given and that either the time for doing so has expired or that an acknowledgment of service has been filed indicating an intention not to defend (in which case the plaintiff is entitled to judgment under Ord. 13 even though the prescribed time for acknowledging so has not expired).

(b) Check that leave to enter judgment (if required) has been given (for example, in actions between husband and wife—see Ord. 89, r.2(3)).

(c) Check that one year has not elapsed since the service of the writ (if it has the plaintiff must produce evidence of giving one month's notice of intention to proceed under Ord. 3, r.6).

(d) Check that the names of the parties, the amount of the judgment debt and the costs (if fixed) are correct in the forms of judgment. (*N.B.* The scale of fixed costs prescribed by Ord. 62, Appendix 3).

(e) Make sure that the claim has been properly pleaded and the appropriate judgment is to be entered according to whether the claim is liquidated or unliquidated. In an unliquidated claim the judgment will be for damages to be assessed.

(f) Seal the judgment forms and affidavit of service.

(g) Return the original writ and one sealed copy of the judgment to the plaintiff's solicitor.

(h) Enter details in court records.

3. Court fees? No fee is payable on entering judgment under Ord. 13.

4. Claims in foreign currency As the court has power to give judgment in foreign currency, a liquidated demand may be made in such a currency: *Miliangos v. George Frank (Textiles) Ltd* [1976] A.C. 443. For some of the factors relevant to the determination of the question as to whether the plaintiff is entitled to judgment in a particular foreign currency, see *Oresudsvarvet Aktiebolag v. Marcos Diamantis Lemos, The Angelic Star* [1988] 1 Lloyd's Rep. 122; *The Lash Atlantico* [1987] 2 Lloyd's Rep. 114; *The Transoceanica Francesca and Nicos V* [1987] 2 Lloyd's Rep. 15.

5. Foreign currency—particular procedural requirements The writ in which a claim is made for payment of a debt or liquidated demand in foreign currency must:

(a) Be indorsed with the following certificate which must be signed by or on behalf of the solicitor for the plaintiff if he is acting in person:

> *Sterling equivalent of amount claimed:*
> I/We certify that the rate current in London for the purchase of (state the unit of the foreign currency claimed) at the close of business on the   day of   19   (being the date next to or most nearly preceding the date of issue of the writ) was … … …
> to the £ Sterling and at this rate the debt or liquidated
> demand claimed herein namely (state the sum of the foreign currency claimed) amounts to … … … or exceeds £600 (as the case may be).
> DATED 19
> signed … … … … … … …
> (the solicitor for the plaintiff)

(b) Expressly state (whether indorsed with a statement of claim or not) that the claim is for payment in a specified foreign currency and unless the facts clearly show this, the facts relied on to support a claim must be pleaded in the statement of claim.

(c) State that the contract under which the debt is claimed in the foreign currency is governed by the law of some country outside the United Kingdom.

(d) State that under that contract the money of account in which the debt was payable was the currency of that country or of some other foreign country (*Practice Direction (Judgment: Foreign currency)*

[1976] 1 W.L.R. 83, as amended by *Practice Direction (No. 2)* [1977] 1 W.L.R. 197).

6. Form of judgment in foreign currency See specimen Form G, Part C, p. 572.

7. Fixed costs in foreign currency The amount of fixed costs is calculated on the sterling equivalent of the amount of the foreign currency claimed as indorsed and certified on the writ.

4 Claims for interest under Order 13

1. Generally indorsed writs Where the writ contains a general indorsement, the plaintiff is entitled to recover interest on entry of judgment under Ord. 13 even thought he writ does not contain a claim for interest. Ord. 18, r.8(4) which states that a party must plead specifically any claim for interest under section 35A of the Supreme Court Act 1981 or otherwise does not apply to a generally indorsed writ which is not a pleading: *Edward Butler Vintners Ltd v. Grange Seymour International Ltd* (1987) 131 S.J. 1188.

2. Other writs—what has to be indorsed Guidance as to the appropriate indorsement on the writ so as to come within Ord. 13, r.1(2) is given in *Practice Note* [1983] 1 W.L.R. 377. The indorsement must show:
  (a) The cause of action with particulars, the sum claimed and the date when payment was due.
  (b) The claim for interest under section 35A of the Supreme Court Act 1981. The indorsement may simply read "Interest pursuant to section 35A of the Supreme Court Act 1981."
  (c) The rate of interest claimed and the amount of interest claimed from the date when payment was due to the date of issue of the writ, not exceeding the rate at the date of issue of the writ.
  (d) A claim for further interest at that rate under the Act from the date of issue of the writ to judgment or sooner payment. This should be shown as a daily rate to assist calculation when judgment is entered.

3. What if no claim for interest indorsed? Generally indorsed writs apart, if there is no claim for interest in the writ or statement of claim, no interest can be awarded.

4. What if claim for interest not properly expressed? If the claim for interest up to the date of judgment is not expressed to be under section 35A of the Supreme Court Act 1981, interlocutory judgment may be entered for the claim with interest to be assessed by the master or district judge.

The same applies where interest claimed is for "such sum by way of interest as the court considers reasonable" or some similar expression or where a higher rate than judgment debt rate is claimed: *Practice Note (Claims for Interest) (No. 2)* [1983] 1 W.L.R. 377. In such a situation, the plaintiff may choose to abandon his claim for any interest so as to be able to sign final judgment for a liquidated sum.

5. Contractual interest If the writ claims interest due under a contract on the sum claimed, the writ should:

- (a) Give sufficient particulars of the contract relied on for the claim for interest.
- (b) Show the date from which interest is payable.
- (c) Show the amount of interest due at the date of issue of the writ.
- (d) Contain a claim for further interest at the contract rate from the issue of the writ to judgment or sooner payment, showing the daily figure for ease of calculation.

If the defendant fails to give notice of intention to defend, the plaintiff may then sign judgment for the principal sum, interest to the date of the writ, further interest calculated to the date of judgment and fixed costs.

6. Contractual interest and penalty clauses Where interest is payable as damages in the event of a breach of contract, it is recoverable and treated as liquidated damages if it represents a genuine pre-estimate of the damage likely to be sustained in the event of a breach. If it is not a genuine pre-estimate or is stipulated *in terrorem* it is a penalty and is irrecoverable: *Dunlop Pneumatic Tyre Co. v. New Garage & Motor Co.* [1915] A.C. 79; *Campbell Discount Co. Ltd v. Bridge* [1962] A.C. 600; *The Angelic Star* [1988] 1 Lloyd's Rep. 122.

7. Interest on bills of exchange By section 57 of the bills of Exchange Act 1882, the holder of a dishonoured cheque or other bill of exchange is entitled to recover the amount of the cheque and interest as liquidated damages from the date of dishonour to the date of judgment or sooner payment. The Act does not prescribe the rate. Short-term investment rate is a good guide although the plaintiff may probably ask for a rate around or somewhat above base rate: *Practice Note* [1983] 1 W.L.R. 377. The writ should give the date of dishonour, the rate of interest claimed, a calculation of the interest to the date of issue of the writ and a claim for further interest until judgment or sooner payment showing the daily figure.

8. Interest on damages—P.I. actions Where judgment is given for a sum in excess of £200 and includes damages for personal injuries, the court must include interest on that award or on such part as it considers appropriate unless satisfied that special reasons exist why no interest should be awarded: Section 35A Supreme Court Act 1981, as amended by Administration of Justice Act, 1982.

9. P.I. actions—how much interest? Special damages will ordinarily attract interest from the date of the accident until the date of trial at half the "appropriate" rate, *e.g.* the average rate of interest allowed on money in court on special account. No interest is awarded on damages for future loss of earnings or earning capacity. Interest on general damages for pain, suffering and loss of amenity is awarded at 2 per cent p.a. from date of service of the writ to the date of trial.

10. Interest on judgment debts Every High Court judgment debt carries interest at the statutory rate from the time of entry of judgment. In section 17 of the Judgments Act 1838, the word "judgment " contemplates a single, final judgment for a quantified sum, rather than an interlocutory judgment or order: *Thomas v. Bunn* [1991] 2 W.L.R. 27. Exceptionally, an order for the payment of costs to be taxed is construed for the purposes of section 17 as a judgment debt even though, until taxation, there is no sum for which execution can be levied: *Hunt v. R. M. Douglas (Roofing) Ltd* [1990] 1 A.C. 398, H.L.

11. Judgment debt interest rate A judgment entered prior to April 1, 1993 carries interest at 15 per cent p.a. regardless of when it is satisfied or a writ of execution issued. A judgment entered on or after April 1, 1993 carries interest at 8 per cent p.a. regardless or when it is satisfied or a writ of execution issued.

12. Interest on judgment debt in foreign currency A judgment entered in foreign currency carries the statutory rate of interest on the amount of the judgment in foreign currency and that interest is added to the judgment debt itself for purposes of enforcement: *Practice Direction (Judgment in Foreign Currency)* [1976] 1 W.L.R. 83 and *Practice Direction (Judgment in Foreign Currency) (No. 2)* [1977] 1 W.L.R. 197.

5 The judgment figure

1. What if the defendant has partly paid? The amount for which judgment is entered should be adjusted to take into account any payments made by the defendants since the date of issue of the writ. If this is not done, the defendant is entitled to have the judgment set aside unless the plaintiff corrects the error: see *Muir v. Jenks* [1913] 2 K.B. 412; *Hughes v. Justin* [1894] 1 Q.B. 667; *Craigmyle v. Inchcape* [1942] 1 Ch. 394; *Chessum v.*

Gordon [1901] 1 K.B. 694; *Moundreas & Co. S.A. v. Navimpex Centrala Novala* [1985] 2 Lloyd's Rep. 515.

2. Examples
   (a) In *Bolt & Nut Co. (Tipton) Ltd v. Rowlands, Nicholls & Co. Ltd* [1964] 2 Q.B. 10, the plaintiffs issued a writ claiming £4,000 for goods supplied. The defendants made payment on account after the writ was issued. A meeting later took place at which the defendants gave a cheque to the plaintiffs for a further sum of £1,179. Two days later the plaintiffs entered judgment by default for a sum which gave credit for the amount previously paid but gave no credit for the amount of the cheque for £1,179 given two days earlier. The cheque was presented and cleared in the normal way. It was held that acceptance of a cheque was a conditional payment of a debt and that it operated to suspend the creditors' remedies in respect of the debt until it was met or dishonoured. So the plaintiffs could not ignore the cheque accepted by them two days before they signed judgment. It was held that the judgment, being entered for too much, was irregular. The defendants were entitled to have it set aside *ex debito justitiae*. The plaintiff may apply to reduce it to the proper sum.
   (b) The importance of not entering judgment in default for too much was illustrated in *Muir v. Jenks* [1913] 2 K.B. 412 where bankruptcy proceedings were dismissed and the judgment set aside because the judgment had been entered for £20 too much even though the judgment creditor acknowledged that he had been paid £20 by the judgment debtor's son and was not pursuing that sum.

3. What if debt paid in full after writ but before judgment?
In *Hughes v. Justin* [1894] 1 Q.B. 667, was held that if the whole debt had been paid prior to judgment, judgment should be entered for costs and interest (if any) only.

4. Relevance of slip rule
If the amount for which judgment is entered in default is too much because of an administrative slip on the part of the court clerk, the court may on application amend the judgment under the slip rule: Ord. 20, r.11; *Armitage v. Parsons* [1908] 2 K.B. 410, C.A. The conditions precedent to the application of the slip rule, in the absence of the defendant's consent, are:
   (a) The plaintiff must show that there has been a slip.
   (b) The application has been made promptly.
   (c) The defendant must not have been notified of the judgment.
   (d) No execution or enforcement proceedings must have been taken.
In other situations, the application must be by *inter parte* summons returnable before the master or district judge. The amended judgment must

show exactly what amendment has been made, when and under what order.

5. What if the judgment entered for too little? If the plaintiff enters judgment for too little, the amendment may be corrected in the manner set out above if the slip rule provisions apply. If they do not, the plaintiff cannot sue again for the shortfall since the matter is *res judicata*. What he should do is apply to have the judgment set aside on the grounds of his own mistake (*Sanders v. Hamilton* [1907] 96 L.T. 679).

E: INTERLOCUTORY JUDGMENT FOR UNLIQUIDATED DAMAGES

1 Introduction

1. How does the procedure work? Ord. 13, r.2 provides that where a writ is indorsed with a claim against a defendant for unliquidated damages only, then, if that defendant fails to give notice of intention to defend, the plaintiff may, after the time for acknowledgment of service has gone by, enter interlocutory judgment against the defendant for damages to be assessed.

2. What must the practitioner do? The plaintiff should lodge (or send by post) the same documents as are required on the entry of the final judgment for a liquidated sum except that the form of judgment is in Form H, p. 572. No fee is payable. One sealed copy of the interlocutory judgment is handed back to the solicitor.

2 Assessment

1. Who assesses? The assessment hearing takes place before the master or district judge unless some other method of assessment is ordered (Ord. 37, r.1). The hearing is in public (*Hesz v. Sotheby (Practice Note)* [1960] 1 W.L.R. 285). Appeal from the master or district judge lies direct to the Court of Appeal: Ord. 58, r.2.

2. The assessment—how to get it The plaintiff should:
  (a) Produce his sealed copy of the interlocutory judgment.
  (b) Lodge two copies of a notice of appointment for the assessment indorsed with a time estimate, and a statement whether counsel is to attend and any dates to be avoided.
  (c) Pay the court fee of £15.

In London, the documents are lodged in the Q.B. Masters' Secretary's Department.

3. Directions Any party may apply to the court for directions prior to the assessment hearing. Common directions relate to the exchange of medical or other expert evidence; discovery and inspection of documents concerning the quantum of damages; schedules and counter-schedules of special damages. Application is by summons before the master or district judge on notice to the other parties.

4. Notification It is imperative that notice of the appointment of the assessment hearing is served on the defendant against whom judgment has been obtained at least seven days before the return date (Ord. 37, r.1(1)). This is so whether that defendant has filed an acknowledgment of service or not and even though he has given no address for service. The court has no power to dispense with this requirement nor to abridge the service period. Ordinary service is permissible (Ord. 65, r.5). Where appropriate, leave to serve the defendant out of the jurisdiction must be obtained under Ord. 11.

5. Judgment—for how much? At the conclusion of the hearing, the master or district judge will certify the amount of damages, calculate interest, if any, and make an appropriate order for costs.

6. What if cause of action continuing (*e.g.* "nuisance")? Where damages are assessed in respect of any continuing cause of action, they are assessed down to the time of assessment (Ord. 37, r.6).

7. Interest—from when? Interest on damages under section 17 of the Judgments Act 1858 runs from the date of assessment not from the date of entry of interlocutory judgment: *Thomas v. Bunn* [1991] 2 W.L.R. 27.

8. Provisional damages—no default judgment It is not possible to enter judgment under Ord. 13 in such action in which the plaintiff claims provisional damages: Ord. 37, r.8(5). The procedure in such cases is regulated by *Practice Direction (Provisional Damages)* [1988] 1 W.L.R. 654. If the defendant does not give notice of intention to defend, the plaintiff should, if he has not already done so, serve a statement of claim. In the absence of any response from the defendant, for an order precluding the defendant from contesting liability unless within a specified time he gives notice of intention to defend and serves a defence.

F: ORDER 13 JUDGMENTS FOR WRONGFUL INTERFERENCE WITH GOODS

1 Introduction

1. What relief is available? The plaintiff seeking an Ord. 13 judgment for wrongful interference with his goods will have to consider which kind of relief most suits his needs. He has the following options:

(a) An order for the value of the goods as assessed and damages for their retention. This is appropriate where the goods are ordinary articles of commerce. The court will not normally order restitution where damages are an adequate remedy: *General and Finance Facilities Ltd v. Cooks Cars (Romford)* [1963] 1 W.L.R. 644. In this situation the defendant can satisfy the claim (apart from damages for detention) by returning the chattel at any time up to judgment. Once such default judgment is entered, however, the defendant is deprived of the option of returning the chattel instead of paying the value: *General Finance Facilities Ltd (ibid.)*.

(b) An order for the return of the goods or their assessed value and damage for their retention.

(c) An order for the specific return of the goods and damages for their retention.

2. The available relief—not available to all Ord. 13, r.3 imposes the following restrictions, namely it applies only:

(a) To a sole owner.

(b) Where the writ is indorsed with a claim relating to wrongful detention only (and where appropriate, damages).

3. Partial owners Where a claim is made by a partial owner (*i.e.* a joint owner—see Ord. 42, r.1A) the only relief he can obtain is damages. He cannot obtain an order for the delivery of the goods unless he has the written authority of every joint owner to sue on that joint owner's behalf (Ord. 42, r.1A).

4. The "wrongful detention" restriction The addition of any other sort of claim over and above that relating to detention of the goods and damages for wrongful detention, such as, for example, a claim for an injunction, prevents the plaintiff from entering judgment under Ord. 13, r.3. In such a case he must proceed under Ord. 13, r.6 (as to which see p. 446). One way round this inconvenient rule is to pray in aid Ord. 29, rr.2 and 2A and seek an order for the interim preservation or delivery-up of the goods.

2 Procedure—judgment for value of goods

1. Requirements on entry of judgment for value of goods The requirements are the same as in the case of the entry of interlocutory judgment with damages to be assessed except that, where a partial owner is seeking judgment, he must produce the written authority of every other joint owner to sue on their behalf.

2. Form The form of judgment is in Prescribed Form 41, the body of it reading "it is this day adjudged that the defendant do pay the plaintiff the value of the goods described in the writ of summons to be assessed and also damages for their detention to be assessed." (See Form J.)

3. The assessment—how to get it The procedure (including the service provisions) for obtaining an appointment for an assessment of damages is exactly the same as in the case of an assessment of damages pursuant to interlocutory judgment (as to which see p. 437).

4. Assessing the damages The master or district judge has a two-part exercise to carry out on the assessment hearing. He must assess separately:
- (a) the value of the goods at the date of the assessment;
- (b) the consequential damages sustained by the plaintiff by their detention up to the date of the assessment (such as, for instance, loss of use or profit on hire during the period of their detention).

The two sums should be separately identified even though included in the same certificate. (For form of final judgment for assessed value of goods and damages, see Form K.)

5. Appeals An appeal from an assessment of the value of goods by the master or district judge lies to the Court of Appeal: Ord. 58, r.2(b).

3 Procedure—judgment for the return of goods or value

1. Judgment for return of goods or their value A judgment in this form gives to the defendant the option of returning the goods instead of paying their value. On the other hand, it gives the plaintiff the right to apply to enforce specific restitution of the goods by writ of delivery, committal or sequestration as well as recovering damages for their detention by writ of *fieri facias*.

2. Requirements on entry of judgment The requirements are as on entry of judgment for the assessed value only, the form of judgment reading "it is this day adjudged that the defendant do deliver to the plaintiff the chattel described in the writ of summons as (a Ford Sierra saloon car registered number ABC 123) or pay the plaintiff its value to be assessed and also damages for its detention to be assessed." (See Form J.)

3. Assessment The procedural requirements (including the service provisions) and the method of assessment are exactly the same as for a judgment for the assessed value only. Once the damages have been assessed, it is important that the judgment should specify separate amounts for the assessed value of the goods and for the damages for detention since if the plaintiff wishes to proceed by writ of delivery, he has the option of distraining for the assessed value of the goods if the goods themselves are not recovered by the sheriff. He will be deprived of this option if the value of the goods were not separately assessed.

4. Advantages of this form of relief The plaintiff may immediately issue without leave either:
- (a) a writ of *fi. fa.* for a sum comprising the assessed value of the goods, damages for detention and costs; or,
- (b) a combined writ (in Prescribed Form 65) of delivery and, (if the goods have been disposed of) in the alternative, execution for the assessed value and damages for detention and costs.

4 Judgment for specific return of goods

1. Rare A judgment in this form is uncommon.

2. A statutory discretion Whereas in the other two types of relief it is the plaintiff who decides which remedy he intends to pursue, in this type of situation the discretion whether to grant an order for specific return without giving the defendant the option of paying its value, remains with the court: section 3(3)(b) of the Torts (Interference with Goods) Act 1977. As Swinfen Eady M.R. said in *Whiteley v. Hilt* [1918] 2 K.B. 808 at 819.:

> "The power vested in the court to order the delivery up of a particular chattel is discretionary, and ought not to be exercised when the chattel is an ordinary article of commerce and of no special value or interest, and not alleged to be of any special value to the plaintiff, and where damages would fully compensate." (And see *Hyman v. Ogden* [1905] 1 K.B. 246.)

3. Example If the plaintiff were seeking the return of a Rembrandt, he would no doubt seek an order for specific delivery. If he were suing in respect of a mass-produced car, damages sufficient to enable him to buy another would normally suffice.

4. No need to assess value In this type of judgment the value of the chattel need not be assessed. Under it the only pecuniary sum recoverable is damages for detention. The plaintiff can only obtain specific restitution of the chattel by writ of delivery, attachment or sequestration. He has no option under the writ of delivery to distrain for the value of the chattel.

5. Procedure The plaintiff must apply by summons returnable before the master or district judge for such a judgment (Ord. 13, r.3(1)(b)). A claim for consequential damages (*e.g.* for loss of profit on hire) may be included: section 3(2)(a) of the Torts (Interference with Goods) Act 1977.

6. How is the application made? The plaintiff should lodge:
(a) Original writ.
(b) Affidavit of due service of the writ (unless the defendant has filed an acknowledgment of service indicating an intention not to defend or the defendant's solicitor has indorsed his acceptance of service of the writ on the plaintiff's copy of the writ in which case that writ should be produced to the court clerk).
(c) The statement of claim, if served separately from the writ.
(d) Two copies of the summons. (In London, one copy only.)
(e) Supporting affidavit. (In London, this is not lodged on issue but handed to the master at the hearing.)
(f) Self-addressed envelope (if by post).
(g) Fee £10.

Both copies of the summons are sealed and one is handed back to the plaintiff's solicitor for service.

7. Specimen form See Form M.

8. Notification A copy of the summons and of the affidavit in support must be served on any defendant against whom such a judgment is sought: Ord. 13, r.3(2). That defendant must be served even though he has not filed an acknowledgment of service and even if he has given no address for service. Postal service will suffice: Ord. 65, r.5. The service period in this case is two clear days before the return date unless the court otherwise orders: Ord. 32, r.3.

G: FINAL JUDGMENT FOR POSSESSION OF LAND

1 Introduction

1. Not the "squatters" provision Quite apart from the summary procedure

442

available under Ord. 113, the plaintiff may seek final judgment for possession of land under Ord. 13, r.4.

2. Procedural requirements The requirements on entry of judgment are, subject to the differences discussed below, the same as on entry of a judgment for liquidated demand. The differences in summary are:

(a) A different form.
(b) The need for two certificates.
(c) Multiple defendants—must be judgment against all.
(d) Service on empty property.
(e) Particular pleading requirements.
(f) Arrears of rent, mesne profits and damages.

These are dealt with below in detail.

2 Investigating these differences

1. Form The form of judgment is in Prescribed Form 42 (see Form L).

2. Two certificates The plaintiff's solicitor must produce two certificates (indorsed on both copies of the form of judgment) to the effect that:

"We, AB & Co., solicitors for the plaintiff, certify that:
1. The plaintiff is not claiming any relief in this action of the kind specified in Ord. 88, r.1 (Mortgage Action), and
2. The plaintiff's claim does not relate to a dwelling house (or the plaintiff's claim relates to a dwelling house the rateable value of which [*state whichever is appropriate*] on the appropriate day was in excess of £400 in Greater London or £200 elsewhere *or* was on March 2, 1973, in excess of £600 in Greater London or £300 elsewhere *or* after April 1, 1973, exceeds £1500 in Greater London or £750 elsewhere)."

In broad terms the plaintiff's solicitor is certifying that the house cannot be the subject of a protected tenancy because its rateable value exceeds £1,500 in Greater London or £750 elsewhere. If the plaintiff is acting in person, this information must be given by affidavit rather than by certificate: Ord. 13, r.4(1) and (2). If the plaintiff's solicitor is unable to give the certificate or if the plaintiff is unable to give the affidavit, final judgment cannot be entered except on *inter partes* application by summons returnable before the master or district judge for leave to enter final judgment for possession. The purpose of this provision is to ensure that the court does not inadvertently deprive a tenant of his protection under section 4 of the Rent Act 1977 by granting judgment for possession to the plaintiff of a

443

house which is subject to the protection of the 1977 Act. The court must be given the opportunity where there is no such certificate to decide whether it is reasonable to grant final judgment for possession. If the court is of the view that the house is protected by the Rent Act it will not give judgment to the plaintiff. The onus is on the plaintiff to satisfy the court that the Rent Act does not apply. A default judgment entered under Ord. 13 without the appropriate certificate and without leave of the master or district judge is a nullity: *Smith v. Poulter* [1947] K.B. 339; *Peachey Property Corporation Ltd v. Robinson* [1967] 2 Q.B. 543.

3. Multiple defendants—must be judgment against all In an action involving more than one defendant, a default judgment for possession under Ord. 13 entered against any defendant is subject to an automatic stay (and thus cannot be enforced) until judgment has been obtained for possession against all defendants: Ord. 13, r.4(5). If some defendants indicate an intention to defend and others do not, the plaintiff may enter default judgment against the latter and proceed to trial in the action against the others. If other defendants cannot be served with the writ, the plaintiff may have to consider seeking an order striking their names out of the action so as to enable him to enforce the judgment against all remaining defendants against whom he has obtained judgment for possession.

4. Service on empty property Where the property is empty and the writ was served by affixing a copy to a conspicuous part of it, the plaintiff cannot seek to enter final judgment under Ord. 13 unless before service he obtained an order for service of the writ under Ord. 10, r.4(a) authorising service in that manner. If he affixed the copy writ to some conspicuous part of the property but did not obtain an order for service in that manner before he affixed it, then he must apply under Ord. 10, r.4(b) for an order that such a course of action adopted by him should be deemed good service. This he may do on *ex parte* application to the master or district judge supported by affidavit showing:

(a) that the property is empty; and

(b) the service of the writ could not have been effected on any defendant; and

(c) what efforts have been made to effect personal, postal or letter-box service.

No attendance before the master or district judge is required. If the application is granted, the plaintiff may enter judgment under Ord. 13 after the expiry of 14 days from the date of such service.

5. Particular pleading requirements Unless the indorsement on the writ or (if served separately) on the statement of claim shows clearly the following matters the plaintiff will not be entitled to enter default judgment under Ord. 13. The matters are:

(a) Whether the claim relates to a dwelling house.

(b) If it does, whether the rateable value on every day specified by section 4(2) of the Rent Act 1977 exceeds the specified sum.

(c) The grounds on which the plaintiff claims to be entitled to possession and in particular:

    (i) Particulars of any alleged breach of the covenant by the tenant in the lease or tenancy agreement giving rise to a right of re-entry.

    (ii) Particulars of any notice of termination of the lease.

    (iii) If the lease has expired by effluxion at the time, particulars of the term of the lease and the date of its alleged expiration.

    (iv) Particulars of any alleged trespass.

6. Arrears of rent, mesne profits and damages More often than not, the plaintiff is not only seeking possession but is also claiming arrears of rent, mesne profits and damages for breach of covenant. In that situation, the action is treated for purposes of Ord. 13 as involving mixed claims. "Mixed claims" are regulated by Ord. 13, r.5 and are dealt with below. In summary, the court has power to enter one judgment under rule 5 split into different parts—final judgment for possession of the land and arrears of rent and interlocutory judgment for mesne profits and damages for breach of covenant to be assessed. The assessment is normally carried out by the master or district judge under Ord. 37 (as to which see p. 437).

3 Mesne profits

1. Meaning Mesne profits are recoverable in a possession action from the date of service of the writ, not from the date of its issue nor from the date of the breach of covenant giving rise to the landlord's right to re-enter: *Elliott v. Boynton* [1924] 1 Ch. 236 and *Canas Property Co. Ltd v. K.L. Television Services Ltd* [1970] 2 Q.B. 433, C.A. So, the plaintiff should claim arrears of rent up to the date of service of the writ and thereafter mesne profits from that date to the date of delivery up of possession *not* to the date of judgment. The plaintiff may well not get possession until a date well after judgment.

2. Calculation There may well be circumstances in which the plaintiff's monetary claims are capable of arithmetical calculation even though involving mesne profits. Such would be the case where the mesne profits are claimed at the same rate as the arrears of rent. In that event final judgment may be sought for possession and a liquidated sum of money

445

continuing until delivery up of possession at a given periodical rate. The body of the judgment dealing with mesne profits would read, "It is further adjudged that the defendant do pay the plaintiff ... pounds for mesne profits at the rate of ... pounds per ... from ... up to the time of obtaining possession".

3. Impossibility of calculation If mesne profits are not capable of arithmetical calculation, the plaintiff will have to content himself with a judgment for final possession of the land and interlocutory judgment for mesne profits to be assessed by the master. This will also be the case where unliquidated damages for breach of covenant are sought.

H: MULTIPLE CLAIMS

1 Mixed claims

1. What are they? If all the claims in the writ are within the scope of Ord. 13, rr.1–4, and there are no other claims, the plaintiff may enter judgment in respect of each such claim as he would be entitled to enter if that were the only claim on the writ: Ord. 13, r.5.

2. Example So, he may obtain final judgment for possession of land together with final judgment for arrears of rent and interlocutory judgment for damages for breach of covenant to be assessed.

2 Other multiple claims

1. The problem Some or all of the plaintiff's claims in the writ are not within the provisions of Ord. 13, rr.1–4.

2. Example The plaintiff who is seeking specific performance of a contract for the sale of a house to a defendant (outside Ord. 13) and damages for its breach (within Ord. 13). The policy of the rules is to prevent the plaintiff from entering judgment by default under Ord. 13 even for that part of the relief sought which is within the scope of the order.

3. What do the rules require? Ord. 13, r.6 requires the plaintiff to proceed as if the defendant had, in fact, given notice of intention to defend. This has the effect of requiring the plaintiff to serve a statement of claim if one has not already been served.

4. And then—if the defendant defaults? If the defendant then fails to serve his defence within the time prescribed by Ord. 18, r.2(1), normally within 14 days after the time limited for acknowledging service of the writ or the date of service of the statement of claim (whichever is the later), the plaintiff may then proceed by summons or motion for judgment under Ord. 19, r.7 (as to which see Chapter 6).

5. Bypassing the problem posed by "other multiple claims" The plaintiff can abandon once and for all those claims in the writ which are not within the scope of Ord. 13. If he does, he may enter default judgment under Ord. 13 for the balance of the claims which are within the scope of the order. A plaintiff is free to elect to abandon a particular form of relief at any time and is free to choose the relief he wishes to pursue. The only requirement is that he must make it plain what remedy he is seeking. He is however under no duty to give prior notice of his election and abandonment to the defendant: *Morley London Developments Ltd v. Rightside Properties Ltd* (1973) 117 S.J. 876, C.A. The body of the judgment would then read:

> "The plaintiff having abandoned his claim to the relief sought in the writ [statement of claim] [for specific performance] it is this day adjudged that the defendant do pay the plaintiff damages to be assessed."

In the *Morley* case above, the plaintiffs abandoned their claim for specific performance and entered interlocutory judgment for damages to be assessed.

6. The *Mareva* exception Can a *Mareva* prevent an Ord. 13 default judgment? This was the problem confronting Goff J. in *Stewart Chartering Ltd v. C. & O. Managements* S.A. [1980] 1 W.L.R. 460. The plaintiffs claimed against each of the two defendants out of the jurisdiction £23,000 for services rendered and a *Mareva*. The plaintiffs were granted leave to serve out of the jurisdiction, and concurrently were granted the *Mareva*. Neither defendant entered an appearance. The chief clerk, however, refused to allow judgment to be entered in default of appearance having regard to the inclusion in the writ of a claim for an injunction. The plaintiff then issued an *ex parte* summons before the judge in chambers seeking leave to enter judgment in default of appearance for the amount claimed on the writ. Robert Goff J. was presented with a paradoxical situation which he explained—and answered thus at 460H–461B:

> "Because the plaintiffs have obtained an injunction designed to prevent the defendants from removing assets from the jurisdiction in order to prevent the plaintiffs from satisfying any judgment, they are inhibited from signing judgment in default of appearance which is, in the

present situation, the next step which would ordinarily be taken by them with a view to enforcing their claim.

The solution to this problem lies, in my judgment, in the inherent jurisdiction of the court to control its own process, and in particular to prevent any possible abuse of that process. If the plaintiffs were unable to obtain a judgment in the present case without abandoning their *Mareva* injunction, it would be open to a defendant to defeat the very purpose of the proceedings simply by declining to enter an appearance. Such conduct would be an abuse of the process of the court; and in my judgment the court has power to take the necessary steps, by virtue of its inherent jurisdiction, to prevent any such use of its process. The appropriate action to be taken by the court in such circumstances is, in my judgment, to grant leave to the plaintiffs, in an appropriate case, to enter judgment in default of appearance, notwithstanding that the writ is indorsed with a claim for an injunction."

I: THE DEFENDANT'S OPTIONS UNDER ORDER 13

1 Introduction

1. First issue What protective steps can a defendant take who admits the debt and cannot pay it all at once?

2. Second issue How and in what circumstances can a default judgment under Ord. 13 be set aside so as to give the defendant the opportunity of defending the action?

2 Admitting the claim and getting time to pay

1. The problem A defendant, sued for a liquidated sum, may not wish to defend the action but yet cannot afford to pay the debt off all at once.

2. The defendant's safety net—the acknowledgment of service In order to stop him from resorting to the device of indicating an intention to defend the action (so as to buy time and cause unnecessary costs to be incurred), the acknowledgment of service gives a defendant who has no intention of defending the action the opportunity of saying so and applying for a stay of execution against any judgment entered by the plaintiff.

3. Procedural steps
   (a) He admits the debt in the acknowledgment of service and asks in

the same form for a stay. Ord. 13, r.8 provides an automatic stay of execution on the judgment by writ of *fi. fa.* for 14 days from the date of receipt of the acknowledgment of service by the court.

(b) The defendant should act promptly by then taking out a summons within that 14-day period under Ord. 47, r.1 seeking a further stay of execution. Once he has issued the summons within the 14-day period the stay originally imposed continues until the summons under Ord. 47 is heard or otherwise disposed of unless the court directs otherwise after giving the parties an opportunity of being heard: Ord. 13, r.8.

3 Order 47 summons—procedure

1. Documents The defendant should lodge in court within the 14-day period:

(a) Two copies of the summons to stay asking for "an order that execution of the judgment herein be stayed on the grounds of the defendant's inability to discharge the judgment debt forthwith."

(b) Supporting affidavit.

In London, only one copy of the summons is lodged and the supporting affidavit is handed to the master at the hearing.

2. Fee? A fee of £10 is payable.

3. What happens then? A hearing date is given before the master or district judge (Ord. 47, r.1(4)). The service period is four clear days' notice before the return date. One sealed copy of the summons and a copy of the affidavit must be served on the plaintiff.

4. What goes into the defendant's affidavit? The affidavit must set out the grounds on which the defendant is seeking a stay and the evidence necessary to substantiate them (Ord. 47, r.1(3)). If the ground of the defendant's application is his inability to pay, he must disclose his income, the nature and value of any property of his and the amount of any other liability of his (Ord. 47, r.1(3)). It must be a full and frank disclosure of his financial position.

3. What can the court do? The court's options under Ord. 47 are:

(a) To dismiss the summons.

(b) To make an absolute order staying execution by writ of *fi. fa.*

(c) To make an order staying execution by writ of *fi. fa.* for such a period and subject to such conditions as it thinks fit. (But note the stay only operates in relation to liquidated debts, and it is restricted to a writ of *fi. fa.* Thus there is nothing to prevent the plaintiff applying, for instance, for a charging order against the defendant's property or embarking on any other method of enforcement; but see *Mercantile Credit Co. v. Ellis, The Times*, April 1, 1987, C.A; and Section 86(1) County Courts Act, 1984.

6. Form of order—instalments Under the last of the options is derived the court's power to make an instalment order. It normally runs:

"1. Stay execution on the writ of *fieri facias* so long as the defendant pays the judgment debt, interest and costs by weekly [monthly] instalments of £   on [*e.g.* Friday of each week] [*e.g.* the first day of each month] commencing on 19

2. If the defendant defaults in the payment of any instalment on the due date:

(a) the whole outstanding balance shall become due immediately;

(b) the stay of execution shall be removed forthwith; and

(c) the plaintiff may issue execution on the writ on *fieri facias* without further order."

4 Setting aside judgment under Order 13

1. Introduction Ord. 13, r.9 gives the court a general and wide discretion to set aside or vary any judgment entered in pursuance of the Order on such terms as it thinks just. So the defendant against whom judgment by default has been entered may apply to have it set aside.

2. Court can act alone The court, too, may set aside a default judgment of its own motion when satisfied that it is null and void and after hearing the parties. So where it was apparent to the court that a Russian bank had been liquidated by government decree following the bolshevik Revolution in October 1917 a default judgment obtained in 1930 against the bank was declared null and void and set aside (*Lazard Brothers & Co. v. Midland Bank Ltd* [1933] A.C. 289). Similarly, where the court was satisfied that an action to enforce a regulated consumer credit agreement had been wrongly brought in the High Court (section 141 of the Consumer Credit Act 1974 giving the county court exclusive jurisdiction), it was entitled of its own motion to set aside a default judgment and transfer the action to the appropriate county court: *A.A. Financial Services Ltd v. Docherty* (Scott J., November 10, 1987; unreported) and see also *Practice Note* of January 21, 1988. (*The Supreme Court Practice (1995)*, Vol. 1, para. 6/2/22); *Sovereign Leasing v. Ali, The Times*, March 21, 1991; [1992] CCLR 1.

3. What if the defendant has not acknowledged service? Where the defendant seeks to set aside the default judgment, it is not necessary for him first to obtain leave to acknowledge service.

4. The court's discretion—to what degree is it fettered? The observations of Lord Atkin in *Evans v. Bartlam* [1937] A.C. 473 at 480 on the court's approach to the exercise of the discretion are helpful. He said:

> "The discretion is in terms unconditional. The courts, however, have laid down for themselves rules to guide them in the normal exercise of their discretion. One is that where the judgment was obtained regularly there must be an affidavit of merits, meaning that the applicant must produce to the court evidence that he has a prima facie defence. It was suggested in argument that there is another rule that the applicant must satisfy the court that there is another rule that the applicant must satisfy the court that there is a reasonable explanation why judgment was allowed to go by default, such as mistaken, accident, fraud or the like. I do not think that any such rule exists, though obviously the reason, if any, for allowing judgment and thereafter applying to set is aside is one of the matters to which the court will have regard in exercising its discretion. If there were a rigid rule that no one could have a default judgment set aside who knew at the time and intended that there should be a judgment signed, the two rules would be deprived of most of their efficacy. The principle obviously is that unless and until the court has pronounced judgment upon the merits or by consent, it is to have the power to revoke the expression of its coercive power where that has only been obtained by a failure to follow any of the rules of procedure.
>
> But in any case in my opinion, the court does not, and I doubt whether it can, lay down rigid rules which deprive it of jurisdiction. Even the first rule as to affidavit of merits could, in no doubt rare but appropriate cases, be departed from. The supposed second rule does not in my opinion exist."

5. Two classes of judgment At this point it is convenient to divide judgments which are sought to be set aside into two classes—irregular judgments and regular judgments.

5 Setting aside irregular judgments

1. What is an irregular judgment? An irregular judgment is one which has been entered otherwise than in strict compliance with the rules or some statute or is as a result of some impropriety which is regarded as so serious as to render the proceedings a nullity.

2. Examples

(a) A judgment entered prematurely, *i.e.* before the expiry of the prescribed time for giving notice of intention to defend.

(b) A judgment entered for more money than is actually due.

(c) Failure to renew a writ for service is a procedural irregularity which constitutes such a fundamental defect in procedure that the court ought not to exercise its discretion to disregard it. The writ is bad and thus ought to be set aside along with the judgment: *Bernstein v. Jackson* [1982] 1 W.L.R. 1082: and see *Westpile v. Collins* [1989] C.L.Y. 3100.

3. The general rule When it is clear that the judgment has been irregularly obtained then, subject to what is said below, the defendant is entitled as of right to have it set aside. In such a situation it would also be wrong for the court to impose any terms on the defendant (such as payment of money into court or as to costs) as a condition of letting him in to defend: *Anlaby v. Praetorious* (1888) 20 Q.B.D. 764; *White v. Weston* [1968] 2 Q.B. 647, but see *Singh v. Atombrook Ltd* [1989] 1 W.L.R. 810; *The Goldean Mariner* [1990] 2 Lloyd's Rep. 215, and compare *R. v. London County Quarter Sessions Appeals Committee, ex p. Rossi* [1956] 1 Q.B. 682; *Charlesworth v. Focusmulti Ltd* (February 17, 1993; unreported).

4. May the plaintiff be put on terms? In *Abbas v. Rudolfer* (September 23, 1986, C.A.T. No. 804; unreported), the plaintiff entered judgment in default (of defence) notwithstanding that the defendant had served a defence and counterclaim. On the defendant's application to set aside the irregular judgment, the master took an unfavourable view of the plaintiff and of the way in which he had behaved in signing judgment. In setting the judgment aside, he ordered that the costs thrown away should be taxed and paid by the plaintiff and that the proceedings be stayed until the plaintiff had paid the defendant £250 on account of those costs. The Court of Appeal held that the master had fallen into error in that he had ordered the equivalent of security for the defendant's costs and accordingly, that part of the order granting a stay until payment of the £250 was deleted.

5. Delay and approbation Notwithstanding the general rule, application to set aside an irregular judgment should be made:

(a) within a reasonable time of the judgment, and

(b) before the defendant has taken any fresh steps after becoming aware of the irregularity: Ord. 2, r.2(1) (and see paragraph 6 immediately below).

Nonetheless, the court still has a discretion to set aside judgment even though there has been delay so long as it is satisfied that:

(a) no one has been prejudiced by the defendant's tardiness;
(b) or that such prejudice as has been sustained can be cured by an appropriate order for costs;
(c) or that to allow the judgment to stand would be oppressive: *Attwood v. Chichester* (1878) 3 Q.B.D. 772; *Harley v. Samson* (1914) 30 T.L.R. 450.

It was held in *Beale v. McGregor* (1886) 2 T.L.R. 311 that there is an inherent power in the court to prevent an abuse of its proceedings and a judgment will be set aside even though the application is out of time if the circumstances of the case require it.

6. "Fresh step"—meaning The defendant must act consistently. He cannot blow hot and cold. If he accepts some benefit given to him by the judgment with full knowledge of his right to apply to have it set aside, he cannot afterwards allege the invalidity of the judgment which conferred the benefit. Having said that, the defendant who asks for and gets a stay of execution does not approbate the judgment so as to prevent him thereafter from applying to set is aside: *Evans v. Bartlem (ibid.)*. "A fresh step" is one which amounts to a waiver of the irregularity: *Rein v. Stein* (1892) 66 L.T. 469; *cf. Re Dulles' Settlement (No. 2)* [1951] Ch. 842, C.A.

7. Procedural requirements Application to set aside an irregular judgment is made under Ord. 2, r.2(1). Although Ord. 2, r.2(2) states that an application may be made by summons or motion, application is almost invariably made by summons returnable before the master or district judge. The grounds of the application should be stated in the summons and the summons should be supported by affidavit. A fee of £10 is payable.

8. Specimen forms See Form P (Summons) and Form Q (Affidavit).

6 Setting aside regular judgments

1. Introduction The essential difference in the approach of the courts to the setting aside of regular judgments from those irregularly obtained is that whereas the irregularly obtained judgment should generally be set aside as of right (*ex debito justitiae*) without terms, the regular judgment may or may not be set aside and if it is set aside it may be set aside on terms.

2. Procedural requirements Order 2, r.2 does not, of course, apply because there is no allegation of irregularity. Nevertheless, application is by summons to the master or district judge and unless supported by affidavit

453

will not be granted except for some very sufficient reason: *Farden v. Richter* (1889) 23 Q.B.D. 124.

3. The affidavit The affidavit should:
(a) Explain why the defendant allowed judgment to be entered in default.
(b) Explain any undue delay in applying to set the judgment aside.
(c) Demonstrate that there is an issue to be tired between the parties.

In satisfaction of requirement (a) above, the defendant may, for example, seek to satisfy the court that he was too ill to attend to his affairs—in which event some written medical evidence ought to be exhibited to the affidavit. If it is clear that the defendant for reasons of his own deliberately ignored the proceedings and purposely allowed judgment to be entered, his subsequent application to set the judgment aside in unlikely to be successful: *Haigh v. Haigh* (1885) 31 Ch.D. 478; *Alpine Bulk Transport Co. v. Saudi Eagle Shipping Co.* [1986] 2 Lloyd's Rep. 221. Requirement (c) above is best satisfied by exhibiting a copy of the proposed defence. As in the case of Ord. 14 (see p. 347), it is useless for the defendant simply to put up a general denial of the plaintiff's claim.

4. The four questions In deciding whether to exercise its discretion in favour of the defendant by letting him in to defend, the court will consider all the circumstances, but, in particular:
(a) The reason why the defendant failed to give notice of intention to defend within the prescribed time.
(b) Whether there has been any undue delay by the defendant in making the application to set aside judgment. Delay itself will not be important unless it prejudices the plaintiff or third party rights have arisen in the intervening period.
(c) Whether any prejudice to the plaintiff or others can be cured by an appropriate order for costs. In this context, the court, in considering whether in all the circumstances it is just to set aside judgment should consider the consequences to both parties if that is done: *Fairhurst v. Tempest Construction Ltd* (May 17, 1984, C.A.T. No. 202; unreported).
(d) Whether the defendant has an arguable case which has a real prospect of success and carries some degree of conviction. Merely to show an arguable case is insufficient. The court must form a provisional view of the probable outcome of the action: *Alpine Bulk Transport Co. v. Sandi Eagle Shipping Co* (above) but see *Allen v. Taylor* [1992] P.I.Q.R. P 255, C.A. The court will consider the merits of the defence first and then, if necessary, the other three factors set out above (see *Ladup Ltd v. Siu* (1984) 81 L.S. Gaz. 283).

The court is entitled to satisfy itself that the defendant has a bona fide intention of defending the action and there is some possibility of him doing so with success; see *"Ruben Martinez Villena,"* [1987] 2 Lloyd's Rep. 621; *Shah v. Woodchester Equipment Leasing Ltd* (unreported) (1994), April 27, C.A.

5. A modern illustration—the *Saudi Eagle* In *Alpine Bulk Transport Co. v. Saudi Eagle Shipping Co.* [1986] 2 Lloyd's Rep. 221, the plaintiff's claim arose out of a charterparty, the plaintiffs being the charterers, the defendants the shipowners. It was a claim for damages for breach of contract by the defendant who refused to load the cargo. The breach took place in November 1981. In October 1982 the plaintiffs arrested the defendants' ship at Rotterdam and the defendants were forced to give security in the form of a bond in order to effect the release of the ship. Later, the plaintiffs issued and served a writ against the defendants. No notice of intention to defend was given and interlocutory judgment was signed. Damages were later assessed and final judgment was entered for $49,000. The defendants had made a deliberate decision not to defend the plaintiffs' claim because the defendant company had no assets having sold its only ship before final judgment. But then someone from the defendants remembered the bond. The plaintiffs' judgment was not valueless after all. Application was made to the judge to set aside judgment. He refused saying that although there was an arguable point that the plaintiffs had sued the wrong defendant, there was not much merit in it, and in any event the defendants were not deserving of the court's discretion since they had deliberately allowed judgment to be entered. The Court of Appeal dismissed the defendants' appeal. In doing so, however, the court stressed that the primary consideration in deciding whether to set the judgment aside is whether the defendant has an arguable defence which carries some degree of conviction. As to the defendants' conduct in allowing the action to proceed by default, Sir Roger Ormrod had this to say (at 225):

> "The conduct of the defendants in this respect and in deliberately deciding not to give notice of intention to defend because it suited the interests of the [defendants] to let the plaintiffs proceed against these defendants is a matter to be taken into account in assessing the justice of the case. While it does not amount to an estoppel at law, the Court can and must consider it. The principle of election and the maxim about approbating and reprobating are, in origin, rules of equity and as such give some indication of where the justice of a case may lie."

6. What if the defendant has lied to the Court? In applying to set the judgment aside, the defendant puts forward a wholly dishonest explanation for his failure to give notice of intention to defend. How should the court react? In *Vann v. Awford* (1986) 130 S.J. 682 the judge refused to grant the defendant an extension of time in which to apply under Ord. 35, r.2 to set aside the judgment. He did so because he said that the defendant had failed to give a reasonable explanation for his delay. The Court of Appeal held that the judge had misdirected himself. The court's major consideration was whether the defendant had a defence on the merits and that was to transcend any reason given by the defendant for his delay. The plaintiff had undoubtedly suffered prejudice because of the delay but the court found that there was an arguable defence. Even for lying to the Court, a penalty of £53,783 (the judgment debt) was excessive. The judgment was set aside conditional upon the defendant fulfilling stringent financial conditions to protect the plaintiff.

7. Plaintiff's contributory negligence If a claim is based on negligence, the defendant should still be deemed to have an arguable case even though he only wishes to argue the plaintiff's contributory negligence. Lord Denning M.R. said so in *Burns v. Kondel* [1971] 1 Lloyd's Rep. 554 at 555:

> "In an accident case it is sufficient if he shows that there is a triable issue of contributory negligence. A plea of contributory negligence, if successful, may reduce the damages greatly."

8. Order 14 contrasted It will have been observed that the test to be applied under Ord. 13 is more stringent than that which obtains under Ord. 14. Whereas the defendant on an Ord. 14 application need only show an arguable or triable issue, the defendant under Ord. 13 needs to go further, according to the principles to be extracted from the *Saudi Eagle*, by showing that the arguable defence has a real prospect of success and carries some degree of conviction.

9. Terms Should the court be minded to set aside the judgment on terms, it would be a wrong exercise of its discretion to impose financial conditions on a defendant (by, for example, requiring him to pay a substantial amount into court when he is impecunious) which he is unable to meet: see *M.V. Yorke Motors v. Edwards* (1982) 1 W.L.R. 444; (1982) 1 All E.R. 1024, H.L. The defendant must, however, satisfy the court by sufficient and proper evidence as to his means that compliance with the condition would be impossible, as opposed to difficult.

10. Security for plaintiff The court may require the defendant to pay money into court as a condition of setting a regular judgment aside where the defendant has not complied with procedural rules even though he has a good arguable defence. The purpose of such a condition is to ensure the proper future conduct of the litigation. The condition should be such as is within the defendant's power to comply: *City Construction Contracts (London) Ltd. v. Adam, The Times,* January 4, 1988, C.A.

11. Setting aside one part and staying execution on another In *National Westminster Bank plc v. Humphrey* (1984) 128 S.J. 81, C.A. the Court of Appeal held in a case decided under the identical powers to set aside judgment entered in default of defence under Ord. 19, r.9 that the wording of the order is wide enough to give the court authority, in a proper exercise of its discretion, to set aside one part of a judgment and to grant a general stay of execution in respect of another part.

12. Setting aside part-variation not substitution Where it is clear that there is no defence to part of the claim but there is a triable issue as to the remainder, the proper course is for the court to vary the default judgment by reducing it to the undisputed amount rather than to set aside the whole of the default judgment and substitute a fresh default judgment for the admitted part. The reason for this is that the plaintiff then will not be deprived of interest under the Judgment Act 1838 on the admitted part between the date of the original default judgment and the date on which it is varied. If it were set aside in its entirety and a fresh default judgment substituted, he would lose that interest: *The Iran Nabuvat* (1990) 1 W.L.R. 1115, C.A.

13. Reasons In *Lennard v. International Institute for Medical Studies, The Times*, April 29, 1985, C.A., the Court of Appeal held that where a judge allows an application to set aside a default judgment, he is obliged to give his reasons otherwise the Court of Appeal will have to exercise its discretion afresh in the matter.

14. Late compliance with terms—the problem Suppose the court makes an order setting aside judgment conditional on the defendant complying with certain terms within a specified period and the defendant fails to comply with them within the prescribed time. Can he ask for an extension of time after the time allowed has elapsed? In *Manley Estates Ltd v. Benedik* [1941] 1 All E.R. 248, C.A. the Court of Appeal said that he could since the court has power to enlarge the time as the action is still in existence. Presumably the court would have to be satisfied that there has been good reason for the defendant's failure to comply with the terms within the time allowed since orders are made to be obeyed, not ignored: see also *Samuels v. Linzi Dresses Ltd* [1981] Q.B. 115.

15. Failure to comply with terms The position of a defendant who does not apply for an extension of time and who fails to comply with any conditions on which the judgment is to be set aside, is clear. Ord. 45, r.10 provides that a defendant is deemed to have abandoned the benefit of the order granting him conditional leave to defend and the plaintiff may enforce the judgment as if the order had not been made.

7 Applications by strangers

1. The problem It frequently occurs that a judgment obtained by the plaintiff affects not only the defendant but others who are not parties to the action. Those others may be placed in great difficulties if a defendant fails to take any steps to defend the action. The most common example is of a defendant motorist who, having been served with a writ, fails to hand it over to his insurers. The plaintiff then enters judgment under Ord. 13 and the insurers may be faced with the possibility of having to pay substantial damages to the plaintiff unless they are permitted to take steps to have the judgment set aside.

2. The *locus classicus* The leading case on the point is *Jaques v. Harrison* (1883) 12 Q.B.D. 165 where Bowden L.J. said (at 167):

> "There are, so far as we can see, only two modes open by which a stranger to an action, who is injuriously affected through any judgment suffered by a defendant by default, can set that judgment aside ... [I]n the first place, obtain the defendant's leave to use the defendant's name, if the defendant has not already bound himself to allow such use of his name to be made ... Or he may, if he is not entitled without further proceedings to use the defendant's name, take out a summons in his own name at chambers to be served on both the defendant and the plaintiff, asking leave to have the judgment set aside, and to be at liberty either to defend the action for the defendant on such terms as indemnifying the defendant as the judge may consider right, or, at all events, to be at liberty to intervene in the action ..."

So in *Windsor v. Chalcraft* [1939] 1 K.B. 279, the defendant's underwriters in a road traffic case were successful in applying as strangers for the judgment entered against their insured defendant to be set aside and for an order that they should be at liberty to acknowledge service in the name of the defendant and to deliver a defence: see also *Harrington v. Pinkey* [1989] 2 Lloyd's Rep. 310; *Hayler v. Chapman* [1989] 1 Lloyd's Rep. 490.

3. Conditions precedent to stranger's application Thus, a stranger may apply to set aside the default judgment against the defendant where:
  (a) the defendant, though served with the writ, chooses not to take steps to defend it; and
  (b) as a result judgment is entered against him by default; and
  (c) the stranger can demonstrate that he will be directly affected either legally or financially by the judgment thus showing that he has an interest in the proceedings.

4. What procedure?

(a) General rule: Application is on summons supported by affidavit returnable before the master or district judge in the defendant's name provided he consents: see *Murfin v. Ashbridge and Martin* [1941] 1 All E.R. 231.

(b) Exception: If the defendant's consent is not forthcoming, the application is on summons supported by affidavit and served on all parties seeking:

  (i) leave to intervene for the purposes of setting aside the judgment;

  (ii) to acknowledge service; and

  (iii) to defend the action (see also Ord. 15, r.6; *Gurtner v. Circuit* [1968] 2 Q.B. at 587).

(c) The fee payable is £10.

J: COSTS ON SETTING ASIDE JUDGMENT

1 "Costs thrown away"

1. Usual order Where the court orders the judgment to be set aside in circumstances where it is clear that the defendant is to blame for allowing the default judgment to be entered in the first place, the judgment will normally only be set aside on condition that the defendant pays the cost thrown away.

2. "Costs thrown away"—meaning? The expression "costs thrown away" (now defined in Ord. 62, r.3(8)) will normally cover all the plaintiff's costs except for the issue and service of the writ and includes all costs reasonably incurred in enforcing the judgment, such as abortive costs and fees of enforcing the judgment. But note:

(a) There is some doubt as to whether the expression includes the costs of the application to set aside the judgment itself and so the order should state that the defendant should pay all the plaintiff's costs thrown away including the costs of and incidental to the application to set aside the judgment.

(b) The costs of bankruptcy proceedings taken on the judgment are not included in the expression but, of course, the court could always make it a condition of setting aside the judgment that the defendant bears them: *Andromeda v. Holme* (1923) 130 L.T. 329, C.A.

459

2 Costs in cause

1. General rule Where a regular judgment has been entered and it is clear that nobody is to blame, the appropriate order on setting aside the judgment is for costs to be in the cause.

2. Example In *Cox (Peter) Ltd v. Thirwell* (1981) 125 S.J. 481, the plaintiff claimed the balance of money due for building work done on the defendant's house. The writ was served by post. The defendant had gone abroad and did not receive the writ. The plaintiff entered judgment in default of entry of appearance. On hearing of the judgment, the defendant applied to have it set aside. The plaintiff refused to consent to an order setting aside the judgment. Forbes J. held that where the post had not been effective and neither party was at fault the appropriate order was costs in the cause.

3 No costs

1. *White v. Weston*—the facts In *White v. Weston* [1968] 2 Q.B. 647, the plaintiff commenced proceedings in the county court against the defendant for damages in negligence. The summons was sent by post to the defendant at an address which he had left some time previously. The plaintiff proceeded to trial, proved his claim in the absence of the defendant and obtained judgment for damages and costs. By chance, sometime later, the defendant discovered what had happened and succeeded in having the judgment set aside, the judge being satisfied that he had never received notice of the proceedings. The judge ordered that there should be no order for costs of the application to set aside judgment but that the costs of the abortive trial should be in the cause. The defendant appealed against this latter order.

2. What did the Court of Appeal say? In the Court of Appeal, Russell L.J. in allowing the appeal said that the judge had misdirected himself in considering that he had any power to visit, even contingently, on the defendant, the plaintiff's costs of a hearing that, as against the defendant, should never have taken place at all, and to which he was a stranger. (See also *R. v. London County Quarter Sessions Appeals Committee, ex p. Rossi* [1956] 1 Q.B. 682 and *Hewitt v. Leicester Corporation* [1969] 1 W.L.R. 855.)

4 The court's discretion on costs

1. The overriding discretion It must be stressed that the court has a general discretion on costs: Supreme Court Act 1981, s.51; Ord. 62, r.2(4).

2. Example of exercise adverse to plaintiff Where it is clear that the plaintiff has entered judgment be default in the circumstances of impropriety or irregularity, it may well be that an order for costs is made against him (see Ord. 62, r.10): see *Abbas v. Rudolfer* (September 23, 1986, C.A.T. No. 804; unreported).

K: THE PRIORITY OF WRITS OF *FIERI FACIAS* ON SETTING ASIDE JUDGMENT

1 Supreme Court Act 1981, section 138

1. Which goods are covered? The writ of *fi. fa.* binds the property in the goods of the execution debtor as from the time when the writ is delivered to the sheriff for execution by him and not when the sheriff obtains possession of the goods under the writ.

2. The sheriff's duty In order:
  (a) to identify which goods are covered by the writ, and
  (b) to establish an order of priorities in a situation where numerous writs of *fi. fa.* have been issued;
the sheriff is under a duty immediately he receives a writ to indorse on the back of it the hour, day, month and year when he received it (S.C.A. 1981, s.138(3)).

3. The execution creditor's duty He must inform the sheriff promptly once the judgment has been set aside. The sheriff cannot then proceed with the execution and must withdraw from possession immediately if he has already taken walking possession. Subject to what is said below, the sheriff can then proceed to execute later writs of *fi. fa.*

2 The order setting aside judgment reversed

1. The problem Imagine that the plaintiff, aggrieved that the judgment has been set aside, appeals the order setting it aside successfully and so gets his judgment restored. Does he have to issue a fresh writ of *fi. fa.* and go through the whole procedure again? Most importantly, is he relegated to the back of the queue in terms of the priority of his writ of *fi. fa.* or can he seek to have his priority restored? This will be of crucial importance should the debtor's goods be of insufficient value to satisfy all the judgments for which execution has been issued.

2. The solution In *Bankers Trust Co. v Galadari* [1987] Q.B. 222, the Court of Appeal held that:

(a) although a writ of *fi. fa.* was only to be treated as valid during periods when the sheriff had instructions to execute it, the enforced withdrawal of those instructions following an erroneous order of the court should not affect the priority of the writ;

(b) in the absence of good reason to the contrary, the court will order that the priority obtained by the plaintiff on delivering the writ should be maintained or restored;

(c) accordingly, the plaintiff's writ would take priority over the writs of *fi. fa.* delivered to the sheriff by other creditors after the time when the plaintiff's writ was first delivered to him; and finally

(d) there is no need for the plaintiff to issue a fresh writ.

3 Intervening

1. Protecting the sheriff The sheriff is protected against any claim by the plaintiff if, in between the time when the judgment is set aside and the time when it is restored, he (the sheriff) has had any dealings with the goods or their proceeds which would have been wrongful as against the plaintiff had the judgment not been set aside; *Bankers Trust Co. v. Galadari* (above); *Davis (P.B.J.) Manufacturing Co. Ltd v. Fahn* [1967] 1 W.L.R. 1059.

2 Directions If the plaintiff whose judgment has been set aside gives notice to the sheriff that the order setting the judgment aside is under appeal and thereafter the sheriff receives another writ for execution in respect of the same goods, he should not proceed beyond possession without applying to the court for directions and giving notice to both creditors of such application.

4 A different set of priorities

1. Voluntary arrangements If the plaintiff voluntarily instructs the sheriff to withdraw from possession because, for example, he (the plaintiff) has reached an amicable arrangement with the debtor, it is most unlikely that he will be allowed to keep his priority over any later writ received by the sheriff: *Hunt v. Hooper* (1844) 12 M. & W. 664.

2. The difference "There is a vast difference between an instruction given as a necessary consequence of an order of the court and an instruction given pursuant to a voluntary bargain between the creditor and the judgment debtor. In the latter case, it would clearly be inequitable to allow the creditor to maintain his priority against subsequent creditors," *per* Parkes L.J. in *Bankers Trust Co. v. Galadari* (above) at 227H.

CHAPTER 6

Judgment in Default of Defence

A: GENERAL PRINCIPLES

1 The basic rule

1. Judgment in default of defence—when? If the defendant fails to serve his defence within the time allowed, the plaintiff can enter judgment in default of defence in some cases and in others can apply to the court for judgment in default of defence. The same result may follow if the defendant's defence has been struck out or he withdraws it. This summary procedure is regulated by Ord. 19.

2. Scope of Order 19 The scope of Ord. 19 is similar in extent to that of Ord. 13 except that Ord. 19 regulates the situation where the defendant is in default of defence. There are, however, two more important differences. These relate to counterclaims and claims within Ord. 13, r.6.

3. Counterclaims Whereas Ord. 13 cannot in the nature of things apply to counterclaims, Ord. 19 does. Ord. 19, r.8 gives the defendant exactly the same rights to enter judgment against the plaintiff in default of him serving a defence to the counterclaim as the plaintiff has on the claim against the defendant. So, what is said in this chapter about the defaulting defendant applies equally to the defaulting plaintiff on the counterclaim: see *Zimmer Orthopaedic LH v. Zimmer Manufacturing Co.* [1968] 1 W.L.R. 852; [1968] 2 All E.R. 309.

4. Claims within Order 13, rule 6 As we have seen, the plaintiff cannot under Ord. 13 enter judgment in default of notice of intention to defend in any action where the relief sought is outside the scope of Ord. 13, rr.1– 4 (liquidated demands; unliquidated damages; wrongful interference with goods; recovery of land or any combination of those claims). In that situation, Ord. 13, r.6 requires the plaintiff to pretend that the defendant has given notice of intention to defend. In this way the plaintiff is pushed on procedurally to Ord. 19 where, as is explained at p. 472 below, he can apply by summons or motion in default of defence. To the extent, then, that the plaintiff can obtain judgment in "Ord. 13, r.6" cases under Ord. 19, the scope of that order is wider than that of Ord. 13.

2 "Default of defence"

1. When is a defendant in default? Before the plaintiff is entitled to seek judgment in default of defence under Ord. 19, the plaintiff must have indorsed a statement of his claim on the duly served writ or served a separate statement of claim and:

(a) the defendant must have failed to serve his defence within the time prescribed; or

(b) the defence must have been struck out for non-compliance with the rules or with an order of the court; or

(c) the defence must have been withdrawn by the defendant.

2. Statement of claim—pleading requirements The obligation to serve a defence only arises after the statement of claim has been served either separately from the writ or by indorsement on it. If no statement of claim has been indorsed or served, the plaintiff cannot proceed to obtain judgment by default under Ord. 19 since the defendant cannot be said to be in default of defence: *Fowler v. White* (1901) 45 S.J. 723. This is still the case where the defendant has given notice to the plaintiff that he does not require a statement of claim to be served: *Wilmott v. Young* (1881) 44 L.T. 331. This is because the court can only give the plaintiff such judgment to which he appears entitled on his statement of claim: see Ord. 19, r.7. No evidence in support of the plaintiff's claim is permitted to be adduced on the hearing.

3 Service of defence

1. The rule of implied admissions The defendant must serve his defence before "the expiration of the period fixed by or under these Rules for service of defence": see Ord. 19, rr.2–7. The failure to serve any defence brings into play the so-called "rule of implied admission" under which everything in the statement of claim is deemed to be admitted by the defendant unless expressly denied. So a failure to serve a defence amounts to an admission by the defendant of everything in the statement of claim: see Ord. 18, r.13 and *Cribb v. Freyberger* [1919] W.N. 22, C.A.

2. When is a defence late? Generally the time limits are:

(a) The defendant must serve his defence within 14 days from the time allowed for giving notice of intention to defend, if the statement of claim:

465

     (i) is indorsed on the writ, or

    (ii) served with the writ, or

   (iii) served within 14 days of service of the writ and the defendant has filed an acknowledgment of service indicating an intention to defend.

(b) If the statement of claim is served more than 14 days after the service of the writ, the time limit for service of the defence is 14 days after service of the statement of claim.

3. Exception to the general rule The principles are:

(a) The plaintiff may grant the defendant an extension of time for service of his defence.

(b) If the plaintiff refuses to grant an extension of time for defence, the defendant may seek an order for an extension of time for the defence under Ord. 3, r.5 in which case time will run in accordance with the terms of the order rather than the general rule.

(c) If, after the defendant has filed acknowledgment of service indicating an intention to defend but before he serves his defence, the plaintiff issues an Ord. 14 or Ord. 86 summons for summary judgment, time does not begin to run for service of the defence until the disposal of the Ord. 14 or Ord. 86 summons. If the defendant is given leave to defend, he has 14 days from the date of the Ord. 14 or Ord. 86 order to serve his defence unless the court gives him a longer or shorter time—Ord. 18, r.2.

4. Time limits—a summary

(a) The time limit for the defence is 28 days (14 days for acknowledgment of service and 14 days for defence) from the date of service of a writ indorsed or served with the statement of claim if it has been served personally or on a limited company, or 35 days if served by post or through the letter-box on an individual.

(b) Where the defendant's solicitor has indorsed his acceptance of the writ on the plaintiff's copy of the writ, the time for defence is 14 days from the lodgement in court of the acknowledgment of service (which is not necessary but desirable) or 28 days from the date of acceptance of the service of the writ exclusive of the date of acceptance, whichever is the later.

(c) If the last day for giving notice of intention to defend falls on a day on which the court office is closed, the defendant has the whole of the next day when the court office is open to lodge the notice and the 14 days for defence is only counted from then (Ord. 3, r.4).

(d) If the last day for serving the defence falls on a day when the court office is closed, then judgment cannot be entered until the morning of the second day after reopening. So, if the last day for serving the defence is Sunday, judgment cannot be entered until the Tuesday (Ord. 3, r.4).

(e) August is included in counting the 14 days for service of the defence since Ord. 3, r.3 has been revoked.

(f) If the plaintiff amends his statement of claim (as he is entitled to do without leave before close of pleadings—see Ord. 20, r.3(1)) before service of the defence, the time for service of the defence is extended by 14 days from the date of service of the amended statement of claim or the time mentioned in 2(a)(i) and (ii) above, whichever is the later (Ord. 20, r.3(2)).

(g) There is no obligation on a defendant to serve an amended defence if, after he has served his defence, the plaintiff amends his statement of claim. So the defendant cannot be said to be in default of filing an amended defence for purposes of Ord. 19. If he does not amend his defence, he is presumed to rely on his original pleading (Ord. 20, r.3(6)).

4 Late service of defence

1. Late service—not necessarily fatal If the defendant serves a defence after the time allowed but before the plaintiff has entered judgment, the plaintiff cannot then enter judgment under Ord. 19. In *Gill v. Woodfin* (1884) 25 Ch.D. 707, C.A., the plaintiff contended that, as the defence was put in after the proper time, he was entitled to treat it as a nullity. The court (Earl of Selborne L.C. at 708) said that that approach was a mistake since there is nothing in the Orders to the effect that such a defence may be so treated. Similarly in *Gibbings v. Strong* (1884) 26 Ch.D. 66, C.A., on a motion to enter judgment by default under Ord. 19 where the defence had been served late the Earl of Selborne said at 69:

> "... and if the defence had been put in, though irregularly, I think the court would do right in attending to what it contains. If it were found to contain nothing, which, if proved, would be material by way of defence, the court would disregard it. If, on the other hand, it discloses a substantial ground of defence, the court will not take the circuitous course of giving a judgment without regard to it, and obliging the defendants to apply to have that judgment set aside on terms, but will take steps to have the case properly tried on the merits."

2. Sham defence—the plaintiff's riposte Should the plaintiff consider that the defence is a sham used by the defendant as a delaying tactic, then he should take out a summons under Ord. 14 for summary judgment. He should take care, however, to do so only where he can clearly demonstrate to the court that despite the defence served, there is in reality no defence. If he cannot do so, he puts himself at risk as to the costs of the Ord. 14 proceedings (see generally p. 384).

5 Striking out of defence and default judgment

1. Application of Order 19 Although by far the greatest use of Ord. 19 is made when the defendant fails to serve a defence, the plaintiff may, under this order, enter judgment in default of defence where the defence has been struck out for non-compliance with an order: *Re Hartley* (1891) 91 L.T.J. 229.

2. Striking out for want of discovery In *Bains v. Patel, The Times*, May 20, 1983, the Court of Appeal held that the effect of an order under Ord. 24, r.16(1) (failure to give discovery) that a defence be struck out and judgment be entered accordingly, was to put the defendant in the position of one who had not put in a defence to the action. So a judgment so entered constitutes a judgment in default of defence. By analogy, a defendant whose defence has been struck out for failure to comply with other rules dealing with default (such as answering interrogatories—(Ord. 26, r.6) and in default of appearance at trial—(Ord. 35, r.1)) operates to place him in the same position as if he had not served a defence.

3. Procedure The normal procedure is for the plaintiff to issue a combined summons asking for the defence to be struck out for non-compliance and, if successful, for judgment to be entered for the relief sought.

6 "Unless" orders

1. What are they? Frequently, a party may seek a peremptory order against a wayward opponent. So, for example, a plaintiff may ask the court to order that unless the defendant takes some specified action (such as supplying the plaintiff with further and better particulars of his defence; supplying a list of his documents) by a prescribed time, the defence should be stuck out and the plaintiff should be permitted to enter judgment in default against him. In this situation, the plaintiff should take care to ensure that the order is precisely worded otherwise he will fall into a trap which is best explained by reference to *Hitachi Sales (U.K.) Ltd v. Mitsui Osk Line Ltd* [1986] 2 Lloyd's Rep. 574.

2. "Unless" order explained For a detailed discussion of *Hitachi* and "unless" orders, reference should be made to p. 516.

7 Withdrawal of defence

1. The principle A defendant may withdraw his defence at any time without the leave of the court: Ord. 21, r.2(2)(a). If he does so, the plaintiff may enter judgment in default of defence under this order: *Cooper Dean v. Badham* [1908] W.N. 100.

2. But what happens in practice? The more usual course is to lodge an order by consent of the parties (rather than under Ord. 19) simply giving judgment to the plaintiff in the terms agreed between them (as to which see Ord. 42, r.5A).

8 Default in defence to counterclaim

1. The general rule Ord. 19, r.8 provides that:

> "A defendant who counterclaims against a plaintiff shall be treated for the purposes of rules 2 to 7 as if he were a plaintiff who had made against a defendant the claim made in the counterclaim and, accordingly, where the plaintiff or any other party against whom the counterclaim is made fails to serve a defence to counterclaim, those rules shall apply as if the counterclaim were a statement of claim, the defence to counterclaim a defence and the parties making the counterclaim and against whom it is made were plaintiffs and defendants respectively, and as if references to the period fixed by or under these rules for service of the defence were references to the period so fixed for service of the defence to counterclaim."

2. "Default in defence to counterclaim"—meaning? The following are the conditions precedent to the defendant's entitlement to seek judgment under Ord. 19, in default of defence to counterclaim:
  (a) he must have served his counterclaim and either,
  (b) the plaintiff must have failed to serve his defence to the counterclaim within the time allowed by or under the rules, or
  (c) the defence to the counterclaim must have been struck out for non-compliance with the Rules or an order of the court, or
  (d) the plaintiff must have withdrawn his defence to the counterclaim.

3. Service of defence to counterclaim—time limits? A plaintiff on whom a defendant serves a counterclaim must, if he intends to defend it, serve on that defendant a defence to the counterclaim within 14 days of the service on him of the counterclaim. The defendant may agree to extend that time. If he refuses, application is made by the plaintiff on summons to the master or district judge. In all other respects, the principles and practice relating to default in defence apply equally to default in the defence to a counter-claim so as to assimilate the position of defence and defence to counterclaim under Ord. 19.

B: TWO CLASSES OF JUDGMENT UNDER ORDER 19

1 Introduction

1. A distinction must be drawn The normal procedure for seeking judgment under Ord. 19 differs according to the kind of relief sought in the statement of claim (or counterclaim). It is convenient to divide those kinds of relief into two broad classes.

2. First class Those kinds of relief within Ord. 19, rr.1–4 which comprise:
  (a) liquidated claims;
  (b) unliquidated damages;
  (c) wrongful interference with goods (except judgment for their specific return without giving the defendant the alternative of paying their assessed value which falls into the second class);
  (d) recovery of land;
  (e) any combination of (a)–(d) above.

3. Second class All other kinds of relief (except those forms of relief such as mortgage and probate actions, etc. (see p. 464) which are not within the scope of the Order).

2 Relief falling within Class 1

1. The Order 13 parallel The relief in this class of case (covered by Ord. 19, rr.1–4) is exactly that covered by Ord. 13, rr.1–4. All that has been said about the law and practice in obtaining such relief under Ord. 13, r.5 applies equally to Ord. 19 and reference should be made to pp. 412 *et seq.*

2. Entering judgment in default—how? The requirements on entry of judgment by default under Ord. 19 are exactly the same as under Ord. 13 except that:
  (a) No search for an acknowledgment of service is required.
  (b) No affidavit of service is required unless the defendant has failed to lodge an acknowledgment of service and the defendant's solicitor has not accepted service by indorsement on the plaintiff's copy of the writ.

(c) The time for entry of judgment is the day after the last day for serving the defence.

(d) A certificate (in the form below) to the effect that the time for serving the defence has expired must be indorsed on the court copy judgment.

3. **Order 19 default judgment check list** The court clerk will require:

(a) To see the original writ.

(b) To see the statement of claim if served separately from the writ (with certificate of date of service indorsed on it).

(c) To see the acknowledgment of service (which will already be on the court file) or the original writ indorsed with the acceptance of service by the defendant's solicitor.

(d) To be satisfied that the prescribed time for defence has expired.

(e) To be satisfied that the proper judgment is to be entered depending on whether the claim is liquidated or unliquidated. If it is unliquidated the judgment is interlocutory with damages to be assessed.

(f) Two top copies of the judgment (see Part C, section 3). The back of the court copy must be indorsed with the following certificate:

"We, A.B. & Co. of ———, solicitors for the plaintiff, certify that the time for service of the defence by the defendant prescribed by the Rules of Court or extended by order of the court or the consent of the parties has expired and that the defendant is in default in serving his defence within such a time.

dated 19

A.B. & Co. ————————

of ————————

Solicitors for the plaintiff."

(See *Practice Direction (Judgment in Default)* [1979] 1 W.L.R. 85.)

(g) To see any order giving leave of the court to sign judgment in cases where leave is required.

(h) To ensure that the details in the forms of judgment (including the amount of fixed costs) are correct.

4. **Sundry practice points** Note:

(a) No fee is payable.

(b) No affidavit of service of the writ is required (because the acknowledgment of service on the court file or the production of the original writ indorsed with acceptance of service by the defendant's solicitor is sufficient proof in itself).

(c) In commercial actions, reference is made in the form of judgment to "points of defence" instead of "defence".

471

(d) Both copies of the judgment are sealed and one sealed copy is handed back to the plaintiff.

5. Payment of claim after acknowledgment of service Should the defendant pay the claim on the writ after acknowledging service and before serving a defence, but does not pay any costs, the plaintiff may enter judgment in default of defence for costs alone stating in the judgment that the debt has been discharged.

3 Relief falling within Class 2

1. What is included? Class 2 includes all other forms of relief within the scope of Ord. 19. Examples of the sort of relief covered here are injunctions and orders for specific performance.

2. The plaintiff's two options Where the defendant is in default of defence in a Class 2 relief case, the plaintiff may:
  (a) Either apply by summons or motion for judgment in default under Ord. 19; or
  (b) Proceed to trial.
Thus, where he has good reason not to proceed under Ord. 19 he can proceed to prove his case at trial in the normal way.

3. Example of second option In *Nagy v. Co-operative Press Ltd* [1949] 2 K.B. 188, C.A., Cohen L.J., speaking about the former Ord. 27, r.11, the predecessor of Ord. 19, r.7, said:

"I think that the purpose of the rule was to provide a cheap method for the plaintiff to obtain in most cases the relief he seeks. But circumstances might well rise in which a real hardship would be inflicted on a plaintiff if he was compelled to proceed by a motion for judgment and could not exercise the right which he would otherwise have had of setting down the case for trial and letting it come on for trial in the usual way. For instance, some of the relief he sought might be relief of a kind which it was not the practice of the Chancery Division to give on motion for judgment, such for instance as a declaration as to the construction of a document (see, *per* Lord Maugham and Lord Russell in *New Brunswick Railway Co. v. British and French Trust Corporation Ltd* [1939] A.C. 1, 22 at 28). That case is a long way from the present case, but it does seem to me to indicate that there may be circumstances in which real hardship would be inflicted on a plaintiff, if he could not pursue the alternative remedy of setting down the case for trial in the usual way and may explain why the word 'may,' which is deliberately permissive, has been used in the terms of Ord. 27, r.11."

See also Austin v. Wildig (Practice Note) [1969] 1 W.L.R. 67; *Practice Direction (Provisional Damages)* [1988] 1 W.L.R. 654.

4. When should the plaintiff elect for second option? The following are examples:

(a) *Publicity:* If the nature of the relief sought by the plaintiff is such as by convention or reason demands the publicity of an open trial, the plaintiff may choose to ignore the semi-private course afforded by Ord. 19. In the *Nagy* case, the plaintiff claimed that the defendant had libelled him. He was seeking damages and injunction. No doubt, he wanted the publicity afforded by going to trial and proving his claim so as to clear his name of any slur caused by the alleged libel. (See also *Grant v. Knaresborough U.D.C.* [1928] Ch. 310.)

(b) *Declaration as to rights:* Case law has settled that certain types of relief are wholly unsuitable for the default procedure. A declaration as to rights is not generally available on summons or motion for judgment under Ord. 19 (*Williams v. Powell* [1894] W.N. 141).

(c) A *departure from convention:* In *Patten v. Burke Publishing Co Ltd* [1991] 1 W.L.R. 541; [1991] 2 All E.R. 821 the court considered the circumstances were such as to warrant a departure from convention. The author and owner of the copyright in a book gave to the defendant publishing company the sole and exclusive right to print and publish his book in return for royalties. The defendants went into receivership and the author brought an action for damages for breach of contract and a declaration that the agreement had been determined by the defendant's breach in failing to pay royalties due. The court held that the fullest justice could not be done by omitting the declaration sought. The author's right to publish the work by offering it to a new publisher would be seriously prejudiced by any contention that the agreement was still subsisting. A declaration that the defendants had repudiated the contract and was no longer subsisting was granted to the author.

5. Beware—the costs risk If the plaintiff does not have a good and substantial reason for proceeding to trial rather than under Ord. 19, he is not only unlikely to get an order for the extra costs of proceeding to trial against the defendant but may well end up with an order that the extra costs incurred by the defendant in having to go to trial should be borne by him.

6. When must the plaintiff proceed to trial? Where provisional damages

473

are part of the relief claimed in an action, entry of judgment with or without leave is not permissible under Ord. 13 or Ord. 19: Ord. 37, r.8(5).

7. What must the plaintiff do? In provisional damages actions, if the defendant has not given notice of intention to defend, the plaintiff must, if he has not already done so, serve a statement of claim. If this provokes the defendant into giving notice of intention to defend and the service of a defence out of time, the action will proceed to trial in the normal way. If the defendant remains inactive, the plaintiff should take out a summons promptly for directions for trial. The summons should include a prayer for an order that the defendant be precluded from contesting the issue of liability unless within a specified time he files notice of intention to defend and serves a defence. A defendant who has filed a notice of intention to defend but fails to serve a defence enables the plaintiff to issue a summons for directions to be issued on default: Ord. 25, r.1(7).

4 Order 19 default judgment—procedure for Class 2 relief

1. Introduction Procedural requirements vary according to whether relief is sought in the Queen's Bench Division or the Chancery Division and whether the hearing is in London or the provinces.

2. Summons or motion? Where the plaintiff seeks to obtain his judgment under Ord. 19 whether in the Queen's Bench Division or the Chancery Division, application is by summons to the master or district judge except in one case—the injunction. Only the judge has the general power to grant an injunction: see *Shell Mex & B.P. Ltd v. Manchester Garages* [1971] 1 W.L.R. 612. Masters and district judges have no such general power (Ord. 32, r.11(1)(d) except in agreed terms (Ord. 32, r.11(2)).

3. Issue of summons—requirements The plaintiff should lodge two copies of the summons for judgment. A fee of £10 is payable (£15 in the case of a judge's summons, *e.g.* for an injunction) and no supporting affidavit is necessary or desirable. Both copies of the summons are sealed and one copy is returned to the plaintiff's solicitor for service on the defendant against whom judgment is being sought. That defendant must be served. He may be served by post. The service period is two clear days before the return date. In London, only the original summons is required in the case of a master's summons since no copy is kept by the court.

4. Issue of motion for judgment—requirements Whereas a summons is an oral application in chambers before a judge, master or district judge, a motion is an oral application made direct to the judge in open court without any prior hearing in front of the master or district judge. Motions are regulated by Ord. 8. They should contain a concise statement of the nature of the relief required (Ord. 8, r.3(2)). The service period is at least two clear days but the motion will not be set down until at least 14 days have gone by since the statement of claim has been served.

5 Chancery Division: London action: hearing in London

1. Documents—what and where? The plaintiff should lodge at the office of the Clerk of the Lists, Room TM8.13, Chancery Chambers, Thomas More Building, Royal Courts of Justice, Strand, London WC2A 2LL:
- (a) Two plain copies of the writ.
- (b) Two plain copies of the statement of claim, one of which is indorsed with a form of certificate that no defence has been served.
- (c) Either:
  - (i) a copy of the acknowledgement of service showing either an intention to defend or an intention not to defend; or
  - (ii) a certificate that the defendant has failed to return any acknowledgment of service in which case an affidavit of service of the writ or other proof of service (for example the plaintiff's copy of the writ indorsed with the defendant's solicitor's acceptance of service on it).
- (d) If the statement of claim was not served with or indorsed on the writ, an affidavit of service of it on the defendant.
- (e) Two plain copies of the notice of motion (see Form N). A return date will be given at least 14 days later than that on which the statement of claim was served. If the defendant does not attend when counsel moves for judgment, an affidavit of service of the notice of motion on the defendant should be sworn and produced.
- (f) (If appropriate) a certificate of counsel that the motion is fit to be heard as "short" and that it is unlikely to exceed 10 minutes.
- (g) Two copies of the minutes of the proposed judgment. If no minutes are proposed, the notice of the motion itself should set out with precision the judgment to be asked for: *De Jongh v. Newman* (1887) 56 L.T. 180.
- (h) If the defendant is an infant, two copies of any affidavits to be used in proving the plaintiff's claim (see later p. 480) and Ord. 80, r.8).

6 Chancery Division: district registry action

1. Chancery trial centres Although proceedings begun in the Chancery Division by writ can be commenced in any district registry (Ord. 6, r.7(2)(c)), the trial of Chancery actions issued in a district registry must take place either in London or one of the eight authorised provincial chancery trial centres (Birmingham, Bristol, Cardiff, Leeds, Liverpool, Manchester, Newcastle-upon-Tyne and Preston). See *Chancery Division Practice Directions, The Supreme Court Practice* (1997) Vol. 2, Part 3B.

2. Hearing in London—documents—when and where? The motion is set down by lodging in the district registry those documents referred to under the previous heading together with a request to have the action set down. The papers are then sent down to London to listing section which enters the action up in the cause list.

7 Chancery Division: district registry action: hearing outside London

1. Venue Here the hearing of the motion must take place at one of the eight authorised provincial Chancery trial centres. See *Chancery Division Practice Directions, The Supreme Court Practice* (1995) Vol. 2, Part 3B.

2. Documents—where? The plaintiff should lodge at the district registry where the action is proceeding all those documents set out at p. 475.

3. When? If the action is already proceeding in a district registry at one of those centres, it will normally be set down in the Motion Day List maintained by the senior Chancery clerk at that centre.

4. What if the district registry not a trial centre? In a district registry other than at one of those trial centres, the papers are lodged in the district registry where the action is commenced and sent on to the Senior Chancery clerk at one of the authorised centres. The papers are then returned to the local district registry after the hearing.

8 Chancery Division: London action: hearing outside London

1. A rarity It is permissible for a motion for judgment in a London Chancery action to be heard outside London at one of the eight authorised centres (*Practice Direction (Chancery: Proceedings outside London)* [1972] 1 W.L.R. 1).

2. Check first Before setting it down, the master will not doubt make enquiries of the relevant court administrator.

9 Queen's Bench Division: London action: hearing in London

1. Which list? A motion for judgment in a Queen's Bench action proceeding in the Royal Courts of Justice is set down in the Non-Jury List (see *Practice Direction (Trials in London)* [1981] 1 W.L.R. 1296 and Ord. 34, r.4).

2. What has to be lodged? The plaintiff should lodge in Room W11, clerk of the Lists Office, Royal Courts of Justice, Strand, London, WC2A 2LL:
  (a) Original writ.
  (b) Copy of the statement of claim indorsed with a certificate that the time of service of the defence has expired and that no defence has been served.
  (c) Two copies of the notice of motion.
  (d) Affidavit of service of statement of claim if served separately from the writ.
  (e) If in default of notice of intention to defend, an affidavit of service of the writ to the original writ indorsed with the defendant's solicitor's acceptance.
  (f) Fee of £10.

3. Notice The notice of motion must be served on the defendant and the service period is two clear days (Ord. 8, r.2(2)).

4. Proof of service—when? If the defendant fails to appear when the plaintiff moves for judgment, evidence of service of the notice of motion on the defendant (such as an affidavit of service) should be made available.

10 Queen's Bench action: district registry: hearing outside London

1. Essentially—as for London The requirements on setting down and service of a motion for judgment for hearing in the provinces are the same as for London cases.

2. The role of the district registry clerk A hearing is obtained by the district registry clerk from the civil listing officer at the trial centre where the hearing is to take place.

3. And then? One copy of the notice is sealed and returned for service with a return date inserted. The court file is then sent to the civil listing office at the trial centre and is returned to the district registry after the hearing.

11 Queen's Bench action: district registry: hearing in London

1. Procedure—the same The requirements in a district registry action for setting down and service of a motion for judgment to be heard in London are as for other Queen's Bench motions for judgment.

2. Role of the district registry clerk After the documents have been lodged at the district registry, they are sent by the district registry court clerk to the address at paragraph 2 of section 9 at p. 477 above.

12 Multiple defendants

1. Class 1 relief If the plaintiff is seeking relief against several defendants under Ord. 19, rr.1–4 ("Class 1" kinds of relief), he may enter judgment against any defaulting defendant and proceed to trial against the rest (Ord. 19, rr.1–4). In this respect the position is exactly the same as under Ord. 13 (as to which see p. 415).

2. Class 2 relief If the plaintiff is seeking relief against several defendants otherwise than under Ord. 19, rr.1–4 ("Class 2" kinds of relief) and any defendant is in default of defence, the plaintiff may:
  (a) if his claim against any defaulting defendant is severable from his claims against the others, apply on motion for judgment against any such defaulter and proceed to trial against the others; or
  (b) if his claim is not so severable, set down the motion for judgment against any defaulter at the same time as setting the action down for trial against the other non-defaulting defendants (Ord. 19, r.7).
If paragraph (a) applies, it is not necessary for the plaintiff to serve notice of motion on any defendant but the defaulters against whom he is seeking judgment: *Cooke v. Gilbert* [1882] W.N. 111 at 128.

3. Judgments both in default and on admissions Similarly, where some defendants are in default of defence and some have pleaded, the plaintiff may wish to move for judgment on the admissions contained in those pleadings. The motions for judgment in default against some defendants and on admissions against the others should be set down at the same time so that they can all be dealt with together: *National & Provincial Bank v. Evans* (1881) 30 W.R. 177.

13 Costs

1. Discretion On the hearing of the summons or motion for judgment, the court has a discretion—to be judicially exercised—to make such orders in relation to the costs as it considers appropriate (section 50 of the Supreme Court Act 1981) and for their taxation or assessment.

2. Restricted application of "fixed" costs The table of fixed costs contained in Ord. 62, Appendix 3 has no application to what we have chosen to call Class 2 kinds of relief. It only applies to claims for debts or liquidated demands of £600 or upwards.

14 Form and carriage of judgment

1. Specimen forms? For forms of judgment on motion for judgment in default of defence, see generally Part C, section 3.

2. Who draws? In Queen's Bench cases, the plaintiff, as the party seeking to have a judgment entered, draws up the judgment (see Ord. 42, r.5: *Masters' Practice Directions (Drawing up Orders in Q.B.D.) Direction No. 30; The Supreme Court Practice (1997)*, vol. 2, para. 743. In the Chancery Division the judgment is drawn up by the court (Ord. 42, r.6).

C: THE HEARING

1 Default of defence

1. Late defence not necessarily fatal A late defence is not a nullity: *Gill v. Woodfine* (1884) 25 Ch.D. 707, C.A. The court will read it to see whether it sets up grounds of defence, which, if proved, will be material. If the defence contains nothing by way of defence, the court will ignore it and proceed. If it raises a substantial ground of defence, the court will make such an order as will enable the case to be tried on its merits: *Gibbings v. Strong* (1884) 26 Ch.D. 66, C.A.

2. Failure to appear What if the defendant has a defence but fails to attend on the motion for judgment? A course taken in the Chancery Division in the past is to give judgment for the plaintiff, but to direct that the order should not be drawn up for a specified period so as to give the defendant the opportunity of applying to discharge it: *Butterworth v. Smallwood* [1924] W.N. 8. The same approach is adopted on a motion for judgment

on the counterclaim as in default of defence: *Graves v. Terry* (1882) 9
Q.B.D. 170 and *Higgins v. Scott* (1888) 21 Q.B.D. 10.

2 Pleadings and evidence

1. No proper pleading—no judgment In *Smith v. Buchan* (1888) 58 L.T.
710, the plaintiff sought judgment in default of defence for the specific
performance of an agreement for the purchase by the defendant from the
plaintiff of "certain hereditaments situate in the Parish of St Peter the
Great in the City of Chichester and described in the schedule to the said
agreement, in fee simple". The schedule was not set out in the statement
of claim. Kerr L.J. said:

> "I cannot give judgment in default of defence for specific performance,
> as the property is not described sufficiently in the statement of claim.
> There was a difference of opinion among the judges, but at a meeting
> the majority of the judges decided that in such cases the court could
> not look at an agreement or receive any evidence but must give a
> judgment accordingly to the pleadings alone. The statement of claim
> must be amended by making it contain a more specific description of
> the property and must be served afresh."

That rule remains intact. The judge will look at the statement of claim
and nothing else. In *Young v. Thomas* [1892] 2 Ch. 135, C.A., Bowen L.J.
explained the reasoning thus at 137:

> "There is no doubt that, in determining the rights of the parties in
> the action, the statement of claim alone is to be looked to, and the
> reason for this rule is obvious, namely, that the facts stated therein
> are taken to be admitted by the defendants; and, as has been decided
> by Lord Justice Kay in *Smith v. Buchan*, no evidence can be admitted
> as to those facts."

2. Are affidavits sufficient? No—in *Jones v. Harris* (1887) 55 L.T. 884, the
plaintiff sought to prove his claim on moving for judgment by affidavits
filed in support. The court not only refused to read them but held that the
costs of their preparation should be disallowed.

3. The "disability" exception The basic rule is displaced where the defendant against whom motion for judgment is sought is a person under
disability, that is, an infant or mental patient. In such cases, there is no
presumption of admissions to be drawn from the fact that the defendant
is in default of defence. So the plaintiff must adduce evidence (which may
be in affidavit form in an appropriate case) so as to prove his claim: see

Re Fitzwater (1882) 52 L.J. Ch. 83; *Cheek v. Cheek* (1910) 45 L.J.N.C. 22 and Ord. 80, r.8.

4. "Disability"—must there always be an affidavit? No—the court does have the power, however, in an appropriate case, to dispense with affidavit evidence even where the defendant is an infant or patient where it is considered unnecessary for the protection of a defendant: *Ripley v. Sawyer* (1886) 31 Ch.D. 494.

5. Drafting the claim The statement of claim must be drafted with such precision that there is no room for doubt as to the exact nature of the relief which you are seeking. Moreover, the kind of relief sought in the statement of claim must not extend beyond the kind of relief sought in the writ because the plaintiff cannot obtain judgment for more than he has claimed on his writ: *Gee v. Bell* (1887) 35 Ch.D. 160. In that case, the plaintiffs brought a foreclosure action against the second mortgagee and the mortgagor. In addition to the relief sought in the writ (an account, foreclosure and the appointment of a receiver), the plaintiff, by his statement of claim, claimed personal payment of the mortgage money from the mortgagor. In the days of *Gee v. Bell* the plaintiff had to file his statement of claim in the court office, not serve it on the defendant and so it is not surprising that North J. asked:

> "How can you have a personal judgment against the mortgagor when you have not claimed it by your writ? The statement of claim has not been delivered to him."

Nowadays, a more relaxed view may be taken since the statement of claim has to be served on the defendant and it cannot therefore be said that he is unaware of the extended relief sought.

3 The relief granted

1. The wording of the rule It is true that Ord. 19, r.7 uses mandatory language "on the hearing of the application (for judgment) the court shall give such judgment as the plaintiff appears entitled to on his statement of claim."

2. The rule—only directory The rule has always been considered directory not mandatory. In *Charles v. Shepherd* [1892] 2 Q.B. 622 the statement of claim alleged that the plaintiff, a merchant in England, having business transactions on the West Coast of Africa, had appointed the defendant as his agent for the collection of money due to him there. The plaintiff claimed payment of £4,462 and an account of what was due to him. The defendant failed to serve a defence. The plaintiff sought final judgment for £4,462 plus interest. The court refused him final judgment and referred the whole claim to the Official Referee to ascertain the real amount due to the plaintiff with leave to the Official Referee to communicate with the defendant in Lagos.

3. The reasoning of the Court of Appeal The Court of Appeal dismissed the plaintiff's appeal. This is how Lord Esher M.R. construed Ord. 27, r.11, the predecessor of Ord. 19, r.7:

> "We are of opinion upon the true construction of that rule—first, that the court is not bound to give judgment for the plaintiff, even though the statement of claim may on the face of it look perfectly clear, if it should see any reason to doubt whether injustice may not be done in giving judgment; it has a discretion to refuse to make the order asked for; and secondly, that the expression 'such judgment as upon statement of claim the court or a judge shall consider the plaintiff to be entitled to,' includes an interlocutory judgment, to be subsequently worked out as well as a final judgment."

4. Rationale Why, if the defendant cannot be bothered to serve a defence, should the court be concerned to exercise a discretion not to grant the relief sought by the plaintiff? In *Wallersteiner v. Moir* [1974] 1 W.L.R. 991, an action in which the defendant sought by his counterclaim, not only money, but declarations against the plaintiff of fraud, misfeasance and a breach of trust, Scarman L.J. said at 1030C–F:

> "The discretion is a valuable safeguard in the hands of the court. Take the instant case: though I entertain grave doubts as to the bona fides and honesty of Dr Wallersteiner both in the financial dealings the court is now considering and in the conduct of this litigation, injustice might well be done to him if without the benefit of trial the court should declare him fraudulent, guilty of misfeasance and of breach of trust. For the very reason that the case reeks of the odour of suspicion, it is, I believe, the duty of the court to exercise caution before committing itself to sweeping declarations: to look specifically at each claim, and to refrain from making declarations, unless justice to the claimant can only be met by so doing. Generally speaking, the court should leave until after trial the decision whether or not to grant declaratory relief, and if so, in what terms: see *Williams v. Powell* [1894] W.N. 141.
>
>   Different considerations, however, apply when what is sought is a money or property judgment. When a defendant fails to plead, it is ordinarily in the interests of justice that the plaintiff should be able without more ado to obtain judgment for the money or property for

which he is suing; the defendant is not without remedy after judgment in default, for , if he can show a bona fide defence, he can get it set aside before it is enforced. But, when what is sought is a declaration, there is the risk of irremediable injustice: the court has spoken and words cannot be recalled, even though later they be negatived: '*nescit vox missa reverti*', (Horace, *Ars Poetica*, line 390). The power of the court to give declaratory relief upon a default of pleading, of course, exists, but, for the reason crystallised by Horace in those four words of his, should be exercised only in cases in which to deny it would be to impose injustice upon the claimant." (But see *Aitbelaid v. Nima*, *The Times*, July 19, 1991, and *Patten v. Burke Publishing Ltd* [1991] 1 W.L.R. 541).

5. Summary Thus, if the relief sought is not appropriate for disposal under Ord. 19 (such as a declaration) or the court considers that it would not be just to give relief in the terms sought, it has a discretion to refuse judgment altogether or give such other relief as it considers meets the justice of the situation or stand the motion over until trial if other defendants are involved or even extend the defendant's time to plead.

D: THE POSITION OF THE DEFAULTING DEFENDANT

1 Introduction

1. Substantially—as for Order 13 The position of the defendant who is in default of defence under Ord. 19 is almost exactly the same as the position of the defaulting defendant under Ord. 13.

2. The alternatives The defendant has two broad choices. If he admits the claim but cannot pay it all at once, he may seek a stay of execution. If he wishes to defend the claim, he may apply to have it set aside.

2 Choice 1—admitting the claim

1. Applying for time to pay If the defendant sued for a liquidated sum admits the plaintiff's claim but wants time to pay, he should file an acknowledgment of service admitting the claim and indicate on the acknowledgment of service his intention to apply for a stay of execution against any judgment entered by the plaintiff.

2. Automatic stay? Yes—such a course will operate to create an automatic stay of execution of the judgment by *fieri facias* for a period of 14 days from the date on which the acknowledgment of service is received t the court office, thus giving the defendant time to apply for a further stay under Ord. 47 on terms, for instance, that he discharges the debt by specified instalments.

3. And if not stay? A defendant who is in default of defence and has failed either to return any acknowledgment of service at all or has returned an acknowledgment of service giving notice of intention to defend, should apply promptly under Ord. 47 for a stay of execution (as to which see p. 449).

3 Choice 2—setting aside judgment

1. As for Order 13 The defendant against whom judgment has been ordered in default of defence may apply to set aside judgment under Ord. 19, r.9. The law and practice for setting the judgment aside is exactly the same as that applicable to Ord. 13 and references should be made to pp. 000 *et seq.* for a detailed discussion of the matter. The jurisdiction to set aside includes the power to set aside an interlocutory judgment in default for damages to be assessed: *City of Westminster v. Reema Construction Ltd* [1990] 20 Con LR 44.

2. The court's discretion—flexible In *National Westminster Bank plc v. Humphrey* (1984) 128 S.J. 81, the Court of Appeal held that the wording of Ord. 19, r.9 is wide enough to give the court authority in the proper exercise of its discretion, to set aside one part of a judgment and to grant a stay of execution in respect of another part. See also the advantage of seeking a variation of the judgment rather than its setting aside where part of the claim is admitted and part is denied, p. 457.

3. Security for costs On an application to set aside judgment in default of compliance with the rules of court or an order of the court, the court's power to make it a condition of setting it aside that the defendant pay a sum into court is not confined to cases where the defence appears shadowy or the defendant's credibility is in doubt or where it is proper to require security for costs. The court has power to impose such a condition even where there is a good arguable case, not to punish the defendant but to encourage the proper future conduct of the litigation and to provide a measure of security for the plaintiff. The amount to be paid in should be fixed in accordance with the defendant's means to pay: *City Construction Contracts (London) Ltd v. Adam, The Times,* January 4, 1988.

4. The case of judgment in default of discovery In *Bains v. Patel*, *The Times*, May 20, 1983, the Court of Appeal held that a defendant whose defence had been struck out for failure to give discovery with judgment entered for the plaintiff was in the same position as a defendant who had failed to serve a defence. Thus the judgment so entered was a judgment in default of defence and like any other such judgment could be set aside or varied on such terms as the court thought just under Ord. 19, r.9.

5. Applications by strangers An application to set aside a judgment against a defendant may be made by strangers to the action in similar circumstances to those which regulate such applications under Ord. 13 (as to which see p. 458).

CHAPTER 7

Dismissal

A: GENERAL

1 The Defendant's Objective

So far we have dealt with those pre-emptive steps which plaintiffs may, in appropriate circumstances, take in order to secure either victory without trial or a strategic procedural advantage over the defendant in the early stages of litigation.

We must now redress the balance by considering those forms of pre-emptive relief which may, in appropriate circumstances, be available to a defendant, the object of which is to secure the dismissal of the plaintiff's action or its more expeditious progress to trial. Whereas speed is usually of the essence to the plaintiff in making his pre-emptive application, historically delay has been a weapon in the defendant's armoury. Since the late 1960s, however, first case law, then significant rule changes and finally, the adoption of a more interventionist role by the courts in the control and management of the conduct of actions have together brought about a much brisker and more businesslike approach to the disposal of litigation. Moreover, not all applications to dismiss necessarily involve proof of indolence on the part of the plaintiff in the conduct of the action.

2 Scope of dismissal

We are not here concerned with the dismissal of an action on its merits at trial, nor with situations in which an action is dismissed by the consent of the parties. We are concerned with the dismissal of actions before trial through the plaintiff's intentional or neglectful default.

3 Jurisdiction to dismiss action

1. Sources The jurisdiction to dismiss actions in case of failure or default is derived from three sources:
    (a) Under the court's inherent jurisdiction to control its own procedures.
    (b) Failure to comply with an order of the court;

(c) Failure to comply with the express provisions of the R.S.C. (in the county court, with the County Court Rules).

2. Concurrent These sources are cumulative not alternative and may be invoked simultaneously: see *Davey v. Bentinck* [1893] 1 Q.B. 185 at 187.

4 Categories of conduct

1. Two types The court's jurisdiction to dismiss actions broadly falls to be exercised in two types of situation:
- (a) Those situations where the failure to prosecute the action expeditiously arises from the plaintiff's inactivity or neglect.
- (b) Those situations in which the failure by the plaintiff to prosecute the action is intentional and contumacious.

We shall consider each of these in turn later (see pp. 489 and 515).

5 Consequences of dismissal

1. No *res judicata* Although an order to dismiss the action for failure to comply with the rules or an order or under the inherent jurisdiction has the consequences of killing off the action, the doctrine of *res judicata* does not apply since there has been no determination of the issues between the parties on the merits.

2. Fresh action Where the dismissal arises as a result of the plaintiff's inactivity or dilatoriness (as opposed to contumacy), there is generally nothing to prevent the plaintiff from commencing a second action, raising the same or similar issues, provided that he does so within any relevant limitation period. We shall discuss this in detail later. Different considerations apply, however, where the first action has been dismissed for failure to comply with a peremptory order of the court (see p. 519).

3. No estoppel For the same reason, the doctrine of estoppel does not apply.

4. Effect on counterclaims—both parties to blame R.S.C. Ord. 15, r.2(3) gives the court a discretion to permit a counterclaim to proceed notwithstanding, *inter alia* that the plaintiff's action is dismissed. In *Zimmer Orthopaedic Ltd v. Zimmer Manufacturing Co.* [1968] 3 All E.R. 449 the defendant applied to have the plaintiff's claim struck out. The plaintiff made a cross-application to have the counterclaim struck out. The Court of Appeal held that both parties were to blame for the delay which had accrued, and since the defendants were in a position throughout the action to bring it on for trial, both parties should be put in the same position. The claim and counterclaim were both dismissed. (See also *Janata Bank v. Noor, The Times*, November 18, 1983.) Where the limitation period has not expired so that the plaintiff and the defendant could each bring a fresh action for their respective claims, the Court of Appeal has reinstated both claim and counterclaim, which had each been struck out for want of prosecution at first instance: *Instrumatic Ltd v. Supabase Ltd* [1969] 1 W.L.R. 519.

5. Plaintiff to blame If, however, the entire fault in failing to get on with the action rests with the plaintiff and not with the counterclaiming defendant, there is no reason why the claim and counterclaim should stand or fall together and on this basis the Court of Appeal in *Westminster City Council v. Clifford Culpin & Partners* (1987) 12 Con LR 117 refused to treat claim and counterclaim on the same footing. It struck out the plaintiffs' claim and allowed the defendants to continue with their counterclaim.

6. Counterclaiming defendant to blame In *Zimmer* the judge described the plaintiffs and the defendants as being like two dogs fighting over the same bone. In *Owen v. Pugh* [1995] 3 All E.R. 345, Otton J. made on important factual distinction between *Zimmer* and the dispute in the case before him at 352:

> "The distinction here is that the parties are not fighting over the same bone. The dispute has two entities; the claim for unpaid professional fees and a claim for damages for breach of contract and negligence."

On the facts the defendant had conceded that his delay was inordinate and inexcusable and it was also clear that the plaintiff had suffered prejudice and that there was a substantial risk that a fair trial of the issues of quantum arising from the counter-claim was no longer possible. Accordingly, he struck out the counterclaim for want of prosecution but saw no reason why the plaintiff's claim should be struck out. He allowed it to proceed.

7. Dismissal of third party proceedings Defendants are not entitled to assume that the interests of themselves and the third party are the same because both may wish that the plaintiff's claim either should not be prosecuted or, if it is, that it should fail. The third party is not an ally of the defendant because he has had proceedings brought against him by the defendant. If a defendant brings in a third party and then because the plaintiff is slow in prosecuting the main action and the defendant thinks it is in his interest not to object to the plaintiff's delay, the defendant does not himself press on with the third party proceedings, he can and should, if he is going to adopt that course without communicating with the third party, ensure that he is always in a position to apply to strike out the plaintiff's action for want of prosecution if the third party should turn nasty by moving to strike out the third party proceedings. On the basis of this reasoning the court struck out the third party proceedings for want of prosecution even though the main action remained ongoing: *Slade v. Kempton (Jewelry) Ltd v. Kayman Ltd* [1969] 3 All E.R. 786—thus providing a good example of the concept of third party proceedings having a life of their own quite independent of the main action. (See also *Stott v. West Yorkshire Road Car Company Ltd* [1971] 2 Q.B. 651; [1971] 3 All E.R. 534.)

8. Multiple applications to dismiss The starting point is that prima facie where two or more defendants apply, for example, to have the plaintiff's action dismissed for want of prosecution, each application should be considered separately. But there may be cases where the prejudice which would be caused to one or more of the parties by his dismissal from the action requires modification of what would otherwise be the appropriate order in relation to him: *Westminster City Council v. Clifford Culpin & Partners* (see above, p. 488). In *Hollis v. Islington L.B.C. v. Peppiatt* (unreported) (1989) C.A.T. January 27, 1989, Stuart Smith L.J. stated that:

> "It is clear that only in exceptional circumstances should an action be struck out against one defendant and continue against another, certainly where, as here, the defendants have rights of contribution or indemnity *inter se*. In this case, if the first defendants remained in the action and it was struck out against the second defendants, they would immediately be joined as third parties, thus reinstating the very injustice that the court seeks to avoid."

9. The aim—broad justice But acquiescence by one defendant does not necessarily disentitle another defendant from having the action struck out for want of prosecution. Considerations of broad justice are relevant in the exercise of the court's discretion and it was said in *Kelly v. Marley Tile* (1978) 122 S.J. 17 that it would need a strong case to persuade the court. (See also *Hatter v. Port of London Authority* (1971) 115 S.J. 950.)

B: DISMISSAL FOR WANT OF PROSECUTION

1 Jurisdiction

The Rules of the Supreme Court contain express provision empowering the High Court to dismiss an action for want of prosecution. So, for example, a plaintiff who fails to issue a summons for directions within the time fixed by the rules runs the risk of having the action so dismissed:

Ord. 25, r.1(4). This and other provisions of the R.S.C. containing similar powers will be considered later (at p. 519). A second source of the court's jurisdiction to dismiss for want of prosecution springs from the court's power to prescribe by order time limits which, if not adhered to, will result in the automatic dismissal of the action for want of prosecution. This jurisdiction will also be examined later (at p. 516). Apart from those two jurisdictional sources, the High Court has an important third source and that is its inherent jurisdiction to dismiss an action for want of prosecution where the plaintiff has defaulted in complying with the rules or has been guilty of culpable delay in prosecuting the action. It is the circumstances in which this inherent power is exercised with which we are now concerned.

2 Historical overview

"To no-one will we deny or delay right or justice." So King John promised the people in 1215 when he assented to Magna Carta. That the Great Charter failed to cure the law's delays is evident from the literature throughout the centuries that followed and from extensive current judicial comment (see, *e.g.* Sir Thomas Bingham in *Sparrow v. Sovereign Chicken Ltd* C.A.T. June 8, 1994 (unreported); and Kerr L.J. in *Westminster City Council v. C. Culpin & Partners* (1987) 12 Con LR 117 at 136; and Mustill L.J. in *Electricity Supply Nominees Ltd v. Longstaff & Shaw Ltd* (1986) C.A.T. 1063). In the nineteenth century, a practice had grown up by virtue of which there was a tacit understanding between plaintiffs' solicitors and defendants' solicitors that, no matter how long the plaintiff had delayed in prosecuting his action, the defendant would do him the courtesy of offering him a further opportunity of taking any necessary steps before seeking to secure the plaintiff's compliance with a rule or previous order. So the plaintiff's solicitor could put a case on one side as long as he pleased without fear of the consequences. Further, certainly by 1882 a deep-rooted convention had been established that no court would dismiss the plaintiff's action on a first application, no matter how dilatory the plaintiff or his solicitor had been. The court would always give the plaintiff one last chance by making an order that the action would be dismissed for want of prosecution unless within a given time the plaintiff took some prescribed action (see for example *Eaton v. Storer* (1882) 22 Ch.D. 91).

3 The 1960s—a sea change

By the 1960s inexcusable dilatoriness and inefficiency by lawyers and others such as insurance companies in the approach to litigation had become scandalous and pernicious. Lord Salmon had this to say about them in *Birkett v. James* [1978] A.C. 297 at 329C:

490

"These delays had become a blot on the administration of justice for it is of great public importance that actions should be brought to trial with reasonable expedition. Defendants' solicitors might no doubt have taken out applications to dismiss for want of prosecution or for pre-emptory orders to compel plaintiffs to get on with their actions. No unnaturally they rarely did so, relying on the maxim that it is wise to leave sleeping dogs lie. They had good reason to believe that a dog which had remained unconscious for such long periods of time might well die a natural death at no expense to their clients; whereas if they were to take the necessary steps to force the action to trial, they would really be waking up a dog for the purpose of killing it at great expense to their clients which they would have no chance of recovering. Accordingly, it was unusual for summonses to dismiss actions for want of prosecution or for peremptory orders to be taken out."

4 Allen v. McAlpine & Sons Ltd

In 1967, Lord Denning, then Master of the Rolls, decided that enough was enough and in a series of cases beginning with *Fitzpatrick v. Batger & Co. Ltd* [1967] 2 All E.R. 657 and *Reggentin v. Beecholme Bakeries Ltd* [1968] 2 Q.B. 276 and *Allen v. Sir Alfred McAlpine & Sons Ltd* [1968] 2 W.L.R. 366; [1968] 1 All E.R. 543, the Court of Appeal set out to cure the law of this malaise. In *Allen*, Lord Denning said (at [1968] 1 All E.R. 547):

"To put right this wrong, we will in this court do all in our power to enforce expedition: and, if need be, we will strike out actions when there has been excessive delay. This is a stern measure; but it is within the inherent jurisdiction of the court, and the rules of court expressly permit it."

5 The basic rule in *Allen*

The basic rule established in *Allen* is that an action may be struck out where the court is satisfied either:
  (a) that there has been default on the part of the plaintiff or his lawyers which was intentional and contumelious as, for example, by disobedience to a peremptory order of the court or conduct amounting to an abuse of the process of the court; or
  (b) that there has been inordinate and inexcusable delay on the part of the plaintiff or his lawyers and such delay will give rise to a substantial risk that it is not possible to have a fair trial of the issues in the action or is such as is likely to cause or to have caused serious prejudice to the defendants either as between themselves and the

491

plaintiff or between each other or between them and a third party: see *Birkett v. James* [1977] 2 All E.R. 801 at 805; [1978] A.C. 297 at 318.

6 The rule in *Birkett v. James*

1. Three unanswered questions Some years later, in 1977, the basic rule in *Allen* was approved by the House of Lords in *Birkett v. James* (see above). The House supplemented the rule by providing answers to three further questions. These three supplementary points which assumed importance in subsequent cases in the years between 1968 when *Allen* was decided and 1977 when *Birkett* was reported were:
  (a) Whether the fact that the limitation period had not expired by the time the application to dismiss for want of prosecution was heard was relevant.
  (b) The relevance of the period which the plaintiff had allowed to elapse before the action had been brought when this was done within the limitation period.
  (c) Whether the judge ought to weigh up the plaintiff's prospects of success in any remedy he might have against his solicitor if the action were dismissed, and, if so, how this estimate should affect the exercise of his discretion.

7 Dismissal within the limitation period

1. No dismissal The House of Lords held in *Birkett* that the power to dismiss an action for want of prosecution other than in a case of contumelious conduct on the plaintiff's part should not normally be exercised within the currency of the limitation period.

2. The rule explained The reasons for this were explained by Lord Diplock (at [1978] A.C. 320A):

> "Crucial to the question whether an action ought to be dismissed for want of prosecution before the expiry of the limitation period is the answer to a question that lies beyond it, *viz.*, whether a plaintiff whose action has been so dismissed may issue a fresh writ for the same cause of action. If he does so within the limitation period, the effect of dismissing the previous action can only be to prolong the time which must elapse before the trial can take place beyond the date when it could have been held if the previous action had remained on foot. Upon issuing his new writ the plaintiff would have the benefit of additional time for repeating such procedural steps as he had already completed before the action was dismissed. This can only

aggravate: it can never mitigate to the prejudice to the defendant from delay ... Where all that the plaintiff has done has been to let the previous action go to sleep, the court in my opinion would have no power to prevent him starting a fresh action within the limitation period and proceeding with it with all proper diligence notwithstanding that his previous action had been dismissed for want of prosecution."

3. Rule generally conclusive And so he concluded (at [1978] A.C. 322D) that in cases where it is likely that if the action were dismissed, the plaintiff would avail himself of his legal right to issue a fresh writ, the non-expiry of the limitation period is generally a conclusive reason for not dismissing the action which is already pending. (See also *Department of Transport v. Chris Smaller (Transport) Ltd* [1989] 1 All E.R. 897.)

8 Pre-writ delay within limitation period

1. Defendants' concern The concern of defendants here was to know whether, if the plaintiff delayed issuing his writ until, say, shortly before the expiry of the time laid down by Parliament under the Limitation Act within which the action must be brought, that pre-writ delay could, when standing alone, be taken into account when applying the basic *Allen* test.

2. Pre-writ delay of itself does not count Since Parliament has given the plaintiff a statutory right to commence his action at any time before the expiry of the time laid down in the statute, the House of Lords held in *Birkett v. James* that time elapsed before the issue of a writ within the limitation period cannot of itself constitute inordinate delay, however much the defendant may already have been prejudiced by the consequent lack of early notice of the claim against him, the fading recollections of his potential witnesses, their death or their untraceability (see, *e.g. Rowe v. Glenister, The Times*, August 7, 1995.

3. Post-writ does count To justify dismissal of an action for want of prosecution, the delay relied upon must relate to time which the plaintiff allows to lapse unnecessarily after the writ has been issued.

4. Late starters beware The House of Lords, however, was at pains to stress in *Birkett v. James* (see Lord Diplock at [1978] A.C. 322G) that a late start makes it the more incumbent upon the plaintiff to proceed with all due speed; a pace which might have been excusable if the action had been started sooner may be inexcusable in the light of the time that has already passed before the writ was issued.

5. Pre-writ delay may count with post-writ delay In setting out this principle for late starters, the House of Lords in *Birkett v. James* expressly approved the principle laid down in *William C Parker Ltd v. F.J. Ham & Son Ltd* [1972] 1 W.L.R. 1583. That case decided that to justify dismissal of an action for want of prosecution, some prejudice additional to that inevitably flowing from the plaintiff's tardiness in issuing his writ must be shown to have resulted from his subsequent delay beyond the period allowed by rules of court in proceeding promptly with the successive steps in the action. The additional prejudice need not be great compared with that which may have been already caused by the time elapsed before the writ was issued; but it must be more than minimal; and the delay in taking a step in the action if it is to qualify as inordinate as well as prejudicial must exceed the period allowed by rules of court for taking that step: see also *Department of Transport v. Chris Smaller (Transport) Ltd* [1989] 1 All E.R. 897.

6. The moral So, the moral is clear. The later the plaintiff issues his writ within the limitation period, the greater the obligation to conduct the litigation more swiftly than if the action had been started sooner.

9 Remedies against solicitor

1. *Birkett*—the majority view The majority of the Law Lords in *Birkett* (Lords Diplock, Edmound-Davies and Russell) concluded that the plaintiff's ability or inability to recover damages in negligence from his own solicitor should never be taken into account when the court is considering whether to dismiss an action for want of prosecution. Lord Diplock put it thus (at [1978] A.C. 324A):

> "Where an action is dismissed for want of prosecution the fault must lie either with the plaintiff or with his solicitors or with both. Which of them is to blame for the inordinate and inexcusable delay does not affect the prejudice caused to the defendant, which is the justification for the dismissal of the action; nor should it, in principle, affect his remedy. If it were a matter which the judge ought to take into account in deciding whether to dismiss the action, the court upon an interlocutory application in an action between different parties would have to embark upon what in effect would be the trial of an action by the plaintiff against his actual or former solicitor for professional negligence. That, clearly, is impossible." (See also *Paxton v. Allsopp* [1971] 3 All E.R. 370.)

2. A minority difference Lord Salmon, whilst not suggesting that it should by any means be a weighty factor to be taken into consideration, nevertheless could not agree that the plaintiff's inability to recover damages from his own solicitor should never deserve consideration. In a case were the pros and cons of dismissing the action for want of prosecution were very evenly balanced, he concluded that the plaintiff's inability to recover in some cases might just tip the scales in the plaintiff's favour (see *Birkett v. James* [1978] A.C. at 330F).

10 The law's delays uncured

It was hoped that the initiative taken by the Court of Appeal in *Allen* and by the House of Lords in *Birkett* would be sufficient to ensure the reasonable dispatch of litigation in the future. This proved not to be the case. In 1987, in a postscript to his judgment in *Westminster City Council v. Clifford Culpin & Partners* (1987) 12 Con LR 117 136, Kerr L.J. expressed his frustration at the then current state of affairs and delivered a stinging criticism of the delays, costs, inefficiency and inexcusable dilatoriness which characterised the litigation system (see also similar misgivings expressed by Mustill L.J. in *Electricity Supply Nominees Ltd v. Longstaff & Shaw Ltd* (1986) C.A.T. 1063; and by Sir Thomas Bingham and Kennedy L.J. in *Sparrow v. Sovereign Chicken Ltd* C.A.T. June 8, (1994) (unreported)).

11 An attempt to modify the rule in *Birkett v. James*

1. *Smaller*—the facts In *Department of Transport v. Chris Smaller (Transport) Ltd* [1989] 1 All E.R. 897, a lorry owned by the defendants and driven by their employee crashed into a motorway bridge in December 1978 killing the driver and badly damaging the bridge. Early in 1979 the plaintiff department, which owned the bridge, notified the defendants that they intended making a claim in respect of the damage to the bridge if it had been caused by the negligence of the defendants' driver. In June 1982 the plaintiffs presented their claim for £334,000, being the cost of the repairs. The defendants' insurers instructed a consulting engineer to advise on the plaintiffs' claim, but he was unable to arrange a meeting to agree the value of the claim. On May 30, 1984, 5-and-a-half years after the accident and six months before the expiry of the six-year limitation period, the plaintiffs issued a writ against the defendants. Six months later, on March 19, 1985, the writ was served on the defendants. The statement of claim was delivered on September 23, 1985 and the defendants filed a defence denying liability. Pleadings closed on December 20, 1985. The plaintiffs failed to issue a summons for directions and instead the defendants did so on June 24, 1986. The summons was heard on July 8, 1986, when the plaintiffs were ordered to give further and better particulars, to answer interrogatories and to set the action down for trial, all within 28 days. The plaintiffs provided further and better particulars and answered interrogatories within that period but failed to set the action down for trial. On April 28, 1987 the defendants applied to have the actions truck out for want of execution.

2. The judge's decision The master struck out the plaintiffs' claim, but the judge reversed his decision on the ground that although the plaintiffs had been guilty of inordinate and inexcusable delay for 13 months in the period following the issue of the writ, there was no real risk that there could not be a fair trial of the action and the defendants had failed to show that they would suffer more than minimal prejudice as a result of the post-writ delay.

3. Court of Appeal affirms On appeal by the defendants the Court of Appeal affirmed the judge's decision.

4. The Issue in House of Lords The defendants appealed to the House of Lords, contending that inordinate and inexcusable delay in the conduct of the litigation *after the expiry of the limitation period* ought to be a ground for striking out, *even though there could be a fair trial and the defendant would suffer no prejudice.*

5. *Smaller*—the rule in *Birkett v. James* intact The House of Lords rejected the defendants' contentions. They held that a plaintiff could not be penalised for any delay occurring between the accrual of the cause of action and the issue of the writ if the writ was issued within the limitation period. Secondly, inordinate and inexcusable delay by the plaintiff in prosecuting an action after the limitation period had expired was not a ground for striking out the action for want of prosecution unless the defendant had suffered prejudice from the delay, or a fair trial of the issues was impossible. Thirdly, where the delay before the issue of proceedings has caused prejudice, the defendant has only to show more than minimum additional prejudice resulting from post-issue delay to justify the court striking out of the proceedings. Fourthly, prejudice is not confined to prejudice affecting the actual conduct of the trial but includes, *inter alia*, prejudice to the defendant's business interests. Fifthly, the court will be cautious before allowing the mere fact of anxiety that accompanies any litigation to be regarded as prejudice justifying the striking out of the proceedings.

6. *Smaller*—the rationale Lord Griffiths justified the decision by asking:

"What would be the purpose of striking out in such circumstances? If there can be a fair trial and the defendant has suffered no prejudice, it clearly cannot be to do justice between the parties before the court. As between the plaintiff and defendant such an order is manifestly an injustice to the plaintiff. The only possible purpose of such an order would be as a disciplinary measure which by punishing the plaintiff will have a beneficent effect on the administration of justice by deterring others from similar delays. I have no faith that the exercise of the power in these circumstances would produce any greater impact on delay in litigation than the present principles."

12 The rule in *Birkett v. James*—closer analysis

1. The components We can now look at the principles established in *Allen, Birkett and Smaller* a little more closely. The component elements of the rule in *Birkett v. James* are

    (a) delay
    (b) which is inordinate
    (c) and inexcusable
    (d) giving rise to a substantial risk of prejudice or likely prejudice to the defendant or of the impossibility of a fair trial.

The first point to consider is the meaning of delay.

2. Does delay equal inactivity? Is there a legitimate distinction to be drawn between total inactivity on the part of the plaintiff and mere dilatoriness? Can the defendant succeed if he establishes either of these factors or must he establish total inactivity? This is what Lord Justice May said in *Lev v. Fagan* (unreported) C.A.T. March 8, 1989:

> "In the light of one of the arguments before us, I make this initial comment in cases where it is sought to dismiss an action for want of prosecution. In my opinion relevant delay does not only mean the passage of time in which nothing is done on either side. I accept that those periods are usually more important and can usually be more precisely identified. But there can be delay, even though things are happening, albeit in a somewhat desultory fashion. There is no need to take months, for instance, in proofing one's case. There is no need to take months in considering papers with counsel, as appears to have happened in the course of this case. The litigation must be considered as a whole and one must ask oneself whether there has been delay of an inordinate and inexcusable kind and whether, as a result, justice can now been done. Thus when considering the facts of this case I think it right to bear in mind, in addition to the two specific major periods in which it is said that nothing was happening, the fact that in other periods quite clearly, although some things were happening, they were happening very slowly."

3. Delay is time wasted It is clear from this passage that delay is not time used, but time wasted. Further, the delay must be in prosecuting *the proceedings*. Obviously delay in *starting* the proceedings within the limitation period may be prejudicial, but of itself it cannot be sufficient to warrant striking out an action for want of *prosecution*. There must be some delay after the issue of the writ.

4. When is delay inordinate? The defendant must show that the delay has been inordinate. In *Allen*, Lord Salmon said (at [1968] 1 All E.R. 561F):

> "It would be highly undesirable and indeed impossible to attempt to lay down a tariff—so many years or more on one side of the line and a lesser period on the other. What is or is not inordinate delay must depend on the facts of each case. These vary infinitely from case to case, but it should not be too difficult to recognise inordinate delay when it occurs."

It has been said that for delay to be inordinate, it must exceed, and probably by a substantial margin, the times prescribed by the rules of court for the taking of steps in the action: *Trill v. Sacher* [1993] 1 All E.R. 961 at 878J. But, as we have seen, in judging whether the delay is inordinate, a stricter approach is adopted the later the plaintiff starts his action. The later he starts, the higher is his duty to prosecute the action with diligence: *Birkett* (1978) A.C. 297 at 322; *Tabata v. Hetherington, The Times,* December 15, 1983; and see above p. 494.

5. When is delay inexcusable? The defendant must also establish that the plaintiff has no excuse for the delay. If the delay is the fault of neither the plaintiff nor his legal advisers, the court will not drive the plaintiff from the judgment seat. So, where the plaintiff was unable to give instructions to his solicitors because he was being held prisoner in Burma and it was impossible to know when he would be released, the court accepted that the plaintiff had given a complete excuse for the delay in the prosecution of his case and the application to dismiss for want of prosecution was refused: *Akhtar v. Harbottle (Mercantile* (1982) 126 Sol. Jo. 643. See also *Spriggs v. Norrard Trawlers Ltd* [1969] 2 Lloyd's Rep. 627, a case concerning trawlermen with very little time ashore and evidence that was difficult to collect).

6. Negotiations—no excuse for delay Litigants who mislead themselves into thinking that fruitless negotiations are going somewhere have only themselves to blame if they allow time to pass by. Sporadic attempts at settlement have been held to be no excuse for letting an action go to sleep. There is generally no reason why negotiations should not be pursued simultaneously with the advancement of the litigation: *Fort Sterling Ltd v.*

South Atlantic Cargo Shipping N.V. ("The Finnrose") [1984] 1 Lloyd's Rep. 559 at 564. Against that, however, if the defendant expressly agrees with the plaintiff that the plaintiff should take no further step in the action pending attempts at settlement, the defendant can hardly be seen to be accusing the plaintiff of inexcusable delay in respect of the negotiation period, since it was he who expressly excused the delay.

7. Uncertain prognosis—a possible excuse In *Marston v. Lee-Leviten* [1968] 1 W.L.R. 1214 the Court of Appeal considered that where the plaintiff's solicitor in good faith and in the client's best interests took the view that it would be wrong to bring the case on to trial until after an assessment could be made of the effect of the injuries on the plaintiff's shoulder after she had commenced work, such delay was excusable.

> "Why should the court be made to listen to conjecture on a matter which would become an accomplished fact? Why should the court be asked to guess when it can calculate? Why, with the light before it, should the court be made to grope in the dark?" *Per* Sachs L.J. in *Marston v. Lee-Leviten* at [1968] 1 W.L.R. 1220.

8. The split trial alternative This was, however, a case in which liability had been admitted. It is doubtful whether the court would adopt that approach where liability remains an issue. Clearly, the plaintiff's solicitor should consider the feasibility of seeking an order under Ord. 33 r.4(2) for a split trial so that the issue of liability could be determined before any issue as to quantum.

9. Delay pending appeal—no excuse In *Thomas Storey Engineers Ltd v. Wailes Dove Bitumastic Ltd, The Times,* January 21, 1988, the court had stayed the proceedings pending the provision of security for costs by the plaintiff company which had gone into receivership. The plaintiff appealed the security for costs order. The plaintiff took no step in the action for two years pending the appeal. The Court of Appeal held that the plaintiff's conduct in doing so was inexcusable. The plaintiff should have considered whether the action was worth pursuing and, if so, it should then have considered what the likely amount of security for costs would be and then make an offer. Alternatively, it should have complied with the order pending the appeal.

10. Legal aid delays—a possible excuse Some support for the proposition that delay caused by the processing of the plaintiff's legal aid application may amount to an excuse is to be found in *Trill v. Sacher* [1993] 1 All E.R. 961.

11. Disability—another excuse Time does not run against a person under disability: section 28 Limitation Act 1980. For that reason, proceedings by a person under permanent disability should not be struck out for want of prosecution: *Turner v. Malcolm Ltd* (1992) 126 S.J. (LB) 236. Neither does it run against an infant: *Tolley v. Morris* [1979] 1 W.L.R. 592; [1979] 2 All E.R. 561, H.L.; and for the same reason an infant's action should not be struck out for want of prosecution.

12. Excuses—evidential burden Although the burden is on the defendant to establish the inexcusable nature of the delay, once he establishes that the delay was inordinate, as a rule, the natural inference is that the delay is also inexcusable until the plaintiff supplies a credible excuse: *Allen* [1968] 1 All E.R. at 561F. The plaintiff should remember, however, that the discretion of the court can only be exercised on material before the court. If no explanation for the delay is given at all, the court has nothing on which to act: *Saville v. Southend Health Authority* [1995] 1 W.L.R. 1255, C.A.

13 Prejudice or impossibility of fair trial

1. No prejudice—no dismissal A defendant who cannot establish that he has been or is likely to be prejudiced by the plaintiff's inordinate and inexcusable delay, or that a fair trial is no longer possible, will not succeed in having the plaintiff's action struck out for want of prosecution: *Marston v. Lee-Leverton* [1968] 1 W.L.R. 1214: *Pryer v. Smith* [1977] 1 All E.R. 218. In refusing to strike out the action, the court has the jurisdiction to make a conditional order requiring the plaintiff to take specified steps to compel him to get on with the action on pain of having it struck out on breach of the time limits imposed by the order: *Pryer v. Smith* (above).

2. Meaning of prejudice "Prejudice" simply means some detriment to the defendant. The existence or otherwise of prejudice is a matter of fact and degree. In addition to any inference that may properly be drawn from the delay itself, prejudice can sometimes be directly proved (see p. 502 below). As a rule, the longer the delay, the greater the likelihood of serious prejudice at the trial: *Allen* [1968] 1 All E.R. at 561.

3. Prejudice through late issue of writ We have seen (at p. 493) that time which has elapsed before the issue of the writ within the limitation period is not by itself relevant delay. It therefore follows that a defendant cannot rely on any prejudice caused to him by the late issue of his writ within the limitation period. Some additional prejudice after the issue of the writ must be shown: *Birkett v. James* [1977] 2 All E.R. 801 at 809.

4. Only more than minimal additional prejudice In *Birkett v. James* [1978] A.C. 297 at 323; [1977] 2 All E.R. 801 at 809 it was said:

> "The additional prejudice need not be great compared with that which may have been already caused by the time elapsed before the writ was issued; but it must be more than minimal; and the delay in taking a step in the action if it is to qualify as inordinate and prejudicial must exceed the period allowed by rules of court for taking that step."

5. Dim memories More often than not, the prejudice will be to the defendant's case itself. The fact and extent of the prejudice may well vary according to the nature of the issues to be decided. So the evidence of an eye witness or a witness who will testify to the words used when an oral representation was made is likely to be much more seriously impaired by the lapse of time than the evidence of someone who can rely on contemporary documents: see, *e.g. Trill v. Sacher* [1993] 1 All E.R. 961 at 980; *National Insurance Guarantee Corporation Ltd v. Robert Bradford & Co. Ltd* (1970) 114 S.J. 436 C.A. Where there has been prolonged culpable delay following a long delay in the service of the writ, the court may readily infer that memories have further deteriorated in the period of that culpable delay: *Benioit v. Hackney Borough Council* (unreported, February 11, 1991). Another frequent form of prejudice occurs were witnesses may have moved away or become untraceable: *Trill v. Sacher* (above).

6. Are bald assertions sufficient? In *Hornagold v. Fairclough Building Ltd, The Times*, June 3, 1995; [1993] P.I.Q.R. P400 Roch L.J. stated that there has to be more than a bold assertion by the defendant that the plaintiff's delay has caused him prejudice or has created a substantial risk that a fair trial would not be possible. He said that the defendant needs to identify and particularise the alleged prejudice. There has to be some indication of the prejudice; for example, that no statement was taken at the time of the material events so that a particular witness who would have been called on a particular issue has no means of refreshing his memory; or that a particular witness who was to be called on a particular issue was of an advanced age and no longer wished to give evidence or had become infirm and unavailable in the period of the inordinate and inexcusable delay. It is, he stated, incumbent on a defendant always to identify the particular respects in which his position has been impaired: *Hornagold v. Fairclough Building Ltd, The Times*, June 3, 1995; [1993] P.I.Q.R. P400; see also *Rowe v. Glenister, The Times*, August 7, 1995.

7. A different view The judgment of Roch L.J. in *Hornagold* was somewhat at variance with the judgment of Glidewell L.J. in the same case. In the course of his judgment as reported in [1993] P.I.Q.R. P400 at 414, Glidewell L.J. said:

> "However, evidence of this specific kind is not essential, nor in my judgment is it always necessary for a defendant in order to succeed in an application to strike out, to identify a specific witness or passage of time. I agree with those judges who have said that there is something faintly ludicrous in the idea that a defendant should be required to put in evidence an affidavit from a witness who says in effect:
>
> > 'My recollection of the events of this accident was reasonably clear after four years, but now that six years have elapsed I have very little recollection.' "

8. A difference resolved This variance was believed to have been resolved in the House of Lords by the speech of Lord Browne-Wilkinson in *Roebuck v. Mungovin* [1994] 2 W.L.R. 290 at 296F where, having referred to the difference of opinion in *Hornagold* as to whether it is necessary to adduce specific evidence that prejudice flowed from a loss of memory in particular period, continued:

> "I have no doubt that such evidence is not necessary and that a judge can infer that any substantial delay at whatever period leads to a further loss of recollection. But even to attempt to allocate prejudice to one rather than another period of delay is artificial and unsatisfactory."

9. Provisional Conclusion—prejudice may be direct or inferred It appears, therefore, on these authorities that on appropriate facts a judge may infer prejudice to a defendant from the mere passage of time if, in all the circumstances, common sense dictates that the passage of time will have weakened the recollection of material witnesses in such a way as to cause prejudice or jeopardise a fair trial: *Sparrow v. Sovereign Chicken Ltd* C.A.T. June 8, 1994, (unreported). In *Sparrow*, Kennedy L.J. stated that what the court should do when faced with the issue of prejudice is to look first at the issues in the case as identified in the statement of claim and in the further and better particulars. Having identified the issues, it should then look at the affidavit evidence to see whether, as a result of delay, the defendant has been more than minimally prejudiced. Finally, he said that a court could be led to the conclusion that there had been more than minimal prejudice either by direct evidence, for example, evidence that a critical witness had died or become unavailable, or as a matter of inference, the inference being drawn from the fact that important witnesses were now saying that as a result of culpable delay they no longer have any clear recollection: see also *Sylvester Alexis v. Fernon Liverpool* (1994) (unreported) C.A.T. June 22.

10. Differences rumble on Notwithstanding the guidance given by Lord Browne-Wilkinson (above), the differences still rumbled on afterwards. In *Slade v. Adco Ltd*, *The Times*, December 7, 1995, the Court of Appeal held (by a majority) that a mere assertion of prejudice caused by inordinate or inexcusable delay was not enough. The individual judge should be left to assess the prejudice, the risk to a fair trial and the adequacy of the evidence in the circumstances of the case and it would be unwise to hamper the exercise of the judge's discretion by strict guidelines.

11. *Shtun v. Zaljeska*—the test in witness recollection cases There is no doubt that confusion abounded on the question as to whether specificity of proof of prejudice to the defendant was always required or whether, in appropriate circumstances, prejudice could be inferred. The authorities showed differences of approach within the Court of Appeal. For instance, the approach adopted by Roch L.J. in *Hornagold* and by Waite L.J. and Sir Christopher Slade in *Rowe v. Glenister* and by Auld L.J. in *Slade v. Adco* appeared to be somewhat at variance with the approach adopted by Stuart-Smith L.J. in *Leniston v. Phipps* (C.A.T. October 21, 1988) and *Behoit* and of Glidewell L.J. in *Hornagold* and *Slade v. Adco*; and of Neill L.J. in *Slade*; and Lord Browne-Wilkinson in *Roebuck v. Mungovin*. A comprehensive review of all the authorities on the need or otherwise of proof of prejudice was conducted by Neill, Gibson and Hobhouse L.JJ. in March 1996 in *Shtun v. Zaljeska*, [1996] 3 All E.R. 411, C.A. After referring to these differences of approach, Peter Gibson L.J. continued:

"But as I read the authorities, all the judges are agreed that in appropriate circumstances inferences can be drawn. Each case must turn on its own particular facts. I reject the submission of [counsel for the plaintiff] that the decision of this court in *Rowe v. Glenister* on its particular facts is determinative of the outcome of this appeal on its different facts. In my judgment, in order to determine whether a defendant has suffered the necessary prejudice when it is in the form of the impairment of witnesses' recollections as a result of inordinate and inexcusable post-writ delay, the court must examine with care all the circumstances of the case, including both the affidavit evidence as well as the issues disclosed by the pleadings. It is not, in my judgment, essential in every case that there should be evidence of particular respects in which potential witnesses' memories have faded, still less that it need be shown that such fading of memories occurred in a particular period. That would be to approve of the classically inept question in cross-examination: 'When did you first forget?' Every court in the land is accustomed to drawing inferences from primary facts. So long as there are primary facts from which inferences can

503

properly be drawn, there is nothing wrong in doing so."

12. *Shtun* test—a matter of fact In *Shtun* Hobhouse L.J., stated that it was unreal to expect a defendant in a witness recollection case to do more at the stage of his application for dismissal than demonstrate the existence of the substantial risk of the unreliability of a witness' recollection. He emphasised that the question in each case remains one of fact: the drawing of inferences and the assessment of risk. He continued:

> "Authorities do not help. The judge has to arrive at his own conclusion on the material before him and the whole of the circumstances of the relevant case."

13. *Shtun*—factors to be considered Neill L.J. agreed that each case will depend upon its own facts and stated that it is not helpful to lay down hard and fast rules. But he attempted to give guidance on those factors to be taken into account in evaluating the defendant's case. These include:
(a) the issues in the case;
(b) the evidence which is or is likely to be available and how far this will be oral or documentary;
(c) the time which has elapsed since the relevant events;
(d) the degree of prejudice which was or is likely to have been suffered in the pre-writ period;
(e) the degree of prejudice which has been or is likely to have been caused by the inordinate and inexcusable delay.
Finally, he stated that it was the "judge's task on a dismissal application to assess the *likely* effect on the trial and on the defendant's ability to put his case forward and the judge must therefore draw inferences based on all the material before him".

14. Lord Browne-Wilkinson's dicta not obiter In *Shtun*, it was contended that Lord Browne-Wilkinson's dicta in *Roebuck v. Mungovin* [1994] 2 W.L.R. 296F, that a judge can infer a further loss of recollection from any substantial delay, were obiter. In *Shtun*, Neill L.J. firmly rejected that contention.

15. *Postscript*—good practice Whilst it must now be regarded as settled that the court may, in appropriate circumstances, infer post-writ prejudice, it is clear that it is for the defendant to set out clearly in his supporting affidavit an explanation of the nature and extent of the likely prejudice which he alleges he will suffer. Except where the existence of prejudice is too plain for argument the onus is on the defendant to lay before the court material on which it is permissible to draw the inference of prejudice. A failure to do so, may well arouse the suspicion that the defendant's application is all Micawberism.

16. Other forms of prejudice Must the defendant establish prejudice in the conduct of his defence, or is he at liberty to establish a form of prejudice beyond the confines of the case itself? In *Antcliffe v. Gloucester Health Authority* [1992] 1 W.L.R. 1044 the defendant health authority sought to rely on prejudice to their organisation of a financial nature, rather than prejudice in the conduct of the case itself. Until January 1990 claims against health authorities arising out of an employed doctors' negligence were met out of the funds of the Doctors' Medical Defence Organisation. Thereafter claims of less than £300,000 including costs fell to be met by the health authorities themselves. The defendants contended that, had the action been concluded by 1989, they would not have been adversely affected by these new insurance arrangements. The judge at first instance drew a distinction between prejudice to the defendant and prejudice to the defendant's case:

> "So, in the present case, if one accepts that the relevant question is not 'has the defendant been prejudiced?' but 'had the defendant's case been prejudiced?' then insurance is irrelevant."

The Court of Appeal said that the judge had misdirected himself and held that prejudice is not confined to the defendant's case but extends to the defendant's financial interests.

17. Examples of other kinds of prejudice This and other authorities establish that other forms of prejudice may be relevant. In *Chris Smaller (Transport) Ltd* [1989] A.C. 1197 Lord Griffiths said (at 1209):

> "... prejudice may be of varying kinds and it is not confined to prejudice affecting the actual conduct of the trial. It would be foolish to attempt to define or categorise the type of prejudice justifying striking out an action but there can be no doubt that if the defendants had been able to establish sufficient damage to their business interest, flowing directly from the culpable delay ... a judge would have been entitled to regard it as prejudice justifying striking out the action."

The decisions in *President of India and Union of India v. John Shaw & Sons (Salford) Ltd, The Times,* October 27, 1977; *Bridgnorth D.C. v. Henry Willcock & Co. Ltd* (1983) C.A.T. 958; *Department of Transport v. Chris Smaller (Transport) Ltd* (above); and *Antcliffe* (above) are all examples of the court accepting business prejudice as a relevant form of prejudice.

18. Anxiety In *Biss v. Lambeth, Southwark and Lewisham Health Authority (Teaching)* [1978] 1 W.L.R. 382 the Court of Appeal considered that the anxiety suffered by nurses whose professional competence was in question was a sufficient prejudice to justify striking the action out.

> "There is much prejudice to a defendant in having an action hanging over his head indefinitely, not knowing when it is going to be brought to trial; like the prejudice to Damocles when the sword was suspended over his head at the banquet. It was suspended by a single hair and the banquet was a tantalizing torment to him": *per* Lord Denning M.R. in *Biss* [1978] 2 All E.R. 125 at 131; see also *Haynes v. Atkins, The Times*, October 12, 1983—the burden of an action hanging over a professional man was relevant prejudice: and also *Electricity Supply Nominees v. Longstaff & Shaw Ltd* (1986) 12 Con LR 1 at 13; and *Ralph v. British Railways Board* (1994) (unreported) C.A.T. May 20.

19. Anxiety—a note of caution The mere existence of litigation neurosis is not of itself a sufficient prejudice to justify striking the action out: *Department of Transport v. Smaller* [1983] 1 All E.R. 897 at 905. In *Eagle Trust Co. Ltd v. Pigott-Brown* [1985] 3 All E.R. 119 at 124, Griffiths L.J. said:

> "... any action is bound to cause anxiety, but it would as a general rule be an exceptional case where that sort of anxiety alone would found a sufficient ground for striking out in the absence of evidence of any particular prejudice. *Biss*'s case is an example of such an exceptional case, the action hanging over for 11 and a half years with professional reputations at stake."

Although the "anxiety" cases are concerned with the anxiety caused to professional people, there is no reason in principle why anxiety cannot equally amount to prejudice to non-professionals.

20. Increase in size of claim An increase in a defendant's liability for damages caused by the plaintiff's inordinate and inexcusable delay in bringing the claim to trial may constitute financial prejudice justifying the dismissal of the action: *Hayes v. Bowman* [1989] 1 All E.R. 293; *Newman v. Hopkins, The Times*, December 28, 1988; *Martin v. Turner* [1970] 1 All E.R. 256 (where the defendant was deprived of the opportunity to pay into court by the plaintiff's delay). On the other hand, in *Gahan v. Szerelmeg (U.K.) Ltd* (1993) 4365 Gaz. 26, the defendant had succeeded in getting the plaintiff action struck out at first instance, having established that the plaintiff's inordinate and inexcusable delay had caused serious prejudice to the defendant in the form of a substantial increase in the damages payable. The Court of Appeal allowed the plaintiff's appeal ([1996] P.I.Q.R. P83) on the ground that the judge had failed to take in to account the value to the defendant of having in hand money, which but for the delay, we would have had to pay the plaintiff by way of damages.

14 Delay and prejudice—causal link

1. Tracing the cause A causal link must be established between the delay and the prejudice to the defendant or the inability to have a fair trial: *Rath v. Lawrence* [1991] 3 All E.R. 679 at 688. When considering the question of prejudice and, if it is raised, the question whether there is a substantial risk that it will not be possible to have a fair trial of the issues in the action, the court will look at all the circumstances. It will look at the periods of inordinate and inexcusable delay for which the plaintiff or his advisors are responsible and will then seek to answer the questions: Has *this* delay caused or is it likely to cause serious prejudice, or is there a substantial risk that because of *this* delay it is not possible to have a fair trial of the issued in the action? *Per* Neill L.J. in *Trill v. Sacher* [1993] 1 All E.R. 961 at 980.

2. Culpable delay linked to relevant prejudice Prejudice is treated differently according to the period when it was suffered. Prejudice caused by the plaintiff's tardiness in issuing the proceedings until shortly before the expiration of the limitation period, taken in isolation, is irrelevant in the sense that it cannot be relied on by the defendant on an application to dismiss for want of prosecution. Relevant prejudice is first that prejudice which may occur after the issue of the proceedings but before the expiry of the limitation period; and secondly, that prejudice which the defendant suffers after the expiry of the limitation period. In *Manama Holdings S.A. v. Marnbeni Corporation* (1994) (unreported) C.A.T. June 24, the Court of Appeal held that the judge, who had taken into account the whole of the delay since the cause of action arose in determining whether the defendants had been prejudiced, had misdirected himself in so doing. The defendants were not entitled to claim prejudice about the whole course of events from the date of the cause of action until the time when the action would come on for trial but only prejudice in respect of culpable delay. Dillon L.J. continued:

> "That is an issue arising as a result of *Birkett v. James*. For the reasons explained in that case and *The Department of Transport v. Smaller*, that is always difficult to apply, but it is clear from the decison of the majority of this court in the unreported case of *Hollis v. Islington L.B.C.* in 1989, which was adopted by all three members of the court in the reported case of *Rath v. C.S. Lawrence* [1991] 1 W.L.R. 399 that it is not necessary to consider the prejudice only in relation to culpable delay which took place after the expiration of the limitation period; it is possible to add together the culpable delay after the issue of the writ, and before the expiration of the limitation period, with further culpable delay after the expiration of the limitation period in

considering whether the culpable delay has caused prejudice. That approach in *Rath v. C.S. Lawrence* seems to be in line with the view expressed by Lord Browne-Wilkinson in *Roebuck v. Mungovin* as to the general discretion that the court has to consider the case in the light of all the circumstances."

Nevertheless, evaluation of the degree of prejudice caused by delay since the issue of the writ is likely to require consideration of the context of such delay and, therefore, of the effect of the total lapse of time since the events giving rise to the dispute: *James Investments (I.O.M.) Ltd v. Phillips Cutler Phillips Troy, The Times*, September 16, 1987.

3. Defendant's own fault It follows that if the prejudice caused or that is likely to be caused to the defendant, or the risk of an unfair trial, has been brought about by the defendant's own conduct, he will not succeed in getting the action struck out: *Austin Securities Ltd v. Northgate & English Stores Ltd* [1969] 2 All E.R. 753; *Trill v. Sacher* (above).

4. Fault on both sides Similarly, where there has been delay on the part of both parties, the court will look at both parties' conduct and the more significant the defendant's contribution to the delay, the less likely he is to succeed in his application to strike out: *Austin* (above); *Banco Popolare Di Novara v. John Levanos & Sons Ltd* (1973) 117 S.J. 509.

5. Letting sleeping dogs lie Speaking in *Birkett v. James* about the delays prior to 1967 (the year in which *Allen* was heard), Lord Salmon commented (at [1978] A.C. 329):

> "Defendants' solicitors might no doubt take out applications to dismiss for want of prosecution or for peremptory orders to compel the plaintiffs to get on with their actions. Not unnaturally they rarely did so, relying on the maxim that it is wise to leave sleeping dogs lie. They had good reason to believe that a dog which had remained unconscious for such long periods of time might well die a natural death with no expense to their client; whereas, if they were to take the necessary steps to force the action to trial they would be merely waking up a dog for the purpose of killing it at great expense to their clients which they would have no chance of recovering."

6. A wiser option So the defendant can with propriety wait until he can successfully apply to the court to dismiss for want of prosecution: *Allen* (above). But a defendant should beware, lest an attempt be made by the plaintiff to show that the defendant was by his inactivity content to allow matters to drift and so has effectively contributed to any prejudice which he alleges he has suffered or is likely to suffer. A wiser course than inactivity would be to warn the plaintiff to get on with the action on pain of a strike out application if he fails to do so. The plaintiff cannot, however, complain if the defendant fails so to warn him: *Zimmer Orthopaedic Ltd v. Zimmer Manufacturing Co. Ltd* [1968] 2 All E.R. 309 at 311.

7. Defendant's further acquiescence We have seen that in an application to dismiss an action for want of prosecution the defendant's conduct of the action is always relevant. So far as he himself has been responsible for unnecessary delay, he obviously cannot rely on it. But also if, after the plaintiff has been guilty of inordinate and inexcusable delay which has prejudiced him, the defendant so conducts himself as to induce the plaintiff to incur further expense in pursuing the action, that conduct of the defendant, whilst not in law constituting an absolute bar preventing him from obtaining a striking out order, is nevertheless a relevant factor to be taken into account by the court in exercising its discretion whether or not to strike out the claim. The weight to be attached to the defendant's conduct will depend on the circumstances of the case: *Roebuck v. Mungovin* [1994] 1 All E.R. 568 overruling *County and District Properties Ltd v. Lyell* [1991] 1 W.L.R. 683. The matter is one of discretion for the court, depending on the balance between the harm done to the defendant by the plaintiff's delay and the expense or other detriment incurred by the plaintiff by reason of the defendant's representation. The introduction into this area of the law of concepts of waiver, acquiescence or estoppel was discouraged in *Roebuck* as being confusing.

8. Need for additional prejudice? It had been held in *Culbert v. Westwell & Co.* [1993] P.I.Q.R. P54 C.A., that when a defendant had been estopped from relying on the plaintiff's inordinate and inexcusable delay which had caused him prejudice, the defendant had to establish not only further (post-estoppel) inordinate and inexcusable delay but that such post-estoppel delay had caused additional prejudice and the defendant could not merely rely on the prejudice caused by the totality of the plaintiff's delay. It was this failure to show such additional prejudice caused by the later delay which defeated the defendant's application to strike out in *Harwood v. Courtaulds Ltd*, *The Times*, February 1, 1993, and in *Roebuck v. Mungovin*. Lord Browne-Wilkinson in *Roebuck* (at [1994] 1 All E.R. 572) went back to the basic principles as laid down in *Allen*, where Lord Diplock had said (at [1968] 1 All E.R. 563):

"But it must be remembered that the evils of delay are cumulative, and even when there is active conduct by the defendant which would debar him from obtaining dismissal of the action for excessive delay by the plaintiff anterior to that conduct, the anterior delay will not be irrelevant if the plaintiff is subsequently guilty of further unreasonable delay. The question will then be whether as a result of the whole of the unnecessary delay on the part of the plaintiff since the issue of the writ there is a substantial risk that a fair trial of the issues in the litigation will not be possible."

It follows that it is not necessary for the defendant to establish that he has suffered additional prejudice following the subsequent (post-estoppel) inordinate and inexcusable delay of the plaintiff in order to succeed in having the action struck out.

15 Limitation Act

1. Basic rule Save in exceptional circumstances, an action will not be struck out for want of prosecution before the expiry of the limitation period: *Birkett v. James* [1977] 2 All E.R. 801 at 807. It is not altogether clear how this rule is best explained. It may be that before the limitation period has expired the delay cannot properly be regarded as inordinate. Alternatively, it may be that, thought the delay is both inordinate and inexcusable, the court would not in the ordinary case exercise its discretion to strike the action out because a fresh writ could be issued at once. To do so would only delay the trial: *per* Neill L.J. in *Trill v. Sacher* [1993] 1 All E.R. 961 at 979. For an exception to this rule, see *Wright v. Morris*, *The Times*, October 31, 1988; and also *Spring Grove Services Ltd v. Deane* (1972) 116 S.J. 844. It should also be remembered that time does not run against an infant or other person under disability (see p. 500).

2. Approach after limitation period Once the limitation period has expired, the court is entitled to take account of all the earlier periods of inexcusable delay since the issue of the writ. These periods can include:
  (a) periods of delay occurring before the expiry of the limitation period which at an earlier stage could not be *treated* as inordinate; and
  (b) periods of delay on which at an earlier stage the defendant could not rely because of his own conduct in inducing the plaintiff to incur further costs in the reasonable belief that the action was going to proceed to trial, but which have been revived by subsequent inordinate and inexcusable delay.

16 Issue of second writ

1. Within limitation period There is generally nothing to prevent the plaintiff from issuing a second writ within the period of limitation following the dismissal for want of prosecution of his first action. As we shall see later (at p. 519), dismissal within the period of limitation on grounds of intentional and contumelious behaviour warrants a different approach.

2. After limitation period If the action is struck out for want of prosecution after the expiry of the limitation period, there is little point in the plaintiff issuing a second writ and seeking the court's discretion under section 33 Limitation Act 1980 to override the time limits imposed by that Act, since the prejudice to the plaintiff which has to be considered under section 33 will normally have been brought about by his own inexcusable and inordinate delay in the previous action. If that is so, he cannot rely upon his own prejudice in seeking the disapplication of section 33: *Walkley v. Precision Forging Ltd* [1979] 1 W.L.R. 606.

17. Originating summonses and official referees' business

The same principles apply to the dismissal for want of prosecution of proceedings commenced by originating summons as those which apply to writ actions: *Halls v. O'Dell* [1992] Q.B. 393 C.A. overruling *United Bank v. Maniar* [1988] Ch. 109. Similarly, Ord. 36, r.6(2) gives the official referee the power to dismiss an action on application in default of the plaintiff making application for directions within 14 days of the notice of intention to defend or the order for transfer.

18 County Court

The principles applicable to applications to dismiss for want of prosecution in the High Court apply equally in the county court: *Kirkpatrick v. The Salvation Army Trustee Co. Ltd* [1969] 1 All E.R. 388. The source of the jurisdiction is to be found in C.C.R. Ord. 13, r.2 which enables the court to give such directions as it thinks proper and includes the power to dismiss the action.

19 Arbitrations

1. Arbitration Act 1950—recent amendment Section 102 of the Court and Legal Services Act 1990, enacted on November 1, 1990, made an amendment to the Arbitration Act 1950 by inserting section 13A which came into force on January 1, 1992. So far as is relevant, section 13A reads:

> "13A—(1) Unless a contrary intention is expressed in the arbitration agreement, the arbitrator or umpire shall have power to make an award dismissing any claim in a dispute referred to him if it appears to him that the conditions mentioned in sub-section (2) are satisfied.
> (2) The conditions are—a)that there has been an inordinate and inexcusable delay on the part of the claimant in pursuing the claim; and b) that the delay—(i) will give rise to a

511

substantial risk that it is not possible to have a fair resolution of the issues in that claim; or (ii) has caused, or is likely to cause or to have caused serious prejudice to the respondent..."

2. Section 13A partially retrospective In *L'Office Cherifien v. Yamashita Ltd (The Boucraa)* [1994] A.C. 486 the House of Lords had to consider whether and if so to what extent the new section applied to delay which occurred prior to January 1, 1992. The House held that Parliament was presumed when enacting legislation not to have intended to alter the law applicable to past events and transactions in a manner which was unfair to those concerned in them unless a contrary intention appeared. Accordingly, the question whether an Act was retrospective was to be determined according to whether in a particular case the consequences of reading the statute with the suggested degree of retrospectivity was, having regard to the degree of retrospectivity involved, the value of the rights affected, the clarity of the language used and the circumstances in which the legislation was enacted, so unfair that the words used by Parliament could not have been intended to mean what they might appear to say. On that approach, section 13A of the 1950 Act was partially retrospective, to the extent that it enabled an arbitrator to exercise the power to dismiss any claim be reference to all the "inordinate and inexcusable delay" which had caused the substantial risk of unfairness, including that which had occurred before section 13A came into force, since the section was directed to the situation where the claimant himself had regarded his claim so poorly that he had taken no trouble to enforce it and had been so remiss in exercising his right to call for an award that the award when ultimately rendered might be the outcome of an unfair process. Accordingly, the arbitrator had been entitled to take into account the owner's inordinate and inexcusable delay prior to January 1, 1992 in dismissing the claim.

3. Birkett applies to arbitrations An argument was advanced in *James Lazenby & Co. v. McNicholas Construction Co. Ltd* [1995] All E.R. 820 that the principles established in *Birkett* should not be extended to arbitrations which are designed to achieve speedy resolutions of disputes. Rix J. rejected the argument and held that the power to dismiss arbitration claims and the corresponding power in litigation were clearly intended to be exercised in the same way.

4. Arbitration appeals It would seem that different considerations apply to applications to dismiss arbitration appeals for want of prosecution. In *Secretary of State for the Environment v. Euston Centre Investments Ltd* [1994] 3 W.L.R. 1081, John Cherryman Q.C. sitting as a deputy judge of the High Court had held that the rule in *Birkett v. James* did not apply to arbitration appeals. Although the judgment was reversed on the facts by the Court of Appeal ([1995] 1 All E.R. 269), it confirmed that the court's inherent power to strike out appeals to the High Court from awards of arbitrators is not limited to cases where the delay had caused serious prejudice, but exercisable whenever there had been a failure to conduct and prosecute the appeal with all deliberate speed. It was held that the object of the Arbitration Act 1979 was to reduce the scope of the supervisory jurisdiction of the English courts and to promote speedy finality in the enforcement of arbitration awards. An application under section 1 of that Act for leave to appeal to the High Court from an arbitration award could be struck out for want of prosecution even if the delay had neither caused nor was likely to cause prejudice to the other party.

20 Practice and procedure

1. Issue and service of application Application to dismiss for want of prosecution in the High Court is made by summons to the master or district judge in chambers and in the county court by notice of application to the district judge in chambers. The application should be supported by affidavit demonstrating the nature and extent of the delay and its inordinate and inexcusable qualities coupled, if possible, with specified prejudice to the defendant. Unless the court otherwise orders, the summons must be served on the plaintiff not less than two days before the day specified in the summons for the hearing of the application. In the High Court it must be served within 14 days of its issue and any evidence relied on in support of the application must be served with the summons: R.S.C., Ord. 32, r.3 as substituted by R.S.C. (Amendment) Rules 1994, r.7.

2. Plaintiff's response If the plaintiff opposes the summons, he should file and serve an affidavit in response addressing the matters raised in the defendant's affidavit and, in particular, explaining the reasons for the delay. There is no rule of law which excludes consideration of without prejudice correspondence in relation to applications to dismiss for want of prosecution and other interlocutory applications: *Family Housing Association (Manchester) Ltd v. Michael Hyde & Partners* [1993] 2 All E.R. 567. Similarly, where there has been a payment into court, the court may be informed of this on an interlocutory application if it is relevant: *Williams v. Boag* [1940] 4 All E.R. 246, C.A.

In the High Court the fee payable is £20. No fee is payable in the county court.

3. Appeals from master An appeal from the decision of a master or district judge lies as a right to a High Court judge in chambers: R.S.C., Ord. 58, r.1(1). The notice of appeal must be issued within five days of the decision appealed against (seven days in the case of an appeal from a district judge: Ord. 58, r.3(2)). This time may be extended by the master and the time limited by the master may be extended by the judge after such time has expired or the five-day period has elapsed. The judge has power to increase the time at the hearing of the appeal without the need to take out a chambers summons beforehand: Ord. 58, r.1(3); *Gibbons v. London Financial Association* (1879) 4 C.P.D. 263. The notice of appeal must be served at least two clear days before the hearing: Ord. 58, r.1(3); three clear days in the case of an appeal from a district judge: Ord. 58, r.3(2). The appeal is by way of re-hearing. The judge may admit additional evidence by affidavit beyond that which was before the master or district judge.

4. County court—appeal from district judge In the county court a right of appeal from the decision of the district judge lies to a circuit judge. An order made on an application to strike the action out for want of prosecution would appear to be an interlocutory order and as such the circuit judge will hear the matter *de novo*: C.C.R. Ord. 13, r.1(10): Ord. 37, r.6. The notice of appeal stating the grounds of appeal must be served within 14 days of the day on which the district judge gave his decision: Ord. 37, r.6(2).

5. Appeals to the Court of Appeal

(a) *Interlocutory character of order:* An order striking out an action or other proceedings or any pleading under Ord. 18, r.19 or under the inherent jurisdiction of the court and orders dismissing or striking out actions or other proceedings for want of prosecution are interlocutory orders for the purpose of appeals to the Court of Appeal: R.S.C. Ord. 59, r.1A(k) and (l).

(b) *Errors in principle only:* The Court of Appeal will not lightly interfere with the exercise by the judge of his discretion: *Birkett*. The court starts with the presumption that the judge has rightly exercised his discretion: *Charles Osenton & Co. v. Johnston* [1942] A.C. 130 at 148.

(c) *A reviewing function:* In *Ward v. James* [1966] 1 Q.B. 273, it was said that the Court of Appeal can and will interfere if it is satisfied that the judge was wrong. An appellate court will regard its function primarily as a reviewing function and will recognise that the decision below involves a balancing of a variety of different considerations upon which the opinion of individual judges may reasonably differ as to their relative weight. Accordingly, unless intervention is necessary or desirable in order to achieve consistency where there appear to be conflicting schools of judicial opinion, the appellate court will only interfere where the judge has erred in principle: Neill L.J. in *Trill v. Sacher* [1993] 1 All E.R. 961 at 980.

(d) *Reasons:* When dealing with an application to strike out for want of prosecution, the judge should give his reasons in sufficient detail to show the Court of Appeal the basic principles on which he has acted and the reasons that have led to his conclusion: *Eagle Trust Co. Ltd v. Piggott-Brown* [1985] 3 All E.R. 119.

C: DISMISSAL FOR FAILURE TO COMPLY WITH COURT ORDERS

1 Contumelious or Contumacious?

1. Meaning The first limb of the rule in *Birkett v. James* gives the court a discretion to strike an action out where the default by the plaintiff or his lawyers had been intentional and contumelious. The noun "contumely" is defined in the *Shorter Oxford English Dictionary* as "insolent reproach or abuse; insulting or contemptuous language or treatment; scornful rudeness." It is not, however, a necessary prerequisite to the operation of this limb of the rule to establish that the default in the party's conduct of his case is characterised by insolence, scorn or rudeness: *Caribbean General Insurance Co. Ltd v. Frizzell* [1994] 2 Lloyd's Rep. 32 at 37. In *Re Jokai Tea Holdings Ltd* [1993] 1 All E.R. 630 at 641, Sir John Megaw contrasted the two nouns "contumely" and "contumacy" and concluded:

> "With all respect, it seems to me that the word 'contumacious' would be more apt than 'contumelious' in the passages in Lord Diplock's discussion of the effect of failure to comply with a peremptory order in *Allen v. Sir Alfred McAlpine & Sons Ltd* [1968] 1 All E.R. 543 at 556; [1968] 2 Q.B. 229 at 259 and in *Birkett v. James* [1977] 2 All E.R. 801 at 807; [1978] A.C. 297 at 321. 'Contumacy' means 'perverse and obstinate resistance to authority'. Surely it is that characteristic, not 'insolent reproach or abuse', which is a frequent hallmark of a litigant's failure to comply with a peremptory order?"

Accordingly, it is submitted that the plaintiff's intentional and contumacious conduct may warrant the striking out of his action, even though the conduct is not contumelious.

515

2 "Unless" orders

1. What are they? Disobedience to a peremptory order of the court is generally to be treated as contumacious conduct: *Tolley v. Morris* [1979] 1 W.L.R. 592, 603. A peremptory order (more usually described as an "unless" order) is one which provides that unless a specified act is done within a time prescribed by the order, unpleasant consequences will follow, as, for example, the dismissal of the action if the defaulter is the plaintiff, or the striking out of the defence if the defaulter is the defendant.

2. The distinction between perversity and neglect There is a fundamental distinction between the case where a plaintiff disobeys a peremptory order of the court regarding the prosecution of an action and then commences fresh proceedings within the limitation period raising the same cause of action, and the case where the plaintiff's action has been struck out for want of prosecution and he subsequently commences fresh proceedings within the limitation period raising the same cause of action. In the first case the plaintiff is in contempt. Commencing the fresh proceedings constitutes contumacious conduct which entitles the court to strike out the fresh proceedings, whereas in the second case the mere failure of the plaintiff to comply with the procedure or rules of court in the first action does not prevent him commencing the fresh proceedings: *Bailey v. Bailey* [1983] 3 All E.R. 495; *Janov v. Morris* [1981] 1 W.L.R. 1389.

3. Unless orders—the underlying principle The underlying principle is simple. Peremptory orders are meant to be obeyed: *Re Jokai Tea Holdings Ltd* [1992] 1 W.L.R. 1196. It is important that breach of such orders should not be incautiously condoned or overlooked, otherwise the notion that the court will readily allow further time would encourage those who have not troubled to comply with its peremptory orders to apply to set aside default judgments and orders striking out the action: *per* Leggatt L.J. in *Caribbean General Insurance Ltd v. Frizzell* [1994] 2 Lloyd's Rep. 32 at 40; *Ratnam v. Camurasamy* [1965] 1 W.L.R. 8; *Saville v. Southend Health Authority* [1995] 1 W.L.R. 1255.

4. Extending time for compliance In *Samuels v. Linzi Dresses Ltd* [1981] Q.B. 115 at 126H, Roskill L.J. acknowledged that the court has the power to grant an extension of time after non-compliance with an unless order. He said:

> "In my judgment, therefore, the law today is that the court has power to extend the time where an 'unless' order has been made but not complied with; but that it is a power which should be exercised cautiously and with due regard to the necessity for maintaining the

principle that orders are made to be complied with and not to be ignored."

5. Is the struck-out action dead or alive? The concept held prior to *Samuels* that where an action had been struck out following a failure to comply with an unless order, the action was dead so as to deprive the court of jurisdiction to extend time, was rejected in *Samuels*. Even an unless order made by consent following which the action is struck out does not deprive the court of its jurisdiction to reinstate and extend time for compliance under R.S.C. Ord. 3, r.5: *Greater London Council v. Rush & Tomkins* (1984) 81 L.S. Gaz. 2624, C.A.; and see *R. G. Carter (West Norfolk) Ltd v. Ham Gray Assoc. Ltd.*

6. Principles of discretion In determining whether the court should excuse the defaulter for non-compliance with a peremptory order and grant a further extension of time, the relevant question is whether the non-compliance was intentional and contumacious. The court will not be astute to find excuses for such failure because obedience to its orders is the foundation of the court's authority: *Samuels v. Linzi Dresses*; (above, at 126H); and see *Re Jokai Tea Holdings Ltd* (above at 516). In *Caribbean General Insurance Co. Ltd v. Frizzell* (above) the Court of Appeal reversed the judge who had set aside a judgment in favour of the defendant and had granted the plaintiff a fourth extension in which to comply with a peremptory order made against the plaintiff. The Court of Appeal held that he had erred in principle in so doing. In concentrating on the prejudice to the defendants and disregarding the plaintiff's persistent failure to comply with the peremptory orders of the court, the judge failed to ask himself the right question. The combination of repeated and persistent failures to comply with the court's peremptory orders, the absence of any credible excuse for non-compliance and the prejudice caused to the defendants should together have compelled the conclusion that the judgment should stand, and see *Hogg v. Aggerwal, The Times*, August 1, 1995.

7. Non-contumacious conduct It follows from what has been said that if the defaulter (and the burden is on him) can clearly demonstrate that there was no intention to ignore or flout the court's order and that the failure to obey was due to extraneous circumstances, that failure is not to be treated as contumacious or contumelious and therefore will not disentitle the litigant to proceed with his claim or defence: *Re Jokai Tea Holdings* (above); *Grand Metropolitan Nominees (No. 2) Co. Ltd v. Evans* [1993] 1 All E.R. 642; and see *Reed v. Reed* (1984) L.S. Gaz. January 18, 123; *Pereira v. Beanlands* [1996] 3 All E.R. 528. Even in the case of a peremptory order the court will consider whether there was a reasonable and plausible cause for disobedience: *Thornburn v. Mansell* (1982) 133 New L.J. 1062 C.A.

517

8. A trap for the unwary Unless orders are orders that "require a person to do an act" within the meaning of Ord. 42, r.2. For this reason care should be taken to ensure that the order is precisely worded and that it expressly states the date from which time begins to run against the party who is required to comply with the order. The problem which arises if care is not taken is best illustrated by *Hitachi Sales (UK) Ltd v. Mitsui Osk Lines Ltd* [1986] 2 Lloyd's Rep. 574.

9. *Hitachi Sales v. Mitsui*—the facts Mustill J. made an order that the defendants should supply the plaintiffs with further particulars of their defence by a specified date. The defendants failed to do so. The plaintiffs then applied for, and on May 16 1985, obtained an order against the defendant in terms that:

> "Unless the defendants do serve within 14 days the Further and Better Particulars of the points of defence ... the points of defence be struck out and the plaintiffs be at liberty to enter judgment against the defendants for damages to be assessed."

The order was served a few days later on the defendants but was not complied with. On May 29, 1985, the plaintiffs entered judgment in default. Later the defendants applied to have the order and the judgment set aside on the ground that the order was invalid since it did not state the date from which the 14 days was to run and that accordingly it did not comply with the terms of Ord. 42, r.2 ("... a judgment or order which requires a person to do an act must specify the time after service of the judgment or order, or some other time within the act is to be done").

10. Hitachi Sales v. Mitsui—the decision The Court of Appeal held that having regard to the terms of Ord. 42, r.12(1) and the decisions of *Van Houten v. Foodsafe Ltd* (1980) 124 S.J. 227 and *Fulcher v. Berthom Boat Co. Ltd* (May 21, 1984; unreported), the order was irregular and consequently the judgment was also irregular. No starting date had been given for the 14-day period and it was difficult to see what starting date should be given. The judgment was thus set aside. A moment's reflection will show that if the rule were otherwise, it would be possible for a party to be in default of the order before he actually became aware of it.

11. Moral In order to comply with Ord. 42, r.2(1) a peremptory order must either:
  (a) specify the time after service of the order within which the act is to be done; or
  (b) specify some other time for compliance.

12. Form If the defendant or his solicitor attends the hearing of the summons, the order should read "unless the defendant by 4 p.m. on [insert date] ..." If neither the defendant nor his solicitor attends the hearing, the order should read "unless the defendant ... within [   ] days of service of this order on him ..." (See Practice Direction (Peremptory Orders: Form) (1986) 1 W.L.R. 948.)

14. Four-day orders If the order fails to fix any time at all, it is not a nullity but can be cured by a supplementary order—sometimes known as a four-day order—which fixes the time for compliance. The time so fixed is not necessarily four days.

15. Issue of second action We have seen (at p. 487) that there is generally nothing to stop the plaintiff from issuing a second writ within the limitation period following the dismissal of the first action for want of prosecution. The position is thought to be different, however, where the first action has been struck out for non-compliance with a peremptory order—at any rate when the failure stems from contumacious behaviour on the plaintiff's part. Unless he can satisfy the court in the second action that his reasons for not complying with the peremptory order in the first action are excusable, the second action is likely to be stayed as an abuse of the process of the court: *Janov v. Morris* [1981] 1 W.L.R. 1389; [1981] 3 All E.R. 780, C.A. approved in *Palmer v. Birks* (1986) 83 L.S. Gaz. 125, C.A.

D: DISMISSAL FOR NON-COMPLIANCE WITH R.S.C.

1. Preamble

Various rules of court prescribe time limits within which certain procedural steps shall be taken and go on to give the court the power to strike out the action, or as the case may be, the defence for non-compliance with the relevant rule. Mention is made of them below. Then we shall consider (at p. 521 *et seq.*) the approach of the courts in dealing with these failures to observe the rules.

2 The various rules stated

1. Failure to serve statement of claim Unless the court gives leave to the contrary, or the statement of claim is endorsed on the writ, the plaintiff must serve a statement of claim on the defendant either when the writ is served on him or before the expiration of 14 days after the defendant gives notice of intention to defend. Ord. 19, r.1 provides:

"**1.**—Where the plaintiff is required by these rules to serve a statement

519

of claim on a defendant and he fails to serve it on him, the defendant may, after the expiration of the period fixed by or under these rules for service of the statement of claim, apply to the court to dismiss the action, and the court may by order dismiss the action or make such other order on such terms as it thinks just."

2. Failure to give discovery or documents Ord. 24, r.16 provides:

"**16.**—(1) If any party who is required by any of the foregoing rules, or by any order made thereunder, to make discovery of documents or to produce any documents for the purpose of inspection or any purpose or to supply copies thereof fails to comply with any provision of that rule or with that order, as the case may be, then, without prejudice, in the case of a failure to comply with any such provision, to rules 3(2) and 11(1) the court may make such order as it thinks just including, in particular, an order that the action be dismissed or, as the case may be, an order that the defence be struck out and judgment be entered accordingly."

3. Failure to answer interrogatories Ord. 26, r.6(1) provides that if a party fails to answer interrogatories, or to comply with an order requiring him to make a further answer where his previous answer was insufficient, or to comply with a request for further and better particulars of a previous answer, then the court may make such order as it thinks just, including in particular, an order that the action be dismissed or that the defence be struck out.

4. Failure to take out summons for directions As a basic rule (and excluding certain exceptions set out in Ord. 25, r.1(2) including actions where automatic directions apply) the plaintiff must take out a summons for directions within one month after pleadings are deemed to be closed: Ord. 24, r.1(1). If he fails to do this then the defendant may do so or apply for an order to dismiss the action: Ord. 24, r.1(4). Ord. 24, r.1(5) gives the court express power to dismiss the action on an application under Ord. 24, r.1(4).

5. Originating summonses If any party in proceedings begun by originating summons (whether on the claim or counterclaim) defaults in complying with R.S.C. Ord. 28 or an order or direction of the court as to the conduct of the proceedings, the court has power under Ord. 28, r. 10 to dismiss the claim or strike out: *Halls v. O'Dell* [1992] 2 W.L.R. 308, C.A. The Court of Appeal had held that the *Birkett v. James* principles were to be applied in proceedings to discuss an originating summons for want of prosecution. The result was that no such application to discuss was likely to succeed if brought within the limitation period. Limitation periods in Ord. 28 are likely to be considerably longer than, for example, in personal injury litigation. Hence, the need for greater judicial control over the conduct of proceedings under Ord. 28.

6. Failure to set down Whenever the court makes an order providing for trial by a judge (with or without a jury), it must provide a time within which the plaintiff has to set the action down for trial: Ord. 34, r.2(1). If the plaintiff fails to do so, the defendant may either set the action down or apply for the action to be dismissed and the court is expressly given the power to dismiss the action on such an application: Ord. 34, r.2(2).

3 Failure to comply with R.S.C.—the courts' approach

1. A clash of two principles The court has the power to extend the time for compliance with the rules. What approach should it adopt on such applications? In *Costellow v. Somerset County Council* [1993] 1 All E.R. 952, Sir Thomas Bingham M.R. set out the correct approach to resolving the problem which arises at the intersection of two principles. He said (at 959):

> "The first principle is that the rules of court and the associated rules or practice, devised in the public interest to promote the expeditious despatch of litigation, must be observed. The prescribed time limits are not targets to be aimed at or expressions of pious hope but requirements to be met. This principle is reflected in a series or rules giving the court a discretion to dismiss on failure to comply with a time limit ... This principle is also reflected in the court's inherent jurisdiction to dismiss for want of prosecution.
>
> The second principle is that a plaintiff should not in the ordinary way be denied an adjudication of his claim on its merits because of procedural default unless the default causes prejudice to his opponent for which an award of costs cannot compensate. This principle is reflected in the general discretion to extend time conferred by Ord. 3, r.5, a discretion to be exercised in accordance with the requirements of justice in the particular case. It is a principle also reflected in the liberal approach generally adopted in relation to the amendment of pleadings.
>
> Neither of these principles is absolute. If the first principle were rigidly enforced, procedural default would lead to dismissal of actions without any consideration of whether the plaintiff's default had caused prejudice to the defendant. But the court's practice has been to treat such prejudice as a crucial and often a decisive, matter. If the second principle were followed without exception, a well-to-do plaintiff

521

willing and able to meet order for costs made against him could flout the rules with impunity, confident that he would suffer no penalty unless or until the defendant could demonstrate prejudice. This would circumscribe the very general discretion conferred by Ord. 3, r.5 and would indeed involve a substantial re-writing of the rule.

The resolution of problems such as the present cannot in my view be governed by a single universally applicable rule of thumb. A rigid, mechanistic approach is inappropriate."

2. Procedural abuse As is said in *Costellow*, prejudice to the defendant by the plaintiff's failure to comply with a time limit may be crucial and often decisive. So, in *Hytrac Conveyors Ltd v. Conveyors International Ltd* [1982] 3 All E.R. 415, the plaintiff company issued a writ claiming an injunction restraining the defendants from infringing their industrial copyright. Some of the defendants had been employees of the plaintiff company and it was alleged that they had acted in breach of covenant to act faithfully to the plaintiff. The plaintiff executed an *Anton Piller* order. Despite repeated requests from the defendants, the plaintiff had neglected to serve a statement of claim three months later. It became apparent that the plaintiff when issuing the writ did not know the form which its statement of claim would take. The Court of Appeal held that such tactics amounted to procedural abuse and dismissed the action. The court said that since the nature of the common law procedure for civil litigation was not inquisitorial but accusatorial, those who made charges had to state right at the beginning what those charges were and on what facts they were based on. They could not use *Anton Piller* orders as a means of finding out what sort of charges could be made but had to deliver their statement of claim within the time specified within the rules, unless the court ordered otherwise.

6. The defaulter's explanation In *Erskine Communications Ltd v. Worthington, The Times*, July 8, 1991, C.A.T. 725 the appellant submitted that a plaintiff who was late in tendering a statement of claim must furnish a convincing excuse for the delay, in his application for an extension of time for it to succeed. Mustill L.J. retorted:

"I do not agree. I go this far with the appellants, that the reference to an 'excuse' in *Price v. Dannimac Ltd* must have meant 'an acceptable explanation', not a mere assertion that the person in charge of the action forgot the statement of claim or was too busy to get on with it. I also accept, what is obvious, that the tendering of an acceptable excuse such as illness, will prompt a more sympathetic response to the application than if the omission was caused by neglect. Furthermore, there is no doubt, as I have already said, that the party guilty of inexcusable delay in complying with the rules, rather than his opponent, has to make the running when the court is asked to exercise discretion. This is, I believe, all that can be extracted by way of principle from *Revici v. Prentice Hall Inc.* [1969] 1 All E.R. 772, a case in which, it may be noted, the applicant sought an extension of time for appealing and was therefore in a situation in which his opponent had obtained an order which on the face of it was final. But it would be absurd to say that every instance of overstepping the time limit without excuse, however short and however lacking in harmful consequence to the defendant, should be punished by the loss of the action. I am confident that the court in *Price v. Dannimac Ltd* intended no such result." See also *Price v. Dannimac Ltd*, *The Independent*, August 3, 1990.

4. Which application is heard first?

Costellow made it clear that in the great mass of cases, it is appropriate to hear both the plaintiff's summons for an extension of time and the defendant's summons to dismiss at the same time since, in considering what justice requires, the court is concerned to do justice to both parties and the case is best viewed in the round. In *Erskine*, Mustill L.J. deprecated attempts which are made to cram the general discretion conferred by the rules into a set of rigid formulae:

> "In some cases, for example where the real vice is not the plaintiff's breach of a rule, but his consistent delay in prosecuting the action, it will be sensible to look at the dismissal first. In others, the total delay may not be long, so that a fair hearing is still feasible; and yet the plaintiff's breach of the rules may be serious enough, and the immediate consequences sufficiently damaging, to justify a course which enables the defendant to have the action disposed of with all the attendant costs even if at some later date a properly prepared and conducted action can be started afresh. In still other cases, the factors weighing in the scales of justice may be substantially the same, which ever of the cross applications is considered."

5. Is there a difference in the standard and burden of proof?

In *Erskine* it was submitted by the defendant appellants that there is a difference between the standards to be applied where the plaintiff requires an extension of time for delivering his statement of claim and that where the defendant seeks to have the action dismissed; and that the burden of proof is different in the two cases. Mustill L.J. was willing to accept that an application to extend time in the context of the failure to comply with rules of court may be approached in a rather different light from an application to dismiss for want of prosecution. He was ready to accept that the principles, so far as there are any, governing the application to extend and the application to dismiss may on occasion require the facts to be looked at in a rather different perspective, but emphasised that what he was talking about was shades of emphasis. In the end the test was what was most fair in the circumstances of the individual case.

6. *Costellow*—the principle stated

Following his review of the relevant authorities, Sir Thomas Bingham M.R. concluded in *Costellow* that cases involving procedural abuse (such as *Hytrac Conveyors Ltd v. Conveyors International Ltd* (above) or questionable tactics (such as *Revici v. Prentice Hall* (above) may call for special treatment. So also would cases of contumelious and intentional default and cases were a default is repeated or persisted in after a peremptory order. But in the ordinary way, and in the absence of special circumstances, a court will not exercise its inherent jurisdiction to dismiss a plaintiff's action for want of prosecution unless the delay, complained of after the issue of the proceedings, has caused at least a real risk of prejudice to the defendant. A similar approach, he said, should govern applications made under Ords.19, 24, 25, 28 and 34. The approach to applications under Ord. 3, r.5 should not in most cases be very different. Save in special cases or exceptional circumstances, it can rarely be appropriate, on an overall assessment of what justice requires, to deny the plaintiff an extension (where the denial will stifle his action) because of a procedural default which, even if unjustifiable, has caused the defendant no prejudice for which he cannot be compensated by an award of costs. In short, an application under Ord. 3, r.5 should ordinarily be granted where the overall justice of the case requires that the action be allowed to proceed. See also *Greek City Co. Ltd v. Demetriou* [1983] 2 All E.R. 91.

E: DISMISSAL FOR NON-COMPLIANCE WITH COUNTY COURT RULES

1 Introduction

1. A stricter regime? The principles of law and procedure in the High Court so far covered in this chapter apply equally in the county court. There are, however, some rules applicable in the county court which have no corresponding provision in the R.S.C. These need to be noted since a stricter regime seems to be emerging in the county court than that which obtains in the High Court—at any rate in relation to securing the parties' compliance with rule-made time limits.

2 C.C.R., Order 9 rule 10

1. Striking out default action after 12 months C.C.R. Ord. 9, r.10 provides:

> "Where 12 months have expired from the date of service of a default summons and—
>
> (i) no admission, defence or counterclaim has been delivered and judgment has not been entered against the defendant, or
>
> (ii) an admission has been delivered but no judgment has been entered under rule 6(1) or, as the circumstances may require, no notice of acceptance or non-acceptance has been received by the proper officer, the action shall be struck out and no enlargement of the period of 12 months shall be granted under Order 13 Rule 4.

2. Is the strike-out automatic? Suppose, after service of the particulars of claim the defendant requests and obtains a general extension of time from the plaintiff in which to serve and file a defence. Suppose further that more than 12 months expire before the plaintiff calls on the defendant to serve a defence. In *Heer v. Tutton* [1995] 1 W.L.R. 1335 the Court of Appeal heard that, although Ord. 9, r. 10 precluded the court from granting retrospective extension of the 12-month period, an agreement reached between the parties before the expiry of that period was effective to oust the operation of the rule; that, since the court could not always know when the 12-month period had expired, the striking out for which Ord. 9, r. 10 provided could not ordinarily take place automatically but on application by the defendant; that it would be repugnant to ordinary principles to accede to such an application where the defendant had agreed, if not sought, an extension; and that, accordingly, the plaintiff's action would not be struck out.

3. No order or agreement extending time for defence Three weeks or so after *Heer v. Tutton* was decided, a differently constituted Court of Appeal decided in *Webster v. Ellison Circlips Group Ltd* [1995] 1 W.L.R. 1447 that on a true construction of Ord. 9, r. 10, where at the end of the 12-month period, no order or agreement extending the time for delivery of defence had been made and judgement had not been entered, the action was struck out automatically on that date. Glidewell L.J. commented (at 1453 B):

> "There may indeed, as Sir Thomas Bingham M.R. said in *Heer v. Tutton*, be an issue as to precisely when the default summons was served. I do not understand that when the Master of the Rolls said at

p. 1346C, 'it would seem unlikely that the striking out for which Ord. 9, r. 10 provides could take place automatically', he was differing from my view that, on an application being made, the court's task is to decide whether, on the facts proved, the action was struck out at the end of the 12-month period."

3 C.C.R., Order 13, rule 3

1. 12 months' adjournment The court has the power to adjourn the hearing; Ord. 13, r.3(1). If the court had adjourned the hearing generally and no application has been made within the following 12 months for a fresh hearing date, the court may warn the parties that if no application for a fresh hearing date is made within 14 days, the action will be struck out. The provision is rarely invoked because pressure on court staff time does not permit a trawl of court files. This provision is mentioned largely because of the recent introduction of computerisation in the county court system which may give the rule a new lease of life in the future. The provision has no relevance to actions where the court itself fixes (and if necessary refixes) the trial date (as in Liverpool County Court where the general adjournment of actions within the deadline listing system is impermissible).

4 Failure to request date for trial

1. The relevant rules C.C.R. Ord. 17, r.11 lays down a system of automatic directions in county court default and fixed date actions with some exceptions which are irrelevant. These directions, covering discovery and inspection of documents and the disclosure of expert and lay evidence within prescribed time limits, take effect automatically when the pleadings are deemed to be closed (which is 14 days after a delivery of defence or 28 days after delivery of a counterclaim: Ord. 17, r.11(11)(a)).

2. The trigger date This date, the date on which the pleadings are deemed to be closed, has come to be known as "the trigger date" since it triggers the operation of the automatic timetable: *Williams v. Globe Coaches, The Times*, January 18, 1995.

3. The duty to request a hearing date Ord. 17, r. 11(3)(d) imposes a further obligation on the plaintiff:

"Unless a day has already been fixed, the plaintiff shall within 6 months request the proper officer to fix a day for the hearing...".

This period may be extended under Ord. 17, r.11(4).

4. The central rule Ord. 17, r.11(9) contains a draconian provision:

> "If no request is made pursuant to paragraph (3)(d) within 15 months of the day on which pleadings are deemed to be closed (or within 9 months of the expiry of any period fixed by the court for making such a request), the action shall be automatically struck out."

So, the plaintiff has six months from the close of pleadings to request a hearing date and if he does not do so within nine months of the expiry of that six-month period (or of any other period which the court may have fixed for making the request), the action is automatically stuck out. The date on which the action is automatically struck out has unsurprisingly come to be known as the guillotine date: see *Williams v. Globe* (*supra*).

5. Trigger date and delivery of defence Pleadings are deemed to be closed 14 days after the delivery of the defence (or 28 days after delivery of any counterclaim). For the purposes of Ord. 17, r. 11(11), the word "deliver" means the lodging by the defendant of his defence with the court. Accordingly, the commencement of the automatic directions timetable should be calculated by reference to the date of the defendant's delivery of the defence to the court and not by reference to a two-stage process, perfected when the proper officer of the court fulfils his duty under Ord. 9, r. 2(7) to send a copy of the defence to the plaintiff: *Lightfoot v. National Westminster Bank PLC, The Times*, January 18, 1995. If the plaintiff is, however, able to show that the proper officer's failure has caused him real prejudice by his action being struck out in circumstances where it would not otherwise have been, the court's powers are sufficiently ample to enable any genuine injustice to be remedied; *ibid*.

6. Which defence is the trigger? Suppose an action is brought originally against more than one defendant? Is the automatic timetable applicable at all? Or is the trigger date calculated from the date of the first defence? Or from the date of the last defence to be delivered? Or is it to be calculated *vis-à-vis* each defendant from the date of delivery of his defence? In *Peters v. Winfield, The Times*, January 19, 1995, the Court of Appeal held that the trigger date is to be calculated by reference to the date on which the last defendant named in the action as originally issued delivered his defence to the court. The Master of the Rolls acknowledged that the preferred solution was not without its drawbacks and difficulties. For example, what happens when a defendant had not been served; or where he had been but had not delivered a defence. Again, there could be further problems where a named defendant blamed an additional party whom the plaintiff had to join and who would then serve a defence, causing delay after the timetable had begun. The solution, it seems, is that any party finding himself

527

embarrassed by this interpretation should seek a variation of the automatic timetable.

7. N450 generally irrelevant County court form N450 (the notice that automatic directions apply) is routinely sent out by the court staff without any judicial intervention to the parties after delivery of the defence. Its purpose is to give guidance on the steps to be complied with under the automatic timetable: the form provides for the insertion of a date and states that the timetable begins 14 days after that date (or 28 days if a counterclaim is delivered). If the date of delivery of the defence is at variance with the date inserted in form N450, from which date does the timetable run? In *Williams v. Globe, The Times*, January 18, 1995, the Court of Appeal held that the timetable presented by Ord. 17, r. 11 prevailed over any different timetable indicated in form N450 sent out by the county court when acting in our administrative capacity. Where, however, the plaintiff has been misled by reliance on form N450 and in consequence has not requested a hearing date within the period specified by the rules as he otherwise would have done so that his action has been automatically struck out under Ord. 17, r. 11(9) the court will ordinarily accede an application to re-instate the action without requiring him to satisfy the *Rastin* tests (see below). In *Computacenter Maintenance Ltd v. Intersolv plc*, C.A.T. May 12, 1995, (unreported), it was held that the absence of any date in form N450 was not such a procedural irregularity as to invalidate the automatic strike out provisions. Further form N450, containing the automatic directions, is not a judgment or order for the purposes of Ord. 22, r. 3 (which requires that "every judgment or order requiring any person to do an act ... shall state the time within which the act is to be done"). Again, N450 is not analogous with an unless order which is fatally flawed if it fails to provide the starting point for the running of time, since the rules themselves provide the starting point for the purposes of the automatic strike-out provisions.

8. Application to re-instate-procedure Application by the plaintiff to reinstate an action strike out under Ord. 17, r.11(9) is made under Ord. 13, r.4.

9. *Rastin*—the issues *Rastin v. British Steel plc* [1994] 2 All E.R. 641 concerned six actions which had fallen foul of Ord. 17, r.11(9) and which has thus been struck out automatically due to the plaintiff's solicitor's failure to apply timeously for a trial date. Two main issues were raised. First, if an action is automatically struck out under Ord. 17, r.11(9), has the county court jurisdiction to extent the time for compliance retrospectively and so, in effect, reinstate the action? Secondly, if a county court has jurisdiction so to act, on what principles should it exercise its jurisdiction?

10. *Rastin*—decision on first issue The Court of Appeal held in answer to the first issue that the county court has the jurisdiction under Ord. 13, r.4 retrospectively to extend the time for requesting a hearing date following the automatic striking out of an action under Ord. 17, r.9.

11. *Rastin*—the second issue—three hurdles In deciding whether to exercise its jurisdiction to reinstate the action and extend the time for compliance with Ord. 17, r.9, the Court of Appeal held that the plaintiff has to satisfy two threshold requirements as a prerequisite. Only if he clears those two hurdles will the court go on to consider what, in effect, is a third hurdle, namely the interests of justice in a more general way, including any prejudice to the defendant: see also *Reville v. Wright, The Times*, January 18, 1995. The burden of proof lies on the plaintiff in relation to both threshold tests. *Reville v. Wright (supra)*.

12. First threshold test The first threshold condition is that the plaintiff (including his advisers) must be able to show that, save for his failure to comply with r.11(3)(d) he had prosecuted his case with reasonable diligence.

13. Second threshold test The second threshold requirement is that the plaintiff must be able to show that his failure to comply with Ord. 17, r.11(3)(d), whilst never justifiable, must in all the circumstances be excusable.

14. *Birkett* and *Allen* irrrelevant It had been argued on behalf of the plaintiffs in *Rastin* that their application to reinstate should be treated either along the principles established in *Costellow v. Somerset C.C.* (see above, p. 524); or alternatively as the obverse of an application to dismiss for want of prosecution so that if the plaintiff could show that there had been no inordinate or inexcusable delay and no prejudice had been sustained by the defendant and that a fair trial was still possible, the court should reinstate the action. The Court of Appeal emphatically rejected that submission. Sir Thomas Bingham M.R. stated (at [1994] 2 All E.R. 647D):

> "That submission [*i.e.* the *Costellow* submission] gives quite inad-
> equate weight to the fact that in this instance the action has been
> struck out. To accede to it would deprive r.11(9) of its intended
> draconian effect. We also reject the submission that retrospective
> applications to extend time after automatic striking out should be
> treated as the obverse of applications to dismiss for want of pros-
> ecution, with particular attention paid to any prejudice suffered by
> the defendant. We would not readily extend the application of the
> rules laid down in *Allen v. Sir Alfred McAlpine & Sons Ltd* [1968] 1
> All E.R. 543; [1968] 2 Q.B. 229 and *Birkett v. James* [1977] 2 All E.R.
> 801; [1978] A.C. 297 into this new field, and it would in any event be

strange to concentrate on the position of the defendant when the object of the rule is to ensure diligent prosecution of the case by the plaintiff."

See also *Jackson v. Slater Harrison & Co. Ltd, The Times*, January 18, 1995.

15. Reasonable diligence explained: In *Rastin* Sir Thomas Bingham M.R. explained that in seeking to establish that he has acted with reasonable diligence, the plaintiff does not have to show that there is no room to criticise any aspect of his conduct of the case, but that overall he is innocent of any significant failure to conduct the case with expedition, having regard to the particular features of the case: see also *Woodfall v. Northamptonshire C.C.*, C.A.T. March 9, 1995 (unreported); *Kramer v. Landugal*, C.A.T. March 28, 1995 (unreported); *Hoskins v. Wiggins Teape (U.K.) Ltd* [1994] P.I.Q.R. P377; *Gardner v. Southwark L.B.C.*, *The Times*, January 18, 1996.

16. Reasonable diligence—the yardstick In the important case of *Gardner v. Southwark L.B.C.*, (above), the Court of Appeal compared what might be described as the *Allen* approach with the *Rastin* approach. Henry L.J. said:

> "It is fair to say in relation to the plaintiff's solicitors, that judged by the standards of what I might call the 'bad old days', those solicitors did act with the diligence that was then tolerated. They were ignorant of the automatic directions and the time limit therein set out. That is an irony in their case, but it is not one that helps us in the decision that we have to reach.
>
> Viewed against the timetable set out in the rules, the plaintiff's solicitors cannot show that they acted with reasonable diligence in this simple case. Reasonable diligence must be tested against the yardstick for progress set out in the rules, unless it can be shown that an extension would have been given if applied for."

Millett L.J. agreed. He said:

> "In this context diligence must be tested, not by the approach adopted by the court on applications to dismiss for want of prosecution, but by the new timetables laid down by Order 17."

In *Gardner*, the Court of Appeal was at pains to emphasise that *Allen and Birkett* had no place in the new scheme of things under Order 17. Henry L.J. emphasised the point (see also, *Beachley Property Ltd, v. Edgar, The Times*, July 18, 1996):

> "As the Master of the Rolls' judgment in *Rastin* emphasises, in personal injury cases in the county court a new regime is in place, a

regime under which the old leisurely and often ruthless way of
conducting these usually simple cases will not be tolerated. The onus
is initially put on the plaintiff and his advisers. If they do not keep
the pressure on, then the court itself should act to control proceedings
to try to ensure that these cases are tried according to the timetable
laid down in the rules unless justice requires some extension to the
time limits."

17. The duty to prosecute case expeditiously In *Kramer v. Landogal (supra)*
Sir Thomas Bingham M.R. asked of the duty to prosecute the case
expeditiously.

> "What does that mean? In the first place it means that they (the
> plaintiff and his advisers) should comply with the Rules of Court.
> Ord. 17, r. 11 provides a clear statement of the steps to be taken and
> the timetable for taking them ... It is not every minor and trivial no-
> compliance which disqualifies the plaintiff from seeking re-instatement
> if he should fall foul of Ord. 17, r. 11(9). On the other hand, it is
> reasonably required of the plaintiff that he should have made every
> effort to do what was required of him under the Rules in the time
> provided.
>
> What is, therefore in issue in a case of this kind is not whether it
> is possible to identify any nit-picking failure to comply with the Rules,
> but whether there is any significant failure to comply with them".

18. What is a "significant" failure? Sir Thomas went on to consider the
meaning of the phrase "significant failure to conduct the case with
expedition". He said:

> "In my judgment, however, the Learned Judge did fall into error in
> his approach to the meaning of significant. Significant means the
> opposite of insignificant, that is, not trivial and not minor. The judge's
> test—a degree of failure which would affect the doing of justice
> between these particular parties in this particular case—is, in my
> judgment, open to objection on two grounds. First of all, it introduces
> a test of prejudice which the Court of Appeal in *Rastin* was at pains
> to eschew at this first stage; second, it overlooks the fact that these
> provisions are not designed for particular parties in particular cases,
> but for the government of county court cases in general. That is why
> the court may not, in my view, reflect its obvious sympathy for the
> plaintiff by upholding the judge's order, but should insist on a
> principled application of the rules which it is hoped will be of lasting
> benefit to countless plaintiffs other than this plaintiff".

19. Limitation irrelevant As the whole object of the new regime under

531

Order 17 is to ensure the diligent prosecution of the case by the plaintiff, by a parity of reasoning, the Court of Appeal also held in *Gardner* that the mere fact that the limitation period had not expired so that the plaintiff could issue a fresh proceedings is *not* a factor to induce the court to reinstate the action in the same way that it would normally preclude the court from dismissing an action for want of prosecution. It was said that that approach would largely stultify the beneficial effects of the new rule and deprive it of all content in the great majority of cases.

20. Defendant's consent to extension Again, it will not necessarily assist the plaintiff to show (as was the case with one of the defendants in *Gardner*) that even if the plaintiff had requested a hearing date, the defendant was not ready for trial and would have consented to an extension of time in which to apply for a trial date. Millett L.J. said:

> "The new provisions for automatic directions are intended to place a heavy responsibility on the plaintiff and his advisers to bring the case on expeditiously. If the defendants are themselves dilatory, and the plaintiff is ready, the responsibility lies upon the plaintiff to apply for a date for the hearing. If the plaintiff needs further time, and can make out a case for it, he may be able to obtain an extension of time for making the application. The mere fact that the defendants themselves support the application, ought not, in my judgment, to be conclusive, otherwise the parties' solicitors can get together by agreement and in effect obtain an extension of time without applying to the court at all. It is not bound to grant an extension of time to a plaintiff who cannot show good reason for it, and it is not a sufficient reason that the defendants have behaved so dilatorily that they too are not ready."

21. Threshold tests consecutive A month after *Gardner*, Sir Thomas Bingham M.R. took the opportunity to explain *Rastin* further in another unreported case, *Hoskins v. Wiggins Teape (U.K.) Ltd* C.A.T. May 16, 1994 (unreported).

Firstly, he re-emphasised that it is a necessary precondition that the plaintiff, in seeking reinstatement and a retrospective extension of time in which to apply for a trial date, should be able to show that the action has been conducted with reasonable diligence and the question as to whether the failure can be excusable only arises if that condition is overcome. So, the two threshold tests are consecutive, not concurrent: see also *Kramer v. Landugal (supra)*.

22. The two threshold tests linked Once the plaintiff has satisfied the reasonable diligence test, the court will then go on to consider whether his failure to apply within the prescribed time limit for a hearing date was excusable. But the two threshold tests, though separate, are linked. In *Hookins*, Sir Thomas said:

> "If a plaintiff, and his advisers, can show that the action has been conducted with appropriate expedition, the court will be the more likely to regard the failure to make the appropriate application to comply with the rule as excusable if the plaintiff can show that the application was in effect a formality because the court would have been bound, or almost bound, to grant an application for an extension had it been made prospectively."

23. Technical failure—an excuse The more technical the plaintiff's failure to comply with the time limit, the more readily will it be excused. "Technical" here refers essentially to the mere passage of time. The sooner after his failure the plaintiff takes steps to remedy it by seeking reinstatement, the readier the court may be to regard the failure as excusable: *per* Simon Brown L.J. in *Hoskins*.

24. Excuses—the test In *Hoskins*, the Court of Appeal, told by counsel that there was some doubt and argument over the second threshold test, declined the invitation to indulge in any process of exegesis. The Master of the Rolls said:

> "I do not, however, wish to attempt any exhaustive catalogue of what may, or may not, on given facts be regarded as excusable since what the court had in mind was a broad and simple test to be applied by the trial judge who, having concluded that the plaintiffs have conducted the action with at least reasonable expedition, simple has to ask himself: 'In all the circumstances do I regard the failure to comply with the setting down rule as excusable?'."

25. Ignorance—no excuse In *Russell v. Dennis, The Times*, January 18, 1995, the Court of Appeal stated that whether a proffered explanation amounted to an excuse depended on all the circumstances and the nature of the forgetfulness or other shortcoming. In that case there was nothing to suggest that the person having the conduct of the plaintiff's case had received any instruction as to the effect of Ord. 17, r. 11 now that she has had the detail of it in mind, nor that anyone else had given any attention to the date from which the timetable ran. The error was not one which might occur in any well run and properly supervised organisation but was a plain failure to institute a proper system to see that this important risk was observed. The application to re-instate was refused. See also *Birch v. Tesco Stores Ltd* (1995) C.A.T. May 11, 1994, (unreported).

26. Too busy—no excuse Nevertheless, the court did give some examples of what would not be accepted as legitimate excuses. It was, for example, anxious to discountenance the view that a failure to comply with the time limit would be regarded as excusable because the plaintiff's solicitor or legal executive had been so busy that he had not had the time to get round to it.

27. Oversight—no excuse Likewise, where the plaintiff's solicitor had simply forgotten to comply with the time limit, that will afford no excuse. It was rejected on the facts in *Hoskins*. That was the excuse proferred in *Hoskins*. See also *Hackwell v. Blue Arrow plc, The Times*, January 18, 1995.

28. Short illness—no excuse Similarly, it would be no excuse that the plaintiff's solicitor had been ill for a short period.

29. Post goes astray—no excuse Yet again, it was said in *Hoskins* that even if the plaintiff's solicitor's letter requesting a trial date had gone astray, that, too, will not afford an acceptable excuse.

30. *Rastin*—third hurdle—justice If, but only if, the plaintiff has passed the two threshold tests, the court then goes on to consider the interests of justice. It is only at this third stage that questions of prejudice become relevant; see *Rastin (supra); Gardner (supra); Hoskins (supra); Woodford v. Northants C.C. (supra); Kramer (supra).*

31. *High Court transfers* The automatic directions regime under Ord. 17, r. 11 applies to actions commenced in the High Court and subsequently transferred to a county court. The timetable is calculated under Ord. 16, r. 6(1A) which had been amended by Rule 7 County Court (Amendment No. 4) Rules 1991. Under that provision, pleadings are deemed to be closed 14 days after the date of transfer. What remains to be decided authoritatively is the pin-pointing of the date of transfer. Is it the date of the High Court Order for transfer or the date of receipt of the relevant documents by the proper officer of the county court? Where directions have been given in the High Court prior to transfer the automatic directions under Ord. 17 take effect subject to the High Court directions.

32. Pre October 1, 1990 cases The automatic directions regime under Ord. 17, r. 11 does not apply to proceedings commenced before October 1, 1990: (County Courts (Amendment No. 3) Rules 1990, Rule 17). Suppose an action is commenced in the High Court before that date and transferred to a county court after that date. Is the action regulated by the automatic regime or not? In *Glud v. Milton Keynes B.C.* (1995) C.A.T. February 6, (unreported), the defendants sought to argue that, for the purposes of Ord. 17, r. 11, proceedings transferred from the High Court to the county court should be treated as having been commenced in the county court on the date of transfer, thus attracting the automatic regime. Saville L.J. firmly rejected that argument saying that there was nothing in the Rules to support that contention. The Court held that, as the proceedings were commenced (albeit in the High Court) before October 1, 1990, the automatic regime did not apply. In *Tarry v. Humberside Finance Ltd, The Times*, January 19, 1995, a three-man Court of Appeal confirmed that conclusion.

33. Requests for hearing dates The plaintiff requests a hearing date even though he has inexcusably failed to comply with the automatic timetable in other respects. Should the request be treated as an abuse of process? In *Ashworth v. McKay Foods Ltd, The Times*, November 16, 1995, the Court of Appeal held that mere failure to comply with the rules could not amount to such abuse. But it may be possible to establish abuse if it can be shown that the plaintiff acted in wilful or contumacious disregard for the rules or in bad faith or for ulterior reasons.

34. Request defective A request which was not processed by the court staff because the wrong plaint number had been quoted was held nevertheless to have been a valid request despite its defective character. *Gayle v. House of Copiers Ltd* (1995) C.A.T. (unreported).

35. Applications for extension of time to request hearing date In *Ferreira v. American Embassy Employees' Assoc., The Times*, June 30, 1995, the plaintiff applied for an extension of time in which to request a hearing date before the guillotine date. The hearing of that application took place after the guillotine date. The Court of Appeal held that the action had been struck out automatically since the plaintiff's application for an extension of time was by implication to be taken as including a request for a hearing date to be fixed in the event of an extension being refused. (See also *Carr v. Northern Clubs Federation Brewery Ltd, The Times*, January 18, 1996; see also *Goodman v. Ryvita Co. Ltd*, June 19, 1995, C.A., (unreported).)

36. Displacement of Ord. 17, r. 11(3)(d) and (g) In *Downer and Downer Ltd v. Brough, The Times*, January 19, 1995, the issue before the Court of Appeal was: what is the effect on the automatic directions and the requirement to request a hearing date within the prescribed period of an interlocutory direction of the judge that the action is to be listed on the joint application of the parties or (in another case before the court) on the filing of certificates of readiness? The court held that such interlocutory directions have the effect of displacing to that extent the automatic directions regime. The effect is that when such a direction has been given, Ord. 17, r. 11(3)(d) and (g) cease to apply.

37. Second Action—an abuse? Given that the plaintiff's action has been struck out automatically under Ord. 17, r. 11(9), is there anything to prevent him from commencing an identical second action so long as it is commenced within any relevant limitation period? Is there an analogy to be drawn between a failure to comply with automatic directions and disobedience to a peremptory order of the court? The relevance of the question is this; in the case of the commencement of a second action following dismissal of the first action for failure to comply with peremptory order one school of thought considers that the second action can be stopped unless the plaintiff gives a satisfactory explanation for his apparently contumacious behaviour (See *Janov v. Morris* [1981] 1 W.L.R. 1389; [1981] 2 All E.R. 780, C.A. approved in *Palmer v. Birks* (1980) 83 L.S. Gaz. 225, C.A.). Could it be argued that, likewise the plaintiff who has had his action struck out automatically for failure to comply with Ord. 17, r. 11 should be placed in the same position? In *Gardner v. Southwark London Borough Council (No. 2) The Times*, January 18, 1995, the Court of Appeal rejected the attempted analogy. The automatic directions are not akin to a peremptory order. Nor is a plaintiff who has failed to comply with automatic directions to be treated as though guilty of contumacious disobedience to a court order. Of course, the court recognised that the discretion to strike out a second action was never excluded but was retained only to deal with exceptional cases. Further, although the plaintiff can not be precluded from bringing a second action within the limitation period, it is open to the defendant to seek an order staying that action until the plaintiff had paid any costs of the first action which he had been ordered to pay.

38. Conclusion These decisions taken as a whole clearly point the way to an altogether tougher regime for the plaintiff's conduct of litigation than that laid down in *Allen* and *Birkett*. Perhaps the time is rapidly approaching where the House of Lords will be invited to look again at the principles established in *Allen* and *Birkett* in the light of changed attitudes to litigation as this century draws to its close.

F: STAY OF PROCEEDINGS

1 Meaning and object

By granting an order staying the action, the court puts a stop on any further steps being taken in it. The order is only sparingly granted in circumstances where the object is to save the costs and expense of a trial in order to prevent an abuse of court occurring or prejudice being sustained by a party to the action.

2 Limited or general

The order granting the stay may be general, that is without limit in point of time; or limited in the sense that it may be removed upon the occurrence of a defined contingency. In the case of a general stay, application must be made for its removal. In the case of a stay pending the occurrence of a future event, the stay is automatically removed upon the occurrence of that event. A stay pending the plaintiff's submission to medical examination by a doctor nominated by the defendant is a common example of a stay automatically being removed upon the plaintiff's compliance with the condition of the stay.

3 Effect of a stay

A stay does not operate as a dismissal, nor does it constitute a discontinuance of the action since the stay may be removed at a later date.

4 High Court jurisdiction

The sources of the High Court's jurisdiction to stay proceedings are threefold:
   (a) the inherent jurisdiction which was expressly preserved by section 49(3) Supreme Court Act 1981;
   (b) under various provisions of the R.S.C.
   (c) by virtue of particular statutes.
These sources may be invoked concurrently.

5 County court jurisdiction

A county court has, by virtue of section 38 County Courts Act 1984 the same power as the High Court to stay proceedings.

6 Inherent jurisdiction—examples

Under its inherent jurisdiction the court may, for example, stay action:
   (a) Until such time as the plaintiff complies with an order for security for costs: *Whiteley Exerciser Ltd v. Gamage* [1898] 2 Ch. 405.
   (b) Until such time as the plaintiff in a personal injuries action submits to an examination by the defendant's doctor. The examination must be of a reasonable character and must be reasonably required: see

537

generally *Edmeades v. Thames Board Mills* [1969] 2 All E.R. 127, C.A.; *Lane v. Willis* [1972] 1 All E.R. 430; *Starr v. N.C.B.* [1977] 1 All E.R. 243; *Aspinall v. Sterling Mansell Ltd* [1981] 3 All E.R. 866; *Prescott v. Bulldog Tools Ltd* [1981] 3 All E.R. 869; *Hall v. Avon A.H.A.* [1980] 1 All E.R. 516; *Megarity v. D.J. Ryan & Sons Ltd* [1980] 2 All E.R. 832; *Lacey v. Harrison, The Times*, April 22, 1992; *Bough v. Delta Water Fittings Ltd* [1971] 3 All E.R. 258; *Larby v. Thurgood, The Times*, October 27, 1992; 136 C.J. L.B. 275, C.A.

(c) Until interlocutory costs which have been assessed or taxed forthwith in the action have been paid.

(d) Until the costs of a previous action have been paid.

(e) Where an abuse of the court has occurred.

(f) Where proceedings are brought or continued without lawful authority: see, *e.g. Daimler Co. Ltd v. Continental Tyre & Rubber Co. (GB) Ltd* [1916] 2 A.C. 307, H.L.

(g) Where a foreign action and an English action relating to the same matter are commenced (*lis alibi pendens*). The court may, instead of staying the English action, put the plaintiff to his election as to which action he wishes to prosecute; or it may enjoin him from prosecuting the foreign action.

(h) Where two English actions are brought in respect of the same matter. The court will prima facie view this as vexatious and stay one or other of the actions.

(i) In actions to which the principles of *forum non conveniens* apply: see generally *Spiliada Maritime Corp. v. Cansulex Ltd, the Spiliada* [1986] 3 All E.R. 843 H.L.; and *Supreme Court Practice* (1995) Volume 1, notes at 11/1/7. A discussion of the principles of *forum non conveniens*, including the Civil Jurisdiction and Judgments Act, 1982 is outside the scope of this work.

7 Stay under R.S.C.

Under the R.S.C. the court may, for example, order a stay of the action:

(a) Under Ord. 18, r.19(1) when satisfied that a pleading or writ endorsement discloses no reasonable course of action or defence; is scandalous, frivolous or vexatious; may prejudice, embarrass or delay a fair trial; or is otherwise an abuse of the process of the court.

(b) Under Ord. 21, r.5 until a party who has discontinued a previous action and commenced a second action has paid the other party's costs of the previous action.

(c) Under Ord. 81, r.2 until the plaintiffs in an action brought by a firm have furnished the defendants with the names and addresses of all the partners of the plaintiff firm after a request to do so.

(d) Under Ord. 4, r.9 where two or more actions are pending in which common issues are raised so that, for example, all but one action are stayed so that that one can proceed as a test case.

8 Stay under statute

Particular statutes give the court power to stay proceedings. Under section 4(1) Arbitration Act 1950, an action may be stayed where the parties have agreed to submit their disputes to arbitration (see also section 1 Arbitration Act 1975). Again, the court has power to stay proceedings under section 49 Civil Jurisdiction and Judgments Act, 1982 on the ground of *forum non conveniens* or otherwise where to do so is not inconsistent with the Brussels or Lugano Conventions.

9 Practice and procedure

Application for a stay is made to the master or district judge in the Queen's Bench Division on summons. In the Chancery Division the application may be made by summons or motion. The application should be supported by affidavit unless under Ord. 18, r.19(1)(a) (no reasonable cause of action).

CHAPTER 8

Security for Costs

A: INTRODUCTION

An application for security for costs is a powerful pre-emptive remedy, particularly useful in cases where the claim cannot be struck out before costs escalate, *e.g.* under Ord. 18, r.19(1)(a) on the ground that a writ or pleading discloses no reasonable cause of action.

The court may in its discretion order security for costs if, but only if, it has jurisdiction to do so. The jurisdiction is derived from statute and from the Rules of the Supreme Court and County Court Rules, which are delegated legislation. In *DSQ Property Co. Ltd v. Lotus Cars Ltd* [1987] 1 W.L.R. 127 Millett J. gave an interesting and useful account of the history of the jurisdiction. At one point in his judgment he referred to "the court's inherent jurisdiction", but he decided the case on how the court should exercise its discretion when exercising jurisdiction conferred by the R.S.C., and it seems extremely unlikely that the High Court would nowadays assert an inherent jurisdiction to order security for costs in a case where they do not have such jurisdiction by statute or under the relevant rules.

The statutory jurisdiction goes back to the Joint Stock Companies Act 1856, so decisions on earlier Acts may be useful. The same point arises under the statutes and under the rules as to who is a plaintiff, and cases decided under each aspect of the jurisdiction may be useful on the other. Any authority must, however, be read with extreme care; in the past the courts have not always distinguished between jurisdiction and discretion with the punctilious clarity of the Court of Appeal in *Europa Holdings Ltd v. Circle Industries (UK) plc* [1993] BCLC 320.

The circumstances in which the court has power to order security for costs have been described as exceptions to a general principle that nobody is prevented by impecuniosity from bringing or resisting a claim in the courts. That proposition is inaccurate in two ways. First, nobody is prevented by impecuniosity from starting or resisting a claim in the courts. Rather—hence the pre-emptive nature of this remedy—there are circumstances in which the court may, on the application of the defendant to a claim which has been started, prevent the plaintiff from pursuing it, because the plaintiff is impecunious, unless security for costs is given. Secondly, it fails to distinguish between cases in which the claimant's impecuniosity is the essential prerequisite to the court's jurisdiction to order security for costs—the jurisdiction under the Companies Act 1985 and, in the High Court, under R.S.C., Ord. 23, r.(1)(b)—and cases in which the claimant's impecuniosity is relevant to whether in its discretion the court will exercise its jurisdiction.

There are circumstances in which the court's jurisdiction to order security depends not on the claimant's impecuniosity but on some other factor. Such other factors may be related to the claimant himself—that it may be difficult to enforce an order for costs against him, irrespective of his means, because he is ordinarily resident outside the jurisdiction or because he is reticent about his address—or may depend on the cause of action.

Where the court would otherwise have jurisdiction to order security for costs it may nevertheless be deprived of jurisdiction because of the cause of action.

B: JURISDICTION

1 Statutory jurisdiction

The current statutory provision is section 726(1) of the Companies Act 1985, which provides:

> "Where in England and Wales a limited company is plaintiff in an action or other legal proceeding, the Court having jurisdiction in the matter may, if it appears by credible testimony that there is reason to believe that the company will be unable to pay the defendant's costs if successful in his defence, require sufficient security to be given for those costs, and may stay all proceedings until the security is given."

1. "A limited company" The subsection does not apply either to corporate bodies other than those incorporated under the Companies Acts or to unincorporated associations.

The Companies Act 1985 applies to Scotland, so "limited company" includes a limited company incorporated there. It does not apply to Northern Ireland. In *Wilson Vehicle Distribution Ltd v. Colt Car Co. Ltd* [1984] BCLC 93, Bingham J. held that security for costs could not be ordered against a limited company incorporated in Northern Ireland. In *DSQ Property Co. Ltd v. Lotus Cars Ltd* [1987] 1 W.L.R. 127 Millett J. agreed that the court does not have jurisdiction under the Act but held that the court has jurisdiction under Ord. 23, r.1(1)(a) (below) to order security for costs against a company incorporated in Northern Ireland if it was also resident there. He said at 132B–C:

"I have not overlooked the fact that a company is not necessarily resident in the country of its incorporation, but resides where its central control and management abide, nor that it is not the plaintiff's residence in Northern Ireland but its incorporation there that precludes the exercise of the statutory jurisdiction. In my judgment, however, this is of little practical significance and can be disregarded. The great majority of companies do reside in the country of their incorporation; ... A company in liquidation must be resident where the liquidation is being carried on, and this can only be the part of the United Kingdom where it is incorporated."

2. "*Plaintiff*" means any claimant A defendant limited company which seeks merely to defend itself, even if its defence is strictly a counterclaim rather than a set off, cannot be ordered to give security: *Accidental and Marine Insurance Co. v. Mercati* (1866) L.R. 3 Eq. 200; but if the counterclaim goes beyond self-defence it can be ordered to give security for the additional costs of the plaintiff in resisting the counterclaim. The same point arises under R.S.C., Ord. 23 and the corresponding county court rule, and decided cases where the claimant was not a limited company are also relevant. In *Neck v. Taylor* [1893] 1 Q.B. 560 at 562 Lord Esher M.R. said:

"Where the counterclaim is put forward in respect of a matter wholly distinct from the claim ... the case may be treated as if that person were a plaintiff and only a plaintiff and an order for security for costs may be made ... Where, however, the counterclaim is not in respect of a wholly distinct matter, but arises in respect of the same matter or transaction upon which the claim is founded, the court ... will ... consider whether the counterclaim is not in substance put forward as a defence to the claim, whatever form in point of strict law and of pleading it may take..."

The test is whether a defendant is "simply setting up some claim by way of defence to an action" or whether he has "in substance taken up the position of plaintiff" (Vaughan Williams L.J. in *New Fenix Compagnie Anonyme D'Assurances de Madrid v. General Accident, Fire and Life Assurance Corporation Ltd* [1911] 2 K.B. 619). If the counterclaim is purely defensive in substance, jurisdiction to order security for costs is not conferred by the mere fact that the amount of the counterclaim is greater than the amount of the claim: *Maplseon v. Masini* (1879) 5 Q.B.D. 144 at 148, approved by Russell L.J. in *Ashworth v. Berkeley-Walbrook Ltd* (1989) C.A.T. 896, *Malcolm Charles Cathery t/a King Cathery partnership v. Lithodomas Ltd* [1987] 41 B.L.R. 76, C.A.

In *Hutchison Telephone (UK) Ltd v. Ultimate Response Ltd* [1993] BCLC 307 at 314h Dillon L.J. said:

"If one is considering whether the counterclaim is indeed a mere defence or a cross-claim in its own right which might well stand and be proceeded with even though the original claim was abandoned, the marked discrepancy in size between the amount claimed in the action and the very much greater amount claimed by the cross-claim must be, in my judgment, a relevant factor."

In the same case Bingham L.J. said at 317g:

"It is again not conclusive that the counterclaim overtops the claim, although I venture to think that the relative quantum of the counterclaim is not in all circumstances irrelevant."

If one party obtains a *Mareva* injunction (or, presumably, any other form of interlocutory relief) against another on the usual undertaking as to damages, that other party is not a plaintiff if it seeks damages under the undertaking: *C.T. Bowring & Co. (Insurance) Ltd v. Corsi & Partners* [1994] 2 Lloyd's Rep. 567 (C.A.).

3. "Other legal proceeding" These include legal proceedings commenced other than by writ, *e.g.* by petition: *Re Unisoft Group (No. 1)* [1993] BCLC 528.

4. "Credible testimony" The fact that a company is in liquidation is sufficient prima facie evidence that it will be unable to pay the defendant's costs: *Northampton Coal, Iron & Waggon Co. v. Midland Waggon Co.* (1887) 7 Ch.D. 500 (C.A.); *Pure Spirit Co. v. Fowler* (1890) 25 Q.B.D. 235. If there is a conflict of evidence it is not sufficient that a credible witness for the applicant has put forward a case of inability to pay; the court must reach a conclusion on the totality of the evidence. In *Re Unisoft Group (No. 2)* [1993] BCLC 532 at 534h (Sir Donald Nicholls V.-C.).

In *Kim Barker Ltd v. Aegon Insurance Company (UK) Ltd and Another* (C.A. September 27, 1989) the defendant applied for security for costs on the basis of inferences to be drawn from the last three balance sheets filed at Companies House by the plaintiff, a company which had a turnover in each year of less than £1m. and therefore did not have to file profit and loss accounts. The plaintiff opposed the application and relied on an affidavit sworn by its accountant and auditor to which were exhibited profit and loss accounts and some material which had not yet been, but would be, filed at Companies House. The accountant expressed the view that the defendant's estimated costs "would not pose a problem for the Plaintiffs and they should be able to meet such costs from their ordinary monthly cash inflow and accumulated profits". At first instance security was ordered by an Official Referee but the plaintiff's appeal was allowed in the Court of Appeal where Russell L.J. (with whom Stuart-Smith L.J. agreed) said:

"The accountant's evidence was unchallenged. It is easy to be wise after the event and for us to say that it could have been challenged by having the accountant called and cross-examined. But the fact of the matter is that his evidence did remain unchallenged..."

5. "Will be unable to pay the defendant's costs" In *Re Unisoft Group (No. 2)* [1993] BCLC 532 at 534h Sir Donald Nicholls V.-C. made two points on the burden which lies upon an applicant for security:

"... the phrase 'the company will be unable to pay the defendant's costs if successful in his defence' is clear and unequivocal. The phrase is 'will be unable', not 'may be unable'.

'Inability to pay' in this context I take to mean inability to pay the costs as and when they fall due for payment. Thus the question is, will the company be able to meet the costs order at the time when the order is made and requires to be met? That is a question to be judged and answered as matters stand when the application is heard by the court, although the court will take into account and give appropriate weight to evidence about what is expected to happen in the interval before the costs order would fall to be met. The court will draw appropriate inferences and here, as elsewhere, it will not let common sense fly out of the window."

A company may show in its balance sheet a surplus of assets over liabilities sufficient to meet the plaintiff's costs but still be unable to meet an order to pay the defendant's costs as and when they fall due because the assets may include real property, work in progress, investment in research and development, shares in subsidiaries which could not be sold quickly so as to realise the sums at which they may, with propriety, be valued in the balance sheet.

A limited company is a legal entity. It may be unable to pay the defendant's costs even though it is a wholly owned subsidiary of another company which would be able to pay those costs.

6. "... if successful in his defence" The amount of any security is a matter of discretion and in that context the court may take into account the possibility of settlement (see below). In relation to jurisdiction, however, the words of the Act seem clear: that the court may order security if the plaintiff will be unable to pay the defendant's costs if the plaintiff is unsuccessful at the end of a full trial.

2 Jurisdiction under Rules of Court

R.S.C., Ord. 23:

"**1.** (1) Where, on the application of a defendant to an action or other proceeding in the High Court, it appears to the Court—

(a) that the plaintiff is ordinarily resident out of the jurisdiction, or

(b) that the plaintiff (not being a plaintiff who is suing in a representative capacity) is a nominal plaintiff who is suing for the benefit of some other person and that there is reason to believe that he will be unable to pay the costs of the defendant if ordered to do so, or

(c) subject to paragraph (2) that the plaintiff's address is not stated in the writ or other originating process or is incorrectly stated therein, or

(d) that the plaintiff has changed his address during the course of the proceedings with a view to evading the consequences of the litigation, then if, having regard to all the circumstances of the case, the Court thinks it just to do so, it may order the plaintiff to give such security for the defendant's costs of the action or other proceeding as it thinks just.

(2) The Court shall not require a plaintiff to give security by reason only of paragraph (1)(c) if he satisfies the Court that the failure to state his address or the mis-statement thereof was made innocently and without intention to deceive.

(3) The references in the foregoing paragraphs to a plaintiff and a defendant shall be construed as references to the person (however described on the record) who is in the position of plaintiff or defendant, as the case may be, including a proceeding on a counterclaim."

C.C.R., Ord. 13, r.8:

"(1) Where, on the application of a defendant to an action or other proceeding, it appears to the court that the plaintiff is ordinarily resident out of England and Wales, then if, having regard to all the circumstances of the case, the court thinks it reasonable to do so, it may order the plaintiff to give such security for the defendant's costs of the action or other proceeding as it thinks just.

(2) The references in paragraph (1) to a plaintiff and a defendant shall be construed as references to the person (however described on the record) who is in the position of plaintiff or defendant, as the case may be, including proceedings on a counterclaim."

1. County court jurisdiction The more limited jurisdiction of the county court is obvious and does not merit comment. Paragraphs 1(1)(c) and (d) and 1(1)(2) of R.S.C., Ord. 23, r.1 are also too clear to need comment. For "plaintiff" and "action or other proceeding", see p. 542 above.

2. "Ordinarily resident out of the jurisdiction"/"out of England and Wales" A plaintiff corporation is ordinarily resident out of the jurisdiction if the central control and management of the company abides and is exercised out of the jurisdiction: *Little Olympian Each Ways Ltd* [1994] 4 All E.R. 561.

3. "Nominal plaintiff who is suing for the benefit of some other person" This means someone who is merely named as plaintiff and is suing only for the benefit of some other person. It includes an equitable assignor who is the named plaintiff only because the assignment is not a legal one; a plaintiff who has charged the whole proceeds of the action (*Semler v. Murphy* [1968] 1 Ch. 183 C.A.) and the trustee under a deed executed by a debtor for the benefit of his creditors and who does not himself have any beneficial interest in the subject-matter of the trust (*Greener v. Kahn & Co* [1906] 2 K.B. 374). It does not include a next friend or a person placed in a representative capacity by a court of competent jurisdiction.

3 Jurisdiction by reason of the cause of action

Under rule 6.17 of the Insolvency Rules 1986 the petitioning creditor may, on the debtor's application, be ordered to give security for the debtor's costs where the debt in respect of which a bankruptcy petition is presented under the Insolvency Act 1986 s.268(2) is for a liquidated sum payable at some time in the future, it being claimed in the petition that the debtor appears to have no reasonable prospect of being able to pay it. When security is ordered under this rule, the petition cannot be heard until the whole amount of the security ordered by the court has been given.

Proceedings under the Chancel Repairs Act 1932 and the Customs and Excise Management Act 1979 Sched. 3 para. 10(2) are outside the scope of this work, as are election petitions.

4 Jurisdiction removed because of the cause of action

By Article 31 para. 5 of the CMR Convention (which has the force of law by the Carriage of Goods by Road Act 1965), security for costs cannot be required in proceedings arising out of carriage under the Convention from nationals of contracting countries resident or having their place of business in one of those countries.

Article 45 of the 1968 Convention on the enforcement of foreign judgments, brought into force by the Civil Jurisdiction and Judgments Act 1982, provides that security for costs shall not be required from a person seeking to enforce a foreign judgment given in a Convention country.

C: DISCRETION

1. The Triplan case *Sir Lindsay Parkinson & Co. Ltd v. Triplan Ltd* [1973] 1 Q.B. 609 is best read as reported in the Law Reports, where the argument of counsel is also reported. Triplan was the "plaintiff" (the fact that it was the claimant in an arbitration is irrelevant). The master found that there was reason to believe that if Parkinson was successful Triplan would be unable to pay Parkinson's costs, a conclusion which was not thereafter challenged, but held that having reached this conclusion he had no discretion and was bound to order security for costs under what was then section 447 of the Companies Act 1948. On appeal, the judge in chambers held that he had an unfettered discretion and in the exercise of that discretion decided not to order security. Parkinson appealed. In the Court of Appeal, counsel for Parkinson abandoned the argument that as a matter of law there was no discretion but contended that the true position was as stated in the Irish case *Peppard and Co. Ltd v. Bogoff* [1962] I.R. 180 at 188; that the relevant statute (which for the Irish court was the Companies Act 1908):

> "does not make it mandatory to order security for costs in every case where the plaintiff company appears to be unable to pay the costs of a successful defendant, but there still remains a discretion in the court which may be exercised in special circumstances."

He submitted that the court ought to order security once it is shown that the claimant company is in financial difficulties, and that the mere fact of impecuniosity is not a "special circumstance". He also argued that offers and payments into court are not "special circumstances". He asked the court to lay down clear guide lines on the *extent* (editors' emphasis) of the discretion in a section which, he submitted, "was intended to prevent 'one man' limited companies from indulging in speculative litigation."

Lord Denning M.R. gave the first judgment. He rejected the argument based on *Peppard and Co. Ltd v. Bogoff* and held (at 626F) that the court has "a discretion which it will exercise considering all the circumstances of the particular case". Cairns L.J. said at 627D–F:

> "... I agree that there is, or at least may be, a discretion in the court in relation to the matter. In my view the highest at which it can be put in favour of the applicants for security is the way in which it was put in ... *Peppard and Co. Ltd v. Bogoff*, where it was said that there

remains a discretion in the court which may be exercised in special circumstances; and assuming that that is a correct statement of law, I am satisfied that there were special circumstances here."

Lawton L.J. regarded Cairns L.J. as having differed from Lord Denning M.R. He said at 628F–629A:

"There are now two judgments in favour of dismissing the appeal. In the ordinary way I would not have thought it appropriate to give further reasons for dismissal, but, having listened to the judgments already given, it seems to me the position is this: Lord Denning M.R. has said that in his judgment section 447 gives a general discretion to the court which is to be exercised having regard to all the circumstances of the case. Cairns L.J., however, has dealt with the problem before us on the basis of the Irish case of *Peppard and Co. Ltd v. Bogoff* ...

There being a difference of emphasis between the two judgments already given, doubt may continue as to the construction of section 447 unless something is said by me. I agree with Lord Denning M.R. that the effect of the section is that once it is established by credible evidence that there is reason to believe that the plaintiff company will be unable to pay the costs of the defendants if they are successful in their defence, the court has a discretion, and that the discretion ought not to be hampered by any special rules or regulations, nor ought it to be put into a straightjacket by considerations of burden of proof. It is a discretion which the court will exercise having regard to all the circumstances of the case."

Having said that the court has a discretion which it will exercise considering all the circumstances of the particular case, Lord Denning M.R. continued:

"So I turn to the circumstances. Mr Levy helpfully suggests some of the matters which the court might take into account, such as whether the company's claim is bona fide and not a sham and whether the company has a reasonably good prospect of success. Again it will consider whether there is an admission by the defendants on the pleadings or elsewhere that money is due. If there was a payment into court of a substantial sum of money (not merely a payment into court to get rid of a nuisance claim), that, too, would count. The court might also consider whether the application for security was being used oppressively—so as to try to stifle a genuine claim. It would also consider whether the company's want of means has been brought about by any conduct by the defendants, such as delay in payment or delay in doing their part of the work.

Mr Tackaberry accepted that most of these were matters proper for consideration, but he urged that it was not legitimate to take into account a payment into court, or, as in the present case, the open offer of a sum. But Mr Levy said it was an important matter which should be taken into consideration ... I am quite clear that a payment into court, or an open offer, is a matter which the court can take into account. It goes to show that there is substance in the claim: and that it would not be right to deprive the company of it by insisting on security for costs."

It is suggested (1) that by holding that the discretion is a general one, to be exercised in the light of all the circumstances of each case, the Court of Appeal was by implication rejecting the suggestion that the section is directed any more at "one-man" companies than at any other companies; and (2) that Lord Denning M.R. was not purporting to provide a list of the most important points to be considered when a court decides how to exercise its discretion; he was merely agreeing with counsel for Triplan Ltd that the discretion is a general one under which the court takes all matters into consideration, rather than that the court should order security unless there are special circumstances (the point made by Lawton L.J. at the end of the extract from his judgment quoted above).

2. Claim bona fide and not a sham; whether the claim has a reasonably good prospect of success The court will usually not entertain a detailed investigation of the merits: *Porzelack KG v. Porzelack (UK) Ltd* [1987] 1 All E.R. 1074 and *Trident International Freight Services Ltd v. Manchester Ship Canal Co.* [1990] BCLC 263. It is suggested, however, that the court should be prepared to investigate the merits in more detail where the plaintiff's argument is that even though there has been no admission, payment into court or offer, there is a very high probability that the claim will succeed and that the application for security is oppressive or will fail.

3. Without prejudice correspondence In *Simaan General Contracting Co. v. Pilkington Glass Ltd* [1987] 1 All E.R. 345 an Official Referee, Judge John Newey Q.C., held that without prejudice correspondence cannot be referred to in an application for security for costs. He cited the judgment of Oliver L.J. in *Cutts v. Head* [1984] Ch. 290 at 306:

"The protection from disclosure of without prejudice negotiations rests in part on public policy and in part on convention (*i.e.* an express or implied agreement that the negotiations shall be protected)."

Cutts v. Head was one of the *Calderbank* line of cases on costs, not a case on security for costs. In the *Simaan* case Judge Newey Q.C. said:

"In striking out applications, it is not the content of 'without prejudice' negotiations but the fact that they took place which may be material as excusing delay."

549

However, since the *Simaan* case the Court of Appeal, in *Family Housing Association (Manchester) Ltd v. Michael Hyde & Partners* [1993] 2 All E.R. 567, has examined the use of without prejudice correspondence in striking out applications (which it approved). Giving the only judgment Hirst L.J. cited an unreported decision of the Court of Appeal, *Taylor v. St Augustine with St George, Brandon Hill, Bristol Parochial Church Council* [1980] C.A.T. 558 and said

"... the content of the negotiation may well be of much more significance in this context than the mere fact that they have taken place, for the reasons given by Megaw L.J. in *Taylor's* case..."

Whether without prejudice correspondence is admissible in applications for security for costs must, therefore, be regarded as an open question.

4. Ability to pay costs if unsuccessful In *Pearson and Another v. Naydler and Others* [1977] 1 W.L.R. 899 at 906G Megarry V.-C. said:

"It seems plain enough that the inability of the plaintiff company to pay the defendant's costs is a matter which not only opens the jurisdiction but also provides a substantial factor in the decision whether to exercise it. It is inherent in the whole concept of the section that the court is to have power to order the company to do what it is likely to find difficulty in doing, namely to provide security for the costs which *ex hypothesi* it is likely to be unable to pay. At the same time, the court must not allow the section to be used as an instrument of oppression, by shutting out a small company from making a genuine claim against a large company ... As against that, the court must not show such a reluctance to order security for costs that this becomes a weapon whereby the impecunious company can use its inability to pay costs as a means of putting unfair pressure on a more prosperous company. Litigation in which the defendant will be seriously out of pocket even if the action fails is not to be encouraged. While I fully accept that there is no burden of proof one way or the other, I think that the court ought not to be unduly reluctant to exercise its power to order security for costs in cases that fall squarely within the section."

The first part of this passage does not stand on its own as a retreat towards the idea, finally laid to rest in *Sir Lindsay Parkinson & Co. Ltd v. Triplan Ltd*, that there is any burden on a claimant company which will be unable to pay costs if unsuccessful, still less that it must show special circumstances why it should not give security. Not only did Megarry V.-C. use the words which followed; he had earlier (at 905E) said:

"Now in the *Parkinson* case the majority of the court rejected the view that under the section there was any burden of proof one way or the other: the discretion is one that has to be exercised having regard to all the circumstances of the case."

5. Who will benefit if the plaintiff's claim succeeds? An assertion by a plaintiff company that an order for security for costs would stifle a bona fide claim which has a reasonably good prospect of success should be supported by evidence not merely of the company's inability to provide security from its own resources without a stifling effect but also evidence that the company cannot raise funds for purpose from directors, share-holders, supporters or others interested in the outcome of the litigation: *Flender Werft AG v. Aegean Maritime Ltd* [1990] 2 Lloyd's Rep. 27, *Kloeckner Co. AG v. Gatoil Overseas Inc.* [1990] 2 Lloyd's Rep. 177, *Okotcha v. Voest Alpine Inter-Trading GmbH* [1993] BCLC 474, *Keary Developments Ltd v. Tarmac Construction Ltd* [1994] C.A.T. 463 and *Paper Properties Ltd v. Jay Benning & Co.* [1995] 1 BCLC 172. Dicta to the contrary in *Trident International Freight Services Ltd v. Manchester Ship Canal Co.* [1990] BCLC 263 C.A. should be regarded as *obiter* or confined to the facts of that case: *Paper Properties Ltd v. Jay Benning & Co.* (above).

6. Two (or more) plaintiffs; no jurisdiction to order one (or some) to give security Security will not be ordered where the case of all the plaintiffs is identical: *Winthorp v. Royal Exchange Assurance Co.* (1775) 1 Dick. 282; *D'Hormusgee v. Grey* (1882) 10 Q.B.D. 13. But if the case of all plaintiffs is not identical, so that a plaintiff against whom the court has jurisdiction to order security might lose but another plaintiff, against whom security could not be ordered, might win, the court may order security to be given by a plaintiff against whom there is such jurisdiction: *John Bishop (Caterers) Ltd and another v. National Union Bank Ltd and others* [1973] 1 All E.R. 707.

7. Plaintiffs ordinarily resident out of the jurisdiction but who are nationals of and resident in a European Union country In *Fitzgerald and Regan and others v. Williams and others* [1996] 2 All E.R. 171, the Court of Appeal held that as a matter of discretion (not jurisdiction), security for costs should not be ordered against a plaintiff ordinarily resident in a country which is a signatory of the 1968 Convention on Jurisdiction and the Enforcement of Judgements in Civil and Commercial Matters who is also a national of a country which is a member of the European Union (not necessarily the same country. The Court left open the possibility of a different exercise of jurisdiction if there were evidence that despite rec-ognition of a foreign (*i.e.* English) costs order in the Convention Country there would be difficult in enforcement there. This case has no effect on the exercise of discretion in the case of an insolvent foreign company resident in a member state of the European Union.

D: PRACTICE

(a) A request should first be made to the plaintiff (if in person) or his solicitor in writing. It should state the amount of security sought.

(b) The summons should follow Practice Form 43 in Volume 2 of *The Supreme Court Practice*, adapted as necessary if the action is in a district registry or a county court. If the action is in the commercial court, in a mercantile list in Birmingham, Bristol, Liverpool or Manchester, or is an official referee action it will be heard by a judge, not by a master or district judge.

(c) The contents of the affidavit in support will depend on the circumstances, but should include:
 (i) the original request ((a) above);
 (ii) the plaintiff's refusal (or notice that the plaintiff did not answer);
 (iii) a skeleton bill of costs (*T. Sloyan & Sons (Builders) Ltd v. Brothers of Christian Instruction* [1974] 3 All E.R. 715), on a party and party basis.

(d) The contents of the plaintiff's affidavit in reply will also depend on the circumstances. Note especially Section C, para. 5 at p. 551 above.

(e) If security is ordered it will often be so framed that the security is provided in stages as the action proceeds towards trial.

(f) The security may take the form of payment into court, but the court will if possible avoid freezing the plaintiff's money in that way and the security may take the form of a guarantee by a suitable guarantor.

(g) If security is ordered the court will stipulate the time within which it is to be provided. The court may, and often does, order that the action be stayed until it is provided, but the defendant may be willing to let the action proceed pending the provision of security, especially if the defendant is anxious to get to trial as quickly as possible and the action is at a stage when it is the plaintiff who is incurring costs.

(h) If security is ordered the amount is in the discretion of the court. There is now no practice of ordering security for any proportion of the likely costs if the action proceeds to trial and judgment, but the court will take into account the possibility of settlement.

(i) If security has been ordered there can be a further application, either because costs have increased significantly above the original estimate or because the first order was only for security for costs up to a particular stage of the action.

(j) In the High Court, appeal from the master or district judge is to the judge in chambers. Leave is not needed. The appeal is a rehearing, but the appellant—whether plaintiff or defendant—opens the appeal. In the county court the appeal is to the county court judge in chambers.

(k) Appeal from a judge (whether on appeal to him or whether he heard the application at first instance ((b) above) is to the Court of Appeal. Leave is necessary and should be sought from the Judge; if it is refused application may be made to leave to a single judge of the Court of Appeal.

(l) Default. If the plaintiff fails to give security within the time ordered, the court may extend the time or dismiss the action with costs. It is unlikely to dismiss the action on the first occasion of default unless the default is contumelious.

(m) Plaintiff successful at trial. The plaintiff will be entitled to an order for the payment out of any money paid into court by way of security and to the release of any security.

E: SECURITY FOR COSTS OF APPEAL

Under R.S.C. Ord. 59, r.10(5) the Court of Appeal can order security for the costs of an appeal. This topic is outside the scope of a work on pre-emptive remedies. See the notes to the rule in *The Supreme Court Practice*.

Forms, Precedents and Practice Direction

Forms, Precedents and Practice Direction

SECTION 1: INJUNCTION FORMS

Contents

Note: for Form of Commencement of Summons—see p. 586

A. Special Indorsement for an Injunction

[*Title as in action*]

1. *Claim against sole defendant:* The plaintiff's claim is for an injunction to restrain the defendant, whether by himself or by his servants or agents or otherwise howsoever from [*specify precisely what it is sought to restrain. Where this appears in the earlier part of the indorsement, the following may suffice to say*: from continuing or repeating the acts above complained of].

2. *Claim against more than one defendant:* The plaintiff's claim is for an injunction to restrain the defendants and each of them, whether by themselves or by either [or any] of them or by their or his [her] servants or agents or otherwise from [*continue as above*].

3. *Claim against a limited company:* The plaintiff's claim is for an injunction to restrain the defendants, whether by themselves or by their directors, officers, servants or agents or otherwise howsoever from [*continue as above*].

4. *Claim against a corporate body:* The plaintiff's claim is for an injunction to restrain the defendants, whether by themselves, their officers, servants or agents [or contractors] or otherwise howsoever from [*continue as above*].

B. Intended Affidavit for *Ex Parte* Injunction before Issue of Writ

                                   i. Plaintiff

                                   ii. G. George

                                   iii. First

iv. GGI

v. [Date sworn]

IN THE HIGH COURT OF JUSTICE

QUEEN'S BENCH DIVISION

[— District Registry]

In the Matter of the Supreme Court Act 1981, section 37.

And in the Matter of Order 29, Rule 1 of the Rules of the Supreme Court.

And in the Matter of an Intended Action

BETWEEN

A.B.	Intended Plaintiff
and	
C.D.	Intended Defendant

[*State full name and residence or workplace and occupation or description of deponent*] make oath and say as follows:

1. The intended plaintiff *A.B.* intends to commence proceedings by issuing a writ out of this Honourable Court against the intended defendant for [*state briefly the nature of the claim*] as appears from the draft writ of summons, a copy of which is now produced and shown to me marked "GG1."

2. [*State lucidly and succinctly the facts generating the claim in the intended action.*]

3. [*State lucidly and succinctly the facts generating the claim for an interlocutory injunction, for example in a "Cyanamid" case:*

(a) *The right allegedly infringed or threatened.*

(b) *Facts showing that the issue to be tried is serious.*

(c) *That damages would not be an adequate remedy for the plaintiff and/or that damages would be an adequate remedy for the defendant.*

(d) *That the balance of convenience lies in favour of granting the injunction.*

If the proceedings fall within one of the exceptions to "Cyanamid", the strength of the plaintiff's claim should be emphasised together with the likelihood of the plaintiff succeeding at trial.)

4. [*If ex parte relief required, state the facts relied on as justifying the application such as:*

(a) *the fact that unless restrained by injunction the defendant threatens and intends to infringe or violate or to continue to infringe or violate the plaintiff's right or to repeat the acts complained of, deposing to those facts which show that the defendant threatens and intends to do so; and*

(b) *facts showing that the plaintiff has suffered and will continue to suffer serious loss or damage and prejudice, which is or will be irreparable*

559

or unlikely to be recovered from or compensated by the defendant and sufficiently serious to justify the application for an ex parte *injunction as a matter of urgency;*

(c) *whether any notice was given to the defendant that application would be made to the court for an* ex parte *injunction and if so when, how and by whom such notice was given and what response if any the defendant made or if no such notice was given, state the reasons for giving none, such as that if the defendant had been given such notice he would or might be likely to destroy or put out of reach the very substratum of the plaintiff's claim.*

(d) *whether the defendant has asserted or is thought likely to assert any answer to the plaintiff's claim in the action or to the claim for an* ex parte *or interlocutory injunction and show if it be the fact that any such answer is frivolous or unfounded.*]

5. [*Here state the precise relief sought by exhibiting a draft minute of the order sought.*]

Sworn [*etc.*]

C. Draft Minute of Order for *Ex Parte* Injunction before Issue of the Writ

[*Title as in B*]

Upon hearing Mr Richard Roe, counsel for the intended plaintiff.

And upon reading the draft affidavit proposed to be sworn by John Doe and the exhibits thereto and the draft writ of summons in the above-mentioned intended action and the draft minute of the order sought.

And upon the said intended plaintiff by his counsel undertaking:

(1) to abide by any order that the court may make as to damages (and interest thereon) in case the court shall hereafter be of opinion that the intended defendant shall have sustained any by reason of this order which the plaintiff ought to pay;

(2) to issue a writ of summons in the form of the said draft writ of summons forthwith; (or — by the — day of — 19—);

(3) to procure the said John Doe to make and file an affidavit in or substantially in the terms of the said draft affidavit [*or in the absence of any draft affidavit, to make and file an affidavit deposing to the facts averred by counsel for the intended plaintiff*];

(4) to notify the defendant forthwith of the terms of this order (*e.g.* by facsimile machine, etc., as appropriate) and to serve upon him as soon as practicable a copy of the affidavit as sworn and a copy of the exhibits thereto together with a copy of this order;

(5) to notify the defendant and any person upon whom notice of this order is served at the time of service of his right, if so advised, to apply to discharge or vary the order.

It is ordered and directed:

1. That the defendant be restrained and an injunction is hereby granted restraining him, whether by himself, or by his servants or agents or any of them or otherwise howsoever from [*specify precisely what it is sought to restrain*]

    (a) until after the trial of this action or until further order; or

    (b) until after the hearing of a summons to continue this injunction [returnable on the — day of —, 19—] [or until the — day of —, 19—]; or

    (c) until further order.

2. That without prejudice to the right to apply *ex parte* there be liberty to apply to discharge or vary this order on (*for example*) 48 hours' notice.

3. That the costs of this application be reserved.

Dated the — day of — 19—.

NOTE: (1) Adapted from Practice Form, PF64. (2) An order for an *ex parte* injunction before the issue of the writ will be in the Forms of the draft minute of order as approved or amended by the judge hearing the *ex parte* application.

D. Certificate by Counsel of Extreme Urgency for *Ex Parte* Injunction

In the Matter of *A.B. v. O.D.* [and others].

I, John Doe, being the counsel instructed by Messrs Careless and Wise, 15 Hatton Garden, Liverpool L2 3SW on behalf of *A.B.* the above-named intended plaintiff hereby certify that, in my opinion, the application for an *ex parte* injunction on behalf of the above-named intended plaintiff in or substantially in the terms of the draft minute of the order which I settled is one of extreme urgency.

Dated the 10th day of June, 1993

                                                (Signed)

NOTE: In the event of counsel not being instructed, such a certificate should be drawn up by the solicitor for the intended plaintiff.

E. Order for *Ex Parte* Discharge or Variation of *Ex Parte* Injunction

[*Title as in action*]

Upon hearing counsel for the plaintiff and the defendant.

And upon reading [*etc.*]

It is ordered that the injunction granted herein by the Honourable Mr Justice Doe on the 6th day of May, 1993 be varied and the same is hereby varied by deleting from paragraph 2 thereof the following words, namely [.........].

And that the costs of this application be reserved.
Dated the 3rd day of June, 1993

NOTE: In the event of discharge rather than variation—adapt accordingly.

F. Summons to Continue *Ex Parte* Injunction

[*Title as in action*]

[*Usual form of summons which then continues*] on the hearing of an application on the part of the plaintiff for an order that the injunction granted herein by the Honourable Mr Justice Bracton on the 6th day of May, 1993, restraining the defendant by himself, his agents or servants, or otherwise howsoever from [as in the injunction] be continued until after the trial of this action, or until further order, and that the costs of this application and of the application made by the plaintiff on the 6th day of May, 1993, be costs in the cause (or as appropriate).

Dated the 10th day of June, 1993
This summons was taken out by Messrs Careless and Wise, 5 South Castle Street, Liverpool 2.

To the defendant and to Messrs Sharp, Wit & Co. of Tower House, The Strand, Liverpool 2, his solicitors.

G. Order to Continue *Ex Parte* Injunction

[*Title as in action*]

Upon hearing Mr Richard Roe, counsel on behalf of the plaintiff and Mr John Doe, counsel on behalf of the defendant.

And upon reading [*the affidavit of the plaintiff*]

And upon the plaintiff by his counsel undertaking to abide by an order that the court may make as to damages in case the court shall hereafter be of the opinion that the defendant shall have sustained any by reason of this order which the plaintiff ought to pay.

It is ordered and directed that the injunction granted by the Honourable Mr Justice Glanvill on the 4th day of May, 1991 restraining the defendant, be continued until after the trial of this action or until further order and that the costs of this application and of the application made by the plaintiff on the 6th day of May, 1993 be costs in the cause [*or as may be*].

Dated the 24th day of May, 1993.

H. Summons by Defendant to Discharge or Vary *Ex Parte* Injunction and for Inquiry as to Damages

[*Title as in action*]

[Usual form of summons to judge in chambers which then continues] on the hearing of an application on the part of the defendant for an order:

1. That the injunction herein granted *ex parte* by the order of the Honourable Mr Justice Coke on the 6th day of May, 1993 be discharged *[if variation sought, specify precisely the alterations proposed.]*

2. That *[if the said injunction be discharged]* an inquiry be made as to the damages sustained by the defendant by reason of the said injunction, according to the undertaking of the plaintiff contained in the said order and for interest thereon pursuant to section 35A of the Supreme Court Act 1981.

3. That the defendant be at liberty to enter judgment against the plaintiff for the amount of such damages and interest.

4. That the costs of this application be the defendant's costs in any event [or, as appropriate].

Dated the 10th day of June, 1993.

This summons was taken out by Messrs Careless and Wise, 5 South Castle Street, Liverpool 2.

To the defendant and to Messrs Sharp, Wit & Co., Tower House, The Strand, Liverpool 2, his solicitors.

I. Order for Discharge and for Inquiry as to Damages

[Title as in action]

Upon hearing counsel for the plaintiff and the defendant.

And upon reading [*etc.*].

It is ordered:

1. That the injunction herein granted by order of the Honourable Mr Justice Doe on the 6th day of May, 1993 be and it is hereby discharged.

2. That an inquiry whether the defendant has sustained any and if so what damages by reason of the said injunction which the plaintiff ought to pay according to his undertaking contained in the said order be referred to a Master of the Queen's Bench Division, who shall assess such damages and interest thereon from the date of the said order until the date of the inquiry pursuant to section 35A of the Supreme Court Act 1981 and that the costs of such inquiry shall be in the discretion of the Master and that the defendant be at liberty to enter judgment against the plaintiff for the amount of the damages and interest so assessed and costs if any.

3. That the costs of this application be the defendant's costs in any event [*or as appropriate*].

Dated the 10th day of June, 1993.

NOTE: For a variation—adapt clause 1, and omit clause 2.

J. Order for Discharge of *Ex Parte* Injunction and of Undertaking as to Damages

[*Title as in action*]

Upon hearing counsel for the plaintiff and for (*e.g.*) the third defendant.

And upon the third defendant by his counsel undertaking to take no steps to enforce the undertaking as to damages given by the plaintiff and embodied in the order of the Honourable Mr Justice Doe dated the 6th day of May, 1993.

It is ordered and directed:

1. That the injunction as against the third defendant granted by the Honourable Mr Justice Doe on the 6th day of May, 1993 be and the same is hereby discharged.

2. That there be no order as to costs as between the plaintiff and the third defendant of the said *ex parte* order dated the 6th day of May, 1993 and of this application.

Dated the 5th day of June 1993.

K. Summons for Interlocutory Injunction

[*Title as in action*]

[*Usual form of summons which then continues*] on the hearing of an application on the part of the plaintiff for an order that the defendant by himself, his agents or servants, or otherwise howsoever be restrained, and that an injunction be granted restraining him from (*specify precisely what it is sought to restrain*) until after the trial of this action, or until further order, and that the costs of this application be costs in the cause.

Dated the 10th day of June, 1993.

This summons was taken out by Messrs Careless and Wise, 5 South Castle Street, Liverpool 2.

To the defendant and to Messrs Sharp, Wit & Co., Tower House, The Strand, Liverpool 2, his solicitors.

L. Order for Interlocutory Injunction until Trial of Action

[*Title as in action*]

Upon hearing counsel for the plaintiff and the defendant.

And upon reading the affidavits of A.B. and O.D. file herein.

And the plaintiff by his said counsel undertaking to abide by any order the Court may make as to damages, in case the Court shall hereafter be of the opinion that the defendant shall have sustained any by reason of this order which the plaintiff ought to pay.

It is ordered and directed that the defendant whether by himself, his servants, or agents or howsoever otherwise be restrained, and an injunction is hereby granted restraining him from [*set out the acts, etc., prohibited*] until after the trial of this action, or until further order.

And it is ordered that there be a certificate for a speedy trial.

And it is ordered that [*here set out the directions given by the Judge as to pleadings, or as to affidavits standing as pleadings, discovery and inspection of documents, place and mode of trial, estimated duration, listing category and setting down*].

And it is ordered that the costs of the application and of that before Mr Justice Doe on the 6th day of May, 1993 be reserved to the Judge at the trial.

[Fit for 2 counsel.]

Dated the — day of —, 19—.

NOTE: Adapted from Practice Form, PF64.

M. Summons for Directions on Inquiry as to Damages

[*Title as in action*]

[*Usual form of summons on application to master which then continues*] on the hearing of an application on the part of the plaintiff for directions on the inquiry as to damages alleged to have been sustained by the defendant pursuant to the order of the Honourable Mr Justice Doe dated the 6th day of May, 1993 [*such directions may, for example, be*]:

1. That the defendant do within 14 days serve on the plaintiff a statement of the particulars of the damages alleged to have been sustained by him by reason of the order of the Honourable Mr Justice Doe dated 6th day of May, 1993 stating:

(a) the quantum of damages claimed;

(b) how such amount is made up; and

(c) the fact relied on as justifying the claim that such damages were sustained by reason of the said order dated the 6th day of May, 1993.

2. That the defendant do within 14 days thereafter serve on the plaintiff a list of documents and file an affidavit verifying such list relating to the damages claimed.

3. That there be inspection of the documents within [7] days thereafter.

4. That the date of the hearing be fixed.

5. That costs of this application be costs in the said inquiry.

Dated the — day of —, 19—.

This summons was taken out by Messrs Careless and Wise, 5 South Castle Street, Liverpool 2.

To the defendant and to Messrs Sharp, Wit & Co., Tower House, The Strand, Liverpool 2, his solicitors.

N. Affidavit for *Ex Parte Mareva* Injunction in intended action

IN THE HIGH COURT OF JUSTICE

QUEEN'S BENCH DIVISION

[COMMERCIAL COURT]

In the Matter of the Supreme Court Act 1981, section 37(3).

And in the Matter of Order 29, rule 1 of the Rules of the Supreme Court.

And in the Matter of an Intended Action

BETWEEN

A.B.	Intended Plaintiff
and	
C.D.	Intended First Defendant
E.F.	Intended Second Defendant
and	
X.Y. Ltd [plc]	Intended Third Defendant
	Intended Plaintiff
	A.B.
	First
	A.B. 1 to 7
	sworn on [date]

I. A.B. a [*occupation*] of [*address*] make oath and say

1. That I am the above-named intended plaintiff.

2. That I intend to start an action in this Court against each of the above-named intended defendants as appears from the draft writ of summons a copy of which is now produced and shown to me and exhibited hereto marked "A.B.1".

3. That except where I say otherwise all the facts to which I depose in this section of this affidavit are true to my own knowledge; and that where I say in this section of this affidavit that I am informed by a named informant of any fact I believe such fact to be true.

Factual basis of the claim

4. There is now produced and shown to me and exhibited hereto marked "A.B.2" a paginated bundle containing true copies of the documents relevant to this section of this affidavit.

5. [*Set out the facts which form the basis of the claim in as many numbered paragraphs as may be appropriate, referring where relevant to documents.*]

Amount of the claim

6. There is now produced and shown to me and exhibited hereto marked

"A.B.3" a paginated bundle containing true copies of the documents relevant to this section of this affidavit.

7. [*Set out the facts and calculations which form the basis of the quantification of the claim in as many numbered paragraphs as may be appropriate, referring where relevant to documents. If the claim is different in amount against two or more of the defendants this must be made clear in the affidavit.*]

Defences

8. There is now produced and shown to me and exhibited hereto marked "A.B.4" a paginated bundle containing true copies of the documents relevant to this section of this affidavit.

9. [*Set out fully and with reference to relevant documents any possible defences which the plaintiff has any reason to believe might be advanced by the defendants or any of them on liability or quantum, together with any facts upon which the plaintiff will rely to rebut such defences.*]

Defendants' assets

10. There is now produced and shown to me and exhibited hereto marked "A.B.5" a paginated bundle containing true copies of the documents relevant to this section of this affidavit.

11. [*Set out, with reference to documents, any information known to the plaintiff about the assets of each of the defendants within the jurisdiction* – e.g. that a defendant has drawn cheques on account number XXX at the YYY branch of ZZZ bank plc.]

12. [*If the plaintiff seeks a world-wide Mareva, set out with reference to documents any facts relevant to show (a) the inadequacy of the defendants' assets within the jurisdiction with which to meet the claim and (b) that any defendant has assets out of the jurisdiction.*]

Risk of dissipation of the defendants' assets

13. There is now produced and shown to me and exhibited hereto marked "A.B.6" a paginated bundle containing true copies of the documents relevant to this section of this affidavit.

14. I believe that unless restrained by this court the defendants will [*dissipate their assets by* etc.] or [*remove their assets out of the jurisdiction of this court to* XXX] with the intention and result that any judgment given against them in this action would remain unsatisfied.

15. [*Set out, with reference to documents, the basis of the plaintiff's belief*].

16. [*Set out, with reference to documents, any facts known to the plaintiff which might suggest that there is no risk, or that the risk is slight, together with the plaintiff's answer.*]

Plaintiff's undertakings

17. There is now produced and shown to me and exhibited hereto marked "A.B.7" a paginated bundle containing true copies of the documents relevant to this section of this affidavit.

567

18. I give to the court the undertakings set out in the draft order in relation to loss incurred by the defendants and costs incurred by anyone other than the defendants as a result of any order which the court may make.

19. My means with which to satisfy any order which may be made against me are [*give full details of assets and liabilities so as to show net asset position and so as to distinguish assets which are and which are not cash or "near cash"*—i.e. saleable at market price at short notice].

SWORN [*etc.*]

O. Summons to Continue *Ex Parte Mareva* Injunction

[*Title as in action*]

[*Usual terms of application to the [Commercial] Judge in Chambers*] on the hearing of an application on the part of the plaintiff for an order that the injunction granted therein by the Honourable Mr Justice Doe on the 6th day of May, 1993 restraining the defendants [*cite injunction*] be continued until judgment herein or until further order and that the costs of this application and of the application made by the plaintiff on the 6th day of May, 1993 be the plaintiff's costs in the cause.

Dated the 10th day of June, 1993.

This summons was taken out by Messrs Careless and Wise, 5 South Castle Street, Liverpool 2.

To the defendant and to Messrs Sharp, Wit & Co., Tower House, The Strand, Liverpool 2, his solicitors.

P. *Ex Parte* or Summons to Continue *Ex Parte Mareva* Injunction until Execution or Satisfaction of Judgment

[*Where judgment has been or will be entered in default of the defendant acknowledging service of the writ or giving notice of intention to defend.*]

[*Title as in action*]

[*Usual form of summons then continue*] on hearing of an application on the part of the plaintiffs for an order that the injunction granted herein by the Honourable Mr Justice Doe on the 6th day of May, 1993 restraining the defendants [*cite original injunction*] be continued until after satisfaction of the judgment herein dated the 10th day of June, 1991 whether by execution, payment or otherwise or until further order and that the costs of this application be the plaintiff's costs in any event.

Dated the 1st day of August, 1993.

This summons was taken out by Messrs Careless and Wise, 5 South Castle Street, Liverpool 2.

To the defendant and to Messrs Sharp, Wit & Co., Tower House, The Strand, Liverpool 2, his solicitors.

Q. Affidavit in support of application for *Anton Piller* Order (writ already issued)

Plaintiff
John Doe
First
J.D. 1
sworn on [date]

IN THE HIGH COURT OF JUSTICE

CHANCERY DIVISION

BETWEEN

A.B. Ltd   Plaintiff

and

C.D.   Defendant

I John Doe a solicitor of the Supreme Court of [*address*] make oath and say

1. I am a solicitor of the Supreme Court. I am a partner in the firm John Doe and Co. of [*address*] the solicitors for the above-named plaintiff. I have conduct of this action on behalf of the plaintiff.

2. The facts to which I depose in this affidavit are derived from information given to me by Richard Roe, the managing director of the plaintiff, from Alan Roe, the marketing director of the plaintiff and from the documents exhibited to this affidavit in a paginated bundle now produced and shown to me and marked "J.D. 1". I believe them to be true.

3. The plaintiff has for 40 years carried on business as a manufacturer of clothing including T-shirts. The plaintiff is the owner of the copyright in a graphic work consisting of a picture of an imaginary animal with a human face known as "Naughty Ned" and has for the last five years used the said picture on T-shirts manufactured and sold by the plaintiff. The said picture has been used on T-shirts with a "balloon" from its mouth containing various humorous remarks.

4. In April 1995 Alan Roe was unable to obtain orders for "Naughty Ned" T-shirts from retailers in various seaside towns including Blackness, Easton Super Flumen and Darkton who had in previous years purchased such T-shirts in large quantities and who had not made any complaint to the plaintiff about their purchases. Pages 1–77 of the bundle show the monthly sales to 14 retailers over the years 1990–1994. Pages 78–79 show the monthly sales to the same retailers for the months January–June 1995. From those pages it will be apparent that sales are made in April and May

for the summer season, and that sales were dramatically lower in 1995 than in the preceding five years.

5. Alan Roe reported this problem to Richard Roe. Richard Roe engaged Blank Mind Ltd, enquiry agents, to investigate whether the plaintiff's T-shirts were being "pirated".

6. Pages 80–95 of the bundle consist of a report by Blank Mind Ltd dated 29th May 1995 from which it appears that in the week 18th to 25th May 1995 deliveries were made to the premises of 13 of the 14 retailers referred to on pages 1–79 of the bundle; that all the deliveries were made in hired vans bearing the name "Brispool Cheep and Ruff Van Hire"; that all the deliveries were made between the hours of 8.00p.m. and 10.00p.m.; that none of the retailers took any other deliveries during those hours; that during shop opening hours of the day on which the delivery was made to each retailer that retailer was not displaying any "Naughty Ned" T-shirts; and that on the day following delivery each retailer displayed "Naughty Ned" T-shirts for sale.

7. As appears from the said report, Blank Minds Ltd made purchases of "Naughty Ned" T-shirts from each of the 13 retailers on the day after the aforesaid deliveries. The purchases cannot conveniently be exhibited but will be available to the court for inspection and will be retained by me as an officer of the court until further order of the court. I am told by Richard Roe and believe that the humorous remarks in the "balloons" do not emanate from the plaintiff. It is also the case for the plaintiff that those humorous remarks are in bad taste and likely to damage the reputation of the plaintiff.

8. As also appears from the said report, Blank Minds Ltd visited the premises of Brispool Cheep and Ruff Van Hire and obtained the name of the hirer of the said vans by asking the cost of hiring a van similar to those let on hire by Brispool Cheep and Ruff Van Hire in the relevant week to a hirer whose name the enquiry agent pretended to have forgotten. The name was that of the defendant. The enquiry agent traced the registered office of the defendant through Companies House (Pages 96–98 of the bundle). He visited the address and found it to be a run-down warehouse and in a skip on some adjacent waste ground he found several torn T-shirts bearing the "Naughty Ned" design with the same humorous remarks as the test purchases previously referred to.

9. I believe that if the defendant were to be served with a writ all evidence of the use of the "Naughty Ned" design and sales of "Naughty Ned" T-shirts would be destroyed or concealed by the defendant. My belief is based upon the facts previously deposed to in this affidavit and on the fact, revealed by the company search, that the defendant has an authorised capital of £100, an issued capital of £2 and though it has been incorporated for three years it has not filed any accounts at all.

10. The plaintiff offers the usual undertaking in damages. Pages 99–105 of the bundle are the accounts of the plaintiff for the financial year to 30th

April 1995, with the comparable figures for the previous year, audited by the well-known firm Cosstt Cutting & Partners. I believe that the plaintiff is well able to meet its undertaking.

11. I have made enquiries of my London agents. They suggested the name of Mr Anthony Pile as a solicitor unconnected with them who is experienced in serving *Anton Piller* Orders. I have spoken to him. He confirmed to me that he has no professional or other connection with the plaintiff, that he has served 18 such Orders as supervising solicitor and that he is willing to serve such an Order if made on this application. Sworn, etc.

R. Summons for Leave to Use Information and Documents Obtained Consequent on Enforcing *Anton Piller* Orders

[Title as in action]

[Formal parts as usual on application to [Commercial] Judge in Chambers] on the hearing of an application on the part of the plaintiff for an order that he do have leave to use information and the documents [*or* the following documents [*specify them*] *or* specified in the Schedule hereto [*specify the same in a Schedule to the Summons*]] obtained as a result of enforcing the order made by the Honourable Mr Justice — on the — day of —, 19— for the purpose of commencing and prosecuting an action against [*state who are the intended defendants*] for [*state the nature of the relief or remedy intended to be claimed in the intended action*] and for an order that the costs of this application be reserved.

Dated the — day of —, 19—.

[Conclude as in Form S below.]

S. Summons for Safe Custody of Subject-matter Pending Trial

[Title as in action]

[Usual form of summons which then continues] on the hearing of an application by the plaintiff that the defendant deliver the Rolls-Royce Corniche saloon car registered number AB 11 to Mancunian Garages Ltd, Oxford Road, Manchester for safe custody pending trial of this action or further order.

And the costs of this application be [borne by the defendant in any event]

Dated the — day of —, 19—.

(Signed)
(Address)
Solicitor for the plaintiff.

This summons was taken out by
[*Name and address of solicitor for plaintiff*].
To [*defendant's name and address for service*].

T. Affidavit in Support of Summons for Safe Custody of Subject-matter Pending Trial

[*Set out title to action*]

I, [*name address and occupation of deponent*], the plaintiff in this action make oath and say as follows:

1. I am the owner of a Rolls-Royce Corniche Saloon car registered number AB 11.

2. On November 22, 1990 I took it to a local garage for a service. When I went to collect it two days later I found that the garage had closed down and my car had gone.

3. On November 29, 1990 as a result of enquiries by the police I was informed that the defendant had acquired my car. The defendant subsequently told me that he had purchased the car in good faith for £37,500 from the garage and that he was not prepared to return it to me.

4. On December 17, 1990 I commenced this action against the defendant for the specific return of the car without giving him the option of paying its value. On receipt of the writ, the defendant telephoned me and said: "You'll get the car back over my dead body."

5. Mancunian Garages Ltd of Oxford Road, Manchester are the main Rolls-Royce Dealers in that area. They have informed me that they would be prepared to assume responsibility for the safe custody of the car under an order of this court pending the trial of the action on their usual terms. In particular, they want my assurance that I shall discharge their storage charges whatever the outcome of the proceedings. I am willing to give that assurance.

6. Accordingly, I ask this honourable court to make an order for the storage of the said car, with Mancunian Garages Ltd pending the trial of this action or further order.

Sworn [*etc.*].

U. Order for Safe Custody of Subject-matter Pending Trial

[*Set out title to action*]

Master [District Judge]—in chambers.

On hearing [counsel for the plaintiff, the defendant not being in attendance although duly served].

And on the plaintiff undertaking to discharge the storage charges of

Mancunian Garages Ltd, [but without prejudice to the right of the plaintiff to seek to be indemnified in respect thereof by the defendant].

It is ordered that the defendant do within [4] days of the date of the service of this order on him deliver to the service manager of Mancunian Garages Ltd, Oxford Road, Manchester the Rolls-Royce Corniche registered number AB 11, to be stored there in safe custody pending the trial of this action or further order.

And it is further ordered that the costs of and occasioned by this application be borne by the defendant in any event.

V. Summons for Injunction Restraining Dealings with Subject-matter Pending Trial

[Note: returnable before judge—not master: Ord. 32, r.11(1)(d)]

[Start as in Form G1 or G2 on p. 586]

[then continue]:

on the hearing of an application by the plaintiff for an order that the defendant by himself, his servants or agents or otherwise howsoever be restrained from disposing of or in any way dealing with [description of subject-matter] the subject-matter of this action until the conclusion of the trial or further order.

And the costs of this application be [provision for costs].

[Conclude as in form S at p. 571]

W. Order Granting Injunction Restraining Dealings with the Subject-matter Pending Trial

[Set out title to action]

[The Honourable Mr Justice — in chambers.]
Dated the — day of —, 19—.

Upon hearing [counsel for the plaintiff and counsel for the defendant].

And upon reading the affidavit of the plaintiff sworn on the — day of —, 19— and the affidavit of the defendant sworn on the — day of —, 19—.

And the plaintiff undertaking by counsel to abide by any order the court or a judge may make as to damages in case the court or a judge should hereafter be of the opinion that the defendant shall have sustained any by reason of this order which the plaintiff ought to pay.

It is ordered that the defendant by himself, his servants or agents or otherwise howsoever be restrained and an injunction is hereby granted restraining him from disposing of or in any way dealing with [description *of subject-matter*] the subject-matter of this action until the conclusion of the trial of this action or further order.

And it is further ordered that the costs of this application [*provision for costs*].

X. Summons for Immediate Sale of Perishable Property

[*Start as in Form G1 or G2, on p. 586*]

[*then continue*]:
   on the hearing of an application by the plaintiff that the cargo of Seville oranges [the subject-matter of this action] at present on board the vessel "Sea Steel" berthed in the Port of Liverpool be sold forthwith for the best price reasonably obtainable and that the proceeds of such sale less the expenses thereof be lodged in court to the credit of this action until further order and that the costs of this application be [*provision for costs*].
[*Conclude as in Form S at p. 571*]

[*Note*: Immediately after sale, the plaintiff should prepare and lodge in court a lodgement schedule [see Form IP.7 below] showing the amount of the net proceeds of sale. This is signed by the master [district judge] and forwarded by the court staff to the Accountant General of the Supreme Court.]

Y. Summons by Third Party for Order by Payment of the Plaintiff of his Costs, Charges, etc.

[*Note*: This summons must be supported by an affidavit, deposing to the fact that the order for the injunction has been served on the applicants specifying the date of service and further deposing to the amount claimed specifying how such sum is made up and stating that such amount was incurred or expended in complying with the injunction.]

   [*Usual summons on application to Judge in Chambers then continue*] on the hearing of an application on behalf of — Bank plc [*or as may be*] of — that they be at liberty to enter judgment against the plaintiff herein for the sum of £—, being the amount of the costs, charges and expenses incurred by them in complying with the order of the Honourable Mr Justice — dated the — day of —, 19— which was served upon them by the plaintiff on the — day of —, 19—, and interest thereon pursuant to section 35A of the Supreme Court Act 1981 at the rate of [—] per cent per annum from the date of service upon them of the said order to the date of judgment [*or as may be*] and for an order that the plaintiff do pay the applicants the costs of this application to be taxed.

   Dated the — day of —, 19—.
[*Conclude as in Form S at p. 571*]

SECTION 2: SUMMARY JUDGMENT FORMS

Contents

Note: for Form of Commencement of Summons—see p. 586

by plaintiff under Order 14

T   Specimen form of affidavit in reply by defendant under   585
Order 14

A. Specimen Form of Notice of Appeal by Defendant under Order 14 from Judge in Chambers to Court of Appeal

IN THE COURT OF APPEAL
On Appeal from the High Court of Justice
QUEEN'S BENCH DIVISION
19— No.—
[or — District Registry — 19— No.—]

BETWEEN

A.B.   Plaintiff
and
C.D.   Defendant

NOTICE OF APPEAL

Take notice that the Court of Appeal will be moved as soon as counsel can be heard on behalf of the above-named defendant on appeal from [the whole of] the judgment herein of the Honourable Mr Justice — given in chambers [at Liverpool] on the — day of —, 19— whereby it was adjudged that the plaintiff be entitled to judgment under Order 14, r.3 for [set out judgment appealed from] for an order that the said judgment may be set aside and that the defendant may be granted unconditional leave to defend the action and that the plaintiff may be ordered to pay to the defendant his costs of the Order 14 proceedings to include the costs of this appeal.

And further take notice that the grounds of this appeal are:

1. [e.g.] that the Learned Judge misdirected himself in holding that the provisions of Order 14 apply to this action, such action being based on an allegation by the plaintiff against the defendant of fraud.

2. [Set out grounds of appeal.]

And further take notice that the defendant proposes to apply to set this appeal down in the [Queen's Bench Division Interlocutory List].

Dated the — day of —, 19—

To   Solicitor for the

B. Affidavit in Support of Application by Plaintiff under Order 14 for Judgment for Liquidated Claim

[Set out title to action]

I, [name, address and occupation of deponent] the plaintiff in this action [*or* legal executive employed by the solicitors acting for the plaintiff *or as may be*] make oath and say as follows:

1. The defendant is and was at the commencement of this action, justly and truly indebted to me [*or* to the plaintiff] in the sum of £— for [the price of goods sold and delivered] [the value of services rendered for and on behalf of the defendant and at his request] [the price of work done and materials supplied] [*or as the case may be*].

2. Particulars of the claim are set out in the statement of claim.

3. It is within my knowledge that the said debt was incurred and still remains due and owing to the plaintiff.

4. I believe that there is no defence to this action.

5. I am authorised to make this affidavit by the plaintiff.

Sworn, etc.

C. Specimen Form of Notice of Appeal by Defendant under Order 14 from Order of District Judge to Judge in Chambers

[*Title as in action*]

Take notice that the defendant intends to appeal against the decision of Mr District Judge — dated the — day of 19— whereby the plaintiff was given judgment under Order 14, r.3 for [*set out judgment given*].

And further take notice that you are required to attend before the judge in chambers [*court address*] where the hearing of the appeal will take place on the — day of —, 19— at — a.m./p.m. on the hearing of the application by the defendant that the said order be discharged and that the defendant be granted unconditional leave to defend the action and that the costs of this application [and before the District Judge] be the defendant's in any event.

And further take notice that it is the intention of the defendant to attend by counsel [*estimated length of hearing—hours*].

Dated the — day of —, 19—.

(Signed)
(Address)
Solicitor of the defendant

To [*plaintiff's name and address for service*].

D. Judgment for Plaintiff under Order 14 for Part of the Claim [or one of Several Claims] with Leave to Defend as to Residue and Directions

[*Set out title to action*]

Master [District Judge] — in Chambers.
The — day of — 19—.
On hearing [*the solicitors for both parties*].

577

It is ordered that judgment be entered for the plaintiff for £— being part of his claim and £— interest.

It is further ordered that:

1. The defendant may defend the residue of the plaintiff's claim.

2. The defendant shall serve his defence within the next — days.

3. [*Any other directions for the conduct of the action—e.g. for discovery and inspection, medical and/or other expert evidence, setting down, mode and place of trial*].

4. The costs of and occasioned by this application be costs in the cause [*or other provision for costs*].

E. Judgment for Plaintiff for Delivery of Goods

[*Title as in action*]

[*then continue*]:

Master [District Judge] — in Chambers.

The — day of —, 19—.

The defendant having given notice of intention to defend the action and the court having under Order 14, r.3, ordered that judgment as hereinafter provided be entered for the plaintiff against the defendant.

It is this day adjudged that:

[*Specify delivery—no option to pay value*]

1. The defendant deliver up to the plaintiff [*description of goods*] mentioned in the statement of claim.

2. The plaintiff do recover against the defendant damages to be assessed for wrongful interference and interest thereon.

3. Costs to be taxed.

[*Or delivery of goods or their value*]

1. The defendant deliver up to the plaintiff [*description of goods*] mentioned in the statement of claim or pay their value to be assessed.

2. The plaintiff do recover against the defendant damages to be assessed for wrongful interference and interest thereon.

3. Costs to be taxed.

[*Or value of goods only*]

1. The defendant do pay to the plaintiff the value to be assessed of [*description of goods*] mentioned in the statement of claim.

2. The plaintiff do recover against the defendant damages to be assessed for wrongful interference and interest thereon.

3. Costs to be taxed.

F. Judgment for Plaintiff under Order 14 for Whole Liquidated Claim [with Stay of Execution on Payment by Instalments] [with Stay of Execution Pending Trial of Counterclaim]

[*Title as in action*]

[*then continue*]:
Master [District Judge] — in Chambers.
The — day of —, 19—.

The defendant having given notice of intention to defend this action and the court having under Order 14, r.3 ordered that judgment as hereinafter provided be entered for the plaintiff against the defendant.

It is this day adjudged that the defendant do pay to the plaintiff £— together with £— interest and £— costs [*or costs to be taxed*].

[*Stay of execution on payment by instalments*]

And it is ordered that execution on the said judgment be stayed so long as the defendant pays to the plaintiff the judgment debt, interest and costs by instalments of £— per week [month] commencing on the — day of — 19— until discharge or further order but this stay of execution shall be removed immediately should the defendant default in the payment of any instalment on the due date.

[*Stay of execution pending trial of counterclaim*]

And it is ordered that:

(i) execution on the said judgment be stayed until the trial of the defendant's counterclaim or further order;

(ii) the defendant shall serve his counterclaim within the next — days;

(iii) the plaintiff shall serve his defence to the counterclaim within — days of the date of service of the counterclaim;

(iv) there shall be mutual discovery of documents by lists within — days of close of pleadings and inspection of documents shall take place within a further — days;

(v) the trial of the counterclaim shall take place before a Judge sitting alone in [Liverpool] Category [A B or C] the estimated length of hearing being — hours [days];

[*Provision for costs of the Order 14 application*].

G. Judgment for Plaintiff on Defendant's Failure to Comply with Order giving him Conditional Leave to Defend

[*Title as in action*]

[*then continue*]:
Master [District Judge] — in Chambers.
The — day of —, 19—.

The court having on the — day of —, 19— ordered that unless the defendant paid £— into court on or before the — day of —, 19— the plaintiff should be entitled to enter judgment for the sum claimed in the statement of claim, interest and costs.

And the defendant having failed to comply with the said order, it is this day adjudged that the defendant do pay the plaintiff:

    (i) £—, and

    (ii) £— interest thereon, and

    (iii) £— costs [*or* costs to be taxed].

H. Order for Payment of Part and in Default Judgment for that Part and Leave to Defend as to Residue

[*Title as in action*]

[*then continue*]:

Master [District Judge] — in Chambers.

The — day of —, 19—.

On hearing [*counsel for the plaintiff and counsel for the defendant*]

It is ordered that:

1. Unless the defendant pays £— to the plaintiff within the next — days, the plaintiff may enter judgment against him for that sum.

2. The defendant may defend the residue of the claim.

[*Specimen directions*]

3. The defendant's affidavit sworn on the — day of —, 19— shall stand as his defence.

4. There shall be mutual discovery of documents by lists within the next — days and inspection of documents within a further — days.

5. By consent, the action shall be tried by a Master [District Judge] pursuant to Order 36, r.11 on a date to be fixed.

6. Provisions for costs.

I. Order giving Defendant Leave to Defend Conditional on Payment of Whole or Part of Claim into Court

[*Title as in action*]

[*then continue*]:

Master [District Judge] — in Chambers.

The — day of —, 19—.

On hearing [*counsel for the plaintiff and solicitor for the defendant*].

It is ordered that:

1. Unless the defendant pays £— into court within the next — days, the plaintiff may enter judgment against him for the amount indorsed on the writ, interest and costs.

2. If the defendant pays that sum into court within the prescribed time:

    (a) he may defend the action;

    (b) he shall serve his defence within the next — days;

    (c) there shall be mutual discovery of documents within — days of the

close of pleadings and inspection thereof within a further — days;
(d) [set out any further directions].

J. Order Dismissing Order 14 Summons

[Title as in action]

[then continue]:
Master [District Judge] — in Chambers.
The — day of —, 19—.
    On hearing [counsel for the plaintiff and counsel for the defendant]
    It is ordered that the application by the plaintiff for summary judgment
be dismissed with costs to be taxed and paid forthwith by the plaintiff to
the defendant.
[Certificate for counsel.]

K. Order giving Defendant Unconditional Leave to Defend

[Title as in action]

[then continue]:
Master [District Judge] — in Chambers.
The — day of —, 19—.
    On hearing [solicitor for the plaintiff and counsel for the defendant]
    It is ordered that:
    1. The defendant may defend the action.
    2. The defendant shall serve his defence within the next — days.
    3. [Set out further directions for the conduct of the action.]
    4. [Provision for costs.]

L. Summons by Defendant under Order 14 for Final Judgment on Counterclaim

[Start as in Form G1 or G2 on p. 586]

[then continue]:
    on the hearing of an application by the defendant against the plaintiff
for:
    1. The sum claimed in the counterclaim.
    2. Interest.
    3. Costs of the counterclaim and of this application.
Dated the — day of —, 19—.

[Signed]
[Address]
Solicitor for the defendant.

581

This summons was taken out by [*name and address of defendant's solicitor*]
To [*plaintiff's name and address for service*].

M. Combined Summons for the Plaintiff under Order 14 for Interlocutory Judgment and an Interim Payment under Order 29, rule 11

[*Start as in Form G1 or G2 on p. 586*]

[*then continue*]:

on the hearing of an application by the plaintiff against the defendant
[*or state which of several defendants, e.g. the third defendant*] for:

1. Interlocutory judgment with damages and interest to be assessed;
and/or

2. An order that the [third] defendant do make an interim payment to
the plaintiff of £— or such other sum as the court thinks fit under Order
29, r.11; and

3. Costs

Take notice etc. [*Conclude as in Form N*].

N. Summons under Order 14 by Plaintiff for Final Judgment for Whole or Part of Liquidated Claim against One or More Defendants

[*Start as in Form G1 or G2 on p. 586*]

[*then continue*]:

on the hearing of an application by the plaintiff for final judgment
against the defendant [*or state which of the several defendants—e.g. the
third defendant*] for:

1. The sum claimed in the statement of claim. [*or*]

1. £— representing that part of the plaintiff's claim [*identify the relevant
part, e.g. set out in paragraph 4(b) of the statement of claim*].

2. Interest.

3. Costs.

Take notice that a party intending to oppose this application or to apply
for a stay of execution should send to the opposite party or his solicitor,
so as to reach him not less than [3] days before the above date of hearing,
a copy of any affidavit intended to be used.

Dated the — day of —, 19—.

[Signed]
[Address]
Solicitor for the plaintiff.

This summons was taken out by [*name and address of solicitor for plaintiff*].
To [*defendant's name and address for service*].

O. Summons under Order 14 by Plaintiff for Interlocutory Judgment with Damages to be Assessed

[*Start as in Form G1 or G2 on p. 586*]

[*then continue*]:
   on the hearing of an application by the plaintiff for interlocutory judgment against the defendant [*or state which of several defendants,* e.g. *the third defendant*] with damages to be assessed, interest and costs.
   Take notice [*conclude as in Form N*].

P. Summons under Order 14 by Plaintiff for Delivery of Goods

[*Start as in Form G1 or G2 on p. 586*]

[*then continue*]:
   on the hearing of an application by the plaintiff for judgment against the defendant [*or state which of several defendants,* e.g. *the third defendant*] for:
[*Either*] [*Specific delivery only*]
   1. The delivery to the plaintiff of [*description of goods*] referred to in the statement of claim.
   2. Damages to be assessed for their wrongful interference.
   3. Interest.
   4. Costs.
[*Or*] [*Delivery or value*]
   1. The delivery to the plaintiff of [*description of goods*] referred to in the statement of claim or their value to be assessed.
   2. Damages to be assessed for their wrongful interference.
   3. Interest.
   4. Costs.
[*Or*] [*Assessed value only*]
   1. A sum representing the value to be assessed of [*description of goods*] referred to in the statement of claim.
   2. Damages to be assessed for their wrongful interference.
   3. Interest.
   4. Costs.
[*then continue*]:
   Take notice [*Conclude as in Form N*].

Q. Summons under Order 14 by Plaintiff for Recovery of Land

[*Start as in Form G1 or G2 on p. 586*]

[*then continue*]:
   on the hearing of an application by the plaintiff for final judgment

583

against the defendant [*or state which of several defendants*—e.g. *the third defendant*] for:

1. Possession of the premises known as [*address of property*] referred to in the statement of claim.
2. Arrears of rent.
3. Mesne profits.
4. Costs.

Dated the — day of —, 19—.

[Signed]
[Address]
Solicitor for the plaintiff.

This summons was taken out by [*name and address of solicitor for plaintiff*]. To [*defendant's name and address for service*].

R. Summons under Order 14 by Plaintiff for Final Judgment for an Injunction

[*Note: returnable before judge—not master: Ord. 32, r.11(1)(d)*]

[*Start as in Form G1 or G2 on p. 586*]

[*then continue*]:

on the hearing of an application by the plaintiff for final judgment against the defendant [*or state which of several defendants, e.g. the third defendant*] for:

1. An injunction in the terms set out in the Schedule to his summons.
2. Costs.

THE SCHEDULE

[*Specify precise terms of proposed injunction, e.g.* that the defendant by himself, his servants or agents or otherwise howsoever be restrained from continuing to enter on and use the premises known as 5, Castle Street, Liverpool for any of the purposes described in a licence between the parties dated July 31, 1992 or from trespassing on the said premises.]

Take notice [*conclude as in Form N*].

S. Further Specimen Form of Affidavit in Support of Application by Plaintiff under Order 14

[*Title as in action*]

I, Iain Saville Goldrein of 1, Wood Park, Kirby, Liverpool, the plaintiff in this action, make oath and say as follows:

1. I am a builder. I was in November 1990 instructed by the defendant to

undertake works of construction and structural alteration at the defendant's house, the Oast House, Chivley Road, Borham, Nr. Ormskirk, Lancashire.

2. No written contract was drawn up. The only arrangement we had was that I was to receive payment on account as the work proceeded, and when the whole was finished, send in my bill, which the defendant promised he would then pay.

3. Accordingly I did the work, the defendant paying me on account £15,000, being about 75 per cent of the whole amount, which is customary in my trade.

4. Towards the end of January 1991, when the work was finished, I was with the defendant on the premises and asked him when it would be convenient for him to receive my account. He asked me to send in my bill which I promised to do, adding that if he would like to, I was willing for any respectable surveyor to survey and value the work, and accept his valuation as binding on both parties. The defendant said that he did not want that, but if I sent in my bill he was ready to settle, or words to that effect.

5. Accordingly, I sent in my bill as requested by the defendant.

6. All items in the bill are fair and reasonable charges and all of the work charged for in the bill has been done by me or at my direction.

7. A Mr Allard, who was recommended to me by a friend as a competent surveyor, has gone over the work and measured it, and valued it at £10,000 or thereabouts.

8. To the best of my knowledge and belief the defendant has no grounds of defence to this action on the merits and there remains owing to me the sum of £5,125.

Sworn, etc.

T. Specimen Form of Affidavit in Reply by Defendant under Order 14 [see Form S]

[*Title as in action*]

I, Kenneth Henry Pinder Wilkinson of the Oast House, Chivley Road, Borham, Near Ormskirk, Lancashire, the defendant in this action, make oath and say as follows:

1. I have read the plaintiff's affidavit in support of an application for judgment in this action under Order 14.

2. In answer to paragraph 2, it is true that no contract as to price was entered into between myself and the plaintiff, with the exception, however, that the plaintiff guaranteed that the total price for such alterations should not exceed £15,000. I deny, however, that I agreed, as stated in that paragraph, to pay the plaintiff any sums on account, although I did subsequently pay him sums in respect of such work amounting to £15,000.

3. Pending the progress of such alterations I frequently remonstrated with the plaintiff upon the additional expense to which he was putting me and consistently asked him when the works would be completed.

4. The account sent in by the plaintiff to me is most excessive and unreasonable and the amount already paid by me was greatly in excess of the amount the plaintiff is entitled to receive for such work. The work carried out has been very badly done, to the extent that an outside wall built by the plaintiff will, as I am advised, have to be pulled down and rebuilt.

5. I am advised and do verily believe that I have a good defence, set-off and counterclaim on the merits. There is now produced and shown to me marked "KHPW1" a copy of the report by Mr Alan Smith, a Chartered Surveyor instructed by me to survey the work for the purpose of giving evidence on my behalf on the trial of this action from which it will be seen that remedial work to the estimated value of £8,326 is required to be executed in order to remedy the defects in the works carried out by the plaintiff.

6. Having regard to the matters aforesaid, I respectfully submit that the summons under Order 14 be dismissed and that I be given unconditional leave to defend the action.

Sworn by Kenneth Henry Pinder Wilkinson at Ormskirk in the County of Lancaster this — day of — 19—.

Before me etc.

Form G1: Commencement of Summons in Chambers in London Action

[Set out title to action]

[Either—if in Q.B.D.]:

Let all parties attend the judge [or Master in Chambers] in Room No. —, Central Office, Royal Courts of Justice, Strand, London, on — day the — day of —, 19— at — o'clock in the [—] noon...

[Or—if in Ch.D.]

Let all parties attend Master — in Room No. —, Chancery Chambers, Royal Courts of Justice, Strand, London, on the — day of —, 19— at — o'clock in the [—] noon...

Form G2: Commencement of Summons in Chambers in District Registry Action

[Set out title to action]

Let all parties attend the Judge [or District Judge] in Chambers at [set out

the full address of the court building where the hearing is to take place] on —
day the — day of —, 19— at — o'clock in the [—] noon...

SECTION 3: DEFAULT JUDGMENT FORMS

Contents

Note: for Form of Commencement of Summons—see Forms G1 and G2
above.

A. Request for Search for Notice of Intention to Defend

[Set out title to action]

Please search for a notice of intention to defend this action filed by or on behalf of [*name of defendant*].

Dated the — day of —, 19—.

[Signed]
[Address]
Solicitors for the plaintiff.

B. Affidavit of Personal Service of Writ

[*Title as in action*]

I, [name, address and description of *deponent*] MAKE OATH and say as follows:-

1. I did on — day the — day of — 19—, at [*state where*] personally serve C.D. the above-named defendant [*or one of the above-named defendants*] with a true copy of the writ of summons in this action.

2. The said copy writ was duly sealed with the seal of the Court office out of which it was issued and was accompanied by a prescribed form of acknowledgment of service.

Sworn etc.

C. Affidavit of Postal Service of Writ on Individual

[*Title as in action*]

I, [*state name, address and description of deponent*] MAKE OATH and say as follows:-

1. That I did serve the above-named defendant, C.D. with a true copy of the writ of summons in this action by posting the same on — day, the — day of — 19—, by ordinary post first class mail in an envelope duly pre-paid and properly addressed to the said defendant at (*state the address in full*).

2. The said copy writ was duly sealed with the seal of the Court office out of which it was issued and was accompanied by a prescribed form of acknowledgment of service.

3. The said letter or envelope has not been returned by the Post Office through the Dead Letter Service.

4. That in my opinion [*or in the case of posting by the plaintiff's solicitor or any employee in his firm* in the opinion of the plaintiff] the said writ of summons so posted to the defendant will have come to his knowledge within seven days after the said date of posting thereof.

Sworn, etc.

D. Affidavit of Service of Writ on an English Limited Company

[*Title as in action*]

I, [*name, address and occupation*], MAKE OATH and say as follows:-

1. I did on — day the — day of — 19—, (date of posting), serve the above-named defendants with a true copy of the writ of summons in this action, by [leaving the same at (*place of service*) or by sending the same by ordinary post first class mail in an envelope duly pre-paid and properly addressed to the company at (*address*)], which is the registered office of the said defendant company. (*See note.*)

2. The said copy writ was duly sealed with the seal of the Court office out of which it was issued and was accompanied by a prescribed form of acknowledgment of service.

Sworn, etc.

Note—The word "post" in section 725 of the Companies Act 1985, is wide enough to include both ordinary and registered post; and therefore a company is properly served with a writ which is sent by registered post to its registered office (*T.O. Supplies (London) v. Jerry Creighton* [1952] 1 K.B. 42). Presumably it also includes recorded post. If the writ was posted by second class mail, the affidavit should so state.

E. Affidavit of Personal Service on a Partner in a Firm

[*Title as in action*]

I, [*name, address and occupation*], MAKE OATH and say as follows:-

1. I did on —day the — day of — 19—, at (*state where*) personally serve C.D., a partner in the above-named defendant firm of C.D. *& Co.*, with a true copy of the writ of summons in this action.

2. The said copy writ was duly sealed with the seal of the Court office out of which it was issued and was accompanied by a prescribed form of acknowledgment of service.

Sworn, etc.

F. Default Judgment in Action for Liquidated Demand

[*Title as in action*]

Date: —, 19—.

No notice of intention to defend having been given [*or no defence having been served*].

It is this day adjudged that the defendant do pay the plaintiff £— and £— interest [*or interest to be assessed*] and £— fixed costs [*or costs to be taxed*]

[*After assessment of interest*]

The Master [*or* District Judge] having assessed interest on the sum due to the plaintiff at £— by this certificate dated the — day of —, 19—.

It is further adjudged that the defendant do pay the plaintiff £— and £— costs [*or* costs to be taxed]

[*After taxing officer's certificate*].

The above costs have been taxed and allowed at £— as appears by the taxing officer's certificate dated the — day of —, 19—.

G. Default Judgment in Action for Liquidated Demand in Foreign Currency

[*Title as in action*]

Date: —, 19—.

No notice of intention to defend having been given [*or no defence having been served*].

It is this day adjudged that the defendant do pay the plaintiff:

1. —Deutsch marks
2. —Deutsch marks in interest [*or* interest to be assessed];
3. —Deutsch marks fixed costs [*or* costs to be taxed]

or the sterling equivalent at the time of payment.

[*After assessment of interest*].

The Master [*or* District Judge] having assessed interest on the sum due to the plaintiff at — Deutsch marks by his certificate dated the — day of —, 19—.

It is further adjudged that the defendant do pay to the plaintiff — Deutsch marks or the sterling equivalent at the time of payment and £— costs [*or* costs to be taxed].

[*After taxing officer's certificate*].

The above costs have been taxed and allowed at £— as appears by the taxing officer's certificate dated the — day of —, 19—.

H. Interlocutory Judgment for Plaintiff with Damages to be Assessed

[*Title as in action*]

Date: —, 19—.

No notice of intention to defend having been given [*or no defence having been served*].

It is this day adjudged that the defendant do pay the plaintiff damages to be assessed.

I. Final Judgment for Plaintiff after Assessment of Damages pursuant to Interlocutory Judgment

[*Title as in action*]

Date: —, 19—.

The plaintiff having on the — day of —, 19— obtained interlocutory judgment against the defendant for damages to be assessed and the amount found due to the plaintiff having been certified at £— as appears by the Master's [*or* District Judge's] certificate filed on the — day of —, 19—.

It is this day adjudged that the defendant do pay the plaintiff £— and costs to be taxed

[*After taxing officer's certificate*]

The above costs have been taxed and allowed at £— as appears by the taxing officer's certificate dated the — day of —, 19—.

J. Default Judgment for Return of Goods or their value [and Damages for Wrongful Detention to be assessed]

[*Title as in action*]

Date: —, 19—.

No notice of intention to defend having been given [*or no defence having been served*].

[*Either*] [*Return or value*]

It is this day adjudged that the defendant do deliver to the plaintiff the goods described in the writ of summons [*or* statement of claim] as [*description of goods*] or pay the plaintiff the value of the said goods to be assessed [*and* also damages for their detention to be assessed].

[*Or*] [*Value only*]

It is this day adjudged that the defendant do pay the plaintiff the value of the goods described in the writ of summons [*or* statement of claim] to be assessed [and also damages for their detention to be assessed].

K. Final Judgment for Assessed Value of Goods [and Damages for Wrongful Detention]

[*Title as in action*]

Date: —, 19—.

The plaintiff having on the — day of —, 19— obtained interlocutory judgment against the defendant for the value of the goods described in the writ [*or* statement of claim] to be assessed [and damages for their wrongful detention to be assessed] and the value of the goods having been assessed at £— [and the damages for the wrongful detention assessed at £— as appears by the Master's [*or* District Judge's] certificate filed on the — day of —, 19—.

591

It is this day adjudged that the defendant do pay the plaintiff £— and costs to be taxed.

[*After taxing officer's certificate*]

The above costs have been taxed and allowed at £— as appears by the taxing officer's certificate dated the — day of —, 19—.

L. Default Judgment for Plaintiff for Recovery of Land

[*Title as in action*]

Date: —, 19—.

No notice of intention to defend having been given [*or no defence having been served*].

It is this day adjudged that the defendant do give the plaintiff possession of the land described in the writ of summons [*or statement of claim*] as [*postal or other description of kind*] and pay the plaintiff £— costs [*or costs to be taxed*].

[*After taxing officer's certificate*]

The above costs have been taxed and allowed at £— as appears by the taxing officer's certificate dated the — day of —, 19—.

[*Add certificate set out at p. 441*]

M. Summons for Default Judgment for Specific Return of Goods Without Giving Defendant Option of Paying their Value

[*Title as in action*]

[*The London Action commences as in Form G1 on p. 586*]

[*The District Registry action commences as in Form G2 on p. 586*]

[*Then continue*]:

on the hearing of the application by the plaintiff for:

1. Judgment for the specific return of the [*describe the goods*] referred to in the statement of claim without the defendant having the alternative of paying their value.

2. Damages for their wrongful detention.

3. Costs [including the costs of this application] to be taxed if not agreed, the defendant having failed to give notice of intention to defend the writ served on the — day of —, 19— [*or no defence having been served*].

Dated the — day of —, 19—.

[Signed]

[Address]

Solicitors for the plaintiff.

This summons was taken out by [*name and address of solicitors for plaintiff*].

To: [*name and address [for service] of defendant*].

N. Notice of Motion for Judgment in Default of Defence

[*Title as in action*]

Take notice that the Court will be moved on —day the — day of —, 19— at — o'clock or soon hereafter as counsel for the plaintiff can be heard, for an Order pursuant to Order 19, r.7 that no defence having been served the plaintiff be at liberty to enter judgment against the defendant in the following terms:

1. [*Set out the precise terms of judgment sought against the defendant.*]
2. [*etc.*]
3. That the plaintiff's costs of this action [including the costs of this application] be taxed and paid by the defendant.

Dated the — day of —, 19—.

> [Signed]
> [Address]
> Solicitors for the plaintiff.

This notice was taken out by: [*name and address of solicitors for the plaintiff*]

To: [*name and address [for service] of defendant*]

O. Judgment on Motion for Judgment in Default of Defence

[*Title as in action*]

Date: —, 19—.

This action having on the — day of —, 19— come before the Court on motion for judgment by the plaintiff, no defence having been served by the defendant.

And upon hearing counsel for the plaintiff [and for the defendant *or* there being no attendance by *or* on behalf of the defendant].

And upon the Court ordering that the plaintiff be at liberty to enter judgment against the defendant in the terms hereinafter set out.

It is this day adjudged that [*set out terms of judgment including any provision for costs*].

[*After issue of taxing officer's certificate*]

The above costs have been taxed and allowed at £— as appears by the taxing officer's certificate dated the — day of —, 19—.

P. Summons to Set Aside Irregular Judgment

[*Title as in action*]

[*In a London Action commence as in Form G1 on p. 586*]

[*In a District Registry action commence as in Form G2 on p. 586*]

[*Then continue*]:
   on the hearing of an application by the defendant for:
   1. An Order that the judgment entered by the plaintiff on the — day of —, 19— in default of notice of intention to defend [*or in default of defence*] [*and execution thereon*] be set aside for irregularity on the ground that [*set out briefly the nature of the alleged irregularity—e.g.* the said judgment was entered prematurely].
   2. An Order that the plaintiff do pay the defendant's costs of and occasioned by the entry of the said judgment [and execution] including the costs of and incidental to this application.
Dated the — day of —, 19—.

[Signed]
[Address]
Solicitors for the defendant.

This summons was taken out by: [*name and address of solicitors for defendant*]
To: [*name and address* [*for service*] *of plaintiff*]

Q. Affidavit in Support of Application to Set Aside Irregular Judgment

[*Title as in action*]

I, [*name, address and occupation*], the above-named defendant, make oath and say as follows:
   1. I make this affidavit in support of my application to set aside judgment [and execution thereon].
   2. The plaintiff's specially indorsed writ was served on me by his solicitor on November 1, 1990.
   3. I gave notice of intention to defend the action to the court in the prescribed form on November 5, 1990.
   4. The plaintiff entered judgment in default of defence on November 26, 1990.
   5. I contend that the said judgment is irregular in that it was entered prematurely, the time for service of my defence being 28 days from the date of service of the writ on me, which time had not expired on the date of entry of judgment.
   6. I respectfully contend that the judgment [and execution thereon]

should be set aside as of right so as to allow me to defend the action and that the plaintiff should bear my costs of and incidental to this application for failure to comply with the rules.

Sworn, etc.

R. Summons to Set Aside Regular Judgment

[*Title as in action*]

[*In a London Action commence as in Form G1 on p. 586*]

[*In a district registry action commence as in Form G2 on p. 586*]

[*And continue*]:

on the hearing of an application by the defendant for an order that:

1. The judgment entered by the plaintiff on the — day of —, 19— in default of notice of intention to defend [*or* in default of defence] [and execution thereon] be set aside.

2. The defendant be at liberty to defend the action.

3. The defendant do have — days in which to serve his defence.

4. The costs of and incidental to this application be borne by — in any event.

Dated the — day of —, 19—.

[Signed]

[Address]

Solicitor for the defendant.

This summons was taken out by: [*name and address of defendant's solicitor*]

To: [*plaintiff's name and address* [*for service*]]

S. Affidavit of Service of Summons through Document Exchange

[*Title as in action*]

I, [*name, address and occupation*], make oath and say as follows:

I did serve — solicitors for the above named — in this action whose address for service is a numbered box [*insert box number*] at [*insert town*] Document Exchange with the summons now produced and shown to me and marked "A" by leaving on —day the — day of — 19—, a true copy of the said summons at that document exchange being a document exchange which transmits documents every business day to the document exchange first mentioned

Sworn, etc.

[*Note*: "Document exchange" means an exchange approved by the Lord Chancellor.]

595

SECTION 4: PRACTICE DIRECTION

Practice Direction (*Mareva* Injunctions and *Anton Piller* Orders) July 28, 1994

(1) The granting of a *Mareva* injunction or *Anton Piller* order is a matter for the discretion of the judge hearing the application. However, it is desirable that a consistent approach should in general be adopted in relation to the form and carrying out of such orders, since they represent serious restrictions on the rights of those persons subjected to them imposed after hearing only the applicant's case on an *ex parte* application. This Practice Direction sets out guidelines for the assistance of judges and those who apply for these orders.

(2) Attached to this Practice Direction are new standard forms of the following orders: annex 1, *Anton Piller* order; annex 2, world-wide *Mareva* injunction; and annex 3, *Mareva* injunction limited to assets within the jurisdiction. These forms, inevitably, are complicated, but their language and layout are intended to make it easier for persons served with these orders to understand what they mean. These forms of order should be used save to the extent that the judge hearing a particular application considers there is a good reason for adopting a different form.

(3) The following matters should be borne in mind in relation to an *ex parte* application for any of these orders.

A. On an application for either a *Mareva* or an *Anton Piller* order

1. Where practicable the papers to be used on the application should be lodged with the judge at least two hours before the hearing.

2. An applicant should be required, in an appropriate case, to support his cross-undertaking in damages by a payment into court or the provision of a bond by an insurance company. Alternatively the judge may order a payment by way of such security to the applicant's solicitor to be held by the solicitor as an officer of the court pending further order.

3. So far as practicable, any application for the discharge or variation of the order should be dealt with effectively on the return date.

B. On an application for an *Anton Piller* order

1. (a) as suggested in *Universal Thermosensors Ltd v. Hibben* [1992] 3 All E.R. 257 at 276; [1992] 1 W.L.R. 840 at 861 the specimen order provides for it to be served by a supervising solicitor and carried out in his presence and under his supervision. The supervising solicitor should be an experienced solicitor, having some familiarity with the operation of *Anton Piller* orders, who is not a member or employee of the firm acting for the applicant. The evidence in support of the application should include the

identity and experience of the proposed supervising solicitor. (b) If in any particular case the judge does not think it appropriate to provide for the order to be served by a supervising solicitor, his reasons should be expressed in the order itself.

2. Where the premises are likely to be occupied by an unaccompanied woman and the supervising solicitor is a man, at least one of the persons attending on the service of the order should be a woman: see para. 2(3) of the standard form of order and footnote b.

3. Where the nature of the items removed under the order makes this appropriate, the applicant should be required to insure them: see Sched. 3, footnote e of the standard form.

4. The applicant should undertake not to inform any third party of the proceedings until after the return date: see Sched. 3, para. 6.

5. In future, applications in the Queen's Bench Division will no longer be heard by the judge in chambers. In both Chancery and Queen's Bench Divisions, whenever practicable, applications will be listed before a judge in such a manner as to ensure that he has sufficient time to read and consider the papers in advance.

6. On circuit, applications will be listed before a High Court judge or a Circuit Judge, sitting as a judge of the High Court specially designated by the Presiding Judge to hear such applications.

(4) If an *Anton Piller* order or *Mareva* injunction is discharged on the return date, the judge should always consider whether it is appropriate that he should assess damages at once and direct immediate payment by the applicant.

(5) This practice direction applies to all Divisions of the High Court.

By direction of the Lord Chief Justice, Lord Taylor, with the concurrence of the President of the Family Division, Sir Stephen Brown, and the Vice-Chancellor, Sir Donald Nicholls.

July 28, 1994

ANNEX 1

[*Heading*]

ORDER TO ALLOW ENTRY AND SEARCH OF PREMISES

IMPORTANT:

Notice to the Defendant
(1) This order orders you to allow the persons mentioned below to enter the premises described in the order and to search for, examine and remove or copy the articles specified in the order. This part of the order is subject

to restrictions. The order also requires you to hand over any of the articles which are under your control and to provide information to the plaintiff's solicitors, and prohibits you from doing certain acts. You should read the terms of the order very carefully. You are advised to consult a solicitor as soon as possible.

(2) Before you the defendant or the person appearing to be in control of the premises allow anybody onto the premises to carry out this order you are entitled to have the solicitor who serves you with this order explain to you what it means in every day language.

(3) You are entitled to insist that there is nobody [or nobody except Mr ...] present who could gain commercially from anything he might read or see on your premises.

(4) You are entitled to refuse to permit entry before 9.30 a.m. or after 5.30 p.m. or at all on Saturday and Sunday.

(5) You are entitled to seek legal advice, and to ask the Court to vary or discharge this order, provided you do so at once, and provided that meanwhile you permit the supervising solicitor (who is a solicitor acting independently of the plaintiff) and the plaintiff's solicitor to enter, but not start to search: see para. 3.

(6) If you ... the defendant disobey this order you will be guilty of contempt of Court and may be [sent to prison or] fined or your assets seized. [*Delete the words "sent to prison" in the case of a corporate defendant. This notice is not a substitute for the indorsement of a penal notice.*]

The Order

An application was made today [date] by counsel [or solicitors] for ... the plaintiff to Mr Justice [...]. Mr Justice [...] heard the application and read the affidavits listed in Sched. 6 at the end of this order.

As a result of the application IT IS ORDERED by Mr Justice [...] that:

Entry and search of premises and vehicles on the premises

1. (1) The defendant must allow Mr/Mrs/Miss ...: ("the supervising solicitor"), together with Mr ... a solicitor of the Supreme Court, and a partner in the firm of the plaintiff's solicitors ... and up to ... other persons being [their capacity] accompanying them, to enter the premises mentioned in Sched. 1 to this order and any vehicles on the premises so that they can search for, inspect, photograph or photocopy, and deliver into the safekeeping of the plaintiff's solicitors to all the documents and articles which are listed in Sched. 2 to this order ("the listed items") or which Mr ... believes to be listed items. The defendant must allow those persons to remain on the premises until the search is complete, and if necessary to re-enter the premises on the same or the following day in order to complete the search.

(2) This order must be complied with either by the defendant himself or

by a responsible employee of the defendant or by the person appearing to be in control of the premises.

(3) This order requires the defendant or his employee or the person appearing to be in control of the premises to permit entry to the premises immediately the order is served upon him, except as stated in para. 3 below.

Restrictions on the service and carrying out of para. 1 of this order

2. Paragraph 1 of this order is subject to the following restrictions.

(1) This order may only be served between 9.30 a.m. and 5.30 p.m. on a weekday.

(2) This order may not be carried out at the same time as any police search warrant.

(3) This order must be served by the supervising solicitor, and para. 1 of the order must be carried out in his presence and under his supervision. [At least one of the persons accompanying him as provided by para. 1 of this order shall be a woman.] [*The words in brackets in (3) are to be included in a case where the premises are likely to be occupied by an unaccompanied woman and the supervising solicitor is a man.*]

(4) This order does not require the person served with the order to allow anyone [or anyone except Mr ...] who could gain commercially from anything he might read or see on the premises if the person served with the order objects.

(5) No item may be removed from the premises until a list of the items to be removed has been prepared, and a copy of the list has been supplied to the person served with the order, and he has been given a reasonable opportunity to check the list.

(6) The premises must not be searched, and items must not be removed from them, except in the presence of the defendant or a person appearing to be a responsible employee of the defendant.

(7) If the supervising solicitor is satisfied that full compliance with sub-para. (5) or (6) above is impracticable, he may permit the search to proceed and items to be removed without compliance with the impracticable requirements.

Obtaining legal advice and applying to the court

3. Before permitting entry to the premises by any person other than the Supervising Officer and the plaintiff's solicitors, the defendant or other person appearing to be in control of the premises may seek legal advice, and apply to the Court to vary or discharge this order, provided he does so at once. While this being done, he may refuse entry to the premises by any other person, and may refuse to permit the search to begin, for a short time (not to exceed two hours, unless the supervising solicitor agrees to a longer period).

599

Delivery of listed items and computer print-outs

4. (1) The defendant must immediately hand over to the plaintiff's solicitors any of the listed items which are in his possession or under his control.

(2) If any of the listed items exists only in computer readable form, the defendant must immediately give the plaintiff's solicitors effective access to the computers, with all necessary passwords, to enable them to be searched, and cause the listed items to be printed out. A print-out of the items must be given to the plaintiff's solicitors or displayed on the computer screen so that they can be read and copied. All reasonable steps shall be taken by the plaintiff to ensure that no damage is done to any computer or data. The plaintiff and his representative may not themselves search the defendant's computers unless they have sufficient expertise to do so without damaging the defendant's system.

Disclosure of information by the defendant

5. (1) The defendant must immediately inform the plaintiff's solicitors: (a) where all the listed items are; and (b) so far as he is aware: (i) the name and address of everyone who has supplied him, or offered to supply him, with listed items; (ii) the name and address of everyone to whom he has supplied, or offered to supply, listed items; and (iii) full details of the dates and quantities of every such supply and offer.

(2) Within ... days after being served with this order the defendant must prepare and swear an affidavit confirming the above information.

Prohibited acts

6. (1) Except for the purpose of obtaining legal advice, the defendant must not directly or indirectly inform anyone of these proceedings or of the contents of this order, or warn anyone that proceedings have been or may be brought against him by the plaintiff until [...] [*The date to be inserted here should be the return date or, if sooner, seven days from the date of the order.*]

(2) [Insert any negative injunctions.]

Effect of this Order

(1) A defendant who is an individual who is ordered not to do something must not do it himself or in any other way. He must not do it through others acting on his behalf or on his instructions or with his encouragement.

(2) A defendant which is a corporation and which is ordered not to do something must not do it itself or by its directors officers employees or agents or in any other way.

Undertakings

The plaintiff, the plaintiff's solicitors and the supervising solicitor gave to the court the undertakings contained in Scheds. 3, 4 and 5 respectively to this order.

Duration of this Order

Paragraph 6(2) of this order will remain in force up to and including [:   :19   ] (which is "the return date"), unless before then it is varied or discharged by a further order of the court. [*The date should be the earliest practicable return date.*] The application in which this order is made shall come back to the court for further hearing on the return date.

Variation or Discharge of this Order

The defendant (or anyone notified of this order) may apply to the court at any time to vary or discharge this order (or so much of it as affects that person), but anyone wishing to do so must first inform the plaintiff's solicitors.

Name and address of Plaintiff's Solicitors

The plaintiff solicitors are: [*name, address and telephone numbers both in and out of office hours.*]

[Interpretation of this Order

(1) In this order "he" "him" or "his" include "she" or "her" and "it" or "its".

(2) Where there are two or more defendants then (unless the context indicates differently) (a) references to "the defendants" means both or all of them; (b) an order requiring "the defendants" to do or not to do anything requires each defendant to do or not to do it; (c) a requirement relating to service of this order, or of any legal proceedings, on "the defendants" means on each of them; and (d) any other requirement that something shall be done to or in the presence of "the defendants" means to or in the presence of one of them.]

Schedule 1

The premises

Schedule 2

The listed items

Schedule 3

Undertakings given by the plaintiff

(1) If the court later finds that this order or carrying it out has caused loss to the defendant, and decides that the defendant should be compensated

601

for that loss, the plaintiff will comply with any order the court may make.

[(2) As soon as practicable to issue a writ of summons [in the form of the draft writ produced to the court] [claiming appropriate relief.]]

(3) To [swear and file an affidavit] [cause an affidavit to be sworn and filed] [substantially in the terms of the draft produced to the court] [*confirming the substance of what was said to the court by the plaintiff's counsel/solicitors*].

(4) To serve on the defendant at the same time as this order is served upon him (i) the writ (ii) a notice of motion/summons for ... 19 and (iii) copies of the affidavits and copiable exhibits containing the evidence relied on by the plaintiff. [*Copies of the confidential exhibits need not be served, but they must be made available for inspection by or on behalf of the defendant in the presence of the plaintiff's solicitors while the order is carried out. Afterwards they must be provided to a solicitor representing the defendant who gives a written undertaking not to permit the defendant to see them or copies of them except in his presence and not to permit the defendant to make or take away any note or record of the exhibits.*]

(5) To serve on the defendant a copy of the supervising solicitor's report on the carrying out of this order as soon as it is received and to produce a copy of the report to the Court.

(6) Not, without the leave of the court, to use any information or documents obtained as a result of carrying out this order except for the purposes of these proceedings or to inform anyone else of these proceedings until after the return date.

[(7)] [*In appropriate cases an undertaking to insure the items removed from the premises shall be included.*]

Schedule 4

Undertakings given by the plaintiff's solicitors

(1) To answer at once to the best of their ability any question whether a particular item is a listed item.

(2) To return the originals of all documents obtained as a result of this order (except original documents which belong to the plaintiff) as soon as possible and in any event within two working days of their removal.

(3) While ownership of any item obtained as a result of this order is in dispute, to deliver the article into the keeping of solicitors acting for the defendant within two working days from receiving a written undertaking by them to retain the article in safe keeping and to produce it to the court when required.

(4) To retain in their own safe keeping all other items obtained as a result of this order until the Court directs otherwise.

Schedule 5

Undertakings given by the supervising solicitor

(1) To offer to explain to the person served with the order its meaning and effect fairly and in everyday language, and to inform him of his right to seek legal advice and apply to vary or discharge the order as mentioned in para. 3 of the order.

(2) To make and provide to the plaintiff's solicitors a written report on the carrying out of the order.

Schedule 6

Affidavits

The judge read the following affidavits before making this order:

(1) ...

(2) ...

ANNEX 2

[Heading]

INJUNCTION PROHIBITING DISPOSAL OF ASSETS WORLDWIDE

IMPORTANT:

Notice to the Defendant

(1) This order prohibits you from dealing with your assets up to the amount stated. The order is subject to the exceptions at the end of the order. You should read it all carefully. You are advised to consult a solicitor as soon as possible. You have a right to ask the court to vary or discharge this order.

(2) If you disobey this order you will be guilty of contempt of court and may be [sent to prison or] fined or your assets may be seized. [*Delete the words "sent to prison" in the case of a corporate defendant. This notice is not a substitute for the indorsement of a penal code.*]

The Order

An application was made today [date] by counsel for [or solicitors] for ... the plaintiff to Mr Justice [...]. Mr Justice [...] heard the application and read the affidavits listed in Sched. 2 at the end of this order.

As a result of the application IT IS ORDERED by Mr Justice [...] that:

1. Disposal of assets

(1) The defendant must not (i) remove from England and Wales any of his assets which are in England and Wales whether in his own name or not and whether solely or jointly owned up to the value of £... or (ii) in

603

any way dispose of or deal with or diminish the value of any of his assets whether they are in or outside England or Wales whether in his own name or not and whether solely or jointly owned up to the same value. This prohibition includes the following assets in particular: (a) the property known as ... or the net sale money after payment of any mortgages if it has been sold; (b) the property and assets of the defendant's business known as ... (or carried on at ...) or the sale money if any of them have been sold; and (c) any money in the accounts numbered ... at ...

(2) If the total unincumbered value of the defendant's assets in England and Wales exceeds £... the defendant may remove any of those assets from England and Wales or may dispose of or deal with them so long as the total unincumbered value of his assets still in England and Wales remains above £... If the total unincumbered value of the defendant's assets in England and Wales remains above £... If the total unincumbered value of the defendant's assets in England and Wales does not exceed £..., the defendant must not remove any of those assets from England and Wales and must not dispose of or deal with any of them, but if he has other assets outside England and Wales the defendant may dispose of or deal with those assets as the total unincumbered value of all his assets whether in or outside England and Wales remains above £...

2. Disclosure of information

(1) The defendant must inform the plaintiff in writing at once of all his assets whether in or outside England and Wales and whether in his own name or not and whether solely or jointly owned, giving the value, location and details of all such assets.

(2) The information must be confirmed in an affidavit which must be served on the plaintiff's solicitors within days after this order has been served on the defendant.

Exceptions to this Order

(1) This order does not prohibit the defendant from spending £... a week towards his ordinary living expenses [and £... a week towards his ordinary and proper business expenses] and also £... a week [or a reasonable sum] on legal advice and representation. But before spending any money the defendant must tell the plaintiff's solicitors where the money is to come from.

[(2) This order does not prohibit the defendant from dealing with or disposing of any of his assets in the ordinary and proper course of business.]

(3) The defendant may agree with the plaintiff's solicitors that the above spending limits should be increased or that this order should be varied in any other respect but any such agreement must be in writing.

Effect of this Order

(1) A defendant who is an individual who is ordered not to do something must not do it himself or in any other way. He must not do it through others acting on his behalf or on his instructions or with his encouragement.

(2) A defendant which is a corporation and which is ordered not to do something must not do it itself or by its directors officers employees or agents or in any other way.

Third Parties

(1) *Effect of this order.* It is a contempt of court for any person notified of this order knowingly to assist in or permit a breach of the order. Any person doing so may be sent to prison, or have his assets seized.

(2) *Effect of this order outside England and Wales.* The terms of this order do not affect or concern anyone outside the jurisdiction of this court until it is declared enforceable or is enforced by a court in the relevant country and then they are to affect him only to the extent they have been declared enforceable or have been enforced UNLESS such a person is. (a) a person to whom this order is addressed or an officer or an agent appointed by power of attorney of such a person; or (b) a person who is subject to the jurisdiction of this Court and (i) has been given written notice of this order at his residence or place of business within the jurisdiction of this Court and (ii) is able to prevent acts or omissions outside the jurisdiction of this Court which constitute or assist in a breach of the terms of this order.

(3) *Set off by banks.* This injunction does not prevent any bank from exercising any right of set off it may have in respect of any facility which it gave to the defendant before it was notified of the order.

(4) *Withdrawals by the defendant.* No bank need inquire as to the application or proposed application of any money withdrawn by the defendant if the withdrawal appears to be permitted by this order.

[Service out of the Jurisdiction and Substituted Service

(1) The plaintiff may serve the writ of summons on the defendant at ... by ...

(2) If the defendant wishes to defend the action he must acknowledge service within ... days of being served with the writ of summons.]

Undertakings

The plaintiff gives to the court the undertakings set out in Sched. 1 to this order.

Duration of this Order

This order will remain in force up to and including : :19 ("the return date") unless before then it is varied or discharged by a further order of the court. [*The date should be the earliest practicable return date.*] The application in which this order is made shall come back to the court for further hearing on the return date.

Variation or discharge of this Order

The defendant (or anyone notified of this order) may apply to the court at any time to vary or discharge this order (or so much of it as affects that person), but anyone wishing to do so must first inform the plaintiff's solicitors.

Name and address of Plaintiff's Solicitors

The plaintiff's solicitors are: [*name, address and telephone numbers both in and out of office hours.*]

[Interpretation of this Order

(1) In this order "he" or "him" or "his" include "she" or "her" and "it" or "its".

(2) Where there are two or more defendants then (unless the context indicates differently) (a) references to "the defendants" mean both or all of them; (b) an order requiring "the defendants" to do or not to do anything requires each defendant to do or not to do it; (c) a requirement relating to the service of the order, or of any legal proceedings, on "the defendants" means on each of them.]

Schedule 1

Undertakings given to the court by the plaintiff

(1) If the court later finds that this order has caused loss to the defendant, and decides that the defendant should be compensated for that loss, the plaintiff will comply with any order the court may make.

(2) As soon as practicable the plaintiff will [issue and] serve on the defendant [a] [the] writ of summons [in the form of the draft writ produced to the court] [claiming appropriate relief] together with this order.

(3) The plaintiff will cause an affidavit to be sworn and filed [substantially in the terms of the draft affidavit produced to the court] [*confirming the substance of what was said to the court by the plaintiff's counsel/solicitors*].

(4) As soon as practicable the plaintiff will serve on the defendant a [notice of motion] [summons] for the return date together with a copy of the affidavits and exhibits containing the evidence relied on by the plaintiff.

(5) Anyone notified of this order will be given a copy of it by the plaintiff's solicitors.

(6) The plaintiff will pay the reasonable costs of anyone other than the defendant which have been incurred as a result of this order including the costs of ascertaining whether that person holds any of the defendant's

assets and that if the court later finds that this order has caused such a person loss, and decides that the person should be compensated for that loss, the plaintiff will comply with any order the court may make.

[(7) The plaintiff will not without the leave of the court begin proceedings against the defendant in any other jurisdiction or use information obtained as a result of an order of the court in this jurisdiction for the purpose of civil or criminal proceedings in any other jurisdiction.

(8) The plaintiff will not without the leave of the court seek to enforce this order in any country outside England and Wales [*or seek an order of a similar nature including orders conferring a charge or other security against the defendant or the defendants assets*].]

Schedule 2

Affidavits

The judge read the following affidavits before making this order:

(1) ...

(2) ...

ANNEX 3

[*Heading*]

INJUNCTION PROHIBITING DISPOSAL OF ASSETS IN ENGLAND AND WALES

IMPORTANT:

Notice to the Defendant

(1) This order prohibits you from dealing with your assets up to the amount stated. The order is subject to the exceptions at the end of the order. You should read it all carefully. You are advised to consult a solicitor as soon as possible. You have a right to ask the court to vary or discharge this order.

(2) If you disobey this order you will be guilty of contempt of court and may be [sent to prison or] fined or your assets may be seized. [*Delete the words "sent to prison" in the case of a corporate defendant. This notice is not a substitute for the indorsement of a penal notice.*]

The Order

An application was made today [date] by counsel [or solicitors] for ... the plaintiff to Mr Justice [...]. Mr Justice [...] heard the application and read the affidavits listed in Sched. 2 to this order.

As a result of the application IT IS ORDERED by Mr Justice [...] that:

1. *Disposal of assets*

(1) The defendant must not (i) remove from England and Wales or in any way dispose of or deal with or diminish the value of any of his assets which are in England and Wales whether in his own name or not and whether solely or jointly owned up to the value of £... This prohibition includes the following assets in particular: (a) the property known as ... or the net sale money after payment of any mortgages if it has been sold; (b) the property and assets of the defendant's business known as ... (or carried on at ...) or the sale money if any of them have been sold; and (c) any money in the accounts numbered ... at ...

(2) If the total unincumbered value of the defendant's assets in England and Wales exceeds £... the defendant may remove any of those assets from England and Wales or may dispose of or deal with them so long as the total unincumbered value of his assets still in England and Wales remains above £...

2. *Disclosure of information*

(1) The defendant must inform the plaintiff in writing at once of all his assets in England and Wales and whether in his own name or not and whether solely or jointly owned, giving the value, location and details of all such assets. The information must be confirmed in an affidavit which must be served on the plaintiff's solicitors within days after this order has been served on the defendant.

Exceptions to this Order

(1) This order does not prohibit the defendant from spending £... a week towards his ordinary living expenses [and £... a week towards his ordinary and proper business expenses] and also £... a week [*or a reasonable sum*] on legal advice and representation. But before spending any money the defendant must tell the plaintiff's solicitors where the money is to come from.

[(2) This order does not prohibit the defendant from dealing with or disposing of any of his assets in the ordinary and proper course of business.]

(3) The defendant may agree with the plaintiff's solicitors that the above spending limits should be increased or that this order should be varied in any other respect but any such agreement must be in writing.

Effect of this Order

(1) A defendant who is an individual who is ordered not to do something must not do it himself or in any other way. He must not do it through others acting on his behalf or on his instructions or with his encouragement.

(2) A defendant which is a corporation and which is ordered not to do something must not do it itself or by its directors officers employees or agents or in any other way.

Third Parties

(1) *Effect of this order.* It is a contempt of court for any person notified of this order knowingly to assist in or permit a breach of the order. Any person doing so may be sent to prison, or have his assets seized.

(2) *Set off by banks.* This injunction doe snot prevent any bank from exercising any right of set off it may have in respect of any facility which it gave to the defendant before it was notified of the order.

(4) *Withdrawals by the defendant.* No bank need inquire as to the application or proposed application of any money withdrawn by the defendant if the withdrawal appears to be permitted by this order.

[Service out of the Jurisdiction and Substituted Service

(1) The plaintiff may serve the writ of summons on the defendant at . . . by . . .

(2) If the defendant wishes to defend the action he must acknowledge service within . . . days of being served with the writ of summons.]

Undertakings

The plaintiff gives to the court the undertakings set out in Sched. 1 to this order.

Duration of this Order

This order will remain in force up to and including   :   : 19 ("the return date") unless before then it is varied or discharged by a further order of the court. [*The date should be the earliest practicable return date.*] The application in which this order is made shall come back to the court for further hearing on the return date.

Variation or Discharge of this Order

The defendant (or anyone notified of this order) may apply to the court at any time to vary or discharge this order (or so much of it as affects that person), but anyone wishing to do so must first inform the plaintiff's solicitors.

Name and address of Plaintiff's Solicitors

The plaintiff's solicitors are: [*name, address and telephone numbers both in and out of office hours.*]

[Interpretation of this Order

(1) In this order "he" "him" or "his" include "she" or "her" and "it" or "its".

(2) Where there are two or more defendants then (unless otherwise stated) (a) references to "the defendants" mean both or all of them; (b) an order requiring "the defendants" to do or not to do anything requires each

defendant to do or not to do it; and (c) a requirement relating to service of this order or of any legal proceedings on "the defendants" means on each of them.]

Schedule 1

Undertakings given to the court by the plaintiff

(1) If the court later finds that this order has caused loss to the defendant, and decides that the defendant should be compensated for that loss, the plaintiff will comply with any order the court may make.

(2) As soon as practicable the plaintiff will [issue and] serve on the defendant [a] [the] writ of summons [in the form of the draft writ produced to the court] [claiming appropriate relief] together with this order.

(3) The plaintiff will cause an affidavit to be sworn and filed [substantially in the terms of the draft affidavit produced to the court] [*confirming the substance of what was said to the court by the plaintiff's counsel/solicitors*].

(4) As soon as practicable the plaintiff will serve on the defendant a [notice of motion] [summons] for the return date together with a copy of the affidavits and exhibits containing the evidence relied on by the plaintiff.

(5) Anyone notified of this order will be given a copy of it by the plaintiff's solicitors.

(6) The plaintiff will pay the reasonable costs of anyone other than the defendant which have been incurred as a result of this order including the costs of ascertaining whether that person holds any of the defendant's assets and that if the court later finds that this order has caused such person loss, and decides that such person should be compensated for that loss, the plaintiff will comply with any order the court may make.

Schedule 2

Affidavits

The judge read the following affidavits before making this order:

(1) . . .

(2) . . .

I *Cyanamid*—Case File

A: SERIOUS ISSUE TO BE TRIED—EXAMPLES

1 *Foseco International Ltd v. Fordath Ltd* [1975] F.S.R. 507

1. The facts The plaintiffs, whose business concerned foundry processes, sold exclusively overseas. The defendants, manufacturers of foundry equipment, and, in particular, core binders, had no satisfactory arrangement for sales overseas, except in France and South Africa. In 1961 the parties agreed in writing that the plaintiffs would set up a Swiss holding company (Foseco-Fordath AG), putting the plaintiffs' overseas sales organisation at its disposal, and the defendants would assign to that holding company all their patents, trade marks, and applications. Further, pursuant to the agreement both parties were to channel all their technical knowledge as to relevant products through the holding company of which the plaintiffs owned 70 per cent and the defendants 30 per cent. The plaintiffs spent large sums in establishing a lucrative world-wide business for the holding company in selling "core-binder" products. In 1971 the defendants were taken over and whilst negotiating with the plaintiffs for termination of the agreement, built a factory in Holland for manufacturing, *inter alia*, core binders and entered into agreements for disclosing know-how and establishing independent sales organisations.

2. What did the plaintiffs seek? The injunctions sought fell into four categories:

(a) *Know-how:* from communicating to or placing at the disposal of any person or corporation other than Foseco-Fordath AG any know-how now in their possession or under their control or which shall come into their possession or under their control during the subsistence of an agreement made between the plaintiffs and the defendants and dated May 2, 1961 and relating to the products therein defined.

(b) *Manufacture:* from manufacturing or causing or permitting to be manufactured during the subsistence of the said agreement in any country outside the United Kingdom [save only Australia] any of the products defined in the said agreement otherwise than by Foseco-Fordath AG.

(c) *Sales:* from selling or distributing or causing or permitting to be sold or distributed during the subsistence of the said agreement in any country outside the United Kingdom [save only Australia] any of the products defined in the said agreement otherwise than selling the same to the plaintiffs or to Foseco-Fordath AG in accordance with the terms of the said agreement.

(d) *Trade marks:* from making application for or otherwise acquiring, owning or controlling in any country outside the United Kingdom [save only Australia] any trade mark used or capable of use in respect of the products defined in the said agreement during the subsistence thereof.

3. The case for the defendants The defendants challenged the validity of the agreement. Their argument had four limbs (reported at 513):
- (a) That the agreement was non-exclusive and Fordath could compete with Foseco-Fordath AG.
- (b) That, if it was exclusive, it had been repudiated by Foseco International.
- (c) If it was exclusive, and had not been repudiated, it was void as being in restraint of trade.
- (d) In any event, so far as Common Market countries were concerned, it was void under Article 85 of the Treaty of Rome.

As to those submissions Foster J. said by way of preliminary observation:
- (a) "The first submission is a matter of construction of the agreement in the light of all the surrounding circumstances in 1961. The subsequent conduct of the parties cannot be taken into account in construing it: see *Wickman Machine Tool Sales Ltd v. Schuler (L.) AG* [1974] A.C. 235. Counsel for the defendants invited me to construe the agreement, but I did not have before me all the evidence of the surrounding circumstances, nor had it been tested in cross-examination."
- (b) "The question whether it is void as being in restraint of trade is ... a question of mixed law and fact."
- (c) "Whether the argument falls foul of Article 85 must be a question of construction of that article and of the other relevant regulations. My tentative view on both the last two questions is that the [plaintiffs are] more likely to succeed at the hearing."

4. Was there a serious issue to be tried? Yes—at 515:

"Counsel for the plaintiff submitted that the defence was bound to fail, but he later withdrew that submission. I do not think that there can be any doubt that the question of exclusivity is not an easy one. I am warned by the House of Lords not to embark on anything resembling a trial, and I say no more on the question of exclusivity than that, on the untested evidence before me, I think that Foseco International is more likely to succeed in its contention that the contract is exclusive."

2 Picketing: *Hubbard v. Pitt* [1976] Q.B. 142

1. Background Social workers in Islington alleged that property developers with the assistance of estate agents were, in a harassing fashion, winkling out tenants, thereby to afford opportunity to refurbish their homes with a view to sell at a very substantial profit to those enjoying a much higher income.

2. The facts Against that background, social workers arranged "pickets," singling out for special treatment "Prebble & Co." There were sometimes four, and occasionally up to eight. They stood about on the pavement in front of Prebble's offices. They only did it for about three hours on Saturday mornings, different persons on different Saturdays. Their placards bore phraseolgy such as "Tenants Watch Out, Prebble's About" and "If Prebble's In—You're Out." Further, they handed leaflets to passers-by which explained their reasons for the pickets. The pickets were arranged with the full knowledge and agreement of the local police and they behaved in a peaceful and orderly manner throughout.

3. The nub of the claim against the pickets Paragraph 4 of the statement of claim read:

"... with the intention of and for the purpose of compelling the plaintiffs to cease acting as aforesaid in the purchase, sale and letting of domestic accommodation in Islington and/or compelling them to conduct their said business in accordance with the demands made in a letter dated March 16, 1974 (to which the plaintiffs will refer at trial) from an organisation called Islington Tenants Crusade to the plaintiffs' firm. Further, the said picketing has been carried out in such a manner as substantially to interfere with the plaintiffs' enjoyment of their said premises and the conduct of their said business and so as to intimidate and deter persons wishing to transact business with the plaintiffs or otherwise seeking access to their premises, including the plaintiffs' employees."

The plaintiffs went on, in their affidavit, to depose in great detail to the interference with their business allegedly caused by the defendants.

615

4. The issue—was it "nuisance"? Although the defendants denied the plaintiffs' allegations, the Court of Appeal found it impossible to hold that the available material failed to disclose that the plaintiffs had no real chance of succeeding. There was, on the contrary, a serious issue to be tried, namely on which side of the dividing line set by the following authorities did the case lie. Was it as in *Lyons (J) & Sons v. Wilkins* [1899] 1 Ch. 255 where it was held to amount to a private nuisance where the activities of the defendants had amounted to a watching or besetting of the plaintiffs' premises with a view to compelling the plaintiffs not to do acts which it was lawful for them to do? Or did the case approximate to *Ward, Lock & Co. Ltd v. Operative Printers' Assistants' Society* [1906] 22 T.L.R. 327 where was held that picketing without violence, obstruction, annoyance or molestation, in the vicinity of the plaintiffs' business premises with a view to persuading the plaintiff's employees to become members of a union, does not amount to a nuisance. In the context of industrial picketing on a large scale, see *Thomas v. National Union of Mineworkers (South Wales Area)* [1986] Ch. 20.

5. Representative defendants In the context of this case, reference should be made to *Micheals (M.) (Furriers) v. Askeur* (1983) 127 S.J. 507, C.A., in which Dunn L.J. is reported as saying:

> "Care had to be taken to ensure that Order 15, rule 12 was not abused. But where a number of unidentified persons were causing injury and damage by unlawful acts of one kind or another, and there was an arguable case that they belonged to a single organisation or class which encouraged actions of the type complained of and their clients could be linked to that organisation, the rule enabled the court to do justice in the particular case. The narrow construction of the rule contended for would deprive the courts in such a situation of a useful remedy. The appeal should be dismissed but the order varied by deleting (v) which it was conceded was unnecessarily wide in its scope and might involve interference with lawful activities."

In this case, having taken the view that following *Cyanamid* the balance of convenience was overwhelming in favour of granting interlocutory relief to the plaintiffs, Stephen Brown J. granted eight interlocutory injunctions restraining eight defendants until the trial of the action, *inter alia*, from:

(a) picketing the plaintiffs' shops at Bristol, Weston-super-Mare and Taunton; and

(b) doing any act calculated to interfere with the plaintiffs' contracted relations with their customers or other persons.

The injunctions against the first defendant and a Ms Pink were expressed to be on their own behalf and on behalf of all other members of Animal Aid (of which unincorporated association Ms Pink was the national organiser).

616

3 Union rule book: *Porter v. National Union of Journalists* [1980] IRLR 404, H.L.

1. The facts Lord Diplock set the factual scene at 406(1):

"... the plaintiffs in the two actions which have given rise to this consolidated appeal are members of the National Union of Journalists (the NUJ) employed on the *Birmingham Post and Mail* and the *Coventry Evening Telegraph* respectively who refused to obey an instruction to take part in a strike beginning on December 4, 1978. This instruction (the strike order) had been issued on December 1 by the National Executive Council (the NEC) of the NUJ and was addressed to all members of the NUJ employed on provincial news-papers whose publishers were members of the Newspaper Society (the NS newspapers) and to all members employed by the Press Association (the PA), a press agency on which the NS newspapers relied for much of their material. Ancillary instructions (the blacking orders) had also been issued before December 4 to members of other sectors of the journalists' profession to supply no material to and to use no material emanating from the NS newspaper or the PA."

2. The run-up to the litigation Prior to the settling of the strike on January 18, 1979, the president of the NUJ had threatened the plaintiffs with expulsion from the union on the basis of "their failure, without reasonable cause, to comply with an instruction of the NEC" such failure being an offence under Rule 18(b) of the NUJ rule book. The plaintiffs in turn contended that the strike order was unlawful because under Rule 20(b) of the NUJ Rule Book:

"No withdrawal from employment affecting a majority of the members of the union shall be sanctioned by the NEC unless a ballot of the whole of the members shows a two-thirds majority of those voting in favour of such action."

3. The issue to be tried Against that backdrop, Lord Diplock identified the following issue to be tried:

"The plaintiffs' contention is that the action called for by the strike order and the blacking orders constituted a 'withdrawal from employ-ment affecting a majority of the members of the union' within the meaning of Rule 20(b); the NUJ's contention is that it did not affect a majority of the members. Which is right will be decisive of the only issue in the two actions that has not by now been overtaken by events."

4. Was that issue serious? Slade J. at first instance had firmly come down in favour of the defendants' contention. The Court of Appeal had with equal firmness come down in favour of the plaintiffs' contention. The House of Lords thus had to advert to the criterion expressed by Lord Diplock in *Cyanamid* at 407G:

> "The court must no doubt be satisfied that the claim is not frivolous or vexatious; in other words, that there is a serious issue to be tried."

5. The rule book To explore the application of the *Cyanamid* criterion, Lord Diplock turned to the defendant union's rule book, and as a canon of interpretation cited the dicta of Lord Wilberforce in *Heatons Transport v. Transport and General Workers' Union* [1973] A.C. 15 at 100:

> "But trade union rule books are not drafted by parliamentary drafts-men. Courts of law must resist the temptation to construe them as if they were: for that is not how they would be understood by the members who are the parties to the agreement of which the terms, or some of them, are set out in the rule book, nor how they would be, and in fact were, understood by the experienced members of the court. Furthermore, it is not to be assumed, as in the case of a commercial contract which has been reduced to writing, that all the terms of the agreement are to be found in the rule book alone: particularly as respects the discretion conferred by the members upon committees or officials of the union as to the way in which they may act on the union's behalf. What the members understand as to the characteristics of the agreement into which they enter by joining a union is well-stated in the section of the TUC Handbook on the Industrial Relations Act which gives advice about the content and operation of unions' rules. paragraph 99 reads as follows:
>
> > 'Trade union government does not however rely solely on what is written down in the rule book. It also depends upon custom and practice, by procedures which have developed over the years and which, although well understood by those who operate them, are not formally set out in the rules. Custom and practice may operate either by modifying a union's rule as they operate in practice, or by compensating for the absence of formal rules. Furthermore, the procedures which custom and practice lay down very often vary from workplace to workplace within the same industry, and even within different branches of the same union.'"

6. Held—the issue was serious Why? With these dicta of Lord Wilberforce to guide him, Lord Diplock then had to establish whether or not there was

618

a serious question as to whether a "majority" was affected by the withdrawal form employment. To this end, he said at 407(13):

> "My Lords, on this approach I do not find it appropriate to seek to dissect Rule 20(a) and (b), by considering separately particular words and phrases of which the sub-rules are composed. I do not find it necessary or desirable in an interlocutory appeal, to discuss whether the phrase 'withdrawal from employment' is limited to complete cessation of work by an employed journalist or includes a refusal by him to do some part on of the work required under his contract of employment, nor whether the word 'employment' includes working as a freelance journalist on one's own account. What your Lordships have to consider is what members of the NUJ an ordinary journalist in 1978 would regard as being affected by the strike of journalists employed on NS newspapers and by the PA that was the subject of the strike order issued by the NEC at the beginning of December 1978."

On the affidavit evidence, Lord Diplock was able to identify three categories of members who would be affected by the "withdrawal from employment" ordered by the NEC:

> "(1) All members employed by NS newspaper and the PA;
> (2) All freelance journalists and staff journalists in any other sector who engaged in linage work and whose normal professional earnings included receipts from NS newspaper or the PA, not so trifling as to be regarded as *de minimis*; and
> (3) All employed journalists for whom compliance with the blacking orders would involve their breaking their contracts of employment in a respect which was not so trifling as to be regarded as *de minimis*."

7. The "issue" splits into two The issue to be tried thus resolved itself to the following questions:

(a) How many members did the union have?

(b) Of those members, how many fell into the three categories?

If it was obvious that less than half fell within the categories, the plaintiffs had to lose. If it was obvious that more than half fell within the categories, then an interlocutory injunction would almost be a certainty. If it was in doubt whether more than half fell within the categories, the court had carefully to consider the balance of convenience. In this regard, Lord Diplock said:

> "The evidence so far available on affidavit at this interlocutory stage of the proceedings is in my view inadequate, inconclusive and conflicting as to the number of members who could have been

reasonably foreseen as likely to fall within categories (2) and (3) when the NEC issued the strike order and the blacking orders. This is because throughout the interlocutory proceedings the NUJ has relied primarily on its contention accepted by the judge, that only members within category (1) were affected; whereas the plaintiffs, for whom the relevant information would in any event have been difficult to obtain, have relied primarily on their contention, accepted by the Court of Appeal, that all members of any sector of the profession to which the blacking orders were addressed were affected."

The "balance of convenience" thus fell to be considered, in which regard, see below, p. 655.

4 Abuse of dominant position—Article 86: *Garden Cottage Foods Ltd v. Milk Marketing Board*[1984] A.C. 130

1. Background 90 per cent of the plaintiff's purchase of bulk butter came from the defendant. By a letter dated March 24, 1982 the defendant advised the plaintiff that it had decided to revise its sales and marketing strategy and would no longer use the plaintiff to handle the distribution of bulk butter.

2. The nub of the plaintiff's claim The plaintiff claimed that the defendant was in breach of Article 86 of the EEC Treaty, in that it had abused its dominant position. By virtue of *Belgische Radio & T.V. v. S.A.B.A.M.* (Case 127/73) [1974] E.C.R. 51 at 313; [1974] 2 C.M.L.R. 238 at 251 such a breach can be categorised in English law as a breach of a statutory duty that is imposed not only for the purpose of promoting the general economic prosperity of the Common Market but also for the benefit of private individuals to whom loss or damage is caused by a breach of that duty.

3. The interlocutory injunction application—what terms did the plaintiff seek? The plaintiff claimed an interlocutory injunction to restrain the defendant by itself, its servants or agents or otherwise:
  (a) from confining its sales of bulk butter to any particular person or persons or body of persons or any particular organisation or corporate body; and
  (b) from imposing significantly different terms in relation to the supply of butter to buyers in the bulk butter market, whether as regards price, quantity, credit terms or otherwise than pursuant to ordinary mercantile and commercial practice, such injunction to remain in force until the trial of the action or further order.

4. The serious issue to be tried Although it was not central to the decision of the House of Lords, it was, *inter alia*, recognised that there was a serious issue to be tried. In this regard, Lord Diplock held that to establish whether or not there was a breach of Article 86, the questions for the full trial of the action were:

(a) "The contravenor must be in a dominant position in a substantial part of the Common Market; and this involves as a preliminary question the identification of the 'relevant market'"—not necessarily as easy task as *Europemballage Corporation & Continental Can Co. Inc. v. E.C. Commission* (Case 6/72R) [1972] E.C.R. 157; [1972] C.M.L.R. 690 shows.

(b) "... there must be shown an 'abuse' of that dominant position. The particular examples in paragraphs (b) and (c) of Article 86 upon which the company principally relies *may* constitute an abuse but do not necessarily do so, and in this connection it may be necessary to take into account the interaction between the Community rules on competition and the C.A.P."

(c) "... Thirdly, it must be shown that the abuse affects trade between member states."

5 Unauthorised telephone tapping: *Francome v. Mirror Group Newspapers Ltd* [1984] 1 W.L.R. 892

1. The facts There had come into the possession of the defendants, 38 tapes which through a bugging device contained conversations of Mr and Mrs Francome which had been recorded contrary to the criminal law. The plaintiffs issued a writ and, *inter alia*, claimed an interlocutory injunction. Park J.:

(a) Ordered a speedy trial.

(b) Granted an injunction restraining all the defendants from publishing or causing to be published any article which was based on or made use of the plaintiffs' telephone conversations.

(c) Ordered the defendants to deliver the tapes, transcripts and any notes of telephone conversations to a third party.

(d) Ordered the defendants to reveal their sources within 24 hours.

The defendants appealed.

2. The serious issue to be tried In the course of his judgment, Stephen Brown L.J. identified the following serious issue to be tried, namely what use, if any, may be made of tape recordings which are known to have been obtained illegally by unauthorised phone tapping.

6 Handmade Films (Productions) Ltd v. Express Newspapers plc [1986] F.S.R. 463

1. The facts Continuity photographs of "Madonna" and her husband taken by an employee of the plaintiff film production company were declared by the *Daily Express* to have been "smuggled" from the film set en route to featuring in that newspaper. Scott J. granted an *ex parte* injunction restraining further infringement by the defendant of the plaintiff's copyright in the photographs.

2. The motion The plaintiff asked for delivery up of the infringing photographs and the following relief:

> "The Defendant do forthwith disclose to the Plaintiff and within four days make and serve an Affidavit upon the Plaintiff setting forth (a) in detail the circumstances by which it obtained possession of the photographs of the Plaintiff, copies of which appeared in the February 28th edition of the *Daily Express*; (b) the identity of the party or parties who allowed the Defendant access to the Plaintiff's private documents and the Plaintiff's private property on the occasion whereby the Defendant obtained possession of the photographs; (c) the identity of the party or parties who took the said photographs from the Plaintiff; and (d) the identity of the party or parties involved in smuggling the said photographs out of the possession of the Plaintiff."

It was this particular relief which was the subject matter of the adjudication before the Vice-Chancellor.

3. Why did the plaintiff seek that relief? Their reasons are recorded at 466:

(a) "The control of publicity by a film company and by the Plaintiffs in this case is of great importance to them."

(b) "[T]he presence on the set (either amongst their employees or otherwise) of unreliable persons who can breach their security (as in the present case) is disruptive both to the staff and, more importantly, to the stars."

4. Case for the defendant

(a) They paid for the photographs, and did not steal them. The Vice-Chancellor went on to say at 466/7:

> "In their evidence the Defendants said that when they purchased the photographs they were not aware that they were the property of the Plaintiffs or that the Plaintiffs owned the copyright in the photographs. The Plaintiffs are sceptical about that evidence, especially bearing in

622

mind that the photographs themselves were on cards with punched holes on the corners and with annotations on the bottom referring to scene numbers. That is a scepticism which I can understand; but it is something which I cannot reserve on motion. I must proceed on the footing, I think, that the evidence sworn by the Defendants is accurate and the copyright in them was the Plaintiffs'. They were certainly aware that the photographs were smuggled and they were not intended to have them."

(b) Section 10 of the Contempt of Court Act 1981 reads:

"No Court may require a person to disclose nor is any person guilty of contempt of Court for refusing to disclose the source of information contained in a publication for which he is responsible unless it is established to the satisfaction of the Court that disclosure is necessary in the interests of justice or national security of for the prevention of disorder or crime."

5. The legal matrix of the plaintiff's case

(a) *Norwich Pharmacal Company:* in *Norwich Pharmacal Company v. Customs and Excise Commissioner* [1974] A.C. 133 Lord Reid said at 175:

"... If through no fault of his own a person gets mixed up in the tortious acts of others so as to facilitate their wrong-doing he may incur no personal liability but he comes under a duty to assist the person who has been wronged by giving him full information and disclosing the identity of the wrong-doer."

Thus it was that the plaintiff's argument was recorded by the Vice-Chancellor in the following terms, at 467:

"So, it is said that the unknown wrong-doer who has misappropriated the continuity photographs of the Plaintiff Company and sold them to the Defendants for the purpose of reproducing them in the *Daily Express* was a wrong-doer in that he infringed the copyright of the plaintiffs indeed."

(b) *Balancing exercise:* The Vice-Chancellor went on to say at 467:

"Then, it is said, the Defendant Company though themselves not parties to the original wrong-doing, on the basis of the *Norwich Pharmacal* case, are bound to disclose to the Plaintiffs the identity of the person from whom they got the photographs. The Plaintiffs accept that whether or not such an order for discovery is made is within the discretion of the court. In exercising that discretion I have to weigh the detriment suffered by the Plaintiffs in this case against the public

623

interest which exists in ensuring the free flow of information to the Press, one of the bastions of such free flow of information being that the source of information given in confidence is not revealed by the Press."

(c) *British Steel Corporation:* By reference to the decision of the House of Lords in *British Steel Corporation v. Granada Television Ltd* [1981] A.C. 1096, the court should order the disclosure of the identity of the wrong-doer as outweighing any public interest in confidentiality of Press sources.

6. The significance of section 10

(a) The decision in the *British Steel Corporation* case antedates section 10, and

(b) section 10 was considered by the House of Lords in *The Secretary of State for Defence v. Guardian Newspapers Ltd* [1985] A.C. 339.

7. Section 10—its application or otherwise to the present case

(a) *Plaintiff's argument:* It is in the interests of justice that the identity of the wrong-doer should be made known—even though the plaintiff had no intention of launching legal proceedings against that wrong-doer— the plaintiff praying in aid as authority for that proposition, the decision of the House of Lords in the *British Steel* case.

(b) *The defendant's argument:* The law laid down in the *British Steel* case had been substantially affected by section 10 of the Contempt of Court Act 1981—as interpreted by the House of Lords in the *Guardian Newspapers* case.

(c) *Judgment:* The Vice-Chancellor referred to the following passages in the judgment of Lord Diplock in the *Guardian Newspapers* case:
   (i) At 350C:

   "I would add that in my view the expression 'justice,' the interests of which are entitled to protection, is not used in a general sense as the antonym of 'injustice' but in the technical sense of the administration of justice in the course of legal proceedings in a court of law..."

   (ii) At 350F:

   "In view of the course that the case took before Scott J., however, it is necessary to say something about another exception: the interests of justice. This, as I have already pointed out, refers to the administration of justice, in particular legal proceedings already in existence, or, in the type of 'bill of discovery' case revived after long disuse and exemplified by *Norwich Pharmacal Co. v. Customs and Excise Commissioners* [1974] A.C. 133 (to which, incidentally, section 10 of the Act of 1981 would not have applied), a particular civil action which is proposed to bring against a wrong-doer whose identity has not yet been ascertained.

I find it difficult to envisage a civil action in which section 10 of the contempt of Court Act 1981 would be relevant other than one for defamation or for detention of goods where the goods, as in the instant case and in *British Steel Corporation v. Granada Television Ltd* [1981] A.C. 1096 consist of or include documents that have been supplied to the media in breach of confidence."

Against that backdrop, the Vice-Chancellor at 470 went on to rule:

"However, I think it is clear that the passages I have quoted indicate that, in order for a claim for disclosure to be brought within the exception as being necessary in the interests of justice, the plaintiff in a *Norwich Pharmacal* type of action has to show that he needs the name of the unknown wrongdoer in another action. It is not apparently any longer sufficient, in order to comply with the requirements of section 10, that the purpose is merely to identify the wrongdoer against whom any action might be brought. If that is right, then, in my judgment, this claim for disclosure at this stage cannot succeed."

8. Subsidiary matters

(a) The plaintiffs had argued that section 10 did not apply to photographs—but the Vice-Chancellor ruled at 468 that it did.

(b) As to the underlying purpose of section 10, the Vice-Chancellor said:

"The House of Lords has shown [the underlying purpose of section 10] to be to protect the public interest by preserving the confidentiality of communications to the media. If in every case in which some wrongdoing by an unknown third party involved the leakage of information to the Press by the use of the *Norwich Pharmacal* type of proceedings the Press could be bound to disclose the source of the leakage, it could in my judgment seriously impair the assurance of confidentiality which lies at the basis of freedom of communication to the Press."

(c) The *Francome* analogy—at 471, the Vice-Chancellor said:

"It seems to me that this is a case which raises the same kind of problem as was considered by the Court of Appeal in *Francome v. Mirror Group Newspapers Ltd* [1984] 2 All E.R. 408. In that case the plaintiff wished to get, by way of interlocutory relief, discovery from the defendant newspaper of the identity of a person who had wrongfully tape recorded the plaintiff's telephone conversations.

625

The judge had ordered on an interlocutory application discovery of his name. The Court of Appeal reversed that saying that it was not a proper order since the discovery of the name once made could never be brought back, and there were facts which at the trial would require further investigation before it was appropriate to treat the case as being an exception to section 10. In my judgment exactly the same features apply in this present case. The evidence as to the Plaintiffs' need for security in their organisation against this kind of leakage and the *bona fides* of the Plaintiffs' assertion through Counsel that they intend to sue the wrongdoer are matters which may very well be investigated at the trial and might very well reflect on the discretion which exists in this case if my judgment on the law is wrong."

7 Employment: *Powell v. Brent London Borough Council* [1988] I.C.R. 176

1. The facts The plaintiff was employed by the Council as a Senior Benefits Officer. She applied for promotion to a post as Principal Benefits Officer (Policy and Training) and after she and others were interviewed she was told that she had been selected. However, one of the unsuccessful candidates submitted a grievance, arguing that the selection procedure was in breach of the Council's equal opportunity code of practice, and a week after her appointment she was told that she could not be appointed and the post would be readvertised.

2. The remedy sought By notice of motion the plaintiff sought an order that the Council should not do any of the following acts, namely:
(a) further advertising the post;
(b) treating the said post as vacant and/or taking any steps to fill the said post; and/or
(c) treating the plaintiff as other than their Principal Benefits Officer (Policy and Training).

3. The issue The plaintiff argued that on the evidence the lack of necessary confidence between employee and employer constituted no bar to the continuation of the injunction until trial. The defendants argued that the necessary confidence was lacking.

4. The Court of Appeal held that there was a serious issue Ralph Gibson L.J. said at 193G:

"First I must state the principle which must, I think, guide our decision. It is clear to me that part of the basis of the general rule against specific performance of contracts of service is that mutual confidence is normally a necessary condition for the satisfactory working of a contract of service. If one party refuses to allow the relationship to continue the mutual confidence is almost certainly missing...

... I prefer to state what I think the applicable principle to be in this way. Having regard to the decision in *Hill v. C.A. Parsons & Co. Ltd* [1972] Ch. 305 and to the long-standing general rule of practice to which *Hill v. C.A. Parsons & Co. Ltd* was an exception, the court will not by injunction require an employer to let a servant continue in his employment, when the employer has sought to terminate that employment and to prevent the servant carrying out his work under the contract, unless it is clear on the evidence not only that it is otherwise just to make such a requirement but also that there exists sufficient confidence on the part of the employer in the servant's ability and other necessary attributes for it to be reasonable to make the order. Sufficiency of confidence must be judged by reference to the circumstances of the case, including the nature of the work, the people with whom the work must be done and the likely effect upon the employer and the employer's operations if the employer is required by injunction to suffer the plaintiff to continue in the work."

The exceptional circumstances of this case were such that there was sufficient confidence. The plaintiff was competent to do the job, and there was no friction at the workplace.

[And see "Damages adequate" at p. 644, below.]

8 *Hughes v. Southwark London Borough Council* [1988] IRLR 55

1. The facts The plaintiffs were social workers employed by the London Borough of Southwark at the Maudsley Hospital. The defendants had an acute shortage of staff in one of their other areas, Area 7. They instructed the plaintiffs to work in Area 7 for three days a week for a temporary period. But the plaintiffs complained that this was not part of their contractual duty and they sought an interlocutory injunction to prevent the Council from requiring compliance with the instruction.

2. The law
   (a) Following *Powell v. London Borough of Brent* [1988] I.C.R. 176 it was accepted that an injunction can be granted in relation to a contract of service where there is sufficient mutual confidence.
   (b) Taylor J. rejected the defendants' submission that the interlocutory

decision would decide the action because the injunction only related to a temporary period of the order of six weeks.

"All I say is that, looking at the issues that are raised, I am by no means persuaded that they will go away with the passage of six weeks to a degree where it could be said that the interlocutory decision is final."

3. What was the serious question

"... I think that the essential matter here for me to consider is whether the instruction is arguably unreasonable. If it is arguably unreasonable, then I think there is an issue to be tried on the allegation of breach of contract. I say that in reliance upon the approach adopted by Scott J. in the case of *Sim v. Rotherham Council* [1986] IRLR 391 to which I was referred. Scott J. adopted the test that it was appropriate for an employer to issue and it was requisite for an employee to obey any lawful and reasonable instruction. The case itself was concerned with school-teachers who were requested to cover for absent school-teachers during their own non-teaching periods."

4. The plaintiffs' argument

"[The plaintiffs] say it is one thing for a school teacher in a non-teaching period to be asked to cover for an absent colleague; it is quite a different matter for social workers who have been engaged to a rather specialist field, and a field in which they are not working individually but working as part of a group, to be taken away from that work for the greater part of a week for six weeks in order to cover a situation elsewhere which is not specifically the sort of work that they were engaged to do."

5. The defendants' argument

"In considering the reasonableness of that injunction [counsel for the defendants] suggests that I really ought to put on as it were contractual blinkers and look at the matter only in relation to the employer-employee relationship."

6. There was a serious question to be tried. Why? Taylor J. said:

"In considering that, I think it is relevant to consider also what impact they would make, where they are going to be moved, and looking at the whole of the circumstances, it seems to me arguable that this robbing of Peter to pay Paul is not actually going to result in any satisfactory resolution of Paul's problems which are more long-standing and difficult than could be resolved by this mere tinkering with the problem."

9 Trade secrets: *Johnson & Bloy (Holdings) Ltd v. Wolstenholme Rink plc* [1987] IRLR 499

1. The facts The plaintiff company manufactured printing inks and had developed a particular combination of two ingredients to make up the "drier" in offset metallic ink. The second defendant, Mr Fallon, had been a director of the plaintiffs, but had left them and agreed to join the first defendant company Wolstenholme Rink plc. When he left, Mr Fallon took with him a number of documents containing information about the formulation of the plaintiffs' inks. The defendants wished to use this information to develop inks which were as good as the plaintiffs' and the plaintiffs wished to restrain them.

2. The relief sought The wording of the injunction sought was modified in the course of the appeal, and the final version as granted by the Court of Appeal protected against the following acts:

"(a) Disclosing or using the information that the two ingredients set out in paragraph 8 [of Exhibit 3 of the plaintiffs' affidavit] may be used in combination in the manufacture of an ink and in particular in the manufacture of a drier for an offset metallic printing ink; or

(b) Manufacturing or arranging for the manufacture of an ink and in particular an offset metallic printing ink containing therein such two ingredients as parts of their drier thereof."

3. The law The Court of Appeal applied the law as summarised by Nourse L.J. in *Roger Bullivant Ltd v. Ellis* [1987] IRLR 491 at 494:

"... the confidential information whose misuse is actionable at the suit of the employer may fall into one of the two distinct classes ... First, there are what this court compendiously described as trade secrets or their equivalent. They may not in any circumstances be used by the employee, either during or after the employment, except for the benefit of the employer ... Secondly, there is information which, although not falling into the first class, must nevertheless be treated as confidential by the employee in the discharge of his general implied duty of good faith to his employer. Such information may not be used by the employee during the employment except for the benefit of the employer but, if and only to the extent that it is inevitably carried away in the employee's head after the employment had ended, it may then be freely used for the benefit either of himself or of others."

629

4. The Court of Appeal held: a serious issue Fox L.J. said:

"I think ... that the plaintiffs have an arguable case for interlocutory protection both under the head of trade secrets and of confidential information."

5. The problem of where to draw the line As Fox L.J. put it:

"It may be that some of the information in the documents which Mr. Fallon removed could be carried in his head..."

Further the defendants argued that to restrain them in the manner sought would be unduly burdensome upon Mr Fallon in that it may prevent his using general chemical knowledge which he had acquired throughout the years in the course of his work or his training and of which he cannot rid himself.

6. The line must be drawn on the plaintiffs' side to afford protection The court was mindful of the need not unjustly to fetter an ex-employee, but Parker L.J. said:

"If an employee is sufficiently ill-advised to remove his employers' property when he leaves and that property contains information which was confidential during the course of his employment, he may by reason of his own wrong thereafter be restrained from doing something which, but for his own wrong, he might be entitled to do. That, as Nourse L.J. said, is only fair."

[And see "Damages adequate" at p. 646, below.]

10 The "Chambourcy" case: Mitchelstown Co-operative Society Ltd v. Société des Produits Nestlé SA [1989] F.S.R. 345

1. The facts By a written licence agreement in 1984 the plaintiffs (Mitchelstown) acquired the right to manufacture food to "Chambourcy" recipes and the exclusive right to sell it in Ireland using that trade mark. That written agreement was between Mitchelstown and the first defendants Société de Produits Nestlé SA (hereafter referred to as Nestlé (Switzerland)), who owned the trade mark. Mitchelstown were not able to start manufacturing the food straight away, and there was an agreement known to all parties that in the meantime Mitchelstown would be supplied "Chambourcy" food by the second defendants (Chambourcy U.K.). In 1988 Nestlé (Switzerland) purported to terminate the licence agreement and arranged for the third defendants, Nestlé (Ireland), to sell "Chambourcy" food in Ireland. Mitchelstown applied for an interlocutory injunction to enforce the written licence agreement and the supply arrangement with Chambourcy U.K.

2. The plaintiffs' cause of action was different against each defendant
  (a) The claim against Nestlé (Switzerland) was primarily for simple breach of contract.
  (b) Against Chambourcy U.K. Mitchelstown alleged that the supply arrangement amounted to a collateral contract involving Mitchelstown, Nestlé (Switzerland) and Chambourcy U.K.
  (c) Against Nestlé (Ireland) Mitchelstown argued that it was procuring and assisting in the other two defendants' breaches.

3. The first issue: the defendants' case The defendants asserted that Nestlé (Switzerland) was entitled to deem the licence agreement "abandoned" by reason of Mitchelstown's failure to begin manufacturing "Chambourcy" food in the four years 1984 to 1988. In the Irish Court of Appeal McCarthy J. pointed out that there had been no previous complaint about this failure or any advance warning of the planned termination. But the court did not expressly find an arguable case on this issue.

4. The principal issue: the collateral contract The trial judge had found that a collateral agreement "has not really been proved to any extent ...". McCarthy J. said in the Court of Appeal:

> "... I am unable to accept this view. Not merely was a collateral agreement proved, but it was proved, so to speak, from the defendants."

This was a reference to a letter written by Nestlé (Switzerland) to Mitchelstown in 1983 which said:

> "Until you can start the manufacture of the desserts, these products can be imported from the U.K."

Finlay C.J. was satisfied that the collateral contract also involved Chambourcy U.K.:

> "I am satisfied that his correspondence which I have partly quoted and the further facts set out in the affidavits filed on behalf of the plaintiff on this application clearly constitute an arguable case that a contractual relationship exists between it and the U.K. company concerning the supply to it of the Chambourcy products from the U.K. company and its sale by it (the plaintiff) in Ireland under the 'Chambourcy' trade mark."

5. The third issue: the conspiracy with Nestlé (Ireland) All the defendants

631

denied that they acted in concert in cutting off the supplies of food to the plaintiff, asserting that each of them is an independent company having its own independent decision-making process and acting independently one of the other, although they conceded that they were associated companies. McCarthy J. said:

> "In my view the plaintiff has made out a clear case of the existence of the oral agreement, its breach, the involvement of all three defendants in its breach, the acting in concert by the defendants such as prima facie to amount to a conspiracy to procure breach of contract..."

[And see "Balance of Convenience" at p. 670.]

11 "One Girl's War": *Att.-Gen. v. Brandon Book Publishers Ltd* [1989] F.S.R. 37

1. The facts The defendants wished to publish in Ireland a book *One Girl's War* written by an MI5 agent (Miss Miller) about her experiences during the Second World War. Shortly before publication the Attorney-General for England and Wales applied in the Irish High Court for an interlocutory injunction to prevent its publication.

2. The plaintiffs' case The plaintiffs' case was based upon Miss Miller's duty of confidentiality as an employee. The book was a clear breach of that duty.

3. The breach of confidence issue Carroll J. said:

> "The publication which is sought to be prevented here is not a private confidence or trade information but information shared between a Government and a private individual. It seems to me that a distinction can and should be drawn between a Government and a private person."

Carroll J. quoted Mason J. in the case of *Commonwealth of Australia v. John Fairfax and Sons Ltd* (1980) 147 C.L.R. 39 at 51, and applied the principle stated by him there:

> "This is not to say that equity will not protect information in the hands of the government, but it is to say that when equity protects Government information it will look at the matter through different spectacles ... Accordingly the court will determine the Government's claim to confidentiality by reference to the public interest. Unless disclosure is likely to injure the public interest it will not be protected."

4. The public interest issue Carroll J. took the view that there was no question of Irish public interest.

> "Mason J. was talking there in the context of the Government of Australia asking the courts of Australia to restrain publication where the question of public interest did arise and which would arise here if the government of Ireland were the plaintiff. But here the plaintiff is the representative of a foreign government. There is no question of the public interest of this state being affected. The considerations which would move the courts in the United Kingdom in this matter are different from the considerations here."

12 *Att.-Gen. v. Turnaround Distribution Ltd* [1989] F.S.R. 169

1. The facts The defendants wished to distribute in the United Kingdom a book *One Girl's War* written by an MI5 agent (Miss Miller) about her experiences during the Second World War. The subject matter of the book ended in 1944 and it was accepted that the contents were not "sensitive". The Attorney-General failed to prevent the book being published in Ireland for reasons connected with the Irish Constitution. (See p. 632) He applied for an interlocutory injunction to prevent distribution in the United Kingdom.

2. The plaintiff's argument It was accepted that the defendants could be in no better position than the agent authoress. The plaintiff argued that by reason of her employment by the Crown the authoress was subject to an implied lifelong condition not to divulge information acquired through that employment.

3. An arguable case? Yes, but a different case was also arguable. Simon Brown J. said:

> "... although it is to my mind a good deal less than self-evident, it is nevertheless clearly arguable that those serving in the security service owe a lifelong obligation of confidence and this founds a contractual right to restrain a breach, irrespective of whether the contents of any proposed publication are intrinsically sensitive or innocuous. But ... prima facie the contrary view—namely that the obligation of confidence is owed only so long as there is a real need to restrain publication in the interests of national security—appears in my judgment at least equally tenable. Why otherwise if national security did not require it, would the courts be prepared to imply a term as to a lifelong duty of confidentiality? It is not after all suggested that any express term was imposed upon Miss Miller. Surely therefore the

implication only arises if there exists a true public interest in restraining publication on a lifelong basis."

[And see "Damages adequate" at p. 646 and "Balance of convenience" at p. 669.]

13 *Fresh Fruit Wales Ltd v. Halbert, The Times,* January 29, 1991, C.A.

1. The facts The plaintiffs had been issued with 22 tickets by the Welsh Rugby Union in respect of matches for the current season. The tickets had come into the possession of the defendants, the trustees of the Cacran (Ely) Sports and Social Club, and the plaintiffs accordingly applied for an interlocutory injunction, a week before the first match, that the defendants should hand over the tickets. The judge ordered the defendants to hand over all the tickets. The defendants unsuccessfully appealed.

2. A strong case The Court of Appeal had no doubt that there was a high degree of probability that the plaintiffs would succeed in the action and dismissed the appeal.

3. The subsidiary point The defendants argued that the trial judge had been wrong in concluding that he had no power to make an order other than one which could finally be made at the end of the trial, for example, give half the tickets to the plaintiffs and half to the defendants.

4. A hollow victory for the defendants The report of Parker J.'s judgment reads:

> "His Lordship could not accept that the judge had no power, if the circumstances justified it, to make the order asked for by [the defendants, *i.e.* halving the tickets]. Section 37(1) of the Supreme Court Act 1981 allowed the court to grant injunctions where it was 'just and convenient to do so' and section 37(2) of the Act conferred jurisdiction on the court to grant an injunction 'on such terms and conditions as the court thinks just.' There was no limitation on the court to make an order at the interlocutory stage which would not be appropriate at the final trial."

So the Court of Appeal exercised its discretion afresh, but exercised it in the same way as the trial judge.

14 *Ciba Geigy plc v. Park Davis & Co. Ltd* (1993) T.L.R. 202

1. The background The plaintiffs had developed and marketed an established non-steroidal anti-inflammatory drug "Voltarol Retard". The defendants then developed and wished to market what they regarded as an equivalent diclofenac painkiller under the name "Diclomax Retard". They placed advertisements in *Pulse* magazine stating in effect that "Diclomax Retard" was just as good as "Voltarol Retard" but cheaper. The plaintiffs at first obtained an *ex parte* interlocutory injunction, but failed at the hearing of the motion.

2. The plaintiffs' three-pronged attack The plaintiffs alleged effectively three causes of action:
  (a) The defendants' advertisement amounted to passing off "Diclomax Retard" as "Voltarol Retard".
  (b) The defendants had falsely represented that its product used the same slow-release formula as "Voltarol Retard".
  (c) The defendants' advertisements falsely claimed that their product was entitled to claim the track-record enjoyed by "Voltarol Retard".

3. Was there a serious issue to be tried? No—Aldous J. held that the plaintiffs had failed to show a serious issue on any of the three causes of action.
  (a) The affidavit evidence failed to establish a serious issue of passing off.
  (b) Since the evidence established that two products enjoyed, for practical purposes, equivalent therapeutic and bio-availability characteristics, it was not reasonably arguable that any reasonable doctor would conclude that the defendants were misrepresenting use of the same slow-release formula.
  (c) There was no serious issue on the claim for the same track-record because the defendants' evidence showed that "Diclomax Retard" had been granted the necessary product licence by the DHSS, to obtain which pharmaceutical equivalence must have been established.

B: EXAMPLES OF CASES RELATING TO ADEQUACY OF DAMAGES

1 *Foseco International Ltd v. Fordath Ltd* [1975] F.S.R. 507 (for the facts, see p. 613)

1. Damages—an adequate remedy
(a) *For the plaintiffs?* No—Foster J. said at pp. 515–516:

"Both counsel urged on me that whichever party lost it would suffer incalculable damage. If pending the hearing of the action Fordath can manufacture, can appoint selling agents to compete in the same market as Foseco-Fordath AG's licensees, can register trade marks and impart know-how, I, for my part, think that Foseco International could not be compensated by an award of damages at the trial if it succeeds. If Fordath is allowed to proceed in total disregard of the terms of the agreement, it will cause, in my judgment, confusion in the market, as two competitors with the same or similar product will be competing in a highly competitive market, and will inevitably result in loss of goodwill built up by Foseco International in its overseas business."

(b) *For the defendants?* Yes—at 515–516:

"On the other hand, the injunction if granted will not stop Fordath from increasing its sales by its own efforts, and only requires it to channel those sales under the agreement through Foseco-Fordath AG. If Fordath succeeds in this action, it will be easy to ascertain the quantity of such sales from the books of Foseco-Fordath AG."

2 Copyright: *Hubbard v. Vosper* [1972] 2 Q.B. 84

1. The background The defendant, having for 14 years been a member of the Church of Scientology, wrote a book which was very critical of the cult of Scientology.

2. The arguments The plaintiff claimed an interlocutory injunction for breach of copyright and confidence and the defendant in turn invoked section 6(2) of the Copyright Act 1956, which provided:

"No fair dealing with a literary ... work shall constitute an infringement of the copyright in the work if it is for purposes of criticism or review, whether of that work or another work, and is accompanied by a sufficient acknowledgment."

3. The Court of Appeal dismissed the application—why? Stephenson L.J. said at 101C:

"Damages appear to be an adequate remedy for any breach of copyright or confidence which may be proved at the trial; indeed any damage which the publication of Mr. Vosper's book may cause to the plaintiffs is less likely to result from what he quotes from their literature or discloses from their material than from the criticism which Mr. Vosper makes of them and of their cult of Scientology as a whole."

This perhaps reflects the principle expressed by Lord Denning M.R. at 96H–97A, with a wider sweep of the judicial pen:

> "But here, although Mr. Hubbard owns the copyright, nevertheless, Mr. Vosper has a defence of fair dealing: and although Mr. Hubbard may possess confidential information, nevertheless Mr. Vosper has a defence of public interest. These defences are such that he should be permitted to go ahead with the publication. If what he says is true, it is only right that the dangers of this cult should be exposed. We never restrain a defendant in a libel action who says he is going to justify. So in copyright action, we ought not to restrain a defendant who has a reasonable defence of fair dealing. Nor in an action for breach of confidence, if the defendant has a reasonable defence of public interest. The reason is because the defendant, if he is right, is entitled to publish it: and the law will not intervene to suppress freedom of speech except when it is abused."

4. Contrast with the *Harman Pictures* case In the interests of completeness, the dicta of Stamp L.J. (recited above) with regard to copyright should be contrasted with the decision in *Harman Pictures NV v. Osborne* [1967] 1 W.L.R. 723. The plaintiffs which owned the copyright in so far as concerned any reproduction in cinematographic form of a book, *The Reason Why* (dealing with the incident of the charge of the Light Brigade), applied for an interlocutory injunction to restrain the defendants from infringing that copyright by means of a screenplay which in part bore a marked similarity. Goff J. granted the injunction (applying the pre-*Cyanamid*—"strong prima facie case"—test) but as to adequacy of damages he said:

> "It is true that if I were to refuse any injunction at this stage, and the plaintiffs ultimately succeeded, they would be entitled to an account of the profits, and I could now put the defendants on terms to keep separate accounts and even to keep all proceeds separately from their other moneys, but as Sir Andrew rightly pointed out, the defendants might not make any, or might not make such as the plaintiffs would hope to secure from their own production. True, on the other hand, that if ultimately the plaintiffs make the film, they may be less successful than the defendants would be, but in my judgment if the plaintiffs are right they are entitled to control the situation and have the play made and cast as they want it."

3 Sales distribution and agency agreement: *Evans Marshall & Co. Ltd v. Bertola SA* [1973] 1 W.L.R. 349, C.A.

1. The facts In 1972 the first defendant purported to terminate a sale distribution and agency agreement pursuant to which the plaintiff was the first defendant's sole agent for the sale of its sherry in England until 1986. The plaintiff contended that such termination was a breach of contract, and applied for an interlocutory injunction. By the time of the hearing before the Court of Appeal, the second defendants had been performing for a number of weeks the role of the plaintiff as sole distributor and agent.

2. Damages held not to be an adequate remedy—why? Sachs L.J. held at 379H–380A–D:

> "I.S.I., by Mr. Butler's affidavit, chose to emphasise the damage to their goodwill and trade reputation that they would suffer if the agency at will which they had held for three weeks was unjustifiably disrupted: he emphasised the difficulty of assessing the resulting damage.
>
> These assertions appear a little naive when one looks in comparison at the loss of goodwill, the disruption in trade, and the litigation with sub-agents which would be inflicted on the plaintiffs by an unjustified abrupt termination of an agreement with 14 years to run—terminated with the aid of allegations of their having failed to carry out their obligations and of having made undue profits.
>
> In my judgment damages would not be an adequate remedy in this case, any more than they were held to be in any of the three cases already cited, *Warner's* case, the *Decro-Wall* case and *Hill v. C. A. Parsons & Co. Ltd.* The courts have repeatedly recognised that there can be claims under contracts in which, as here, it is unjust to confine a plaintiff to his damages for their breach. Great difficulty in estimating these damages is one factor that can be and has been taken into account. Another factor is the creation of certain areas of damage which cannot be taken into monetary account in a common law action for breach of contract: loss of goodwill and trade reputation are examples—see also, in another sphere, the judgment of Jenkins L.J. in *Vine v. National Dock Labour Board* [1956] 1 Q.B. 658 at 676 which, albeit a dissenting judgment, was unanimously adopted *in toto* in the House of Lords. Generally, indeed, the grant of injunctions in contract cases stems from such factors."

4 Trade dispute: *Hubbard v. Pitt* [1976] 1 Q.B. 142 (see p. 615 for the facts)

1. On the basis of an undertaking by the defendants Orr L.J. held at 189E–F:

"The next question to be asked is whether, if the plaintiffs were to succeed at the trial, they would be adequately compensated for the interim continuance of the defendants' activities. In my judgment, the answer is that they plainly would not, because such continuance might well cause very serious damage to their business, and the judge was entitled, on this issue, to have regard to any doubts he might have felt as to the defendants' ability to satisfy any award of damages made against them. Mr Turner-Samuels has claimed that it would be wrong to do so in the absence of any evidence that the defendants would be unable to pay; but I think that the boot was on the other foot and that in the absence of any evidence as to ability to pay what could amount to very substantial damages the judge would have been entitled to put in the balance any doubts he may have felt as to that matter."

2. On the basis of an undertaking given by the plaintiffs Orr L.J. went on to say at 189G–190A:

"The next question to be asked is the converse question whether if the defendants were to succeed at the trial they would be adequately compensated for the interim restriction on their activities which the grant of an interlocutory injunction would have imposed, I have no doubt that they would be, since the only restriction imposed by the injunction would be in respect of activities in front of the plaintiffs' premises, leaving the defendants free to conduct their campaign by lawful means elsewhere and if, as some at least of the defendants assert and as I am for the present purposes prepared to assume, their object has not been to damage the plaintiffs but simply to impart information, it seems to me that the disadvantage involved would be minimal, and in any event I see no reason to suppose that the plaintiffs would be unable to pay any damages properly recoverable."

3. What happened? The Court of Appeal granted an interlocutory injunction, reflecting the following dicta of Lord Diplock in *N.W.L. Ltd v. Wood* [1979] I.C.R. 867 at 880:

"... there is the risk that if the interlocutory injunction is granted but the plaintiff fails at the trial the defendant may in the meantime have suffered harm and inconvenience which is similarly irrecompensable. The nature and degree of harm and inconvenience that are likely to be sustained in these two events by the defendant and the plaintiff respectively in consequence of the grant or the refusal of the injunction are generally sufficiently disproportionate to bring down, by themselves, the balance on one side or the other..."

5 Copyright: *Radley Gowns Ltd v. Costas Spyrou (t/a "Touch of Class" and "Fiesta Girl")* [1975] F.S.R. 455, *per* Oliver J. (for the facts, see p. 812, below)

1. Were damages an adequate remedy for plaintiffs? No.:

> "On the one hand I have the plaintiffs, who complain that their styles are being poached. This has a dual effect, they say: in the first place, because of the changes of fashion, the lifespan of a new style is necessarily limited, and the probability is that if it is unprotected in the meantime, by the time the trial takes place its value will have passed with the current season, so that the damage which the plaintiffs suffer is immediate damage. Secondly, they say that their goodwill suffers because their customers, finding the same articles being sold more cheaply elsewhere, tend to become resentful. This damage is not readily quantifiable in financial terms."

2. Were damages an adequate remedy for the defendant? Yes—the defendant had set out the stock he presently held and declared that he did not in any event intend to make any of these styles. Against that backdrop, Oliver J. said:

> "So far as the fur models are concerned—and that is all I am concerned with on this motion—the defendant has a loss which is finite and quantifiable if he is right, and it is the selling price of the stock that he has. The plaintiffs are a substantial public company; if they turn out to be wrong at the trial the defendant will be compensated by the undertaking as to damages."

6 Contract for specific and ascertained goods: *Perry (Howard E.) & Co. Ltd v. British Railways Board* [1980] I.C.R. 743

1. The facts The defendant refused to deliver (or allow the plaintiff to collect) 500 tons of steel belonging to the plaintiff which lay at two of the defendant's depots. The defendants's refusal was prompted by members of the National Union of Railwaymen refusing to transport steel, in aid of the steelworkers' strike. The defendant feared the inception and escalation of industrial disruption affecting the conduct of its business.

2. For what did the plaintiff apply? The plaintiff applied for an interlocutory order that the defendant permit the plaintiff, with its own vehicles, equipment and employees to enter the defendant's depots and remove the steel itself.

640

3. Why the urgency? The reasons for the plaintiff's sense of urgency were two-fold:

(a) by virtue of the steelworkers' strike, there was a strong demand for steel; and

(b) the 500 tons of steel could not be kept for any long period without the risk of it becoming too hard and unmalleable to work.

4. The "damages on adequate remedy" criterion—the defendant's argument. One of the arguments advanced by the defendant in resisting the plaintiff's application was that damages would be an adequate remedy. The defendant placed reliance upon the principle on which courts have long acted, namely not to order delivery of goods which are ordinary articles of commerce with no special value or interest, whether to the plaintiff or others, when damages would fully compensate: *Whiteley Ltd v. Hilt* [1918] 2 K.B. 808 at 819, *per* Swinfen-Eady M.R.; *General and Finance Facilities Ltd v. Cooks Cars (Romford) Ltd* [1963] 1 W.L.R. 644 at 649–650, *per* Diplock L.J.

5. The principle *Per* Sir Robert Megarry at 751D:

"If a plaintiff can easily replace goods detained by purchasing their equivalent on the market, then the payment of damages out of which the price of the equivalent may be paid is adequate compensation to the wronged plaintiff, and there is little or not point in making an order for the delivery of the goods. Far better to let the plaintiff fend for himself with the defendant's money."

6. Damages held not an adequate remedy—why? Sir Robert Megarry went on to distinguish the circumstances prevailing in the instant case from an available market for steel, and also took into account the effect of a refusal to make the order applied for on the plaintiffs' customers:

(a) *No available market:*

"In normal times, the steel here in dispute might indeed be in this category; but these times are not normal, and at present steel is obtainable on the market only with great difficulty, if at all. If the equivalent of what is detained is unobtainable, how can it be said that damages are an adequate remedy? They plainly are not. Counsel for the plaintiff observed that at present 'Steel is gold,' and one can see what he meant. Yet even that may not do justice to his cause, since as far as I know gold is still available on the open market to those who pay the price." (751 E–F.)

641

(b) *Balance of commercial convenience:*

> "In one sense, I suppose, it can be said that as those who trade do so for profit, damages of a sufficient amount may compensate for any wrong. All that the plaintiffs are losing, said counsel for the defendants, is the sale of some steel, and damages will adequately compensate them for that. I do not think that this is by any means the whole picture. Damages would be a poor consolation if the failure of supplies forces a trader to lay off staff and disappoint his customers (whose affections may be transferred to others) and ultimately forces him towards insolvency. On the facts of the present case the perils of the plaintiffs may well not be so great as that at present, but such elements cannot be ignored. In any case, I think that what matters is the adequacy of damages in place of the thing that ought to have been delivered. Under this head I think that my discretion ought to be exercised in favour of making the order that the plaintiffs seek." (at 751 F–H.)

7 Building works—noise: *Smith v. Nottingham County Council* (1983) New L.J., January 7

1. The facts With the financial support of the students' union, four students of Trent Polytechnic sought an injunction against the defendants to enjoin them from continuing with building works at their hall of residence that were of such a major character as greatly to interfere with the students' studies. Lord Denning M.R. held there to be implied into the students' licence to occupy, a covenant for quiet enjoyment in respect of which the building work was a breach, and without just cause or excuse.

2. Adequacy of damages for the defendants? Yes—Oliver L.J. held:

> "Certainly the result of an injunction would put severe financial penalties on the defendants. Those were catered for by the existence of funds which would be available on any cross-undertaking by the plaintiffs, and the judge was satisfied, as she said in her judgment, that they were suffering uncompensatable damage which could only be dealt with, if it were to be dealt with at all, by an injunction."

8 Abuse of dominant position—Article 86: *Garden Cottage Foods Ltd v. Milk Marketing Board* [1984] A.C. 130 (for the facts, see p. 620)

1. Would damages be an adequate remedy for the plaintiff? Yes—held Lord Diplock, in the following terms at 142:

"So far as the business of the company, conducted as it was entirely by Mr and Mrs. Bunch from their own home, consisted of dealing in bulk butter, it appears to have involved no more than acting as a middleman who transferred to traders in the bulk market immediately on delivery by the board of ex creamery or ex cold store consignments of butter that the company had itself bought on seven-day credit terms, and taking its own 'cut' out of the price at which it passed on the consignment to the trader. If it were compelled to buy bulk butter from one or other of four distributors referred to in the letter of March 24, 1982 instead of directly from the board this would be likely to reduce the amount of the company's cut, or even to eliminate the possibility of retaining one, so that the sensible course could be to suspend until trial of the action this part of the company's business. But, if that were the course adopted, all that the company would lose by such suspension of business would be the opportunity of obtaining the sums of money represented by that cut. There could hardly be a clearer case of damages being an adequate remedy unless insuperable difficulties of estimation could be foreseen; but any difficulties of estimation would be greatly reduced by the fact that the company had only one substantial customer, the Dutch company with whom 95 per cent. of the company's business in bulk butter was transacted, and that one customer, as appears from the affidavit of Mr J. Wijffels that was before the Court of Appeal, during the period that the company was obtaining butter from the board, purchased from the company about one-third of its requirement for bulk butter originating in the United Kingdom."

2. Would damages have been an adequate remedy to the defendant? No—held Lord Diplock at 143E in the following terms:

"I should refer to another aspect of the difficulty of estimating damages, which the judge also took into account in exercising his discretion in favour of refusing to grant an interlocutory injunction. That was the damage that would be caused to the business of the board and the business of the four distributors to whom it had already made commitments. For that disturbance, in the event of the company failing in the action, the board's only remedy would be the recovery of damages from the company under the cross-undertaking which it would be required to give."

9 *Francome v. Mirror Group Newspapers Ltd* [1984] 1 W.L.R. 892 (for the facts, see p. 621)

1. What was the position as to adequacy of damages? Fox L.J. held:

"If the *Daily Mirror* is permitted to publish the tapes now, the consequent harm to Mr Francome might be such that he could not be adequately compensated in damages for any wrong thereby done to him whatever the result of subsequent proceedings. Unless Mr Francome is given protection until the trial, I think that a trial might be largely worthless from his point of view even though he succeeded." (P. 900E.)

10 Employment: *Powell v. Brent London Borough* [1988] I.C.R. 176 (see p. 626 for the facts)

1. An additional point—would damages be an adequate remedy for the plaintiff? The plaintiff argued that:

"... if Brent were allowed to advertise again and to fill the post, she could not then be confirmed in the post, even if she won the case. She could recover damages for estimated loss of earnings. The common law relating to damages would preclude recovery for her disappointment at losing this important promotion and for the loss of her pleasure and satisfaction in doing more demanding and responsible work."

2. What the court held Ralph Gibson L.J. said at 196B:

"Damages would not in my judgment be adequate compensation for the plaintiff if she were to succeed at the trial in respect of what she would suffer if the defendants were free to exclude her from the post and proceed to fill it after advertisement. She could now be compensated, of course, for loss of earnings between now and then, but she would have the lost the satisfaction of doing this more demanding and rewarding job, and I accept that damages for estimated future financial loss would not be full compensation to her."

So the court granted the injunction.

[And see "Serious issue" at p. 626.]

11 *Hughes v. Southwark London Borough Council* [1988] IRLR 55 (see p. 627 for the facts)

1. Would damages be an adequate remedy—for the plaintiffs? No—Taylor J. said:

"I do not think it has been seriously disputed that there are heads of damage, of loss, of grievance, on the part of the plaintiffs which at common law could not be compensated by damages ... I am not

644

impressed by the suggestion that they will suffer in their careers. I think that that is an overstatement. But I do think that there will be a loss of job satisfaction, distress and other factors, which are not compensatable at common law, and the whole objection to this is nothing to do with money, it is to do with what their job is, what they feel they ought to be doing and their distress at being taken away from what they regard as important work. That is not capable of being compensated in damages."

2. Would damages be an adequate remedy—for the defendants? Yes.

"All that I have to consider under this head is whether, if the defendants suffer any damage themselves in any way it is damage capable of being compensated by an award of damages. I have not found it easy to see how this particular element in the *Cyanamid* case is likely to arise in the present case unless, as I indicated in the course of argument, the defendants required to be indemnified against any claims for negligence or failure to carry out statutory duties resulting, it may be said, from the plaintiffs' unwillingness to carry out the instruction. However that may be, it seems to me that here the plaintiffs are backed by their union, both in terms of costs and damages, and any damages of that kind which may be suffered by the defendants would be adequately compensated by an award."

[And see "Balance of convenience" at p. 664.]

12 *Jakeman v. South West Thames Regional Health Authority* [1990] IRLR 62 (for the facts, see p. 965)

1. Would damages be an adequate remedy for the plaintiffs? Yes. Auld J. said:

"The governing principle was to consider whether, if the plaintiffs were to succeed at trial, they would be adequately compensated by an award of damages. The plaintiffs might well suffer some hardship from the shortfall of about £300 in their take-home pay, with Christmas approaching. However, temporary hardship was a feature in any case where an employer withheld wages ... Such hardship as might flow from the deduction, the legality of which had yet to be determined, was not such that it could not be adequately compensated in damages if the plaintiffs were successful in the end."

This was a further reason for refusing an injunction.

13 Trade secrets: *Johnson & Bloy (Holdings) Ltd v. Wolstenholme Rink plc* [1987] IRLR 499 (see p. 629 for the facts and background)

1. Damages an adequate remedy for the defendants? Yes. Fox L.J. said:

"I have no reason to suppose that the plaintiffs are not good for any damages which would be payable under the implied undertaking in damages if an injunction were granted."

2. Damages adequate for the plaintiffs? The defendants argued so:

"It is said that damages are an adequate remedy. The defendants have since the hearing before Whitford J. been developing their trade, subject only to the limited undertaking extracted by the judge. In effect it is said that the 'bird has flown'."

3. The Court of Appeal held: not adequate for the plaintiffs Fox L.J. said:

"For myself I do not feel able to accept that approach. It may be that some harm has already been done, but it seems to me that that is no reason why the damage should not be limited between now and the trial by protecting the plaintiffs until trial. Damages are not necessarily a satisfactory remedy in these circumstances. If the information is in truth a trade secret, the plaintiffs are entitled to have their trade connection protected and it is the protection of a trade connection, not damages, which the plaintiffs or any other trader in these circumstances is primarily concerned to obtain and needs to obtain."

14 "One Girl's War": *Att.-Gen. v. Turnaround Distribution Ltd* [1989] F.S.R. 169 (see p. 633 for the facts)

1. Were damages adequate for the plaintiff? The plaintiff argued not. The defendants argued:

"... that damages would afford the plaintiff adequate compensation if at the trial he was to establish his right to relief at all. Analysis of the plaintiff's claim based on the interests of national security indicates ... that only the principle of publication is at stake and that this principle is itself invoked essentially *pour encourager les autres*. This need ... will adequately be served and thus the principle sufficiently be vindicated, by making the defendants disgorge their profits and no doubt pay damages in addition, if and when the plaintiff succeeds at trial."

2. The judge held: damages would not be adequate for the plaintiff Simon Brown J. said:

"... damages would not in my judgment provide an adequate remedy to the Crown in respect of the loss to the public interest by such distribution in the United Kingdom as would occur between today and trial. That loss is in truth incalculable—which is certainly not to say that it is necessarily great. [Counsel for the defendants] asserts that the principle contended for the Crown would be sufficiently protected if the plaintiff wins at trial and thereby establishes the inviolability of the principle and moreover robs the defendants of any profits meanwhile made. That may or may not be so: one cannot assess what adverse short-term consequences may follow in the way of loss of confidentiality. As [counsel for the plaintiff] to my mind convincingly observes, one cannot assume that relations in and with other security services will remain on ice pending trial."

3. Would damages be adequate for the defendants? The plaintiff argued so:

"To the extent (which may be doubted) that there is really any historical value in this work, let alone any public purpose to be served by exposing Miss Miller's long past unlawful acts, those interests, having waited upwards of 40 years can surely wait ... another few months until trial."

4. The judge held: damage would be adequate for the defendants Simon Brown J. said:

"What disadvantage or damage will accrue to the defendants by a delay in the United Kingdom distribution of this book by the six months or so that would elapse prior to the speedy trial of the action to which the defendants are, if they desire, entitled? To this question [counsel for the defendants] offered no effective reply. Any damage to his clients would in any event be compensated for under the Crown's continuing cross-undertaking in damages, quite apart from the no doubt immense commercial boost which would be given to the book sales were the defendants hereafter to succeed."

So the judge granted an injunction.

[And see "Balance of Convenience" below.]

C: EXAMPLES OF CASES DEMONSTRATING THE "BALANCE OF CONVENIENCE" CRITERION

1 Reorganising schools: *Bradbury v. Enfield London Borough Council* [1967] 1 W.L.R. 1311

1. The facts Several ratepayers brought proceedings against the borough pursuant to a plan which it had prepared to reorganise education on a comprehensive basis. The local authority, contrary to statutory requirements, had not issued public notices in relation to eight schools which were to be enlarged to the extent of fundamentally changing their character. The question, *inter alia*, arose—should the local authority be enjoined from pursuing their proposals until compliance with the statutory provisions?

2. The education authority resisted the application for the injunction—why? The chief education officer suggested that in the event of an injunction being granted, chaos would supervene. All the arrangements had been made for the following term. The teachers had been appointed to the new comprehensive schools. The pupils had been allotted places. He contended that it would be next to impossible to reverse all these arrangements without complete chaos and damage to teachers, pupils and the public.

3. Lord Denning M.R. rejected the "chaos" argument At 1324H–1325C he held:

> "I must say this: If a local authority does not fulfil the requirements of the law, this court will see that it does fulfil them. It will not listen readily to suggestions of 'chaos.' The Department of Education and the local education authority are subject to the rule of law and must comply with it, just like everyone else. Even if chaos should result, still the law must be obeyed. But I do not think that chaos will result. The evidence convinces me that the 'chaos' is much over-stated. If an injunction is granted now, there will be much less chaos than if it were sought to reverse the situation in a year or so. After all the injunction will only go to the eight schools, and not as to the remaining 20 or so schools in the borough.
>
> And in regard to these eight schools, it will only affect the new intake coming in at the bottom forms. I see no reason why the position should not be restored, so that the eight schools retain their previous character until the statutory requirements are fulfilled. I can well see that there may be a considerable upset for a number of people, but I think it far more important to uphold the rule of law. parliament has

laid down these requirements so as to ensure that the electors can make their objections and have them properly considered. We must see that their rights are upheld.

I have only to add this: It is still open to the education authority to fulfil the statutory requirements, that is, to give the public notice so that objections can be submitted to and considered by the Minister. I will not venture to predict what the results will be, but that is the least that must be done in order that the law should be observed.

I would therefore vary the judge's order and grant an injunction in respect of the eight schools."

Such proceedings would now, it is submitted, be more appropriate for judicial review.

2 Noise—breach of covenant: *Hampstead & Suburban Properties Ltd v. Diomedous* [1969] 1 Ch. 248

1. Balance of convenience—how did the defendant frame his argument? At p. 257 E–F, the defendant argued that:

"The grant of an injunction was discretionary, and that here the balance of convenience favoured the refusal of an injunction. To the plaintiffs, he said, the case was 'essentially trivial,' whereas an injunction would inflict 'incalculable loss' on the defendant. The inconvenience to the landlords of refusing an injunction would be 'nil,' whereas the inconvenience of an injunction to the defendant would be 'enormous'; and he referred feelingly to the contribution which music made to the atmosphere of a restaurant and its effect on the clientele."

2. The argument—flatly rejected Megarry J. swept aside the suggestion that if there was any loss, it was that of the tenants and not of the plaintiff landlords:

(a) *The defendant's hands—not clean:*

"Finally, there is the balance of convenience. To say that the inconvenience to the plaintiffs is 'nil', and that to them the case is 'essentially trivial,' seems to me as much an exaggeration as to say that the loss to the defendant will be 'incalculable.' I have already dealt with the injury to the plaintiffs, and I need say no more about it. The defendant's claim is, in essence, that he will suffer an 'incalculable loss' if he is not permitted to continue his plain breach of the obligations which he so recently entered into and

649

voluntarily undertook when he became an assignee of the lease. Stripped of the persuasions of Mr Weeks's advocacy, the proposition is: 'I am making handsome profits by doing what I covenanted and undertook not to do: therefore it would be wrong for the court to stop me.' I can conceive few propositions calculated to appeal less to equity." (at 260B–D.)

(b) *The defendant's argument—undermined:*

"In this connection I must mention Mr Weeks's emphasis on the fact that this was an action brought not by the tenants but by the landlords, and his contention that I ought to disregard any injury or damage to those who are not parties to these proceedings. The case, he urged, was one between the plaintiffs and the defendant, and I must consider the hardship to the defendant, and disregard any hardship to other tenants of the plaintiffs. I do not consider this to be a correct analysis of the position." (at 260D–E.)

(c) *Social values:*

"The plaintiffs are making money by letting their property to tenants. The defendant is making money by providing a restaurant to which customers come for food, drink and music. The plaintiffs' tenants object to the music when played as loudly as it is; the defendant's customers like the music (or so I assume) when played at that volume. The case for each party is based in large degree not on any direct personal benefit or injury, but on the benefit or injury to that party's tenants or customers (as the case may be), and so to that party. In these circumstances, it seems to me that I am entitled to pay some regard to the social values involved. The point has not been argued, and I do not rest my decision upon it. But it seems to me that it is of some relevance to consider whether it is more important for the plaintiffs' tenants to have the relative peace and quiet in their homes to which they have become accustomed, or for the defendant's customers to have the pleasure of music while they eat, played at high volume. When this comparison is made, it seems to me that it is the home rather than the meal table which must prevail. A home in which sleep is possible is a necessity, whereas loud music as an accompaniment to an evening meal is, for those who enjoy it, relatively a luxury. If, of course, the two can peacefully co-exist, so much the better; but if there is irreconcilable conflict, as there is at present in this case, I think it is the home that should be preferred." (at 260F–261B.)

650

3 Supply—sale of goods: *Comet Radiovision Services Ltd v. Farnell-Tandberg Ltd* [1971] 1 W.L.R. 1287

1. The background The plaintiff, a "hi-fi" dealer, sought an interlocutory injunction restraining the defendant suppliers from withholding supplies—on the basis that the suppliers were in breach of section 2 of the Resale Prices Act 1964, which provided: "... it shall be unlawful for any supplier to withhold supplies of any goods from a dealer seeking to obtain them for resale ... on the ground that the dealer (a) has sold ... at a price below the resale price ... or (b) is likely, if the goods are supplied to him, to sell them ... at a price below that price ..." On facts in relation to which there was "no real dispute", Goulding J. found the defendants to be in breach of their statutory obligation to supply and went on to grant the injunction. (The statute has since been repealed—but the case is analysed to explore the "injunction" aspect.)

2. Why was the injunction granted? The grounds for the decision of Goulding J. were:

(a) The mandatory element of the order sought—consistent with the policy of the Act:

> "It seems to me that if the Act is susceptible of interlocutory enforcement at all, as I think it must have been intended to be, any injunction will be of mandatory effect, and indeed the whole scheme of the Act is to order people actually to supply goods that they may be unwilling to supply, and that takes one rather out of the ordinary sphere in which injunctions operate. I do not think that the mere objection that the order would be of a mandatory character takes one very far." (at 1292G–H.)

(b) *The laches argument:*

> "Then it is said the plaintiff has been guilty of inordinate delay; it has been slow to seek a remedy. There was a definite refusal of supplies in December 1969, the writ and the notice of motion did not appear until March 1971 and the maxim *'vigilantibus non dormientibus jura subveniunt'* is prayed in aid; it is said that the plaintiff slept on its rights. This is one of the matters on which in the present state of the evidence it is not possible to form a very definite conclusion on the merits of the contending parties.
>
> It is clear that there was some continued contact between the parties during the year 1970, and indeed they were doing considerable business together in goods other than in Tandberg items which had caused trouble. The plaintiff asserts that it hoped to get the decision to

651

withhold supplies modified without litigation and that it was reasonable for it to go on trying for a long time. The defendants say that either that assertion on the part of the plaintiff is insincere or the hope was quite unreasonable. The correspondence does not, I think, contain the full story as there were a number of conversations during 1970, so that I cannot, as I have said, form a final opinion on the merits of that branch of the controversy." (at 1292H–1293C.)

(c) *Balance of convenience:*

"Again with regard to the balance of convenience, I find it difficult to be decisive on the evidence before me. The giving of the supplies in question, or the withholding of those supplies, is hardly likely to be a matter of commercial life or death to either party. If no injunction is granted and then the plaintiff succeeds at the trial, the assessment of damages may well be very difficult. Similarly, if an injunction is granted and then the defendants succeed at the trial, there may be equal difficulty in assessing damages under the plaintiff's usual undertaking in damages." (at 1293D.)

(d) *The final weighing-up process:*

"On those matters of delay and balance of convenience I think, although Mr Threlfall ably argued the contrary, I am entitled to take into account that others besides the parties, namely, the purchasing public, will be affected by my conclusion. As I take the view on the facts that the true ground of withholding supplies is not in doubt, and on the law that such ground is one falling within the prohibition imposed by Parliament, I think so far that I ought to secure supplies to the plaintiff and thereby to its potential customers until the trial of the action proves me either right or wrong." (at 1293E.)

4 Market: *Birmingham Corporation v. Perry Barr Stadium Ltd* [1972] 1 All E.R. 725

1. The background Pennycuick V.-C., as a matter of law, held that on agreed facts the plaintiff had a statutory monopoly of the holding of markets within the boundary of the city, which it was entitled to enforce by whatever form of action was available in the courts. Against that backdrop he granted to the plaintiff an interlocutory injunction restraining the defendant from operating an unlicensed market.

2. Why was the injunction granted? The following were the bases for the decision:

(a) There was evidence of the likelihood of loss on the part of the Corporation:

As Pennycuick V.-C. said at 730G–H:

"In order to obtain relief, the plaintiff corporation will have to show damage at the trial of the action. For the purposes of this motion, it is sufficient—and this is accepted by counsel for the second defendant—that the plaintiff corporation should show a likelihood of damage. It seems to me that the passages I have read from the affidavit of Mr Pitt do establish the likelihood of damage. It is really apparent that if some other party, unauthorised by the plaintiff corporation, establishes a market within the city of Birmingham, the value of the plaintiff corporation's monopoly right must be reduced. Obviously, if it is known that traders can get away with establishing a market without recourse to the licence of the plaintiff corporation, other traders are less likely to spend their money on obtaining a licence from the plaintiff corporation. There is also the point as to interference with the existing markets carried on by the plaintiff corporation itself."

In this regard, the following, *inter alia*, had been deposed to on behalf of the plaintiff:

"The [plaintiff corporation] in addition to the various markets they run, license seven markets within the city of Birmingham. For the privilege of being allowed to run these markets, the proprietors pay licence fees. If it appears that [the second defendant] can hold a market unlicensed, the [plaintiff corporation's] licenses fees from these licensed markets will be endangered. This is particularly important at the moment when negotiations are under way but have not been concluded for the grant of a licence for a market to be held At Corporation Square, Bull Street, Birmingham. The fees payable in respect of licences to hold markets are considerable and in the case of some licences payment is calculated by reference to the turnover of the market. ... [The plaintiff corporation's] loss stems not only from the fall in trade at their existing markets, but also from the damage to the value of their franchise, the decrease in turnover at their licensed markets and the loss of the opportunity to collect the tolls to which they are entitled." (at 727G–J.)

(b) *As to balance of hardship:*

"There is evidence of the likelihood of loss on the part of the plaintiff corporation and there is really no reason to suppose that the second defendant will suffer greater hardship by an injunction should be ultimately succeed in the action, than would the plaintiff corporation

653

from the refusal of the injunction should the plaintiff corporation succeed in the action. As I have said, the second defendant's business is not, in the nature of things, a business involving much capital outlay." (at 732G.)

(c) *The undertaking as to damages:*

"... the plaintiff corporation will certainly be good for any damages that might ultimately be awarded to the ... defendant ..." (at 732H.)

3. Market: contrast with the *Elwes* case   The *Birmingham Corporation* case should be contrasted with *Elwes v. Payne* (1879) 12 Ch.D. 468. There, the plaintiffs were the owners of the tolls of an ancient market held weekly on Thursday. The defendants, who were auctioneers, filled up with stalls and pens a neighbouring piece of ground, and issued circulars stating that weekly sales of cattle by auction would be held there on Mondays. The plaintiffs brought their action to restrain the defendants from holding their proposed sales as being an interference with the plaintiffs' market. The Court of Appeal rejected the application, prompting James L.J. to say:

"... this is the first time that I have ever heard of an interlocutory injunction being granted in respect of such a right as this..."

James L.J. went on to explain the rationale of the court's decision, thus:

"The only question that it seems to me right to decide at the present moment is whether there has been such a case made out as to induce the court before the rights are finally determined to do something which shall interfere with the prima facie rights of the defendants [*i.e.* the right to trade] ... The order of the Master of the Rolls is not in accordance with my view of what ought to be done, having regard to the greater amount or less amount of damage to be sustained by these parties. If the defendants are stopped from beginning a trade which may become a very valuable trade, then, supposing they should turn out to be right, they will have been prevented from carrying out a trade which they had a perfect right to carry on, and there would be great difficulty in determining the amount of damage they would have sustained. I do not know how they would be compensated if it should turn out that they are right. On the other hand, if the plaintiffs succeed at trial it does not seem to me that there will be the slightest difficulty in giving them full compensation for everything they can shew that they have lost." (at 476–477.)

5 *Foseco International Ltd v. Fordath Ltd* [1975] F.S.R. 507 (for the facts, see p. 613)

1. Balance of convenience—material considerations Foster J. said at 516, "This raises the question: what [have the defendants] done to date?"

(a) *Manufacture:* They had acquired a company in Holland and built a factory. On the evidence, Foster J. concluded that an interlocutory injunction would only postpone the start of such manufacture.

(b) *Trade marks:* Though applied for, trade marks had not been registered in any jurisdiction. As above, the grant of an interlocutory injunction would only postpone any successful application for registration.

(c) *Know-how and selling:* In the evidence for the defendants it was stated:

> "The defendant company has negotiated or is shortly likely to conclude agreements in five overseas countries."

Such agreements were already concluded, and put in evidence.

2. Ruling Foster J. said at 517:

> "In my judgment, it is of great importance to maintain the status quo in so far as I am able until the trial of the action; and the balance of convenience is all on the side of the F.I., if I except from the relief effective contracts made by Fordath before the writ was issued."

6 Industrial dispute: *Porter v. National Union of Journalists* [1980] IRLR 404, H.L. (for the facts, see p. 617)

1. Interaction of "balance of convenience" and "status quo" Having found that there was a serious issue to be tried, Lord Diplock said at 407(14):

> "... the balance of convenience would appear clearly to lie in favour of maintaining the status quo until the trial. To lose their union cards upon expulsion from the NUJ could not fail to be a serious handicap to the plaintiffs if they should want to move on to work on other newspapers in London or the provinces or in other sectors of the journalists' profession, and would debar them from any employment in establishments where there are closed shop agreements. Although these are not widespread throughout the newspaper industry, they do include the *Daily Express*, the *Mirror* and the *Star*. On the other side of the balance there would appear to be no more than the understandable desire on the part of those members of the NUJ who suffered financial hardship by participating loyally in the strike, for

speedy vengeance on those who went on working and earning. But if the strike order was issued contrary to the rules, the plaintiffs were entitled to disregard it, while if at the trial it is held to have been lawful, vengeance will have only been postponed."

2. "Status quo"—meaning See p. 162.

7 *Romalpa* clause: *Feuer Leather Corporation v. Johnston (Frank) & Sons Ltd* [1983] Com. L.R. 12, C.A.

1. The background P sold good to M subject to a *romalpa* type clause. M sold on to D, and subsequently went into liquidation, owing large sums of money to P. At trial on August 16, 1981, Neill J. gave judgment for the defendant on the basis that title in the goods passed, D having at all times acted in good faith.

2. Application for injunction pending appeal P gave notice of appeal on September 17 and on September 25 applied for an injunction restraining D until after judgment in the appeal (effectively) from disposing of the goods.

3. The application failed—why? The Court of Appeal held that on the balance of convenience, D should be free to deal with all the goods without accounting to P further, for otherwise D's trade would be seriously restrained for many more months.

8 Trespass: *Savoy Hotel Plc v. British Broadcasting Corporation, The Times,* December 18, 1982; reversed by (1983) 133 New L.J. 1100, C.A.

1. The facts The plaintiff applied for an interlocutory injunction to restrain the defendant until trial of the action or further order from transmitting a television film which disclosed that the plaintiff had sold short measure in its American Bar.

2. What were the grounds for the application? The grounds for the application were that irrespective of the defendant's knowledge that permission on terms was required for such filming, it had introduced the television equipment surreptitiously.

3. Comyn J. granted the injunction—why? Applying the principles in *Cyanamid,* he held that in the light of the following, the balance of convenience lay in granting the injunction:

"... (i) all the circumstances of the case including the entry to the hotel and what went on there and the presence of the Inspectors of Weights and Measures; (ii) the fact that, subject to fuller argument at the trial, there was no general principle that the press could use information, however obtained; and (iii) a finding that, subject to argument at the trial, the corporation's entry with concealed cameras and television equipment could well be said to amount to a trespass." (P. 105.)

4. Sequel The Court of Appeal (December 20, 1982) allowed the defendant's appeal on the basis that it had seen not only the whole film (in two parts) taken by the BBC in the American Bar of the Savoy Hotel, but also the revised and much more restricted version of that film which the BBC proposed, if given leave, to televise that evening (1982, C.A.T. No. 514).

9 *Harrington v. Brannigan* (1983) 133 New L.J. 1133

1. The facts The plaintiff issued a writ claiming a declaration that the entitlement of the defendant to retain the office of Secretary of the Film Artistes Association (of which the plaintiff was a member) had lapsed, and he sought an interlocutory injunction restraining the defendant from purporting to act as Secretary and from performing any of the Secretary's powers or functions.

2. The relevant rule Rule 21 provided:

"(1) The General Secretary shall be elected by a postal ballot of the member ... (2) Any member shall be eligible provided ... (b) he is at least 25 years of age. In no case shall a member be elected to or retain the office after reaching the age of 70 years ... (6) The General Secretary may be dismissed by the Executive Committee without notice if he is proved guilty of fraud or other grave misconduct. Should the post of General Secretary become vacant through dismissal, resignation, death or other reason, the Executive Committee shall, pending a further election, appoint an acting secretary to fill the place."

3. Injunction refused—why? Judge Mervyn Davies sitting as a deputy judge founded his decision on the "status quo". The report, *inter alia*, reads:

"If ever there was a case for maintaining the status quo, the present case was that case. Convenience and order required that B should remain in office while he had the confidence of the majority of the

657

Executive Committee, particularly at a time when the Association had been negotiating with another trade union to join it and an application was about to go before the Certification Office shortly. It would be wholly wrong to throw the whole administrative arrangements for the Association into confusion a day or so before that important appointment. (*American Cyanamid Co. v. Ethicon Ltd* [1975] A.C. 396 applied.)"

10 Banks' breach of duty of confidence: *XAG v. A Bank* [1983] 2 All E.R. 464, *per* Leggatt J.

1. Who were the parties? The first plaintiff was incorporated in Switzerland and conducted its business wholly outside the USA. The second plaintiff was a subsidiary of the first, was also incorporated in Switzerland, but had a major branch in New York. The third plaintiff was a company associated with the first plaintiff, was incorporated in Panama, and had its headquarters in Switzerland. The plaintiffs had account with the London branch of the defendant, an American Bank.

2. The intervention of the United States Department of Justice Pursuant to criminal investigations, the United States Department of Justice served a subpoena on the American bank to produce all documents relating to any account maintained by the plaintiffs at the defendant's London branch.

3. What prompted the plaintiffs' application for an interlocutory injunction? The defendant bank declared its intention to comply with the subpoena, whereupon the plaintiffs sought and were granted an *ex parte* injunction in the High Court to restrain the bank from producing the documents.

4. The basis of the plaintiffs' case The grounds were that if the bank were to produce the documents it would hereby be in breach of the duty of confidentiality it owed to the plaintiffs.

5. The backdrop against which Leggatt J. applied the *Cyanamid* criteria The proceedings before Leggatt J. were an application by the plaintiffs to continue the injunction. Leggatt J. took the view that the relationship between banker and customer was centred in London, and further found powerful support for the proposition that the New York court would not exact a penalty upon the bank in the event that compliance with the subpoena was enjoined by the High Court in England. Following *Cyanamid*, Leggatt J. held:

(a) Indisputably there is a serious issue to be tried (*i.e.* whether, as a matter of law, the bank could, in breach of its duty of confidence to the plaintiffs, justify production of the documents pursuant to the subpoena).

(b) Damages would not be an adequate remedy to the plaintiffs, because the non-continuation of the injunction would cause potentially very considerable commercial harm to the plaintiffs, which could not be disputed.

(c) It was not established that the bank would suffer any detriment were the injunction to continue, even allowing for the probability that contempt proceedings that might be brought would be dealt with before the trial of the action.

(d) Thus, the balance of convenience firmly favoured granting the plaintiffs' application.

6. *Obiter*—Leggatt J. went beyond *Cyanamid* It is worthy of note that Leggatt J. went to considerable lengths to assess the respective strengths of the legal arguments for both sides, prompting him to say in conclusion:

> "If an in so far as it is necessary for me to pay any regard to the merits of the matter at this stage, I am firmly on the side of the plaintiffs." (at 480D.)

Thus it may be contended that as a counsel of prudence, it would behove a plaintiff even at the interlocutory stage to be prepared to argue the merits, always of course keeping to the forefront of one's mind the following dicta of Lord Diplock in *Cyanamid*:

> "It is no part of the court's function at this stage of the litigation to try to resolve conflicts of evidence on affidavit as to facts on which the claims of either party may ultimately depend nor to decide difficult questions of law which call for detailed argument and mature consideration."

11 Unauthorised telephone tapping: *Francome v. Mirror Group Newspapers* [1984] 1 W.L.R. 892 (for the facts, see p. 621)

1. Balance of convenience Stephen Brown L.J. held at 902A–C:

(a) *Authenticity:*

> "... publication by the defendants of the contents of the tape recordings in advance of the trial of the action and before the tape recordings have been authenticated would be likely to prejudice a fair trial of the plaintiffs' claim."

659

(b) *Deposit with police, etc.:*

> "So far as the defendants are concerned, it is open to them to serve the public interest, if they so wish, by seeking the appropriate authority to place the tapes in the hands of the police or the stewards of the Jockey Club."

(c) *Postponed only:*

> "An order restraining publication by them until the trial of the action would merely postpone for a time the publication of a sensational story."

(d) *Criminal:*

> "The fact that coincidentally publication would be a criminal offence which the defendants say they are prepared to commit strongly reinforces the case for an injunction."

2. What happened to the application that the defendants do disclose their source of information? Sir John Donaldson M.R. held, at 898G:

> "In the present case, assuming that the plaintiffs are entitled to an order that the defendants reveal their source, I cannot see that they will be substantially prejudiced if they have to wait until after trial of the action, particularly as a speedy trial has been ordered. On the other hand, if we allow the judge's order to stand, any argument by the defendants at the trial that the plaintiffs are not entitled to seek an order would be wholly academic. I would therefore quash this part of the judge's order."

3. The terms of the injunction The Court of Appeal granted an injunction in the following (revised) terms:

> "... the defendants, by themselves, their servants or agents [be restrained] from disclosing, otherwise than under the authority of the appropriate minister of the Crown as the successor of the Postmaster General or in the course of legal proceedings, any information as to the contents, sender or addressee of any telephone messages passing to or from telephones at the home of the plaintiffs, being information which would not have come to the knowledge of the defendants, but for the use of wireless telegraphy apparatus by the defendants or any of them or by another person." (898H–899A.)

4. Why adopt that wording? Sir John Donaldson M.R. said at 899C:

> "Assuming that the tapes reveal evidence of the commission of a criminal offence or a breach of the rules of racing—and I stress that

this is an assumption—it may well be in the public interest that the tapes and all the information to be gleaned therefrom be made available to the police and the Jockey Club. Accepting the defendants' expressed desire to promote the public interest it will be open to them to apply to the appropriate minister of the Crown for authority to disclose all the information to one or other or both of the authorities. Furthermore, if the defendants wish to publish statements which are prima facie defamatory of Mr Francome—and they have disavowed any intention of making such statements about Mrs Francome—the exception contained in the injunction which I propose and in the section of the Act of 1949 will leave them free to use the tapes as evidence in support of a plea of justification."

12 Scottish coal power station: *British Coal Corporation v. South of Scotland Electricity Board* [1991] S.L.T. 302

1. The facts In 1965 the National Coal Board (predecessors of the pursuers) agreed to supply the coal required for a new power station of the defenders at Longannet, in an arrangement whereby they were obliged to meet all Longannet's requirements throughout its life. The defenders wished to buy their coal for Longannet elsewhere, so the pursuers sought an interim interdict to prevent the defenders from purchasing or taking from any other source coal which was necessary for the operation of their Longannet Power Station.

2. The defenders failed to address the balance of convenience Lord Prosser said:

"Even if the SSEB's case on the point of law had appeared strong, no other argument on balance of convenience was advanced in their favour.

The pursuers had contended that rejection of their supplies even for a short period would have an irreversible and catastrophic effect upon the Scottish coal industry. If that were so, and it appeared to his Lordship that it would well be so, then cogent reasons existed for granting interim interdict, even if it had appeared that the pursuers' prospects were slender.

If there were any reasonable prospect of success for the pursuers it would be premature to embark on a course with such a potential for disaster for the Scottish coal industry.

In his Lordship's opinion the pleadings and arguments disclosed that there was a reasonable prospect that the pursuers would prove to be right. They were entitled to the interim interdict sought."

The pursuers won the day.

13 Rival London evening newspaper: *Evening Standard Co. Ltd v. Henderson* [1987] I.C.R. 588

1. The facts The defendant had worked for the *Evening Standard* newspaper for 17 years and had become its productions manager. Mr Robert Maxwell planned to publish a new London evening newspaper called the *Daily News* and the defendant intended to join that newspaper as productions manager. He only gave the *Evening Standard* two months' notice instead of the required one year. The *Evening Standard* sought an injunction to prevent him from going to work for the *Daily News* until the one year had expired.

2. The defendant's contract His contract contained an express term:

> "In accordance with the usual terms of our service contracts, it is understood that your entire services are to be devoted to the interests of the company, its subsidiary and associated companies, or as the directors may decide, and that on no account are you to engage in work outside, unless special permission has first been obtained for you to do so."

3. The relief sought The writ claimed an injunction restraining the defendant from:

(a) undertaking or continuing employment with or providing information, advice, assistance or services to any present or intended future competitors of the plaintiffs including the owner of the *Daily News* or otherwise acting in breach of his duty of loyalty, fidelity and good faith owed to the plaintiffs and implied into his contract of employment with them [for one year commencing with the defendant's notice]; and

(b) disclosing to any present or intended future competitor of the plaintiffs or any other person any confidential information belonging to the plaintiffs.

4. The balance of convenience The Court of Appeal held that there was a serious issue of liability. Lawton L.J. summarised the balance of convenience:

> "What we have to ask ourselves is: what, in the circumstances of this case, is the balance of convenience? If the defendant leaves the employment of the plaintiffs today, as he says he intends to do, and takes himself off straightaway or very shortly to the rival newspaper,

the plaintiffs, in my judgment, will undoubtedly suffer damage but, as I have already said and the judge at first instance found, it will be almost impossible to quantify that damage. It follows, on the face of it, that the defendant ought not, pending trial, to be allowed to do the very thing which his contract was intended to stop him doing namely, working for somebody else during the period of his contract. But that has got to be balanced against what I have said is the trite law. The injunction must not force the defendant to work for the plaintiffs and it must not reduce him, certainly, to a condition of starvation or to a condition of idleness, whatever that may mean to the authorities on this topic." (at 549B.)

5. The plaintiffs made an offer which tipped the balance

"But all that, in my judgment, is overcome by the fact that the plaintiffs have made the offer they have. The defendant can go back to work for them. If he elects not to go back (and it will be matter entirely for his election: there will be nothing in the judgment which forces an election on him) he can receive his salary and full contractual benefits under his contract until such time as his notice would have expired had it been for the proper period.

Thus it follows, in my judgment, that at this stage, as a matter of interlocutory proceedings, the balance of convenience is in favour of granting the kind of injunction asked for by the plaintiffs." (at 594D.)

14 Solicitors as estate agents: *Nixon v. Wood* (1987) 248 EG 1055

1. The facts The plaintiffs and the defendants were all partners in the same firm of solicitors, but each of the firm's three offices was allowed substantial autonomy. The defendants were the partners at the Stony Stratford office and the plaintiffs were the partners at the other two offices. The defendants intended to take advantage of the 1985 change in the Law Society's rules of conduct so as to start a business of selling property, and they intended to do so without the consent of the partners at the other offices.

2. The relief sought The plaintiffs sought an injunction to restrain the defendants from using the firm name "E.T. Ray & Co." or the property or assets of the firm, in connection with the proposed property-selling venture. They applied for an interlocutory injunction in those terms until judgment or further order in the meantime.

3. The plaintiffs' argument The plaintiffs argued that the defendants were in breach of the terms of the partnership deed by embarking upon property dealing because the business was there defined as a solicitors' practice and at the time it was so defined it was not in contemplation that a solicitors' practice could include selling property.

4. The defendants' argument The defendants replied that property dealing was a legitimate part of a solicitors' business and all they were seeking to do was to carry on a type of business which as a result of the changes in the rules of the profession, had become something which was a legitimate part of any solicitors' business and therefore a type of business which they, the defendants, were entitled to carry on at the Stony Stratford office as part of their business as solicitors practising under the partnership deed.

5. The judge weighed the balance correctly Sir Denys Buckley said in the Court of Appeal:

> "The learned judge ... came to the conclusion that there was the possibility that, if the injunction were granted, the defendants would be put at risk of being prevented from carrying out valuable business which, on one view of the possible outcome of the action, they were perfectly entitled to carry on, and that the damage involved in their being excluded from the possibility of carrying on that business pending the trial might be substantial damage which would be difficult to assess. He also came to the conclusion that, if the injunction were refused, the plaintiffs might consequently suffer damage during the period pending the trial and that that damage might be difficult to assess ... He came to the conclusion that the balance of convenience lay in refusing the injunction."

15 Employment: *Hughes v. Southwark London Borough Council* [1988] IRLR 55 (for the facts and law, see p. 627: "Serious Issue")

1. The defendants' argument The defendants strongly relied upon the principle that it must be for an employer to decide on priorities and, having made the necessary inquiries and investigations, it was for the managers of the defendants' social service staff to manage.

2. The flaw in the defendants' argument Taylor J. said:

> "There is no suggestion at all anywhere that the plan to remove social workers for substantial parts of the week for six weeks was ever put to the [Maudsley] hospital for its consideration as to what impact that would have and whether that was sustainable, and whether there

would be any cover, and so on. So that I am of the view in regard to balance of convenience that the principle of managers being left to manage is flawed in this case by their failure to inform themselves of the relevant considerations before deciding on priorities."

3. The balance lay with the plaintiffs—for three reasons:

(a) "... on the balance of convenience it seems to me that ... this move of the plaintiffs to Area 7 may well only be at best a temporary palliative to a problem that needs, as everyone agrees, a more thorough-going and permanent solution."

(b) "Meanwhile, a situation which at present is satisfactory at the Maudsley Hospital would itself be put in crisis."

(c) "There are other factors here. There is the statutory duty on the defendants to co-operate with the Special Health Authority and to provide social workers for any hospital run by them within the local authority's area. Those statutory duties may very well be in peril of being breached if this instruction which was not taken in consultation with the Special health Authority at all, is allowed to operate."

[And see "Damages adequate" at p. 644.]

16 Irregular disciplinary action: *Loosely v. National Union of Teachers* [1988] IRLR 157

1. The facts The plaintiff was a secretary of a division of the defendant union. He organised a strike without the prior approval of the union's national executive committee in breach of the union's rules and was duly disciplined by a reprimand. However, the union's officers thought this was an insufficient penalty and took the view that they could appeal to the union's appeal committee (which they themselves normally composed). The appeal committee excluded the plaintiff from union office for two years and he brought an action to contest the committee's jurisdiction within the union rules.

2. The relief sought The order of Knox J. the subject of the instant appeal was:

"... that the defendants be restrained until after judgment in this action from doing, whether by themselves or by their servants or agents or any of them, or otherwise howsoever, the following acts or any of them, that is to say, acting upon the decision of the appeals committee which was made upon April 9, 1987 in so far as it relates to the plaintiff."

3. The question of the balance of convenience was subsidiary The principal ground upon which Knox J. granted, and the Court of Appeal continued, the relief sought was a detailed construction of the union rules. But the judge also considered the balance of convenience.

4. The defendants' argument Stocker L.J. said:

> "[Counsel for the union] says that the offence committed by the plaintiff and others was so great that the potential and administrative difficulties and the position of the executive and the officers was rendered particularly difficult in the face of serious challenge to union authority. The factors in favour of the [plaintiff] are of far less weight since they involve no financial penalty on himself, he still continuing to be paid as a schoolteacher. He says that the union has a legitimate interest, as the judge found, but that it went further than a legitimate interest and could properly be described as an important duty. [Counsel for the union] argues that those factors so heavily outweigh any factors in favour of the [plaintiff] that on balance of convenience the injunction should have been discharged."

5. The plaintiff's argument

> "Before this court the [plaintiff has] said that it is not only a case of professional stigma, to which the judge referred in the light of the case of *Lawlor v. Union of Post Office Workers* [1965] 1 Ch. 712, but we are further told that the plaintiff is in fact a candidate for the [union] elections, which would take place during the period of his suspension, and is also a candidate for the conference business committee which is an important committee of the union."

6. The Court of Appeal unhesitatingly preferred the plaintiff

> "Therefore in my view I cannot see that the judge's ruling on balance of convenience, if it arises, is seriously open to challenge."

17 The "Batteries" case: *Duracell International Inc. v. Ever Ready Ltd* [1989] F.S.R. 71

1. The facts Both parties made batteries. The defendants published an advertisement which suggested that their own batteries lasted longer than the plaintiffs'. They identified the plaintiffs' batteries (a) by referring to "Duracell Batteries Ltd" and (b) by a black and white photograph of a mock-up designed to look like a battery of the plaintiffs. Both the word "Duracell" and the get-up of the batteries (copper and black) were registered trade marks. The plaintiffs applied for an interlocutory injunction to prevent the defendants repeating the advertisement.

2. The causes of action The plaintiffs' case was framed in trade libel and infringement of trade mark. The defendants pleaded justification in response to the allegation of trade libel, and it was accepted that for that reason no interlocutory relief would be forthcoming in that cause of action. The claim for infringement of the trade mark was under section 4(1)(b) of the Trade Marks Act 1938.

3. The parties' primary submissions The plaintiffs argued that the case was, on the admitted facts, clear and that their entitlement to an injunction was, on those facts, made out. The defendants, similarly, argued that on the common ground facts the plaintiffs' case was unarguable and could not succeed. Scott J. noted that Mackinnon L.J. had referred to section 4(1)(b) of the Trade Marks Act 1938 as being of "fuliginous obscurity" and heeded Lord Diplock's warning in *American Cyanamid* against deciding difficult questions of law or fact on applications for interlocutory injunctions.

4. The get-up—a non-starter However, the judge decided that when a get-up consisted of only two colours, a black and white picture suggesting two colours could never amount to infringement of the trade mark in the get-up.

5. The balance of convenience The judge dealt with the adequacy of damages compendiously under the heading of the balance of convenience. He summarised the plaintiffs' first argument that damages would be an inadequate remedy for them, as follows:

> "Assume that the plaintiffs establish at trial that the advertisement constitutes an infringement of its word mark, and assume that there is no injunction. Until trial—and, even if there is a speedy trial, that cannot take place, I imagine, much sooner than six to nine months from now—the defendants will have been using wrongly an advertisement designed and, they would suppose, effective for the purpose of drawing custom away from the plaintiffs and to themselves. In the nature of things, the extent to which that happens will be impossible to establish with any certainty at all."

6. Were damages adequate for the plaintiffs? Yes. Scott J. said:

> "The matter has not been argued out before me, but I would have thought there was a fair and firm argument, if the plaintiffs succeed and have difficulty in establishing loss , for them to ask to be awarded

667

as damages some capital sum—which, of course, would be highly arbitrary in amount—to be awarded to reflect the expropriation against their wishes of their right to a monopoly use of their mark."

7. The defendants' mirror argument The defendants argued that if they were entitled to use the comparative advertisement that had led to the litigation, but were restrained from doing so for a period of over six months, it was impossible to tell what sales they would have been deprived of, that they would otherwise have obtained.

8. The judge held: damages not adequate for defendants Referring to the method of quantifying damages he had suggested for the plaintiffs (see paragraph 6 above) Scott J. said:

"On the other hand, I do not see any possibility of the defendants' remedy on the cross-undertaking being dealt with on that footing. They would I think have to satisfy the judge of the loss they had suffered and for which they ought to be compensated."

9. The freedom of speech issue The judge summarised the defendants' argument thus:

"[Counsel for the defendants] draws attention to the nature of the purpose sought to be served by the injunction. He says this case is really a trade libel case, with trade mark allegations hitched on to the end of it in order to justify interlocutory relief that could not have been obtained if the case had rested simply as one of trade libel. He puts the case, indeed, as one involving freedom of speech."

The judge accepted that this point was in the defendants' favour.

10 The status quo The judge also accepted the plaintiffs' argument on the status quo, which he summarised thus:

"[Counsel for the plaintiffs'] second point was that the status quo ought to be held. Once I am satisfied that there is an arguable case and that the plaintiffs do not fail *in limine*, the *status quo ante*, which does not involve any infringement, arguable or otherwise, of their mark by the defendants, ought to be maintained by an injunction."

11. The judge's instinct Scott J. said:

"In the end, it seems to me that this is a case which can be brought on for trial quite quickly. It is a case between ... two giants in the field of battery sales ... In a case of this sort, my instinct is to permit the competition that the defendants want to engage in pending trial on the footing that they will have to pay damages, which would no doubt, if assessed on a capital basis, be substantial, if they fail at trial."

18 "One Girl's War": *Att.-Gen. v. Turnaround Distribution Ltd* [1989] 1 F.S.R. 169 (for the facts, see p. 633).

1. The balance of convenience This involved consideration of some three issues.

2. The first issue: the publication in Ireland The defendants argued:

"In striking the balance, counsel says, the court is bound to have regard to the existing state of publication ... Here, [counsel for the defendants] asserts, no further harm would be caused by re-publication and certainly none sufficient to justify continuation of the injunction. After all, he says, this is not a contents claim and the principle of publication has already been breached."

3. The plaintiff's argument The judge summarised the plaintiff's argument thus:

"... while recognising that the Irish decision with its inevitable consequence of partial publication creates a factor to be brought into the balance when considering injunctive relief, no doubt permanently as well as interlocutorily, of itself it neither is nor could be a decisive consideration. Were it otherwise, anyone could secure release from the constraints against revelation simply by publishing first in Dublin or indeed in the English language any where in the world, including no doubt Moscow."

4. The judge held: a factor, but outweighed Simon Brown J. said:

"... although [counsel for the plaintiff] describes the existing lawful publication of this book in Ireland as an adventitious circumstance, it is nonetheless a potent factor now in play. But whilst I accept [counsel for the defendants'] submission that regard must indeed now be had to this factor and as a corollary of this that no inflexible rule operates invariably to restrain all such unauthorised publication, I cannot accept his further submission that the balance of convenience accordingly at this stage tips in his favour."

5. The second issue: the public interest of national security The plaintiff argued that despite the fact that the contents of the book were not "sensitive": (a) friendly foreign intelligence services would lose confidence in the British intelligence; and (b) other British intelligence officers would be tempted to publish.

6. The judge accepted that such a factor was arguable Simon Brown J. said

"... although in my judgment it is ... by no means obvious that the publication of the book—let alone its further publication, given the existing extent of distribution—will damage the work of the security service in either or both of the respects [referred to at paragraph 5(a) and (b) above], that too, I accept, is properly arguable. I emphasise that it will clearly need to be argued, since the court at the trial will certainly not accept any mere *ipse dixit* to this effect."

7. The third issue: the public interest in freedom to publish The defendants argued that the freedom to publish was properly to be regarded as a valuable free-standing public interest. The plaintiff said that it could not be invoked, at least at the interlocutory stage, to outweigh a prima facie claim to enforce a contractual duty of confidence; *a fortiori* it cannot overbear a prima facie claim to restraint in the interest of national security.

8. The judge held: a slight matter

"... relatively slight although at present I perceive to be the public interest in favour of continued restraint of publication of this book, even slighter do I regard the public interest in favour of publication at this stage."

The judge granted the injunction.

[See "Damages Adequate" at p. 646.]

19 The "Chambourcy" case: *Mitchelstown Co-operative Society Ltd v. Société des Produits Nestlé SA* [1989] 1 F.S.R. 345 (for the background, see p. 630)

1. The defendants' argument The defendants (who had cut off the plaintiff's supplies of "Chambourcy" food in respect of which it previously had enjoyed exclusive rights in Ireland) argued that damages were a completely adequate remedy for the plaintiff.

2. The plaintiff's case The plaintiff said that if the defendants were permitted to continue to distribute food under the "Chambourcy" trade mark in Ireland to the exclusion of the plaintiff, the plaintiff would suffer a loss not capable of being compensated in money damages. They had asserted in their affidavits that they had taken irreversible steps in pursuance of the agreements:

(a) winding down and phasing out its existing products in favour of "Chambourcy" products;

(b) purchasing land for factory premises and applying for planning permission;

(c) purchasing machinery necessary for the production of "Chambourcy" food.

3. The Court held: damages would not be adequate for the plaintiffs Finlay C.J. said:

"I have come to the conclusion that the plaintiff in its affidavits has made out a case for a form of loss which would not be reasonably quantifiable and not reasonably capable of being repaired or compensated for by money damages."

4. The balance of convenience: in the plaintiff's favour

"Having regard to the situation which has been permitted by these defendants to continue from the date of the agreement in 1984 as far as the plaintiff is concerned, and having regard to the fact that the activity which it is sought to restrain on the part of the defendants is one commenced by them as recently as July or August of this year [it was then October], the balance of convenience is in favour of granting an injunction."

20 *Wadcock v. Brent London Borough Council* [1990] IRLR 223

1. The facts The plaintiff was employed as a social worker with experience in both child care and special needs. Following a reorganisation of the social services department the defendants allocated the plaintiff to special needs. The plaintiff refused, but made it clear that he would carry out his usual work. The council dismissed him and he brought proceedings for a declaration that their termination of his contract was unlawful.

2. The relief sought The plaintiff applied for an injunction restraining the council from acting on its purported determination of his contract and for payment of his salary pending trial.

3. The preliminary considerations were inconclusive Mervyn Davies J. said:

"There was a serious question to be tried: whether the council was justified in dismissing the plaintiff having regard to grievance and disciplinary procedures and to the fact that the plaintiff said his duties were altered in a way outside the terms of his contract. If the plaintiff did not get an interlocutory order, damages at trial would not be an adequate remedy. Equally, the council would not be compensated by damages if it failed to withstand an order and yet won at trial. The question became one of the 'balance of convenience'."

4. The balance of convenience

"The 'status quo' guidelines suggested that an interlocutory order should be made in the plaintiff's favour. But account must be taken of the fact that an order would in effect decree specific performance, pending trial, of a master and servant contract. The court generally refused to so decree, while accepting that in exceptional circumstances the court would grant an injunction in aid of a contract of personal services ... The plaintiff was now willing to work in special needs."

But:

"Having taken into account the evidence, it was impossible to conclude that if an injunction was made there would arise between the parties a 'workable situation'."

5. The plaintiff himself tipped the balance in his favour

"On the other hand, the plaintiff was a competent social worker well able to work in special needs if he were minded to obey the order of his team leader and other supervisors ... His Lordship proposed to make the order unless the plaintiff was not willing to give the undertaking unreservedly."

The undertaking was "to work in accordance with the orders of his team leader or any other person having authority over him."

21 *Cambridge Nutrition Ltd v. British Broadcasting Corporation* [1990] 3 All E.R. 523

1. The facts The plaintiffs manufactured and marketed a very low calorie diet. The Government Committee on the Medical Aspects of Food (COMA) was due shortly to publish a report on very low calorie diets, and the BBC wanted to make a programme about them. The plaintiffs co-operated with the BBC in making the programme. They said the BBC had agreed not to broadcast the programme until after the COMA Report was published, but the BBC disputed this and wished to broadcast before publication. At first instance the judge applied *American Cyanamid* and granted the injunction. The BBC successfully appealed.

2. Did *Cyanamid* apply? In the Court of Appeal Kerr L.J. said that the cases in which the subject matter concerned the right to publish an article, or to transmit a broadcast, whose importance may be transitory but whose impact depends on timing, news value and topicality, did not lend themselves easily to the application of the *Cyanamid* guidelines; he did not apply that case. But Ralph Gibson L.J. and Eastham J. did.

3. Damages were not adequate for the plaintiffs Ralph Gibson L.J. put this in two ways:

    (1) "I confess that I am not confident that a premature broadcast of the programme would have the grave effect which the plaintiffs feared; but that, in my view, is nothing to the point. The plaintiffs know their business. The judge was entitled to accept that in all probability damage would be caused to the plaintiffs in their trade by a premature broadcast of the programme, and that an award of damages at trial, which damages would be difficult to prove and to quantify, would not be adequate compensation."

    (2) "Further, as counsel for the plaintiffs pointed out, if the substantial damage which, in their case, would be caused to the plaintiffs by premature broadcast of the programme could not be recovered at law as damages, there is thereby established the more reason for holding that damages would not be an adequate remedy for the plaintiffs."

4. Nor would damages be adequate for the defendants Ralph Gibson L.J. said:

"But once the point is raised in its proper place, namely is the loss which the BBC would suffer from the grant of the injunction if the plaintiffs should fail to prove the right to it adequately compensated by an award of damages, and in particular for the money thrown away by the unusable parts of the programme and by other financial loss, coupled with such estimate as the court could make in respect of the loss of the right to publish at the time chosen by them, then, as it seems to me, the answer must be that the BBC's loss would not be adequately compensated."

5. The principle which applied Ralph Gibson L.J. quoted the relevant principle from Lord Diplock in *American Cyanamid*:

"... if the extent of the compensatable disadvantage to each party would not differ widely, it may not be improper to take into account in tipping the balance the relative strength of each party's case...".

The main problem for the plaintiffs was that the BBC's alleged agreement not to broadcast was oral.

6. The public interest The other thing which Ralph Gibson L.J. said tipped the balance was the public interest in the exercise by the BBC of their rights and duties in communication to the people of this country.

7. In a nutshell Kerr L.J. said:

"I can summarise the position by saying that in a context such as the present a doubtful contract should never prevail over the right of free speech, all other things being even."

22 *The Post Office v. Interlink Express Parcels Ltd* [1989] 1 F.S.R. 369

1. The background The plaintiffs owned the registered trade mark "Datapost" and had been operating an express delivery service using that name for 18 years when the defendants launched a directly competitive service called "Datamail" run by their 116 franchisees, using "knocking" advertisements.

2. The relief sought The plaintiffs sued for infringement of their registered trade mark, and sought an injunction pending judgment or further order restraining the defendants whether acting by their servants, agents or otherwise howsoever from using in connection with the provision of a service for collecting and/or delivery packages or parcels the mark "Datamail" or any other mark so resembling "Datapost" as to be likely to deceive or cause confusion.

3. Serious issue to be tried Aldous J. identified the issue as being whether "Datamail" so nearly resembled "Datapost" as to be likely to deceive or cause confusion. He held that it would be wrong for him to attempt to resolve this question unless absolutely necessary, and it was not necessary. Nevertheless there was a serious issue to be tried.

4. Damages were not an adequate remedy Since the defendants' "knocking" advertisements actually used the similarity of the trade names to suggest that the same service was being provided, not surprisingly the judge held that damage would be bound to be done to the plaintiffs—and such damage as could not be quantified. Conversely the grant of an injunction would waste the effect of the defendants' advertising, disrupt their business, and damage their credibility, also in an unquantifiable way.

5. But an interlocutory injunction was likely to be final Instead of trying to determine the case on the merits, the judge decided that the fact that the grant of an injunction was likely to be determinative of the dispute between the parties was simply a factor to be taken into account:

> "Counsel for the defendants, relying on *Athletes Foot Marketing Associates Inc. v. Cobra Sports Ltd* [1980] R.P.C. 343 and *Cayne v. Global Natural Resources plc* [1984] 1 All E.R. 225 submitted that when considering whether to grant an injunction I should take into account that the grant of an injunction would decide the case in the plaintiffs' favour in that the defendants, pending trial, would have to give up using DATAMAIL and would have to use another trade mark with the consequence that they could not in practice return to using DATAMAIL. I believe that this submission is correct. The *American Cyanamid* case was concerned with doing justice when an interlocutory injunction was sought in a patent action. The crux of the speech of Lord Diplock was that the courts ought not, when considering applications for interlocutory injunctions, to carry out a mini trial, but should grant or refuse to grant relief so that justice was and could be done. In a case where an interlocutory injunction would in substance decide the subject of the case in one party's favour it may be necessary for the court to take that into account and if necessary to assess the strength of the parties' cases before deciding where the balance of justice lies. In the present case, I consider it right, as suggested by Eveleigh L.J. in the *Cayne* case at page 232H, to endeavour to avoid injustice, and in so doing I must take into account the fact that an injunction would decide the main part of the case in the plaintiffs' favour. In so doing I do not believe I am dissenting from the reasoning of the *American Cyanamid* case but believe I am applying the general principles to particular facts."

6. The balance of convenience The judge decided the case on the balance of convenience. He refused an injunction, considering two factors to be critical on each possible eventuality:

> "In my view, this is not a case where an interlocutory injunction should be granted. If the damage to the plaintiffs by the refusal to grant an injunction is weighed against the damage and injustice which would be caused by the wrongful grant of an injunction the scales are clearly in favour of the refusal to grant the injunction."

675

If an injunction were wrongly refused:

> "In the present case no passing off is likely and although I accept that some damage will be caused by infringement of the plaintiffs' trade mark this will not be of the same order as that which would be caused to the defendants. The grant of injunction will completely disrupt the defendants' business and damage their reputation and goodwill.
>
> Further, this action does not entail lengthy discovery or other matters which would prevent it from coming to trial quickly and if the plaintiffs are right they will obtain an injunction and the court wielding the proverbial broad axe will be able to order compensation in damages."

If an injunction were wrongly granted:

> "On the other hand, if an injunction be wrongly granted the defendants and their franchisees can never go back as they cannot in practice return to using the trade mark DATAMAIL.
>
> I also see more difficulty in assessing the damages which will be payable under the cross-undertaking as to damages than damages for infringement of trade mark. Such an assessment would require the court to come to some conclusion as to what proportion of the defendants' and their 116 franchisees' advertising and launch costs have been thrown away and what diminution of goodwill and general reputation has been suffered by them. The task of doing this for 117 parties would be complex to say the least."

23 *Rafique v. The Trustees of the Walton Estate* (1992) 65 P. & C.R. 356

1. Background The plaintiffs were four out of some 380 house owners on the St George's Hill Estate. The defendants were trustees of the Walton Estate over which the plaintiffs used a road to gain access to their houses. The plaintiffs brought proceedings against the defendants in which the issue was the status of the plaintiffs' right of way.

2. The defendants' second bite at the interlocutory cherry An interlocutory injunction had already been granted restraining the defendants from interfering with the plaintiffs' use of the road until trial. But since then the defendants had become anxious that the continuing absence of any obstruction along the road meant that the other 376 inhabitants of the St George's Hill Estate might be acquiring rights of the same kind as the plaintiffs by the passage of time. The defendants wished to be permitted to place a locked barrier across the road and give the four plaintiffs keys.

3. The only question—the balance of convenience For the plaintiffs was urged the obvious inconvenience of a locked barrier, in terms of locking and unlocking and the lack of access for visitors. Although there were five other access roads to the estate, the relevant road was the busiest and most convenient.

4. The defendants' argument On the other side the defendants could point to the potential injustice to them if other house owners acquired prescriptive rights in the meantime—and there was evidence that many of the houses had been built in the last 20 years.

5. The Gordian knot cut The plaintiffs suggested that the potential injustice to the defendants could be avoided by the simple expedient of putting up a notice on the road stating unequivocally that anybody using the road was using it only be permission of the defendants and that that permission might be withdrawn at any time.

6. The injunction continued Although neither side could cite any authority for or against the efficacy of such a notice in preventing rights of way arising by prescription, Warner J. felt that it rendered the defendants' objections insufficient:

> "It is difficult to see what the answer would be to a claim by the Trustees that their notice rendered the use of the road by anyone while it was there a use with their permission. It would not be use, as it seems to me, with their acquiescence, because the notice would unequivocally state otherwise."

24 Newsgroup Newspapers Ltd v. The Mirror Group Newspapers (1986) Ltd [1991] F.S.R. 487

1. The background An interlocutory injunction had been granted by Aldous J. two years earlier (see p. 850 below) preventing the defendants from publishing advertisements in a certain form which, it was alleged, infringed the plaintiffs' trade marks. But the action had thereafter gone to sleep. In the meantime the editor of the *Daily Mirror* changed and the new editor, in ignorance of the interlocutory injunction, published the same sort of advertisement. The plaintiffs threatened to apply to the court. The defendants applied to discharge the injunction.

2. The principle Hoffmann J. identified the principle as that stated by Buckley L.J. in *Chanel Ltd v. Woolworth & Co* [1981] 1 W.L.R. 485:

> "Even in interlocutory matters a party cannot fight over again a battle

which has already been fought unless there has been some significant change of circumstances, or the party has become aware of facts which he could not reasonably have know, or found out, in time for the first encounter."

3. The principle applied Hoffmann J. went on to apply the principle to the case before him:

"This is not a case in which the defendant is seeking to refight matters which could have been fought in 1988. The question is whether the inordinate and inexcusable delay since 1988 constitutes a change of circumstances within the meaning of Buckley L.J.'s statement which would justify an application for discharge. In my view, for the reasons which I have given, it does. [Counsel for the plaintiffs] submitted that the defendants have suffered no real prejudice from the order remaining in place for the last 2 and a half years. The fact that the editor of the *Daily Mirror* in July 1990 was unaware of its existence shows, in his submission, that the *Daily Mirror* could not previously have wanted to do anything which would infringe the order. But in my view the fact that the *Daily Mirror* found itself in July 1990 tripped up by an order made at an interlocutory stage in an action which appeared long to have gone to sleep was in itself prejudice caused by the existence of the order. Nor do I think it is necessarily incumbent upon a defendant in a case like this to show that, for example, the circulation of his newspaper has been hampered by his being unable to place advertisements which are restricted by the terms of the order. It is in my view sufficient that the order has constituted a longstanding restriction on the defendants' freedom to use the forms of advertisement which they wish. These litigants are parties between whom quarter is neither given nor sought and in my view there would be no injustice in depriving the plaintiffs of the interlocutory protection which was intended to preserve their position until trial but which they have been content to treat as if it already represented a final victory.
The injunction will therefore be discharged."

4. The underlying reason? Delay before the trial greatly affects the balance of convenience. Hence it will often be in a plaintiff's interest, in persuading the court to grant an interlocutory injunction, to submit to a tight schedule directed towards a speedy trial.

25 *Dalgety Spillers Foods Ltd v. Food Brokers Ltd* (1993) T.L.R. 618

1. The background The plaintiffs manufactured a range of products called "Pot Noodle". The defendants introduced a competitor range called "Cup Noodles".

2. The relief sought The plaintiffs applied for an interlocutory injunction restraining the defendants from importing, advertising, exposing for sale or supply, selling or supplying or otherwise dealing in any snack soup or other snack product in any container in the same shape or form as the plaintiffs' "Pot Noodle" range of products.

3. Was there a serious issue to be tried? The plaintiffs' evidence of the risk of confusion took the form of 24 affidavits of shoppers in Manchester who were shown the two products in various sequences and asked for their reactions. Blackburne J. felt unable to attach very much weight to the affidavits because of the circumstances in which they had been obtained. But he did not feel able, on an interlocutory motion, simply to brush them aside. Accordingly he concluded that he could not say there was no serious issue to be tried as to the risk of confusion. (Interestingly, *The Times* reports the judge as using this inverted form of the test.)

4. The balance of convenience—two major factors

(a) *The undertaking:* The defendants were prepared to give an undertaking to maintain until trial, full and accurate records of all sales of "Cup Noodles" in their current get-up.

(b) *The plaintiffs' behaviour:* Nearly a year before the defendants launched "Cup Noodles", on the advice of leading counsel they wrote to the plaintiffs frankly informing them that they had set up a company to manufacture "Cup Noodles" for supply to the United Kingdom and enclosing sample containers. Yet the plaintiffs never answered the letter.

5. The plaintiff's behaviour—how was it relevant? In writing their warning letter the defendants had demonstrated a wish to act with proper regard for the rights of others. The plaintiffs had ignored that warning and in the meantime the defendants had expended time, trouble and expense in launching their product in that container.

6. The principle Blackburne J. quoted the words of Hoffmann J. in *Films Rover International Ltd v. Cannon Film Sales Ltd* [1987] 1 W.L.R. 670 at

679

680, as a statement of principle which had been approved by Lord Jauncey in *R. v. Secretary of State for Transport, ex parte Factortame Ltd (No. 2)* [1991] 1 A.C. 603 at 683:

> "The principal dilemma about the grant of interlocutory injunctions ... is that there is by definition a risk that the court may make a 'wrong' decision ... A fundamental principle is therefore that the court should take whichever course appears to carry the lower risk of injustice, if it should turn out to be 'wrong'."

Applying this principle Blackburne J. refused any injunction.

26 *R. v. Inspectorate of Pollution, ex parte Greenpeace Ltd* [1994] 4 All E.R. 321

1. The background The respondent government departments granted to British Nuclear Fuels plc (BNFL) authorisation under the Radioactive Substances Act 1960:

- (a) to operate a radioactive waste reprocessing plant at Sellafield; and
- (b) to carry out a 10-week commissioning test of the reprocessing plant before it went into operation.

The tests involved some discharge of radioactive waste into the air and sea. Instead of applying for an interlocutory injunction against BNFL, the environmental organisation Greenpeace applied for certiorari to quash the government departments' authorisation, and then, interlocutorily, for a stay of the authorisation pending the hearing. BNFL were not a party to the proceedings, but were represented.

2. The principles to be applied The judge (Brooke J.) treated the application for a stay as if it were an application for an interlocutory injunction against BNFL and applied the *Cyanamid* principles. The Court of Appeal held that this was the right approach. Glidewell L.J. said:

> "If a third party would be affected by a decision on an application for a stay but is not made a party to the proceedings as a respondent to an application for an injunction, then, in my view, nevertheless, the same principles should be followed."

3. Damages an adequate remedy? Obviously damages would not be an adequate remedy for the "pseudo-plaintiff" (Greenpeace). On the other side, BNFL alleged that its losses if the commissioning test were held up would be £250,000 a day. Not only would Greenpeace be unable to afford such sums, but they had not even offered any undertaking as to BNFL's damages.

4. The balance of convenience—at first instance In favour of granting the stay was the very real concern of Greenpeace backed by their scientific evidence challenging the government departments: all emissions are harmful, and cannot be justified merely by BNFL's wish to make money. Against the stay were three factors:
- (a) The authorisation had been granted by the government departments charged with the task of deciding whether the emissions would be safe.
- (b) The level of radioactive discharge would be very small indeed, and required no alteration of BNFL's existing permitted limits.
- (c) BNFL's losses would be very considerable if the commissioning were held up.

5. The balance of convenience—on appeal The judge held that the balancing exercise resulted in refusing relief. On appeal BNFL produced details of the various "phases" of emission. This enabled Greenpeace to suggest a compromise—a shorter stay of only six days beginning only at the start of the higher-level emissions. But the majority of the Court of Appeal refused to accept that this new evidence invalidated the judge's exercise of his discretion (within the principle of *Hadmor Productions Ltd v. Hamilton* [1983] 1 A.C. 191 at 220, [1982] 1 All E.R. 1042 at 1046.) The appeal was accordingly dismissed.

D: THE STRENGTH OF THE CASE

Series 5 Software Ltd. v. Clarke [1996] 1 All E.R. 853

1. The facts The plaintiff company developed computer software for use in the publishing industry, its main product being a software package, QC 2000. The defendants were employees of the plaintiff, who had become disaffected. They resigned and took with them computer equipment, a full set of QC 2000 software, company accounts and client mailing lists. The plaintiff claimed that the defendants were making use of the client lists to sell a version of QC 2000 as their own, and estimated their loss at £50,000.

2. The relief sought At an earlier hearing the defendants had been ordered to return the equipment. But the plaintiffs also claimed interlocutory orders restraining the defendants from:
- (i) contacting any of the plaintiff's customers; and
- (ii) using or disclosing to any third party certain of the plaintiff's alleged trade secrets.

681

3. The plaintiff's preferred position The plaintiff did not urge the court to consider the apparent strength or weakness of its case, preferring the lesser hurdle of demonstrating at least an arguable case. But there was a difficulty:

> "It is a matter of common knowledge and frequent comment that there was an apparent sea-change in the courts' approach to the grant of this form of relief in 1975 as a result of the speeches of the House of Lords in *American Cyanamid Co. v. Ethicon Ltd* [1975] 1 All E.R. 504, [1975] A.C. 396. Since then it has been suggested on a number of occasions that it is now no longer appropriate to consider as a significant factor the apparent strength or weakness of the plaintiff's case as disclosed by the affidavit evidence filed on the application for interlocutory relief. At an early stage in the hearing before me, I asked Mr Staddon whether he was submitting that the court could take account of the relative strength of the parties' cases in deciding whether or not to grant interlocutory relief in view of that decision of the House of Lords. It was clear that Mr Staddon's preferred position was that all that his client had to overcome was the lesser hurdle of demonstrating at least an arguable case on its claims. However, he also said that, whatever the strict interpretation of *American Cyanamid*, it is known that some courts still pay regard to the relative strengths of the parties' cases. I am not sure that he was prepared to accept that this was legitimate, even though it is common knowledge that it happens frequently in practice.
>
> I understand Mr Staddon's reluctance to come off the fence on this issue. However, I do not believe it is satisfactory to exercise the court's discretion to grant an interlocutory injunction by paying lip-service to the guidance given in *American Cyanamid* while in practice applying different criteria. The courts must know what the ground rules are and then apply them. Therefore, before deciding whether or not an interlocutory injunction of any sort should be ordered in this case, it is necessary to consider what factors are relevant to the court's exercise of its discretion and how those factors should be assessed."

4. A reappraisal of American Cyanamid Laddie J. reconsidered *American Cyanamid* in the context of other decisions, particularly *F. Hoffmann-La Roche & Co. AG v. Secretary of State for Trade and Industry* [1975] A.C. 295 and came to the following conclusions:

> "Accordingly, it appears to me that in deciding whether to grant interlocutory relief, the court should bear the following matters in mind. (1) The grant of an interlocutory injunction is a matter of discretion and depends on all the facts of the case. (2) There are no fixed rules as to when an injunction should or should not be granted. The relief must be kept flexible. (3) Because of the practice adopted

on the hearing of applications for interlocutory relief, the court should rarely attempt to resolve complex issues of disputed fact or law. (4) Major factors the court can bear in mind are (a) the extent to which damages are likely to be an adequate remedy for each party and the ability of the other party to pay, (b) the balance of convenience, (c) the maintenance of the status quo, and (d) any clear view the court may reach as to the relative strength of the parties' cases."

5. Applying those principles The judge then went on to apply these principles and refused the plaintiff an injunction. The headnote explains the reasons as follows:

"In the circumstances, the plaintiff's case, while arguable in the sense that the facts at trial could possibly support the allegations made, was weak in relation to some claims, and in relation to others it was impossible at an interlocutory stage to come to a conclusion as to whether there was substance in the claim or the defence. As far as the balance of convenience was concerned, while it was clear that either of the injunctions sought could effectively deprive the defendants of their means of earning a living, the plaintiff's assertion of substantial and immediate damage was unsubstantiated and, moreover, was inconsistent with the delay evident in the issue of proceedings. In view of the financial difficulties facing both parties it was likely that neither side would be able to meet an order for damages, and having regard to the fact that, by the time proceedings were commenced, the defendants were well advanced in their attempt to create a new livelihood and would not be the only competitors to the plaintiff's market, to allow the defendants to enter that market would not significantly affect the status quo. On that basis it would not be appropriate to grant the relief sought by the plaintiff and its application would accordingly be dismissed."

II *Cyanamid*—Case File—Special Factors

A: PASSING OFF

1 Introduction

1. Are "passing off" cases an exception to *Cyanamid*?

(a) *Sometimes—yes:* As Walton J. said in the *Athletes Foot Marketing Associates Inc. v. Cobra Sports Ltd* [1980] R.P.C. 343 at 348–349:

> "I now turn to the law applicable. Mr Anthony Evans, for the plaintiffs, argued that on the foregoing facts there was an arguable case to the effect that the plaintiffs did indeed have the goodwill which they assert, and that therefore, following *American Cyanamid v. Ethicon* [1975] A.C. 396, I should forthwith proceed to consider the balance of convenience which he submitted came down heavily in favour of the plaintiffs. I am not, however, prepared to take that simple course, and that for two reasons. The first is that, in matters involving trade restrictions, it is not possible to apply the general procedure of the case in precisely the same manner as in other cases. The reason is simple: the decision on the motion, whichever way it goes, profoundly affects the rights of the parties in a way which cannot easily be undone if at the trial a different result is reached. If, for example, an injunction were granted as sought by the plaintiffs, then the defendants would have to change the name of their Mail Order and Bargain Basement Operations. It would be idle to say that they could change back—possibly years later after there has been a trial and appeals from the decision therein—because in the meantime they will, of necessity, have invested time, money and effort in a totally different direction, and, obviously, they would not wish to throw all that away. It has therefore been clearly recognised that in the present type of case it is necessary to consider rather more than in the usual case the strength of the plaintiffs' case in law: see *Office Overload v. Gunn* [1977] F.S.R. 39; and *per* Lord Diplock in *N.W.L. Ltd v. Woods* [1979] 1 W.L.R. 1294 at 1307A–B."

(b) *Sometimes—no:* As Peter Gibson J. explained in *Home Box Office Inc.*

684

v. Channel 5 Home Box Office Ltd [1982] F.S.R. 449 at 459:

"I turn next to Mr Baldwin's submission that the present case falls within a recognised exception to the applicability of the principle of the *American Cyanamid* case. He referred me to *Newsweek Inc. v. British Broadcasting Corporation* [1979] R.P.C. 441, where Lord Denning M.R., at 447, expressed the view that in passing off cases the practice is still to see whether the plaintiff has a strong prima facie case. That was a case, unlike the present, where all the essential facts had been ascertained, so that the issues of law could be determined at the interlocutory stage. An example of a passing off case where the *American Cyanamid* principles were still applied was *Dunhill (Alfred) Ltd v. Sunoptic SA* [1979] F.S.R. 337 in which the *Newsweek* case in the Court of Appeal was cited. Mr Baldwin also referred me to *N.W.L. Ltd v. Woods* [1979] 1 W.L.R. 1294, which laid down that it was appropriate to consider the degree of likelihood of a permanent injunction being granted, where the grant or refusal of an interlocutory injunction would dispose of the action finally, there being nothing left on which it would be in the interests of the unsuccessful party to proceed to trial. The *Athlete's Foot* case was an illustration of the application of that principle, all the relevant facts being virtually undisputed. But I cannot see that the present is such a case. There are relevant facts in dispute, and I do not see that the grant or refusal of the injunction, whichever way it goes, will mean the end of this action. Mr Baldwin submitted that a case (such as he submitted was the present) where the defendant would suffer serious damage by the grant of the injunction was a fortiori one where a strong prima facie case had to be made out. Whilst I accept that in such a case this factor is a very important one in assessing the balance of convenience, I do not see it as a reason for not applying the principles of *American Cyanamid*, intended as they were as principles of general application."

(c) *In any event—it is a matter of fact:* As Sir John Donaldson said in *Elan Digital Systems Ltd v. Elan Computers Ltd* [1984] F.S.R. 373:

"He submitted that as a matter of law in passing off actions something more than a triable issue is required. He made that submission because, he says, it is rare in cases of this sort that cases go beyond an interim hearing. I do not for my part think that this is a point of law at all. I think it is a point of fact that if a product is about to be launched and there is an injunction, it may well be that it is not worthwhile for the launcher to wait for a trial because the disruptive effects will be so great that the sensible commercial course would be to adopt another name. Those are factors which have to be taken into account when balancing the consequences of an interim injunction. If the

685

consequence on the facts of a particular case is that the defendant will have to abandon his projected course of action, that is a factor which has to be taken into account and to which due weight must be given. There is no principle of law involved."

In this context however, reference should also be made to *Parnass/Pelly v. Hodges* [1982] F.S.R. 329, *per* Whitford J. which is authority for the proposition that in an application for an interlocutory injunction the plaintiff in a passing off action must show more than that there is an arguable case, because the defendant will often adopt a different name in order to continue in business once the injunction is granted and the injunction will be final in effect if not in name.

2. Passing off check list

(a) *As to establishing goodwill:* In *Erven Warninck BV v. Townend (J.) & Sons (Hull) Ltd* [1979] A.C. 731 at 755, Lord Fraser said:

"It is essential for the plaintiff in a passing off action to show at least the following facts: (1) that his business consists of, or includes, selling in England a class of goods to which the particular trade name applies; (2) that the class of goods is clearly defined, and that in the minds of the public, or a section of the public, in England, the trade name distinguishes that class from other similar goods; (3) that because of the reputation of the goods there is goodwill attached to the name; (4) that he, the plaintiff, as a member of the class of those who sell the goods, is the owner of goodwill in England which is of substantial value; (5) that he has suffered, or is really likely to suffer, substantial damage to his property in the goodwill by reason of the defendants selling goods which are falsely described by the trade name to which the goodwill is attached."

(b) *"My Kinda Town Ltd" (t/a Chicago Pizza Pie Factory) v. Lauren Sabin Soll and Grunts Investments Ltd (t/a L. S. Grunts Chicago Pizza Co.)* [1981] Com LR 194: Slade J. at 195 listed the relevant principles which should guide the courts in approaching the evidence in a passing off case:

"(1) If a plaintiff in a passing off action can show that the defendant has had the intent to mislead members of the public, the court will readily infer that deception has indeed resulted or is likely to result (see for example *Office Cleaning Services Ltd v. Westminster Windows and General Cleaners Ltd* (1946), 63 R.P.C. 39 at 42 (lines 38–41) *per* Lord Simonds). Nevertheless, it is not essential to establish fraudulent intention in order to obtain relief in a passing off action. ... Proof of *mala fides* merely lightens the burden of proof falling on the plaintiff in other respects.

(2) If a trader adopts as part of his title a 'fancy' word or phrase which has no relation to the character or quality of the services or goods offered by him and a competitor subsequently takes that word of phrase as part of his trade name, the court will be very ready to infer both an intention on the part of the second to mislead members of the public and the likelihood of actual deception occurring (see for example the *Office Cleaning Services* case, 63 R.P.C. at 42 (lines 31–35) *per* Lord Simonds, who asked 'why else did he adopt it?').

(3) If, however, a trader adopts as part of his trading name a word or phrase which is apt simply to describe to the ordinary member of the public the character or quality of the services or goods offered by him and a competitor subsequently takes that word of phrase as part of his trade name, the court will, in the absence of proven bad faith be very slow to infer that confusion is likely to result. ...

(4) It is not, however, a rule of law that a trader who had adopted as part of his trading name a descriptive word or phrase of the nature referred to in (3) above can never, in the absence of proof of bad faith, succeed in an action in passing off against a competitor who has subsequently adopted the same descriptive word or phrase as part of his title. One particular instance in which he may still succeed in such circumstances is if he can show the word or phrase has acquired such a subsidiary or secondary meaning that it has come to connote in the minds of the public not only the nature or quality of the goods or services offered but also the identity of the persons offering them.

(5) However, it is not an essential condition of success in a passing off case that the plaintiff should establish that the disputed descriptive words should have acquired such a secondary meaning.

(6) There is no rule that a name is not so like another as to be calculated to deceive where the words common to the two names come first in the one and last in the other. ...

(7) Though the decided cases afford valuable guidelines to which the court has to pay due weight in approaching the evidence, the ultimate issue is always one of fact."

2 *Alltransport International Group Ltd v. Alltrans Express Ltd* [1976] F.S.R. 13

1. The facts The plaintiffs, international carriers, had a reputation in the names "Alltransport" and "Alltransport International." The defendants, also international carriers, began using the name "Alltrans International".

2. What did the plaintiffs seek? By their notice of motion they applied to secure an injunction which would have stopped the defendants using the trading style of Alltrans International, and further, to secure relief which would have stopped the defendants using any other name which included the word "Alltrans," at least as the initial word in the name.

3. Was there a serious issue to be tried?

(a) *Alltrans International:* Yes—at 15, *per* Whitford J.:

> "The plaintiffs as I say, having established, as accepted for present purposes, this reputation as Alltransport International, it seems tome really to be beyond dispute that there is an arguable case for saying that the use of the expression Alltrans International in relation to a transport business is likely to lead to confusion and dissension. I do not go into the question as to whether they have effectively established cases of confusion and deception. The instances they put forward have been challenged and there is some substance in the challenges that have been made, but I think there is undoubtedly a very arguable case."

(b) *Any name beginning with "Alltrans":* No—at 15:

> "So far as any wider injunction is concerned, what the plaintiffs want is an injunction which will stop the use of the name 'Alltrans' in conjunction with any other name, and they only begin to establish an arguable case if they can show reputation. I doubt myself whether they have even begun to establish an arguable case on the evidence at present before me so far as reputation in 'Alltrans' is concerned. There are some faint indications, which again are very much open to criticism, that others may use an abbreviation of this kind as indicating the business of the plaintiffs. Certainly the word 'Alltrans' is used as part of the telegraphic address of the plaintiffs, but so far as the evidence in the main goes it really all goes to reputation in the names Alltransport or Alltransport International. The name Alltrans Express Ltd. is in my view upon a very different footing from the name Alltrans. I need not go so far as to consider the effect, if any, of the addition of words such as 'Express.' The truth of the matter is that all these terminations have got descriptive elements and may serve very little to distinguish if the initial word in both cases are the same. But I am so little satisfied that the plaintiffs have an arguable case so far as any wider injunction be concerned and I am so little satisfied that there is any real probability of damage accruing to them on the present evidence if the defendants are allowed to continue to use the name Alltrans Express Ltd. and having regard to the fact that there is no evidence that anybody is likely to be interested in any other name incorporating or consisting of the word 'Alltrans,' I do not think it would be right for me to grant the plaintiffs any relief over

and above that which I think they are in fact entitled to, and to that extent their application by way of motion succeeds."

4. Damages—not an adequate remedy for the plaintiff Whitford J. held at 15–16:

(a) *The "passing off" factor:*

"I think that in businesses of this kind, if one is considering names in relation to the business which are likely to bring about confusion, it is all too likely that damage may result which will never even be known to the one party or the other. There is no doubt that when persons are considering employing the services of organisations like the organisation of the plaintiffs or either of the defendants they do so probably very often on personal recommendation or because they have seen the services advertised in some appropriate journal and it seems to me all too likely that anybody who has been recommended to go to the plaintiffs, who are known as Alltransport International, going away and coming across a company calling itself Alltrans International might well come to the conclusion that they had been recommended to employ and business would be lost, although at the end of the day nobody could know anything about it at all."

(b) *The "only recently established" factor:*

"Then there is this to be borne in mind: it stands accepted on the defendants' side that they have only started using this particular style of Alltrans International very recently indeed. There is a case for saying that Alltrans Express Limited has been used, albeit only in a sort of secondary connotation with the business of Kwickasair for a little bit longer, but Alltrans International came into use very recently indeed, when the decision was taken, in some respects a sensible enough decision, too, by TNT that it would be desirable to standardise the names used by the companies within the group throughout the world. I do not say that that was not a perfectly sensible decision to take and, if at the end of the day, they are able to satisfy the court that they ought to be allowed to do this then so well and good. The next question that I am really concerned with is whether, if they are stopped from extending their activities in that way between now and the hearing of the action the defendants are going to suffer any very serious damage, and I would only say that I am not satisfied that they are."

689

3 *Fisons Ltd v. Godwin (E.J.) (Peat Industries) Ltd* [1976] R.P.C. 653

1. Background A "moron in a hurry" case—see the judgment of Brightman J. in *Morning Star Co-operative Society Ltd v. Express Newspapers Ltd* [1979] F.S.R. 113. In the *Fisons* case, Brightman J. at 657 said at line 25:

> "On this motion I am not concerned with infringement of trademark or breach of copyright, but only with passing off. Infringement of trademark has hardly been argued and breach of copyright not at all."

2. The facts The plaintiffs manufactured plastic "growing bags" partly overprinted with horticultural decoration, instructions and the mark "Fisons Gro-bag." Growing bags similar in function and size had been manufactured by others for some time. The defendants, peat merchants, obtained a plastic bag identical in size to those of the plaintiffs and marked "Godwin's Crop-bag" and bearing similar instructions and decorations. The plaintiffs had always relied on prominent display of their name on their products and the defendants' bags had yet to be marketed.

3. No serious issue to be tried Brightman J. said at 657(45)–652(15):

> "I am of course aware of the guidelines laid down in recent cases by the House of Lords and the Court of Appeal for the proper approach to an interlocutory application of this sort and of the important part played by balance of convenience. In all the circumstances, I have reached the conclusion that this motion ought to be dismissed. There is a great volume of evidence before me, some of it admissible and some obviously inadmissible, as to the probability or improbability of confusion. I prefer to trust to my own eyes. There are obvious similarities between the two bags, but it seems to me inconceivable that anyone seeing a growing bag described in very bold letters as 'Godwin's Crop-bag' could possible suppose that it was a 'Gro-bag' produced by Fisons, or that anyone buying a growing bag of the Fison design could fail to observe that it was a Fison product, so prominently displayed is the name 'Fisons.' If the Fison 'Gro-bag' had not contained the name 'Fisons' or if the name 'Godwins' had not been so promi-nently displayed, I might well have reached a different conclusion, but I doubt whether the defendants could have done much more to signify to a buyer that he was looking at a product of Godwins and not at a product of Fisons. I suspect that the deponents who have professed to discern a possibility of confusion have been directing their minds

690

to similarities in design and neglecting the clear message conveyed by the dissimilarity of the two names. I am wholly unconvinced on the evidence presented to me and the arguments so far deployed, that any buyer of normal mental capacity with the remotest conception of what he was seeking to purchase could be misled."

4. Balance of convenience—against an injunction Brightman J. said at 657 (30–40):

"The issue which I must decide is whether on the balance of convenience, the use by the defendants of Godwin's 'Crop-bag' ought to be restrained pending trial of the action, because there is an appreciable possibility or a likelihood of confusion resulting. Fisons' present design of bag was extensively marketed in 1975 and will, I am told, be marketed in 1976. It has no doubt acquired a get-up reputation. The defendants' bag has not yet been marketed to the public, but it has been shown extensively to retailers who have put in orders on the faith of it. It would, no doubt, be possible for the defendants' bag to be redesigned. It would take perhaps four to eight weeks, or maybe a little more, for a different bag to be produced. If that were done it would be possible for the defendants to catch at least a part, and perhaps a major part, of the 1976 market from the point of view of time, but I think that there is no doubt that the defendants' sales to retailers would be disrupted and that loss would be occasioned to them which might be very difficult to assess."

4 *Lyngstad v. Anabas Products Ltd* [1977] F.S.R. 62

1. The facts The plaintiffs were well-known Swedish pop musicians known as "Abba". The first defendant manufactured various articles bearing photographs of Abba. The second defendant had offered these for sale. The plaintiffs alleged that the defendants were using Abba's reputation for their own gain and the public would suppose that Abba was associated with the defendants.

2. The law Oliver J. invoked the following principles at 66:

"First and foremost, the action is based on misrepresentation, conscious or unconscious, calculated to lead to confusion between the goods or business of the plaintiffs and those of the defendants. Secondly, the rationale of the action is that the law will not permit the plaintiffs' legitimate business interests to be prejudiced by the exploitation by another person of the plaintiffs' goodwill. The goodwill is of course an essentially localised concept and the court does not

691

interfere to protect against exploitation by a foreign business which has established no goodwill here."

3. The case for the plaintiffs Oliver J. explained at 65:

"There is no question that the plaintiffs themselves or indeed I think any company connected with them, have at any time marketed in this country any of the articles to which the notice of motion refers. It cannot be claimed on the evidence that what the defendants are doing is causing goods of their manufacture to be confused with goods of the plaintiffs' manufacture, and that indeed is not claimed. What is said here is that the plaintiffs, as entertainers, have built up a reputation which is associated in the public mind with the name and image of the plaintiffs, and that the defendants are exploiting that reputation for their own commercial purposes. This, it is said, is properly the subject-matter of an action for passing off."

4. Was it a "serious issue to be tried"? Oliver J. was able to avoid answering the question, by showing that in any event the balance of convenience was against the grant of an injunction. However, he voiced the following view at 66:

"I do not think that there is any English authority which goes so far as to justify the cause of action upon which the plaintiffs rely in this case...."

5. Damages—an adequate remedy?

(a) *For the plaintiffs?* No—as Oliver J. explained at 69:

"In the ultimate analysis, if the plaintiffs are right, their loss is a loss of royalties on goods of any particular description sold which bear their names or images—if they are right—and the possible and really wholly hypothetical loss, in the present state of law, which might arise from their being unable to guarantee a licensee exclusivity. That is not of course easily quantified."

(b) *For the defendants?* No—as Oliver J. went on to explain at 69:

"No doubt that may be true, but equally the loss which the defendants may sustain if an injunction is granted is equally difficult to quantify because it cannot be predicted how many articles they could sell between now and the trial and what the loss of profit would be. Mr Balcombe suggested that it is merely a case of making projections on existing sales, but that again is purely a matter of guesswork, because one does not know how the market is going to go. The plaintiffs' popularity might wane or it might increase. On either side it seems to me that the quantification of damages is largely a matter of guesswork."

Oliver J. went on to explain at 70:

"The defendants who, as it seems to me, are not in a large way of business and who make relatively small profits on the items sold will suffer an equally unquantifiable loss which they cannot easily mitigate. For them indeed the loss of potential profit is likely to be a much more serious matter because they are an existing business with an existing goodwill which is likely to be damaged if an injunction is granted."

6. Balance of convenience As to "status quo", Oliver J. said at 70:

"Furthermore, the *American Cyanamid* decision directs me to pay some attention to the status quo. I have to bear in mind here that this is an existing business of the defendants which has been carried on, so far as they knew at any rate, quite legitimately up to date. It is the plaintiffs here who are seeking to interfere with an existing situation, because they say that they want to break now into the market which the defendants have."

5 *Hayter (John) Motor Underwriting Agencies Ltd v. R.B.H.S. Agencies Ltd* [1977] 2 Lloyd's Rep. 105

1. The facts The plaintiffs carried on the business of motor insurance underwriting under the style of "J.S.B. Motor Policies at Lloyd's". They applied in proceedings commenced by writ to restrain the defendants from passing off their business (B.J.S. Motor Syndicate at Lloyd's) as that of the plaintiffs.

2. Passing off—a definition Goff L.J. summarised the law thus at 110:

"... it will be seen that the essence of the action is not merely confusion but deception which leads to injury to the goodwill. I would refer to a passage in the speech of Lord Morris in the *Parker-Knoll* case, [1962] R.P.C. at 279 in the paragraph numbered 6:

'If it is proved on behalf of a plaintiff that a name or a mark has acquired such a secondary meaning, then it is a question for the court whether a defendant, whatever may be his intention, is so describing his goods that there is a likelihood that a substantial section of the purchasing public will be misled into believing that his goods are the goods of the plaintiff.'

693

And Lord Hodson at 285:

> 'All relevant circumstances must be taken into account, and the question whether or not there is a real likelihood of deception of the public is ultimately for the court and not for the witness to decide.'

And also see *per* Lord Guest at 287:

> 'The court must make up its own mind. It must, of course, regard the evidence as to the nature of the plaintiff's business and its name or style and exactly what the defendant is doing, but not the opinion of witnesses. Therefore, the fact that in this case the Committee at Lloyd's approved of the use of the defendants' name and the fact that the defendants have been admitted to membership of Lloyd's Motor Underwriters Association and the Motor Insurance Bureau are irrelevant considerations.' "

In this regard it is useful to keep in mind that in *Erven Warninck BV v. Townend (J.) & Sons (Hull) Ltd* [1979] A.C. 731 the House of Lords laid down the following essential ingredients to establish a claim for passing off:

(a) a misrepresentation;
(b) made by a trader in the course of trade;
(c) to customers or potential customers;
(d) that was calculated to injure another trader's business or goodwill in the sense that that was a reasonably foreseeable consequence; and
(e) that caused damage to the trader or might do so.

3. The issue Goff L.J. thereafter identified the issue at 110:

> "Now the similarity of the initials, which are the same serve that the last is placed first, does seem to me to be something which may well cause confusion. But is it calculated to deceive, and so to damage the plaintiffs' goodwill? The defendants say in truth there is no possibility of damaging the business. When it comes to dealings there will be no mistake or, if there be, it will be detected and put right at the box or at any rate before the business is completed."

4. Was that issue proved to be sufficiently serious? Goff L.J. identified three potential fields of confusion:

(a) The position of Lloyd's brokers.
(b) The position of non-Lloyd's brokers.
(c) The position of the public.

5. First field—Lloyd's brokers The plaintiffs' evidence was very weak.

Against that, there was a very strong body of evidence from Lloyd's brokers saying they would not be misled and one, Mr Smeaton, went so far as to say "no self-respecting broker ever would be." Against that backdrop, Goff L.J. held at 111:

"Considering only Lloyd's brokers and having in mind the evidence as to the way in which business is conducted at Lloyd's, I agree with the learned judge that the plaintiffs' evidence fails to show a reasonable prospect of success such as required by the *Cyanamid* case."

6. Second field—non-Lloyd's brokers Goff L.J. said at 111–112:

"Then I turn to the question of outside brokers. Here it is submitted that owing to the necessary guarantee arrangements they must have a close personal relationship with any syndicate with whom they deal and must know fully what they are doing. If they have arrangements with both J.S.B. and B.J.S. they must, as it seems to me, inevitably know the difference, but if they have a guarantee arrangement with one only and they go to the wrong one then the matter must inevitably be passed on or referred back, it could not be processed.

On the evidence at the moment, the absence of likelihood of any injury to the business under this branch seems to me to be well established. There are outside brokers without such arrangements but they would have to go to Lloyd's brokers and so one is back to that aspect of the case and the outside broker adds nothing."

7. Third field—the public This was the real issue and was narrowed down to the question: How frequently do individual members of the public specify a Lloyd's syndicate? The thrust of the defendants' evidence was as follows:

"Mr Dowlen in his affidavit says:

'... it will be exceedingly rare for a member of the public to specify a particular Lloyd's syndicate.'

Mr Pratt said:

'In all normal cases the public does not instruct the broker to go to a particular syndicate.'

Mr Kosviner said:

'Very rare indeed; in vast majority of cases they do not.'

Then in the additional evidence which the defendants put in following the admission (by our leave) of additional evidence put in by the plaintiffs, we have an affidavit from a Mr Fleck, an associate partner

695

with the defendants' solicitors, and he refers to two inquiries which he had made and the answers. First:

> 'J. B. Lloyd Taylor & Company Limited—I spoke to a Mr Lloyd, and he informed me that: (i) Members of the public almost always ask the broker to obtain insurance cover and never name a particular Lloyd's syndicate. (ii) To his knowledge, there have been no instances of confusion having arisen or mistakes having been made as a result of the alleged similarity in the names of the two syndicates, JSB and BJS.' "

The plaintiffs' evidence to the contrary was weak and led Goff L.J. to hold at 113:

> "Here I think, apart from special schemes where the inherent nature of the business will prevent deception, there is, in my judgment, no risk of confusion leading to deception and to injury of the goodwill."

In the third judgment of the court, Buckley L.J. at 114 broadened the ambit of judicial approach thus:

> "Not only does the evidence indicate (as I think it does) that the plaintiffs have no reasonable prospect of succeeding in obtaining a permanent injunction at the trial; it also indicates, in my judgment, that, even if that were for any reason thought to be putting the matter too highly, there is no reasonable and substantial prospect of the plaintiffs suffering loss of business or other damage to their goodwill in consequence of any confusion resulting from such similarity as exists between the names under which the parties respectively carry on their business during the limited period until trial. The injunction which is sought would undoubtedly, I think, inhibit the defendants severely in the conduct of their business and accordingly, if the balance of convenience were here a relevant consideration, as it seems to me, the circumstances do not warrant the grant of interlocutory relief to avoid injury to the plaintiffs during the interlocutory period. ..."

8. Summary No serious issue to be tried—the application for the injunction failed *in limine*.

6 John Walker & Sons Ltd v. Rothmans International Ltd and John Sinclair Ltd [1978] F.S.R. 357, per Brightman J.

1. The facts The plaintiffs had a reputation in "Red Label" whisky. The defendants intended to produce "Red Label" cigarettes. The plaintiffs alleged passing off, and sought an interlocutory injunction.

2. Was there a serious issue to be tried? Yes—on the following basis:
   (a) In the case of alleged name confusion, there are two essential
       ingredients of the tort:
       (i) there must be proof or prospect of confusion;
       (ii) there must be proof of prospect of damage (at 360).
   (b) "If the defendants' cigarette packet does to a discernible extent wear
       the livery of the plaintiffs' whisky bottle ... the possibility of such
       confusion is heightened by the fact that sources which sell whisky
       often sell cigarettes side by side and by the fact that these two plea-
       sures tend to be indulged together by their devotees. ..." (at 361).
   (c) "There is no positive evidence before me that the name confusion,
       which arguably exists, will or may damage the reputation of the
       plaintiffs' Red Label Whisky. ... Such damage by association will
       presumably only occur if the Red Label cigarettes acquire at some
       time in the future the reputation of being an inferior commodity."
       (at 361).

3. Damages—adequate compensation for the plaintiffs? No—by virtue of
the impossibility of quantifying the damages in any realistic way, as
conceded by the defendants: (at 362).

4. Damages—adequate compensation for the defendant? No—there would
be a large element of unquantifiable damage as Brightman J. explained at
362:

> "The effect of an injunction will be that the defendant will have to
> stop marketing Red Label cigarettes in their existing pack. They will
> then have a choice. They can drop the proposed product until the
> conclusion of the trial of the action or they can continue with the
> product but adopt a different name and/or design. If they adopt the
> first course they will suffer an unquantifiable loss of profits pending
> the lifting of the injunction at the conclusion of the action, because
> of course the hypothesis is that the injunction goes. If they adopt the
> second course they will suffer an unquantifiable loss of profit pending
> the launch of the cigarette under its new mark. At the end of the
> action, which *ex hypothesi* the defendants have won, they will have
> to choose whether to abandon the new mark and revert to the Red
> Label mark, involving more expense and unquantifiable loss of profit,
> or they will stick to the new mark which is not the mark of their
> choice and which may well be less advantageous to them commercially.
> I reach the conclusion in the face of these imponderables that the
> defendants' potential loss, if an interim injunction is granted but if
> they succeed at trial, is not capable of being adequately measured by
> any monetary award."

5. Balance—against injunction The factors which Brightman J. at 363 held weighed against an injunction were:

(a) *Only small risk of damage:*

> "If the plaintiffs are refused an injunction but succeed at the trial they will in the meantime run only a risk, and not a certainty, of damage and it is a risk which in the short term appears to me somewhat remote, having regard to the reputation of the Rothman Group of Companies. *Per contra*, if the plaintiffs are granted an injunction but fail at the trial the defendants incur the certainty of unquantifiable damage."

(b) *Merits:*

> "Furthermore, I suspect that the defendants will in practice be permanently deprived of their Red Label mark in relation to this particular product and it is likely that they will be compelled to market the cigarette in the meantime under a different mark in order to catch the low tar market which they now have the opportunity to exploit."

6. Undertakings Brightman J. rounded off his judgment at 363, *inter alia,* thus:

> "I should mention that three undertakings have been offered by the defendants and I think that, if they are desired by the plaintiffs, the court should accept them. First, the defendants have offered to co-operate to the maximum feasible extent in a speedy trial. Secondly, they have offered to undertake to retain the Red Label get-up in their hands, and not part with it in favour of others who might abuse it pending the trial of the action. Thirdly, I understand that the parent company of the group will underwrite any award of damages which may be made at the trial of the action."

7 *Morny Ltd v. Ball & Rogers (1975) Ltd* [1978] F.S.R. 91, *per* Goulding J.

1. Background Goulding J. said at 91:

> "This motion marks another step along the road by which the proprietors of well established businesses are constantly striving to enlarge the utility of the action for passing off as the activities of their less well-known competitors assume novel and varied forms."

2. The facts The plaintiff had a very well established reputation in respect of perfume, soaps and other toilet articles. The defendant was selling and advertising commercially, a gift package made up as follows:

(a) Rectangular box of transparent plastic ("I should think a very cheap one"—*per* Goulding J.).

(b) A genuine bottle of the plaintiff's perfumed foam bath.

(c) A light cardboard container—having within, a bottle of scent.

3. The issue Goulding J. said at 92:

"The plaintiff is afraid that the public will think that the plaintiff has either produced the package of scent or has at least authorised the product to be sold with its own and that consequently the plaintiff will suffer damage in its commercial reputation and business."

4. The law Goulding J. cited the following:

(a) *Per* Buckley L.J. in *Bulmer (H.P.) Ltd v. Bollinger (J.)* [1977] 2 C.M.L.R. 625:

"I will, however, venture as far as this: if the defendant's conduct has been such as to mislead members of the public into a mistaken belief that the goods or services of the defendant or the defendant's business are or is either (a) the goods or services or business of the plaintiff, or (b) connected with the plaintiff's business in some way which is likely to damage the plaintiff's goodwill in that business, the defendant will be liable to be held to have committed the tort of passing off. This formulation has two necessary elements; first a misrepresentation, express or implied but not necessarily fraudulent, and secondly, a consequent likelihood of damage of the plaintiff's goodwill."

(b) *Per* Goff L.J. in the same case:

"Not every kind of connection claimed will amount to passing off; for example if one says that one's goods are very suitable to be used in connection with the plaintiff's. On the other hand in my view there can be a passing off of goods without representing that they are actually the well-known goods which the plaintiff produces or a new line which he is supposed to have started. It is sufficient in my view if what is done represents the defendant's goods to be connected with the plaintiff's in such a way as would lead people to accept them on the faith of the plaintiff's reputation. Thus for example it would be sufficient if they were taken to be made under licence, or under some trading arrangement which would give the plaintiff some control over them, and I think Harman J. had such ideas on his mind as appears from the passage at 93 of the

> *Treasure Cot* case (1950) 67 R.P.C. 89 when he spoke of 'something for which the plaintiffs were responsible.'"

5. Was the issue to be tried serious? Yes—*per* Goulding J. at 93:

> "It seems to me that there is a substantially arguable case that the packaging and get-up do represent that the plaintiff has authorised the scent to be sold in conjunction with its own foam bath and it is also, in my view, strongly arguable that such a representation carries with it, in the words of Buckley L.J. a consequent likelihood of damage to the plaintiff's goodwill."

6. Damages—an adequate remedy? *Per* Goulding J. at 93:

> "If the plaintiff succeeds at the trial no injunction has been granted meanwhile, it will be impossible for the plaintiff to quantify whatever damage its goodwill may have suffered. Similarly, if an injunction is granted and turns out to have been wrongly granted because the plaintiff fails at the trial, it may well be extremely difficult to quantify what loss the injunction has imposed on the defendant."

7. Ability of the parties to pay *Per* Goulding J. at 93:

> "When one comes to compare the financial status of the parties, as appears from the evidence, there is a very great contrast. The plaintiff is a well established company and the member of a very large group internationally known. The defendant, so far as appears, is a company with no particular connections having an authorised and paid up capital of £100."

8. What happened? Injunction granted, in that the plaintiffs had acted as soon as the gift pack appeared in the advertisements, and the granting of relief would preserve the status quo.

8 *Morning Star Co-operative Society Ltd v. Express Newspapers Ltd* [1979] F.S.R. 113

1. The facts The plaintiffs, publishers of the *Morning Star* newspaper, applied for an interlocutory injunction to restrain *quia timet* the publication by the defendants, of the *Daily Star*.

2. The issue to be tried Foster J. identified the issue thus, at 114:

> "... will the defendants' proposed paper deceive members of the public into buying the defendants' new paper thinking that it is the plaintiffs' paper?"

Against that backdrop, Foster J. virtually incorporated into his judgment by reference the decision of Megarry J. in *Thomson (D.C.) & Co. Ltd v. Kent Messenger Ltd* [1975] R.P.C. 191, in which context he said, at 117:

> "In that case *The Sunday Post* tried to stop the *South East Sunday Post* being started. The differences are of course not exactly the same but the learned judge concluded that the two publications were totally different in appearance, content, price and availability and were not likely to be confused one with the other, except by a very small, unobservant section of society, and refused to grant interlocutory relief."

3. No injunction—why? "... only a moron in a hurry would be misled" said Foster J. in holding that there was no serious issue to be tried. In so ruling, he took into account the following factors:

(a) *Name* (at 115):

> "... that word [Star] is ... a descriptive and popular rather than a fancy or distinctive word. It has a long established meaning in general use as a title for newspapers."

(b) *Get-up:*
- (i) *Morning Star*: Continental broadsheet (only slightly smaller than, say, *The Times*) text newspaper, simple style of print for title— small headlines.
- (ii) *Daily Star*: Tabloid, headlines and pictures newspaper. Complex style of print for title—dramatic headlines.

(c) *Contents:*
- (i) *Morning Star*: Left wing, out of a total circulation of 35,000, 21,000 copies in the U.K.
- (ii) *Daily Star*: Target circulation—over 1 million, "Most of its front page will consist of startling large headlines and within there will be pictures of nearly nude models."

(d) *Readership:*
- (i) *Morning Star*: Circulation—declining (24,000 copies, January 1, 1977; just under 21,000 on July 1, 1978).
- (ii) *Daily Star*: Sought the readership of the *Mirror* and *Sun*.

(e) *Sales techniques:*
- (i) *Morning Star*: Many sales effected at the factory gate, usually exclusively by order from newsagents. "I do not think that if one without warning asked for a copy from a news vendor, it would be available except in a minimal number of cases." (at 117).

701

(ii) *Daily Star*: Massive advertising campaign.

(f) *Price:*
   (i) *Morning Star*: 12 pence.
   (ii) *Daily Star*: six pence.

(g) *Size:*
   (i) *Morning Star*: six/eight pages.
   (ii) *Daily Star*: 32 pages.

4. Damages—an adequate remedy? No—Foster J. ruled that there was no serious issue to be tried. But even if there had been he would have refused an injunction because:

(a) *Unquantifiable loss* (at 118):

> "... if they were to be stopped now from publishing the *Daily Star* and succeeding at the trial cannot be quantified. It is true that the amount which the defendants have expended to date in promoting the new newspaper can be quantified and it is not large. But when they announced they were considering publishing a new national daily newspaper, the venture received considerable free publicity on its own account in national newspapers and on television and no wonder, as, apart from the *Daily Worker*, there has been no new national daily paper for 71 years. If it has to change its name now it will suffer heavy loss; and the loss of confidence in the venture and of that publicity cannot in my judgment be quantified."

(b) *Plaintiffs' financial position* (at 118):

> "On the other hand, the business of the plaintiff society in its newspaper is at present of little or no value. A search at the Register of Friendly Societies on September 28, 1978 shows the plaintiffs' assets amounted to some £170,000 and its liabilities to some £260,000 and of course it has to find some £9,000 a month to keep going. An undertaking as to damages if the plaintiff loses the action is the price which a person asking for an interlocutory injunction has to pay and it is only in very exceptional circumstances that the court will dispense with such an undertaking. No special circumstances were suggested here. But where the damage cannot be quantified and it is clear that the plaintiff is unlikely to be able to pay any appreciable damages, no interlocutory relief should be given."

702

9 *Mothercare Ltd v. Robson Books Ltd* [1979] F.S.R. 466

1. The facts The plaintiff sought to enjoin the defendant from publishing a book called "Mothercare" on the basis that this would be a passing off—the plaintiff having in conjunction with *Readers' Digest*, already published the "Readers' Digest Mothercare Book." The plaintiff's case was not primarily based on similarities between the two books but on the defendant's book being thought to be connected in some way with that of the plaintiff.

2. Was there a serious issue to be tried? Yes—the Court took into account:
- (a) An action for passing off is based on the likelihood of injury to goodwill: *Bulmer (H.P.) Ltd v. Bollinger (J.) SA* [1978] R.P.C. 79 at 93–95 *per* Buckley L.J.
- (b) Although the plaintiff's "Mothercare" looked different and dealt with babycare, whereas the defendant's "Mothercare" dealt primarily with looking pre-and post-natally after mother, it was at least possible that purchasers of the defendant company's book would buy it in the belief that it was in some way the product of the plaintiff company or associated with them in some way.

3. Were damages an adequate remedy? The court balanced the factors of adequacy of damages on the one hand, and ability to pay on the other:
- (a) As to adequacy of damages for the plaintiffs, the Vice-Chancellor held at 475:

  "If an interlocutory injunction is refused, but the plaintiff company wins at the trial, there would plainly be considerable difficulty in assessing the damages. The injury to the plaintiff company's good-will, and the loss of sales of its book, would be hard to assess."

- (b) As to the defendant's ability to pay—also at 475:

  "Furthermore, the defendant company does not appear to be in a financial condition to meet a heavy burden of damages. The company is still struggling to establish itself with an adequate catalogue of books. It has an insurance policy against 90 per cent. of certain claims, but it is far from clear that this policy would operate to cover an award of damages in this case. In the result, I cannot say that an award of damages would adequately compensate the plaintiff company if it wins at the trial after failing to get an interlocutory injunction."

- (c) As to the disadvantage to the defendant in granting an injunction and the plaintiff's ability to pay, the Vice-Chancellor went on to say:

703

"On the other hand, if an interlocutory injunction is granted, but the defendant company succeeds at the trial, there is a substantially greater prospect of damages proving an adequate recompense. There has been no suggestion that the plaintiff company would be unable to meet even a large award of damages. Further, a substantial part of the damages, relating to expenditure thrown away in promoting the book and the loss of the use of money tied up in its production, is likely to be calculable without any great difficulty. Other elements of damages are likely to be more difficult to assess. Thus there is a proposed publication of the book by a book club, and this is unlikely to proceed at least until this litigation has ended. There are also possible injuries to the reputation of the defendant company as a rising book publisher in respect of the failure to proceed with the publication of a book which, in the company's catalogue, was announced for February 1979. There may also be difficult questions about whether the defendant company would be able to alter the title of the book, and the effect of doing this, or refraining from doing it. However, when these and all other facts are added together, it seems clear that it is the defendant company that can best be compensated by an award of damages. Furthermore, if an injunction is granted, the injury to the defendant company will mainly (though by no means exclusively) be merely one of delay; and the status quo would be preserved by granting the injunction."

4. Result—injunction granted Its terms were:

"Injunction—to restrain the defendants until judgment in the action or further order in the meantime from (whether by their directors officers servants or agents or any of them or otherwise howsoever) advertising, publishing or distributing or causing to be advertised, published or distributed in Great Britain, whether for the purpose of review or any other purpose, the book entitled 'Mother Care' by Lyn Delli Quandri and Kati Breckenridge, or any other publication under or by reference to the title 'Mother Care' or any other colourable imitation of the plaintiffs' name and trade mark 'Mothercare' or otherwise passing off or attempting to pass off or causing or enabling or assisting others to pass off any book or other publication not being a publication of or associated with the plaintiffs as and for a book or publication of or assisted with the plaintiffs."

10 *Tetrosyl Ltd v. Silver Paint & Lacquer Co. Ltd* [1979] C.A.T. No. 599

1. The facts One manufacturer produced tubs, which both parties used for their filler products. The plaintiff had the name "Tetrion" in white lettering upon an orange base impressed on the lid and also around the tub itself. The defendant's tubs were also white, but with a red band— very much larger than the plaintiff's orange band. The defendant's logo was: "SP2 Homecharm All-Purpose Filler".

2. The ruling at first instance At first instance the plaintiff successfully obtained an injunction restraining the defendant from advertising, offering for sale, selling or distributing any product in identical containers to those of the plaintiff and/or so closely resembling the plaintiff's product in get-up as to be likely to cause confusion between the plaintiff's and the defendant's products. The justification for the injunction was apparently evidence of confusion discovered by two market researchers.

3. The case went on appeal—with what result? What distinguished the hearing before the Court of Appeal from that at first instance was a large amount of additional evidence (which the Court of Appeal gave leave to adduce) arguing against the possibility of confusion. In that context, Roskill L.J. held that when balancing the evidence from the defendant against the very tenuous evidence available from the plaintiff, it was very difficult to state that there was a serious issue to decide. Lawton L.J. said:

> "The court has to consider whether the evidence provides the essential backing ... the real evidence in the case, namely, the articles which are in dispute, provide no backing at all for the alleged serious question."

11 *Rolls-Royce Motors v. Zanelli* [1979] R.P.C. 148, *per* Browne-Wilkinson J.

1. The facts This case, *inter alia*, involved section 4 of the Trade Marks Act 1938. The plaintiffs sought an order restraining the defendants from buying second-hand "Shadow" saloons and converting the bodywork so that the cars looked like the more expensive "Corniche," modified. The vehicles were to be sold under the name "Rolls-Royce Panache." The defendants stated that they intended only to offer the service of conversion to existing owners of Silver Shadows (the cheaper models, in relative terms).

2. The case for the plaintiffs It had three limbs—at 150:

(a) *Trade marks:*

> "... they being the registered owners of the trade marks, the words 'Rolls-Royce,' the badge, the logo RR and the radiator shape."

(b) *Passing off:*

"... the defendants are passing off the converted motor car as being a Rolls-Royce when in fact it had been substantially altered."

(c) *Copyright:*

"... they are infringing the copyright which belongs to the plaintiffs in the design of the Corniche motor car because they say that this new motor car is designed to be substantially similar in appearance to the Corniche."

3. Serious issue to be tried Browne-Wilkinson J. ruled:

(a) *Trade marks* (at 150(25–45), 151(0–10)):

"Their first claim based on infringement of their trade mark is, if I may say so, rather bold. It may prove to be correct after full argument, but at this stage I think it would be very dangerous for me to accept the proposition which they put forward that, even after an outright sale of a Rolls-Royce motor car to a private individual, Rolls-Royce have the right to object to any substantial alteration to that vehicle by the absolute owner who has acquired it. That would seem, at first sight, to be a very extreme claim by the owner of the trade mark impinging upon what a purchaser in the open market would have regarded as his absolute purchase of the vehicle. However, it does seem to me certainly much more likely, even accepting the defendants' story, that they must necessarily be going to infringe section 4(1)(b) of the Trade Marks Act 1938, which provides, so far as is relevant for this purpose:

'... the registration ... of a person ... as proprietor of a trade mark ... in respect of any goods shall, if valid, give or be deemed to have given to that person the exclusive right to the use of the trade mark in relation to those goods and, without prejudice to the generality of the foregoing words, that right shall be deemed to be infringed by any person who ... uses a mark identical with it or so nearly resembling it as to be likely to deceive or cause confusion, in the course of trade, in relation to any goods in respect of which it is registered, and in such manner as to render the use of the mark likely to be taken either ... (b) in the case in which the use is use upon the goods or in physical relation thereto or in an advertising circular or other advertisement issued to the public, as importing a reference to some person having the right either as a proprietor or as registered user to use the trade mark or to goods with which such a person as aforesaid is connected in the course of trade.'

It seems to me inevitable that by advertisement in the press the defendants are bound to hold themselves out as using 'Rolls-Royce' as a name and 'Rolls-Royce Panache' as part and parcel of their trade and so indicating to the outside world that they are authorised to do so. The whole conversion is designed to be a conversion of a Rolls-Royce and in those circumstances, as at present advised, I find it difficult to see how they would carry out their trade otherwise than by using the words Rolls-Royce in the course of so doing. As such, prima facie, it seems to me that there would be an infringement of the trade mark."

(b) *Passing off* (151(15–25)):

"On passing off it seems to me arguable again, although I am far from saying that this will prove eventually to be the law, that although on the defendants' present evidence they are not proposing to sell the converted car, they are by converting it to a form which, on their own evidence, the general public will be likely to think it is a Rolls-Royce motor car which will be seen in public and generally, they are by so doing passing off something as being a Rolls-Royce which is not a Rolls-Royce. They have altered it in a substantial degree but in such a way that to the public at large it will appear still to be a Rolls-Royce. Again I say that is an arguable passing off of something as being the product of the plaintiffs which is not the plaintiffs' and as such they are putting into circulation an instrument of fraud as something which can be used to deceive and confuse the public. Therefore, I think there is an arguable case on passing off."

4. Damages—an adequate remedy?

(a) *To the plaintiff:* No—as Browne-Wilkinson J. said at 151 (25–35):

"When I come to consider the balance of convenience I am satisfied that the damage which may be done to the plaintiffs, if inferior work is put out as being the work of Rolls-Royce, is quite incalculable and of very great financial harm to Rolls-Royce. On this aspect of the case they are certainly in a very unusual position in that a large part of the goodwill of Rolls-Royce does depend on their reputation for immaculate finish and engineering. Anything which might impinge on that reputation could do incalculable harm."

(b) *To the defendant?* Probably—at 151(35–40):

"So far as the defendants are concerned, if I grant an injunction they will be kept out of business until the trial judge deals with the matter. If it then proves that the defendants should have been entitled to go on, they will be entitled to recover damages under the cross-undertaking from the plaintiffs. I do not think the cross-undertaking is wholly adequate to cover them because it is impossible to quantify the loss in the market which has been or may have been caused by them being kept out of the market for a period of some duration. However, I think the uncompensatable loss is likely to be minor compared with that which might be suffered conversely by Rolls-Royce."

And even if damages had not been an adequate remedy Browne-Wilkinson J. would still have refused the injunction, as he explained at 151(40–45):

"In any event, in considering what is the right order to make in the interim, I think it is most relevant to bear in mind that the defendants have chosen after having approached Rolls-royce and having been refused permission to start to carry out this work without further reference to Rolls-Royce, thereby seeking to enter into the market and change the status quo."

5. The order The order made by first instance, as modified (on a peripheral issue) by the Court of Appeal, provided:

"THIS COURT DOTH ORDER that the defendants be restrained until after Judgment in this Action or until further order in the meantime from doing (as regards the Defendant Companies whether by their directors servants or agents or any of them or otherwise howsoever and as regards the other Defendants whether by themselves or by their servants or agents or any of them or otherwise howsoever) the following acts or any of them that is to say:

(a) Exhibiting in public by use or otherwise than for exclusively domestic purposes offering for sale or otherwise disposing of any motor vehicle being a vehicle originally manufactured by the Plaintiff Rolls-Royce Motors Limited or their predecessors in title the design whereof has been modified.

(b) Without the licence of the Plaintiffs Rolls-Royce Motors Limited making a reproduction or substantial reproduction of any one or more of the drawings entitled 'Silver Shadow Two Door Saloon' a copy whereof is exhibited as exhibit 'G5' to the said affidavit of Allan James Michael Grant sworn August 11, 1978.

(c) Enabling causing procuring and/or assisting any other person or concern to execute any of the acts set out in (a) and (b) hereinabove.

AND the costs of the Plaintiffs of the said Motion are to be their costs in the cause."

12 *Metric Resources Corporation v. Leasemetrix Ltd* [1979] F.S.R. 571

1. The facts The plaintiffs were, in the USA and Canada, well known in the business of hiring electronic equipment under the name "Leasametric." They claimed they were well-known in the United Kingdom because of advertising in USA journals circulating here, and through dealings with U.K. companies. The defendants were set up in 1977, and commenced trading in March 1979. In April the plaintiffs moved for interlocutory relief, alleging passing off. The defendants sought by cross-motion for interlocutory relief to restrain the plaintiffs from trading in the United Kingdom, prompted by the plaintiffs revealing in evidence that it was their intention by the autumn of that year to enter the U.K. market trading as Leasametric.

2. The law Sir Robert Megarry V.-C. took as his starting point the dicta of Lord Diplock in the Privy Council case of *Star Industrial Company Ltd v. Yap Kwee Kor* [1976] F.S.R. 256 at 269:

> "A passing off action is a remedy for the invasion of a right of property not in the mark, name or get-up improperly used, but in the business or goodwill likely to be injured by the misrepresentation made by passing off one person's goods as the goods of another. Goodwill, as the subject of proprietary rights, is incapable of subsisting by itself. It has no independent existence apart from the business to which it is attached. It is local in character and divisible; if the business is carried on in several countries a separate goodwill attaches to it in each. So when the business is abandoned in one country in which it has acquired a goodwill the goodwill in that country perishes with it although the business may continue to be carried on in other countries."

The Vice-Chancellor added, at 576:

> "It will be observed that this passage is expressed in terms which recognise that although there is to be a separate goodwill for each country, there may be a single business carried on in two or more countries."

The defence however referred to several other authorities to substantiate the following argument, recited by the Vice-Chancellor at 575:

> "On behalf of the defendants, Mr Aldous's basic proposition was that if a trader carries on no business in this country, then even if the name under which he trades is well known here and he had acquired a considerable reputation for it here, anyone is at liberty to set up a

709

rival business under that trader's name in this country. The trader need have no place of business here, but if he is entitled to protect his trading name here, he must carry on his business here. This follows, Mr Aldous said, from the fact that what is protected by the action for passing off is goodwill. This cannot subsist by itself, but only as an asset of a business, or part of that business; goodwill is local in character, and a separate goodwill exists for every country in which the business is carried on. Consequently, if no business is carried on in a country, no goodwill can exist in that country; and so, no matter how great the trader's reputation in that country, any claim by him for passing off must fail."

Further authorities referred to were:
(a) *Erven Warninck BV v. Townend (J.) & Sons (Hull) Ltd* [1979] A.C. 731—the *Advocaat* case.
(b) *La Société Anonyme des Anciens Etablissements Panhard et Levassor v. Panhard-Levassor Motor Co. Ltd* (1901) 18 R.P.C. 405.
(c) *Spalding (A.G.) & Bros. v. A.W. Gamage Ltd* (1915) 32 R.P.C. 273.
(d) *Bulmer (H.P.) Ltd v. Bollinger (J.) SA* [1978] R.P.C. 79 at 95.
(e) *Poiret v. Jules Poiret Ltd* (1920) 37 R.P.C. 177.
(f) *Sheraton Corporation of America v. Sheraton Motels Ltd* [1964] R.P.C. 202.
(g) *Bernadin (A.) et Cie v. Pavilon Properties Ltd* [1967] R.P.C. 581—the *Crazy Horse* case.
(h) *Amway Corporation v. Eurway International Ltd* [1974] R.P.C. 82.
(i) *Maxims Ltd v. Dye* [1977] 1 W.L.R. 1155.

3. Was there a serious issue to be tried? Yes—at 579:

"... it was no part of the court's function at this stage of the litigation 'to decide difficult questions of law which call for detailed argument and mature consideration.' I feel no doubt that the point arising from the cases I have mentioned falls into this category, and that it is fully arguable on either side. ..."

Against that backdrop, the Vice-Chancellor said at 580:

"On the facts, the plaintiff company's case is thin. There are many difficulties in a hiring business, particularly when much of the hiring is on a short-term basis: for the goods have to be returned at the end of the hire, and the Atlantic lies between the point of hire and any point of use in this country. As Mr Aldous emphasised, there is a strong element of locality in the business of hiring. Furthermore, the servicing and calibration of the instruments hired is local in nature; and full duty has to be paid on imported equipment, and there is no 'clawback' for duty paid. If equipment is hired from the plaintiff company, the hirer has to make his own arrangements to transport it from the United States to this country. The evidence of actual transactions is relatively slender also; with the best instance for the plaintiff company being certain substantial transactions with Plessey Co. Ltd which carries on business here. The field, of course, is relatively narrow and specialised, and the number of potential customers limited. There seems, however, to be some attraction for customers from outside North America in the range of instruments that are outside North America in the range of instruments that are available from the plaintiff company and are not readily obtainable elsewhere, and in the option to purchase instruments that have been hired. Mr Aldous made some telling criticisms of the extent of the reputation of the plaintiff company in this country. Nevertheless, in the end I reached the conclusion that I could not say that the plaintiff company had no real prospect of success at the trial; and I certainly do not regard the claim as being frivolous or vexatious. Instead, I think that although the plaintiff company has undoubted difficulties, there is a serious issue to be tried."

4. Defendants' arguments—that damages an adequate remedy for the plaintiffs

(a) *First argument:*

  (i) Case for the defence (at 580):

> "If the plaintiff company succeeds at the trial in obtaining a permanent injunction, would damages provide adequate compensation if an interlocutory injunction is refused now? Mr Aldous said that the answer was yes. The refusal of an injunction to the plaintiff company would merely delay the commencement of its proposed new business here; and it would be possible to find out how many customers had come to the defendant company because they thought it was the plaintiff company, and in this way assess the loss to the plaintiff company. On the other hand, if the defendant company was to be restrained by an interlocutory injunction, but won at the trial, the defendant company would have irretrievably lost the business of those customers who would have come to the defendant company because they believed it to be the plaintiff company, and would thus deprive the defendant company of the advantage that it would have obtained by taking a name so close to the name used by the plaintiff company."

  (ii) Ruling (at 580):

> "This latter contention, which Mr Aldous called his 'extreme

argument,' seemed to me to be remarkably unattractive. After the midday adjournment on Day 3, Mr Aldous told me that the second defendant also found it unattractive, and did not wish to trade on any confusion in the names, though he said that it would never happen. But Mr Aldous did not withdraw the argument, and said that, if it did happen, the argument necessarily fell to be taken in to account on the balance of convenience."

(b) *Second argument:*

(i) Case for the defence (at 581):

"Mr Aldous also relied on the serious effect that an interlocutory injunction would have on the defendant company, which was struggling to establish itself in a specialist field with what, at the moment, was a limited range of equipment; and he relied on *Potters-Ballotini Ltd v. Weston-Baker* [1977] R.P.C. 202."

(ii) Ruling (at 581):

"That seems to me to have a little relevance in the present case. The injunction sought there would have closed down the defendants' factory altogether: the injunction sought here will not in any way stop the defendant company from trading, but only affect the style under which it trades. The second defendant and his associate, Mr Munday, have admittedly a considerable reputation in this field, and even if the injunction were to be granted, they could carry on the business without interruption, although they would have to do so under their own names, or under some name not confusingly similar to the name used by the plaintiff company. Undoubtedly some expenditure on publicity and printing would have been largely thrown away if the interlocutory injunction is granted but the defendants succeed at the trial; but that can be assessed with relative ease, and there has been no suggestion at all that the plaintiff company would be unable to pay the damages for this or anything else."

5. Reason why damages not an adequate remedy for plaintiffs At 581:

"On the other hand I think there would be real difficulty in assessing the loss to the plaintiff company if the injunction is refused but the plaintiff company succeeds at the trial. Furthermore, I am not at all sure how far the defendants could be relied upon to meet the claim for damages. I know nothing about the resources of the second defendants; and, as for the first defendant, the picture painted by Mr Aldous of a company struggling to establish itself is not reassuring. He referred to evidence which, he said, showed that the company had

£30,000 free, and the right to call on another £40,000, but I have little idea how much of this would still be available to satisfy the plaintiff company after the trial. The equipment is plainly expensive, and such figures as are in evidence (that is, not much beyond a monthly balance sheet for May 1979) do not inspire any great confidence. It is stated that there was a trading profit of just over £100 in May, with a cumulative trading loss for the first three months of a little over £10,000; but of course it may be important to see how that trading profit was arrived at."

6. Balance of convenience—in favour of injunction

(a) *Preserving status quo* (at 581–582):

"As for preserving the status quo, there is the familiar difficulty of saying what that phrase means. Mr Aldous says it must mean the state of affairs existing at the time the court is hearing the case, so that the status quo that ought to be preserved was that of the defendant company carrying on its business under the name 'Leasemetrix,' and of the plaintiff company having a mere intention to begin a business in this country under the name 'Leasametric.' On that footing it was desirable to keep the first defendant in business under its present name. One problem in this approach is that the status quo may materially change between the hearing at first instance and a hearing on appeal. The term 'status quo' is plainly incomplete on the face of it; and as I suggested in *Robbie v. Fulham Football Club Ltd* (unreported) March 26, 1979, I think the full term is *'status quo ante bellum.'* If the issue of the writ is the notional equivalent of the outbreak of war, that would require matters to be tested when the writ was issued, which sometimes would be capricious or unfair. If the metaphor is pursued, then it may well be that the true *status quo ante bellum* is the state of affairs which existed immediately before the act which constitutes the *casus belli*, unless hostilities are delayed so long that the act becomes part of the status quo. I would, I think, regard the act of the defendants in commencing business under a name closely resembling that used by the plaintiff company as constituting the *casus belli*, and the status quo to be preserved (since the plaintiff company moved so promptly) as being the state that existed immediately before the defendants began business in this way. However, this does not arise unless the other factors are evenly balanced, and I do not think that they are."

(b) *Not a case for cross-injunctions* (at 582):

"The case is not easy; but on the whole I think that damages are more likely to prove an adequate recompense for the defendants than

713

for the plaintiff company. I have not expanded this judgment by setting out every material factor, but after rereading my notes and considering again all the submissions made on each side, I have reached the conclusion that the injunction claimed by the plaintiff company against the first defendant should be granted; and I have heard nothing to persuade me that in this event the injunction sought against the second defendant should not also be granted. On the other hand, I think that I ought to dismiss the cross-motion for an injunction by the first defendant. Theoretically, as Mr Kentridge pointed out, both sides could get an injunction, thereby preserving both the disputed names unused in this country until the trial. But I do not think that the evidence makes out a sufficient case for this, and in any case I am not satisfied that the first defendant's undertaking in damages would sufficiently protect the plaintiff company. Accordingly, I dismiss the cross-motion by the first defendant and grant the injunctions claimed by the plaintiff company against each of the defendants."

7. Caveat As to the "status quo" factor—the dicta of Sir Robert Megarry V.-C. should be contrasted with those of Peter Gibson J. in *Home Box Office Inc. v. Channel 5 Home Box Office Ltd* [1982] F.S.R. 449 at 462:

"Mr Kentridge relied upon certain *obiter dicta* of the Vice-Chancellor, Sir Robert Megarry, in *Metric Resources Corporation v. Leasemetrix Ltd* [above] at 581 and 582, in which the Vice-Chancellor said that the term 'status quo' meant the *status quo ante bellum* and that a true status might well be the state of affairs which existed immediately before the act which constitutes the *casus belli*. In that case, he regarded the status quo as being the status that existed immediately before the defendant began business under a name resembling that of the plaintiff; but on the facts of that case the adoption of the name by the defendant appeared to be a deliberate attempt to take advantage of the plaintiff's reputation. It would, in my view, favour plaintiffs unduly to take that point of time as the appropriate moment in every case."

[See also pp. 162 and 655 above, for further references to "status quo."]

13 *Athletes Foot Marketing Associates Inc. v. Cobra Sports Ltd* [1980] R.P.C. 343, *per* Walton J.

1. The facts The plaintiffs supplied footwear called "The Athlete's Foot" to stores in the USA and elsewhere under franchise agreements. They had no business in the United Kingdom. In September 1979 the first defendants opened "Athlete's Foot Bargain Basement". The second defendant, a director of the first defendant, had earlier registered "Athlete's Foot" for sports shoes and goods retail and "Athlete's Foot (Mail Order)" in respect of sports shoes and goods mail order. The plaintiffs knew of the registrations, but sought relief only when they saw the advertisements.

2. The law relating to "goodwill" in a passing off action involving a foreign plaintiff Walton J. conducted an exhaustive review of the authorities, perhaps summarised in the following citations from his judgment. At 349(30–45)–350(5):

> "The next question of law—namely, what connection with this country is required before a plaintiff can successfully maintain an action for passing off? There appear, on the cases, to be two schools of thought about this. There is what was described in argument as a 'hard line' school of thought, which maintains that it is essential for the plaintiff to have carried on a trade in this country (best, perhaps, exemplified by *Bernardin (A.) et Cie v. Pavilon Properties Ltd* [1967] R.P.C. 581, the well known *Crazy Horse* case) and a much less demanding approach, which suggests that something less than that will do (well exemplified by *Maxim's Ltd v. Dye* [1977] 1 W.L.R. 1155, the case concerning the famous restaurant). *In limine*, I can only echo the first part of the holding as set out in the headnote to *Metric Resources Corporation v. Leasemetrix Ltd* [1979] F.S.R. 571 to the effect that the final decision between these two schools of thought is a difficult matter requiring mature consideration and detailed argument, and is not best dealt with on motion. However, I have a wide variety of cases cited to me by both Mr Evans and Mr Toulmin, and of course duly criticised by each in turn, and so far as I can see, whatever the strict theoretical position may be, the cases are all within a fairly small compass when one comes to look at the actual facts concerning which the court was at the time directing its attention."

At 357(15–25):

> "Having therefore commented upon all the cases on this point which were cited to me, unless the 'hard line' alleged to have been taken by the Privy Council in the *Star Industrial* case, and by the House of Lords in the *Advocaat* represents the law—in which case the plaintiffs' case is even more wholly unarguable than I think it to be—the position in law appears to be relatively clear. That is to say, it does not matter that the plaintiffs are not at present actually carrying on business in this country, provided that they have customers here. Equally, it is of no moment, if they have no customers here, that they have a reputation in the general sense of the word in this country. It is also of no moment that that reputation may have been brought about by

715

advertising: this can be of no moment, unless (as it did in the C. &
A. case) it brings in customers, when, of course, once again there is
no need to rely upon it."

3. The ruling In dismissing the motion, Walton J. in effect held that there
was no serious issue to be tried (and thus this text could equally feature
in Part DI, A: "Serious issues to be tried—examples (See pp. 613 *et seq*)).
He said at 357:

"Now in the present case the most remarkable fact of all is that the
plaintiffs disclose not one single solitary transaction by way of trade
with anybody in this country at all. The nearest they get to this
essential requirement is to show that they had entered into some kind
of negotiations with Ravel with a view to the grant of a franchise to
that company. But, to date, this has not come to anything. But the
matter does not rest there. There is not even one single instance given
of a transaction by one of the plaintiffs' franchisees in the USA (or
Australia or Japan, for that matter) with anybody normally resident
in England or Wales at all. Whether such an instance by itself would
be of any assistance to the plaintiffs may well be a moot point on
several different grounds; but there is not even one such offered.

In these circumstances, it is simply not possible to say that the
plaintiff company has any goodwill in this country whatsoever,
whatever the strength of its more general reputation might be."

14 *News Group Newspapers Ltd v. The Rocket Record Company Ltd* [1981] F.S.R. 89

1. The facts The plaintiffs published the *Sun* newspaper. They published
a feature of a scantily clad girl on page three of each issue. They registered
the mark "Page Three" in Part B of the register in respect of "tapes and
discs, all bearing audio and video recordings." They marketed and sold
goods under the mark for three years. The defendants, an independent
record company, were planning to release:
  (a) An album, one track of which was called "Page Three".
  (b) A single entitled "Page Three".

2. The issues There were four relating to the question, was there a serious
issue to be tried?

(a) *Trade marks:*
  (i) Album.
  (ii) Single.

(b) *Passing off:*
  (i) Album.
  (ii) Single.

3. Law relating to trade marks The relevant provisions of the Trade Marks Act 1938 were:

(a) *Section 4(1):*

"Subject to the provisions of this section, and of sections 7 and 8 of this Act, the registration (whether before or after the commencement of this Act) of a person in Part A of the Register as proprietor of the trade mark (other than a certification trade mark) in respect of any goods shall, if valid give or be deemed to have given to that person the exclusive right to the use of the trade mark in relation to those goods and, without prejudice to the generality of the foregoing words, that right shall be deemed to be infringed by any person who, not being the proprietor of the trade mark or a registered user thereof using by way of the permitted use, uses a mark identical with it or so nearly resembling it as to be likely to deceive or cause confusion in the course of trade, in relation to any goods in respect of which it is registered, and in such manner as to render the use of the mark likely to be taken either (a) as being used as a trade mark; or (b) in a case in which the use is use upon the goods or in physical relation thereto or in an advertising circular or other advertisement issued to the public, as importing a reference to some person having the right either as proprietor or as registered user to use the trade mark or to goods with which such a person as aforesaid is connected in the course of trade."

(b) *Section 5:*

"(1) Except as provided by subsection (2) of this section, the registration (whether before or after the commencement of this Act) of a person in Part B of the Register as proprietor of a trade mark in respect of any goods shall, if valid, give or be deemed to have given to that person the like right in relation to those goods as if the registration had been in Part A of the Register, and the provisions of the last foregoing section shall have effect in like manner in relation to a trade mark registered in Part B of the Register as they have effect in relation to a trade mark registered in Part A of the Register.

(2) In any action for infringement of the right to the use of a trade mark given by registration as aforesaid in Part B of the Register, otherwise than by an Act that is deemed to be an infringement by virtue of the next succeeding section, no injunction or other relief shall be granted to the plaintiff if the defendant establishes to the

717

satisfaction of the court that the use of which the plaintiff complains is not likely to deceive or cause confusion or to be taken as indicating a connection in the course of trade between the goods and some person having the right either as proprietor or as registered user to use the trade mark."

(c) *Section 68—defining a trade mark:*

"A mark used or proposed to be used in relation to goods for the purpose of indicating, or so as to indicate, a connection in the course of trade between the goods and some person having the right as proprietor or as registered user to use the mark, whether with or without any indication of the identity of that person. ..."

4. Law relating to passing off Slade J. said at 103:

"I now turn to consider the plaintiffs' claim so far as it is concerned with passing off. In *Erven Warninck BV v. Townend Ltd* [1979] A.C. 731 at 742, Lord Diplock summarised the five features which have to be present in order to create a valid cause of action for passing off: (1) A misrepresentation; (2) made by a trader in the course of his trade; (3) to prospective customers of his or ultimate consumers of goods or services supplied by him; (4) which is calculated to injure the business or goodwill of another trader in the sense that this is a reasonably foreseeable consequence; and (5) which causes actual damage to a business or goodwill of the trader by whom the action is brought or, in a *quia timet* action will probably do so.

The argument in the present case has effectively centred round points (1), (4) and (5). On this motion, there is no evidence that anyone has yet actually been misled by the get-up of the album record. The single record is of course not yet on the market."

5. First and second issues—trade mark

(a) *First argument:*

(i) For the plaintiffs (at 97):

"Section 5(1) of the Act of 1938, read in conjunction with the opening limb of section 4(1) (ending with the words 'in relation to those goods') gives the plaintiffs the exclusive right to the use of the trade mark 'Page Three' in relation to discs bearing audio recordings. The defendants, he said, are using or intending to use this mark in relation to both the relevant discs, even though 'Page Three' is not actually the title of the album record. Since this is something which the plaintiffs have a statutory exclusive right to do, the defendants' activities, he submitted, constitute an infringement of the plaintiff's rights."

(ii) Ruling (at 98):

"The phrase 'the exclusive right to the use of the trade mark' appearing in section 4(1) of the Act of 1938, when read in conjunction with the definition of a trade mark contained in section 68(1) of that Act, must in my judgment refer to the use of a mark in relation to goods for the purpose of indicating or so as to indicate a connection in the course of trade between the goods *and the user of the mark*.

The defendants are, in my judgment, manifestly not using their mark 'Page Three' in this trade mark sense. Their use of the mark 'Page Three' is clearly not for the purpose of indicating a connection in the course of trade between the relevant records and the defendants themselves, the users of the mark. For this reason, I hold that the plaintiffs have not established a seriously arguable case in respect of the first of their three alternative submission on the trade mark issue, in respect of either record."

(b) *Second argument:*

(i) For the plaintiffs (at 98):

"As a second alternative, Mr Mummery relied on section 5(1) of the Act of 1938, read in conjunction with the second limb of section 4(1), beginning with the words 'and without prejudice to the generality of the foregoing words,' and paragraph (a) thereof. He submitted that the plaintiffs' rights are deemed to be infringed by the defendants, because the defendants are using a mark identical with the plaintiffs' trade mark 'Page Three' in the course of trade in relation to goods in respect of which it is registered, and in such a manner as to render the use of the mark likely to be taken as being used as a trade mark."

(ii) Ruling (at 98–99):

"I must however reject this second submission in respect of both the records, substantially on the same grounds as I have rejected the first. As Sir Wilfred Greene M.R. said in *Bismag Ltd v. Amblins (Chemists) Ltd* [1940] 57 R.P.C. 209 at 233, the use mentioned under head (a) of section 4(1) is 'quite clearly a use by the alleged infringer in relation to his own goods which is likely to be taken as being used as a trade mark for his own goods, that is, to use Lord Tomlin's words "as indicating in relation to" those goods "the origin of" them "in the user of the mark," that is, the alleged infringer. This, therefore, is the old type of infringement.' As I have already said, I do not see how the defendants' use of the name 'Page Three' on their two records would be likely to be taken as use for a trade mark for their own goods."

719

(c) *Third argument:*

(i) For the plaintiffs (at 99):

"Mr Mummery relied on section 5(1) of the Act of 1938, read in conjunction with the second limb of section 4(1) and paragraph (b) thereof. He submitted that the plaintiffs' rights are deemed to be infringed by the defendants, because the defendants are using or threatening to use a mark identical with the plaintiffs' trade mark 'Page Three' in the course of trade upon records or in physical relation thereto, in such manner as to render the use of the mark likely to be taken as importing a reference to the plaintiffs, who have the right as proprietors to use the trade mark."

(ii) Cases referred to: *Bismag Ltd v. Amblins (Chemists) Ltd* [1940] 57 R.P.C. 209; *Autodrome Trade Mark* [1969] R.P.C. 564; *Pompadour Laboratories Ltd v. Frazer* [1966] R.P.C. 7; *British Northrap Ltd v. Texteam Blackburn Ltd* [1974] R.P.C. 57.

(iii) Ruling: "single"—yes; "album"—no (at 101–102):

"In my judgment, it is at least strongly arguable that, having regard to the definition of a trade mark contained in section 68(1) of the Act of 1938, any use of a trade mark constitutes user in a trade mark sense within the authorities relating to section 4(1)(b) if it is likely to be taken as indicating a connection in the course of trade between the goods in question and the proprietor of the trade mark. ... I think it must be at least arguable that the use of the name 'Page Three' as the title of a single record, appearing as the sole or principal title on the sleeve of the record and as one of two titles on the labels of the record itself, would be likely to be regarded by a number of persons as indicating a connection in the course of trade between the record and the plaintiff proprietors of *The Sun* newspaper. The position might be different if the plaintiffs were not already offering a wide variety of consumer goods on the market. I must, however, assume that by now at least a substantial number of readers of *The Sun* would be well aware that the proprietors market a number of goods under the name 'Page Three.' If they were to see a record being offered for sale under the sole or principal name 'Page Three,' which was predominantly displayed on the sleeve, then, in the absence of evidence to the contrary, it seems to me by no means inconceivable that at least some readers would infer that there was some connection in the course of trade between the record and the plaintiffs. In other words, they might infer that the plaintiffs had had something to do with the making, publication or distribution of it.

The points of law and of fact and mixed law and fact arising in the context of section 5 and 4(1)(b) will all fall to be ventilated on fuller evidence and argument at the trial. In the meantime, however, the plaintiffs have satisfied me that, in relation to the defendants' projected single record, there is a serious issue to be tried on the trade mark issue.

In relation to the album record however, the position seems to me to be quite different on the facts. There, as I have said, the name 'Page Three' appears in a relatively inconspicuous position on the sleeve and, on the record itself, merely as one of a number of titles of songs. On the evidence before me, I think it more or less conceivable that any member of the public, whether a reader of *The Sun* or not, on seeing that name in this particular context, would deduce from its appearance that the defendants' album record had any connection in the course of trade with the plaintiffs. I can see no likelihood at all of any person wrongly inferring that the plaintiffs had anything to do with the making, publication or distribution of the record, even if he knew of the plaintiffs' other marketing activities."

6. Third and fourth issue—passing off

(a) *Album:*

"In relation to Lord Diplock's point (1) Mr Mummery has submitted that, by the use of the expression 'Page Three' in relation to their records, the defendants are or will be falsely representing to the public that their records are connected with the plaintiffs and that accordingly they are guilty of passing off. In relation to the album record, I have already said enough to indicate my view that it is not seriously arguable that the defendants, merely by including the name 'Page Three' as one of 12 titles of songs on the sleeve and on the record itself, are representing that the plaintiffs had anything to do with either the making, publication or distribution of the record. Accordingly, on this ground alone, the plaintiffs in my judgment have failed to establish a triable issue on the passing off claim in relation to the album record." (at 103)

(b) *Single:*

"Again, however, the position is in my judgment very different in relation to the proposed single record. For reasons which I have indicated, and making the assumptions that I do make in relation to the proposed appearance of the single record and its sleeve, I think it will be arguable that the use of the name 'Page Three' on the record and on its sleeve as one of only two titles—or, in the case of the sleeve as the sole title—will constitute a false representation that there is some connection in the course of trade between the record and the plaintiffs." (at 103.)

7. Damages—an adequate remedy in relation to the "single"?

(a) *Adequate for the defendants:* On the basis of the following evidence, the defendants argued that if distribution and sale of the proposed single were to be prevented by interlocutory injunction, the damage to the defendant would be likely to be substantial and incapable of assessment for the purpose of any award of damages pursuant to the cross-undertaking:

> "In his affidavit, though he accepts that it is impossible to give an accurate prediction, he expresses the view that, in view of the success of The Lambrettas' last two singles, the defendants can reasonably estimate that their new single will sell 250,000 copies. He says that the defendants have selected the song 'Page Three' for release as a single as it is considered to be the best track on the album and the one likely to be the most successful. He says he is confident that the song 'Page Three' is capable of having a considerable effect on the sales of the album and that if the marketing of the single is prevented, the chances of the album being successful are greatly reduced. He says that if the new single including the song 'Page Three' was delayed by even a few months, the single would have no commercial value to the defendants, since by that time the group's music would have developed, fashions would have changed and the song 'Page Three' would be an old track; and quite possibly by then, the Lambrettas would no longer be a successful group. Mr Hall further makes the point that if the new single is not released on July 18, which in the defendants' commercial judgment is the best date for the release, it will be impossible to tell what effect the release would have on The Lambrettas' careers and, consequently, on the defendants' profits." (at 105–106.)

(b) *Adequate for the plaintiffs?* The plaintiffs' argument was:
   (i) The issue of a record by the defendants under the name "Page Three" at the present stage would, for practical purposes, prevent the plaintiffs from ever making such a record under the same name in the foreseeable future.
   (ii) If the single was a great success, the plaintiffs could perhaps be compensated for loss of their commercial opportunity by reference to the actual profits made by the defendants from their record.
   (iii) But if the single was published and was a failure, not only would the potential damage to the plaintiffs' goodwill be the greater, but

722

any profits earned by the defendants from the single would be a quite unsatisfactory yardstick for the purpose of measuring the plaintiffs' loss of commercial opportunity.

8. Balance of convenience—the single Having found that damages would not be an adequate remedy for either party, Slade J. granted the injunction in relation to the single on the following grounds:

(a) There was no evidence that the single had been actually pressed or that its sleeve had been printed.

(b) "... the defendants, embarking on this single record project before they had either obtained the plaintiffs' consent or ascertained their reactions, must be taken to have done so at their own risk and with their eyes open as to the possible consequences." (at 107).

(c) "It cannot be suggested that the plaintiffs have in any way lulled them into a false sense of security." (at 107).

(d) The proper course was to preserve the status quo.

15 *Miss World (Jersey) Ltd v. James Street Productions Ltd* [1981] F.S.R. 309, C.A.

1. The facts The plaintiffs were proprietors of goodwill in the title "Miss World" for a beauty contest. The defendants proposed releasing a film entitled "Miss Alternative World," which satirised and caricatured the theme. Prompted by the following critique the plaintiffs alleged that it might become associated in the public's mind with their own:

"Junket in which contestants of all shapes, sizes, and sexes clad in *outré* dress or undress, trod the dais.... The appalling apparel ranges from alien chic—a spike-studded costume with reptilian face-covering—to leather beach wear ... the oversize cherry on the camp cake is America's drag supreme 'Divine' lording it over the evening, with woozy and wobbly charisma as the show's leopard-skinned compere."

2. Held—no serious issue to be tried Lord Denning M.R. said at 311–312:

(a) *No confusion:*

"The question is: Is that likely to cause confusion in the minds of a substantial number of people? There is no evidence of any confusion whatsoever. No one going to one of these cinemas and seeing the film would in any way be confused. They would know that the film had nothing to do with the real 'Miss World.' The only possibility of confusion would be if somebody—seeing the advertisement outside the cinema for 'The Alternative Miss World' certified 'X'—thought

723

that the real 'Miss World' was getting involved in making 'X' certificate films. But there is no evidence that anyone has thought that; and for myself, I think it is too far-fetched to warrant a claim being brought for passing off."

(b) *No copyright* (at 311):

"It seems to me that the judge was right. You must remember that there is no copyright in a title. There is no property in a title such as 'Miss World.' The only way in which the plaintiffs could complain is that they have a goodwill in the name 'Miss World.' If that goodwill is likely to be damaged by passing off, then there might be grounds for an injunction. But for myself I would agree with the judge."

16 *Home Box Office Inc v. Channel 5 Home Box Office Ltd* [1982] F.S.R. 449 (Peter Gibson J.)

1. The facts The plaintiff had since 1972 carried on business in the USA concerning the programming and marketing of pay television and production and manufacture of television programmes. It had sold a number of programmes in the United Kingdom, but had no place of business here despite its regularly advertising in *The Economist*. In 1979 it sought registration of "Home Box Office" as a trade mark for video cassettes and tapes, and such applications were still pending at the date of trial as were the defendants' applications made in September 1980, for the following trade marks in respect of tape cassettes and video cassettes, namely: "Channel 5" and "Home Box Office". The plaintiff sought an interlocutory injunction to restrain the defendants from marketing "Home Box Office" tapes.

2. The terms of the injunction sought

"Advertising or offering for sale or hire, selling, hiring or otherwise dealing in any video tapes or cassettes, films, video recorders or similar goods or carrying on the business of selling or hiring any such goods or any other business in relation to any such goods under or by reference to the name 'Home Box Office' or any other name including the name 'Home Box Office' as to be likely to deceive or cause confusion."

3. Was there a serious issue as to passing off to be tried? The question involved the following factors:
  (a) The extent, if any, of the plaintiff's goodwill.
  (b) Confusion.
  (c) Likelihood of damages.

4. The extent if any of the plaintiff's goodwill

(a) *Plaintiff's argument:*
   (i) The plaintiffs must establish that they had goodwill in England.
   (ii) The plaintiff's trade in the United Kingdom was not *de minimus* (four of eight programmes sold were in excess of $150,000).

(b) *Defendants' argument:*
   (i) The plaintiff had no relevant goodwill in England.
   (ii) Eight sales of programmes to English television companies were *de minimus* and irrelevant in that they were not retail sales of video cassettes to the general public from whom the defendants' customers were drawn.
   (iii) The plaintiff's reputation was limited to that of being an American Pay Television Company and was only known to executives in the entertainment field.

(c) *Ruling* (at 455–456):

   "Mr Kentridge was content to proceed on the basis that the plaintiff must establish that it has goodwill in England. That this is the correct basis is, in my view, established by the preponderance of the authorities, which were comprehensively reviewed and analysed by Walton J. in *The Athlete's Foot Marketing Associates Inc. v. Cobra Sports Ltd* [1980] R.P.C. 343. It is not sufficient to have a reputation abroad; there must be some business activity conducted by the plaintiff by which that English goodwill is established; though it is not necessary that the plaintiff should have a business establishment in this country, nor it seems, need the business activities here be very extensive. Thus in *Sheraton Corporation of America v. Sheraton Motels Ltd* [1964] R.P.C. 202 it was sufficient that bookings had been taken in this country for the plaintiff company's hotels abroad. In *Metric Resources Corporation v. Leasemetrix Ltd* [1979] F.S.R. 571 evidence of certain substantial transactions by a foreign plaintiff with an English company was the main evidence of an English goodwill. Moreover, goodwill established by English activities in one field may found an action against a defendant operating in England in a different field (*Harrods Ltd v. R. Harrod Ltd* (1924) 41 R.P.C. 74) *a fortiori* of the fields are close or overlap.

   In the present case, on the facts before me I am not prepared to say that the plaintiff has no properly arguable case on goodwill."

Peter Gibson J. also relied upon the view expressed by Templeman J. in *Globelegance BV v. Sarkissian* [1974] R.P.C. 603 at 613 that an English reputation once established can be supplemented by evidence of a foreign reputation and activities abroad.

5. Confusion

(a) *Case for the defendants:* The first defendant, unlike the plaintiff, sells or hires out to the general public video cassettes and hardware from its shops, to which the public must come to acquire those items.

(b) *Ruling* (at 457):

    (i) The plaintiff and defendants were operating in the same field:

> "It seems to me that both are operating in the same broad field of providing home entertainment by use of the television set, and that the natural extension of the activities of each would bring them into closer competition. Thus, it is natural that the plaintiff, as the producer of original programmes recorded on tape, which it sells to television companies should also be considering going into the business or providing such tapes for sale or hire to the general public. I have already referred to the negotiations with the Thames Television subsidiary. The defendants, according to Mr Robinson, are preparing a three-hour film package under the name 'Channel 5 Home Box Office Video Pack,' whilst one of the promotional documents refers to the second defendant as 'producing a variety of software programmes for home video systems.'"

    (ii) There was evidence from which an inference could properly be drawn that the defendants had "deliberately sought to filch" the name of the plaintiff.

6. Likelihood of damage

(a) *Case for the plaintiff:* The damage that the plaintiff apprehended was the damage caused by the injurious association of the first defendants with the plaintiff. That is because a plaintiff who establishes the existence of goodwill ought not to be put in jeopardy by another person using the same or similar name over which the plaintiff had no control and from which something adverse may rub off on to the plaintiff: *British Legion v. British Legion Club (Street) Ltd* [1928] R.P.C. 555.

(b) *Case for the defendants:* The likelihood of the plaintiff suffering damage did not exist taking into account the different business activities carried on by the plaintiff and the defendants.

(c) *Ruling* (at 458–459):

> "It is sufficient to say at this point that the issue of whether there is a likelihood of damage arising as a result of confusion of the plaintiff with the first defendant, particularly in view of the expansion plans of the plaintiff and the defendants and the possibility that at the trial

726

it will be found that the defendants sought deliberately to make use of the plaintiff's name, is one which, in my view, cannot be dismissed as unarguable."

7. Summary thus far At 459 Peter Gibson J. said:

"Accordingly, I conclude that the plaintiff's claim does raise serious issues fit to go to trial, and that this application cannot on that account be dismissed *in limine*."

8. Factors relevant to the adequacy of damages *vis-à-vis* the plaintiff *Per* Peter Gibson J.:
  (a) Reservations on the evidence of the defendants' ability to pay.
  (b) There was a real risk that the defendant might prove a financial disaster and that this might affect the plaintiff, through the public associating the first defendant with the plaintiff (at 461). The inference as to the existence of such risk was strengthened by the absence in evidence of any separate accounts or balance sheets.

9. Factors relevant to adequacy of damages *vis-à-vis* the defendants "Home Box Office" featured predominantly in the first defendant's trading and as an integral and important part of the defendants' promotion. (It was a significant part of what attracted Debenhams and Rymans.)

10. Factors relevant to the balance of convenience
  (a) The risk of uncompensatable damage to the defendants was greater if the injunction was granted than to the plaintiff if the injunction was refused.
  (b) As to the status quo, at 463:

"Mr Baldwin referred me to the observations of Lord Justice Megaw in the *Alfred Dunhill* case at 376, to the effect that the relevant point of time may vary in different cases and be one of various moments between the first allegedly wrongful act and the issue of the writ. For my part, I think that the appropriate point of time in the present case, where I cannot be sure that the defendants were deliberately attempting to take advantage of the plaintiff's reputation, is the time when the plaintiff gave a warning to the defendants by its letter before action. From then on, the defendants were on notice. At that time the defendants had incurred substantial expenditure in connection with the launching and promotion of their business, and had been trading from the King's Road premises for nearly two months. As against that, an injunction would prevent the further planned extension to the use of the name 'Home Box Office' according to the defendants' expansion plans. I do not find

727

the consideration of the preservation of the status quo greatly assists me in the determination of this motion."

11. Ruling
(a) "... the plaintiff has not discharged the onus laid upon it of satisfying me that it is an appropriate case for interim relief" (at 463).
(b) "I shall hold Mr Baldwin (for the defendants) to his offer, on behalf of Mr Blackman at Bestpor Ltd, to supply a bond by way of security."
(c) "Directions for a speedy trial."

17 *Sodastream Ltd v. Thorn Cascade Co. Ltd* [1982] R.P.C. 459, C.A.

1. The facts The action concerned refillable metal cylinders which contained carbon dioxide gas for use in machines for making "fizzy" drinks in the home. By the time the plaintiffs issued a writ, both parties marketed their own cylinders. The plaintiffs applied for an interlocutory injunction to restrain the defendants from re-marking, refilling and marketing the plaintiff's cylinders pending trial. As to the size of the respective footholds in the market (and there were no other manufacturers or distributors):
(a) The plaintiffs were the sole manufacturers and distributors from 1974 to 1980, and by the time of the hearing they had in circulation 150,000 blue cylinders and about 1.6 million grey cylinders. Each cylinder was marketed with red and white label denoting that it was a Sodastream cylinder and had been filled by the plaintiffs. Many of the cylinders had the trade-mark 'Sodastream' embossed on them, this name was stamped on many of the valves;
(b) By agreement with the plaintiffs, the defendants from 1980 had been marketing an identical and competing product whose cylinders were originally stone coloured, but later black. The defendant had 160,000 stone coloured and 50,000 black cylinders in circulation, and their trade was not much more than 10 per cent of the plaintiffs' volume.

2. Serious issue to be tried There were two points:
(a) What evidence could the plaintiffs call?
(b) Had the plaintiffs achieved a reputation that the grey cylinders were associated with them?

3. First point—evidence The plaintiffs' evidence was mainly contained in affidavits from persons dealing from the retailer's and consumer's point of view with the plaintiffs' refilled cylinders and in particular with the distinctive quality of the colour. The evidence was virtually uncontradicted—and admissible. Kerr L.J. said:

> "It is perfectly proper and admissible for someone in the trade to express opinions about the likely reaction of others in relation to matters which are within his or her sphere of work; indeed, it is part of their responsibility to form a view on such matters. In particular it seems to me that this kind of evidence must be admissible in affidavits in interlocutory proceedings, although at the trial the witnesses will of course be cross-examined about the opinions expressed by them."

Similarly, contrary to the view of Whitford J. at first instance, Kerr L.J. held that at the introductory stage, it was not a justifiable criticism of the plaintiffs to say they had adduced no evidence from the general public:

> "All the cases which have been cited to us, concerning the need for evidence as to confusion among the general public, were reports of trials, not of interlocutory applications. Moreover, we are here dealing, as I have already explained, with a situation where the contentious article is at present not on the market. ... Therefore, members of the public cannot be usefully asked—at least, not usefully to the same extent—about their reaction if both kinds of grey cylinders were on the market. In my view it was therefore excusable to confine the evidence at this stage to that of persons in the trade."

4. Second point—passing off At first instance, Whitford J. had expressed the view that a grey gas cylinder had no inherent capacity to generate a sufficient reputation. Kerr L.J. disagreed:

> "Of course, it may not in itself be of distinctive colour, but it may nevertheless be distinctive to the plaintiffs. That must be a question of evidence."

5. Would damages be an adequate remedy? There were two factors:
(a) The application was *quia timet*.
(b) Status quo.

6. First point—*quia timet* At 470(45)–471(5): Kerr L.J. concluded that the plaintiffs had established a serious issue to be tried. Turning to the balance of convenience, he said, citing Lord Diplock in *Warnink v. Townend & Sons (Hull) Ltd* [1979] A.C. 731 at 742, that in a *quia timet* action for an injunction the plaintiffs must show a probability of damage, and despite the defendants' submissions to the contrary, he was far from convinced that damages would be an adequate remedy. He continued: "Indeed, this must be rare in cases in which one of the allegations is the likelihood of confusion in the trade."

7. Second point—status quo At 472: Kerr L.J. said an important point to which the judge had not given any real weight, was that the plaintiffs were not asking for an injunction to prevent the defendants from carrying on business in the way they were already doing, but were merely seeking to preclude them from doing something new which they were not yet doing at all. Having cited Lord Diplock in the *Cyanamid* case, at 408F, he said:

> "It seems to me that on the question of balance, one must ask oneself: If the plaintiffs have an arguable case ... why should the status quo not be preserved pending the trial? What harm would it do to the defendants if it is preserved? Why do the defendants really want to do what they propose doing, and reject all alternatives?
>
> To my mind there is not the beginning of a satisfactory answer to any of these questions. On the contrary, if the defendants are not restrained, the plaintiffs' chances of obtaining a permanent injunction at the trial, which in my view is at any rate an arguable possibility, will be seriously prejudiced. On the other hand, thee is no suggestion that the defendants will suffer any substantial, or perhaps, any financial damage if an injunction is granted.
>
> For all those reasons I conclude that the balance of convenience, or justice, is wholly in favour of granting the injunction applied for pending the trial in order to preserve the status quo." (at 472(5)–472(17).)

18 *Century Electronics Ltd v. CVS Enterprises Ltd* [1983] F.S.R. 1, *per* Dillon J.

1. The facts The plaintiffs manufactured interchangeable games systems for video machines under the mark "CVS" (Century Video Systems). The plaintiffs sought interlocutory relief to restrain the defendants from carrying on business using the name "CVS" (Computer Video Service).

2. The relevant law At 3 Dillon J. invoked the judgment of Megaw L.J. in *Jarman & Platt v. Barge (I.) Ltd* [1977] F.S.R. 260:

> "The first is the particular name or style on which he is relying has become distinctive of his goods. The second is that the use of that name by the defendant amounts to a misrepresentation in that it was likely to lead people to suppose that the defendant's goods are the plaintiff's goods, and confusion is the normal way in which the misrepresentation is shown. As Lord Justice Megaw pointed out, the question of confusion does not arise unless the plaintiffs get over their first hurdle in establishing a monopoly in the name on which they are relying."

will have difficulties in establishing and quantifying the damage which they will have suffered between now and the hearing if the defendant were allowed to operate as he intends to do. If they were to prove any such loss it is unlikely that the defendant could satisfy any money judgment which the plaintiffs obtained, he being unemployed and on state benefits. On the other side, the defendant does not suggest that he will have any particular difficulty in quantifying his loss if he succeeds at the trial, nor does he suggest that the plaintiffs are not good for any damages which the court may award him under their undertakings. It is still open to the defendant to operate his business on the basis that the advertising material is delivered at the same time as but not interleaved with the plaintiffs' newspapers. Thus the injunctions do not entirely prevent the defendant carrying on his business as counsel for Mail Newspapers pointed out. Their action began in December 1985 and an interlocutory injunction was granted on 12 December 1985. The defendant has not sought to accelerate the trial of this action or to isolate the questions of law that he has raised before me as preliminary issues. Nor did the defendant seek to vary or discharge the interlocutory injunctions until July 1986. That in my judgment is an indication of where the balance of convenience lies in this case."

8. In case the status quo was relevant ...

"Finally, in my view the *status quo ante* is preserved by the continuation of these interim injunctions restraining the defendants from inserting or procuring the insertion of advertising material in the plaintiffs' newspapers."

32 Scott Ltd v. Nice-Pak Products Ltd [1989] F.S.R. 100

1. The background Both parties were American-owned manufacturers of baby wipes (pre-moistened disposable towelettes used primarily for cleaning babies when they have their nappies changed.) The plaintiffs were the market leader, but for six years the plaintiffs and the defendants had marketed their baby wipes in the USA side by side, in similar but not identical tubs with blue labels showing a mother and baby. The plaintiffs' baby wipes were called "Baby Fresh" and the defendants' "Nice 'n Clean". For three years the plaintiffs had marketed their baby wipes in Britain in substantially the same get-up as in the USA. Then the defendants resolved to enter the British market, also using substantially the same get-up as in the USA.

2. The relief sought Nine months before the defendants first started selling their product in Britain the plaintiffs carried out a poll survey of mothers of young children in an attempt to show that the new product would be confused with the plaintiffs' existing one. They then issued proceedings seeking to prevent the defendants entering the British market using their American get-up, and applied for an interlocutory injunction.

3. At first instance At the time of the hearing the defendants had still not introduced their product to Britain. Walton J. refused to grant an interlocutory injunction, on the ground that the plaintiffs had not established that there was a serious issue to be tried. They had failed to show that degree of misrepresentation which is necessary to establish passing off.

4. On appeal The Court of Appeal (Fox L.J. and Sir Frederic Lawton) dismissed the appeal on the same ground as the trial judge, rejecting the five arguments put forward by the plaintiff as showing misrepresentation.

5. No serious issue to be tried—why?

    (a) "First it is said, look at the tubs themselves. They are all in blue and of a similar shade though in fact the shades are not the same. As to the difference in the shade of the blue it is said that the difference although it exists is not great enough to distinguish them effectively in the public's mind. I would agree that the similarities which undoubtedly exist cannot be brushed aside, but one has to consider the entirety of shape and get-up of the respective objects. The fact is that all the tubs are labelled. The plaintiff's boxes are labelled, both on the side and on the top; the defendant's boxes are labelled on the side. The labels of the two products are different. A glance at the labels would differentiate the goods."

    (b) Secondly the plaintiff relied on new evidence placed before the Court of Appeal which the judge had not had, in the form of an internal memorandum of the defendants clearly showing an intention right at the start of the defendants' marketing in the USA to copy the plaintiffs' product. Fox L.J. accepted that the court can normally infer from copying, an intention to gain some adhesion of the other's goodwill. But in circumstances where the two products had been on sale in the USA side by side for six years, yet there was no evidence whatever of any confusion there, the copying argument lost all its force.

    (c) "Thirdly, it is said that the plaintiff's advertising emphasises the size and shape of the tub. The advertising, it seems to me, does not give emphasis to the size and shape of the tub. Of course, if you advertise a tub and give a photograph or representation of it, its shape will in some degree be apparent. In the present case no particular emphasis seems to me to be given to the shape or size of the tub, but rather to the name 'Baby Fresh'."

(d) "Fourthly, the plaintiff asserts that Mr Hodges, in his evidence for the defendant, states that the public sometimes have the false impression that private label goods are in fact all made by the market leader. That, it is said, shows that confusion is a possibility. But in the immediately preceding sentence of Mr Hodges' affidavit, however, he says there is no evidence that that is an idea which would occur to the mother when buying baby wipes. The point regarding a single origin of products from the market leader was not, it seems to me, really examined in any depth in the evidence and I do not think that the plaintiff can hang anything upon it."

(e) Finally, the poll survey of shoppers had been conducted in a way that was so flawed that it could not be relied upon. Most of the flaws stemmed from the survey's failure to make sufficient allowance for the fact that, at the time of the survey, the defendants' product was not on the market in Britain, and the plaintiffs' product was the only one of its kind in British shops.

33 *Island Trading Company v. Anchor Brewing Company* [1989] R.P.C. 287a

1. Steam beer—the background One year after the plaintiff company launched its "Newquay Steam beer" range in Britain the defendants (who had been making "steam beer" in the USA since the nineteenth century) introduced their "Anchor Steam beer" in Britain. By the time of the hearing, the defendants' sales in Britain were in bottles from its "Majestic" warehouses—rather than in kegs for use in public houses. The plaintiffs commenced proceedings for passing off and moved for an interlocutory injunction.

2. Was there a serious issue of confusion? Knox J. made a distinction between the customer who selects off a shelf in a warehouse and the customer who makes a verbal order in a public house or off-licence.

"In relation to sales where the consumer selects the articles off a shelf or its equivalent, I do not consider that the plaintiffs have shown more than a weak case on probability of confusion and thereby a real likelihood of suffering substantial damage. That covers the great bulk of the sales in Majestic warehouses for the cartons, and cases are no less distinctive than the bottles. In relation to sales where the customer puts in a verbal order which may be one for "Steam Beer" or the like, the plaintiffs do in my judgment show a serious issue to be tried on the issue of substantial damage. This covers the great bulk of sales in public houses and off-licences. Of course, there will be exceptions to both. There will be customers who go into a warehouse and ask the vendor behind the counter for "Steam Beer" and there will be customers in public houses who go in and point to a bottle and say, "I will have one of those", but in general, the distinction is a clearly defined one."

3. Would damages be an adequate remedy? The judge held that both sides could show a prospect of unquantifiable loss should the interlocutory decision go against them followed by success at trial—though such losses might not be very substantial.

4. The judge granted a partial injunction The balance of convenience was determined by two main factors:
  (a) The defendants' bottles were not easily confused with the plaintiffs'; and
  (b) Almost all of the defendants' imported beer was in bottles rather than any other form.

"My conclusion overall, taking the above consideration into account, is that I should refuse an injunction in relation to sales of bottles of Anchor Steam Beer but grant one in relation to sales of kegs. I draw that distinction because the sales of bottles by the defendants are, in the very great majority, from warehouses direct to the end consumer, where it seems to me that the circumstances of sale are such as largely to eliminate the risk of confusion. Some bottles have in the past found their way into public houses, and doubtless will continue to do until trial, but the small proportion of what is anyway a very small amount as compared with the plaintiffs' sales tips the balance against granting an injunction on that score. In relation to the sale of kegs which the defendants have not embarked upon in this country, disregarding as I do the 15 kegs sent gratuitously for promotional purposes. I consider the scales tip the other way, partly because the risk of confusion is much greater in public houses than in the defendants' warehouses and partly because the defendants show no significant unquantifiable loss if they are restrained until trial from selling their beer in kegs. I propose to accept the defendants' offer to supply the plaintiffs' solicitors with monthly sales figures of bottles of Anchor Steam beer because my decision has been significantly influenced by the evidence of the volume of sales."

34 *Stacey v. 2020 Communications plc* [1991] F.S.R. 49

1. The "20/20" fight Both parties carried on business in the tele-communications field, though arguably in different areas. The plaintiff had traded as "20/20 Telecom" for two years. The defendants had traded for 18 months when they changed their business name to "2020 Communications". Despite having started trading later, the defendants' business had about ten times the turnover of the plaintiff. Any confusion between the two businesses appeared to be the opposite from the usual way, so that it was customers of the defendants who inadvertently telephoned the plaintiff, rather than vice versa. The plaintiff had therefore been able to correct the confusion.

2. Damages not an adequate remedy Having established that there was clearly a serious question to be tried as to whether there was a risk of confusion between the two businesses, Millett J. went on to consider whether damages would be an adequate remedy for the plaintiff:

"Clearly damages are not a fully adequate remedy for the plaintiff. They rarely are in a case of this kind, for if there is a risk of loss of sales through confusion the damage would be unquantifiable. More-over, there is always the added risk that there will not only be a loss of recommendations from satisfied customers whose recommendations have gone awry because the recipients of the recommendations have mistaken the parties, but that there will be actual positive rec-ommendations not to use 20/20 Telecom from dissatisfied customers of the defendant. That is often an argument that is put forward in these cases. I think it has relatively little force in the present case, where it appears that the defendant's work is strictly regulated and its standards are supervised and monitored by Mercury. The real risk of loss which Mr Stacey identifies is the loss of referrals from satisfied customers."

3. Damages—a remedy for the defendants? The plaintiff argued that the only effect of an injunction would be to compel the defendants to revert to their previous trading name, the reputation of which had not yet been completely lost. That may cause the defendants some loss in the temporary inability to use the name of their choice, but the plaintiff argued that was not great. The judge disagreed because the interlocutory decision would effectively dispose of the substantive issue. Millett J. disposed of the plaintiff's argument in this way:

"I do not think it is as easy as that. If I grant the injunction now and the defendant changes its name and adopts a new name or reverts to Extel Communications, that will be that. It may be that a trial will still take place but it will largely be about costs. I cannot think that the defendant, having changed its name, will want to change it back again. The real dispute between the parties is as to the right to use this name. The defendant plainly cannot prevent Mr Stacey from continuing to use it. Can Mr Stacey stop the defendant from using it?

4. The balance of convenience The judge came to his decision on the balance of convenience on the basis that if an injunction were granted the probable effect would be to deprive the defendants permanently of the right to use their chosen name, whereas he doubted whether there was a real risk of significant loss to the plaintiff until the trial if no injunction were granted. He therefore refused an injunction.

5. The plaintiff would suffer insignificant loss—why? The judge gave four reasons for his conclusion that the plaintiff would probably not suffer significant loss if no injunction were granted:

"The reason I say that is first that I am minded to grant a speedy trial, so that I am considering a period of perhaps nine months to, at worst, a year.

Secondly, Mr Stacey is in a small way of business and the number of telephone systems which he is likely to install in the course of a year is, while not insignificant, not enormous, and the number of occasions on which referrals may be made and go awry is not likely to be very great.

Thirdly, the installation of a telephone system is a significant investment. The customers include substantial public companies. The mechanism of apprehended loss it that a satisfied customer recommends 20/20 Telecom for the installation of a telephone system, meaning Mr Stacey, and there is then an error or confusion on the part of the person who receives the recommendation so that he takes his business to the defendant. Should that occur between now and the trial—I think it is not likely to occur very often—but should it occur it seems to me that appropriate orders for discovery should make it possible to track down the cases where it has occurred so that the loss may be susceptible to some quantification.

Fourthly, if there is error and confusion of that kind it is just as likely to occur the other way round, and insofar as there is competing business in this overlapping field, it will be the satisfied customers of the defendant who will recommend the defendant with the result that the business will go to the plaintiff. It is true that the defendants cannot complain of that, but there is much force in the submission that, if there is confusion, then given the comparative sizes of the businesses it is more likely on the whole to enure to the advantage of Mr Stacey than of the defendant."

35 *Mirage Studios v. Counter-Feat Clothing Co. Ltd* [1991] F.S.R. 145

1. Teenage Mutant Ninja Turtles The plaintiffs, an American partnership, owned the copyright in drawings of four cartoon-character "Turtles" and exploited them commercially by licensing their reproduction on goods sold by third parties. The unhappily-named defendant company ("CCCL") made drawings of turtles which were similar but not identical to the plaintiffs' and began to license these drawings to various clothing manufacturers. The effect of what the defendants had done was to copy the idea of Turtles and to use the name "Ninja Turtles", but not in terms of line reproducing the drawings as a copy.

2. The battles lines The plaintiffs' first reaction had been to report the matter to the trading standards authorities, but that method of enforcement proved abortive because the defendants claimed to own the original copyright. Eventually the plaintiffs brought an action alleging breach of copyright and passing off, and seeking interlocutory relief. The defendants' riposte was that the plaintiffs did not have an arguable case under either head, asserting that there were no intellectual property rights in either the name or the concept of turtles.

3. The adequacy of damages Sir Nicholas Browne-Wilkinson V.-C. held that the plaintiffs had an arguable case on both grounds, and moved on, applying *American Cyanamid*, to consider the adequacy of damages. The plaintiffs' loss of royalties could be quantified, but their loss of reputation through bad-quality products was more difficult. In the event it was conclusive that the defendants were a very small company with no assets. It meant both that damages were an inadequate remedy for the plaintiffs, and also that a cross-undertaking in damages would be inadequate protection for the defendants, who would undoubtedly cease to exist if the injunction were granted.

4. The significance of the delay in suing The plaintiffs' delay in bringing proceedings whilst they relied on the trading standards authorities to enforce their rights made it very hard to see where the status quo lay. The defendants argued that the delay had lulled them into a false sense of security, as a result of which they had decided to concentrate on their one

769

new Turtle line. The judge thought that would have been a very important factor if the delay had been unexplained:

> "However, I do not think that that is a proper reflection of what occurred in this case. The plaintiffs were seeking to enforce their rights, as they thought them to be, through the trading standards authorities. The defendants were well-aware of that and when that proved to be abortive then no further delay, as far as I can see, occurred. I do not think the defendants were entitled to feel secure when they were in fact being pursued through the trading standards authorities route."

5. Balance of convenience: David and Goliath On behalf of the defendants it was urged that the defendants were a small-time operation which could not bear the loss flowing from an injunction, whereas the plaintiffs were extremely prosperous and wealthy. Given the relative damage to be done to the one side and the other, the right course was to allow the defendants to go on trading and so to diversify their business and indeed finance the action. The judge was not impressed:

> "In all cases of small defendants getting close to the line of copyright or passing off cases, it could always be said that the defendant is a small operator and the person seeking to enforce his rights is normally the big operator. But that cannot in general be determinative of the matter since in cases such as these it is often critical to put an end to the infringement speedily since if that is not done the value of the intellectual property which the plaintiff is seeking to enforce is lost. For example, in the present case the defendant himself puts a life on the craze for Mutant Turtles of only some further six months. I also find the whole suggestion of diversification slightly unrealistic. I can see no real grounds for thinking that if the defendants were allowed to go on they would be in a position both to pay the costs of fighting the action and to pay the damages in full. I asked whether the defendants were prepared to put the royalties into the joint names of solicitors, but the only offer forthcoming from the defendants was to put 20 per cent of the royalties into joint names."

6. The balance was even The judge was driven to decide the interlocutory application on the strength of the relative cases and in due course granted an injunction.

> "Putting all these factors together, I really am very unclear where the justice of the case lies on the interlocutory application. On the one side, to grant the injunction will almost certainly close down the defendant company for good, on the other hand not to grant the

relief will mean that the plaintiff is without effective redress for an infringement of its rights. In those circumstances, I believe that I am entitled under the *American Cyanamid* decision to look at the strength of the relative cases of the two sides. It seems to me extremely desirable that I should because, for practical purposes, it seems almost certain that this is the end of the litigation and that what I decide today is in fact going to be determinative of the action."

36 *Consorzio del Prosciutto di Parma v. Marks & Spencer plc* [1991] R.P.C. 351

1. The Parma ham case The plaintiffs were a consortium of producers of Parma ham. Under Italian law Parma ham cannot be described as such unless it is sliced in the presence of the customer, but that law had not been incorporated into English law either directly or via European law. The defendants had for a time been content to comply voluntarily with the Italian rules and sell their Parma ham under the description "Italian dry cured ham". They then decided to call it "Parma ham" and the plaintiffs applied for an interlocutory injunction to stop them doing so. The only cause of action to which the plaintiffs could resort was passing off.

2. Was there a serious issue to be tried? In the Court of Appeal Nourse L.J. summarised the elements of the tort of passing off on each of which the plaintiffs had to establish a case:

> "In order to obtain a permanent injunction at the trial, the producers will have to establish, first, that they have acquired in England a reputation in the trade description "Parma ham" as one connoting ham sliced in the presence of the retail purchaser from a leg bearing the Parma crown, secondly, that the defendants have represented that Marks & Spencer's ham is ham of that description in such a way as to confuse ordinary, sensible members of the public or a section of them, and, thirdly, that such confusion has caused or is likely to cause damage to the producers. In order to obtain an injunction at this interlocutory stage, the consortium must establish that there is a serious question to be tried as to each of those three matters. If they do not do that, the balance of convenience does not become an issue and no injunction is appropriate."

3. No serious issue because no misrepresentation The Court of Appeal agreed with Morritt J. at first instance, who pithily summarised the plaintiffs' difficulty thus:

771

"Notwithstanding the valiant and patient efforts of counsel for the plaintiffs, I am unable to see how it can be a misrepresentation to sell as Parma ham a slice of ham carved from what the Consortium accepts is a Parma ham merely because the purchaser is not present. The truth of the matter is that the crown on the ham is a mark of authenticity. To apply it to a ham which is not produced in accordance with Italian law may well amount to passing off. But to take it off a ham which was so produced by the operation of carving, in my judgment, cannot do so."

37 *Drayton Controls (Engineering) Ltd. v. Honeywell Control Systems Ltd* [1992] F.S.R. 245

1. The facts The background to this dispute about the defendants' introduction of a thermostatic radiator valve which competed with the plaintiffs' is at p. 856 below.

2. No serious issue to be tried Knox J. applying *Cyanamid*, refused an injunction on the grounds that the plaintiffs had not established that there was a serious issue to be tried. They could not establish that the defendants' valve made any misrepresentation. His conclusion was based on two aspects of the case.

3. First aspect—the circumstances of the sale Most sales of radiator valves are by builders' merchants selling to tradesmen, who order by name not visual appearance.

"The suggestion that a significant body of purchasers would make purchases on the strength of a visual recollection of the general appearance of a valve whether seen on a relative's or friend's installation or in an advertisement (and I take into account the advertisement aimed by Drayton at end users) without also remembering or taking the trouble to find a quite prominent name, seems to me fanciful."

4. Second aspect—misrepresentation by shape is difficult The judge put it in this way:

"The second aspect which I find compelling is that it requires an exceptionally strong case to justify the conclusion that a particular configuration of an article such as a chrome body, white plastic bezel and chrome dome for a thermostatic radiator valve has become so identified with a particular manufacturer and seller of such an article as to give him the right to claim that such a configuration conveys the message to the relevant section of the public that such a configuration

772

indicates his goods and his goods alone. Neither chrome dome nor white plastic bezels are the exclusive preserve of Drayton."

B: APPLICATION FOR INTERLOCUTORY RELIEF IN PATENT CASES

1 *Hoffman-La Roche AG v. D.D.S.A. Pharmaceuticals Ltd* [1965] R.P.C. 503

1. Background Harman L.J. explained at 513(9–14):

"This is another round in the war being carried out by a number of comparatively small pharmaceutical companies in this country against the great monopolies. It having been discovered that there are no royalties payable in Italy on these drugs which are therefore obtainable from that source very much more cheaply, enterprising groups of persons have imported the drugs and have advertised and circularised the trade promising to supply them at cheaper prices."

2. The facts The plaintiffs, producers of the drug "librium", claimed that the defendants were marketing a tablet which infringed the "librium" patent. The defendants admitted that claim 3 in the patent was narrow enough to cover the drug's constituents—but averred that claims 1 and 2 of the patent were so widely framed as to be invalid.

3. Was there a prima facie case? Yes—held the Court of Appeal, in this pre-*Cyanamid* decision, but the following dicta of the Master of the Rolls at 512(13–16) would probably carry equal weight today:

"It seems to me that when you have, as he had, a patent of such long standing, widely used and much respected throughout the world, with no citation against it and not challenged over all these years until now, there is prima facie evidence of validity of the patent."

4. If claims 1 and 2 were invalid, would they defeat claim 3—assuming that were valid? No—Lord Denning M.R. said at 512(33–42):

"I may add that even if claims 1 and 2 are so wide that the probability is that they are invalid, nevertheless it is plain that claim 3 is valid. This brings me to section 62 of the Patents Act 1949 which provides in subsection 1: 'If in proceedings for infringement of a patent it is found that any claim of the specification, being a claim in respect of which infringement is alleged, is valid, but that any other claim is

773

invalid, the court may grant relief in respect of any valid claim which is infringed.' It seems to me that under that section an interlocutory injunction can be granted in respect of the valid claim. It is not necessary for the court at an interlocutory stage to consider whether an amendment should be made to the specification (under subsection 3). That can be considered at the trial. It is sufficient for an interlocutory injunction that a prima facie case of validity is established in respect of claim 3 in the letters patent, and of the infringement of it."

5. Would damages be an adequate remedy? No—particularly because it would be wrong to allow the defendants a head-start in the compulsory licence stakes. As Lord Denning M.R. said at 512 (45–56), 513 (1–5):

"There is one remaining matter, namely, the balance of convenience. Mr Graham says that the defendants are ready to keep an account of profits and to put the money aside, and so no harm will be done by letting them carry on until they get a compulsory licence. There would be no damage done to the plaintiffs, he says, because they would be recompensed just as if a licence were given. But I think that a person who is entitled in proper circumstances to a compulsory licence ought not to anticipate the grant of that licence. He must not take the law into his own hands. He is not allowed to say: 'I will get a licence before very long, therefore I will anticipate it, I will supply the goods now and keep an account.' A person who wants a licence must make his application and await the time until he has got his licence with all the conditions attached to it."

2 *Hoffman-La Roche (F.) & Co. AG v. Inter-Continental Pharmaceutical Ltd* [1965] Ch. 795, C.A.

1. The facts The defendant admittedly infringed the plaintiff's patent by marketing drugs of which the plaintiff was patentee. In response to the plaintiff's application for an interlocutory injunction to restrain the infringement the defendant contended that it had applied under section 41 of the Patents Act 1949 for a compulsory licence and that the Comptroller-General had power under that section to backdate any licence which he might grant.

2. The Court of Appeal granted the injunction—why? The grounds for its decision were:
  (a) As a matter of law, section 41 did not provide a power to backdate (one may square this with *Cyanamid* on the basis that this decision did not constitute a "difficult question of law").

(b) As to adequacy of damages, Russell L.J. held:

> "For such a patentee, it is said, it ought to be sufficient that he be entitled to monetary reward or compensation in the form of damages or an account of profits. I cannot accept that his should be regarded as sufficient protection of his patent rights. Those rights forbid the exploitation of the invention by others unless and until the proper terms of a licence, giving the patentee any necessary rights of supervision for the purpose at least of ascertaining the true figures for royalty, and a commensurate and proper reward, have been settled. Refusal of an injunction against the wrongdoer achieves none of these things, and, in particular, the patentee is faced with the difficulties of establishing at some later date the true measure of the harm done to him." (P. 815F.)

3 *Zaidener v. Barrisdale Engineers Ltd* [1968] R.P.C. 488

1. The facts The plaintiff sought by interlocutory injunction to restrain the defendants from allegedly infringing her patent for a vehicle anti-theft device, which she had patented two years before.

2. The case for the defendants The defendants argued that the plaintiff's claim was invalid, invoking the usual grounds of:
   (a) Prior publication.
   (b) Obviousness.
   (c) Lack of inventive merit.
The defence also offered the usual undertaking to keep an account pending trial.

3. The real issues In this pre-*Cyanamid* decision, the Court of Appeal found a prima facie case. *Inter alia,* the court took into account:
   (a) Previously, no-one had produced the device as patented by the plaintiff.
   (b) The plaintiff's patent withstood the test of examination at the time when it was registered.
   (c) The plaintiff had been granted patents in respect of her invention in a number of other countries.
The real issue to adequacy of damages.

4. Were damages an adequate remedy? Yes—for the following reasons:

(a) *Scale:*
   (i) If the defendants were operating on a small scale, the infringement would be almost minimal.

775

(ii) If the defendants were operating on a large scale, the plaintiffs would recover substantial damages and there would be no doubt as to the ability of the defendant to pay.

(b) *Patent—only recent:* An interlocutory injunction was inappropriate to enforce a recent patent. In arriving at that conclusion, the court took into account the following judgments of Scrutton L.J. and Atkins L.J. in *Smith v. Grigg Ltd* (1924) 41 R.P.C. 149:

"... where the patent which you are seeking to enforce is a recent patent, an interlocutory injunction is not granted where there is a genuine case to be decided. Parker J. put it very shortly in *Trautner v. Patmore* (1912) 29 R.P.C. 60 at 63: 'I cannot grant an interim injunction. It is very unusual if the patent has not been established.' It is put at greater length by this court in the case of *Jackson v. Needlee*, which was decided just after the Patents, Designs and Trade Marks Act 1883, where both Baggallay L.J. and Cotton L.J. state that, where it is a new patent, or a recent patent, the court is not in the habit of granting these injunctions until the title has been established. I take the principle that underlies to be this, that the court leans against monopolies. Where you find a respectable and old-established monopoly which has been in existence for years and not challenged, there is no reason for the court to lean too badly against it, but when you find a recent monopoly which there has not yet been time to challenge sought to be enforced, the court is inclined to take the view as a general rule, unless there are special circumstances to overcome it, that the title to the monopoly must be established before it interferes by interlocutory injunction. It is not a universal rule; there may easily be facts which will lead the court in a particular case to depart from it, but as a general rule that is the practice of the court."

Atkin L.J. at 154 said:

"I think the reason for the principle which has been adopted in respect of a person claiming an interlocutory injunction restraining the infringement of a patent is that the plaintiff has always to establish at any rate a prima facie case of having a right which has been infringed by the defendant, and according to our patent law, which in this respect differs from that of some other countries, the mere fact of the granting of a patent is not in itself an indication that the plaintiff has established to the satisfaction of any authority that he had the right to the monopoly which he claims. In the case of a patent, therefore, the mere fact that a patent has been granted does not show that those conditions have been performed which alone entitle a plaintiff to a conclusive right, and therefore the courts, when they are approached by a plaintiff who said: 'I am the owner of a patent and the defendant has infringed it,' say, where the patent is of recent date: 'Your right is not established sufficiently by the mere fact that a patent has been granted to you; and unless there is some kind of substantial case evidenced before the court that there is in fact a valid patent, then the court refuses to grant an injunction.'"

5. What if the patent were about to expire *Zaidener* should be contrasted with the pre-*Cyanamid* case of *Fomento (Sterling Area) v. Refill Improvements (RICO) Co. Ltd* [1963] R.P.C. 163 which is authority for the principle that the balance of convenience is against the grant of an interlocutory injunction where the patent relied on will expire before the action can be heard.

6. The unanswered question Does *Zaidener* survive *Cyanamid*?

4 *Carroll v. Tomado Ltd* [1971] R.P.C. 401

1. The facts The plaintiff by notice of motion sought to restrain the defendants by their directors, officers, servants or agents or otherwise, howsoever, from infringing letters patent relating to domestic clothes carriers. The patent was applied for in 1958 and published in 1961. Between such publication and the motion, several competitors (including the defendant) had withdrawn competing articles after their attention had been drawn to the patent.

2. The chronology
(a) Patent applied for—1958.
(b) Patent published—1961.
(c) Defendant withdrew an airer from the market, after objection by the plaintiffs—1969.
(d) Plaintiffs heard of a modified design advertised by the defendants—November 1970.
(e) Plaintiffs immediately sought to obtain a sample—acquired January 11, 1971.
(f) Proceedings commenced—January 21, 1971.

3. A pre-*Cyanamid* decision Graham J. held at 405:

"The principles upon which an interlocutory injunction may be granted in a patent action are the same as in any other action, namely the plaintiff must show a prima facie case and also that the balance of convenience, as it is called, is in his favour. In patent actions it very frequently happens that the defendant is able to show that there are substantial grounds for disputing the validity of the patent and often also that there are good reasons for saying that his apparatus does not infringe the plaintiff's claim. If either of these circumstances is shown to be present it is not the practice of the court to grant an interlocutory injunction because these are not the issues which can conveniently be tried on motion by affidavit. Indeed in some of the cases, such as *Marshall and Lace Web Spring Co. Ltd v. Crown Bedding Company Ltd* [1929] 46 R.P.C. 267, the courts appear to have gone as far as saying that, at any rate in the case of a recently granted patent, it was sufficient in order to prevent the grant of an interlocutory injunction for the defendant's counsel to assert that the validity of the patent would in due course be attacked. I doubt myself if these cases really were intended to go much further than to indicate that in a patent action the onus of showing a prima facie case justifying the grant of an injunction which lies on the plaintiffs is a heavy one and that it is comparatively easy for the defendant to establish a defence sufficient to prevent the grant of such an injunction. (See, for example, the remarks of Lord Evershed in *Newman v. British International Proprietaries Ltd* [1962] R.P.C. 90, a case in the Court of Appeal in this country, and *Beecham Group Ltd v. Bristol Laboratories Pty. Ltd (Australia)* [1968] R.P.C. 301, a case in the High Court of Australia, that the principles governing the grant of an interlocutory injunction in patent cases are no different from the principles governing the grant of such an injunction in any other case.)"

4. **Post-*Cyanamid*—do these dicta still apply?** It is submitted that:
   (a) The proposition that the principle upon which an interlocutory injunction may be granted in a patent action was the same as in any other action probably applies as equally as it did in 1971—only that cross the jurisprudential spectrum, such principle has to be viewed through the Cyanamid prism.
   (b) Subject to the dicta of the Court of Appeal in *Smith (T.J.) & Nephew Ltd v. 3M United Kingdom plc* [1983] R.P.C. 92, C.A. (see below, p. 000) it may be open to argument that when considering a grant of an interlocutory injunction in a patent action, the courts should weigh in the balance those factors recited by Graham J. above (*e.g.* how recent was the grant of the patent, etc.).

5. **The adequacy of damages criterion** At 411, Graham J. held in the following terms that damages would not be an adequate remedy:

"The damages [*sic*] to the plaintiffs which may occur if the defendants are allowed to proceed with their sales are not limited to multiplicity of actions clearly liable to be caused but is irreparable in the sense that such sales are likely to disrupt the plaintiffs' present business and future plans and thereby cause damage which is very difficulty to quantify and which would not be adequately met by the offer to keep an account which the defendants have made."

Graham J. held that damages would not be an adequate remedy to the plaintiff, but would be to the defendant, and made an interlocutory injunction accordingly.

6. The relevance of "balance of convenience" Graham J. implicitly found confirmation for his approach by reference to the "balance of convenience," which he explained thus at 410–411:

(a) *Plaintiffs—long established*

"It is clear that the plaintiffs' trade has been going on for a good many years and they have built up a large and expanding business in the article in question, and until very recently, when the defendants' article appeared, had a practical monopoly in the field. The evidence shows that they have just built a new plant with a view to further expansion. The defendants on the other hand have only recently started selling their particular articles and between September 1970 and the end of January 1971, as appears from Mr Edwards' first affidavit, paragraph 4, they have only sold about 3,675 articles."

(b) *Defendant went in with eyes open:*

"In addition here the circumstances are similar to the circumstances in the *Beecham* (Australian) case in that the defendants have known for a long time of the plaintiffs' patent and their monopoly in the field in question. The best evidence of this is, of course, the defendants' earlier abandoned attempt to introduce a competing airer on the market in 1969. Further, the plaintiffs' brochure clearly refers, albeit in small print, to a number of patents of which the subject of the present action is one. It is, therefore, clear that the defendant in the present case have entered this market with their eyes open and knowing perfectly well that the plaintiffs have a patent and have up to the present been vigilant in endeavouring successfully to stop others entering the market. They have, therefore, only themselves to blame if they now find they are in a position where they are liable to be held to have infringed the patent and, if the plaintiffs turn out to be right, must put up with the fact that they have expended money in advertising and sales promotion which will be wasted. This is, of course, not the whole of the matter because if thereafter it eventually turns out that the defendants are right they will be protected by the cross-undertaking in damages."

(The *Beecham* reference is *Beecham Group Ltd v. Bristol Laboratories Pty Ltd* (Australian) [1968] R.P.C. 301.)

779

In similar vein, in the copyright case of *Merchant-Adventurers v. Grew &
Co.* [1972] 1 Ch. 242, Graham J. held at 256C:

> "The balance of convenience is in the plaintiffs' favour since the
> defendants' trade is quite new and indeed has hardly got started at
> all. In such circumstances, it is right to preserve the status quo by
> granting an injunction rather than to refuse it. It would not be right
> to allow the defendants, pending the trial, to build up a business in
> these fittings and inevitably to some extent disrupt the established
> business of the plaintiffs, such disruption being a matter which it is
> extremely difficult to quantify in damages."

5 *American Cyanamid Co. v. Ethicon Ltd* [1975] A.C. 396

1. Background The plaintiffs owned a patent covering certain sterile
absorbable surgical sutures and issued proceedings to restrain the defendants from launching on the British market a suture which the plaintiffs
claimed infringed their patent.

2. The case for the defendants The defendants argued (as defendants so
regularly do in patent cases) that:
  (a) If the wording of the patent was taken in its narrow sense, there
  was no infringement.
  (b) If the wording of the patent was taken in its broad sense, then it is
  invalid by reason of inutility, insufficiency, unfair basis and false
  suggestion.

3. The approach of an appeal court in such a case Graham J. heard
the case at first instance. In the words of Lord Diplock at 409F–
511H:

> "As patent judge he has unrivalled experience of pharmaceutical
> patents and the way in which the pharmaceutical industry is carried
> on. Lacking in this experience, an appellate court should be hesitant
> to overrule his exercise of his discretion, unless they are satisfied that
> he has gone wrong in law."

4. The relevant factors in the interlocutory application The factors which
Graham J. took into account, the propriety of which the House of Lords
affirmed, were:

(a) *Status quo—defendant not yet started:*

> "The defendants' XLG sutures were not yet on the market, so they
> had no business which would be brought to a stop by the injunction;

no factories would be closed and no work-people would be thrown out of work." (at 409G, 511J.)

(b) *No injunction—irreparable damage to plaintiff:*

"[The defendant] held a dominant position in the United Kingdom market for absorbent sutures and adopted an aggressive sales policy. [The plaintiffs] on the other hand were in the course of establishing a growing market in PHAE surgical sutures which competed with the natural catgut sutures marketed by [the defendants]. If [the defendants] were entitled also to establish themselves in the market for PHAE absorbable surgical sutures until the action is tried, which may not be before two or three years yet, and possibly thereafter until the case is finally disposed of on appeal [the plaintiffs], even though ultimately successful in proving infringement, would have lost its opportunity of continuing to increase its share in the total market in absorbent surgical sutures which the continuation of an uninterrupted monopoly of PHAE sutures would have gained for it by the time of the expiry of the patent in 1980." (at 409G–410A.)

(c) *The peculiar character of pharmaceutical products:*

"It is notorious that new pharmaceutical products used exclusively by doctors or available only on prescription take a long time to become established in the market, that much of the benefit of the monopoly granted by the patent derives from the fact that the patented product is given the opportunity of becoming established and this benefit continues to be reaped after the patent has expired." (at 410A.)

(d) *A foot in the surgical suture door now would have the commercial effect of permanency:*

"Once doctors and patients had got used to [the defendants'] product in the period prior to the trial, it might well be commercially impracticable for [the plaintiff] to deprive the public of it by insisting on a permanent injunction at the trial, owing to the damaging effect which this would have upon its goodwill in this specialised market and thus upon the sale of its other pharmaceutical products." (Pp. 410B, 512C.)

6 *Roussel-Uclaf v. Searle (G. D.) & Co. Ltd* [1978] R.P.C. 747; [1977] F.S.R. 125

1. Background The case concerned two drugs used for treating cardiac diseases and in particular diseases involving the several kinds of arrhythmias for which previously Quinidine was commonly prescribed. The drugs were

781

very similar. Both shared the same active ingredient, mainly disopyramide— so that once in the bloodstream the drugs had the same effect. But as to getting the drugs into the bloodstream, there were dissimilarities:

(a) *Amide based:*
    (i) Insoluble in water.
    (ii) Could not be made into tablets.
    (iii) Could not be made into an injectable product.

(b) *Phosphate salt:*
    (i) Soluble in water.
    (ii) Could be made into tablets.
    (iii) Could be made into an injectable product.

2. Section 63(1) of the Patent Act 1949

"Subject to the provisions of this section, the holder of an exclusive licence under a patent shall have the like right as the patentee to take proceedings in respect of any infringement of the patent committed after the date of the licence, and in awarding damages or granting any other relief in any such proceedings, the court shall take into consideration any loss suffered or likely to be suffered by the exclusive licensee as such or, as the case may be, the profits earned by means of the infringement so far as it constitutes an infringement of the rights of the exclusive licensee as such."

3. The facts The plaintiffs contended that by an agreement with the second defendant dated February 3, 1964, they were granted an exclusive licence under letters patent and had exclusive rights in Britain to sell both the base and the phosphate salt. The first defendant (an English subsidiary of the second defendant) commenced marketing in Britain the phosphate salt (which the plaintiffs had intended to market the following year). It was the case for the defendants that the licence agreement covered only the base, not the phosphate salt.

4. What made the case special? Graham J. explained at 126:

"The case raises in an acute form, I think for the first time, the question as to whether the court ought to prevent the public from receiving the benefit of an admittedly life-saving drug and, if so, in what circumstances."

5. Was there a serious issue to be tried? Yes—were the plaintiffs correct in arguing that the licence agreement was broad enough to cover both the base and phosphate salt, or were the defendants justified in arguing that it was confined to the base?

782

6. Were damages an adequate remedy? Yes—for the following reasons:

(a) *Past estimates:* There were past estimates which, when compared with subsequent facts, proved to have been remarkably accurate. Thus evidence as to the actual and projected sales of the phosphate salt could be relied upon. Graham J., in this context said at 129:

> "The defendants and plaintiffs both kept accurate accounts of all they sell and from such accounts, showing the defendants' actual sales, the graph of projected sales by the plaintiffs, and other undisputed figures, such as the likely total market, a reasonably accurate commercial assessment of the plaintiffs' loss is likely to be easily obtained."

(b) *The "head-start" argument:*

    (i) Case for the plaintiffs (which failed) reported at 129–130:

> "The plaintiffs ... put their case on the difficulty of assessing the future position if the defendants are allowed now to enter the market before they are legally entitled to. They will ... be able to build up a business from an unjustifiably early start, and the creation of the monopolisation position which the plaintiffs could reasonably be expected to establish by the date of the expiry of the patent if they were to remain the only people in the market until then, will be prevented. This would mean that at the expiry of the patent, they would have to contend not only with the competition of the defendants, but also with that of third parties who may enter the market, perhaps importing from countries where no patents exist."

    (ii) Ruling: The percentage of the plaintiffs' sales represented by this drug was 2.2 per cent. The relevant market was only 450,000. The maximum anticipated share for both drugs was only 25 per cent. Graham J. thus considered it doubtful whether it would be worth the while of other drug companies to try to force their way into this small market in which the plaintiffs and defendants were already well established. Thus Graham J. continued at 130:

> "I consider that as a commercial matter damages here should be an adequate remedy, or as Sachs L.J. put it in *Evans Marshall v. Bertola* [1973] 1 W.L.R. 349 the plaintiffs ought here 'to be confined to their remedy in damages.' I use the words 'as a commercial matter,' because I apprehend that the question must be looked at from such a point of view, rather than treated as a matter of precise mathematics, brooking no approximations or allocations."

7. Balance of convenience Even if damages would not have been an adequate remedy for the plaintiffs, Graham J. would have declined an interlocutory injunction. Why?

(a) First: He set the scene with the following words at 131:

"I come to the interesting and, I think, novel point as to whether this court ought ever and, in particular in this case, to exercise its discretion to grant an injunction the effect of which will be, temporarily at any rate, to deprive members of the public of the benefit of a life-saving drug which may be prescribed for otherwise fatal heart diseases."

(b) Secondly: He then narrowed down the issue:

"I think this must be a question for decision in the particular circumstances of each case, though I feel that the onus in such cases must be very heavily on the plaintiffs to show that there is little, if any, likelihood of the public being injured by their inability to obtain the drug in question when necessary."

(c) Thirdly: He went on to demonstrate the position at either end of the scale (at 131–132):
(i) At one end:

"There are often cases where a number of drugs exist alongside each other and are in general all equally efficacious for a particular ailment or disease. If the evidence shows it to be the fact that there may well be cases where it would make little, if any, difference to the public, apart from satisfying personal preference, whether a particular drug was no longer available or not, then in such a case it may well be proper to grant an injunction."

(ii) At the other end:

"there is the unique life-saving drug, where, in my judgment, it is at least very doubtful if the court in its discretion ever ought to grant an injunction and I cannot at present think of any circumstances where it should."

(d) Finally, he explained the particular sensitivity of those suffering from cardiac disease (at 132):

"There are infinite variations between these two limits. The present case is very near to the unique end, because the soluble salt has at present no precise equivalent, the base not having, on the evidence, the same biological activity even though the active disopyramide once in the blood will have the same effect, other things being equal, in both cases. To add to this, there is uncontradicted evidence that heart patients are peculiarly sensitive to and fearful of changes in drugs and their régime.

Giving the matter the best consideration I can, I am not prepared to accept the argument that in the present case the base is a sufficiently good and equivalent alternative to the phosphate salt to justify my granting an injunction even if I were otherwise prepared to do so. It follows that even if I were in the plaintiffs' favour on all points up to the stage of the question of the balance of convenience, I would be against them on this final point and would refuse an injunction in this case."

7 *Polaroid Corporation v. Eastman Kodak Co.* [1977] R.P.C. 379

1. The facts By several patents the plaintiffs protected their 100 per cent world-wide monopoly in the manufacture of instant print cameras and associated films. Upon the defendants announcing their intention to manufacture and sell rival products in Europe, the plaintiffs sought by way of interlocutory injunction *quia timet* to restrain the defendants until trial from launching their product in the United Kingdom.

2. The respective arguments The arguments of each party are cited at 380 and 381 in the R.P.C. report:

(a) *By the plaintiffs:*

   (i) Irreparable damage to goodwill: That the loss of their 100 per cent monopoly in the field of instant photography pending the trial would cause irreparable damage to their goodwill and to the growth and prosperity of their business in the United Kingdom.

   (ii) Vulnerability: That interlocutory relief was needed because the plaintiffs' "integral" system was only just beginning to be profitable.

   (iii) General adverse effects: That competition from the defendants would adversely affect not only the plaintiffs' "integral" business but also their business in the "peelapart" field.

   (iv) Damages—not an adequate remedy: That competition from the defendants would seriously disrupt the plaintiffs' expanding business, occasioning damage which would be difficult to quantify.

   (v) The particular problem of United Kingdom manufacture: That competition abroad from the defendants' products manufactured abroad might be much less damaging than such competition from the defendants' products if manufactured in the United Kingdom.

(b) *By the defendants:*

   (i) Minimal damage: That since the defendants were free to compete

785

with the plaintiffs world-wide and no interlocutory injunction could be obtained in any other country, the only relevant trade in respect of which the plaintiffs could complain of loss was trade in the United Kingdom, and that, this trade being very small, the effect of competition from the defendants in the United Kingdom would be very slight in relation to the plaintiffs' total turnover.

(ii) Ready calculation of loss: That the loss which would be caused to the plaintiffs if an interlocutory injunction were refused would be readily quantifiable by reference to the defendants' sales, and that the plaintiffs had not shown that they would suffer irreparable damage and had therefore failed to demonstrate the need for interlocutory protection.

(iii) Irreparable damage to defendant: That the damage which would be caused to the defendants by the granting of an interlocutory injunction would be very difficult to assess, and would continue beyond the trial by reason of the fact that every sale of the plaintiffs' cameras in the meantime would give rise to a tied outlet for the plaintiffs' film, since the films of the parties were not interchangeable.

(iv) Good faith: That the defendants had been careful to avoid infringement of any valid claim of the plaintiffs' patents, and that it ought not to be incumbent upon the defendants, when seeking to enter a new field, and at the same time to avoid an interlocutory injunction, so to design their products that the plaintiffs had no arguable case of infringement, thereby effectively conceding to the plaintiffs a wider monopoly than that to which they are entitled by virtue of the patents.

The arguments were recited in greater detail in the judgment of Buckley L.J. at 391–393.

3. The real issue The following was accepted by the Court of Appeal:
  (a) On the evidence, interlocutory relief would not be available otherwise than in the United Kingdom.
  (b) At 391(36–40), *per* Buckley L.J.:

"It is accepted that there are serious issues to be tried in the action [and in so holding Buckley L.J. held at 396(10–15) that the issue to be tried was not less serious merely because the defendant declares that it has taken all reasonably necessary steps to ensure that it has avoided infringement]. It is accepted that the trial will not be for about two years at least and it may be considerably more delayed than that. There is no doubt about the financial ability of either the plaintiffs or the defendants to pay any sum which may be awarded in damages in respect of what occurs during the period between the present time and the trial."

Thus the real issue was: Would damages be an adequate remedy?

4. Damages—an adequate remedy for the plaintiffs? Yes—for the following reasons:

  (a) Competition in the world-wide market would readily occur, injunction or no injunction. The competition in the United Kingdom would thus be comparatively minor (at 393(27–30)).

  (b) The reputation of the plaintiffs' product in the United Kingdom as well as elsewhere would depend substantially on how they would compete with the defendants abroad as upon conditions in the United Kingdom. An injunction in the United Kingdom would thus not freeze that reputation (at 393(32–34)).

  (c) The value of the business lost to the plaintiff would be capable of fairly easy quantification—and any damage to goodwill would not defy quantification (at 393(40–43)).

  (d) If the plaintiff won a final injunction, they should quickly recover their command of the United Kingdom market (at 394(1–3)).

  (e) If the injunction were granted the defendants may well have suffered damage which would have been difficult, if not impossible, to quantify (at 395(32–35)).

8 *Corruplast Ltd v. George Harrison (Agencies) Ltd* [1978] R.P.C. 761, C.A.

1. The facts The plaintiffs claimed interlocutory relief by way of injunction in a patent infringement action. The relevant patent had 14 months to run (although there were also two improvement patents with several years to run) and related to extruded plastic cellular board. The proceedings arose through imports of such product effected by the defendants from Austria. There was no dispute as to there being a "serious issue to be tried".

2. Would damages have been an adequate remedy for the plaintiff? No— for the following reasons, given by Buckley L.J.:

(a) *Investment* (at 763(35)):

> "So on the one hand we have a company already engaged in manufacture in the United Kingdom, having invested substantial funds, which has now reached a point, as the judge observed, when the market is turning in their favour for the first time. On the other hand, we have a company who, when the motion came before the court,

787

appeared to have been just launching upon trade in the United Kingdom in the allegedly infringing product; they do not manufacture it themselves."

(b) *Crucial stage of development—the "bridgehead" point* (at 764(20–25)):

"If the plaintiffs are right about infringements, they are entitled to be protected by their patents against competition by the defendants until those patents expire. They are struggling to establish a new market and to establish themselves in that market; they are, or they appear to be, at a crucial stage of that development, and if the defendants are allowed to compete with the plaintiffs, not only will the plaintiffs' present efforts be hindered, but also at the expiry of their patents, when other competitors may come on the market as well as the defendants, they will find that instead of being the only known and established suppliers in this country, they will have to compete with the defendants, who may then have built a significant bridgehead in the market, giving them an advantage over other suppliers, and the plaintiff company will find itself confronted by stronger competition than would otherwise be the case."

(c) *Size of market* (at 764(30–40)):

"The learned judge seems to have considered that because there is a good and expanding market which could not be fully supplied by the plaintiffs' own present production, the defendants' competition would not much harm the plaintiffs. With respect to him, I cannot agree with this. The existence of the market is the very circumstance which will help the plaintiffs to strengthen their position and perhaps to expand their production, and at any rate they will be able to take advantage of any business in that market which they consider to be of value to them, by importing what they cannot themselves make from foreign sources of supply. If they are deprived of this opportunity it would, as it seems to me, be well-nigh impossible to assess the continuing damage which they may suffer by loss of competition strength when the patents expire."

(d) *Impossibility of quantification* (at 764(45)–765(5)):

"But I think it would be much easier to arrive at a measure of that damage than it would be to arrive at a measure of the continuing damage which would be suffered by the plaintiff company in the way I have described; and moreover, that damage, so far as it relates to the possible loss of business after the expiry of the patents would seem, arguably at least, to be damage which could not be recovered under the heading of infringement, so that the plaintiff company might be without relief in that respect."

3. Would damages be an adequate remedy for the defendants? Yes—*per* Buckley L.J.:

(a) *Investment* (at 763(25)):

> "The defendants, on the other hand, do not manufacture the allegedly infringing product. They buy it, as I have said, from an Austrian manufacturer and put it on the market in this country, presumably with comparatively little capital expenditure; we have no information about that."

(b) *Capacity of plaintiff to pay* (at 763(25–30)):

> "There is no question in this case of the financial inadequacy of either side to meet any liability in damages. Although the plaintiff company is a relatively small company and is concerned only with one form of activity, it is a wholly owned subsidiary of Ruberiod Ltd., which is a very substantial concern and backs the plaintiff company in this action."

(c) *Ease of calculation of loss* (at 764(40–45)):

> "... all that an injunction will occasion for the defendants is a delay for a time in embarking upon their infant new business in a market where it would seem that they have not had to make any substantial capital investment. It is quite true that it may not be easy to estimate the amount of business which the defendant company would have obtained but for an injunction if it is granted, if they succeed at the trial of the action."

4. Balance of convenience In favour of injunction, Buckley L.J. said at 765(10–15):

> "It is true, as submitted by Mr Walton, that if the defendant company is restrained from now pursuing their infant business, they may to some extent lose opportunities of building up contacts and building up goodwill in a market where at present they and the plaintiff company are the only competitors. That, as it seems to me, as was submitted by Mr Everington, would be a circumstance of a kind which would be common in very many infringement cases where an injunction is sought, and it cannot be any kind of complete barrier to the granting of an injunction. In every case of this kind the function of the court must, I think, be to consider which course, either the granting or withholding of an injunction, is the one which is likely to make it most easy for the trial court, when the issues in the action have been decided, to adjust the rights of the parties and do justice to them; and in the present case it seems to me that the balance of

789

convenience is substantially in favour of granting an injunction."

Goff L.J. said at 766(35):

> "So that on that evidence, whilst it is clear that the plaintiffs hope
> that they will be able to maintain a monopoly until the end of their
> improvement patents, and indeed they may be able to do so, that
> remains to be seen they certainly rely upon the effect which will be
> produced during the residue of the life of this patent. Thus it seems
> to me that during that time, on the balance of convenience, it would
> not be right that the defendants should be allowed to build up a
> business which they are only just starting, and create a bridgehead to
> enable them, when the one patent expires, to start off from a position
> of an established business, instead of starting off as a new competitor
> just coming into the market."

9 *Netlon v. Bridport-Grundy Ltd* [1979] F.S.R. 530, C.A.

1. The facts The plaintiffs were the patentees and the sole manufacturers
in the English market of a particular type of extruded plastic netting,
invented by an Italian licensee company. When the licence was determined,
some of the "moving lights" among the Italian licensees formed a new
concern (RDB), which continued manufacturing in Italy by the use of the
patented process—such manufacturing being prima facie an infringement
of the plaintiffs' equivalent Italian patent. The defendants sought to enter
the English market and compete with the plaintiffs. In so doing, they
admitted that initially they would have to use some of the netting supplied
by RDB and made by use of the patented process. They disputed infringement, however, by (a) challenging the validity of the patent, and (b) claiming
to have a number of defences under European Economic Community law.
At the hearing, the defence (for the purposes of the motion) limited its
case to the following argument (at 533):

> "... there is an express or implied concerted practice between [the
> plaintiffs] and their licensees which is an infringement of Article 85
> of the Treaty of Rome."

2. The plaintiffs' case on this line of defence The plaintiffs denied any
such practice and argued:
  (a) Modification: Although the licenses were originally exclusive, they
      had been modified (to render them non-exclusive) thereby to secure
      the freedom of trade required by Article 85.
  (b) "Confess and avoid" in the alternative: Even if there were a concerted
      practice, it was not contrary to Article 85 by virtue of the terms of
      clause 3.

"The provisions of paragraph 1 may, however, be declared inapplicable in the case if: Any agreement or category of agreements ... which contributes to improving the production or distribution of goods or to promoting technical or economic progress, while allowing customers a fair share of the resulting benefit and which does not: (a) impose on the undertakings concerned restrictions which are not indispensable to the attainment of these objects; (b) afford such undertakings the possibility of eliminating competition in respect of a substantial part of the products in question."

3. Was there a serious issue to be tried? Yes—at 533:

"... it is impossible to resolve the question whether that Article affords any defence on this motion. It would be necessary to embark upon that mini-trial which the *Cyanamid* case points out is not to be adopted. ..."

4. Would damages have been an adequate remedy for the plaintiffs? No:

(a) *The head-start factor:* Goff L.J. said at 537:

"The respondents say that any damage that the appellants would suffer by not obtaining an injunction, if they ultimately prove right at the trial, is capable of being calculated with reasonable certainty and so damages are an adequate remedy. They say that the amount of the respondents' sales will be known, so also will those of Netlon in previous years, so that the measure of the diminution of business as the result of their activities can be ascertained and the damages quantified by calculation on a royalty basis. For my part, I am unable to accept this argument. The first year would be a building-up one so that one would have to look at least to the second, but then, I think, it would be impossible to distinguish sales due to the early start with the assistance of the patented material and sales which the respondents would have made anyway. The truth, in my judgment, is that it is quite impossible to calculate the adverse effect upon the appellants of their having to face competition a year earlier than they would have to do if the respondents had to wait for supplies of unquestionably unoffending material."

(b) *The investment factor:* Goff L.J. said at 537–538:

"The appellants also rely on the fact that they are embarked upon a research programme involving an expenditure of 3.6 million pounds in respect of which they have a Government loan covering about one half, and they rely on their profits to finance the loan and to provide the balance. The respondents say that is nonsense. The royalty basis they submit on which the appellants work is quite small and cannot be adequate for such a purpose and in any case the appellants being a seven million pound company they would have no difficulty in borrowing the balance. The appellants counter that by saying that the argument ignores their manufacturing profits and in any event they would of course have to finance any further loans.

The respondents say that the figures which the appellants have given in evidence must be exaggerated because they would have known by February of last year that competition was likely to be encountered and they would not have embarked on such a programme if the envisaged competition was likely to wreck it, but as they are not foolhardy, their figures must be wrong. But the appellants say that that is a fallacious argument because, though they knew there would be competition, they would be protected by their monopoly of the square cut mesh and they rely upon the insistence by the respondents on the necessity of having such mesh to enable them to launch their own campaign this year.

As at present advised, I think the appellants may have exaggerated the prospective injury to their research programme, but even so, I think, that injury might be very real and I cannot, at all events, for the purposes of a motion, accept the respondents' further argument that insomuch as licensees are free, as it is submitted, if for no other reason by virtue of the Treaty of Rome, to compete here, the appellants' damages must be measured not by their manufacturing profits or profits on sales, but by the very much lower standard of royalties. In my judgment therefore, damages would not be an adequate remedy for the appellants."

5. Would damages have been an adequate remedy for the defendants? No—at 538:

"Conversely, the appellants say that damages are an adequate remedy for the respondents. They concede that they cannot get a true picture in the first year, but they submit within a year or two one could get a reasonably accurate picture of the share of the market they have been able to capture and so be able fairly to evaluate the loss of the first year. I cannot accept that either, for in my view, it is impossible to see what the respondents may suffer in their attempts to break into the market by having to wait a year and so give other competitors an opportunity to come in on even terms.

Mr Jeffs argued that one must consider only what is known now and the possibility of others coming in is but speculation. In my view, however, it is of the essence in delaying one's start that one should thereby lose an advantage over other potential customers, and the respondents, who have gone ahead in making their start, are entitled to rely on that as a head of damage if they be improperly restrained.

There is, however, in my judgment another head of incalculable damage which the respondents will suffer, which is general injury to their goodwill. The appellants have offered to limit the injunction they seek by a proviso allowing the respondents to use the patented square mesh to fulfil all orders placed not only down to 1 November when the warning letter was written, but thereafter down to the service of the writ. So, they say, the respondents would not be exposed to the risk of having to break contracts made before they had knowledge of the appellants' objections. This, however, cannot in any case go far enough because the respondents have advertised their intentions to the trade, orders will be coming in, and it may be very damaging to them if they cannot meet them."

Thus Goff L.J. went on to consider the "balance of convenience," having ventilated the following view at 538–539:

"The question of adequacy of damages still has to be borne in mind from a somewhat different angle. If it be much more difficult to arrive at an assessment with reasonable accuracy in the case of one party than that of the other, or possibly the damage suffered by one be much greater than that suffered by the other, that will be a balancing act to be considered with any others there may be. Mr Jacob, indeed, argued at length that such is the position in this case. He said it will be much more difficult to assess the damage suffered by the respondents than that of the appellants, and indeed I think he also argued that the respondents' damage would be greater. In my judgment, I do not think there are any differences in this respect sufficient to sway the balance of convenience."

6. Balance in favour of plaintiffs Goff L.J. held that the balance of convenience weighed in favour of an injunction because in the evidence: (543 *et seq.*):

(a) The defendants "walked into this" with their eyes open and took a calculated risk.

(b) It was conceded that the offending material was made pursuant to the patented process. Thus, unless the Treaty of Rome defence applied, there was an infringement.

(c) The plaintiffs were manufacturers with plant and machinery, and this type of trading was their entire business. In contrast, the defendants were importers, this was a new venture and constituted a comparatively small part of their business.

(d) Status quo. Goff L.J. said at 544:

793

"Finally, as Lord Diplock said in the *Cyanamid* case at 408: 'Where other factors appear to be evenly balanced it is a counsel of prudence to take such measures as are calculated to preserve the status quo.' That seems to me, if I am wrong in thinking that the scales are already in favour of the appellants on a balance of convenience sufficient clearly to bring the scales down on that side. Further, although this may be merely another way of stating the status quo argument, I think that there is further weight in support of the appellant's case in that the respondents are seeking to use the patented material as a spring-board to give them an advantage which they cannot, in my view of Mr Budden's evidence, secure if they wait for material which cannot give rise to any complaint. Nor does it seem to me that the undertakings offered by the respondents afford any reason why an injunction which in my view ought to be granted to the appellants, should be refused."

10 E.A.R. *Corporation v. Protector Safety Products (U.K.) Ltd* [1980] F.S.R. 574, *per* Graham J.

1. Background Graham J. explained at 575–576:

"... related to earplugs which are of particular value, as I understand it, nowadays in factories and other places where there is much noise. Recently considerable emphasis has been placed on the necessity to reduce noise in order to prevent damage not only to ears but also to health. As is known, there has recently been passed a Health and Safety Act and there has been set up a Health and Safety Executive which is very active now in these matters.

The result of course is that a really effective earplug which does have the effect of reducing noise is considered a valuable article. Obviously from the figures which are before me it has been a commercial success and is being sold in larger and larger quantities."

2. The facts The patent in suit was an earplug of polymenic foam which expanded slowly from compression to fit the ear. The defendant imported an earplug of different plastic but with the claimed physical characteristics. In this regard, Graham J. said at 576:

"It will be seen that the claim covers any plug which has those physical characteristics and it can be made of any plastic which enables those characteristics with suitable manufacturing processes to be obtained. The claim, therefore, is a wide claim and in fact here, as I understand it, the defendants' articles which they sell, at any rate some of them, fall within the words of that claim because they have

There was also discussion as to the extent of previous use by the defendants of the initials CVS. In this regard reference was made to *Hammond & Champness Ltd v. H.A.C. Lifts Ltd* [1975] F.S.R. 131, where Templeman J. took the view that previous use by the defendants of certain initials of their name did not preclude the granting of an interlocutory injunction for a combination of two reasons. First, on the evidence the previous use was no more than peripheral and *de minimus*; and, secondly, because what the defendants had gone on to do was not a mere continuance or expansion of the business relating to a former use, but a new step.

3. Was there a serious issue to be tried? Yes—Dillon J. said at p. 3:

"It seems to me that, although there is undoubtedly for the purposes of this doctrine enunciated in *American Cyanamid v. Ethicon* [1975] A.C. 396 an arguable case, it is by no means crystal clear that the plaintiffs are going to establish the reputation on which they must rely at the trial of the action. It is not all that easy to acquire a monopoly reputation in a group of letters."

4. Balance of convenience—against an injunction Dillon J. took into account the following factors:
  (a) Drastic nature of relief sought (complete change of defendants' trading title).
  (b) The need for the plaintiffs to establish their monopoly reputation in the letters "CVS."
  (c) The defence of honest concurrent trading.
  (d) The question whether what was done was no different from what had been legitimately done before.
  (e) Delay.

19 *I.P.C. Magazines Ltd v. Black and White Music Corporation* [1983] F.S.R. 348, *per* Goulding J.

1. The facts The plaintiffs published a weekly science-fiction magazine with a feature cartoon character called "Judge Dredd." The plaintiffs also supplied a weekly cartoon to a daily newspaper and published an annual "Judge Dredd" book. The first and second defendants produced and published without the plaintiffs' permission a "Judge Dredd" record. The plaintiffs sought an interlocutory injunction to restrain the defendant from dealing in the "Judge Dredd" record or any other records including any song so entitled or otherwise featuring the character known as "Judge Dredd."

731

2. The issue Goulding J. explained at 350:

"It is common ground that if the plaintiff has any legal reasons for complaint it can only be asserted in the form of an action for passing off the defendants' products as the plaintiff's. There is no infringement of copyright alleged and there is no question of a registered trade mark being infringed; it is passing off or nothing. The whole business of 'character merchandising' as it is called, where use is made of the reputation of a well-known fictitious character like Mickey Mouse or Superman to give a name to, and add tot he popularity of, goods not otherwise connected with that character, is one, if not wholly of recent origin, at least of considerable recent commercial development; and the application of the familiar principles of a passing off action to such transactions is still far from settled."

In that context, the authorities invoked were:

(a) *By the plaintiff:*
   (i) *Lego System v. Lego M. Lemelstrich Ltd* [1983] F.S.R. 155 (where the manufacturers of the toy "Lego" were held entitled to restrain the use of that name in connection with garden irrigation equipment).
   (ii) *News Group Newspapers Ltd v. Rocket Record Company* [1981] F.S.R. 89 (The *Page Three* case—see p. 716).

(b) *By the defendant:*
   (i) *Lyngstad v. Anabas* [1977] F.S.R. 62 where the pop-group Abba failed in its application for interlocutory relief against the defendants who were using their name and likenesses in connection with goods wholly unrelated to their musical performance, such as T-shirts and key-rings.
   (ii) *Wombles Ltd v. Wombles Skips Ltd* [1977] R.P.C. 99, where publishers and copyright owners failed in their application for interlocutory relief to prevent the use of the name "Wombles" in the manufacture of builders' skips. The *ratio decidendi* was that in order to establish passing off it was necessary for there to be a common field of activity and in this case, there was no such common field. This case should be contrasted with *Harrods Ltd v. Harrod (R.) Ltd* [1924] R.P.C. 74 and *Dunlop Pneumatic Tyre Co. Ltd, The v. Dunlop Lubricant Co., The* (1889) 16 R.P.C. 12. As Russell L.J. said in *Annabel's (Berkeley Square) Ltd v. Schock (G.) (t/a Annabel's Escort Agency)* [1972] R.P.C. 838 at 844:

"In this question of confusion, of course, as a matter of common sense, one of the important considerations is whether there is any kind of association ... between the field of activities of the plaintiff and the field of activities of the defendant—as it is sometimes put: Is there an overlap in the fields of activity? But, of course, when one gets down to brass tacks, this is simply a question which is involved in the ultimate decision whether there is likely to be confusion. If there is no overlapping ... then of course it is in the highest degree relevant in considering whether there is a case for an injunction based on the likelihood of confusion."

(iii) *Tavener Rutledge Ltd v. Trexapalm Ltd* [1977] R.P.C. 275, where the plaintiffs—who had rights with regard to the television presentation of "Kojak"—sought unsuccessfully to claim a propriety right against the manufacturer of sweets who called their lollipops "Kojak pops."

3. Was that issue "serious"? Yes—Goulding J. said at 351:

"Those cases and others were decided on particular evidence, most of them at an interlocutory stage, and I think it is undesirable, as happily I think it is unnecessary for me to make any observations on the law today. It should be done, I think, at trial when the facts of the present case will be fully ascertained by *viva voce* evidence before the court."

4. Damages—an adequate remedy for the plaintiff? Yes—because:

(a) *No real risk of damage to reputation:*

"It can do the plaintiff no harm to have thought that it has licensed a record by Loose Talk. Loose Talk are not yet a famous group, but nothing has been said against them except their lack of experience and perhaps limited skill ... musically it seems to me that the record is no worse, if anything, slightly above average, in comparison with compositions of a similar class that weekly come into the charts." (at 352–353.)

(b) *No real risk of encouragement:*

"[It would be 'somewhat fanciful' to argue that the conduct of the defendants would] be an encouragement to other entrepreneurs to appropriate the names of Judge Dredd or of other characters in the plaintiff's magazines without coming to any agreement with the plaintiff or paying money. ... Judge Dredd has been in the magazine for several years now. The merchandising arrangements made by the plaintiff are not very extensive and they cannot be more than trivial in relation to the whole scale of the plaintiff's business. I find it fanciful to think that over the period from now to the trial any substantial damage will be done to the plaintiff in that way either. ..."

733

(c) *Royalty basis of assessing compensation:* At 354:

> "Accordingly, having considered the whole matter, I think that if on a favourable view of the law and on a consideration of live evidence at the trial the plaintiff succeeds, almost certainly it will be adequately compensated by damages worked out as the equivalent of a reasonable royalty in accordance with prevailing rates. I gather the defendants are willing to undertake to keep full accounts of the production and sale of the record, and can provide, since their company is of apparently no financial substance, some security for the payment of possible damages in a form acceptable to the plaintiff, or if agreement cannot be reached, to the court. Subject to those safeguards I would refuse any interlocutory injunction."

20 *Elan Digital Systems Ltd v. Elan Computers Ltd* [1984] F.S.R. 373

1. The facts The plaintiffs manufactured Eprom programs and sold them under the name Elan. The defendants prepared to launch a home computer under the name Elan Enterprise.

2. Case for the defendant The respective markets of the parties were so different that no confusion could result from the use of the name Elan.

3. Was there a serious issue to be tried? Vivian Price Q.C. at first instance held at 380–381:

> "I do not think that it can be said that the plaintiff does not have a triable case. I do not think that it can be said that the business of manufacturing and dealing in Eproms is so completely divorced from the business of manufacturing and dealing in home computers that no confusion could arise when both businesses operate under the same name Elan. I do not think that it can be said that the goodwill of the first business could not be damaged by the activities of the second business. These are all matters which should go to trial. In my judgment, therefore, the plaintiff has overcome the first hurdle in the way of this application."

And on appeal, Browne-Wilkinson L.J. said at 386:

> "Secondly, Mr Silverleaf's argument, as I understood it, was that the judge was not entitled to come to the conclusion that there was an arguable case that the plaintiffs had any goodwill capable of being protected in the field which the defendants were about to enter with

their new home computers. That seems to me to involve a consideration of factual matters which are outside what this court should be invited to do. There was here, as my Lord has said, plainly an arguable question as to whether or not the plaintiffs' existing field of business was or was not wholly separate from that group of customers which the defendants are proposing to sell to. That is a question of fact, that the judge has held it to be an arguable question, and in my judgment he was fully entitled to do so on the material before him."

21 *Rizla Ltd v. Bryant & May Ltd* [1986] R.P.C. 389

1. The facts The plaintiff had (to all intents and purposes) a monopoly in cigarette papers, which they marketed as follows:
  (a) Blue: Fine weight;
  (b) Green: Medium weight—adapted for a mechanical rolling machine;
  (c) Red: Medium weight.
The packages containing these papers were marked under the name "Rizla", together with a cross and (strangely) were intended to be kept under the counter, rather than displayed over the counter. And so it was that over the years customers became accustomed to asking for packets of "reds" or "blues" or "greens". The defendants sought to challenge such monopoly by marketing three separate (and slightly different) coloured sets of cigarette papers, the packages being marked with the words "Swan," such manufacture expressly being for display over the counter.

2. What did the plaintiff seek? Alleging passing off, the plaintiff moved for an order restraining the defendant:

> "From advertising, offering for sale, inviting offers to acquire, selling or supplying cigarette papers in packaging which is the same as the packaging of the cigarette papers which forms exhibit H.G. 9 to the affidavit of Hadrian Gower to be sworn herein, or any colourable imitation thereof."

The motion was prompted by fear of "passing off by substitution"—as Walton J. explained at 391(3–8):

> "What is suggested is that those who order red, green and blue, are so careless as to what they are given and are so careless as to the manner in which they will cheerfully acquire a couple of packets of cigarette papers perhaps with the evening paper and a packet of sweets for the kids, that they will not notice if in fact they are given a Bryant & May packet of papers instead of the plaintiff's papers."

Moreover, what apparently also concerned the plaintiff was the prospect

735

of retailers offering Swan rather than Rizla to customers asking for (*e.g.*) "red", such retailer attracted by the discount which Swan were proposing. But as Walton J. said at 391:

> "It seems to me that that is not something, if it happens, for which the defendant ought to be held responsible."

3. Walton J. applies *Cyanamid*—**subject to the passing off "special factor"** At 391(20–25):

> "This, of course, is only an interlocutory motion and therefore I have to make up my mind to some extent upon the familiar *Cyanamid* principles. But it seems to be, and there are many cases to this effect, that in actions of this nature, especially if the plaintiff is the successful party, that puts an end to the action. Therefore it is not sufficient to say that there is a serious case to be tried. One must go somewhat further and take a view as to the plaintiffs' success at the trial, bearing in mind that of its nature there can be no real evidence as to confusion because the plaintiffs have commendably commenced their action in time before the defendants have got their product on the market."

4. The relevant law Walton J. prayed in aid paragraph 175 from Volume 48 of Halsbury's *Laws of England*—which provides:

> "A trader is not permitted to use any mark, device or other means whereby, although he does not make a false representation to a direct purchaser of his goods, he enables such a purchaser to make a false representation to ultimate purchasers of those goods. Where goods are sold to trade customers who are not themselves deceived but the goods are so marked or got up as to be calculated to deceive ultimate purchasers, the plaintiff's cause of action for passing off is regarded as complete, both at law and in equity, as soon as the goods are disposed of to the trade customer.
>
> It is not enough that the goods are merely capable of being used by dealers to perpetrate frauds on their customers; the goods, or leaflets or other material supplied with them, must be intended or must be of such a nature as to suggest, or readily or easily lend themselves to, such passing off, as otherwise the consequence is too remote to be attributed to the supplier of the goods."

5. Was there a serious issue to be tried? No—

(a) *No confusion:* At 392(35–40) Walton J. said:

> "If in fact the goods are sold as, on their face, they are intended by Bryant and May to be sold, that can be no conceivable ground upon

which any purchaser of the Swan Cigarette papers who intended to buy the Rizla Cigarette papers can be deceived. That is, I think, a completely unique feature of the present case."

(b) *Self help:* At 392(40–45) Walton J. went on to say:

"But the present case has another equally unique feature which I cannot imagine has been the subject matter of any case of this nature before. That is this: That if there is any such danger as the plaintiffs apprehend, the remedy is entirely in their own hands. At the moment they supply their cigarette papers in boxes which, whilst adequate for the purposes for storing the booklets, are not adapted in any way so far as one can see for easy display on a counter. Rizla have only to package their goods in the same kind of way—I am not inviting them to copy—as the Bryant & May cigarette papers are packaged so that both of them will be available on the counter together for there to be not the slightest possibility that anybody, even the most besotted smoker, will be deceived for a single second."

In summary, Walton J. said at 393(9–10):

"That the plaintiffs have no monopoly of any description in that and therefore it seems to me that they have no real cause of complaint there."

6. Damages—in any event, an adequate remedy for the plaintiff? Yes— held Walton J., on the basis that such loss could readily be calculated in the sum of about £81,000, by reference to the 2.7 million users of cigarette papers.

7. Damages—an adequate remedy for the defendant? No—for if the defendants were enjoined:
  (a) they would have to revamp completely their colour-coding; and
  (b) by reason of such revamping, they would be conceding an effective monopoly to the plaintiff.

22 *Harrods Ltd v. Schwartz-Sackin & Co. Ltd* [1986] F.S.R. 490

1. The facts For 15 years the defendant operated the fine art department on the third floor of the plaintiff's premises. The relationship between the parties was regulated by contract, by Clause 2(b) of which the defendant agreed:

"Not to advertise or to indicate its association with Harrods or to use Harrods' name directly or by inference in its advertising without obtaining Harrods' prior permission to do so."

737

The plaintiff's managing director deposed to the purpose of such provision, in the following paragraphs of his affidavit:

(a) *Paragraph 5:*

> "It is fundamental to the relationship between the concessionaires and Harrods, that Harrods should retain ultimate control of their activities, and that the concessions should remain firmly part of Harrods. Were this not so, Harrods would degenerate into a mere Bazaar consisting of numerous traders operating independently under one roof. So far as the customer is concerned, therefore, all his dealings are with Harrods. All payments are made by customers to Harrods, the concessionaire's staff wear Harrods' badges, and invoices etc. are issued on Harrods stationery. Harrods remain responsible for customer complaints, and we retain the right to veto the sale of any goods which we consider unsuitable."

(b) *Paragraph 6:*

> "It is also fundamental to the relationship that it is aimed at increasing trade within Harrods' store. Obviously, by selling another's goods, Harrods are conferring on those goods some of the prestige which is associated with Harrods. By making a special feature of those goods, Harrods confer considerable prestige upon them. If the seller of those goods were to make use of this prestige to sell goods *outside* Harrods, Harrods would get no benefit from the relationship."

After the cessation of the concession, the defendant opened new premises, which he advertised *inter alia* by reference to his previous association with the plaintiff.

2. The issues

    (a) Clause 2(p)—did it lapse on termination of the contract?
    (b) Clause 2(p) Was it an unreasonable restraint of trade?
    (c) Infringement of trade mark?
    (d) Passing off?
    (e) Unfair competition?

3. First issue—did clause 2(p) lapse?

(a) *Defendant's case:*

    (i) Clause 2(p) did not survive the termination of the contract—had the plaintiff wanted an indefinite period, it should have contracted for it. In contrast, in the "binding out" provision (clause 2(x), the plaintiff had stipulated two years); and if there was any doubt, the contra-preferentem rule should militate against the plaintiff's interpretation.

738

(ii) As a matter of law, the termination of the contract brought to an end its provisions—unless there were some special provision to the contrary.

(b) *Plaintiff's case:*
   (i) The defendant's argument could be turned on its head—the defendant was seeking to imply into clause 2(p) the words: "During the term of this agreement."
   (ii) There were other clauses in the agreement which manifestly, by their nature, had survived the termination of the period of the agreement but in which no express reference to that fact was made;
   (iii) the significance of clause 2(p)—to protect Harrods—would be of equal significance after the termination of the contract, as before.

(c) *Judgment: at 498, Warner J. said:*

"So, on balance, it seems to me that Mr Burton has made good his claim to be entitled to enforce clause 2(p), but, if that is wrong, he has certainly made out that there is a triable issue as to that. It must be a triable issue because, to a substantial extent, the construction of the contract depends upon the circumstances surrounding its conclusion, or, as it is now fashionable to say, its 'matrix of fact.'"

4. Second issue—unreasonable restraint of trade

(a) *Defendant's case:*
   (i) Clause 2(p) "restricts the way in which the defendant can advertise, and ... that amounts to a restriction of restraint on trade, having regard to the importance of advertising in the modern world and particularly in the world of antique dealers." (at 498.)
   (ii) By reference to the case of *Hepworth Manufacturing Company Ltd v. Ryott* (1920) 1 Ch. 1, the defendant's reputation had been built up in the fine art department of Harrods and it could not be deprived of it (the defendant also referred to *Petrofina (Gt. Britain) Ltd v. Martin* (1966) Ch. 146).
   (iii) If clause 2(p) were perpetual, it must be unreasonable.

(b) *Plaintiff's case:*
   (i) A restraint on advertising was not a restraint of trade.
   (ii) Clause 2(p) was not unreasonable in all the circumstances—see paragraph 5 and 6 of the managing director's affidavit.

(c) *Judgment:* At the very least, there was a triable issue.

739

5. Third issue: infringement of trade mark

(a) *Case for the plaintiff.* Section 4(1)(b) of the Trade Marks Act 1938 provides:

"... the registration ... in respect of any goods shall, if valid, give or be deemed to have given to that person the exclusive right to the use of the trade mark in relation to those goods and, without prejudice to the generality of the foregoing words, that right shall be deemed to have been infringed by any person who, not being the proprietor of the trade mark ..., uses a mark identical with it or so nearly resembling it as to be likely to deceive or cause confusion, in the course of trade, in relation to any goods in respect of which it is registered, and in such manner as to render the use of the mark likely to be taken. ..." "In a case in which the use is use upon the goods or in a physical relation thereto or in an advertising circular or other advertisement issue to the public, as importing a reference to some person having the right as proprietor ... to use the trade mark...."

(b) *Defendants case:*

  (i) First point:

"The use of the word 'Harrods' otherwise than in the familiar modern script (which was registered) or that in an earlier Victorian form, as amended in 1920 or thereabouts (which is also registered), whilst it might be passing off, could not be an infringement of any trade mark, because the mere word 'Harrods' was not registered as a trade mark." (at 495.)

  (ii) Second point:

"... the user proposed by the defendant of the word 'Harrods' was not a user in relation to any goods: It was user in relation to a business. Mr Thompson submitted that there was here the same sort of distinction which one has between passing off as a business and passing off goods." (at 495.)

  (iii) Third point:

"... as was established ... in particular by the decision of the Court of Appeal in *Bismag Ltd v. Amblins (Chemists) Ltd* (1940) 57 R.P.C. 209, use of a mark does not come within section 4(1)(b) of the Act, unless it is in use in what Lord Greene M.R. called 'a trade mark sense'."

Here, said Mr Thompson, the use was not in a trade mark sense, because the use of the word "Harrods" proposed by the Defendant was used to describe Harrods' store, not any of the goods in it. He relied on *Pompadour Laboratories Ltd v. Stanley Frazer* [1966] R.P.C. 7.

(c) *Plaintiff's case:*
   (i) First point: there was a triable issue as to whether the use proposed would be "a mark so nearly resembling the registered mark as to be likely to cause confusion."
   (ii) Second point: plaintiff's case—not reported.
   (iii) Third point: "Mr Burton contrasted that [the *Pompadour* case] with the case of *News Group Newspapers Ltd v. The Rocket Record Co. Ltd* [1981] F.S.R. 89." For the facts of the *News Group* case, see p. 716.

(d) *Judgment:*
   (i) First point: triable issue.
   (ii) Second point: "Mr Thompson submitted that for there to be infringement of the trade mark, as distinct from passing off, the use of the mark had to relate to specific goods. It seems to me that that must be right." (at 495).
   (iii) Third point: as to the *News Group* case

   "there the mark 'Page 3' was used on the records on themselves and on the sleeves, and it was arguably used in a trade mark sense so far as one of the records was concerned, the single. It was a case of 'use upon the goods' not of use for advertising. There is no point in speculating as to what Slade J. might have said if he had had before him an advertisement which in some way referred to 'page 3.' Here, I think that Mr Thompson is right in saying that, just as in the Pompadour case, the use of the mark was to identify the plaintiff company, so here the use of the mark is to identify Harrods' store, not any particular goods in it." (at 496.)

In summary, Warner J. said at 495:

   "As to the claim based on the trade marks, despite Mr Burton's very attractive argument, I do not think it is a cock that can fight."

6. Fourth issue—passing off
   (a) The problem. The defendant had sent to customers, letters advertising its previous association with Harrods—the phraseology differing between various batches of such letters.
   (b) Warner J. at 495 said:

   "As to passing off, it may be that some of the formulae suggested in correspondence, particularly that suggested in the letter of the 12th March 1985, would not be close enough to the truth to prevent the defendant from being guilty of passing off. But we now have in evidence the defendant's letters to customers of 17th July and 25th September 1985 and I cannot see that there is any untruth in either of these."

(c) The significance of the defendant's undertaking: Warner J. went on to say:

"I also now have Mr Thompson's assurance, on behalf of the defendant, that it does not intend to say anything more than that it did operate that department during that period. The defendant does not propose to say that it operated 'as' that defendant, which is a formula that Mr Burton particularly objects to, nor as I understand it, does it propose to describe itself as 'formerly known as Harrods Fine Art Department' or to say that it was for 15 years the fine art department of Harrods. In those circumstances, I hardly think I would be justified in granting an injunction to restrain the defendant from using formulae that it had not in fact used and now says that it does not propose to use."

7. Fifth issue—unfair competition

(a) *Case for the plaintiff*

"Mr Burton relied upon what was said by the Privy Council in *Cadbury Schweppes Pty v. Pub Squash Company Pty* [1981] 1 W.L.R. 193 at 200–201 about the decision of the Supreme Court of the United States in *International News Services v. Associated Press* (1918) 248 U.S. 215. In reliance on that Mr Burton suggests that there may be in English law a tort of unfair competition which could be committed if one trader misappropriated the goodwill of another, even though he did not utter any falsehood." (at 494.)

(b) Judgment: *Warner J. said at 494:*

"... I should have thought that the way in which Lord Scarman expressed the opinion of the Privy Council in the *Cadbury-Schweppes* case would have been enough to discourage most judges of this Court from holding that there was any such tort as Mr Burton suggests, but the matter is to my mind put beyond doubt by two authorities. One is *Hookham v. Pottage* (1872) L.R. 8 Ch.App. 91, where, clearly, both Vice-Chancellor Mallins and Lords Justices of Appeal took the view that the defendant there was entitled to say that he was a former partner of the plaintiff, provided that he did so in a way that could not be misleading. That was echoed by Plowman J. in *Pompadour Laboratories Ltd v. Stanley Frazer* [1966] R.P.C. 7 (at 10). ... So, in my judgment, so far as the English law of tort is concerned, the defendant, provided it states nothing but the truth, is entitled to say that it operated the fine art department of Harrods during the period when it did so."

8. Balance of convenience The defendant *inter alia* prayed in aid the "delay" argument. Without prejudice to that, the defendant also made the point that 30 letters to shippers and agents, and one for one letters to customers all over the world had already been despatched—and that "the cat is out of the bag, and there is no point in trying to close the bag now by means of an injunction." (at 489). Warner J. was unimpressed with that argument on the basis that:
  (a) Such dissemination did not mean that further dissemination would not harm Harrods.
  (b) Advertisements in magazines or newspapers might reach people whom the present information had not yet reached.
The damage to Harrods which Warner J. identified had two limb, namely:
  (a) It might impair the trade which Harrods continued to operate, in the "Fine Art" field, and
  (b) The fear which Harrods had, which generated clause 2(p)—namely that it would be "looked upon as a Bazaar."
Warner J. substantiated this approach to the case by referring to the submission of defence counsel in another part of his argument, namely that:

"If further disclosures were restrained, the damage to the defendant would be unquantifiable, and would be heavy."

Warner J. hoist the defendant by this petard—in the following terms:

"That shows that there is something material to restrain."

23 *C.P.C. (United Kingdom) Ltd v. Keenan* [1986] F.S.R. 527

1. The facts The defendant produced "Oxbridge" marmalade. The second plaintiff was the registered user of "Oxford" marmalade and sought interlocutory relief alleging infringement of the trademark and passing off. The salient features of the case were:
  (a) Products sold under the Frank Cooper "Oxford" brand name were made from a bitter Seville orange having a distinctive taste, and was sold not just in the United Kingdom, but also abroad.
  (b) In 1985, £200,000 had been spent in advertising—particularly emphasising the link between the marmalade, and the University City of Oxford.
  (c) The defendant's product was described by Peter Gibson J. in the following terms, at 529:

"Mrs. Keenan started to trade in July 1985. Her business has expanded rapidly. Her products consist of gift sets primarily comprising miniature jars of marmalades, sometimes with other things such as coffee included, and 12 ounce gift jars of marmalade and jams, all of the 12 ounce jars being octagonal in shape and attached to each lid being an eye-catching black plastic mortar-board with a dark or light blue tassel. 'Oxbridge' products are now sold in many stores, including Selfridges in Oxford, Harrods, Liberty's and other famous stores. She has already been successful in obtaining export orders."

2. *Cyanamid*—"special factors" considered At 530–531, Peter Gibson J. reaffirmed the particular significance of interlocutory relief to restrain passing off; namely that it may well have the effect of being final:

"It is common ground that I should apply the guidelines provided by *American Cyanamid Co. v. Ethicon Ltd* [1975] A.C. 396 in determining whether or not to accede to the plaintiff's application. Accordingly I must first consider whether or not there is a serious issue to be tried. In cases of this sort it is the practical experience of the courts that few cases come to full trial because the interlocutory decision, particularly if it is adverse to the defendant, often entails the repackaging of a product and the commercial decision may then be taken that it is not worthwhile trying to re-use a name in respect of which an injunction has been obtained even if the defendant were successful at the trial. That, as Sir John Donaldson M.R. said in *Elan Digital Systems Ltd v. Elan Computers Ltd* [1984] F.S.R. 373 at 386, is a factor which has to be taken into account and to which due weight must be given by the court, but it does not involve any principle of law."

3. The issues Peter Gibson J. identified the following issues—(which he subsequently dealt with together, rather than separately) namely:
- (a) The infringement alleged under section 4(1) of the Trade Mark Act 1938; and
- (b) Passing off.

4. The law relating to those issues

(a) *Trade marks:* Section 4(1) of the Act (since amended by the Patents, Designs and Marks Act 1986) *inter alia* provides that the trade mark is to be:

"deemed to be infringed by any person who, not being the proprietor of the trade mark or a registered user thereof ... uses a mark identical with it or so nearly resembling it as to be likely to deceive or cause confusion, in the course of trade, in relation to any goods in respect of which it is registered, and in such manner as to render the use of the mark likely to be taken either (a) as being used as a trade mark; or (b) in a case in which the use is use upon the goods ... or is an advertising circular or other advertisement issued to the public, as importing a reference to some person having the right either as proprietor or as a registered user to use the trade mark or to goods with which such a person is connected in the course of trade."

Peter Gibson J. then went on to say at 531:

"In looking at that issue the court must bear in mind that it is only the words as distinct from, for example, the get-up to which regard must be had; nor is it material that the manufacturer's name appears on the label of the goods. One must look at all the surrounding circumstances including the nature of the goods and the sort of customer likely to buy the goods. It is relevant too to have regard to what is known as the idea of the mark, that is to say the idea which is given by the mark to a person who sees it, and if the mark gives rise to a particular association that association may be important in relation to the question of deception or confusion."

(b) *Passing off:* Peter Gibson J. invoked the "leading authority" of *Erven Warnink BV v. J. Townend (Hull) Ltd* [1979] A.C. 731, and said at 531:

"... one is looking for a misrepresentation made by a trader in the course of trade to prospective customers of his or of goods or services supplied by him which is calculated to injure the business or goodwill of another trader in the sense that it is a reasonably foreseeable consequence and which causes actual damage to a business or goodwill of the trader by whom the action is brought. The question of confusion is relevant because of sales lost to the plaintiff through purchasers making purchases of the defendant's products or which they have bought assuming that the defendant's products were associated with the plaintiff or his products because of a similarity in name or get-up."

5. The confusion argument

(a) *Case for defendant:* No real risk of confusion—on the following bases:
  (i) The words "Oxford" and "Oxbridge" shared only the two initial letters;
  (ii) The first defendant had deposed to her own personal research that one in two people know "Oxbridge" to be a construct of Oxford and Cambridge, and that they were two Universities;
  (iii) The first defendant denied any intention to benefit from the Frank Cooper "Oxford" trade mark;

(iv) Three retailers deposed to their not being confused.

(b) *Judgment:* There was a possibility of appreciable damage resulting from confusion (and thus a "serious issue to be tried") in that:
  (i) There was evidence before the court of actual confusion—not only of a customer, but also of the opinion of persons of experience in the trade;
  (ii) "Oxford" and "Oxbridge" each conjured up the idea of excellence, associated *inter alia* with the University of Oxford.

Peter Gibson J. came to such a conclusion, against the backdrop of the following dicta which he ventilated at 532:

> "It is always difficult for a defendant in an action like this to establish the negative proposition of non-confusion, and I must bear in mind that confusion amongst a not insignificant number of people must be shown so that damage of an appreciable amount can be established."

6. Were damages an adequate remedy for the plaintiff? No—the defendant conceding:
  (a) The difficulty of calculating damage to goodwill.
  (b) The defendant had exhausted all her capital in getting the business going in the first place.

7. Were damages an adequate remedy for the defendant? Not entirely—in that again, there was the difficulty in quantifying damage to goodwill. But Peter Gibson J. took into account, on the other hand, the following:
  (a) The financial strength of the plaintiffs—rendering it well able to compensate the defendant for any loss.
  (b) The loss resulting from the defendant being forced to change labels and withdraw promotional material was susceptible to ready calculation.

8. Balance of convenience

(a) *The defendant's case:*
  (i) First argument: The difficulty a new trader would encounter in having to market its products under a new name, particularly taking into account the risk of losing the existing market and the lack of capital available to continue business under a new name.
  (ii) Second argument: Alterations to the brochures and gift packaging would be very expensive.

(b) *Judgment:*
  (i) First argument—at 534–535:

"But one of the problems that Mrs. Keenan's evidence poses is that she has been extremely unspecific as to her volume of business, as to her stocks and as to when it was that she incurred the expenditure that she has incurred in relation to promoting 'Oxbridge' as her brand product. If, for example, she had gone ahead incurring expenses at a time when she had been put on notice by the plaintiffs that they were challenging her right to use 'Oxbridge,' the court would not have too much sympathy with her in taking the calculated risk that she did. I simply do not know such details."

(ii) Second argument—at 535:

"No advertising expenditure has been incurred, though brochures have been issued, including one very handsome one which Mrs. Keenan describes as having recently had produced. Mr Hill-Smith submitted that the alterations that would be needed if an injunction were granted were very extensive. It appears that on the gift packages the word 'Oxbridge' is written over and over again but it is written in such small and unnoticeable print that I certainly did not observe this until it was drawn to my attention, nor apparently did the plaintiffs, and they are content that if an injunction is granted those packages can go out with only the name 'Oxbridge' removed where it appears prominently. It is a frequent occurrence, unhappily, that those who are resisting such applications do have to put new stickers over that which has already been printed. For my part I am not satisfied that there would be that enormous a disruption if such stickers were to be applied."

The defendant unavailingly sought to invoke the "delay" and "status quo" arguments above—and Peter Gibson J. granted the injunction.

9. The defendant's riposte Not to be beaten, the first defendant shortly thereafter applied for a stay pending an expedited appeal. The basis of the application was (at 535):

"... she will effectively be prevented from trading under the name 'Oxbridge' and from disposing from stocks which she now possesses and in which her monies are tied up, unless a stay is granted, and that this may render the appeal nugatory because she will not be able to keep her name in front of her retailers."

Peter Gibson J. allowed the application, for reasons which he expressed at 535–536:

"But I am troubled that if the appeal is successful then the fruits of that victory would largely be denied to Mrs. Keenan. Mrs. Keenan

747

has offered to pay 10 per cent of her gross takings into a joint account. She has also undertaken to proceed diligently with the appeal.

In all the circumstances I think it right to grant a stay accepting those undertakings, but giving liberty to apply should circumstances warrant a further application to this court by either party.

24 *Mothercare U.K. Ltd v. Penguin Books Ltd* [1988] R.P.C. 113, C.A.

1. The facts Penguin Books Ltd published a serious sociological study of the problems faced by working mothers who delegated the care of their children to others, with the title "Mother Care/Other Care". Mothercare U.K. Ltd's business included the publication of books such as the "Complete Mothercare Manual," which contained sensible and useful advice for mothers on the problems during pregnancy.

2. The relief sought Mothercare U.K. Ltd wanted to restrain the publication of "Mother Care/Other Care" in the United Kingdom because it was polemic and controversial whereas Mothercare U.K. Ltd had a policy of avoiding all matters of controversy in their publications. The claim was brought in passing off and as an infringement of trade mark.

3. The first issue: passing off Dillon L.J. with whom the rest of the Court of Appeal agreed, said that in making out their claim in passing off Mothercare would have to establish at the trial the five factors listed by Lord Diplock in *Warnink v. Townend & Sons (Hull) Ltd* [1979] A.C. 731, at 742, which had to be present in order to create a valid cause of action in passing off. These factors included misrepresentation, which meant showing that Penguin were representing that their book was issued or sponsored by or associated with Mothercare.

4. Passing off: was there a serious question to be tried?

"In considering whether there was a misrepresentation, the court had to consider the name "Mother Care/Other Care" as a whole. So considering the name, his Lordship was wholly unable to see any basis for saying that there was a misrepresentation in the title of the book. The book, taken as a whole, did not begin to suggest that the book had been issued or sponsored by, or was in any way associated with Mothercare.

Accordingly the claim in passing off was, in his Lordship's judgment, bound to fail. Mothercare did not get over the first hurdle of establishing that there was a serious question to be tried."

5. The second issue: infringement of trade mark The plaintiff's argument. The allegation of infringement of trade mark depended on section 4 of the Trade Marks Act 1938 and the leading authority was still *Bismag Ltd v. Amblins (Chemists) Ltd* [1940] Ch. 667. The plaintiffs argued that Mothercare suffered damage because the value and exclusivity of its mark was diminished by any use by anyone else of the words "mother care."

6. Infringement of trade marks: was there a serious question to be tried? No

> "That, in his Lordship's judgment, could only be so if those words were used by the offender as a trade mark or in a trade mark sense; if descriptive words were merely used descriptively the mark was unaffected.
>
> In the present case the words 'Mothercare' in the title of the book were not, in his Lordship's judgment, used as a trade mark or in any trade mark sense. They were merely used descriptively, as describing, with the words 'other care' what the book was about.
>
> Accordingly, on the trade mark aspect of the case also, Mothercare did not get over the first hurdle of establishing that there was a serious issue to be tried. His Lordship would discharge the order of Mr Justice Falconer."

25 *Dalepak Foods plc v. Frezmet Daily Pack Ltd* [1987] 2 N.I.J.B. 1

1. The facts The plaintiffs manufactured and marketed in Northern Ireland "steakettes" under the name "Dalepak." They had mounted a vigorous advertising campaign in Northern Ireland and said that their products were "extremely popular and successful." Some eight months after the plaintiffs had started to market "steakettes" the defendants launched their own "steakettes" on the Northern Ireland market under the name "Daily Pack". Like the plaintiffs the defendants' packaging was a deep blue, and the plaintiffs argued that the whole get-up was very similar.

2. The relief sought The plaintiffs sought interlocutory relief as follows:

> "An injunction to restrain the defendant, whether by its directors, officers, servants or agents or any of them or otherwise howsoever, until the trial of this action or until further order from doing the following acts, that is to say:
> (a) passing off or attempting to pass off goods not the goods of the plaintiff as and for the goods of the plaintiff and a business not the business of the plaintiff as and for the business of the plaintiff;

749

(b) using in connection with its business the words 'Daily Pack' or any other words so closely resembling the title of the plaintiff as to be calculated to lead to the defendant's goods or business being confused by members of the public with those of the plaintiff."

3. The law Lord Lowry C.J. sitting in the Chancery Division of the High Court of Northern Ireland summarised the law at the interlocutory stage:

"In all cases, including patent cases and [it would seem] passing off cases, the court must determine an application for an interlocutory injunction on a balance of convenience, there being no rule against granting relief unless satisfied that if the case went to trial on the evidence then available the plaintiff would obtain a permanent injunction: see *American Cyanamid v. Ethicon* [1975] A.C. 396, at 406–8. The passage at 140 of *Garden Cottage Foods v. Milk Marketing Board* [1984] A.C. 130 shows that what may be called the 'status quo' doctrine is variable in its application, according to circumstances."

4. The balance of convenience favoured the plaintiff Lord Lowry C.J. said:

"I note that the plaintiff issued a warning on 29th October and moved promptly after the defendant marketed its products on 26th November. There are reasonable grounds for believing that through the defendants' activities the plaintiff *could* suffer very serious damages which will be impossible to estimate and perhaps very difficult to recoup. And, whether the defendant is in the right or not, it cannot at this stage have built up much goodwill for the products in regard to which it is in competition with the plaintiff, nor (interestingly enough) does the defendant allege that it has spent money on advertising.

Therefore, even if restrained from using a certain get-up, the defendant could, if it wished, switch to a different and undeniably distinct format. This option, it seems likely, could not be adopted by the plaintiff without serious loss of money and goodwill. The balance of convenience in all the circumstances is in favour of granting an injunction."

5. The status quo also favoured the plaintiff

"As for the status quo, its classic meaning is the *status quo ante bellum* and, if there is a war, it started, not on 12th December with the issue of a writ, but on 26th November when the defendants' marketing commenced. That is the status quo which in my estimation ought to be restored (not preserved) pending trial."

26 *British Association of Aesthetic Plastic Surgeons v. Cambright Ltd* [1987] R.P.C. 549

1. The facts The plaintiff was a charitable company whose principal objects were the promotion of knowledge into, and the advancement of, cosmetic plastic surgery. It did not carry on any trade. Some seven years after the plaintiffs had been in existence (as a body) the defendants started to advertise for business under the name "The Association of Aesthetic Plastic Surgery." The plaintiffs applied for an interlocutory injunction to restrain the use of this name.

2. Was the "Association" issue arguable? No—Scott J. said:

"I see a good deal of force in the criticism advanced by [the plaintiffs] to the effect that the description of Cambright Limited as an 'Association' was spurious. Prima facie that seems to me to be a justified criticism. The company is not an association; it is a trading company. [But] That criticism does not establish passing off. It may or may not be something which the advertising standards authority would think it right to question, but it is not a matter which assists the plaintiff association, in my view, in its passing off claim."

3. The balance of the risk of injustice Scott J. weighed the balance (without using that word). He stated the test thus:

"These three elements in the plaintiff's case, reputation, confusion and risk of damage, may at trial be established. I would not wish to say that the plaintiff has not a case which may succeed at trial. But for the purposes of interlocutory relief it must, in my view, not only be shown that there is a case which may succeed at trial, but it must also be shown that until trial an injunction is needed in order to avoid risk of serious damage to the plaintiff."

4. The balancing exercise The judge considered four matters and concluded that this was not a case for interlocutory relief:

"[1] As to [the risk of serious damage to the plaintiff] I am unpersuaded. I can see that there may be some damage to the plaintiff's reputation if everything that the plaintiff needs to establish for its cause of action is at trial established; but I am bound to say I do not regard the risk of damage as being a substantial one.

[2] I must bear in mind that if I grant an interlocutory injunction restraining until trial the first defendant from trading as 'The Association of Aesthetic Plastic Surgery,' it will for the next year or so have to adopt a different trading style. Even if it succeeds in the action it

751

will probably not then be worth its while to revert to its current trading style and the effect of the interlocutory injunction will be to deprive it permanently of the advantage, if it is an advantage, of trading under the style of its choice.

[3] I find somewhat distasteful the spectacle of a trading company trying to dignify itself by calling itself an 'Association'; but it is entitled to choose that style and trade under it provided it avoids misrepresentation to the public ... and provided it avoids committing tort to others.

[4] The issues in the case are not complex ... ; the parties are not faced with an elaborate, long trial. The pleading should be short and I would have supposed the trial could be quite quickly brought on. But although nearly three months have elapsed since the writ was issued ... the progress of the action has not been processed at all since the issue of the writ ... The duration of an interlocutory injunction would therefore continue for three months longer than it need have done."

27 *Reckitt and Colman Products Ltd v. Borden Inc.* [1987] F.S.R. 228

1. **The facts** The plaintiffs had for 30 years sold lemon juice under the name "Jif" in a plastic container resembling a lemon. For some years the plaintiffs had allowed two other competitors to sell lemon juice in plastic containers resembling a lemon, but only on condition that the containers were four times the size of Jifs; these were "Lazy Lemon" and "Supercook". The defendants were now making efforts to market the same sort of thing. Their three variant containers (Marks I, II and III) were the subject of two actions. The Mark I action was pending. In the present action the plaintiffs sought an interlocutory injunction in respect of Marks II and III.

2. **The plaintiffs' case** In order to succeed at trial the plaintiffs had to establish:
   (1) that the Jif lemon was distinctive of the plaintiffs; and
   (2) that use of the Mark II or III lemon was likely to give rise to deception. In support of the deception the plaintiffs adduced evidence including surveys and affidavits from members of the public tending to show actual confusion between the defendants' lemons and Jifs.

3. **The defendants' three-pronged defence** Nicholls L.J. summarised it (at 234–236) as follows:

"[1] Borden's first line of defence was that, as a matter of law, there can be no proprietary rights in the lemon-shaped squeeze packs in question in this case. The argument was that in this field the lemon-shaped container is primarily descriptive but also, in part, functional.

[2] Borden's second line of defence was to the effect that the necessary reputation could not be established here by Colman because not only was the container of a descriptive and partly functional character, but it was used by Colman during a time of monopoly or virtual monopoly when there was no other article from which to distinguish it. Hence distinctiveness would not grow out of trading, members of the public having no occasion to distinguish this container from any other.

[3] A further point was taken by Borden, based on the terms of settlement of the actions against the 'Lazy Lemon' and 'Supercook' traders. It was submitted that, having by those terms licensed the use of other lemon-shaped containers unconnected in the course of trade with Colman, Colman could not be heard to say that its 'Jif' lemon get-up was distinctive of its own goods. ..."

4. The Court of Appeal held: an arguable case Nicholls L.J. said at 236:

"... taking into account in particular the heavy burden lying on Colman on question (1) [that the Jif lemon was distinctive of Colman], my overall conclusion on Colman's prospects in the action accords with the conclusion of the judge expressed in his judgment, that for the purposes of the motion the matter is to be considered as standing in the balance, but if the scales are tipped at all, they are tipped against Colman."

5. Were damages an adequate remedy for the plaintiffs? No—the plaintiffs put their potential damage under four heads.

(a) Loss of sales. The Court of Appeal differed from Whitford J. at first distance, and held that this would be very hard to assess. Nicholls L.J. felt that the most difficult part of the exercise was:

"ascertaining what percentage of the Mark II and Mark III sales are to be regarded as sales made as a result of passing off. For my part, I have to say that I think that if this inquiry ever had to be made in this case, the court could easily find itself having to make little more than a guess at this figure. If Borden were to sell its Mark II and Mark III lemons at outlets not currently selling Jif lemons, it might be very difficult to arrive at a figure fairly, if roughly, representing sales acquired by deception." (at 239.)

(b) Reduced profit margins from having to reduce its prices if the expected "price war" should break out. The Court of Appeal also though this would be difficult:

753

"The difficulty here is that a wide range of possibilities exist, with widely differing possible outcomes for the future for Colman, without any real clue at this stage on which possibilities are most likely. One can expect Borden to price its lemon-shaped containers at less than Jif lemons, but how much less?" (at 239.)

(c) The "snowball" effect of others entering the lemon-shaped container field pending the trial.

(d) Loss of goodwill. The Court did not attach much weight to these last two types of loss.

6. The balance of convenience favoured the plaintiffs—why? Nicholls L.J. said:

"Turning to the balance of convenience, this is a case in which the desirability of preserving the status quo is, obviously and clearly, an important consideration. ... I have in mind Borden's evidence concerning the urgent commercial need for it to be able to enter the lemon-shaped container market. I also have in mind the views I have expressed regarding Colman's [limited] prospects of success in the action and that damages will not provide a satisfactory remedy for Borden if it succeeds at the trial. But, to my mind, despite these matters, the balance of convenience tilts firmly in this case towards preserving the status quo pending trial. Borden has been contemplating entering, and has been trying to enter, this particular market for some time. It has designed and introduced the Mark II and Mark III containers, knowing full well that those containers would be objected to, and it has done so whilst there awaits trial an action which it is defending and in which substantially the same issues in the present action arise on the extent to which the Jif lemon is distinctive of Colman." (at 240.)

7. The ruling The Court of Appeal granted the injunction and gave directions designed to secure that this action caught up with the Mark I action.

28 *Nationwide Building Society v. Nationwide Estate Agents Ltd* [1987] F.S.R. 579

1. The facts In October 1986 the defendants opened four branches and began trading as estate agents. In November 1986 the plaintiff building society issued a writ claiming that the defendant company was passing itself off as being associated with the building society. The Building Societies Act 1986 came into force on January 1, 1987 and enabled the plaintiffs for the first time to act as estate agents. Since that date they had purchased 380 existing estate agents which then carried on business under both their original names and the name "Nationwide Estate Agency".

2. A preliminary skirmish The plaintiffs issued a notice of motion which had been stood over upon the defendants undertaking not to use the name "Nationwide" except in connection with the four existing branches. Meanwhile the plaintiffs had gone ahead as fast as possible to establish their estate agency business.

3. The relief claimed The plaintiffs sought an injunction:

"(a) restraining the defendant company from using or advertising or displaying or promoting the name and style 'Nationwide' or any colourable imitation of the same, in or in connection with a business which is not a business of, or connected with, the plaintiffs;

(b) using or advertising or displaying or promoting the name and style 'Nationwide' or any colourable imitation of the same, in or in connection with provision of estate agency, mortgage broking, or other ancillary service, not provided or approved by the plaintiffs."

They also sought mandatory relief requiring:

"the obliteration of any material which would offend an order in those terms."

4. Did *American Cyanamid* apply? Yes—Browne-Wilkinson V.-C. said:

"There are certainly passing off cases in which the *American Cyanamid* approach in all its rigour is not appropriate; in the ordinary case of one trader with goodwill in a particular trade seeking to close down a competitor the outcome of the interlocutory motion is likely to be decisive of the whole case. For myself, I do not think that is true of the present case. Both plaintiff and defendant are very newly into the field; they have gone into it with their eyes open; if an injunction is granted, the only result will be to postpone the further development of an embryo goodwill in the name 'Nationwide' in connection with estate agents until after the trial of the action." (at 585.)

5. Did the plaintiff have an arguable case? Yes.

"In my judgment the plaintiffs clearly have an arguable case that the word 'Nationwide,' in the context of dealings with house purchase, is extremely widely known and uniquely associated with the plaintiff building society ... As a matter of impression, I would expect that there would be confusion in the public mind between estate agents

755

conducted under the same 'Nationwide Estate Agents' and estate agents conducted under their own name in conjunction with the word 'Nationwide' ... [And there] is very strong evidence indeed of actual confusion."

6. Had the plaintiffs suffered damage? The judge decided that they had.

"Then, still considering whether there is an arguable case, has it been shown that the plaintiff building society has suffered damage? The damage relied upon is that the plaintiff society would be impaired in its ability to enter into the estate agency business using its own name if the defendant company is allowed also to use the name 'Nationwide' in connection with estate agency. That, I think is real damage. More seriously, what is said is that the plaintiff building society's reputation and the good name on which it depends is put at risk if you allow somebody not under its control to carry on a business in a field with which it is closely associated—the buying and selling of houses—since the shortcomings of the defendant company, if any, would reflect on the good name of the plaintiff society." (at 590–591.)

7. The injunction was refused as a matter of discretion The judge held that damages would certainly not be an adequate remedy to either side at the trial, because the losses could not be quantified.

"In all those circumstances, were it not for one factor to which I will come, I would myself have granted an injunction against the defendants until trial and have directed speedy trial. ... But there is this very strange feature of this case which I have mentioned which would render it unjust to grant such an injunction. ... The application for an injunction is designed ... to tie one of two competitors to the starting post while the other one gets rather more than a head start. The objective appears to be not to protect the plaintiffs' name (the only right it has) but to build the building societies Nationwide Estate Agency chain from scratch whilst the defendants are disabled from competing in the same field." (at 592.)

8. An injunction upon the plaintiffs' undertakings?

"If the plaintiff society is prepared to agree to a speedy trial and to undertake pending trial not to use the word 'Nationwide' in conjunction with the agencies that it has taken over, I would if necessary grant the injunction against the defendants. But unless that undertaking is forthcoming from the plaintiffs, I am not prepared to enjoin the defendants alone from competing in this field pending trial." (at 593.)

No undertaking was forthcoming, so there was no injunction.

29 *Unidoor Ltd v. Marks and Spencer plc* [1988] R.P.C. 275

1. The facts The plaintiffs had registered "Coast to Coast" as a trade mark which they used on the clothes they manufactured. Marks and Spencer plc began to sell T-shirts with slogans on the front reading "Marine Girl" and "Coast to Coast". The plaintiffs sought an interlocutory injunction to prevent Marks and Spencer plc continuing to sell these T-shirts.

2. The causes of action The plaintiffs' claim was based on infringement of their trade mark and passing off. For the purposes of the interlocutory hearing it had to be assumed that the trade mark was validly registered, although that would be disputed at trial.

3. The trade mark issue The plaintiffs would have to establish that Marks and Spencer plc were using "Coast to Coast" as a trade mark. The plaintiffs said it was clear use of a registered mark.

4. The judge had grave doubts—for two main reasons Whitford J. said:

> "[1] This is not a case where any steps have ever at any time been taken to acquaint the public at large, and by that I mean the purchasing public, with the fact that these words 'Coast to Coast' are a trade mark of the plaintiffs. ... Nothing has been done to acquaint anybody with the fact that these words 'Coast to Coast' are in truth not just some sort of decoration or some sort of slogan on the goods in question but a trade mark of the plaintiff company.
> [2] So far as the question of infringement is concerned, whatever the position might have been if what Marks and Spencer had done was to use these words 'Coast to Coast' on a small label of the type found used by he plaintiffs themselves on the exhibit SCR. 9, the question which is going to have to be decided is whether in fact the form of usage on the actual articles the subject of complaint is in truth used as a trade mark. For my part, I am bound to say that, although inevitably when the action comes to be tried, it may well be that evidence on this matter will prove decisive one way or the other, if I just had to decide it on a sight of the garment in question I have the gravest doubts as to whether it would ever be possible ... to persuade me that this was in fact a trade mark usage."

5. The passing off issue The plaintiffs argued that by reason of their extensive use of "Coast to Coast" they had a reputation which could be protected in a passing off action. Whitford J. saw considerable difficulties in the plaintiffs' way—again for two main reasons:

"[1] Here I find the plaintiffs, on the evidence as it at present stands, in some great difficulty because, although there have been sales of goods spoken to, ... they are in my experience, in connection with the sales of articles of this kind, figures of sales of a very moderate number of garments.

[2] As I have said, there is nothing to indicate that any step has ever been taken by the plaintiffs to identify these words as being words which are to be understood in the garment field as having a trade mark connotation, indicating that the garments in question come from them. There has been no advertising and I can see that there may be some considerable difficulty, so far as the plaintiffs are concerned, in establishing the necessary reputation."

6. Were damages adequate for the plaintiffs? Yes.

"Is it really a case where there ought to be an interlocutory injunction because, unless an interlocutory injunction be granted the damage that is going to be suffered will be irreparable? In my opinion it cannot conceivably be said that that is the case. I do not think that, as matters stand at present, and as I have said there is really only the one outstanding batch so far as the defendants are concerned, if these goods are sold it will be beyond the wit of the court to arrive at some appropriate figure when the question of damage falls to be considered, if it ever does. I do not myself feel that the damage that is likely to be suffered by the plaintiffs, if an injunction be not granted, is very significant."

7. Were damages adequate for the defendants? No.

"It may be that the grant of an injunction would not produce very substantial damage in purely financial terms so far as the defendants are concerned, but it might I think quite seriously damage their reputation and their standing, particularly with some of their trade customers."

The judge declined to grant an injunction.

30 *The Boots Company Ltd v. Approved Prescription Services Ltd* [1988] F.S.R. 45

1. The facts The plaintiffs had for some time sold the drug Ibuprofen under the "Brufen" in the form of magenta coloured pills of a particular shape. After the plaintiffs' patent on Ibuprofen had expired, the defendants wished to market a generic version of the drug, but using the same colour and shape as Brufen. The plaintiffs applied for an interlocutory injunction in a passing off action based on get-up.

2. The appeal Whitford J. had refused an injunction. He applied *American Cyanamid* and found that although the plaintiffs had an arguable case, they would have an adequate remedy in damages at the trial if a permanent injunction were granted then, and the balance of convenience lay in favour of not granting any interlocutory relief. In dismissing the plaintiffs' appeal the Court of Appeal heard argument only from the plaintiffs, on adequacy of damages and the balance of convenience.

3. Damages would be an adequate remedy for the plaintiffs—why? The plaintiffs advanced four arguments to the effect that Boots would suffer unquantifiable loss if not protected immediately.

(a) The defendants would be bound to argue that the plaintiffs' loss of profit until trial should not be measured by reference to the defendants' entire profits over that period, because the defendants would have secured some orders in any event as a result of a prescription describing the drug generically, and the profits from those orders should be deducted from the account of the profits from the passing off; yet that calculation was very difficulty. But Templeman L.J. said:

> "It seems to me, however, that, if the defendants tried to raise such a claim, they would be given short shrift and that if magenta pills bear all the insignia of Boots and magenta pills are sold, and wrongly sold, by the defendants, then the measure of damages would be the profits on the magenta pills which were sold by the defendants and ought to have been sold by Boots." (at 47)

(b) Boots would have suffered loss of goodwill causing loss of profit to them after the grant of a permanent injunction; such loss of profit would be impossible to calculate. Templeman L.J. said:

> "The high reputation of champagne emanating from that district of France would be damaged if, even as a matter of interim relief, the distinction were blurred in the minds of the public, so that, for example, a beginner, taking champagne type wine, might acquire a dislike to it and never realise how intoxicated and euphoric he could become if only he would confine his attention to the genuine champagne which comes from the appropriate district in France. This case is plainly distinguishable, because there is, therapeutically, no difference between the drug which the defendants will manufacture and the drug which Boots manufacture under the trade name 'Brufen'." (at 48.)

(3) If an interlocutory injunction was refused other competitors would

be encouraged into the same market, whereupon there could be a blurred distinction as with the drinker of champagne type wine.

"The learned judge considered that and dismissed it. He thought that competitors would be frightened off until the action was decided, at any rate. ... Again, the learned judge pointed out that there is quality control in this country. ... I agree with him. ..." (at 49.)

(4) Patients might become irritated and disillusioned with Boots if they took the defendants' tablets thinking they were made by Boots, and then discovered that they had been deceived.

"In those circumstances, it seems to me, if this rather far-fetched hypothesis is correct, the patient might well berate his chemist or his doctor, but that, if he goes through life thinking that nobody can prescribe drugs except Boots and he is irritated and annoyed because he is deprived of a product manufactured by Boots, he will turn back with relief to the situation which obtains after the grant of a permanent injunction. ... I cannot see, for myself, that Boots can suffer in the long term as a result of this submission." (at 49.)

4. Damages would not be an adequate remedy for the defendants Templeman L.J. said:

"Turning then to the other side, ... namely, if an injunction is granted against the defendant but at the trial it is found that this action of Boots fails, on the cross-undertaking for damages the defendants will be in a difficulty, because they will never be able to prove with any certainty how many pills they would have sold if the injunction had not been granted." (at 50.)

5. Finally, the balance of convenience Whitford J. had considered the balance of convenience as well. Templeman L.J. summarised it thus in refusing relief:

"The factors which (the judge) did accept as being in favour of Boots were that there was no evidence of any capital expenditure by the defendants, no evidence of stocks or embarrassment about contracts, except a general statement without particulars. But there would be some embarrassment to the defendants, who have already launched into this business on however small a scale. The thing which finally weighed with the judge was this:

'I think the difficulty of the defendants is that, if they are stopped at this juncture, it will effectively mean the end of the road so far as pills of this shape, size and colour are concerned. ...'

In addition, there is the present evidence that, to put it at its lowest, the principal witness of APS considers that, if an injunction is granted, it will be impossible or difficult for them to continue to resist the action by Boots, simply on the ground that it will not be economically worth it." (at 50–51.)

31 *Associated Newspapers Group plc v. Insert Media Ltd; Express Newspapers plc v. Arnold (No. 2)* [1988] 1 W.L.R. 509, [1987] R.P.C. 521

1. The background These two consolidated actions raised exactly the same issue, in relation to the Mail newspapers and Express newspapers respectively, against the same defendant. Mr Arnold, who had formerly operated as Insert Media Ltd, had the idea of adding advertising inserts to the plaintiffs' colour supplements extra to those already inserted by the plaintiffs themselves but limited to any geographical requirements of the particular advertiser. The plaintiffs objected on the grounds that the inserts which they themselves permitted were very carefully scrutinised on the basis of numerous criteria, whereas the defendants' were not.

2. The principal cause of action The main thrust of the plaintiffs' case was that inserting the extra advertising material amounted to passing off the material as having been inserted with the authority or approval of the newspapers. Initially both plaintiffs obtained interlocutory injunctions against the defendants' inserts.

3. The defendants' new offer It was the defendants' new argument that they could circumvent the difficulties of the plaintiffs' allegations of passing off by offering to include on all of their extra advertising material a clear warning that the material did *not* appear with the approval or knowledge of the publishers of the newspapers. No reader could then be misled. With this suggestion in mind the defendants applied to vary the original injunction.

4. The proposed additional cause of action In the mean time the plaintiffs had applied to amend their pleadings to allege a further tort of deliberate act calculated to damage the plaintiffs' goodwill. They alleged that they had a right which the law would recognise and enforce, that their goods should reach the purchaser without any addition or alteration not authorised by them. Roch J. in the end rejected the existence of such a cause of action, but more interesting is the fact that he decided, after argument, that he should consider the unpleaded cause of action even though the amendment was resisted. It may have been a critical factor that the writs were widely drafted. Roch J. said:

761

"The plaintiffs point out that the endorsements of the writs are not confined to the first ground but are in terms capable of embracing both alleged causes of action. In my judgment I must consider both grounds advanced by the plaintiffs as founding their entitlement to an injunction and damages when deciding these applications, in spite of the fact that the plaintiffs have yet to obtain leave to amend their statement of claim."

5. Did *Cyanamid* apply? The defendants argued that, in passing off, a plaintiff had to establish more than simply that there was a serious issue to be tried. Roch J. applied *Cyanamid*:

"It may be that there is such a special rule in a case where the issue is 'Does the business name or trade mark chosen by the defendant infringe the rights of the plaintiffs to their business name or trade mark?' and where an interlocutory injunction will in reality resolve the whole issue. In the present case the interlocutory injunction does not have that consequence and accordingly I apply the test as stated by Lord Diplock. ... I add that the same principles must apply where the applications are, as they are before me, to discharge or vary interlocutory injunctions already made."

6. The defendants' new offer—what effect on the serious issue to be tried? The effect of the defendants' offer was on the face of it to prevent any misrepresentation that the defendants' inserts were authorised by the newspapers. But the judge held that the plaintiffs' ripostes had substance and there remained a serious issue to be tried.

(a) If the defendants really meant not to confuse they would be happy with simultaneous delivery of their material but not interleaved in the newspapers—yet they were not.

(b) The proffered disclaimer would come too late: by the time it is read the tort has already been committed—upon sale.

(c) The existence of the disclaimers would have suggested that the newspapers were no longer concerned with protecting their readers and wished to exclude liability.

7. Where lay the balance of convenience? Although the defendants' new argument actually affected different issues and the balance of convenience had already been considered by other judges at the interlocutory stage, Roch J. considered the balance again:

"Should the injunction be permitted to remain? This depends on the balance of convenience. In my judgment the balance of convenience is in favour of the interlocutory injunctions remaining in force until the trial of this action. The plaintiffs, if they succeed in this action,

those physical characteristics, but in fact they are made from a plastic which is different from that of the plaintiffs' articles. What is essential, therefore, is that those characteristics should be present irrespective of how they are obtained, or what material the plug is made of."

And he continued:

"There is nothing wrong in a patentee who has made a discovery of this sort, namely, that an object with certain physical characteristics is valuable and who has shown by his specification how to make that object, claiming it in general and functional terms as has been done here. A claim of that type which generally results from good advice is very valuable since it enables him to claim the object however it is made. That is sufficient for his purposes and does give him a wide claim so far as the monopoly is concerned. There has so far been no argument, as I understand it, that if you carry out the examples in the specification you can obtain a satisfactory plug."

3. Was there a triable issue? Yes—Graham J. said at 577–578:

(a) *Propounding the approach:*

"I want to make it quite clear that in anything I say in these proceedings I am not attempting to decide (a) validity of their patent, or (b) whether there is infringement. All I am doing is giving what I think fairly my prima facie view on matters on the material which is before me and I do not think that any judge who has had experience of trying patent cases, who has got the exhibits and the prior art in front of him, can help, to some extent at any rate, evaluating what he thinks the likely strength of the cases of both parties will be in due course at the trial. Of course he is not making up his mind and of course he has not got all the material which is available. All he can do is the best he can do in the circumstances on the material which he does have."

(b) *Applying that approach to the facts:*

"The plaintiffs here say that they think they have a valid patent, that the patent would be likely to be held to be infringed by the defendants and, so far as the prior art cited so far is concerned, there is nothing really which can fairly be said to anticipate or make the plaintiffs' claim obvious. That is prima facie argument which, from what I see of the material before me, looks as if it might eventually be accepted. That being the position, it seems to me that the first hurdle of the *American Cyanamid* case is got over by the plaintiffs and one then has to go on and consider other matters."

4. Damages—an adequate remedy for the plaintiffs? No—Graham J. explained at 578–579:

(a) *Expanding market:*

(i) Argument for the defendants:

"The defendants say that damages are perfectly adequate here because there would be no difficulty in ascertaining how many earplugs the defendants would sell in the coming period before the trial, if they are allowed to continue, and that really is all that matters. They do add however that, as far as their sales are concerned, they are only planning to sell some 400,000 earplugs during the coming year in 1980 that when one sees the figures it is only a flea-bite as far as the plaintiffs' overall sales are concerned and that, therefore, they are not likely to do the plaintiffs any damage anyway. The patent has another 11 years to run and, therefore, even if the defendants are stopped by injunction in due course there is plenty of time for the plaintiffs to build up their business and recover all that they may have lost by reason of the defendants' activities in the meantime."

(ii) Ruling—rejecting defendants' argument:

"I am not satisfied about that argument in this case because it does seem to me that the defendants here, if they are allowed to go on, will be an example to other potential infringers, who are no doubt standing on the sidelines and seeing how the present proceedings go. If the defendants were allowed to continue it seems to me quite probable that others may be encouraged to enter the market and that there will be a considerable build-up against the plaintiffs and their business at this, as they say, very critical time in the establishment of their business here."

(iii) Ruling—going on to accept plaintiffs' argument:

"The plaintiffs also say that if they are not allowed to develop their business on the scale and with the expedition which they are at present planning, considerable damage will be caused and the business (though this is inference of course) may well not be as profitable as it otherwise would be. It will not be as large, overheads will be greater and, as the evidence shows, less numbers of people will be able to be employed."

(b) *"Catnic"—distinguished:* The defendants contended on the basis of *Catnic Components Ltd v. Stressline Ltd* [1976] F.S.R. 157 that if both plaintiffs and defendants are large companies, good for the money which might arise on the cross-undertakings, then in a patent action

796

in those circumstances normally an injunction will not be granted. Graham J. distinguished *Catnic* however, to rule in favour of the plaintiffs.

(i) First distinguishing factor: The plaintiffs had preserved the monopoly, at 579–580:

> "First of all, Mr Everington said that if a plaintiff has taken every step which he can to preserve his monopoly then the court ought not in any way to be reluctant to assist him when he asks for an injunction against an outstanding defendant. To do otherwise, argues Mr Everington, is in effect to say that in a patent action one can of course obtain what really is a licence of right, that is to say, a right to manufacture an infringing article, whether the plaintiff likes it or not. The object of granting letters patent is to encourage manufacture in this country and to enable people who have valid patents to build up their business in the early years under the umbrella of those patents and, in those circumstances, while we have the system that we have, I think the court ought to be ready to assist the plaintiff if, on the whole, the facts appear to justify it.
>
> In the *Catnic* case it was pointed out that the plaintiffs had failed at the date of the hearing of the interlocutory injunction to preserve their monopoly and there were on the market at least two infringers, or alleged infringers, other than the defendants."

(ii) Second distinguishing factor—knowledge of patent:

> "It is also clear that in that case the particular defendants sued had no reason for thinking that the plaintiffs had any monopoly which would stop them, the defendants, setting up here. They sated that on making a search they did not find any patent in the plaintiffs' name, and no doubt they took account of the presence of the other two infringers on the market. On the contrary here, the evidence, prima facie, satisfies me that the defendants here knew perfectly well not only of the plaintiffs' product but also of the fact that it was being manufactured under patents in various places in the world, not necessarily in the United Kingdom. At any rate they knew perfectly well that patents were involved and there was evidence of a director, a Mr Danilo, who is a director of both the Australian parent company and of the defendants' company here. He wrote letters to the plaintiffs about the plugs.
>
> In those circumstances, at this stage at any rate, where there has so far been no cross-examination, I am not prepared to hold that the defendant did enter on their business of selling their competing earplugs otherwise than in the knowledge that they did so at their own risk."

797

5. Damages an adequate remedy for the defendants? No—Graham J. said at 580:

> "Here it seems to me that damages, in view of the circumstances which I am reciting, are not likely to be an adequate remedy. I am certainly in a position at the moment of doubt as to whether they would be. This being so it is necessary for me to consider the balance of convenience and the strength of the parties' case. It is laid down in the *American Cyanamid* case that where the matter is one of doubt, that is sufficient to make such consideration necessary.

6. Merits, etc. In this regard, at 577, Graham J. had already contrasted the respective scales of investment of the parties:

> "The plaintiffs are a corporation which is a subsidiary of the Cabot Corporation, a Boston based company. The parent has a very large business and sells a large number of articles. The plaintiffs themselves, though they may make some other protective articles, are in this country at any rate, as I understand it, primarily concerned with these earplugs. They form some 90 per cent, as the evidence shows, of their business in this country.
>
> The defendants have a large business in safety devices in the United Kingdom of which, as I understand it, the plugs which they sell only form a very small part. These plugs they do not manufacture here but import from Germany where they are made by a company named Tech Med."

11 *Brupat Ltd v. Sandford Marine Products Ltd* [1983] R.P.C. 61

1. The facts The plaintiff manufacturer of the "Bruce" anchor sought an interlocutory injunction to restrain the defendants, a £2m. company from allegedly infringing their patent by manufacture of the "Sea Claw" anchor. The evidence established that both products were good anchors.

2. Was there a serious issue to be tried? Yes—at first instance, Falconer J. decided that the plaintiffs had established a triable issue on the question of infringement and the appeal did not touch upon that finding. As Templeman L.J. said at 62(35):

> "We do not know, therefore, whether the plaintiffs are innocent possessors of a valid patent valiantly resisting the attacks of a base infringer or whether, on the other hand, the defendants are the public champions of private enterprise and freedom resisting the attempts of a monopolist to extend the area of his monopoly."

3. Narrowing the issue In that there was a triable issue, Templeman L.J. at 62(40)–63(5) identified the questions thrown up by such an issue:

"... we are only concerned with two questions. The first question is whether damages will be an adequate remedy if the plaintiffs succeed at the trial in establishing that their patent has been infringed by the Sea Claw. The second question is whether damages would be an adequate remedy if the defendants succeed at the trial in establishing that they have every right to manufacture the Sea Claw and they have, alas, been wrongly subjected to an injunction which has restrained them from carrying on their business in the meantime."

4. Would damages be an adequate remedy to the defendant? No—for the following reasons:

(a) The defendants were beginning on the venture of selling the Sea Claw—thus there was no past history on which to base estimates. It could not be established how many sales the defendants would have made if they had not been restrained from manufacturing the anchor. The analogy of the "War Loss" cases (Patent Act 1949, s.24) was misconceived because, in most if not all cases, there would be evidence of the number of sales made before the war began and the number of sales which were made after the effects of the hostilities had passed off. As Oliver L.J. said in *SKM S.A. v. Wagner Spraytech (U.K.) Ltd* [1982] R.P.C. 497:

"... that the likelihood of any damages being an adequate remedy if they prove right at the trial is very much less, for in their case there are virtually no certainties. They have not been selling their equipment long enough to establish a clear sales pattern; there will be no actual sales which can be used to assess the demand that there might have been if the defendants had been free to sell. The answer given, that they have their own estimates of future sales to go on, seems to me to be an inadequate one because, without the experience of the market, it is really quite impossible to say whether or not these estimates are well-founded."

(b) If the defendants were prevented from continuing production, there was a real risk that one of its financial backers would withdraw.

5. Would damages be an adequate remedy for the plaintiffs? Yes—for the following reasons:

(a) The plaintiff was well in the field and the defendant was just starting. In such circumstances it is easier to assess the damages of the plaintiffs than it is to assess the damages of the defendant. As Oliver L.J. said in *SKM S.A. v. Wagner Spraytech (U.K.) Ltd* [1982] R.P.C. 497:

"... the assessment of damages, if the plaintiffs succeed at the trial and no injunction is granted in the meantime, has features of difficulty. For instance, how many [articles] would the plaintiffs have sold if their total monopoly had been preserved? How many spares and how many subsidiary equipment would they have sold? What prices would they have been able to command if there had been no competition in the market? And what is the impact of reduced sales on their other business and overheads? I agree that there are inevitable difficulties of this sort, but nothing in the evidence has convinced me that they are so formidable as to preclude the court from arriving at a reasonably accurate assessment of any loss suffered. There will, after all, be a substantial number of known factors. The past sales of the plaintiffs are known; the ratio of spares and so on; their estimates of future sales volumes are known."

(b) The defendants could provide a form of security, namely, by putting aside a percentage (which was held to be sufficient at 7 per cent) in relation to all sales on the Sea Claw:
  (i) such money to be paid into a joint account of the solicitors; and
  (ii) such moneys to be set aside on the basis of the defendants keeping proper records (in this regard, the court was following the precedent set in *Coco v. Clark (A.N.) (Engineers) Ltd* [1969] R.P.C. 41).

(c) As Templeman L.J. went on to say at 66(30):

"There is one other point. The plaintiffs are buttressed against misfortune by having a very large interest in large anchors, whereas the defendants are limiting their activities so far as to the smaller anchor. In those circumstances, the defendants have agreed to submit to a limitation of the Sea Claw anchors and are prepared not to produce or sell Sea Claw anchors which weigh more than 50kg."

6. The *Catnic Components* case The position in *Catnic Components Ltd and Robinson v. Stressline Ltd* [1976] F.S.R. 157, C.A. was not dissimilar to the *Brupat* case. Here the plaintiffs moved to restrain the defendants from selling joists of a design similar to that patented by the plaintiff and in which the plaintiffs had invested about £140,000. The injunction was refused on appeal because:

(a) *Damages an adequate remedy:* The plaintiffs admitted that the defendants were in a position to pay any damages assessed against them and in the circumstances the plaintiffs would be adequately compensated in damages for any loss suffered if an injunction was withheld.

(b) *Balance of commercial convenience:* An injunction would debar the defendants from selling their stock of joists in hand and from establishing their footing in the market as early as they might.

7. A copyright parallel In the *Staver Co. Inc. v. Digitext Display Ltd* [1985] F.S.R. 512, the plaintiffs alleged that the defendants were in breach of their copyright in digital display unites. The trial judge upon interlocutory application restrained the defendants from "infringing the plaintiff's copyright in six specified drawings". After the order the defendants redesigned certain units and sought, *inter alia*, a declaration that their units now fell outside the scope of the injunction. Scott J., *inter alia*, held that the order should be varied to permit the defendants to manufacture and sell their redesigned units upon deposit into a joint account of a percentage of sales receipts as security for damages. He said at 522:

> "At the previous hearing I decided that a deposit of 15 per cent would be appropriate. Mr Pumfrey has addressed me on the figures and has suggested that eight per cent would now be appropriate. He suggested his argument by referring to *Brupat Ltd v. Sandford Marine Products Ltd* [1983] R.P.C. 61 where, on the basis of a gross profit of around 40 per cent the Court of Appeal ordered a deposit of eight per cent of the retail price. In addition, Mr Pumfrey submitted that in considering the appropriate level of the deposit conversion damages should be ignored since those damages did not represent any element of loss to the plaintiff. I can see a good deal of logic and force in that submission but, on the figures in the present case, it does not lead me to think that a reduction of the 15 per cent figure is called for. On the evidence the plaintiff's loss of profit figure may well exceed 15 per cent of the defendant's price for its units. Further, the defendant has not put before me any figures relevant to its business on which a submission that a 15 per cent deposit would place it in difficulties could be based or from which its own profit margin could be assessed.
>
> In my judgment therefore the deposit level should be 15 per cent."

12 *Smith (T.J.) and Nephew Ltd v. 3M United Kingdom plc* [1983] R.P.C. 92, C.A.

1. The facts The defendants were the wholly-owned subsidiary of an American corporation—such corporation being far larger than the plaintiff's which was a well-known British company with branches in many parts of the world and which had acquired a well-earned reputation for making dressings of one kind or another for the treatment of surgical or other wounds. The plaintiffs claimed to have invented a surgical dressing which revolutionised the treatment of wounds, which they had marketed from 1974. Lawton L.J. said at 94(37–45):

> "They had a difficult task in front of them, because they knew from their long experience in this field that the medical and nursing professions tend to be conservative in their methods and, very understandably, if they are asked to change them, they want to know why they should and have to be convinced that the reasons they are given are sound medical reasons. This means that the plaintiffs had to educate the medical and nursing professions. They did it through their representatives calling at hospitals. They did it by organising demonstrations for doctors and nurses. They made educational films which were shown to doctors and nurses. After some years at long last they began to convince doctors and nurses of the value of their new kind of surgical dressing."

The plaintiffs launched proceedings for an interlocutory injunction when learning of the defendants' intention to market a competing dressing in the United Kingdom. In addition, the plaintiffs wrote to hospital officers in the following terms:

> "Dear Sir, You are, of course, familiar with our British-made dressing 'Op-Site.' 'Op-Site' is protected by our British patent No. 1,280,631. It has come to our attention that 3M United Kingdom plc has recently begun to import into this country, and offer for sale, its dressing Tegaderm which infringes our patent and particularly claim 28 of that patent. It will probably come as no surprise to you to learn that we have issued proceedings against 3M United Kingdom plc for an injunction. We thought it right to let you know of our actions."

The letter prompted a cross-application by the defendants to restrain a trade libel.

2. The decision at first instance Falconer J. dismissed the defendants' application but granted an injunction to restrain the defendants by their officers, servants, agents or otherwise until after judgment in the action or until further order in the meantime, from making, disposing of, offering to dispose of, using, importing or keeping whether for disposal or otherwise, adhesive dressings identified by the trade mark TEGADERM or otherwise infringing claim 28 of letters patent No. 1,280,631.

3. Was there a serious issue to be tried? Yes.

4. In a patent action—how much need the defendant aver, to establish a serious issue?

802

(a) *The policy problem:* Lawton L.J. said at 99(13–18):

"The problem we have to consider, having regard to Mr Blanco White's cross-notice, is what in this class of case has to be shown in order to enable the court to say that thee is a serious issue to be tried. Mr Gratwick told us—the thoroughness of his researches was not queried by Mr Blanco White—that to date there has been no case indicating the extent to which a defendant on an interlocutory motion of this kind is expected to reveal his case."

(b) *The patentee's problem:* Lawton L.J. explained at 99(29–39):

"Mr Blanco White's argument is understandable, if I may be allowed to say so, because in this class of litigation it would be very easy for an infringer to put forward a bare denial of the infringement so as to enable him to go on dealing with the subject of the patent until trial, probably making a great deal of money in the meantime, and then submitting to judgment but content with the profits he had already made. We know from experience in this court that often there is a good deal of profitable infringement going on in relation to patented products which are copied in other parts of the world and imported into this country. Sometimes those who do the importing are very difficult to reach for the purposes of executing any money judgment. In that class of case an interlocutory judgment is a very valuable aid to the administration of justice."

(c) *How much was the defence prepared to concede?* Lawton L.J. said at 99(19–29):

"I remind myself that in our system of litigation those who claim have to prove their case. Defendants normally do not have to reveal to the court before trial, save in their pleadings, what their case is. There are two well known exceptions to that rule—one under Order 14, the other under Order 86. Mr Gratwick pointed out that, as a matter of leading, all he had to do so far as there was an allegation of infringement of the plaintiffs' patent was concerned, was to deny that the defendants had infringed the patent. That is so. He conceded, however, that, in so far as he was challenging the validity of the plaintiffs' patent—and he says that the defendants are challenging the validity—he would have to give particulars of the grounds on which he was going to say that the patent was invalid."

(d) *The solution—"good faith":* The question of good faith arose because the plaintiffs advanced the following argument: the patent was dated 1969. The plaintiffs' monopoly was to end in 1985. Thereafter, under the Patents' Act, the plaintiffs would have to grant licences to other parties who wished to use the patent, on such terms as may be agreed

803

or the Patent Officer decides. Thus, the argument developed, the inference could be drawn that the defendants were engaged in a ploy whereby they were pretending that they had a defence to the infringement action when they had not, but they knew that, if they could keep the litigation going for two-and-a-half years, they would have built up during that time a considerable amount of goodwill for themselves; and even if they lost in the end, they could then claim that they were entitled to be granted a licence. Against that background, Lawton L.J. said at 99(40–45):

"It follows, in my judgment, that in this kind of case it behoves a defendant to show that he genuinely does intend to defend the plaintiffs' claim. How he does it will depend upon the facts of each case. The defendants in this case were able to do so easily, because the history of the dispute, starting as it did in September 1981, shows a consistent attitude on the part of the defendants towards the plaintiffs' claim that they had a valid patent and their allegation that the defendants had infringed it. In other cases a different kind of evidence may be required, but I am satisfied, for the reason I shall be pointing out later, that it is not necessary for the defendants to reveal the claims of their defence to a claim for infringement."

And Lawton L.J. went on at 101(5–9):

"It seems to me, therefore, that in this class of case, although the defendants, according to the circumstances, will have to show that they genuinely intend to defend the action and are not merely playing for time so as to get a further opportunity of infringing the plaintiffs' patent, it is not necessary for them to reveal in detail what their case is."

5. Were damages an adequate remedy for the plaintiff? No—Lawton L.J. said at 102(16–24):

"It suffices, I think, now for me to say that I am satisfied that the amount of time, energy and money which the plaintiffs have put into the marketing of Op-Site does justify them taking up the attitude that from now on, pending the trial of the action, if the defendants, or indeed any others who are minded to come into this market—and there are others—are allowed to do so, irreparable damage would be done to the plaintiffs, and that is particularly so having regard to the time interval between the present date and 1985 when the plaintiffs' monopoly position runs out."

6. The "hot furnace" point The defendant had argued that during formal discussion, the plaintiffs had expressed a willingness to accept a royalty

payment—and relied on the "hot furnace" case of *Neilson v. Thompson &
Forman* (1841) 1 W.P.C. 275 in support of the principle that in such
circumstances, where plaintiffs have indicated willingness to give up their
monopoly position, they cannot now say that money cannot compensate
for any damage that may be done between now and trial. Lawton L.J.
accepted that as a general principle but held on the facts of the case that
there was insufficient evidence of willingness to accept a royalty payment.

7. What happened to the defendant's application? The Court of Appeal
rejected the defendant's appeal against Falconer J.'s refusal to restrain the
alleged "trade libel". Lawton L.J. said at 103(1–14):

> "I do not find it necessary to review the law in any detail, because it
> has long been accepted, ever since the case of *Bonnard v. Perryman*
> [[1891] 2 Ch. 269] in the last century, that where there is a libel—this
> would include a trade libel—if the party publishing it says he intends
> to justify, then no injunction restraining the republication of the libel
> will be issued. If it is necessary to bring that proposition up to date
> with a more recent case, it is to be found in the judgment of Oliver
> J. (as he then was) in *Bestobell Paints Ltd v. Bigg* [1975] F.S.R. 421.
> In that case Oliver J. was of the opinion that injunctions should not
> be granted to restrain the publication of trade libels unless they were
> obviously untruthful and libellous. This letter was libellous but the
> plaintiffs say that it was not untruthful and they propose at the trial,
> if it becomes necessary, to justify every word they have put in it.
> That, in my judgment, they are entitled to do if they can. If they fail,
> then of course they might find themselves having to pay very substantial
> damages. That is the risk they must be prepared to take if they raise
> a plea of justification."

13 *Conder International Ltd v. Hibbing Ltd* [1984] F.S.R. 312, C.A.

1. The facts The defendants produced a petrol interceptor tank which
had features which bore a fairly pronounced degree of similarity to the
features of the plaintiffs' interceptor tank. However, what prompted the
plaintiffs moving for interlocutory relief to restrain the defendants from
counselling or procuring others to infringe the patent in suit was that the
defendants' product was accomplished by instructions recommending the
tank to be embedded in concrete—a feature of the subject matter of one
of the plaintiffs' patents. Buckley L.J. put it at 313:

> "The plaintiffs do not complain that in so doing the defendants have
> themselves infringed the patent, but that they are counselling and

procuring others—that is to say, that those who buy their interceptor tank from them—to infringe the patent, and the plaintiffs seek an injunction to restrain such counselling and procuring. It is not suggested that by counselling and procuring others to infringe the patent, the defendants themselves infringe the patent."

In contrast to the plaintiffs who were financially sound, the defendants were a very young business operating on a very small scale and there was doubt as to whether they could meet any liability in damages. There was clearly a serious issue to be tried. This appeal turned on the decision at first instance not to grant an injunction.

2. The "adequacy of damages" criteria For different reasons, damages were not an adequate remedy for either party: for the plaintiffs, by virtue of the defendant's potential inability to pay; for the defendants, by reasons of the difficulty of assessment necessarily associated with the very incipient state of the business. It was thus necessary to turn to the "balance of convenience."

3. Balance of convenience

(a) *First factor—alternative business:*
   (i) Plaintiffs' argument: If the injunction is granted, the defendants would not be put out of business—they could concentrate on developing that side of their business which related to the sale of plastic septic tanks and cesspools.
   (ii) Ruling: Buckley L.J. said at 315:

   "This does not appeal to me as being at all a strong argument. If the defendants are entitled to deal in interceptor tanks, they are entitled to develop that side of their business either in preference to, or side by side with, the rest of their business; if they are not so entitled they will of course be liable in damages, when the matter has been determined at the trial, for any infringements that are proved to have taken place. But the fact that the defendants may have other activities to which they could turn their minds and resources does not seem to me to be a strong ground for saying that they should therefore be the more readily restrained from carrying on what may turn out to be a perfectly legitimate business."

And Goff L.J. said at 317:

   "It had to be borne in mind, and the learned judge did bear it in mind, that the defendants were at the outset of their business and that therefore they were, and are, in a very vulnerable position. It is not, as my Lord has said, an answer to say that they had other aspects of their business to which they could turn. Just starting their business as they are it must be very important that they should be able to develop it whichever way they might wish to go."

(b) *Second factor—the "snowball" effect:*

(i) Plaintiffs' argument: At 315:

"What is meant by that expression is that the plaintiffs conceive themselves to be open to the depredations of infringers in this case because of the simplicity of their invention and because of the comparative cheapness of its manufacture and the ease of its installation by the purchaser. They have had to fight off four to five infringers already, apart from the defendants, and they say that if the defendants are not restrained, other infringers will be encouraged to come into the market and infringe their patent. This is called the snowball effect. It is not suggested that that would itself be an element in assessing damage for which the plaintiffs could hold the defendants liable, but it is said that it is a proper consideration to take into account in arriving at the balance of convenience in determining whether or not this is a case in which an interlocutory injunction should be granted."

(ii) Ruling: At 315–316:

"I would not say that that is not a proper consideration to take into account, or that it might not be a proper consideration to take into account in a suitable case; but prima facie it must surely be for the plaintiff company to protect itself against all infringers, and it does not appeal to me at all as an argument for holding that the defendants in the present case should be subjected to an injunction which would otherwise not be granted against them."

Injunction refused.

14 *Fleming Fabrications Ltd v. Albion Cylinders Ltd* [1989] R.P.C. 47

1. The facts When Messrs Carruthers and Warburton were employees of the plaintiffs, Mr Carruthers had invented a self-priming device for use in domestic central heating and hot water systems, which was called "Spartan". The plaintiffs were the registered proprietor of the patent in suit of the "Spartan". Subsequently Messrs Carruthers and Warburton had joined the defendants and produced for the defendants a similar device called "Ventank". The plaintiffs applied for an interlocutory injunction to stop the defendants marketing it.

807

2. The appeal Falconer J. found that both sides were good for such damages as would be quantifiable, and granted the injunction to preserve the status quo. The defendants appealed.

3. The first issue: were damages adequate for the plaintiffs? The defendants argued that if an injunction was wrongly withheld the plaintiffs would suffer a loss of sales, but that loss would be quantifiable by reference to their own (the defendants') sales. Moreover, the patent was not about to expire: it had eight more years to run for the plaintiffs to recover their position if they succeeded at trial. The plaintiffs replied that the defendants were not offering an undertaking that their loss was quantifiable by reference to their own sales. And the eight years' monopoly which the plaintiffs would enjoy if successful at trial was meaningless in the light of the fact that both sides accepted that the present time was absolutely critical for marketing the devices in question.

4. The Court of Appeal held: in the circumstances damages would not be adequate for the plaintiffs May L.J. said:

> "I respectfully agree with the view expressed by the learned judge below that, if the plaintiffs were merely paid by way of damages by the defendants if they do not get an interlocutory injunction but are held to be entitled to a permanent injunction at the trial, that would not be full compensation for what they would in those circumstances have lost. ... In the end I also agree with the learned judge ... that, so far as these respondents are concerned, to be debarred from marketing their 'Spartan' might have a catastrophic effect on their business if their opportunity to develop their main product were to be jeopardised."

5. The second issue: were damages adequate for the defendants? The defendants contended that the evidence when properly scrutinised plainly showed that the plaintiffs were not good for damages. The plaintiffs argued that the judge was right to hold that the plaintiffs would be able to meet any liability under the cross-undertaking; and even if they would not, the court should not too stringently examine a plaintiff's ability to meet any liability unless it amounted to a situation where the plaintiff was not able to provide a credible cross-undertaking at all. The plaintiffs were allowed to adduce further evidence of their finances.

6. The Court of Appeal held: damages would not be adequate for the defendants, but that was not the end of it May L.J. said:

> "It is quite apparent, in my view, particularly when one analyses the fresh evidence which was put before the court on the hearing of this

appeal, that the plaintiff respondents have not cleared the previous debt situation. It has been tidied up and it has been resolved in a particular transaction whereby, in effect, the bank has been substituted for the previous creditor. ... It is true that they have been able to arrange a fresh injection of working capital amounting to some £55,000, but that has only been achieved as a result of the chairman ... of the plaintiff company ... mortgaging the family home ... I for my part doubt very much if the plaintiff respondents could in 18 months' time find £100,000 by way of damages to the appellants without going under. I think it probable that they could not."

7. Why then an injunction? Because the adequacy of damages is only part of the balance of convenience. May L.J. said:

"I fully appreciate that if one simply does the damages exercise, to which reference is so often made when *American Cyanamid* is quoted, the result might seem to be that no interlocutory injunction should go in the circumstances of the instant case. On the other hand, when one bears in mind that that is only part of the balance of the risk of doing an injustice and looks at all the other considerations ... I think that that balance in the circumstances of the instant case does require the grant of an interlocutory injunction against the appellants."

8. And there were other factors in the balance

"What are the factors to take into account in the instant case in addition to those financial ones to which I have already referred?

I think it is material to remember that the appellants only very recently began marketing their 'Ventank'. ... The plaintiff respondents quite clearly spent a lot of time and money in developing the 'Spartan'. ... I need say no more than that there is more than significant evidence on the affidavits before the court that at least since leaving the employ of the respondents, and probably before, Mr Carruthers and Mr Warburton acted against the interests of their then employers, and have been since acting against the interests and in derogation of the interests of the respondents, the licensed proprietors of the patent.

There is, I think, also force in [counsel for the plaintiffs'] submission that, if nothing were done, the public—and, in particular, the customers for these devices—might well be led to conclude that the appellants' 'Ventank' has the Gas and Water Board approval which the 'Spartan' has and which the 'Ventank' does not in fact have."

809

15 *Improver Corporation v. Remington Consumer Products Ltd* [1989] R.P.C. 69, C.A.

1. The facts The plaintiffs were the proprietor and licensees of a European patent in a women's depilatory device called "Epilady," which worked by means of a rotating helical coil. The defendants were the manufacturers and retail sellers of a depilatory device called "Lady Remington Smooth and Silky" which worked by means of a rotating arced rubber rod with slits in. The plaintiffs brought an action for infringement of their patent and sought an interlocutory injunction to stop the defendants marketing their device.

2. The relief sought The notice of motion sought to restrain the defendants and each of them from importing into the United Kingdom, selling, advertising for sale, offering for sale, exposing for sale, supplying, dealing in for the purposes of trade or disposing of the item now called by the defendants "Smooth and Silky", an example of which is exhibited to an affidavit in the pleadings. The Court of Appeal granted the injunction omitting the words "advertising for sale, offering for sale, exposing for sale."

3. The unfortunate background The plaintiffs' application for an interlocutory injunction was coupled with an application by the defendants to strike the action out as frivolous, vexatious and an abuse of the process of the court. Falconer J. had acceded to the defendants' application on the footing that there was no basis on which it could be said that the defendants' device infringed the patent. Five days later a West German court, which was referred to Falconer J.'s decision, did not accede to an application to strike the action out, and granted the injunction. Both courts were applying the same European Patent Convention and the same principle of construction.

4. The plaintiffs' case Dillon L.J. summarised it as follows:

> "The plaintiffs put their case in two ways. They say that the rod of elastomeric material, though solid and merely having slits on its circumference, is in truth, if you consider the positioning of the slits and the solid areas of circumference left, a helical spring: alternatively they say—and this, to my mind, is a much simpler and more attractive way of presenting their case—that the rod of elastomeric material is merely a mechanical equivalent for the helical spring."

5. Was there a serious question to be tried? Yes. The Court of Appeal applied *American Cyanamid*, quoting extensively from Lord Diplock's judgment at each stage. Having considered the English authorities on infringement of patents Dillon L.J. observed:

> "The fact that their Lordships had differed in those cases indicates that how far variants do or do not infringe can often be a matter of considerable difficulty."

And later,

> "Against this background it seems to me that the question of whether on a purposive construction this particular mechanical equivalent does or does not infringe the patent is a question of considerable difficulty. It is wholly inappropriate for a striking-out application. ... In the present case I have no doubt, considering the matters I have already rehearsed, that there is a serious question to be tried. It certainly cannot be said that the plaintiffs are bound to fail."

6. Would damages be adequate for the defendants? No.

> ". ... it would be extremely difficult to quantify the damages which the defendants will suffer if an interlocutory injunction is granted and if the defendants succeed at the trial, because until the trial the defendants will have been kept out of a market which they are only just entering and it would be impossible to calculate satisfactorily what sales in the market they would otherwise have achieved."

7. Would damages be adequate for the plaintiffs? Possibly not.

> "So far as the damage to the plaintiffs is concerned, if they are refused an interlocutory injunction but succeed at the trial, one possible measure of the damage might be to say that the maximum would be the value of all sales which any of the defendants effected until judgment in the action. But it is not as simple as that, partly because of a possible knock-on effect with other infringers.
>
> ... as it seems to me, the conclusion must be that there is a risk that the plaintiffs would not be adequately compensated by an award of damages for the loss to be sustained as a result of the defendants continuing to do what is sought to be enjoined between the time of the present application and the time of the trial."

8. The status quo

The Court of Appeal noted that if there is doubt as to the adequacy of the respective remedies in damages available to either party or to both, it should then consider the balance of convenience, and where other factors appear to be evenly balanced it is a counsel of prudence to preserve the status quo. The Court therefore granted an injunction.

> "So far as the status quo is concerned, the plaintiff moved as soon as

the defendants' device came on the market. They actually found one of the defendants' devices for sale only a few days before the issue of the writ."

C: COPYRIGHT

1 *Radley Gowns Ltd v. Costas Spyrou* [1975] F.S.R. 455, *per* Oliver J.

1. The facts The plaintiff manufacturer of ladies' dresses applied for an interlocutory injunction in a breach of copyright action concerning the production by the defendant of certain dresses which were substantially the same as patterns designed by the plaintiff's designers. The terms of the injunction sought were to restrain breaches in relation to:
  (a) A prototype dress.
  (b) The cutting patterns.
  (c) The design sketches.
The defendant contended there was no serious issue to be tried on the basis that cutting patterns could not be the subject of copyright and a dress could not be a "reproduction" of an original sketch.

2. Statute Section 3(1) of the Copyright Act 1956 provided:

> "In this Act 'artistic work' means a work of any of the following descriptions, that is to say—(a) the following, irrespective of artistic quality, namely paintings, sculptures, drawings, engravings and photographs; (b) works of architecture, being either buildings or models for buildings; (c) works of artistic craftsmanship, not falling within either of the preceding paragraphs."

3. Injunction granted—why?

(a) *First issue:* was the prototype dress a work of artistic craftsmanship?
  (i) Case for defence: The prototype no longer exists, and thus it was impossible to predicate if it was a work of artistic craftsmanship. Further, to be such a work the artistry and the craftsmanship have to be united in the author of the work: *Burke and Margo-Burke Ltd v. Spicers Dress Designs* [1936] Ch. 400. And in any event, whether a work is of artistic craftsmanship is one of fact to be determined in the light of the evidence—and here, there was no evidence bearing on this issue in support of the motion, only by way of affidavit in reply.
  (ii) For the plaintiffs, *inter alia*: The plaintiff initially is entitled to

rely upon the statutory presumption in section 20(1) of the Act that copyright subsisted in the matter to which the action related until that was challenged in the defendant's affidavit in answer.

(iii) Ruling: Not necessarily a valid criticism that the prototype no longer existed. *Burke v. Spicers (ibid.)* was not conclusive on the point taken with regard to the separate contributions: see *Hensher (G.) Ltd v. Restawhile Upholstery (Lancs.) Ltd* [1976] A.C. 64. Section 20(1) of the Act—a point validly taken by the plaintiff.

(b) *Second issue:* can and did copyright subsist in the cutting patterns?
   (i) Case for the defence: The only conceivable applicable heading in the Act is section 3(1)(a), namely "drawing" and even as expanded by section 48(1), this includes only a "diagram, map, chart or plan." In contract, the cutting patterns are merely functional objects, individual instruments in respect of which no copyright can subsist—as was the case of the pattern sleeve: *Hollindrake v. Traswell* (1894) 3 Ch.D. 420.
   (ii) Ruling:

"As regards the cutting patterns, I do not happily have to decide on this motion the question of whether they are or are not drawings. It is in fact obvious from inspection, even if it were not almost self-evident, that the patterns have been cut along the lines drawn on the larger sheet of brown paper of which they originally formed part. At the moment I am not sure that I see why that which was a drawing beyond dispute on the virgin sheet ceases to be a drawing because it is cut out. I would be surprised, for instance, if a silhouette did not fall within the description of a drawing. It does not really seem to me to be an answer to say that the cut-out serves a functional rather than an artistic purpose. It is, however, sufficient for present purposes to say that the question appears to me to be clearly an arguable one, and I cannot accept that there is any solution which is so obvious that it can be said that there is no serious question to be tried."

(c) *Third issue:* Can a made-up dress which assumes the shape only when filled up with a dummy or a model, or being on a hanger, be by itself a reproduction of a sketch?
   (i) Case for defence: The sketches are original works of art in which copyright subsists. But by reference to section 9(8) of the Act, and *Burke v. Spicers (ibid.)* the dresses cannot be classified as reproductions from the sketches.
   (ii) Ruling: By reference to *Gleeson v. Denne* [1975] R.P.C. 471, the court was unable to derive any very general principle or guidance from Clauson J.'s inability on the facts of *Burke v. Spicers* to

813

discern a resemblance between the dress in that case and the sketch of the lady. Oliver J. went on to say that he could not draw from it any principle that a dress cannot be a three-dimensional copy of a sketch."

"I have seen the clothes which are exhibits AL3 to AL6 inclusive, and I have compared them with the sketches CC1, MW5, MW9 and MW13. Such comparison, I am bound to say, leaves me in no doubt at all as to their derivation."

Injunction granted.

2 *Slick Brands (Clothing) Ltd v. Jollybird Ltd* [1975] F.S.R. 470

1. The facts The plaintiffs, specialists in fashion garments, had produced an original design sketch for denim jeans, which they had termed Z4 and which were to be labelled under their logo "Made in Heaven". The defendants acquired a pair of jeans manufactured to the Z4 design and they in turn ordered a sample to that design from Hong Kong manufacturers, with a follow-up order for 4,000 pairs to go under the logo "Jollyjeans". The plaintiffs placed a "trap" order on April 9, 1974 and issued a writ and notice of motion on April 21, prompting the defendants to cancel their follow-up order. The plaintiffs claimed a *quia timet* injunction on the basis that the copying of the jeans produced from that design was an indirect copying and the defendant conceded that there was a serious issue to be tried. The case turned upon "adequacy of damages" and "balance of convenience".

2. Damages not an adequate remedy for the plaintiff—arguments

(a) *First argument—unfair competition:* In their affidavit, the plaintiffs deposed:

"I have very little doubt that many of our customers or potential customers for style Z4 will see the copy garments to be sold by the defendants and believe that they had come from us. The clothing trade is plagued with manufacturers, many of them of little financial standing, who copy successful designs produced by the major companies and sell them at a very low price. This has two effects: it is very likely that we shall receive complaints from our own customers who will consider that they have been overcharged for their purchases or that we have deliberately sold the same garment to other outlets at a lower price. Of course, nearly always a copied design is made in inferior materials and with very cheap, back-street labour but the damage to companies such as my own is nevertheless very considerable.

Furthermore the presence of the copy garments upon the market is likely to have a very dampening effect on sales of our own products."

(b) *Second argument—loss of goodwill:* Oliver J. said at 475:

"There is also a further possible loss of goodwill—I have not had much evidence about it but it is a matter of common-sense deduction— that if the style is a popular one and pleasing to the public, then the potential goodwill attached to the 'Made in Heaven' label will also be diluted. Such loss is not readily provable or capable of precise assessment in damages. Therefore if the plaintiffs prove to be right at the trial and no injunction is now granted, their immediate and ascertainable loss from competition can be readily compensated, provided the defendant company are good for the damages, but there is a possible loss of goodwill, which is not easily quantifiable, for which it would not be altogether easy to compensate them."

(c) *Third argument—damages would be an adequate remedy for the defendants:* Oliver J. said at 475:

"Turning to the defendants, if an injunction is granted and the plaintiffs fail at the trial, with the result that the defendants really ought to have been free all the time to produce the jeans which they want to produce, the position would be that no stocks have been in fact held on which a loss has been sustained; the defendants have not lost anything in the way of material because the material which was brought in for the purpose of cutting these jeans has been diverted to other purposes; and there is no evidence before me of any orders for jeans which have been lost as a result of these proceedings so far. It seems to me that the loss which will be sustained by the defendants, in the event which I have indicated of there being an injunction which is not held at the trial, will be simply the loss of potential profit which may be sustained by the inability of the defendants to trade in this particular style. Theoretically I suppose it would be possible for the defendants to produce other jeans incorporating the same or perhaps all the features of the plaintiffs' jeans without actually copying, but I think there is force in Mr Fysh's submission that in practice they would never be quite certain if they did that whether they were infringing or not. Again that is a loss which is altogether not easily ascertainable."

3. The defendants' riposte—plaintiffs not good for the money Oliver J. said at 476:

"A good deal of evidence has been directed to the question whether in the event of an injunction being granted the plaintiffs are in a

815

position to meet any cross-undertaking which would, as a matter of ordinary course, be extracted from them on the grant of an injunction. The plaintiffs are a £100 company formed apparently in August 1972. The evidence before me indicates that no annual return has been filed. There are no accounts filed but there have been produced by Mr Sergeant, who is a chartered accountant and a partner in the company's auditors, draft accounts which go up to November 30, 1974."

And Oliver J. went on to say at 478:

"I have been somewhat concerned about the plaintiffs' ability to meet the undertaking in damages which they would have to give if such an injunction were granted."

4. The plaintiffs parry the riposte The plaintiffs were granted an injunction——and three bases therefore emerge from the judgment of Oliver J. at 478:

(a) *Payment-in:*

"Mr Laddie has told me, and I think with some force, that in the absence of any evidence before me indicating any way in which that damage could be quantified it is really very difficult for me to suggest any amount which could be paid into court by way of security in respect of the cross-undertaking, though he indicates that his clients would be willing to make such a payment-in and he is instructed to offer an undertaking in damages not only on behalf of the plaintiff company but also on behalf of the other company I have mentioned, Slick Brands Limited."

(Although, in the result, a payment-in was not ordered.)

(b) *Status quo:*

"The status quo here was that the plaintiffs were first in the field with this particular design. It was the defendants who were threatening to change the position."

(c) *Merits:*

"I think I am entitled, if there is a state of equilibrium with regard to the balance of convenience, to consider the probabilities when the action comes to trial. If the matter rested simply on Exhibit LAT.1 alone, it seems to me that there is a good deal of argument whether that exhibit can reasonably be said to be a substantial copy of the drawings which were produced for the design of Z4 by Mrs. Jenner in August 1974, but the production now of the order which was referred to in paragraph 11 of Mr Shah's affidavit leaves it I think beyond doubt that what was intended by the defendants at the time when the writ was issued was that there should be produced by their manufacturers in Hong Kong as faithful a copy of the plaintiffs' Z4 jeans as could be produced. As it seems to me that there is a strong case for arguing that that would be an indirect copying of the original sketch, in those circumstances it seems to me that the balance rests somewhat in the plaintiffs' favour."

3 Potters-Ballotini Ltd v. Weston-Baker [1977] R.P.C. 202

1. The background The plaintiffs were the exclusive U.K. manufacturers of tiny glass beads used to make white lines on roads. They had employed the defendants Weston-Baker and Cramphorn as general manager and works manager respectively. The latter was particularly well informed as to the plaintiffs' manufacturing processes, having helped construct production facilities for such beads in Germany and Brazil, and having supervised the construction of the plaintiffs' plant. Both these defendants were subject to terms in their contracts of employment binding them not to divulge any secrets or other information—and not, for one year after their appointments terminated, to use any secrets relating to the production of such beads ("ballotini").

2. The facts The defendants, Weston-Baker and Cramphorn terminated their employment with the plaintiffs, as from March 1975. However, from 1974, the defendants (including a Mr Boylin, who had constructed the plaintiffs' U.K. plant) planned the construction of a rival and strikingly similar factory, which was ready to produce as from the end of 1975. The plaintiffs issued a writ against all three defendants, on December 4, 1975 and applied for an interlocutory injunction. The hearing was adjourned for the defence to file evidence, upon the defendants' undertaking not to commence production until March 1, 1976. Neild J. refused the injunction on February 14, and production started on February 26.

3. The plaintiffs' problem They had to rely on the restrictive covenant, and the "confidential information" argument, because the plaintiff had no patent for any part of their machines, their processes or their products; and they had no claim to any copyright in any sketch, design or drawing which was used in making the plant or any part of it.

4. Were there serious issues to be tried? Yes—namely:
  (a) After the period of "one year" had expired, how free were the first and second defendants to use confidential information? Lord Denning M.R. said at 205(20–35):

"Potters had made express agreements with Mr Weston-Baker and Mr Cramphorn by which each agreed not for one year to use for himself, confidential information. What is the effect of the 'one year'? Does it mean that after the year has ended, these men can use the information freely? We have been referred to passages from Lord Greene's statement in *Vokes Ltd v. Heather* (1945) 62 R.P.C. 135, and his later statement in *British Celanese Ltd v. Moncrieff* [1948] Ch. 564. I do not think it is necessary or desirable to give any final ruling, but I must say that these clauses seem to me designed to cover the period for which the company is seeking to protect confidential information. It can well be said that, after the men had left for one year, they were free from an obligation as to the use of confidential information. ... The employment of these two men certainly came to an end in March 1975. If the obligation as to confidence is governed by the contract—and was only for one year after the service ended—it would come to an end in March 1975, that is, next month. If either of them broke it in the past there might be a remedy in damages, but there would not be a remedy by way of injunction for the future, seeing that they will soon be free to use it as they please."

(b) To what extent was the information confidential? Lord Denning M.R. said at 206(5–10) after citing *Stephenson Jordan & Harrison Ltd v. MacDonald v. Evans* (1952) 69 R.P.C. 23:

"In this case it seems to me there would be great difficulty in determining to what extent the features of this plant or this process were confidential, especially when one remembers that there are other rival plants making ballotini in Germany and Austria, and have done for many years. There is a great deal of information which may be said to be in the public domain. But apart from that, if not in the public domain, how far was it confidential to Potters— so as to belong to them—as distinct from the man's own knowledge and expertise, which he certainly is not to be prevented from using. ..."

(c) if there were a "springboard", for how long was it to last? Lord Denning said at 206(37)–207(2):

"Assuming that the point is overcome, there is the problem, which has been discussed, and much discussed of late, of what is called the 'springboard' doctrine, whereby it is said that a servant or any other person who has got confidential information ought not to save himself the time of working it out for himself or getting it from some other people without paying for it. I need not go through all the cases. They are all well summarised by Megarry J. in his valuable judgment in *Coco v. Clark (A.N.) (Engineers) Ltd* [1969] R.P.C. 41. Although a man must not use such information as a springboard to get a start over others, nevertheless that springboard does not last for ever. If he does use it, a time may come when so much has happened that he can no longer be restrained."

5. Damages—an adequate remedy to the defendants? No:
(a) *per* Lord Denning M.R. at 207(15–20):

"But then, in considering the balance of convenience, so far as the defendants are concerned, the effect of an injunction at this stage might be disastrous, even though it was only for a limited number of months until trial. Here is a great plant (I agree that it was erected surreptitiously and secretly, as far as one could see) but it cost a quarter of a million pounds. The money has been raised on loan, on security of debentures, and men are working there now. I agree that the defendants ought not to be allowed to gain any advantage by any unlawful conduct, but the effect of an injunction might be disastrous."

(b) *per* Scarman L.J. at 209(5–10):

"But one has to consider further circumstances in this connection. Mr Sandys has submitted that it would be a catastrophe for the defendants now to be put out of business, since the chances of them being able to resume business later, if they should be successful at the trial, would be imperilled. I think there is substance in that point. I very much doubt whether the only sacrifice that would thereby be imposed upon the defendants would be the payment of the interest charges on unused plant. The risk that an interim injunction would put them permanently out of business is a factor, the weight of which it is not easy to assess; but it would be catastrophic if it should arise."

6. Balance of convenience

(a) *Injunction sought—too broad: Per* Lord Scarman L.J. at 209(20–25):

"The injunction sought in this case is an injunction to restrain the defendants from using or assisting others to use all or any of the knowledge acquired by them or any of them in the course of their employment by or dealings with the plaintiffs or their associated companies or any of them concerning any trade secrets, design specifications, technical information or other confidential information relating to the production and marketing of ballotini."

(b) *Merits: Per* Scarman L.J. at 210(5):

"For reasons which my Lord the Master of the Rolls has already given, reasons associated with the service contracts under which Mr Weston-Baker and Mr Cramphorn were at one time employed, I would expect this case to sound rather in damages than in injunction. Of course, that could well be an estimate that is proved wrong in the event, but the contract, particularly the time limit of one year imposed by clause 2(c) in the contract, the clause which deals with the use of confidential information, is a pointer to the likelihood of damages rather than an injunction."

4. *Aljose Fashions Ltd (trading as Fiona Dresses) v. Alfred Young & Company Ltd* [1978] F.S.R. 364, C.A.

1. The facts The plaintiffs (large purchasers of ladies' dresses and a subsidiary of a very substantial company) alleged that the defendants (a subsidiary also of a very substantial company) had copied one of their dress designs—the work of one well known in the fashion world. At first instance Slade J. said that the dresses in similarity were "so close that they must be copies." He granted an injunction which restrained the defendant from "selling, distributing or disposing of ladies' dresses which are substantially copies from the plaintiffs' designs."

2. Was there a serious issue to be tried? The issue was—did the plaintiffs have copyright in their sketches and the underlying designs? And the issue had to be tried—by virtue of the case advanced by the defendants, summarised by Lord Denning M.R. at 365:

"The defendants then put in an affidavit. It is plain that they completely controvert the allegation which is made by the plaintiffs. The defendants say that they supply the mass market with dresses in this country. They follow trends and adopt features made fashionable by specialist dress houses and designers mostly from Paris, London and New York. In other words, they say that both the plaintiffs and the defendants get their designs and trends from the same sources. Mr Bury, who speaks for the defendants, goes on to say that the exhibits produced—that is, the dresses produced—'are neither innovative nor original but are variations of dresses currently sold by a large number of dress manufacturers.' He says that the particular design was the result of a visit by a consultant to Cannes in France where he saw lots of suits and dresses similar to those in question in this action. He is therefore asserting that these were not copies from Pat Farrell, but they came from a common source and were the sort of designs which people working separately would produce."

820

3. Were damages an adequate remedy? Yes:

(a) *Per* Lord Denning M.R. at 366:

> "In those circumstances, as both concerns are amply provided with finance, it seems plain to me that this is not a case for stopping the trade of the defendants but it is a matter which can properly be dealt with in damages. After all, the defendants have to take the risk: if they have been copying the plaintiffs' dresses, if they are copying them and continue to copy them, there will no doubt be very substantial damages which they will have to pay. That is the proper remedy, it seems to me, for the plaintiffs in this case. In view of the big contest on the affidavits I do not think now at this stage it is a proper matter for an injunction."

(b) *Per* Lawton L.J. at 367:

> "I agree entirely that the balance of convenience is that these parties should fight it out for a money stake. The court should not help either of them by granting an injunction."

4. Balance of convenience Against an injunction. As Lord Denning M.R. said at 366:

> "I can see that the continuance of this injunction against the defendants would make things very difficult for them. It is in such wide terms that it would be most difficult and embarrassing for them to comply with it. They would not know the bounds of what they could do nor not do. They would be in the greatest difficulty in knowing what they could legitimately do."

5 *Monet of London Ltd v. Richards (Sybil) Ltd, Desilu Dresses Ltd and C & A Modes* [1978] F.S.R. 368, *per* Browne-Wilkinson J.

1. The facts The plaintiffs, a comparatively young company in a moderate scale of business, alleged that the second defendants had copied and manufactured, and the third defendants retailed (at a price substantially lower than the normal retail price of the dress produced by the plaintiffs), a dress designed by the plaintiff. As to the similarity between the dresses, Browne-Wilkinson J. said at 370–371:

> "I express no view on it and nor am I able to beyond saying this: to the untutored eye, and no eye is less tutored than mine, there is a very strong similarity at first sight between the two dresses. The differences, and there are differences, between the two dresses relate

to what my eye appears to be matters of detail rather than of the main features of the design. Beyond expressing the tentative view that if they are two separate designs there has been an unusual coincidence in two such designs occurring at much the same time I express no further view on the facts at all."

2. Was there a serious issue to be tried? Yes—for the second defendant alleged that the similarity was mere coincidence.

3. Damages—an adequate remedy for the plaintiff? No—at 372:

(a) *Impossibility of quantification:*

"I am quite satisfied that so far as the plaintiff company is concerned damages will not be an adequate remedy at the trial. Is it true that some estimate will be able to be made as to the number of sales which the plaintiff company will have lost by reason of the competitive selling at a lower price by the defendant Desilu. However, that at best will only be an approximation. It is never possible to say how many sales might have been made if things had been different."

(b) *Goodwill:*

"More important to my mind is the effect which the continued existence of the alleged copy will have on the plaintiff company's relations with its critical customers, namely the buyers from the large retailers. They are a design house selling original designs. If the buyers from the large retailers find that they have bought at a higher price a design from Monet only to find the market flooded by their rival retailers selling the same or similar dresses at a much lower price, those buyers are going to be unhappy about the position and are likely, and so the evidence shows, in the future to wait and see whether the copy comes on the market at a cheaper price rather than buying the original design from the plaintiffs. All that is on the basis that there is here copying and as I emphasise, it is not found that there is copying. However, if it is proved that there is here a copy in my judgment it is quite impossible to assess how much goodwill, how much trade generally, the plaintiff company will have lost by the existence of rival, cheaper designs being on the market in the interim."

4. Damages—an adequate remedy for the defendants? No—at 373:

(a) *Desilu:*

"If Desilu is at this stage injuncted from producing and marketing a successful line in dresses nobody can say how many dresses they would have sold if they had not been injuncted, or their profit margin on it, or the harm done to their goodwill by disrupting their relationship with their customers."

(b) *C & A Modes:*

"Similarly, in relation to C & A, if it be a good selling line and they are injuncted how many more dresses would they have been able to sell had an injunction not been granted? Therefore I do not think that it is a case of simply looking at damage by themselves, where it can be said that either plaintiffs or the defendants can be adequately covered by damages."

5. Balance of convenience Browne-Wilkinson J. followed *Aljose Fashions* (see p. 820, above), but reluctantly he said at 373–375:

(a) *The significance of the plaintiffs' head-start:*

"It is therefore a question of trying to see where the balance of convenience lies between the two sides. Were it not for authority I would feel that a very important feature in this case is this: the plaintiff company's dress was on the market from October onwards. It had been advertised, shown, and it was in the shops. The defendant Desilu's evidence goes at some length into the care with which Desilu follows the market in fashion goods. They say how important it is to follow closely what has happened, in particular in going to Paris on frequent occasions and in going to fashion shows in London. The plaintiff company's dress having been on the market for four months in this country one would have expected that the evidence put in by the second defendants would have said one way or another whether they were aware when they started to market their similar looking dress that the plaintiff's dress was on the market and of its similarity. Their evidence is totally silent on this matter. When I asked counsel what view I should take on that in the absence of any direct evidence, it was accepted that in the light of the evidence as it stood I must draw the inference that they were aware of the plaintiff's product before they started marketing their own."

(b) *Risk—should be the intruders':*

"In my judgment if in a competitive field like the fashion field it is decided to market a dress which is known to be very similar to another dress already on the market then the person who chooses to come into that market at a later stage ought really to accept that they do sell at their own risk, if it is thought and shown that thee is a real opportunity of it being a copy and an infringing copy. Otherwise I do not see any way in which it can fairly be said that the court can grant an injunction to prevent, what is not in this case, even outright piracy."

(c) *Summary thus far:*

> "In my judgment the court ought not to allow piracy, or the possibility of piracy, to take place in a case where the original design has been on the market for some time and the alleged infringer chooses to come into that market at a later stage. I do not think that the balance of convenience lies equally between those two. I think that the person who chooses to come in with the second confusing garment is in a less strong position than the first. That of course cannot be a general rule; but, in my judgment, it is a factor to be borne in mind."

(d) *Binding authority:*

> "However, I was referred to authority in the Court of Appeal in the case of *Aljose Fashions Ltd (trading as Fiona Dresses) v. Young (Alfred) & Co. Ltd* [1978] F.S.R. 364, also a case in which dress manufacturers had claimed and obtained from the judge at first instance an injunction designed to restrain the copying of the plaintiff company's dresses by the defendants. In that case both the companies involved were substantial companies ... there is no reference there to the defendant company having chosen to come into a market in which the plaintiffs were already marketing. Again that must have been a feature, although we do not know the exact dates on which it took place. In the circumstances I do not feel that it is right for me, as a judge of first instance, to depart from a principle which seems to be laid down that, in the normal case, the remedy in damages is adequate to cover a case where there is alleged copying of a dress design by one dress designer from another. I reach this conclusion, as I think is apparent from what I have said already, with some regret because I do not think that it is a credit to the legal system that in a case of such short-life property as the design of a dress, an alleged infringer, who at the trial has been found to be an actual infringer, can obtain all the benefits of the infringement before relief is given, taking only the risk of being liable to pay damages which are, in the majority of cases, unquantifiable as to a substantial amount. It seems to me that there should be a consistent practice in these matters and for me to seek to draw distinctions which I suspect are not really present on the facts between this case and the *Aljose* case in the Court of Appeal is undesirable. Therefore, with some regret, I refuse the injunction against Desilu Dresses Ltd."

6. Residuary factor—the position of *C & A Modes* Browne-Wilkinson J. explained at 375:

> "It follows in those circumstances that it would be to my mind quite impossible to make an order against C & A Modes. In any event I

would not have granted an injunction against C & A Modes in this case since, if it had been appropriate to grant relief against Desilu Dresses Ltd. C & A Modes had offered an undertaking not to part with the 900 dresses which they retain—save by returning them to the second defendants, Desilu Dresses—on the plaintiffs giving a cross-undertaking in damages secured by a bank guarantee up to the sum of £15,000. However, as I do not think that it is appropriate to grant relief against Desilu Dresses Ltd. I cannot and do not require that undertaking from C & A Modes in this case."

6 Vernon & Co. (Pulp Products) Ltd v. Universal Pulp Containers Ltd [1980] F.S.R. 179

1. The motions

(a) By the plaintiffs: They moved for an interlocutory injunction to restrain the defendants from manufacturing and selling disposable bedpans and male urine bottles identical with or similar to those of the plaintiffs.

(b) By the defendants: They moved to restrain the plaintiffs from giving effect to, or enforcing, or purporting to enforce clause 4.2 of an agreement between the parties made on April 21, 1971.

2. Clause 4.2 It provided:

"In consideration of its position as exclusive supplier in the United Kingdom, Universal agrees that it will not directly or indirectly manufacture or sell Vernaid products for any party anywhere other than V. and will not manufacture or sell any product in fibre or other similar material which may be used in competition with any of the Vernaid products during the continuance of this agreement and for the period of two years after the termination thereof."

3. Clause 4.2—its background

The plaintiffs produced bedpans and urine bottles based on production drawings in which they owned the copyrights (the patents had expired in 1976). To assist their production, they engaged the defendants as sub-contractors in 1964 and some years thereafter supplied the defendants with machines to improve their rate of production. It was the case for the plaintiffs that during an initial period of their relationship they gave to the defendants much technical advice and assistance of a confidential nature for the purpose of producing the bedpans and bottles. Only in 1971 did the parties enter into a formal written agreement in which clause 4.2 featured. The plaintiffs did not renew the agreement upon its expiration after 10 years and launched the interlocutory motion upon being informed by the defendants of their intention to tender for contracts to supply disposable bedpans to hospitals.

4. The case for the plaintiffs The plaintiffs' claim to relief rested on the following heads:

(a) *The contract:* They sought to enforce clause 4.2

(b) *Copyright:* They relied on the copyright in the drawings of the bedpans, and also on separate drawings of the moulds for making the bedpans.

(c) *Confidential information: i.e.* the imparting of technical expertise during the earlier part of their relationship.

5. Contract—a serious issue to be tried? Yes—for the following reasons:
  (a) It was not obviously void as being in restraint of trade, as Sir Robert Megarry V.-C. said at 185.

> "If clause 4.2 is valid, clearly Vernons can restrain what UPC propose to do. Whether or not UPC will succeed in their attack on the clause as being void because it is an unreasonable restraint of trade is something that must await the trial. I certainly cannot say, on the evidence before me, that the sub-clause is so plainly bad that Vernons have no fairly arguable right to enforce it."

  (b) Were clauses 4.1 and 4.2 of the agreement caught by the Restrictive Trade Practices Act 1976? If they were, the agreement would have been void for want of due registration. Adopting the words of Lord Diplock in *Cyanamid*, there were involved "difficult questions of law which called for detailed argument and mature consideration."

  (c) The strength of the plaintiffs' argument was not affected by the Treaty of Rome, taking into account that the purpose of Article 85 was to inhibit the prevention, restriction or distortion of trade within the Common Market, and that the purpose of Article 86 was to deal with abuse of a dominant position so far as it affected trade between Member States. In contract, the agreement the subject matter of the litigation appeared exclusively internal in operation.

6. Copyright—a serious issue to be tried? Yes—for the following reasons:
  (a) The court had regard to the following statutory provisions: Copyright Act 1956, ss.3, 9(8), such of section 10 as it stood before it was amended by the Design Copyright Act 1968 and section 1 of the Registered Designs Act 1949. Section 1(3) of the Act of 1949 provides:

> "In this Act the expression 'design' means feature of shape, configuration, pattern of ornament applied to an article by any industrial

826

process or means, being features which in the finished article appear to and are judged solely by the eye, but does not include a method or principle of construction or features of shape or configuration which are dictated solely by the function which the article to be made in that shape or configuration has to perform."

(b) The essence of the arguments on either side were as follows:
   (i) The plaintiffs claimed that the relevant copyright was "artistic"—not design, therefore justifying a life of 50 years.
   (ii) The defendants argued to the contrary—the life of the design copyright being only 15 years (and which would by then have expired).

(c) How was section 1(3) to be interpreted? With considerable difficulty, concluded the Vice-Chancellor at 189:

"Even with the aid of the authorities, I find considerable difficulty both in ascertaining the meaning of the subsection and in the application of the possible meanings to the facts of this case. Mr Jeffs, of course, contended that the features of the bedpan did not appeal to the eye, nor were they judged solely by the eye: they were purely fictional, he said. Mr Southwell, on the other hand, tended to be lyrical in his description of the appeal to the eye of what he called the figure-of-eight shape of the bedpans, the setting of this shape within the surrounding border, the shape of that border, and the notch at the broader end; and he said that these features would be judged solely by the eye."

The authorities considered were: *A.M.P. Incorporated v. Utilux Proprietary Ltd* [1972] R.P.C. 103 (authority for the proposition that it is the eye of the customer and not of the court, that must be considered); *Dorling v. Honnor Marine Ltd* [1964] Ch. 570; *Gleeson v. Denne (H.A.) Ltd* [1975] R.P.C. 471 and *Lamson Industries Limited's Application* [1978] R.P.C. 1.

7. Confidentiality—a serious issue to be tried? Just—in that, as the Vice-Chancellor said at 190:

"Some items do not seem to me to be confidential in any real sense of the word. Others are connected with the V.V.M.M.s that Vernons sold to UPC; and a purchaser of a machine of this sort is entitled, I think, to expect to receive from the vendor some degree of information and advice about the operation of the machine without being told that it is confidential. Other information UPC say they already have."

8. Damages—an adequate remedy? Yes—the court adopted the approach taken in *Coco v. Clark (A.N.) (Engineers) Ltd* [1969] R.P.C. 41 and 54 (see p. 819 above).

9. A similar case In *Constable v. Clarkson* [1980] F.S.R. 123, the plaintiffs manufactured and sold latex moulds in the shape of fruit for use in making candles resembling fruit and six designs were registered under the Registered Designs Act 1949, in August 1977. The plaintiffs claimed injunctions against the defendants who were in infringement of copyright in registered designs and in sculptures or artistic works for which the plaintiffs' moulds had been produced. The injunctions were refused despite the fact that the plaintiffs had been selling the moulds for some time and the defendants had just come into the market. The reasoning of the Court of Appeal was:

(a) Since damages would not have been an adequate remedy for either party in the circumstances, the court could consider:

  (i) the desirability of maintaining the status quo (which the court suggested was the plaintiff's previous monopoly in the field); and

  (ii) the merits of the claim to protection of the design.

(b) As to the merits, Brandon L.J. is reported as saying:

> "The plaintiffs might have difficulty in establishing the validity of their designs and difficulties in respect of common articles like fruit. Under section 3(1) of the 1949 Act 'design' meant 'features ... judged solely by the eye' whereas quality depended on functionality. All moulds of oranges would have a great deal in common and even if there was a registered design the defendants' moulds might only have to be marginally different to escape the stigma of infringement. The plaintiffs were trying to preserve a very narrow monopoly. On the balance it would be better to refuse to grant an interlocutory injunction rather than to grant it."

7 *Mondaress Ltd v. Bourne and Hollingsworth Ltd* [1981] F.S.R. 118

1. The facts The plaintiffs manufactured and sold high quality ladies' dresses. The defendants manufactured and sold a dress identical to one of the plaintiffs', but of inferior quality. It was common ground that there was a serious issue as to infringement of copyright to be tried.

2. Damages—an adequate remedy for the plaintiffs? No—for the following reasons:

(a) *Goodwill:* The plaintiffs contended that they would suffer irreparable damage in respect of their reputation, and particularly in respect of their reputation for exclusivity of design, if the defendants were permitted to go on selling their dresses in large numbers, particularly in the market with which the defendants did business. The plaintiffs exhibited two letters from irate customers, which read respectively:

"Re: Style 1055. Dear Sir, I must protest most strongly at your business ethics. We purchased from you in good faith 100 X 1055 dresses to wholesale at £22.50 with a further delivery of 100 for completion by November 30. To our horror and amazement customers have pointed out to us the same dress is in the *Woman's Own* magazine, with a retail selling price of £17.95. Needless to say our sales of this style have stopped completely. As we stock several of your numbers, what sort of assurance can you give to us that this situation will not occur again? Your comments on this ludicrous matter are eagerly awaited. P.S. Will you please cancel our next order of style 1055."

"Dear Sirs, It has come to my notice during the past month that your style 1055 has virtually stopped selling with my company. As this has been an exceptionally good number I was most puzzled by this situation. I have found out since that there is an identical suit being produced by Davies & Field which appears to have been retailing for the amount that I have been paying for the wholesale garment. In view of this situation I have no alternative but to cancel all my present orders on this style. Since seeing this suit in question there appear to be several other copies of your garments in circulation and as I am receiving numerous complaints, I have decided to cancel all my orders on all the other pleated styles. I am sure that the situation at present is equally distressing for you as myself and I will have to consider very carefully before placing any more orders."

(b) *The fickleness of the fashion trade:* Buckley L.J. said at 121:

"The plaintiff company has apparently effected sales of upwards of 10,000 of their dress 1055. Apart from the damage to their reputation, if the defendants continue their present course of action, it is likely that the plaintiffs will suffer considerable losses in loss of sales in the future. As has been pointed out, a lady's dress has a relatively short period of popularity on the market and therefore any loss occurring at the present time is likely materially to affect the value of the plaintiff company's business."

3. Damages—would they be an adequate remedy for the defendants? No—Buckley L.J. rehearsed their argument at 121:

"The second defendants have obtained orders for 6,555 of the allegedly infringing dresses, which include as I understand the evidence, 3,200 ordered by the first defendants and 1,600 ordered by the well-known mail order firm of Littlewoods. The evidence filed on behalf of the second defendants avers that if the dress sells well it would not be

829

impossible that their sales through Littlewoods could amount to between 30 and 40 thousand dresses. So they have large sales at risk and they say that their loss of sales would be very difficult to quantify. The first defendants say that if they are unable to satisfy orders placed by customers who have read their advertisements within a reasonable period of time, they will lose the whole benefit of their investment in the advertisement in *Woman's Own* and *Vogue* magazines. Those advertisements appear to have cost the first defendants something approaching £14,000. They say that in both advertisements they have indicated that they hope to satisfy orders within 14 days of receipt but that it might go as far as 28 days and that if it becomes known among the public that they do not satisfy an order within 28 days this could have a substantially adverse effect, which would be incalculable, on any future advertising that they might make. They would, they say, lose credibility among the buying public."

4. Balance of convenience At p. 122 Buckley L.J. explained that the court had to weigh the damage that might be suffered by one party if an injunction is granted against the damage which may be suffered by the other if an injunction is refused. Against that backdrop, Buckley L.J. said at 123:

"But the real distinction in the present case seems to me to be that the risk to which the plaintiffs are exposed if the injunction is withheld may be irreparable, whereas the risk to which the granting of the injunction may subject the defendants, although perhaps difficult to quantify, is not likely to be of a kind which is irreparable by pecuniary compensation. It is not inconceivable that the plaintiffs' business might be destroyed if their reputation for genuine exclusivity of design were compromised, and it is not improbable that their goodwill might be severely and indefinitely impaired by the continued sale of the defendants' allegedly infringing dress. Such damage would be incalculable and irreparable. On the other hand, the defendants may lose their valuable business and the extent of their loss may be difficult to quantify, but the effect, I think, is likely to be transient and of a kind which, so far as it can be quantified, can be compensated by a pecuniary award. What they would be likely to suffer would be a loss of turnover, not a loss of reputation. There is no suggestion that either party would be unable to meet any foreseeable award of damages."

5. The significance of section 17(3) of the Copyright Act 1956 In resisting the grant of an injunction, the defendants sought, *inter alia*, to rely upon section 17(3) which provides:

"Where, in an action under this section an infringement of copyright is proved or admitted, and the court, having regard (in addition to all other material considerations) to—(a) the flagrancy of the infringement, and (b) any benefit shown to have accrued to the defendant by reason of the infringement, is satisfied that effective relief would not otherwise be available to the plaintiff, the court, in assessing damages for the infringement, shall have the power to award such additional damages by virtue of this subsection as the court may consider appropriate in the circumstances."

Thus, the argument ran:
  (a) If no injunction—the plaintiffs can be awarded additional damages under section 17(3).
  (b) But, if an injunction is granted, the defendants would not enjoy—pursuant to the cross-undertaking as to damages—the equivalent measure of damages.
Buckley L.J. held at 122:

"The defendants, counsel points out, would not have any similar additional remedy under an undertaking in damages given by the plaintiffs in consideration of the grant of any injunction.

That subsection seems to me to confer a wide discretion on the court to award additional damages, which would presumably not be recoverable under the usual rules about remoteness and proof of damage. But it cannot, as it seems to me, relieve the court of the difficulty of assessing what would be fair compensation in circumstances in which there is great difficulty in quantifying the damage suffered by the injured party. Nor, as it seems to me, can the subsection enable the court to compensate an injured party who has suffered irreparable damage. Where irreparable damage is in question an award of pecuniary damages may palliate the position but it cannot fully compensate the injured party.

In my opinion, the learned judge was right to regard section 17(3) as matter proper to be taken into account in assessing the balance of convenience, but in treating it, as he did, as 'a very material factor' I think, with deference, that he placed undue emphasis upon it, for it seems to me that he did not really appreciate the inequality which, in my view, exists between the kind of risk to which the plaintiffs will be subject if an injunction is refused and that to which the defendant will be subject if an injunction is granted."

An injunction was granted, accordingly.

8 *The Quaker Oats Company v. Alltrades Distributors Ltd*
[1981] F.S.R. 9

1. The facts The plaintiffs claimed the copyright in drawings related to articles making up a toy medical kit. They sought an injunction to prevent the defendants importing them from Hong Kong and selling and distributing in the U.K. kits which they alleged infringed their copyright. The plaintiffs did not communicate with the defendants until nearly two months after purchasing a toy, and the defendants had meanwhile ordered several thousand more.

2. Serious issue to be tried? Yes—Buckley J. said at 11:

> "In his judgment the learned judge drew attention to the marked similarity between the plaintiffs' product and that dealt in by the defendants; he observed that the evidence indicated that the defendants' goods were inferior in quality—in fact, the learned judge said that they were very inferior in quality—to the plaintiffs' products, and it is not in dispute in this case that the plaintiffs have an arguable case for infringement of copyright. They make no claim in passing off."

3. Damages—an adequate remedy for the plaintiffs? No—for the following reasons expressed at 12–13:
  (a) Damage to the plaintiffs' goodwill—by virtue of the inferior quality of the defendants' items.
  (b) Losses of sales "which are matters that are generally recognised as being extremely difficult to quantify in cases of this kind."
The court thus rejected an offer by the defendants to undertake not to import any more items pending the trial and to keep an account of all those in the United Kingdom and the sales thereof, and to pay the whole of the proceeds of those sales into a joint account.

4. Damages—an adequate remedy for the defendants? No—for reasons also expressed at 13, *per* Buckley L.J.:

> "In the same way the defendants find themselves in a position in which, if they are restrained by an injunction, they are likely to suffer damage because they have accepted orders from a large number of wholesalers for these kits and, if they are restrained by the injunction as the learned judge has restrained them, they will be unable to fulfil those orders, and that will be not at all good for their reputation and goodwill in the trade. Moreover, their evidence is that in Hong Kong, if they were to sue the suppliers, the probability is that the particular suppliers, who apparently are small companies, would discontinue

business and it would be found that some other company was making
these kits in Hong Kong from then onwards, and the people whom
the defendants might sue are likely to be found of little substance."

5. Merits

(a) *Cyanamid* followed—*per* Buckley L.J. at 14:

"In my judgment, in the circumstances of the case, this was a case
in which it was legitimate for the judge to take into account the
probable outcome of the action. In so doing, I think he was loyally
observing the principles which have been enunciated by the House
of Lords in the *American Cyanamid* decision relating to granting
interlocutory injunctions, and I think that he was exercising his
judicial discretion in a way which was fully open to him to do so."

(b) The approach of Oliver J. at first instance—referred to by Buckley
L.J. at 13:

"In these circumstances, the learned judge thought, the matter
resting in that way on damages on each side of the dispute, that it
was a case in which it was justifiable for him to take into account
what appears to be the likely result of the action and the apparent
probability of the plaintiffs' succeeding in obtaining a permanent
injunction. He thought that upon the evidence the plaintiffs were
almost certain to succeed; indeed, I think that it is true that the
evidence put in by the defendants does not disclose any viable
defence to an action for infringement if in fact the plaintiffs make
good their right to copyright, and of course the defendants at this
stage are not in a position to dispute the plaintiffs' title to the
copyright in any drawings that exist for the manufacture of the
plaintiffs' article."

(c) The significance, or otherwise, of *Aljose Fashions*—*per* Buckley L.J.
at 14:

"I only mention that case because it was followed with some
reluctance by Browne-Wilkinson J. in the next case reported in the
same volume, *Monet of London Ltd v. Sybil Richards Ltd* [1978]
F.S.R. 368, also a dispute between dealers in ladies' dresses. I
mention these cases to say that, as far as I am concerned, it does
not seem to me that this court laid down any rule on principle in
Aljose Fashions Ltd v. Young (Alfred) & Co. Ltd but was merely
dealing with the case on its particular facts. I do not think we get
any assistance in the present case out of either of these two
decisions."

833

9 *Brigid Foley Ltd v. Elliott* [1982] R.P.C. 433

1. The facts The plaintiff alleged that artistic copyrights in knitting guides and a prototype garment had been infringed by garments made and sold by the defendant. There was no evidence to show that the defendants had seen the plaintiff's prototype garment. The plaintiff argued two points— in order to establish a serious issue to be tried: the first, it lost on law, the second, it lost by lack of evidence.

2. First point Could it be argued that garments made in accordance with knitting guides reproduced such goods in a material form?

(a) *Statutory provisions:* "The acts restricted by copyright in an artistic work are—(a) reproducing the work in any material form ..." (section 3(5)(a) of the Copyright Act 1956).

(b) *Case for the plaintiff:* The plaintiff had produced knitting guides (*i.e.* pieces of paper embracing detailed instructions—intelligible in the trade— stating how the garments are to be produced). Garments produced in accordance with those instructions reproduce such knitting guides in a material form.

(c) *Ruling per Sir Robert Megarry V.-C.* (at 434(30–35)):

> "I did not call upon Mr Pumphrey to argue this point, since it seems to me quite plain that there is no reproduction of the words and numerals in the knitting guide in the knitted garments produced by following the instructions. The essence, I think, of a reproduction (and I do not attempt to be exhaustive) is that the reproduction should be some copy of or representation of the original. I do not see how anyone looking at the knitted garment could then say, 'Well, that is a copy of, or a reproduction of the words and numerals to be found in the knitting guide.' By a process of counting up the number of stitches, and so on, in the knitted garment one might be able to work back and produce the knitting instructions: but that is a very different matter from saying that the garment is a reproduction of those instructions. Accordingly, that point fails."

3. Second point The garments themselves constitute artistic works.

(a) *Statutory provisions:* Section 3(1)(c) of the Copyright Act 1956:

> "In this Act, 'artistic work' means a work of any of the following descriptions, that is to say" [omit (a) and (b) and to on to (c):] "works of artistic craftsmanship, not falling within either of the preceding paragraphs."

(b) *Ruling:*

   (i) The legal issue (at 434(45)–435(10–20)):

> "There has been for some while a matter of considerable uncertainty in relation to the copying of dresses where there is no copying from drawings or anything of that kind but a copying of the dress in its finished forms. ... I do not think that I ought on motion to attempt to decide this somewhat difficult point that has been lurking in the law of copyright for many years. Looking at the matter from the outside, one would have thought that if there is a direct copying from a garment which one person has designed and produced by herself, doing all the cutting, stitching and so on, there was a considerable case to be made for saying that there would be a breach of copyright in doing that. However, I do not decide that point."

  (ii) The importance of evidence (at 435(15)):

> "The case before me is one where I think an important factor is that the evidence of there ever having been produced specific prototypes of the garments of which complaint is made is thoroughly unsatisfactory. If there had been clear and specific evidence of the production of prototype garments, of which the defendants' garments could be said to be copies, then the case might have been somewhat different."

 (iii) The significance of knitting guides preceding prototypes (at 435(20–24)):

> "There is not only the unsatisfactory nature of the evidence as to the production of the prototypes in question. There is the further difficulty in the plaintiff's path that the process of manufacture appears to be not that the prototype is manufactured first, and then the knitting guide giving instructions how to produce the garment is produced second, but that it is the other way round: the knitting guide is produced first, and then the prototype, if one is made, is produced second. If necessary, after the prototype has been produced, the knitting guide may be revised, but it is the knitting guide that comes first."

 (iv) No evidence of copying from prototype—plaintiff fails (at 435(25–35)):

> "In this case there is nothing whatever to suggest that any of the defendants ever had any access to any prototype which they could have copied. The first defendant, as a former employee of the plaintiff, undoubtedly had access to various knitting guides. If,

therefore, there is any case of copying from those knitting guides, there cannot be a process of copying from the prototype; it is merely a case of copying from the guide, and that falls under the first head under which Mr DeLacey claims. In other words, it seems to me that no satisfactory evidence has been adduced in this case, even on motion, for their being a sufficient connection between the alleged offending garment on the one hand and any prototype manufactured by the plaintiff on the other hand. There is further point taken by Mr Pumphrey, that if the prototype is merely copied from the knitting guide, then there is no originality in the prototype: for it is merely produced in a mechanical manner from the instructions contained in the guide."

4. Damages—an adequate remedy? Yes—Sir Robert Megarry V.-C. said at 436(5–10):

"There is one matter that I should add, and that is this. The operations of the first defendant, producing these garments in her home, are obviously on a small scale. It seems to me that there is no real peril to the plaintiff in what she is doing that would not be compensable in damages. At any rate, I do not think that she poses any major threat. Further, after the hearing of this motion it is plain that she will have a care as to what garments she produces so as to run no risk of an allegation of any further breach of copyright being made by the plaintiff."

10 *Sega Enterprises Ltd v. Richards (No. 2)* [1983] F.S.R. 73

1. The facts The plaintiff manufactured computer programs for electronic games. It was alleged that the defendants had infringed the copyright in a game called "Frogger" in:
  (a) The program.
  (b) The drawings produced when the program was in use.
  (c) The visual images recorded on the board holding the program.
As Goulding J. explained at 74:

"It is alleged that the defendants, trading under the name of Competitive Video, have infringed the copyright in a game of the kind known as an electronic game, of the plaintiff, called 'Frogger,' by offering for sale conversion kits for setting up an imitation of 'Frogger' on machines belonging to their customers. That is done by selling what is known as a logic board which is placed in the apparatus in place of a board that originally contained some other game. The plaintiff says that the board offered in trade by the defendants is simply an imitation with minor alterations of its own 'Frogger' board.

The board contains a small computer. It has, I understand, a central processing unit and memory and parts (that have been referred to as ports) for receiving and giving out information and other essentials of a computer on a very small scale.

The plaintiff claims copyright under a number of different heads. It claims first and foremost copyright in the computer program, which is the essence of the game. Secondly, it claims artistic copyright in the drawings which, by the electronic apparatus within the unit, are reproduced on the display panel, both in the course of the game and what is known as the attract mode when the apparatus is not in use because no one is playing the game. Thirdly, the plaintiff submits that it has copyright under section 13 of the Copyright Act of 1956 in sequences of visual images recorded in the board which constitute, it says, cinematograph film within the meaning of the definition in that section."

2. The issue Is there copyright in a computer program?

3. The case for the defendant The defendant acted in person. Goulding J. recorded his arguments at 74–75:

"Mr Richards admitted that the defendants' program was based on a 'Frogger' machine code program, but contends, as he will hope to prove at the trial, that considerable work was done by the defendants upon it. He says that only in the early stages of development of a game of this sort is there anything that has the necessary attributes of originality and of labour or skill to make it a literary work within the meaning of the Copyright Act. The idea of a game is developed and its details thought out by the originator. It is set down on paper as what he calls a general overview, and at that stage a drawing of the decision and action processes involved in the game can be made as a large flow chart. He says that that is as far as any original work goes because of the very large part played by automatic means, that is to say by the computer itself, in the subsequent development of the program."

4. Ruling At 75 (after having declared that he was only expressing a provisional opinion):

"On the evidence before me in this case I am clearly of the opinion that copyright under the provisions relating to literary works in the Copyright Act 1956 subsists in the assembly code program of the game 'Frogger.' The machine code program derived from it by the operations of part of the system of the computer called the assembler is to be regarded, I think, as either a reproduction or an adaptation of the assembly code program, and accordingly for the purposes of deciding this motion I find that copyright does subsist in the program. It is not necessary for me to say anything at this stage about the other heads of copyright claimed, because if there is copyright in the program there is enough prima facie evidence of infringement for me to have to consider whether the plaintiff should have interlocutory relief."

11 *Associated Newspapers Group plc v. News Group Newspapers Ltd* [1986] R.P.C. 515

1. The facts This was an action by the owners of the *Daily Mail* newspaper against the owners of the *Sun* newspaper. The *Daily Mail* had purchased the copyright for a limited time in an exchange of letters between the Duke and Duchess of Windsor. Before the period of the *Daily Mail*'s rights had expired the *Sun* newspaper published one of the letters. The *Daily Mail* applied for an interlocutory injunction to prevent a repetition.

2. The injunction would dispose of the issues Because the period of the *Daily Mail*'s rights had only 18 more days to run at the time of the interlocutory hearing, for all practical purposes for granting of an interlocutory injunction would settle one way or another the rights of the parties. Therefore *American Cyanamid* did not apply.

> "Therefore (and this of course applies to a great many actions besides the present type of action) it is necessary for the court to consider in some detail what the actual chances of success by the plaintiffs in the action when it comes to trial will be."

3. Copyright Act 1956, s.6(2) (3)

> "(2) No fair dealing with a literary, dramatic or musical work shall constitute an infringement of the copyright in the work if it is for purposes of criticism or review, whether of that work or of another work, and is accompanied by a sufficient acknowledgment.
>
> (3) No fair dealing with a literary, dramatic or musical work shall constitute an infringement of the copyright in the work if it is for the purpose of reporting current events—(a) in a newspaper, magazine or similar periodical, or ... and, in a case falling within paragraph (a) of this subsection, if accompanied by a sufficient acknowledgment."

4. The first issue: was the defendants' dealing "fair"? Walton J. considered what was meant by "fair" dealing:

> "Let us just see what might be fair. I do not think it depends upon

any one criterion, that is to say, whether large chunks of the copyright material have been used as opposed to small chunks; probably it does not depend upon the precise ratio of the chunks used to the surrounding material, although I must point out that in the present case the matters of which complaint is made represent no less than one-third of the totality of the material that the *Sun* has put out relating to the letters. The question of fairness must at bottom depend upon the motive with which the material has been copied."

5. The judge held: purely to attract readers is not fair Walton J. applied *Hubbard v. Vosper* [1972] 2 Q.B. 84 at 93 and said:

"That seems to me to be exactly what has happened in the present case. There is no blinking the fact that the *Sun* is trying to attract readers by means of printing these letters or extracts from these letters. That seems to me not to be fair."

6. The second issue: was there criticism or review within s.6(2)? No— Walton J. said:

"There is a sufficient acknowledgment but it does not seem to me that what the *Sun* has printed can be said to be a criticism or review of any work at all. They are not criticising the letters in any way, they are not reviewing them in any way, they are merely presenting them and are saying: 'Look at these passionate love letters passing between the Duke and the Duchess.' That, it seems to me, is not what the framers of subsection (2) had in mind. I think they had in mind the kind of case I alluded to in my hypothetical *Times* article where the letters themselves are criticised for their style, orthography or what have you."

7. The third issue: were there current events within s.6(3)? The defendants' argument was summarised by the judge:

"[Counsel] for the *Sun* submitted to me that the current events are the death of the Duchess, her motives and intentions in seeking publication of her letters, and the fact that the undisclosed letters themselves have been published casting, as he says, light on matters of historical interest."

8. The plaintiffs' argument The plaintiffs argued that, although there was no requirement in s.6(3) of the Copyright Act 1956, it was a good starting point to ask the question: is it reasonably necessary to refer to these matters in order to deal with current events? The plaintiffs said that it was not.

9. The judge found against the defendants Walton J. dealt with the defendants' arguments thus:

> "The death of the Duchess is a current event. Whether her motives and intention in wanting publication is a current event seems to be dubious, but one will let that pass. It does not seem to me that the actual publication of the letters is the sort of current event of which subsection (3) is speaking."

And accepted the plaintiffs' arguments:

> "It seems to me that although of course there is no requirement, as [counsel] for the plaintiffs has freely admitted, of necessity in sub-section (3), that at any rate is a good start. If one asks the question: is it reasonably necessary to refer to these matters in order to deal with current events? it seems to me that the answer is no. The death of the Duchess does not require the publication of the contents of the letters. Her motive and intention in wanting publication, still less so. The mere fact that undisclosed letters have now been published do not require that one should go further and go into those matters by breaching the plaintiffs' copyright."

10. The ruling The judge concluded that the plaintiffs had made out a very strong case at trial and granted the injunction sought until the end of the plaintiffs' period of copyright.

12 *Mail Newspapers plc v. Express Newspapers Ltd* [1987] F.S.R. 90

1. The facts Mrs Bell had suffered a brain haemorrhage while 24 weeks pregnant and had been kept on a life-support machine ever since, in the hope that the baby would be born alive. It was not known whether Mrs Bell was clinically dead. Meanwhile Mr Bell purported to enter into a contract with the plaintiffs for the exclusive use of his wedding photographs. The defendants had obtained the photographs and refused to agree not to use them, so the plaintiffs applied for an interlocutory injunction to restrain them.

2. The law If Mr Bell was the joint owner of the copyright in the wedding photographs together with his wife, he would not be able to grant an exclusive licence in its use without his wife's consent, so the plaintiffs would only have the right to sue for infringement of copyright by virtue of the contract if:
  (a) Mr Bell had always been the sole owner of the copyright;
  (b) Mrs Bell had died and Mr Bell had inherited the copyright, either by right of survivorship or otherwise.

3. Was there an arguable case? The evidence was that Mr Bell had asked Mrs Bell to make the arrangements with the photographers, but had himself paid for them. The plaintiffs argued:

"there was at least an arguable case that Mr Bell alone holds the copyright, that in so far as Mrs. Bell commissioned the photographs she did so as agent for him, and accordingly the copyright is vested in Mr Bell alone and the agreement was valid to grant an exclusive licence to the plaintiffs."

The defendants argued that the overwhelming likelihood was that Mr and Mrs Bell together commissioned the photographs, and were therefore both owners. Their argument that the plaintiffs had no real prospect of succeeding at the trial therefore depended on Mrs Bell still being alive.

4. The judge held: a serious question to be tried The judge accepted the defendants' contention that Mr and Mrs Bell were originally joint tenants, and it followed that the question was whether the right of survivorship had operated yet. Millett J. said:

"I have no doubt at all that there is at the very least a serious question to be tried whether Mrs. Bell is alive or dead. Indeed, so far as the evidence before me goes, it supports the conclusion that she is probably already legally dead."

5. Would damages be an adequate remedy? The judge held that the losses potentially to be suffered by both sides would be "unquantifiable and quite imponderable."

6. The balance of convenience The judge took account of two factors, which decided him in favour of granting the injunction.

"The first is that the damage which would be sustained by the plaintiffs should the injunctions be wrongly refused would be caused by the infringement of a legal right, whereas the damage which would be sustained by the defendants should the injunction be wrongly granted would be caused by being prevented from committing what would unarguably constitute a legal wrong, the only reason for their not being prevented being that the plaintiffs were not the persons entitled to complain of that wrong. In my judgment, such latter damage should either not weigh at all in the balance, or should be given very much less weight than the former."

7. The other factor in the balance Realistically the defendants would not lose if an injunction were granted. Up to the birth of the child they would

841

not want to publish the photographs, and after the birth Mrs Bell would be dead and Mr Bell could give the plaintiffs undeniable authority to prevent infringement of copyright.

13 *Williamson Music Ltd v. The Pearson Partnership Ltd* [1987] F.S.R. 97

1. The facts The plaintiffs were the owners of the copyright in the works of Rodgers and Hammerstein. The first defendants were an advertising agency who acted for the second defendants National Express Ltd (the coach company). Channel 4 and Thames Television broadcast an advertisement for National Express Ltd's "Rapide" Coach Service which included a song which sounded like "There is Nothin' Like a Dame" from Rodgers and Hammerstein's *South Pacific*. The plaintiffs applied for an interlocutory injunction to stop the advertisement appearing.

2. The words and the music Judge Baker Q.C. found it convenient to deal with the words and the music separately, although:

> "It is, I think, misleading to think of them in mutually exclusive compartments. The words by themselves are or may be the subject of literary copyright. But those same words when sung are to me part of the music."

3. The test for both The judge reviewed the authorities and summarised the test for breach of copyright as defined in section 2 of the Copyright Act 1956 as follows:

> "What I have to consider is whether the parody, on the one hand, conjures up the idea of the original work and no more than the idea, or, on the other hand, whether it uses a substantial part of the expression of the original work."

4. Was there an arguable case in respect of the words? No—Judge Baker Q.C. said:

> "Coming to this case and applying the test of substantiality to the alleged infringement of the literary copyright I am unable to say that there is a serious question to be tried. [Counsel for the plaintiffs] stressed the importance of the words 'We got', repeated several times, the only common expression in the two versions. It is not, in my judgment, a substantial part of the original— certainly not quantitatively, but nor is it qualitatively. In themselves the words would not be copyright as a literary work. The most the words do when combined with the other words in the new

version is to conjure up the original: the idea of it, not the substance of it."

5. The second issue: the music The plaintiffs relied on two types of argument:
    (a) Expert evidence of similarities of:
        (i) rhythmic pattern;
        (ii) melodic shape;
        (iii) harmony;
        (iv) structure.
    (b) A survey conducted at a theatre in a city where the advertisement had not been broadcast. Nine people out of 130 either thought that the parodying music (played without the words) was "There is Nothin' Like a Dame" or were reminded of it.

6. The defendants' composer replied The composer (Denis King) swore an affidavit which said that of course the harmony of the parody was similar to the harmony of the original, but that was because the harmony was very simple. The affidavit included the following:

> "This sequence ... is very nearly the simplest and most obvious that could possibly have been chosen; no musician would claim it was the invention of Richard Rodgers and I believe Rodgers himself would have been the last man to put forward such a claim; and in so far as it introduces minor sophistications by way of variety, I have not used these in 'National Express Rapide'. ... The position may be summarised by saying that the two chord progressions are obviously different, and that if one nevertheless deliberately ignores the differences there is not much left which is common to both, and what little remains is commonplace and certainly not originated by Richard Rodgers."

7. The judge held: there was an arguable case on the music

> "From my hearing of the tunes and a consideration of these two reports, it seems to me that even allowing for the undoubted original contribution of Mr King, it could be arguable that a substantial part of 'There is Nothin' Like a Dame' is present in the advertisement."

8. The balance of convenience in the plaintiffs' favour The judge therefore granted the injunction.

> "I am not satisfied at all that any harm will fall on the National Express if they are prevented from running their advertisement for the short space of time that it will take for this trial to come on."

843

14 *Radio Telefís Éireann v. Magill T.V. Guide Ltd* [1988] I.R. 97

1. The facts The plaintiff regularly published the Irish equivalent of the "Radio Times" listing all its weekly television and radio schedules. They claimed copyright in the schedules but granted licences to publish excerpts subject to conditions. The defendants published the full listings for one week, thereby infringing the conditions. The plaintiff sought an injunction to restrain a recurrence.

2. The main issue was the adequacy of damages The defendants conceded that there was a serious question to be tried. Costello J. proceeded in accordance with *American Cyanamid v. Ethicon Ltd* [1975] A.C. 396 to consider the adequacy of damages.

3. Damages adequate for the plaintiff? No—there were two reasons. Costello J. said:

> "The plaintiff publishes, pursuant to its statutory powers, a magazine known as the 'RTE Guide' whose purpose is to inform the public of the programme schedules on radio and television to be broadcast by the plaintiff and to promote and advertise such programmes. ... The profit from its sales allows a reduction to be made in the annual licence fee payable by the public and contributes to the financing of radio and television programmes. The defendant company has asserted ... that there is a strong public demand for the sort of compendious publications which it now wishes to produce, and if its continued publication was permitted I am satisfied that this would adversely affect the sales of the plaintiff's guide. The public interest in the level of licence fees is a matter which the court could, I think, legitimately take into account at the trial of this action, and this factor together with the difficulty of quantifying the loss sustained by the continued publication would strongly suggest that an injunction rather than damages is the proper remedy should a breach of copyright be established.
>
> But there is a further consideration to which the court could legitimately have regard. The plaintiff has a statutory duty towards the presentation and development of the national culture. ... The impairment of this effort, which would follow from a continued breach of the plaintiff's copyright and a consequent decline in the circulation of the 'Guide' could not be compensated for by an award of damages and is a further reason why the court would grant an injunction if the plaintiff is successful."

4. Damages adequate for the defendants? Yes.

> "The plaintiff's counsel has stated that the plaintiff is prepared to grant a licence to Magill T.V. Guide Ltd. ... Undoubtedly the sales of the [defendants'] 'Guide' which included programme listing unrestricted by the conditions of the licence ... would be higher than the sales of the original [licensed] 'Guide' which contained restricted information. In these circumstances damages would be assessed by references to the difference between actual sales from now to the date of trial of the 'Guide' with the restricted listings, and sales which it would have achieved during this period had the 'Guide' contained full listings. Evidence to establish this difference could obviously be obtained and the resulting financial loss could be adequately catered for by an award of damages should the plaintiff's claim be dismissed."

The judge therefore granted the injunction.

15 *M.S. Associates Ltd v. Power* [1988] F.S.R. 242

1. The facts The action concerned computer programs which translate "Basic" computer language into "C" computer language. Such programs consist of a translator section and a library section. Whilst employed by the plaintiffs the first defendant had been involved in writing the detailed code for part of the library section of the plaintiffs' translation program "C-Gen," and when he subsequently left the plaintiffs he and his company (the second defendant) were licensed distributors of "C-Gen." The defendant wrote a translation program of his own called "B-tran" which was similar to "C-Gen," and the plaintiffs brought an action for breach of copyright, breach of confidence and breach of contract.

2. The relief sought The plaintiffs sought an interlocutory injunction to restrain the defendants from:
> "(i) reproducing or authorising the reproduction of copies or substantial copies of any part of the plaintiffs' C-Gen computer programs or a substantial part thereof or
>
> (ii) selling or leasing or licensing or offering to sell or lease or license or exporting any such copies or substantial copies or
>
> (iii) transmitting outside the jurisdiction or to third parties any collection of data which represents or comprises such a copy or substantial copy or
>
> (iv) otherwise infringing the plaintiffs' copyright in any of their said C-Gen computer programs."

They sought a similar injunction in relation to B-tran.

3. Did the plaintiffs have an arguable case? Yes. The plaintiffs relied upon "many objective similarities in structure and in detail" between the two programs, including two identical errors. The defendants denied copying and relied upon their expert's view that there were "major and fundamental differences." The plaintiffs replied that they relied on the similarities. Falconer J. said:

> "Giving the matter the best consideration I can, on the materials now before me, it seems to me that the plaintiffs have shown that they have an arguable case that they have a real prospect of succeeding in obtaining a permanent injunction at the trial."

4. Would damages be an adequate remedy? No, not for either party.

> "As to damage in the interim period to trial, the parties seem to be in agreement that whichever way the matter goes now, one party is likely to suffer severe damage, the plaintiffs if no injunction is granted now and the defendants if an injunction is granted now. It also seems to be common ground that on either side the likely damage would be quantifiable, but there is a question on both sides as to the ability of the party liable to pay the likely damage of the other party in the interim period."

The plaintiffs seemed to have slightly more assets.

> "On damages, I think the balance is in favour of the plaintiffs, but not greatly so."

5. There were three matters to weigh in the balance of convenience
  (a) "B-tran is the defendants' only product, according to the evidence. ... The plaintiffs do have a number of products. ..."
  (b) Falconer J. quoted from one of the defendants' affidavits:

> " 'Computer technology changes so fast that both computers and computer programs are soon obsolete. This causes the market for particular programs to be short-lived. My estimate is that B-tran will cease to be in demand in two to three years. This means that if the second defendant is prevented from entering the market now until trial in this action, which I am advised could be as much as two years from now, the demand for the product will have ceased.'

> If an injunction were granted now and there were to be any substantial passage of time before the outcome of the trial ... the motion would be likely to be decisive of whether B-tran would ever come on to the market. That is plainly a matter to be taken into account in assessing where the balance lies."

(c) Falconer J. quoted from the same affidavit:

> "'If we are prevented from selling B-tran, since it is the defendants' only product I would almost certainly be made redundant along with the other employee Mr Bill Joyce', that is the other employee of the defendant company. That likely effect on the employment of two employees is a factor which I take into account in assessing where the balance of convenience lies."

6. The ruling The judge therefore declined to grant an injunction and ordered a speedy trial.

16 *Raindrop Data Systems Ltd v. Systemics Ltd* [1988] F.S.R. 354

1. The facts The plaintiff company marketed computer programs and negotiated with the defendant company for purchase of the copyright of an accounting programme "Cross-Cast" developed by the defendants' two directors Mr and Mrs Healy. A signed document dated November 13, 1987 came into existence, which the defendants denied was binding on them. Before the date of this document the plaintiffs had already entered into speculative contracts with third parties which involved the use of "Cross-Cast," and after it they entered into further such contracts on the basis that the document was a binding agreement. The plaintiffs sought interlocutory relief against the defendants so as to enable them to perform these contracts with third parties.

2. The relief sought The notice of motion asked for:
- (a) an order that the defendants, Systemics, provide to Raindrop the software modules listed in Schedule 1 of the agreement dated November 13, 1987, between the plaintiff and the defendants, and the source code and object code for the said modules and each of them; and
- (b) an injunction in such terms as may be just and appropriate restraining the defendants, whether by themselves, their servants or agents or otherwise howsoever, from reproducing or creating copies of the modules or any of the modules or any part of a module save with the consent of the plaintiff.

3. Was there a serious issue? Yes. The judge applied *American Cyanamid* and held that there was an arguable case either way:

> "There is obviously an issue between the parties as to how far that document constitutes a binding, legal contract. [Counsel for the

847

plaintiffs] submitted that there was more than an arguable case here and that this was not just a case where it was purely a matter of balance of convenience, but that the scales effectively tipped very strongly in favour of the plaintiffs on the issue: does this constitute a binding, legal document? I am not satisfied that this is so. It seems to me that there are sufficient arguments apparent to make the case an arguable one either way; notably, although a commencement date is contemplated—in fact there is not one—there is no provision for determining the agreement and there is generally an air of incompleteness about the document."

4. The balance of convenience on the second order sought The judge refused to prevent the defendants from using "Cross-Cast". Knox J. said:

"That would involve removing from [Mr and Mrs. Healy], pending the trial of the action, a significant part of the way in which they earn their living. I would require a very strong case to make such an order at a time when I regard matters as open to argument in either direction."

5. The balance on the first order sought favoured the plaintiffs The judge ordered the defendants to hand over "Cross-Cast" to the plaintiffs. He considered two matters that weighed in favour of the plaintiffs and three matters which were advanced on behalf of the defendants.

(a) The plaintiffs' contracts with third parties before November 13, 1987. Knox J. said:

"There was an element of speculation as at that date in entering into those contractual arrangements in that they provided for the supply of matters that were not entirely within the control of the plaintiffs. In that respect the plaintiffs took what may have been a calculated risk. Negotiations were, however, proceeding with the defendants and one of the objects of these negotiations, I would be prepared to assume, was to cover that risk. ... This seems to me to have been perhaps, in some circumstances, potentially an imprudent operation, but commerce involves risk in many cases; and it seems to me not an illegitimate operation. ... So I take the view that this is something that I am entitled to have regard to."

(b) "So far as subsequent contracts are concerned, [Counsel for the defendants] did not address any great degree of argument to me that I was not in a position to take any account at all of subsequent contracts. As I say, if I were satisfied that they had been entered into with a view to bolstering up the balance of convenience position, I would disregard them. But I am not satisfied that that was the nature of the plaintiffs' activities."

For the defendants three main matters were advanced, which Knox J. dealt with as follows:

(a) "... It was said that if the plaintiffs developed Cross-Cast they may thereby taint the reputation of the defendants, putting it crudely, by making a mess, and that the defendants' reputation which is closely allied to Cross-Cast will thereby be adversely affected. That does seem to me to be a risk which certainly in principle is there. ... But I am not satisfied that there is a significant risk on this score on the evidence before me."

(b) "Next it was said by [Counsel for the defendants] that the way to cure that particular problem was not what I am proposing to do but by requiring the plaintiffs to use a different name from Cross-Cast in marketing this product. I am not satisfied that this is really a realistic solution to that particular problem. There are undoubtedly contractual arrangements on foot which I suspect may very easily include that use of the Cross-Cast name. ... One cannot undo the past. ..."

(c) "Next it was said—and this I accept—that the defendants should be compensated properly for the use of this software. An undertaking has been offered on behalf of the plaintiffs to put into immediate effect from the handing over of the source code the royalty provision that is in that document I have read dated 13th November 1987."

17 *Video Arts Ltd v. Paget Industries Ltd* [1988] F.S.R. 501

1. The facts A search pursuant to an *Anton Piller* order had unearthed copies of seven training films in the defendants' possession, of which the plaintiffs claimed to be the copyright owners. On a motion for an interlocutory injunction the defendants were prepared to give an undertaking in relation to the seven films but the plaintiffs wanted wider protection.

2. The disputed part of the claim The plaintiffs sought the further protection of an injunction to restrain the defendants from:

"... otherwise infringing a copyright in any cinematograph film the copyright in which belongs to or under the copyright in which the plaintiffs are exclusive licensees."

3. The defendants' argument The defendants relied on the decision of Scott J. in *The Staver Company Inc. v. Digitext Display Ltd* [1985] F.S.R. 512. That was a case in which at an earlier stage an order had been made that the defendant be restrained from infringing "the plaintiffs copyright" in six specified drawings and a subsequent issue arose as to whether or not activities which the defendants were proposing to embark upon would or would not constitute an infringement of that order. Scott J. observed that there were grave objections in principle to the granting of interlocutory injunctions in a form that appears to anticipate the plaintiffs' success at trial and he said that interlocutory injunctions ought in cases like that to identify the prohibited acts in a manner which is not dependent on the resolution of factual triable issues.

4. The plaintiffs' arguments The plaintiffs put forward two main arguments:
  (a) One should take into account the likelihood of the need for protection. It was like the distribution of feature films which if restrained piecemeal might leave a distributor in infringement of copyright in a position to continue to infringe in relation to other films that had not specifically been mentioned in the form of order.
  (b) In the *Staver* case there was a serious dispute likely as to ownership and whether there was an infringing event, whereas it really is a completely open and shut matter in relation to the copying of someone else's film.

5. The judge decided: no further protection Knox J. said:

"In my judgment the question comes essentially down to one whether there is sufficient evidence of prospective probable infringement to warrant the court making an order in wider terms than the actual proved activities of the defendant. ... Secondly, it is necessary in any interlocutory order for the maximum degree of certainty to be provided for a defendant ... as to what is or what is not permitted pending the trial of the action. ... On balance I propose to follow the general guidance of Scott J.'s judgment and to restrict the order that is made to the ambit of what has factually been established as being the defendants' conduct and which plainly would be very proper subject of interlocutory relief . . ."

18 *News Group Newspapers Ltd v. Mirror Group Newspapers (1986) Ltd* [1989] 1 F.S.R. 126

1. The facts The defendant publishers of the *Daily Mirror* had published an advertisement on hoardings which was split in two and displayed the masthead of the *Sun* with the names of other newspapers under the heading "Yes, Prime Minister," while that of the *Daily Mirror* appeared under the heading, "No, Prime Minister." The defendants wished to continue their campaign, bringing to the attention of the public in a light- hearted way the fact that the *Daily Mirror* was the only tabloid newspaper which was committed to the support of Labour Party policies.

2. The plaintiffs' argument The plaintiffs, who were the publishers of the *Sun*, sought an interlocutory injunction to prevent the defendants from authorising or printing any further advertisements using the words the *Sun* or its masthead. The plaintiffs contended that damages would not be adequate compensation if they won at trial because it was a "knocking" advertisement, suggesting that the *Sun* blindly followed the views of the Prime Minister. Its intention was to increase the sales of the *Daily Mirror* and reduce the sales of the *Sun*. The effect of the defendants' infringement of copyright, if proved, could not be quantified.

3. The defendants' argument The defendants submitted that if an injunction were granted, it would be difficult to quantify their loss if the plaintiffs lost the action and the cross-undertaking in damages were enforced. The purpose of their advertisement was two-fold: to increase sales and advertising revenue. It was hard to attribute a loss of sales and a consequent drop in advertising revenue directly to restrictions on their advertising campaign.

4. The injunction was granted Aldous J. applied the principles of *American Cyanamid v. Ethicon* [1975] A.C. 396 and accepted the plaintiffs' argument. The defendants were not prevented from using other advertisements. His Lordship could not see that an injunction would cause the defendants as much damage as not granting it might cause to the plaintiffs.

19 *Missing Link Software v. Magee* [1989] 1 F.S.R. 361

1. The facts The plaintiffs were a computer company which owned the copyright in a computer program called "The Personnel Assistant" (TPA). There were two individual defendants who had both been employed by the plaintiffs. Mr Magee as a programmer, the second defendant as a salesman. They then left the plaintiffs' employment, and six months later wished to market an equivalent program called "Human Resources Planner" (HRP). The plaintiffs applied for an interlocutory injunction to stop them.

2. The plaintiffs' case The plaintiffs did not argue that HRP was copied from TPA. Their case was that the defendants had composed HRP while in the employment of the plaintiffs and therefore they had the copyright in it by virtue of s.4(4) of the Copyright Act 1956:

"Where ... a work is made in the course of the author's employment

851

by another person under a contract of service or apprenticeship, that other person shall be entitled to any copyright subsisting in that work by virtue of this part of this Act."

3. Was there an arguable case? The judge did not think that the defendants were likely to have written HRP on the plaintiffs' equipment in the plaintiffs' time. The plaintiffs argued that s.4(4) of the Act would give them the copyright to HRP even if it was written in the defendants' spare time on the defendants' own equipment. There was no authority and the plaintiffs relied on the analogy with patents, in relation to which it was accepted that if an employee engaged to make an invention had an idea at home in the bath it still resulted in the employer's patent. The plaintiffs relied on the following factors:

"... first, that Mr Magee was a software development manager in charge of a small team of programmers; secondly, he was employed to write programs of this nature, say personnel management programs; and thirdly; whilst so employed he wrote for a competitor; and the submission is that, if that was satisfied, then it would be in the course of his employment he was doing that and would be caught by section 4."

4. The defendants' argument The judge summarised the defendants' answer thus:

"[Counsel for the defendants] called my attention to two matters, first of all, that the new Patents Act 1977, s.39 may be in somewhat narrower terms than the previous Act on which those authorities were based, but secondly he said that patents were not a safe analogy because one can have an idea at any time whereas copyright is not dependent on ideas but on the form in which they are expressed. He said that, if an employee writes in his own time and not for an existing competitor but with a view to setting up in competition, those acts are not done in the course of employment."

5. The judge held:

"In short, I could not say that as a matter of law the proposition which is contended for by [counsel for the plaintiffs] is unarguable."

6. Were damages an adequate remedy for the plaintiff? No—Judge Baker Q.C. said:

"... if the plaintiffs were to establish the case at trial, and in the meantime the defendants had been selling their products at rates substantially below the price of the plaintiffs' product, then damages would not provide an adequate remedy to the plaintiffs. Also it would appear from the evidence that the defendants were not in a position to pay the damages, even if they were adequate, save by generating income from selling their product. The only evidence about the sort of income that could be generated are cash flow forecasts, to which my attention has been called, and which I do not find very persuasive."

7. The balance of convenience favoured the plaintiffs Judge Baker Q.C. continued:

"In those circumstances, it seems to me that, on the balance of convenience, those are strong points in the plaintiffs' favour. On the defendants' side, it is contended, first of all, that the grant of an interlocutory injunction may result in them not being able to go on with the litigation. Secondly, their product may in the end, even if they went on and won the litigation, become useless because it may be overtaken by later products. All that is true. I have to notice, however, that they have not started in business yet and that is often a factor taken into account in the plaintiffs' favour in these cases. So on the tests marked out by Lord Diplock, the balance of convenience comes down on the plaintiffs' side."

8. The injunction prohibited:

"The selling or hiring or offering for sale or hire exposing for sale or for hire distributing or parting with possession of the computer software package known as 'The Human Resource Planner' or the system overview thereof."

20 *Waterlow Directories Ltd v. Reed Information Services Ltd* [1992] F.S.R. 409

1. The background The plaintiffs published, and owned the copyright in, the *Solicitors and Barristers Directory*. Under an agreement with the Law Society and the Bar Council the plaintiffs alone had access to those bodies' records for the purpose of compiling a directory. The defendants published *Butterworths Law Directory*.

2. The facts In 1990 the defendants made more extensive use of the plaintiffs' directory than in previous years. In the first place the defendants identified 1,600 firms of solicitors who appeared in the *Solicitors and Barristers Directory* but not in their own directory and wrote to them inviting them to appear in *Butterworths Law Directory*. And secondly the defendants extracted 2,500 names and addresses from the *Solicitors and*

Barristers Directory with a view to including in their own directory for the first time a section listing solicitors and barristers in public authorities and industry. The plaintiffs discovered the defendants' intentions and applied for an interlocutory injunction to stop them.

3. The defendants proffered undertakings The defendants disposed of the issue over the 1,600 solicitors in private practice by agreeing not to use their responses to the invitations to appear in *Butterworths Law Directory*. But the plaintiffs rejected their undertaking in respect of the employed solicitors and barristers—which was not to put into their directory responses from any organisation which was listed only in the plaintiffs' directory.

4. Was there a serious issue to be tried? The plaintiffs submitted that the defendants had infringed their copyright by:
    (a) copying names and addresses of solicitors onto a data processor;
    (b) copying the names and addresses of organisations into a computer;
    (c) copying the names and addresses during mailing; and
    (d) copying them into their directory.
Under the Copyright Designs and Patents Act 1988 unauthorised reproduction of a substantial part of a literary work in any material form is an infringement. Since the defendants had undoubtedly copied the plaintiffs' names and addresses, the question was whether the amount reproduced constituted a substantial part of the work. Aldous J. answered that question at 414:

> "What is a substantial part of a work is a question of degree, depending on the circumstances, and it is settled law that the quality of that which is taken is usually more important than quantity. In the present case, it is a reasonable inference that the parts reproduced by the defendant were important in that they enabled the defendant to carry out a comprehensive mailing. At trial the matter will be more fully investigated, but on the evidence it would appear that the plaintiff's directory is the most complete and that the copying by the defendant was for the purpose of overcoming difficulties and was of benefit to it. That benefit was perceived to be substantial and at this stage of the action I hold that there is a strong case that the part taken by the defendant was a substantial part."

5. Damages an inadequate remedy for both parties Aldous J. reached the conclusion that damages would not be an adequate remedy for the plaintiffs if no injunction were granted and also would not be an adequate remedy for the defendants if an injunction were wrongly granted.

(a) *For the plaintiffs* (at 417):

854

"It is reasonable to conclude that the plaintiff's remuneration is derived from the work involved in compiling its directory and from its reputation as being the most comprehensive directory of its kind, thereby giving to the plaintiff a competitive advantage over its rivals. This competitive advantage could be lost if the defendant is allowed to continue to publish its 1991 directory as it intended to do. That would give to the defendant an advantage manifest by an increased reputation in its directory. I believe that it would be very difficult for that advantage and the resulting loss to the plaintiff to be quantified if the plaintiff succeeded at trial. I therefore hold that damages after trial would not be an adequate remedy for the plaintiff."

(b) *Nor for the defendants* (at 418):

"If the defendant is right and it has done nothing unlawful, then it is entitled to the advantage that it seeks to obtain by publishing its 1991 directory in the form intended. I believe that if that be taken away by an injunction, then it would be difficult to quantify the defendant's loss and any remedy under the cross-undertaking as to damages might prove to be inadequate."

6. Where did the balance of justice lie? Aldous J. compared the position if he accepted the defendants' undertaking not to use material exclusively contained in the plaintiffs' directory, with the position if he granted a wider injunction preventing the defendants from including any list of organisations and businesses. He summarised the balance at 419:

"If an injunction is granted which would have the effect of preventing the defendant including any list of organisations and businesses, it would damage the defendant and on an enquiry as to damage the amount would be difficult to quantify. If, however, I accept the undertaking not to infringe until trial, it seems likely that for the 1992 directory the defendant will take steps to ensure that its list of organisations and businesses will be compiled without recourse to the plaintiff's directory. If so, at trial the substantive relief which the plaintiff would obtain would be damages. Thus the question for me is: should I grant an injunction with the consequence that the defendant will suffer damage which, if it wins at trial, will not be readily quantifiable, but the plaintiff will be safeguarded, or should I accept the undertaking, with the consequence that very little damage will be suffered by the defendant, but the plaintiff (if it wins) will have difficulty in quantifying the damage that it has sustained?"

7. The critical factors In deciding to grant an injunction Aldous J. held that the critical factors were the strength of the plaintiffs' case and the fact that the granting of an injunction in terms wider than the undertaking would have the effect of preserving the status quo.

21 *Drayton Controls (Engineering) Ltd v. Honeywell Control Systems Ltd* [1992] F.S.R. 245

1. The facts The plaintiffs and the defendants both manufactured and marketed thermostatic radiator valves, but in different sectors of the market: the plaintiffs at the top-quality end and the defendants middle-quality. The defendants' introduction of their "Classic" valve to compete with the plaintiffs' "TRV 3" valve at the top end of the market prompted the plaintiffs to apply for an interlocutory injunction to try to prevent them. They framed their case in breach of copyright and in passing off.

2. The judge refused an injunction—why? Knox J. applied *Cyanamid* and held that in neither cause of action had the plaintiffs established that there was a serious issue to be tried.

3. No serious issue in copyright The judge identified the issues as whether the essential features and substance of the drawings of the plaintiffs' "TVR 3" had been copied—a question of the shape of the valve, not of its colour or the materials of which it is made. He accepted that this was a question of fact, and that it was not appropriate to decide at the interlocutory stage whether the defendants' evidence established that there had been no copying. But it was appropriate to decide whether the shape of the "Classic" design was in itself close enough to the shape of the "TRV 3" to establish a prima facie case of copying which the defendants had to answer. The judge held that it was not.

D: APPLICATIONS FOR INJUNCTIONS IN TRADE DISPUTE CASES—EXAMPLES

1 *BBC v. Hearn* [1977] 1. W.L.R. 1004, C.A.

1. The facts Most of the plaintiffs' 20,000 employees belonged to the Association of Broadcasting Staff, which threatened to prevent the beaming by satellite of a Wembley cup final, thereby to prevent its reception in South Africa.

2. For what did the plaintiffs apply? The plaintiffs sought an injunction which in substance was to restrain the defendants (the general secretary, the chairman and the members of the executive committee of the Union) by themselves their servants or agents, from obstructing the broadcasting to the satellite.

3. The framework of the court's decision Scarman L.J. explained at p. 1016F:

> "... one has to have regard to the various matters set out in the speech of Lord Diplock in *American Cyanamid Co. v. Ethicon Ltd* [1975] A.C. 396, and to the statutory matter to which I have just referred [*i.e.* the Trade Union and Labour Relations Act 1974 as amended]."

4. The plaintiffs won—why? The Court of Appeal held:
(a) There was a serious issue to be tried.
(b) There was no likelihood of the defendants establishing the statutory defence. *Per* Lord Denning M.R. at 118A:

> "There was not a trade dispute 'in contemplation.' It was coercive interference and nothing more."

(c) It was plain on the facts that damages would not be a satisfactory or adequate compensation if the defendants did what they threatened to do.

2 *Express Newspapers v. McShane* [1980] A.C. 672

1. The background In 1978 there was a pay dispute between the proprietors of provincial newspapers and those of their employees who were members of the National Union of Journalists.

2. The facts In order to bring pressure upon the proprietors the Union took the following steps:
(a) It called out on strike the Union's journalists on provincial papers.
(b) When the proprietors sought to supplement their sources of news by greater recourse to the Press Association, the Union called out on strike those of their members employed by the Press Association.
(c) When about half of the Union journalists at the Press Association rejected the strike call, the Union called on all its members working for national newspapers to "black" newscopy sent out by the Press Association. This last step precipitated the injunction application.

3. Held—no injunction The House of Lords refused the plaintiffs' application on the basis of its finding that the "blacking" was done in furtherance of a trade dispute (see also p. 000 where the law relating to injunctions in the context of trade dispute is further considered).

3 *Hadmoor Productions Ltd v. Hamilton* [1983] 1 A.C. 191

1. The background The plaintiff's business consisted of producing films for inclusion in the regular programmes transmitted by television stations. Towards the end of 1980 the plaintiff embarked on the production of a series of programmes lasting approximately half an hour each featuring popular musicians of the 1950s and 1960s and entitled "Unforgettable". Two such films were broadcast, and negotiations were underway with a view to a further 15.

2. Where was the threat as perceived by the union? At this juncture, the union (ACTT), fearful that recourse to private enterprise might result in redundancies at the "in-house" studios, threatened to black any such further programmes.

3. The issue of legal confrontation The attitude of the Union prompted the plaintiff to apply for an interlocutory injunction, which in turn threw up the following questions:
- (a) Had the defendants committed any tort at common law? (*i.e.* was there a serious issue to be tried?)
- (b) If so, were they acting in contemplation or furtherance of a trade dispute?
- (c) If so, did they enjoy statutory immunity from liability in connection with those torts?

4. The ruling Lord Diplock answered these three questions, thus:

(a) *A serious issue to be tried* Yes: namely, were a union member to disobey his employer's order to transmit a programme produced by the plaintiff, would such disobedience be an "unlawful act" of which a threat to do it or procure it was capable of constituting the common law tort of intimidation? (at 224H–225C.) It was, however, a close-run thing. Lord Diplock said:

> "I would therefore hold, although not without considerable misgivings, that *Hadmor* does manage to scramble over the first hurdle in its path. ..."

(b) *Trade dispute?* Yes:

> "... this appears to me to present a classic instance of a trade dispute arising out of fears for job security in a period of high unemployment. The evidence is all one way." (at 226C.)

Thus Hadmor is also authority for the principle that a dispute can relate wholly or mainly to "termination or suspension of employment" even though the cause of it is merely the fear of future redundancies. In other words, an argument that there could not be a trade dispute based on this ground until redundancy notices had already been issued or threatened by the employer was unsuitable.

(c) *Statutory immunity?* Yes—Lord Diplock said at 233E:

> "I agree with Dillon J. that the likelihood of [the defendants] establishing at the trial that they are entitled to immunity under section 13 from liability in tort for all the acts which the evidence before him or the Court of Appeal discloses that they did is very high, and I add, for good measure, that I think that he was entitled to take the view and to attach great weight to it and that, whatever the result of the trial might ultimately be, the grant of the interlocutory injunction sought would have been of no practical use to the plaintiff."

4 *Marina Shipping Ltd v. Laughton* [1982] Q.B. 1127

1. Background The vessel, the *Antama*, was under time charter. The following were the relevant clauses in the New York Produce Exchange Form:

(a) *Clause 2:*

> "That the charterers shall provide and pay for all the fuel except as otherwise agreed, port charges, pilotages, agencies, commission, consular charges (except those pertaining to the crew), and all other usual expenses except those before stated, but when the vessel puts into a part for causes for which the vessel is responsible then all such charges incurred shall be paid by the owners."

(b) *Clause 8:*

> "That the captain shall prosecute his voyages with the utmost despatch, and shall render all customary assistance with ship's crew and boats. The captain (although appointed by the owners) shall be under the orders and directions of the charterers as regards employment and agency; and charterers are to load, stow, trim the cargo at their expense under the supervision of the captain, who is to sign bills of lading for cargo as presented, in conformity with mate's or tally clerk's receipts."

(c) *Clause 30:*

> "The charterers shall not be held responsible for loss or damage to the vessel and/or cargo through the negligence of pilots, tugboats.

859

The owners to remain responsible for the navigation of the vessel, insurance, crew and all other matters same as when trading for their own account."

At the time of litigation, the owners were Marina Shipping Ltd, the plaintiffs. The flag was Maltese, the beneficial owner was a Turk, and the crew were predominantly Turkish.

2. The docking arrangement Lawton L.J. explained at 1137E–G:

"On November 18 a firm of shipping agents at Hull, named General Freight Co. Ltd ('General Freight'), were apprised by the charterers' agents that the vessel was in home waters and approaching Hull. Thereupon General Freight, as agents, got in touch with the port authority at Hull, alerted them that the vessel was shortly due and arranged a berth for her in the Alexandra Dock. There is no evidence before the court at the present time as to whether General Freight, as agents, told the port authority at Hull for whom they were acting. The inference is that the port authority at Hull knew General Freight and were willing to deal with them without making enquiries as to whom they were acting for. I draw that inference from the form in which certain invoices for pilotage services were subsequently rendered, the port authority and its agents making out the invoices to General Freight."

3. The intervention of the ITF The ITF (International Transport Workers' Federation) has for some years conducted a campaign against the use of vessels under flags of convenience in maritime trade to and from ports in Western Europe. The object of this campaign, its consequences on the employment of Asian seamen and the way in which it has hitherto been conducted were explained by Lord Diplock in *N.W.L. Ltd v. Woods* [1979] 1 W.L.R. 1294 at 1297B–H:

"ITF endeavours to exert such 'industrial muscle' as its affiliated national unions are prepared to exercise at its behest in order to compel the owners of vessels sailing under flags of convenience (in this extended sense) to employ their officers and seamen on terms of standard articles prepared by ITF and providing for wages at rates said to be the middle rates paid to ships' crews under collective agreements negotiated by national trade unions for ships on their national registries in European countries outside the communist bloc. An alternative way of buying off industrial action inspired by ITF is to change the vessel's flag by transferring her registry to that of the country of domicile of her beneficial owner, whereupon he will be obliged to negotiate terms of employment and wages of crews with the National Seamen's Union affiliated to the ITF. The ultimate aim is to abolish throughout the world the use by shipowners of flags of convenience as ITF defines them.

Your Lordships are in no way concerned with the economic wisdom or the moral justification of this policy. The evidence in the instant appeals confirms what the evidence in *The Camilla M* suggested, that the policy does not command the approbation of seamen and their national trade unions in those countries of Asia which have traditionally formed the recruiting grounds for many thousands of seamen eager to serve under articles that provide wages which, although lower than those demanded by their European, North American and Australasian counterparts, are, nevertheless, much higher than anything that they could hope to earn in land-based work in their own countries. Their competitiveness as candidates for manning the merchant navies of the world depends upon their cheapness. Their natural fear, as indicated by the evidence, is that if their competitiveness is reduced by forcing shipowners who employ them to pay to them wages at the middle rate paid to European seamen, their chances of sea-faring employment will be very much reduced. This readily accounts for the attitude taken up by the Indian crew in *The Camilla M* and by the Hong Kong crew in the instant case."

4. The ITF The Turks in the crew, at Hull, sought the assistance of the ITF as to their pay and conditions. The ITF in turn made extensive demands of the plaintiffs. When such demands were not met, the ITF took steps to "black" the ship. As Lawton L.J. explained at 1138 E–F:

"The form the blacking was to take was to inform the appropriate affiliated unions, that is to say, the National Union of Seamen, the National Union of Railwaymen and the Transport and General Workers' Union. The object of informing them that the vessel was being blacked was to deprive her of the services of the members of those three unions which would be required for moving the vessel out of port. The Transport and General Workers' Union members worked the tugs which would be necessary to get the vessel out of the dock. The National Union of Railwaymen members operated the lock gates."

5. The plaintiffs won—why? Taking the three-stage process (more fully explained in *Dimbleby & Sons Ltd* at pp. 868–872):
  (a) *First stage:* There was clearly a trade dispute within the meaning of section 29 of the Act of 1974.
  (b) *Second stage:* There was immunity, within the meaning of section 13 of the Act of 1974 as amended.

(c) *Third stage:* That immunity was withdrawn by section 17 of the Act of 1980.

6. Why did the Act of 1980 withdraw the immunity? The Court of Appeal held that:

(a) There was secondary action within the meaning of section 17(2). As Brightman L.J. said at 114C:

> "It is common ground for the purposes of this motion that there has been, and is, secondary action in relation to a trade dispute. The extraneous contract of employment is the contract between the port authority and the lock-keepers employed by them. The ITF is inducing the lock-keepers to break their contract of employment or interfering with it or threatening to do so."

(b) To come within the statutory immunity, it must be shown that the contract for the supply of services which has been disrupted by the secondary action is a contract between the ship owner and port authority (the port authority being the employer of the lock-keeper).

(c) Thus the question, as identified by Lawton L.J. was:

> "In my judgment, everything in this case turns upon this question: on whose behalf did General Freight make such contract (if any) for the provision of the port authority's services? Mr Hoffmann has submitted that the contract was made on behalf of the owners. Mr Buckley, on behalf of the owners, has said it was not made on their behalf, it was made on behalf of the charterers."

(d) On the facts, the contract was between the port authority and the agents—not between the port authority and the plaintiffs.

7. Contract only with the agents—on what grounds? The grounds for the decision of the Court of Appeal were:

(a) *First ground:*

(i) Defendant's argument: Where a vessel is on time charter, the master, prima facie, is the agent of the owners. As such, he has ostensible authority to authorise expenditure on their behalf.

(ii) Ruling: By virtue of the prevalent use of charter parties, there can be no certainty as to who is controlling a particular ship until enquiries have been made. When a master comes into port he may well have, and probably has, ostensible authority to pledge the credit for dock charges on behalf of whoever is in control of the ship. But whoever is in control is not necessarily the owner. No port authority ought to assume in every case that the master of a ship is pledging the credit of the owner: at 1140B–G.

(b) *Second ground:*
(i) Defendant's argument: All the agents were doing was giving the port authority information about the arrival of a ship.

(ii) Ruling: On the evidence before the court, the shipping agents were well known to the port authority and they were content to deal with them and in the ordinary course of their work as shipping agents, agreed with the port authority that the vessel should be admitted into the dock and that the general agents would be, prima facie at any rate, responsible for all dues and charges: at 1141H–1142A.

(c) *Third ground:*
(i) Defendant's argument: On the basis of the Harbours, Docks and Piers Clauses Act 1847, the port authority would be entitled to infer on such information as they had, that they would look to the owners of the ship for the payment of dock charges and dues.

(ii) Ruling: Lawton L.J. said at 1142C:

> "There is one particular section, section 44, which was relied on specifically by Mr Hoffmann as showing that, in the ordinary way, if nothing was said to a port authority, that authority would expect an agent to be contracting on behalf of the owners of a vessel. The section is concerned with the recovery of tonnage rates by distraint and the sale of ships and tackle. The substance of the provision is that, if dock charges and dues are not paid, then, whilst the ship is in the dock and the charges are still unpaid, the port authority can arrest the ship. This is a form of statutory relief, but, as was pointed out by Oliver L.J. in the course of the argument, the Act does not say who is to be responsible for the payment of dock charges and dues. It merely provides in section 44 for a particular kind of relief."

(d) *Fourth ground:*
(i) Defendant's argument: The port authority's standard conditions were more likely to apply to the owners of vessels than to the charterers, and in certain circumstances under what is now section 20 of the Supreme Court Act 1981 [section 3(4) of the A.J.A. 1956] a port authority can take proceedings *in rem* in the Admiralty jurisdiction against owners for failing to pay dock charges—but not against charterers.

(ii) Ruling: There was no holding out by the owners at all that the ship's master had any authority from them to incur expenses for port dues. So the agents had no authority from the owners of any kind to contract on their behalf: at 1142G.

863

(e) *Fifth ground:*
  (i) Defendant's argument: In the absence of ostensible authority, there was ratification by the owners upon the ship's arrival at Hull.

  (ii) Ruling: No—Lawton L.J. said at p. 1143A:

> "... Mr Hoffmann's case, namely, that the master at all material times had ostensible authority from the owners to pledge their credit for harbour dues. As I have already stated, I find that a very difficult proposition to accept and I do not accept it as a general rule of law. Mr Hoffmann was unable, despite the long history of maritime litigation, to refer to any case which supported that proposition.
>
> The master did not ratify, and could not ratify, that which had been done by General Freight. It follows that, so far as the port authority were concerned, if the dues and charges were not paid, they would have to look to General Freight. If they did not get the money from General Freight, as they clearly expected to do, they would then have to find out, as best they could, who were the unidentified principals for whom General Freight were acting. They could not have gone, in my judgment, against the owners, because they had no contract with them."

5 *Merkur Island Shipping Corporation v. Laughton* [1983] 2 A.C. 570

1. Background The plaintiff shipowners flew a flag of convenience under which they engaged a Filipino crew. The ship was sub-chartered under a time charter which, *inter alia*, provided that the charterers would:

> "Provide and pay for all ... port charges, pilotages, agencies, commissions, consular charges ... and all other usual expenses ... when the vessel puts into a port for causes for which vessel is responsible, then all such charges incurred shall be paid by the owners."

2. How did the ITF intervene in *Merkur*? The sub-charterers had a running contract with the tug-owners for the provision of tugs to all their vessels using the port of Liverpool. They made through their agent a specific contract with the tugmen for the provision of tugs to take the ship into and out of the dock at which the ship was to be loaded upon arrival at Liverpool on July 15, 1982. ITF, having previously learnt that the shipowners were paying less than the rate of wages approved by the ITF, persuaded the tugmen employed by the tug-owners to refuse, in breach of their contract of employment, to move the ship out of the dock so as to enable her to sail.

3. The writ The shipowners' writ included claims in tort for damages under two alternative heads:

"(1) Damages for deliberate interference with and/or threat to the performance of a time charter dated February 12, 1982, between the plaintiffs and Leif Hoegh and Co. Atkieselskab, such interference and/or threat being brought about by unlawful means, namely wrongfully procuring and/or inducing and/or threatening to procure or induce lock-keepers and/or tugmen and/or pilots and/or boatmen and/or linemen and/or others concerned with the free passage and operation of vessels at Liverpool to refuse to assist the free passage of working the *Hoegh Apapa* at Liverpool.

(2) Damages for deliberate interference with and/or threat to the trade and business of the plaintiffs, such interference and/or threat being brought about by unlawful means namely wrongfully procuring and/or inducing and/or threatening to procure or induce lock-keepers and/or tugmen and/or pilots and/or linesmen and/or others concerned with the free passage and operations of vessels at Liverpool to refuse to assist the free passage or working of the *Hoegh Apapa* at Liverpool."

The stages of the argument in relation to the interlocutory injunction application—founded on the writ—are set out below.

4. Stage 1—the argument for the plaintiff
  (a) The contract with the performance on which the case turned, was interference with the charter.
  (b) The form of the interference was by immobilising the ship at Liverpool, to prevent the captain from performing the contractual obligation of the shipowners under clause 8 of the charter to "prosecute his voyages with utmost dispatch."
  (c) The unlawful means by which the interference was effected was by procuring the tugmen and the lockmen to break their contracts of employment by refusing to carry out the operations on the part of the tug owners and port authority that were necessary to enable the ship to leave the dock.

5. Stage 1—the approach of Lord Diplock
  (a) He explained why the plaintiffs had pinned their colours to the mast of "interference" and not breach, at 607C–D:

"The reason why the shipowners relied upon interference with the performance of the charter rather than procuring a breach of it was the presence in the charter of clauses 51 and 60 which were in the following terms:

865

'*Clause 51 Blockade/boycott.* In the event of loss of time due to boycott of the vessel in any port or place by shore labour or others, or arising from government restrictions by reason of the vessel's flag, or arising from the terms and conditions on which the members of the crew are employed, or by reason of the trading of this vessel, payment or hire shall cease for time hereby lost.'

'*Clause 60 Cancellation.* Should the vessel be prevented from work for the reasons as outlined in clauses 40/50/51 and 52 for more than 10 days, charterers shall have the option of cancelling this contract.'"

In other words, these *force majeure* provisions would have resulted in there being no breach.

(b) Lord Diplock then invoked the dicta of Jenkins L.J. at 679 in *Thomson (D.C.) & Co. Ltd v. Deakin* [1952] Ch. 646; thereby to define the essential element in the tort of actionable interference with contractual rights by "blacking":

"First, that the person charged with actionable interference knew of the existence of the contract and intended to procure its breach; secondly, that the person so charged did definitely and unequivocally persuade, induce or procure the employees concerned to break their contracts of employment with the intent I have mentioned; thirdly, that the employees so persuaded, induced or procured did in fact break their contracts of employment; and fourthly, that breach of the contract forming the alleged subject of interference ensued as a necessary consequence of the breaches by the employees concerned of their contracts of employment."

(c) Lord Diplock demonstrated how the dicta of Jenkins L.J. apply not only to procuring a breach of contract. At 786G, he cited the dicta of Lord Denning M.R. at p. 138 in *Torquay Hotel Company Ltd v. Cousins* [1969] 2 Ch. 106:

"There must be *interference* in the execution of a contract. The interference is not confined to the procurement of a *breach* of contract. It extends to a case where a third person *prevents* or *hinders* one party from performing his contract, even though it be not a breach." [The emphasis is that of Lord Denning.]

(d) He found statutory confirmation for such interpretation, at 608E:

"Parliamentary recognition that the tort of actionable interference with contractual rights is as broad as Lord Denning M.R. stated in the passage I have just quoted is, in my view, to be found in section 13(1) of the Act of 1974 itself which refers to inducement not only 'to break a contract,' but also 'to interfere with its performance,' and treats them as being *pari materia*."

(e) Lord Diplock found all four elements of the tort satisfied—in that:
   (i) The overwhelming inference to be draws was that ITF knew of the charter—and Lord Diplock quoted the Master of the Rolls at [1983] 2 A.C. at 591E–G:

"Whatever the precise degree of knowledge of the defendants at any particular time, faced with a laden ship which, as they well knew, was about to leave port, the defendants must in my judgment be deemed to have known of the almost certain existence of contracts of carriage to which the shipowners were parties. The wholly exceptional case would be that of a ship carrying the owner's own goods. Whether that contract or those contracts consisted of a time charter, a voyage charter or one or more bill of lading contracts or some or all of such contracts would have been immaterial to the defendants. Prima facie their intention was to immobilise the ship and in so doing to interfere with the performance by the owners of their contract or contracts of carriage—immobilising a laden ship which had no contractual obligation to move would have been a pointless exercise, since it would have brought no pressure to bear on the owners."

   (ii) "The fulfilment of the second and third requirements, that ITF successfully procured the tugmen and lock-keepers to break their contracts of employment and that ITF's intention in doing so was to interfere with the performance by the shipowners of their primary obligations to the charterers under the charter, is beyond dispute." (at 609E.)
   (iii) "So is the fulfilment of the fourth requirement, that the prevention of performance by the shipowners of their primary obligation under the charter to secure through the captain that the ship, as soon as she had completed loading, should proceed from the port of Liverpool on her voyage with utmost dispatch, was a necessary consequence of the breaches by the tugmen and the lock-keepers of their contracts of employment." (at 609E–F.)

6. Stage 2 There was no dispute that the "blackleg" fell within the immunity afforded by section 13 of the Act of 1974 as amended.

7. Stage 3 Lord Diplock held that section 17 of the Act of 1980 cut down the statutory immunity, thereby justifying the court at first instance in refusing an injunction. His reasoning was:

867

   (a) To establish immunity, the defendants, to come within section 17(3)(a), had to overcome three hurdles:

      (i) *First*: The purpose or principal purpose of the "blacking" (*i.e.* secondary action) was to prevent or disrupt, during the trade dispute, the supply of services between parties to a contract.

     (ii) *Second*: That contract had at the material time to be subsisting between the shipowners and the tugmen.

    (iii) *Third*: The prevention or disruption of the supply of services between the shipowners and the tugmen had to be brought about by some means other than preventing or disrupting the supply of services by or to any other person other than a party to such contract.

   (b) The defendant fell at the second hurdle. Lord Diplock said at 611B:

> "My Lords, in the instant case the contract concerned was the charter. The employers who were parties to the trade dispute were the shipowners. The charter was a contract for the supply of services, to which the shipowners and the charterers alone were parties. The shipowners were not parties to any subsisting contract with the tugowners. The tugowners were the employers under the contract of employment to which the secondary action related. So the requirements of subsection (3)(a) were not satisfied."

8. The ruling—its effect Lord Diplock, after giving the judgment of the House, drew back to afford a wider perspective:

> "I appreciate that this will have the consequence of making it more difficult for ITF to continue to apply its policy of 'blacking' vessels sailing under flags of convenience without ah blue certificate from ITF. It may also make blacking more difficult in other industries where contracts and sub-contracts are common, but your Lordships have not needed to go into that in the instant appeal. One thing is plain as to the intention of Parliament in enacting section 17 of the Act of 1980; it was to impose restrictions upon the circumstances in which 'blacking' could be procured without incurring liability in tort. The only function of this House in its judicial capacity is to ascertain from the language that the draftsman used the extent of those restrictions." (at 612B–C.)

6 *Dimbleby & Sons Ltd v. National Union of Journalists* [1984] 1 W.L.R. 427, H.L.

1. The background Dimbleby & Sons Ltd (the respondents) were the publishers of several local weekly newspapers circulating in suburban areas to the west of London. The respondents did not print their newspapers themselves. That was done by another associated company, Dimbleby Printers Ltd. Dimbleby Printers were at the material time engaged in a trade dispute with the National Graphical Association. This resulted in a strike by members of the National Graphical Association employed by Dimbleby Printers Ltd—which in turn stopped Dimbleby Newspapers appearing after August 19, 1983. The respondents had recourse to alternative printers, namely TBF. TBF had a common shareholding with T. Bailey Foreman Ltd, with which the NUJ had been engaged in a long-running trade dispute, which was continuing.

2. The contractual relationship At the beginning of October 1983, the respondents entered into an oral contract with TBF for the provision by the respondent to TBF of copy for the Dimbleby Newspapers and the printing of the necessary quantities of those newspapers by TBF.

3. The NUJ's mistake The NUJ apparently was unaware that TBF was a corporate entity, separate from T. Bailey Foreman Ltd. It accordingly instructed its journalists employed by the respondents to refuse to provide copy to the respondent for printing by TBF—and the journalists complied with such instructions.

4. The appellant (the NUJ) lost—why?

(a) *First argument:*
  (i) Case for NUJ: the journalists' refusal to provide copy to the respondents constituted in itself a trade dispute between workers and their employer as to the terms and conditions of their employment, within the meaning of section 29 of the Act of 1974 as amended by section 18 of the Act of 1982.

  (ii) Why use that argument? The simplicity of the argument was that by invoking "primary action" it obviated the necessity of entering into the legislative maze created by section 17 of the Act of 1980 as to secondary action: *Merkur Island Shipping Corporation v. Laughton* [1983] 2 A.C. 570.

  (iii) The ruling: Lord Diplock held at 480B–C that there was no vestige of any claim by the NUJ itself or by the journalists that their current contracts of employment with the respondent contained a term entitling them to refuse to comply with instructions given to them by the respondents to provide copy of the kind that they were employed to obtain, if they received contrary instructions from the NUJ.

(b) *Second argument:*
  (i) Case for the NUJ: There existed a trade dispute between the

869

respondents and the NUJ, namely "the allocation of work or the duties of employment between workers or groups of workers" within the meaning of section 29(1)(c) of the Act of 1974. The allocation sought to be relied upon was that between the workers employed by Dimbleby Printers Ltd (not the respondents) and workers employed by TBF.

(ii) Ruling—*per* Lord Diplock at 434C–E:

> "This contention does not appear to have been advanced on behalf of the NUJ before either the judge or the Court of Appeal. Even if an argument to this effect could have been advanced with any degree of plausibility before the amendment of section 29 of the Act of 1974 by section 18 of the Act of 1982, all vestige of plausibility is removed by the amended definitions of 'trade dispute' and 'worker' found in subsections (2) and (6) respectively. The effect of subsection (2) is to redefine 'trade dispute' as a dispute between workers and their employer wholly 'or mainly related to ' one or more of the matters listed in section 29(1). Subsection (6), so far as relevant, provides that 'worker' in relation to a trade dispute with an employer means a worker employed by that employer.
>
> So allocation of work or duties of employment between workers or groups of workers as a possible subject of a trade dispute is now limited to demarcation issues between workers or groups of workers employed by the same employer. The likelihood of the NUJ succeeding in this particular defence is, in my view, nil."

(c) *Third argument:*

(i) Case for the NUJ: The tort of actionable interference was not made out because the evidence before the judge did not disclose that the failure by the respondent to provide copies to be printed by TBF would constitute a breach of any primary obligation of the respondents to TBF under the oral printing contract.

(ii) Ruling: Lord Diplock said at 434G–435A:

> "It is the fact that the particulars of the primary obligations of each party under that contract which are deposed to in the affidavits before the judge are scanty; but since the avowed intention of the NUJ was to prevent the printing contract from being performed at all, the likelihood of the NUJ's succeeding at the trial upon its argument on this issue is, in my view, small unless at the trial further evidence can be adduced to show that the printing contract was not a synallagmatic contract at all but a mere unilateral or 'if' contract without any obligations on the part of Dimbleby as to its duration. In any event there was sufficient evidence before the judge of contracts between Dimbleby and various advertisers under which Dimbleby undertook primary obligations to publish advertisements

in particular positions in consecutive weekly issues of Dimbleby Newspapers extending long beyond October 1983, which would be broken if the NUJ journalists refused to provide the necessary copy for such issues. Neither the printing contract nor the advertising contracts were contracts of employment; and I do not think that the evidence before the judge discloses any perceptible likelihood of a defence by the NUJ upon this ground turning out to be successful at the trial of the action."

(d) *Fourth argument:*

(i) Case for the NUJ: as a matter of statutory construction, TBF, although a separate corporate entity from T. Bailey Foreman Ltd, was nevertheless a party to the trade dispute between the NUJ and T. Bailey Foreman Ltd.

(ii) Ruling: Lord Diplock rejected the argument, notwithstanding that TBF and T. Bailey Foreman Ltd had identical shareholdings—and his decision was also founded on statutory constructions; at 435C–436A:

"The 'corporate veil' in the case of companies incorporated under the Companies Act is drawn by statute and it can be pierced by some other statute if such other statute so provides; but in view of its *raison d'être* and its consistent recognition by the courts since *Salomon v. Salomon and Co. Ltd* [1897] A.C. 22, one would expect that any parliamentary intention to pierce the corporate veil would be expressed in clear and unequivocal language. I do not wholly exclude the possibility that even in the absence of express words stating that in specified circumstances one company, although separately incorporated, is to be treated as sharing the same legal personality of another, a purposive construction of the statute may nevertheless lead inexorably to the conclusion that such must have been the intention of Parliament. It was argued for the NUJ in the instant case that because TBF and T. Bailey Foreman Ltd were operating companies with identical shareholding and were companies of which a single holding company had control, TBF as well as T. Bailey Foreman Ltd was an 'employer who is party to the dispute' between the NUJ and T. Bailey Foreman Ltd within the meaning of that phrase where it is used in section 17(3) of the Act of 1980.

My Lords, this seems to be a quite impossible construction to put upon the phrase 'an employer who is a party to the dispute' in the context in which it appears in subsection (3). This subsection is followed immediately by subsection (4) which deals with secondary action against an 'associated employer.' By subsection (7), the definition of the expression 'associated employer' in the Act of 1974 is adopted for the purposes of section 17 of the Act of 1980. That

871

definition in section 30(5) of the Act of 1974 provides that:

'Any two employers are to be treated as associated if one is a company of which the other (directly or indirectly) has control, or if both are companies of which a third person (directly or indirectly) has control; and in this Act 'associated employer' shall be construed accordingly.'

TBF is thus an associated employer of T. Bailey Foreman Ltd. Section 17(4), read in conjunction with section 17(1)(b), legalises a particular kind of secondary action if it is directed against an 'associated employer of an employer who is a party to the dispute,' although it would be unlawful if it were directed against any other person. If one were to accept the construction of section 17(3) of the Act of 1980 for which the NUJ contends, subsection (4) would be entirely otiose; and if an associated employer were *ipso facto* an employer who is a party to the suit, the phrase in subsection (4), which I have quoted, would make nonsense."

(e) *Fifth argument:*

(i) Case for the NUJ: The NUJ argued that the respondents were estopped from denying that the printing contract was entered into with T. Bailey Foreman Ltd because (so it was alleged) when Mr Dimbleby first told the NUJ that he had made arrangements for the printing of the Dimbleby Newspapers in Nottingham, he left them with the impression that the contract under which this was to be done was a contract with T. Bailey Foreman Ltd.

(ii) Ruling: Lord Diplock said at 436D–E:

"Any misapprehension under which the N.U.J. may have originally laboured, however, as to which company was the party to the printing contract had been removed before the date when the interlocutory injunctions were granted; so no estoppel, even if there might have been one previously, could still be relied upon then. At the most, estoppel might go to damages, recoverable at the trial for the period before the N.U.J. discovered the mistake under which they had been labouring if they prove that the mistake was induced by a representation by Dimbleby."

7 *Mercury Communications Ltd v. Scott-Garner* [1984] 1 Ch. 37

1. Background Sir John Donaldson set the scene at 73A–C:

"For many years the Post Office enjoyed a monopoly in the operation of telecommunications systems within the United Kingdom. Then, in 1981, Parliament passed the British Telecommunications Act. This established British Telecommunications (B.T.) and transferred it to the telecommunications business of the Post Office. It also empowered the Secretary of State to license rival telecommunications systems. This latter provision met with very strong disapproval from the union and many of its members, the vast majority of whom are employed by B.T. It was probably also unwelcome to the management of B.T. However, neither the union nor B.T. were or are in a position to prevent the Secretary of State issuing such licences and on February 22, 1982 he issued a licence the effect of which was to authorise Mercury to establish a telecommunications system within the United Kingdom on the terms set out in the licence."

2. What was industrial action The sequence of events was as follows:

(a) *March 1982:* The union's national executive committee resolved to instruct the membership not to connect Project Mercury to the British Telecom system.

(b) *October 1982:* A "day of action."

(c) *April 1983:* A series of selective strikes.

(d) *June 20, 1983 and after:* The union called its members to action, *inter alia*, through the medium of an "Industrial Action Bulletin". The British Telecom management responded by themselves effecting some inter-connection. The union thereupon:
  (i) Instructed its members to "black" Mercury shareholders and British Telecom's services at Mercury's own premises.
  (ii) In September 1983 threatened to take industrial action against any customer of Mercury.

3. What was not in issue? It was accepted by all parties that there was a serious issue to be tried as to whether the defendant had committed the tort of inducing a breach of contract and interference with business by unlawful means, within the meaning of paragraph (a) or (b) of section 13(1) of the Act of 1974 as amended.

4. What was in issue? Were the acts complained of by Mercury and which are alleged to have constituted those torts done in contemplation or furtherance of a trade dispute within the statutory immunity afforded by section 13(1) of the Act of 1974?

5. Ruling at the interlocutory hearing—probably Why?

(a) *Was there a dispute?*
  (i) Plaintiff's argument: No—in the present case, the union's primary

873

dispute is with Mercury and in furtherance of that dispute it is doing the equivalent of stopping suppliers of goods and services to Mercury. Thus there is no dispute properly so called, between British Telecom and the union, still less between British Telecom and its employees.

(ii) Held—there was a dispute: As May L.J. said at 87E and 88E:

> "In the instant case the dispute relied on by the union before the judge and before us was the one which it was contended existed between B.T. and its engineers when the latter complied with their union's instructions to black the interconnection with the Mercury and B.T. equipment, and the maintenance and installation work at Mercury's offices and the other shareholders' buildings, thus disobeying the lawful and reasonable instructions of their employer, B.T. Indeed on the facts of this case there was no other dispute upon which the union could rely. ... [I]n my opinion if one asks any reasonable man in the street whether at the material times in the present case there was a 'dispute' between British Telecom and its employers who were refusing the foreman's instructions, his answer would almost certainly be in the affirmative."

(b) *Was the dispute a "trade dispute" as statutorily defined?* That is, did the dispute relate wholly or mainly to one or more of the matters specified in section 29(1) of the Act of 1974—which in the present context was narrowed to: "termination of employment"? Held—no.

6. Why was the dispute not a "trade dispute?" The Court of Appeal held that taking the evidence as a whole, it was impossible to conclude that the risk to jobs was a major part of what the dispute was all about. The grounds for its conclusion were:

(a) The union had not approached B.T. asking for a guarantee of job security. Similarly, there was no evidence before the judge nor before the Court of Appeal that there had been any discussion between the union and B.T. about the effect that the arrival of Mercury on the telecommunications scene might or would have on redundancies, nor about the effect of the Job Security Agreement in these circumstances.

(b) The union did not originally regard a "Job Security Agreement," previously entered into with B.T., as relevant to the instant proceeding.

(c) There was massive evidence that the union was waging a campaign against the political decision to hive off part of its monopoly, and privatise.

(d) The evidence was sufficient to lead to the conclusion that to the knowledge of the union, B.T. clearly anticipated being able to accommodate any job losses that might result either from competition or from technological advance, by natural wastage and retirement.

7. Applying *Cyanamid*. With this as the background the Master of the Rolls applied the *Cyanamid* criteria, as at 83A–C:

"Q. Has Mercury shown that there is a serious question to be tried?
A. Yes.
Q. Has Mercury shown that it has a real prospect of succeeding in its claim for a permanent injunction at the trial?
A. Yes.
Q. If Mercury succeeded, would it be adequately compensated by damages for the loss which it suffered as the result of the union being free to continue to take industrial action pending the trial?
A. No. Mercury is in a relatively frail condition as a newcomer to the field and has very large sums invested in the project. New customers cannot be attracted whilst industrial action is threatened and the losses will vastly exceed the maximum liability which can be imposed upon the union, namely £250,000 (see section 16 of the Employment Act 1982).
Q. If the union were to succeed at the trial in establishing its defence under section 13 of the Act of 1974, would it be adequately compensated by an award under the cross-undertaking?
A. Yes. The union would suffer no loss since, on this hypothesis, the dispute is wholly or mainly about redundancy and there is no suggestion that a temporary cessation in the industrial action would cause or hasten any redundancy.
Q. Where does the balance of convenience lie?
A. It lies in protecting Mercury pending the trial of the action."

8 *Barretts and Baird (Wholesale) Ltd v. Institution of Professional Civil Servants* [1987] 1 FTLR 121

1. Definition of terms

(a) IBAP: Intervention Board for Agricultural Products. This was created to administer subsidies under the Common Agricultural Policy.

(b) MLC: Meat and Livestock Commission—set up under the Agriculture Act 1967 to help maintain guaranteed prices for livestock. The MLC also performs the delegated powers of the IBAP. It employed at the material time 650 fatstock officers who carried out at private abattoirs the certification procedures necessary to obtain subsidy and export meat.

(c) IPCS: Institution of Professional Civil Servants—the fatstock officers' union. It called its members out on strike—in respect of the restraint of which, the plaintiffs applied for an injunction. The plaintiffs were innocent third parties whose business was adversely affected by such strike.

875

2. The relevant statutory provisions

(a) Section 13(1) of the Trade Union and Labour Relations Act 1974 (as amended by the Trade Unions and Labour Relations (Amendment) Act 1976, s. 3(2)):

"An act done by a person in contemplation or furtherance of a trade dispute shall not be actionable in tort on the ground only—

(a) that it induces another person to break a contract or interferes or induces any other person to interfere with its performance; or

(b) that it consists in his threatening that a contract (whether one to which he is a party or not) will be broken or its performance interfered with, or that he will induce another person to break a contract or to interfere with its performance."

(b) Section 10 of the Trade Union Act 1984:

"(1) Nothing in section 13 of the 1974 Act shall prevent an act done by a trade union without the support of a ballot from being actionable in tort (whether or not against the trade union) on the ground that it induced a person to break his contract of employment or to interfere with its performance.

(2) Nothing in section 13 of the 1974 Act shall prevent an act done by a trade union from being actionable in tort (whether or not against the trade union) on the ground that it induced a person to break a commercial contract or to interfere with its performance where—

(a) one of the facts relied upon for the purpose of establishing liability is that the union induced another person to break his contract of employment or to interfere with its performance; and

(b) by virtue of subsection (1) above, nothing in section 13 of the 1974 Act would prevent the act of inducement referred to in Paragraph (i) above from being actionable in tort.

(3) For the purposes of subsection (1) above, an act shall be taken as having been done with the support of a ballot if, but only if—

(a) the trade union has held a ballot in respect of the strike or other industrial action in the course of which the breach of interference referred to in subsection (1) above occurred;

(b) the majority of those voting in the ballot have answered 'Yes' to the appropriate questions;

(c) the first authorisation of endorsement of any relevant act, and in the case of an authorisation the relevant act itself,

876

took place after the date of the ballot and before the expiry of the period of four weeks beginning with that date; and

(d) section II of this Act has been satisfied in relation to the ballot.

(4) In subsection (3)(ii) above 'appropriate question' means

(a) Where the industrial action mentioned in subsection 3(1) above is, or includes, a strike, the question referred to in subsection (4)(a) of section II and

(b) in any other case, that referred to in subsection (4)(b) of that section.

(5) In this part—

(a) 'the 1974 Act' means the Trade Union and Labour Relations Act 1974;

(b) 'authorisation or endorsement' means an authorisation or endorsement of an act which, by virtue of Section 15 of the Employment Act 1982, causes the act to be taken, for the purposes mentioned in that section, to have been done by the trade union;

(c) 'commercial contract' means any contract which is not a contract of employment;

(d) 'contract of employment' has the same meaning as it has in the 1974 Act by virtue of Section 30;

(e) 'the date of the ballot' means, in the case of a ballot in which votes may be cast on more than one day, the last of those days;

(f) 'relevant act' means an act (done in the course of the action mentioned in subsection (3)(a) above) of inducing a person to break his contract of employment or to interfere with its performance;

(g) 'trade union' has the same meaning as it has in the 1984 Act by virtue of section 28;

and any reference to a breach or interference occurring in the course of a strike or other industrial action includes a reference to a breach or interference which, taken together with any corresponding action relating to other contracts of employment, constitutes that action."

(c) Section 16 of the Act of 1974:

"No court shall, whether by way of—

(a) An order for specific performance or specific implement of a contract of employment, or

> (b) An injunction or interdict restraining a breach or threatened
> breach of such a contract,
>
> compel an employee to do any work or attend at any place for
> the doing of any work."

3. The plaintiffs' problem It was—to find a cause of action which had not been rendered immune by section 13(1) of the Act of 1974 as amended.

4. The plaintiffs' line of attack The plaintiffs sought to establish the existence of any one of three torts which were not caught by the Act, namely:

- (a) Interference with the plaintiffs' trade, business or employment contracts by unlawful means, namely:
  - (i) The inducement or procurement of a breach by the IBAP or MLC of their statutory duty under the Agriculture Act 1967 and the European Communities Act 1972, and
  - (ii) The actual breach by a fatstock officer of his contract of employment with the MLC.
- (b) Interference with the plaintiffs' contracts by the same unlawful means.
- (c) Inducement of breach of the same statutory duties as a tort on its own.

5. Line of attack in relation to (a)(i)—were the means unlawful? Henry J. said:

> "Dealing with (a) and (b) together, the threatened strikes would undoubtedly interfere with the plaintiffs' business, but were the means unlawful?
>
> The statutory duty under (i) was to provide a proper system for the inspection and certification of live and dead stock. It was in performance of that duty that the MLC had trained and appointed the 630 fatstock officers.
>
> It was eminently arguable that the duty was owed to the plaintiffs. But it was difficult to see how the MLC could be under a duty to provide the plaintiffs with a strike-free system and there was nothing to that effect in the legislation.
>
> Moreover, there was no evidence to suggest that the proposed industrial action would bring the certification system to a grinding halt. On the evidence as it stood, there was therefore no arguable case under (i) based on breach of statutory duty."

6. Line of attack in respect of (a)(ii)—were the means unlawful? Henry J. said:

"The point taken under (i) had excited academic speculation but had not apparently been before the Courts. If correct, its effect would be that any employee could not obey his union's strike call without leaving himself personally open to a claim in tort by a Third Party whose business happened to be affected by the strike.

It meant that while union officials were covered by statutory immunity for the giving of strike instructions, those who obeyed those instructions, or faced the possibility of losing their union cards if they refused, might still be personally liable in tort. Most strikes interfered with the business not just of the company which employed them but also of others not involved in the dispute. It was clear that strike action by the fatstock officers would interfere with the plaintiffs' (a) trade or business, or (b) contracts.

The Trade Union and Labour Relations Act 1974 declared by section 13(3) 'for the avoidance of doubt' that a striker's breach of his own service contract should not be regarded as an unlawful means of furthering a dispute, but section 17(8) of the Employment Act 1980 provided that section 13(3) 'shall cease to have effect.'

In the circumstances, there was clearly an arguable case sufficient for interlocutory purposes, that a striker's breach of his contract of employment might be unlawful means in the present situation.

But to make an individual striker liable in tort to a third party damaged by the strike, it had to be shown that the striker's predominant purpose was injury to the plaintiff and not the furtherance of his own self-interest.

Although the union had referred with apparent satisfaction to the major disruption caused by the first one-day strike, it seemed plain on the evidence before his Lordship that the purpose of the industrial action being taken was a perfectly straightforward claim for more pay.

The fatstock officers were based at abattoirs nationwide, and there was no evidence of any independent, let alone predominant, desire to injure any of the plaintiffs, at whose premises they worked."

7. **Sweeping up dicta** Henry J. thus discharged the injunction which had been granted *ex parte* by telephone—but went on to add:

"In any event, by virtue of section 16 of the 1974 Act, the Court was precluded from granting an injunction to prevent a breach of contract of employment or compel an employee to attend work.

It followed that the injunction could not be maintained on either of the unlawful means relied on for torts (a) and (b). The plaintiffs' case under tort (c) also failed in the light of his Lordship's finding that there was no arguable case under means (i) of breach of statutory duty, actual or threatened."

E: EXAMPLES OF NON-INDUSTRIAL DISPUTE CASES WHERE INTERLOCUTORY RELIEF HAD EFFECT OF BEING FINAL

1 The principle

1. *Cyanamid*—not all-embracing Kerr L.J. said in *Cayne v. Global Natural Resources plc* [1984] 1 All E.R. 225 at 234:

"It may well be self-evident that the decision in *Cyanamid* cannot be treated as laying down rules of law which are applicable to all cases in which an interlocutory injunction is claimed, but it may be helpful to mention two matters in this regard. First, a literal application of the well-known passages in the speech of Lord Diplock (see [1975] A.C. 396 at 408) would lead to the result that whenever a plaintiff puts forward a serious issue to be tried, and whenever he is able to show that any inconvenience, let alone injustice, to the defendant by the grant of injunction is capable of being compensated in damages against the plaintiff's cross-undertaking, the court will be bound to grant an injunction. The question whether the defendant can be adequately compensated in damages normally arises if the case is in fact taken to trial by the plaintiff. True, if the plaintiff does not do so, the defendant could still claim damages against the plaintiff's cross-undertaking on the ground that no injunction should ever have been granted. But this is no answer, since it is for the plaintiff to make out a case for the exercise of the court's discretion in his favour; and in any event, defendants rarely proceed to a trial of issues whose investigation they had not sought, but were concerned to resist. The test for the application of *Cyanamid* is therefore whether the case is one where the court can see that it is likely to go for trial at the instance of the plaintiffs, and whether the grant of an injunction is therefore appropriate or not, as a way of holding the situation in the interim."

2. *Cyanamid* does not apply where the case is unlikely to go for trial— rationale Lord Diplock clarified the principle in *N.W.L. Ltd v. Woods* [1979] 1 W.L.R. 1294 at 1307A–B:

"Where, however, the grant or refusal of the interlocutory injunction will have the practical effect of putting an end to the action because the harm that will have been already caused to the losing party by its grant or its refusal is complete and of a kind for which money cannot constitute any worthwhile recompense, the degree of likelihood that the plaintiff would have succeeded in establishing his right to an injunction if the action had gone to trial is a factor to be brought into the balance by the judge in weighing the risks that injustice may result from his deciding the application one way rather than the other."

3. The "trade dispute" example Applications for an interlocutory injunction in the context of a trade dispute constitute the classic example of a case where interlocutory relief has the effect of being final: As Lord Diplock said in *N.W.L. Ltd v. Woods* [1979] 1 W.L.R. 1294 at 1305G: "... the grant or refusal of an interlocutory injunction generally disposes finally of the action; in practice actions of this type seldom if ever come to actual trial." By way of contrast where *N.W.L.* was distinguished, see *Porter v. National Union of Journalists* [1980] IRLR 404. However, because such "trade dispute" type cases have attracted a statutory gloss peculiar to themselves, they are dealt with separately, at p. 856.

2 *Woodford v. Smith* [1970] 1 W.L.R. 806

1. The issue The rules of a ratepayers' association provided that any person agreeing with the objects of the association should be "eligible for membership". The annual subscription per member was five shillings. The first plaintiff filled in a "membership form" and paid five shillings. Was he a member?

2. Interlocutory relief granted—why? On the evidence before him, Megarry J. held that the plaintiff was a member on the basis that the phrase "eligible for membership" did not mean "eligible for election to membership." He went on to grant an interlocutory injunction acknowledging that it would have the practical effect of amounting to the sole relief claimed.

3. Why would such relief have had the effect of being final? By implication, Megarry J. based his decision to grant the relief on the balance of convenience factor:

> "In breach of their contract, the defendants and others have been excluding the first plaintiff and others from the benefits of membership to which they are entitled. No doubt the value of any property rights of a member are small, and perhaps negligible; but the case is one which has manifestly aroused strong feelings amongst a large number of those affected, and the association is concerned with matters of public importance in the district. It accordingly seems proper that the matter should be resolved at the earliest possible moment. Further, unless the court intervenes, the first plaintiff and the others of the 57 will be denied their rights as members at the adjourned annual general meeting. The wrongful deprivation of a right to vote even at a meeting

of a mere private association is, in my judgment, no trivial matter. It may not be possible to put any real monetary value on it, any more than it may be possible in the case of a parliamentary vote (see *Ashby v. White* (1703) 2 Ld. Raym. 938); but that does not mean that the court must abstain from intervention. If an injunction be refused now, the election can take place without the 57 having an opportunity to take part in or vote at the adjourned annual general meeting, so that by the time this action is heard, unwelcome changes may have taken place in the association which the 57 may be powerless to put right. Leaving the matter until the trial of the action may thus fail to achieve justice." (at 817C–F.)

3 *News Group Newspapers Ltd v. The Rocket Record Company Ltd* [1981] F.S.R. 89 (for the facts, see p. 716)

1. A half-way house case If the injunction were not granted, that interlocutory decision would have the effect (as far as injunctive relief was concerned) of being final. As Slade J. said at 107:

"If I refuse the injunction sought in respect of the single record, it will be too late for the plaintiffs to obtain any injunction at the trial. If I grant it, and the defendants then succeed at the trial, it will still be open to them then to release a single entitled 'Page Three,' though I appreciate that the somewhat ephemeral nature of records of this kind would render this a less attractive proposition if the trial were to be long delayed."

That notwithstanding, Slade J. did not consider the merits, save to the extent that he applied the criteria stipulated by *Cyanamid*.

4 *Fulwell v. Bragg* (1983) 127 S.J. 171, *per* Nourse J.

1. The facts The plaintiff, a solicitor, committed his firm to a substantial indemnity without informing his partners then or subsequently. The defendant purported to expel him under the terms of the partnership deed for grave or persistent breach. The expulsion provisions stipulated that the defendant acquired the plaintiff's share of goodwill, and required the defendant to circularise only three limited categories of clients about the change. The plaintiff alleged the expulsion to be invalid but accepted it as repudiation, thereby dissolving the partnership. He claimed to be entitled to circularise all clients.

2. Cyanamid Nourse J. is reported as ruling:

"The question of circularisation was important and must be decided at the interlocutory stage. It could not be left until trial. It must be decided, on the evidence as it stood, what side was more likely to succeed at trial, and an injunction granted or refused accordingly. That approach did not really conflict with *American Cyanamid Co. v. Ethicon* [1975] A.C. 396, since it would finally decide the extent to which clients should be canvassed. Of the authorities cited his Lordship preferred *N.W.L. Ltd v. Woods* [1979] 1 W.L.R. 1294."

3. Held The plaintiff was not entitled to an interlocutory injunction giving full circularisation since it seemed more likely than not that his failure to disclose the matter was a grave breach. He was only entitled to circularise the three limited categories of client.

5 *Cayne v. Global Natural Resources* [1984] 1 All E.R. 225 (hearing dates: August 24/25, 1982)

1. The background At the time of the hearing the state of the shareholding in the defendant company was as follows:
(a) Out of 25 million shares that were authorised, 21 million had been issued. Nearly all the shares were bearer shares, transferable by delivery and so there were special arrangements for shareholders to be able to vote by proxy at meetings or depositing their shares with a bank or certain other bodies. Only seven of the shares were registered rendering communication with shareholders difficult.
(b) 600,000 shares were retained to meet second stock options.
(c) 3.35 million shares were to be issued under a contract made two months prior to the hearing—the "June Contract"—and these were at the centre of the litigation. They represented virtually all the shares in the defendants which were unissued and available.
(d) 3,000 shares remained unallocated and unissued.
(e) As between the directors of the defendant company and the plaintiffs, the directors had only 67,000 shares whereas on June 22, 1982, the "concert party" had over 1.2 million. Eveleigh L.J. explained at 226E:

> "The shareholders on whose behalf Mr Cayne sues are members of what is termed a 'concert party,' namely those who have joined in an agreement directed towards obtaining certain changes in the control of Global whereas the second plaintiff, Mr Munro Bank, is a shareholder in Global who is not included in the concert party. ...."

2. The run-up to the injunction application On June 21, 1982 the defendants entered into an agreement with the N.R.C. Properties of Texas Inc. (a

wholly-owned subsidiary of the defendants) and MacFarlane Oil Co. Inc.—
the "June Contract". This provided for the merger of the oil company
with N.R.C. in consideration of the shareholders in the oil company being
entitled to receive from the defendants, *inter alia*, 3.25 million common one
cent shares in the defendants. The contract contained complex provisions
including the following:

    (a) It stipulated two relevant dates:

        (i) First date: the "closing" date—*i.e.* completion date. This was to
be August 17, 1982—but it was not immutable for under section
1.3 of the contract, "closing" was to take place on that date, or
at such other time as the parties may mutually agreed, or "if
any condition of the closing has not been fulfilled or waived by
such date, as soon as practicable thereafter, subject to the
provisions of section 10" (for which, see below).

        (ii) Second date: The "effective time of merger"—this being the
close of business on the date the Secretary of State of Texas was
to issue the relevant statutory certificate of merger, whereupon
the oil company would cease to exist and would be merged with
N.R.C.

    (b) Section 10 of the contract allowed the contract to be "terminated
and abandoned before the effective time of merger" by mutual
consent, or by written notice—but such a notice could be given only
in two stipulated cases:

        (i) First case: If the merger was not consummated prior to August
31, 1982 solely by reason of a "legal restraint" (as defined), the
oil company could give to the defendants on or after August 31,
1982 and prior to September 4, 1982 written notice of its election
to terminate the contract ("legal restraint" was defined so as to
include an injunction of a court in proceedings based on a claim
that the dominant motive of the defendants' directors in making
the contract was to gain an advantage in the dispute at the
forthcoming general meeting).

        (ii) Second case: Either the oil company or the defendants could
give notice to the other if either the merger had not been made
effective on or before November 1, 1982, or else, before then,
"a final non-appealable judgment" had been given by a court of
competent jurisdiction enjoining the merger or the payment of
the consideration to the oil company's shareholders.

3. Who applied for what? Against that backdrop, the "concert party" and
the second plaintiff, by notice of motion, applied to restrain the defendants
from doing two acts:

    (a) *First act*: Completing or implementing the "June Contract" without
first obtaining approval in general meeting.

(b) *Second act*: The issuing and allotting of any shares in Global to shareholders of the oil company or anyone else on their behalf or at their discretion, or to anyone to whom such shareholder has assigned his right to such share.

4. The case for the plaintiffs Eveleigh L.J. explained at 226F–G the plaintiffs' purpose in moving the court:

"The plaintiffs' case, in broad outline, is that the issue of the 3.25 million shares is being made in order to maintain the present directors in office. The holders of over five per cent of the voting rights have required the company to give notice of resolutions to remove all the existing directors and to appoint others, and these are intended to be moved at the annual general meeting of Global, which is now fixed for 13 September next. If the 3.25 million shares in Global are issued in time for the new shareholders to vote at the annual general meeting, they are likely, say the plaintiffs, to vote to support the existing board of Global, being the board which has entered into the June contract with MacFarlane under which the shares are to be issued; and the plaintiffs contend that this was the dominant motive for Global entering into that contract."

5. The defendants' case Conversely, Eveleigh L.J. said:

"Global, on the other hand, deny this and say that the dominant motive was to strike a bargain which was for the true benefit of Global."

6. Was there a triable issue? As to whether or not there was a triable issue, Eveleigh L.J. said at 230C–D:

"In the present case, if this is to be approached as one in which a triable issue has to be established, I myself would come to the conclusion that there was here a triable issue. The plaintiffs' evidence, as I have said, clearly pointed to the inference which they asked the court to draw. Global's evidence, if true and accepted, of course clearly destroyed that inference. But the great question that has to be determined is whether the defendant's case is accepted or not. The mere fact that it is deposed to does not make it incontrovertible. Therefore, when the evidence is not accepted by the plaintiffs, I am left in no doubt as to the outcome of the trial on that issue. If I am in doubt and if the issue seems to be one that is not frivolous, in other words is one for which there is supporting material, then I would conclude that there was a triable issue."

Sir Robert Megarry V.-C. at first instance had come to a different conclusion, by reference to *Re Smith & Fawcett Ltd* [1942] Ch. 304 at 308–309. But Eveleigh L.J. distinguished this authority on the basis that it clearly referred to the assessment of affidavit evidence in the context of a final hearing—and not as here, an interlocutory application.

7. The proceedings parted company from *Cyanamid*—why? At this juncture, the case parted company with the guidelines for which *Cyanamid* is authority, because it was clear that the grant or refusal of an interlocutory injunction would have the practical effect of putting an end to the action. Eveleigh L.J. explained the position thus, at 232B–C:

> "[Sir Robert Megarry V.-C.] said:
>
> > 'In the present case, what really matters to the parties is whether or not the 3.25 million shares in Global should be issued; and the possibility of proceeding to trial for damages is but a pale shadow of the real claim.'
>
> With that I agree. If the injunction is granted the general meeting will be the next step. The plaintiffs will succeed or they will not succeed in mustering the support that they seek to remove the directors from the board. If an injunction is refused then the agreement will be implemented and there will be no point in seeking an injunction thereafter. It will not be possible to unscramble the situation, so that whichever way this decision goes it seems highly likely that it will finally determine the issue."

8. If *Cyanamid* did not guide—what did? Without assistance from *Cyanamid*, Eveleigh L.J. approached the problem thus, at 232G:

> "Having asked myself the various questions referred to in *Cyanamid* I have reached the conclusion that this case is one that the court has to approach on a broad principle: what can the court do in its best endeavour to avoid injustice?"

9. The plaintiffs lost—why? Approaching the case on such broad principle, the court ruled against the plaintiffs and its grounds for so doing were based on the proposition that to grant interlocutory relief would have the effect of being final and denying the defendants a right of trial. The decision of the Court of Appeal in this regard may be split into three parts:

(a) *Per* Eveleigh L.J. at 232J:

> "... it is necessary to look a little into the background of this application. It is submitted in this court that the plaintiffs are seeking to preserve the voting value of their shares; and indeed that is right, they are. But the voting value of the shares in this particular case, if taken

in isolation, is really very little indeed. The shares which are intended to be issued to MacFarlane are available for issue at some time or another. They may legitimately be issued, and indeed the directors say that they are being or are intended to be legitimately issued to MacFarlane; but they may legitimately be issued to others and then the voting power of the plaintiffs' shares will to that extent be diminished. The importance of the voting power from the plaintiffs' point of view is not its value as voting power generally speaking but its value at the moment in order to enable the plaintiffs to achieve a particular object which they have in mind."

(b) As to what precisely that particular object was, Eveleigh L.J. said at 233A–C:

"It is not necessary to go into all the evidence that one has seen in this matter. Suffice it to say that it would appear that shareholders come on the scene introduced by the finance house of Bear Stearns & Co. in America with the view to persuading the company to adopt a policy of realisation of assets. That policy is one to which the present board of directors is opposed, and that is what this application is all about. It is in order that the policy of the board may be changed to accord with the wishes and intentions of the holders of 10 per cent of the equity. The court in that situation is not simply being asked to preserve the voting rights or the strength of the plaintiffs (that cannot be done anyway) but to prevent an issue of shares to MacFarlane as part of a financial manoeuvre. The plaintiffs are perfectly entitled to make such an application to this court and ask the court to enforce the plaintiffs' rights. However, in an application for an injunction when the court is being asked to exercise its discretion in enforcing those rights, regard may be had to all the circumstances. The real aim of Global is to change the policy of the Board. We are not concerned with the rights and wrongs of that policy. The question, it seems to me, is: should the court exercise its discretion bearing in mind all the circumstances of the case, when to decide in favour of the plaintiffs would mean giving them a judgment in the case against Global without permitting Global the right of trial? As stated that way, it seems to me that would be doing an injustice to the defendants."

(c) As to the loss to the plaintiffs if an injunction is not granted, Eveleigh L.J. said at 233D–E:

"On behalf of the plaintiffs it is submitted that to refuse to make an order will be depriving the plaintiffs of the right to trial. It may well be that it will deprive the plaintiffs of the opportunity on September 13 at the annual general meeting of achieving the ends in the way in which they now might be able to achieve them, that is right, but the plaintiffs come to this court and ask the court to exercise its discretion, it is not Global which is making that application. It seems to me that, with the risk that this decision will produce an injustice on one side or the other, it would be wrong to run the risk of causing an injustice to a defendant who is being denied the right to trial where the defence put forward has been substantiated by affidavits and a number of exhibits in this case."

(d) As to the strengths of the cases for each side, Eveleigh L.J. said at 233F:

"... I wish to express no view as to the strength of [the] defence. What I can safely say is that on the evidence before the court the case for the plaintiffs is not overwhelming. It does not mean it is not a good one, but counsel for the plaintiffs quite properly could not contend in this case that he was presenting an overwhelming case. If that was so, it may be that the court would be entitled to come to a different conclusion."

May L.J. said at 238F–G:

"There may be cases where the plaintiff's evidence is so strong that to refuse an injunction and to allow the case to go through to trial would be an unnecessary waste of time and expense and indeed do an overwhelming injustice to the plaintiff. But those cases would, in my judgment, be exceptional."

See also *Neptune Navigation Corporation v. Ishikawajima-Harima Industries Co.* [1987] 1 Lloyd's Rep. 24.

6 *Re Channel Four Television Company Ltd* v. *The Times,* February 2, 1988, C.A.

1. The facts During the hearing of a criminal appeal, *R. v. Callaghan,* Channel Four Television wished to broadcast an enactment of the hearing. On the application of the Attorney-General the court itself granted an injunction restraining any such broadcast. The television company appealed.

2. The television company's argument The company argued that a broadcast of an enactment of proceedings was no more than the television equivalent of ordinary press reports of cases heard in court.

3. The court decided that issue: such a broadcast would be a contempt Lord Lane C.J. said:

"... it seemed to the court that the television programme proposed was not analogous to press reports. Press comment did not pretend to be more than comment. The proposal here was for the portrayal of the court by actors. The portrayal of witnesses was of particular significance as it was pretending to be the real thing and was subtly inviting the viewer to sit in the judgment seat and make what he would think was his own comment on actual events when in reality what the viewer saw would be conditioned by the way the actor had played the part of the witness. The actor had it in his power to make a truthful witness seem untruthful and vice versa."

7 *Cambridge Nutrition Ltd v. British Broadcasting Corporation* [1990] 3 All E.R. 523

1. The facts The plaintiffs were the originators of the Cambridge Diet, a very low calorie diet. Very low calorie diet was going to be the subject of the Committee on Medical Aspects of Food Report which was to be published shortly. The BBC had prepared a programme to be transmitted before the publication of the report. The plaintiffs sought an injunction to prevent the BBC broadcasting the programme before the report.

2. The plaintiffs' argument The plaintiffs submitted that if the injunction granted by the High Court were discharged it would be quite catastrophic from their point of view, and they relied on *American Cyanamid v. Ethicon* [1975] A.C. 396.

3. The BBC's argument The defendants argued that the grant of the injunction would render the programme out of date and all the efforts and money spent would go to waste. They submitted that *American Cyanamid* did not apply: there was no status quo to be preserved, and the grant of the injunction would amount to putting an end to the action.

4. The Court of Appeal refused an injunction Kerr L.J. said:

"His Lordship did not think that *American Cyanamid* applied here. The judge had granted an injunction on the basis that if it turned out that there was no contract that the programme should not be transmitted before the Committee on Medical Aspects of Food report was out then the BBC would be compensated.

But in such circumstances the BBC would suffer uncompensatable damage. It was the BBC's duty to broadcast on subject of public interest. The consequence of granting the injunction would be to deprive the BBC of an opportunity to transmit a discussion on matters of public interest."

F: THE SPECIAL CASE OF INJUNCTIONS TO THWART WINDING-UP PETITIONS

1 *Bryanston Finance Ltd v. de Vries (No. 2)* [1976] 1 Ch. 63

1. The facts The defendant held 62 of over seven million issued shares in the plaintiff company and felt animosity to the plaintiff's chairman. In summary, the defendant had threatened to present a winding-up petition under the "just and equitable" provisions (section 222(f) of the Companies Act 1948) which in turn prompted the plaintiff's motion for an injunction to restrain him.

2. The plaintiff's procedure In *Bryanston* it was stated to be the practice for the company seeking relief to go by way of writ claiming an injunction to restrain presentation of the petition followed immediately by a motion expressed to claim an interlocutory injunction in the same terms: see *Coulson Sanderson & Ward Ltd v. John Francis Ward* (C.A.T. October 15, 1985) for a recent example.

3. The effect of such procedure Sir John Pennycuick explained at 80:

> "The issue between the intending petitioner and the company which would arise upon presentation of the petition is whether or not the company shall be compulsorily wound up. The motion seeks a summary order restraining the defendant from starting the process which would raise the issue for litigation in the Companies Court. The order sought upon the motion, if made, will from its very nature conclude once and for all, so far of course as concerns the ground upon which the petition is based, the summary issue raised by the motion: that is to say, the defendant is either free to present his petition or he is prohibited from doing so. It is no doubt procedurally necessary under the present practice to bring the application for an injunction before the court by way of motion commenced by writ seeking the same relief, the order sought upon the motion being expressed in interlocutory form. But whether the application succeeds or fails, the order upon it is the end of the action. The only issue in the action has been determined once and for all upon the motion and there can be no question of the action itself being brought on for a hearing at some later date on the same issue. The notion of a full hearing with oral examination and cross-examination of an application to stop proceedings *in limine* is altogether at variance with the principles upon which the court acts."

In other words, although the procedure is in form for an interlocutory injunction, in substance it is for a final order. And the court's jurisdiction to grant such final order is a facet of its inherent jurisdiction to prevent an abuse of its process: *Forte (Charles) Investments Ltd v. Amanda* [1964] Ch. 240 and *Mann v. Goldstein* [1968] 1 W.L.R. 1091. Stephenson L.J. summed up the position at 79D–E:

> "But the method of applying does not transform the substance of the proceeding or the nature of what the applicant has to prove. If he applied to strike out the petition under the inherent jurisdiction or under R.S.C., Ord. 18, r. 9(1)(d) and (3) he would not be able to rely on anything said by the House of Lords in the *American Cyanamid* case [1975] A.C. 396 or on the balance of convenience. Nor can he do so because consideration of the irretrievable damage to a company from advertising a baseless petition had led to the practice of applying for an injunction to restrain the would-be petitioner from presenting it."

4. Would there have been such "abuse" in *Bryanston* within the meaning of Ord. 18, r. 9(1)(d)? No—for the following reasons:

(a) The defendant's shareholding was not so small that he did not qualify as a petitioner. As Buckley L.J. said at 75B–C:

> "In my judgment, the smallness of a minority shareholder's holding is no bar to his petitioning for a winding-up order if what he may hope to recover in a liquidation of the company is likely to be appreciable in relation to the size of his shareholding. If it would be *de minimis*, he might well be treated as having no *locus standi*, but otherwise he should be treated as having as good a right to seek a winding-up order as any other contributor. He must have what Sir George Jessel M.R. called a 'tangible interest' in the winding-up: see *Re Rica Gold Washing Co.* (1879) 11 Ch.D. 36 at 43."

(b) The defendant's motive, even if prompted by malice, was irrelevant:

> "If a petitioner has a sufficient ground for petitioning, the fact that his motive for presenting a petition, or one of his motives, may be antagonism to some person or persons cannot, it seems to me, render that ground less sufficient. If, on the other hand, he has no sufficient ground, his petition will be an abuse, whether he be actuated by malice or not." (at 75D–E.)

(c) The defendant had no other remedy (if he had, *Forte (Charles) Investments Ltd v. Amanda* [1964] Ch. 240 at 251 would have applied, where Willmer L.J. expressed the view that a winding-up petition was not justified where a minority shareholder had other more satisfactory remedies available to him). Furthermore, in the present case, Buckley L.J. discounted the following as constituting sufficient alternative remedies:

    (i) An investigation (which was already on foot) under section 164 of the Companies Act 1948, and

    (ii) a minority shareholder's action, and

    (iii) proceedings under section 210 of the Act of 1948, which provides an alternative remedy to winding-up in cases of oppression.

(d) Counsel for the plaintiff had conceded that a petition based upon allegations already advanced by the defendant might succeed (at 77F–G).

(e) It was not established that upon a winding-up, no surplus would be available to shareholders.

(f) As a matter of policy, Buckley L.J. said at 78D–F:

> "It has long been recognised that the jurisdiction of the court to stay an action *in limine* as an abuse of process is a jurisdiction to be exercised with great circumspection and exactly the same considerations must apply to a *quia timet* injunction to restrain commencement of proceedings. These principles are, in my opinion, just as applicable to a winding-up petition as to an action. The right to petition the court for a winding-up order in appropriate circumstances is a right conferred by statute. A would-be petitioner should not be restrained from exercising it except on clear and persuasive grounds. I recognise that the presentation of a petition may do great damage to a company's business and reputation, though I think that the potential damage in the present case may have been rather exaggerated. The restraint of a petitioner may also gravely affect the would-be petitioner and not only him but also others, whether creditors or contributors. If the presentation of the petition is prevented the commencement of the winding-up will be postponed until such time as a petition is presented or a winding-up resolution is passed. This is capable of far-reaching effects."

5. Could the plaintiff have salvaged something? Probably yes—as Buckley L.J. explained at 78F:

> "We have not been invited to substitute for the injunction granted by the judge an injunction restraining advertisement without the leave of the court of any petition which the defendant may present which might, it seems to me, have been a possible via media."

6. *Bryanston* applied In *Re A Company* [1983] 1 W.L.R. 927 Vinelott

J. invoked *Bryanston* as *inter alia*, being authority for the following proposition:

> "It is as much an abuse of the process of the court to persist in a petition which, because of a subsequent offer, is bound to fail as it would be to present a petition which, on the facts existing at the time of the petition, is bound to fail."

If through lack of time for filing evidence, etc., the court is asked to make an interim injunction pending the full interlocutory hearing, the company must produce sufficient prima facie evidence to show that the presentation of a winding-up petition would constitute an abuse of the process of the court: *Coulson Sanderson & Ward Ltd v. John Francis Ward* (C.A.T. October 15, 1985). In that case the court *inter alia* considered the following sections of the Companies Act 1985: sections 459(1), 461(1), 461(2)(a), 517(g) and 520(2).

2 *Holt Southey Ltd v. Catnic Components Ltd* [1978] 1 W.L.R. 630

1. The facts The plaintiff company sought to restrain the defendant from presenting a winding-up petition in respect of an alleged debt of £39,000 for which the defendant had made formal demand. The plaintiff contended, *inter alia*, that £20,000 of the alleged debt was not yet payable by virtue of a credit arrangement with the defendant.

2. Assuming the plaintiff denied the debt in its entirety—what would have happened? On this premise, Goulding J. would have allowed the motion, because:
(a) the plaintiff disputed the debt on a substantial ground (and not just on some ground which was frivolous or without substance and which the court should therefore ignore), and
(b) the company was solvent (the solvency of the company was not something which has to be proved in order to restrain the prosecution of a petition based on a substantially disputed debt).
In respect of both these rulings, Goulding J. would have followed the judgment of Ungoed-Thames J. in *Mann v. Goldstein* [1968] 1 W.L.R. 1091 who went on to say at 1098–1099:

> "For my part, I would prefer to rest the jurisdiction direction on the comparatively simple propositions that a creditors' petition can only be presented by a creditor, that the winding-up jurisdiction is not for the purpose of deciding a disputed debt (that is, disputed on substantial and not insubstantial ground), since, until a creditor is established as a creditor he is not entitled to present the petition and has no *locus*

893

standi in the Companies Court; and that, therefore, to invoke the winding-up jurisdiction when the debt is disputed (that is, on substantial grounds) or after it has become clear that it is so disputed is an abuse of the process of the court."

3. Why did the plaintiff's argument that the £20,000 was a prospective debt, thwart the injunction application?

(a) The relevant provisions of the Companies Act 1948 read:
  (i) Section 222(c): A company may be wound up by the court if the company is unable to pay its debts.
  (ii) Section 223(d): A company shall be deemed to be unable to pay its debts if it is proved to the satisfaction of the court that the company is unable to pay its debts, and, in determining whether a company is unable to pay its debts, the court shall take into account the contingent and prospective liabilities of the company.
  (iii) Section 224(1): "... an application to the court for the winding-up of a company shall be by petition ..." and the petition may be presented by, among other, "any creditor or creditors (including any contingent or prospective creditor or creditors)." Then there is proviso (c) under section 224(1), that "the court shall not give a hearing to winding-up petition presented by a contingent or prospective creditor until such security for costs has been given as the court thinks reasonable and until a prima facie case for winding-up has been established to the satisfaction of the court."

(b) Whereas *Mann v. Goldstein* lays down that it is an abuse for a person who is not qualified as a petitioner under the terms of the Companies Act 1948 to present a petition, here the defendant was qualified as a prospective creditor at least subject to the provisions of section 224(1)(c). As to the operation of that provision, that was a matter to be left to the Companies Court itself to weigh up and decide by its own process all the allegations that may be made in the petition. As Goulding J. said at 634G–H:

"It was said by Sir William James V.-C. in *Re Imperial Guardian Life Assurance Society* [1869] L.R. 9 Eq. 447, 450, quoted in the report of *Mann v. Goldstein* [1968] 1 W.L.R. 1091, 1097, that 'A winding-up petition is not to be used as machinery for trying a common law action,' and that of course is the whole basis of the application before me. But that does not mean that the Companies Court may not have to decide on the validity or terms of an alleged liability once the petitioner has established his *locus standi* to petition before that court."

G: IMPOSSIBILITY OF DEVISING SUITABLE WORDING

1 *Bower v. Bantam Investments Ltd* [1972] 1 W.L.R. 1120

1. The contractual background The plaintiff sold to the first defendant (for the purposes of selling on to the second defendant) parcels of land for the purposes of development of a marina, the consideration for the transaction being paid partly in cash and partly in fully paid-up shares in the second defendant. It was further agreed that the plaintiff enter into a service contract with the second defendant in the capacity as managing director for a period of 10 years.

2. The mutual grievances No progress was made on the marina. The plaintiff claimed this to be the fault of the defendants, or at any rate of the first defendant, on the basis that it had lost interest largely following the takeover of an associated company. The defendants, conversely, blamed the plaintiff, on the basis that his ideas had been too grandiose, and that despite strenuous efforts, they were unable to raise the necessary finance for any scheme which would satisfy the plaintiff. That, as Goff J. recognised at 1123F, was a serious issue to be tried.

3. What precipitated the litigation Approximately four years after the execution of the transaction, the defendants offered part of the land for sale (thereby apparently acknowledging the failure of the marina project) thus precipitating the plaintiff's application for an injunction to restrain the sale.

4. The plaintiff's problem The problem confronting the plaintiff was— what were the defendants doing wrong? There was nothing in the terms of the contracts the subject-matter of the overall transaction to render such a sale a breach of contract.

5. Taking the plaintiff's case at its highest, how high was it? Goff J. suggested that the only relevant term capable of implication into the contractual relationship between the parties was that the defendants use their best endeavours to procure if practicable the development of the property for the purposes of a marina with associated recreational facilities. And this in turn posed the insuperable problem—expressed thus by Goff. J.:

> "I ask myself, could anything be less specific or more uncertain? There is absolutely no criterion by which best endeavours and practicability are to be judged. If it be said indeed that the injunction ought to be against parting with the land without using best endeavours, and so

long as it is practicable to develop all the land, then in my judgment that must be too uncertain."

6. The headnote Against that backdrop, the headnote reads:

"... that in order to found a claim for relief by way of injunction it was necessary to point to something specific which the defendant had by implication agreed not to do and that the mere fact that his conduct was inconsistent with his obligations was not sufficient."

7. "Uncertainty"—not a licence to breach contracts It should be borne in mind that there is a limit beyond which the "uncertainty" argument cannot be advanced. This was made clear by Megarry J. in *Hampstead & Suburban Properties Ltd v. Diomedous* [1969] 1 Ch. 248 where the plaintiff landlords brought proceedings for an interlocutory injunction against the assignee of a lease in respect of noise. Clause 2(18) of the lease and the licence to assign respectively provided:

"... not to use or suffer the demised premises or any part thereof to be used for any sale by auction or for any offensive or noisy trade, business, manufactory or occupation or for any illegal or immoral purpose or for the sale of wine, beer, spirits or as a dwelling-house or club or so as to cause, in the opinion of the landlord, any nuisance, damage or annoyance (particularly by wireless or television apparatus or any musical instrument)."

"Without prejudice to the provisions of clause 2(18) of the lease, the assignee will not play music or musical instruments or permit music or musical instruments to be played within the premises in such a manner as to be audible to the extent of causing a nuisance or annoyance to the occupiers of any adjoining or neighbouring premises (including the flats situated above the premises) and in the event of any complaints being received by the landlords from the owner or occupier of any adjoining or neighbouring premises, the assignee will, at the request of the landlords (such request to be made only if, in the opinion of the landlords, the said complaint was reasonable) forthwith discontinue the playing of music or musical instruments within the premises until such time as effective soundproofing works to the premises (to be carried out in accordance with plans to be approved by the landlords and subject to such reasonable conditions as the landlords may impose) have been completed."

The defendant, *inter alia*, contended that the covenants were too uncertain for an injunction. As Megarry J. explained the argument at 256:

"What, asks Mr Weeks, is the standard of audibility 'to the extent of causing a nuisance or annoyance' to neighbours, and what is 'effective' soundproofing? Damages, he says, are the proper remedy, not an injunction."

In respect of the uncertainty argument, Megarry J. held:

"The court is always slow to repose on the easy pillow of uncertainty; and there have been many instances on the grant of interlocutory injunctions to restrain the commission of nuisances, despite the difficulty that there often is in defining precisely what degree of smell or noise or vibration amounts to a nuisance. In the celebrated phrase of Knight-Bruce V.-C. in *Walter v. Selfe* [(1851) 4 De G. & Sm. 315 at 322] which I put to Mr Weeks in argument, 'nuisance' is a term which must be construed according to 'plain and sober and simple notions among the English people'; and the courts are not unaccustomed to this standard.

The fact that a defendant enjoined from committing a nuisance may have some difficulty in going as close as he can to the dividing line without crossing it is in my judgment no reason for not enjoining him in a case where it is plain that wherever the line ought to be drawn he is overstepping it by a wide margin. I have no doubt that what is a nuisance or annoyance will continue to be determined by the courts according to robust and common-sense standards. Nor have I any hesitation in assuming that where there has been a breach of an injunction because of a genuine and understandable uncertainty about what is or what is not licit, the court will continue to exercise a proper discretion in dealing with the breach. Similar considerations apply to the argument on effective soundproofing. In the context I feel little doubt that 'effective soundproofing' is soundproofing which is effective in preventing a nuisance or annoyance to neighbours. In my judgment, there is nothing in the point on uncertainty. In this I am comforted by the decision of the Court of Appeal in *Tod-Heatly v. Benham* (1888) 40 Ch.D. 80 which shows the court enforcing a covenant where the phrase in question was 'annoyance, nuisance, grievance or damage of the lessor,' and so on."

8. "Certainty"—and the "undertaking to the court" analogy *Bower v. Bantam Investments Ltd* reflects the decision of Plowman J. in *Wilson & Whitworth Ltd v. Express & Independent Newspapers Ltd.* [1969] R.P.C. 165. He explained the background at 168:

"The plaintiffs alleged that since the year 1886 they and their predecessors had published in suburban Essex a newspaper known as the 'Stratford Express' and that for a somewhat, although not substantially, shorter period the defendants and their predecessors had published, also in suburban Essex,local newspapers under the title 'Express & Independent,' prefixed by the name of the locality in which they circulated, such as Leytonstone, Woodford and so on. The plaintiffs alleged that the defendants were guilty of passing off by representing that there was an association or connection between the plaintiffs and the defendants."

The parties compromised by recourse to a Tomlin Order in the following terms:

"... the plaintiffs and the defendants having agreed to the terms set forth in the schedule hereto and by their counsel consenting to this order this court doth order [amongst other things] that all further proceedings in this action be stayed except for carrying the said terms into effect and for that purpose the parties are to be at liberty to apply."

Then the schedule to the order was as follows:

"1. The plaintiffs agree that within the common area of circulation they will not in their newspapers, advertisements, signs, contents, bills, circulars or other matter use the word 'Express' with any greater prominence or drop the word 'Stratford' to any further extent than at the commencement of this action.

2. The defendants agree that within the common area of circulation they will not in their newspapers, advertisements, signs, contents, bills, circulars or other matter use the word 'Express' with any greater prominence or drop the prefix of the district name or names or the word 'Independent' to any further extent than at the commencement of this action.

3. The above agreement shall be construed as independent.

4. The common area of circulation is shown approximately by the shaded area in the plan initialled for identification by Soames Edwards & Jones and Stanley Evans & Co. the respective solicitors for the parties and dated July 3, 1936."

The Court of Appeal however refused to sanction an undertaking to the court in the terms of the agreement reached by the parties, on the ground that the terms were too vague to be enforced by the court. The motion before Plowman J. was brought by the defendants who complained that the plaintiffs had broken their agreement contained in paragraph 1 of the schedule to the order. Plowman J. dismissed the motion. The headnote reads:

"Held, that as the Court of Appeal had refused to sanction an undertaking to the court because the terms of the agreement made by the parties were too vague to be enforced, the court would not then have been prepared to grant an injunction in that form, and an injunction could not now be granted in terms which the Court of Appeal had been unwilling to accept. The evidence failed to establish satisfactorily the common area of circulation in 1936, and without reaching a decision on the merits of the defendants' complaints, an injunction was refused."

2 *Woodward v. Hutchins* [1977] 1 W.L.R. 760

1. The facts Thomas John Woodward, Arnold George Dorsey, Raymond O'Sullivan and Gordon William Mills are better known as Tom Jones, Engelbert Humperdinck, Gilbert O'Sullivan and Gordon Mills. The defendant to their claim had been their public relations officer, consultant, press representative and literary agent. In 1972, the defendant covenanted not "to make any statement or give any interview or pass any information to any third party ... touching or concerning the principals in the group, either during the employment or at any time afterwards." There was an issue of fact as to whether that provision was subsequently rescinded. After the amicable cessation of his employment, the defendant wrote about the group for the *Daily Mirror* newspaper—*inter alia* saying:

> "This accurate record of an amazing decade will put straight the fallacies and half-truths of the lives and careers of four of the most interesting men British show business has ever produced."

The publicity flowing from the *Daily Mirror* article was less than favourable—culminating on the day of the hearing with:

> "Tom Jones superstud. More shortly. Secrets of the Family by Chris Hutchins."

The plaintiffs launched their application for an injunction. Slynn J. granted it, hearing the case between 2.15 p.m. and 4.20 p.m. The terms were:

> "An injunction restraining the defendants and each of them from disclosing, divulging or making use of or from writing, printing, publishing or circulating any confidential information acquired during the course of employment with the plaintiffs or any of them relating to the private lives, personal affairs or private conduct of the plaintiffs or any of them."

The defendants were dismayed. They were ready for press. They went within 10 minutes to the Court of Appeal, who heard the case from 4.30 p.m. to 6.30 p.m.

2. What did the plaintiffs claim? The relief sought by the plaintiffs in the writ sounded in:

(a) libel;
(b) breach of contract;
(c) breach of confidence.

3. Injunction to restrain libel? No—Lord Denning M.R. said at 763D:

"So far as libel is concerned, the *Daily Mirror* and Mr Hutchins intimate that they are going to plead justification. They are going to say that the words in the article are true in substance and in fact. In these circumstances it is clear that no injunction would be granted to restrain the publication. These courts rarely, if ever, grant an injunction when a defendant says he is going to justify. The reason is because the interest of the public in knowing the truth outweighs the interest of a plaintiff in maintaining his reputation."

4. Injunction restraining the alleged breach of contract? No—Lord Denning M.R. said at 763E–F:

"So far as the cause of action for breach of contract is concerned, it is based on the letter in 1972 which I have read. Even if that letter still stood, I doubt whether the promise in it would be enforced. A serious question would arise as to whether it was reasonable to impose such a fetter on freedom of speech. But I need not pursue the point. On the evidence as it stands at the moment as to the tearing up of the letter it is a permissible view that the promise was rescinded."

5. Injunction to restrain breach of confidence? No—the reason given by the court for refusing the injunction can be discerned as having three limbs:

(a) *First limb—an exceptional case:* Lord Denning M.R. said at 736H– 764C:

"No doubt in some employments there is an obligation of confidence. In a proper case the court will be prepared to restrain a servant from disclosing confidential information which he has received in the course of his employment. But this case is quite out of the ordinary. There is no doubt whatsoever that this pop group sought publicity. They wanted to have themselves presented to the public in a favourable light so that audiences would come to hear them and support them. Mr Hutchins was engaged so as to produce, or help to produce, this favourable image, not only of their public lives but of their private lives also. If a group of this kind seek publicity which is to their advantage, it seems to me that they cannot complain if a servant or agent of theirs afterwards discloses the truth about them. If the image which they fostered was not a true image, it is in the public interest that it should be corrected. In these cases of confidential information it is a question of balancing the public interest in maintaining the confidence against the public interest in knowing the truth. That appears from *Initial Services Ltd v. Putterill* [1968] 1 Q.B. 396; *Fraser v. Evans* [1969] 1 Q.B. 349 and *D v. National Society for the Prevention of Cruelty to Children* [1976] 3 W.L.R. 124. In this case the balance comes down in favour of the truth being told, even if it should involve some breach of confidential information. As there should be 'truth in advertising' so there should be truth in publicity. The public should not be misled. So it seems to me that the breach of confidential information is not a ground for granting an injunction."

(b) *Second limb—difficulty of devising suitable wording:* Lord Denning M.R. said at 764D–E:

"The injunction is so vaguely worded that it would be most difficult for anyone—Mr Hutchins, or the newspaper or any court afterwards— to know what was prohibited and what was not. It speaks of 'confidential information.' But what is confidential? As Bridge L.J. pointed out in the course of the argument, Mr Hutchins, as a press agent, might attend a dance which many others attended. Any incidents which took place at the dance would be known to all present. The information would be in the public domain. There could be no objection to the incidents being made known generally. It would not be confidential information. So in this case the incident on this Jumbo Jet was in the public domain. It was known to all the passengers on the flight. Likewise with several other incidents in the series. The injunction is framed in such wide terms that it would be impossible for the newspaper of Mr Hutchins to know where the line should be drawn."

(c) *Third limb—the case was really one of libel, camouflaged as breach of confidence:* Per Lord Denning M.R. at 764E–G:

"There is a parallel to be drawn with libel cases. Just as in libel, the courts do not grant an interlocutory injunction to restrain publication of the truth or of fair comment. So also with confidential information. *If there is a legitimate ground for supposing that it is in the public interest for it to be disclosed, the courts should not restrain it by an interlocutory injunction, but should leave the complainant to his remedy in damages.* Suppose that this case were tried out and the plaintiffs failed in their claim for libel on the ground that all that was said was true. It would seem unlikely that there would be much damages awarded for breach of confidentiality. I cannot help feeling that the plaintiffs' real complaint here is that the words are defamatory: and as they cannot get an interlocutory injunction on that ground, nor should they on confidential information."

901

The passage italicised was adopted in *Lion Laboratories Ltd v. Evans* [1985] Q.B. 526 as constituting the criterion by which in such a case a court should decide whether or not an interlocutory injunction should be granted. *Per* Lawton L.J. at 765C in the *Woodward* case:

> "What then is the position? The allegation and confidentiality is interwoven with the claim for damages for libel and, once that is understood, it seems to me that the balance of convenience is entirely on the side of allowing the publication to go on. The defendants should know and possibly do, that if they fail in their plea of justification, the damages are likely to be heavy. They may be heavier still by reason of the fact that the offence—because that is what libel is—has been made worse by the circumstances in which Mr Hutchins has come to reveal what he knows about the plaintiffs. I find it impossible in this case to extricate the libel aspect from the confidentiality aspect. In those circumstances, it seems to me that it would be wrong to allow this injunction to continue."

6. Balance of convenience Lord Denning, at 764G said:

> "At this late hour, when the paper is just about to go to press, the balance of convenience requires that there should be no injunction. Any remedy for Mr Tom Jones and his associates should be in damages and damages only."

3 *Khashoggi v. Smith* (1980) 124 S.J. 149

1. The facts The plaintiff was very wealthy. She had employed a housekeeper, who after the cessation of her employment sought through the medium of the second defendant newspaper to publish allegedly confidential information concerning the plaintiff's private affairs which had been disclosed to the first defendant during her employment.

2. The case for the plaintiff The plaintiff relied, *inter alia*, on an implied duty of confidentiality arising out of the relationship of master and servant, and she contended that the information sought to be disclosed had been received in confidence, and that no recognised exception applied.

3. The relevant law Roskill L.J. preferred the narrower definition of the servant's duty of confidentiality laid down in *Woodward v. Hutchins* [1977] 1 W.L.R. 760 to the wide proposition adopted by Lord Denning M.R. in *Initial Services Ltd v. Putterill* [1968] 1 Q.B. 396.

4. Analysing the evidence The evidence fell into two categories:

(a) Allegations of criminal misconduct which the newspaper wished to investigate.
(b) Allegations involving men who were said to have had affairs with the plaintiff.

5. Case for the defendants The defence argued that there could be no confidence as to the disclosure of iniquity. This doctrine was expressed thus, by Page Wood V.-C. in *Gartside v. Outram* (1857) 26 L.J. Ch. 113:

> "The true doctrine is, that there is no confidence as to the disclosure of iniquity. You cannot make me the confidant of a crime or a fraud, and be entitled to close up my lips upon my secret which you have the audacity to disclose to me relating to any fraudulent intention on your part. Such a confidence cannot exist."

6. Impossibility of devising suitable wording The judgment of Roskill L.J. in the *Solicitors' Journal* is, *inter alia*, reported thus:

> "There could not be any confidence where it was desired to exploit information for investigation into the commission of alleged offences. That matter, and the issues arising from the plaintiff's private life, were closely interwoven. It was not possible to draw a line between the two. Even if matters ought to be separated, and different considerations applied to those relating to the plaintiff's private life, then applying *Woodward v. Hutchins*, the plaintiff was a person who had allowed herself to get into the public eye to such an extent that she ran the risk of the whole story being made public."

Whilst recognising that sexual misconduct might be covered by a duty of confidence, Sir David Cairns followed Roskill L.J.:

> "... in so far as what the defendants sought to disclose and publish involved allegations of criminal behaviour, the plaintiff was not entitled to relief. He was by no means satisfied that the duty of confidentiality was inappropriate to protect matters involving the plaintiff's sexual misconduct. But as certain details had already been disclosed, it would be difficult to distinguish, in relation to anything published, how much was derived from information given by the first defendant and how much had been obtained from other sources. He was not satisfied that any injunction could be framed which would at the same time protect the plaintiff against some disclosure which ought not to be made, while not being unreasonably restrictive of the right of publication, and which would be capable of enforcement."

However, the difficulty in the instant case of unscrambling the defamation element from the breach of confidence element should not generate the

903

impression that there was little conceptual distinction between them. As the Court of Appeal transcript of the dicta of Sir David Cairns shows:

> "It seems to me that there is a fundamental distinction between the two types of action, in that in the one case the plaintiff is saying 'Untrue and defamatory statements have been made about me,' and in the other case the plaintiff is saying 'Statements which are about to be published are statements about events which have happened and have been disclosed as a result of a breach of confidence.'"

And thus the plaintiff lost. As to *Woodward v. Hutchins (ibid.)* see p. 899.

4 *Garden Cottage Foods Ltd v. Milk Marketing Board* [1984] A.C. 130 (For the facts, see p. 620)

1. The injunction made by the Court of Appeal The injunction granted by the Court of Appeal was set out by Lord Diplock at 145H–146A:

> "... there be an injunction herein and an injunction is hereby granted restraining the defendants whether by themselves or by their servants or agents or otherwise from: (i) confining its sales of bulk butter to any particular person or persons or body of persons or any particular organisation or corporate body; (ii) from imposing significantly different terms in relation to the supply of butter to buyers in the bulk butter market whether as regards price, quantity, credit terms or otherwise, otherwise than pursuant to ordinary mercantile and commercial practice until the trial of this action or further order."

2. Terms of the injunction—indefensible Lord Diplock said at 146C–D:

> "It is sufficient to say of this that counsel for the company conceded that an injunction in these terms was indefensible. He submitted to your Lordships an alternative form in which paragraphs (i) and (ii) were replaced by:
>
> > '(i) from refusing to supply the plaintiffs with bulk butter, and (ii) in supplying such bulk butter from applying to such supply dissimilar conditions, whether as to price, quantity or credit terms or otherwise from those applied to equivalent transactions with other traders to whom the defendants supply bulk butter.'
>
> This draft, unlike the injunction granted by the Court of Appeal, is at least restricted to restraining the conduct of the M.M.B. towards the company, but it still suffers from a similar lack of precision as to what the M.M.B. may and may not do without infringing it."

3. Impossibility of devising suitable wording—perhaps only a temporary problem Lord Diplock explained that one of the problems was a potential lack of sufficient information. He said at 146E–F:

"... I would accept that if this action were to proceed to trial before any positive step had been taken by the Commission of the EEC under Council Regulations (EEC) No. 17/62 and the company were to succeed in establishing a continuing contravention by M.M.B. of Article 86, the High Court would have to do its best to devise a suitable form of words for a permanent injunction; but the court by then would have a great deal more evidence of the operation of the bulk butter market in the EEC and its task, which in the present state of detailed evidence I regard as being impossible, would at least be thereby facilitated."

4. The powers of the Commission Recourse to the High Court was not the only avenue of redress open to the plaintiffs. As Lord Diplock explained at 146F–G:

"... your Lordships have been informed that the company has made a complaint to the Commission under Regulation No. 17, which will entitle the Commission to investigate the behaviour of M.M.B. that is complained of and either make an order under Article 3 of the Regulation requiring M.M.B. to bring such behaviour to an end if the Commission finds that it constitutes an infringement of Article 86, or grant negative clearance under Article 2 if the Commission finds that there has been no infringement. Continuance of the behaviour after an order to cease and desist under Article 3 may be visited with penalties imposed by the Commission under Article 15(2)(b). From decisions of the Commission under Regulation No. 17 there lies an appeal to the European Court of Justice."

5. Two avenues of redress can run concurrently Lord Diplock continued by explaining that recourse to the Commission does not oust the jurisdiction of the national court. He said at 146H-147D:

"As was held by the European Court of Justice in *Belgische Radio en Televisie v. S.V. S.A.B.A.M.* (Case 127/73) [1974] 1 E.C.R. 51, 313; [1974] 2 C.M.L.R. 238 at 251, the initiation of proceedings by the Commission under Regulation No. 17 does not deprive the national court of jurisdiction to continue with an action brought by an individual citizen based on the same behaviour that is concurrently the subject of investigation by the Commission, and, in continuing that action, to refer a request for a preliminary ruling by the European Court of Justice under Article 177 of the Treaty. ... So it may be that, as the company is now pursuing also a remedy under Regulation No. 17, the High Court will be spared the problem of devising a suitable form of words for a permanent injunction if the company is ultimately successful in this action."

6. The results? Interlocutory injunction granted by the Court of Appeal—set aside.

5 *Lawrence David Ltd v. Ashton* [1989] I.C.R. 132 (for the facts, see p. 924)

1. The breach of confidence issue The plaintiff sought to restrain Mr Ashton from working for their competitor by means of an interlocutory injunction in these terms:

"An order that the defendant be restrained under judgment in this action or further order in the meantime from doing, whether by himself, his servants or agents or otherwise howsoever the following acts or any of them, namely:

(i) Disclosing to any person or making use of any confidential information or trade secret belonging to the plaintiff, knowledge of which has been acquired by the defendant during the course of his employment with the plaintiff as sales director—region 2

That is intended to rely on the general law.

(ii) Disclosing to any person whomsoever any information relating to the plaintiff or its customers or any trade secrets of the plaintiff of which the defendant has become possessed while acting as the plaintiff's sales direction—Region 2.

That is intended to rely on clause 5 of the contract."

2. The court would not make the order Balcombe L.J. said:

"On this aspect of the case I agree unhesitatingly with the view of the judge. I have always understood it to be a cardinal rule that any injunction must be capable of being framed with sufficient precision so as to enable a person injuncted to know what it is he is to be prevented from doing. After all, he is at risk of being committed for contempt if he breaks an order of the court. The inability of the plaintiff to define, with any degree of precision, what they sought to call confidential information of trade secrets militates against an injunction of this nature. That is indeed a long-recognised practice."

H: COVENANTS IN RESTRAINT OF TRADE

1 *Clifford Davis Management Ltd v. W.E.A. Records Ltd* [1975] 1 W.L.R. 61

1. The facts The plaintiffs managed a pop group. Two of the group were songwriters who entered into an agreement with the plaintiffs, the terms of which are summarised in the headnote thus:

> "They each signed, on cyclo-styled forms, publishing agreements assigning to the plaintiffs the copyright throughout the world in all their compositions for a period of five years which the plaintiffs could extend to ten. One writer agreed to deliver to the plaintiffs a minimum of one complete musical composition a month and the plaintiffs agreed to use their best endeavours to exploit the compositions to the fullest, but the plaintiffs gave no positive undertaking to publish any of their works. Payment was based on royalties and the price of sheet music. The plaintiffs had the right to assign their rights under the agreement to any third party."

The group broke off from their manager and worked under new management—pursuant to which the two songwriters composed an album, the release of which the plaintiffs sought to restrain.

2. Was there a serious issue to be tried? The Court of Appeal adopted the pre-*Cyanamid* "prima facie" case test—the hearing being just days before the deliberation of the House of Lords. However, the arguments can still with propriety be deployed for they would also bear relevance to the "serious issue to be tried" approach. The court held that there was a prima facie case, on the following grounds:

(a) *The terms of the contract were manifestly unfair:*

> "... the tie of 10 years for a composer seems to me just as unfair as a tie of 21 years in a solus agreement for a garage in *Esso Petroleum Company Ltd v. Harper's Garage (Stourport) Ltd* [1968] A.C. 269." (at 65C.)

(b) *The consideration for the copyright (one shilling per item of work) was grossly inadequate:*

> "It is true that if the publisher chose to exploit a work, he was to pay royalties; but if he did not do so, he got the copyright for one shilling." (at 65D.)

(c) *Inequality of bargaining power:*

907

"He was skilled in business and finance. ... In negotiation, they could not hold their own." (at 65E.)

(d) *Undue influence:*

"... one thing is clear from the evidence. The composer had no lawyer and no legal advisers. It seems to me that, if the publisher wished to exact some onerous terms or to drive such unconscionable bargain, he ought to have seen that the composer had independent advice." (at 65H: *Instone v. Schroeder Music Publishing Company* [1974] 1 W.L.R. 1308.)

As to undue influence and inequality of bargaining power, also see *National Westminster Bank plc v. Morgan* [1985] A.C. 686, H.L.

3. Damages—an adequate remedy? Yes—Browne L.J. said at 66C:

"I assume that the offer made in the letter from the solicitors to the first defendants dated October 1974, that all royalties arising from the sales of this album will be paid to a suspense account and held there until the dispute has been settled still stands."

2 *Fellowes & Son v. Fisher* [1976] Q.B. 122

1. The facts The defendants had for nearly 10 years, from the age of 20, worked for the plaintiff firm of solicitors rising to a conveyancing and probate clerk. He agreed in the course of that employment to be bound by a restrictive covenant binding him from being "employed, interested or concerned in the legal profession with the postal districts of Walthamstow and Chingford for a period of five years." The relevant zone was about six miles in length and two miles in width; and contained about 150,000 people. About six months after leaving the employ of the plaintiffs, the defendant took up employment with a firm of solicitors in the street next to that in which the plaintiffs' office was situated.

2. Should *Cyanamid* apply?
   (a) *Per* Lord Denning M.R.—No (for he considered "restrictive covenants" to be one of the exceptions to the *Cyanamid* rule): at 133B–D.
   (b) *Per* Browne L.J.—Yes: at 138G–H.
   (c) *Per* Sir John Pennycuick—with reluctance, yes: at 141C.

3. Applying *Cyanamid*

(a) *Was there a serious issue to be tried?* Yes—there was a conflict of evidence as to the nature and extent of the defendant's contacts with the plaintiffs' clients in the course of his work with them, and this was a relevant factor in considering the validity of the clause: *Fitch v. Dewes* [1921] 2 A.C. 158 at 164–165.

(b) *As to adequacy of damages:*

 (i) The plaintiffs had not proved that they would not be adequately compensated in damages if the injunction was not granted.

 (ii) There was no evidence whether or not damages would be an adequate remedy for the defendant if an injunction were granted.

(c) *Balance of convenience:* It was because there was doubt (through lack of evidence) as to the adequacy of the respective remedies in damages that the Court of Appeal went on to consider the balance of convenience:

 (i) *Per* Browne L.J. at 139H–140A:

> "If an injunction is granted, the defendant will lose his present job and may find himself with no job at all. He might well have difficulty in getting any job with a solicitor while this action is hanging over him. If he ultimately succeeds at the trial, there is no evidence that he could or would be reinstated by his present employers ..."

 (ii) *Per* Sir John Pennycuick at 142A:

> "On the other hand, the possible inconvenience to the plaintiffs in that they might lose a few clients appear to be much less than the certain inconvenience to the defendant being prevented from continuing his present employment ..."

4. Could the court provisionally review the merits? Yes—was the unanimous ruling:

(a) *Per* Browne L.J. at 140B (adopting the word "improper" from the dicta of Lord Diplock in *Cyanamid* [1975] 2 W.L.R. at 324):

> "If it is not 'improper' in this case to take into account the relative strengths of the cases of the parties, my view on the material before us is that the strength of the plaintiffs' case is certainly not 'disproportionate' to that of the defendant; my provisional view is that ... the defendant is here the more likely to succeed."

(b) *Per* Sir John Pennycuick at 142C:

> "I think it right to express my own view that the restriction in clause 10(a) of the contract of service is rather (but not much) too wide when one takes into account the terms of the defendant's employment, the nature of the prohibited activities, which amount in effect to doing legal work, the prohibited area and the duration of the prohibition. For myself I find difficulty in reaching a just

conclusion on this interlocutory application without considering the likelihood or otherwise of the court taking the view on the trial of the action, and I should welcome further guidance from the House of Lords on the application of the principles laid down in the *American Cyanamid* case to a restriction of the present nature."

3 *Consolidated Agricultural Supplies Ltd v. Rushmere and Smith* (1976) 120 S.J. 523

1. The facts In 1972 the plaintiff bought out the company in which the defendant, R, had been a shareholder. In the agreement for the sale of the shares there were covenants in restraint of trade whereby R and S covenanted for five years not to enter into competition with the plaintiff in nine East Anglian and adjacent counties. Concurrently with that agreement the defendant entered into service agreements with the plaintiff for three years and then on notice of not less than six months—and those agreements were renewed in 1974. In February 1976, R was wrongly and summarily made redundant and he thereupon formed a new company together with S, to pursue their original trade in animal health products. It was this activity which the plaintiff sought to restrain.

2. The plaintiff lost—why? Because:
  (a) All the agreements in the present case (sale of shares, service, covenants in restraint of trade) were interdependent.
  (b) The plaintiff did not come to equity with clean hands because:
    (i) The plaintiff had been running down its activities in East Anglia, and
    (ii) R was wrongfully dismissed.

4 *Standex International Ltd v. C.B. Blades & C.B. Blades Ltd* [1976] F.S.R. 114

1. Background The first defendant had entered into a restraint of trade covenant with the first plaintiff, which was a subsidiary of the second plaintiff. In breach of that covenant he had launched a business of his own, through the second defendant.

2. The covenant It read:

"(A) Mr Blades shall not within the area of Great Britain and Northern Ireland (1) for a period of five years from the date of the termination of his engagement hereunder be engaged in or concerned with either directly or indirectly the business of mould engraving; (2) for a period of three years from the date of termination of his engagement hereunder be engaged in or concerned with either directly or indirectly the business of roller and plate engraving. (B) Mr Blades shall not at any time solicit for himself or on behalf of others the custom of any person or firms who shall have been customers of the company. (C) Mr Blades shall not at any time divulge any trade secrets whatsoever of the company to any persons or firms whomsoever."

The first defendant was apparently taking independent legal advice when he executed the agreement.

3. The relief sought The plaintiffs sought injunctions to restrain:
  (a) The first defendant from engaging in or being concerned with the business of mould engraving in Great Britain and Northern Ireland.
  (b) Both defendants from disclosing confidential information relating to a certain process employed by the plaintiffs in their business directly or indirectly acquired by the defendants from the first plaintiff, and in particular any such information relating to the transfer paper, wax, acid resist applied to the mould prior to the etching and acid formulation used for the etching.
  (c) The defendants from using or otherwise turning to account any such confidential information.

4. The special nature of the case The first plaintiff was engaged in the business of mould engraving, *i.e.* operating a process for producing a certain pattern on the inside of a tool to be used as a mould by an engraving or etching technique. The process was patented, and thus in the public domain. But the technique for conducting the process was, claimed the plaintiffs, one of particular skill and specialised knowledge. The first plaintiff had gone to considerable length to preserve the secrecy of such technique and the first defendant was in charge of the security arrangements. In consequence, as Buckley L.J. said at 118:

> "In consequence of the position which he held, Mr Blades had an intimate knowledge of all the Mould-Tech business. He was in close touch with and had an intimate knowledge of all the company's customers for the products of the Mould-Tech business. I think it would be quite legitimate to say, if I may be allowed to borrow the expression used by Scarman L.J. in the course of the argument, that Mr Blades was really the embodiment of the trade connections of the company in respect of this part of their business."

The mould engraving business was particularly lucrative, and what made the facts of the case very special was that the plaintiffs (apart from the

911

defendants) were the only practitioners in the country of the art of mould engraving.

5. Was there an arguable case (this being a pre-*Cyanamid* decision)? There were two issues:
- (a) Was the covenant in restraint of trade obviously void?
- (b) Was the first defendant seised of trade secrets, within the meaning of the second limb of the covenant?

6. First issue: was the covenant obviously in restraint of trade? No:

> "It might well be that ... a covenant as wide as covenant 11(A)(1) in the present case would be held to be too wide as excluding the covenantor from any part in the art in which he was skilled anywhere in the United Kingdom, but I cannot satisfy myself that in the present case there is not at least an arguable case and I think it is not by any means a negligible case to be argued, that in the special circumstances which obtain here the only effective sort of covenant that the plaintiff company could subject Mr Blades to, which would protect their trade connection and their process so far as it was a confidential process, would be one by which Mr Blades was barred from the mould engraving field of activity altogether for a space of time." (at 121.)

7. Trade secrets: was the point arguable? Yes:

(a) *The case for the defendants:*

> "So far as the process has been published in the complete specification of the patent relating to the process, there is no secrecy about it. He says that the know how which the plaintiff company possesses in relation to the carrying out of the process is of a kind which is really part of the knowledge of any skilled engraver employed in this type of work."

(b) *Ruling:* If the defence were right, "why on earth did the [plaintiffs] go to all the trouble to which they did go to keep the process secret?"

8. Damages an adequate remedy for the plaintiffs? No—as Buckley L.J. said at 122–123:

> "It seems to me at the present stage that it is impossible to say how great damage the disclosure of secret processes might do or how much harm it might occasion to the plaintiff company. Moreover in a trade which is I think an expanding trade, it seems that is the position here, the whole future of the business may be affected by a 12 months' interference with its successful prosecution due to competition which ought not to have been permitted to take place. ... On the other side

912

... the English company is evidently a company of substance and would be able to answer any damages and any liability which they might incur under an undertaking in damages forming part of an order restraining Mr Blades. The effect of an injunction in the terms asked for may be substantially to inhibit the business of the defendant company, but it will not I think mean that the defendant company's business will have to be brought entirely to a halt or that Mr Blades will not be able to continue to earn a living in the exercise of his skill as a mechanical engineer. There are other types of commercial engraving which will open to the defendant company, roller engraving and plate engraving, but not mould engraving."

And Scarman L.J. said at 127:

"I can imagine nothing more disruptive of the plaintiffs' successful business venture in the application of this Mould-Tech process than that their trusted manager, with all the knowledge at his fingertips, should be in that very limited business as their principal competitor and using, if the plaintiffs are right, the confidential information about the process obtained by him during his time with them. It may be that if this relief is not granted now, the plaintiffs' business might be irreparably damaged before the trial."

5 *Office Overload Ltd v. Gunn* [1977] F.S.R. 39

1. The facts The defendant had originally (as their agent) worked the Croydon area for the plaintiff which was a multinational company running an extensive employment agency. In the plaintiff's "licensing agreement" with the defendant, there was the following covenant:

"For one year after the termination of this agreement the licensee agrees not to be connected directly or indirectly as employee, proprietor, stockholder, partner or officer in the operation of any business competitive with Overload within the licensed area."

The plaintiff terminated that agreement, but even before the 60-day contractual notice period had elapsed, the defendant commenced in competition with the plaintiff.

2. Was there any dispute on the affidavit evidence? From the report—apparently none.

3. What was the validity of the restrictive covenant? The approach of the court can be analysed thus:

913

(a) "One-year": reasonable in point of time (at 40).

(b) *"Six-mile radius"*: reasonable in point of area (at 40).

(c) *"Any business connected directly or indirectly"*:
   (i) Defendant's argument: the clause was expressed more widely than was reasonable.

   (ii) Held: *per* Lord Denning M.R. at 41–2:

> "In master-and-servant cases the court will not restrain a servant from competing; but in a vendor-and-purchaser case, it will restrain the vendor from competing. This case is somewhat betwixt and between. The nearest to it is the case of the canvasser in *Manson v. Provident Clothing and Supply Co. Ltd* [1913] A.C. 724. Lord Moulton said:
>
>> 'Such being the nature of the employment, it would be reasonable for the employer to protect himself against the danger of his former servant canvassing or collecting for a rival firm in the district in which he had been employed. If he were permitted to do so before the expiry of a reasonably long interval, he would be in a position to give to his new employer all the advantages of that personal knowledge of the inhabitants of the locality, and more especially of his former customers, which he had acquired in the service of the respondents and at their expense. Against such a contingency, the master might reasonably protect himself, but I can see no further or other protection which he could reasonably demand.'
>
> So here, if Mr Gunn were allowed, in this very area, to use his knowledge of and connection with employers and workers, so as to get business for himself, he would be taking unfair advantage of information which he acquired in his service with Industrial Overload. This is something against which Industrial Overload are entitled to protection."

   (iii) *Per* Lawton L.J. at 44:

> "The next problem is: Was there anything which it was reasonable for the clause to protect in the interests of the plaintiffs? And the answer, in my judgment, comes from the defendant's own affidavit sworn on June 30, 1975. Paragraph 12 of that affidavit starts in this way: 'While I was trading under the plaintiffs' name in Croydon I realised that 90 per cent of my work came from 10 per cent of the employers in the area. Most of this 10 per cent is contained in the lists given to Industrial Overload.' In other words, he was admitting that there was a trading connection of considerable value to the

plaintiffs, and which was likely to be of considerable value to him."

(d) *"Stockholder":*

(i) Case for the defendant: It might prevent the defendant from holding stock in a company in which he has no influence at all.

(ii) Held—no: "It has often been said that a covenant in restraint of trade is not to be rendered invalid simply by putting forward unlikely or improbable contingencies in which it might operate unreasonably." (*Commercial Plastics v. Vincent* [1965] 1 Q.B. 623 at 644, *per* Pearson L.J.) in the same vein, in *Edwards v. Worboys* [1984] A.C. 724 Dillon L.J. said at 727H–728A:

> "The other, and for present purposes, much more important point, is that the validity of a covenant is not to be tried by the improbabilities that might fall within its wording. The fact that on the literal reading of a covenant the wording may prohibit a person doing something in circumstances which are highly improbable or unlikely, or whatever the appropriate word may be, does not indicate in any way necessarily that the covenant is unreasonable. This was explored particularly by Salmon and Cross L.JJ. in *Home Counties Dairies Ltd v. Skilton* [1970] 1 W.L.R. 526."

(e) *Repudiation:*

(i) Case for defendant: The plaintiffs had repudiated the licence agreement of 1975 by giving notice to determine it before it had been signed by both parties.

(ii) Held: "That this is not a repudiation. By giving notice, Office Overload were insisting that the agreement was in existence, and that its existence could be determined by reasonable notice: *Sweet & Maxwell v. Universal News Services* [1964] 2 Q.B. 699."

4. Balance of convenience? The defendant argued that there were serious issues to be tried, the defendant had money and damages were an adequate remedy. Lord Denning M.R. however held at 43:

> "But as we pointed out in *Fellowes v. Fisher* [1975] 3 W.L.R. 184 covenants in restraint of trade are in a special category. The practice also has been that, if they are prima facie valid and prima facie there is an infringement, the courts will grant an injunction. These cases are very rarely fought out to the bitter end. They are invariably decided at the interlocutory stage. Moreover, as Bridge L.J. pointed out, if this case were to go to trial, the whole year would be up and over before the case was tried. So the *American Cyanamid* case does not apply."

So as not apparently to flout the authority of the House of Lords, Bridge L.J. added at 44:

> "I would not wish to be thought to treat with anything less than the respect due to it the decision of the House of Lords in the case of the American Cyanamid Company. That decision considered the principle which ought to govern the grant of interlocutory injunctions where either there is an unresolved dispute on the affidavit evidence before the court, or a question of law to be decided. I cannot see that either of those conditions are applicable here.
>
> All the relevant matters which the parties have chosen to put before the court are plain and uncontroversial—indeed, it is upon the affidavits which have been submitted by the interlocutory that the plaintiffs are primarily in a position to rely to show clearly that the contravention of the restriction in the covenant which the defendant entered into will be destructive of a legitimate interest of the plaintiffs which the plaintiffs are entitled to have protected. Similarly it seems to me, though, of course, this being an interlocutory decision we must formally state that we do not finally determine the issue, on the application to the terms of this restrictive covenant in relation to the situation of these parties of the well-known principles which govern the validity of restrictive covenants, that this is a valid covenant.
>
> If it were not possible for the court to grant interlocutory relief to enforce a restrictive covenant of limited duration such as this, then, in cases like the present, such covenants could never be enforced by the courts, the parties entitled to the benefit of them would always be left to their remedy in damages, which in such cases might frequently be an indeterminate remedy."

6 *Curson and Poole v. Rash* (1982) 263 EG 518

1. The facts The defendant had been employed by the plaintiff firm of estate agents as a senior sales negotiator in whose service contract there featured the following covenant:

> "For a period of one year next after the determination of the Associate's employment hereunder whether by effluxion of time or in any other way whatsoever the Associate shall neither:
>
> (a) On behalf of himself or of any person, firm or company solicit or act for any person, firm or company who shall at the time of such determination have been a client of the firm, nor
> (b) Directly or indirectly be concerned in the business of that of an Estate Agent, Surveyor or Valuer within a radius of three miles from the Branch."

Having left the firm, the defendant set up a rival business within 400 yards of the plaintiffs' branch in which he had been last employed.

2. Triable issues Vinelott J. identified the following triable issues:
  (a) Evidently, to what "branch" did the covenant refer?
  (b) As a matter of law, was clause 15 valid or void as in restraint of trade?

3. Analysing clause 15 The following parts of clause 15 were subjected to judicial scrutiny:
  (a) "Any person, firm or company who shall at the time of such determination have been a client of the firm" (the "client restriction").
  (b) "Within a radius of three miles" (the "area restriction").
  (c) The soliciting part of the covenant (the "soliciting restriction").

4. The "client restriction" Vinelott J. held at 519:

"Subparagraph (a) of clause 15 in so far as it purports to restrict the defendant from acting for 'any person, firm or company who shall at the time of such determination have been a client of the firm.' That, as I see it, is hopelessly wide—far wider than would be necessary for the protection of any legitimate interest of the plaintiffs. The firm, as I said, has a very wide geographical spread, and I think I am entitled to infer that it has been in existence for some considerable time. To prohibit the defendant from acting for anyone who at any time had been a client of the firm is in effect to prohibit competition, and not merely to protect the legitimate interest of the plaintiffs."

5. The "area restriction"

(a) *Arguments:*
    (i) By the defendant: The area was 17 square miles, contained a population of 250,000 and was serviced by 70 other firms and had a variety of housing.

    (ii) By the plaintiffs: the tendency of clients was to return to the estate agent who acted for them previously and that is a connection which the plaintiffs were entitled to protect—just as they were entitled to protect the connection which the defendant, as their manager and in effect their representative at the Southgate office was likely to have built up on behalf of the firm with persons likely to be able to influence vendors and purchasers of houses in the area (*i.e.* solicitors, bank managers, building society representatives etc.).

(b) *Judgment:*

"It has been recognised in many cases that a firm of estate agents can acquire, and in fact does normally acquire, a connection of this kind

917

which it is entitled to protect, more particularly against a senior employee who, like the defendant, is the representative of the firm in a particular office. I do not propose to refer in detail to any of the cases; the facts of one case can never usefully be compared with the facts of another case. But there is a useful analysis of the principles in the judgment of Graham J. in *Calvert, Hunt & Barden v. Elton* (1975) 233 EG 391 which, like this case, was a three-mile restriction, though in an area further from the more populous part of London. I do not think it is possible to say that an area of three miles is *ex facie* wider than is reasonable to protect a connection of this kind. It must be borne in mind that part of this wider area comprises different kinds of housing development running from detached rural houses to the north to the more modest houses on the south and west, and that the surrounding area is homogeneous in the sense that once you get beyond the three-mile limit you continue with similar kinds of housing. There is nothing to stop the defendant, subject to the soliciting covenant, from starting just over the three-mile border where he would be dealing with houses not very different from those with which he would be dealing in that part inside the three-mile border, so that he would not be deprived of the opportunity of exploiting the knowledge, skill and experience he has acquired in dealing with property of the kind he dealt with in the plaintiffs' employment. He does in fact live in Enfield and he could practise there without infringing the covenant. It must be borne in mind also that it is quite a short period of restriction. ... It is not, of course, for me to decide on this occasion whether the restriction is or is not wider than is reasonably necessary to protect the plaintiffs' connection. It is sufficient to say that I am wholly unpersuaded that it is obviously too wide. Indeed, it seems to me on the evidence I have seen to be nothing more than (as was expressed by counsel for the plaintiffs) a restriction which will provide protection by imposing a 'cooling-off' period during which the defendant's successor can do whatever lies within his power to keep the connection, particularly with building societies and the like, within the area, and to make sure that he does not have to build or retain that connection against unfair competition."

6. The "soliciting restriction" A triable issue—just. Vinelott J. said at 519 (column 2):

"Then there is the soliciting covenant. That seems to me rather near the borderline. It has been pointed out in more than one case that it is difficult, where a soliciting covenant is drawn as widely as this, extending as it does to all persons who have been clients of the firm, for the covenantor to know whether he is breaching the covenant or not. The answer that has been given, in particular in *Plowman (G. W.) & Son Ltd v. Ash* [1964] 1 W.L.R. 568, is that a defendant in these circumstances must act with circumspection (in this case for a period of only seven months); if he does so, and inadvertently solicits former clients, he will not be at risk of being committed. On the whole, although with some diffidence, I think there is at least a triable issue whether the soliciting part is not also valid."

7. Balance of convenience Having established triable issues, Vinelott J. found assistance from the judgment of Buckley L.J. in *Office Overload Ltd v. Gunn (ibid.)* at 44:

"If it were not possible for the court to grant interlocutory relief to enforce a restrictive covenant of limited duration such as this, then, in cases like the present, such covenants could never be enforced by the courts, and parties entitled to the benefits of them would always be left to their remedy in damages, which in such cases might frequently be an indeterminate remedy."

8. Balancing the risks Vinelott J. identified the following conflicting interests:
  (a) "The risk that the plaintiffs would be deprived, by the refusal of an injunction, of the whole benefit of the covenant (which only had seven months to run)."
  (b) "The possible damage to the defendant if the injunction is granted and it transpires either that it was not a term of the contract of employment or was too wide to be enforced."

9. Analysing the "damage" Vinelott J. explored the "damage" to the defendant if the injunction were granted. He said at 520:

"If the business started by his brother survives, then there will be no irreparable damage, and to the extent that the defendant has an interest in that business, any damage suffered by his exclusion for seven months from participating in it should be capable of being measured, as also the damage to him of being perhaps left without employment for seven months. The defendant says that the business may 'go under' if he is not there to help. I confess that I find this claim exaggerated. We are dealing with a period of only seven months; one brother (who gave no covenant) will be there all the time, and can employ other staff for seven months when the defendant can rejoin him."

10. The "clean hands" factor Vinelott J. granted the injunction taking into account the "provocation" of the defendant:

919

"I must weigh the fact that the defendant and his brother chose to set up business in what seems to me a position provocatively close to the plaintiffs' office, and negotiated and completed their arrangements over a period of several months, and gave no indication even when they left of how close that office would be to the Southgate office. I think it lies ill in their mouth to complain that enforcement of the covenant might mortally injure their business."

7 *Oswald Hickson Collier & Co. v. Carter-Ruck* [1984] A.C. 720

1. The facts The plaintiff partnership dissolved, pursuant to which the defendant solicitor set up his own account. The plaintiff sought to restrain the defendant from acting for a previous client of the firm, and invoked Clause 24 of the partnership deed:

"In the event of retirement or determination [it is 'retirement' in this case] any partner retiring or in respect of whom the partnership with the firm shall not be renewed shall not either in his own name alone or as managing clerk to or as agent for or on behalf of or in partnership with any other person or persons for a period of two years from such retirement or determination or non-renewal approach solicit or act for any clients of the firm except (a) in connection with business appertaining to relations by blood or marriage or business concerns in which the partner had or there is a family interest, or (b) any client introduced to the firm by such partner whom he elects by notice in writing to the other partners to retain as a client of his ..."

2. Was the client in question introduced to the firm? No—the client was introduced in August 1944, when the defendant was the sole partner of the plaintiff. In other words, at the material time, there was no firm. Section 4 of the Partnership Act 1890 provides:

"Persons who have entered into partnership with one another are for the purposes of this Act called collectively a firm and the name under which their business is carried on is called the firm-name."

3. Ruling

(a) *No breach:* No injunction.

(b) *Public policy: Per* Lord Denning M.R. at 723:

"I cannot see that it would be proper for a clause to be inserted in a partnership deed preventing one of the partners from acting for a client in the future. It is contrary to public policy because there is a fiduciary relationship between them. The client ought reasonably to be entitled to the services of such solicitor as he wishes. That solicitor no doubt has a great deal of confidential information available to him. It would be contrary to public policy if the solicitor were prevented from acting for him by a clause of this kind."

But the public policy argument was a fact misconceived, as the Privy Council pointed out in *Bridge v. Deacons* [1984] 1 A.C. 705 at 719F–720B:

"If these dicta were intended to state a general rule, their Lordships must respectfully but emphatically decline to agree with it. It is unsupported by authority, and appears to have been made without any reference to the fact that it was directly contrary to a considerable volume of authority including a decision of the House of Lords in *Fitch v. Dewes* [1921] 2 A.C. 158. It also seems to be unjustified in principle. For one thing a solicitor is always (except to some extent in legal aid cases) entitled to refuse to act for a particular person, and it is difficult to see any reason why he should not be entitled to bind himself by contract not to act in future for a particular group of persons. For another thing, the relationship of solicitor and client is not unique in being confidential; the relationships of medical men with their patients and of many other professional men with their clients are also confidential. If there were a general rule that they could not bind themselves not to act for former clients of the firm after they had retired from a partnership, the results would be very far reaching. It must be remembered that the clients are clients of the firm, rather than of an individual partner. These and other objections to treating the dicta in the *Carter-Ruck* case as being of general application were pointed out by Walton J. in *Edwards v. Worboys* (unreported), March 18, 1983. When *Worboys'* case reached the Court of Appeal [1984] A.C. 724, Dillon L.J. and Sir John Donaldson M.R. both treated the obiter dicta in the *Carter-Ruck* case as not being of general application. Their Lordships agreed with that view."

8 *Faccenda Chicken Ltd v. Fowler* [1987] Ch. 117, C.A.

1. Background This case involves the extent to which a former employee can use information deriving from his erstwhile employer. As such, it must be the authority by which courts of first instance will decide whether or not there is a serious issue to be tried in "confidentiality" cases.

2. The facts The plaintiffs, who marketed fresh chicken, employed the defendant as their sales manager, adopting a system suggested by the defendant. The defendant left the plaintiffs and set up a similar business in the same area employing a number of the plaintiffs' staff. There was no contractual agreement governing the activities of employees after ceasing employment.

3. Ruling An injunction to restrain the defendant from using sales information was refused. The Court of Appeal held:
- (a) An ex-employee did not owe the same duty of fidelity as an employee, and confidential information short of a trade secret was not protected, so long as the ex-employee had not abused his duty of fidelity whilst an employee by memorising it or recording it then. Furthermore, such information short of a trade secret could not be protected by a restrictive covenant.
- (b) In considering whether information was a trade secret or the equivalent of a trade secret, the court should have regard to:
  - (i) the nature of the employment and the status of the employee;
  - (ii) the nature of the information;
  - (iii) whether the employer had stressed the confidentiality of the information to the employee; and
  - (iv) whether the information could be isolated from other nonconfidential information.

See also *Evening Standard Company Ltd v. Henderson* [1987] I.C.R. 588.

9 *John Michael Design Plc v. Cooke* [1987] I.C.R. 445

1. The facts The two defendants had been employed by the plaintiffs, one as a director and one as a senior designer, and their terms of employment included a restrictive covenant. They left the plaintiffs' employment and set up a new firm which in due course wished to do business with Hornes Menswear, who were former clients of the plaintiffs. The plaintiffs sought an injunction to enforce the covenant.

2. The judge had granted the injunction but excepted Hornes At first instance Swinton Thomas J. came to the conclusion that prima facie the covenant was binding—obviously there had been a breach of it, or there was about to be a breach of it—and therefore that the plaintiffs were entitled to an injunction. But having regard to the balance of convenience he decided to exclude Hornes Menswear from the scope of the injunction, because if the injunction covered Hornes Menswear,
- (a) the defendants would probably not get the contract; and
- (b) the plaintiffs would probably not get the contract either.

3. The clause

"At no time within two years of the termination of this contract (howsoever ended and whether or not John Michael shall be in breach of this contract) shall the employee directly or indirectly canvass, solicit or accept from any client who is or was in the four years prior to the termination of his employment a client of John Michael any business in competition to or similar to that of John Michael."

4. The Court of Appeal deleted the exclusion of Hornes—why? As to the judge's reason referred to at 2(a) above Nicholls L.J. said:

"[The learned judge] mentioned the overwhelming likelihood that, if the injunction should cover the proposed contract with Hornes, the defendants would fail to get the contract at all. That factor goes to adequacy of damages as a remedy for the defendants if ultimately they should succeed at the trial, and that is of course a matter properly to be brought into account in deciding whether it is just to grant an interlocutory injunction."

5. Reason 2(b) was bad The fact that the plaintiffs would not have got the contract is no good reason for excluding that contract from the scope of the injunction. O'Connor L.J. said:

"There are, I think, at least two good reasons for it. First of all, any such covenant restraining competition by an ex-employee is always looked at with care, but where it falls within the accepted limits of time and area, not to enforce it against a particular customer who comes forward and says that he has no intention of any further business dealings with the plaintiff but is proposing to give his allegiance to the defendants, is the very class of case against which the covenant is designed to give protection ... The second one advanced by [the plaintiffs is] ... that the court ought not to support the situation where a party aware of a term of a contract such as this, so to speak deliberately promotes a breach of it; and that he may be embarking on a course of conduct which amounts to the tort of inducing breach of contract. It seems to me that that is not a desirable matter which the court should support ..."

6. *American Cyanamid* does not really apply O'Connor L.J. said:

"When the learned judge had the matter before him he contemplated a speedy trial, and he gave a stringent timetable for the interlocutory proceedings to be completed within a month and the case to be set down. But the reality of the case is, as has been presented to us, that really these interlocutory proceedings are in fact conclusive of the case ... So it seems to me that in these cases the court, as the learned judge I think did, has to make up its mind—is the covenant prima facie good? If it is prima facie good, then in the ordinary course of events it is right to restrain the offending defendant."

10 *Lawrence David Ltd v. Ashton* [1989] I.C.R. 123

1. The facts Lawrence David Ltd were a company which manufactured side-opening bodies for lorries. They employed Mr Ashton as a sales director, but he was not successful and they terminated his employment without giving proper notice. After the end of his employment Mr Ashton wished to work for a competitor of the plaintiffs. The plaintiffs sought an interlocutory injunction to prevent him from doing so, in two ways. (See p. 000 for the breach of confidence point.)

2. The restraint of trade issue By clause 13 of his contract,

> "For a period of two years after the determination of this agreement for any reason whatsoever Mr Ashton shall not without the written consent of the board, either alone or in partnership undertake to carry on or be employed in any capacity or be interested directly or indirectly in the design and development, manufacture or supply of any sliding door vehicle body, tension or sliding curtain vehicle body or any other vehicle body for which a patent or any part of the aforementioned vehicle bodies within the United Kingdom."

3. The principles applicable The plaintiffs applied for an order in the terms of clause 13. The Court of Appeal held that *American Cyanamid v. Ethicon Ltd* [1975] A.C. 396 applied. Balcombe L.J. said:

> "... both counsel appear to have been of the view that that approach is not relevant where an interlocutory injunction is sought to enforce a contractual obligation in restraint of trade. We were told that this is a view widely held in the profession. If so, it is time that the profession is disabused."

4. Is there a serious question to be tried? Yes. Balcombe L.J. said that this issue breaks down into two parts:

> "... first, was there here a repudiatory breach of the contract which has been accepted by the defendant [Mr Ashton]? This raises issues of fact, for example, the precise manner of his dismissal, how and when the defendant left, and whether he has now been paid that to which he is entitled. It also raises an issue of law: was this a repudiatory breach?—since not every breach of contract is repudiatory. ... On this point there is clearly a serious question to be tried.
>
> Secondly, under this head, comes the construction of clause 13 itself.

924

At this stage I do not think it appropriate to say anything more than that it is clear to me that there is a serious question to be tried. It is quite impossible to say that this covenant is obviously bad."

5. Would damages be an adequate remedy for the plaintiffs? No:

"It seems to me that [the plaintiffs] have made out a prima facie case for having trade secrets in a number of areas ... It is accepted that if the plaintiffs do suffer damage, the defendant would be quite unable to pay any such damages. There is no doubt in my mind that here, as is usual in this type of case, damages would not be an adequate remedy for the plaintiffs."

6. Would damages be an adequate remedy for the defendant? Yes—on two conditions:

"Turning to the defendant's ability to recover any damages from the plaintiffs on their cross-undertaking (if it turns out that any interlocutory injunction should not have been granted) he undoubtedly can be compensated by the plaintiffs for being kept out of work during the period he is wrongly injuncted. There is no question but that the plaintiffs are clearly able to pay any such damages."

"More difficult is any long-term damage which he may suffer by being kept out of the employment market for a period. He is 48, and his evidence that he may find difficulty in obtaining suitable employment, although not tested in cross-examination, is prima facie credible. This may not be easy to establish or, if established, to assess in monetary terms. Much depends on the period for which the interlocutory injunction operates. As we said in *Dairy Crest Ltd v. Pigott* ([1989] I.C.R. 92), cases of this type are singularly appropriate for a speedy trial."

7. *American Cyanamid* **does not always apply**

"It is only if the action cannot be tried before the period of the restraint has expired, or has run a large part of its course, that the granting of an interlocutory injunction will effectively dispose of the action, thus being the case within the exception to the rule in *American Cyanamid*, such as was considered by the Lord in *N.W.L. Ltd v. Woods* [1979] IRLR 478 ..."

925

11 *Unigate Dairies Ltd v. Bruce, The Times*, March 2, 1988

1. The facts The defendant milkman had been employed by the plaintiffs under a contract preventing him from serving the plaintiffs' customers after termination of his employment. After leaving the plaintiffs' employment the defendant nevertheless did serve some customers of the plaintiffs. The plaintiffs applied for an interlocutory injunction.

2. At first instance The judge at first instance used his discretion and granted an interlocutory injunction restraining the defendant from committing further alleged breaches, but permitting him to continue to serve such customers as he had already started to serve.

3. On appeal The Court of Appeal reasoned that since the judge must have concluded that an injunction was necessary to restrain the alleged breaches and that damages would not be an adequate remedy for the plaintiffs, it was *Wednesbury* unreasonable of the judge to refuse also to restrain the defendant from continuing with the breach which was already occurring.

4. The status quo In restraint of trade cases the Court of Appeal said that the court should preserve the status quo position it had been before the alleged breaches—not the position as at the date of the hearing. The latter necessarily involved permitting the former employee to continue to do acts which were alleged to constitute breaches of the covenant.

I: CASES INVOLVING A CONFLICT BETWEEN PUBLIC AND PRIVATE INTERESTS

1 *Distillers Company (Biochemicals) Ltd v. Times Newspapers Ltd* [1975] Q.B. 613

1. Preamble This pre-*Cyanamid* case—turning as it did on "prima facie" arguments, may at first blush appear to have been superseded. But in *Lion Laboratories Ltd v. Evans* [1985] Q.B. 526 the issue of the balance between public and private interests arose at an interlocutory stage—and the Court of Appeal explored extensively the merits of the claim. This is a warning to practitioners that in such cases, gathering only sufficient material to show a "triable issue" may not be enough. Against that backdrop, caution warrants consideration of the *Distillers* case.

2. The facts Doctor Phillips was a chemist. He was retained by the claimants in the Thalidomide litigation to advise them on the documents produced by Distillers (10,000 of them). Subsequent to such advice but prior to his undertaking not to divulge, Dr Phillips entered into an agreement with Times Newspapers Ltd to sell to them documentary information concerning the litigation. Upon the defendants indicating in March 1974 that they intended to publish an article based on the documents, the plaintiffs claimed interlocutory relief founded on a writ claiming an overriding protection from publication and that the documents were subject to copyright by section 4 of the Copyright Act 1956. It should be recorded that at all material times, no case of negligence had been made out against the plaintiffs. The Thalidomide claim had settled without prejudice to liability.

3. What Talbot J. found as established He said at 617H–618A–B:

"Perhaps the principal reason why the plaintiffs complain of the defendants' use of their material is that the defendants are unfairly critical, that they have misreported the documents which they have used, that they have selected information from the documents to support their criticism of the plaintiffs and that they have suppressed other material which has relevance to the matters contained in the defendants' critical article. The plaintiffs further point out that the defendants knew that Dr. Phillips had been retained in the litigation by the defendants as an expert adviser, that they knew that Dr. Phillips had access to the documents in question in his capacity as such adviser, that they knew that the documents were discovery documents and that it must follow that the defendants were prepared to pay and did pay for these documents and so procure a breach of confidence on the part of Dr. Phillips. It seems to me that, on the evidence, all these matters have been proved."

4. The case for the defendants The defendants claimed entitlement to publication, by reference to four arguments:
  (a) The publication would not constitute any breach of any duty which they might owe as a result of the disclosure to them by Dr Phillips of the documents.
  (b) Publication of the proposed article based on these documents was in the public interest.
  (c) Publication would not constitute a breach of copyright.
  (d) If publication did constitute a breach of copyright, it would be fair dealing with a literary work within section 6(2) and (3) of the Act of 1956.

927

5. The plaintiffs' arguments The plaintiffs advanced the following submissions:

(a) It was an established principle that a party to litigation was under an obligation not to make improper use of documents disclosed in an action pursuant to discovery.

(b) Disclosure of such documents for purposes other than the litigation in question was an improper use.

(c) The protection of discovery documents was paramount in the public interest in the proper administration of justice. If discovery were to result in documents becoming public the process of discovery would be in danger. Thus when one considered the need that the litigants who made discovery should feel that their interests would be fully protected, there was no room for a higher public interest.

It was on the third submission that the principal issue between the parties lay.

6. Balancing the interests Talbot J. marked out the field of battle thus:

(a) It is a matter of importance to the public that documents disclosed on discovery should not be permitted to be put to improper use and that the court should give its protection in the right case.

(b) Thus as to the public interest factor, the only competing factor which the defendants could advance was that there was a public interest which was so high as to override the public interest which would otherwise protect documents disclosed on discovery.

7. How did the defendants pitch their case? Taking as his theme "Is the administration of justice so important that everything else has to be swept aside?" counsel for the defendants argued:

(a) If the administration of justice was so important, then the documents would be shut up forever.

(b) There had never been a public enquiry. He then listed 16 questions which would have had to be put to such enquiry—and justified such questions by reference to parts of the contents of the documents in dispute. Against that backdrop, he explained that the defendants wished to:

(i) publish either a series of articles or a book based on the material which they had;

(ii) seek to put the material before Lord Pearson's Commission on Compensation;

(iii) make the documents available to claimants who did not get them from the plaintiffs, for example, claimants outside the country.

8. Talbot J. found for the plaintiffs At 625C–D, he said:

"Whilst, as I have said, the public have a great interest in the thalidomide story (and it is a matter of public interest) and any light which can be thrown on to this matter to obviate any such thing happening again is welcome, nevertheless the defendants have not persuaded me that such use as they proposed to make of the documents which they possess is of greater advantage to the public than the public's interest in the need for the proper administration of justice, to prevent the confidentiality of discovery of documents. I would go further and say that I doubt very much whether there is sufficient in the use which the defendants have proposed to raise a public interest which overcomes the plaintiffs' private right to the confidentiality of their documents. In any event I consider that the plaintiffs have established their right (this is not really disputed) and have an arguable case for its protection by an injunction."

2 *Schering Chemicals Ltd v. Falkman Ltd* [1982] Q.B. 1

1. The facts Pursuant to suspicion that its pregnancy test drug might cause foetal abnormalities, the plaintiff withdrew it from the market and engaged the first defendant to advise it as to how to limit the damage to their commercial reputation. Such engagement necessarily involved putting the first defendant into possession of all the information the plaintiff could offer as to the manufacture and marketing of the drug. The information so provided necessarily included much that was then justifiably regarded as confidential. Accordingly, the terms of the plaintiff's contract with the first defendant expressly imposed on it the obligation to preserve the confidentiality of the information imparted. The first defendant in turn recruited a Mr Elstein (the second defendant) to advise it. "E" then approached Thames Television (the third defendant) with a view to making a film about the drug—and went ahead, notwithstanding the plaintiff's declining to grant consent.

2. The case for the second defendant, Elstein "E" argued that:
   (a) the information which he supplied to the third defendant (Thames Television) was in any event available from public sources, and
   (b) that as a matter of law, there was no power in the court to restrain publication of information which is not confidential information but is available from public sources: *Seager v. Copydex Ltd* [1967] 1 W.L.R. 923; *Fraser v. Evans* [1969] 1 Q.B. 349 at 361 and *Coco v. Clark (A.N.) Engineers Ltd* [1969] R.P.C. 41 at 46 *et seq.*

3. Was there a serious issue to be tried? Yes:
   (a) The first defendant (through a Mr Bernard Falk) deposed to having

told "E" "that he must not use any confidential information the source of which [was] any ... training sessions in which he participated... This was accepted by Mr Elstein."

(b) "E" deposed that he made no promise, he knew nothing of the first defendant's promise to the plaintiff, and therefore he was not bound.

(c) It was conceded on behalf of "E" that if "E" had promised the plaintiff not to make use for his own purposes of information, whether confidential or not, which he received from the plaintiff for the purposes of the training course, then he would be bound by that promise.

(d) The triable issues were therefore:

    (i) Whether "E" saw the proposals made in December 1978 whereby the first defendant acknowledged that information which it received from the plaintiff "some of which is public and some of which is private, remains strictly confidential" and guaranteed that such information "will never be used in the future by a broadcasting associate of ETT."

    (ii) Whether "E," if he did not see the proposals, saw any other document which disclosed the promise made by the first defendant on "E's" behalf or whether by reason of earlier employment by the first defendant he was aware that such a promise would be made.

Templeman L.J. went further, and expressed a very strong view that whether express or by implication, the information by which "E" came was impressed with a sufficient degree of confidentiality—to his knowledge—as to warrant his being restrained from exploiting it.

4. Where did the balance of convenience lie? Templeman L.J. at 38G held that the balance was all one way:

"If the film 'The Primodos Affair' were shown, damages would be a grossly inadequate remedy for Schering. It is impossible to quantify the damage caused by bad publicity."

5. Did a "journalist's immunity" affect the balance? There were a number of factors to be considered:

(a) Was "E" a journalist?

(b) If he was—was that sufficient to afford immunity? As Templeman L.J. said at 39E:

"The questions then arise as to whether a journalist or a newspaper is entitled as of right to immunity from an injunction against publication and whether, if there is no absolute immunity, nevertheless in the circumstances of the present case the court should in the exercise of its discretion decline to grant an injunction."

Templeman L.J. posed the question on the basis that Thames Television was entitled to all the protection afforded to a newspaper.

6. Was Elstein a journalist? On balance, Templeman L.J. thought not, but gave him the benefit of the doubt (at 39A–B):

"It is not abundantly clear that Mr Elstein is to be regarded as a part-time or full-time journalist for present purposes. He resists compliance with a rule of professional conduct laid down by the National Union of Journalists for the purpose of maintaining high professional standards amongst journalists on the ground that he is not a member of the union. When Mr Elstein took part in the training programme, he was not acting as a journalist but as a confidential adviser. But, assuming for present purposes that Mr Elstein is entitled to cast over himself the cloak and protection of journalism, he is claiming an immunity from the remedy of an injunction in circumstances in which other persons not claiming to be journalists would not be immune."

7. Defining the ambit of the immunity In this regard, the following principles were enunciated:

(a) Journalists and the press were not entitled to absolute immunity from injunctions to restrain the publication of confidential information: *British Steel Corporation v. Granada Television Ltd* [1980] 3 W.L.R. 774, recited at 39F;

(b) The court should consider the consequences to the public of withholding or granting an injunction—*i.e.* a balance is to be drawn between preserving confidentiality and the freedom of the press. As Templeman L.J. said at 40A:

"It is important in the present case that, if the injunction is withheld the court will enable a trusted adviser to make money out of his dealing in confidential information. These consequences must be weighed against the argument that, if an injunction is granted, the public will be deprived of information."

(c) The obligation of confidentiality may in some circumstances be overborne—but not here. As Shaw L.J. said at 27C–D:

"If the subject-matter is something which is inimical to the public interest or threatens individual safety, a person in possession of knowledge of that subject-matter cannot be obliged to conceal it although he acquired that knowledge in confidence. In some situations it may be his duty to reveal what he knows. No such consideration has existed in this case since the time that Primodos was withdrawn from the market. Neither the public nor any individual stands in need of protection from its use at this stage in

931

the history. There is no occasion to beat the drum again. As to any rights of liability which may have arisen from the use of Primodos in the past, these will be determined by the outcome of the pending litigation. Mr Elstein and Thames can offer no valid or effective assistance in this regard; they are without any legitimate justification for canvassing the issues in flagrant breach of an elementary duty to honour confidences acquired by Mr Elstein in the guise of a professional adviser."

8. The ruling The appeal against the grant of the injunction in the first instance was dismissed.

3 *Lion Laboratories v. Evans* [1985] Q.B. 526

1. The facts Two ex-employees of the plaintiff manufacturers of intoximeters sought to have published through the medium of the *Daily Express*, adverse publicity as to the Lion Intoximeter flowing from the plaintiffs' internal correspondence. The plaintiffs issue a writ against the two ex-employees and against the proprietors and the editor of the newspaper seeking an injunction restraining the defendants from disclosing or making use of any confidential information belonging to the plaintiffs and damages for breach of confidence and/or breach of copyright. The appeal was launched by the defendants against an interlocutory injunction in the terms of the writ, namely:

"(A) Until the 15th day of March 1984 or further order the defendants and each of them be restrained from: (1) Disclosing or making use of any confidential information being the property of the plaintiffs for any purpose whatsoever. (2) Infringing the plaintiffs' copyright in their internal or other documents. (B) The defendants and each of them should within 14 days deliver up all documents or copies thereof containing such confidential information or being the subject of such copyright in the defendants' possession, power or control. (C) The defendants and each of them should within 14 days disclose the identity of the supplier of any such confidential information or supplier of any such documents. (D) That the first and second defendants should within five days disclose by list verified by affidavit all persons to whom they have supplied any such documents or confidential information."

2. Agreed evidence There was no dispute as to the following:
   (a) That the documents which were the subject-matter of the appeal were confidential.

(b) They were taken by the ex-employees without authority and handed over to the newspapers.

(c) Publication would be a breach of confidence by all four defendants subject to a defence that it was in the public interest that they should be published now.

(d) The copyright of these documents was in the plaintiffs and to publish them would infringe the plaintiffs' copyright, subject to the same public interest being a just cause or excuse for their publication.

3. The documents The documents, the publication of which was in issue, were as follows:

(a) The documents fell into three categories:
  (i) Four documents exhibited to the first affidavits sworn by the Chairman and Managing Director of the plaintiffs (who had certified the intoximeters).
  (ii) A number of reports exhibited to an affidavit of a journalist.
  (iii) A report from the plaintiffs' marketing director.
(b) Of these documents:
  (i) The defendants did not press for disclosure of a long report in the first category.
  (ii) There was no issue that some of the documents in the second category were entitled to protection.

4. The interlocutory problem Stephenson L.J. explained that the problem before the court was how best to resolve before trial, a conflict of two competing public interests, namely, on the one hand:

"... the preservation of the right of organisations, as with individuals, to keep secret confidential information. The duty of confidence, the public interest in maintaining it, is a restriction on the freedom of the press which is recognised by our law as well as by article 10(2) of the European Convention for the Protection of Human Rights and Fundamental Freedoms (1953) (Cmnd. 8696)."

On the other hand:

"The countervailing interest of the public to be kept informed of matters which are of real public concern, is an inroad on the privacy of confidential matters. This is by virtue of there being confidential information which the public may have a right to receive and others, in particular the press, now extended to the media, may have a right or even a duty to publish, even if the information has been unlawfully obtained in flagrant breach of confidence and irrespective of the motives of the informer."

In advancing such propositions, the Court of Appeal expressly referred as authority to the judgment of Lord Denning M.R. in *Initial Services Ltd v.*

933

Putterill [1968] 1 Q.B. 396; *Fraser v. Evans* [1969] 1 Q.B. 349; *Hubbard v. Vosper* [1972] 2 Q.B. 84; *Woodward v. Hutchins* [1977] 1 W.L.R. 760 and *Schering Chemicals Ltd v. Falkman Ltd* [1982] Q.B. 1. In addition, there was prayed in aid the speeches of Lord Wilberforce, Lord Salmon and Lord Fraser in *B.S.C. v. Granada Television Ltd* [1981] A.C. 1096.

5. The additional factors When weighing the respective public interests in the balance, the court also had regard to the following factors:

  (a) "There is a wide difference between what is interesting to the public and what is in the public interest to make known." (*Per* Lord Wilberforce in *B.S.C. v. Granada Television Ltd (ibid.)* at 1168.)

  (b) "The media have a private interest of their own in publishing what appeals to the public and may increase their circulation or the number of their viewers and listeners" (at 546G of the *Lion Laboratories* case); "... they are peculiarly vulnerable to the error of confusing the public interest with their own interests." (*Per* Sir John Donaldson in *Francome v. Mirror Group Newspapers* [1984] 1 W.L.R. 892 at 898.)

  (c) "There are cases in which the public interest is best served by an informer giving the confidential information not to the press but to the Police or some other responsible body." (*Per* Lord Denning M.R. in *Initial Services Ltd v. Putterill* [1968] 1 Q.B. 396 at 405–406.)

  (d) "There is no confidence as to the disclosure of iniquity" (*Gartside v. Outram* (1856) 26 L.J.Ch. 113 at 114, subject to the gloss on those words expressed by Salmon L.J. in *Initial Services Ltd v. Putterill* [1968] 1 Q.B. 396 at 410—which Stephenson L.J. in the present case interpreted to mean at 537E: "... in 1984 [iniquity] extends to serious misdeeds or grave misconduct.")

6. The issue Stephenson L.J. adopted the following yardstick—invoking the dicta of Lord Denning M.R. in *Woodward v. Hutchins* [1977] 2 W.L.R. 760 at 764:

> "To be allowed to publish confidential information, the defendants must do more than raise a plea of public interest—they must show 'a legitimate ground for supposing it is in the public interest for it to be disclosed.' Then, the courts should not restrain it by interlocutory injunction, but should leave the complainant to his remedy in damages, after considering and weighing in the balance all relevant matters, such as whether damages would be an adequate remedy to compensate the plaintiffs if they succeeded at the trial."

7. Could the court look at the evidence? Yes—"to see if there is a serious defence of public interest which may succeed at the trial, we have to look at the evidence and, if we decided that there is such a defence, to perform a balancing exercise, as indicated for instance in the judgment of Lord Denning M.R. in *Woodward v. Hutchins* [1977] 1 W.L.R. 760 at 764, and in the speech of Lord Fraser in *British Steel Corporation v. Granada Television Ltd* [1981] A.C. 1096 at 1202."

8. What did Lord Fraser say? Motives were irrelevant:

"The answer to the question therefore seems to me to involve weighing up the public interest for and against publication. The balance does not in my opinion depend on the use made of the leaked information by the appellants in this particular case. Anyone who hands over to the press a bundle of confidential documents belonging to someone else must surely expect, and intend, that, if they contain information of topical interest, it will be published in some form. The informer's motives are, in my opinion, irrelevant. It is said, and I am willing to accept, that in this case the informant neither asked for nor received any money, or other reward, but that he acted out of a keen sense of indignation about the dealings between B.S.C. and the government before and during the strike. No doubt there is a public interest in maintaining the free flow of information to the Press, and therefore against obstructing informers. But there is also I think a very strong public interest in preserving confidentiality within any organisation in order that it can operate efficiently, and also be free from suspicion that it is harbouring disloyal employees. There is no difference in this respect between a public corporation like B.S.C. and an ordinary company."

9. The balancing exercise The respective arguments for the parties were:

(a) *By the plaintiffs:*
   (i) The importance of uninhibited evaluations and criticisms by the plaintiffs of their own intoximeter and of any troubles it may have had in the early stages or developed later, and that this should not be abused for the creation out of context of one-sided, ill-informed and unjustified doubts (this argument did not prove to be "live" by virtue of the court's agreeing not to allow disclosure of the documents recited at (3)(b) above).
   (ii) The importance of not weakening confidence in the machine if it is a reliable aid to protecting the public from drunken driving.
   (iii) The advantage that disclosure may give to trade competitors and the irreparable damage it may do to the plaintiffs and that it would bring final ruin to the plaintiffs because there would be no trial if the documents were disclosed.

935

(b) *By the defendants:*

    (i) The public should know, and the press should give them now, any material which may indicate that the intoximeter was either inherently defective or incorrectly operated, contrary to the denials of the plaintiffs or the Home Office. The gravity of the matter was underlined by the following facts.

    (ii) The intoximeter was by law providing the sole evidence on which many members of the public had been, and were being, prosecuted to convictions.

    (iii) There was a police "crack-down" on drunken drivers, shortly before, at Christmas 1983.

10. The court held that balance in favour of disclosure—why?

(a) Damages were an adequate remedy to the plaintiffs in that:

> "... I cannot see that any damage from consequent loss of sales in this country or overseas cannot be compensated for by an award of damages if the plaintiffs succeed at trial; and the damage caused by what has already been published without objection, or make it any more unlikely that the plaintiffs' action for breach of confidence and copyright will ever be tried ... The judge never referred to the damage directly done to the reputation of the plaintiffs and their intoximeter by what had already been published ... It may be distasteful to let damage done by a newspaper weigh in support of its application to be allowed to do more damage in breaking confidence. Nevertheless, the existing damage is, in my view, a matter which the court must now take into account." (at 545D–G.)

(b) As to "balance of convenience"—there was inadequate evidence to challenge the force of the defendants' case. For example, there was no evidence from the plaintiffs from the plaintiffs' Dr. King to explain a memorandum he wrote on December 15, 1982 which, *inter alia*, said:

> "I can no longer write certificates for instruments which I know are not operated properly and I cannot ignore a failure on one day of 65 per cent."

Nor was there an affidavit from Dr King to explain the following passage in the affidavit of the "*Express* journalist," Mr Rees, who said, in paragraph 8:

> "When I saw Dr. King on the morning of Wednesday, March 7, 1984, I showed him the two memoranda from himself and Dr. Jones. Of the first he said, 'Oh yes, that was mine. I wrote that memorandum and received the other one. There were problems, with calibration

but any machine that left my hands after a week was calibrated and working—whether it continued to work was another matter.' He used those or very similar words. In addition, as reported in Friday's *Daily Express*, he asked me whether this was what I would call 'blowing the whistle,' confirmed that he was unhappy with his situation about the intoximeter and said that he had resigned; confirmed that there were difficulties with the machine; and he said 'I have no doubt that the police will be disturbed by what you have uncovered.' " (at 543D–F.)

Against that backdrop, Stephenson L.J. said that:

"The issue raised by the defendants is a serious question concerning the matter which affects the life, and even the liberty, of an unascertainable number of Her Majesty's subjects, and though there is no proof that any of them has been wrongly convicted on the evidence of the plaintiffs' intoximeter, and we certainly cannot decide that any has, we must not restrain the defendants from putting before the public this further information how the Lion Intoximeter 3000 has worked, and how the plaintiffs regard and discharge their responsibility for it, although the information is confidential and was unlawfully taken in breach of confidence." (at 546A–C.)

11. For what else is the case significant? The following matters also feature in the judgment—which show the case to bear an importance over and beyond its immediate facts:
  (a) An attempt at invoking a defamation analogy was rejected.
     (i) *Per* O'Connor L.J. at 548D:

"[Counsel] on behalf of the third and fourth defendants, has submitted that just as a plea of justification operates to block restraint by injunction in defamation, so too a plea that it is in the public interest to publish should block relief in breach of confidence. I cannot accept this proposition."

     (ii) *Per* Griffiths L.J. at 550E–551B:

"I do not accept the submission that there is so close an analogy between an action for libel or slander and an action for breach of confidence, that the courts should adopt a similar approach to a defence of justification and a defence of public interest. If a newspaper says that it intends to plead justification, the court will not, as a general rule, restrain publication. The court makes no attempt to evaluate the defence at the interlocutory stage: it leaves the plaintiff to his remedy in damages if the newspaper fails to justify the libel. Any other rule would involve an unacceptable gag upon the press, and if the press cannot justify, the plaintiff's reputation can be restored by verdict or apology and he can be properly compensated in damages.

But if the same approach was adopted in actions for breach of confidence it would, to use [counsel for the plaintiffs] colourful phrase, indeed be a mole's charter. There is a public interest of a high order in preserving confidentiality within an organisation. Employers must be entitled to discuss problems freely, raise their doubts and express their disagreements without the fear that they may be used to discredit the company and perhaps imperil the existence of the company and the livelihood of all those who work for it. I am old-fashioned enough to think that loyalty is a virtue that it is in the public interest to encourage rather than to destroy by tempting disloyal employees to sell confidential documents to the press, which I am sure would be the result of allowing the press to publish confidential documents under cover of a shadowy defence of public interest.

When there is an admitted breach of confidence and breach of copyright, there will usually be a powerful case for maintaining the status quo by the grant of an interlocutory injunction to restrain publication until trial of the action. It will, I judge, be an exceptional case in which a defence of public interest which does not involve iniquity on the part of the plaintiff will justify refusing the injunction. But I am bound to say that I think this is such a case."

(b) Section 2(1) of the Copyright Act of 1956 did not feature in the judgment—yet the granting of copyright in all original works under that section is absolute and there is no statutory exception for infringement on the grounds of public interest. (*Quaere*: should Lion Laboratories have proceeded only in respect of breach of copyright?)

(c) The court allowed disclosure notwithstanding that the defence has not been able to find any case where a defendant had been able to rely on public interest in defiance of a claim for breach of confidence—when the plaintiff had not been guilty of iniquity, serious misdeeds or grave misconduct. But as Griffiths L.J. said at 550C–D:

"I can see no sensible reason why this defence should be limited to cases in which there has been wrong-doing on the part of the plaintiffs. I believe that the so-called iniquity rule evolved because in many cases where the facts justified a publication in breach of confidence the plaintiff had behaved so disgracefully or criminally that it was judged in the public interest that his behaviour should be exposed. No doubt it is in such circumstances that the defence will usually arise, but it is not difficult to think of instances where, although there has been no wrong-doing on the part of the plaintiff, it may be vital in the public interest to publish a part of his confidential information. Stephenson L.J. has given such an example, in the course of his judgment."

4 *Att.-General v. Observer and Guardian Newspapers* (1986) 136 New L.J. 799, C.A.

1. The facts A former member of the British Security Service (W) published in Australia allegations of serious wrong-doing by the Service based on the disclosure of confidential information. The defendants published articles outlining the allegations contained in W's memoirs, thus prompting the Attorney-General to launch proceedings and apply for interlocutory relief to prevent further publication until trial.

2. Balance of convenience/likelihood of success at trial Sir John Donaldson M.R. said:

"There is undoubtedly a balancing exercise to be performed. It is what is referred to in *American Cyanamid Co. v. Ethicon Ltd* [1975] 1 All E.R. 504 at 509 and other decisions as 'the Balance of Convenience,' although I have always thought this to be an unhappy phrase. 'Balance of Inconvenience' better describes what is essentially a damage limitation exercise. In special circumstances the formulation in *Lion Laboratories Ltd v. Evans* and that in *American Cyanamid*, 'has the plaintiff any real prospects in succeeding in his claim for a permanent injunction at the trial,' may need modification. This was recognised by the House of Lords in *N.W.L. Ltd v. Nelson and Laughton* [1979] 3 All E.R. 614 where account was taken, *inter alia*, of the fact that an interlocutory injunction restraining industrial action would make it very difficult for it to be resumed at a later date. Similarly, in the instant appeal account must be taken not only of the total inadequacy of damages as an alternative to injunctive relief, but of the relative seriousness of the consequences of on the one hand an unjustified restraint on the defendants' freedom to publish and on the other an unjustified publication of confidential material. An assessment of this relativity might lead a court properly to conclude that, in the context of the confidentiality of the work of the security service, a proper approach is that 'the conflict ... should be resolved in favour of restraint, unless the court is satisfied that there is a serious defence of public interest which is *very likely* to succeed at the trial.'"

3. Common ground
(a) As to how far equity extends: the protection afforded by equity to

the maintenance of confidentiality extends beyond trade and domestic secrets to what Lord Widgery C.J. described as "public secrets" in *Attorney-General v. Jonathan Cape Ltd* [1976] Q.B. 752 (the "Cross-man Diaries Case").

(b) The special character of public secrets: Prior restraint of the disclosure of public secrets has to be considered in a somewhat different context from that of the prior disclosure of private secrets.

(c) The position of the Attorney-General: He is not personally the beneficiary of the right to confidentiality which he asserts, nor is the Executive. His claim is made on behalf of the State, that is to say, the general community.

(d) Newspapers can and do assert a public interest:
  (i) In the exposure of wrong-doing, which may be stronger in the case of wrong-doing by Offices of the State than in the case of wrong-doing by private individuals.
  (ii) In being informed what is being done by the State and its Executive on behalf of the public (which would not usually arise in the context of private secrets).

4. The nature of the claim by the Attorney-General It had two potential limbs:
  (a) the contractual obligation of confidence accepted by Officers of the Security Services; and
  (b) an independent cause of action based purely on the supremacy of the public interest which could be invoked in extreme cases where public disclosure would imperil National Security—a proposition which Lord Widgery C.J. seemed to accept in the Jonathan Cape case.

5. The two principal arguments

(a) *First:*
  (i) Case for the defendants: The right of confidence is lost forever once the information which theretofore was impressed with confidentiality emerges into the public domain.
  (ii) Sir John Donaldson M.R. said:

> "It is undoubtedly the law that no one is entitled to seek the assistance of the courts to maintain a confidence, if he has himself allowed it to become common knowledge (see Lord Buckmaster in *O Mustad & Son v. Dosen, (1928)* [1964] 1 W.L.R. 109). In reliance on the same principle, counsel for the defendants complains that no liberty has been given to the defendants to republish the allegations already made by them which precipitated the application for these injunctions. The short answer to this is that if the original

publications were in breach of the Crown's right to confidence, acceptance of this plea would enable the defendants to profit by their own wrong. This cannot be permitted. Whether or not the original publications were justified turns on the public interest in the exposure of alleged wrongdoing, which I have yet to consider.

Allied to this complaint is a plea that it is unjust that the defendants should be restrained from re-publishing allegations made by them whilst every other publisher is free to do so. The short answer to this is that if the original publications were unlawful, other publishers are *not free* to republish. It is true that the consequences of their doing so would be less serious, but that is another matter."

(b) *Secondly:*
   (i) Case for the defendants: There is no confidence in wrong-doing.
   (ii) Judgment:

"I now turn to the alleged justification for the defendants being free to publish any allegation of serious wrong-doing by the security service. The basis of this submission is that the security service is as much subject to the law as any ordinary citizen and that, in as much as it is a public service, the public has a legitimate interest in knowing of, and being able to bring pressure to bear to restrain, any breach by it of the law or of this Country's treaty obligations. That the service is subject to the law is not in doubt and was reaffirmed by a direction of then Home Secretary the Rt Hon. Sir David Maxwell Fyfe Q.C., M.P., made on September 24, 1952 which is still in force. Furthermore, it is beyond argument that a security service which is de facto able to depart from its obligations under the law as and when it sees fit would constitute a major and quite unacceptable threat to democratic freedoms as we know them. So there can be no doubt of the public interest in ensuring that allegations of wrong-doing are investigated and that, if they are established, appropriate action is taken to prevent repetition and to punish those responsible. What is more difficult is how this is to be achieved.

Counsel for the defendants submits that the more serious the alleged wrong-doing, the greater the public interest and this is no doubt right. But from this he argues that, given a sufficiently serious *allegation*, publication of the allegation with a view to forcing an investigation is automatically justified in the public interest. It is at this point that I part company from him. Where there is confidentiality, the public interest in its maintenance has to be overborne by a countervailing public interest, if publication is not to be restrained. In some cases the weight of the public interest in the

941

maintenance of the confidentiality will be small and the weight of the public interest in publication will be great. But in weighing these countervailing public interests or, perhaps more accurately, those countervailing aspects of a single public interest, both the nature and circumstances of the confidentiality and the nature and circumstances of the proposed publication have to be examined with considerable care. This is what is sometimes referred to as the principle of proportionality—(that) is the restraint or lack of restraint proportionate to the overall assessment of the public interest. Thus it by no means follows that, because the public interest in the exposure of wrong-doing would justify the communication to the police or some such authority of material which has been unlawfully obtained, it would also justify wholesale publication of that material in a national newspaper (see *Francome v. Mirror Group Newspapers Ltd* [1984] 1 W.L.R. 892).

The defendants seek freedom to publish in their newspapers ... It is thus solely with this, the widest and most indiscriminate, form of publication that we are concerned. Given the special nature of the confidentiality which applies to any aspect of the work of the security service, such publication could not possibly be justified on the evidence at present available and I regard it as in the highest degree unlikely that it could be justified on further evidence which may be available at the trial."

6. Subsidiary issues

(a) First, the situation of dual sources. The Master of the Rolls said:

"It will be remembered that the injunction restrain publication of information which the defendants know, or have reasonable grounds for believing, to have come or been obtained, whether directly or indirectly, from (W). The complaint here is that this may prevent the defendants from publishing allegations from an independent source, merely because remotely (W) may have been *a*, but not necessarily the *only*, primary source. Examples of such an independent source which were suggested were a retired CIA agent and a defector from the service of a foreign power. This argument is superficially attractive, but it does not bear examination. The public interest in restraining publication of information obtained from (W) is not removed by the fact that an 'independent' source has some knowledge of that information..."

(b) Secondly: the extent of the restraint—the Master of the Rolls said:

"Curiously, the defendants have made no complaint that the injunctions might restrain them from publishing fair and accurate reports of proceedings in Parliament, if a member said something which could be said to constitute information obtained by (W) in his official capacity and which the defendants knew, or had reasonable grounds to believe, had been obtained, directly or indirectly, from him. This is understandable if they did not raise the matter with the Judge and could, in any event, have been the subject of an application to vary. Nevertheless for the sake of completeness, I would add that if they had made such a complaint, I would have been minded to add an appropriate proviso, because in my judgment, it is for Parliament and not for the courts to safeguard the public interest by restricting what can and cannot be published by way of reporting what is said. Similarly I would, if asked, have been minded to add a proviso permitting fair and accurate reports of proceedings in the Courts of this Country in addition to the Courts of New South Wales, since it is a salutory right that anything can be reported which occurs in open court, leaving it to the courts to ensure that the proceedings are closed or restrictions imposed on an *ad hoc* basis insofar as the public interest so requires."

See also *Att.-Gen. v. Turnaround Distribution Ltd* [1989] F.S.R. 169.

5 *Att.-Gen. v. Guardian Newspapers Ltd* [1987] 1 W.L.R. 1248

1. The facts A former member of the British Security Services, Wright, published in Australia allegations of serious wrong-doing by the Service based on the disclosure of confidential information *Spycatcher*. The defendants published articles outlining the allegations contained in Wright's memoirs, thus prompting the Attorney-General to launch proceedings and apply for interlocutory relief to prevent further publication until trial.

2. The background A year after Millett J. had granted the Attorney-General injunctions against the *Guardian* and *Observer* newspapers restraining them from disclosing or publishing any information obtained by Wright in his capacity as a member of the British Security Service, those newspapers applied for the discharge of the injunctions on the grounds that there had been a significant change of circumstances. The Vice-Chancellor discharged the injunctions. The Court of Appeal allowed the appeal but modified the injunctions by allowing the newspapers to publish a summary in very general terms of Wright's allegations. The newspapers appealed to the House of Lords and the Attorney-General cross-appealed.

3. Common ground For all practical purposes it was not in dispute that Mr Wright owed a fundamental duty to the Crown not to disclose confidential information; that he had committed a most serious breach of his duty of confidentiality by publishing *Spycatcher* abroad; that the Attorney-General had an arguable point of law; if an interlocutory injunction were not granted it would deprive the Attorney-General for ever of the benefit of that arguable point of law; and that conversely the granting of an interlocutory injunction would not rule out the possibility that after a full trial the newspapers would be allowed to publish in full.

4. The defendants' argument Three defences were put forward by the appellant newspapers; first, that Mr Wright intended his treachery to be helpful to the British public, secondly, that damage to the Security Service arising from Mr Wright's treachery had already been fully inflicted, and thirdly, that the public interest in receiving information entitled the press to publish treachery at home provided it had been published abroad.

5. The public interest factor Lord Ackner said at 1303F–H:

"This case involves an entirely new and highly significant factor which is of the greatest relevance to the exercise of the courts' discretion in considering whether to grant or refuse an injunction pending trial. Both Millett J., in granting the original injunction, and the Vice-Chancellor, in discharging it, proceeded on the same principle which I understand your Lordships accept, that when there is a conflict between the public interest of preserving confidentiality and some other public interest, then the court should favour the preservation of confidentiality, unless that other public interest outweighs it. But in this case there is more than the public interest of preserving confidentiality. Here, unlike the not infrequent case where a company wishes to prevent, to its financial detriment, the publication of its trade secrets, there is the following additional public interest factor accepted by the Vice-Chancellor and stated in these words:

'There remains what Mr Mummery urges is the persisting public interest, namely, to prevent general dissemination of the contents of this book through the press within the United Kingdom. By discouraging general dissemination those who are tempted to follow Mr Wright's example in the future and write their memoirs hot from the Security Service will not find it such a satisfactory or profitable business.' "

6. The Convention for the Protection of Human Rights and Fundamental Freedom (1953) Article 10: the right to freedom of expression Lord Templeman applied *The Sunday Times v. United Kingdom* [1979] 2 E.H.R.R. 245 in which the European Court of Human Rights held that in applying the right to freedom of expression a court is faced not with a choice between two conflicting principles, but with a principle of freedom of expression that is subject to a number of exceptions which must be narrowly interpreted. One exception was where the court is satisfied that the interference is necessary having regard to the facts and circumstances prevailing in the specific case before it. Lord Templeman said at p. 1297E:

"The question is therefore whether the interference with freedom of expression constituted by the Millett injunctions was, on 30 July 1987 when they were continued by this House, necessary in a democratic society in the interests of national security, for protecting the reputation or rights of others, for preventing the disclosure of information received in confidence or for maintaining the authority and impartiality of the judiciary having regard to the facts and circumstances prevailing on 30 July 1987 and in the light of the events which had happened. The continuance of the Millett injunctions appears to me to be necessary for all these purposes."

6 *Sierbein v. Westminster City Council* (1987) 86 L.G.R. 431

1. The facts The plaintiffs had run sex encounter establishments in Soho before the Local Government (Miscellaneous Provisions) Act 1982 and they had applied for licences under that Act but had been refused them by the defendants. They intended to apply for judicial review of the defendants' decisions on the ground of bias and had obtained leave to move.

2. The relief sought When leave to move was granted the plaintiffs applied for an interlocutory injunction to restrain the defendant authority from enforcing against them the provisions of the 1982 Act pending the hearing of their application for judicial review.

3. Public interest and the balance of convenience The public interest element arose from the fact that the 1982 Act provides a criminal means of enforcement. Dillon L.J. said:

"I myself feel that in a case were what is sought to be restrained is the act of a public authority in a matter of public law, the public interest is very important to be considered and the ordinary financial considerations in an *American Cyanamid* case, though no doubt to some extent relevant, must be qualified by a recognition of the public interest. A *fortiori* is that so when the injunction is sought to permit the party concerned to do or continue something which will be in breach of the criminal law."

4. The balance favoured the public interest Nicholls L.J. said:

"In short, therefore, on the one hand, is the applicants' interest in carrying on their lawful business at least until a valid determination of their application is made by the authority. Arising out of this is the further and important factor that the applicants have no remedy in damages if their trading is now stopped and yet their judicial review applications succeed after a period probably of two or more months. In that event, the applicants would have suffered significant and unrecoverable financial loss in the meantime.

Against this is to be weighed the public interest in the applicants not carrying on their business in Soho when they ought not to be doing so for the period in question. The existence and extent of the public interest in this are shown by the serious criminal sanctions which are laid down."

7 X v. Y [1988] 2 All E.R. 648

1. The facts The plaintiffs were a health authority in which two doctors worked who had contracted AIDS. The defendants were a national newspaper who had obtained, in breach of the confidentiality of hospital records, the identity of the two doctors. The defendants wished to publish an article identifying the doctors. The plaintiffs sought *inter alia* an injunction restraining the defendants from publishing the identities of the two doctors.

2. The legal background The plaintiff health authority's cause of action lay not just in breach of confidence, but also in procurement of breach of contract, because the newspaper had paid £100 for the information. Once the tort of interference with contractual rights is established, the onus of proving justification is on the defendants (*South Wales Miners' Federation v. Glamorgan Coal Co. Ltd* [1905] A.C. 239 at 246, 251–252, 254). Accordingly, the defendants had to justify publication of information obtained in breach of confidence.

3. The competing public interests Rose J. said at 600H–661G:

"On the one hand, there are the public interests in having a free press and an informed public debate; on the other, it is in the public interest that actual or potential AIDS sufferers should be able to resort to hospitals without fear of this being revealed, that those owing duties of confidence in their employment should be loyal and should not disclose confidential matters and that, prima facie, no one should be allowed to use information extracted in breach of confidence from hospital records even if disclosure of the particular information may not give rise to immediately apparent harm.

... I keep in the forefront of my mind the very important public interest in freedom of the press. And I accept that there is some public interest in knowing that which the defendants seek to publish. ... But in my judgment those public interests are substantially outweighed when measured against the public interest in relation to loyalty and confidentiality both generally and with particular reference to AIDS patients' hospital records. There has been no misconduct by the plaintiffs. The records of hospital patients, particularly those suffering from this appalling condition, should, in my judgment, be as confidential as the courts can properly keep them in order that the plaintiffs may 'be free from suspicion that they are harbouring disloyal employees.' The plaintiffs have 'suffered a grievous wrong in which the defendants became involved ... with active participation.' The deprivation of the public of the information sought to be published will be of minimal significance if the injunction is granted; for, without it, all the evidence before me shows that a wide ranging public debate about AIDS generally and about its effect on doctors is taking place among doctors of widely differing views, within and without the BMA, in medical journals, and in many newspapers including the *Observer*, *The Sunday Times* and the *Daily Express*.

... These are the considerations which guide me, whether my task is properly described as a balancing exercise, or an exercise in judicial judgment, or both. No one has suggested that damages would be an adequate remedy in this case."

8 *Megaphone International Ltd v. British Telecommunications plc, The Independent*, March 1, 1989

1. The facts The plaintiffs operated chatline services on the telephone network for which the defendants charged callers at such a high rate that uncontrolled use by teenagers ran up huge telephone bills. This gave rise to subscriber complaints and bad publicity for the defendants, who therefore decided to suspend all chatline services under a term in their contracts. The plaintiffs applied for interim injunctions to prevent the defendants from disconnecting their chatlines.

2. The plaintiffs argued that there was a serious issue to be tried Drake J. said:

"The plaintiffs' case was that BT had no right to terminate the chatline services, that the term of their contracts under which BT claimed to terminate the contract was in breach of the Unfair Contract Terms Act 1977; and BT was abusing its dominant position contrary to article 86 of the E.C. treaty."

947

3. The defendants argued unsuccessfully that the plaintiffs were bound to fail

"Although his Lordship was attracted by BT's argument that the chatline service was subject to an inherent flaw, which could not be cured by a code of practice or monitoring, the plaintiffs' case still contained serious issues to be tried. Nor was his Lordship satisfied that the plaintiffs would inevitably fail to get a permanent injunction at the trial on the ground that BT could by then have lawfully terminated their contracts by giving notice."

4. Public interest was critical

"In this case, public interest was a paramount influence on the exercise of his Lordship's discretion. The plaintiffs pointed to the loss of jobs which would arise from discontinuation of their services, but while that was a factor, it did not have as great an influence as the effect of further abuses of the chatline services. Taking everything into account, the public interest was best served by refusing the injunctions sought."

9 *Femis-Bank (Anguilla) Ltd v. Lazar* [1991] 3 W.L.R. 80; [1991] 2 All E.R. 865; *The Times*, February 11, 1991

1. The facts The defendant had published a series of serious allegations against the plaintiffs alleging that they were financially unsound, dishonest and were conducting their business in breach of the laws or regulations of certain jurisdictions. The plaintiff bank brought an action based on a conspiracy the sole or dominant purpose of which was to injure, and sought an injunction restraining the defendant from publishing libellous statements pending trial.

2. Justification did not prevent an injunction Because the action was framed in conspiracy with the sole or dominant purpose of injury, rather than in defamation, the fact that the defendant intended to prove that the words used were true did not prevent the court granting an injunction and Browne-Wilkinson V.-C. applied the *American Cyanamid* principles.

3. The plaintiffs' argument The plaintiffs argued that *Gulf Oil (Great Britain) Ltd v. Page* [1987] Ch. 327 at 332H was authority for the proposition that the public interest in preventing freedom of speech as a right generally was not a relevant matter to be taken into account when the case was founded on conspiracy to injure.

4. The judge held: two relevant public interests Browne-Wilkinson V.-C. identified two elements of public interest:
  (a) the public interest in preserving freedom of speech as a right generally; and
  (b) the public interest in allowing allegations to be made and published alerting investors and others concerned and the regulatory authorities to the possibility of malfeasance in the conduct of a financial institution.

5. Both public interests were important *The Times'* summary of the judgment reads:

> "The fact that an injunction in the present case would interfere with free speech was an important factor and should be taken into account. It was only in the clearest cases, like *Gulf Oil*, that an injunction would be justified.
>
> In his Lordship's judgment there was a real public interest ... that investors should know what was being alleged about the plaintiffs and that there should not be a choking off of matters which were inconvenient to persons running financial institutions.
>
> This particular institution was still inviting subscriptions and its affairs were being looked into by certain authorities in Holland and Anguilla and there was at least some corroboratory evidence in support of some of the allegations.
>
> This was a case where in the exercise of one's discretion one would not preclude Mr Lazar from exercising this freedom of speech since there was an element of public interest in the allegations being known and the case against him was not strong."

10 *Att.-Gen. v. British Broadcasting Corporation, The Times,* December 18, 1987

1. The facts The Attorney-General applied to prevent the BBC broadcasting on Radio 4 a series about the British Security Services entitled "My Country Right or Wrong". The BBC did not disclose the script and deliberately limited information as to what the series contained.

2. On what basis did the plaintiff sue? The Attorney-General alleged that the series would constitute a breach of the security agents' life-long obligation of confidentiality and that that obligation extended to third parties receiving information in breach of it.

3. The BBC's defence The defendants raised three defences:
  (a) They said that the material was not confidential.

949

(b) The information to be communicated by the agents was already in the public domain.

(c) The public interest would be better served by revelation of the material. The Press and the BBC were in a privileged position in that, so far as they were concerned, the only confidentiality to be respected by them as that which was proved to be necessary in a democratic society. Otherwise there was an overriding public right of citizens to freedom of expression in the Press.

4. The plaintiff's riposte—accepted as arguable by the court

(a) The material was confidential: the fact that an agent was an agent was confidential, and any statement by a secret agent about his job involved a breach of confidentiality.

(b) The restrictions and obligations of confidentiality still applied even if the material was already in the public domain.

(c) It was impossible for the Government to say more without seeing the transcript of the broadcast.

5. Was there a serious issue to be tried?—yes

Owen J. held that the plaintiff's case was fairly and properly arguable, and it was a matter which should not be decided upon the say-so of the legal adviser of the defendant. No question of adequacy of damages arose.

6. The balance of convenience

The judge weighed the balance as follows:

"On the hypothesis that the Attorney-General's claim, if tried, would succeed, the effect of discharging the temporary injunction now would be to deprive him, summarily and without a trial, of all opportunity of achieving that success and might do harm to the security of the realm. On the alternative hypothesis that the Attorney-General's claim, if tried, would fail, the effect of continuing the temporary injunction until trial would only be to postpone, not to prevent, the exercise by the BBC of the right to publish which it would in that event have been established that it had. Having regard to the above, the discharge of the temporary injunction now was capable of causing much greater injustice to the Attorney-General and harm to this country than continuation of the injunction until trial was capable of causing to the BBC."

11 Att.-Gen. v. Barker and Another [1990] 3 All E.R. 257

1. A flagrant breach The first defendant, an ex-employee in the royal household, had written a book entitled *Courting Disaster* about his experiences during that time. Before entering his employment he had signed an undertaking not to disclose, publish or reveal any incident, conversation or information which came to his knowledge during his employment. The book was therefore admittedly a flagrant breach of the contractual undertaking. The Queen in her private capacity applied for a worldwide interlocutory injunction to prevent publication of the book by the first defendant or by the second defendant publishing company, which was simply the alter ego of the first defendant.

2. Closing the stable door The book had been published in Canada, the United States and Bermuda and had been serialised in *Paris Match* (except in its British edition). At first instance Wright J. granted the plaintiff an injunction against the first defendant which applied worldwide. But he was told incorrectly that the second defendant publisher was independent of the first defendant and for that reason limited his injunction against the second defendant to the United Kingdom.

3. Did *Cyanamid* apply? On appeal Lord Donaldson M.R. (with whom Parker L.J. agreed) applied *Cyanamid*, albeit in a somewhat perfunctory way because the *Cyanamid* questions could realistically only be answered one way, as was largely admitted.

4. The European Convention on Human Rights The defendants sought to argue that the injunction should be restricted to the jurisdiction of the court in the case of both defendants on the grounds that foreigners, unlike the citizens of this country, have a right to be informed which overrides contractual rights. Article 10 of the Convention for the Protection of Human Rights and Fundamental Freedoms is in these terms:

> "(1) Everyone has the right to freedom of expression. This right shall include freedom to hold opinions and to receive and impart information and ideas without interference by public authority and regardless of frontiers. ...
>
> (2) The exercise of these freedoms, since it carries with it duties and responsibilities, may be subject to such formalities, conditions, restrictions or penalties as are prescribed by law and are necessary in a democratic society, in the interests of national security, territorial integrity or public safety, for the prevention of disorder or crime, for the protection of health or morals, for the protection of the reputation or rights of others, for preventing the disclosure of information received in confidence, or for maintaining the authority and impartiality of the judiciary."

951

5. The defendants' argument failed—why? Lord Donaldson M.R. dismissed this appeal to the European Convention on Human Rights with these trenchant observations:

"For my part, I would have thought that much more relevant was the question of whether a man's word is his bond and whether contractual obligations freely entered into shall be maintained. It is not a question of what foreigners are entitled to read, but what somebody subject to the jurisdiction of this court is entitled to publish and it is an incidental result that, if he cannot publish, foreigners cannot read. I am bound to say, having read this book, I do not think they will miss anything at all, but that is merely a personal view. I cannot believe that there is a foreign country which would regard the sanctity of contract as not being of enormous importance and central to the necessities of a democratic society."

12 R. v. Secretary of State for Transport, ex parte Factortame (No. 2) [1990] 3 W.L.R. 818, [1991] 1 All E.R. 70

1. Interlocutory suspension of an Act of Parliament—how to do it Spanish fishing boats had the cunning, if parasitic, idea of registering as British thereby to take the pressure off the Spanish fishing quotas at the expense of the British quotas. Parliament tried to regulate this by the Merchant Shipping Act 1988 and regulations made under it, by which a fishing vessel could only qualify for entry on the British Register if the whole of its legal title and at least 75 per cent of its beneficial ownership was vested in British citizens or companies. The President of the European Court in *E.C. Commission v. U.K.* (Case 246/89R) [1989] E.C.R. 3125; [1989] 3 C.M.L.R. 601 held that this was in breach of the non-discrimination obligations of Articles 7, 52 and 221 of the EEC Treaty. Therefore the House of Lords disapplied Parliament's 1988 measures, *pro tem.*

2. The dilemma The fishing quotas were set by the EEC by reference to nations. Yet discrimination in terms of nations is contrary to European law. Women may catch 100 fish a year. Men may catch 100 fish a year. But there is to be no rule preventing women becoming men or vice versa.

3. Did *American Cyanamid* apply?—Yes Lord Goff, who gave the leading judgment in the House of Lords, went out of his way to make it clear that he was not putting any gloss on *Cyanamid*. But for obvious reasons the question of a serious issue to be tried and the adequacy of damages would almost never be relevant in these circumstances.

952

4. The *Cyanamid*/public interest interface Lord Goff said:

> "Turning then to the balance of convenience, it is necessary in cases in which a party is a public authority performing duties to the public [*sc.* Parliament] that 'one must look at the balance of convenience more widely, and take into account the interests of the public in general to whom these duties are owed': see *Smith v. Inner London Education Authority* [1978] 1 All E.R. 411 at 422 *per* Browne L.J. and see also *Sierbien v. Westminster City Council* (1987) 86 L.G.R. 431. Like Browne L.J., I incline to the option that this can be treated as one of the special factors referred to by Lord Diplock. ..."

5. What difference does it make when the Crown is a party? Lord Goff continued:

> "In this context, particular stress should be placed on the importance of upholding the law of the land, in the public interest, bearing mind the need for stability in our society, and the duty placed on certain authorities to enforce the law in the public interest. This is of itself an important factor to be weighed in the balance when assessing the balance of convenience. So if a public authority seeks to enforce what is on its face the law of the land, and the person against whom such action is taken challenges the validity of that law, matters of considerable weight have to be put into the balance to outweigh the desirability of enforcing, in the public interest, what is on its face the law, and so to justify the refusal of an interim injunction in favour of the authority, or to render it just or convenient to restrain the authority for the time being from enforcing the law."

6. The actual decision disapplying an Act—irrelevant? The decision of the European Court upon which the House of Lords acted had a Delphic quality:

> "Community law must be interpreted as meaning that a national court which, in a case before it concerning Community law, considers that the *sole obstacle* which precludes it from granting interim relief is a *rule of national law* must set aside that rule."

It is not necessarily obvious what a "sole obstacle" could be, in terms of the "balance" of convenience. And the House of Lords do not expressly say that they are treating the sovereignty of Parliament as a "rule of national law". Nevertheless Lord Goff's speech is clearly the pre-eminent authority.

953

13 *Secretary of State for the Home Department v. Central Broadcasting Ltd* (1993) T.L.R. 33

1. The Nilsen interview Nilsen was a convicted serial killer serving a prison sentence. It was Home Office policy never to grant consent to a broadcast of an interview of a convicted prisoner. The defendants had nevertheless obtained permission and filmed a four-minute interview between Nilsen and a psychiatrist, which they wished to include as part of an hour-long programme on serial murderers and rapists.

2. The legal background The plaintiff alleged breach of copyright in the film and breach of an agreement not to broadcast the interview without the plaintiff's consent. Armed with these causes of action the plaintiff applied for an interlocutory injunction to prevent the interview being broadcast.

3. Serious issues to be tried? The defendants conceded that there were serious issues to be tried, and the arguments at first instance and on appeal concerned the balance of convenience—mostly by reference to various matters of public interest.

4. The balance of convenience was in favour of refusing an injunction—why?
- (a) The plaintiff firstly argued that the broadcast would be likely to distress the relatives of Nilsen's victims. But the Court of Appeal accepted the defendants' riposte, that the relatives could always switch off their television sets.
- (b) It was said that the broadcast would enhance Nilsen's notoriety. But Aldous J. at first instance thought it difficult to believe that the sight of Nilsen, in prison garb and plainly locked up for the rest of his life, would make him a role model for anyone to consider emulating. On the contrary the broadcast might be salutary in educating the public into appreciating how ordinary-looking and intelligent such a killer could appear, and yet be both cunning and wicked.
- (c) To refuse an injunction was to condone the defendants' unlawful behaviour in obtaining a copy of the film in breach of their agreement. But the Court of Appeal indicated that it could not reach a concluded view as to any impropriety by the defendants in that respect.
- (d) The plaintiff argued that the public interest was likely to be damaged, in that the failure to grant an injunction rendered Home Office policy futile.
- (e) The plaintiff said the broadcast might damage valuable scientific research into profiling serial killers and rapists which could lead to

their earlier detection. The Court of Appeal accepted that it might damage such research by the Home Office in *conjunction* with broadcasting companies, but it would not do so if the research were carried out by the Home Office or some other body on its own.

5. The additional reason Both Aldous J. at first instance and the Court of Appeal indicated that one extra factor to be taken into account in the balance was the harm that would be done to the defendants if the film were not shown and, some considerable time later, they were found to have been entitled to show it. The Master of the Rolls referred to "irreparable harm".

J: MANDATORY INTERLOCUTORY INJUNCTIONS

1 Introduction

1. General principles underlying grant of a mandatory injunction In a general context, but against the backdrop of an application for *quia timet* relief, Lord Upjohn held in *Morris v. Redland Bricks Ltd* [1970] A.C. 652 at 665–6:

> "1. A mandatory injunction can only be granted where the plaintiff shows a very strong probability upon the facts that grave damage will accrue to him in the future. As Lord Dunedin said in 1919 it is not sufficient to say *"timeo"* [*Att.-Gen. for the Dominion of Canada v. Ritchie Contracting and Supply Co.* [1919] A.C. 999 at 1005, P.C.]. It is a jurisdiction to be exercised sparingly and with caution but in the proper case unhesitatingly.
> 2. Damages will not be a sufficient or adequate remedy if such damage does happen. This is only the application of a general principle of equity; it has nothing to do with Lord Cairns' Act or *Shelfer's Case* [1895] 1 Ch. 287.
> 3. Unlike the case where a negative injunction is granted to prevent the continuance or recurrence of a wrongful act the question of the cost to the defendant to do works to prevent or lessen the likelihood of a future apprehended wrong must be an element to be taken into account:
>
> > (a) Where a defendant has acted without regard to his neighbour's rights, or has tried to steal a march on him or has tried to evade the jurisdiction of the court or, to sum it up, has acted wantonly and quite unreasonably in relation to his neighbour he may be ordered to repair his wanton and unreasonable acts by doing

positive work to restore the status quo even if the expense to him is out of all proportion to the advantage thereby accruing to the plaintiff. As illustrative of this we see *Woodhouse v. Newry Navigation Co.* [1898] I.R. 161;

(b) but where the defendant has acted reasonably, though in the event wrongly, the cost of remedying by positive action his earlier activities is most important for two reasons. First, because no legal wrong has yet occurred (for which he has not been recompensed at law and in equity) and, in spite of gloomy expert opinion, may never occur or possibly only upon a much smaller scale than anticipated. Secondly, because if ultimately heavy damage does occur the plaintiff is in no way prejudiced for he has his action at law and all his consequential remedies in equity."

So the amount to be expended under a mandatory order by the defendant must be balanced with these considerations in mind against the anticipated possible damage to the plaintiff and if, on such balance, it seems unreasonable to inflict such expenditure upon one who for this purpose is no more than a potential wrongdoer then the court must exercise its jurisdiction accordingly. Of course, the court does not have to order such works as upon the evidence before it will remedy the wrong but may think it proper to impose upon the defendant the obligation of doing certain works which may upon expert opinion merely lessen the likelihood of any further injury to the plaintiff's land. Sargant J. pointed this out in effect in the celebrated "Moving Mountain" case, *Kennard v. Cory Bros. & Co. Ltd* [1922] 1 Ch. 265 at the foot of 274 (his judgment was affirmed by the Court of Appeal [1922] 2 Ch. 1):

"If in the exercise of its discretion the court decides that it is a proper case to grant a mandatory injunction, then the court must be careful to see that the defendant knows exactly in fact what he has to do and this means not as a matter of law but as a matter of fact, so that in carrying out an order he can give his contractors the proper instructions."

Thus, unless the work to be done is so simple that the defendant can be ordered, for example, "to restore the right of way to its former condition," the court must in fairness tell the defendant precisely what he has to do—for example, by reference to plans prepared by a surveyor. Also see *Hooper v. Rogers* [1975] 1 Ch. 43.

2. A *fortiori*—if the proceedings are interlocutory *The Supreme Court Practice* (1997) vol. 1 states at 29/1/5:

"The Court has jurisdiction to grant a mandatory injunction upon an interlocutory application (*per* Fry L.J. in *Bonner v. Great Western*

Railway (1883) 24 Ch.D. 1, at 10; and see *Collison v. Warren* [1901] 1 Ch. 812 (application by defendants) but it is a very exceptional form of relief (*Canadian Pacific Railway v. Gaud* [1949] 2 K.B. 239 (C.A.))."

In this latter case, Sellers J. made an order directing that a Canadian crew (which was on strike) should depart a Canadian ship in London, after the Master had terminated the crew's licence to remain on board.

3. Significance of applying for interim relief One of the factors justifying the court in refusing a mandatory injunction in *Wrotham Park v. Parkside Homes* [1974] 1 W.L.R. 799, *per* Brightman J., was the failure of the plaintiffs to seek an interlocutory mandatory injunction (by the time of the hearing, the housing estate had been erected to completion, and damages were a reasonable substitute remedy under Lord Cairns' Act). See also *Locobail International v. Agroexport* [1986] 1 W.L.R. 657, and *Films Rover International Ltd v. Cannon Films Sales Ltd* [1986] 3 All E.R. 772.

2 Examples from the cases

1. Valuing chattels on house purchase The headnote in *Smith v. Peters* (1875) L.R. 20 Eq. 511 reads:

> "Where an agreement had been entered into for the sale of a house at a fixed price, and of the fixtures and furniture therein at a valuation by a person named by both parties, and he undertakes the valuation, but is refused permission by the vendor to enter the premises for that purpose, the court will make a mandatory order to compel the vendor to allow the entry to enable the valuation to proceed. The court has jurisdiction to make an interlocutory order which is reasonably asked as ancillary to the administration of justice at the hearing."

2. Protection of ancient lights

(a) *Smith v. Day* (1880) 13 Ch.D. 651: The headnote provides:

> "An order having been made restraining the defendant from proceeding with certain buildings, he appealed, offering an undertaking to abide by any order the court might make at the hearing as to pulling down or altering any buildings erected by him. The Court of Appeal being of opinion that the right to an interlocutory injunction was not established, discharged the order, taking from the defendant an under-taking in the terms of his offer."

Jessel M.R. went on to say at 651–2:

> "I wish to express my decided opinion that, without any undertaking,

957

the court has jurisdiction to order the pulling down of anything erected after the commencement of the action, or after notice given to the defendant that his erecting it is objected to."

(b) *Daniel v. Ferguson* (1891) 2 Ch.D. 27: The defendant, upon receiving notice of motion for an injunction in an action to restrain him from building so as to darken the plaintiff's lights put on a number of extra men, and by working night and day built a wall to 39 feet in height. There was an issue as to whether the plaintiff had easement of light—it could have gone either way. The Court of Appeal upheld the decision at first instance, which:

  (i) restrained the defendant from further building, and

  (ii) directed the wall to be pulled down.

Kay L.J. said at 30:

> "Whether he turns out at the trial to be right or wrong, a building which he has erected under such circumstances ought to be at once pulled down, on the ground that the erection of it was an attempt to anticipate the order of the court."

(c) *Von Joel v. Hornsey* [1895] 2 Ch. 774: In circumstances not dissimilar to *Daniel v. Ferguson (ibid.)* the defendant erected a building near the plaintiff's house (thereby, according to the plaintiff, obstructing his ancient lights). The defendant continued building notwithstanding the plaintiff's bringing action—and for several days evaded service. A mandatory order was made, that the building be pulled down, Lopes L.J. saying at 776:

> "The evidence is conclusive, in my opinion; attempts were over and over again made to serve him with that writ, and excuses of all sorts were made with regard to the absence of the defendant. In the meantime instructions are proved to have been given to the foreman, as the foreman states, to hurry on the building, and to do that in defiance of the plaintiffs and of the proceedings before the court. Under these circumstances the principle in *Daniel v. Ferguson* applies to this case."

(d) *Pugh v. Howells* (1984) 48 P. & C.R. 298: The defendant erected an extension to his home which interfered with the daylight into the plaintiff's kitchen. The court granted a mandatory injunction to pull down the extension, its grounds for so doing being:

  (i) The defendant had, prior to construction, been professionally advised that the extension would interfere with the plaintiff's ancient light.

  (ii) The defendant embarked hastily upon construction, refusing to accept a recorded delivery letter of the plaintiffs.

(iii) In *Shelfer v. City of London Electric Lighting* Co. [1895] 1 Ch. 287, A. L. Smith L.J. said:

"Many judges have stated, and I emphatically agree with them, that a person by committing a wrongful act, whether it be a public company for public purposes or a private individual is not thereby entitled to ask the court to sanction his doing so by purchasing his neighbour's rights, by assessing damages in that behalf, leaving his neighbour with the nuisance, or his lights dimmed, as the case may be. ..."

These dicta should not be read to the exclusion of the following passage, in the same case:

"(1) If injury to the plaintiff's legal rights is small. (2) And is one which is capable of being estimated to money. (3) And is one which can be adequately compensated by a small money payment. (4) And the case is one in which it would be oppressive to the defendant to grant an injunction. Then damages in substitution for an injunction may be given."

3. Redirecting mail In *Hermann Long v. Bean* (1884) 26 Ch.D. 306, the defendant was dismissed from the plaintiff's employ. Upon such dismissal, D gave notice to the Post Office to forward to his residence, letters addressed to him at the plaintiff's office. The Court of Appeal held that:

"The defendant had no right to give a notice to the Post Office the effect of which would be to hand over to him, letters of which it was probable that the greater part related only to L's business; and that the case was one in which a mandatory injunction compelling the defendant to withdraw his notice could properly be made, the plaintiff being put under an undertaking only to open the letters at specified times, with liberty for the defendant to be present at the opening."

4. Breaching solus agreements—*Esso Petroleum Co. Ltd v. Kingswood Motors (Addlestone) Ltd* [1974] 1 Q.B. 142 In 1972 in breach of a "solus agreement", with the intention of defeating it, the second defendants acquired the shares of the first defendant and without entering into a solus tie agreement with the plaintiffs. The second defendants procured the transfer of the legal title to the land on which the garage premises were situated, to the third defendant. The plaintiff applied for relief—in the nature of an unscrambling of these transactions. In essence, they sought, *inter alia* injunctions against the third defendant requiring the retransfer of the site to the plaintiffs, in whose hands it would still be bound by the terms of the 1969 agreement which Esso sought to enforce by prohibitory injunctions. In this pre-*Cyanamid* case Bridge J. held in favour of the plaintiffs, on the following grounds:

(a) As to the covenant in the solus agreement there was a strong
probability that the plaintiff would establish its validity because:

  (i) it was not prohibited by the provisions of Article 85 of the EEC
  Treaty, as applied by the European Communities Act 1972 (see
  Case 23/67, *Brasserie de Haecht S.A. v. Wilkin* [1967] E.C.R. 407;
  [1968] C.M.L.R. 26: Case 48/72, *Brasserie de Haecht S.A. v.
  Wilkin (No. 2)* [1973] E.C.R. 77; [1973] C.M.L.R. 287 and Case
  43/69, *Brauerei A. Bilger Söhne GmbH v. Jehle,* [1970] E.C.R.
  127; [1974] 1 C.M.L.R. 382).

  (ii) the solus tie did not constitute a clog on the equity of redemption—the third defendant having charged the land to a finance
  company.

(b) The court could in principle grant a mandatory interlocutory injunction, on the basis that all three defendants conspired to induce a
breach of contract between the first defendant and the plaintiff.
Bridge J. drew upon the following dicta of Lord Denning M.R. in
Acrow (Automation) Ltd v. Rex Chainbelt Inc. [1971] 1 W.L.R. 1676
at 1682:

> "I think that this court has the power to, and should relieve Rex
> Chainbelt and Rex International of the embarrassing situation in
> which they find themselves. I take the principle of law to be that
> which I stated in *Torquay Hotel Co. Ltd v. Cousins* [1969] 2 Ch.
> 106, namely, that if one person, without just cause or excuse,
> deliberately interferes with the trade or business of another, and
> does so by unlawful means, that is, by an act which he is not at
> liberty to commit, then he is acting unlawfully. He is liable to
> damages: and, in a proper case an injunction can be granted against
> him." (at 155H–156A.)

(c) Discretion should be exercised in favour of the grant of mandatory
relief on the following grounds expressed by Bridge J. at 157A–E:

> "So I turn to the final question, which perhaps is the easiest of
> those which I have to decide. Given that I have a discretion and a
> power to make the mandatory injunction sought, is this a proper
> case for its exercise? Of course it is accepted that I have been taken
> through the authorities that a mandatory injunction of the kind
> here sought on an interlocutory application is not lightly to be
> granted, it requires a very strong case indeed. In a number of cases
> to which I have been referred, the phrase used to describe the kind
> of situation in which the court might be expected properly to grant
> a mandatory injunction on an interlocutory application is 'stealing
> a march.' I ask myself: what clearer case could there be of defendants
> stealing a march on plaintiffs than this case? It is as strong a case

calling for the exercise of the power which I hold the court possesses to order the consequences of unlawful action to be undone, as it is well possible to imagine. But if I had any doubt on other grounds whether this was a proper case for the exercise of discretion, one consideration above all would convince me that it is a case which cries out for the exercise of the court's power. The very history of this case strongly suggests that tie-breaking, by acquiring petrol stations the subject of solus agreements, then disregarding those agreements and acting in breach of them, must be a profitable activity, if you can get away with it subject only to a liability to pay damages. That calculation has clearly motivated the defendants in this case, and if that is a correct calculation, it affords the strongest possible reason why others who may be tempted to make it, should be shown that it is a calculation based on a false premise, namely, the premise that the only liability the tie-breaker incurs is a liability to pay such damages as the supply company can eventually prove. It is quite clear from the evidence before me that damages in a case of this kind would be a wholly inadequate remedy to protect the plaintiffs from the consequences of this sort of tie- breaking."

5. Occupation of a building site In *London Borough of Hounslow v. Twickenham Garden Developments Ltd* [1971] Ch. 233, the defendant builder had a licence to enter upon the plaintiff's land for the purpose of performing a major construction contract which he had with the plaintiff. Labour disputes finally prompted the plaintiff to seek to terminate the defendant's employment under the contract and when the defendant refused to accept such termination the plaintiff sought to eject them from the land, as a trespasser. Megarry J. held:
  (a) The licence was irrevocable so long as the contract was running.
  (b) The plaintiff had discharged the high burden of proof upon it to show its terminating of the contract had been valid thereby to justify an injunction having in part, mandatory effect.
It should be noted that this, of course, was a pre-*Cyanamid* decision.

6. Delivery of mail In *Harold Stephen & Co. Ltd v. The Post Office* [1977] 1 W.L.R. 1172 postal workers at a North London Postal Centre "blacked" mail. The plaintiffs, three associated business companies in the area, issued a writ framed in an action in detinue or bailment and applied for mandatory interlocutory relief requiring the defendant forthwith to deliver up all postal packets addressed to them in its possession or under its control at two offices in the area. The Court of Appeal held that:
  (a) The Post Office had immunity under section 29 of the Post Office Act 1969.
  (b) Even if it did not have immunity, mandatory relief would not be

ordered because it would require the Post Office to discriminate between users of the mail services, to aid and abet the criminal offence by the postal workers of wilfully detaining the mails and to undermine disciplinary measures and other steps taken with the object of limiting the dispute in the interest of the public as a whole. Geoffrey Lane L.J. added, at 1180D–E:

> "This court plainly should not make any mandatory order unless it is in a position to enforce it. If through no fault of the Post Office it was unable to comply with the order which we have made, what sanction could be properly imposed upon it? One asks that question, and so far as I can see there is no proper answer.
>
> Finally, and most seriously as I see it, the ground on which I would primarily base my decision would be this. It can only be in very rare circumstances and in the most extreme circumstances that this court should interfere by way of mandatory injunction in the delicate mechanism of industrial disputes and industrial negotiations. It is likely, if mandatory injunctions are imposed in these circumstances, that more damage might be done than good...."

7. Trespass to land *Trenberth (John) Ltd v. National Westminster Bank* (1980) 253 EG 151 (see p. 988).

3 *De Vos v. Baxter* [1987] 11 N.I.J.B. 103

1. The facts The plaintiff ran a business from his premises, which included a yard. He had enjoyed access to the yard by the same road for some 23 years until the two defendants partially obstructed it. The plaintiff sought a mandatory injunction to make the defendants remove the obstruction, alleging a right of way. (The facts are as inferred from the judgment of Lord Lowry C.J. sitting in the Chancery Division of the High Court of Northern Ireland, but the judgment does not contain a statement of the facts or the relief sought.)

2. Three issues Lord Lowry C.J. considered the application of three principles:
  (a) the balance of convenience;
  (b) the status quo; and
  (c) the fact that this injunction would be mandatory.

3. The balance of convenience Lord Lowry C.J. stated the principle thus:

> "A guiding principle is to do justice to all parties according to law and the phrase 'the balance of convenience' must be understood in

the light of that principle. May L.J. has called it in *Cayne v. Global Natural Resources plc* [1984] 1 All E.R. 225 at 237H 'the balance of the risk of doing an injustice'."

4. The defendants' argument was rejected

"[Counsel for the defendants] made the ... point that in the meantime the plaintiff could easily overcome the effect of the alleged torts by widening the entrance of his yard. If there is some obvious and easy step that a party can take, even though perhaps adding the expense of that step to the amount of an eventually successful claim, well and good, it should be considered, but it is, like most things connected with ancillary relief, a question of degree. In this case it appears to me that the step, though reasonably simple, that it is suggested that the plaintiff should take in his own interests, is not so cheap or simple as that which the first defendant is asked to take and certainly no cheaper and no simpler."

5. The first issue: resolved in the plaintiff's favour

"The facts stated suggest that if the plaintiff's use of the alleged right of way is not restored he will suffer financial loss and, although some of the loss foreseen is quantified, the facts also indicate that some of the loss will be difficult to quantify. ... If the right of way is restored now during the less busy time for coal deliveries [*sc.* summer], the plaintiff's loss so far as not quantifiable will be kept to a minimum between now and the final adjudication of the parties' rights. The loss and inconvenience to each of the defendants caused by granting the injunction will be very slight and the situation pending trial will be the same as it has been for many years."

6. The second issue: the status quo

"As I observed in *Dalepak Foods plc v. Frezmet Daily Pack Ltd* the status quo is strictly speaking the *status quo ante bellum* and, as such, normally falls to be restored rather than preserved. The doctrine expounded by Lord Diplock [in *American Cyanamid v. Ethicon* [1975] A.C. 396 at 408F] can best be understood and applied by considering whether the realistic status quo is represented by the situation the plaintiff seeks to have restored (as when the alleged tort is recent) or consists of the allegedly tortious situation (as it does when the plaintiff has stood by and allowed that situation to exist for some time). ... Here the status quo must be regarded as the situation just before the alleged tort took place, and therefore it should, in my opinion, be restored."

963

7. The third issue: a mandatory injunction

"This will involve a mandatory injunction, and again there is a question of degree. The court is generally less ready to grant a mandatory interlocutory injunction than a restrictive one. On the other hand the court will be more likely to grant a mandatory injunction if what is required to be done by a defendant is simple and cheap and if the allegedly offending situation has been of short duration, and less likely to grant it if it would be expensive to carry out, for example by pulling down an established building, and still less likely if the alleged tort has been tolerated for some time by the plaintiff."

4 *Leisure Data v. Bell* [1988] F.S.R. 367

1. The facts The plaintiffs engaged the defendant to develop computer programs to monitor the performance of coin operated games machines installed in places such as public houses. The plaintiffs would market the programs to the machine operators of breweries and the defendant would receive a royalty. The parties fell out, and the major dispute was as to the ownership of the copyright in the source code version of the programs, which was the means of access to the programs for purposes of repair and improvement.

2. The order of Whitford J. The plaintiffs were granted an interlocutory injunction of a mandatory nature upon giving various undertakings as to confidentiality. The order against the defendant obliged him to allow the plaintiffs to use the relevant source codes for maintenance and improvement of the programs pending trial.

3. The defendant's grounds of appeal The defendant contended:
 (a) that a mandatory injunction should not have been granted at an interlocutory stage where it is not clear that the plaintiffs will succeed at trial; and
 (b) that although some form of order might be appropriate to enable mistakes in the programs to be corrected, the order was in any event unduly wide in permitting improvements.

4. The first issue: the defendant lost It was common ground that where what is in question is the grant of an interlocutory mandatory injunction, the *American Cyanamid* guidelines are not really relevant. The Court of Appeal accepted the principles set out by Megarry J. in *Shepherd Homes Ltd v. Sandham* [1971] Ch. 340 at 351:

"In a normal case the court must *inter alia* feel a high degree of assurance that at the trial it will appear that the injunction was rightly granted; and this is a higher standard that is required for a prohibitory injunction."

However, the Court of Appeal held that the present case was one in which practical considerations overrode this principle. Dillon L.J. said at 372:

"The court is required, as Lord Diplock pointed out in *N.W.L. Ltd v. Woods* [1979] 3 All E.R. 614 at 625, to give full weight to the practical realities of the situation and weigh the respective risks that injustice may result from a decision one way or another. The court has to keep firmly in mind the risk of injustice to either party. Beyond that, there are many cases where there is a salvage element involved, and where it is necessary that some form of mandatory order shall be made to deal with a situation which cannot on the practical realities of the situation be left to wait until the trial. Here the court will act whether or not the high standard of probability of success indicated by Megarry J. is made out."

5. The second issue: the defendant succeeded in extracting more undertakings Dillon L.J. said:

"... it is possibly necessary for the purpose of preserving the copyright as a valuable asset for one or other of the parties after the trial has been held, because otherwise in a highly competitive market there is the risk that customers will have turned elsewhere and the parties will be found to have been fighting over a dead body. ... At the end of the argument on this appeal certain further undertakings were offered by the plaintiffs. ... These fresh undertakings to my mind go so far as in the circumstances can at present be reasonably devised to meet the damages to the defendant and enable the asset the parties are fighting about to be preserved as a valid commercial asset."

5 *Jakeman v. South West Thames Regional Health Authority* [1990] IRLR 62

1. The facts The plaintiffs were ambulancemen employed by the defendant health authority. As part of industrial action they refused to comply with one of the health authority's instructions (to report from hospitals), as a result of which the health authority treated them as absent from work for part of their shifts and withheld some of their pay. The ambulancemen sought an interlocutory mandatory injunction to require the health authority to make payment of full pay in spite of the industrial action.

965

2. The law Auld J. said that:

"The starting point for interlocutory relief was that the plaintiffs must establish that they had at least a good arguable claim or a serious question to be tried. A more onerous test generally applied where, as here, a mandatory injunction requiring a party to act was sought: *Locobail International Finance Ltd v. Agroexport* [1986] 1 W.L.R. 657. In the absence of special circumstances a mandatory injunction would not normally be granted unless the case was clear and one which should be decided at once."

3. The plaintiffs' argument

"The plaintiffs said that the authority was not entitled [to withhold pay] because their breach of contract in failing to report from hospitals was a minor matter; they could be contacted at any time, they had otherwise done what was expected of them, and the authority had accepted the position by keeping them in employment and requesting them to return to work daily. They said the authority had waived such breach and was therefore not entitled to make deductions from their wages."

4. The defendant's argument

"The authority said that the plaintiffs were not ready to carry out an important part of their duties and their failure to do so impeded efficient central control and deployment of its ambulances, and that it had made it plain that it would treat such partial performance as absence from the shift."

5. The judge refused an interlocutory injunction—why? Auld J. said:

"While there was undoubtedly a serious question to be tried it could not be said that the plaintiffs' case was a clear one. As it was a claim for mandatory relief and the grant of it would amount to substantially the whole of the relief sought in the action, following the approach in *Locobail*, the application would be refused on that ground alone. ...

A further reason was that the court generally would not grant interlocutory injunctions, as opposed to prohibitory injunctions, in cases arising from industrial disputes."

K: DEFAMATION

1 Introduction

1. The primary dicta In the following cases, the courts have classically explained how their discretion will be exercised in respect of applications for injunctions in defamation actions:

(a) *William Coulson & Sons v. Coulson (James) & Co.* (1887) 3 T.L.R. 846, C.A., *per* Lord Esher M.R.:

> "It could not be denied that the court had jurisdiction to grant an interim injunction before trial. It was, however, a most delicate jurisdiction to exercise, because, though Fox's Act only applied to indictments and informations for libel, the practice under that Act had been followed in civil actions for libel, that the question of libel or no libel was for the jury. It was for the jury and not for the court to construe the document and to say whether it was a libel or not. To justify the court in granting an interim injunction it must come to a decision upon the question of libel or no libel before the jury decided whether it was a libel or not. Therefore, the jurisdiction was of a delicate nature. It ought only to be exercised in the clearest cases, where any jury would say that the matter complained of was libellous, and where, if the jury did not so find, the court would set aside the verdict as unreasonable. The court must also be satisfied that in all probability the alleged libel was untrue, and, if written on a privileged occasion, that there was malice on the part of the defendant. It followed from those three rules that the court could only on the rarest occasions exercise the jurisdiction."

These dicta founded the decision not to grant an interlocutory injunction in the libellous effigy case: *Monson v. Tussauds Ltd* [1894] 1 Q.B. 671.

(b) *Liverpool Household Stores Association v. Smith* (1887) 37 Ch.D. 170: Where application was made to restrain publication in a newspaper of reports and correspondence containing unfavourable statements as to the position and solvency of a joint stock company. Lopes L.J. said at 184:

> "And as regards future letters of the description mentioned in the notice of motion, it clearly is not so apparent that a jury will find them libels as to justify the court in interfering in the way asked. It could be most inconvenient to have the question of libel or no libel tried by a judge on a motion to commit instead of being tried by a jury."

(c) *Quartz Hill Consolidated Gold Mining Company v. Beall* (1882) 20

Ch.D. 501: In holding that great caution is needed before granting inter-locutory relief where the impugned document is prima facie a privileged communication, Jessel M.R. said at 509:

> "The circular appears on the face of it to be private in the nature of a privileged communication. It is issued by one shareholder to his brother shareholders, asking for their co-operation either in putting an end to the company or reconstituting it. As I said before, it may be answered that it is malicious and not entitled to protection, but that is very difficult to try upon interlocutory application. In the present case the defendant says he is acting bona fide, and there is no evidence against him. But if there were, I think a judge should hesitate long before he decides so difficult a question as that of privilege upon an interlocutory application, the circular being on the face of it privileged, and the only answer being express malice. Those are questions which really cannot be tried upon affidavit, or in the mode in which an interlocutory application is disposed of."

(d) *Bonnad v. Perryman* [1891] 2 Ch. 269, *per* Lord Coleridge at 283–284:

> "But it is obvious that the subject-matter of an action for defamation is so special as to require exceptional caution in exercising the jurisdiction to interfere by injunction before trial of an action to prevent an anticipated wrong. The right of free speech is one which it is for the public interest that individuals should possess, and, indeed, that they should exercise without impediment, so long as no wrongful act is done; and, unless an alleged libel is untrue, there is no wrong committed; but, on the contrary, often a very wholesome act is performed in the publication and repetition of an alleged libel. Until it is clear that an alleged libel is untrue, it is not clear that any right at all has been infringed; and the importance of leaving free speech unfettered is a strong reason in cases of libel for dealing most cautiously and warily with the granting of interim injunctions. We entirely approve of, and desire to adopt as our own, the language of Lord Esher M.R. in *Coulson v. Coulson.*"

(e) *Fraser v. Evans* [1969] 1 Q.B. 349 at 360, *per* Lord Denning M.R.:

> "The court will not restrain the publication of an article, even though it is defamatory, when the defendant says he intends to justify it or to make fair comment on a matter of public interest. That has been established for many years ever since *Bonnar v. Perryman.* The reason sometimes given is that the defences of justification and fair comment are for the jury, which is the constitutional tribunal, and not for the judge. But a better reason is the importance in the public interest that the truth should out. As the court said in that case: 'the right of free

speech is one which it is for the public interest that individuals should possess, and, indeed, that they should exercise without impediment so long as no wrongful act is done.' There is no wrong done if it is true, or if it is fair comment on a matter of public interest. The court will not prejudice the issue by granting an injunction in advance of publication."

(f) *Bestobell Paints Ltd v. Bigg* [1975] F.S.R. 421 (a malicious falsehood case):

"There is an old and well-established principle which is still applied in modern times and which is in no way affected by the recent decision by the House of Lords in *American Cyanamid Corpn v. Ethicon*, that no interlocutory injunction will be granted in defamation proceedings, where the defendant announces his intention of justifying, to restrain him from publishing the alleged defamatory statement unless its truth or untruth has been determined at the trial, except in cases where the statement is obviously untruthful and libellous. That was established towards the end of the last century and it has been asserted over ad over again. ... [A]n interlocutory restraint in any case that is not obvious would operate as an unjust fetter on the right of free speech and the defendant's liberty (if he is right) to speak the truth."

(g) *Trevor (J.) Sons (a firm) v. Solomon (P.R.)*, *The Times*, December 16, 1977: The headnote reads:

"The principle of *Bonnar v. Perryman* ([1891] 2 Ch. 269) that an interlocutory injunction ought not to be granted to restrain what is alleged to be a libel which the defendant genuinely intends to justify, and the court is not satisfied that he might not be able to do so, has not been affected by the House of Lords' decision in the *American Cyanamid* case ([1975] A.C. 39)."

(h) *Harakas v. Baltic Mercantile and Shipping Exchange* [1982] 1 W.L.R. 958, *per* Lord Denning M.R. at 960F–G:

"This court never grants an injunction in respect of libel when it is said by the defendant that the words are true and that he is going to justify them. So also, when an occasion is protected by qualified privilege this court never grants an injunction to restrain a slander or libel—to prevent a person from exercising that privilege—unless it is shown that what the defendant proposes to say is known by him to be untrue so that it is clearly malicious. As long as he proposes to say what he honestly believes to be true, no injunction should be granted against him."

Hereafter is set out an analysis of those cases in recent times, showing how the courts exercise their discretion in cases touching upon defamation.

2 *Losinka v. Civil and Public Services Association* [1976] I.C.R. 473

1. The facts The plaintiff was the president of the defendant association and in an article in a magazine, critically referred to 10 per cent of the members of the association as being supporters of the "Militant Left". The National Executive of the defendant passed a resolution deploring the improper use of the office of president to attack the properly authorised activities of some members. It issued a writ seeking an interlocutory injunction restraining the publication of the article in the association's journal.

2. The relevant rule Rule 26 (Discipline of the Association) stated:

> "3. Members ... (b) Action by the National Executive Committee. Where the N.E.C. considers that the conduct of a member appears to be detrimental to the interests of the association, the N.E.C. may refer the matter for investigation by an enquiry tribunal under paragraph (f) of this clause."

3. The plaintiff won—by reference to the rules The report of the decision of the Court of Appeal reads:

> "L had to show a threatened breach of contract, a contract—which existed within the terms of the association's rules. She said that if the resolutions were published, the N.E.C. were failing to apply rule 26(3)(b). She contended that the terms of the resolution asserted that she had been guilty of conduct detrimental to the Association's interests and that she should be dealt with by the appropriate procedure. This procedure had not in fact been observed, and publication of the resolution must be restrained. (*American Cyanamid Corp. v. Ethicon Ltd* [1975] A.C. 396 applied.)"

3 *Harakas v. Baltic Mercantile Shipping Exchange Ltd* [1982] 1 W.L.R. 958

1. The facts The second defendant, the International Maritime Bureau, claimed to have received some evidence suggesting that one Costas Kamateros was behind some of the operations of Grecian Lines. As a result, it caused to be published in the Baltic Exchange, the following notice:

"*Grecian Lines.* Members contemplating business with the above named company whose agents are, it is understood, called 'Maritime Tradition' may be interested in information available from the Secretary."

The first plaintiff, the owner of Grecian Lines, swore an affidavit stating such suggestions to be untrue. A director of the second defendant deposed in answer:

"The ICC International Museum Bureau does not at present contend that it is true that Costas Kamateros is behind the plaintiffs' operation: such evidence of that as is set out herein is included in an attempt to demonstrate that there are reasonable grounds for an honest belief that he may be."

2. Injunction refused—why? The Court of Appeal allowed an appeal against the injunction granted by Boreham J. at first instance. Lord Denning M.R. held at 960G–H:

"When there is a bureau of this kind—which is specially charged with the responsibility of obtaining information and giving it to those interested, to warn them of possible dangers—it is very important that they should be able to give information to people who are properly interested: so long as it is done honestly and in good faith. That is all the bureau wish to do in this case. They should not be prevented from doing so by an injunction unless it is clearly shown that they are dishonestly and maliciously saying what they know to be untrue. There is not a shred of evidence to support a suggestion of that kind. In my opinion this injunction should never have been granted: and should be discharged here and now."

4 *Herbage v. Pressdram Ltd* [1984] 1 W.L.R. 1160

1. The facts The defendants were *Private Eye*—which published of the plaintiff (an investment adviser) defamatory material including the fact of his conviction for certain offences under the Companies Act 1948—despite the fact that such convictions were spent pursuant to the provision of the Rehabilitation of Offenders Act 1974. On the plaintiff's application for injunctive relief, the defendant editor declared his intention to justify the contents of their article and denied that they had published them maliciously.

2. The case for the plaintiff The plaintiff argued that *Cyanamid* should apply—and not *Trevor v. Solomon* (above, at p. 969)—and that an injunction should lie. Lord Denning M.R. explained the argument thus:

"... but now, says counsel for the plaintiff, a new factor is introduced into the equation to which the court must give weight and which justifies a radical departure from its practice in other defamation actions. The manifest overall purpose of the 1974 Act, he says, is to allow a man to live down his past and put it behind him, and now the court must throw into the balance on the side of the individual that intention of Parliament when balancing it against the value of free speech or of a free Press. This so tips the scale, he submits, that the court should in such cases apply the approach for which guidance is found in the *American Cyanamid* case, rather than to apply its present practice in other defamation actions."

3. The statutory provisions Section 4(1) of the Act of 1974 provides:

"Subject to sections 7 and 8 below, a person who has become a rehabilitated person for the purposes of this Act in respect of a conviction shall be treated for all purposes in law as a person who has not committed or been charged with or prosecuted for or convicted of or sentenced for an offence or offences which were the subject of that conviction."

Section 8(3) of the Act of 1974 provides:

"Subject to subsections (5) and (6) below, nothing in section 4(1) ... shall prevent the defendant in an action to which this section applies from relying on any defence of justification or fair comment or of absolute or qualified privilege which is available to him, or restrict the matters he may establish in support of any such defence."

Section 8(5) goes on to state:

"A defendant in any such actions shall not by virtue of subsection (3) above be entitled to rely upon the defence of justification if the publication is proved to have been made with malice."

4. What is the effect of those statutory provisions? Lord Denning M.R. said:

"The effect of these two subsections is to place a person who has rehabilitated himself in a more advantageous position than a person who has been convicted and has not rehabilitated himself by avoiding further conviction for the requisite period required under the 1974 Act. If a man has rehabilitated himself and his conviction is to be regarded as 'spent' and that conviction is publish of him, he can recover damages if he is able to show that it was maliciously published. I take 'malice' in this subsection to mean published with some irrelevant, spiteful, or improper motive. If it is so published, even though it is true he has a 'spent' conviction, that conviction is to be disregarded. He is to be treated as though no such conviction had taken place and accordingly the publication is libellous. That is a great advantage over another man who may have had a conviction a number of years ago, but who has not yet fulfilled the qualifying period, and of whom, no matter how maliciously, it may be published that he has been convicted, since the defendants will have an absolute defence of justification. The rehabilitated person, for the purposes of the law of libel, is placed at a real advantage by virtue of the fact that he has kept clear of crime for the requisite period. It seems to me that this very closely equates the position with the case where a defendant relies on a defence of qualified privilege."

5. Thus did *Cyanamid* apply here? No—as Lord Denning explained:

"In such a case, the law is now well settled. Only if, at the interlocutory stage, the evidence of malice is absolutely overwhelming will the court intervene to restrain publication by way of an interlocutory injunction: see *William Coulson & Sons v. James Coulson & Co.* (1887) 3 T.L.R. 864.

Parliament having so provided, I can see no reason why this court should approach the resolution of the problem in this case in any different manner to that which it would be in any other defamation action where the real issue to be tried is one of malice. That is the issue in this case exactly in the same way as it is in every case where qualified privilege is pleaded as a defence."

5 *Gulf Oil (G.B.) Ltd v. Page* [1987] Ch. 327

1. The facts The defendants owned a number of petrol filling stations which had been supplied with petrol by the plaintiff under an agreement which had given rise to litigation. In that litigation the High Court held *inter alia* that the plaintiff had been in fundamental breach of the agreement. During a race meeting at Cheltenham on the day before the Gold Cup the defendants flew a light aircraft over the race course towing a banner "Gulf exposed in fundamental breach." They intended to do the same the next day during the Gold Cup itself.

2. The relief sought Gulf Oil (G.B.) Ltd, immediately applied in the Chancery Division for an interim injunction in these terms:

"... that until trial or further order in the meantime the defendants and each of them, in the case of the third defendant by its director and officers and in the case of all defendants by themselves their servants or agents or otherwise howsoever be restrained from exhibiting or publishing on any airborne sign or otherwise howsoever the legend 'Gulf exposed in fundamental breach' or any words to the like or similar effect."

3. The plaintiff's argument The plaintiff did not seek to challenge the principle that in a libel action if a defendant intends to justify, interim relief is, as a matter of principle, never granted. But they contended that where the writ is also indorsed with a claim for damages for conspiracy and there is clear evidence of conspiracy to injure, the principle has no application.

4. The defendants' argument The defendants asserted that if interim relief could be granted in such a case as this it would in effect reverse the long-standing principle because it would often be open to a plaintiff in a libel action to claim also in conspiracy against the reporter, editor, printers and publishers of the libel.

5. Injunction granted by the Court of Appeal Parker L.J. said at 333G–334A:

> "It is true that there is no wrong done if what is published is true provided that it is not published in pursuance of a combination and, even if it is, there is still no wrong unless the sole or dominant purpose of the combination and publication is to injure the plaintiff. If, however, there is both combination and purpose or dominant purpose to injure there *is* a wrong done. When a plaintiff sues in conspiracy there is, therefore, a potential wrong even if it is admitted, as it is in the present case, that the publication is true and thus that there is no question of a cause of action in defamation. In such a case the court can, and in my view should, proceed on the same principles as it would in the case of any other tort.
>
> The prospect that this would open the floodgates and reverse the principle applicable in libel action, is, in my view, unreal. A plaintiff in an action against the author and publisher of a newspaper article, for example, might well establish a combination, but it appears to me that it would only be in the rarest case that sufficient evidence of a dominant purpose to injure could be made out to warrant the grant of interlocutory relief. ...."

L: NO UNRESOLVED DISPUTE ON THE AFFIDAVIT EVIDENCE—EXAMPLES

1 *Dublin Port & Docks Board v. Britannia Dredging Co. Ltd* [1968] I.R. 136

1. The background The defendant agreed with the plaintiff to undertake dredging work in the Port of Dublin. Clause 53 of the contract stipulated that all equipment brought to the site by the defendant should be deemed to be the property of the plaintiff and that such equipment should not be removed by the defendant without the written consent of the plaintiff's engineer, which would not be withheld unreasonably.

2. The defendant threatens a breach The defendant threatened to abandon the work (probably by virtue of its having sustained through the bargain, a heavy loss). This precipitated the plaintiff into claiming, *inter alia*, an injunction to restrain the defendant's apprehended removal of the dredging equipment.

3. Injunction granted—why? The Irish Supreme Court held:
   (a) "... that Clause 53 of the contract was designed to enable the plaintiffs to have the works completed in the event of the defendants ceasing to perform their part of the contract, and that, accordingly, the injunction sought by the plaintiffs would not be equivalent to ordering the defendants to perform their contract."
   (b) "That, as the defendants had agreed to the negative term relating to removal of equipment and a breach of the contract was imminent, the court should hold the defendants to their bargain, pending the trial, by an interlocutory injunction without considering the balance of hardship or damage. ...."

4. Reliance on English authority In making its ruling, the Irish Court, *inter alia*, prayed in aid the following dicta from *Doherty v. Allman* (1878) 3 App.Cas. 709 at 720:

"If parties, for valuable consideration, with their eyes open, contract that a particular thing shall not be done, all that a court of equity has to do is to say, by way of injunction, that which the parties have already said by way of covenant, that the thing shall not be done; and in such case the injunction does nothing more than give the sanction of the process of the court to that which is already the contract between the parties. It is not then a question of the balance of convenience or inconvenience, or of the amount of damage or of

975

injury—it is the specific performance, by the court, of that negative bargain which the parties have made, with their eyes open, between themselves." (*Per* Lord Cairns L.C.)

5. Megarry J. would probably have decided similarly In *Hampstead and Suburban Properties Ltd v. Diomedous* [1969] 1 Ch. 248 at 259 Megarry J. held:

> "Where there is a plain and uncontested breach of a clear covenant not to do a particular thing, and the covenantory promptly begins to do what he has promised not to do, then in the absence of special circumstances it seems to me that the sooner he is compelled to keep his promise the better."

2 *Woollerton & Wilson Ltd v. Richard Costain Ltd* [1970] 1 W.L.R. 411

1. Dates are relevant In September 1969 the defendant builders erected a tower crane on a building site which at times overhung the plaintiff's premises 50 feet above roof level.

2. The plaintiff takes a hard line After abortive negotiations during which the plaintiff had refused the defendant's offer of £250 the plaintiff launched proceedings in respect of the (admitted) trespass.

3. The court accepted, in principle, the plaintiff's argument Stamp J. found both of the following arguments of the plaintiff to be well-founded:
  (a) The absence of any damage caused by the trespass, either present or apprehended, is no reason for refusing an injunction.
  (b) Since the tort of trespass was admitted, and was threatened to be continued there was no good reason for refusing interlocutory relief on the ground of balance of convenience.
In respect of these points, Stamp J. said at 413F–H:

> "It is in my judgment well established that it is no answer to a claim or an injunction to restrain a trespass that the trespass does no harm to the plaintiff. Indeed, the very fact that no harm is done is a reason for rather than against the granting of an injunction: for if there is no damage done the damage recovered in the action will be nominal and if the injunction is refused the result will be no more nor less than a licence to continue the tort of trespass in return for a nominal payment. Furthermore, the very fact that the plaintiff is the owner of the property:
>
> > '... that no interference of this kind can lawfully take place without

his consent, and without a bargain with him, gives him interest in
this land, even in a pecuniary point of view, precisely the value
which the power of veto upon its use creates, when such use is to
any other person desirable and an object sought to be obtained.'
(See the judgment of Lord Selbourne L.C. in *Goodson v. Richardson*
(1874) 9 Ch.App. 221 at 224.)

Sir George Jessel M.R. in *Eardley v. Granville* (1876) 3 Ch.D. 826 at
832, remarked of the defendant in that case:

'... he is a mere trespasser and he being a trespasser comes
within the well established doctrine of *Goodson v. Richardson* and
Rochdale Canal Company v. King (1851) 14 Q.B.D. 122, where
damages would be no compensation for a right to property, and
the plaintiffs are entitled to prohibit him by injunction. There may
be little or no injury to the estate, but if they restrain him he will
be glad to pay a way-leave.'"

4. The real issue—not "whether" but "when"? The issue effectively
confronting the court was not whether an injunction should be granted,
but when it should come into effect, taking into account that the building
work was expected to be completed within the ensuing 12 months. In the
event Stamp J. ordered the injunction to come into effect in November
1970.

5. Why was Stamp J. lenient to the defendants? The grounds for Stamp
J.'s ruling were:
   (a) There was uncontradicted evidence that:
      (i) "... a tower crane was a practical necessity for reasons connected
          with the fact that the site is a most restricted one and that a
          mobile crane would cause a complete blockage in Clyde Street
          and the installation of other types of crane would be imprac-
          ticable. The only place in which the tower crane can be placed
          is precisely where it is."
      (ii) "There is also uncontradicted evidence that if the tower crane
          was required to be removed from where it is, all building
          operations would be brought to a halt while the job was
          replanned."
   (b) Were the injunction to have effect forthwith, it was the opinion of
       the defendants' contract manager that the building would have had
       to be redesigned and that this would have resulted in the contract
       period being extended by at least six months and probably 12
       months.
   (c) The plaintiffs were offered £250 for the right to continue to trespass
       while the crane was there; and although as a matter of law the

977

plaintiffs were entitled to exploit to the full the fact that the air space in which the jib of the crane swings has by reason of these defendants' vital requirements suddenly assumed an artificial value, the court could properly take into account in considering whether an immediate injunction ought to be granted the fact that they have been offered a sum of money which is at least substantial so that when they started this action they were not in the position of a plaintiff whose only remedy other than an injunction was nominal damages.

(d) As to the conduct factor, Stamp L.J. said:

"In considering whether or not an injunction should be granted and, if so, on what terms, the court may consider the behaviour of the parties. Nor do I think I ought to ignore in considering whether an immediate injunction ought to be granted the fact that the air space in question has only assumed any value at all by reason of those particular defendants' necessities. This is not a case such as was before McNair J. in *Kelsen v. Imperial Tobacco Co.* [1957] 2 Q.B. 334: where the air space could be let to a party other than the defendant company which was trespassing on it and it is not a case where the defendants have been insisting upon the right to swing the crane over the plaintiffs' land as a matter of right."

(e) It was the evidence of Mr Waters, the general manager employed by the defendants, that on no occasion in his experience had any neighbouring proprietor over whose property the jib of a tower crane had passed sought to obtain an injunction to prevent this happening or to claim compensation for the crane swinging over his air space. Nor, said Mr Waters, was he aware that any other contractor had encountered difficulties of this nature. He said that on previous occasions the Costain Group had provided neighbouring proprietors with insurance cover against the possibility of any damage being caused and this had always satisfied them (and on no occasion had any claim been made against that insurance cover).

6. The "commercial"/"private" trespass distinction There is an interesting contrast between the *Woollerton* case, involving what may be called "commercial" trespass, and *Behrens v. Richards* [1905] 2 Ch. 614—very much a case of a private trespass. In that case, the plaintiff had bought land on an unfrequented part of the coast, and stopped up several paths which the defendants asserted were public highways. The plaintiff brought an action against them for an injunction to restrain them from trespassing, upon the plaintiff removing the obstructions, Buckley J. held that there were no public rights of way, but refused an injunction. He said:

"It would, in my judgment, be a disastrous thing, not for the public only, but for the landowners also, if this court, at the caprice of the landowner, not because circumstances have altered, but merely because he was minded that it should be so, entertained every trivial application to restrain persons by injunction from using paths which, though not public highways, have in fact been used by the permission of the owners of the land. The landowner, if he be wise, will rather erect upon the road or path a notice expressive of permission or even of invitation to persons who make use of the way so long as they conduct themselves in an orderly and reasonable manner."

7. Summary In *Shelfer v. City of London Electric Lighting Company* [1895] 1 Ch. 287, A. L. Smith L.J. at 322 advanced the following working rule in the context of an interlocutory injunction in respect of a proved nuisance:

"(1) If the injury to the plaintiff's legal rights is small,
(2) and is one which is capable of being estimated in money,
(3) and is one which can be adequately compensated by a small money payment.
(4) and the case is one in which it would be oppressive to the defendant to grant an injunction"

then damages in substitution for an injunction may be given. Reference should also be made to *Pugh v. Howells* (1984) 48 P. & C.R. 298, and *Patel v. Smith* [1987] 1 W.L.R. 853.

3 *Birmingham Corporation v. Perry Barr Stadium Ltd* [1972] 1 All E.R. 725 (for the facts, see p. 652)

1. No factual dispute At 726, Pennycuick V.-C. said:

"The evidence on matters of fact is quite short, and really, I think nothing turns on it. Mr Griffith, a deputy general manager employed by the plaintiff corporation, gives an account of what took place on October 17."

Then after recruiting the material part of the affidavit, Pennycuick V.-C. went on to say at 727C:

"Then there is evidence on the part of the second defendant that he conducts markets elsewhere, and as I have said there is no suggestion that this market is not properly conducted. The real question on the notice of motion is, I think, almost wholly one of law."

2. The legal issues Pennycuick V.-C. went on to consider the legal issues, namely whether the plaintiff had a monopoly and if it did, whether it had been infringed. Both questions he answered in the affirmative after full consideration of the authorities, reflected in the extensive recitation of law in the judgment.

3. Pennycuick V.-C. does the inevitable Having found as a matter of law that there was an infringement of a monopoly, Pennycuick V.-C. realistically had no alternative but to grant an injunction. In so doing he, *inter alia*, prayed in aid the "balance of justice"—which necessarily was all one way:

> "It seems to me that, the plaintiff corporation having established disturbance of its monopoly right, the balance of justice and convenience is in favour of putting an end to that disturbance at once. I do not see any ground for saying otherwise. This is not a case of delay on the part of the plaintiff corporation, nor, I think, is it a case where the second defendant is likely to have incurred capital expenditure, or anything like that, and I cannot see any special circumstances which would make it right to allow him to go on carrying on his market to the detriment of the plaintiff corporation pending the trial of this action."

4. How does *Cyanamid* affect this approach? The extensive recitation of law in the judgment should be contrasted with the following dicta of Lord Diplock in *Cyanamid*:

> "It is no part of the court's function at this stage of the litigation to try to resolve conflicts of evidence on affidavit as to facts on which the claims of either party may ultimately depend nor to decide difficult questions of law which call for detailed argument and mature considerations. These are matters to be dealt with at the trial."

5. Post-*Cyanamid*—what would happen now? The questions which necessarily present themselves, and which presently cannot be authoritatively answered, are:

(a) If the *Birmingham Corporation* case were to be litigated today, would the court undertake extensive legal investigation, if, for example, it were unable to strike a ready balance by reference to the "adequacy of damages" criterion?

(b) If the court would not today conduct such investigation, how would it assess the "balance of convenience"?

Such questions are also prompted by the pre-*Cyanamid* case of *Comet Radiovision Services Ltd v. Farnell-Tandberg Ltd* [1971] 1 W.L.R. 1287 where there was little dispute of fact, but a question of law fell for full consideration (for the facts, see p. 651).

4 *Granada Group Ltd v. Ford Motor Company Ltd* [1972] F.S.R. 103

1. Background Although this pre-*Cyanamid* case was decided by Graham J., *inter alia*, on the basis of "no prima facie case" it may still be considered persuasive in that there was no effective dispute on the evidence and would thus have probably been decided similarly today.

2. The issue the dispute arose out of the defendant's declared intention to call their new top-line model the "Granada".

3. The plaintiffs' case The plaintiffs' case as reported at 104 rested on two contentions:

   (a) "... that, having regard to the quite exceptional requirements of the plaintiffs' name 'Granada,' the public seeing the name 'Granada' used on motor cars to denote the maker's mark or model type, and seeing the word in literature and other advertising and business matter used in the sale and marketing of such cars, would associate such cars with the plaintiffs, and would as a result think that the business of the defendants was associated or in some way connected with the business of the plaintiffs. It was not really suggested that the public would think that the cars in question were actually made by the plaintiffs."

   (b) "That irrespective of any actual direct association of the defendants' motor cars and business with the plaintiffs and their business, brought about the use of the name 'Granada' on such cars, the plaintiffs have a legal right in the commercial exploitation of the name, for example by way of licence or franchise in return for money or money's worth. This legal right they are entitled to protect by injunction when it is actually, or likely to be, infringed. If the defendants' activities are not stopped *in limine* the effect, it is said, will be irreparable damage to the plaintiffs and in a metaphorical sense the gold attaching to their name 'Granada' will rub off and embellish their defendants' products without their paying anything for it or even asking the plaintiffs' permission."

4. The defendants' case The defendants' case, as reported at p. 105, rested on the following contentions:

   (a) "... that the matter must be tested by looking at the proposed use of the name in its context, that is on the car itself and in literature and advertising matter used in the marketing of the car. When so tested ... they do not believe that there can or ever will be any confusion between their cars or business and the business of the plaintiffs if they use the name 'Granada' as they intend to use it, on and in connection with the marketing of their motor cars in question."

(b) "... they chose the name as the result of an extensive market survey both in this country and on the Continent, in Germany, France, Italy and the Netherlands, in which the merits from various points of view of some 25 possible names for the proposed new car were closely evaluated. In the end, for various reasons which are set out in their evidence, the name 'Granada' was chosen. This, of the 25 names tested, was in fact the best liked in Germany, the largest potential market for the car in question, the second best liked in all six markets combined, and the fourth best liked in the United Kingdom."

(c) "The name was chosen ... without it ever crossing the mind of those concerned with the choice of the name that, if used by the defendants, anyone would think that there was any connection between the plaintiffs and the defendants."

(d) "It follows ... that ... they can use the name freely without asking the permission of or paying any tribute to the plaintiffs. The latter have no right of property which will be infringed by such use, since their goodwill in the name can only extend to goods or businesses which are the same as their own or so closely related to be liable to be confused with them, and it is only in cases where such conditions are fulfilled that a legal right to protect goodwill or a right of property in a franchise can exist."

5. How did the court approach the problem? Graham J. said at 105(108):

"There is, therefore, no substantial disagreement, as to the principles of law applicable to the case, the real dispute being as to how broadly on the facts of the present case the goodwill of the plaintiffs' name can be extended, and how tenuous the connection between the fields of activity in which both the plaintiffs and the defendants are engaged can be and yet still entitle the plaintiffs to the grant of an interlocutory injunction to protect their rights. ... In the present case the onus is on the plaintiffs to make out their prima facie case and to show that there is a likelihood of confusion between the defendants' business and their business, if the defendants proceed as they at present intend to do."

6. The relevant law As to the legal principles to be applied, Graham J. substantially adopted the dicta of James L.J. in *Singer Manufacturing Co v. Loog* (1880) 18 Ch.D. 395 at 412:

"No man ... is entitled to represent his goods as being the goods of another man; and no man is permitted to use any mark, sign or symbol, device or means, whereby, without making a direct false representation himself to a purchaser who purchases from him, he enables such purchaser to tell a lie or to make a false representation to somebody else who is the ultimate customer. That being, as it appears to me, a comprehensive statement of what the law is upon the question of trade mark or trade designation, I am of the opinion that there is no such thing as a monopoly or a property in the nature of a copyright, or in the nature of a patent, in the use of any name. Whatever name is used to designate goods, anybody may use that name to designate goods; always subject to this, that he must not, as I said, make, directly or through the medium of another person, a false representation that his goods are the goods of another person."

Graham J. continued:

"To this statement must also be added, as is accepted by counsel on both sides, that it is enough also if the false representation relates to the existence of a connection or an association between the businesses of the plaintiffs and the defendants. This is amply established by such cases as the *Kodak* case, *Eastman Photographic Materials Co. Ltd v. The John Griffiths Cycle Corporation Ltd* (1898) 15 R.P.C. 105, *Parker-Knoll Ltd v. Knoll International Ltd* [1962] R.P.C. 265, and the two persuasive authorities cited by Mr Finer, *Yale Electric Corporation v. Robertson* 26 Federal Reporter, Second Series, 972, a judgment of Mr Justice Learned Hand, and *Henderson v. Radio Corporation Pty Ltd* [1969] R.P.C. 218, a judgment of the High Court of Australia, consisting of Mr Justice Evatt, Mr Justice Myers and Mr Justice Manning."

7. Application of the law to the *Granada* facts Graham J. contrasted, adversely to the plaintiffs, the evidence to which both sides deposed. He said at 106–107:

"It will be seen, on the other hand, that the plaintiffs have produced no evidence whatever from motor dealers, garages or members of the motoring or general public to suggest that, if the name 'Granada' is used upon and in connection with the marketing of the defendants' motor cars, having regard to the way cars are used, bought and sold, it is considered that there is likely to be any confusion as to the origin of such cars, or that it is likely to be thought that the businesses of the plaintiffs and the defendants are in some way connected or associated. It is, of course, true that, as the cars have not yet been sold in this country, there could not be evidence of actual confusion of the defendants' goods with those of the plaintiffs. Nevertheless, it

983

seems to me that, if there is really a danger that the public will be likely to confuse the business of the Ford Motor Company with that of one or more of the plaintiff companies, it would be possible to produce some useful evidence to assist the court to come to a conclusion to that effect. None is so far forthcoming."

As to the defendants evidence he said, at 107:

"The evidence of the defendants shows how the name 'Granada' was chosen for the new car after a very extensive market research operation spoken to by Messrs. Batty, Moulson, Orton and Dobbs....

In addition, there is some evidence on the part of the defendants' witnesses already mentioned, and a further witness, Mr Huggins, the chairman of Hartwell Group Limited, who has five Ford main dealerships and five British Leyland main distributorships, that they do not for a moment believe that anyone is likely to think that a motor car called the 'Granada' is likely to lead to confusion between the businesses of the plaintiffs and of the defendants."

8. The plaintiffs lost—why? In summary, Graham J. at 108–109 dismissed the motion because the plaintiffs failed to show that if the word 'Granada' was used in its proposed context, the public were likely to confuse:

  (a) a Ford car called and marketed "Granada" and any goods of any of the plaintiffs, or
  (b) to think that the plaintiffs or any of them have entered the business of making or marketing cars, or that the defendants are by their proposed actions likely to make anyone think that the plaintiffs or any of them have in some way sponsored or approved the Ford Motor Company's new product or its proposed name, "Granada".

5 *Bentley-Stevens v. Jones* [1974] 1 W.L.R. 638

1. The facts The third defendant company was a wholly owned subsidiary of H. Ltd. The plaintiff, the first and second defendants were directors of both companies. The first and second defendants sought to remove the plaintiff from his directorship in the third defendant. However, it was probably the case that the first and second defendants failed to adhere to strict procedure.

2. What did the plaintiff want? The plaintiff, by notice of motion, asked for an injunction:

"... restraining the defendants and each of them until the trial of the action or further order from acting upon the resolution purported to have been passed by the defendant company at a purported extra-ordinary general meeting thereof held at 9.30 a.m. on February 26, 1974, removing the plaintiff as a director of the defendant company."

3. The plaintiff failed—why? Plowman J. refused the injunction, *inter alia*, ruling:

"In my judgment, even assuming that the plaintiff's complaint of irregularities is correct, this is not a case in which an interlocutory injunction ought to be granted. I say that for the reason that the irregularities can all be cured by going through proper processes and the ultimate result would inevitably be the same. In *Browne v. La Trinidad* (1887) 37 Ch.D. 1 at 17, Lindley L.J. said:

'I think it is most important that the court should hold fast to the rule upon which it has always acted, not to interfere for the purpose of forcing companies to conduct their business according to the strictest rules, where the irregularity complained of can be set right at any moment.'

It seems to me that the motion which is before me falls within the principle stated by Lindley L.J."

6 *Newsweek Inc. v. British Broadcasting Corporation* [1979] R.P.C. 441, C.A.

1. *Newsweek*—extent of circulation Lord Denning M.R. expressed the background at 447:

"Newsweek Inc. is an American corporation. It brings out a weekly magazine called *Newsweek*. It circulates all over the world. It has a United States edition, an Atlantic edition, a Pacific edition, and so forth. Its circulation world-wide is over 3,000,000: but in this country it is about 38,000 copies per week. Comparatively few people in this country see it."

2. What prompted the litigation? The plaintiff applied for an injunction in passing off proceedings against the defendant on the basis that the defendant's proposed news programme, "Newsweek" would cause confusion with their magazine.

3. Passing off, the test As to the legal principle, Lord Denning said at 447:

"The law of this subject was stated by Buckley L.J. in the recent case of *Bulmer H.P. Ltd and Showerings ltd v. Bollinger (J.) SA* [1978] R.P.C. 79 at 99. In order to obtain an injunction there must be something in the nature of a representation, express or implied, however unintentional, that the BBC programme is in some way connected with the American company's concern; and that there is, as a consequence, a probability of confusion which is likely to do damage to the American company. The test is whether the ordinary, sensible members of the public would be confused. It is not sufficient that the only confusion would be to a very small, unobservant section of society: or, as Foster J. put it recently, if the only person who would be misled would be 'a moron in a hurry': [1979] F.S.R. 117."

4. The plaintiff lost—why? Counsel for the plaintiff identified five possible grounds for confusion, which are set out below, together with the respective ruling:

(a) *First ground:*

(i) Case for the plaintiff: The viewers, namely those who watch the programme, may think that it has some connection with the plaintiff's magazine.

(ii) Ruling: No—"None of the ordinary people in England know anything about the American periodical at all. The most likely people to know about it are American tourists, or people who often travel by air. They form such a small section of the viewers in the country that they can be put on one side." (at 447.)

(b) *Second ground:*

(i) Case for the plaintiff—the sources: The plaintiff contended that a reporter might go to a source of information and by announcing himself as being from "Newsweek", thus cause the source to think that the reporter was from the American corporation, not from the BBC.

(ii) Ruling: No—"That person might think the reporter was from the American corporation, whereas in truth he was from BBC 2. It seems to me that there is very little likelihood of confusion. After the first introduction the person interviewed would soon get to know in what guise the reporter came." (at 448.)

(c) *Third ground:*

(i) Case for the plaintiff—the quotations: The plaintiff argued that after it published an important article, there is usually a "follow- up" in the press—with the risk of the story being cited as being from "Newsweek"—without distinguishing between them.

(ii) Ruling: No—"If this should cause confusion, it seems to me very unlikely to cause any damage."

(d) *Fourth ground:*

(i) Case for the plaintiff—television: The plaintiff contended that it was negotiating entry into the U.K. television market and was seeking to make arrangements with Thames Television whereby its magazine and Newsweek goodwill would be made use of in that channel's programmes.

(ii) Ruling; No—"They may have some difficulty in doing this. They will have to be careful not to offend against the Independent Broadcasting Act 1973. They will have to avoid anything of an advertising nature. I think the possibility of confusion in that field is too speculative to be taken into account." (at 448.)

(e) *Fifth ground:*
 (i) The case for the plaintiff—alter the name: The plaintiff argued that the BBC could make some alteration in the word, in some little way or other, and that would be sufficient.

(ii) Ruling: No—"This word 'Newsweek' is very largely a descriptive word. It is 'News of the Week,' shortened for commercial and publicity purposes to 'Newsweek.' I do not think we should give one publication virtually a monopoly in that largely descriptive word. It would stretch all over the English-speaking countries. We certainly should not do it when the great majority of the ordinary folk of England who watch television would not have the slightest idea or slightest knowledge of the American periodical 'Newsweek' ... [T]here are not many choices available. It has to convey the idea of 'news' and the idea of 'week.' There are very few short and snappy titles available. It seems to me that the likelihood of confusion, and the likelihood of damage, is not sufficient to warrant the court granting an injunction to stop the BBC going on with their programme." (at 447.)

5. An overview Shaw L.J., in the third judgment of the court, drew back to achieve what may be described as a strategic overview (at 449(10–20)):

"... it seems to me that there are two crucial factors. One is that an invented word, 'newsweek,' is very little removed from being an ordinary descriptive phrase; and the other is that since the parties operate through totally different media, although in the same field of disseminating current news, any confusion which may arise is more likely to be quickly dissipated and not preserved, let alone increased. As time goes on the distinction between Newsweek magazine and Newsweek on the BBC will become so apparent that any danger in relation to sources or quotation will be eliminated. I therefore see no likely detriment to the plaintiffs if the injunction they seek is refused. I agree ... that this appeal should be dismissed."

7 *Trenberth (John) Ltd v. National Westminster Bank Ltd* (1980) 253 EG 151 (see further *Anchor Brewhouse Developments v. Berkley House (Docklands) Developments Ltd* [1987] 2 EGLR 173 at p. 993)

1. The facts The first defendant engaged the second defendant to undertake works of reconstruction on the first defendant's bank premises to prevent serious structural fault resulting in collapse on to the highway. the plaintiff refused the defendants access to its neighbouring land, which was essential to the conduct of the works of reconstruction. This had the following effect, explained by Walton J. thus:

> "There was on the one hand the Scylla of the dangerous building and there was on the other hand the Charybdis of trespassing upon the plaintiff's land, and they chose, says Mr Powell-Jones, to go ahead and trespass."

The hearing before Walton J. arose from the plaintiff's application for mandatory interlocutory orders to direct the defendants to remove scaffolding and building materials, and to vacate the plaintiff's land.

2. Did the plaintiff act in good faith? Apparently yes—Walton J. said:

> "It may be or it may not be, and I do not think I am really concerned with that, that the refusal of the plaintiffs to grant permission was irrational. But it was certainly made in good faith and it certainly was not made, as the evidence makes perfectly clear, as a bargaining counter in order to extract concessions from the defendants. It was a genuine belief and desire on the part of the plaintiff, they did not want their property to be trespassed upon by the defendants."

3. Did the defendants act from any commercial motive? Yes—held Walton J., although they wished to render the building safe, they could have achieved that by pulling down.

4. Could the plaintiff be compensated in damages? No—as Walton J. said at 152:

> "But it is perfectly clear that the actual damage, apart from any question of aggravation, caused by the mere trespass, both by oversailing the front of the plaintiffs' property and by actually resting upon the rear of the plaintiffs' property, is comparatively slight; so slight that if an action were brought of it, it would hardly command the smallest coin in the realm. But so far from that being a reason why an injunction should not be granted, it has been said in many of

the cases to which Mr Munby drew my attention that the fact that any damage would be trifling is the very reason why an injunction should be granted. People are not to infringe the property rights of others and then say 'And I am entitled to go on doing it because I am really doing you no tangible harm, and five pence will amply compensate you for that harm."

5. What about a suspension of the injunction—as in the _Tower Crane_ case? No—as Walton J. said at 152:

"I think I must refer in this connection to the case of _Woollerton & Wilson Ltd v. Richard Costain Ltd_ [1970] 1 W.L.R. 411 where, on facts which in some ways bear a great resemblance to the present case, Stamp J. (as Stamp L.J. then was) granted an injunction, but then suspended it for a couple of years. I find that that case is not one which on the question of suspensions, has received universal approbation; and, indeed, in _Charrington v. Simons & Co. Ltd_ [1971] 1 W.L.R. 598, there occurs in the judgment of Russell L.J. (as the third Lord Russell of Killowen then was) these words:

'Further, we wish to reserve our opinion whether the decision in _Woollerton & Wilson Ltd v. Richard Costain Ltd_ [1970] 1 W.L.R. 411 was correct. Neither counsel seemed to think that it was. I therefore think that this must be a case where Homer nodded, and that that case cannot be relied upon so far as suspension is concerned. And I think the reason it cannot be relied upon was well illustrated by Mr Munby in his submissions to me when he said that in a sense, when one is dealing with the direct physical invasion of a right of property by trespass one is very close to the line of cases stemming from _Doherty v. Allman_ (1878) 3 App.Cas. 709, which decide that an injunction to enforce a negative stipulation in a contract goes almost of course. The parties, having agreed that something shall not be done, the court simply says that what the parties have agreed shall not be done.'"

6. Taking another perspective—what if the application had been _quia timet_? Walton J. said at 152:

"The matter can be tested, I think, very simply in this way. Supposing that instead of putting up that scaffolding, as the second defendants doubtless did, taking their time about it in the normal way, supposing they had signalled notice of their intention well in advance so that it was quite clear what was going to happen if it was not restrained, and the plaintiffs had applied to the court for an injunction _quia timet_; what conceivable ground could have been put forward by the defendants in answer to the claim for such an injunction? There is not the faintest shadow of reason they could have advanced why they should not be restrained from committing the trespass. Can it then be any better that they have actually committed it? Does the fact of their having committed it and it being, I doubt not from a structural point of view and commercially, highly advantageous to them that they should be able to go on and complete their building, make the matter better from their point of view? Does that give them any right at all to have a suspension of the injunction which, if the plaintiffs had been able to come realising what was going to happen earlier, they would have got without the faintest difficulty at all? The answer must clearly be 'No,' there can be no conceivable reason for any such postponement at all."

8 *Laws v. Florinplace Ltd* [1981] 1 All E.R. 659

1. The facts The defendants opened a "sex" establishment in the immediate vicinity of a residential enclave in a commercial area of London. The plaintiffs brought proceedings in nuisance and sought interlocutory relief.

2. Was there a serious issue to be tried? Yes—after evidence from the plaintiffs and, *inter alia*, from a "behavioural psychotherapist" on behalf of the defendants, and also the dicta of Lord Evershed M.R. in *Thompson-Schwab v. Costaki* [1956] 1 W.L.R. 335 at 339. In arriving at his conclusion on this issue, Vinelott J. said at 665J, 667C–D:

> "Lord Evershed M.R. did not have in mind the danger that the plaintiffs might suffer material inconvenience by being accosted or the danger that criminals and other undesirable people might be attracted into the immediate neighbourhood... Further, I cannot disregard the fact that, however discreetly conducted, the business will, in fact, be the sale of hard pornography and will be a business deeply repugnant to the reasonable sensibilities of most ordinary men and women... Lastly, the argument founded on the defendants' evidence as to the character of 80 per cent of the customers even if it transpired to be correct, means that there are a substantial number of others, 20 per cent, some of whom may be, or are likely to be, persons who are unbalanced and perhaps perverted and who would be an embarrassment and might be a danger to visitors and residents. That risk is not, I think, one which can be easily brushed aside."

3. Balance of convenience

(a) *Damages—an adequate remedy to the defendants, particularly by virtue of their expertise:*

990

"I turn, therefore, to consider the balance of convenience. Counsel for the defendants accepted, rightly I think, that the damage that would be suffered by the defendants if an interlocutory injunction were granted, and if it were held at the trial that the plaintiffs were not entitled to injunctive relief, would not extend beyond the loss of profit which the defendants might otherwise have earned, and that the plaintiffs are persons from whom such damages, when assessed, would be recoverable. He submitted the loss of profit may be difficult to ascertain if the business is closed at a time when it has no record of profit on which an assessment can be based. I find that argument unconvincing. The defendants are, and assert that they are, experienced in this trade and there should be no real difficulty in estimating profits that might have been earned by reference to earnings in similar establishments. Further, this is not a case where the defendants will suffer irreparable and possibly unquantifiable damage to goodwill by the loss of momentum in the promotion of a new business, the launching of which is delayed by an interim injunction." (at 667F–G.)

(b) *Damages—not an adequate remedy to the plaintiffs:*

"On the one hand, therefore, it seems to me that the damage might be suffered by the defendants by the grant of interim relief which is afterwards found to be unjustified is quantifiable and will be recoverable. On the other hand, there are features which, to my mind favour the grant of interim relief, notwithstanding the undertakings that have been offered. First, the plaintiffs know the nature of the business carried on. They have seen, as I have, some of the hard pornography which is purveyed and they feel, to my mind reasonably, a profound repugnance at the possibility that such a trade will continue to be carried on on their very doorstep. I do not think I should lightly compel them to accept the continued existence of this trade, however discreetly conducted, until the trial. Second, there must be a danger that in such a small residential area, which is, as it were, perched insecurely on the edge of the environs of Victoria Station, the continued existence of this business will slowly and insensibly erode the quality of the immediate neighbourhood, even during the period between now and the trial." (at 667H–J.)

4. Special factors Although not expressly referring to *Cyanamid* special factors, Vinelott J. also threw into balance the "criminal" feature, at p. 668A–C:

"Last, I am, I think, entitled to bear in mind that the business which the defendants carry on, and which will be stopped if an injunction

991

is granted, is one which operates at least near the boundary of the criminal law. The material I have seen is, I think, patently capable of corrupting and depraving any ordinary member of the public into whose hands it might come. Some has been seized by the police and a prosecution is, I understand, pending. The defence, as I understand it, will be that those persons who resort to the shop and ask for the hidden material, and who are therefore, the only persons likely to read, see or hear this material, are persons who are mature and aware of the nature of the material they are buying, and therefore, unlikely to be corrupted or depraved by it. The question whether that is so or not will in due course be a question for a jury to decide, but I think I am entitled to weigh in the scales the fact that the trade that will be interrupted by an injunction is one of selling material of a kind which is, in the ordinary sense of the word obscene, even though its sale may not involve the commission of a criminal offence, if the particular defence to which I have referred is ultimately established."

The only realistic justification for this judicial approach is that there was no substantial dispute on the affidavit evidence.

9 *Redler Grain Silos Ltd v. B.I.C.C. Ltd* [1982] 1 Lloyd's Rep. 435, C.A.

1. The facts Pursuant to a construction contract which the plaintiffs had with the Iranian authorities, it purchased a large quantity of electrical cable and equipment from the defendants which was to be shipped to Iran and paid for under a divisible letter of credit that the Iranian authorities had supplied to the plaintiffs. The Iranian authorities thereafter sought to terminate the construction contract, whereupon the plaintiffs paid the defendants from their own resources, without recourse to the letter of credit. Throughout, the defendants retained possession of the equipment initially acknowledging the plaintiffs as owners but subsequently purporting to acknowledge either the plaintiffs or the Iranian authorities as owner.

2. What was the defendants' motive? The motive behind the defendants' apparent volte face was a fear of Iranian sanctions against them if the equipment was not delivered.

3. The plaintiffs' riposte The plaintiffs issued proceedings in conversion and sought by way of interlocutory relief an order under the provisions of R.S.C., Ord. 29, r. 2 for the preservation of the property.

4. The Court of Appeal granted the relief—why? The ruling of Kerr L.J. has two limbs:

(a) The ordinary case was where the defendants had some prima facie propriety or possessory claim to the goods which the plaintiffs sought to recover or to preserve. In the case before the court the defendants did not seek to raise any such claim but by resisting the injunction sought to deprive the plaintiffs of the right to ask the court at trial to exercise its discretion (on the assumption that the plaintiffs succeeded) between awarding delivery or damages under section 3(2)(a) of the Torts (Interference with Goods) Act 1977.

(b) It was settled law that the English courts would not recognise anything in the nature of penal or confiscatory measures on the part of a foreign government as would affect proprietary rights in assets situated in England. There was nothing before the court which supported, on any basis recognised by English law, the Iranian claim to ownership or possession and the Iranian authorities had not sought to make any representations to the court as they easily could have done.

5. Distinguishing *Cyanamid* Stephenson L.J. highlighted the contrast between the instant case and *American Cyanamid* in the following terms:

"I do not think that the House of Lords in the *American Cyanamid* case had in mind a case of this exceptional kind, where a defendant is not asserting any right of his own against the plaintiff and the plaintiff could have applied for an order for detention or preservation of property, or for delivery up of the goods, under either rule 2 or rule 2A of Order 29 of the Rules of the Supreme Court." (at 440–441.)

10 *Anchor Brewhouse Developments Ltd v. Berkley House (Docklands Developments) Ltd* [1987] 2 EGLR 173; (1987) 284 EG 173

1. The facts The defendants were the owners of a development site south of Tower Bridge and they or their contractors were using a number of tower cranes. These cranes swung, either freely or on operational use, over the plaintiffs' land. The plaintiffs suffered no damage, but applied for interlocutory injunctions to prevent the trespasses.

2. Not an *American Cyanamid* **case** Scott J. said:

"In my view, the defendant is committing trespass by its use of its oversailing cranes. This is not a case, in my judgment, in which there is any issue on liability which must await trial. It is not a case, therefore, in which balance of convenience as to what should be done

993

at this interlocutory stage is relevant. The plaintiffs are, in my judgment, entitled now to the injunctive relief to which, in accordance with the view of the law that I take, they would be entitled at trial."

3. The defendants' rejected submissions The defendants put forward four special circumstances at 177M–178E:

"I do not think [counsel for the defendants'] point that the trespass is causing no harm is a sound one except in the sense that the oversailing booms are causing no physical harm or interference with present plans. One of the rights of an owner of property is the right to allow others on terms acceptable to the owner to use the property; another right is the right to prevent others from using the property. The use by the defendant of the oversailing cranes deprives the plaintiffs of these rights. It deprives the plaintiffs of the right to bargain as they wish for the grant of rights over their property. It is not, in my view, accurate to say that no harm is being done to the plaintiffs by the trespassing cranes. ...

[Counsel for the defendants'] second point is that the tower cranes stand high above the ground and their oversailing booms do not interfere with any ordinary use of the plaintiffs' properties. That, as a fact, I accept. But if, as I think, the booms are trespassing, their height above the ground is not, in my view, a special circumstance of any relevance.

Third [counsel for the defendants] submitted that the defendant, if it was trespassing by its use of tower cranes with oversailing booms, was trespassing through inadvertence and not culpably. I am not impressed by that point. ... Ever since the judgment of Stamp J. in *Woollerton and Wilson v. Costain* ([1970] 1 W.L.R. 411), which was reported in 1970, developers have been on notice of the potential risks arising from trespass from oversailing cranes.

Finally, a special circumstance relied on by [counsel for the defendants] was that each of the plaintiffs had stood by and allowed the tower cranes to be built and used without complaint. ... In my opinion, however, an owner of land against whom no more can be said than that he has not intervened to prevent a neighbour from erecting a tower crane on the neighbour's land, does not thereby lose the right to claim an injunction to prevent the cranes from trespassing."

11 *Attorney-General v. Barker and Another* [1990] 3 All E.R. 257

1. Background The first defendant and his publishing company (of which he was sole director and company secretary) wished to publish a book,

Courting Disaster, about his experiences whilst a member of the royal household. In doing so he was compelled to admit that he was acting in flagrant breach of his contractual undertaking not to do so. The facts are set out more fully on p. 950 above.

2. Did *Cyanamid* apply? Lord Donaldson M.R. (and Parker L.J., who agreed with his judgment) purported to apply *Cyanamid*, although the exercise did not take very long. But Nourse L.J. treated it as a case where the principles to be applied at the hearing for a final injunction were so clear-cut that you do not ask if there is a serious issue to be tried, but its *converse*:

> "In a case where the validity of the covenant cannot sensibly be attacked it is difficult to see what practical difference there can be at the interlocutory stage. Applying the converse of the *American Cyanamid* principles to the present case, I would say that there is no real prospect that the first defendant will succeed in resisting the grant of a perpetual injunction at the trial. On that footing an injunction ought to be granted until that time."

3. The defendants argued there was a public policy defence Nourse L.J. dismissed the suggestion of a public policy defence thus:

> "What then is said to be so special about the present case? Counsel for the defendants submits that at the trial it will be open to the first defendant to contend that the undertaking is void on grounds of public policy. He submits that it is contrary to public policy for the English court to make an order whose effect would be to decide what people abroad may or may not read. That, he says, is something which ought to be left to the decision of the local courts.
>
> I know of no principle of our law by which that submission can be supported. A valid covenant restricting freedom of expression abroad is just as much enforceable as a valid covenant restricting freedom of action abroad, for example a valid covenant in restraint of trade. True it is that the local courts may or may not enforce the covenant if it is sued on in the foreign country. But that has nothing at all to do with the question whether it is or is not right for the English court to grant an injunction to restrain a breach of a worldwide undertaking entered into in an English contract between persons who are amenable to the jurisdiction of the English court."

12 *Waverley Borough Council v. Hilden* [1988] 1 W.L.R. 246

1. The background Gypsies had bought some land and proceeded to lay it out as an encampment for gypsy caravans. Hardcore was laid and pitches were sold to individual gypsies. Planning permission was required for the change of use and for the works, but not obtained. The Council issued four enforcement notices requiring discontinuance of the use of the land as a caravan site and removal of the hardcore.

2. The relief sought The Council brought proceedings under section 222(1) of the Local Government Act 1972 for injunctions in support of their enforcement notices, and applied for those injunctions to be granted interlocutorily.

3. The key to the judge's approach Scott J. did not mention the *Cyanamid* principles—perhaps because it was obvious that the balance of convenience test would be overwhelmingly in the defendants' favour, so that the only way in which the Council could succeed was by invoking a "special factor", in particular that there was no real dispute because there was no real defence. The judge put the issue thus:

> "I have already remarked that the relief sought on motion is the same relief as is ought in the action. Mr Katkowski accepts that in order to obtain this relief on motion the council must satisfy me that the defendants have no arguable defence. If there is no arguable defence then, he submits, correctly in my opinion, the balance of convenience is irrelevant and the council should be granted now the injunctions to which it would be entitled at trial: see *Manchester Corporation v. Connolly* [1970] Ch. 420."

4. The gypsies' main defence—*Wednesbury* unreasonableness The defendants argued that the Council's decision to institute these civil proceedings was *Wednesbury* unreasonable, but the judge held that whilst that may provide grounds for judicial review, it was not a defence to the action.

> "In the present case the council's decision to institute and prosecute this action in its own name is open to challenge. But the defendants' allegation that the decision was unreasonable in a *Wednesbury* sense is not an allegation of a defence to the action. It is an allegation first that the action was commenced without proper authority and, second, that the council lacks *locus standi* to bring this action in its own name. An attack of this nature ought, in my view, to be conducted by means of judicial review procedure."

5. Since no defence, did that mean an injunction granted? Although the judge found no arguable defence, special principles applied to injunctions in aid of the criminal law:

> "Injunctions in aid of the criminal law are remedies of last resort. They ought not to be granted if other less Draconian means of securing obedience to the law are available."

Section 91 of the Town and Country Planning Act 1971 enables planning authorities themselves to take steps to remedy non-compliance with enforcement notices. This meant that *some* of the injunctions the plaintiffs applied for could be carried out by the plaintiffs pursuant to their section 91 power—for example, removing the hardcore. But it would be impractical for the Council to use that power to discontinue the use of the land as a caravan site. The judge therefore made only that order interlocutorily—though he suspended it for three months to allow the defendants a reasonable time to comply.

M: DOCUMENTARY CREDITS AND PERFORMANCE BONDS

1 Introduction

1. What contractual relationships are locked into a documentary credit? There are four, namely (in the context, for example, of a contract for the sale of goods):
   (a) "The underlying contract for the sale of goods, to which the only parties are the buyer and seller."
   (b) "The contract between the buyer and the issuing bank under which the latter agrees to issue the credit and either itself or through a confirming bank to notify the credit to the seller and to make payments to or to the order of the seller (or to pay, accept or negotiate bills of exchange drawn by the seller) against presentation of stipulated documents; and the buyer agrees to reimburse the issuing bank for payment made under the credit. For such reimbursement the stipulated documents, if they include a document of title such as a bill of lading, constitute a security available to the issuing bank."
   (c) "If payment is to be made through a confirming bank the contract between the issuing bank and the confirming bank authorising and requiring the latter to make such payment and to remit the stipulated documents to the issuing bank, when they are received, the issuing bank in turn agreeing to reimburse the confirming bank for payments made under the credit."

997

(d) "The contract between the confirming bank and the seller under which the confirming bank undertakes to pay to the seller (or to accept or negotiate without recourse to drawer, bills of exchange drawn by him) up to the amount of the credit against presentation of the stipulated document." (*Per* Lord Diplock in *United City Merchants (Investments) Ltd v. Royal Bank of Canada* [1983] A.C. 168 at 182–184).

2. Rationale of the documentary credit Lord Diplock went on to explain at 183D–G:

"Again, it is trite law that in contact, with which alone the instant appeal is directly concerned, the parties to it, the seller and the confirming bank, 'deal in documents and not in goods,' as article 8 of the Uniform Customs puts it. If, on their face, the documents presented to the confirming bank by the seller conform with the requirements of the credit as notified to him by the confirming bank, that bank is under a contractual obligation to the seller to honour the credit, notwithstanding that the bank has knowledge that the seller at the time of presentation of the conforming documents is alleged by the buyer to have, and in fact has, already, committed a breach of his contract with the buyer for the sale of the goods to which the documents appear on their face to relate, that would have entitled the buyer to treat the contract of sale as rescinded and to reject the goods and refuse to pay the seller the purchase price. The whole commercial purpose for which the system of confirmed irrevocable documentary credits has been developed in international trade is to give to the seller an assured right to be paid before he parts with control of the goods that does not permit of any dispute with the buyer as to the performance of the contract of sale being used as a ground for non-payment or reduction or deferment of payment."

In other words, the very *raison d'être* of the documentary credit is its autonomy—the seller's right to payment by the confirming bank is not dependent upon the buyer's right against the seller under the terms of the contract for the sale of goods—because of the terms of that contract, the confirming bank will have no knowledge.

3. The effect of the Uniform Customs and Practice for Documentary Credits (1974) revision of the International Chamber of Commerce The following parties to the contracts locked into a documentary credit transaction owe a particular duty, in relation to the documents in which they deal:

(a) As between the confirming bank and the issuing bank.
(b) As between the issuing bank and the buyer.

(c) As between the confirming bank and the seller.

4. What is that duty? It is to examine with reasonable care all documents presented in order to ascertain that they appear on their face to be in accordance with the terms and conditions of the credit, and, if they do so appear to pay to the seller/beneficiary by whom the documents have been presented the sum stipulated by the credit, or to accept or negotiate without recourse to drawer drafts drawn by the seller/beneficiary if the credit so provides.

5. Practical effect of the operation of that duty Pursuant to article 9 of the Uniform Customs, confirming banks and issuing banks assume no liability or responsibility to one another or to the buyer "for the form, sufficiency, accuracy, genuineness, falsification or legal effect of any document." Thus in *Gian Singh & Co. Ltd v. Banque de l'Indochine* [1974] 1 W.L.R. 1234, the customer was held liable to reimburse the issuing bank for honouring a documentary credit upon presentation of an apparently conforming document which was an ingenious forgery—a fact that the bank had not been negligent in failing to detect upon examination of the document.

6. Injunction proceedings—in any event, usually misconceived This point arose in *Discount Records Ltd v. Barclays Bank Ltd* [1975] 1 W.L.R. 315. The plaintiff buyers signed instructions to the first defendants for a documentary credit with full cash cover, the credit being made through the second defendants. On the day on which the credit was taken out the second defendants sent telex instructions to the third bank directing the opening of an irrevocable credit with the fourth bank. By its original motion against the first two banks, the plaintiffs sought an injunction restraining the following:

> "(i) Paying a draft drawn upon them or either of them in the sum of 44,175 French francs being equivalent to or alternatively 4,000 pounds sterling by Promodisc S.A./BYG Records, their servants or agents, and/or (ii) paying out either to Promodisc S.A./BYG Records or to Discount Bank or to any party at all any sums pursuant to the irrevocable credit requested by the plaintiffs to be opened on their behalf by the first and/or second defendants in favour of Promodisc S.A./BYG Records."

Megarry J. without demur, appeared unreservedly to have accepted the arguments advanced by counsel for the defendants at 319:

> "For his part Mr Thomas did not seek to deal with the points on fraud or a lack of correspondence between the goods and the documents. His case was that the claim for an injunction was misconceived. He said

that what would happen was this. Somewhere there is a bill of exchange which has already been accepted by the Discount Bank. That bill may well have been negotiated; it may indeed have passed into the hands of a holder in due course. That bill will be presented for payment and the Discount Bank is due to pay it on July 20. The Discount Bank will then debit Barclays Bank S.A. Barclays Bank S.A. will then debit the second defendants and the second defendants will the debit the first defendants. The injunction against the two defendants, if granted, would not achieve Mr Pain's avowed purpose, which was to prevent Promodisc from being paid. Promodisc, indeed, may already have obtained payment by discounting the bill. All that the injunction would do would be to prevent the banks concerned from honouring their obligations. As regards the two defendants (as distinct from whatever claim there may be against Promodisc) the plaintiffs' only real claim, Mr Thomas said, was against the first defendants alone, and there was, and could be, no suggestion that the first defendants were not good for the money."

This theme of damages being an adequate remedy is referred to in the dicta of Kerr L.J. in *Harbottle (R. D.) (Mercantile) Ltd v. National Westminster Ltd* [1978] Q.B. 146 at 155B–D:

"However, let it be assumed in the plaintiffs' favour that these considerations would not by themselves preclude the court from continuing injunctions against the bank. The plaintiffs then still face what seems to me an insuperable difficulty. They are seeking to prevent the bank from paying and debiting their account. It must then follow that if the bank pays and debits the plaintiffs' account, it is either entitled to do so or not entitled to do so. To do so would either be in accordance with the bank's contract with the plaintiffs or a breach of it. If it is in accordance with the contract, then the plaintiffs have no cause of action against the bank and, it seems to me, no possible basis for an injunction against it. Alternatively, if the threatened payment is in breach of contract, which the plaintiffs' writs do not even allege and as to which they claim no declaratory relief, then the plaintiffs would have good claims for damages against the bank. In that event the injunctions would be inappropriate, because they interfere with the bank's obligations to the Egyptian banks, because they might cause greater damage to the bank than the plaintiffs could pay on their undertakings as to damages, and because the plaintiffs would then have an adequate remedy in damages. The balance of convenience would in that event be hopelessly weighed against the plaintiffs."

As a fact, the consignment constituted not records—but rubbish. The unresolved question arises—could not that fraud have unravelled all?

2 Fraud

1. The fraud exception Again, *per* Lord Diplock at 183G–184B in *United City Merchants (Investments) Ltd v. Royal Bank of Canada* [1983] 1 A.C. 168:

> "To this general statement of principle as to the contractual obligations of the confirming bank to the seller, there is one established exception: that is, where the seller, for the purpose of drawing on the credit, fraudulently presents to the confirming bank documents that contain, expressly or by implication, material representations of fact that to his knowledge are untrue. Although there does not appear among the English authorities any case in which this exception has been applied, it is well established in the American cases of which the leading or 'landmark' case is *Sztejn v. Henry (J.) Schroder Banking Corporation* (1941) 31 N.Y.S. 2d 631. This judgment of the New York Court of Appeals was referred to with approval by the English Court of Appeal in *Edward Owen Engineering Ltd v. Barclays Bank International Ltd* [1978] Q.B. 159, though this was actually a case about a performance bond under which a bank assumes obligations to a buyer analogous to those assumed by a confirming bank to the seller under a documentary credit. The exception for fraud on the part of the beneficiary seeking to avail himself of the credit is a clear application of the maxim *ex turpi causa non oritur actio* or, if plain English is to be preferred, 'fraud unravels all.' The courts will not allow their process to be used by a dishonest person to carry out a fraud."

And also see *Etablissement Esefka International Anstalt v. Central Bank of Nigeria* [1979] 1 Lloyd's Rep. 445, where such a fraud was discussed in the context of a *Mareva* application.

2. What if the documents were not necessarily a nullity—but a forgery? Lord Diplock said at 188A–B:

> "I would prefer to leave open the question of the rights of an innocent seller/beneficiary against the confirming bank when a document presented by him is a nullity because unknown to him it was forged by some third party; for that question does not arise in the instant case. The bill of lading with the wrong date of loading placed on it by the carrier's agent was far from being a nullity. It was a valid transferable receipt for the goods giving the holder a right to claim them at their

1001

destination, Callao, and was evidence of the terms of the contract under which they were being carried."

3. How do you prove fraud? In *Owen (Edward) Engineering Ltd v. Barclays Bank International Ltd* [1978] Q.B. 159 Browne L.J. said:

"It is certainly not enough to allege fraud; it must be 'established,' and in such circumstances I should say very clearly established."

And on the facts, Geoffrey Lane L.J. said:

"I disagree that that amounts to any proof or evidence of fraud. It may be suspicious, it may indicate the possibility of sharp practice, but there is nothing in those facts remotely approaching true evidence of fraud or anything which makes fraud obvious or clear to the bank."

4. Only the risk of future fraud is relevant Plaintiffs are not entitled to an injunction restraining a bank making payments under an irrevocable letter of credit on the ground of fraud where they could not show that a further fraudulent demand would be made notwithstanding that fraudulent demands had already been made: *Tukan Timber Ltd v. Barclays Bank plc* [1987] 1 Lloyd's Rep. 171. In that case the plaintiffs were engaged in the timber trade with a Brazilian company. At the plaintiffs' request the defendants issued a letter of credit in favour of the Brazilian company that included provision for advance payment upon receipt by the defendants of a simple receipt from the Brazilian company countersigned by a director of the plaintiffs. The letter of credit was issues in substitution for earlier letters of credit. The Brazilian company had threatened to issue receipts to obtain advance payments using signatures of the plaintiffs' directors supplied previously for other purposes. The new letter of credit provided for different signatures from the directors of the plaintiffs. After the issue of the letter, on two occasions the Brazilian company sought advance payments using receipts countersigned by a director of the plaintiffs in its original as opposed to new form. The defendants refused to pay the Brazilian company. The plaintiffs commenced proceedings against the defendants and sought an interlocutory injunction to restrain the defendants from making any advance payments under the letter of credit. On the facts, Hirst J. held that there was a heavy burden of proof on the plaintiffs to show that there was fraud on the part of the Brazilian company. The second attempt to obtain an advance payment was only consistent with fraud. Notwithstanding that, the relief sought would not be granted because the plaintiffs had failed to show that a further fraudulent demand for advance payment would be made using signatures in the new form. In any event, it would not be a proper case in which to grant an interlocutory injunction because the damage the defendants might sustain to their reputation could not be properly compensated by the plaintiffs if the injunction should not have been granted. He said, *inter alia*:

"It is of course very clearly established by the authorities that a letter of credit is autonomous, that the bank is not concerned in any way with the merits or demerits of the underlying transaction, and only in the most extremely exceptional circumstances should the court interfere with the paying bank honouring a letter of credit in accordance with its terms bearing in mind the importance of the free and unrestricted flow of normal commercial dealings. The importance of the free and unrestricted flow of normal commercial dealings. The importance of these aspects to banks generally and to Barclays Bank in particular in the present case are very clearly and fairly spelt out in the passage from Mr Pardy's affidavit which I have quoted.

As stated in the leading case of *Edward Owen Engineering Ltd v. Barclays Bank International Ltd* [1978] 1 Lloyd's Rep. 166; [1978] Q.B. 159, only if the bank has notice of a clear fraud committed by the beneficiary is the court entitled to interfere. ...

This seems to me to be manifestly a crude and plainly dishonest attempt to get round the difficulties encountered with the first receipt. I am therefore prepared to hold that the only realistic inference is that Unibanco S.A. could not have honestly believed that this document purportedly emanating from its subsidiary, Unibanco Trading S.A., was valid, and that this is known to the bank.

If therefore Barclays were intending to honour the red clause in the letter of credit on the strength of this second receipt, I should have been prepared to hold that this was one of those very, very rare cases wherein the strict burden of proof was satisfied subject of course to the overriding discretionary aspects. But Barclays is not going to pay on this second receipt.

What is in issue in the ultimate analysis is whether the plaintiffs have proved, with the high burden which rests upon them, that a yet further demand will be made on the strength of a yet further fraudulent receipt bearing the purported signature of Mr Franklin in its new form.

This in my judgment is a fatal difficulty to the plaintiffs here also. Indeed, I think it much more probable that Unibanco and/or Unibanco Trading, having been twice bitten, will be thrice shy, particularly as they would then have to produce a different signature for Mr Franklin. Thus in my judgment the plaintiffs have failed to clear the first hurdle. ...

May I say in conclusion that I think it most improbable that the loss of this application will do any practical harm to the plaintiffs. It is quite obvious that Barclays, having been twice put on enquiry, will exercise the very utmost circumspection before honouring an

1003

application based on a third receipt or purported receipt, in the unlikely event that such is submitted, bearing the new form of signature of Mr Franklin."

3 Analogous commercial transactions

1. Documentary credit and performance bonds The parallel between documentary credit and performance bonds was highlighted in *Potton Homes Ltd v. Coleman Contractors* (1984) 81 L.S.Gaz. 1044. There, the plaintiff sellers unsuccessfully sought to restrain the defendant buyers from making a demand upon the performance bond for £68,816 given under the sale contract for the supply of prefabricated building units in Libya. Although the defendant had failed to pay part of the purchase price, Eveleigh L.J. held that despite the wide powers afforded to the court under section 37 of the Supreme Court Act 1981, "the plaintiffs could raise no objection to a demand upon the bonds." One of the objects of giving the bond was that the defendants should be entitled to obtain the money without first establishing any breach of contract by the plaintiffs. The court should not order what in effect would be a variation of the parties' agreement in relation to the bond. May L.J. went on to say:

> "The defendants' entitlement to payment under the bond was not within the scope and proper construction of Order 29. Notwithstanding the court's wide powers under section 37, as the circumstances did not justify the grant of a *Mareva* injunction, the judge erred in attempting to freeze the proceeds of the bond."

As Lord Denning M.R. said in *Edward Owen Engineering Ltd v. Barclays Bank International Ltd (ibid.)*:

> "The performance guarantee stands on a similar footing to a letter of credit. A bank which gives a performance guarantee must honour that guarantee according to its terms. It is not concerned in the least with the relations between the supplier and the customer; nor with the question whether the supplier has performed his contracted obligation or not; nor with the question whether the supplier is in default or not. The bank must pay according to its guarantee, on demand, if so stipulated, without proof or conditions."

2. The documentary credit/guarantee interface In *Harbottle (R. D.) (Mercantile) Ltd v. National Westminster Bank Ltd* [1978] Q.B. 146 the plaintiff sellers as part of the sale contract negotiations with the defendants, agreed to establish a guarantee confirmed by a bank at five per cent of the price in favour of the buyers. As Kerr J. said at 149:

"These were in effect to be performance bonds. They were called guarantees *simpliciter*, but their purpose was to provide security to the buyers for the fulfilment by the plaintiffs of their obligations under the contracts. They were to be established with the respective Egyptian banks. The machinery was that the plaintiffs instructed the bank to confirm the guarantees to the respective Egyptian bank, which therefore became the bank's correspondent in Egypt for this purpose. The Egyptian banks in turn confirmed the guarantees to the buyers. The guarantees were backed by counter-indemnities by the plaintiffs to the bank. The plaintiffs agreed to indemnify the bank in the widest terms and gave authority for payment under the guarantees and to debit the plaintiffs' account accordingly."

The guarantee simply provided that payment would be made on the buyers' "first demand" without any safeguard. Momentarily, perhaps, disconcerted, Kerr J. explained the rationale, at 150A–C:

"Performance guarantees in such unqualified terms seem astonishing, but I am told that they are by no means unusual, particularly in transactions with customers in the Middle East. In effect, the sellers rely on the probity and reputation of their buyers and on their good relations with them. But this trust is inevitably sometimes abused, and I understand that such guarantees are sometimes drawn upon, partly or wholly, without any or any apparent justification, almost as though they represented a discount in favour of the buyers. In such cases the sellers are then left merely with claims for breaches of contract against their buyers and the difficulty of establishing and enforcing such claims."

4 The Practice Note of the Master of the Rolls

Sir John Donaldson M.R. in *Bolivinter Oil SA v. Chase Manhattan Bank NA* [1984] 1 W.L.R. 392 gave the following Practice Note:

"*Injunction—Interlocutory—Irrevocable credit—Ex parte injunctions—Circumstances in which such injunctions to be granted to restrain bankers from paying under terms of letter of credit*

INTERLOCUTORY APPEAL from Staughton J.

By contract of affreightment dated June 8, 1982 the plaintiffs Bolivinter Oil S.A., agreed to transport a cargo of crude oil for the third defendant, the General Company of Homs refinery, from Iran to Syria. The plaintiffs also agreed to furnish the third defendant with a bank guarantee for U.S. 1 million dollars, the plaintiffs requested the first

1005

defendant, Chase Manhattan Bank N.A., to arrange the guarantee. In consequence the second defendant, the Commercial Bank of Syria gave a guarantee of U.S. 1 million dollars to the third defendant and the first defendant opened an irrevocable letter of credit in favour of the second defendant. Disputes over the performance of the contract arose between the plaintiffs and the third defendant and subsequent to the issue of a writ the plaintiffs on October 31, 1983 obtained *ex parte* injunctions (1) restraining the third defendant from claiming on the guarantee; (2) restraining the second defendant from paying under that guarantee or claiming on the letter of credit; and (3) restraining the first defendant from paying under the letter of credit.

On November 30, 1983 after an *inter partes* hearing the judge discharged the injunctions against the first and second defendants. By a notice of appeal dated December 5, 1983 the plaintiffs appealed. The judgment on the appeal does not call for report.

December 9, Sir John Donaldson M.R. handed down the judgment of the court which stated the court's reasons for dismissing the appeal and continued: Before leaving this appeal, we should like to add a word about the circumstances in which an *ex parte* injunction should be issued which prohibits a bank from paying under an irrevocable letter of credit or a purchase bond or guarantee. The unique value of such a letter, bond or guarantee is that the beneficiary can be completely satisfied that whatever disputes may thereafter arise between him and the bank's customer in relation to the performance or indeed existence of the underlying contract, the bank is personally undertaking to pay him provided that the specified conditions are met. In requesting his bank to issue such a letter, bond or guarantee, the customer is seeking to take advantage of this unique characteristic. If, save in the most exceptional cases, he is to be allowed to derogate from the bank's personal and irrevocable undertaking, given be it again noted at his request, by obtaining an injunction restraining the bank from honouring that undertaking, he will undermine what is the bank's greatest asset, however large and rich it may be, namely its reputation for financial and contractual probity. Furthermore, if this happens at all frequently, the value of all irrevocable letters of credit and performance bonds and guarantees will be undermined.

Judges who are asked, often at short notice and *ex parte*, to issue an injunction restraining payment by a bank under an irrevocable letter of credit or performance bond or guarantee should ask whether there is any challenge to the validity of the letter, bond or guarantee itself. If there is not or if the challenge is not substantial, prima facie no injunction should be granted and the bank should be left free to honour its contractual obligation, although restrictions may well be imposed upon the freedom of the beneficiary to deal with the money after he has received it. The wholly exceptional case where an injunction may be granted is where it is proved that the bank knows that any demand for payment already made or which may thereafter be made will clearly be fraudulent. But the evidence must be clear, both as to the fact of fraud and as to the bank's knowledge. It would certainly not normally be sufficient that this rests upon the uncorroborated statement of the customer, for irreparable damage can be done to a bank's credit in the relatively brief time which must elapse between the granting of such an injunction and an application by the bank to have it discharged. The appeal will be dismissed."

N: CONTRACTS FOR PERSONAL SERVICES

1 *Warren v. Mendy* [1989] 3 All E.R. 103

1. The background Mr Frank Warren had been manager of a boxer Mr Nigel Benn under a management agreement which included a clause whereby Mr Benn agreed to be exclusively managed and directed by Mr Warren. Within a few months Mr Benn had become disillusioned with Mr Warren's management and asked Mr Ambrose Mendy to act as his agent and adviser on matters concerning his career.

2. The novelty of the case Instead of suing Mr Benn, thereby to prevent him going elsewhere for management, Mr Warren brought proceedings against his rival Mr Mendy alleging that he had induced a breach of the management agreement. Mr Warren applied for an interlocutory injunction.

3. The relief sought Mr Warren sought injunctions restraining Mr Mendy from inducing a breach by Mr Benn of his management contract, and, *inter alia*, from acting as Mr Benn's agent or manager in respect of boxing activities and other related engagements.

4. The principle It is well settled that an injunction to restrain a breach of contract for personal services will not be granted where the effect is to order performance of the contract.

5. At first instance Phillips J., in considering whether to grant the injunctions, asked himself if the effect of their being granted would be to compel Mr Benn to perform the obligation imposed on him by the management agreement to be exclusively managed by Mr Warren. He refused an interlocutory injunction on the ground that it would have that effect.

6. On appeal The Court of Appeal (Purchas, Nourse and Stuart-Smith L.JJ.) dismissed the appeal, stating that even in this novel context of an action against the third party rather than the "servant", injunctive relief ought usually to be refused against the third party if on the evidence its effect would be to compel performance of the contract.

7. An added comment Nourse L.J. giving the judgment of the Court, said that the Court had in mind that an injunction was a discretionary remedy, particularly at the interlocutory stage, and that the discretion was to be exercised by the judge of first instance. That discretion could not be faulted.

O: PLANNING

1 *Runnymede Borough Council v. Harwood* [1994] EGCS 23

1. The background The defendant made applications for planning permission to change the use of part of a farm in Surrey to use (a) for residential purposes and (b) for repairs to commercial vehicles. While his planning applications were pending, he went ahead with the conversion to residential use and his family moved in.

2. The law By section 187B of the Town and Country Planning Act 1990:
  "(1) Where a local planning authority consider it necessary or expedient
      for any actual or apprehended breach of planning control to be
      restrained by injunction, they may apply to the court for an
      injunction, whether or not they have exercised or are proposing to
      exercise any of their other powers under this Part.
  (2) On an application under subsection (1) the court may grant such
      an injunction as the court thinks appropriate for the purpose of
      restraining the breach."

3. Did *Cyanamid* apply?—at first instance, yes Although the plaintiffs succeeded in obtaining an injunction against the defendant *ex parte*, at the hearing on notice Colman J. discharged it. Colman J. attached particular importance to the fact that the application before him was for interlocutory relief. He was therefore concerned that if by the time of the trial the defendant was no longer using the land for residential purposes it would militate against his chances of resisting injunctions at the trial.

4. On appeal—*Cyanamid* did not apply Dillon L.J. in the Court of Appeal is reported as having said:

"By [section 187B of the 1990 Act] Parliament had granted the Court a clear power to grant injunctions to enforce planning control over actual as well as apprehended breaches of planning control, and it could not have been the intention, where there had been an actual breach, that the power should only be exercisable at the trial of the action, with interlocutory applications confined to preserving the status quo until trial."

5. The twist in the tail But the order made by the Court of Appeal nevertheless did not treat the grant of an interlocutory injunction as automatically following from proof of breach of planning control. The fact that the defendant was appealing the refusal of both planning applications (residential and motor) meant that the Court of Appeal *suspended* the injunction against residence until that planning appeal had been determined.

PART E

Case Digest

All cases digested in this Part relate to Part B which covers:

Cases are listed chapter by chapter and appear in chronological order.

CASE	CITATION	JUDGE(S)	FACTS	ISSUES	ADJUDICATION
Rundell v. Murray	(1821) Jac.311			Plea of acquiescence.	Acquiescence by one of several plaintiffs may preclude interlocutory relief.
Greenhalgh v. Manchester and Birmingham Railway Co.	(1838) 3 My. & Cr. 783; 8 L.J.Ch. 75	Cottenham L.C.	Railway co. empowered by parliament to enter land.	Plea of acquiescence.	Questionable whether plaintiff prejudiced by acquiescence if both parties unaware of material factor.
Saunders v. Smith	(1838) 3 My. & Cr. 711; 7 L.J.Ch. 227			Plea of acquiescence.	Acquiescence by one of several plaintiffs may preclude interlocutory relief.
Hilton v. Earl of Granville	(1841) Cr. & Ph. 283		Application to restrain working of a mine.	Whether defendant could be ordered to make admissions.	Injunction refused on condition defendant made certain admissions.
Gordon v. Cheltenham and Great Western Union Railway Co.	(1842) Beav. 565; 2 Ry. & Can.Cas. 800	Lord Langdale M.R.		Plea of acquiescence.	Defence if plaintiff led to believe violation temporary.

CASE	CITATION	JUDGE(S)	FACTS	ISSUES	ADJUDICATION
Rigby v. Great Western Railway Co.	(1849) 2 Ph. 44.	Cottenham L.C.		Whether defendant may be ordered to keep accounts, pending trial.	Court required defendant to keep accounts pending trial.
Rigby v. Great-Western Railway Co.	As above.			What if injunction is granted and decision turns out to be wrong?	Order framed so that neither party will lose benefit he is entitled to.
Marker v. Marker	(1851) 9 Hare 1; 20 L.J.Ch. 246			Plea of acquiescence.	Acquiescence by one of several plaintiffs may preclude interlocutory relief.
Att.-Gen. v. Council of the Borough of Birmingham	(1858) 4 K. & J. 528; 22 J.P. 561			Plea of acquiescence.	Defence for plaintiff if led to believe by defendant that evil would be remedies.
Ford v. Gye	(1858) 6 W.R. 235		Application to prevent building/demolish building.	Plea of acquiescence.	Defendant required to undertake to abide by any order concerning demolition of structure built after a certain date.

CASE	CITATION	JUDGE(S)	FACTS	ISSUES	ADJUDICATION
Laird v. Birkenhead Railway Co.	(1859) John. 500; 29 L.J.Ch. 218			Plea of acquiescence.	Effect of knowledge/acquiescence same for company as for individual.
Bankart v. Houghton	(1860) 27 Beav. 425; 28 L.J.Ch. 473			Whether defence available to plea of acquiescence.	Plaintiff not barred by acquiescence if it can be accounted for.
Davis v. Marshall	(1861) 10 C.B.(N.S.) 697; 31 L.J.L.P. 61	Erle C.J.		(i) Effect of passive acquiescence by plaintiff. (ii) Whether defence for plea of acquiescence.	(i) Plaintiff need not induce changes in defendant's position for plea of acquiescence. (ii) Defence if defendant falsely represented that injury would not result from his acts.
Newby v. Harrison	(1861) 3 De G.F. & J. 287	Turner L.J.		(i) Nature of undertaking in damages. (ii) Effect of delay.	(i) Undertaking is between party making it and the court. (ii) Inquiry ordered despite delay of four months.

1015

CASE	CITATION	JUDGE(S)	FACTS	ISSUES	ADJUDICATION
Clarke v. Clark	(1864) 13 W.R. 133		Application for injunction.	Whether defendant could give undertaking in lieu of injunction.	Court required defendant to give undertaking.
Wakefield v. Duke of Buccleugh	(1865) 12 L.T. 628			How much investigation of the issues should the court undertake?	Court should refrain from opinion on the merits until the hearing.
Colebourne v. Colebourne	(1876) Ch.D. 690				Plaintiff should indorse writ with claim for injunction.
Bolton v. London School Board	(1878) 7 Ch.D. 766			Duration of interlocutory injunction.	Can be dissolved before date specified but extension requires new order.
Graham v. Campbell	(1878) 7 Ch.D. 490; 47 L.J.Ch. 593	James L.J.		Nature of undertaking in damages.	Except under special circumstances effect ought to be given to the undertaking.
Newcomen v. Coulson	(1878) 2 Ch.D. 764; 47 L.J.Ch. 429	Malins V.-C.	Undertaking in damages. Delay of 11 months.	Whether to order inquiry following delay.	Inquiry ordered.

CASE	CITATION	JUDGE(S)	FACTS	ISSUES	ADJUDICATION
Sturla v. Freccia	(1879) 12 Ch.D. 438; 41 L.T. 173	Cotton L.J. James L.J. Jessel M.R.	Application for *ex parte* injunction to stay all dealings with a fund pending appeal.	Whether Court of Appeal has jurisdiction to grant *ex parte* injunction pending appeal to the House of Lords.	The Court of Appeal has jurisdiction similar in principle to the above.
Re Myers Patent	(1882) 26 S.J. 371				Ideally the exact terms of the order sought should be indorsed on the writ.
Smith v. Day	(1882) 21 Ch.D. 421; 28 W.R. 712	Cotton L.J. Brett L.J. Sir George Jessel M.R.	Undertaking in damages.	(i) Will court always order an inquiry in damages if plaintiffs fail? (ii) Quantum of damages. (iii) When should application for inquiry be made?	(i) Inquiry in damages in the discretion of the court. Trivial loss will not justify inquiry. (ii) Quantum ascertained by analogy to breach of contract/duty claim. (iii) Proper time for application depends on circumstances.
Re Wood, ex p. Hall	(1883) 23 Ch.D. 644		Undertaking in damages.	Whether to order inquiry into damages following delay.	Inquiry refused as a matter of discretion on the ground of delay.

CASE	CITATION	JUDGE(S)	FACTS	ISSUES	ADJUDICATION
Ex p. Abrams	(1884) 50 L.T. 184; 1 Marr. 32			Duration of *ex parte* order in Chancery.	*Ex parte* order in Chancery usually until first motion day for which defendant can be properly served.
Griffith v. Blake	(1884) 27 Ch.D. 474; 53 L.J.Ch. 965	Baggallay L.J. Cotton L.J. Lindley L.J.	Inquiry as to damages following undertaking in damages.	Is it relevant that plaintiff was without fault in his application for injunction?	Fault is irrelevant.
Newson v. Pender	(1884) 27 Ch.D. 43; 52 L.T. 9		Undertaking to prosecute with due diligence by plaintiff.	Whether ancillary order binding the plaintiff should be made.	Ancillary order made as a condition of granting injunction.
Harrison v. McSheehan	[1885] W.N. 207		Undertaking in damages. *Anton Piller* application.	Costs?	It is contrary to the practice of the courts to give as damages the difference between party and party and a higher scale of costs.

CASE	CITATION	JUDGE(S)	FACTS	ISSUES	ADJUDICATION
Green v. Prior	(1886) W.N. 50			(i) Role of affidavit in interlocutory applications. (ii) How "serious" must issue to be tried be? (iii) How much evidence should be adduced?	If affidavit sworn before writ issued, can be order following undertaking to reswear.
Sheppard v. Gilmore	[1887] W.N. 242; 57 L.J.Ch. 6		Interlocutory injunction granted with undertaking—defendant died—action later dismissed.	Whether undertaking survived defendant's death.	Inquiry granted as to whether deceased defendant/heirs had suffered loss.
Ross v. Buxton	[1888] W.N. 55	Stirling J.		*Ex parte* injunction sought. Material fact suppressed.	Suppression of material fact may taint plaintiffs' hands.
Ross v. Buxton	As above.		Material fact withheld on an *ex parte* application.	(i) Is defendant entitled to an inquiry on damages? (ii) Who pays costs of inquiry?	(i) Defendant so entitled even though order giving undertaking discharged as *inter partes* hearing. (ii) Costs of the inquiry reserved.

CASE	CITATION	JUDGE(S)	FACTS	ISSUES	ADJUDICATION
Manchester and Liverpool Banking Co. v. Parkinson	(1888) 60 L.T. 47		Plaintiffs were a limited company.	Can undertaking be properly given by plaintiff company's counsel?	Yes.
United Telephone Co. v. Equitable Telephone Association	(1888) 5 R.P.C. 233		Patent case. Delay advised by solicitor until defendants financially sound enough to manufacture infringing articles.	Delay.	Delay satisfactorily explained.
Silber v. Lewin	(1889) 33 S.J. 757			Affidavits.	Affidavits should be sworn after the writ is issued.
Mexican Co. v. Maldonado	[1890] W.N. 8			*Ex parte* injunction: whether plaintiff should inform court of defendant's intention to defend.	Court should be informed of defendant's notice of intention to defend.

CASE	CITATION	JUDGE(S)	FACTS	ISSUES	ADJUDICATION
Tucker v. New Brunswick Trading Company of London	(1890) 44 Ch.D. 249, C.A.; 59 L.J.Ch. 551			By whom can undertaking in damages be enforced?	Undertaking can be enforced by all defendants not just those restrained by undertaking.
Spanish General Agency Corp. v. Spanish Corp.	(1891) 63 L.T. 161			(i) Role of affidavit in interlocutory applications. (ii) How "serious" must issue to be tried be? (iii) How much evidence should be adduced?	Injunction may be dissolved if plaintiff fails to fulfil condition re. amendment of writ.
East Molesey Local Board v. Lambeth Waterworks Co.	[1892] 3 Ch.D. 289; 62 L.J.Ch. 82		Plaintiff was local authority.	Undertaking in damages?	Undertaking can properly be given by local authority itself.
Schmitten v. Faulkes	[1893] W.N. 64; 37 S.J. 389		Inquiry as to damages following undertaking in damages.	Is it relevant that plaintiff was without fault in his application for injunction?	Fault is irrelevant.

CASE	CITATION	JUDGE(S)	FACTS	ISSUES	ADJUDICATION
Fenner v. Wilson	[1893] 2 Ch. 656; 62 L.J.Ch. 984			Nature of undertaking in damages.	Undertaking should be given on every interlocutory injunction except where it is effectively a final order.
Carter v. Fey	[1894] 2 Ch. 541; 63 L.J.Ch. 723	Lindley L.J.	Application for relief by defendant. Covenant in restraint of trade.	Cross-application for injunction.	If defendant applies for relief by injunction other than incidental to plaintiff's action and the time for delivery of the counterclaim has not arrived a writ must be issued in a cross-action.
Smith v. Baxter	[1900] 2 Ch. 138	Stirling J.	Application for injunction to prevent building.	How to protect rights of plaintiff.	Defendant required to undertake to give plaintiff reasonable notice of his intention to build as well as copy of plans.
Re Young J.L. Manufacturing Co. Ltd	[1900] 2 Ch. 753	Rigby L.J.	Affidavits including hearsay but without specifying source.	Hearsay in affidavits.	A ground for information or belief must be stated.

CASE	CITATION	JUDGE(S)	FACTS	ISSUES	ADJUDICATION
Arthur v. Consolidated Collieries Corp.	(1905) 49 S.J. 403			Motion practice in Chancery.	Motion by special leave cannot be saved without leave of the court.
Oberrheinische Metalwerke v. Cocks	[1906] W.N. 127			Undertaking in damages.	In Chancery, undertaking is automatic where defendant makes undertaking in lieu of injunction. Should be stipulated in Q.B.D.
Jones v. Pacaya Rubber & Produce Co. Ltd	[1911] 1 K.B. 455, C.A.; 80 L.J.K.B. 155		Action against a company for the rescission of a contract to buy shares.	Whether defendant company could forfeit plaintiff's shares.	Company restrained from forfeiting on payment in of sum by plaintiff.
Amber Size & Chemical Co. Ltd v. Menzel	[1913] 2 Ch. 239; 82 L.J.Ch. 573	Astbury J.	Possible improper use of information gleaned while defendant was plaintiff's servant.	Can injunction be granted even if information not disclosed?	Injunction available in this situation.
Att.-Gen. of Canada v. Ritchie Contracting Co.	[1919] A.C. 999	Lord Dunedin Viscount Haldane Lord Buckmaster	Canada. Question of vesting territory and whether a bay was a public harbour.	*Quia timet* injunctions.	Plaintiff must prove that act, etc., is calculated to infringe his rights.

1023

CASE	CITATION	JUDGE(S)	FACTS	ISSUES	ADJUDICATION
Cavenagh v. Coker	(1919) 147 L.T. 252		Plaintiff's claim for, *inter alia*, a sum of money.	Ancillary order binding plaintiff.	Injunction granted conditional on payment into court.
Thompson v. Park	[1944] 1 K.B. 408	Goddard L.J. Du Parcq L.J.	Agreement to amalgamate schools revoked by plaintiff. Plaintiff sought to exclude defendant from plaintiff's premises.	What was status quo?	Status quo was that existing before illegal acts by defendant (trespass).
Cutler v. Wandsworth Stadium Ltd	[1945] 1 All E.R. 103; 172 L.T. 207	Finlay L.J. Morton L.J.	Plaintiff was bookmaker excluded from greyhound track.	Applying to vary or discharge an undertaking.	Defendant should apply for release coupled (if appropriate) with offer of different undertaking.
Baxter v. Claydon	[1952] W.N. 376	Roxburgh J.	Undertaking in damages.	Whether undertaking should be fortified.	Plaintiff ordered to pay sum into joint names of solicitors for each party.
Kangol Industries Ltd v. Alfred Bray	[1953] 1 All E.R. 444; 70 R.P.C. 15	Danckwerts J.	Commercial confidentiality.	Undertaking/injunction.	An affidavit may be ordered verifying compliance with an undertaking.

CASE	CITATION	JUDGE(S)	FACTS	ISSUES	ADJUDICATION
Super-Rax v. Broadfoot	[1961] R.P.C. 61	Cross J.	Defendant undertook not to infringe plaintiffs' letters patent. Four years later plaintiff brought new action for breach of letters patent on similar facts.	(i) Can defendant argue in the second action that his act were not an infringement of patent? (ii) Since this bringing of new action cannot disguise the laches, should court grant interim injunction?	(i) Not in interlocutory proceedings. His undertaking and admission prima facie bind him. (ii) On the balance of convenience the laches was insufficient to prevent an injunction.
Morecambe and Heysham Corp. v. Mecca Ltd	[1962] R.P.C. 145	Wilberforce J.	Delay effectively for over a year.	Example of delay.	Injunction refused.
Pictograph Ltd v. Lee-Smith Photomechanism Ltd	[1964] 1 W.L.R. 402; [1964] R.P.C. 376	Pennycuick J.	Passing off proceedings. Direct conflict of facts.	Could plaintiff have the motion stood over until trial?	Plaintiff must either abandon or move motion on the evidence as it stood or file further evidence in reply and then move.

CASE	CITATION	JUDGE(S)	FACTS	ISSUES	ADJUDICATION
Hoffman-La Roche & Co. A.G. v. Inter-Continental Pharmaceuticals Ltd	[1965] Ch. 795; [1965] 2 W.L.R. 1045.	Harman L.J. Diplock L.J. Russell L.J.	Passing off/patent case.	Should application to comptroller for compulsory licence under patent thwart injunction application?	Court of Appeal disapproved thwarting of application in this way.
Pfizer Corp. v. Inter-Continental Pharmaceuticals Ltd	[1966] R.P.C. 565; [1966] F.S.R. 249	Lloyd-Jacobs J.	Plaintiffs delayed about 18 months before seeking removal of stay on injunction/drug patent case.	Example of delay.	Stay remained two more months to avoid undue difficulties for defendants.
Regent Oil Co. Ltd v. J.T. Leavesley (Lichfield) Ltd	[1966] 1 W.L.R. 1210; [1966] 2 All E.R. 454	Stamp J.	Restraint of trade—petrol stations.	Has court power to discharge injunction obtained otherwise than by consent?	Court has power to discharge if decision shown subsequently to be clearly wrong in law.
Ronson Products Ltd v. Ronson Furniture Ltd	[1966] Ch. 603; [1966] 2 W.L.R. 1157	Stamp J.	Passing off.	Order enforceable?	Prohibitory order enforceable if notice of making of order proved.

1026

CASE	CITATION	JUDGE(S)	FACTS	ISSUES	ADJUDICATION
Harman Pictures N.V. v. Osborne	[1967] 1 W.L.R. 723; [1967] 2 All E.R. 324	Goff J.	Plaintiffs seeking injunction were outside the jurisdiction.	Should there be security for the undertaking in damages?	Injunction conditional on giving security for the undertaking.
Re N (No 2)	[1967] Ch. 512; [1967] 2 W.L.R. 691	Stamp J.	Wardship action.	Documents required in *ex parte* application.	In emergency a draft writ will suffice in an *ex parte* application.
Re N (No. 2)	As above.	Stamp J.	Application re. children who were abroad with father.	*Ex parte* procedure. Sunday applications.	In a case of sufficient urgency an interlocutory injunction may be granted on a Sunday. Notional date of issue of writ is date of undertaking to issue (Q.B.D.).
Coco v. Clark A.N. (Engineers) Ltd	[1969] R.P.C. 41; [1968] F.S.R. 415	Megarry J.	Patent case.	How could defendant circumvent ability to pay criterion?	Injunction refused on defendant's undertaking to pay funds into account in joint names of parties' solicitors.
Beese v. Woodhouse	[1970] 1 W.L.R. 586; [1970] 1 All E.R. 769	Davies L.J. Sachs L.J. Fenton Atkinson L.J.	Use of motor racing track near school.	Whether *ex parte* injunction should be granted.	Utmost good faith must be shown in *ex parte* application.

CASE	CITATION	JUDGE(S)	FACTS	ISSUES	ADJUDICATION
London City Agency (J.C.D.) Ltd v. Lee	[1970] 1 Ch. 597; [1970] 2 W.L.R. 136	Megarry J.	Application to restrain defendant from dealing with a bank account.	Application to vary or discharge order.	Preferable that application to vary/discharge should be on notice but can be *ex parte* in suitable case.
Redland Bricks Ltd v. Morris	[1970] A.C. 652; [1969] 2 W.L.R. 1437	Lord Reid Lord Morris Lord Hodson Lord Upjohn Lord Diplock	Excavation with actual/possible landslip.	*Quia timet* injunctions.	Unqualified obligations should specify acts to be performed.
Woollerton and Wilson v. Costain Ltd	[1970] 1 W.L.R. 411; 114 S.J. 170	Stamp J.	Tower crane overhung plaintiffs' premises.	Does absence of actual/apprehended damage prevent injunction?	Injunction granted.
Carroll v. Tomado Ltd	[1971] F.S.R. 218; [1971] R.P.C. 401	Graham J.	Patent case. No action until plaintiff had inspected defendant's article.	Delay.	Delay here was inevitable. Plaintiff's actions reasonable.
Comet Radiovision Services Ltd v. Farnell-Tandberg Ltd	[1971] 1 W.L.R. 1287; [1971] 3 All E.R. 230	Goulding J.	Withholding supplies to maintain resale price.	(i) Discretion. (ii) Mandatory injunctions.	Exercise of discretion to grant mandatory injunction.

CASE	CITATION	JUDGE(S)	FACTS	ISSUES	ADJUDICATION
Charrington v. Simons & Co. Ltd	[1971] 1 W.L.R. 598; [1971] 2 All E.R. 588	Russell L.J. Cross L.J. Cairns L.J.	Breach of covenant not to build road.	Discretion to grant mandatory injunction.	Decision in *Silber v. Lewin* (1889) 33 S.J. 757 doubted.
Shepherd Homes Ltd v. Sandham	[1971] Ch. 340; [1970] 3 W.L.R. 348	Megarry J.	Breach of restrictive covenant.	Delay and its effect on the status quo.	The status quo may be altered by delay.
Bates v. Lord Hailsham of St Marylebone	[1972] W.L.R. 1373; [1972] 3 All E.R. 1019	Megarry J.	*Ex parte* application. Action concerning regulation of solicitors' fees.	(i) When is *ex parte* application appropriate? (ii) When effect of delay on *ex parte* may be fatal?	(i) Where delay may cause irreparable damage or need for secrecy. (ii) Delay fatal unless overwhelming case on merits or delay.
Hubbard v. Vosper	[1972] 2 Q.B. 84; [1972] 2 W.L.R. 389	Lord Denning Megaw L.J. Stephenson L.J.	Infringement of literary copyright of Church of Scientology.	Whether injunction to protect confidentiality.	Injunction refused: not clean hands. Deplorable methods of protecting secrets.
G.C.T. (Management) Ltd v. Laurie Marsh Group Ltd	[1972] F.S.R. 519; [1973] R.P.C. 432	Whitford J.	Passing off concerning cinemas. Defendants undertook to change name pending trial. Initially accepted by plaintiffs, then further order sought.	Could plaintiffs "change their minds?"	Subsequent application refused.

CASE	CITATION	JUDGE(S)	FACTS	ISSUES	ADJUDICATION
Granada Group Ltd v. Ford Motor Co. Ltd	[1972] F.S.R. 103	Graham J.	Copyright. Defendants wanted to call new model "Granada".	Were damages an adequate remedy?	If necessary, damages could be calculated on a "royalties" basis.
Pickwick International Inc. (G.B.) Ltd v. Multiple Sound Distributors Ltd	[1972] 1 W.L.R. 1213; [1972] 3 All E.R. 384	Megarry J.	Passing off action.	(i) Costs of *ex parte* hearing. (ii) Procedure at "opposed *ex parte*".	(i) If defendant voluntarily attends *ex parte* hearing and plaintiff loses, plaintiff may be ordered to pay defendant's costs of hearing. (ii) Better to treat "opposed *ex parte*" as *inter partes* hearing.
Royal Insurance Co. Ltd v. G. & S. Assured Investment Co. Ltd	[1972] 1 Lloyd's Rep. 267	Whitford J.	Contract-unit trust life assurance policy.	Undertakings/ injunction.	Injunction can be ordered/volunteered.
Ushers Brewery Ltd v. King P.S. & Co. (Finance) Ltd	[1972] Ch. 148; [1971] 2 W.L.R. 1411	Plowman J.	Action concerning a lease of premises.	When does undertaking in damages become enforceable?	(i) Plaintiff has failed at trial. (ii) Established before trial that injunction ought not to have been granted. (iii) Unsuccessful defendant establishes after trial that undertaking ought not to have been given.

CASE	CITATION	JUDGE(S)	FACTS	ISSUES	ADJUDICATION
Evans Marshall & Co. Ltd v. Bertola S.A.	[1973] 1 W.L.R. 349; [1976] 2 Lloyd's Rep. 17, H.L. (reversing above decision)	Viscount Dilhorne Lord Simon Lord Kilbrandon Lord Russell	Defendant sought to terminate sale/distribution agreement. Plaintiff applied for injunction to restrain.	(i) Are damages an adequate remedy? (ii) Could defendant satisfy a judgment in damages?	(i) Question is whether it is just that plaintiff should be confined to damages. (ii) If not, damages may not be an adequate remedy.
Erinford Properties Ltd v. Cheshire County Council	[1974] Ch. 261; [1974] 2 W.L.R. 749	Megarry J.	Application for injunction pending appeal, *ex parte*	Whether court has jurisdiction pending appeal having refused interlocutory injunction.	Court has jurisdiction to grant limited *ex parte* injunction preserving status quo in these circumstances.
American Cyanamid Co. Ltd v. Ethicon Ltd	[1975] A.C. 396; [1975] 2 W.L.R. 316	Lord Diplock Viscount Dilhorne Lord Cross Lord Salmon Lord Edmund-Davies	Dispute over patent between U.S. companies; injunctions.	Principles concerning grant of interlocutory injunctions.	Main principle: balance of convenience; remedy discretionary.
Fosesco International Ltd v. Fordath Ltd	[1975] F.S.R. 507	Foster J.	Patent action involving core binders.	Plea of delay.	Defence defeated because delay was during negotiations.

1031

CASE	CITATION	JUDGE(S)	FACTS	ISSUES	ADJUDICATION
Landi den Hartog N.V. v. Sea Bird (Clean) Air Fuel Systems) Ltd	[1975] F.S.R. 502	Whitford J.	Patent case.	Nature of interlocutory injunction.	An exceptional remedy.
Hoffman-La Roche A.-G. v. Secretary of State for Trade and Industry	[1975] A.C. 295	Lord Diplock Lord Reid Lord Morris Lord Cross Lord Wilberforce	Undertaking in damages	Quantum of damages.	Assessed on contractual basis.
Radley Gowns Ltd v. Costos Spyrou	[1975] F.S.R. 455; (1975) 119 S.J. 626	Oliver J.	Copyright case concerning clothing styles.	Delay.	Delay may prove fatal where it has caused defendant materially to alter his position.
Secretary of State for Trade and Industry v. Hoffman-La Roche A.G.	[1975] A.C. 295	Lord Reid Lord Morris Lord Wilberforce Lord Diplock Lord Cross	Plaintiff was the Crown. Application for declaration that statutory order was invalid.	Undertaking in damages required?	Generally yes, but not when seeking to enforce what was prima facie the law of the land.
Bryanston Finance Co. v. de Vries (No. 2)	[1976] 3 Ch. 63; [1975] 2 W.L.R. 41	Lord Denning Lord Diplock Lawton L.J.	Libel and slander—publication to clerical staff.	(i) Privilege as between employer/employee. (ii) Do concessions made at first instance bind on interlocutory appeal?	(i) This privilege indefeasible except by proven malice. (ii) Generally yes.

CASE	CITATION	JUDGE(S)	FACTS	ISSUES	ADJUDICATION
Celanese Corp. v. Akzo Chemie U.K. Ltd	[1976] F.S.R. 273	Whitford J.	Patent case.	Nature of interlocutory injunction.	An exceptional remedy.
Celanese Corp. v. Akzo Chemie U.K. Ltd	As above.			Whether defendants should be restrained from infringing letter patent.	Applications for interlocutory injunctions governed by *American Cynamid* principles.
Celanese Corp. v. Akzo Chemie U.K. Ltd	As above.			Nature of interlocutory injunction.	If apparent there is an arguable case, may waste time to deal with liability at interlocutory application.
Fellowes v. Fisher	[1976] Q.B. 122; [1975] 3 W.L.R. 184	Sir John Pennycuick Lord Denning M.R. Browne L.J.	Restraint of trade action	What was status quo?	Status quo was situation existing when defendant embarked on activities sought to be restrained.
Fior (London) Ltd v. Schemilt (Eric) Designs Ltd	[1976] F.S.R. 107	Brightman J.	Cross-applications.	Order in which counsel should move.	Plaintiff should move his motion first.

CASE	CITATION	JUDGE(S)	FACTS	ISSUES	ADJUDICATION
Gloverall Ltd v. Durworth Ltd and Bodner Elan Ltd	[1976] F.S.R. 543	Walton J.	Passing off in duffle coat alleged.	(i) Could motion be stood over to trial? (ii) Costs?	(i) Motion stood over. (ii) If motion is hopeless, should be dismissed even if defence not served. If not hopeless, costs should be reserved to trial.
Hubbard v. Pitt	[1976] 1 Q.B. 142; [1975] 3 W.L.R. 201	Lord Denning Stamp L.J. Orr L.J.	Picketing case. Claim in nuisance and libel.	Whether interlocutory injunction appropriate.	Interlocutory injunction upheld.
Société Française v. Electronic Concepts Ltd	[1976] 1 W.L.R. 51; [1975] 3 All E.R. 425	Oliver J.		(i) Effect of delay? (ii) Costs? (iii) Whether motion may be stood over until trial.	(i) (ii) No distinction between delay in instituting proceedings and delay in prosecuting proceedings—plaintiff penalised in costs. (iii) Whether to stand over is a matter in discretion of court.
Steepleglade Ltd v. Stratford Investments Ltd	[1976] F.S.R. 3	Oliver J.	Copyright.	Costs order.	If plaintiff succeeds, usual order is plaintiff's costs in the cause.

CASE	CITATION	JUDGE(S)	FACTS	ISSUES	ADJUDICATION
Standex International Ltd v. C.B. Blades and C.B. Blades Ltd	[1976] F.S.R. 114	Buckley L.J. Scarman L.J.	Plaintiff alleged breach of covenant in restraint of trade. Defendant was new company.	(i) Could defendant satisfy judgment in damages? (ii) What was status quo?	(i) Probably not, as only recently launched. Injunction granted. (ii) Status quo was situation before disturbed by defendant to detriment of plaintiff.
Polaroid Corp. v. Eastman Kodak Co.	[1977] R.P.C. 379; [1977] F.S.R. 25	Buckley L.J. Goff L.J. Bridge L.J.	Patents case.	(i) Are damages an adequate remedy? (ii) Could defendant satisfy a judgment in damages?	If plaintiff can be compensated in damages, defendant should only be restrained in exceptional circumstances.
Potters-Ballotini Ltd v. Weston Baker	[1977] R.P.C. 202	Lord Denning	Commercial confidentiality.	Form of interlocutory injunction.	Interlocutory injunction should be precise and specific.
Solihull M.B.C. v. Maxfern	[1977] 1 W.L.R. 127; [1977] 2 All E.R. 177	Oliver J.	Local authority proceeding to prevent public market.	Undertakings/ injunction.	Injunction can be ordered despite undertaking to act lawfully.

CASE	CITATION	JUDGE(S)	FACTS	ISSUES	ADJUDICATION
Simon Jeffrey Ltd v. Shelana Fashions Ltd	[1977] R.P.C. 103	Walton J.	Plaintiffs applied to stand motion over until trial. Defendant applied for "pictograph" order.	Could motion be stood over until trial?	Motion stood over to trial.
Morny Ltd v. Ball & Rogers Ltd (1975)	[1978] F.S.R. 91	Goulding J.	Passing off.	*Ex parte* affidavits—principles.	Promptness important—*ex parte* may be granted on terms as to costs.
Harbottle (R.D.) (Mercantile) Ltd v. National Westminster Bank Ltd	[1978] Q.B. 146; [1977] 3 W.L.R. 752	Kerr J.	International contract case.	Discharge of *ex parte*.	Court can discharge an *ex parte* order even if the defendant has not entered an appearance.
Dunhill (Alfred) Ltd v. Sunoptics S.A.	[1979] F.S.R. 337	Roskill L.J. Megan L.J. Browne L.J.	Passing off case.	(i) Role of affidavits in interlocutory applications. (ii) How "serious" must issue to be tried be? (iii) How much evidence should be adduced?	(i) Affidavits are vehicles for fact not law. (ii) Plaintiff must have some chance of success, however small. (iii) May lead to consideration of merits.

CASE	CITATION	JUDGE(S)	FACTS	ISSUES	ADJUDICATION
Dunhill (Alfred) Ltd v. Sunoptics S.A.	As above.	Megan L.J. Roskill L.J. Browne L.J.	Passing off case.	(i) Whether non-disclosure by defendants material. (ii) What was status quo?	(i) Non-disclosure by defendants may assist plaintiffs. (ii) Relevant point in time of status quo may vary in different cases.
Hepworth Plastics Ltd v. Naylor Bros (Clayware) Ltd	[1979] F.S.R. 521	Buckley L.J.	Passing off of manhole covers.	Whether interlocutory injunction should be specific.	Interlocutory injunction should be to prevent a particular thing.
Mothercare Ltd v. Robson Books Ltd	[1979] F.S.R. 466	Sir Robert Megarry V.-C.	Passing off case.	(i) Whether interlocutory injunction should be specific. (ii) How serious is "serious"?	(i) Hoped that expression "frivolous and vexatious" would disappear in this context as it encouraged misunderstanding. (ii) Plaintiff's prospects of success must exist in substance and reality.
Netlon v. Bridport-Grundy Ltd	[1979] F.S.R. 530	Goff L.J.	Patent case concerning plastic netting.	Delay.	No material delay where plaintiff brought proceedings as soon as aware of seriousness of situation.

CASE	CITATION	JUDGE(S)	FACTS	ISSUES	ADJUDICATION
Tetrosyl Ltd v. Silver Paint and Lacquer Co. Ltd	(1979) C.A.T. No. 599; New L.J. Aug. 28, (1980) 786	Lawton L.J. Roskill L.J.	Passing off.	Was question to be tried serious?	A serious question can only arise if there is evidential backing for it.
Siskina, The	[1979] A.C. 210; [1977] 3 W.L.R. 818	Lord Diplock Lord Simon Lord Hailsham Lord Russell Lord Keith	Claim to restrain removal from jurisdiction of insurance moneys for loss of ship.	Whether interlocutory injunction can stand alone.	Interlocutory injunction depends on pre-existing cause.
Allen v. Jambo Holdings Ltd	[1980] 1 W.L.R. 1252; [1980] 2 All E.R. 502	Lord Denning M.R. Shaw L.J. Templeman L.J.	*Mareva* injunction to prevent removal of aircraft.	(i) Hearing of *ex parte* application. (ii) Undertaking in damages.	(i) Hearing of *ex parte* application can be made by telephone. (ii) Undertaking applies even where plaintiff impecunious.
Dellborg v. Corix Properties and Blissfield Corp. N.V.	(June 26, 1980 C.A.T. No. 541)	Lawton L.J.	Application for *Mareva*.	Whether Court of Appeal should interfere with decision.	A note should be taken of the judge's reasons for making his decision.
E.A.R. Corp. v. Proctor Safety Products (U.K.) Ltd	[1980] F.S.R. 574	Graham J.	Delay of six weeks.	Example of delay.	No unreasonable delay.

CASE	CITATION	JUDGE(S)	FACTS	ISSUES	ADJUDICATION
Porter v. National Union of Journalists	[1980] IRLR 404	Lord Diplock Viscount Dilhorne Lord Salmon Lord Russell Lord Keith	Plaintiffs expelled from union for refusing to strike.	(i) Whether *American Cyanamid* criteria must be/had been invoked. (ii) Consequence of failure to invoke criteria.	(i) Criteria must be invoked whenever appropriate and had not been. (ii) Failure to invoke purported exercise of discretion.
Revlon Inc. v. Cripps & Lee Ltd	[1980] F.S.R. 85; (1979) 124 S.J. 184	Buckley L.J. Bridge L.J. Templeman L.J.	Passing off case. Plaintiff and defendant companies part of same world-wide group.	Whether group-structure a factor.	Marks or get-up distinctive of the whole group available to every company in the group.
Simons Records Ltd v. W.E.A. Records Ltd	[1980] F.S.R. 35	Brightman L.J. Brandon L.J.	Action to restrain distribution of circulars to plaintiffs customers.	Decision in *Dunhill (Alfred) Ltd v. Sunoptics S.A.* [1979] correct?	Court of Appeal expressed no view.
Stewart Chartering Ltd v. C. & O. Managements S.A.	[1980] 1 W.L.R. 460; [1980] 1 All E.R. 718	Robert Goff J.	Shipping contract case.	Interrelation of Ord. 13 and *Mareva*.	Ord. 13 judgment may be entered while *Mareva* in force.

1039

CASE	CITATION	JUDGE(S)	FACTS	ISSUES	ADJUDICATION
Vernon & Co. (Pulp Products) Ltd v. Universal Pulp Containers Ltd	[1980] F.S.R. 179	Sir Robert Megarry V.-C.	Copyright.	Is ability to pay a rich man's charter?	Courts must be astute to prevent unfairness of ability to pay criterion if possible without injury to plaintiff. Damages would be adequate remedy if defendant is rich.
Allied Collection Agencies v. Wood	[1981] 3 All E.R. 176; (1980) 124 S.J. 498	Neill J.	Application to correct alleged clerical error in an order.	Costs order.	Plaintiff may be awarded costs of interlocutory application with immediate taxation— but only in exceptional cases.
Chanel Ltd v. Woolworth (F.W.) & Co.	[1981] 1 W.L.R. 485; [1981] 1 All E.R. 745	Buckley L.J. Shaw L.J. Oliver L.J.	Infringement of trade mark/passing off case. Defendants gave undertakings then sought to have them discharged.	Whether court can vary an interlocutory consent order.	Motion disposed of by consent. Court has power to vary on application to discharge undertakings but refused here because no significant change in circumstances or new knowledge by defendants.
Gallery Cosmetics Ltd v. Number 1	[1981] F.S.R. 556 (European Court)	Nourse J.	Passing off of perfumes.	Whether material non-disclosure.	Non-disclosed facts insufficiently material to set order aside.

CASE	CITATION	JUDGE(S)	FACTS	ISSUES	ADJUDICATION
My Kinda Town Ltd (t/a Chicago Pizza Pie Factory) v. Lauren Sabin Soll and Grunts Investments Ltd (t/a L.S. Grunts Chicago Pizza Co.)	[1981] Com.L.R. 194; [1983] R.P.C. 407 (reversing above decision)	Slade J.	Passing off case.	Plea of acquiescence.	Test is whether it had become unconscionable for plaintiff to insist on rights. Insufficient acquiescence here.
Thermax Ltd v. Schott Industrial Glass Ltd	[1981] F.S.R. 289	Browne-Wilkinson J.	Alleged infringement of registered design.	Would court set aside Anton Piller?	Yes. Plaintiffs had failed to disclose material facts.
Wilmot-Breedon Ltd v. Woodcock Ltd	[1981] F.S.R. 15	Slade J.	Passing off action. Ex parte application.	Delay.	Delay may prevent relief in an ex parte action.
Quaker Oats Co. v. Alltrades Distributors Ltd	[1981] F.S.R. 9	Buckley L.J. Geoffrey Lane L.J. Goff L.J.	Infringement of copyright alleged. Delay of two months.	Delay.	Delay was not, on closer examination, culpable. Plaintiffs examining their position. Defendants not prejudiced.
Foley (Brigid) Ltd v. Ellott	[1982] R.P.C. 433	Sir Robert Megarry V.-C.		Could plaintiff meet an undertaking in damages?	When applying for interlocutory injunction plaintiff must normally tender evidence of financial status.

CASE	CITATION	JUDGE(S)	FACTS	ISSUES	ADJUDICATION
Curson and Poole v. Rash	(1982) 263 EG 518	Vinelott J.	Covenant in restraint of trade. Plaintiff sought to enforce.	Delay of one month material?	One month not undue delay and defendant suffered no detriment.
Fletcher Sutcliffe Wild v. Burch	[1982] F.S.R. 64	Gibson J.	Copyright case.	(i) How is defendant to be compensated for loss arising from injunction which is discharged? (ii) When does cause of action on undertaking arise?	(i) Cross-undertakings in damages by plaintiff. (ii) Not until court has made an award of damages pursuant to the undertaking.
I.T.C. Film Distributors Ltd v. Video Exchange Ltd (No. 2)	(1982) 126 S.J. 672	Lawton L.J.	Video piracy case.	Whether poorly drafted affidavit fatal to application.	Poor drafting did not necessarily bar relief.
Idmac Industrial Designers and Management Consultants B.V. v. Midland Bank Ltd	*The Times,* October 8, 1982	Templeman L.J.	Company used as cloak for fraud sought injunction	Should injunction be granted?	Court could refuse injunction where application unmeritorious.

CASE	CITATION	JUDGE(S)	FACTS	ISSUES	ADJUDICATION
Siebe Gorman & Co. Ltd v. Pneupac Ltd	[1982] 1 W.L.R. 185; [1982] 1 All E.R. 377	Lord Denning M.R. Eveleigh L.J. Templeman L.J.	Application for discovery order.	Variation of consent order.	Court has discretion to grant extension of time for compliance with consent order.
Tigner-Roche & Co. v. Spiro	(1982) 126 S.J. 525	Cumming Bruce L.J. Templeman L.J. O'Connor L.J.	Action in restraint of trade against former employees.	Variation of consent order.	Where consent order embodies contract, court will only interfere on normal grounds for interfering with contract.
Walt Disney Productions v. Gurvitz	[1982] F.S.R. 446	Vinelott J.	Copyright.	Whether trap orders with a defendant legitimate after under-taking in *Anton Piller* proceedings.	Plaintiff entitled to place trap orders.
C.B.S. United Kingdom Ltd v. Lambert	[1983] 1 Ch. 37; [1982] 3 W.L.R. 746	Lawton L.J. Templeman L.J.	Breach of copyright in musical recordings.	General protective powers of the court.	*Mareva* order for delivery up and *Anton Piller* combined.
Century Electronics Ltd v. C.V.S. Enterprises Ltd	[1983] F.S.R. 1	Dillon J.	Delay of five months.	Effect of delay.	Delay prejudicial. Defendants, in false sense of security, had expanded business.

CASE	CITATION	JUDGE(S)	FACTS	ISSUES	ADJUDICATION
Computer Machinery Company Ltd v. Drescher	[1983] 1 W.L.R. 379; [1983] 3 All E.R. 153	Sir Robert Megarry V.-C.	Allegation that defendant was wrongfully using confidential information.	(i) If interlocutory costs reserved, are they included in taxed costs relating to final injunction if defendant offers to submit? (ii) On issue of costs, is only evidence used at hearings admissible?	(i) Court should enforce terms on which "without prejudice" offer is made, to encourage compromise. (ii) No rule that only previously adduced evidence is admissible regarding costs.
Hadmor Productions Ltd v. Hamilton	[1983] 1 A.C. 191; [1982] 2 W.L.R. 322	Lord Diplock Lord Fraser Lord Scarman Lord Bridge Lord Brandon	Trade dispute	(i) To what extent may an appellate court interfere with the exercise of a judge's discretion? (ii) How should the Court of Appeal view fresh evidence?	(i) Principles governing an appellate court's limited right to interfere laid down. (ii) Fresh evidence only examined to determine whether it invalidates reasons given by the judge for his decision.
Max Factor & Co. v. M.G.M./U.A. Entertainment Co.	[1983] F.S.R. 577	Vinelott J.	Passing off.	Motion practice in Chancery.	Judge had discretion to save motion where counsel for applicant wants to save motion rather than opening it.

CASE	CITATION	JUDGE(S)	FACTS	ISSUES	ADJUDICATION
P.C.W. (Underwriting Agencies) Ltd v. Dixon (P.S.)	[1983] 2 All E.R. 158; (1983) 133 New L.J. 204	Lloyd J.	Allegation that director made secret profits.	Duration of ex parte order in Q.B.D.	Most ex parte Marevas settle the action. Usual duration until trial or further order.
Smith (T.J.) & Nephew Ltd v. 3M United Kingdom plc	[1983] R.P.C. 92	Lawton L.J. Dillon L.J.	Patent case concerning surgical dressings.	How much evidence must defendants adduce?	Defendants must show genuine intention to defend but need not reveal detail.
W.E.A. Records Ltd v. Visions Channel 4 Ltd	[1983] 1 W.L.R. 721	Sir John Donaldson M.R. Dunn L.J. Purchas L.J.	Video piracy case. Application for Anton Piller.	(i) Ex parte procedure. (ii) Disclosure by plaintiff.	(i) Application accompanied only by draft writ and counsel's instructions. (ii) Confidential information if secret, but disclosed to defendant's solicitors.
Hytrac Conveyors Ltd v. Conveyors International Ltd	[1983] 1 W.L.R. 44; [1982] 3 All E.R. 415	Lawton L.J. Templeman L.J. Fox L.J.	Plaintiff had failed to serve statement of claim within Ord. 19 time limit despite execution of Aton Piller.	Effect of delay in service.	Statement of claim must be issued in time unless court orders otherwise.

1045

CASE	CITATION	JUDGE(S)	FACTS	ISSUES	ADJUDICATION
Cayne v. Global Natural Resources plc	[1984] 1 All E.R. 225	May L.J. Eveleigh L.J. Kerr L.J.	Case involving contract to merge companies and transfer shares.	(i) What was the "balance of convenience"? (ii) How rigid are American Cyanamid guidelines?	(i) Should be "balance of risk of doing an injustice". (ii) Discretion of court cannot in general be fettered.
Conder International Ltd v. Hibbing Ltd	[1984] F.S.R. 312	Whitford J. (first instance) Buckley L.J. Goff L.J.	Patent case.	Is it open to express a view on merits?	Judge said did not think plaintiff's case was a strong one. Court of Appeal ruled judge did not allow his view unduly to influence his decision.
Digital Equipment Corp. v. Darkcrest Ltd	[1984] Ch. 512; [1984] 3 W.L.R. 617	Falconer J.	Plaintiff obtained Anton Piller. Defendant sought to argue plaintiffs had misled court and counterclaimed.	(i) Whether counterclaim lay. (ii) Category of damages awarded on undertaking.	(i) No counterclaim in abuse of process, negligence or trespass. (ii) If fraud or malice in application for injunction, exemplary/aggravated damages may be awarded.
Elan Digital Systems Ltd v. Elan Computers	[1984] F.S.R. 373	Sir John Donaldson M.R.	Passing off case.		Heavy burden on an appellant to show that a judge has erred in principle.

CASE	CITATION	JUDGE(S)	FACTS	ISSUES	ADJUDICATION
Francome v. Mirror Group Newspapers	[1984] 1 W.L.R. 892; [1984] 2 All E.R. 408	Sir John Donaldson M.R. Fox L.J. Stephen Brown L.J.	Tapes of plaintiffs' conversation obtained by means contrary to criminal law	(i) What was the balance of convenience? (ii) How rigid are *American Cyanamid* guidelines?	Should be "balance of justice".
Garden Cottage Foods v. Milk Marketing Board	[1984] A.C. 130; [1983] 3 W.L.R. 143	Lord Diplock Lord Wilberforce Lord Keith Lord Bridge Lord Brandon	Defendant terminated distribution agreement with plaintiff.	What was status quo?	Duration of period since circumstances last changed must be more than minimal. If not, status quo is situation before last change.
Harrington v. Polytechnic of North London	[1984] 1 W.L.R. 1293; [1984] 3 All E.R. 666	Sir John Donaldson M.R. Griffiths L.J. Browne-Wilkinson L.J.	Student prevented by other students from attending lectures.	Whether jurisdiction to order lectures to identify students.	An order requiring identification could be made.
Refson (P.S.) & Co. Ltd v. Saggers	[1984] 1 W.L.R. 1025; [1984] 3 All E.R. 111	Nourse J.	*Ex parte* applications.	*Ex parte* procedure.	Laid down procedure for *ex parte* injunction application in Chancery Division. Writ dated from actual issue, not undertaking.

CASE	CITATION	JUDGE(S)	FACTS	ISSUES	ADJUDICATION
Savings and Investment Bank Ltd v. Gasco Investments (Netherlands) B.V.	[1984] 1 W.L.R. 271	Peter Gibson J.		Hearsay in affidavits.	Hearsay of admissible evidence allowed in interlocutory proceedings.
Bank of Mellat v. Nikpour (Mohammed Ebrahim)	[1982] Com.L.R. 158; [1985] F.S.R. 87	Lord Denning M.R. Donaldson L.J. Slade L.J.	Action by bank against former chief executive.	*Ex parte* application for *Mareva*: principles of utmost good faith.	Injunction discharged— not full and frank disclosure.
Barclays Bank Ltd v. Rosenberg	*Financial Times*, June 12, 1985; (1985) 135 New L.J. 633	Anthony Evans J.	Plaintiff won damages at trial but had wrongly obtained injunction.	Nature of undertaking in damages.	If impecunious plaintiff wins damages, assets available to fulfil undertaking.
International Bank & Trust Corp. Ltd. v. Joacs Luis Perestrello	(C.A.T. October 15, 1985)	Slade L.J.	Battle for control of management of a bank.	Whether material non-disclosure.	Non-disclosure need not be intentional.
Rogers (Jeffrey) Knitwear Productions Ltd v. Vinola (Knitwear) Manufacturing Co. Ltd	[1985] F.S.R. 184	Whitford J.	Copyright.	*Ex parte* application for *Anton Piller*. Whether sufficient inquiries necessary.	*Anton Piller* set aside: insufficient inquiries by plaintiff.

CASE	CITATION	JUDGE(S)	FACTS	ISSUES	ADJUDICATION
Staver Company Inc. v. Digitext Display Ltd	[1985] F.S.R. 512	Scott J.	Copyright in drawings.	Form of interlocutory injunctions.	Interlocutory injunctions should not anticipate plaintiff's success at trial.
C.P.C. (United Kingdom) Ltd v. Keenan	[1986] F.S.R. 527	Peter Gibson J.	Some months spent seeking negotiated solution in passing off case.	Delay.	Delay reasonable.
C.P.C. (United Kingdom) Ltd v. Keenan	As above.		Passing off action involving marmalade.	What was status quo?	Argument for retaining status quo rejected.
Deborah Building Equipment Ltd v. Scaffio	*The Times*, November 5, 1986	Potts J.	Committal sought for breach of order.	Form of interlocutory injunctions.	If order not absolute no breach unless deliberate disobedience proved.
Harrods Ltd v. Schwartz-Sackin & Co. Ltd	[1986] F.S.R. 490	Warner J.	Covenant in restraint of trade: not to use plaintiff's name without permission.	Was delay by plaintiff unreasonable?	Delay reasonably explained.

1049

CASE	CITATION	JUDGE(S)	FACTS	ISSUES	ADJUDICATION
Hawke Bay Shipping Co. Ltd v. First National Bank of Chicago	[1986] 1 Lloyd's Rep. 244	O'Connor L.J. Purchas L.J. Mustill L.J.	Appeal against refusal to stay proceedings on the basis of *forum non conveniens*.	Can Court of Appeal interfere with decision?	Appeal refused: Court of Appeal could review only.
Locobail International Finance v. Agro Export	[1986] 1 W.L.R. 657; [1986] 1 All E.R. 901	Mustill L.J. Balcombe L.J.	Shipping contract case.	Whether mandatory injunction appropriate.	Mandatory injunction only in clear case and where enforceable.
News Group Newspapers Ltd v. Society of Graphical and Allied Trades	[1986] IRLR 337	Stuart-Smith J.	Picketing.	Whether new premises of former employers are pickets' place of work.	New premises not place of work.
Thomas v. N.U.M. (South Wales) Area	[1986] Ch. 20; [1985] 2 W.L.R. 1081	Scott J.	Picketing.	Whether mass picketing amounts to tortious intimidation.	Mass picketing can be tortuous intimidation.
United Kingdom Nirex Ltd v. Barton	*The Times*, October 14, 1986	Henry J.	Disposal of low level radioactive waste.	Representative injunctions.	Where conflict of interest, inappropriate to sue representatives.

CASE	CITATION	JUDGE(S)	FACTS	ISSUES	ADJUDICATION
Bradford Metropolitan City Council v. Brown	(1987) 19 H.L.R. 16	May L.J. Nourse L.J. Woolf L.J.	Council sought injunction to prevent gypsies from camping.	Injunctions granted?	If no arguable defence, the balance of convenience does not apply.
Butt v. Butt	[1987] 1 W.L.R. 1351; [1987] 3 All E.R. 657	Mustill L.J. Nourse L.J.	Property dispute—*Mareva* granted. Undertaking by deed.	Should defendant be relieved from undertaking on ground of material non-disclosure?	Yes.
Columbia Picture Industries Inc. v. Robinson	[1987] Ch. 38; [1986] W.L.R. 542	Scott J.	Undertakings in damages: *Anton Piller* application.	Category of damages.	Example of award of aggravated damages.
Evening Standard Co. v. Henderson	[1987] I.C.R. 588; [1987] IRLR 64	Lawton L.J. Balcombe L.J.	Covenant in restraint of trade. Contract not at an end. Employer undertook to honour it.	Could interlocutory injunction lie to restrain employee from working for employer's rival?	Yes.
Hunter and Partners v. Welling and Partners	[1987] F.S.R. 83	May L.J. Hollings J.	Opposed *ex parte* hearing.	Appeal from grant of interlocutory injunction on an "opposed *ex parte*" hearing.	Generally unsatisfactory for Court of Appeal to adjudicate an appeal when only one side's evidence filed.

CASE	CITATION	JUDGE(S)	FACTS	ISSUES	ADJUDICATION
McDonald's Hamburgers Ltd v. Burgerking (U.K.) Ltd	[1987] F.S.R. 112	Fox L.J. Kerr L.J. Sir Denys Buckley	Passing off injunction obtained at trial. Pre-trial offer on basis of no order as to costs.	(i) Plaintiffs entitled to inquiry as to damages? (ii) Plaintiffs reasonable to reject offer?	(i) Not automatically. (ii) Yes.
Nationwide Building Society v. Nationwide Estate Agents Ltd	[1987] F.S.R. 579	Sir Nicholas Browne-Wilkinson V.-C.	Passing off. Plaintiff refused to undertake not to use "Nationwide" concerning newly acquired estate agency business.	Would court enjoin defendants from using "Nationwide"?	No.
Patel v. Smith (W.H.)	[1987] 1 W.L.R. 853; [1987] 2 All E.R. 569	May L.J. Neill L.J. Balcombe L.J.	Land dispute.	Injunction?	Yes. If no arguable defence other factors not relevant.
R. v. Westminster City Council, ex p. Costi	The Independent, March 12, 1987	Buckley L.J.		Is it open to express a view on merits?	Judge apparently did not allow his view of strength of plaintiff's case to influence decision.
R. v. Westminster City Council, ex p. Sierbien	The Times, March 30, 1987	Dillon L.J. Nicholls L.J.	Licence for sex encounter establishment refused.	"Public interest" factor.	"Public interest" could be special factor.

CASE	CITATION	JUDGE(S)	FACTS	ISSUES	ADJUDICATION
Associated Newspapers Group v. Insert Media	[1988] 1 W.L.R. 509	Hoffmann J.	Passing off action.	Will injunction lie without a legal right?	No.
Att.-Gen. v. Wright	[1988] 1 W.L.R. 164; [1987] 3 All E.R. 579	Hoffmann J.	Action against headmaster/trustees of educational charity. Receiver appointed.	Should Att.-Gen. give or procure cross-undertaking in damages?	Cross-undertaking by receiver.
C.B.S. Songs v. Amstrad Consumer Electronics	[1988] A.C. 1013	Fox L.J. Nicholls L.J. Sir Denys Buckley	Copyright.	Was there a serious issue to be tried?	No, therefore application for interlocutory injunction failed.
Financiera Avenida S.A. v. Shiblaw	*The Times*, November 21, 1988	Saville J.	*Mareva*, Cross undertaking in damages.	Burden of proving loss caused by *Mareva?*	On party seeking to enforce cross-undertaking.
Hughes v. Southwark London Borough Council	[1988] IRLR 55	Taylor J.	Hospital social workers.	Injunction to restrain employers from instructing employees to carry out abnormal duties?	Yes.

CASE	CITATION	JUDGE(S)	FACTS	ISSUES	ADJUDICATION
K.M.S. Advertising plc & Another v. Singer	(March 24, 1988; unreported)		Contested *Mareva*, appeal to Court of Appeal.	Judge under duty to give detailed analysis of evidence/detailed reasons?	No duty—though may indicate to C.A. that some aspect of evidence has been overlooked.
National Dock Labour Board v. Sabah Timber Co. Ltd	*The Times*, January 5, 1988, C.A.	May L.J. Ewbank J.	Dock Workers Employment Scheme 1967—interlocutory injunction granted.	Injunction to continue after industrial tribunal decision (pending appeal)?	No.
Powell v. Brent London Borough	[1988] I.C.R. 176; [1987] IRLR 446	Ralph Gibson L.J. Nicholls L.J. Sir Roger Ormrod	Employment/promotion case.	Would court grant injunction requiring employer to treat employee as if appointed to post?	Yes.
Rochdale Borough Council v. Anders	[1988] 3 All E.R. 490; (1988) 138 New L.J. 212	Caulfield J.	Action under Shops Act 1950. Local authority sought injunction.	Cross-undertaking in damages by local authority?	Yes, in court's discretion.

CASE	CITATION	JUDGE(S)	FACTS	ISSUES	ADJUDICATION
Savings and Investment Bank Ltd v. Gasco Investments (Netherlands) B.V. (No. 2)	[1988] Ch. 422; [1988] 2 W.L.R. 1212	Purchas L.J. Nicholls L.J. Russell L.J.	Defendant company had undertaken not to dispose of assets. Plaintiffs, applied to commit directors for contempt for breach.	(i) Were these contempt proceedings 'interlocutory', so as to permit hearsay within Ord. 41, r. 5(2)? (ii) Were these contempt proceedings 'civil proceedings' within the hearsay system of the Civil Evidence Act 1968?	(i) Yes. (ii) Yes.
T.R. Technology Investment Trust, Re	[1988] 4 BCC 244; [1988] BCLC 256	Hoffman J.	Section 216 of Companies Act 1985 allows court to freeze shares if the owner fails to give full particulars in response to request for information.	(i) Does company applying for a freezing order have to show damages inadequate remedy, or loss if information not provided? (ii) Is a takeover bid a defence to a freezing order?	(i) No. It is enough to show that insufficient information was given. (ii) No.

CASE	CITATION	JUDGE(S)	FACTS	ISSUES	ADJUDICATION
Unigate Dairies Ltd v. Bruce	*The Times*, March 2, 1988	Waite J.	Covenant in restraint of trade.	Status quo?	Position before alleged breaches.
Walsh v. National Union of Public Employees	*The Times*, March 22, 1988, C.A.	May L.J. Waite J.	Industrial disciplinary case.	Will court restrain hearing before domestic disciplinary case?	Only if (a) No reasonable tribunal could entertain application; (b) Bias/prejudice; (c) Previous misapplication of rules likely to be repeated.
Att.-Gen. v. Turnaround Distribution	[1989] F.S.R. 169	Simon Brown J.	Memoirs of M.I.5 employee—no longer sensitive.	Injunction to prevent/deter publication by other former employees?	Yes.
London Underground v. National Union of Railwaymen	[1989] IRLR 341.	Simon Brown J.	Injunction granted *inter partes*.	Could court discharge injunction on defendant's application?	Yes, but would not do so if justice could be equally served by appeal.

CASE	CITATION	JUDGE(S)	FACTS	ISSUES	ADJUDICATION
Town and Country Building Society v. Daisystar Ltd	*The Times,* October 16, 1989	Dillon L.J. Farquharson L.J.	Plaintiff sat on *Mareva* injunction for two years.	What are the plaintiff's duties if he no longer wishes to prosecute an action in which he has obtained a *Mareva* injunction?	Either prosecute the action or apply himself to discharge it, even temporarily.
Derby & Co. Ltd v. Weldon (No. 8)	*The Times,* August 29, 1990	Dillon L.J. Butler-Sloss L.J. Leggatt L.J.	Plaintiffs mistakenly disclosed obviously privileged documents.	Injunction that defendant should return mistakenly disclosed documents?	Yes, except where it is too late to restore the status quo.
Dubai Bank v. Galadari (No. 2)	[1990] 1 W.L.R. 731; [1990] 2 All E.R. 738	Morritt J.	Plaintiff obtained injunction against one of several defendants—gave undertaking in damages.	Does undertaking apply to other defendants?	Yes.

CASE	CITATION	JUDGE(S)	FACTS	ISSUES	ADJUDICATION
Eldan Services Ltd v. Chandag Motors Ltd	[1990] 3 All E.R. 459	Millett J.	Dispute about price payable for sale of stock. Part of payment was post-dated cheque, and part was a solicitor's undertaking.	Should the court (i) restrain presentation of the cheque? (ii) release the solicitor's undertaking?	(i) No. (ii) No.
Elliott v. Islington Borough Council	*The Times*, July 6, 1990	Lord Donaldson M.R. Ralph Gibson L.J. Taylor L.J.	Defendants' tree was damaging plaintiffs' property.	Did the public amenity value of the tree prevent court granting injunction?	No. Public hardship is no obstacle to enforcing a private right.
Jakeman v. South West Thames R.H.A.	[1990] IRLR 62	Auld J.	Claim for wages withheld. Injunction would settle action.	Injunction?	No, only available in clear case where effectively resolves case.
Marcus Publishing v. Hutton-Wild Communications	[1990] R.P.C. 576	Dillon L.J. Staughton L.J. Mann L.J.	Passing off.	May court grant injunction to defendant even before service of counterclaim?	Yes, if undertaking to issue writ or serve counterclaim.

CASE	CITATION	JUDGE(S)	FACTS	ISSUES	ADJUDICATION
Newport Borough Council v. Khan	[1990] 1 W.L.R. 1185	Lloyd L.J. Beldam L.J.	Application for injunction in support of tree preservation order.	Did county court have jurisdiction?	Yes.
Oxy Electric v. Zainuddin	[1990] 2 All E.R. 902	Hoffmann J.	Restrictive covenant benefiting land—injunction sought.	Injunction?	Yes, plaintiff unwilling to accept compensation/unable to give cross-undertaking in damages.
Factortame Ltd. v. Secretary of State for Transport (No. 2)	[1991] 1 All E.R. 70; [1990] 3 W.L.R. 818	Lord Bridge Lord Brandon Lord Oliver Lord Goff Lord Jauncey	Defendants argued that statute was invalid as contrary to E.C. law.	Is the possible invalidity of a statute fatal to application for injunction based on it?	No, but in a clear case it is one factor in the balance of convenience.
Femis-Bank (Anguilla) Ltd v. Lazar	*The Times,* February 11, 1991	Browne-Wilkinson V.-C.	Conspiracy to injure by libelling a financial institution.	Is the interest of potential investors a relevant factor?	Yes. It is part of public interest, just as free speech is.

CASE	CITATION	JUDGE(S)	FACTS	ISSUES	ADJUDICATION
Financiera Avenida S.A. v. Shiblaq	(1991) T.L.R. 21	Lloyd L.J. Stocker L.J. Sir George Waller	Enforcing the cross-undertaking accompanying a *Mareva* injunction.	(i) What are the factors relevant to the exercise of the discretion to enforce? (ii) On what principles are damages assessed?	(i) (a) The circumstances in which the injunction has been obtained; (b) the success or otherwise of the plaintiff at trial; (c) the subsequent conduct of the defendant; (d) all the circumstances. (ii) The ordinary principles of law of contract both as to causation and quantum
Fresh Fruit Wales Ltd v. Halbert	*The Times,* January 29, 1991	Parker L.J. Balcombe L.J. Ralph Gibson L.J.	Defendants had tickets to imminent rugger match.	Did court have power to make interlocutory order it could not make at trial?	Yes.
Lagenes Ltd v. It's At (U.K.) Ltd	*The Times,* March 12, 1991	Ferris J.	*Ex parte* injunction had been granted upon material non-disclosure.	Where non-disclosure is not innocent, must the court discharge injunction?	No. It is a matter for the court's discretion.

CASE	CITATION	JUDGE(S)	FACTS	ISSUES	ADJUDICATION
Lansing Linde Ltd v. Kerr	[1991] 1 All E.R. 418	Butler-Sloss L.J. Staughton L.J. Beldam L.J.	Covenant in restraint of trade.	Should court take into account the strength of plaintiff's case?	Yes, if action cannot be heard until after expiry of period of restraint.
Laurence (David) Ltd v. Ashton	[1991] 1 All E.R. 385	Fox L.J. Balcombe L.J.	Covenant in restraint of trade, and covenant not to disclose confidential information.	(i) Does *American Cyanamid* apply? (ii) Injunction to prevent trade? (iii) Injunction to prevent disclosure?	(i) Yes, if the action can be tried quickly. (ii) Yes. (iii) No. Too imprecise.
Mirage Studios v. Counter-Feat Clothing Co. Ltd	[1991] F.S.R. 145	Browne-Wilkinson V.-C.	Passing-off and copyright in Teenage Mutant Ninja Turtles	Could the defendants rely upon the plaintiff's two-month delay in issuing a writ?	No, because it was explained by the fact that the plaintiffs were trying to enforce their rights via trading standards authority.
Newsgroup Newspapers Ltd v. The Mirror Group Newspapers (1986) Ltd	[1991] F.S.R. 487	Hoffmann J.	Trade mark and copyright action by the *Sun* against the *Daily Mirror*.	What is the effect of a delay of two years following an interlocutory injunction?	Injunction discharged.

CASE	CITATION	JUDGE(S)	FACTS	ISSUES	ADJUDICATION
Pickering v. Liverpool Daily Post	[1991] 2 A.C. 370	Lord Bridge Lord Brandon Lord Templeman Lord Goff Lord Lowry	Murderer's application for injunction to prevent publication of proceedings in Mental Health Tribunal.	The breadth of the court's powers under section 37 of the Supreme Court Act 1981.	The court's powers are limited by authority.
Southway Group Ltd v. Wolff	(1991) T.L.R. 251	Mustill L.J. Nourse L.J.	*Mareva* injunction where plaintiff gave undertaking	Where defendant suggests that cross-undertaking should be "fortified" by a certain level of security, can the judge require more security?	No.
Bhimji v. Chatwani (No. 2)	[1992] 1 W.L.R. 1158	Knox J.	Claim for fraud.	When will the Court "fortify" a cross-undertaking in damages by ordering security?	(i) Defendant must show likelihood of significant loss. (ii) Plaintiff insolvent.

CASE	CITATION	JUDGE(S)	FACTS	ISSUES	ADJUDICATION
Re Capital Expansion & Development Corporation Ltd	(1992) T.L.R. 570	Millet J.	Injunction preventing a secured creditor from enforcing his security.	Court can find time quickly for short *ex parte* application to grant injunction. What about the longer hearing *inter partes* to discharge it?	Court must expedite the *inter partes* hearing if it expedited the *ex parte* hearing.
City of London Corporation v. Bovis Construction Ltd	[1992] 3 All E.R. 697	O'Connor L.J. Bingham L.J. Taylor L.J.	Noise nuisance by building works in contravention of notice under the Control of Pollution Act s. 60.	(i) Can injunction be granted even though criminal contravention of the notice had not been established? (ii) What is the test for granting an injunction?	(i) Yes (ii) Can it be inferred that the defendants' unlawful activities will continue unless restrained by injunction?
EMI Records Ltd v. The C.D. Specialists Ltd	[1992] F.S.R. 70	Hoffmann J.	*Anton Piller* order in proceedings for copyright infringement.	In an application to discharge for non-disclosure, what procedure should be followed?	Give notice of the precise non-disclosures relied upon.

CASE	CITATION	JUDGE(S)	FACTS	ISSUES	ADJUDICATION
Graham v. Delderfield	[1992] F.S.R. 313	Dillon L.J. Stocker L.J. Butler-Sloss L.J.	Misuse of confidential information in invention for repair of roads.	When is the status quo in a case where there was no letter before action and delay after issue of writ before service?	Service of writ fixes the status quo.
National Bank of Sharjah v. Dellborg	(1992) T.L.R. 643	Lloyd L.J. Ralph Gibson L.J. Sir Michael Kerr	*Mareva* injunction for fraud.	Is the obligation to disclose all material facts equivalent to disclosing all relevant documents?	No. Do not exhibit all relevant documents.
Ocean Software Ltd v. Kay	[1992] 1 Q.B. 583	Scott L.J. Sir David Croom-Johnson	*Mareva* injunction in respect of the royalties from the sale of a computer game.	Where the Court of Appeal refused an injunction granted at first instance, to whom does a party apply to discharge?	A judge.
Polly Peck International plc v. Nadir (No. 2)	[1992] 4 All E.R. 769	Lord Donaldson M.R. Stocker L.J. Scott L.J.	Fraudulent transfer of funds offshore.	(i) *Mareva* against a bank? (ii) *Mareva* when tracing remedy available?	(i) Not normally, particularly if it would interfere with normal banking business. (ii) No.

CASE	CITATION	JUDGE(S)	FACTS	ISSUES	ADJUDICATION
Universal Thermosensors Ltd v. Hibben	[1992] 1 W.L.R. 840	Nicholls V.-C.	Claim for misuse of confidential information.	(i) Is defendant entitled to damages on the cross-undertaking even if he consented to the injunction? (ii) Safeguards for the execution of *Anton Piller* orders?	(i) Yes. The defendant is not prejudiced by his consent. (ii) Guidelines given.
Re All Starr Video Ltd	(1993) T.L.R. 171	Dillon L.J. Leggatt L.J.	Petition under section 459 Companies Act 1985	*Ex parte Mareva* injunction during *inter partes* hearing?	No. Application should be *inter partes*.
Channel Tunnel Group Ltd v. Balfour Beatty Construction Ltd	[1993] A.C. 334	Lord Keith Lord Goff Lord Jauncey Lord Browne-Wilkinson Lord Mustill	Building contract containing provision for arbitration abroad.	(i) Can the court grant an interlocutory injunction where there is a foreign arbitration clause? (ii) Injunction to prevent defendants stopping work?	(i) Yes. (ii) No, because it would pre-empt the very issue at the arbitration.

1065

CASE	CITATION	JUDGE(S)	FACTS	ISSUES	ADJUDICATION
Cheltenham and Gloucester Building Society v. Ricketts	[1993] 4 All E.R. 276	Neill L.J. Mann L.J. Peter Gibson L.J.	Mortgage fraud by overvaluing properties and obtaining mortgages using false names.	When will the Court enforce a cross-undertaking as to damages?	Discretion exercisable on ordinary equitable principles by any convenient means at any stage of the action.
Dalgety Spillers Foods Ltd v. Food Brokers Ltd	(1993) T.L.R. 618	Blackburne J.	Passing off as "Pot Noodles". The plaintiffs had ignored a letter warning them of the defendants' planned product.	Is the behaviour of the parties relevant?	Yes.
Re J (a Minor) (Child in Care: Medical Treatment)	[1993] Fam. 15	Lord Donaldson M.R. Balcombe L.J. Taylor L.J.	Baby with severe brain damage could be kept alive by hospital until late adolescence.	What are the principles on which a court should act to allow a child to die?	A balancing exercise.
Kirklees M.B.C. v. Wickes Building Supplies Ltd	[1993] A.C. 227	Lord Keith Lord Ackner Lord Goff Lord Jauncey Lord Lowry	Council applied for injunction to restrain criminal offences under the Shops Act 1950	(i) Did the Crown's exemption from the need to give a cross-undertaking in damages *qua* law-enforcer extend to local authority law-enforcers? (ii) What is the relevance of the defendant's defence? (iii) What about a	(i) Yes. (ii) A defence went to the Court's discretion whether to grant relief. (iii) A Euro-defence is no reason to require a cross-undertaking.

CASE	CITATION	JUDGE(S)	FACTS	ISSUES	ADJUDICATION
M. v. Home Office	[1993] 3 All E.R. 537	Lord Keith Lord Templeman Lord Griffiths Lord Browne-Wilkinson Lord Woolf	The Home Secretary was guilty of contempt of Court in an immigration case	Can the Court grant an injunction against a minister of State?	Yes.
Moran v. University College, Salford	(1993) T.L.R. 528	Glidewell L.J. Evans L.J. Waite L.J.	N/A	Is leave to appeal required against the grant or refusal of an interlocutory injunction?	Court of Appeal gave guidelines. Leave is required.
Securities and Investments Board v. Lloyd-Wright	[1993] 4 All E.R. 210	Morritt J.	World-wide *Mareva* injunction under Financial Services Act 1986	Is there a discretion not to require a cross-undertaking from a designated agency discharging statutory law enforcement functions?	Yes, in spite of draconian effect of *Mareva* injunction.

CASE	CITATION	JUDGE(S)	FACTS	ISSUES	ADJUDICATION
Balkanbank v. Taber (No. 2)	(1994) T.L.R. 615	Staughton L.J. Beldam L.J. Waite L.J.	Cross-undertaking in damages accompanying *Mareva* injunction.	Where Court orders an enquiry as to damages "which the plaintiff ought to pay", what issues arise on the enquiry?	(i) Discretion whether to enforce the undertaking; (ii) causation; (iii) quantum.
Re C (Audit: Refusal of Medical treatment)	[1994] 1 W.L.R. 290	Thorpe J.	Adult mental patient would not consent to operation to amputate gangrenous foot.	Can the Court grant an injunction to the effect that a mental patient was incapable of refusing or consenting to medical treatment?	Yes, but evidence is necessary.
Deutsche Ruckverischëring Aktiengesellschaft v. Walbrook Insurance Co Ltd	[1994] 4 All E.R. 181; *The Times*, May 6, 1994	Phillips J. 250	Plaintiffs alleged that defendants had obtained letters of credit from them fraud, and applied for injunction to prevent them drawing upon them.	Can affidavit in support of application for interlocutory injunction exhibit intermediate sources of information (a DTI report)?	Yes.

CASE	CITATION	JUDGE(S)	FACTS	ISSUES	ADJUDICATION
Hong Kong Toy Centre Ltd v. Tomy UK Ltd	(1994) T.L.R. 24	Aldous J.	Infringement of patents.	Where plaintiff obtains injunction *ex parte* and the court does not fix a return day, can the plaintiff enjoy the delay and do nothing?	No. The plaintiff's relief will be withdrawn if he does not apply for earliest hearing date.

CASE	CITATION	JUDGE(S)	FACTS	ISSUES	ADJUDICATION
Roberts v. Death	(1881) 8 Q.B.D. 319; (1881–5) All E.R. 849			Must assets be held by defendant *qua* defendant?	Yes—not in any other capacity.
Lister & Co. v. Stubbs	(1890) 45 Ch. D. 1; 59 L.J.Ch. 570	Cotton L.J.	Agency case— payment in of claim sought.	Traditional view of ordering restraint on defendant's dealing.	Such restraint wrong in principle.
Apollinaris Company's Trade Mark, Re	[1891] 1 Ch. 1; 63 L.T. 502		Plaintiff made defendant to counterclaim.	Order for security for costs?	Not against foreign plaintiff with substantial assets permanently available within jurisdiction.
Seward v. Paterson	[1897] 1 Ch. 545		Injunction obtained.	May party (not servant/agent) be committed for assisting other to disobey injunction?	Yes.
Hubbard v. Woodfield	(1913) 57 S.J. 729		Injunction obtained.	May court restrain non-parties from assisting in breach?	Yes.

CASE	CITATION	JUDGE(S)	FACTS	ISSUES	ADJUDICATION
R. v. Kensington Income Tax Commissioners, ex p. Princess Edmond de Polignac	[1917] 1 K.B. 486; (1917) 86 L.J.K.B. 257	Viscount Reading C.J. Ridley J. Low J. (K.B.D.) Lord Cozens-Hardy M.R. Warrington L.J. Scrutton L.J.	Tax case. Profits from foreign possessions. Application for rule *nisi* for writ of prohibition. Affidavit of applicant not full/frank.	Could rule *nisi* be granted?	No. *Uberrimae fides* required from applicant.
Hudson's Concrete Products Ltd v. Evans (D.B.) (Bilston) Ltd	(1961) 105 S.J. 281, C.A.	Willmer L.J. Donovan L.J.	Judgment creditors obtained garnishee order.	Garnishee order set aside?	Yes—or would give judgment creditor priority over the creditors.
Chic Fashions (West Wales) Ltd v. Jones	[1968] 2 Q.B. 299; [1968] 2 W.L.R. 201	Lord Denning M.R. Diplock L.J. Salmon L.J.	Search for stolen goods under warrant.	Could constable seize only goods reasonably believed to be covered by warrant?	No. Property seized could include that reasonably believed to be stolen/evidence.
Usher's Brewery Ltd v. King (P.S.) & Co. (Finance) Ltd	[1972] Ch. 148; [1971] 2 W.L.R. 1411	Plowman J.	Action involving lease/mortgage. Interlocutory injunction?	Should court dissolve injunction/inquire into damages suffered by reason of injunction?	Inquiry only when plaintiff failed at trial or it was shown pre-trial that injunction should not have been granted.

CASE	CITATION	JUDGE(S)	FACTS	ISSUES	ADJUDICATION
Nippon Yusen Kaisha v. Karageorgis	[1975] 1 W.L.R. 1093; [1975] 3 All E.R.	Lord Denning M.R. Browne L.J. Geoffrey Lane L.J.	Shipping case.	Could *ex parte* injunction restraining defendant from removing assets be granted under s.45 of Supreme Court of Judicature (Consolidation) Act 1925?	Yes.
Rainbow v. Moorgate Properties Ltd	[1975] 1 W.L.R. 788; [1975] 2 All E.R. 821	Buckley L.J. Ormrod L.J.	Nuisance action. Defendant co. in voluntary liquidation.	(i) Should charging order be made on debtor's land? (ii) Direct appeal to Court of Appeal from district judge?	(i) Not if substantial doubt about defendant's solvency. (ii) Yes.
Wilson (D.) (Birmingham) Ltd v. Metropolitan Property Developments Ltd	[1975] 2 All E.R. 814	Buckley L.J. Thompson J.	Winding up of company; garnishee order *nisi*.	Garnishee order absolute?	Court must bear in mind position of all creditors of judgment debtor.

CASE	CITATION	JUDGE(S)	FACTS	ISSUES	ADJUDICATION
Anton Piller K.G. v. Manufacturing Processes Ltd	[1976] Ch. 55; [1976] 2 W.L.R. 162	Lord Denning M.R. Ormrod L.J. Shaw L.J.	Alleged disclosure of confidential information to commercial rivals.	(i) Does *Anton Piller* order give plaintiff right to enter defendant's premises/take his property without his consent?	(i) No.
				(ii) Does court have jurisdiction to grant order *ex parte* requiring defendant to allow the plaintiff to enter his premises/take property?	(ii) Yes.
Cybil Inc. v. Timpuship	1978 (C.A.T. No. 478)	Stamp J.	Grant of *Mareva* would effectively put defendants out of business.	What was "balance of convenience"?	If hardship to defendant outweighed advantage to plaintiff this would militate against *Mareva*.
Cretanor Maritime Co. Ltd v. Irish Marine Management Ltd	[1978] 1 W.L.R. 966; [1978] 3 All E.R. 164	Buckley L.J. Goff L.J. Sir David Cairns	Dispute between foreign shipowner and foreign charterer going to arbitration in London. Injunction against charterer.	Could receiver under debenture of charter apply for discharge of injunction?	Yes. By virtue of position as debenture holder.

CASE	CITATION	JUDGE(S)	FACTS	ISSUES	ADJUDICATION
Howe Richardson Scale Co. Ltd v. Polimex-Cekop	[1978] 1 Lloyd's Rep. 161	Roskill L.J. Cumming-Bruce L.J.	Contract buyers alleged non-delivery.	(i) Bound to honour guarantee to sellers?	(i) Yes. Similar principle to irrevocable letters of credit.
				(ii) Should injunction restraining sellers for claiming guarantee be granted?	(ii) No. Balance of convenience was against injunction.
Rasu v. Maritima S.A. v. Perusahaan	[1978] 1 Q.B. 644; [1977] 3 W.L.R. 578	Lord Denning M.R. Orr L.J.	Claim for breach of charter party. Defendants outside court's jurisdiction sought to remove assets from England.	Did court have jurisdiction to issue injunction restraining removal?	Yes. Under s.45 of 1925 Act.
Negocios del Mar S.A. v. Doric Shipping Corp. S.A.; Assios, The	[1979] 1 Lloyd's Rep. 331	Lord Denning M.R. Stephenson L.J. Shaw L.J.	Ship sale—contract case.	Could sale proceeds be frozen in seller's hands as security for damages for faults with ship?	*Mareva* initially granted, then discharged—not full and frank disclosure.

CASE	CITATION	JUDGE(S)	FACTS	ISSUES	ADJUDICATION
Etablissement Esefka International Anstalt v. Central Bank of Nigeria	[1979] 1 Lloyd's Rep. 445	Lord Denning M.R. Lawton L.J. Brandon L.J.	Letter of credit. Allegation that documents forged.	Would court order *Mareva* against defendant's bank?	No *Mareva* granted against reputable bank.
Fary-Jones (Insurance) Ltd v. I.F.M. Funding	(April 10, 1979; unreported)			Good arguable case?	To obtain/retain *Mareva*, plaintiff must establish good arguable case and also that court which deals with matter entitled/bound to look at both parties' cases.
Montecchi v. Shimco (U.K.) Ltd	[1979] 1 W.L.R. 1180, C.A.; (1978) 123 S.J. 551	Roskill L.J. Lane L.J. Bridge L.J.	Italian plaintiffs sold goods to English defendant company. Action to recover dishonoured bills of exchange.	Would court grant stay of execution/*Mareva* against plaintiffs?	Court had jurisdiction to make *Mareva* order but here no evidence of intention to avoid future liability.
Rena K, The	[1979] 1 Q.B. 377; [1978] 3 W.L.R. 431	Brandon J.	Action against shipowners by owners of ruined cargo.	Was *Mareva* order an alternative to arrest of ship?	Yes.

1075

CASE	CITATION	JUDGE(S)	FACTS	ISSUES	ADJUDICATION
Third Chandris Shipping Corp. v. Unimarine S.A.	[1979] Q.B. 645; [1979] 3 W.L.R. 122	Lord Denning M.R. Lawton L.J. Cumming-Bruce L.J.	Charter party case.	Court's jurisdiction to grant *Mareva*?	High Court had jurisdiction if evidence that debtor intended to transfer assets outside jurisdiction to defeat debt.
Visionair International Inc. v. Euroworld California Inc.	(November 30, 1979, C.A., unreported)	Lord Denning M.R. Goff L.J.	Plaintiff claimed to own aircraft at Exeter airport. Injunction preventing defendants from flying aircraft out. Defendants applied to discharge.	Did plaintiffs have "good" arguable case?	No. Injunction discharged.
Bakarim v. Victoria P. Shipping Co. Ltd; Tatiangela, The	[1980] 2 Lloyd's Rep. 193	Parker J.	Defendant outside the jurisdiction wanted to make payment to another within jurisdiction.	To what extent did defendant have to justify payment? See *Intraco Ltd v. Notis Shipping Corp. of Liberia.*	Payment prima facie justified, provided not a disguised method of removing assets from jurisdiction.

CASE	CITATION	JUDGE(S)	FACTS	ISSUES	ADJUDICATION
Bakarim v. Victoria P. Shipping Co.; Tatiangela, The	As above.		Charter of ship vessel sank with plaintiff's cargo. See *Avant Petroleum Inc. v. Catoil Overseas Inc.*, below.	Could plaintiff obtain *Mareva* over hull insurance policy held by defendants?	No. Plaintiff failed to show good arguable case.
Bankers Trust Co. v. Shapira	[1980] 1 W.L.R. 1274	Lord Denning M.R. Waller L.J. Dunn L.J.	Money obtained by forgery.	Would court order disclosure of confidential information concerning banker/customer relationship?	Such order justified where plaintiffs sought funds which in equity belonged to them.
Barclay-Johnson v. Yuill	[1980] 1 W.L.R. 1259; [1980] 3 All E.R. 190	Sir Robert Megarry V.-C.	*Mareva* application. English defendant domiciled in England.	Was *Mareva* jurisdiction restricted to preventing foreigners from removing assets from jurisdiction?	Defendant's nationality/domicile were material factors but *Mareva* was not barred simply because defendant not a foreigner/foreign-based.
Barker v. Wilson	[1980] 1 W.L.R. 884; [1980] 2 All E.R. 81	Bridge L.J. Caulfield J.	Alleged deficiencies in company's books.	What is a "book" for the purposes of the Bankers' Books Evidence Act 1879?	Books include microfiche, magnetic tape and other data retrieval systems.

CASE	CITATION	JUDGE(S)	FACTS	ISSUES	ADJUDICATION
Dellborg v. Corix Properties and Blissfield Corp. N.V.	June 26, 1980 (C.A.T. No. 541)	Lawton L.J.	*Mareva* ordered.	Would *Mareva* inhibit defendant companies' objects?	In practice, no, because defendants would arrange alternative security.
Kirby v. Banks	1980 (C.A.T. No. 624)			Land an asset included in *Mareva* jurisdiction?	Yes.
Rahman (Prince Abdul) bin Turki al Sudairy v. Abu-Taha	[1980] 1 W.L.R. 1268; [1980] 3 All E.R. 409	Lord Denning M.R. Waller L.J. Dunn L.J.	*Mareva* application. English defendant.	Was *Mareva* jurisdiction restricted to preventing foreigners from removing assets from jurisdiction?	Defendant's nationality/domicile were material facts but *Mareva* was not barred simply because defendant not a foreigner/foreign-based.
Sanko Steamship Co. Ltd v. D.C. Commodities (Australasia) Pty Ltd	[1980] W.A.R. 51		Shipping.	Ships' bunkers included in *Mareva* jurisdiction?	Yes.
Stewart Chartering v. C. & O. Managements S.A.; Venus Destiny, The	[1980] 1 W.L.R. 460; [1980] 1 All E.R. 718	Goff J.	Shipping case. Application for liquidated sum and *Mareva*.	Could plaintiffs enter judgment in default?	Yes. By court's inherent jurisdiction to prevent abuse of its process.

CASE	CITATION	JUDGE(S)	FACTS	ISSUES	ADJUDICATION
Stolt Filia, The	L.M.L.N. Issue No. 15, 1980	Sheen J.	Spare parts/services provided for ship. Owners did not pay. Mortgagees arrested vessel. Nothing seemed left for plaintiffs.	Could plaintiffs obtain *Mareva*?	No. Only action *in rem* against ship. No service out of jurisdiction under Ord. 11.
A. v. C. (No. 2)	[1981] 2 W.L.R. 654	Goff J.	Defendant to *Mareva* claimed assets required for purpose not contrary to policy underlying *Mareva* jurisdiction (legal costs).	Could *Mareva* injunction be qualified in this situation?	Not in this case. Defendants failed to show they had no other assets to pay legal costs.
A. v. C. (Note)	[1981] Q.B. 956	Goff J.	*Mareva* injunction. Defendants resisted disclosure of sums in bank accounts.	Did court have jurisdiction to order discovery/interrogatories?	Yes.
Bekhor (A.J.) & Co. Ltd. v. Bilton	[1981] 1 Q.B. 923; [1981] 2 W.L.R. 601; [1981] 2 All E.R. 565	Ackner L.J. Stephenson L.J. Griffiths L.J.	Claim for liquidated sum.	Could court order discovery or interrogatories in aid of *Mareva* injunction?	Yes, pursuant to Judicature (Consolidation) Act 1925, s.45(1).

1079

CASE	CITATION	JUDGE(S)	FACTS	ISSUES	ADJUDICATION
Clipper Maritime Co. Ltd. of Monrovia v. Mineralimport-export; The Marie Leonhardt	[1981] 1 W.L.R. 1262; [1981] 3 All E.R. 644	Goff J.	Third party vessel chartered under time charter.	Could plaintiff indemnify third party?	Yes. Charter with third party was time charter. Loss more likely to fall on defendants.
Clipper Maritime Co. Ltd. of Monrovia v. Mineralimport-export; The Marie Leonhardt	As above.	Goff J.	*Mareva*. Innocent third party affected.	How should *Mareva* jurisdiction be implemented?	Implementation should take account of innocent third party's interests.
Hitachi Shipbuilding and Engineering Co. Ltd v. Viafel Compania Naviera S.A.	[1981] 2 Lloyd's Rep. 498, C.A.	Donaldson L.J. Ackner L.J.	Shipbuilding contract. Plaintiffs obtained *Mareva* at arbitration. Plaintiffs applied for security for costs of arbitration.	Interaction of *Mareva*/security for costs.	*Mareva* for benefit of plaintiffs. Security for costs sought by defendants/respondents in arbitration. No interaction unless a counterclaim.
Intraco Ltd v. Notis Shipping Corp. of Liberia; Bhoja Trader, The	[1981] Com.L.R. 184; [1981] 2 Lloyd's Rep. 256	Ackner L.J. Donaldson L.J.	See *Barker v. Wilson* [1980].		

CASE	CITATION	JUDGE(S)	FACTS	ISSUES	ADJUDICATION
Iraqi Ministry of Defence v. Arcepey Shipping Co. S.A. and Gillespie Brothers and Co.; Angel Bell, The	[1981] Q.B. 65; [1980] 2 W.L.R. 488	Goff J.	Shipping case. Creditors intervening to seek variation of *Mareva* to allow defendants to make loan repayments.	Court's jurisdiction to vary *Mareva*.	Variation allowed.
Johnson v. L. & A. Philatelics	[1981] F.S.R. 286	Goff J.	Plaintiff claimed defendants owed him money and sought orders to prevent defendants from dealing with their stocks and allowing plaintiff's solicitors to search for and take the stock (stamps).	Should injunctions be granted?	Order granted. Evidence that defendants about to close business/leave jurisdiction.
Panton (Faith) Property Plan Ltd v. Hodgetts	[1981] 1 W.L.R. 927	Waller L.J. Brandon L.J. Sir David Cairns	Passing off case. Interlocutory order for payment of taxed costs. Defendant threatened to sell assets/make himself bankrupt. Plaintiff sought order restraining defendant.	Did court have jurisdiction under Supreme Court of Judicature (Consolidation) Act 1925 or *Mareva* decisions to grant injunction restraining disposal of assets before trial?	Court granted injunction under 1925 Act.

CASE	CITATION	JUDGE(S)	FACTS	ISSUES	ADJUDICATION
Power Curber International Ltd v. National bank of Kuwait SAK	[1981] 1 W.L.R. 1233; [1981] 3 All E.R. 607	Lord Denning M.R. Griffiths L.J. Waterhouse J.	Irrevocable letter of credit. Credit conflict of laws.	Which was proper law of letter of credit? Which was *lex situs* of debt? Stay of execution of summary judgment?	Proper law and lexsins were both U.S. (plaintiff's base). No stay of execution.
Searose Ltd v. Seatrain U.K. Ltd	[1981] 1 W.L.R. 894; [1981] 1 All E.R. 806	Goff J.	Contract. Application for *Mareva*.	Position of banks.	Plaintiff must identify defendant's accounts, etc. with as much precision as reasonably practicable. Plaintiff must initially bear bank's costs.
Thermax v. Schott Industrial Glass	[1981] F.S.R. 289	Foster J.	Copyright in engines. Defendant bought/reconditioned such engines.	Interlocutory injunction to prevent reconditioning using pistons not made by plaintiffs?	No—In absence of express conditions.
Bank Mellat v. Nikpour (Mohammed Ebrahim)	[1982] Com.L.R. 158; [1985] F.S.R. 87	Lord Denning M.R. Donaldson L.J. Slade L.J.	Banking case.	Basis of *Mareva* order.	Exceptional remedy. Full and frank disclosure required.

CASE	CITATION	JUDGE(S)	FACTS	ISSUES	ADJUDICATION
Darashah v. U.F.A.C. U.K. Ltd	*The Times*, March 30, 1982	Lord Denning M.R. Ackner L.J. O'Connor L.J.	Contract Animal nutrition consultant.	Can damages lie for loss of business goodwill?	Yes. Goodwill can be valuable commodity.
Galaxia Maritima S.A. v. Mineral Importexport; Eleftherios, The	[1982] 1 W.L.R. 539; [1982] 1 All E.R. 796	Eveleigh L.J. Kerr L.J.	Plaintiff claimed demurrage under charter party. *Mareva* included cargo on third party vessel chartered under voyage charter.	Could plaintiff indemnify third party?	No. Plaintiff could not buy off a third party's rights.
Project Development Co. S.A. v. K.M.K. Securities	[1982] 1 W.L.R. 1470; [1983] 1 All E.R. 465.	Parker J.	Innocent third party affected by *Mareva* successfully applied for variation.	To what costs was third party entitled?	Entitled to all reasonable costs. Burden of establishing reasonableness is on third party.
Z. v. A–Z and AA–LL	[1982] 1 Q.B. 558; [1982] 2 W.L.R. 288	Lord Denning M.R. Kerr L.J. Eveleigh L.J.	Allegation of fraud by forged telexes, etc.	*Mareva* orders generally. "Maximum sum" orders. Special difficulties of banks.	Plaintiff should give undertakings in damages to defendant/third parties. "Maximum sum" orders preferable.

CASE	CITATION	JUDGE(S)	FACTS	ISSUES	ADJUDICATION
A. v. B. (X intervening)	[1983] 2 Lloyd's Rep. 532; (1983) 133 New L.J. 725	Parker J.	Mareva obtained against defendant. Defendant indebted to interveners.	Whether interveners' application to vary injunction should be granted.	Mareva should not be used to prevent a defendant meeting a debt of honour.
C.B.S. United Kingdom Ltd v. Lambert	[1983] Ch. 37; [1982] 3 W.L.R. 746	Lawton L.J. Templeman L.J. Fox L.J.	Copyright case.	Court's jurisdiction to grant Mareva?	Court had jurisdiction if it appeared "just and convenient."
Chief Constable of Kent v. V	[1983] Q.B. 34; [1982] 3 W.L.R. 462	Lord Denning M.R. Donaldson L.J.	V arrested/charged. Attempt to restrain V from dealing with alleged proceeds.	Could court order injunction restraining V?	Yes. Chief Constable had interest because of duty to recover stolen goods.
Home Office v. Harman	[1983] A.C. 280; [1982] 2 W.L.R. 338	Lord Diplock Lord Simon Lord Keith Lord Scarman Lord Roskill	Solicitor allegedly disclosed confidential documents.	What is basis of production of documents to solicitor?	Implied undertaking by solicitor that documents will not be used for collateral/ulterior purposes.
Ninemia Maritime Corp. v. Trave Schiffabrtsgesellschaft mbH & Co. K.G., (Niedersachsen, The)	[1983] 1 W.L.R. 1412; [1983] 2 Lloyd's Rep. 660	Eveleigh L.J. Kerr L.J. Dillon L.J.	Ship purchase contract.	Basis for Mareva order.	Order where just and convenient on good arguable case.

CASE	CITATION	JUDGE(S)	FACTS	ISSUES	ADJUDICATION
Ninemia Maritime Corp. v. Trave Schiffahrtsgesellschaft mbH & Co. K.G., (Niedersachsen, The)	As above.		Ship sale. Plaintiff buyers alleged non-conformity with contract. Paid for ship but sought *Mareva*.	Could *Mareva* be granted in respect of sum to cover alleged deficiencies?	*Mareva* not intended to provide security for claims. Test was whether just and convenient (was there real risk that judgment for plaintiff would remain unsatisfied?).
Oceanica Castelana S.A. of Panama v. Mineral Importexport	[1983] 1 W.L.R. 1294	Lloyd J.	Shipping case.	Difficulties created for banks *et al* by *Mareva* applications.	Banks should be able to look to plaintiffs for cooperation.
PCW (Underwriting Agencies) Ltd v. Dixon (P.S.)	[1983] 2 All E.R. 158; (1983) 133 New L.J. 204	Lloyd J.	Allegation that director made unauthorised profits.	What was purpose of *Mareva*?	Purpose was to prevent plaintiff being cheated out of proceeds of judgment, not to give plaintiff priority over defendant's assets.
Campbell Mussels v. Thompson	(1984) 81 L.S.Gaz. 2140	Sir John Donaldson M.R.	Defendant's application to qualify injunction granted.	Was test in *A. v. C. (No. 2)* valid?	Every case must be dealt with on merits. *Mareva* not designed to put plaintiff in position of secured creditor.

CASE	CITATION	JUDGE(S)	FACTS	ISSUES	ADJUDICATION
Continental Airlines Inc. v. Aviation and Tourist Marketing A.G.	(January 18, 1984, Webster J. Com. Ct, unreported)	Webster J.	Plaintiff had good arguable case for certain sum. Defendants had arguable counterclaim for most of it.	For what sum would Mareva be granted, if at all?	If granted, Mareva for balance only.
K/S A/S Admiral Shipping v. Portlink Ferries Ltd	[1984] 2 Lloyd's Rep. 166; (1984) 81 L.S.Gaz. 1676	Sir John Donaldson M.R. May L.J. Purchas L.J.	Ship lease: Mareva injunction for plaintiffs.	Should plaintiffs be treated as unsecured but established creditors?	Courts could not give plaintiffs quasi-secured status.
Orwell Steel (Erection and Fabrication) v. Asphalt & Tarmac (U.K.) Ltd	[1984] 1 W.L.R. 1097; [1985] 3 All E.R. 747	Farquharson J.	Claim for liquidated sum.	Did High Court have power to grant Mareva in aid of execution?	Yes. Where plaintiff can adduce evidence of usual kind in Mareva application.
Sanders Lead Co. Inc. v. Entones Metal Brokers Ltd	[1984] 1 W.L.R. 452; [1984] 1 All E.R. 857	Stephenson L.J. Kerr L.J.	Dispute over alleged purchase of lead.	Could third party have financial interest in outcome of action intervene?	Third party intervener's interest must be directly related to subject matter of action.

CASE	CITATION	JUDGE(S)	FACTS	ISSUES	ADJUDICATION
Stockler v. Fourways Estates Ltd	[1984] 1 W.L.R. 25; [1983] 3 All E.R. 501	Kilner Brown J.	Landcharge.	Could *Mareva* injunction be registered in land register?	No.
C.B.S. United Kingdom Ltd v. Perry	[1985] F.S.R. 421	Falconer J.	Copyright.	In what circumstances may oral examination of a defendant be ordered?	Before order for cross-examination, court must be reasonably satisfied that subject has relevant knowledge.
Chief Constable of Hampshire v. A.	[1985] Q.B. 132; [1984] 2 W.L.R. 954	Waller L.J. Oliver L.J. Purchas L.J.	Application to restrain criminal defendants from dissipating alleged proceeds of crime. Funds only partly such proceeds.	Did court have jurisdiction?	Yes, but only if proceeds identified.
Hill Samuel & Co. v. Littaur (No. 2)	(1985) 129 S.J. 433	Bingham J.	Loans on security of defendant's stamp collection.	(i) Injunction interlocutory if between judgment/execution?	(i) Yes: If an aid of court's procedure/to safeguard rights of parties.
				(ii) Nature of *Mareva* in aid of execution?	(ii) Does not interfere with insolvency law/make beneficiary a secured creditor.

CASE	CITATION	JUDGE(S)	FACTS	ISSUES	ADJUDICATION
House of Spring Gardens Ltd v. Waite	(1985) 129 S.J. 64; [1985] F.S.R. 173	Slade L.J. Cumming-Bruce L.J.	Copyright case.	In what circumstances may oral examination of a defendant be ordered?	If defendant determined to put assets beyond plaintiff's reach and conceal them from court.
International Bank and Trust Corp. Ltd v. Joao Luis Perestrello	(October 15, 1985 C.A.T.)		*Mareva/Anton Piller* orders.	Principle of full/frank disclosure.	Discharge of orders.
Lipkin Gorman (a firm) v. Cass	*The Times*, May 29, 1985	Walton J.	Plaintiff sought to recover stolen money. Needed information regarding defendant's accounts/deposits.	Could writ *ne exeat regno* be granted?	Yes. To assist plaintiff in tracing funds.
SCF Finance Co. Ltd. v. Masri	[1985] 1 W.L.R. 876; [1985] 2 All E.R. 747	Webster J.	*Mareva* application. Some assets in hands of third party. Plaintiff alleging defendant trading through wife's bank a/c.	Was court obliged to accept account of defendant/third party intervening that assets belonged to third party?	Court was not so obliged.

1088

CASE	CITATION	JUDGE(S)	FACTS	ISSUES	ADJUDICATION
X. Bank v. G.	(1985) 82 L.S.Gaz 2016 (D.C.); *The Times*, April 13, 1985	Cumming-Bruce L.J. Hollings J.	Commercial case.	Extent of court's jurisdiction to make interlocutory orders.	Extends to disclosure/restraint of foreign Cos./trusts.
Al Nahkel for Contracting and Trading v. Lowe	[1986] Q.B. 235; [1986] 2 W.L.R. 317	Tudor Price J.	Defendant employed by plaintiff company outside jurisdiction, detained at Gatwick. Handed some funds out, kept others and intended to leave jurisdiction.	Could *Mareva* be combined with writ *ne exeat regno?*	Yes.
Avant Petroleum Inc. v. Gatoil Overseas Inc.	[1986] 2 Lloyd's Rep. 236	O'Connor L.J. Neill J.	Contract for sale of crude oil. Plaintiff obtained *Mareva*.	Would *Mareva* be discharged?	*Mareva* not discharged.
Bayer AG v. Winter (No. 2)	[1986] 1 W.L.R. 540; [1986] 2 All E.R. 43	Scott J.	Passing off action.	In what circumstances may oral examination of a defendant be ordered?	Difficult to envisage circumstances in which oral examination right.

CASE	CITATION	JUDGE(S)	FACTS	ISSUES	ADJUDICATION
Hispanica de Petroles S.A. v. Vencedora Oceania Navegacion S.A.; Kapetan Markos, The	[1986] 1 Lloyd's Rep. 211	Ackner L.J. Stephen Brown L.J.	Carriage of goods by sea. Explosion on vessel. Salvage costs. Plaintiffs claimed indemnity.	Was mistake in framing cause of action fatal to *Mareva*?	No, when factual substances of the case remained unaltered.
Siporex Trade S.A. v. Comdel Commodities Ltd	[1986] 2 Lloyd's Rep. 146; (1986) 136 New L.J. 538	Hirst J.	Contract case. Letters of credit. Performance bond.	Was performance bond an absolute obligation?	Yes. Bank strictly liable to pay.
Steamship Mutual Underwriting Association (Bermuda) Ltd v. Thakbur Shipping Co. Ltd	[1986] 2 Lloyd's Rep. 439	Sir John Donaldson M.R. May L.J. O'Connor L.J.	Shipping. No existing cause of action other than for declaration.	*Mareva* available to support declaratory relief?	No.
T.D.K. Tape Distributors (U.K.) Ltd v. Videochoice Ltd	[1986] 1 W.L.R. 141; [1985] 3 All E.R. 345	Skinner J.	*Mareva* against defendant. Affidavit of means. Defendant acquired further asset and used it to pay Q.C. to defend him in criminal matters.	Could defendant/his solicitor be committed for contempt?	Asset was not after-acquired but even if it was it was caught by injunction. Q.C.'s fees an exceptional expense and not an ordinary living expense.

CASE	CITATION	JUDGE(S)	FACTS	ISSUES	ADJUDICATION
T.D.K. Tape Distributors (U.K.) Ltd. v. Videochoice Ltd.	As above.	Skinner J.	See Galaxia Maritime S.A. v. Mineral Importexport; Eleftherios, The, [1982] above.		
Block v. Nicholson (t/a Limascue Stud)	[1987] C.L.Y. 3064; (April 17, 1986, C.A.T. No. 409)		Plaintiff obtained Mareva but did not disclose his arrest for fraud.	Contents of affidavit.	Must be full/frank, including criminal charge/conviction against applicant.
Eastglen International Corp. v. Monpare S.A.	(1987) 137 New L.J. 56	Sir John Donaldson M.R. Ralph Gibson L.J. Nicholls L.J.	Business dispute. Plaintiff obtained Mareva.	Non-disclosure through fault of plaintiff's solicitor. Automatic discharge?	Yes.
Al Mohamed Shorafa Al Hamadi & Another v. Tarik Alfred Alsa Samra & Another	(November 17, 1987, unreported)		Mareva application.	Is failure to disclose a defence?	Generally yes, but not if non-disclosure immaterial.

CASE	CITATION	JUDGE(S)	FACTS	ISSUES	ADJUDICATION
American Express Bank Ltd v. Ali and Fahd Shoboksh Group Ltd	(April 1, 1987; unreported)		*Mareva* sought.	Can overdrawn bank account be basis for *Mareva*?	Yes.
Bebbehanie v. Salem	(September 11, 1987, unreported)		*Ex parte* order discharged for non-disclosure.	Order re-granted?	Not if non-disclosure due to deliberate lack of candour.
British Air Ferries Ltd v. Svenska Aktie Bolvet for Direkta Kompetition-Saffaver	(April 22, 1987, unreported)		*Mareva* case.	Ownership?	Must be sufficiently certain.
Commodity Ocean Transport Corp. v. Basford Unicorn Industries Ltd; Mito, The	[1987] 2 Lloyd's Rep. 197	Hirst J.	Application by defendants for security for plaintiffs in damages (*Mareva*).	Security order following discharge of *Mareva*?	No. Court would not impose additional term *ex post facto*.
Deutsche Schachtbau-und-Tiefbohrgesellschaft mbH v. The R'As Al Khaimah National Oil Co	[1987] 3 W.L.R. 1023; [1987] 2 All E.R. 769	Sir John Donaldson M.R. Woolf L.J. Russell L.J.	Exploration for oil contract.	Debt owing to defendants by English company payable in America. Asset within jurisdiction?	Yes.

CASE	CITATION	JUDGE(S)	FACTS	ISSUES	ADJUDICATION
Laffey (J.J.) & Co. Ltd v. Wrightson	(November 13, 1987, unreported)		*Mareva* application.	Legal/equitable right necessary?	Yes—But not to support possible future action.
Law Society v. Shanks	(1987) 131 S.J. 1626; [1988] 1 FLR 504	Sir John Donaldson M.R. Neill L.J. Sir Roualeyn Cumming-Bruce	Costs order against defendant: *Mareva.* Employers refused to pay gratuity/pension.	Should *Mareva* be set aside?	Yes. No evidence defendant intended to dissipate funds.
National Bank of Greece v. Constantinos Dimitriou	*The Times,* November 16, 1987 C.A.	Parker L.J. Caulfield J.	Defendant had unfrozen/undisclosed assets outside jurisdiction.	*Mareva* varied to release funds to pay solicitor?	No.
Unicorn Shipping v. Demet Navy Shipping Co.	[1987] 2 FTLR 109		Time charter. Injunction restraining charterer from removing bunkers from jurisdiction.	Injunction discharged after charter period?	Yes. Would unfairly prejudice owners of ship.
Allied Arab Bank v. Hajjar	[1988] Q.B. 787; [1988] 2 W.L.R. 942; [1987] 3 All E.R. 739	Legatt J.	Defendant was guarantor of loan.	Writ *ne exeat regno.* Would defendant's absence prejudice plaintiff's claim?	No writ if only prejudice is to execution.

CASE	CITATION	JUDGE(S)	FACTS	ISSUES	ADJUDICATION
Allied Arab Bank Ltd v. Hajjar	As above.		Commercial *Mareva*.	Should wife's account be frozen?	No. Even though defendant could draw on it.
Babanaft International Co. S.A. v. Bassatne	[1989] 2 W.L.R. 232, C.A.; (1988) 138 New L.J. 203	Kerr L.J. Neill L.J. Nicholls L.J.	Commercial *Mareva*.	Unqualified *Mareva* freezing assets abroad justified?	No, never. No objection to personal order binding defendant only.
Bir v. Sharma	*The Times*, December 7, 1988	Vinelott J.	*Mareva* obtained on basis of fabricated evidence.	Costs of application/discharge?	Against plaintiff on indemnity basis.
Brink's-Mat Ltd v. Elcombe	[1988] 1 W.L.R. 1350; [1988] 3 All E.R. 188; [1989] F.S.R. 211	Slade L.J. Balcombe L.J. Ralph Gibson L.J.	*Mareva* application arising from robbery.	Would *ex parte* order be set aside?	No. Non-disclosure not material.
Chief Constable of Leicestershire v. M.	[1988] 3 All E.R. 1015	Hoffmann J.	Application for interlocutory injunction restraining dealing by defendants.	Police entitled to injunction?	Not to restrain dealing with alleged profits of fraud. Can detain money obtained by fraud.

CASE	CITATION	JUDGE(S)	FACTS	ISSUES	ADJUDICATION
Chief Constable of Surrey v. A.	*The Times*, October 27, 1988	Ognall J.	Application by police to restrain defendants from dealing with assets.	Did police have *locus standi*?	No.
Dormeuil Frères S.A. v. Nicolian International (Textiles)	[1988] 1 W.L.R. 1362; [1988] 3 All E.R. 197	Sir Nicholas Browne-Wilkinson V.-C.	Trade mark.	Would *Anton Piller* be set aside on ground of non-disclosure?	No.
Felixstowe Dock & Railway Co. v. United States Lines Inc.	[1988] 2 All E.R. 77	Hirst J.	Shipping *Mareva*.	Weight to be attached to interest of foreign court?	Recognised, but not permitted to remove English assets outside English courts' control.
Guinness plc v. Saunders	[1988] 1 W.L.R. 863; [1988] 2 All E.R. 940	Fox L.J. Glidewell L.J. Sir Frederick Lawton	Alleged breach of fiduciary duty by company directors.	Duty of full/frank disclosure by plaintiff?	Yes, even if prejudice thereby to plaintiff.
Leisure Data v. Bell	[1988] F.S.R. 367	Dillon L.J. Neill L.J.	Copyright.	High probability of success always necessary for mandatory interlocutory injunction?	Yes (also general guidelines *re* mandatory interlocutory injunctions).

CASE	CITATION	JUDGE(S)	FACTS	ISSUES	ADJUDICATION
Lloyds Bank plc v. Hurst	(January 22, 1988, unreported)		Breach of *Mareva*.	Should FLA grant breach lead to committal for contempt?	Yes.
Lloyds Bowmaker Ltd v. Britannia Arrow Holdings	[1988] 1 W.L.R. 1337; [1988] 3 All E.R. 178	Dillon L.J. Glidewell L.J.	Leasing telecommunication equipment. Defendants applied *ex parte* for *Mareva* against third party.	(i) Should *Mareva* be discharged for material non-disclosure?	(i) Yes.
				(ii) Was delay in applying for discharge fatal?	(ii) No.
				(iii) Delay in pursuing action after grant of injunction fatal to fresh injunction?	(iii) Such delay a factor.
Pospischal v. Phillips	*The Times*, January 20, 1988	Glidewell L.J. Taylor L.J.	Property sold/assets dissipated in defiance of *Mareva*.	Punishment?	Immediate imprisonment.

CASE	CITATION	JUDGE(S)	FACTS	ISSUES	ADJUDICATION
Reilly v. Fryer	(1988) 138 New L.J. 134, C.A.; [1988] 2 FTLR 69	Mustill L.J. Ralph Gibson L.J.	Judgment for plaintiff, *Mareva* granted. Defendant not to remove assets from jurisdiction.	Will court order disclosure of defendant's assets outside jurisdiction?	No.
Tucker (A Bankrupt), Re	[1988] 1 W.L.R. 497; [1988] 2 All E.R. 339	Millett J.	Action involving land.	Does interlocutory claim require some substantive right?	Yes.
Arab Monetary Fund v. Hashim	[1989] 1 W.L.R. 565; [1989] 3 All E.R. 466	Morritt J.	Application to discharge *ex parte* order.	Possibility of self-incrimination a factor in exercising discretion?	Yes.
A. v. B.	[1989] 2 Lloyd's Rep. 423	Saville J.	Sale of ship at pre-delivery stage. Buyers suspected delivery would be in breach of contract because of condition.	Could *Mareva* injunction issue before the breach which would constitute the cause of action?	Yes. A *Mareva* injunction can come into effect upon delivery of ship.

1097

CASE	CITATION	JUDGE(S)	FACTS	ISSUES	ADJUDICATION
Bank Mellat v. Kazmi	[1989] Q.B. 541; [1989] 2 W.L.R. 613	Purchas L.J. Nourse L.J. Stuart Smith L.J.	*Mareva.* Secretary of State for Social Services has notice.	How should arrears of benefit be paid?	To claimant's bank account which was aware of *Mareva*—not to claimant himself.
Commercial Bank of The Near East v. A.B.C. & D.	[1989] 2 Lloyd's Rep. 319	Saville J.	*Ex parte* application. New matters later became known.	Duty on plaintiff to furnish court with full facts?	Yes. But here, not material.
Derby Co. Ltd v. Weldon (No. 1)	[1989] 2 W.L.R. 276	May L.J. Parker L.J. Nicholls L.J.	Action in contract, negligence, breach of fiduciary duty.	Principle of arguing for a *Mareva.*	(i) No attempts to resolve disputed facts. (ii) No detailed arguments. (iii) *Mareva* could apply outside jurisdiction (See *Nos. 3/4*).
Derby & Co. Ltd v. Weldon (No. 3) and (No. 4)	[1989] 2 W.L.R. 412	Lord Donaldson M.R. Neill L.J. Butler-Sloss L.J.	One defendant was a Luxembourg company and one was a Panama company. Neither had assets within English jurisdiction.	Could the court make a *Mareva* injunction: (i) despite no assets within jurisdiction?	(i) Yes.

CASE	CITATION	JUDGE(S)	FACTS	ISSUES	ADJUDICATION
D.P.R. Futures, Re	[1989] 1 W.L.R. 778; (1989) 5 B C C 603	Millett J.	Liquidators sought *Mareva* against respondents.	(ii) despite not being directly enforceable in Panama?	(ii) Yes.
				Level of cross-undertaking in damages by liquidators?	Commensurate with company's assets.
Maclaine Watson & Co. Ltd v. International Tin Council (No. 2)	[1989] Ch. 286 [1988] 3 W.L.R. 1190	Kerr L.J. Nourse L.J. Ralph Gibson L.J.	Contract. International organisation.	Would defendant be ordered to disclose assets worldwide?	Yes, in aid of execution.
Republic of Haiti v. Duvalier	[1989] 2 W.L.R. 261; [1989] 1 All E.R. 456	Fox L.J. Stocker L.J. Staughton L.J.	*Mareva* worldwide.	Should *Mareva* be generally subject to a time-limit?	Yes.
Securities and Investments Board Ltd v. Pantell S.A.	[1989] 3 W.L.R. 698; [1989] 2 All E.R. 673	Sir Nicholas Browne-Wilkinson V.-C.	*Mareva* application. Foreign company was defendant.	Did court have power to grant *ex parte Mareva*?	Yes. Strong argument that defendant had illegally offered financial services in U.K.
Town & Country Building Society v. Daisystar	(1989) 139 New L.J. 1563; *The Times*, October 16, 1989, C.A.	Dillon L.J. Farquharson L.J.	Party obtained *Mareva*.	Must party proceed swiftly with action?	Yes, or seek discharge of order.

CASE	CITATION	JUDGE(S)	FACTS	ISSUES	ADJUDICATION
X v. Y and Y Establishment	[1989] 3 W.L.R. 910; [1989] 3 All E.R. 689	Diamond Q.C.	Banking case. Parties were foreign.	Could court grant leave for service out of jurisdiction?	Yes, whether claim for substantive or ancillary relief.
Arab Monetary Fund v. Hashim (No. 2)	[1990] 1 All E.R. 673	Hoffmann J.	Arab banking organisation.	Could affidavit in support of Mareva contain references to previous proceedings?	Yes, if necessary for narrative/full and frank disclosure.
Babanaft International Co SA v. Bassatne	[1990] Ch. 13	Kerr L.J. Neill L.J. Nicholls L.J.	Defendants were Lebanese and had assets abroad as well as in the U.K.	Jurisdiction to grant a Mareva injunction over foreign assets after judgment?	Yes, but should be qualified by an express proviso that the injunction did not seek to control third parties.
Brink's-Mat Ltd. v. Elcombe (No. 2)	The Independent, April 24, 1990		Application by defendant to release assets to meet legal expenses.	Should the court take account of effect of legal aid if assets were not released?	Yes. Effect on public funds, and on plaintiff, are both relevant.
Charles Church Developments plc v. Cronin	[1990] F.S.R. 1	Edward Nugee Q.C.	Passing off.	Basis of assessing compensation damages for purposes of Mareva.	Mareva sum reduced.

CASE	CITATION	JUDGE(S)	FACTS	ISSUES	ADJUDICATION
Derby & Co. Ltd v. Weldon (Nos 3 & 4)	[1990] Ch. 65	Lord Donaldson M.R. Neill L.J. Butler-Sloss L.J.	One defendant was a Luxembourg company and one was a Panama company. Neither had assets within English jurisdiction.	Could the court make a *Mareva* injunction: (i) despite no assets within jurisdiction?	Yes.
				(ii) despite not being directly enforceable in Panama?	Yes.
Derby & Co. v. Weldon (No. 6)	[1990] 1 W.L.R. 1139; [1990] 3 All E.R. 263	Dillon L.J. Taylor L.J. Staughton L.J.	Claim for damages for deceit, breach of fiduciary duty and conspiracy to defraud. *Mareva* sought.	Could English court order transfer of assets from one foreign jurisdiction to another?	Yes, in appropriate circumstances.
Dubai Bank Ltd v. Galadari	[1990] 1 Lloyd's Rep. 120; [1989] 3 All E.R. 769	Dillon L.J. Staughton L.J. Mann L.J.	Plaintiffs were guilty of non-disclosure in obtaining *Mareva*.	Discharge automatic for non-disclosure?	No. A matter for judge's discretion.

CASE	CITATION	JUDGE(S)	FACTS	ISSUES	ADJUDICATION
Investment and Pensions Advisory Service v. Gray	[1990] BCLC 38	Morritt J.	Barlow Clowes link.	Payment of debts by defendant.	Defendant could pay genuine debts—but not from property subject to a proprietary claim.
Rosseel NV v. Oriental Commercial & Shipping Ltd	[1990] 3 All E.R. 545	Lord Donaldson M.R. Parker L.J.	*Mareva* in support of foreign judgment.	Worldwide *Mareva*?	No: normally limited to assets within the jurisdiction.
Atlas Maritime Co SA v. Avalon Maritime Ltd, The Coral Rose (No. 1)	[1991] 4 All E.R. 769	Neill L.J. Stocker L.J. Staughton L.J.	Oral contract that defendant would buy ship from plaintiff. Existing *Mareva* injunction.	Should *Mareva* to varied to enable defendant to repay loan to its parent company?	No.
Atlas Maritime Co SA v. Avalon Maritime Ltd, The Coral Rose (No. 2)	[1991] 4 All E.R. 781	Lord Donaldson M.R. Nicholls L.J. Farquharson L.J.	Sale of ship.	Order granting or refusing application to vary a *Mareva* injunction. Is leave to appeal required?	No.

CASE	CITATION	JUDGE(S)	FACTS	ISSUES	ADJUDICATION
Atlas Maritime Co SA v. Avalon Maritime Ltd, The Coral Rose (No. 3)	[1991] 4 All E.R. 783	Lord Donaldson M.R. Nicholls L.J. Farquharson L.J.	Oral contract that defendant would buy ship from plaintiff. Existing *Mareva* injunction.	Defendant with wealthy parent company. Should *Mareva* be varied to allow defendant to pay legal expenses?	No. There were reasonable grounds to believe defendant could obtain funds to pay legal expenses.
Sociedade national de Combustiveis de Angola v. Lundqvist	[1991] 2 W.L.R. 280; [1990] 3 All E.R. 280	Browne-Wilkinson V.-C. Staughton L.J. Beldam L.J.	Fraud.	How privilege against self-incrimination bears on *Mareva* direction for affidavit disclosing world-wide assets.	Defendant must disclose nature and situation of assets, but not value.
Tate Access Floors Inc. v. Boswell	[1991] 2 W.L.R. 304; [1990] 3 All E.R. 303	Browne-Wilkinson V.-C.	Fraud.	Can plaintiffs use information revealed by British *Mareva* in foreign proceedings?	No. Form of words of *Mareva* implied an undertaking not to start proceedings elsewhere.

CASE	CITATION	JUDGE(S)	FACTS	ISSUES	ADJUDICATION
Capital Cameras Ltd v. Harold Lines Ltd	[1991] 1 W.L.R. 54		Post-trial *Mareva* in force against defendant.	Are administrative receivers appointed pursuant to a debenture granted by defendant entitled to a variation of *Mareva* to allow disposition?	Yes. Receivers' property rights were superior to personal rights under the injunction.
Financiera Avenida SA v. Shiblaq	*The Times*, January 14, 1991	Lloyd L.J. Stocker L.J. Sir George Waller	Application by defendant to enforce cross-undertaking in damages.	(i) Should the undertaking be enforced at all?	(i) Depends on all the circumstances.
				(ii) Has the defendant suffered any damage by the grant of the injunction?	(ii) Ordinary principles of law of contract apply.
Atlas Maritime Co. SA v. Avalon Maritime Ltd. (No. 2)	*The Times*, May 21, 1991	Lord Donaldson M.R. Nicholls L.J. Farquharson L.J.	Application to vary *Mareva* injunction.	Is leave to appeal required?	No.

1104

CASE	CITATION	JUDGE(S)	FACTS	ISSUES	ADJUDICATION
Southway Group Ltd v. Wolff	*The Times*, May 21, 1991	Mustill L.J. Nourse L.J.	*Mareva*: plaintiff sought added protection of a guarantee in a certain amount.	Could judge set for himself the amount of guarantee?	No. Judge should decline to grant injunction unless fortified to the extent he had in mind.
Polly Peck International plc v. Nadir (No. 2)	[1992] 4 All E.R. 269	Lord Donaldson M.R. Stocker L.J. Scott L.J.	Fraudulent transfer of funds offshore.	(i) *Mareva* against bank? (ii) *Mareva* when tracing remedy available?	(i) Not normally, particularly if it would interfere with normal banking business. (ii) No.
Gidrxslme Shipping Co. Ltd v. Tantomar-Transporters Maritimos	[1994] 4 All E.R. 507	Colman J.	In an action for unpaid charter hire the plaintiffs had obtained two arbitration awards (not converted into judgments of the court) and had a further arbitration pending. Existing *Mareva* confined to assets within the jurisdiction.	Jurisdiction to order disclosure of assets worldwide, even though (i) no *Mareva* or	(i) Yes.

CASE	CITATION	JUDGE(S)	FACTS	ISSUES	ADJUDICATION
				(ii) *Mareva* limited to assets within the jurisdiction or	(ii) Yes.
				(iii) no judgment?	(iii) Yes.
Mercantile Group (Europe) AG v. Aiyela	[1994] 1 All E.R. 110	Bingham M.R. Steyn L.J. Hoffmann L.J.	Judgment debtor avoiding paying by placing funds in his companies and his wife.	Can a *Mareva* injunction extend to third parties against whom the plaintiff has no cause of action?	Yes, if it is arguable that the third parties hold funds on trust for the defendant.

CASE	CITATION	JUDGE(S)	FACTS	ISSUES	ADJUDICATION
Shaw v. Smith	(1886) 18 Q.B.D. 193; 56 L.J.Q.B. 174			Who may apply for interim preservation order?	Any opposite party.
Velati & Co. v. Braham & Co.	(1887) 46 L.J.Q.B. 415		Action for recovery of jewellery.	Would court order delivery up to an officer of the court?	Yes.
Scott v. Mercantile Accident Insurance Co.	(1892) 8 T.L.R. 320	Cave J.	Jeweller was allegedly burgled. Insurance co. refused to pay out. Later some of jewellery was handed to police.	Defendants (insurers) sought order preserving jewellery until trial.	Order refused.
Chaplain v. Barnett	(1912) 28 T.L.R. 256			When is interim preservation order available?	Whenever security of property between parties is threatened.
Wilder v. Wilder	(1912) 56 S.J. 571			When will interim preservation order be made?	Only if it is shown that relevant party has property in his possession/control.

CASE	CITATION	JUDGE(S)	FACTS	ISSUES	ADJUDICATION
Whitely v. Hilt	[1918] 2 K.B. 808	Swinfen Eady M.R. Warrington L.J. Duke L.J.	Hire purchase of a piano.	Will delivery up be ordered of items of no special value if damages will adequately compensate?	No.
Tudor Accumulator Co. Ltd v. China Mutual Co.	[1930] W.N. 201; 74 S.J. 596			Does "property" include details of a process?	No.
Saxton, Re	[1962] 1 W.L.R. 968; (1962) 106 S.J. 668	Wilberforce J.	Plaintiffs claimed that defendants had excluded certain assets from administration of deceased's estate.	Were documents "property"?	Yes.
General and Finance Facilities Ltd v. Cooks Cars (Romford)	[1963] 1 W.L.R. 644; [1963] 2 All E.R. 314	Pearson L.J. Diplock L.J.	Plaintiff successful in action in detinue.	Will delivery up be ordered of items of no special value if damages will adequately compensate?	No.

CASE	CITATION	JUDGE(S)	FACTS	ISSUES	ADJUDICATION
Norwich Pharmacal Co. v. Customs and Excise Commissioners	[1974] A.C. 133; [1973] 3 W.L.R. 164	Lord Denning M.R. Buckley L.J. Roskill L.J. (C.A.) Lord Reid Lord Morris Viscount Dilhorne Lord Cross Lord Brandon (H.L.)	Patent case.	Was there a duty of disclosure on third party innocently involved in tortious act?	Yes.
E.M.I. v. Pandit	[1975] 1 W.L.R. 302; [1975] 1 All E.R. 418	Templeman J.	Defendant attempted to forge letter from one of plaintiffs.	Sufficient evidence for order for delivery up?	Yes.
University City Studios Inc. v. Mukhter & Sons	[1976] 1 W.L.R. 568; [1976] 2 All E.R. 330; [1976] F.S.R. 252	Templeman J.	Copyright.	Who should serve *Anton Piller* order?	Qualified solicitor for applicant or equivalent person.
Vapormatic Co. Ltd v. Sparex Ltd	[1976] 1 W.L.R. 939; [1976] F.S.R. 451	Graham J.	Fear that former employee would disclose confidential information to commercial rivals.	(i) Should applicant produce specific evidence of his ability to carry out undertaking in damages?	(i) Yes.

1109

CASE	CITATION	JUDGE(S)	FACTS	ISSUES	ADJUDICATION
				(ii) Should persons accompanying solicitor to execute order be identified?	(ii) Yes.
E.M.I. Ltd v. Sarwar & Haidar	[1977] F.S.R. 146	Lord Denning M.R. Stevenson L.J. Shaw L.J.	Copyright case.	What material should be produced?	Relevant material included names/address of suppliers, order book indicating source of illicit material.
Hallmark Cards Inc v. Image Arts Ltd	[1977] F.S.R. 150	Buckley L.J. Goff L.J. Shaw L.J.	Copyright.	Should order for inspection be suspended where application ex parte or without affidavit/oral evidence?	No.
Protector Alarms Ltd v. Maxim Alarms Ltd	[1978] F.S.R. 442	Goulding J.	Patent case.	Terms of order.	Material to be delivered into custody of applicant's solicitor. Precise premises should be identified.

CASE	CITATION	JUDGE(S)	FACTS	ISSUES	ADJUDICATION
Bestworth Ltd v. Wearwell Ltd	[1979] F.S.R. 320	Slade J.	Application for leave to appeal grant of *Anton Piller*.	Order executed—bar to challenge?	No.
Centri-Spray Corp. v. Cera International Ltd	[1979] F.S.R. 175	Whitford J.	Copyright.	Can confidential drawings be inspected?	Yes, but plaintiff may be required to undertake not to remove/take copies/use information.
Cook Industries Inc. v. Galliher	[1979] Ch. 439; [1978] 3 W.L.R. 637	Templeman J.	Alleged fraudulent share dealings. Defendant within jurisdiction. Premises outside.	Could *Anton Piller* order be made in principle?	Court may be prepared to grant *Anton Piller* order.
Howard Perry & Co. Ltd v. British Railways Board	[1980] I.C.R. 743; [1980] 1 W.L.R. 1375; [1980] 2 All E.R. 579	Sir Robert Megarry V.-C.	Strike plaintiffs sought delivery up of strike-bound goods.	Can delivery up include merely transferring authority over something *in situ*?	Yes.
International Electronics Ltd v. Weigh Data Ltd	[1980] F.S.R. 423	Graham J.	Patent.	Should evidence support *Anton Piller* application be served on defendant?	Yes.

CASE	CITATION	JUDGE(S)	FACTS	ISSUES	ADJUDICATION
Malone v. Metropolitan Police Commissioner	[1980] Q.B. 49; [1978] 2 W.L.R. 936	Stephenson L.J. Roskill L.J.	Plaintiff was suspected handler of stolen goods.	Could police retain property lawfully seized from accused if not stolen but the subject of charges.	Only if retention justified on ascertainable grounds. Could be retained until trial in public interest if necessary as evidence.
Yousif v. Salama	[1980] 1 W.L.R. 1540; [1980] 3 All E.R. 405	Lord Denning M.R. Donaldson L.J. (dissenting)	*Anton Piller* application. Evidence of forgery in endorsement of cheque.	Was there sufficient evidence for order for delivery up?	Yes.
A.B. v. C.D.E.	[1981] 2 W.L.R. 629; [1980] 2 All E.R. 347; [1982] R.P.C. 509			Can order be made against defendant's employer?	No. No cause of action against him.
Gallery Cosmetics Ltd v. Number 1	[1981] F.S.R. 556	Nourse J.	Passing off/infringement of trademark.	Was non-disclosure sufficiently material?	No.
Roberts v. Jump Knitwear	[1981] F.S.R. 527	Falconer J.	Plaintiff designed knitwear and alleged infringement of copyright.	Could defendants be ordered to reveal persons to whom garments supplied?	Discovery order refused. No action in conversion against those who received garments.

CASE	CITATION	JUDGE(S)	FACTS	ISSUES	ADJUDICATION
Sony Corp. v. Anand (R.S.)	[1981] Com.L.R. 55; [1981] F.S.R. 398	Browne-Wilkinson J.	Patent case.	In what ways could documents seized be used against third parties?	Information in documents could be used against third parties involved with the same infringing goods and also to bring criminal proceedings against third parties outside the jurisdiction.
Thermax v. Schott Industrial Glass	[1981] F.S.R. 289	Browne-Wilkins J.	Alleged infringement of registered design.	What if defendant objects to execution of *Anton Piller* order?	No force can be used. Order is not a search warrant.
Wilmot Breedon Ltd v. Woodcock	[1981] F.S.R. 15	Slade J.	Copyright. Plaintiff delayed.	Were defendants to be ordered to disclose names of those supplied?	No.
Dunlop Holdings Ltd and Dunlop Ltd v. Staravia Ltd	[1982] Com.L.R. 3, C.A.	Oliver L.J.	Plaintiffs designed/manufactured brake systems for aircraft. Defendants were aircraft repairers. Copyright action.	Could order for delivery up be made without actual evidence of risk of destruction?	If defendant engaged in nefarious activities/not trustworthy, actual evidence may not be required.

1113

CASE	CITATION	JUDGE(S)	FACTS	ISSUES	ADJUDICATION
Gates v. Swift	[1982] R.P.C. 339; [1981] F.S.R. 57	Graham J.	Copyright.	Material stored on computer—how should it be produced?	Material should be produced in readable form.
ITC Film Distributors Ltd v. Video Exchange Ltd (No. 2)	(1982) 126 S.J. 672; (1981) 125 S.J. 863, C.A.	Lawton L.J.	Copyright.	Can forcible entry be used to execute order?	No.
Sega Enterprises Ltd v. Alca Electronics	[1982] F.S.R. 516	Templeman L.J.	Defendant's customers were established brewers. No reason to suppose they would try to evade plaintiffs.	Would order be made ex parte requiring defendant to disclose customers?	No order made.
Walt Disney Productions v. Gurvitz	[1982] F.S.R. 446	Vinelott J.	Defendant made undertaking not to deal in illicit material.	Could plaintiff place trap order with defendant?	Yes.
West Mercia Constabulary v. Wagener	[1982] 1 W.L.R. 127; [1981] 3 All E.R. 378	Forbes J.	Criminal case. Police applied for order restraining withdrawals from an account.	Could order be made?	Yes.

CASE	CITATION	JUDGE(S)	FACTS	ISSUES	ADJUDICATION
E.M.I. Records Ltd v. Kudhail	[1983] Com.L.R. 280; [1985] F.S.R. 36	Sir John Donaldson M.R.	Breach of recording copyright.	Could order be made against defendants representing a group?	Yes, if sufficient common interest.
Hazel Grove Music Co. v. Elster Enterprises	[1983] F.S.R. 379	Warner J.	Plaintiff had reasonable suspicion that locked cabinet could contain offending material.	Could defendant be ordered to deliver up key or allow removal of cabinet?	Yes.
HPSI v. Thomas and Williams	(1983) 133 New L.J. 598	Woolf J.	Application to commit for breach of Anton Piller.	Should defendants be committed?	No. Breach unintentional/insignificant.
Hytrac Conveyers Ltd v. Conveyors International Ltd	[1983] 1 W.L.R. 44; [1983] 3 All E.R. 415; [1983] F.S.R. 63	Lawton L.J. Templeman L.J. Fox L.J.	Industrial copyright.	Terms of Anton Piller.	Order could not be used to "fish" for potential charges.
Systematica Ltd v. London Computer Centre Ltd	[1983] F.S.R. 313	Whitford J.	Defendant acting openly.	Could plaintiff get costs of Anton Piller application?	No. Plaintiff had made insufficient inquiries.

1115

CASE	CITATION	JUDGE(S)	FACTS	ISSUES	ADJUDICATION
W.E.A. Records Ltd v. Visions Channel 4 Ltd	[1983] 1 W.L.R. 721; [1983] 2 All E.R. 589	Sir John Donaldson M.R. Dunn L.J. Purchas L.J.	Copyright action.	Could information be revealed to judge *ex parte* but be permanently withheld from the defendants?	No.
Customs and Excise Commissioners v. Hamlin (A.E.) & Co.	[1984] 1 W.L.R. 509; [1983] 3 All E.R. 654	Falconer J.	Film copyright case.	Applicant's undertakings.	Applicant must normally undertake not to allow any person to have access to property seized.
Digital Equipment Corp. v. Darkcrest	[1984] Ch. 512; [1984] 3 W.L.R. 617	Falconer J.	Copyright/passing off case.	To whom was plaintiff's duty of full/frank disclosure owed?	Duty owed to the court.
General Nutrition Ltd v. Pradip Pattni	[1984] F.S.R. 403; (1984) 81 L.S.Gaz. 2223	Warner J.	Police sought discovery of documents.	Should documents be produced?	In certain circumstances but not solely on basis that documents might disclose a criminal offence.

CASE	CITATION	JUDGE(S)	FACTS	ISSUES	ADJUDICATION
Universal City Studios Inc. v. Hubbard	[1984] Ch. 225; [1984] 2 W.L.R. 492	Cumming-Bruce L.J. Fox L.J.	Copyright proceedings involving films. Production of pornographic films exposed.	Could defendant oppose orders on basis that criminal offence would be revealed.	No.
Wardle Fabrics Ltd v. Myristis (G.) Ltd	[1984] F.S.R. 263	Goulding J.	Copyright.	(i) Non-disclosure. (ii) Was contempt in refusing to comply with *Anton Piller* affected by subsequent discharge?	(i) Yes. (ii) No.
Yardley & Co. Ltd v. Higson	[1984] F.S.R. 304	Lawton L.J. Oliver L.J. Slade L.J.	Passing off/copyright. Non-disclosure. *Ex parte* disclosure at subsequent hearing.	Non-disclosure material?	No.

1117

CASE	CITATION	JUDGE(S)	FACTS	ISSUES	ADJUDICATION
Altertext Inc. v. Advanced Data Communications	[1985] 1 W.L.R. 457; [1985] 1 All E.R. 395	Scott J.	Some property referred to in application outside the jurisdiction.	Could *Anton Piller* order be made in principle?	Only if defendant outside the jurisdiction has opportunity to challenge service of writ.
Booker McConnell v. Plascow	[1985] R.P.C. 425	Park J.		What is nature of *Anton Piller* order?	Exceptional and extreme remedy.
Chief Constable of Hampshire v. A.	[1985] Q.B. 132; [1984] 2 W.L.R. 954	Waller L.J. Oliver L.J. Purchas L.J.	Police sought order to prevent defendant dealing with money believed to be fruits of crime.	Could order be made?	Yes, unless proceeds of crime cannot be identified or separated from legitimate funds.
Distributori Automatici Italia SpA v. Holford General Trading Co. Ltd	[1985] 1 W.L.R. 1066; [1985] 3 All E.R. 750	Leggatt J.	Action for liquidated sum. Judgment in default.	Could court grant *Anton Piller* for purpose of eliciting documents essential for execution?	Yes. Under broad principle of ensuring that ends of justice are not defeated.

CASE	CITATION	JUDGE(S)	FACTS	ISSUES	ADJUDICATION
Fields (Randolph) v. Watts	(1985) 129 S.J. 67; (1985) L.S.Gaz. 364	O'Connor L.J. May L.J.	*Anton Piller* against practising Members of the Bar and their clerk.	Should order be discharged?	Yes. Plaintiff had shown no reasonable risk that relevant documents would be concealed or destroyed.
Rogers (Jeffrey) Knitwear Productions v. Vinola (Knitwear) Manufacturing Co.	[1985] F.S.R. 184	Whitford J.	Copyright.	Discharge of *Anton Piller*?	Yes. Plaintiffs had failed to disclose all relevant knowledge.
Unilever v. Pearce	[1985] F.S.R. 475	Falconer J.	Patent case.	Is machinery used to carry out a process "property"?	Yes.
E.M.I. Records Ltd v. Spillane	[1986] 1 W.L.R. 967; [1986] 2 All E.R. 1016	Sir Nicholas Browne-Wilkinson V.-C.	Copyright recordings. Customs and Excise sought production of documents seized following order.	Should documents be produced?	No.

CASE	CITATION	JUDGE(S)	FACTS	ISSUES	ADJUDICATION
Columbia Picture Industries v. Robinson	[1987] Ch. 38; [1986] 3 W.L.R. 542; [1986] 3 All E.R. 338	Scott J.	Video piracy case, *Mareva* and *Anton Piller*. Execution put defendant out of business.	Could order be set aside?	Plaintiff's solicitor had not made full/frank disclosure and had acted oppressively. No purpose in setting orders aside so compensation instead.
Films Rover International Ltd v. Cannon Film Sales Ltd	[1987] 1 W.L.R. 670; [1986] 3 All E.R. 772	Hoffmann J.	Film distribution contract.	Would court make order for delivery up of films?	Test was whether potential injustice to defendant out-weighed potential injustice to plaintiff. Reversed on appeal. See *Financial Times*, June 10, 1988, C.A.
Piver (L.T.) Sarl v. S. & J. Perfume Co.	[1987] F.S.R. 159	Walton J.	Counterfeiting.	Injunction lay to prevent further prosecution of counterfeiters?	No.
Japan Capsule Computers (U.K.) Ltd v. Sonic Games Sales	[1988] F.S.R. 256	Fox L.J. Croom-Johnson L.J. Mustill L.J.	Copyright contempt. Motion for committal.	Would court dismiss motion for want of prosecution?	No.

CASE	CITATION	JUDGE(S)	FACTS	ISSUES	ADJUDICATION
O'Regan v. Iambic Productions	(1989) 139 New L.J. 1378	Peter Pain J.	*Anton Piller* order.	(i) Duty of disclosure to court on party obtaining *Anton Piller*?	(i) Yes.
				(ii) Can *Anton Piller* be discharged after execution?	(ii) Yes, if it appears it should have never been granted.
Swedac Ltd v. Magnet & Southerns	[1989] F.S.R. 243	Harman J.	Copyright. Plaintiff obtained *Anton Piller* without evidence *re* copyright and with non-disclosure.	Should order be discharged?	Yes.
Tate Access Floors Inc. v. Boswell	[1991] 2 W.L.R. 304; [1990] 3 All E.R. 303	Browne-Wilkinson V.-C.	Fraud.	Does privilege against self-incrimination prevent grant of *Anton Piller* order?	Yes, against individual defendant, if documents may lead to fraud charge.

CASE	CITATION	JUDGE(S)	FACTS	ISSUES	ADJUDICATION
Bhimji v. Chatwani	[1991] 1 All E.R. 705	Scott J.	*Anton Piller* order granted but not executed.	Can defendant refuse to allow search and instead apply to discharge order?	Yes, if defendant offers to protect documents.
IBM United Kingdom Ltd v. Prima Data International Ltd	[1994] 1 W.L.R. 719	Sir Mervyn Davies	Plaintiff sellers sued defendant buyers for conspiracy to extract goods without payment.	Can a defendant claim privilege against self-incrimination at any stage before delivering up items pursuant to an *Anton Piller* order?	No. If the proper warning is given before execution of the order, the defendant cannot claim privilege at some later stage, even if danger of criminal proceedings.

CASE	CITATION	JUDGE(S)	FACTS	ISSUES	ADJUDICATION
Morgan v. Richardson	(1806) 7 East 482n; 1 Camp. 40n		Action on bill of exchange. Defendant alleged goods inferior.	Defence?	No.
Charles v. Marsden	(1808) 1 Taunt 224; 127 E.R. 818		Defendant contended he had received no value for a bill.	Ord.14 judgment?	Yes.
Trickey v. Larne	(1840) 6 M. & W. 278; 9 L.J.Ex. 141		Action on bill of exchange. Defendant alleged goods inferior.	Defence?	No.
Rawson v. Samuel	(1841) Cr. & Ph. 161; 10 L.J.Ch. 214			Did defendant's equitable right undermine plaintiff's legal claim?	Yes.
Sheels v. Davis	(1874) 4 Camp 119, N.P.		Cross-claim in respect of cargo.	Did cross-claim extinguish/diminish claim for freight?	No.
Lloyd's Banking Co. v. Ogle	(1876) 1 Ex.D. 263; 2 Char.Pr.Cas. 252		Action against guarantor.	Ord.14 judgment?	No—liability unclear.

CASE	CITATION	JUDGE(S)	FACTS	ISSUES	ADJUDICATION
Standard Discount Co. v. La Grange	(1877) 3 C.P.D. 67; 47 L.J.Q.B. 3	Bramwell L.J. Brett L.J. Cotton L.J.	Order "empowering" plaintiff to sign judgment under Ord. 14.	Is such an order interlocutory or final?	Interlocutory, because plaintiff was still to take the formal step of signing judgment.
Anglo Italian Bank v. Davies	(1878) 38 L.T. 197, C.A.		Action on bill of exchange. Defendant alleged goods inferior.	Defence?	No.
Begg v. Cooper	(1878) 40 L.T. 29; 27 W.R. 224, C.A.		Liquidated demand.	May court allow plaintiff to cure defective affidavit with supplemental affidavit?	Yes.
Davy v. Garrett	(1878) 7 Ch.D. 473; 47 L.J.Ch. 218		Action in fraud.	May charge of fraud be made without using the word "fraud"?	Yes.
Harrison v. Bottenheim	(1878) 26 W.R. 362, C.A.		Plaintiff's case showed he had acted harshly.	Trial of action?	Yes, if judgment obtained, should be full publicity.

CASE	CITATION	JUDGE(S)	FACTS	ISSUES	ADJUDICATION
Dennis v. Seymour	(1879) Ex.D. 80; 42 L.T. 31		Defence to part of Ord.14 claim.	Leave to defend disputed part conditional on payment of non-disputed part?	No.
Muirhead v. Direct U.S. Cable Co. Ltd	(1879) 27 W.R. 708		Action against limited company.	Ord.14 applicable?	Yes.
Rotherham v. Priest	(1879) 28 W.R. 277; 49 L.J.Q.B. 104		Action for rent. Ord.14 judgment.	Could defendant set up counterclaim in libel unconnected with action?	No.
Yorkshire Banking Co. v. Beatson	(1879) 4 C.P.D. 321		Defendant given conditional leave. Unconditional leave on appeal.	Is defendant entitled to return of money paid in as condition?	Yes.
Stooke v. Taylor	(1880) 5 Q.B.D. 569; 49 L.J.Q.B. 857		Cross-claim.	Should plaintiff give credit for cross-claim in his action?	Yes, taken to know of existence/amount of set-off.

1125

CASE	CITATION	JUDGE(S)	FACTS	ISSUES	ADJUDICATION
Wallingford v. Mutual Society	(1880) 5 App.Cas. 685	Lord Blackburn		Detail required in defendant's affidavit?	General denial not enough. Must satisfy judge of reasonable grounds.
Aboulaff v. Oppenheimer	(1882) 30 W.R. 429; 10 Q.B.D. 295; [1881–5] All E.R.Rep. 307		Action on judgment obtained in Russia.	Fraud arguments ventilated in Russia?	No. Question of whether Russian court misled could not have been submitted to them.
Fuller v. Alexander	(1882) 52 L.J.Q.B. 103			Bills of Exchange Act 1882, s.30(2).	Some evidence of fraud required—sufficient to require a trial.
Warner v. Bowlby	(1882) 9 T.L.R. 13		Ord.14 application. Plaintiff knew of defence.	Ord.14 summons dismissed?	Yes, with costs.
Hobson v. Monks	[1884] W.N. 8 Bitt.Rep. In Ch. 161		Ord.14 application.	If no defence served after Ord.14 notice of intention to defend, can plaintiff enter judgment in default?	No.

CASE	CITATION	JUDGE(S)	FACTS	ISSUES	ADJUDICATION
Millard v. Baddeley	[1884] W.N. 96; (1884) Bitt.Rep. In Ch. 125			Oral evidence in Ord.14 procedure?	No, expensive and would lead to Ord.14 trials.
Ochse v. Duncan	(1886) 3 T.L.R. 220, C.A.		Ord.14 application. Allegation by defendant that claim excessive.	Unconditional leave to defend?	Yes, one reason was apparent good faith of defendant's allegation.
Desart (Earl of) v. Townsend	(1887) 22 L.R.Ir. 389	Lord Ashbourne Fitzgibbon L.J. Barry L.J.	Judgment for rent arrears.	Will court stay execution on the sole ground of inability to pay?	No.
Jackson v. Murphy	(1887) 4 T.L.R. 91		Action on bill of exchange. Defendant alleged goods inferior.	Defence?	No.
Wardens of St. Saviour's Southwark v. Grey	(1887) 3 T.L.R. 667		Ord.14 action appeal.	Approach of the Court of Appeal?	If Divisional Court gave leave to defend, Court of Appeal reluctant to interfere. If leave refused, Court of Appeal would look for plausible defence.

CASE	CITATION	JUDGE(S)	FACTS	ISSUES	ADJUDICATION
Read v. Brown	(1888) 22 Q.B.D. 128; 58 L.J.Q.B. 120		Action by assignee of debt.	Assignee has title to sue?	Only if avers written assignment/notice of it to defendant. See Law of Property Act 1925, s.134.
Smith v. Edwardes	(1888) 22 Q.B.D. 10; 58 L.J.Q.B. 227		Action on solicitor's bill of costs.	Order?	Bill of costs referred to taxing master. Credit by plaintiff for all sums received from/on account of defendant. Judgment of amount of taxing masters allocatur and costs (Taxed if not agreed).
Derry v. Peek	(1889) 14 App.Cas. 337; 58 L.J.Ch. 864		Fraud action.	Meaning of fraud in Ord.14 context?	Deceit in *Derry v. Peek* sense.
Manger, etc. v. Cash	(1889) 5 T.L.R. 271, D.C.		Conditional leave to defend.	May condition be imposed such as would deprive defendant of right to defend?	No.
Manger v. Cash	As above.		Foreign judgment obtained by fraud, allegedly.	Judgment vitiated by fraud?	Yes.

CASE	CITATION	JUDGE(S)	FACTS	ISSUES	ADJUDICATION
Millar v. Keane	(1889) 24 L.R.Ir. 49		Action against deceased's estate—Ord.14 application. Administration completed.	Order?	Judgment with costs against P.R.s to be levied against estate/effects. Plaintiff to pay P.R.'s costs.
Saw v. Hakim	(1889) 5 T.L.R. 72			Leave to defend in Ord.14 proceedings.	Leave—unless clear that defendant has nothing worthwhile to say.
Sheppards & Co. v. Wilkinson & Jarvis	(1889) 6 T.L.R. 13, C.A.		Action by stockbrokers on loan. Defendants counter-claim for breach of agreements.	Ord.14 judgment?	Yes, but subject to a stay.
Griffiths v. Ystradyfodwg School Board	(1890) 24 Q.B.D. 307; 59 L.J.Q.B. 116		Ord.14 application. Defence of tender before action.	Ord.14 judgment?	Not if clear that defendant's plea/payment in is correct. Plaintiff ordered to pay defendant's costs.
McLardy v. Slateum	(1890) 24 Q.B.D. 504; 62 L.T. 151		Application for Ord.14 made after defence delivered.	Ord.14?	Only if plaintiff shows circumstances justifying delay.

CASE	CITATION	JUDGE(S)	FACTS	ISSUES	ADJUDICATION
Ward v. Plumbley	(1890) 6 T.L.R. 198			Leave to defend in Ord.14 proceedings?	Leave—unless clear that defendant has nothing worthwhile to say.
Court v. Sheen	(1891) 7 T.L.R. 556		Unliquidated cross-claim. Whole of liquidated claim admitted.	Ord.14 judgment?	No—counter-claim might exceed claim. Unconditional leave.
Slater v. Cathcart	(1891) 8 T.L.R. 92, D.C.		Solicitor secured defendant's release from lunatic asylum. Defendant alleged negligence.	Order?	*Smith v. Edwardes* order, but with stay after taxation pending counter-claim.
Western National Bank of New York v. Perez Triana & Co.	(1891) 6 T.L.R. 366		Question as to law of New York.	Triable on Ord.14 affidavit?	No.
London Chatham and Dover Railway Co. v. South Eastern Railway Co.	[1892] 1 Ch. 120; 61 L.J.Ch. 294; [1893] A.C. 429, H.L.	Lord Herschell L.C. Lord Watson Lord Morris Lord Shand	Joint traffic agreement.	Object of interest/payment in Ord.14 application?	To compensate plaintiff for having been kept out of money.

CASE	CITATION	JUDGE(S)	FACTS	ISSUES	ADJUDICATION
Satchwell v. Clarke	(1892) 66 L.T. 641; 8 T.L.R. 592		Plaintiff wishes to amend statement of claim.	Amendment between issue/hearing of Ord.14 summons without fresh summons?	Yes—plaintiff should obtain fresh hearing date/warn defendant (unless defendant agrees to original date).
Sheba Gold Mining Co. Ltd v. Trubshawe	[1892] 1 Q.B. 674; [1891–4] All E.R.Rep. 626	Lord Coleridge C.J.	Claim for liquidated sum.	Can defect in statement of claim be cured by simple averment in Ord.14 affidavit?	No.
Bradley v. Chamberlyn	[1893] 1 Q.B. 439; 68 L.T. 413		Plaintiff wishes to amend statement of claim.	Amendment between issue/hearing of Ord.14 summons without fresh summons?	Yes—plaintiff should obtain fresh hearing date/warn defendant (unless defendant agrees to original date).
Electric & General Contract Corp. v. Thompson Houston	(1893) 10 T.L.R. 103			Leave to defend in Ord.14 proceedings?	Leave—unless defendant has nothing worthwhile to say.
Fenner v. Wilson	[1893] 2 Ch. 656; 62 L.J.Ch. 984		Ord.14 injunction.	Undertakings as to damages by plaintiff?	No—this was final, not interlocutory injunction.

CASE	CITATION	JUDGE(S)	FACTS	ISSUES	ADJUDICATION
Wing v. Thurlow	(1893) 10 T.L.R. 53		Bill of exchange. Defendant alleged lack of consideration.	Ord.14 judgment?	No.
Jones v. Stone	[1894] A.C. 122; 63 L.J.P.C. 68	Lord Halsbury Lord Watson Lord MacNaughton Lord Morris Sir Richard Couch Davey L.J.	Action in ejectment.	Leave to defend in Ord.14 proceedings?	Leave—unless clear that defendant has nothing worthwhile to say.
May v. Chidley	[1894] 1 Q.B. 451; 63 L.J.Q.B. 347	Wills J. Lawrence J.	Liquidated claim on dishonoured cheque.	May verification of cause of action be made in affidavit by general reference to statement of claim?	Yes.
Lynde v. Waithman	[1895] 2 Q.B. 180; 64 L.J.Q.B. 762	Kay L.J. Smith (A.L.) L.J.	Action for mortgage debt. Ord.14 application.	Leave to defend if clear accounts necessary to determine claim?	Yes.

CASE	CITATION	JUDGE(S)	FACTS	ISSUES	ADJUDICATION
Roberts v. Plant	[1895] 1 Q.B. 597; 64 L.J.Q.B. 347	Lord Esher M.R. Lopes L.J. Rigby L.J.	Action upon cheque.	May verification of cause of action be made in affidavit by general reference to statement of claim?	Yes.
Burke v. Rooney	(1897) 4 C.P.D. 226; 48 L.J.Q.B. 601		Appeal under Ord.14.	Leave to appeal out of time?	Possible, but application must be to judge.
Hallett v. Andrews	(1897) 42 S.J. 68		Ord.14 affidavit.	Can solicitor's clerk swear plaintiff's affidavit?	Yes.
United Gutta Percha Co. v. Welch & Co.	(1897) 14 T.L.R. 154, C.A.		Unliquidated cross-claim. Whole of liquidated claim admitted.	Ord.14 judgment?	No—counter-claim might exceed claim. Unconditional leave.
Pemberton v. Hughes	(1899) 1 Ch. 781; 68 L.J.Ch. 287		Foreign judgment obtained. Minor local procedural irregularity alleged by defendant.	Ord.14 available?	Yes, so long as English views of substantial justice unaffected.

CASE	CITATION	JUDGE(S)	FACTS	ISSUES	ADJUDICATION
General Railway Syndicate, Re, Whiteley's Case.	[1900] 1 Ch. 365; 69 L.J.Ch. 250	Vaughan Williams L.J.	Share call case.	Establishing a defence.	General denial in an affidavit is inadequate.
Jacobs v. Booths Distillery Co.	[1901] 85 L.T. 262; 50 W.R. 49, H.L.	Lord Halsbury L.C.	Action on two promissory notes. Ord.14 judgment.	(i) Nature/appropriateness of Ord.14 proceedings? (ii) Leave to defend in Ord.14 proceedings?	(i) Ord.14 proceedings should not be used lightly. (ii) Leave—unless clear that defendant has nothing worthwhile to say.
County Theatres & Hotels Ltd v. Knowles	[1902] 1 K.B. 480; 71 L.J.K.B. 351	Collins M.R. Romer L.J.	Contract: arbitration clause.	Stay for defendant to allow arbitration?	No—defendant had taken steps in action by attending on summons for directions taken out by plaintiff.
Bankes v. Jarvis	[1903] 1 K.B. 549; 72 L.J.K.B. 267	Lord Alverstone C.J. Wills J. Channell J.	Plaintiff suing as trustee defendant owed unliquidated sum.	Monetary cross-claim a defence?	Generally yes, to amount due under set-off.

CASE	CITATION	JUDGE(S)	FACTS	ISSUES	ADJUDICATION
Morel Brothers & Co. Ltd v. Earl of Westmorland	[1903] 1 K.B. 64; [1904] A.C. 11	Collings M.R. Romer L.J. Mathew L.J.	Claim against husband and wife.	Could plaintiff seek Ord.14 judgment against one defendant and proceed to trial against the other?	No—judgment against one bars proceedings against the other.
Richardson v. Le Maitre	[1903] 2 Ch. 222; 72 L.J.Ch. 779	Swinfen Eady J.	Contract: arbitration clause.	Stay for defendant to allow arbitration?	No—defendant had taken step in action by attending on summons for directions taken out by plaintiff.
Cross v. Matthews and Wallace	[1904] 91 L.T. 500		Alternative defendants.	Can plaintiff seek to set aside judgment against one defendant to remove bar against proceedings against the other?	No.
Codd v. Delap	(1905) 95 L.T. 510, H.L.		Foreign judgment. Fraud alleged.	Approach of courts on Ord.14 application.	Great caution. No Ord.14 unless allegation obviously frivolous.

CASE	CITATION	JUDGE(S)	FACTS	ISSUES	ADJUDICATION
Lazarus v. Smith	[1908] 2 K.B. 266; 77 L.J.K.B. 791	Cozens Hardy M.R. Kennedy L.J.	Money-lender's action. Defence under Money Lenders Act 1900, but a certain sum admitted.	Whether summary judgment should be granted?	Summary judgment for sum admitted. Leave to defend *re* residue.
Dendy v. Evans	[1909] 2 K.B. 894; [1910] 1 K.B. 263	Cozens Hardy M.R. Fletcher Moulton L.J. Farwell L.J. (Appeal)	Forfeiture case.	Effect of relief?	Restores lease as if never forfeited.
Chirgwin v. Russell	(1910) 27 T.L.R. 21; 55 S.J. 10 C.A.		Ord.14 affidavit.	Can plaintiff's solicitor swear his Ord.14 affidavit?	Yes.
Lagos v. Grunwaldt	[1910] 1 K.B. 41; [1908–10] All E.R.Rep. 939	Cozens Hardy M.R. Farwell L.J.	Liquidated demand.	Must sources of hearsay be stated in Ord.14 affidavit?	Yes.
Mosenthal, ex p. Marx	(1910) 54 S.J. 751, C.A.		Defendant absent from Ord.14 proceedings.	Discretion to set aside?	Yes, but may be set aside as to part only.

CASE	CITATION	JUDGE(S)	FACTS	ISSUES	ADJUDICATION
Symons & Co. v. Palmers' Stores (1903) Ltd	[1912] 1 K.B. 259; 81 L.J.K.B. 439	Vaughan Williams L.J. Buckley L.J. Kennedy L.J.	Ord.14 application. Affidavit.	Does court have jurisdiction?	No, defendant entitled to costs.
Pathé Frères Cinema Ltd v. United Electric Theatres Ltd	[1914] 3 K.B. 1253; 84 L.J.K.B. 245	Buckley L.J. Kennedy L.J. Phillimore L.J.	Liquidated claim.	Should Ord.14 deponent state that to best of his knowledge/belief debt remains unpaid?	Yes.
Nash v. Rochford R.D.C.	[1917] 1 K.B. 384; 86 L.J.K.B. 370	Lord Cozens Hardy M.R. Warrington L.J. Scrutton L.J.	Road traffic accident.	Principle on which further evidence received?	Further evidence must be apparently credible.
Jones & Son v. Whitehouse	[1918] 2 K.B. 61; [1918–19] All E.R.Rep. 708	Pickford L.J. Warrington L.J.	Solicitor suing for costs by specially indorsed writ. Defendant objected to some items. Bill delivered for more than 12 months.	Summary judgment sought. Should whole bill be taxed?	Not whole bill; leave to defend *re* few items disputed.

CASE	CITATION	JUDGE(S)	FACTS	ISSUES	ADJUDICATION
Russian Commercial & Industrial Bank v. British Bank for Foreign Trade	[1921] 2 A.C. 438; 90 L.J.K.B. 1089	Viscount Finlay Lord Dunedin Lord Sumner Lord Parmoor Lord Wrenbury	Loan by Russian bank to English bank.	(i) Was loan repayable in Roubles?	(i) Yes.
				(ii) Was action brought in wrong court?	Yes, but not ground for interfering with Court of Appeal's discretion.
Smith v. Howes	[1922] 1 K.B. 591; 91 L.J.K.B. 388	Bankes L.J. Scrutton L.J. Atkin L.J.	If proceedings for taxation of costs are commenced by the client, disbursements made before commencement of taxation can be allowed.	Ord.14 proceedings for costs. Have "proceedings for taxation" commence?	Yes. Such Ord.14 proceedings are *both* an action by solicitor for costs *and* an application by client to tax.
Everett v. Islington Guardians	[1923] 1 K.B. 44; 92 L.J.K.B. 250	Avory J.	Plaintiff claimed right to trial by jury.	Right to jury?	Only if issue of fraud must be decided to determine action.
Powszechny Bank Zwiazkowy W. Polsce v. Paros	[1932] 2 K.B. 353, C.A.	Scrutton L.J. Greer L.J. Slesser L.J.	Bill of exchange. Defence that bill negotiated in fraud of him.	Was defendant entitled to leave to defend?	Yes, triable issue of fraud.

CASE	CITATION	JUDGE(S)	FACTS	ISSUES	ADJUDICATION
Dott v. Brown	[1936] 1 All E.R. 543; 154 L.T. 484	Lord Roche Scott L.J.	Payment of debt by instalments. Income tax case.	Proper to use Ord.14 for tactical purpose with little prospect of success?	No.
Simmons v. Wiltshire	[1938] 3 All E.R. 403	Greer L.J. Slesser L.J. Mackinnon L.J.	Goods sold and delivered. Transfer from High Court to county court.	County court judge's powers *re* costs.	Costs up to transfer on High Court scale.
Contract Discount Corp v. Furlong	[1948] 1 All E.R. 274; 64 T.L.R. 201	Lord Greene M.R. Asquith L.J. Harman J.	Commercial contract case. Claim for £19,000. About £10,000 admitted.	Leave to defend?	Conditional leave on payment in of £8,000.
Cow v. Casey	[1949] 1 K.B. 474; [1949] 1 All E.R. 197	Lord Greene M.R. Wynn-Parry J.	Landlord and tenant.	Leave to defend in Ord.14 proceedings?	Leave unless defendant has nothing worthwhile to say.
Morgan & Son Ltd v. Martin Johnson & Co. Ltd	[1949] 1 K.B. 107; [1948] 2 All E.R. 196, C.A.	Tucker L.J. Cohen L.J.	Claim for sum owed for storage of vehicles. Ord.14 claim.	Cross-claim a defence?	Yes, unconditional leave to defend.

1139

CASE	CITATION	JUDGE(S)	FACTS	ISSUES	ADJUDICATION
Lamont v. Hyland	[1950] 1 K.B. 585; [1950] 1 All E.R. 341	Tucker L.J. Asquith L.J. Roxburgh J.	Action on bill of exchange.	Could plaintiff obtain summary judgment?	Yes, if defendant has no defence under the Bills of Exchange Act.
Cumbes v. Robinson	[1951] 2 K.B. 83; [1951] 1 All E.R. 661	Somervell L.J. Singleton L.J. Denning L.J.	Landlord and tenant.	Can notice of appeal incorporate application for leave?	No.
Pocock (M.) v. A.D.A.C. Ltd; Pocock (K.B.) v. A.D.A.C.	[1952] 1 T.L.R. 29; [1952] 1 All E.R. 294n	Lord Goodard C.J.	Contract of service. Plaintiff of Ord.14 application knew of arguable defence.	Proper course?	Dismiss application with costs.
Dummer v. Brown	[1953] 1 Q.B. 710; [1953] 2 W.L.R. 984	Singleton L.J. Jenkins L.J. Morris L.J.	Road traffic case. Ord.14 application.	(i) Was Ord.14 procedure available for a fatal accident claim?	(i) Yes.
				(ii) Was a faulty affidavit necessarily fatal?	(ii) No.

CASE	CITATION	JUDGE(S)	FACTS	ISSUES	ADJUDICATION
Krakauer v. Katz	[1954] 1 W.L.R. 278; [1954] 1 All E.R. 244	Denning L.J. Romer L.J.	Contract.	Did appellant in interlocutory matter have right to adduce further evidence by affidavit?	No, matter for court's discretion.
Ladd v. Marshall	[1954] 1 W.L.R. 1489; [1954] 3 All E.R. 745	Denning L.J. Hodson L.J.	Contract case. Appeal to Court of Appeal.	Principle on which further evidence received.	Further evidence must be apparently credible.
Thynne (Bath Marchioness) v. Thynne (Bath, Marquess)	[1955] P.272; [1955] 3 W.L.R. 465; [1955] 3 All E.R. 129	Singleton L.J. Hodson L.J. Morris L.J.	Parties married in secret and then later in public (to no effect).	Can court vary decrees of divorce?	Yes, so as to ensure the purpose of justice and express the intention of the court's order.
Gill v. Lewis	[1956] 2 Q.B. 1; [1956] 2 W.L.R. 962	Singleton L.J. Jenkins L.J. Hodson L.J.	Landlord and tenant.	Possession or relief from forfeiture?	Generally relief is rent/costs paid up, but may be exceptional cases such as tenant keeping disorderly house.
Hanak v. Green	[1958] 2 Q.B. 9; [1958] 2 W.L.R. 755	Hodson L.J. Morris L.J. Sellers L.J.	Building contract.	Did defendant's equitable right undermine plaintiff's legal claim?	Yes.

1141

CASE	CITATION	JUDGE(S)	FACTS	ISSUES	ADJUDICATION
Les Fils Dreyfus v. Clarke	[1958] 1 W.L.R. 300	Parker L.J. Sellers L.J.	Liquidated demand.	May court allow plaintiff to cure defective affidavit with supplemental affidavit?	Yes.
Fieldrank Ltd v. Stein	[1961] 1 W.L.R. 1287; [1961] 3 All E.R. 681	Sellers L.J. Davies L.J. Danckwerts L.J.	Liquidated claim.	Should leave to defend be conditional, even if possible triable issue?	If doubt defendant's good faith, may be proper to order payment into court.
International General Electric Co. of New York v. Customs and Excise Commissioners	[1962] Ch. 784; [1962] 3 W.L.R. 20	Upjohn L.J. Diplock L.J.	Commercial case. Declaration sought.	(i) Nature of declaration? (ii) Position of action against Crown.	(i) Declaration is a final order. (ii) No interim injunction declaration against Crown.
General and Finance Facilities Ltd v. Cooks Cars (Romford) Ltd	[1963] 1 W.L.R. 644; [1963] 2 All E.R. 314		See Evans v. Bartlam [1937] A.C. 473.		

CASE	CITATION	JUDGE(S)	FACTS	ISSUES	ADJUDICATION
Brown Shipley & Co. Ltd v. Alicia Hosiery Ltd	[1966] 1 Lloyd's Rep. 668	Lord Denning M.R. Harman L.J.	Action on bill on exchange: counterclaim.	Could plaintiff obtain summary judgment?	Yes.
Barclays Bank Ltd v. Cole	[1967] 2 Q.B. 738; [1967] 2 W.L.R. 166	Lord Denning M.R. Diplock L.J.	Plaintiff bank sued convicted bank robber.	Was defendant entitled to have civil action tried by jury?	No, no issues of fraud involved.
Beswick v. Beswick	[1968] A.C. 58; [1967] 3 W.L.R. 932	Lord Reid Lord Hodson Lord Guest Lord Pearce Lord Upjohn	Contract to transfer coal round. Action by widow of party.	Privity of contract. Would specific performance be granted?	Widow entitled to specific performance as administratrix but not in personal capacity.
Fielding & Platt Ltd v. Selim Najjar	[1969] 1 W.L.R. 357; [1969] 2 All E.R. 150, C.A.	Lord Denning M.R. Davies L.J. Widgery L.J.	Bill of exchange.	Basis for suing on promissory note?	Total failure of consideration and illegality were defences to bad cheque.
Ionian Bank Ltd v. Couvreur	[1969] 1 W.L.R. 781 [1969] 2 All E.R. 651, C.A.	Lord Denning M.R. Davies L.J. Widgery L.J.	Claim involving purchase of wine.	Very "shadowy" defence. Security to defend?	Payment in of full claim was condition for defending.

CASE	CITATION	JUDGE(S)	FACTS	ISSUES	ADJUDICATION
Miles v. Bull	[1969] 1 Q.B. 258; [1968] 3 W.L.R. 1090	Megarry J.	Action for possession of property: Ord.14 application. Estranged husband of defendant sold matrimonial home to plaintiff.	No defence. Disclosed: leave to defend?	Yes, possible conspiracy was good reason for trial.
Revici v. Prentice Hall Inc.	[1969] 1 W.L.R. 157; [1969] 1 All E.R. 772, C.A.	Lord Denning M.R. Edmund Davies L.J. Widgery L.J.	Libel proceedings.	Extension of time for appeal?	Must be good explanation for any delay in notice of appeal.
Van Lynn Developments Ltd v. Pelias Construction Co. (formerly Jason Construction Co.)	[1969] 1 Q.B. 607; [1968] 3 W.L.R. 1141	Lord Denning M.R. Davies L.J. Widgery L.J.	Assignment of debt.	Amount of security?	Full amount of claim.
Manchester Corp. v. Connolly	[1970] Ch. 420; [1970] 2 W.L.R. 746	Lord Diplock Widgery L.J. Megaw L.J.	Defendants occupied plaintiff's land.	Would court grant interlocutory injunction and make order for possession?	Injunction granted, but no possession order on interlocutory application.

CASE	CITATION	JUDGE(S)	FACTS	ISSUES	ADJUDICATION
Bank für Gemeinwirtschaft Aktiengesellschaft v. City of London Garages	[1971] 1 W.L.R. 149; [1971] 1 All E.R. 541	Davies L.J. Phillimore L.J. Cairn L.J.	Action on bill of exchange. Defence of fraud affecting the bill.	Was defendant entitled to leave to defend on Ord.14 application?	Not if plaintiff can show bill taken in good faith and for value.
Dawnays Ltd v. Minter Ltd (F.G.) and Troloppe and Colls	[1971] 1 W.L.R. 1205; [1971] 2 All E.R. 1389	Lord Denning M.R. Edmund Davies L.J. Stamp L.J.	R.I.B.A. building contract.	Defence of set-off applicable to R.I.B.A. contract?	Possibly not.
Shell Mex & B.P. Ltd v. Manchester Garages Ltd	[1971] 1 W.L.R. 612; 115 S.J. 111	Lord Denning M.R. Widgery L.J. Buckley L.J.	Licence to occupy petrol filling station. Defendants claimed tenancy.	Would plaintiff be granted injunction on Ord.14 application?	Yes, agreement was a licence.
Skone v. Skone	[1971] 1 W.L.R. 812; [1971] 2 All E.R. 582, H.L.	Lord Hodson Viscount Dilhourne Lord Wilberforce Lord Diplock Lord Cross	Divorce Court Appeal.	Principle on which further evidence received?	Further evidence must be apparently credible.

CASE	CITATION	JUDGE(S)	FACTS	ISSUES	ADJUDICATION
National Westminster Bank Ltd v. Halesowen Presswork & Assemblies Ltd	[1972] A.C. 785; [1972] 2 W.L.R. 455	Viscount Dilhorne Lord Simon Lord Cross Lord Kilbrandon	Banking case.	Were provisions of s.31 of Bankruptcy Act 1914 mandatory?	Yes.
Sullivan v. Henderson	[1973] 1 W.L.R. 333; [1973] 1 All E.R. 48	Megarry J.	Shares transfer.	Purpose of Ord.14 procedure?	Summary judgment without trial, thus no oral evidence.
Gilbert-Ash (Northern) Ltd v. Modern Engineering (Bristol) Ltd	[1974] A.C. 689; [1973] 3 W.L.R. 421	Viscount Dilhorne Lord Reid Lord Morris Lord Diplock Lord Salmon	R.I.B.A. Building contract.	Rights of set-off eroded in R.I.B.A. contracts?	No.
Starside Properties Ltd v. Mustapha	[1974] 1 W.L.R. 816; [1974] 2 All E.R. 567	Edmund Davies L.J. Cairns L.J. Lawton L.J.	Forfeiture case.	Was there a distinction between forfeiture for non-payment of rent and other breaches?	No.
Wallersteiner v. Moir	[1974] 1 W.L.R. 991; [1974] 3 All E.R. 217, C.A.	Lord Denning M.R. Buckley L.J. Scarman L.J.	Action involving purchase of shares.	Would declaratory relief be granted?	Declaratory relief will not be granted on pleadings, by consent or in default of defence.

1146

CASE	CITATION	JUDGE(S)	FACTS	ISSUES	ADJUDICATION
Cebora S.N.C. v. S.I.P. (Industrial Products) Ltd	[1976] 1 Lloyd's Rep. 271, C.A.	Buckley L.J. Stephenson L.J.	Bills of exchange: counter-claim Ord.14 judgment.	Stay?	No.
Dymond v. Britton (G.B.) & Sons (Holdings) Ltd	[1976] F.S.R. 330; (1976) I C.M.L.R. 133	Oliver J.	Patent case.	Ord.14 application. Leave to defend following Community Law plea?	Yes, conditional, with some misgivings.
Ellis Mechanical Services Ltd v. Wates Construction Ltd	(1976) 120 S.J. 167, C.A.; (1976) 2 Build. L.R. 57	Lord Denning M.R. Lawton L.J. Bridge L.J.	R.I.B.A. contract. Part of claim admitted but not quantified.	Should Ord.14 be granted?	Ord.14 judgment on sum clearly due to plaintiff.
Temple v. Temple	[1976] 1 W.L.R. 701; [1976] 3 All E.R. 12	Cairns L.J. Orr L.J.	Action by wife under maintenance agreement. Ord.14 application.	Should Q.B.D. proceedings be transferred to Family Division: Ord.14 appropriate?	There was jurisdiction to transfer, but should stay in Q.B.D. to allow wife Ord.14 relief.
Aries Tanker Corp. v. Total Transport; Aries, The	[1977] 1 W.L.R. 185; [1977] 1 All E.R. 398	Lord Wilberforce Viscount Dilhorne Lord Simon Lord Salmon Lord Edmund Davies	Voyage charter party.	Breach of warranty claim a valid defence?	Yes, to scale of goods/contract of works claim.

CASE	CITATION	JUDGE(S)	FACTS	ISSUES	ADJUDICATION
Edward Owen Engineering Ltd v. Barclay Bank International Ltd and Another	[1977] 3 W.L.R. 764; [1978] 1 All E.R. 976	Lord Denning M.R. Browne L.J.	Letter of credit. Performance bond.	Was performance bond similar to letter of credit?	Yes.
Nova (Jersey) Knit v. Kammgarn Spinnerei Ltd GmbH	[1977] 1 W.L.R. 713; [1977] 2 All E.R. 463	Lord Wilberforce Viscount Dilhorne Lord Salmon Lord Fraser Lord Russell	Action on bill of exchange by appellants.	Were respondents entitled to a stay?	No; claim for unliquidated damages could not be raised as defence, counter-claim or set-off in action on bill of exchange.
A.B. Contractors Ltd v. Flaherty Bros Ltd	(February 22, 1978, unreported)		Defendant's cross-claim unconnected with plaintiff's claim.	Must cross-claim form subject of separate action?	Yes.
Associated Bulk Carriers Ltd v. Koch Shipping Inc.; Fuohsan Maru, The	[1978] 2 All E.R. 254; [1978] 1 Lloyd's Rep. 24	Lord Denning M.R. Browne L.J. Geoffrey Lane L.J.	Time charter of motor vessel. Ord.14 application.	Ord. 14 Judgment?	Not granted. Impossible to identify particular parts of claim to which no defence.
Customs and Excise Commissioners v. Holvey	[1978] 1 Q.B. 310; [1978] 2 W.L.R. 155	Peter Pain J.	Revenue case.	Defence sought to be raised open to defendants?	No, therefore judgment for plaintiffs.

CASE	CITATION	JUDGE(S)	FACTS	ISSUES	ADJUDICATION
Howe Richardson Scale Co. v. Polimex-Cekop & National Westminster Bank Ltd	[1978] Lloyd's Rep. 161, C.A.	Roskill L.J.	Contract for sale of goods. Bank guarantee.	Injunction preventing payment under guarantee?	No.
Metzger v. Department of Health and Social Security	[1978] 1 W.L.R. 1046; [1978] 3 All E.R. 753, C.A.	Stamp L.J. Orr L.J. Eveleigh L.J.	Action against D.H.S.S. claiming declarations.	Would declaratory relief be granted?	Declaratory relief will not be granted on pleadings, by consent or in default of defence.
Jefferson v. Bhetcha	[1979] 1 W.L.R. 898; [1979] 2 All E.R. 1108, C.A.	Megaw L.J. Brandon L.J.	Action against former employee for appropriated cheques. Ord.14 application.	Was defendant excused from swearing Ord.14 affidavit to preserve criminal defence?	No right of silence in civil action but stay might be granted in appropriate circumstances.
Tennant (Lady Anne) v. Associated Newspapers Group Ltd	[1979] F.S.R. 298	Sir Robert Megarry V.-C.	Copyright of photographs.	Ord.14 judgment?	Yes, defendant had failed to establish plausible defence.
Montecchi v. Shimco Ltd (U.K.); Navone v. Same	[1979] 1 W.L.R. 180; (1978) 123 S.J. 551	Roskill L.J. Geoffrey Lane L.J. Bridge L.J.	Bill of exchange action.	Would court grant stay?	No; counter-claim for unliquidated sum was no defence to bad cheque.

1149

CASE	CITATION	JUDGE(S)	FACTS	ISSUES	ADJUDICATION
Sable Contractors Ltd v. Bluett Shipping Ltd	[1979] 2 Lloyd's Rep. 33, C.A.	Lord Diplock Lord Russell	Building contracts; Ord.14 application. Counter-claim alleged.	Leave to defend?	Leave to defend, *re* part of claim.
C.S.I. International Co. Ltd v. Airway Personnel (Middle East) Ltd	[1980] 1 W.L.R. 1069; [1980] 3 All E.R. 215, C.A.	Roskill L.J. Eveleigh L.J. Walton J.	Action by foreign company on dishonoured cheque.	Could defendant serve counter-claim after satisfying plaintiff's judgment?	No.
Holden v. Trent Regional Health Authority	(November 17, 1980; unreported)		Application by defendant to transfer proceedings.	Test?	Balance of interlocutory convenience.
Hyundai Heavy Industries Co. Ltd v. Papadopoulos	[1980] 1 W.L.R. 1129; [1980] 2 All E.R. 29	Viscount Dilhorne Lord Edmund Davies Lord Fraser Lord Russell Lord Keith	Letter of guarantee.	Position of guarantors?	Liable, irrespective of position between other parties.
Schofield v. River Don Stamping Ltd and Woodhouse & Rixon Ltd	(1980, unreported)	Lincoln J.	Application by defendant to transfer proceedings.	Test?	Balance of interlocutory convenience.

1150

CASE	CITATION	JUDGE(S)	FACTS	ISSUES	ADJUDICATION
Allied Collection Agencies Ltd v. Wood	[1981] 3 All E.R. 176; (1980) 124 S.J.	Neill J.	Restrictive covenant in employment contract. Ord.14 application for defendant's costs.	Defendant's costs taxable immediately?	Yes, no need to await outcome of action.
I.B.A. v. E.M.I. Electronics Ltd	(November 13, 1981; unreported)		Interim payment.	Can court order interest on interim payment?	Yes.
Intraco v. Notis Shipping Corp. of Liberia; Bhoja Trader, The	[1981] Com.L.R. 184; [1981] 2 Lloyd's Rep. 256, C.A.	Donaldson L.J. Ackner L.J.	Sale of ship. *Mareva*: bank guarantee.	Would *Mareva* against money obtained under guarantee be discharged?	Yes.
Montebianco Industrie Tessili S.p.A. v. Carlyle Mills (London)	[1981] 1 Lloyd's Rep. 509, C.A.	Stephenson L.J. Ackner L.J. Sir Stanley Rees	Bill of exchange action. Counterclaim. Ord.14 judgment.	Unconditional leave? Stay?	No.
Power Curber International v. National Bank of Kuwait SAK	[1981] 1 W.L.R. 233; [1981] 3 All E.R. 607	Lord Denning M.R. Griffiths L.J. Waterhouse J.	Documentary credits; conflict of laws.	(i) What was proper law of documentary credit?	(i) That to which it was most closely connected.

CASE	CITATION	JUDGE(S)	FACTS	ISSUES	ADJUDICATION
				(ii) Would execution of Ord.14 judgment be stayed?	(ii) No, letter of credit was equivalent to cash.
Stafford Winfield Cook & Partners v. Winfield	[1981] 1 W.L.R. 458; [1980] 3 All E.R. 759	Sir Robert Megarry V.-C.	Action in Chancery for a declaration, payment up of trust moneys and damages.	Was defendant entitled to have civil action tried by jury?	Not in Chancery Division.
Standard Chartered Bank v. Wymark Plant Hire Ltd	(1981, unreported)		Multiple defendants; fraud alleged only against one.	Ord.14 applicable to any/all of defendants?	Ord.14 proceedings barred against each defendant.
Verrall v. Great Yarmouth Borough Council	[1981] 1 Q.B. 202; [1980] 3 W.L.R. 258	Lord Denning M.R. Roskill L.J. Cumming-Bruce L.J.	Hiring of hall by National Front. Later repudiation by defendants.	Would specific performance be granted on Ord.14 application?	Proper case for Ord.14 when issues clear and could be determined summarily. Specific performance granted.
Clovertogs v. Jean Scenes	[1982] Com.L.R. 88, C.A.		Import/purchase of clothing cheques "stopped".	Did allegation of misrepresentation raise triable issue?	Yes.

1152

CASE	CITATION	JUDGE(S)	FACTS	ISSUES	ADJUDICATION
GMS Syndicate v. Elliot (Gary) Ltd	[1982] 1 Ch. 1; [1981] 2 W.L.R. 478	Nourse J.	Forfeiture case.	Could relief be granted in respect of part of demised premises?	Yes, in appropriate cases.
Langdale v. Danby	[1982] 1 W.L.R. 1123; [1982] 3 All E.R. 129	Lord Diplock, Lord Fraser, Lord Roskill, Lord Bridge, Lord Brightman	Sale of cottage. Option to re-purchase.	Appeal under Ord.14. Can Court of Appeal hear further evidence on questions of fact?	Yes.
Leco Instruments (U.K.) Ltd v. Land Pyrometers	[1982] R.P.C. 140	Fox L.J.	Plaintiffs sought declaration: granted.	Appeal against declaration.	Upheld, but only because defendants showed arguable defence appropriate to trial.
Standard Chartered Bank Ltd v. Walker	[1982] 1 W.L.R. 1410; [1982] 3 All E.R. 938	Lord Denning M.R., Watkins L.J.	Guarantors' Ord.14 application.	Appeals by guarantors against summary judgment.	Leave to defend. Triable issues of law/fact.
Yorke (M.V.) Motors v. Edwards	[1982] 1 W.L.R. 444; [1982] 1 All E.R. 1204, H.L.	Lord Diplock, Lord Fraser, Lord Russell, Lord Scarman, Lord Roskill	Purchase of second-hand Rolls Royce. Ord.14: leave to defend conditional on payment of £12,000 into court.	Condition wrong?	Condition could be difficult though not impossible.

CASE	CITATION	JUDGE(S)	FACTS	ISSUES	ADJUDICATION
Academy Sound & Vision Ltd v. WEA Records Ltd	[1983] I.C.R. 586	Vinelott J.	Restrictive practices *re* sale of copyright recordings.	Ord.14 judgment?	Yes.
Centrovincial Estates v. Merchant Investors Assurance Co. Ltd	(1983) 127 S.J. 443; [1983] Com.L.R. 158, C.A.	Harman J.	Assignment of lease. Assignor sued for unpaid rent.	Unilateral mistake.	Where unambiguous offer, offeror bound by acceptance.
Chakravorty v. Braganza	*The Times*, October 12, 1983	Comyn J.	Application for committal for breach of injunction.	Detail needed in supporting affidavit?	Specific breaches to be identified.
European Asian Bank A.G. v. The Punjab Sind Bank (No. 2)	[1983] 1 W.L.R. 642; [1983] 2 All E.R. 508	Slade L.J. Goff L.J.	Banking. Irrevocable credit. Court of Appeal.	Question of fact.	Court of Appeal reluctant to interfere with findings of fact.
Lloyds Bank v. Ellis Fewster	[1983] 1 W.L.R. 559; [1983] 2 All E.R. 424, C.A.	Sir John Donaldson M.R. Dillon L.J.	Defendants were guarantors. Plaintiff applied for Ord.14 judgment.	Was leave to defend correctly granted?	If triability of issue depended on question of fact not law, judge's discretion unlikely to be interfered with.

CASE	CITATION	JUDGE(S)	FACTS	ISSUES	ADJUDICATION
Banque de Paris et des Pays-Bas (Suisse) S.A. v. Costa de Naray	[1984] 1 Lloyd's Rep. 21, C.A.	Ackner L.J. O'Connor L.J.	Banking guarantee.	Summary judgment?	Yes; assertion in affidavit not sufficient for leave to defend.
Bremar Holdings Ltd v. de Roth	(1984) 134 New L.J. 550; The Times, February 28, 1987	Beldam J.	Defendant's advisers knew defendant unable to raise substantial sum.	Master's position on Ord.14 application?	Should know all facts, re ability to satisfy condition as to leave to defend.
Cadogan v. Dimovic	[1984] 1 W.L.R. 609; [1984] 2 All E.R.	Waller L.J. Fox L.J. Robert Goff L.J.	Forfeiture case.	Relief available in Ord.4 proceedings to sub-lessee?	Yes.
Coastal (Bermuda) v. Esso Petroleum Co.	[1984] 1 Lloyd's Rep. 11, C.A.	Sir John Donaldson M.R. May L.J.	Sale of cargo of oil. Ord.14 judgment.	Appeal by defendants.	Appeal refused.
Extraktionstechnik Gesellschaft für Anlagenbau mbH v. Oskar	(1984) 128 S.J. 417; (1984) 81 L.S.Gaz. 1362, C.A.	Watkins L.J. Slade L.J.	Dishonoured cheques. Ord.14 application. Conditional leave.	Unconditional leave?	Yes, appearance of bad faith by both parties.
Fabre (Pierre) v. Ronco Teleproducts	[1984] F.S.R. 148	Peter Gibson J.	Passing off. Direction for speedy trial.	Ord.14 application consistent with directions?	No.

CASE	CITATION	JUDGE(S)	FACTS	ISSUES	ADJUDICATION
Halvanon Insurance Co. v. Central Reinsurance Corp.	[1984] 2 Lloyd's Rep. 420	Neill J.	Reinsurance case.	Interim payment order?	Order made.
Heyes v. (Earl of) Derby	(1984) 272 EG 939, C.A.	Watkins L.J. Slade L.J.	Action for damage to land. Ord.14 judgment to plaintiff tenant.	Appeal by defendant landlord.	Unconditional leave to defend.
Israel Discount Bank of New York v. Hadjipateras	[1984] 1 W.L.R. 137; [1983] 3 All E.R. 129	Stephenson L.J. O'Connor L.J. Robert Goff L.J.	Foreign judgment.	Would English court enforce judgment?	Undue influence, duress and coercion were reasons for English court to refuse to enforce a foreign judgment.
Jones v. Barnett	[1984] 1 Ch. 500; [1984] 3 W.L.R. 333	Judge Paul Baker Q.C.	Forfeiture case.	Relief available in county court?	No.
Kiu May Construction Co. v. Wai Cheong Co.	(1983) 29 Build.L.R. 137	High Ct. of Hong Kong	Hong Kong standard building contract. Ord.14 appeal.	Additional evidence on appeal.	Yes, subject to costs unless judge exercises discretion to exclude.

CASE	CITATION	JUDGE(S)	FACTS	ISSUES	ADJUDICATION
K/S A/S Oil Transport v. Saudi Research and Development Corp.	[1984] 1 Lloyd's Rep. 5, C.A.	Sir John Donaldson M.R. May L.J. Purchas L.J.	Ship lease: Mareva.	Principle on which further evidence received?	Further evidence must be apparently credible.
Mechanical & Electrical Engineering Contracts Co. v. Christy & Norris Ltd	(1984) 134 New L.J. 1017, D.C.	Neill J.	Iraqi judgment.	Summary judgment for sum claimed.	Yes.
Messenger Newspaper Group v. National Graphical Association	[1984] I.C.R. 345			Plaintiff's right to couple Ord.14/interim payment applications.	Recognised.
Northern Regional Health Authority v. Crouch (Derek) Construction Co. Ltd	[1984] 1 Q.B. 644; 2 W.L.R. 676	Sir John Donaldson M.R. Dunn L.J. Browne-Wilkinson L.J.	Standard form building contract arbitration clause.	Would court interfere with contractual provisions?	No.

CASE	CITATION	JUDGE(S)	FACTS	ISSUES	ADJUDICATION
Paclantic Financing Co. Inc. v. Moscow Narodny Bank Ltd	[1984] 1 W.L.R. 930; (1984) 128 S.J. 349	Waller L.J. Fox L.J. Robert Goff L.J.	Commercial case. Ord.14 application.	Is a "shadowy defence" enough to defeat an Ord.14 application?	Often yes.
Potton Homes v. Coleman Contractors (Overseas) Ltd	(1984) 128 S.J. 282; (1984) 81 L.S.Gaz. 1044, C.A.	Eveleigh L.J. May L.J.	Performance bond.	Stay of execution of summary judgment?	No.
Rapid Building Group Ltd v. Ealing Family Housing Association	The Times, December 5, 1984, C.A.	Stephenson L.J. Lloyd L.J.	Appeal by Housing Association against Ord.14 judgment.	Leave to appeal neccessary?	No.
Redpath Dorman Long Ltd v. Tubeworking Ltd	(March 15, 1984; unreported)		Defendants' cross-claim unconnected with plaintiff's claim.	Must cross-claim form subject of separate action?	Yes.
R.H. & D. International v. Ias Animal Air Services Ltd	[1984] 1 W.L.R. 573; [1984] 2 All E.R. 203	Neill J.	Freight contract.	Could cross-claim re cargo extinguish/diminish freight claim?	No.

CASE	CITATION	JUDGE(S)	FACTS	ISSUES	ADJUDICATION
Rosengrens v. Safe Deposit Centres Ltd	[1984] 1 W.L.R. 1334; [1984] 3 All E.R. 198	Sir John Donaldson M.R. Parker L.J.	Liquidated claim. Order for security pending appeal.	What form should security take?	Least disadvantageous to defendant so long as plaintiff adequately protected.
Schindler Lifts (Hong Kong) v. Shui On Construction Co. Ltd	(1984) 29 Build.L.R. 95, C.A.	Hong Kong case	Standard Hong Kong building contract. Ord.14 application.	Ord.14 judgment?	No; complex chain of contracts (despite fact that questions were of construction).
Stern v. Wolf	[1984] C.L.Y. 2574; *The Times*, November 6, 1984, C.A.	Sir John Donaldson M.R.	Appeal from decision of Official Referee.	Leave necessary?	Yes.
White v. Brunton	[1984] Q.B. 570; [1984] 3 W.L.R. 105	Sir John Donaldson M.R. Fox L.J. Stephen Brown L.J.	Agreement to sell land.	Will Court of Appeal raise question of leave?	Yes, where it considers leave.
Willment Brothers v. North West Thames Regional Health Authority	(1984) 26 Build.L.R. 51, C.A.	Ackner L.J. O'Connor L.J.	Standard form building contract to build hospital wing; stage payments. Action on "stopped cheque".	Ord.14?	No. Bankruptcy Act 1914 gave defendant statutory right to set-off.

CASE	CITATION	JUDGE(S)	FACTS	ISSUES	ADJUDICATION
Avon Display Co. v. Wainwright & Harmer Properties	[1985] C.L.Y. 277	Kennedy J.	Action for recovery of money. Ord.14 judgment. Statement of claim alleged fraud.	Appeal against Ord.14 judgment.	Allegation of fraud does not prevent reliance on Ord.14.
Giles (Electrical Engineers) Ltd v. Plessey Communications Systems Ltd	[1985] 1 W.L.R. 243; [1985] 1 All E.R. 499	Sir John Donaldson M.R. Slade L.J. Lloyd L.J.	Application to consolidate actions.	Leave needed to appeal from Official Referee's decision?	Principles same as for High Court judge's decision.
Liverpool Properties v. Oldbridge Investments	[1985] 2 EGLR 111; (1985) 276 EG 1352, C.A.	Parker L.J. Croom-Johnson L.J.	Repairing covenant. Proceedings for possession.	Right to relief against forfeiture a defence to Ord.14 application?	Yes.
Markbolme Ltd v. Braithwaite	(April 14, 1985; unreported)		Defendant allowed to defend on payment on money into court. Money not paid.	Can defendant apply under C.C.R. Ord.37, r.4 to have judgment against him set aside?	No.

1160

CASE	CITATION	JUDGE(S)	FACTS	ISSUES	ADJUDICATION
Palata Investments v. Burt and Sinfield	[1985] 1 W.L.R. 942; [1985] 2 All E.R. 517	Ackner L.J. Robert Goff L.J. Browne-Wilkinson L.J.	Nuisance.	Does Court of Appeal have unfettered discretion to extend time for appealing?	Yes, will normally exercise if delay short/excuse good.
Pillings (C.M.) & Co. Ltd v. Kent Investments Ltd	(1985) 30 Build.L.R. 80; (1985) 1 Const.L.J. 393		Architect's certificate of value of work done. Defendant says overvalued.	Arbitration?	If contract contains arbitration clause, this is correct approach.
Pinemain Ltd v. Welbeck International Ltd	(1985) 129 S.J. 66; (1985) 81 L.S.Gaz. 3426	Lawton L.J. Kerr L.J.	Application for Ord.14 judgment.	Ord.14 judgment?	No; defence arguable on point of law. Not suitable case.
Pumfrey Construction Ltd v. Childs	*The Times,* July 12, 1985	May L.J. Stephen Brown L.J.	Appeal against Ord.14 judgment.	Role of Court of Appeal?	If question wholly/partly factual, Court of Appeal should not disturb decision.
Sethia Liners Ltd v. State Trading Corp. of India Ltd	[1985] 1 W.L.R. 1398	Kerr L.J. Ralph Gibson L.J. Sir Denys Buckley	Contract of sale. Ord.14 judgment.	If issue raised can be dealt with summarily should trial be ordered?	No, judge in chambers/Court of Appeal can deal with whole matter at once.

CASE	CITATION	JUDGE(S)	FACTS	ISSUES	ADJUDICATION
Turner & Goudy v. McConnell	[1985] 1 W.L.R. 898; [1985] 2 All E.R. 34	Dillon L.J. Mustill J.	Liquidated claim. Arbitration clause.	Stay of judicial proceedings step in proceedings by defendant?	Defendants had filed affidavit opposing Ord.14. No stay.
Wiltshire London v. Mayor Burgess of Lambeth London Borough	June 5, 1985 C.A.T. No. 258		Order other than unconditional leave to defend.	May either party appeal without leave?	Yes; if unconditional leave to defend, plaintiff needs leave to appeal.
Yarnold v. Radio Wyvern	(1985) 11 C.L.R. 6		Ord.14.	Assessment of damages carried out at Ord.14 hearing?	No.
Anglian Building Products v. French Construction Ltd	(1972) 16 Build.L.R. 1		Defendant's cross-claim unconnected with plaintiff's claim.	Must cross-claim form subject of separate action?	Yes.
Barstow v. Roberts & Co. (Building)	June 11, 1985, C.A.T. No. 272		Interim payment application.	Service period of supporting affidavit?	Ten clear days before return date (not necessary for supplemental affidavits).

CASE	CITATION	JUDGE(S)	FACTS	ISSUES	ADJUDICATION
Belsham v. W. Dawson & Son Ltd	*The Times*, November 27, 1986, C.A.	Purchas L.J. Nourse L.J.	At beginning of trial, court asked to enter judgment for plaintiff then try counter-claim.	Correct approach?	Treat as if Ord.14 application.
Breeze v. McKennon (R) & Son	(1986) 130 S.J. 16; (1986) 83 L.S.Gaz. 123	Parker L.J. Croom-Johnson L.J.	Negligence/breach of contract application for interim payment/Ord.14 application.	Was Ord.14 affidavit sufficient for interim payment application?	No.
Case Poclain Corp. v. Jones	[1986] E.C.C. 569, C.A.; *The Times*, May 7, 1986	Gibson L.J. Stocker L.J.	Action on a cheque. Defendant counter-claimed for partial failure of consideration.	Leave to defend following Ord.14 application?	No, not liquidated damages.
Continental Illinois National Bank and Trust Company of Chicago v. Papanicolaou; Fedora, Tatiana and Eretrea II, The	[1986] 2 Lloyd's Rep. 441; (1986) 83 L.S.Gaz. 2569, C.A.	Parker L.J. Nourse L.J. Sir Roger Ormrod	Guarantor of debt had Ord.14 judgment awarded against him.	Stay, pending cross-claims against creditor?	Only in exceptional circumstances.

1163

CASE	CITATION	JUDGE(S)	FACTS	ISSUES	ADJUDICATION
Di Palma v. Victoria Square Property Co. Ltd	[1986] Fam. 150; [1985] 3 W.L.R. 207; [1985] 2 All E.R. 676	Lawton L.J. Fox L.J. Neill L.J.	Forfeiture case.	Relief available in county court?	No.
Edmunds v. Lloyds Italico l'Ancora Compagnia di Assicurazioni & Riassicurazione S.p.A.	[1986] 1 W.L.R. 492; [1986] 2 All E.R. 249	Sir John Donaldson M.R. Stephen Brown L.J. Parker L.J.	Insurance underwriting. Debt paid before issue of proceedings.	Interest payable?	No power to award in absence of contractual right.
Forestal Mimosa Ltd v. Oriental Credit Ltd	[1986] 1 W.L.R. 631; [1986] 2 All E.R. 400	Croom Johnson L.J. Balcombe L.J. Sir John Megaw	Commercial case, involving Ord.14 application.	Nature of letters of credit?	Letters of credit inviolable.
Midland Bank v. Phillips	The Times, March 28, 1986		Ord.14 judgment sought against guarantor.	Ord.14 judgment?	Only if liability of guarantee.
Posner v. Scott-Lewis	[1986] 3 W.L.R. 531; [1986] 3 All E.R. 513	Mervyn Davies J.	Plaintiffs sought specific performance of covenants in leases.	Would specific performance be granted?	Yes, if covenant sufficiently definite and enforceable without unacceptable superintendence by court.

CASE	CITATION	JUDGE(S)	FACTS	ISSUES	ADJUDICATION
Potato Marketing Board v. Drysdale (John M.)	[1986] 3 C.M.L.R. 331, C.A.			Denial in defendant's affidavit.	General denial not enough.
Refidain Bank v. Agom Universal Sugar Trading Co. Ltd	*The Times*, December 23, 1986	Lawton L.J. Nourse L.J.	Banking case involving civil war in Iraq.	Leave to defend?	Conditional leave, despite unusual circumstances.
Tubeworkers v. Tilbury Construction Ltd	(1986) 4 Com.L.R. 13		Contract expressly restricted defendants' right of set-off. Defendants failed to comply with conditions.	Ord.14 judgment for full claim?	Yes.
Williams & Humbert v. W. & H. Trade Marks (Jersey); Rumasa S.A. v. Multivest (U.K.)	[1986] A.C. 368; [1986] 2 W.L.R. 24	Lord Scarman Lord Bridge Lord Brandon Lord Templeman Lord Mackay	Conflict of laws.	Would English courts recognise, without considering merits of, compulsory acquisition laws of a foreign state?	Yes.
World Star, The	[1986] 2 Lloyd's Rep. 274	Sheen J.	Charter party: arbitration clause.	Stay on action?	Yes.

1165

CASE	CITATION	JUDGE(S)	FACTS	ISSUES	ADJUDICATION
Archital Luxfer v. Dunning & Son	(1987) 1 F.T.L.R. 372, C.A.		Arbitration clause.	Relationship Ord.14/arbitration?	Summary judgment on part of claim, rest to arbitration.
Bath Press Ltd v. Rose	*The Times*, July 13, 1987, C.A.	May L.J. Bush L.J.	Plaintiff did not apply under Ord.14 until after issuing summons for directions.	Ord.14 application prevented?	No.
Chatbrown Ltd v. Alfred McAlpine Construction (Southern)	(1986) 35 Build.L.R. 44		Ord.14 application, *re* arbitration clause.	Will court decide questions of law under Ord.14 summons?	Yes, if proper arbitration clause makes no difference.
Famous v. GE Im Ex Italia SRL	*The Times*, August 3, 1987, C.A.		Bad cheque. Payer alleged misrepresentation by payee that he would supply more goods in future.	Leave to defend in these circumstances?	Very doubtful.
Grey v. Durham County Council	[1987] C.L.Y. 3109		Application by defendant to transfer proceedings.	Test?	Balance of interlocutory convenience.

1166

CASE	CITATION	JUDGE(S)	FACTS	ISSUES	ADJUDICATION
Guinness v. Saunders, sub nom. Guinness v. World Tukan; Timber v. Barclays Bank	[1987] 1 Lloyd's Rep. 171; [1987] 1 FTLR 154	Hirst J.	Letter of credit.	Should bank be restrained from paying under letter of credit?	No, court would only interfere if bank had notice of clear fraud by beneficiary.
Imodco Ltd v. Wimpey Major Projects Ltd	(1987) 40 Build.L.R. 1, C.A.		Application under Ord.14 for interim payment.	Does court have jurisdiction to order interim payment before ordering stay?	Yes.
Nichimen Corp. v. Gatoil Overseas Inc.	[1987] 2 Lloyd's Rep. 46, C.A.	Keer L.J. Woolf L.J. Sir John Megaw	Sale of goods. Letter of credit. Application for Ord.14 refused.	Ord.14 judgment on appeal?	Yes.
Shearson Lehman Brothers Inc. v. Maclaine, Watson & Co.	[1987] 1 W.L.R. 480; [1987] 2 All E.R. 181	Lloyd L.J. Nicholls L.J.	Contract.	Interim payments— standard of proof?	Civil burden: balance of probabilities.
Shell International Petroleum Co. v. Transnor (Bermuda)	[1987] 1 Lloyd's Rep. 363	Steyn J.	Contract for supply of oil. Ord.14 judgment sought.	Summary judgment?	Yes.

CASE	CITATION	JUDGE(S)	FACTS	ISSUES	ADJUDICATION
Taddale Investments v. Banque Hypothécaire du Canton de Genève	*The Times,* February 26, 1987, C.A.	O'Connor L.J. Nicholls L.J. Sir Edward Eveleigh	Claim relating to loan agreement. Allegation amounting to fraudulent conspiracy.	Summary judgment case?	Not if court had to make adverse inferences from affidavits/weigh probabilities.
Wales Tourist Board v. Roberts	*The Times,* January 10, 1987, C.A.	May L.J. Lincoln L.J.	Application for leave to appeal summary judgment out of time.	Position of fresh evidence?	Judge cannot refuse to hear on basis should have been put before district judge. But such evidence considered circumspectly.
Zakhem International Construction v. Nippon Kokkam KK (No. 2)	[1987] 2 Lloyd's Rep. 661	Staughton J.	Oil development contract.	Ord.14 refused. Would case be transferred from Commercial to Chancery?	Yes.
Bhogal v. Punjab National Bank; Basna v. Same	[1988] 2 All E.R. 296	Dillon L.J. Bingham L.J.	Case involving bank accounts.	Question of ownership of funds in bank account suitable for Ord.14?	No.
Gibbons v. Wall	*The Times,* February 24, 1988, C.A.	May L.J. Balcombe L.J.	Personal injury.	Standard of proof *re* interim payment?	Civil standard.

CASE	CITATION	JUDGE(S)	FACTS	ISSUES	ADJUDICATION
Heath (C.E.) v. Ceram Holding Co.	[1988] 1 W.L.R. 1219, C.A.	Kerr L.J. Neill L.J.	Commercial case.	Can defendant obtain summary judgment on a counter-claim against a co-defendant?	No.
Hereford and Worcester County Council v. National Association of Schoolmasters/Union of Women Teachers	*The Times,* March 26, 1988, D.C.		Council claimed damages from Union following half day strike.	Suitable for Ord.14?	Yes, except on issue of damages: Union admitted liability.
Jet Holdings v. Patel	[1988] 3 W.L.R. 295, C.A.	Nicholls L.J. Staughton L.J.	Conflict of laws. Default judgment.	Was default judgment abroad enforceable in U.K.?	No; issue of fraud to be tried.
Morgan Guaranty Trust Co. of New York v. Hadjiantonakis (Demetre)	[1988] 1 Lloyd's Rep. 381; [1987] 2 F.T.L.R. 398, C.A.	Mustill L.J. Nourse L.J.	Loan guarantees. Alleged agreement that no enforcement in U.K.	Should Ord.14 judgment be set aside/stay ordered?	Yes, case returned in both aspects to Commercial Court.

1169

CASE	CITATION	JUDGE(S)	FACTS	ISSUES	ADJUDICATION
British and Commonwealth Holdings v. Quadrex Holdings Inc.	[1989] 3 W.L.R. 723, C.A.	Sir Nicholas Browne-Wilkinson V.-C. Woolf L.J. Staughton L.J.	Contract.	Could interim damages order be made?	If unconditional leave to defend, no. If conditional yes, if court satisfied plaintiff would win substantial damages.
Cadogan v. Muscatt	(1990) T.L.R. 372	Nourse L.J. Ward J.	Tenant lowered a wall in flagrant breach of covenant. Landlord applied for a mandatory injunction to reinstate the wall.	Summary mandatory injunction?	Yes.
Express Newspapers v. News (UK) Ltd	[1990] 1 W.L.R. 1320; [1990] 3 All E.R. 376	Sir Nicholas Browne-Wilkinson V.-C.	Copyright. Ord.14 application on counter-claim.	Summary judgment for defendant?	Yes.
Express Newspapers plc v. News (UK) Ltd	As above.		Defendant applied for summary judgment on counterclaim. Defence to counterclaim was inconsistent with plaintiff's claim.	Defence to counterclaim was arguable. Did the inconsistency matter?	Yes. Plaintiff cannot approbate and reprobate judgment on the counterclaim.

CASE	CITATION	JUDGE(S)	FACTS	ISSUES	ADJUDICATION
House of Spring Gardens Ltd v. Waite	[1990] 3 W.L.R. 347	Fox L.J. Stuart-Smith L.J. McCowan L.J.	Proceedings in the English courts to enforce a foreign judgment as a debt at common law.	Can defendants take point that foreign judgment obtained by fraud?	Not when they have already taken the point in the foreign court: estopped.
Hunt v. R.M. Douglas (Roofing) Ltd	[1990] A.C. 398; [1988] 3 All E.R. 823	Lord Bridge Lord Brandon Lord Griffiths Lord Ackner Lord Jauncey	Interest on costs.	From when does interest run on costs?	From date of judgment.
Nestle v. National Westminster Bank plc	(1990) T.L.R. 242	Neill L.J. Nicholls L.J. Butler-Sloss L.J.	Action for mismanagement of a trust fund.	Extension of time for appeal 3 months late?	Yes, if appellant's case not unarguable.
O'Connor v. Amus Bridgman Abbatoirs	*The Times*, April 13, 1990	Scott Baker J.	Personal injury. Summary judgment awarded to plaintiff.	Was possibility of plaintiff receiving an unfairly large amount of interest a return for depriving him of Ord. 14 judgment?	No.

CASE	CITATION	JUDGE(S)	FACTS	ISSUES	ADJUDICATION
Putty v. Hopkinson; Putty v. Barnard	[1990] 1 All E.R. 1057		Personal injury: liability admitted. Quantum at issue.	Judgment available in such a way to avoid defendant paying interest?	Yes, in court's discretion.
R.G. Carter Ltd v. Clarke	[1990] 1 W.L.R. 578; [1990] 2 All E.R. 209	Lord Donaldson M.R. Stocker L.J. Woolf L.J.	Triable issue of law.	Should issue of law be decided in Ord.14 hearing?	Yes, if decisive of all issues between the parties.
Rudge v. Rudge	*The Times*, March 21, 1990		Personal injury claim. Defendant could show no arguable defence to claim for unliquidated damages.	Order?	Judgment with damages to be assessed (not declaratory relief).
Andrews v. Schooling	[1991] 1 W.L.R. 783	Balcombe L.J. Beldam L.J. Sir Denys Buckley	House purchaser suing for defective building construction.	What test for an interim payment?	*Will* the plaintiff succeed in his claim? Not, Is he *likely* to succeed?
Europa Property and Finance Services Ltd v. Stubbert	(1991) T.L.R. 533	Balcombe L.J. Beldam L.J.	Defendant appealed against master's order giving conditional leave to defend.	On defendant's appeal, does plaintiff need to cross-appeal?	No.

CASE	CITATION	JUDGE(S)	FACTS	ISSUES	ADJUDICATION
Fowkes v. Dulthie	[1991] 1 All E.R. 337	Macpherson of Cluny J.	Summary judgment hearing adjourned by consent; letter of consent delivered day before hearing.	Costs?	Could be ordered against solicitors, because of effect in delaying other cases.
Mallory v. Butler	[1991] 2 All E.R. 889	Lord Donaldson M.R. McCowan L.J. Leggatt L.J.	Collision between boats on the River Thames.	Which is the leading judgment in the *Norwich & Peterborough B/S* case? (see below)	That of Lord Donaldson M.R.
Norwich & Peterborough Building Society v. Steed	[1991] 1 W.L.R. 449	Lord Donaldson M.R. McCowan L.J. Leggatt L.J.	Mortgagees' action for possession.	Extension of time to appeal?	Yes because: (i) Arguable case; (ii) Delay caused by legal aid; (iii) No prejudice to plaintiffs.
Schott Kem Ltd v. Bentley	[1991] 1 Q.B. 61	Neill L.J. Glidewell L.J.	Business fraud action in relation to installation of glass (non-corrosive) drains. Application for interim payment.	Does applicant for interim payment need to show: (i) Need;	(i) No.

CASE	CITATION	JUDGE(S)	FACTS	ISSUES	ADJUDICATION
				(ii) Prejudice if he does not obtain interim payment?	(ii) No.
Thomas v. Bunn	[1991] 2 W.L.R. 27; [1991] 1 All E.R. 193	Lord Keith Lord Brandon Lord Brightman Lord Templeman Lord Ackner	Judgment on liability split from assessment of damages.	From when does interest run?	Interest runs from date of assessment of damages.
Axel Johnson Petroleum AB v. MG Mineral Group AG, The Obelix	[1992] 1 W.L.R. 270	Fox L.J. Staughton L.J. Leggatt L.J.	Plaintiffs bought oil from the defendants under a joint venture agreement.	Ascertainable counterclaim for liquidated sum, amounting to set-off defence. Summary judgment?	No. And the state of the law on set-off is unsatisfactory in not allowing any counterclaim to be a defence.
Bulli Trading Ltd v. Afalona Shipping Ltd, The Coral	[1993] 1 Lloyd's Rep 1	Nourse L.J. Stocker L.J. Beldam L.J.	Cargo owners sued ship owners for damage to cargo.	When is a case which turns on construction of documents suitable for summary judgment?	When (i) Not a difficult or long point; (ii) No issue of fact on *either* party's construction.

CASE	CITATION	JUDGE(S)	FACTS	ISSUES	ADJUDICATION
Macmillan Publishers Ltd v. Thomas Reed Publications Ltd	(1993) F.S.R. 455	Mummery J.	Infringement of copyright in the plaintiff's charts of the coastline.	In an application for a summary injunction, is it equivalent to an *American Cyanamid* situation?	No. The balance of convenience is irrelevant.
Stringman v. McArdle	(1993) T.L.R. 578	Butler-Sloss L.J. Stuart-Smith L.J. Sir Tasker Watkins	Road traffic accident.	Should the court be concerned with what the plaintiff would do with interim damages?	No.
National Westminster Bank plc v. Daniel	[1994] 1 All E.R. 156	Glidewell L.J. Butler-Sloss L.J.	Bank sued on personal guarantee.	(i) If defendant's affidavits conflict, can the court conclude that no fair or reasonable probability of defence?	(i) Yes.
				(ii) What order if no fair or reasonable probability of defence?	(ii) Judgment for the plaintiff.

1175

CASE	CITATION	JUDGE(S)	FACTS	ISSUES	ADJUDICATION
Virgin Group Ltd v. De Morgan Group plc	(1994) T.L.R. 137	Bingham M.R. Steyn L.J. Rose L.J.	Leave to appeal to the Court of Appeal on a question of fact.	What is the test?	Has the ground of appeal got a reasonable prospect of success?

CASE	CITATION	JUDGE(S)	FACTS	ISSUES	ADJUDICATION
Hunt v. Hooper	(1844) 12 M. & W. 664; 1 D.C.W. & L. 626		Plaintiff voluntarily instructs sheriff to withdraw from possession.	Plaintiff allowed to keep priority over later writs received by sheriff?	Most unlikely.
Attwood v. Chichester	(1878) 3 Q.B.D. 722; 47 L.J.Q.B. 300		Delay in application to set irregular judgment aside.	Discretion still to set aside?	Yes, if to allow judgment to stand would be oppressive.
Jacques v. Harrison	(1883) 12 Q.B.D. 136; 53 L.J.Q.B. 137		Judgment in default; application to set aside by stranger.	Modes by which stranger can have judgment set aside?	(i) Obtain defendant's leave to use his name. (ii) Ask leave by summons with notice to plaintiff/defendant, to defend action/intervene.
Knight v. Abbott	(1883) 10 Q.B.D. 11			Is claim for unliquidated damages a liquidated demand?	No, calculation not merely arithmetical.
Haigh v. Haigh	(1885) 31 Ch.D. 478; 55 L.J.Ch. 190		Regular judgment.	Judgment set aside if defendant deliberately ignored proceedings?	Very unlikely.

1177

CASE	CITATION	JUDGE(S)	FACTS	ISSUES	ADJUDICATION
Beale v. Macgregor	(1886) 2 T.L.R. 311, C.A.; 47 L.J.C.B. 300		Delay in application to set irregular judgment aside.	Discretion still to set aside?	Yes, if circumstances require it; inherent power of court to prevent abuse of process.
Murray v. Stephenson	(1887) 19 Q.B.D. 60; 56 L.J.Q.B. 647			Can writ be served during August?	Yes, but not pleadings. Writ not a pleading even if indorsed with statement of claim.
Anlaby v. Praetorious	(1888) 20 Q.B.D. 764; 57 L.J.Q.B. 287		Judgment irregularly obtained.	Defendant entitled as of right to set aside?	Yes, and no condition to be imposed on defendant.
Farden v. Richter	(1889) 23 Q.B.D. 124; 58 L.J.Q.B. 244		Irregular judgment.	Procedural requirements for setting aside. Affidavit necessary?	Yes, unless sufficient reason.
Lysaght v. Clark & Co.	(1891) 1 Q.B. 552; 64 L.T. 776		Partnership carried on within jurisdiction. Partners resident abroad.	Valid service on partner temporarily within jurisdiction?	Yes.

CASE	CITATION	JUDGE(S)	FACTS	ISSUES	ADJUDICATION
Rein v. Stein	(1892) 66 L.T. 469; (1892) 1 Q.B. 753		Judgment irregularly obtained.	What is "fresh step" by defendants, preventing subsequent application to set judgment aside?	One which amounts to waiver of irregularity.
Weall v. James	(1893) 68 L.T. 515		Ord. 13. Multiple defendants.	Can default judgment be obtained against any of the defendants?	So long as all/part of debt unsatisfied.
Hughes v. Justin	[1894] 1 Q.B. 667; 63 L.J.Q.B. 417		Default judgment: part of claim paid post-writ.	Should judgment sum be adjusted?	Yes, or judgment may be set aside.
Chessum & Sons v. Gordon	[1901] 1 K.B. 694	A.L. Smith M.R. Collins L.J. Romer L.J.	Element of costs accidentally omitted from order.	Coul order be amended to allow for costs accidentally omitted?	Yes.
Morel Brothers & Co. Ltd v. Earl of Westmoreland	[1903] 1 K.B. 64; [1904] A.C. 11		Claims in alternative.	Must plaintiff elect one defendant before entering judgment in default?	Yes, entering judgment against one bars proceedings against other.

CASE	CITATION	JUDGE(S)	FACTS	ISSUES	ADJUDICATION
Pim Bros Ltd v. Coyle	[1903] 2 I.R. 457		Ord. 13. Multiple defendants.	Can default judgment be obtained against any of defendants?	So long as all/part of debt unsatisfied.
Cross v. Matthews and Wallace	[1904] 91 L.T. 500		Action for goods supplied.	Must plaintiff elect one defendant before entering judgment default?	Yes, entering judgment against one bars proceedings against other.
Hymas v. Ogden	[1905] 1 K.B. 246; 74 L.J.K.B. 101	Collins M.R. Stirling L.J. Mathew L.J.	Judgment for delivery of specific chattel. Wilful refusal to deliver.	Did county court judge have jurisdiction to order warrant of attachment?	Yes.
Sanders v. Hamilton	[1907] 96 L.T. 679; 23 T.L.R. 389, D.C.		Judgment entered for too small a sum.	May amendment be made?	Yes, if slip rule applies. If not, plaintiff should apply to set aside.
Armitage v. Parsons	[1908] 2 K.B. 410; 77 L.J.K.B. 850	Sir Gorell Barnes Fletcher Moulton L.J.	Bill of exchange case. Judgment amount too large.	Could defendant have judgment set aside?	No, judgment should be amended.

CASE	CITATION	JUDGE(S)	FACTS	ISSUES	ADJUDICATION
Muir v. Jenks	[1913] 2 K.B. 412; 82 L.J.K.B. 703	Buckley L.J. Kennedy L.J.	Liquidated claim; reduction by payment. Default judgment amount greater than that actually due.	Judgment set aside or amount reduced?	In a proper case, plaintiff can apply for amendment. Delay will not necessarily deprive defendant of right to have judgment set aside.
Harley v. Samson	(1914) 30 T.L.R. 450		Delay in application to set irregular judgment aside.	Discretion still to set aside?	Yes, if to allow judgment to stand would be oppressive.
Dunlop Pneumatic Tyre Co. Ltd v. New Garage & Motor Co. Ltd	[1915] A.C. 79			Liquidated claim if not a genuine attempt to assess damages, or stipulation *in terrorem*?	No, and not recoverable if in any event a penalty clause.
Whiteley v. Hilt	[1918] 2 K.B. 808	Swinfen Eady M.R. Warrington L.J. Duke L.J.	Hire-purchase of piano. Action in detinue, after hirer sold piano to defendant.	Measure of damages?	Measure was unpaid instalments. No return of piano/its value.

CASE	CITATION	JUDGE(S)	FACTS	ISSUES	ADJUDICATION
Andromeda v. Holme	(1923) 130 L.T. 329; [1923] W.N. 250		Setting aside judgment.	Meaning of "costs thrown away" order?	Does not include costs of bankruptcy proceedings brought on judgment (though court can order defendant to pay these).
Elliott v. Boynton	[1924] 1 Ch. 236; 93 L.J.Ch. 122	Pollock M.R. Warrington L.J.	Breach of covenant in lease: forfeiture.	Date from which mesne profits should be assessed?	From the date of the writ in the action.
Lazard Brothers & Co. v. Midland Bank Ltd	[1933] A.C. 289; [1932] 2 All E.R. 571	Lord Buckmaster Lord Blanesburgh Lord Warrington Lord Russell Lord Wright	Defendant owed debt to Russian bank before revolution.	Who decides question of foreign law?	Question of fact, decided by judge, not jury.
Evans v. Bartlam	[1937] A.C. 473; [1937] 2 All E.R. 646	Lord Atkin Lord Thankerton Lord Russell Lord Wright Lord Roche	Appellant owed sums to bookmaker (respondent).	Basis for setting aside default judgment?	Matter for judge's discretion. Court of Appeal would not interfere unless discretion wrongly exercised.
Windsor v. Chalcraft	[1939] 1 K.B. 279; [1938] 2 All E.R.	Greer L.J. Slesser L.J. Mackinnon L.J.	Running down action. Application by insurers to set aside judgment.	Were insurers entitled to be heard?	Yes, injuriously affected by judgment.

CASE	CITATION	JUDGE(S)	FACTS	ISSUES	ADJUDICATION
Manley Estates Ltd v. Benedik	[1941] 1 All E.R. 248, C.A.	Mackinnon L.J. du Parcq L.J.	Conditional leave to defend. Condition not fulfilled.	Did court have power to enlarge time?	Yes, action still in existence.
Murfin v. Ashbridge and Martin	[1941] 1 All E.R. 231	Sir Wilfred Greene M.R. Goddard L.J.	Running down action. Insurers had control of proceedings but not party to action.	Could insurers apply in own name to have order set aside?	No, not party to action.
Craigmyle v. Inchcape	[1942] 1 Ch. 394; [1942] 2 All E.R. 157	Morton J.	Summons to determine domicile of testator.	Could order be amended to allow for costs accidentally omitted?	Yes.
Smith v. Poulter	[1947] K.B. 339; [1947] 1 All E.R. 216	Denning J.	Landlord and tenant: judgment for possession signed in defendant's absence.	Judgment valid?	No, court had not considered reasonableness of giving possession. Cost order wrong as action should have been in county court.

CASE	CITATION	JUDGE(S)	FACTS	ISSUES	ADJUDICATION
Dulles' Settlement (No. 2), Re Dulles v. Vidler	[1951] Ch. 842; [1951] 2 All E.R. 69	Evershed M.R. Denning L.J.	Infant's application for maintenance (American father).	Had father submitted to jurisdiction of court?	No.
Grimshawe v. Dunbar	[1953] 1 Q.B. 408; [1953] 2 W.L.R. 332	Jenkins L.J. Morris L.J. Roxburgh J.	Landlord and tenant. Judgment in defendant's absence.	Should there have been new trial?	Party has prima facie right to have action tried in his presence.
Hesz v. Sotheby & Co. (Practice Note)	[1960] 1 W.L.R. 285; (1960) 104 S.J. 271	Master Diamond	Writ for return of picture lost by auctioneers.	Summary judgment; proceedings public?	Yes.
Bridge v. Campbell Discount Co. Ltd	[1962] A.C. 600; [1962] 2 W.L.R. 439	Viscount Simonds Lord Morton Lord Radcliffe Lord Denning Lord Devlin	Hire-purchase agreement.	Was sum payable to terminate a penalty?	Yes.
General and Finance Facilities Ltd v. Cooks Cars (Romford)	[1963] 1 W.L.R. 644; [1963] 2 All E.R. 314	Pearson L.J. Diplock L.J.	Hire-purchase of a crane. Crane sold in breach of agreement.	Summary judgment in detinue— separate assessment of value and damages?	Yes.

CASE	CITATION	JUDGE(S)	FACTS	ISSUES	ADJUDICATION
Bolt & Nut Co. (Tipton) v. Rowland Nicholls & Co.	[1964] 2 Q.B. 10; [1964] 2 W.L.R. 98	Harman L.J. Danckwerts L.J.	Payment of part of debt by cheque. Judgment for full sum.	Costs in having irregular judgment set aside.	Defendant's costs in application and costs thrown away.
Davis Manufacturing Co. Ltd v. Fabn	[1967] 1 W.L.R. 1059	Lord Denning M.R. Danckwerts L.J. Winn L.J.	Writ of execution. Wife claimed goods seized were hers. Appeal by execution creditor.	Was creditor entitled to special appointment for hearing?	Yes. Master could determine issue himself but not forthwith.
Peachey Property Corp. Ltd v. Robinson	[1967] 2 Q.B. 543; [1966] 2 W.L.R. 1386	Sellers L.J. Salmon L.J. Winn L.J.	Landlord and tenant: judgment for possession signed in defendant's absence.	Judgment valid?	No, court had not considered reasonableness of giving possession. Cost order wrong as action should have been in county court.
Gurtner v. Circuit	[1968] 2 Q.B. 587; [1968] 2 W.L.R. 668	Lord Denning M.R. Diplock L.J. Salmon L.J.	Road traffic accident. M.I.B. involved.	(i) Did M.I.B. have sufficient interest to be added as defendant? (ii) Substituted service on defendant's insurers valid?	(i) Yes. (ii) No, wrong insurers but allowed to stand. No purpose in setting aside.

1185

CASE	CITATION	JUDGE(S)	FACTS	ISSUES	ADJUDICATION
White v. Weston	[1968] 2 Q.B. 647; [1968] 2 W.L.R. 1459	Russell L.J. Sachs L.J.	Summons by post to wrong address; defendant had no knowledge.	Costs when default judgment set aside in circumstances.	Order for plaintiffs' costs set aside. Summons not served.
Camas Property Co. v. K.L. Television Services Ltd	[1970] 2 Q.B. 433; [1970] 2 W.L.R. 1133	Lord Denning M.R. Fenton Atkinson L.J. Megan L.J.	Forfeiture of lease.	Date from which mesne profits should be assessed?	From date of service of writ for possession.
Burns v. Kondel	[1971] 1 Lloyd's Rep. 554	Lord Denning M.R. Fenton Atkinson L.J. Sir Gordon Willmer	Personal injury case.	Should judgment in default be set aside?	Yes, defence need only be arguable, not good. Can include arguable contributory negligence claim.
Morley London Developments Ltd v. Rightside Properties Ltd	(1973) 117 S.J. 876; (1973) 231 EG 235	Edmund Davies L.J. Stephenson L.J. Bagnall J.	Action for specific performance/damages arising from contract for sale. Judgment in default.	Was notice of withdrawal of specific performance claim necessary?	No.

1186

CASE	CITATION	JUDGE(S)	FACTS	ISSUES	ADJUDICATION
Milangos v. George Frank (Textiles) Ltd	[1976] A.C. 443; [1975] 3 W.L.R. 758	Lord Wilberforce Lord Simon Lord Cross Lord Edmund-Davies Lord Fraser	Debt. Contract payable in Swiss Francs.	Could English judgment be expressed in foreign currency?	Yes.
Stewart Chartering Ltd v. C. & O. Managements S.A.; Venus Destiny, The	[1980] 1 W.L.R. 460; [1980] 1 All E.R. 718	Robert Goff J.	Claim for liquidated damages and *Mareva. Mareva* granted.	Could plaintiffs enter judgment in default?	Yes, *Mareva* continued after judgment in aid of execution.
Cox (Peter) Ltd v. Thirwell	(1981) 125 S.J. 481	Forbes J.	Claim for money due for building work. Service of writ by post ineffective. Judgment in default.	Costs order after judgment set aside?	Costs in cause.
Samuels v. Linzi Dresses Ltd	[1981] Q.B. 115; [1980] 2 W.L.R. 836	Roskill L.J. Lawton L.J. Sir Stanley Rees	Delay in compliance with "unless" order.	Did court have jurisdiction to extend time following "unless" order?	Yes, but should be exercised cautiously.

CASE	CITATION	JUDGE(S)	FACTS	ISSUES	ADJUDICATION
Afro Continental Nigeria v. Meridan Shipping Co. S.A.; Vrontados, The	(1982) 126 S.J. 331; [1982] 2 Lloyd's Rep. 241	Lord Denning M.R. Ackner L.J. O'Connor L.J.	Shipping. Foreign defendants, but had address at Lloyds and three directors resident in London.	Leave required for service out of jurisdiction?	Yes, though in law service was in jurisdiction. Judge's discretion as to whether purported service should stand.
Bernstein v. Jackson	[1982] 1 W.L.R. 1082; [1982] 2 All E.R. 806	Dunn L.J. Slade L.J.	Failure to renew writ.	Could this be cured under Ord.2, r.1?	No.
Drayton Giftware v. Varyland Ltd	(1982) 132 New L.J. 558	Waller L.J. Oliver L.J. Griffiths L.J.	Commercial contract.	Should judgment in default be set aside?	Yes, discrepancies between facts stated in contract/actual facts.
Fairhurst v. Tempert Construction Ltd	May 17, 1984, C.A.T.		Regular judgment.	Judgment set aside?	Court should consider consequences to both parties of setting aside.
Ladup v. Siu	(1984) 81 L.S.Gaz. 283, C.A.	Dunn L.J. May L.J.	Dishonoured cheque in payment for gaming chips.	Should judgment in default be set aside? Delay by defendants.	Consider merits of defence first, then delay, etc.
National Westminster Bank v. Humphrey	(1984) 128 S.J. 81; (1984) 81 L.S.Gaz. 123	Slade L.J. Sir David Cairns	Defendant was guarantor. Judgment in default.	Court's jurisdiction to grant stay?	Wide enough to set aside one part of judgment/grant general stay in respect of another.

CASE	CITATION	JUDGE(S)	FACTS	ISSUES	ADJUDICATION
Lennard v. International Institute for Medical Studies	*The Times*, April 29, 1985	Slade L.J. Griffiths L.J.	Felling of trees without licence. Application to set aside default judgment.	Must judge state reasons for granting application?	Yes.
Moundreas & Co. S.A. v. Navimpex Xentrala Navala	[1985] 2 Lloyd's Rep. 515	Saville J.	Shipbuilding contract. Action for commission for introducing buyers.	Were defendant shipbuilders liable to pay commission even where buyers had cancelled orders?	Yes, because term implied that defendants would not break contract so as to deprive plaintiffs of commission.
Abu Dhabi Helicopters Ltd v. International Aeradio plc	[1986] 1 W.L.R. 312; [1986] 1 All E.R. 395	Dillon L.J. Sir George Waller	Deemed service of writ.	When could writ be deemed served?	Unless contrary shown by plaintiff or defendant.
Alpine Bulk Transport Co. Inc. v. Saudi Eagle Shipping Co. Inc.; Sauchi Eagle, The	[1986] 2 Lloyd's Rep. 221, C.A.	O'Connor L.J. Sir Roger Ormrod	Charter party. Judgment in default; application to set aside.	Judgment set aside?	No; one factor was defendant's initial deliberate decision not to defend.
Austin Rover Group Ltd v. Crouch Butler Savage Associates	[1986] 1 W.L.R. 1102; [1986] 3 All E.R. 50	May L.J. Lloyd L.J. Sir John Megaw	Service writ by post on partnership: incorrectly addressed but redirected to principal place of business.	Writ validity served?	Yes.

1189

CASE	CITATION	JUDGE(S)	FACTS	ISSUES	ADJUDICATION
Bankers Trust Co. v. Galadari	[1987] Q.B. 222; [1986] 3 W.L.R. 1099; (1986) 130 S.J. 986	Kerr L.J. Parker L.J. Balcombe L.J.	Writ of *fi.fa.* See also *Knight v. Abbott* (1883)	Priority.	Writ of *fi.fa.* granted and withdrawn. Regains priority when restored.
Hodgson v. Hart District Council	[1986] 1 W.L.R. 317; [1986] 1 All E.R. 400	Kerr L.J. Dillon L.J. Sir George Waller	Writ served by post, arrived before expiry but deemed date after expiry.	Deemed service date or actual service date valid?	Actual date received was date of service.
Vann v. Awford	(1986) 130 S.J. 682	Dillon L.J. Nicholls L.J.	Action in negligence/contract arising from building work	Should judgment in default be set aside?	Yes, despite lies by defendant, arguable defence disclosed.
Butler (Edward) Vinters Ltd v. Grange Seymour Internationale	(1987) 131 S.J. 1188, C.A.	Kerr L.J. Glidewell L.J. Sir George Waller	Action for breach of contract/duty: default judgment.	Interest, even though not indorsed on writ/mentioned in judgment?	Yes; no need to plead interest on generally indorsed writ.
Huddleston v. Control Risks Information Services Ltd	[1987] 1 W.L.R. 701; (1987) 2 All E.R. 1035	Hoffmann J.	Alleged documentary defamation, South Africa.	Can documents be property?	If actual physical medium is important, yes.

CASE	CITATION	JUDGE(S)	FACTS	ISSUES	ADJUDICATION
Lash Atlantico, The	[1987] 2 Lloyd's Rep. 114, C.A.	Kerr L.J. Croom-Johnson L.J. Mustill L.J.	Collision of ships. Plaintiff ship was owned by a Panamanian company but managed by a Greek company.	Should damages be in U.S. dollars, or Greek drachmas (the currency of the ship's accounts)?	Dollars. The plaintiff's investment and trading venture was in dollars.
Ruben Martinez Villena, The	[1987] 2 Lloyd's Rep. 621	Hobhouse J.	Action involving cargo. Default judgment.	Should judgment be set aside?	Yes, good arguable defences.
Transoceanica Francesca and Nicos V, The	[1987] 2 Lloyd's Rep. 155	Sheen J.	Collision of ships. Plaintiff ship was owned by Italian company.	(i) Should damages be in U.S. dollars or Italian lire? (ii) How should the U.S. dollar counterclaim be set off?	(i) The plaintiffs 'felt their loss' Italian lire. (ii) The smaller claim should be converted into currency of larger claim at rate on day claims were agreed.
Angelic Star, The	[1988] 1 FTLR 94; [1988] 1 Lloyd's Rep. 122, C.A.	Sir John Donaldson M.R. Gibson L.J.	Shipbuilding contract: default clause.	Was default clause a penalty clause?	No: capital sum merely became immediately payable.

1191

CASE	CITATION	JUDGE(S)	FACTS	ISSUES	ADJUDICATION
City Construction Contracts (London) Ltd v. Adam	*The Times*, January 4, 1988	May J. Eubank J.	Regular judgment, good arguable defence but defendant did not comply with procedure.	Judgment set aside?	Court may require payment in as condition.
National Bank of Greece S.A. v. Pinios Shipping Co. (No.1); Maira, The (No. 3)	[1988] 2 FTLR 9	O'Connor L.J. Lloyd L.J. Nicholls L.J.	Shipping. Loan agreement: relation changed from contractual to creditor debtor.	Can plaintiff charge compound interest after change?	No.
Ozer Properties v. Ghaydi	(1988) 03 EG 87, C.A.	Sir John Donaldson M.R. Stocker L.J.	Possession action. Judgment in default by defendant in separate action.	Did default judgment render present action *res judicata*?	No, unless rights of parties necessarily/precisely determined.
Singh v. Atombrook Ltd	[1989] 1 All E.R. 385	Kerr L.J. Sir John Megaw	Writ was not in fact sent to company's registered office.	Nullity or irregularity?	Mere irregularity.
Golden Ocean Assurance Ltd v. Martin	[1990] 2 Lloyd's Rep. 215	Lloyd L.J. McCowan L.J. Sir John Megaw	Writs were served in error on the wrong defendants, but true defendants not in doubt that plaintiff intended to sue them.	Nullity or irregularity.	Irregularity.

CASE	CITATION	JUDGE(S)	FACTS	ISSUES	ADJUDICATION
Hunt v. R.M. Douglas (Roofing) Ltd	[1990] 1 A.C. 398	Lord Bridge Lord Brandon Lord Griffiths Lord Ackner Lord Jauncey	Interest on costs.	Does interest on costs run from date of judgment or date of taxation?	Date of judgment.
Iran Nabuvat, The	[1990] 1 W.L.R. 115; [1990] 3 All E.R.9		Reduction of judgment sum on appeal.	Should court vary default judgment to reduce sum, or substitute fresh judgment in correct sum?	Vary the old judgment, so as not to deprive plaintiff of interest.
Bondy v. Lloyds Bank plc	(1991) T.L.R. 132	Woolf L.J. Stuart-Smith L.J.	Writ served on last day of limitation period without form of acknowledgment of service.	Was a technical error sufficient to set aside writ?	Not in 1887 and not now.
India Videogram Association Ltd v. Patel	[1991] 1 All E.R. 214	Hoffmann J.	Writ 'served' through letterbox of defendant's English house. Plaintiff failed to swear affidavit that in his opinion writ would have come to knowledge of defendant within 7 days.	(i) Is an affidavit essential for letterbox service? (ii) If foreign plaintiff returns to his English address where writ is, service?	(i) Yes. (ii) Plaintiff is deemed to be served on date of return.

1193

CASE	CITATION	JUDGE(S)	FACTS	ISSUES	ADJUDICATION
Kenneth Allison Ltd v. A.E. Limehouse & Co.	[1991] 4 All E.R. 500	Lord Bridge Lord Templeman Lord Goff Lord Jauncey Lord Lowry	Writ 'served' by being handed to partner's secretary who was specifically authorised to accept it.	(i) Is service on partner's authorised secretary service on partner? (ii) Valid service?	(i) No. (ii) Yes by agreement.
Paragon Group Ltd v. Burnell	[1991] 2 W.L.R. 854	Lloyd L.J. Nourse L.J. Ralph Gibson L.J.	Sale of shares. Contractual deadline for claim for misrepresentation. Plaintiffs could not effect service by any method prescribed by the Rules.	Substituted service requires that prescribed methods be "impracticable" Was service "practicable" here?	Yes. The fact that service could easily be effected after the deadline meant that it was "practicable even though vain."
Sovereign Leasing v. Ali	(1991) T.L.R. 148	Judge Kershaw Q.C.	Action to enforce regulated credit agreement commenced in High Court in spite of rule that such actions "shall not be brought" elsewhere than county court.	Abuse of process?	No, because rule says "shall not be treated as improperly brought."

CASE	CITATION	JUDGE(S)	FACTS	ISSUES	ADJUDICATION
Thomas v. Bunn	[1991] 2 W.L.R. 27	Lord Keith Lord Brandon Lord Brightman Lord Templeman Lord Ackner	Split trial	Does Judgment Act interest run from judgment on liability or damages?	Judgment on damages.
Sage v. Double A Hydraulics Ltd	(1992) T.L.R. 165	Lord Donaldson M.R. Stocker L.J. Farquharson L.J.	Defendant's waiver of right to set aside writ.	(i) Test for waiver? (ii) Can defendant waive even after summons to set aside writ? (iii) Even after refusal of summons at first instance and before appeal?	(i) Acting inconsistently with challenge to validity of writ. (ii) Yes. (iii) Yes.
Lawson v. Midland Travellers Ltd	[1993] 1 All E.R. 989	Bingham M.R. Stuart-Smith L.J. Simon Brown L.J.	Personal injuries writ not served within 4 months of issue. Plaintiff consented to extension of time for Defence.	Does plaintiff's consent to extension of time for Defence imply extension of time for defendant to set aside writ?	Yes.

1195

CASE	CITATION	JUDGE(S)	FACTS	ISSUES	ADJUDICATION
Ward-Lee v. Linehan	[1993] 2 All E.R. 1006	Bingham M.R. McCowan L.J. Hirst L.J.	Tenant's action for a new business tenancy. County court failed to serve proceedings within 2 months of issue.	Can the court extend time for service retrospectively?	Yes.
Al-Tobaishi v. Aung	(1994) T.L.R. 138	Stuart-Smith L.J. Kennedy L.J.	Court order was 'served' on defendant at his London address.	Is London address a "last known address" within R.S.C. Ord. 67, r.7 (deemed service)?	Not if the defendant is known to be abroad.
Willowgreen Ltd v. Smithers	[1994] 2 All E.R. 533	Nourse L.J. Thorpe J.	County court summons "served" at defendant's flat sub-let to another.	Is a flat which is sub-let an "address" of the sub-lessor?	No.

CASE	CITATION	JUDGE(S)	FACTS	ISSUES	ADJUDICATION
National & Provincial Bank v. Evans	(1881) 30 W.N. 117		Motions for judgment in default against some defendants. One admission.	Should motions be set down to be dealt with together?	Yes.
Wilmott v. Young	(1881) 44 L.T. 331		No statement of claim. Defendant gave notice that one not required.	Can plaintiff enter judgment in default of defence?	No.
Fitzwater, Re	(1882) 52 L.J.Ch. 83		Defendant under disability.	Must plaintiff adduce evidence to support claim?	Yes, by affidavit or otherwise.
Graves v. Terry	(1882) 9 Q.B.D. 170; 15 L.J.Q.B. 464		As above (but judgment on counterclaim)	Order?	Judgment for plaintiff not to be drawn up for specified period. (Allowing opportunity for application to discharge).
Gill v. Woodfin	(1884) 25 Ch.D. 707		Defence put in after proper time.	Was defence a nullity?	No.
Gibbings v. Strong	(1884) 26 Ch.D. 66; 50 L.T. 578		Defence served late.	Could court ignore substantial evidence?	No.

CASE	CITATION	JUDGE(S)	FACTS	ISSUES	ADJUDICATION
Ripley v. Sawyer	(1886) 31 Ch.D. 494; 55 L.J.Ch. 407		Defendant under disability.	Must there always be an affidavit if defendant under disability?	No, if unnecessary for protection of defendant.
De Jongh v. Newman	(1887) 56 L.T. 180; 35 W.R. 403		No minutes of proposed judgment. Chancery Division.	How should notice of motion be set out?	Defining precisely the judgment asked for.
Gee v. Bell	(1887) 35 Ch.D. 160; 56 L.J.Ch. 718			May relief sought in statement of claim extend beyond relief sought in writ?	No.
Jones v. Harris	(1887) 55 L.T. 884		Plaintiff sought to prove claim by filling affidavits.	Are affidavits sufficient?	No.
Higgins v. Scott	(1888) 21 Q.B.D. 10; 58 L.J.Q.B. 97	Pollock B. Charles J.	Plaintiff failed to deliver a Defence to Counterclaim, and his action was dismissed by the Master.	How should the defendant obtain judgment on the counterclaim?	The defendant should apply on motion for judgment on the counterclaim.

CASE	CITATION	JUDGE(S)	FACTS	ISSUES	ADJUDICATION
Smith v. Buchan	(1888) 58 L.T. 710; 36 W.R. 631	Kerr L.J.	Agreement for purchase of hereditaments. Plaintiff sought specific performance.	Schedule not set out in statement of claim. Judgment in default?	No, property insufficiently described.
Re Hartley	(1891) 9 L.T.J. 229		Defence struck out for non-compliance with an order.	Could plaintiff enter judgment in default of defence?	Yes.
Charles v. Shepherd	[1892] 2 Q.B. 622; 61 L.J.Q.B. 768	Lord Esher M.R.	Action against an agent.	Ord.19, r.7 directory or mandatory?	Directory.
Young v. Thomas	[1892] 2 Ch. 135, C.A.			Will judge look at anything other than statement of claim?	No.
Williams v. Powell	[1894] W.N. 141			Declaration as to rights available under default procedure?	No.
Fowler v. White	(1901) 45 S.J. 723		No statement of claim indorsed/served.	Can plaintiff enter judgment in default of defence?	No.

CASE	CITATION	JUDGE(S)	FACTS	ISSUES	ADJUDICATION
Cooper-Dean v. Badham	[1908] W.N. 100		Defendant withdraws defence without leave of court.	Position of plaintiff?	May enter judgment in default of defence.
Cheek v. Cheek	(1910) 45 L.J.N.C. 22		Defendant under disability.	Must plaintiff adduce evidence to support claim?	Yes, by affidavit or otherwise.
Cribb v. Freyberger	[1919] W.N. 22, C.A.		Failure to serve defence.	Admission by defendant of everything in the statement of claim?	Yes.
Butterworth v. Smallwood	[1924] W.N. 8; (1924) 68 S.J. 478		Defendant has defence but fails to attend on motion for judgment.	Order?	Judgment for plaintiff, not to be drawn up for specified period. (Allowing opportunity for application to discharge).
Grant v. Knaresborough U.D.C.	[1928] Ch. 310; 97 L.J.Ch. 106		Default judgment. Class 2 Case.	Should plaintiff opt to proceed to trial?	Yes, if publicity desirable.

CASE	CITATION	JUDGE(S)	FACTS	ISSUES	ADJUDICATION
New Brunswick Railway Co. v. British and French Trust Corp. Ltd	[1939] A.C. 1	Lord Maugham L.C. Lord Russell Lord Thankerton Lord Wright Lord Romer	Mortgage bond. Judgment in default.	Default judgment. Estoppel defence to subsequent action?	Generally no; only if defence precisely/definitively ruled on in previous judgment.
Nagy v. Co-operative Press Ltd	[1949] 2 K.B. 118; [1949] 1 All E.R. 1019	Cohen L.J.	Plaintiff alleged libel. Sought damages/injunction.	Could plaintiff proceed to trial, despite default of defence?	Yes.
Shell-Mex and BP Ltd v. Manchester Garages Ltd	[1971] 1 W.L.R. 612	Lord Denning M.R. Sachs L.J. Buckley L.J.	Action to eject licensee from business premises.	Injunction only available from judge, yet summary relief should be from master. To whom should plaintiff go?	Judge.
Wallersteiner v. Moir	[1974] 1 W.L.R. 991	Lord Denning M.R. Buckley L.J. Scarman L.J.	Counterclaim for fraud included claim for declarations.	Does the court retain a discretion whether to enter judgment in absence of Defence?	Yes.

CASE	CITATION	JUDGE(S)	FACTS	ISSUES	ADJUDICATION
Bains v. Patel	*The Times*, May 20, 1983 C.A.	Eveleigh L.J.	Defence struck out for want of discovery.	Type of judgment entered accordingly?	Judgment in default of defence.
City Construction Contracts (London) Ltd v. Adam	*The Times*, January 4, 1988	May L.J. Ewbank J.	Application to set aside judgment in default. Condition that defendant pay money into court.	(i) Is the Court's discretion to order payment in confined to shadowy defences?	(i) No. Court can impose condition to encourage proper conduct of the litigation.
				(ii) How should the amount be fixed?	(ii) In accordance with defendant's means.
Mason v. Desnoes and Geddes Ltd	[1990] 2 W.L.R. 1273, P.C.	Lord Bridge Lord Brandon Lord Templeman Lord Oliver Lord Goff	Negligence action. Judgment in default set aside by master (Jamaican case).	Could master set default judgment aside?	Yes, but more appropriate for judge. Wrong decision by master here.
Aitbelaid v. Nima	(1991) T.L.R. 350	Leonard J.	Claim for declaration relating to documents and shares.	Declaration granted without full hearing?	Yes, because impossible to do justice without it.

CASE	CITATION	JUDGE(S)	FACTS	ISSUES	ADJUDICATION
Patten v. Burke Publishing Co. Ltd	[1991] 2 All E.R. 821	Millett J.	Claim for declaration that contract had been terminated.	Rule that no declaration without full hearing. Ever exceptions?	Yes, if justice cannot be done without declaration.

CASE	CITATION	JUDGE(S)	FACTS	ISSUES	ADJUDICATION
Martin v. Turner	[1970] 1 All E.R. 256	Davies L.J. Winn L.J. Karminski L.J.	Road traffic accident 9 years before it was struck out.	Prejudice to defendant from absence of information from which to calculate special damages and pay into court?	Yes.
Paxton v. Allsopp	[1971] 3 All E.R. 370	Davies L.J. Edmund Davies L.J. Karpinski L.J.	Road traffic accident	(i) Will admission of liability prevent strike-out? (ii) Ten years' delay but contemporary documents. Prejudice? (iii) Should a plaintiff offer to limit claim?	(i) No. (ii) Yes. (iii) No. Improper way of conducting litigation.
Stott v. West Yorkshire Road Car Company Ltd	[1971] 2 Q.B. 651	Lord Denning M.R. Salmon L.J. Megaw L.J.	Third party proceedings	The action settles. What happens to third party proceedings?	They proceed as if a separate action.
William C. Parker Ltd v. F.J. Ham & Son Ltd	[1972] 1 W.L.R. 1583	Russell L.J. Buckley L.J. Orr L.J.	Breach of contract for sale of welding rods.	(i) Is pre-writ delay relevant? (ii) Is pre-writ prejudice enough?	(i) Yes. (ii) No.

CASE	CITATION	JUDGE(S)	FACTS	ISSUES	ADJUDICATION
Pryer v. Smith	[1977] 1 All E.R. 218	Megaw L.J. Scarman L.J. Browne L.J.	Plaintiff was injured falling off bales of hay.	Where judge does not strike out, is there any remedy available?	Yes. The court can impose a strict "unless" timetable.
Birkett v. James	[1978] A.C. 297	Lord Diplock Lord Edmund-Davies Lord Russell Lord Salmon	Delay in prosecuting action.	Principles for striking out for want of prosecution?	(i) Not if limitation period running. (ii) Time before action brought is relevant. (iii) Remedy against solicitor irrelevant.
Biss v. Lambeth, Southwark & Lewisham Health Authority	[1978] 1 W.L.R. 382	Lord Denning M.R. Geoffrey Lane L.J. Eveleigh L.J.	Hospital patient contracted bed sores	Prejudice from sword of Damocles over professional man?	Yes if 11 years.
Tolley v. Morris	[1979] 1 W.L.R. 592	Lord Wilberforce Viscount Dilhorne Lord Diplock Lord Edmund-Davies Lord Keith	Delay by infant	Can action by infant be struck out for want of prosecution within the limitation period?	No.
Walkley v. Precision Forging Ltd	[1979] 1 W.L.R. 606	Lord Wilberforce Viscount Dilhorne Lord Diplock Lord Edmund-Davies Lord Keith	Personal injury action struck out after expiry of primary limitation period.	Can plaintiff invoke court's discretion to disapply time bar in a fresh action?	No.

1205

CASE	CITATION	JUDGE(S)	FACTS	ISSUES	ADJUDICATION
Janov v. Morris	[1981] 1 W.L.R. 1389.	Dunn L.J. Watkins L.J.	First action struck out for non-compliance with peremptory order. Second action brought within the limitation period.	Is second action an abuse of the process?	Not necessarily. Court has a discretion.
Samuels v. Linzi Dresses Ltd	[1981] Q.B. 115	Roskill L.J. Lawton L.J. Sir Stanley Rees	Party failed to comply with a peremptory order.	When should extend time retrospectively?	Cautiously.
Hytrac Conveyors Ltd v. Conveyors International Ltd	[1982] 3 All E.R. 415	Lawton L.J. Templeman L.J. Fox L.J.	Action for infringement of copyright, breach of confidence and conspiracy. Plaintiffs applied for interlocutory injunctions two and a half months after writ but before Statement of Claim.	Appropriate to dismiss in default of Statement of Claim?	Yes.

CASE	CITATION	JUDGE(S)	FACTS	ISSUES	ADJUDICATION
Bailey v. Bailey	[1983] 3 All E.R. 495	Dunn L.J. Purchas L.J.	First action dismissed for want of prosecution. Plaintiff commenced second action within limitation period.	Could second action be struck out for abuse of process?	No.
Greek City Co. Ltd v. Demetriou	[1983] 2 All E.R. 921	Goulding J.	Plaintiff failed to serve Statement of Claim, with inordinate and inexcusable delay and prejudice to defendant.	Strike-out for failure to comply with R.S.C.?	No, because limitation period still ran.
Haynes v. Atkins	*The Times,* October 12, 1983	Cumming-Bruce L.J. Drake J.	Action against professional man.	Prejudice from action hanging over head needs affidavit of oppression?	No. It can be inferred.
Janata Bank v. Noor	*The Times,* November 18, 1983	Ackner L.J. Oliver L.J.	Claim and counterclaim. Delay in both.	Can claim be struck out but not counterclaim?	Yes.

CASE	CITATION	JUDGE(S)	FACTS	ISSUES	ADJUDICATION
Tabata v. Hetherington	*The Times,* December 18, 1983	Cumming-Bruce L.J. Browne-Wilkinson L.J.	Delay before proceedings brought	Is a plaintiff who delayed before issuing proceedings under a heavier duty to prosecute?	Yes.
Eagil Trust Co Ltd v. Pigott-Brown	[1985] 3 All E.R. 119	Arnold P. Griffiths L.J.	Action against businessman.	Is seven and-a-half years' anxiety enough prejudice?	No.
James Investments (IOM) Ltd v. Phillips Cutler Phillips Troy	*The Times,* September 16, 1987	Purchas L.J. Sir Roualeyn Cumming-Bruce	Negligence 9 years before writ. Five years elapsed after writ.	Is the pre-writ delay relevant?	Yes. The post-writ delay is in context of pre-writ delay.
Newman v. Hopkins	*The Times,* December 28, 1988	May L.J. Croom-Johnson L.J. Glidewell L.J.	Delay had increased damages by £11,420 in a claim worth £153,080.	Financial prejudice sufficient to strike out?	Not here.
Thomas Storey Engineers Ltd v. Wailes Dove Bitumastic Ltd	*The Times,* January 21, 1988	Glidewell L.J. Taylor L.J.	Defendant applied for costs – granted – appeal.	Do an application for security for costs and a subsequent appeal excuse delay?	No.

1208

CASE	CITATION	JUDGE(S)	FACTS	ISSUES	ADJUDICATION
Wright v. Morris	*The Times*, October 31, 1988	Millet J.	Passing-off action brought by pop-group "Paper-Lace."	When will the Court strike out *within* the limitation period?	Very rarely, but here where action was not for damages and had been overtaken by events.
Hayes v. Bowman	[1989] 2 All E.R. 293	Slade L.J. Croom-Johnson L.J. Lloyd L.J.	Road traffic accident.	Prejudice where the quantum has increased by the delay?	Possible, but not here.
Department of Transport v. Chris Smaller (Transport) Ltd	[1989] 1 All E.R. 897	Lord Keith Lord Roskill Lord Griffiths Lord Oliver Lord Goff	Defendant's lorry damaged bridge.	(i) Should plaintiff be penalised for delay pre-writ? (ii) Strike out for delay without prejudice? (iii) Are the categories of prejudice closed?	(i) No. (ii) No. (iii) No.
Erskine Communications Ltd v. Worthington	(1991) T.L.R. 330	Mustill L.J. Balcombe L.J. Woolf L.J.	Cross-applications for extension of time for Statement of Claim and dismissal in default of Statement of Claim.	Which application should be heard first?	There is no fixed rule. Sometimes both together.

CASE	CITATION	JUDGE(S)	FACTS	ISSUES	ADJUDICATION
Rath v. C.S. Lawrence & Partners	[1991] 3 All E.R. 679	Slade L.J. Nicholls L.J. Farquharson L.J.	Negligent survey of house. Five years passed after issue of writ.	Does the delay have to *cause* the prejudice?	Yes.
Antcliffe v. Gloucester Health Authority	[1992] 1 W.L.R. 1044	Butler-Sloss L.J. Scott L.J.	Medical negligence action. During the action the method of funding the defendant hospital altered.	Financial prejudice from changed method of funding?	Yes.
Halls v. O'Dell	[1992] 1 Q.B. 393	Balcombe L.J. Taylor L.J. McCowan L.J.	Proceedings begun by Originating summons.	Do the same rules for striking out apply?	Yes.
Lacey v. Harrison	(1992) T.L.R. 213	Judge Dobry Q.C.	Defendant was the only witness of road traffic accident.	Can the Court strike out Defence unless defendant has expert test of memory?	Yes.
Larby v. Thurgood	(1992) T.L.R. 493	May J.	Personal injuries action. Loss of earnings. Evidence from employment consultant.	Employment consultant's expert evidence admissible on motivation and willingness to seek better job?	No. A matter for the judge.

CASE	CITATION	JUDGE(S)	FACTS	ISSUES	ADJUDICATION
Turner v. W.H. Malcolm Ltd	(1992) T.L.R. 417	Glidewell L.J. Stocker L.J. Staughton L.J.	Brain damage caused by road traffic accident patient.	Since no limitation period runs against a patient, can his action ever be struck out for want of prosecution?	No.
Costellow v. Somerset County Council	[1993] 1 All E.R. 952	Bingham M.R. Stuart-Smith L.J. Simon Brown L.J.	Failure to serve a Statement of Claim within time allowed by R.S.C. Defendant applied to dismiss. Plaintiff applied for extension of time.	(i) Dismiss for breach of R.S.C.? (ii) Which summons should be heard first?	(i) Not unless prejudice to opponent. (ii) Neither. Both should be heard together.
Family Housing Association (Manchester) Ltd v. Michael Hyde & Partners	[1993] 2 All E.R. 567	Balcombe L.J. Mann L.J. Hirst L.J.	Architects' negligence action.	Can "without prejudice" correspondence be read in an application to strike out?	Yes.
Grand Metropolitan Nominee (No. 2) Co. Ltd v. Evans	[1993] 1 All E.R. 642	Purchas L.J. Mann L.J.	Failure to comply with "unless" order.	Test for striking out for non-compliance with peremptory order?	Contumacy.

1211

CASE	CITATION	JUDGE(S)	FACTS	ISSUES	ADJUDICATION
Re Jokai Tea Holdings Ltd	[1993] 1 All E.R. 630	Browne-Wilkinson V.-C. Parker L.J. Sir John Megaw	Lord Diplock's malapropism	Test for striking out for non-compliance with an "unless" order?	Was the failure intentional and contumacious?
Trill v. Sacher	[1993] 1 All E.R. 961	Neill L.J. Glidewell L.J.	Action for breach of contract. Six years had passed since writ.	(i) If plaintiff serves notice of intention to proceed, must defendant apply to strike out within one month? (ii) Is delay relevant after writ but before expiry of limitation period? (iii) Is three years inordinate?	(i) No. (ii) Yes. (iii) Yes.
Caribbean General Insurance Co. Ltd v. Frizzell	[1994] 2 Lloyd's Rep. 32	Neill L.J. Beldam L.J. Leggatt L.J.	Scandalous lack of application by solicitors, without excuse, prejudicing the defendant.	How can a party in breach of an "unless" order avoid strike-out?	He must show that breach was excusable.

CASE	CITATION	JUDGE(S)	FACTS	ISSUES	ADJUDICATION
L'Office Cherifien des Phosphates v. Yamashita-Shinnihen Steamship Co. Ltd, The Boucraa	[1994] 1 All E.R. 20	Lord Templeman Lord Goff Lord Jauncey Lord Browne-Wilkinson Lord Mustill	Arbitration proceedings before January 1992 (before Arbitration Act 1950, s. 13A).	Can a pre-1992 arbitration be dismissed for want of prosecution?	Yes.
Rastin v. British Steel plc	[1994] 2 All E.R. 641	Bingham M.R. Beldam L.J. Saville L.J.	Automatic strike-out under C.C.R. Ord. 17, r. 11(9). Retrospective application to extend time for requesting hearing date.	When will the Court extend time (sometimes called "re-instating the action")?	(i) If the plaintiff has prosecuted the case with reasonable diligence and failure is excusable. (ii) And if the balance of hardship is in plaintiff's favour.
Roebuck v. Mungovin	[1994] 2 W.L.R. 290	Lord Goff Lord Jauncey Lord Lowry Lord Browne-Wilkinson Lord Slynn	Road traffic accident. Delay of 7 years since the accident.	(i) Can defendant be estopped from applying to strike out by his conduct? (ii) Does there need to be evidence of prejudice from long delay?	(i) No, but conduct is relevant. (ii) No. It can be inferred.

1213

CASE	CITATION	JUDGE(S)	FACTS	ISSUES	ADJUDICATION
Secretary of State for the Environment v. Easton Centre Investments Ltd	[1994] 2 All E.R. 415	Cherryman Q.C.	Appeal from arbitration.	Do the striking out rules apply to an *appeal* from an arbitration?	No.
Heer v. Tutton	[1995] 4 All E.R. 547	Bingham M.R. Peter Gibson L.J. Saville L.J.	More than a year since county court summons served, but no Defence. But plaintiff agreed to extension of time for Defence.	Does the C.C.R. Ord. 9, r. 10 strike-out take precedence over an agreement to extend time?	No. An extension agreement precludes strike-out.
Webster v. Ellison Circlips Group Ltd	[1995] 4 All E.R. 556; [1995] P.I.Q.R. P544	Glidewell L.J. Simon Brown L.J. Peter Gibson L.J.	More than a year since county court summons served but no Defence.	Is C.C.R. Ord. 9, r. 10 an automatic strike-out?	Yes.
Carr v. Northern Clubs Federation Brewery Ltd	(1996) T.L.R. 19	Bingham M.R. Waite L.J. Otton L.J.	Automatic strike-out under C.C.R. Ord. 17, r. 11. Plaintiff's prospective application to extend time for requesting hearing.	Does application to extend time imply, in the alternative, a request for a hearing?	Yes – following *Ferreira* (1995) T.L.R. 378.

CASE	CITATION	JUDGE(S)	FACTS	ISSUES	ADJUDICATION
Downer v. Brough	(1996) T.L.R. 23	Bingham M.R. Waite L.J. Otton L.J.	Automatic strike-out under C.C.R. Ord. 17, r. 11.	What sort of directions displace the automatic directions?	(i) Action listed for trial on joint application of the parties. (ii) Direction for pre-trial review.
Gardner v. Southwark L.B.C.	(1996) T.L.R. 17	Bingham M.R. Waite L.J. Otton L.J.	First action automatically struck out under C.C.R. Ord. 17, r. 11. Second action within limitation period.	Second action an abuse of process?	No.
Hackwell v. Blue Arrow plc	(1996) T.L.R. 19	Bingham M.R. Waite L.J. Otton L.J.	Automatic strike-out under C.C.R. Ord. 17, r. 11.	Excusable failure within *Rastin* if solicitor's oversight?	No.
Jackson v. Slater Harrison Ltd	(1996) T.L.R. 20	Bingham M.R. Waite L.J. Otton L.J.	Automatic strike-out under C.C.R. Ord 17, r. 11. The *Rastin* "double threshold" test of diligence and excusability.	Should the judge apply the principles of dismissal for want of prosecution?	No.

1215

CASE	CITATION	JUDGE(S)	FACTS	ISSUES	ADJUDICATION
Lightfoot v. National Westminster Bank plc	(1996) T.L.R. 18	Bingham M.R. Waite L.J. Otton L.J.	Automatic strike-out under C.C.R. Ord. 17, r. 11.	Automatic directions start 14 days after "delivery" of Defence.	Delivery means to the Court not to the plaintiff.
Peters v. Winfield	(1996) T.L.R. 22	Bingham M.R. Waite L.J. Otton L.J.	Automatic strike-out under C.C.R. Ord. 17, r. 11. More than one defendant.	When do the automatic directions bite?	Date *last* Defence delivered.
Reville v. Wright	(1996) T.L.R. 20	Bingham M.R. Waite L.J. Otton L.J.	Automatic strike-out under C.C.R. Ord. 17, r. 11. The *Rastin* "double threshold" test of diligence and excusability.	Onus of proof?	On the plaintiff.
Russell v. Dennis	(1996) T.L.R. 21	Bingham M.R. Waite L.J. Otton L.J.	Automatic strike-out under C.C.R. Ord. 17, r. 11. The *Rastin* test of "excusability".	The test for an "excusable" failure to request hearing.	(i) Depends on all the circumstances and the nature of the short-coming relied upon. (ii) Gross mis-apprehension of the start of the automatic directions is no excuse.

CASE	CITATION	JUDGE(S)	FACTS	ISSUES	ADJUDICATION
Tarry v. Humberside Finance Ltd	(1996) T.L.R. 24	Bingham M.R. Waite L.J. Otton L.J.	County court automatic directions. Actions commenced in the High Court before October 1, 1990.	Do the county court directions apply?	No.
Williams v. Globe Coaches	(1996) T.L.R. 15	Bingham M.R. Waite L.J. Otton L.J.	County Court automatic strike-out.	Does the automatic directions timetable run from the date specified in the rules or the date in the N450?	The rules take precedence, but re-instatement if plaintiff misled.

CASE	CITATION	JUDGE(S)	FACTS	ISSUES	ADJUDICATION
John Bishop (Caterers) Ltd v. National Union Bank Ltd	[1973] 1 All E.R. 707	Plowman J.	Two plaintiffs: an insolvent company and a natural person. Their claims were not identical.	Consider the incidence of costs if the plaintiff company lost?	Yes. If the company lost, the natural plaintiff may not be ordered to pay all the defendant's costs.
Sir Lindsay Parkinson & Co. Ltd v. Triplan Ltd	[1973] Q.B. 609	Lord Denning M.R. Cairns L.J. Lawton L.J.	Small company would not be able to pay large company's costs.	How should the court's discretion be exercised?	All the circumstances of the case.
T. Sloyan & Sons (Builders) Ltd v. Brothers of Christian Instruction	[1974] 3 All E.R. 715	Lane J.	Building dispute. Builders claimed £10,500. Employers counterclaimed for £65,000 and sought security from builders.	Should the quantum of the security take into account the costs of the counterclaim?	Not to the extent that it exceeded the claim.
Pearson v. Naydler	[1977] 1 W.L.R. 899	Megarry V.-C.	Two plaintiffs: one a natural person, one a company.	Can the court order security where one plaintiff is a natural person?	Yes.

CASE	CITATION	JUDGE(S)	FACTS	ISSUES	ADJUDICATION
Cutts v. Head	[1984] Ch. 290	Oliver L.J. Fox L.J.	Letter "without prejudice" except as to costs.	Effect of such a letter?	Admissible and effective on costs, except where a payment into court could have been made.
Porzelack KG v. Porzelack (UK) Ltd	[1987] 1 All E.R. 1074	Browne-Wilkinson V.-C.	Passing-off action by West German company	What factors are relevant to the Court's discretion?	(i) Improved enforcement under Civil Jurisdiction and Judgements Act 1982. (ii) Security would stifle the claim. (iii) Preliminary view of merits.
Simaan General Contracting Co. v. Pilkington Glass Ltd	[1987] 1 All E.R. 345	Judge Newey Q.C., O.R.	Building dispute.	Can "without prejudice" correspondence be referred to?	Not without consent.
Family Housing Association (Manchester) Ltd v. Michael Hyde & Partners	[1993] 2 All E.R. 567	Balcombe L.J. Mann L.J. Hirst L.J.	Architect's negligence action.	Can "without prejudice" correspondence be used in application to dismiss for want of prosecution?	Yes.

CASE	CITATION	JUDGE(S)	FACTS	ISSUES	ADJUDICATION
Re Little Olympian Each Ways Ltd	[1994] 4 All E.R. 561	Lindsay J.	Company incorporated in Jersey.	When is a company "ordinarily resident" out of the jurisdiction?	If its central control and management are overseas.

INDEX